P9-DDL-476

BARRON'S
FOREIGN LANGUAGE GUIDES

501 FRENCH VERBS

SIXTH EDITION

Fully conjugated in all the tenses in a new, easy-to-learn format, alphabetically arranged

by

Christopher Kendris
B.S., M.S., Columbia University
M.A., Ph.D., Northwestern University
Diplômé, Faculté des Lettres, Sorbonne

Former Chairman,
Department of Foreign Languages
Farmingdale High School,
Farmingdale, New York

and

Theodore Kendris
B.A., Union College
M.A., Northwestern University
Ph.D., Université Laval

Former *Chargé de cours*
Université Laval, Québec, Canada

BARRON'S

© Copyright 2007, 2003, 1996, 1990, 1982, 1970 by Barron's Educational Series, Inc.

All rights reserved.
No part of this book may be reproduced in any form, by photostat, microfilm, xerography, or any other means, or incorporated into any information retrieval system, electronic or mechanical, without the written permission of the copyright owner.

All inquiries should be addressed to:
Barron's Educational Series, Inc.
250 Wireless Boulevard
Hauppauge, New York 11788
www.barronseduc.com

Library of Congress Catalog Card No. 2006047715

Book ISBN-13: 978-0-7641-3554-5
Book ISBN-10: 0-7641-3554-6
Book/CD-ROM package ISBN-13: 978-0-7641-7983-9
Book/CD-ROM package ISBN-10: 0-7641-7983-7

Library of Congress Cataloging-in-Publication Data

Kendris, Christopher.
501 French verbs fully conjugated in all the tenses and moods in a new easy-to-learn format, alphabetically arranged / by Christopher Kendris and Theodore Kendris.—6th ed.
p. cm.
Spine title: 501 French verbs
ISBN-13: 978-0-7641-3554-5
ISBN-10: 0-7641-3554-6
1. French language—Verb—Tables. I. Kendris, Theodore. II. Title. III. Title: Five hundred and one French verbs fully conjugated in all the tenses and moods in a new easy-to-learn format, alphabetically arranged. IV. Title: Five hundred and one French verbs fully conjugated in all the tenses and moods in a new easy-to-learn format, alphabetically arranged. V. Title: 501 French verbs.

PC2271.K378 2007
448.2′421—dc22 2006047715

PRINTED IN CANADA
9 8 7 6 5 4 3

Contents

About the authors iv

Preface to the sixth edition v

Introduction 1

Present and past participles in French—Formation 3

Derivation of tenses: Verbs conjugated with *avoir* and *être* 4

Verbs conjugated with *avoir* or *être* to form a compound tense 6

Principal parts of some important verbs (Les Temps primitifs) 7

Sample English verb conjugation 8

A summary of French verb tenses and moods 10

Formation of the tenses 22

A summary of sequence of verb tenses—**Si** clauses 26

The subjunctive 26

Orthographically changing verbs (Spelling changes) 32

Definitions of basic grammatical terms with examples 35

Verb drills and tests 50

Answers to verb tests with explanations 81

Essential 55 verb list 103

Subject pronouns 103

Abbreviations 103

Alphabetical listing of 501 French verbs fully conjugated in all tenses and moods 107

Appendixes 663

Defective and impersonal verbs 665

Guide to French pronunciation 686

Verbs used in weather expressions 688

Verbs with prepositions 690

Index of common irregular French verb forms 701

English-French verb index 705

Index of 2,600 additional verbs keyed to listing of 501 French verbs 733

To St. Sophia Greek Orthodox Church
of Albany, New York, our parish

and

to the eternal memory of our beloved
YOLANDA FENYO KENDRIS
who is always by our side

With love

About the Authors

Dr. Christopher Kendris has worked as interpreter and translator of French for the U.S. State Department at the American Embassy in Paris. He earned his B.S. and M.S. degrees at Columbia University in the City of New York, where he held a New York State Scholarship, and his M.A. and Ph.D. degrees at Northwestern University in Evanston, Illinois, where he held a Teaching Assistantship and Tutorial Fellowship during four years. He also earned two diplomas with *Mention très Honorable* at the Université de Paris (en Sorbonne), Faculté des Lettres, École Supérieure de Préparation et de Perfectionnement des Professeurs de Français à l'Étranger, and at the Institut de Phonétique, Paris. In 1986 he was one of 95 teachers in the United States awarded a Rockefeller Foundation Fellowship for Teachers of Foreign Languages in American High Schools. He has taught French at the College of the University of Chicago as visiting summer lecturer, at Colby College, Duke University, Rutgers—The State University of New Jersey, and the State University of New York at Albany. He was Chairman of the Department of Foreign Languages and Supervisor of 16 foreign language teachers on the secondary level at Farmingdale High School, Farmingdale, New York, where he was also a teacher of all levels of French and Spanish, and prepared students for the New York State French and Spanish Regents, SAT exams, and AP tests. Dr. Kendris is the author of 22 school and college books, workbooks, and other language guides of French and Spanish. He is listed in *Contemporary Authors* and the *Directory of American Scholars*.

Dr. Theodore Kendris earned his B.A. degree in Modern Languages at Union College, Schenectady, New York, where he received the Thomas J. Judson Memorial Award for modern language study. He went on to earn his M.A. degree in French Language and Literature at Northwestern University, Evanston, Illinois, where he held a Teaching Assistantship. He earned his Ph.D. degree in French Literature at Université Laval in Quebec City, where he studied the Middle Ages and Renaissance. While at Université Laval he taught French writing skills as a *chargé de cours* in the French as a Second Language program and, in 1997, he was awarded a doctoral scholarship by the *Fondation de l'Université Laval*. He has also taught in the Department of English and Foreign Languages at the University of St. Francis in Joliet, Illinois, as well as the Hazleton Campus of Penn State University.

Preface to the Sixth Edition

This new edition of ***501 French Verbs*** has been completely rearranged to help you find the information that you need more quickly. We have also updated the verb lists to account for the ever-changing technological advances in our modern world. We have therefore added to both the French-English and English-French lists of verbs conjugated like model verbs. The model verbs themselves have been revised and include extra material for certain Essential Verbs. These are verbs that we believe will be helpful to students because they represent an important conjugation group or because they are useful in many everyday situations and idiomatic expressions. If you have used ***501 French Verbs*** in the past, you will notice that you can now find all the learning material before the list of 501 fully conjugated verbs. We have also placed the defective and impersonal verbs in a separate section immediately following the 501 fully conjugated verbs. The numerous verb lists can be found in the back part of the book with handy tabs to help you save time as you study. Don't forget to take advantage of the verb drills and tests with answers explained, beginning on page 50. You will need a lot of practice in French verb forms and tenses in a variety of tests to determine your strengths and weaknesses and to make some things clearer in your mind. You should also review the section on definitions of basic grammatical terms. Many students who study a foreign language are at a disadvantage because they do not understand certain grammatical terms. If you understand these terms you will be able to communicate better in French.

If you can't remember the French verb you need to use, don't forget to refer to the English-French verb index, which starts on page 705. We have made it more comprehensive so that you will rarely need to look elsewhere for what you need.

We are very pleased to offer our new ***501 French Verb*** CD-ROM activities, which you will find in the back of the book. Have some fun while you practice conjugating French verbs!

We hope that you will make full use of all the features of this new edition and that you will enjoy your exploration of French language and culture.

C.K. and T.K.

Introduction

This self-teaching book of 501 commonly used French verbs for students and travelers provides fingertip access to correct verb forms.

Verb conjugations are usually found scattered in French grammar books and they are difficult to find quickly when needed. Verbs have always been a major problem for students no matter what system or approach the teacher uses. You will master French verb forms if you study this book a few minutes every day.

This book has been compiled in order to help make your work easier and at the same time to teach you French verb forms systematically. It is a useful book because it provides a quick and easy way to find the full conjugation of many French verbs.

The 501 verbs included here are arranged alphabetically by infinitive at the top of each page. The book contains many common verbs of high frequency, both reflexive and non-reflexive, which you need to know. It also contains many other frequently used verbs which are irregular in some way. Beginning on page 733 you can find an additional 2,600 French verbs that are conjugated in the same way as model verbs among the 501. If the verb you have in mind is not given among the 501, consult this list.

The subject pronouns have been omitted from the conjugations in order to emphasize the verb forms. You can find the subject pronouns on page 103. Turn to that page now and become acquainted with them.

The first thing to do when you use this book is to become familiar with it from cover to cover—in particular, the front and back pages where you will find valuable and useful information to make your work easier and more enjoyable. Take a minute right now and familiarize yourself with the following features:

(a) On page 6 there is an explanation of which verbs are conjugated with *avoir* or *être* to form a compound tense. Study page 6 and refer to it frequently until you master those verbs.

(b) On page 3 you will find how to form a present participle regularly in French and we give you examples. We also give you the common irregular present participles.

(c) On page 3 we do the same for past participles, with examples. The present and past participles of each verb are at the top of the page where verb forms are given for a particular verb.

(d) On page 7 you will find the principal parts of some important verbs, which, in French, are called *Les Temps primitifs.* This is useful because if you know these you can easily form all the tenses and moods from them.

(e) On pages 4 and 5 there are two tables showing the derivation of tenses of a typical verb conjugated with *avoir* and another conjugated with *être*. These are presented as in a picture so that you can see what tenses are derived from the principal parts.

(f) On pages 8 and 9 a sample English verb conjugation gives you an idea of the way a verb is expressed in the English tenses. Many people do not know one tense from another because they have never learned the use of verb tenses in a systematic and organized way—not even in English! How can you know, for example, that you need the conditional form of a verb in French when you want to say "*I would go* to the movies if . . ." or the pluperfect tense in French if you want to say "*I had gone* . . ."? The sample English verb conjugation with the names of the tenses and their numerical ranking will help you to distinguish one tense from another so that you will know what tense you need to express a verb in French.

(g) Beginning on page 10 is a summary of meanings and uses of French verb tenses and moods as related to English verb tenses and moods. That section is very important and useful because the seven simple tenses are separated from the seven compound tenses. The name of each tense is given in French and English starting with the present indicative, which is called tense No. 1, because it is the tense most frequently used. A number is assigned to each tense name so that you can fix each one in your mind and associate the tense names and numbers in their logical order. There is a brief explanation of what each tense is and when you use it, and there are examples using verbs in sentences in French and English.

(h) On page 21 is a summary of all the fourteen tenses in French with English equivalents, which have been divided into the seven simple tenses and the seven compound tenses. After referring to that summary frequently, you will soon know that tense No. 1 is the present indicative, tense No. 2 is the imperfect indicative, and so on.

(i) On page 22 you are shown how to form the seven simple tenses for regular verbs and here, again, the same number has been assigned to each tense name. We also explain how each compound tense is based on each simple tense in the table on page 23 and on page 24. Try to see these two divisions as two frames, two pictures, with the seven simple tenses in one frame and the seven compound tenses in another frame. Place them side by side in your mind, and you will see how tense No. 8 is related to tense No. 1, tense No. 9 to tense No. 2, and so on. If you study the numerical arrangement of each of the seven simple tenses and associate the tense number with the tense name, you will find it very easy to learn the names of the seven compound tenses, how they rank numerically according to use, how they are formed, and when they are used. Spend at least ten minutes every day studying these preliminary pages to help you understand better the fourteen tenses in French.

Finally, in the back pages of this book there are useful indexes, an additional 2,600 French verbs that are conjugated like model verbs among the 501, as well as verbs that require certain prepositions. If you refer to these each time you look up verb tense forms for a particular verb, you will increase your knowledge of French vocabulary by leaps and bounds.

Note that each verb that is listed in the Alphabetical Listing of 501 French Verbs is followed by a number in parentheses. This number is the verb number for the purpose of easy cross-referencing in this book.

We sincerely hope that this book will be of some help to you in learning and using French verbs.

Christopher Kendris and Theodore Kendris

Present and past participles in French—Formation

Formation of the present participle in French

The present participle is regularly formed in the following way. Take the **nous** form of the present indicative of the verb you have in mind, drop the ending **-ons** and add **-ant**. That ending is the equivalent to *-ing* in English. Examples:

chantons, chantant	**vendons, vendant**	**allons, allant**
finissons, finissant	**mangeons, mangeant**	**travaillons, travaillant**

Common irregular present participles

The three common irregular present participles are: **ayant** from **avoir**; **étant** from **être**; **sachant** from **savoir**.

Formation of the past participle in French

The past participle is regularly formed from the infinitive:

-er ending verbs, drop the **-er** and add **é**: **donner, donné**
-ir ending verbs, drop the **-ir** and add **i**: **finir, fini**
-re ending verbs, drop the **-re** and add **u**: **vendre, vendu**

Common irregular past participles

INFINITIVE	PAST PARTICIPLE	INFINITIVE	PAST PARTICIPLE
apprendre	**appris**	naître	**né**
asseoir	**assis**	offrir	**offert**
avoir	**eu**	ouvrir	**ouvert**
boire	**bu**	paraître	**paru**
comprendre	**compris**	permettre	**permis**
conduire	**conduit**	plaire	**plu**
connaître	**connu**	pleuvoir	**plu**
construire	**construit**	pouvoir	**pu**
courir	**couru**	prendre	**pris**
couvrir	**couvert**	promettre	**promis**
craindre	**craint**	recevoir	**reçu**
croire	**cru**	revenir	**revenu**
devenir	**devenu**	rire	**ri**
devoir	**dû, due**	savoir	**su**
dire	**dit**	suivre	**suivi**
écrire	**écrit**	taire	**tu**
être	**été**	tenir	**tenu**
faire	**fait**	valoir	**valu**
falloir	**fallu**	venir	**venu**
lire	**lu**	vivre	**vécu**
mettre	**mis**	voir	**vu**
mourir	**mort**	vouloir	**voulu**

Derivation of tenses: Verbs conjugated with *avoir* and *être*

Verbs Conjugated with *avoir*

INFINITIF
donner

PARTICIPE PRÉSENT
donnant

PARTICIPE PASSÉ
donné

PRÉSENT DE L'INDICATIF
je donne

PASSÉ SIMPLE
je donnai

FUTUR
donnerai
donneras
donnera
donnerons
donnerez
donneront

CONDITIONNEL
donnerais
donnerais
donnerait
donnerions
donneriez
donneraient

IMPARFAIT DE L'INDICATIF
donnais
donnais
donnait
donnions
donniez
donnaient

PASSÉ COMPOSÉ
ai donné
as donné
a donné
avons donné
avez donné
ont donné

PLUS-QUE-PARFAIT DE L'INDICATIF
avais donné
avais donné
avait donné
avions donné
aviez donné
avaient donné

PASSÉ ANTÉRIEUR
eus donné
eus donné
eut donné
eûmes donné
eûtes donné
eurent donné

PRÉSENT DE L'INDICATIF
donne
donnes
donne
donnons
donnez
donnent

IMPÉRATIF
donne
donnons
donnez

PRÉSENT DU SUBJONCTIF
donne
donnes
donne
donnions
donniez
donnent

PASSÉ SIMPLE
donnai
donnas
donna
donnâmes
donnâtes
donnèrent

IMPARFAIT DU SUBJONCTIF
donnasse
donnasses
donnât
donnassions
donnassiez
donnassent

FUTUR ANTÉRIEUR
aurai donné
auras donné
aura donné
aurons donné
aurez donné
auront donné

CONDITIONNEL PASSÉ
aurais donné
aurais donné
aurait donné
aurions donné
auriez donné
auraient donné

PASSÉ DU SUBJONCTIF
aie donné
aies donné
ait donné
ayons donné
ayez donné
aient donné

PLUS-QUE-PARFAIT DU SUBJONCTIF
eusse donné
eusses donné
eût donné
eussions donné
eussiez donné
eussent donné

INFINITIF
arriver

PARTICIPE PRÉSENT
arrivant

PARTICIPE PASSÉ
arrivé

PRÉSENT DE L'INDICATIF
j'arrive

PASSÉ SIMPLE
j'arrivai

FUTUR
arriverai
arriveras
arrivera
arriverons
arriverez
arriveront

CONDITIONNEL
arriverais
arriverais
arriverait
arriverions
arriveriez
arriveraient

IMPARFAIT DE L'INDICATIF
arrivais
arrivais
arrivait
arrivions
arriviez
arrivaient

PASSÉ COMPOSÉ
suis arrivé(e)
es arrivé(e)
est arrivé(e)
sommes arrivé(e)s
êtes arrivé(e)(s)
sont arrivé(e)s

PLUS-QUE-PARFAIT DE L'INDICATIF
étais arrivé(e)
étais arrivé(e)
était arrivé(e)
étions arrivé(e)s
étiez arrivé(e)(s)
étaient arrivé(e)s

PASSÉ ANTÉRIEUR
fus arrivé(e)
fus arrivé(e)
fut arrivé(e)
fûmes arrivé(e)s
fûtes arrivé(e)(s)
furent arrivé(e)s

PRÉSENT DE L'INDICATIF
arrive
arrives
arrive
arrivons
arrivez
arrivent

IMPÉRATIF
arrive
arrivons
arrivez

PRÉSENT DU SUBJONCTIF
arrive
arrives
arrive
arrivions
arriviez
arrivent

PASSÉ SIMPLE
arrivai
arrivas
arriva
arrivâmes
arrivâtes
arrivèrent

IMPARFAIT DU SUBJONCTIF
arrivasse
arrivasses
arrivât
arrivassions
arrivassiez
arrivassent

FUTUR ANTÉRIEUR
serai arrivé(e)
seras arrivé(e)
sera arrivé(e)
serons arrivé(e)s
serez arrivé(e)(s)
seront arrivé(e)s

CONDITIONNEL PASSÉ
serais arrivé(e)
serais arrivé(e)
serait arrivé(e)
serions arrivé(e)s
seriez arrivé(e)(s)
seraient arrivé(e)s

PASSÉ DU SUBJONCTIF
sois arrivé(e)
sois arrivé(e)
soit arrivé(e)
soyons arrivé(e)s
soyez arrivé(e)(s)
soient arrivé(e)s

PLUS-QUE-PARFAIT DU SUBJONCTIF
fusse arrivé(e)
fusses arrivé(e)
fût arrivé(e)
fussions arrivé(e)s
fussiez arrivé(e)(s)
fussent arrivé(e)s

Verbs conjugated with *avoir* or *être* to form a compound tense

(a) Generally speaking, a French verb is conjugated with *avoir* to form a compound tense.
(b) All reflexive verbs, for example, *se laver*, are conjugated with *être*.
(c) The following is a list of common non-reflexive verbs that are conjugated with *être*. The verbs marked with asterisks (*) are conjugated with *avoir* when used with a direct object.

1. **aller** to go
   Elle est allée au cinéma.
2. **arriver** to arrive
   Elle est arrivée à une heure.
3. ***descendre** to go down, come down
   Elle est descendue vite. *She came down quickly.*
   BUT: ***Elle a descendu la valise.** *She brought down the suitcase.*
4. **devenir** to become
   Elle est devenue docteur.
5. **entrer** to enter, go in, come in
   Elle est entrée dans l'école. *She entered the school.*
   BUT: ***Elle a entré la clé dans la serrure.** *She put the key in the lock.*
6. ***monter** to go up, come up
   Elle est montée vite. *She went up quickly.*
   BUT: ***Elle a monté l'escalier.** *She went up the stairs.*
7. **mourir** to die
   Elle est morte hier.
8. **naître** to be born
   Elle est née hier.
9. **partir** to leave
   Elle est partie vite.
10. ***passer** to go by, to pass by
    Elle est passée chez moi. *She came by my house.*
    BUT: ***Elle m'a passé le sel.** *She passed me the salt.*
    AND: ***Elle a passé un examen.** *She took an exam.*
11. ***rentrer** to go in again, to return (home)
    Elle est rentrée tôt. *She returned home early.*
    BUT: ***Elle a rentré le chat dans la maison.** *She brought (took) the cat into the house.*
12. **rester** to remain, to stay
    Elle est restée chez elle.
13. **retourner** to return, to go back
    Elle est retournée à sa place.
14. **revenir** to come back
    Elle est revenue hier.
15. ***sortir** to go out
    Elle est sortie hier soir. *She went out last night.*
    BUT: ***Elle a sorti son mouchoir.** *She took out her handkerchief.*
16. **tomber** to fall
    Elle est tombée.
17. **venir** to come
    Elle est venue ce matin.

Principal parts of some important verbs

(*Les Temps primitifs de quelques verbes importants*)

The principal parts of a verb are very important to know because from them you can easily form all the tenses. See the following pages where two tables are given, one showing the derivation of tenses of a verb conjugated with **avoir** and the other with **être**. Note that the headings at the top of each column are the same as the following headings.

INFINITIF	PARTICIPE PRÉSENT	PARTICIPE PASSÉ	PRÉSENT DE L'INDICATIF	PASSÉ SIMPLE
aller	allant	allé	je vais	j'allai
avoir	ayant	eu	j'ai	j'eus
battre	battant	battu	je bats	je battis
boire	buvant	bu	je bois	je bus
craindre	craignant	craint	je crains	je craignis
croire	croyant	cru	je crois	je crus
devoir	devant	dû, due	je dois	je dus
dire	disant	dit	je dis	je dis
écrire	écrivant	écrit	j'écris	j'écrivis
être	étant	été	je suis	je fus
faire	faisant	fait	je fais	je fis
lire	lisant	lu	je lis	je lus
mettre	mettant	mis	je mets	je mis
mourir	mourant	mort	je meurs	je mourus
naître	naissant	né	je nais	je naquis
ouvrir	ouvrant	ouvert	j'ouvre	j'ouvris
porter	portant	porté	je porte	je portai
pouvoir	pouvant	pu	je peux *or* je puis	je pus
prendre	prenant	pris	je prends	je pris
recevoir	recevant	reçu	je reçois	je reçus
savoir	sachant	su	je sais	je sus
venir	venant	venu	je viens	je vins
vivre	vivant	vécu	je vis	je vécus
voir	voyant	vu	je vois	je vis
voler	volant	volé	je vole	je volai

Tip

In the Present indicative (*Présent de l'indicatif*) and the simple past (*Passé simple*) columns above, only the 1st person singular (**je**) forms are given just to get you started. If you cannot recall the remaining verb forms in the *Présent de l'indicatif* and the *Passé simple* of the verbs listed above in the first column under Infinitive (*Infinitif*), please practice them by looking them up in this book, where the infinitive form of the verb is listed alphabetically at the top of each page from verb 1 to 501. When you find them, say them aloud at the same time you practice writing them in French. This is a very useful exercise to do.

Sample English verb conjugation

INFINITIVE **to go—aller**
PRESENT PARTICIPLE **going** *PAST PARTICIPLE* **gone**

Tense no.	The seven simple tenses
1 *Present indicative*	I go, you go, he (she, it) goes; we go, you go, they go
	or: I do go, you do go, he (she, it) does go; we do go, you do go, they do go
	or: I am going, you are going, he (she, it) is going; we are going, you are going, they are going
2 *Imperfect indicative*	I was going, you were going, he (she, it) was going; we were going, you were going, they were going
	or: I went, you went, he (she, it) went; we went, you went, they went
	or: I used to go, you used to go, he (she, it) used to go; we used to go, you used to go, they used to go
3 *Passé simple*	I went, you went, he (she, it) went; we went, you went, they went
	or: I did go, you did go, he (she, it) did go; we did go, you did go, they did go
4 *Future*	I shall (will) go, you will go, he (she, it) will go; we shall (will) go, you will go, they will go
5 *Conditional*	I would go, you would go, he (she, it) would go; we would go, you would go, they would go
6 *Present subjunctive*	that I may go, that you may go, that he (she, it) may go; that we may go, that you may go, that they may go
7 *Imperfect subjunctive*	that I might go, that you might go, that he (she, it) might go; that we might go, that you might go, that they might go

INFINITIVE **to go—aller**
PRESENT PARTICIPLE **going** *PAST PARTICIPLE* **gone**

Tense no.		The seven compound tenses
8	*Passé composé*	I have gone, you have gone, he (she, it) has gone; we have gone, you have gone, they have gone
		or: I went, you went, he (she, it) went; we went, you went, they went
		or: I did go, you did go, he (she, it) did go; we did go, you did go, they did go
9	*Pluperfect or Past perfect indicative*	I had gone, you had gone, he (she, it) had gone; we had gone, you had gone, they had gone
10	*Past anterior*	I had gone, you had gone, he (she, it) had gone; we had gone, you had gone, they had gone
11	*Future perfect or Future anterior*	I shall (will) have gone, you will have gone, he (she, it) will have gone; we shall (will) have gone, you will have gone, they will have gone
12	*Conditional perfect*	I would have gone, you would have gone, he (she, it) would have gone; we would have gone, you would have gone, they would have gone
13	*Past subjunctive*	that I may have gone, that you may have gone, that he (she, it) may have gone; that we may have gone, that you may have gone, that they may have gone
14	*Pluperfect or Past perfect subjunctive*	that I might have gone, that you might have gone, that he (she, it) might have gone; that we might have gone, that you might have gone, that they might have gone
	Imperative (Command)	Go! (sing.) Let's go! Go! (pl.)

A summary of French verb tenses and moods

A verb is where the action is! A verb is a word that expresses an action (like *go*, *eat*, *write*) or a state of being (like *think*, *believe*, *be*). Tense means time. French and English verb tenses are divided into three main groups of time: past, present, and future. A verb tense shows if an action or state of being took place, is taking place, or will take place.

French and English verbs are also used in three moods (or modes). Mood has to do with the *way* a person regards an action or a state. For example, a person may merely make a statement or ask a question—this is the Indicative Mood, which we use most of the time in French and English. A person may say that he *would do* something if something else were possible or that he *would have done* something if something else had been possible—this is the Conditional Tense. A person may use a verb *in such a way* to indicate a wish, a fear, a regret, a supposition, or something of this sort—this is the Subjunctive Mood. The Subjunctive Mood is used in French much more than in English. A person may command that something be done—this is the Imperative Mood. (There is also the Infinitive Mood, but we are not concerned with that here.)

There are six tenses in English: Present, Past, Future, Present Perfect, Past Perfect, and Future Perfect. The first three are simple tenses. The other three are compound tenses and are based on the simple tenses. In French, however, there are fourteen tenses, seven of which are simple and seven of which are compound.

In the pages that follow, the tenses and moods are given in French and the equivalent name or names in English are given in parenthesis. Each tense name has been numbered for easy reference and recognition. Although some of the names given in English are not considered to be tenses (there are only six), they are given for the purpose of identification as they are related to the French names. The comparison includes only the essential points you need to know about the meanings and uses of French verb tenses and moods as related to English usage.

The examples serve to illustrate their meanings and uses. See page 22 for the formation of the seven simple tenses for regular verbs.

THE SEVEN SIMPLE TENSES

Tense No. 1 Le Présent de l'indicatif (Present indicative)

This tense is used most of the time in French and English. It indicates:

(a) An action or a state of being at the present time.

EXAMPLES:

1. Je **vais** à l'école maintenant. I *am going* to school now.
2. Je **pense**; donc, je **suis**. I *think*; therefore, I *am*.

(b) Habitual action.
EXAMPLE:
1. Je **vais** à la bibliothéque tous les jours.
2. I *go* to the library every day, or I *do go* to the library every day.

(c) A general truth, something which is permanently true.
EXAMPLES:
1. Deux et deux **font** quatre. Two and two *are* four.
2. Voir c'**est** croire. Seeing *is* believing.

(d) Vividness when talking or writing about past events. This is called the *historical present*.
EXAMPLE:
Marie-Antoinette **est** condamnée à mort. Elle **monte** dans la charrette et **est** en route pour la guillotine.
Marie-Antoinette *is* condemned to die. She *gets* into the cart and *is* on her way to the guillotine.

(e) A near future.
EXAMPLE:
Il **arrive** demain. He *arrives* tomorrow.

(f) An action or state of being that occurred in the past and *continues up to the present*. In English, this tense is the Present Perfect, which is formed with the present tense of *to have* (*have* or *has*) plus the past participle of the verb you are using.
EXAMPLES:
1. Je **suis** ici depuis dix minutes.
   I *have been* here for ten minutes. (I am still here at present)
2. Elle **est** malade depuis trois jours.
   She *has been* sick for three days. (She is still sick at present)
3. J'**attends** l'autobus depuis dix minutes.
   I *have been waiting* for the bus for ten minutes.

NOTE: In this last example the formation of the English verb tense is slightly different from the other two examples in English. The present participle (*waiting*) is used instead of the past participle (*waited*).
NOTE ALSO: For the formation of this tense for regular verbs see page 22.

Tense No. 2 L'Imparfait de l'indicatif (Imperfect indicative)

This is a past tense. It is used to indicate:

(a) An action that was going on in the past at the same time as another action.
EXAMPLE:
Il **lisait** pendant que j'**écrivais**. He *was reading* while I *was writing*.

(b) An action that was going on in the past when another action occurred.
EXAMPLE:
Il **lisait** quand je suis entré. He *was reading* when I came in.

(c) An action that a person did habitually in the past.
EXAMPLE:
Nous **allions** à la plage tous les jours. We *used to go* to the beach every day.
OR:
We *would go* to the beach every day.

(d) A description of a mental or physical condition in the past.
EXAMPLES :

(mental condition)	Il **était** triste quand je l'ai vu. He *was* sad when I saw him.
(physical condition)	Quand ma mère **était** jeune, elle **était** belle. When my mother *was* young, she *was* beautiful.

(e) An action or state of being that occurred in the past and *lasted for a certain length of time* prior to another past action. In English, it is usually translated as a pluperfect tense and is formed with *had been* plus the present participle of the verb you are using. It is like the special use of the **Présent de l'indicatif** described in the above section (Tense No. 1) in paragraph (f), except that the action or state of being no longer exists at present.
EXAMPLE:
J'**attendais** l'autobus depuis dix minutes quand il est arrivé.
I *had been waiting* for the bus for ten minutes when it arrived.
NOTE: For the formation of this tense for regular verbs see page 22.

Tense No. 3 Le Passé simple
(Past definite or Simple past)

This past tense is not ordinarily used in conversational French or in informal writing. It is a literary tense. It is used in formal writing, such as history and literature. You should be able merely to recognize this tense when you see it in your French readings. It should be noted that French writers use the **Passé simple** less and less these days. The **Passé composé** (Tense No. 8) is taking its place in literature, except for **avoir** and **être**, which you must know in this tense.

EXAMPLES:
(a) Il **alla** en Afrique. He *went* to Africa.
(b) Il **voyagea** en Amérique. He *traveled* to America.
(c) Elle **fut** heureuse. She *was* happy.
(d) Elle **eut** un grand bonheur. She *had* great happiness.

NOTE: For the formation of this tense for regular verbs see page 22.

Tense No. 4 Le Futur
(Future)

In French and English this tense is used to express an action or a state of being which will take place at some time in the future.

EXAMPLES:
(a) J'**irai** en France l'été prochain.
I *shall go* to France next summer.
OR:
I *will go* to France next summer.

(c) Je **partirai** dès qu'il arrivera.
I *shall leave* as soon as he arrives

(d) Je te **dirai** tout quand tu seras ici.
I *shall tell* you all when you are here.

(b) J'y **penserai**.
I *shall think* about it.
OR:
I *will think* about it.

If the action of the verb you are using is not past or present and if future time is implied, the future tense is used when the clause begins with any of the following conjunctions: **aussitôt que** (as soon as), **dès que** (as soon as), **quand** (when), **lorsque** (when), and **tant que** (as long as).

NOTE: For the formation of this tense for regular verbs see page 22.

Another way to express the future is **le Futur proche** (the Near Future). As one may guess, the **Futur proche** is used when talking about something that will take place in the near future. In French, the near future is formed by using **aller** with the infinitive of the verb that you want to use. In English you use *to go* with the infinitive of the verb that you want to use.

Demain, je **vais acheter** un ordinateur.
Tomorrow I *am going to buy* a computer.
Nous **allons manger** en ville.
We are *going to eat* downtown.

Tense No. 5 Le Conditionnel présent (Conditional)

The Conditional is used in French and English to express:

(a) An action that you would do if something else were possible.
EXAMPLE:
Je **ferais** le travail si j'avais le temps.
I *would do* the work if I had the time.

(b) A conditional desire. This is the Conditional of courtesy in French.
EXAMPLES:
J'**aimerais** du thé. I *would like* some tea.
Je **voudrais** du café. I *would like* some coffee.

(c) An obligation or duty.
EXAMPLE:
Je **devrais** étudier pour l'examen. I *should* study for the examination.
OR: I *ought* to study for the examination.

NOTE (1): The French verb **devoir** plus the infinitive is used to express the idea of *should* when you mean *ought to*.

NOTE (2): When the Conditional of the verb **pouvoir** is used in French, it is translated into English as *could* or *would be able*.
EXAMPLE:
Je **pourrais** venir après le dîner. I *could come* after dinner.
OR: I *would be able* to come after dinner.

NOTE: For the formation of this tense for regular verbs see page 22.

Tense No. 6 Le Présent du subjonctif (Present subjunctive)

The Subjunctive Mood is used in French much more than in English. It is disappearing in English, except for the following major uses:

(a) The Subjunctive is used in French and English to express a command.
EXAMPLE:
Soyez à l'heure! *Be* on time!
NOTE: In English, the form in the Subjunctive applies mainly to the verb *to be*. Also, note that all verbs in French are not in the Subjunctive when expressing a command. See **l'Impératif** on pages 20–21.

(b) The Subjunctive is commonly used in English to express a condition contrary to fact.
EXAMPLE:
If I *were* you, I would not do it.
NOTE: In French the Subjunctive is not used in this instance. Instead, the **Imparfait de l'indicatif** is used if what precedes is *si* (*if*). Same example in French: Si j'**étais** vous, je ne le ferais pas.

(c) The Present subjunctive is used in French and English after a verb that expresses some kind of insistence, preference, or suggestion.
EXAMPLES:
1. Je préfère qu'il **fasse** le travail maintenant. I prefer that *he do* the work now.
2. J'exige qu'il **soit** puni. I demand that *he be* punished.

(d) The Subjunctive is used in French after a verb that expresses doubt, fear, joy, sorrow, or some other emotion. Notice in the following examples that the Subjunctive is not used in English but it is in French.
EXAMPLES:
1. Je doute qu'il **vienne**.
   I doubt that he *is coming*. OR: I doubt that he *will come*.
2. Je suis heureux qu'il **vienne**.
   I'm happy that he *is coming*.
3. Je regrette qu'il **soit** malade.
   I'm sorry that he *is* sick.
4. J'ai peur qu'il ne **soit** malade.
   I'm afraid that he *is* sick.

NOTE: After a verb that expresses fear (used in the affirmative), you should add *ne* before the verb that is in the subjunctive. If the statement is negative, do not add *ne*.

(e) The Present subjunctive is used in French after certain conjunctions. Notice, however, that the Subjunctive is not always used in English.
EXAMPLES:
1. Je resterai **jusqu'à ce qu'il vienne**.
   I shall stay until he *comes*.
2. **Quoiqu'elle soit** belle, il ne l'aime pas.
   Although she *is* beautiful, he does not love her.
3. Je l'explique **pour qu'elle comprenne**.
   I'm explaining it *so that she may understand*.
4. Je partirai **à moins qu'il ne vienne**.
   I shall leave unless he *comes*.

NOTE: After a verb that expresses the possibility of an obstacle (or of a precaution), you may add *ne* before the verb that is in the subjunctive.

(f) The Present subjunctive is used in French after certain impersonal expressions that show a need, doubt, possibility or impossibility. Notice, however, that the Subjunctive is not always used in English in the following examples:

1. Il est urgent qu'il **vienne**.
   It is urgent that he *come*.
2. Il vaut mieux qu'il **vienne**.
   It is better that he *come*.
3. Il est possible qu'il **vienne**.
   It is possible that he *will come*.
4. Il est douteux qu'il **vienne**.
   It is doubtful that he *will come*.
5. Il est nécessaire qu'il **vienne**.
   It is necessary that he *come*. OR: He must come.
6. Il faut qu'il **vienne**.
   It is necessary that he *come*. OR: He must come.
7. Il est important que vous **fassiez** le travail.
   It is important that you *do* the work.
8. Il est indispensable qu'elle **fasse** le travail.
   It is required that she *do* the work.

NOTE: For the formation of this tense for regular verbs see page 23.
See also the note about the Subjunctive which begins on page 26.

Tense No. 7 L'Imparfait du subjonctif (Imperfect subjunctive)

L'Imparfait du subjonctif is used for the same reasons as the **Présent du subjonctif**—that is, after certain verbs, conjunctions, and impersonal expressions which were used in examples above under the section, **le Présent du subjonctif**. The main difference between these two is the time of the action. If present, use the **Présent du subjonctif** (Tense No. 6). If the action is related to the past, the **Imparfait du subjonctif** (this tense) is used, provided that the action was *not* completed. If the action was completed, the **Plus-que-parfait du subjonctif** is used. See below under the section, **Plus-que-parfait du subjonctif** (Tense No. 14).

Since the Subjunctive Mood is troublesome in French and English, you may be pleased to know that this tense is rarely used in English. It is used in French, however, but only in formal writing and in literature. For that reason, you should merely be familiar with it so you can recognize it when you see it in your French readings. In conversational French and in informal writing, **l'Imparfait du subjonctif** is avoided. Use, instead, the **Présent du subjonctif**.

Notice that the **Imparfait du subjonctif** is used in French in both of the following examples, but is used in English only in the second example (b):

EXAMPLES:

(a) Je voulais qu'il **vînt**. I wanted him to come.
(action not completed; he did not come while I wanted him to come)
NOTE: The Subjunctive of **venir** is used because the verb that precedes is one that requires the Subjunctive *after* it—in this example it is **vouloir**. In conversational French and informal writing, the **Imparfait du subjonctif** is avoided. Use, instead, the **Présent du subjonctif**: Je voulais qu'il **vienne**.

(b) Je le lui expliquais **pour qu'elle le comprît.**
I was explaining it to her *so that she might understand it.*
(action not completed; the understanding was not completed at the time of the explaining)

NOTE: The Subjunctive of **comprendre** is used because the conjunction that precedes is one that requires the Subjunctive *after* it—in this example it is **pour que**. In conversational French and informal writing, the **Imparfait du subjonctif** is avoided. Use, instead, the **Présent du subjonctif**: Je le lui expliquais pour qu'elle le **comprenne**.

NOTE: For the formation of this tense for regular verbs see page 23.
See also the note about the Subjunctive which begins on page 26.

THE SEVEN COMPOUND TENSES

Tense No. 8 Le Passé composé
(Past indefinite or Compound past)

The past tense is used in conversational French, correspondence, and other informal writing. The **Passé composé** is used more and more in literature these days and is taking the place of the **Passé simple** (Tense No. 3). It is a compound tense because it is formed with the **Présent de l'indicatif** (Tense No. 1) of *avoir* or *être* (depending on which of these two auxiliaries is required to form a compound tense) plus the past participle. See page 6 for the distinction made between verbs conjugated with *avoir* or *être*.

EXAMPLES:

1. Il **est allé** à l'école. He *went* to school.
2. Il **est allé** à l'école. He *did go* to school.
3. Il **est allé** à l'école. He *has gone* to school.
4. J'**ai mangé** dans ce restaurant beaucoup de fois.
   I *have eaten* in this restaurant many times.

NOTE: In examples 3 and 4 in English the verb is formed with the Present tense of *to have* (*have* or *has*) plus the past participle of the verb you are using. In English, this form is called the Present Perfect.

5. J'**ai parlé** au garçon. I *spoke* to the boy. OR: I *have spoken* to the boy.
   OR: I *did speak* to the boy.

Tense No. 9 Le Plus-que-parfait de l'indicatif
(Pluperfect or Past perfect indicative)

In French and English this tense is used to express an action which happened in the past *before* another past action. Since it is used in relation to another past action, the other past action is expressed in either the **Passé composé** (Tense No. 8) or the **Imparfait de l'indicatif** (Tense No. 2) in French. This tense is used in formal writing and literature as well as in conversational French and informal writing. The correct use of this tense is strictly observed in French. In English, however, too often we neglect to use it correctly. It is a compound tense because it is formed with the **Imparfait de l'indicatif** of *avoir* or *être* (depending on which of these two auxiliaries is required to form a compound tense) plus the past participle. See page 6 for the distinction made between verbs conjugated with *avoir* or *être*. In English, this tense is formed with the Past Tense of *to have* (*had*) plus the past participle of the verb you are using.

EXAMPLES:

(a) Je me suis rappelé que j'**avais oublié** de le lui dire.
I remembered that I *had forgotten* to tell him.

NOTE: It would be incorrect in English to say: I remembered that I *forgot* to tell him. The point here is that *first* I forgot; then, I remembered. Both actions are in the past. The action that occurred in the past *before* the other past action is in the Pluperfect. And in this example it is *I had forgotten* (**j'avais oublié**).

(b) J'**avais étudié** la leçon que le professeur a expliquée.
I *had studied* the lesson which the teacher explained.
NOTE: *First* I studied the lesson; then, the teacher explained it. Both actions are in the past. The action that occurred in the past *before* the other past action is in the Pluperfect. And in this example it is *I had studied* (**j'avais étudié**). If you say **J'ai étudié la leçon que le professeur avait expliquée**, you are saying that you *studied* the lesson which the teacher *had explained*. In other words, the teacher explained the lesson first and then you studied it.

(c) J'étais fatigué ce matin parce que je n'**avais** pas **dormi**.
I was tired this morning because I *had* not *slept*.

Tense No. 10 Le Passé antérieur (Past anterior)

This tense is similar to the **Plus-que-parfait de l'indicatif** (Tense No. 9). The main difference is that in French it is a literary tense; that is, it is used in formal writing, such as history and literature. More and more French writers today use the **Plus-que-parfait de l'indicatif** instead of this tense. Generally speaking, the **Passé antérieur** is to the **Plus-que-parfait** what the **Passé simple** is to the **Passé composé**. The **Passé antérieur** is a compound tense. In French, it is formed with the **Passé simple** of *avoir* or *être* (depending on which of these two auxiliaries is required to form a compound tense—see page 6) plus the past participle. In English, it is formed in the same way as the Pluperfect or Past Perfect. This tense is ordinarily introduced by conjunctions of time: **après que**, **aussitôt que**, **dès que**, **lorsque**, **quand**.

EXAMPLE:

Quand il **eut mangé** son dessert, il partit. When he *had eaten* his dessert, he left.

NOTE: In conversational French and informal writing, the **Plus-que-parfait de l'indicatif** is used instead: Quand il **avait mangé** son dessert, il est parti. The translation into English is the same.

Tense No. 11 Le Futur antérieur (Future perfect or Future anterior)

In French and English this tense is used to express an action which will happen in the future *before* another future action. Since it is used in relation to another future action, the other future action is expressed in the simple Future in French, but not always in the simple Future in English. In French, it is used in conversation and informal writing as well as in formal writing and in literature. It is a compound tense because it is formed with the **Futur** of *avoir* or *être* (depending on which of these two auxiliaries is required to form a compound tense—see page 6) plus the past participle of the verb you are using. In English, it is formed by using *shall have* or *will have* plus the past participle of the verb you are using.

EXAMPLES:

(a) Elle arrivera demain et j'**aurai fini** le travail.
She will arrive tomorrow and I *shall have finished* the work.

NOTE: First, I shall finish the work; then, she will arrive. The action that will occur in the future *before* the other future action is in the **Futur antérieur**.

(b) Quand elle arrivera demain, j'**aurai fini** le travail.
When she arrives tomorrow, I *shall have finished* the work.

NOTE: The idea of future time here is the same as in example (a) above. In English, the Present tense is used (*When she arrives . . .*) to express a near future. In French, the **Futur** is used (**Quand elle arrivera . . .**) because **quand** precedes and the action will take place in the future. Study Tense No. 4 on pages 12–13.

Tense No. 12 Le Conditionnel passé (Conditional perfect)

This is used in French and English to express an action that you *would have done* if something else had been possible; that is, you would have done something *on condition* that something else had been possible. It is a compound tense because it is formed with the **Conditionnel présent** of *avoir* or *être* plus the past participle of the verb you are using. In English, it is formed by using *would have* plus the past participle. Observe the difference between the following examples and the one given for the use of the **Conditionnel présent** which was explained and illustrated in Tense No. 5 above.

EXAMPLES:

(a) J'**aurais fait** le travail si j'avais étudié.
I *would have done* the work if I had studied.

(b) J'**aurais fait** le travail si j'avais eu le temps.
I *would have done* the work if I had had the time.

NOTE: Review the **Plus-que-parfait de l'indicatif** which was explained above in Tense No. 9 in order to understand the use of *if I had studied* (**si j'avais étudié**) and *if I had had the time* (**si j'avais eu le temps**).

NOTE FURTHER: The French verb **devoir** plus the infinitive is used to express the idea of *should* when you mean *ought to*. The past participle of **devoir** is **dû**. It is conjugated with **avoir**.

EXAMPLE:
J'aurais dû étudier.
I *should have* studied. OR: I *ought to have* studied.

Tense No. 13 Le Passé du subjonctif (Past or Perfect subjunctive)

This tense is used to express an action which took place in the past in relation to the present time. It is like the **Passé composé**, except that the auxiliary verb (*avoir* or *être*) is in the **Présent du subjonctif**. The Subjunctive is used (as was noted in the previous sections of verb tenses in the Subjunctive) because what precedes is a certain verb, a certain conjunction, or a certain impersonal expression. The **Passé du subjonctif** is also used in relation to a future time when another action will be completed. This tense is rarely used in English. In French, however, this tense is used in formal writing and in literature as well as in conversational French and informal writing. It is a compound tense because it is formed with the **Présent du subjonctif** of *avoir* or *être* as the auxiliary plus the past participle of the verb you are using.

EXAMPLES:

(a) A past action in relation to the present
Il est possible qu'elle **soit partie**.
It is possible that she *may have left*. OR: It is possible that she *has left*.
Je doute qu'il **ait fait** cela.
I doubt that he *did* that.

(b) An action that will take place in the future
J'insiste que vous **soyez rentré** avant dix heures.
I insist that you *be back* before ten o'clock.

See also the note about the Subjunctive which begins on page 26.

Tense No. 14 Le Plus-que-parfait du subjonctif (Pluperfect or Past perfect subjunctive)

This tense is used for the same reasons as the **Imparfait du subjonctif** (Tense No. 7)—that is, after certain verbs, conjunctions, and impersonal expressions which were used in examples previously under **le Présent du subjonctif**. The main difference between the **Imparfait du subjonctif** and this tense is the time of the action in the past. If the action was *not* completed, the **Imparfait du subjonctif** is used. If the action was completed, this tense is used. It is rarely used in English. In French, it is used only in formal writing and in literature. For that reason, you should merely be familiar with it so you can recognize it in your readings in French literature. In conversational French and in informal writing, this tense is avoided. Use, instead, the **Passé du subjonctif** (Tense No. 13).

This is a compound tense. It is formed by using the **Imparfait du subjonctif** of *avoir* or *être* plus the past participle. This tense is like the **Plus-que-parfait de l'indicatif**, except that the auxiliary verb (*avoir* or *être*) is in the **Imparfait du subjonctif**. Review the uses of the Subjunctive Mood in Tense No. 6.

EXAMPLES:

(a) Il était possible qu'elle **fût partie**.
It was possible that she *might have left*.

NOTE: Avoid this tense in conversational and informal French. Use, instead, **le Passé du subjonctif**:
Il était possible qu'elle **soit partie**.

(b) Je ne croyais pas qu'elle **eût dit** cela.
I did not believe that she *had said* that.

NOTE: Avoid this tense in conversational and informal French. Use, instead, **le Passé du subjonctif**:
Je ne croyais pas qu'elle **ait dit** cela.

(c) Je n'ai pas cru qu'elle **eût dit** cela.
I did not believe that she *had said* that.

NOTE: Avoid this tense in conversational and informal French. Use, instead, **le Passé du subjonctif**:
Je n'ai pas cru qu'elle **ait dit** cela.

(d) J'ai craint que vous ne **fussiez tombé**.
I was afraid that you *had fallen*.

NOTE: Avoid this tense in conversational and informal French. Use, instead, **le Passé du subjonctif**:
J'ai craint que vous ne **soyez tombé**.

NOTE: After a verb that expresses fear (used in the affirmative), you should add *ne* before the verb that is in the subjunctive. If the statement is negative, do not add *ne*.

See also the note about the Subjunctive which begins on page 26.

L'Impératif
(Imperative or Command)

The Imperative Mood is used in French and English to express a command or a request. It is also used to express an indirect request made in the third person, as in (e) and (f) below. In both languages it is formed by dropping the subject pronoun and using the present tense. Remember that you must drop the final *s* in the second person singular of an *-er* verb (**Tu danses—Danse!**) There are a few exceptions in both languages when the **Présent du subjonctif** is used.

EXAMPLES:

(a) **Sortez!** Get out!

(b) **Entrez!** Come in!

(c) **Buvons!** Let's drink!

(d) **Soyez** à l'heure! *Be* on time! (Subjunctive is used.)

(e) Dieu le **veuille!** May God *grant* it! or *God willing!* (Subjunctive is used.)

(f) Qu'ils **mangent du** gâteau! Let them *eat* cake! (Subjunctive is used.)

(g) **Asseyez-vous!** Sit down!

(h) **Levez-vous!** Get up!

(i) **Ne vous asseyez pas!** Don't sit down!

(j) **Ne vous levez pas!** Don't get up!

NOTE: The Imperative is not a tense. It is a mood.

NOTE FURTHER: If you use a reflexive verb in the Imperative, drop the subject pronoun but keep the reflexive pronoun. Example: **Lavez-vous!** Wash yourself! See also examples (g) through (j).

Summary of verb tenses and moods in French with English equivalents

	Les sept temps simples *The seven simple tenses*		**Les sept temps composés** *The seven compound tenses*
Tense No.	Tense Name	Tense No.	Tense Name
1	**Présent de l'indicatif** *Present indicative*	8	**Passé composé**
2	**Imparfait de l'indicatif** *Imperfect indicative*	9	**Plus-que-parfait de l'indicatif** *Pluperfect indicative*
3	**Passé simple** *Past definite or Simple past*	10	**Passé antérieur** *Past anterior*
4	**Futur** *Future*	11	**Futur antérieur** *Future perfect*
5	**Conditionnel** *Conditional*	12	**Conditionnel passé** *Conditional perfect*
6	**Présent du subjonctif** *Present subjunctive*	13	**Passé du subjonctif** *Past subjunctive*
7	**Imparfait du subjonctif** *Imperfect subjunctive*	14	**Plus-que-parfait du subjonctif** *Pluperfect subjunctive*

The imperative is not a tense; it is a mood.

ɔrmation of the tenses

In French there are seven simple tenses and seven compound tenses. A simple tense means that the verb form consists of one word. A compound tense is a verb form that consists of two words (the auxiliary verb and the past participle). The auxiliary verb is also called a helping verb and in French it is any of the seven simple tenses of **avoir** or **être**.

FORMATION OF THE SEVEN SIMPLE TENSES FOR REGULAR VERBS

Tense No. 1 **Présent de l'indicatif**
(Present indicative)

-er verbs: drop **-er** and add **e, es, e; ons, ez, ent**

-ir verbs: drop **-ir** and add **is, is, it; issons, issez, issent**

-re verbs: drop **-re** and add **s, s, -; ons, ez, ent**

Tense No. 2 **Imparfait de l'indicatif**
(Imperfect indicative)

For **-er, -ir, -re** verbs, take the "**nous**" form in the present indicative of the verb you have in mind, drop the ending **-ons** and add: **ais, ais, ait; ions, iez, aient**

Tense No. 3 **Passé simple**
(Past definite or Simple past)

For all **-er** verbs, drop **-er** and add **ai, as, a; âmes, âtes, èrent**
For **-ir** and **-re** verbs, drop the ending of the Infinitive and add **is, is, it; îmes, îtes, irent**

Tense No. 4 **Futur**
(Future)

Add the following endings to the whole infinitive, but for **-re** verbs drop **e** in **-re** before adding the future endings, which are: **ai, as, a; ons, ez, ont**. Note that these endings are based on the Present indicative of **avoir**.

Tense No. 5 **Conditionnel**
(Conditional)

Add the following endings to the whole infinitive, but for **-re** verbs drop **e** in **-re** before adding the conditional endings, which are: **ais, ais, ait; ions, iez, aient**. Note that these endings are the same as those for the Imperfect indicative (Tense No. 2).

Tense No. 6 **Présent du subjonctif** (Present subjunctive)

Drop **-ant** ending of the present participle of the verb you have in mind and add **e, es, e; ions, iez, ent**

Tense No. 7 **Imparfait du subjonctif** (Imperfect subjunctive)

There is a shortcut to finding the forms of this difficult tense. Go straight to the 3d person, singular, **Passé simple** tense of the verb you have in mind. If the ending is **-a**, as in **parla (parler)**, drop **-a** and add **-asse, -asses, -ât; -assions, -assiez, -assent**. If the ending is **-it**, as in **finit (finir)** or **vendit (vendre)**, drop **-it** and add **-isse, -isses, -ît; -issions, -issiez, -issent**. If you find the ending **-ut**, as in many irregular **-re** verbs **(lire/lut)**, drop **-ut** and add **-usse, -usses, -ût; -ussions, -ussiez, -ussent**. Note the accent mark (^) on **-ât, -ît**, and **-ût**.

NOTE:

(a) For the forms of irregular verbs, *e.g.*, **avoir, être, faire, aller**, and many others, turn to the page where the verb you have in mind is given in this book. All verbs are listed alphabetically at the top of each page.

(b) For the uses of the seven simple tenses, see pages 10–16.

(c) For the formation of the seven compound tenses and their uses, see pages 16–20 and the section below.

FORMATION OF THE SEVEN COMPOUND TENSES

An Easy Way to Form the Seven Compound Tenses in French

avoir or **être*** in the following simple tenses + PLUS the past participle of the verb you have in mind** = EQUALS the following compound tenses

1. **Présent de l'indicatif**
2. **Imparfait de l'indicatif**
3. **Passé simple**
4. **Futur**
5. **Conditionnel**
6. **Présent du subjonctif**
7. **Imparfait du subjonctif**

8. **Passé composé**
9. **Plus-que-parfait de l'indicatif**
10. **Passé antérieur**
11. **Futur antérieur**
12. **Conditionnel passé**
13. **Passé du subjonctif**
14. **Plus-que-parfait du subjonctif**

* To know if avoir or être is required, see page 6.
** To know how to form a past participle, see page 3.

Each compound tense is based on each simple tense. The fourteen tenses given on page 23 are arranged in a logical order, which is numerical.

Here is how you form each of the seven compound tenses:

Tense No. 8 is based on Tense No. 1 of **avoir** or **être**; in other words, you form the **Passé composé** by using the auxiliary **avoir** or **être** (whichever is appropriate) in the **Présent de l'indicatif** plus the past participle of the verb you have in mind. Examples: **j'ai parlé**; **je suis allé(e)**.

Tense No. 9 is based on Tense No. 2 of **avoir** or **être**; in other words, you form the **Plus-que-parfait de l'indicatif** by using the auxiliary **avoir** or **être** (whichever is appropriate) in the **Imparfait de l'indicatif** plus the past participle of the verb you have in mind. Examples: **j'avais parlé**; **j'étais allé(e)**.

Tense No. 10 is based on Tense No. 3 of **avoir** or **être**; in other words, you form the **Passé antérieur** by using the auxiliary **avoir** or **être** (whichever is appropriate) in the **Passé simple** plus the past participle of the verb you have in mind. Examples: **j'eus parlé**; **je fus allé(e)**.

Tense No. 11 is based on Tense No. 4 of **avoir** or **être**; in other words, you form the **Futur antérieur** by using the auxiliary **avoir** or **être** (whichever is appropriate) in the **Futur** plus the past participle of the verb you have in mind. Examples: **j'aurai parlé**; **je serai allé(e)**.

Tense No. 12 is based on Tense No. 5 of **avoir** or **être**; in other words, you form the **Conditionnel passé** by using the auxiliary **avoir** or **être** (whichever is appropriate) in the **Conditionnel** plus the past participle of the verb you have in mind. Examples: **j'aurais parlé**; **je serais allé(e)**.

Tense No. 13 is based on Tense No. 6 of **avoir** or **être**; in other words, you form the **Passé du subjonctif** by using the auxiliary **avoir** or **être** (whichever is appropriate) in the **Présent du subjonctif** plus the past participle of the verb you have in mind. Examples: **que j'aie parlé**; **que je sois allé(e)**. This tense is like the **Passé composé** (tense number 8), except that the auxiliary verb **avoir** or **être** is in the present subjunctive.

Tense No. 14 is based on Tense No. 7 of **avoir** or **être**; in other words, you form the **Plus-que-parfait du subjonctif** by using the auxiliary **avoir** or **être** (whichever is appropriate) in the **Imparfait du subjonctif** plus the past participle of the verb you have in mind. Examples: **que j'eusse parlé**; **que je fusse allé(e)**.

If you ever expect to know or even recognize the meaning of any of the seven compound tenses, or to know how to form them, you certainly have to know **avoir** and **être** in the seven simple tenses. If you do not, you cannot form the seven compound tenses—and they are the easiest to form. This is one perfect example to illustrate that learning French verb forms is a cumulative experience because in order to know the seven compound tenses, you must first know the forms of **avoir** and **être** in the seven simple tenses. They are verbs 62 and 211 in this book.

To know which verbs are conjugated with **avoir** or **être** to form the seven compound tenses, see page 6. To understand the uses of the seven simple tenses, see pages 10–16. To understand the uses of the seven compound tenses, see pages 16–20. To know the translation of all fourteen tenses into English, see pages 8–9.

A Note about the *Passé surcomposé* verb tense

There is another verb tense in French but it is rarely used. It is called ***le Passé surcomposé***. It gets its name from the fact that the auxiliary (helping) verb is already stated in a ***Passé composé*** form. In other words, it is "extra" passé composé, just as **surchauffé** means *overheated* or **surnatural** means *supernatural*. The ***Surcomposé*** contains two auxiliary verbs and it is used in the subordinate clause when the verb of the main clause is in a compound tense. Examples: **j'ai eu** (*I have had*, or *I had*); **j'ai été** (*I have been*, or *I was*). To change the compound form into a ***Surcomposé***, the past participle of the verb you have in mind is stated with the double helping verb. Examples: **Mon ami est arrivé quand j'ai eu fini la leçon** / *My friend arrived when I (have had) finished the lesson*. The verb form in the subordinate clause with a double helping verb (**j'ai eu fini**) is what makes the form ***Surcomposé***. In English, some people call it *double* or *super compound*. It has also been used in other compound tenses with **avoir** or **être** as the helping verb. Nowadays, one hardly ever hears this unusual verb form, but it's worth being aware of in case you come across it in your readings in French literature.

A summary of sequence of verb tenses—*Si* clauses

WHEN THE VERB IN THE SI CLAUSE IS:	THE VERB IN THE MAIN OR RESULT CLAUSE IS:
(a) present indicative	present indicative, or future, or imperative
(b) imperfect indicative	conditional
(c) pluperfect indicative	conditional perfect

NOTE: By **si** we mean *if*. Sometimes **si** can mean *whether,* and in that case this summary of what tenses are used does not apply. When **si** means *whether,* there are no restrictions about the tenses. By the way, the sequence of tenses with a **si** clause in French is the same as it is in English with an *if* clause.

Example:

(a) Si elle arrive, je pars. If she arrives, I'm leaving.
Si elle arrive, je partirai. If she arrives, I will leave.
Si elle arrive, partez! If she arrives, leave!

(b) Si elle arrivait, je partirais. If she arrived, I would leave.

(c) Si elle était arrivée, je serais parti. If she had arrived, I would have left.

The Subjunctive

The subjunctive is not a tense; it is a mood, or mode. Usually, when we speak in French or English, we use the indicative mood. We use the subjunctive mood in French for certain reasons. The following are the principal reasons.

After certain conjunctions

When the following conjunctions introduce a new clause, the verb in that new clause is normally in the subjunctive mood:

à condition que on condition that; **Je vous prêterai l'argent à condition que vous me le rendiez le plutôt possible.**
à moins que unless; **Je pars à six heures précises à moins qu'il (n') y ait un orage.** [Expletive **ne** is optional]
afin que in order that, so that; **Je vous explique clairement afin que vous compreniez.**
attendre que to wait until; **Attendez que je finisse mon dîner.**
au cas que in case; **Au cas qu'il vienne, je pars tout de suite.**
autant que **Autant que je le sache . . .** As far as I know . . .
avant que before; **Ne me dites rien avant qu'il vienne.** [Expletive **ne** is optional]
bien que although; **Bien que Madame Cartier soit malade, elle a toujours bon appétit.**
de crainte que for fear that; **La mère a dit à sa petite fille de rester dans la maison de crainte qu'elle ne se fasse mal dans la rue.** [Expletive **ne** is required]
de façon que so that, in a way that, in such a way that; **Barbara étudie de façon qu'elle puisse réussir.**

de manière que so that, in a way that, in such a way that; **Joseph travaille dans la salle de classe de manière qu'il puisse réussir.**

de peur que for fear that; **Je vous dis de rester dans la maison aujourd'hui de peur que vous ne glissiez sur la glace.** [Expletive **ne** is required]

de sorte que so that, in a way that, in such a way that; **Nettoyez la chambre de sorte que tout soit propre.**

en attendant que until; **Nous allons rester ici en attendant qu'elle vienne.**

jusqu'à ce que until; **Je vais attendre jusqu'à ce que vous finissiez.**

malgré que although; **Malgré que Madame Cartier soit malade, elle a toujours bon appétit.** (NOTE: It is preferable to use **bien que,** as in the example given with **bien que** above on this list)

pour autant que as far as, as much as; **Pour autant que je me souvienne . . .** As far as I remember (NOTE: It is preferable to use **autant que,** as in the example given with **autant que** above on this list)

pour que in order that, so that; **Expliquez-vous mieux, s'il vous plaît, pour que je comprenne.**

pourvu que provided that; **Vous pouvez parler librement pourvu que vous me laissiez faire de même.**

que . . . ou non whether . . . or not; **Qu'il vienne ou non, cela m'est égal.**

quoique although; **Quoiqu'il soit vieux, il a l'agilité d'un jeune homme.**

sans que . . . ou que whether . . . or; either . . . or; **Soit qu'elle comprenne ou qu'elle ne comprenne pas, cela m'est égal.**

soit que . . . soit que whether . . . or whether; **Soit que vous le fassiez, soit que vous ne le fassiez pas, cela m'est égal.**

tâcher que to try to, to attempt to; **Tâchez que le bébé soit bien nourri.**

veiller à ce que to see to it that; **Veillez à ce que la porte soit fermée à clef pendant mon absence.**

After indefinite expressions

où que wherever; **Où que vous alliez, cela ne m'importe pas.**

quel que whatever; **Je vous aiderai, quelles que soient vos ambitions** / I will help you, whatever your ambitions may be. (NOTE that the appropriate form of **quel** is needed in this indefinite expression because you are dealing with a noun (**ambitions**) and **quel** functions as an adjective)

qui que whoever; **Qui que vous soyez, je ne veux pas vous écouter** / Whoever you are (Whoever you may be), I don't want to listen to you.

quoi que whatever, no matter what; **Quoi que cet homme dise, je ne le crois pas** / No matter what this man says, I do not believe him.

Si + adj. + que however; **Si bavarde qu'elle soit, elle ne dit jamais de bêtises** / However talkative she may be, she never says anything stupid.

After an indefinite antecedent

The reason why the subjunctive is needed after an indefinite antecedent is that the person or thing desired may possibly not exist; or, if it does exist, you may never find it.

(a) **Je cherche une personne qui soit honnête** / I am looking for a person who is honest.
(b) **Je cherche un appartement qui ne soit pas trop cher** / I am looking for an apartment that is not too expensive.
(c) **Connaissez-vous quelqu'un qui puisse réparer mon téléviseur une fois pour toutes?** / Do you know someone who can repair my TV set once and for all?
(d) **Y a-t-il un élève qui comprenne le subjonctif?** / Is there a student who understands the subjunctive?

BUT IF THE PERSON OR THING YOU ARE LOOKING FOR DOES EXIST, USE THE INDICATIVE MOOD:

(a) **J'ai trouvé une personne qui est honnête.**
(b) **J'ai un appartement qui n'est pas trop cher.**
(c) **Je connais une personne qui peut réparer votre téléviseur.**

After a superlative expressing an opinion

Those superlatives expressing an opinion are commonly: **le seul, la seule** (the only), **le premier, la première** (the first), **le dernier, la dernière** (the last), **le plus petit, la plus petite** (the smallest), **le plus grand, la plus grande**, *etc.*

(a) **A mon avis, Marie est la seule étudiante qui comprenne le subjonctif parfaitement.**

(b) **A mon opinion, Henriette est la plus jolie élève que j'aie jamais vue.**

After **Que**, meaning *let* or *may* to express a wish, an order, a command in the 3d person singular or plural

(a) **Qu'il parte!** / Let him leave!

(b) **Que Dieu nous pardonne!** / May God forgive us! (NOTE that the form ***pardonne*** is the same in the 3d pers. subjunctive as in the indicative)

(c) **Qu'ils s'en aillent!** / Let them go away!
(NOTE that what is understood in front of **Que** here is **(Je veux) que . . .**)

After certain impersonal expressions

c'est dommage que it's a pity that; it's too bad that; **C'est dommage qu'elle soit morte.**
il est à souhaiter que it is to be desired that; **Il est à souhaiter qu'elle soit guérie.**
il est bizarre que it is odd that; **Il est bizarre qu'il soit parti sans rien dire.**
il est bon que it is good that; **Il est bon que vous restiez au lit.**
il est convenable que it is fitting (proper) that; **Il est convenable qu'il vienne me voir.**
il est douteux que it is doubtful that; **Il est douteux qu'il soit présent au concert ce soir.**
il est essentiel que it is essential that; **Il est essentiel que vous veniez me voir le plus tôt possible.**

il est étonnant que it is astonishing that; **Il est étonnant qu'elle soit sortie sans rien dire.**

il est étrange que it is strange that; **Il est étrange qu'il n'ait pas répondu à ta lettre.**

il est faux que it is false (it is not true) that; **Il est faux que vous ayez vu ma soeur dans ce cabaret.**

il est heureux que it is fortunate that; **Il est très heureux que Madame Piquet soit guérie.**

il est honteux que it is shameful (a shame) that; **Il est honteux que vous trichiez.**

il est important que it is important that; **Il est important que vous arriviez à l'heure.**

il est impossible que it is impossible that; **Il est impossible que je sois chez vous avant trois heures.**

il est juste que it is right that; **Il est juste que le criminel soit puni pour son crime.**

il est naturel que it is natural that; **Il est naturel qu'on ait peur dans un moment dangereux.**

il est nécessaire que it is necessary that; **Il est nécessaire que tu finisses la leçon de français avant d'aller au cinéma.**

il est possible que it is possible that; **Il est possible que Madame Paquet soit déjà partie.**

il est rare que it is rare that; **Il est rare qu'elle sorte.**

il est regrettable que it is regrettable that; **Il est regrettable que cet homme riche ait perdu tout au jeu.**

il est surprenant que it is surprising that; **Il est surprenant que tu n'aies pas fait ton devoir aujourd'hui.**

il est temps que it is time that; **Il est temps que tu fasses tes devoirs tous les jours.**

il est urgent que it is urgent that; **Il est urgent que le docteur vienne immédiatement.**

il faut que it is necessary that; **Il faut que tu sois ici à neuf heures précises.**

il importe que it is important that; **Il importe que tu me dises toute la vérité.**

il se peut que it may be that; **Il se peut qu'elle soit sortie.**

il semble que it seems that, it appears that; **Il semble que Madame Gervaise soit déjà partie.**

il suffit que it is enough that, it suffices that; **Il suffit qu'il soit informé tout simplement.**

il vaut mieux que it is better that; **Il vaut mieux que vous soyez présent quand le docteur est ici.**

After the following impersonal expressions (in English, the subject is *It*) used in the negative or interrogative because they suggest some kind of doubt, uncertainty, hesitation . . .

Il ne me semble pas que . . .
Me semble-t-il que . . . ?

Il ne paraît pas que . . .
Paraît-il que . . . ?

Il n'est pas clair que . . .
Est-il clair que . . . ?

Il n'est pas vrai que . . .
Est-il vrai que . . . ?

Il n'est pas évident que . . .
Est-il évident que . . . ?

Il n'est pas certain que . . .
Est-il certain que . . . ?

Il n'est pas sûr que . . .
Est-il sûr que . . . ?

Il n'est pas probable que . . .
Est-il probable que . . . ?

After certain verbs expressing doubt, emotion, wishing

aimer que . . .
to like that . . .
aimer mieux que . . .
to prefer that . . .
s'attendre à ce que . . .
to expect that . . .
avoir peur que . . .
to be afraid that . . .
[expletive **ne** is required]
craindre que . . .
to fear that . . .
[expletive **ne** is required]
défendre que . . .
to forbid that . . .
désirer que . . .
to desire that . . .
douter que . . .
to doubt that . . .
empêcher que . . .
to prevent that . . .
s'étonner que . . .
to be astonished that . . .
s'étonner de ce que . . .
to be astonished at the fact that . . .
être bien aise que . . .
to be pleased that . . .
être content que . . .
to be glad that . . .
être désolé que . . .
to be distressed that . . .
être étonné que . . .
to be astonished that . . .

être heureux que . . .
to be happy that . . .
être joyeux que . . .
to be joyful that . . .
être malheureux que . . .
to be unhappy that . . .
être ravi que . . .
to be delighted that . . .
être surpris que . . .
to be surprised that . . .
être triste que . . .
to be sad that . . .
exiger que . . .
to demand that . . .
se fâcher que . . .
to be angry that . . .
ordonner que . . .
to order that . . .
préférer que . . .
to prefer that . . .
regretter que . . .
to regret that . . .
souhaiter que . . .
to wish that . . .
tenir à ce que . . .
to insist upon . . .
trembler que . . .
to tremble that . . .
[expletive **ne** is required]
vouloir que . . .
to want that . . .

SOME EXAMPLES:

J'aimerais que vous restiez ici / I would like you to stay here.
J'aime mieux que vous restiez ici / I prefer that you stay here.
Je m'attends à ce qu'elle vienne immédiatement / I expect her to come immediately.

J'ai peur qu'il ne soit malade / I am afraid that he may be sick. [expletive **ne** is required]

Je crains qu'elle ne soit gravement malade / I fear that she may be seriously ill. [expletive **ne** is required]

Je m'étonne qu'elle ne soit pas venue me voir / I am astonished that she has not come to see me.

Je m'étonne de ce qu'il ne soit pas parti / I am astonished (at the fact that) he has not left.

Ta mère est contente que tu sois heureux / Your mother is glad that you are happy.

Madame Poulet est désolée que son mari ait perdu toute sa fortune / Mrs. Poulet is distressed that her husband has lost his entire fortune.

After verbs of believing and thinking, such as **croire**, **penser**, **trouver** (meaning *to think, to have an impression*), and **espérer** when used in the negative OR interrogative but not when both interrogative AND negative . . .

EXAMPLES:

Je ne pense pas qu'il soit coupable / I don't think that he is guilty. **Croyez-vous qu'il dise la vérité?** / Do you believe he is telling the truth?

BUT: **Ne croyez-vous pas qu'il dit la vérité?** / Don't you think that he is telling the truth?

Trouvez-vous qu'il y ait beaucoup de crimes dans la société d'aujourd'hui? Do you find (think) that there are many crimes in today's society?

BUT: **Ne trouvez-vous pas que ce livre est intéressant?** / Don't you think (*or*: Don't you find) that this book is interesting?

Note: The subjunctive forms in Tense No. 6 (**présent du subjonctif**), Tense No. 7 (**imparfait du subjonctif**), Tense No. 13 (**passé du subjonctif**), and Tense No. 14 (**plus-que-parfait du subjonctif**) of any verb are normally preceded by **que** (that); for example, **que je sois** / that I may be, **que tu ailles** / that you may go.

Orthographically changing verbs—verb forms that change in spelling

Verbs that end in **-cer** in the infinitive form change **c** to **ç** when in front of the vowels **a**, **o** or **u** in order to keep the **s** sound in the infinitive form and retain its identity. That little mark under the **c** (**ç**) is called **une cédille**. Actually it is the lower part of the letter **s** which is used in order to tell the reader that the **ç** should be pronounced as an **s**. Without that mark, the letter **c** in front of the vowels **a**, **o** and **u** must be pronounced as a **k** sound. Since the **c** in the ending **-cer** is pronounced like an **s**, the same sound must be retained in all its forms.

(1) Some common verbs that end in **-cer** in the infinitive form are:

annoncer / to announce
avancer / to advance
commencer / to begin, to start
divorcer / to divorce
effacer / to erase, to efface
lancer / to launch, to hurl
menacer / to threaten
placer / to place, to set
prononcer / to pronounce
remplacer / to replace

(2) Examples of when this change occurs:

Present indicative: nous annonçons, nous avançons, nous commençons, nous divorçons, nous effaçons, nous lançons, nous menaçons, nous prononçons, nous remplaçons.

Imperfect indicative: j'annonçais, tu annonçais, il (elle, on) annonçait; ils (elles) annonçaient [You do the same for the other **-cer** type verbs given above in (1).]

Passé simple: j'annonçai, tu annonças, il (elle, on) annonça; nous annonçâmes, vous annonçâtes [You do the same for the other **-cer** type verbs given above in (1).]

Imperfect subjunctive: que j'annonçasse, que tu annonçasses, qu'il (qu'elle, qu'on) annoncât; que nous annonçassions, que vous annonçassiez, qu'ils (qu'elles) annonçassent [Now you do the same for the other **-cer** type verbs given above in (1).]

(3) Verbs that end in **-ger** in the infinitive form change **g** to **ge** in front of the vowels **a**, **o** or **u** in order to keep the soft sound of **g** in the infinitive form and retain its identity; otherwise, **g** in front of **a**, **o** or **u** is normally pronounced hard, as in **go**.

(4) Some common verbs that end in **-ger** in the infinitive form are:

arranger / to arrange
changer / to change
corriger / to correct
déranger / to disturb
manger / to eat
nager / to swim
neiger / to snow
obliger / to oblige
partager / to divide, to share
plonger / to dive, to plunge
ranger / to arrange by row, put in order
songer / to think, to dream
voyager / to travel

(5) Examples of when this change occurs:

Present indicative: nous arrangeons, nous changeons, nous corrigeons, nous dérangeons [Now you do the same for the other **-ger** type verbs given above in (4).]

Imperfect indicative: j'arrangeais, tu arrangeais, il (elle, on) arrangeait; ils (elles) arrangeaient [Now you do the same for the other **-ger** type verbs given above in (4).]

Passé simple: j'arrangeai, tu arrangeas, il (elle, on) arrangea; nous arrangeâmes, vous arrangeâtes [Now you do the same for the other **-ger** type verbs given above in (4).]

Imperfect subjunctive: que j'arrangeasse, que tu arrangeasses, qu'il (qu'elle, qu'on) arrangeât; que nous arrangeassions, que vous arrangeassiez, qu'ils (qu'elles) arrangeassent [Just for the fun of it, do the same for the other **-ger** type verbs given above.]

(6) Verbs that end in **-oyer** or **-uyer** in the infinitive form must change **y** to **i** in front of mute **e**.

(7) Common verbs that end in **-oyer** or **-uyer** in the infinitive form are:

-OYER	-UYER
choyer / to fondle, to coddle	**ennuyer** / to bore, to annoy
employer / to employ, to use	**essuyer** / to wipe
envoyer / to send	
nettoyer / to clean	

(8) Verbs that end in **-AYER** in the infinitive form may change **y** to **i** or may keep **y** in front of mute **e**.

Two common verbs that end in **-ayer** in the infinitive form are: **essayer** / to try, to try on; and **payer** / to pay, to pay for.

(9) Examples of when this change occurs:

Present indicative: j'emploie, tu emploies, il (elle, on) emploie; ils (elles) emploient.

Future: j'emploierai, tu emploieras, il (elle, on) emploiera; nous emploierons, vous emploierez, ils (elles) emploieront.

Conditional: j'emploierais, tu emploierais, il (elle, on) emploierait; nous emploierions, vous emploieriez, ils (elles) emploieraient.

Present subjunctive: que j'emploie, que tu emploies, qu'il (qu'elle, qu'on) emploie; qu'ils (qu'elles) emploient.

(10) Verbs that contain a mute **e** in the syllable before the infinitive ending **-er**:

acheter / to buy	lever / to raise, to lift
achever / to complete	se lever / to get up
amener / to bring, to lead	mener / to lead
élever / to raise	peser / to weigh
emmener / to lead away, to take away	promener / to walk (a person or an animal)
enlever / to remove, to take off	se promener / to take a walk (for yourself)
geler / to freeze	

(11) These verbs, given above in (10), change mute **e** to **è** when, in a verb form, the syllable after it contains another mute **e**.

(12) This change occurs because that mute **e** in the stem of the infinitive now becomes pronounced clearly in some verb forms. Examples:

Present indicative: j'achète, tu achètes, il (elle, on) achète; ils (elles) achètent.

Future: j'achèterai, tu achèteras, il (elle, on) achètera; nous achèterons, vous achèterez, ils (elles) achèteront.

Conditional: j'achèterais, tu achèterais, il (elle, on) achèterait; nous achèterions, vous achèteriez, ils (elles) achèteraient.

Present subjunctive: que j'achète, que tu achètes, qu'il (qu'elle, qu'on) achète; qu'ils (qu'elles) achètent.

(13) Instead of changing like the verbs above in (10)–(12) the following verbs double the consonant in the syllable that contains the mute **e** in the stem:

appeler / to call
rappeler / to recall
se rappeler / to remember
jeter / to throw
rejeter / to throw again, to throw back

Examples of when this spelling change occurs:

Present indicative: je m'appelle, tu t'appelles, il (elle, on) s'appelle; ils (elles) s'appellent.

Future: je m'appellerai, tu t'appelleras, il (elle, on) s'appellera; nous nous appellerons, vous vous appellerez, ils (elles) s'appelleront.

Conditional: je m'appellerais, tu t'appellerais, il (elle, on) s'appellerait; nous nous appellerions, vous vous appelleriez, ils (elles) s'appelleraient.

Present subjunctive: que je m'appelle, que tu t'appelles, qu'il (qu'elle, qu'on) s'appelle; qu'ils (qu'elles) s'appellent.

(14) Verbs that contain **é** in the syllable before the infinitive ending **-er**:

céder / to cede, to yield, to give up
célébrer / to celebrate
concéder / to concede, to give up
considérer / to consider
espérer / to hope
posséder / to possess, to own
préférer / to prefer
protéger / to protect
répéter / to repeat
suggérer / to suggest

(15) These verbs, given above in (14), change **é** to **è** when, in a verb form, the syllable after it contains mute **e**.

Examples of when this spelling change occurs:

Present indicative: je préfère, tu préfères, il (elle, on) préfère: ils (elles) préfèrent.

Present subjunctive: que je préfère, que tu préfères, qu'il (qu'elle, qu'on) préfère; qu'ils (qu'elles) préfèrent.

Definitions of basic grammatical terms with examples

active voice When we speak or write in the active voice, the subject of the verb performs the action. The action falls on the direct object.

*Everyone loves Janine / **Tout le monde aime Janine.***

The subject is *everyone*. The verb is *loves*. The direct object is *Janine*. See also *passive voice* in this list. Compare the above sentence with the example in the passive voice.

adjective An adjective is a word that modifies a noun or a pronoun. In grammar, to modify a word means to describe, limit, expand, or make the meaning particular.

*a beautiful garden / **un beau jardin; she is pretty / elle est jolie.***

The adjective *beautiful/**beau*** modifies the noun *garden/**jardin***. The adjective *pretty/**jolie*** modifies the pronoun *she/**elle***. In French there are different kinds of adjectives. *See also* comparative adjective, demonstrative adjective, descriptive adjective, interrogative adjective, limiting adjective, possessive adjective, superlative adjective.

adverb An adverb is a word that modifies a verb, an adjective, or another adverb. An adverb says something about how, when, where, to what extent, or in what way.

*Jane runs swiftly / **Jeanne court rapidement.***

The adverb *swiftly/**rapidement*** modifies the verb *runs/**court***. The adverb shows *how* she runs.

*Jack is a very good friend / **Jacques est un très bon ami.***

The adverb *very/**très*** modifies the adjective *good/**bon***. The adverb shows *how good* a friend he is.

*The boy is eating too fast now / **Le garçon mange trop vite maintenant.***

The adverb *too/**trop*** modifies the adverb *fast/**vite***. The adverb shows *to what extent* he is eating *fast*. The adverb *now/**maintenant*** tells us *when*.

*The post office is there / **Le bureau de poste est là.***

The adverb *there/**là*** modifies the verb *is/**est***. It tells us *where* the post office is.

*Mary writes carefully / **Marie écrit soigneusement.***

The adverb *carefully/**soigneusement*** modifies the verb *writes/**écrit***. It tells us *in what way* she writes.

affirmative statement, negative statement A statement in the affirmative is expressed positively. To negate an affirmative statement is to make it negative.

Affirmative: *I like chocolate ice cream / **J'aime la glace au chocolat.***

Negative: *I do not like chocolate ice cream / **Je n'aime pas la glace au chocolat.***

agreement of adjective with noun Agreement is made on the adjective with the noun it modifies in gender (masculine or feminine) and number (singular or plural).

*a white house / **une maison blanche.***

The adjective **blanche** is feminine singular because the noun **une maison** is feminine singular.

*two white houses / **deux maisons blanches.***

The adjective **blanches** is feminine plural because the noun **maisons** is feminine plural.

agreement of past participle of a reflexive verb with its reflexive pronoun Agreement is made on the past participle of a reflexive verb with its reflexive pronoun in gender (masculine or feminine) and number (singular or plural) if that pronoun is the *direct object* of the verb. The agreement is determined by looking at the subject to see its gender and number, which is the same as its reflexive pronoun. If the reflexive pronoun is the *indirect object*, an agreement is *not* made. *See* **se laver** and **se lever**.

She washed herself / Elle s'est lavée.

There is a feminine agreement on the past participle **lavée** (added **e**) with the reflexive pronoun **se** (here, **s'**) because it serves as a direct object pronoun. What or whom did she wash? Herself, which is expressed in **se** (**s'**).

But:

She washed her hair / Elle s'est lavé les cheveux.

There is no feminine agreement on the past participle **lavé** here because the reflexive pronoun (**se**, here, **s'**) serves as an *indirect object*. The direct object is **les cheveux** and it is stated *after* the verb. What did she wash? She washed her hair *on herself* (*s'*). *See also* reflexive pronoun and reflexive verb.

agreement of past participle with its direct object Agreement is made on the past participle with its direct object in gender (masculine or feminine) and number (singular or plural) when the verb is conjugated with **avoir** in the compound tenses. Agreement is made when the direct object, if there is one, *precedes* the verb.

Where are the little cakes? Paul ate them / Où sont les petits gâteaux? Paul les a mangés.

The verb **a mangés** is in the *passé composé*; **manger** is conjugated with **avoir**. There is a plural agreement on the past participle **mangés** (added **s**) because the *preceding* direct object *them/les* is masculine plural, referring to *les petits gâteaux*, which is masculine plural.

Who wrote the letters? Robert wrote them / Qui a écrit les lettres? Robert les a écrites.

The verb **a écrites** is in the *passé composé*; **écrire** is conjugated with **avoir**. There is a feminine plural agreement on the past participle **écrites** (added **e** and **s**) because the *preceding*-direct object *them/les* is feminine plural, referring to *les lettres*, which is feminine plural. A past participle functions as an adjective.

An agreement in gender and number is *not* made with *an indirect object*. *See* indirect object noun, indirect object pronoun. Review the regular formation of past participles and irregular past participles on page 3. *See also* direct object noun, direct object pronoun.

agreement of past participle with the subject Agreement is made on the past participle with the subject in gender (masculine or feminine) and number (singular or plural) when the verb is conjugated with **être** in the compound tenses.

She went to Paris / Elle est allée à Paris.

The verb **est allée** is in the *passé composé*; **aller** is conjugated with **être**. There is a feminine agreement on the past participle **allée** (added **e**) because the subject **elle** is feminine singular.

The boys have arrived / Les garçons sont arrivés.

The verb **sont arrivés** is in the *passé composé*; **arriver** is conjugated with **être**. There is a plural agreement on the past participle **arrivés** (added **s**) because the subject **les garçons** is masculine plural.

Review page 6 to find out about verbs conjugated with either **avoir** or **être** to form the seven compound tenses. *See* **aller** and **arriver**. *See also* past participle and subject.

agreement of verb with its subject A verb agrees in person (1st, 2d, or 3d) and in number (singular or plural) with its subject.

*Does he always tell the truth? / **Dit-il toujours la vérité?***

The verb **dit** (of **dire**) is 3d person singular because the subject *il/he* is 3d person singular.

*Where are they going? / **Où vont-ils?***

The verb **vont** (of **aller**) is 3d person plural because the subject *ils/they* is 3d person plural. For subject pronouns in the singular and plural, review page 103.

antecedent An antecedent is a word to which a relative pronoun refers. It comes *before* the pronoun.

The girl who is laughing over there is my sister /
La jeune fille qui rit là-bas est ma soeur.

The antecedent is *girl/la jeune fille*. The relative pronoun *who/qui* refers to the girl.

*The car that I bought is expensive / **La voiture que j'ai achetée est chère.***

The antecedent is *car/la voiture*. The relative pronoun *that/que* refers to the car. Note also that the past participle ***achetée*** is fem. sing. because it refers to ***la voiture*** (fem. sing.), which precedes the verb. Review **acheter** and **rire**. *See also* relative pronoun.

auxiliary verb An auxiliary verb is a helping verb. In English grammar it is *to have*. In French grammar it is **avoir** (to have) or **être** (to be). An auxiliary verb is used to help form the seven compound tenses.

*I have eaten /**J'ai mangé; she has left / elle est partie.***

Review page 6 to find out about verbs conjugated with **avoir** or **être** as helping verbs. Also, review **manger** and **partir**.

cardinal number A cardinal number is a number that expresses an amount, such as *one*, *two*, *three*, and so on. *See also* ordinal number.

causative faire In English grammar a causative verb causes something to be done. In French grammar the idea is the same. The subject of the verb causes the action expressed in the verb to be carried out by someone else.

Mrs. Roth makes her students work in French class /
Madame Roth fait travailler ses élèves dans la classe de français.

*Mr. Smith is having a house built / **Monsieur Smith fait construire une maison.***

Review **construire**, **faire**, and **travailler**.

clause A clause is a group of words that contains a subject and a predicate. A predicate may contain more than one word. A conjugated verb form is revealed in the predicate.

Mrs. Coty lives in a small apartment /
Madame Coty demeure dans un petit appartement.

The subject is *Mrs. Coty/Madame Coty*. The predicate is *lives in a small apartment/demeure dans un petit appartement*. The verb is *lives/demeure*. *See also* dependent clause, independent clause.

comparative adjective When making a comparison between two persons or things, an adjective is used to express the degree of comparison in the following ways.

Same degree of comparison:

*Raymond is as tall as his father / **Raymond est aussi grand que son père.***

Lesser degree of comparison:

*Monique is less intelligent than her sister / **Monique est moins intelligente que sa soeur.***

Higher degree of comparison:

This apple is more delicious than that apple /
Cette pomme-ci est plus délicieuse que cette pomme-là.

See also superlative adjective.

comparative adverb An adverb is compared in the same way as an adjective is compared. *See* comparative adjective.

Same degree of comparison:

Mr. Bernard speaks as fast as Mr. Claude /
Monsieur Bernard parle aussi vite que Monsieur Claude.

Lesser degree of comparison:

Alice studies less seriously than her sister /
Alice étudie moins sérieusement que sa soeur.

Higher degree of comparison:

Albert works more slowly than his brother /
Albert travaille plus lentement que son frère.

See also superlative adverb.

complex sentence A complex sentence contains one independent clause and one or more dependent clauses.

One independent clause and one dependent clause:

Jack is handsome but his brother isn't / ***Jacques est beau mais son frère ne l'est pas.***

The independent clause is *Jack is handsome*. It makes sense when it stands alone because it expresses a complete thought. The dependent clause is *but his brother isn't*. The dependent clause, which is introduced by the conjunction *but*, does not make complete sense when it stands alone because it *depends* on the thought expressed in the independent clause.

One independent clause and two dependent clauses:

Mary gets good grades in school because she studies but her sister never studies /
Marie reçoit de bonnes notes à l'école parce qu'elle étudie mais sa soeur n'étudie jamais.

The independent clause is *Mary gets good grades in school*. It makes sense when it stands alone because it expresses a complete thought. The first dependent clause is *because she studies*. This dependent clause, which is introduced by the conjunction *because*, does not make complete sense when it stands alone because it *depends* on the thought expressed in the independent clause. The second dependent clause is *but her sister never studies*. That dependent clause, which is introduced by the conjunction *but*, does not make complete sense either when it stands alone because it *depends* on the thought expressed in the independent clause. *See also* dependent clause, independent clause.

compound sentence A compound sentence contains two or more independent clauses.

Mrs. Dubois went to the supermarket, she bought some groceries, and then she returned home / ***Madame Dubois est allée au supermarché, elle a acheté des provisions, et puis elle est rentrée chez elle.***

This compound sentence contains three independent clauses. They are independent because they make sense when they stand alone. Review the *passé composé* on page 16. *See also* independent clause.

conditional perfect tense In French grammar the conditional used to be considered a mood. Grammarians now regard it as a tense of the indicative mood. This tense is defined with examples on pages 18 and 19.

conditional present tense In French grammar the conditional used to be considered a mood. Grammarians now regard it as a tense of the indicative mood. This tense is defined with examples on page 13.

conjugation The conjugation of a verb is the fixed order of all its forms showing their inflections (changes) in the three persons of the singular and plural in a particular tense.

conjunction A conjunction is a word that connects words or groups of words.

and/et, or/ou, but/mais

*You and I are going downtown / **Toi et moi, nous allons en ville.***

You can stay home or you can come with us /

Tu peux rester à la maison ou tu peux venir avec nous.

declarative sentence A declarative sentence makes a statement.

*I have finished the work / **J'ai fini le travail.***

Review **finir**.

definite article The definite article in French has four forms and they all mean *the*. They are: **le, la, l', les**, as in:

le livre/the book, la maison/the house, l'école/the school,

les enfants/the children

The definite articles are also used as direct object pronouns. *See* direct object pronoun.

demonstrative adjective A demonstrative adjective is an adjective that points out. It is placed in front of a noun.

*this book/**ce livre**; this hotel/**cet hôtel**; this child/**cet enfant**; this house/**cette maison**;*

*these flowers/**ces fleurs***

demonstrative pronoun A demonstrative pronoun is a pronoun that points out. It takes the place of a noun. It agrees in gender and number with the noun it replaces.

I have two apples; do you prefer this one or that one?

J'ai deux pommes; préférez-vous celle-ci ou celle-là?

*Sorry, but I prefer those / **Je regrette, mais je préfère celles-là.***

*Do you like the ones that are on the table? / **Aimez-vous celles qui sont sur la table?***

For demonstrative pronouns that are neuter, *see* neuter.

dependent clause A dependent clause is a group of words that contains a subject and a predicate. It does not express a complete thought when it stands alone. It is called *dependent* because it depends on the independent clause for a complete meaning. Subordinate clause is another term for dependent clause.

Mary is absent today because she is sick /

Marie est absente aujourd'hui parce qu'elle est malade.

The independent clause is *Mary is absent today*. The dependent clause is *because she is sick*.

See also clause, independent clause.

descriptive adjective A descriptive adjective is an adjective that describes a person, place, or thing.

*a pretty girl/**une jolie jeune fille**; a handsome boy/**un beau garçon**;*

*a small house/**une petite maison**; a big city/**une grande ville**;*

*an expensive car/**une voiture chère**.*

See also adjective.

direct object noun A direct object noun receives the action of the verb *directly*. That is why it is called a direct object, as opposed to an indirect object. A direct object noun is normally placed *after* the verb.

*I am writing a letter / **J'écris une lettre.***

The subject is *I/Je*. The verb is *am writing/écris*. The direct object is the noun *letter/une lettre*. *See also* direct object pronoun.

direct object pronoun A direct object pronoun receives the action of the verb *directly*. It takes the place of a direct object noun. In French a pronoun that is a direct object of a verb is ordinarily placed *in front of* the verb.

*I am reading it [the letter] / **Je la lis.***

A direct object pronoun is placed *after* the verb and joined with a hyphen *in the affirmative imperative*.

*Write it [the letter] now / **Écrivez-la maintenant.***

The direct object pronouns are:

Person	Singular	Plural
1st	*me (m') me*	*nous us*
2d	*te (t') you (fam.)*	*vous you (sing. polite or pl.)*
3d	*le (l') him, it (person or thing)* *la (l') her, it (person or thing)*	*les them (persons or things)*

Review **écrire** and **lire**. *See also* imperative.

disjunctive pronoun In French grammar a disjunctive pronoun is a pronoun that is stressed; in other words, emphasis is placed on it.

*I speak well; he does not speak well / **Moi, je parle bien; lui, il ne parle pas bien.***

*Talk to me / **Parlez-moi.***

A disjunctive pronoun is also object of a preposition:

*She is talking with me / **Elle parle avec moi.***

*I always think of you / **Je pense toujours à toi.***

The disjunctive pronouns are:

Person	Singular	Plural
1st	*moi me, I*	*nous us, we*
2d	*toi you (fam.)*	*vous you (sing. polite or pl.)*
3d	*soi oneself* *lui him, he* *elle her, she*	*eux them, they (m.)* *elles them, they (f.)*

ending of a verb In French grammar the ending of a verb form changes according to the person and number of the subject and the tense of the verb.

For example, to form the present indicative tense of a regular **-er** type verb like **parler**, drop **er** of the infinitive and add the following endings: **-e**, **-es**, **-e** for the 1st, 2d, and 3d persons of the singular; **-ons**, **-ez**, **-ent** for the 1st, 2d, and 3d persons of the plural. You then get:

je parle, tu parles, il (elle, on) parle;
nous parlons, vous parlez, ils (elles) parlent

Review pages 22 and 23. *See also* stem of a verb.

feminine In French grammar the gender of a noun, pronoun, or adjective is feminine or masculine, not male or female.

Masculine			Feminine		
noun	pronoun	adjective	noun	pronoun	adjective
le garçon	***il***	***grand***	***la femme***	***elle***	***grande***
the boy	*he*	*tall*	*the woman*	*she*	*tall*
le livre	***il***	***petit***	***la voiture***	***elle***	***petite***
the book	*it*	*small*	*the car*	*it*	*small*

See also gender.

futur proche, le In English the **futur proche** is called the near future. As one may guess, the near future is used when talking about something that will take place in the near future. The formation is similar in French and English. In French, the near future is formed by using **aller** with the infinitive of the verb that you want to use. In English, you use *to go* with the infinitive of the verb that you want to use.

Demain, je **vais acheter** un ordinateur.
Tomorrow, I *am going to buy* a computer.

future perfect tense This tense is defined with examples on page 18.

future tense This tense is defined with examples on pages 12–13.

gender In French grammar gender means masculine or feminine.

Masculine: *the boy/**le garçon**; he, it/**il**; the rooster/**le coq**; the book/**le livre***
Feminine: *the girl/**la jeune fille**; she, it/**elle**;*
*the hen/**la poule**; the house/**la maison***

gerund In English grammar a gerund is a word formed from a verb. It ends in *ing*. Actually, it is the present participle of a verb. But it is not used as a verb. It is used as a noun.

*Seeing is believing / **Voir c'est croire.***

However, in French grammar the infinitive form of the verb is used, as in the above example, when the verb is used as a noun. In French, *seeing is believing* is expressed as *to see is to believe*.

The French gerund is also a word formed from a verb. It ends in ***ant***. It is also the present participle of a verb. As a gerund, it is normally preceded by the preposition **en**.

***En partant, il a fait ses excuses** / While leaving, he made his excuses.*

See also present participle.

***if* (si) clause** An "if" clause is defined with examples at the top of page 26. *See also* clause.

imperative The imperative is a mood, not a tense. It is used to express a command. In French it is used in the 2d person of the singular (**tu**), the 2d person of the plural (**vous**), and in the 1st person of the plural (**nous**). Review the imperative with examples on pages 20 and 21. Also review the three imperative forms of **donner**. *See also* person (1st, 2d, 3d).

imperfect indicative tense This tense is defined with examples on pages 11 and 12.

imperfect subjunctive tense This tense is defined with examples on pages 15 and 16.

indefinite article In English the indefinite articles are *a*, *an*, as in *a book*, *an apple*. They are indefinite because they do not refer to any definite or particular noun.

In French there are two indefinite articles in the singular: one in the masculine form (**un**) and one in the feminine form (**une**).

Masculine singular: ***un ami**/a friend*

Feminine singular: ***une pomme**/an apple*

In French they both change to **des** in the plural.

*I have a brother/**J'ai un frère**; I have brothers/**J'ai des frères**.*

*I have a sister/**J'ai une soeur**; I have sisters/**J'ai des soeurs**.*

*I have an apple/**J'ai une pomme**; I have apples/**J'ai des pommes**.*

See also definite article.

indefinite pronoun An indefinite pronoun is a pronoun that does not refer to any definite or particular noun.

*something/**quelque chose**; someone, somebody/**quelqu'un, quelqu'une**;*
*each one/**chacun, chacune**; anything/**n'importe quoi***

independent clause An independent clause is a group of words that contains a subject and a predicate. It expresses a complete thought when it stands alone.

*The cat is sleeping under the bed / **Le chat dort sous le lit.***

See also clause, dependent clause, predicate.

indicative mood The indicative mood is used in sentences that make a statement or ask a question. The indicative mood is used most of the time when we speak or write in English or French.

*I am going home now/**Je vais chez moi maintenant.***

*Where are you going?/**Où allez-vous?***

indirect object noun An indirect object noun receives the action of the verb *indirectly*. *I am writing a letter to Mary or I am writing Mary a letter / **J'écris une lettre à Marie.*** The subject is *I/**Je***. The verb is *am writing/**écris***. The direct object noun is *a letter/**une lettre***. The indirect object noun is *Mary/**Marie.*** An agreement is not made with an indirect object noun. *See also* indirect object pronoun, direct object noun, direct object pronoun.

indirect object pronoun An indirect object pronoun takes the place of an indirect object noun. It receives the action of the verb *indirectly*. In French a pronoun that is the indirect object of a verb is ordinarily placed *in front of* the verb.

I am writing a letter to her or *I am writing her a letter / **Je lui écris une lettre.***

The indirect object pronoun is *(to) her/**lui***. An agreement is not made with an indirect object pronoun.

An indirect object pronoun is placed *after* the verb and joined with a hyphen *in the affirmative imperative*.

*Write to her now / **Écris-lui maintenant.***

The indirect object pronouns are:

Person	Singular	Plural
1st	*me (m') to me*	*nous to us*
2d	*te (t') to you (fam.)*	*vous to you (sing. polite or pl.)*
3d	*lui to him, to her*	*leur to them*

See also indirect object noun.

infinitive An infinitive is a verb form. In English it is normally stated with the preposition *to*, as in *to talk, to finish, to sell*. In French the infinitive form of a verb consists of three major types: those of the 1st conjugation that end in **-er**, those of the 2d conjugation that end in **-ir**, and those of the 3d conjugation that end in **-re**.

parler/to talk, to speak; ***finir/to finish***; ***vendre/to sell***

All the verbs in this book are given in the infinitive form at the top of each page where they are arranged alphabetically.

interjection An interjection is a word that expresses emotion, a feeling of joy, of sadness, an exclamation of surprise, and other exclamations consisting of one or two words.

*Ah!/**Ah!** Oh!/**Oh!** Darn it!/**Zut!** Whew!/**Ouf!** My God!/**Mon Dieu!***

interrogative adjective An interrogative adjective is an adjective that is used in a question. It agrees in gender and number with the noun it modifies.

*What book do you want? / **Quel livre désirez-vous?***
*What time is it? / **Quelle heure est-il?***

interrogative adverb An interrogative adverb is an adverb that introduces a question. As an adverb, it modifies the verb.

*How are you? / **Comment allez-vous?***
*How much does this book cost? / **Combien coûte ce livre?***
*When will you arrive? / **Quand arriverez-vous?***

interrogative pronoun An interrogative pronoun is a pronoun that asks a question. There are interrogative pronouns that refer to persons and those that refer to things.

*Who is on the phone? / **Qui est à l'appareil?***
*What are you saying? / **Que dites-vous?***

interrogative sentence An interrogative sentence asks a question.

*What are you doing? / **Que faites-vous?***

intransitive verb An intransitive verb is a verb that does not take a direct object.

*The professor is talking loudly / **Le professeur parle fort.***

An intransitive verb takes an indirect object.

*The professor is talking to us / **Le professeur nous parle.***

See also indirect object pronoun.

irregular verb An irregular verb is a verb that does not follow a fixed pattern in its conjugation in the various verb tenses.

Basic irregular verbs in French:

aller/to go *avoir/to have* *être/to be* *faire/to do, to make*

Review these verbs. *See also* conjugation, regular verb.

limiting adjective A limiting adjective is an adjective that limits a quantity.

*three tickets/**trois billets**; a few candies/**quelques bonbons***

main clause Main clause is another term for independent clause. *See* independent clause.

masculine In French grammar the gender of a noun, pronoun, or adjective is masculine or feminine, not male or female. *See also* gender and feminine.

mood of verbs Some grammarians use the term *the mode* instead of *the mood* of a verb. Either term means *the manner or way* a verb is expressed. In English and in French grammar a verb expresses an action or state of being in the following three moods (modes, *ways*): the indicative mood, the imperative mood, and the subjunctive mood. In French grammar there is also the infinitive mood when the whole infinitive is used, *e.g.*, **voir**, **croire**, as in **Voir c'est croire**/*Seeing is believing (to see is to believe)*. Most of the time, in English and French, we speak and write in the indicative mood.

near future See *futur proche, le.*

negative statement, affirmative statement

see **affirmative statement, negative statement**

neuter A word that is neuter is neither masculine nor feminine. Common neuter demonstrative pronouns are **ce (c')**/*it*, **ceci**/*this*, **cela**/*that*, **ça**/*that*. They are invariable, which means they do not change in gender and number.

*It's not true/**Ce n'est pas vrai**; it is true/**c'est vrai**; this is true/**ceci est vrai**; that is true/**cela est vrai**; what is that?/**qu'est-ce que c'est que ça?***

For demonstrative pronouns that are not neuter, *see* demonstrative pronoun. There is also the neuter pronoun **le**, as in: ***Je le crois** / I believe it*; ***Je le pense** / I think so.*

noun A noun is a word that names a person, animal, place, thing, condition or state, or quality.

*the man/**l'homme**, the woman/**la femme**, the horse/**le cheval**, the house/**la maison** the book/**le livre**, happiness/**le bonheur**, excellence/**l'excellence***

In French the noun **le nom** is the word for name and noun.

number In English and French grammar, number means singular or plural.

Masc. sing.:

*the boy/**le garçon; the arm/le bras; the eye/l'oeil***

Masc. pl.:

*the boys/**les garçons; the arms/les bras; the eyes/les yeux***

Fem. sing.:

*the girl/**la jeune fille**; the house/**la maison**; the hen/**la poule***

Fem. pl.:

*the girls/**les jeunes filles**; the houses/**les maisons**; the hens/**les poules***

ordinal number An ordinal number is a number that expresses position in a series, such as *first*, *second*, *third*, and so on. In English and French grammar we talk about 1st person, 2d person, 3d person singular or plural regarding subjects and verbs. *See also* cardinal number and person (1st, 2d, 3d).

orthographical changes in verb forms An orthographical change in a verb form is a change in spelling.

The second letter **c** in the verb ***commencer****/to begin* changes to **ç** if the letter after it is **a**, **o**, or **u**, as in ***nous commençons****/we begin*. The reason for this spelling change is to preserve the sound of *s* as it is pronounced in the infinitive form **commencer**. When **a**, **o**, or **u** follow the letter **c**, the **c** is pronounced as in the sound of **k**. The mark under the letter **ç** is called ***une cédille****/cedilla*. Some linguists say it is the lower part of the letter **s** and it tells you to pronounce **ç** as an **s** sound. Other linguists say that **ç** was borrowed from the Greek alphabet, which represents the sound of **s** when it is the last letter of a Greek word.

The verb ***s'appeler****/to call oneself, to be named* contains a single **l**. When a verb form is stressed on the syllable containing one **l**, it doubles, as in ***je m'appelle*** *. . ./I call myself . . . , my name is . . . .*

partitive In French grammar the partitive denotes a *part* of a whole. In English we express the partitive by saying *some* or *any* in front of the noun. In French we use the following partitive forms in front of the noun:

Masculine singular: **du** or **de l'** Feminine singular: **de la** or **de l'**

Masculine or feminine plural: **des**

I have some coffee / ***J'ai du café.***

I'd like some water / ***J'aimerais de l'eau.***

I'd like some meat / ***J'aimerais de la viande.***

Do you have any candies? / ***Avez-vous des bonbons?***

In the negative, these partitive forms change to **de** or **d'**:

I don't have any coffee / ***Je n'ai pas de café.***

I don't want any water / ***Je ne veux pas d'eau.***

I wouldn't like any meat / ***Je n'aimerais pas de viande.***

No, I don't have any candies / ***Non, je n'ai pas de bonbons.***

passive voice When we speak or write in the active voice and change to the passive voice, the direct object becomes the subject, the subject becomes the object of a preposition, and the verb becomes *to be* plus the past participle of the active verb. The past participle functions as an adjective.

Janine is loved by everyone / ***Janine est aimée de tout le monde.***

The subject is *Janine*. The verb is *is/est*. The object of the preposition *by/de* is *everyone/****tout le monde****. See also* active voice. Compare the above sentence with the example in the active voice.

past anterior tense This tense is defined with examples on page 17.

past definite or simple past tense This tense is defined with examples on page 12. In French it is the *passé simple*.

past indefinite tense This tense is defined with examples on page 16. In French it is the *passé composé*.

past participle A past participle is derived from a verb. It is used to form the compound tenses. Its auxiliary verb in English is *to have*. In French the auxiliary verb is **avoir**/to *have* or **être**/*to be*. It is part of the verb tense.

With **avoir** as the auxiliary verb: ***Elle a mangé*** */ She has eaten.*

The subject is *elle/she*. The verb is *a mangé/has eaten*. The tense of the verb is the *passé composé*. The auxiliary verb is *a/has*. The past participle is *mangé/eaten*.

With **être** as the auxiliary verb: ***Elle est arrivée / She has arrived.***
The verb is *est arrivée/has arrived*. The tense of the verb is the *passé composé*. The auxiliary verb is *est*. The past participle is *arrivée/arrived*.

Review page 3 for the regular formation of a past participle and a list of basic irregular past participles. Review page 6 to find out about verbs conjugated with either **avoir** or **être**. *See also* auxiliary verb and agreement of past participle with the subject.

past perfect tense This tense is also called the pluperfect indicative tense. Review pages 16 and 17 for a definition with examples.

past simple tense This tense is defined with examples on page 12. It is also called the simple past tense or past definite tense. In French it is the *passé simple*.

past subjunctive tense This tense is also called the perfect subjunctive tense. It is defined with examples on page 19.

person (1st, 2d, 3d) Verb forms in a particular tense are learned systematically according to person (1st, 2d, 3d) and number (singular, plural).
Present indicative tense of the verb **aller**/to go:

Singular	Plural
1st person: ***je vais***	1st person: ***nous allons***
2d person: ***tu vas***	2d person: ***vous allez***
3d person: ***il, elle, on va***	3d person: ***ils, elles vont***

personal pronoun A personal pronoun refers to a person. The pronoun *it/il* or *elle* is in this category. Review the subject pronouns on page 103. For examples of other types of pronouns, *see also* demonstrative pronoun, direct object pronoun, disjunctive pronoun, indefinite pronoun, indirect object pronoun, interrogative pronoun, possessive pronoun, reflexive pronoun, relative pronoun.

pluperfect indicative tense This tense is also called the past perfect indicative tense. It is defined with examples on pages 16–17.

pluperfect subjunctive tense This tense is also called the past perfect subjunctive tense. It is defined with examples on pages 19–20.

plural Plural means more than one. *See also* person (1st, 2d, 3d) and singular.

possessive adjective A possessive adjective is an adjective that is placed in front of a noun to show possession. In French their forms change in gender (masculine or feminine) and number (singular or plural) to agree with the noun they modify.

*my book/**mon livre*** *my books/**mes livres*** *my dress/**ma robe***

possessive pronoun A possessive pronoun is a pronoun that shows possession. It takes the place of a possessive adjective with the noun. Its form agrees in gender (masculine or feminine) and number (singular or plural) with what it is replacing.

English:

mine, yours, his, hers, its, ours, theirs

French:

Possessive adjective	Possessive pronoun
*my book/**mon livre***	*mine/**le mien***
*my dress/**ma robe***	*mine/**la mienne***
*my shoes/**mes chaussures***	*mine/**les miennes***

predicate The predicate is that part of the sentence that tells us something about the subject. The main word of the predicate is the verb.

*The tourists are waiting for the tour bus / **Les touristes attendent l'autocar.***

The subject is *the tourists/**les touristes***. The predicate is *are waiting for the tour bus/**attendent l'autocar***. The verb is *are waiting/**attendent***. The direct object is *the tour bus/**l'autocar***.

preposition A preposition is a word that establishes a rapport between words.

English:

with, in, on, at, between

French:

*with me/**avec moi**; in the drawer/**dans le tiroir**; on the table/**sur la table***
*at six o'clock/**à six heures**; between him and her/**entre lui et elle***

Review verbs with prepositions beginning on page 690.

present indicative tense This tense is defined with examples on pages 10 and 11.

present participle A present participle is derived from a verb form. In French it is regularly formed like this: take the **nous** form of the present indicative tense of the verb you have in mind, then drop the ending **ons** and add **ant**. In English a present participle ends in *ing*.

Infinitive	Present Indicative **nous** form	Present participle
chanter	***nous chantons***	***chantant***
to sing	*we sing*	*singing*
finir	***nous finissons***	***finissant***
to finish	*we finish*	*finishing*
vendre	***nous vendons***	***vendant***
to sell	*we sell*	*selling*

For the regular formation of present participles and to find out what the three common irregular present participles are, review page 3.

present subjunctive tense This tense is defined with examples on pages 14 and 15.

pronoun A pronoun is a word that takes the place of a noun.

l'homme/il	***la femme/elle***	***l'arbre/il***	***la voiture/elle***
the man/he	*the woman/she*	*the tree/it*	*the car/it*

reflexive pronoun and reflexive verb In English a reflexive pronoun is a personal pronoun that contains *self* or *selves*. In French and English a reflexive pronoun is used with a verb that is called reflexive because the action of the verb falls on the reflexive pronoun.

In French there is a required set of reflexive pronouns for a reflexive verb.

se laver	***Je me lave.***	***Se blesser***	***Elle s'est blessée.***
to wash oneself	*I wash myself.*	*to hurt oneself*	*She hurt herself.*

In French a reflexive verb is conjugated with **être** to form the compound tenses. The French term for a reflexive verb is **un verbe pronominal** because a pronoun goes with the verb. Review the reflexive verbs **s'appeler** (verb 39), **se blesser** (verb 74), **se laver** (verb 277), and **se lever** (verb 279). *See also* agreement of past participle of a reflexive verb with its reflexive pronoun.

regular verb A regular verb is a verb that is conjugated in the various tenses according to a fixed pattern. For examples, review pages 22 to 25. *See also* conjugation, irregular verb.

relative pronoun A relative pronoun is a pronoun that refers to its antecedent.

The girl who is laughing over there is my sister /
La jeune fille qui rit là-bas est ma soeur.

The antecedent is *girl/la jeune fille*. The relative pronoun *who/qui* refers to the girl. *See also* antecedent.

sentence A sentence is a group of words that contains a subject and a predicate. The verb is contained in the predicate. A sentence expresses a complete thought.

The train leaves from the North Station at two o'clock in the afternoon /
Le train part de la Gare du Nord à deux heures de l'après-midi.

The subject is *train/le train*. The predicate is *leaves from the North Station at two o'clock in the afternoon/part de la Gare du Nord à deux heures de l'après-midi*. The verb is *leaves/part*. *See also* complex sentence, compound sentence, simple sentence.

simple sentence A simple sentence is a sentence that contains one subject and one predicate. The verb is the core of the predicate. The verb is the most important word in a sentence because it tells us what the subject is doing.

*Mary is eating an apple from her garden / **Marie mange une pomme de son jardin.***

The subject is *Mary/Marie*. The predicate is *is eating an apple from her garden/mange une pomme de son jardin.* The verb is *is eating/mange*. The direct object is *an apple/une pomme*. *From her garden/de son jardin* is an adverbial phrase. It tells you from where the apple came. *See also* complex sentence, compound sentence.

singular Singular means one. *See also* plural.

stem of a verb The stem of a verb is what is left after we drop the ending of its infinitive form. It is necessary to add to it the required endings of a regular verb in a particular verb tense.

Infinitive	Ending of infinitive	Stem
donner/to give	*er*	*donn*
choisir/to choose	*ir*	*chois*
vendre/to sell	*re*	*vend*

See also ending of a verb.

subject A subject is that part of a sentence that is related to its verb. The verb says something about the subject.

*Clara and Isabel are beautiful / **Clara et Isabel sont belles.***

subjunctive mood The subjunctive mood is the mood of a verb that is used in specific cases, *e.g.*, after certain verbs expressing a wish, doubt, emotion, fear, joy, uncertainty, an indefinite expression, an indefinite antecedent, certain conjunctions, and others. The subjunctive mood is used more frequently in French than in English. Review the uses of the subjunctive mood with examples on pages 26 to 31. *See also* mood of verbs.

subordinate clause Subordinate clause is another term for dependent clause. *See* dependent clause.

superlative adjective A superlative adjective is an adjective that expresses the highest degree when making a comparison of more than two persons or things.

Adjective	Comparative	Superlative
bon/good	*meilleur/better*	*le meilleur/best*
mauvais/bad	*plus mauvais/worse*	*le plus mauvais/worst*

See also comparative adjective.

superlative adverb A superlative adverb is an adverb that expresses the highest degree when making a comparison of more than two persons or things.

Adverb	Comparative	Superlative
vite/quickly	*plus vite/more quickly*	*le plus vite/most quickly*
	moins vite/less quickly	*le moins vite/least quickly*

See also comparative adverb.

tense of verb In English and French grammar, tense means time. The tense of the verb indicates the time of the action or state of being. The three major segments of time are past, present, and future. In French there are fourteen verb tenses, of which seven are simple tenses and seven are compound. Review pages 21 and 23 for the names of the fourteen tenses in French and English.

transitive verb A transitive verb is a verb that takes a direct object.

*I am closing the window / **Je ferme la fenêtre.***

The subject is *I/**Je***. The verb is *am closing / **ferme***. The direct object is *the window/**la fenêtre***.

See also intransitive verb.

verb A verb is a word that expresses action or a state of being.

Action: ***Les oiseaux volent** / The birds are flying.*

The verb is *volent/are flying*.

State of being: ***La jeune fille est heureuse** / The girl is happy.*

The verb is *est/is*.

Verb drills and tests with answers explained

The hundreds of verb forms in this part of the book will immerse you in the practice and improvement of your knowledge of French verb forms, tenses, and uses. You will find a variety of types of questions to make your experience interesting, challenging, and rewarding. All verb forms used in the drills and tests are found in the preliminary pages, among the 501 verbs, and in the back pages of this book.

The answers and explanations begin on page 81. The explanations are brief and to the point, including references to pages in this book for study and review.

Tips: To figure out the correct verb form of the required tense, examine each sentence carefully. Take a good look at the subject of the verb. Is it 1st, 2d, or 3d person? Is it singular or plural? Is it masculine or feminine? Look for a possible preceding noun or pronoun direct object, agreement on the past participle if necessary, and key elements that precede or follow the verb to determine the verb form and tense.

Also, look for other key words, such as yesterday, last week, today, at this moment, tomorrow, next year, certain conjunctions, and other key elements that indicate the need for the indicative or subjunctive moods in the required tense. The correct verb form depends on the sense and grammatical structure of the sentence. The best way to learn irregular forms in the seven simple tenses is from study, practice, and experience. For the formation of present and past participles, including irregulars, consult page 3. As for the formation of regular verb forms, consult pages 22 to 25. From time to time study and review pages 10 to 21.

Verb Test 1

SENTENCE COMPLETION

Directions: *Each of the following sentences contains a missing verb form. From the choices given, select the verb form of the tense that is required, according to the sense of the sentence, and write the letter of your choice on the line. At times, only the infinitive form is needed or a present or past participle. Answers and explanations begin on page 81.*

1. Hier, Marguerite _____ allée au théâtre avec ses amis.
A. a B. est C. avait D. était

2. Madame Céléstine ne _____ pas lire parce qu'elle a besoin de ses lunettes.
A. pouvons B. peuvent C. peux D. peut

3. Quand j'étais enfant, j' _____ beaucoup de camarades à l'école.
A. ai B. eus C. avais D. aurai

4. La petite fille _____ parce qu'elle est heureuse.
A. sourit B. souris C. ait souri D. eût souri

5. Hier soir, j'ai bien ri pendant que je _____ un film comique à la télé.
A. regardait B. regardais C. ai regardé D. regarderais

6. À cause du grand bruit qui vient de la rue, je ne peux pas _____ .
A. dormir B. dors C. dormant D. dormirai

7. Asseyez-vous, s'il vous plaît. Le docteur _____ d'arriver.
A. viens B. vient C. est venu D. était venu

8. Robert, je te demande de _____ ta chambre parce qu'elle est bien sale.
A. nettoie B. nettoyant C. nettoyer D. nettoyez

9. Le tonnerre va _____ peur aux enfants.
A. faire B. faisant C. fait D. font

10. Il commence à pleuvoir et Hélène a _____ son parapluie.
A. oublié B. oubliée C. oublie D. oublia

11. Chéri, aimes-tu les chaussures que j'ai _____ aujourd'hui?
A. acheté B. achetée C. achetés D. achetées

12. La semaine prochaine j' _____ en France.
A. irai B. alla C. allais D. irais

13. Si j'avais assez d'argent, j' _____ en Italie.
A. irai B. irais C. allais D. aille

14. Si j'ai assez d'argent, j' _____ au Canada.
A. irai B. irais C. allais D. aille

15. Ce matin Paulette _____ .
A. s'est lavé B. s'est lavée C. se sont lavés D. se sont lavées

16. Ce matin Gertrude _____ les cheveux.
A. s'est lavé B. s'est lavée C. se sont lavés D. se sont lavées

17. Je _____ à l'école en ce moment.
A. suis allé B. étais allé C. vais D. serais allé

18. Je _____ à la bibliothèque tous les jours.
A. vais B. étais allé C. serai allé D. serais allé

19. Deux et deux _____ quatre.
A. fait B. font C. feraient D. faisaient

20. Depuis combien de temps êtes-vous ici? Moi? Je _____ ici depuis dix minutes.
A. étais B. serai C. serais D. suis

DIALOGUE

Directions: *In the following dialogue there are blank spaces indicating missing verb forms. Select the appropriate verb form according to the sense of what the speakers are saying and write the letter of your choice on the line. The situation is given below. First, read the entire selection once. During the second reading, make your choices.*

Situation: You just got off an airplane. You go to the baggage room to claim your suitcase but you can't find it. An employee talks to you.

L'employé: Y a-t-il quelque chose qui ne va pas, mademoiselle?
Vous: Je ne _____ pas ma valise.

1. A. trouve B. trouverai C. trouverais D. trouvais

L'employé: Donnez-moi votre ticket de bagages, s'il vous plaît.
Vous: Une seconde, s'il vous plaît. _____ qu'il est dans ma poche.

2. A. J'ai cru B. Je croirai C. Je croirais D. Je crois

L'employé: Une minute. Je vais voir ce qui se passe.
Vous: J' _____ que ma valise n'est pas perdue!

3. A. espère B. espérer C. espères D. espérais

L'employé: Votre valise est dans l'avion qui arrive cet après-midi.
Vous: _____ bien contente.

4. A. J'ai été B. J'avais été C. J'aurais été D. Je suis

L'employé: Votre valise sera ici vers cinq heures, mademoiselle.
Vous: Je _____ la chercher. Merci bien, monsieur.

5. A. viendrai B. suis venue C. suis venu D. viendrais

PATTERN RESPONSES

Directions: *Answer the following questions in French in complete sentences in the affirmative, using a pronoun for the subject. Add* ***aussi*** *(also).*

Model: **François apprend bien. Et vos frères?**
You write: **Ils apprennent bien aussi.**

1. Pierre comprend bien. Et vos frères?

_____

2. Robert écrit bien. Et vos soeurs?

_____

3. Anne va bien. Et ses amis?

_____

4. Juliette lit un livre dans le lit. Et toi?

_____

5. Catherine voit bien. Et tes amis?

_____

6. Richard est allé au cinéma. Et Suzanne?

_____

7. Jean a bien mangé. Et nous?

_____

8. Jeanne s'est assise. Et les autres jeunes filles?

_____

9. Monsieur Dufy s'est lavé. Et sa femme?

_____

10. Monsieur Durand s'est lavé les cheveux. Et sa femme?

_____

11. Tu as rougi. Et les enfants?

_____

12. Monsieur Bertrand choisit une auto. Et Monsieur et Madame Duval?

_____

13. Tu finis la leçon. Et Pierre?

_____

14. Les enfants ont fait les devoirs. Et toi?

_____

15. Ce soldat défend la patrie. Et les autres soldats?

_____

16. Vous répondez à la question. Et Jacques?

_____

17. Vous vous couchez à dix heures. Et vos parents?

_____

18. Les enfants se sont amusés. Et Marie?

_____

19. Jacqueline s'est reposée. Et vous?

_____

20. Annie s'est levée tôt. Et nous?

_____

Verb Test 4

SENTENCE COMPLETION

Directions: *Each of the following sentences contains a missing verb form. From the choices given, select the verb form of the tense that is required, according to the sense of the sentence, and write the letter of your choice on the line.*

1. Je partirai quand mon amie _____ .
A. arrive B. arrivera C. est arrivé D. est arrivée

2. Je voudrais vous _____ ces fleurs.
A. donnez B. donner C. donnerais D. donnerez

3. Avez-vous lu les deux livres que je vous ai _____ la semaine dernière?
A. donner B. donné C. donnés D. donnez

4. Voici la lettre que _____ hier.
A. je reçois B. j'ai reçu C. je recevrais D. j'ai reçue

5. Hier _____ une lettre à des amis en France.
A. j'ai envoyé B. j'ai envoyée C. j'enverrai D. j'enverrais

6. J'irais en France si _____ assez d'argent.
A. j'ai B. j'aurais C. j'aurai D. j'avais

7. J'irai en France quand _____ assez d'argent.
A. j'aurai B. j'aurais C. j'ai eu D. j'avais

8. J'insiste que tu _____ ici avant cinq heures.
A. es B. sois C. soit D. soyez

9. Quand un enfant grandit, cela _____ dire qu'il devient plus grand.
A. veuille B. voulût C. veux D. veut

10. Pour bien apprendre dans la classe de français, _____ faire attention.
A. il faut B. il est C. il pleut D. il fend

11. Mon frère lisait pendant que j' _____ .
A. écris B. écrive C. ai écrit D. écrivais

12. Les étudiants lisaient quand _____ dans la salle de classe.
A. je suis entré B. j'entre C. j'étais entré D. j'entrerai

13. Quand j'étais petit, ma famille et moi _____ à la plage en été.
A. allons B. allions C. allaient D. irons

14. Richard _____ triste quand je l'ai vu.
A. est B. sera C. était D. serait

15. Quand ma mère était jeune, elle _____ jolie.
A. était B. est C. a été D. serait

16. À minuit, Pierre _____ et il a dit à son frère: "Lève-toi!
A. se réveille B. s'est réveillé C. s'est réveillée D. se réveillera

17. J'entends _____ quelqu'un en bas dans la salle à manger!
A. marchant B. marché C. marcher D. a marché

18. En général, on _____ froid en hiver.
A. est B. fait C. tient D. a

19. L'année dernière nous _____ en France.
A. est allé B. est allée C. sommes allés D. irons

20. Voici les livres que vous avez _____ .
A. désiré B. désirée C. désirés D. désirer

Verb Test 5

DIALOGUE

Directions: *In the following dialogue there are blank spaces indicating missing verb forms. Select the appropriate verb form according to the sense of what the speakers are saying and write the letter of your choice on the line. The conversation is taking place at the present time. First, read the entire selection once. During the second reading, make your choices.*

Situation: It's the morning of the year-end French exam in school. You and Jeanne are talking about the exams and your plans for summer vacation.

Jeanne: Il me reste encore un examen pour demain, puis les vacances vont commencer.
Vous: Mon dernier examen _____ lieu après-demain.

1. A. est B. sera C. aura D. avait

Jeanne: J'espère réussir à tous mes examens.
Vous: Il n'y _____ rien à craindre. Tu reçois toujours de bonnes notes.

2. A. ait B. soit C. a eu D. a

Jeanne: Ma famille et moi nous allons faire un voyage à Québec en juillet.
Vous: Moi, je devrai _____ ici à travailler.

3. A. reste B. rester C. restera D. resterai

Jeanne: L'été passé nous sommes allés dans les montagnes.
Vous: Alors, tu _____ faire un voyage tous les étés!

4. A. pouvez B. puis C. peux D. put

Jeanne: Alors, je te souhaite bonne chance dans tes examens.
Vous: Merci. Et je te _____ la même chose!

5. A. souhaite B. souhaites C. souhaité D. souhaitai

Verb Test 6

CHANGING FROM ONE VERB TO ANOTHER

Directions: *The verb forms in the following statements are all in the imperative. Change each sentence by replacing the verb with the proper form of the verb in parentheses, keeping the imperative form. The verb form you write must be in the same person as the one you are replacing. In other words, you must recognize if the given verb form is 2d person singular (tu), 1st person plural (nous), or 2d person plural, polite singular (vous). See the index of common irregular French verb forms, in the Appendixes, for irregular verb forms that you cannot identify.*

Model: **Prononcez le mot. (écrire)**

You write: **Écrivez le mot.**

1. Lisez la phrase. (dire)

_____

2. Prends le lait. (boire)

_____

3. Venez tout de suite. (partir)

_____

4. Ouvre la fenêtre. (fermer)

_____

5. Mets la valise là-bas. (prendre)

_____

6. Lisons la lettre. (écrire)

_____

7. Apprenez le poème. (lire)

_____

8. Partons maintenant. (sortir)

_____

9. Soyez à l'heure! (revenir)

_____

10. Voyons la leçon. (faire)

_____

11. Asseyez-vous, s'il vous plaît. (se lever)

_____

12. Accepte l'argent. (refuser)

_____

13. Vends le vélo. (acheter)

_____

14. Venez à l'heure. (être)

_____

15. Reste dans la maison. (aller)

_____

16. Lave-toi. (se lever)

_____

17. Cachons-nous. (se dépêcher)

_____

18. Arrête-toi. (s'amuser)

_____

19. Vends la maison. (acheter)

_____

20. Mange. (venir)

_____

CHANGING FROM ONE TENSE TO ANOTHER

Directions: *The following verb forms are all in the* ***future tense****. Change them to the* ***conditional****, keeping the same subject. See the index of common irregular French verb forms, in the Appendixes, for irregular verb forms that you cannot identify.*

Model: J'aurai **You write: J'aurais**

1. J'irai _____

2. Je partirai _____

3. J'aurai _____

4. Je serai _____

5. Tu aimeras _____

6. Tu feras _____

7. Il aura _____

8. Il sera _____

9. Il ira _____

10. On dira _____

11. Vous serez _____

12. Elle lira _____

13. J'ouvrirai _____

14. Nous saurons _____

15. Ils viendront _____

16. On boira _____

17. Ils courront _____

18. Ils liront _____

19. Elle mettra _____

20. Il apprendra _____

21. Je couvrirai _____

22. Il deviendra _____

23. Nous devrons _____

24. Vous direz _____

25. Vous irez _____

26. J'aimerai _____

27. Il faudra _____

28. Ils seront _____

29. Elles feront _____

30. On choisira _____

PATTERN RESPONSES

Directions: *Answer the following questions in the negative in complete French sentences. In answer (a), use* ***non****. In answer (b), use* ***non plus*** *(either). Study models (a) and (b) carefully. Use a pronoun as subject in your answers. Place* ***non plus*** *at the end of the sentence.*

Models: (a) **Est-ce que vous dansez?** (Do you dance?) — **You write:** (a) **Non, je ne danse pas.** (No, I don't dance.)

(b) **Et Charles?** (And Charles?) — **You write:** (b) **Il ne danse pas non plus.** (He doesn't dance either.)

1. (a) Est-ce que vous travaillez?

_____

(b) Et Paul?

_____

2. (a) Est-ce que Jacqueline étudie?

_____

(b) Et les grands garçons?

_____

3. (a) Est-ce qu'Anne va au match?

_____

(b) Et toi?

_____

4. (a) Est-ce que les enfants crient?

_____

(b) Et toi et tes amis?

_____

5. (a) Est-ce que l'avion arrive?

_____

(b) Et les trains?

_____

6. (a) Est-ce que tu es occupé?

_____

(b) Et tes parents?

_____

7. (a) As-tu fermé la fenêtre?

_____

(b) Et Pierre?

_____

8. (a) Avez-vous assisté à la conférence?

_____

(b) Et vos amis?

_____

9. (a) Monsieur Durand est-il allé au supermarché?

_____

(b) Et sa femme?

_____

10. (a) Madame Coty est-elle allée à la piscine?

_____

(b) Et les enfants?

_____

Verb Test 9

DIALOGUE

Directions: *In the following dialogue there are blank spaces indicating missing verb forms. Select the appropriate verb form according to the sense of what the speakers are saying and write the letter of your choice on the line. The situation is given below. The conversation is taking place at the present time. First, read the entire selection once. During the second reading, make your choices.*

Situation: You are seated in a train about to leave for Paris. A young man approaches and asks if he can sit next to you.

Le jeune homme: Vous permettez?
Vous: Mais, bien sûr! Je vous en _____ .

1. A. prie B. priez C. pries D. prions

Le jeune homme: J'espère que nous _____ un voyage agréable.

2. A. faisons B. fassions C. avons fait D. ferons

Vous: Je l' _____ bien aussi.

3. A. espérer B. ai espéré C. avais espéré D. espère

Le jeune homme: Savez-vous à quelle heure le train _____ à Paris?

4. A. est arrivé B. arriverait C. arrivera D. arrivait

Vous: Vers une heure et quart.
Le jeune homme: Il semble qu'il _____ beau temps.

5. A. a fait B. va faire C. faisait D. fasse

Vous: Oui, on _____ une belle journée pour aujourd'hui.

6. A. prévoit B. prévois C. prévoira D. prévoie

Le jeune homme: Je suppose que le train _____ bientôt.

7. A. est parti B. sera parti C. va partir D. partir

Vous: En effet, je _____ que nous sommes déjà en route.

8. A. crus B. croit C. croyais D. crois

Verb Test 10

SENTENCE COMPLETION

Directions: *Each of the following sentences contains a missing verb form. From the choices given, select the verb form of the tense that is required, according to the sense of the sentence, and write the letter of your choice on the line. At times, only the infinitive form is needed or a present or past participle.*

1. J'ai besoin de _____ mais je n'ai pas de savon.
A. laver B. se laver C. me laver D. me laverai

2. Quand Lisa _____ dans le salon, elle a vu un vase de jolies fleurs.
A. entre B. entrera C. est entré D. est entrée

3. Si j'ai le temps, _____ le travail.
A. j'ai fait B. je ferai C. je ferais D. je faisais

4. Si j'avais le temps, _____ le travail.
A. je ferais B. je ferai C. j'aurais fait D. j'ai fait

5. Si j'avais eu le temps, _____ le travail.
A. j'ai fait B. j'aurai fait C. j'aurais fait D. je faisais

6. Mademoiselle, un café pour mon ami, s'il vous plaît. Moi, _____ un thé.
A. j'aimerais B. j'ai aimé C. j'aimai D. j'aimais

7. À quelle heure pourriez-vous venir? Je _____ venir après le dîner.
A. pouvais B. pourrais C. pouvons D. puisse

8. Si j'étais vous, je ne le _____ pas.
A. ferai B. ferais C. faisais D. fasse

9. Je doute que Jeanne _____ ce soir.
A. viendra B. vienne C. viendrait D. vient

10. J'ai peur qu'il ne _____ malade.
A. sois B. soit C. sera D. serait

11. Je regrette que tu _____ malade.
A. es B. est C. soit D. sois

12. Je partirai à moins qu'il ne _____ .
A. vienne B. viennent C. viendra D. vient

13. Quoiqu'elle _____ belle, il ne l'aime pas.
A. est B. soit C. serait D. sera

14. Je le lui explique pour qu'elle _____ .
A. comprendra B. comprenne C. comprennent D. comprend

15. Je partirai dès qu'elle _____ .
A. arrive B. arrivera C. arriverait D. est arrivée

16. Il est urgent que vous _____ .
A. pars B. partez C. partiez D. partirez

17. Tout d'un coup, je me suis rappelé que _____ de le lui dire.
A. j'ai oublié B. j'oublie C. j'oublierai D. j'avais oublié

18. J'étais fatigué ce matin parce que _____ dormi.
A. je n'ai pas B. je n'aurai pas C. je n'avais pas D. j'ai

19. Je suis fatigué maintenant parce que _____ dormi.
A. j'ai B. je n'ai pas C. je vais D. je n'avais pas

20. Quand elle arrivera demain _____ le travail.
A. j'aurai fini B. j'ai fini C. j'avais fini D. je finisse

CHANGING FROM ONE TENSE TO ANOTHER

Directions: *The following verb forms are all in the present indicative tense. Change them to the* ***passé composé****, keeping the same subject. Consult the index of common irregular French verb forms, in the Appendixes, for irregular verb forms that you cannot identify. Keep in mind that to form the* ***passé composé*** *you need to use the present indicative tense of either* ***avoir*** *or* ***être*** *(depending on which of the two helping verbs is required) plus the past participle of the verb you are working with. If you feel uncertain about this, consult page 6 about when to use* ***avoir*** *or* ***être*** *as a helping verb.*

Model: **Elle mange.**

You write: **Elle a mangé.**

1. Elle va. _____

2. Il a. _____

3. Je m'assieds. _____

4. Ils ont. _____

5. Tu es. _____

6. Il va. _____

7. Nous allons. _____

8. Nous avons. _____

9. Je parle. _____

10. Elles viennent. _____

11. Je bois. _____

12. Ils boivent. _____

13. Vous buvez. _____

14. Je crois. _____

15. Tu dis. _____

16. Je peux. _____

17. Il faut. _____

18. Vous lisez. _____

19. Vous dites. _____

20. Tu mets. _____

21. Elle naît. _____

22. Elle meurt. _____

23. Elle vend. _____

24. Ils s'amusent. _____

25. Elle entre. _____

26. On finit. _____

27. Elles courent. _____

28. Ils prennent. _____

29. On apprend. _____

30. Elles arrivent. _____

COMPLETION OF VERB FORMS
(in the Seven Simple Tenses)

Directions: *Complete each verb form in the tenses indicated by writing the correct letter or letters on the blank lines.*

Présent de l'indicatif (Tense No. 1)

1. (aimer) J'aim _____
2. (chanter) Tu chant _____
3. (étudier)Il/elle/on étudi _____
4. (choisir) Janine chois _____
5. (entendre) J'entend _____
6. (attendre) Nous attend _____
7. (manger) Vous mang _____
8. (vendre) Ils/elles vend _____
9. (finir) Richard et moi fin _____
10. (donner) Marie et Jeanne donn _____

Imparfait de l'indicatif (Tense No. 2)

1. (parler) Je parl _____
2. (finir) Tu finiss _____
3. (vendre) Il/elle/on vend _____
4. (être) Madeleine ét _____
5. (avoir) Il/elle/on av _____
6. (venir) Nous ven _____
7. (faire) Vous fais _____
8. (aller) Ils/elles all _____
9. (jouer) Paul et Henri jou _____
10. (donner) Tu donn _____

Passé simple (Tense No. 3)
(*This tense is not used in conversation. It is used in literary style.*)

1. (parler) Je parl _____
2. (finir) Tu fin _____
3. (vendre) Il/elle/on vend _____
4. (écrire) Catherine écriv _____
5. (aller) Ils/elles all _____
6. (donner) Nous donn _____
7. (choisir) Vous chois _____
8. (comprendre) Ils/elles compr _____
9. (désirer) Hélène et Raymond désir _____
10. (danser) Il/elle/on dans _____

Futur (Tense No. 4)

1. (manger) Je manger _____
2. (finir) Tu finir _____
3. (vendre) Il/elle/on vendr _____
4. (écrire) La femme écrir _____
5. (aller) J'ir _____
6. (donner) Nous donner _____
7. (choisir) Vous choisir _____
8. (comprendre) Ils/elles comprendr _____
9. (jouer) Les garçons jouer _____
10. (avoir) J'aur _____

Conditionnel (Tense No. 5)

1. (aller) J'ir _____
2. (finir) Tu finir _____
3. (faire) Il/elle/on fer _____
4. (manger) Je manger _____
5. (pouvoir) Vous pourr _____
6. (parler) Nous parler _____
7. (être) Vous ser _____
8. (avoir) Ils/elles aur _____
9. (prendre) Je prendr _____
10. (dîner) Vous dîner _____

Présent du subjonctif (Tense No. 6)

1. (parler) que je parl _____
2. (donner) que tu donn _____
3. (oser) qu'il/elle/on os _____
4. (choisir) que je choisiss _____
5. (manger) que tu mang _____
6. (partir) que nous part _____
7. (vendre) que vous vend _____
8. (prendre) qu'ils/elles prenn _____
9. (finir) que nous finiss _____
10. (fermer) qu'il/elle/on ferm _____

Imparfait du subjonctif (Tense No. 7)

1. (parler) que je parl _____
2. (donner) que tu donn _____
3. (ouvrir) qu'il/elle/on ouvr _____
4. (partir) que nous part _____
5. (vouloir) que vous voul _____
6. (finir) qu'ils/elles fin _____

Verb Test 13

PAST PARTICIPLES

Directions: *In this crossword puzzle (**mots-croisés**) write the past participle for each of the verbs given below. Most of them are irregular. Past participles are important to know because they are needed to form the seven compound tenses, for example, the **passé composé**.*

Horizontalement

1. donner
5. pouvoir
7. fuir
8. rire
9. devoir (*backwards*)
10. taire
11. savoir
13. lire
15. savoir
18. naître
19. rire (*backwards*)
21. taire
22. tuer

Verticalement

1. devoir
2. naître
3. lire
4. vendre
5. prendre
6. dire
7. falloir
12. user
14. finir
16. mourir
17. être
20. avoir

Verb Test 14

DRILLING THE VERB *AVOIR*
(in the Seven Simple Tenses)

Note: You definitely must know the verb **avoir** in the seven simple tenses because they are needed to form the seven compound tenses of verbs conjugated with **avoir**, for example, the **passé composé** (Tense No. 8), as in **j'ai mangé** (I have eaten). Practice these by writing them every day until you know them thoroughly. If you don't know them, see verb 62. Also, read about **avoir** verbs on page 6. Review pages 23 to 25.

Directions: *Write the verb forms of* ***avoir*** *in the seven simple tenses indicated.*

1. Présent de l'indicatif (Tense No. 1)

Singular	Plural
j' _____	nous _____
tu _____	vous _____
il/elle/on/(*or a noun*) _____	ils/elles/(*or a noun*) _____

2. Imparfait de l'indicatif (Tense No. 2)

j' _____	nous _____
tu _____	vous _____
il/elle/on/(*or a noun*) _____	ils/elles/(*or a noun*) _____

3. Passé simple (Tense No. 3)

j' _____	nous _____
tu _____	vous _____
il/elle/on/(*or a noun*) _____	ils/elles/(*or a noun*) _____

4. Futur (Tense No. 4)

j' _____	nous _____
tu _____	vous _____
il/elle/on/(*or a noun*) _____	ils/elles/(*or a noun*) _____

5. Conditionnel (Tense No. 5)

j' _____	nous _____
tu _____	vous _____
il/elle/on/(*or a noun*) _____	ils/elles/(*or a noun*) _____

6. Présent du subjonctif (Tense No. 6)

que j' _____	que nous _____
que tu _____	que vous _____
qu'il/elle/on/(*or a noun*) _____	qu'ils/elles/(*or a noun*) _____

7. Imparfait du subjonctif (Tense No. 7)

que j' _____	que nous _____
que tu _____	que vous _____
qu'il/elle/on/(*or a noun*) _____	qu'ils/elles/(*or a noun*) _____

DRILLING THE VERB *ÊTRE*
(in the Seven Simple Tenses)

Note: You must know the verb **être** in the seven simple tenses because they are needed to form the seven compound tenses of verbs conjugated with **être**, for example, the **passé composé** (Tense No. 8), as in **elle est arrivée** (she has arrived). Practice these by writing them every day until you know them thoroughly. If you don't know them, see verb 211. Also, read about **être** verbs on page 6. Review pages 23 to 25.

***Directions**: Write the verb forms of **être** in the seven simple tenses indicated.*

1. Présent de l'indicatif (Tense No. 1)

Singular	Plural
je _____	nous _____
tu _____	vous _____
il/elle/on/(*or a noun*) _____	ils/elles/(*or a noun*) _____

2. Imparfait de l'indicatif (Tense No. 2)

j' _____	nous _____
tu _____	vous _____
il/elle/on/(*or a noun*) _____	ils/elles/(*or a noun*) _____

3. Passé simple (Tense No. 3)

je _____	nous _____
tu _____	vous _____
il/elle/on/(*or a noun*) _____	ils/elles/(*or a noun*) _____

4. Futur (Tense No. 4)

je _____	nous _____
tu _____	vous _____
il/elle/on/(*or a noun*) _____	ils/elles/(*or a noun*) _____

5. Conditionnel (Tense No. 5)

je _____	nous _____
tu _____	vous _____
il/elle/on/(*or a noun*) _____	ils/elles/(*or a noun*) _____

6. Présent du subjonctif (Tense No. 6)

que je _____ que nous _____
que tu _____ que vous _____
qu'il/elle/on/(*or a noun*) _____ qu'ils/elles/(*or a noun*) _____

7. Imparfait du subjonctif (Tense No. 7)

que je _____ que nous _____
que tu _____ que vous _____
qu'il/elle/on/(*or a noun*) _____ qu'ils/elles/(*or a noun*) _____

Verb Test 16

CHANGING FROM ONE TENSE TO ANOTHER

Directions: *The following verb forms are all in the* ***passé composé*** *(Tense No. 8). Change them to the* ***plus-que-parfait de l'indicatif*** *(Tense No. 9), keeping the same subject. Keep in mind that to form the* ***plus-que-parfait de l'indicatif*** *you need to use the imperfect indicative tense of either* ***avoir*** *or* ***être*** *(depending on which of the two helping verbs is required) plus the past participle of the verb you are working with. If you feel uncertain about this, consult page 6 about when to use* ***avoir*** *or* ***être*** *as a helping verb. Review the formation of the past participles on page 3. Also, review Verb Tests 14 and 15.*

Passé composé	Plus-que-parfait de l'indicatif
Model: Elle a mangé. (She has eaten.) **Elle est arrivée.** (She has arrived.)	**You write: Elle avait mangé.** (She had eaten.) **Elle était arrivée.** (She had arrived.)

1. Elle est allée. _____
2. Il a eu. _____
3. Je me suis assis. _____
4. Ils ont eu. _____
5. Tu as été. _____
6. Il est allé. _____
7. Nous sommes allés. _____
8. Nous avons eu. _____
9. J'ai parlé. _____
10. Elle est venue. _____
11. J'ai bu. _____
12. Ils se sont tus. _____
13. J'ai fait. _____
14. Tu as dû. _____
15. Vous avez dit. _____
16. J'ai pu. _____
17. Il a fallu. _____
18. Vous avez lu. _____
19. Vous avez dit. _____
20. Tu as mis. _____
21. Elle est née. _____
22. Elle est morte. _____
23. Elle s'est lavée. _____
24. Elles se sont lavées. _____
25. Je suis entré. _____
26. On a parlé. _____
27. Ils ont couru. _____
28. Ils ont pris. _____
29. On a dit. _____
30. J'ai compris. _____

SENTENCE COMPLETION

Directions: *Each of the following sentences contains a missing verb form. From the choices given, select the verb form of the tense that is required, according to the sense of the sentence, and write the letter of your choice on the line. At times only the infinitive form is needed or a present or past participle.*

1. Il est possible qu'elle _____ partie.
A. est B. soit C. a D. ait

2. Je doute que Laurent _____ fait cela.
A. a B. est C. ait D. soit

3. Je ne peux pas _____ maintenant parce qu'll fait un temps affreux.
A. sort B. sortant C. sortir D. sors

4. Joséphine est tombée en _____ dans la cuisine.
A. entrer B. entrant C. entrée D. entre

5. Simone a _____ la table.
A. essuyer B. essuyé C. essuyée D. essuyant

6. Françoise s'est _____ à écrire une lettre à sa tante.
A. mis B. mise C. mettre D. mettant

7. Les enfants _____ dire bonsoir aux invités.
A. vouloir B. voulu C. voulus D. veulent

8. Voici les fleurs que j'ai _____ .
A. acheté B. achetés C. achetées D. acheter

9. Quand Raymond eut mangé, il _____ .
A. partit B. partis C. partir D. partira

10. J' _____ fait le travail si j'avais eu le temps.
A. aurait B. aurais C. avais D. ai

Verb Test 18

PRESENT PARTICIPLES

Directions: *In this word puzzle, find the present participle of each of the verbs listed below and draw a line around each one. To get you started, the first verb on the list (**aller**), whose present participle is **allant**, is already done. The present participles are written horizontally, vertically, or backwards.*

aller
avoir
chanter
choisir
croire
dire
être
faire
finir

C	H	A	N	T	A	N	T	A	T
H	F	Y	T	N	V	E	A	P	N
O	A	A	N	A	E	F	V	R	A
I	I	N	A	N	A	I	E	E	Y
S	S	T	Y	E	N	N	N	N	O
I	A	A	O	T	T	I	D	A	V
S	N	N	R	D	I	S	A	N	T
S	T	T	C	T	E	S	N	T	N
A	L	L	A	N	T	A	T	O	A
N	A	I	S	S	A	N	T	S	N
T	N	O	S	A	N	T	F	A	E
L	I	S	A	N	T	T	A	N	V

lire
naître
oser
prendre
tenir
vendre
venir
voir

Verb Test 19

DIALOGUE

Directions: *In the following dialogue there are blank spaces indicating missing verb forms. Select the appropriate verb form according to the sense of what the speakers are saying and write the letter of your choice on the line. The situation is given below.*

Situation: You are a tourist in Paris. You are talking with the desk clerk in a hotel about a room.

L'employé: Bonjour. Vous désirez une chambre?
Vous: Oui, je désire _____ une petite chambre avec salle de bains.
1. A. louer B. loué C. louée D. louant

L'employé: C'est pour combien de personnes, s'il vous plaît?
Vous: _____ pour moi seulement.
2. A. C'était B. C'est C. Ce fut D. Ce fût

L'employé: Il me reste seulement une chambre à 150 euros la nuit, petit déjeuner compris.
Vous: D'accord. Je la _____ .
3. A. prend B. prends C. pris D. prenne

L'employé: C'est pour combien de temps?
Vous: Probablement pour une semaine, je _____ .
4. A. croit B. crus C. croie D. crois

L'employé: Bon. Signez ici et _____-moi votre passeport, s'il vous plaît.
5. A. montres B. montez C. montrez D. montrerez

Verb Test 20

CHANGING FROM ONE VERB TO ANOTHER

Directions: *The verb forms in the following statements are all in the* ***passé composé.*** *Change each sentence by replacing the verb in the sentence with the proper form of the verb in parentheses. Keep the* ***passé composé,*** *of course. Rewrite the statement in French.*

Models: Madeleine *est arrivée.* (partir) **You write: Madeleine *est partie.***
Simone *a mangé* le gâteau. (faire) **Simone *a fait* le gâteau.**

1. Richard *a appris* la leçon. (écrire)

_____

2. Elle *s'est assise.* (se lever)

_____

3. J'*ai écrit* la lettre. (lire)

_____

4. Elle *a fermé* la fenêtre. (ouvrir)

_____

5. Hélène *est arrivée.* (mourir)

_____

6. *Avez-vous acheté* un cadeau? (offrir)

_____

7. Marguerite *est sortie.* (venir)

_____

8. *Nous avons écouté* l'histoire. (croire)

_____

9. *Ils ont visité* Paris. (voir)

_____

10. Les enfants *ont pleuré.* (rire)

_____

11. *As-tu commandé* les frites? (prendre)

_____

12. *Ils sont allés* à Paris. (rester)

_____

13. L'étudiant *n'a pas compris* la réponse. (savoir)

_____

14. L'enfant *a mangé* un bon repas. (avoir)

_____

15. J'*ai envoyé* la lettre. (recevoir)

_____

16. *Avez-vous voyagé* en France? (être)

_____

17. *A-t-il ouvert* la boîte? (couvrir)

_____

18. Les enfants *se sont lavés*. (se taire)

_____

19. Louise *a désiré* venir chez moi. (vouloir)

_____

20. Qui *a entendu* le bruit? (faire)

_____

Verb Test 21

TRANSLATING VERB FORMS OF *ALLER*

Directions: *Translate the following verb forms of* ***aller*** *with their subjects into English. Keep in mind that some verb tenses can be translanted into English in more than one way. For example, depending on the thought expressed in a particular situation,* ***Je vais*** *can mean I go, I do go, or I am going.*

1. Nous allons	_____	**8.** Elle est allée	_____
2. Tu allais	_____	**9.** Elles étaient allées	_____
3. Il alla	_____	**10.** Nous fûmes allés	_____
4. Nous irons	_____	**11.** Tu seras allé	_____
5. Vous iriez	_____	**12.** Vous seriez allé	_____
6. Que j'aille	_____	**13.** Qu'il soit allé	_____
7. Que j'allasse	_____	**14.** Qu'elle fût allée	_____

Now, let's try a few other verbs. The infinitive form is given in parentheses in case you do not recognize the verb form. Remember that all verb forms used in these drills and tests are in this book among the 501 French verbs, in the preliminary pages, and in the back pages.

15. (savoir) Je sais _____
16. (être) Il fut _____
17. (avoir) Elle aura _____
18. (avoir) Nous aurions _____
19. (être) que je sois _____
20. (avoir) Il eut _____
21. (avoir) J'ai eu _____
22. (mettre) J'ai mis _____
23. (faire) Nous ferons _____
24. (venir) Je serais venu _____
25. (s'en aller) Allez-vous-en! _____
26. (vendre) Vous avez vendu _____
27. (finir) Nous aurons fini _____
28. (boire) Tu avais bu _____
29. (monter) Elle est montée _____
30. (rester) Nous sommes restés _____

Verb Test 22

PRESENT INDICATIVE

Directions: *In this word puzzle, find the verb form in the present indicative tense for each infinitive given in parentheses in the sentences below. When you find them, draw a line around each one. The verb form in the present tense of* ***faire*** *in the first statement given below is* ***faites****. It has already been done to get you started. The words are written horizontally, vertically, diagonally, or backwards.*

- Que (**faire**)-vous ce soir?
- Que me (**dire**)-vous?
- J' (**aimer**) danser.
- Moi, je (**aller**) chez moi.
- Les garçons (**avoir**)-ils assez d'argent pour aller au cinéma?
- Nous (**aller**) en France l'été prochain.
- Quand (**partir**)-tu?
- Et vous, (**être**)-vous heureux?
- Tes parents (**pouvoir**)-ils venir avec nous?
- Que (**devoir**)-tu faire maintenant?
- Pourquoi (**courir**)-tu?
- (**Vendre**)-ils leur maison?
- Est-ce que nous (**finir**) le travail aujourd'hui?

A	I	M	E	B	A	L	I	T	A
C	D	A	L	O	S	E	T	I	D
O	O	E	F	I	O	A	E	G	I
U	I	E	A	A	L	L	O	N	S
R	S	V	S	I	O	U	E	A	U
S	A	I	R	E	U	Ê	T	E	S
I	L	N	A	P	S	U	V	L	O
A	E	I	P	E	U	V	E	N	T
E	O	N	T	N	E	D	N	E	V
L	U	I	A	L	L	E	Z	O	N
F	A	T	E	Z	V	A	V	A	I
F	I	N	I	S	S	O	N	S	S

TRANSLATING VERB FORMS
(from English into French)

Directions: *Translate the following verb forms with their subjects into French. In Test 21 you did the opposite. This is good practice because it helps you to master verb forms in French and English.*

1. We are going

_____

2. You (*tu*) were going

_____

3. He went (*Tense No. 3*)

_____

4. We will go

_____

5. You (*vous*) would go

_____

6. that I may go

_____

7. that I might go (*Tense No. 7*)

_____

8. She has gone

_____

9. They (*fem.*) had gone

_____

10. We had gone (*Tense No. 10*)

_____

11. You (*tu*) will have gone

_____

12. You (*vous*) would have gone

_____

13. that he may have gone

_____

14. that she might have gone (*Tense No. 14*)

_____

15. I know (*savoir*)

_____

16. He was (*Tense No. 3*)

_____

17. She will have

_____

18. We would have

_____

19. that I may be

_____

20. He had (*Tense No. 3*)

_____

21. I have had

_____

22. I have put

_____

23. We will do

_____

24. I would have come

_____

25. Go away! (*vous*)

_____

26. You (*vous*) sold

_____

27. We will have finished

_____

28. You (*tu*) had drunk

_____

29. She went up

_____

30. We stayed

_____

DRILLING THE VERB *AVOIR* AGAIN
(in the Seven Simple Tenses)

Note: In Test 14 you drilled the verb **avoir** in the seven simple tenses. Now, do it again here because you must know them in order to form the seven compound tenses of verbs conjugated with **avoir**. Practice these by writing them every day until you know them thoroughly. If you don't know them yet, see verb 62. Also, read about **avoir** verbs on page 6. Review pages 23 to 25 again.

Directions: *Write the verb forms of* ***avoir*** *in the tenses indicated.*

Singular	Plural

1. Présent de l'indicatif (Tense No. 1)

j' _____ nous _____
tu _____ vous _____
il/elle/on/(*or a noun*) _____ ils/elles/(*or a noun*) _____

2. Imparfait de l'indicatif (Tense No. 2)

j' _____ nous _____
tu _____ vous _____
il/elle/on/(*or a noun*) _____ ils/elles/(*or a noun*) _____

3. Passé simple (Tense No. 3)

j' _____ nous _____
tu _____ vous _____
il/elle/on/(*or a noun*) _____ ils/elles/(*or a noun*) _____

4. Futur (Tense No. 4)

j' _____ nous _____
tu _____ vous _____
il/elle/on/(*or a noun*) _____ ils/elles/(*or a noun*) _____

5. Conditionnel (Tense No. 5)

j' _____ nous _____
tu _____ vous _____
il/elle/on/(*or a noun*) _____ ils/elles/(*or a noun*) _____

6. Présent du subjonctif (Tense No. 6)

que j' _____ que nous _____
que tu _____ que vous _____
qu'il/elle/on/(*or a noun*) _____ qu'ils/elles/(*or a noun*) _____

7. Imparfait du subjonctif (Tense No. 7)

que j' _____ que nous _____
que tu _____ que vous _____
qu'il/elle/on/(*or a noun*) _____ qu'ils/elles/(*or a noun*) _____

Verb Test 25

DRILLING THE VERB *ÊTRE* AGAIN
(in the Seven Simple Tenses)

Note: In Test 15 you drilled the verb **être** in the seven simple tenses. We would like you to do it again here because you must know them in order to form the seven compound tenses of verbs conjugated with **être**. Practice these by writing them every day until you know them thoroughly. If you don't know them yet, see verb 211. Also, read the statement about **être** verbs on page 6. Review again pages 23 to 25.

Directions: *Write the verb forms of* ***être*** *in the tenses indicated.*

1. Présent de l'indicatif (Tense No. 1)

Singular	Plural
je _____	nous _____
tu _____	vous _____
il/elle/on/(*or a noun*) _____	ils/elles/(*or a noun*) _____

2. Imparfait de l'indicatif (Tense No. 2)

j' _____ nous _____
tu _____ vous _____
il/elle/on/(*or a noun*) _____ ils/elles/(*or a noun*) _____

3. Passé simple (Tense No. 3)

je _____ nous _____
tu _____ vous _____
il/elle/on/(*or a noun*) _____ ils/elles/(*or a noun*) _____

4. Futur (Tense No. 4)

je _____ nous _____
tu _____ vous _____
il/elle/on/(*or a noun*) _____ ils/elles/(*or a noun*) _____

5. Conditionnel (Tense No. 5)

je _____ nous _____
tu _____ vous _____
il/elle/on/(*or a noun*) _____ ils/elles/(*or a noun*) _____

6. Présent du subjonctif (Tense No. 6)

que je _____ que nous _____
que tu _____ que vous _____
qu'il/elle/on/(*or a noun*) _____ qu'ils/elles/(*or a noun*) _____

7. Imparfait du subjonctif (Tense No. 7)

que je _____ que nous _____
que tu _____ que vous _____
qu'il/elle/on/(*or a noun*) _____ qu'ils/elles/(*or a noun*) _____

LE PASSÉ COMPOSÉ

Directions: *This crossword puzzle (**mots-croisés**) tests your knowledge of the **passé composé**. The missing words in the sentences below are the present tense of **avoir** or **être**, or the correct form of the past participle, or a subject pronoun.*

Horizontalement

1. Hier, je _____ allé au cinéma.
3. Marie est _____ (aller) à Paris.
8. Pierre _____ lu un livre.
9. Ils ont _____ (vouloir) partir.
11. _____ avez bien parlé.
13. La lettre? Je l'ai _____ (lire).
14. Paul s'est _____ (taire).
15. J'ai _____ (mettre) du sucre dans le café.
17. J'ai _____ (devoir) (*backwards*) partir.
18. Les lettres? Je les ai _____ (mettre) sur le bureau.
21. Nous avons bien _____ (rire).
22. Avez-vous _____ (savoir) la réponse?
23. Victor a-t- _____ compris?
24. Qu'a-t-elle _____ (dire)?

Verticalement

1. Je _____ tombé en montant l'escalier.
2. J'ai _____ (savoir) la réponse.
3. Hier soir, j' _____ beaucoup mangé.
4. Simone a _____ (lire) un livre.
5. Ce matin j'ai _____ (avoir) un petit accident.
6. Nous _____ pris le train.
7. Les enfants ont _____ (pouvoir) venir.
10. Nous avons _____ (vendre) la maison.
12. A-t-il _____ (savoir) (*backwards*) la réponse?
15. Madame Durand est _____ (mourir) hier soir.
16. Tu as _____ (finir) la leçon?
19. Jacqueline _____ restée à la maison.
20. Tu as _____ (savoir) cela, n'est-ce pas?

IDENTIFYING VERB FORMS
(in a Passage from French Literature)

Directions: *Read the following literary passage twice. Then, identify the verb forms with their subjects printed in* ***bold face*** *by giving (a) the infinitive of the verb form, (b) the name of the tense in French, and (c) the person and number of the verb form.*

Example: je vois You write: (a) voir
(b) présent de l'indicatif
(c) 1st person singular

Pourquoi donc ne vous **vois-je** pas, mon cher ami? **Je suis** inquiète de vous. **Vous** m'**aviez** tant **promis** de ne faire qu'aller et venir de l'Hermitage ici! Sur cela **je** vous **ai laissé** libre; et point du tout, **vous laissez** passer huit jours. Si **on** ne m'**avait** pas **dit** que **vous étiez** en bonne santé, **je** vous **croirais** malade. **Je** vous **attendais** avant-hier ou hier, et **je** ne vous **vois** point arriver.

Mon Dieu! qu'**avez-vous** donc? **Vous** n'**avez** point d'affaires; **vous** n'**avez** pas non plus de chagrins, car **je me flatte** que **vous seriez venu** sur-le-champ me les confier. **Vous êtes** donc malade! **Tirez**-moi d'inquiétude bien vite, **je** vous en **prie**. Adieu, mon cher ami.

Lettre de Madame d'Épinay à Jean-Jacques Rousseau,
Selection from *Les Confessions* by Jean-Jacques Rousseau

1. vois-je
(a) _____
(b) _____
(c) _____

2. je suis
(a) _____
(b) _____
(c) _____

3. vous aviez promis
(a) _____
(b) _____
(c) _____

4. j'ai laissé
(a) _____
(b) _____
(c) _____

5. vous laissez
(a) _____
(b) _____
(c) _____

6. on avait dit
(a) _____
(b) _____
(c) _____

7. vous étiez
(a) _____
(b) _____
(c) _____

8. je croirais
(a) _____
(b) _____
(c) _____

9. vous avez

(a) _____

(b) _____

(c) _____

10. j'attendais

(a) _____

(b) _____

(c) _____

11. je vois

(a) _____

(b) _____

(c) _____

12. avez-vous

(a) _____

(b) _____

(c) _____

13. vous avez

(a) _____

(b) _____

(c) _____

14. je me flatte

(a) _____

(b) _____

(c) _____

15. vous seriez venu

(a) _____

(b) _____

(c) _____

16. vous êtes

(a) _____

(b) _____

(c) _____

17. tirez

(a) _____

(b) _____

(c) _____

18. je prie

(a) _____

(b) _____

(c) _____

Answers to verb tests with explanations

Test 1

1. B The verb **aller** is conjugated with **être** to form a compound tense. Review page 6. A and C are not correct because they are forms of **avoir**. You need the *passé composé* because of **hier**/yesterday. In D, **était** is imperfect indicative, which makes the verb form **était allée** pluperfect indicative. Review the uses of the *passé composé* on page 16 and the *plus-que-parfait de l'indicatif* on pages 16 to 17. Review **aller**.

2. D The subject is 3d person sing. In D, **peut** is 3d person sing. A, B, and C are not 3d person sing. Review **pouvoir**.

3. C The tenses of **avoir** in A, B, and D would not make sense here because you need the imperfect indicative, which is in C. Review the imperfect tense on pages 11 and 12. Review **avoir**.

4. A You need the 3d person sing., present tense, of **sourire** because the subject is 3d person sing. The tenses in C and D do not make any sense here because there is nothing in the sentence to require the subjunctive. The verb form in B is not 3d person sing. Review **sourire**.

5. B The tenses of **regarder** in C and D would not make sense here because you need the imperfect indicative, which is in B. The verb form in A is 3d person sing. and you are dealing with the subject **je**, which is 1st person, sing. Besides, C is not a good choice because **je** would be **j'** in front of **ai regardé**. Review the uses of the imperfect indicative tense on pages 11 and 12. Review **regarder**.

6. A You need the infinitive form **dormir** because it is right after the verb form **peux** in **je ne peux pas** (I am not able to sleep). The forms in B, C, and D would make no sense. Review those forms of **dormir**.

7. B The situation is in the present. The subject, **le docteur**, is 3d person sing. and so is **vient** in B. In A, **viens** is not 3d person sing. C and D are not in the present tense. Review **venir** and **venir de**. Also review *Verbs with prepositions* in the Appendixes, specifically **venir de + inf.**

8. C The infinitive **nettoyer** is needed because of the preposition **de** in front of it. Review *Verbs with prepositions* in the Appendixes, specifically **demander de + inf.** Review the other forms of **nettoyer** in A, B, and D.

9. A The infinitive **faire** is needed because **va** (a form of **aller**) precedes it. Review **aller + inf.** in the section on *Verbs with prepositions* in the Appendixes, and the other forms of **faire** in B, C, and D.

10. A You need the past participle to complete the *passé composé* where you see the helping verb **a** in front of the blank space. The past participle in B is feminine but there is no preceding feminine direct object. Review the forms of **oublier** in C and D.

11. D You need the fem. pl. form of the past participle (**achetées**) because there is a preceding fem. pl. direct object noun (**les chaussures**). The other past participles are masc. sing. in A, fem. sing. in B, and masc. pl. in C.

12. A The subject is 1st pers. sing. **j'** and it requires **irai**, the future of **aller**. **La semaine prochaine** indicates future time. Review the other tenses of **aller** in B, C, and D.

13. B You need the 1st pers. sing. conditional of **aller** because the subordinate clause begins with **si** (if) and the verb in that clause is imperfect indicative (**j'avais**). Review **si** clauses, a summary of sequence of verb tenses at the top of page 26 where there are examples. Review the other tenses of **aller** in A, C, and D. Study, practice, and experience will help you recognize French verb forms and tenses.

14. A You need the 1st pers. sing. future of **aller** because the subordinate clause begins with **si** (if) and the verb in that clause is present indicative (**j'ai**). Review **si** clauses, a summary of sequence of verb tenses at the top of page 26 where there are examples. Review the other tenses of **aller** in B, C, and D.

15. B You need the fem. sing. form of the past participle (**lavée**) because the verb is reflexive (**se laver**/to wash oneself) and the fem. sing. agreement on the past participle is made with the reflexive pronoun **s'** (herself). We know it's fem. because the subject is **Paulette**. The reflexive pronoun **s'** in this sentence serves as a preceding direct object because Paulette washed *herself*. However, if there were a direct object *after* the verb, e.g., her feet, hair (as in sentence 16 below), there would be no agreement on the past participle. The other past participles in this sentence are masc. sing. in A, masc. pl. in C, and fem. pl. in D. Review also page 6.

16. A You need the masc. sing. form of the past participle (**lavé**) because in this sentence the reflexive pronoun **s'** in **s'est lavé** is an indirect object, not a direct object. A past participle never agrees in gender (masc. or fem.) or number (sing. or pl.) with an indirect object. In other words, Gertrude washed her hair (**les cheveux**), which is *on herself*. Compare this sentence with number 15 above.

17. C You need the present indicative of **aller** because the sentence states **en ce moment**/at this moment. Review the other tenses of **aller** in A, B, and D. Review the uses of the present indicative tense and the examples on pages 10 and 11.

18. A You need the present indicative of **aller** because the sentence states **tous les jours** (every day), which is habitual action. Review the uses of the present indicative tense and the examples on page 10, in particular, the example in (b) at the top of page 11.

19. B You need the present tense, 3d person pl. of **faire** because the subject is 3d person pl. Review the examples in (c) at the top of page 11. Also, review the other tenses of **faire** in A, C, and D.

20. D You need the present tense, 1st person sing. of **être** because the subject is 1st person sing. Review the examples in (f) on page 11. Also, review the other tenses of **être** in A, B, and C.

Test 2

1. A The situation is in the present. Review the other tenses of **trouver** in B, C, and D.

2. D You need the present tense because the action is going on in the present. Do you recognize the other tenses in A, B, and C? Review **croire**.

3. A Again, the present tense. Review the forms of **espérer**.

4. D If you cannot identify the tenses, review **être**.

5. A You need the future tense of **venir** because the clerk says that the suitcase will be available around five o'clock. You will come to get it at that time. Review the tenses of **venir**.

Test 3

1. **Ils comprennent bien aussi.** Study the forms of **comprendre**.
2. **Elles écrivent bien aussi.** Study the forms of **écrire**.
3. **Ils vont bien aussi.** Study the forms of **aller**.
4. **Je lis un livre dans le lit aussi.** Study the forms of **lire**.
5. **Ils voient bien aussi.** Study the forms of **voir**.
6. **Elle est allée au cinéma aussi.** You need to add **e** on the past participle for fem. agreement with the subject **elle**. Study the nonreflexive verbs conjugated with **être** to form the compound tenses on page 6. Also, study the forms of **aller**.
7. **Nous avons bien mangé aussi.** Study the *passé composé* of **manger**.
8. **Elles se sont assises aussi.** You need the fem. pl. agreement on the past participle of this reflexive verb **s'asseoir** because the reflexive pronoun **se** is a preceding direct object and the subject is **elles**. In other words, they *sat themselves*. Review the explanation in number 15 in Test 1. Review the forms of **s'asseoir**.
9. **Elle s'est lavée aussi.** Review the explanation in number 15 in Test 1. It's the same idea here. Review the *passé composé* of **se laver**.
10. **Elle s'est lavé les cheveux aussi.** Review the explanation in number 16 in Test 1. It's the same idea here.
11. **Ils ont rougi aussi.** Review the *passé composé* of **rougir**.
12. **Ils choisissent une auto aussi.** Study the present tense of **choisir**.
13. **Il finit la leçon aussi.** Study the present tense of **finir**.
14. **J'ai fait les devoirs aussi.** Study the *passé composé* of **faire**.
15. **Ils défendent la patrie aussi.** Study the present tense of **défendre**.
16. **Il répond à la question aussi.** Study the present tense of **répondre** and **répondre à** + noun, in the section on *Verbs with prepositions* in the Appendixes.
17. **Ils se couchent à dix heures aussi.** Study the forms of the reflexive verb **se coucher**.
18. **Elle s'est amusée aussi.** She amused *herself.* Review the explanation in number 15 in Test 1. It's the same idea here. Also, study the *passé composé* of the reflexive verb **s'amuser**.
19. **Je me suis reposé(e) aussi. Je** tells you if it is fem. or masc., depending on the context. If **me** (myself) is fem., add **e** to the past participle for fem. agreement with it. The idea here is the same as in the explanation in number 15 in Test 1. Study the *passé composé* of **se reposer**.
20. **Nous nous sommes levés tôt aussi.** Same idea here as in number 19 above. Review **se lever**.

Test 4

1. B You need the future tense because **quand** introduces the clause and the verb in the main clause is future tense. Review the uses and examples of the future tense on pages 12–13 and the formation of the future on page 22. Study the verb forms of **arriver** in A, C, and D.
2. B You need the infinitive form because there is no subject preceding the blank space. Here, **vous** is an indirect object pronoun meaning *to you.* (I would like to give these flowers to you.) Study the verb forms of **donner** in A, C, and D.

3. C You need the masc. pl. form of the past participle because **donner** is conjugated with **avoir** to form the *passé composé*, a compound tense, and it must agree with the preceding direct object **livres**. Here, **que** is a relative pronoun (*that* or *which*) and it refers to **les deux livres**. In other words, *Did you read the two books that I gave (to) you last week?*

4. D Same idea here as in number 3 above. Do you think you understand this construction by now? You need the fem. sing. form of the past participle because it refers to **que**, which relates to **la lettre**. In other words, *Here is the letter that I received yesterday*. Review the forms of **recevoir**.

5. A You need the *passé composé* because the sentence begins with **hier**/yesterday. In B the past participle is fem. because of the added **e**. There is no need for a fem. past participle because there is no *preceding* fem. direct object. The direct object is **une lettre**, which comes *after* the verb. Review the verb forms in C and D of **envoyer**.

6. D The clause where a verb form is needed begins with **si**/if. The verb in the main clause is conditional (**j'irais**/I would go). For those two reasons you need the imperfect indicative in D. Review **si** clauses where there are examples at the top of page 26. If you reversed the two clauses, the idea would be the same: **Si j'avais assez d'argent j'irais en France**/If I had enough money I would go to France. Review the verb forms in A, B, and C of **avoir**.

7. A You need the future tense of **avoir** because **quand** (when) precedes the required verb form and the verb in the main clause is future (**j'irai**). Review the uses and examples of the future on pages 12–13, in particular, example (d). Also, review the other forms of **avoir** in B, C, and D.

8. B You need the present subjunctive of **être** (**que tu** *sois*) because the verb in the preceding main clause is **j'insiste**. Here, the need for the subjunctive is the same in English, too, when we say: *I insist that you be here before five o'clock*. Review the uses and examples of the present subjunctive on page 14, especially example (c). Study the other forms of **être** in A, C, and D.

9. D You need the 3d person sing. present tense **veut** because the subject (**cela**/that) is 3d person sing. The form **veux** in C is 1st or 2d person sing. present tense of **vouloir.** There is nothing in the sentence to require the present subjunctive in A or the imperfect subjunctive in B. Review the forms of **vouloir**.

10. A You must know the impersonal expression **il faut**/it is necessary. Review the forms of **falloir** in the section on *Defective and impersonal verbs* in the Appendixes, and the expressions on the bottom of that page. Also, review the section on *Verbs with prepositions* in the Appendixes, in particular, **falloir** + inf. In B review **être**. In C review **il pleut (pleuvoir)** in the section on *Defective and impersonal verbs*, in the Appendixes, and the examples on the bottom of that page. In D review **il fend (fendre)**.

11. D The conjunction **pendant que** (while) precedes the subject and required verb form. This indicates that two actions were going on at the same time in the past: *My brother was reading while I was writing*. For that reason the imperfect indicative is needed. Review the imperfect tense on pages 11 and 12, especially example (a). Also, review the other forms of **écrire** in A, B, and C. See page 22 for the regular formation of the imperfect.

12. A An action was going on in the past when another action occurred: *The students were reading when I entered the classroom.* Review the imperfect tense on pages 11 and 12, especially example (b). Review the other forms of **entrer** in B, C, and D.

13. B You need the imperfect indicative tense because a habitual action took place in the past: *When I was little, my family and I used to go to the beach in the summer.* Review the imperfect tense on pages 11 and 12, especially example (c). Review the other forms of **aller** in A, C, and D.

14. C You need the imperfect indicative tense because the sentence contains a description in the past: *Richard was sad when I saw him.* Review the imperfect tense on pages 11 and 12, especially example (d). Also, review the other forms of **être** in A, B, and D.

15. A The reason for the imperfect indicative tense here is the same as in number 14 above. Do you think you understand this construction now?

16. B You need the *passé composé* because the action took place in the past: *At midnight, Peter woke up and said to his brother: "Get up!"* In C the past participle is fem. sing., but there is no need for it because the subject is masc. Review agreement on the past participle of a reflexive verb in numbers 15 and 16, Test 1. Review the other forms of **se réveiller** in A, C, and D.

17. C You need the infinitive form **marcher** because it is right after the verb **entendre**. Review **entendre** + inf. in the section on *Verbs with prepositions* in the Appendixes. Review the other forms of **marcher** in A, B, and D.

18. D You are dealing with **avoir froid**/to feel cold. Review the verb **avoir**. Review the forms of **avoir**. In A review **être**, **faire** in B, **tenir** in C, and the idiomatic expressions on the bottom of those pages.

19. C The subject of the verb is **nous**, 1st person pl. You need the *passé composé* because of **l'année dernière**/last year. The plural **s** is needed on **allés** because it is conjugated with **être** and the subject is plural. Review the other forms of **aller** in A, B, and D. Also, review page 6.

20. C The explanation here is the same as in numbers 3 and 4 above in this test.

Test 5

1. C You are dealing with **avoir lieu**/to take place. Review the verb **avoir**, especially **avoir lieu**. You need the future of **avoir** because the exam will take place after tomorrow. Review **avoir** and the forms of **être** in A and B.

2. D You are dealing with **avoir** in the idiomatic expression **il y a**/there is . . ., there are: *There is nothing to fear.* Review the verb **avoir**, especially **il y a**. Review the other forms of **avoir** in A and C. Review also **être** for **soit** in B.

3. B You need the infinitive form **rester** because it is right after the verb **devrai (devoir)**. Review **devoir** and **devoir** + inf. in the section on *Verbs with prepositions* in the Appendixes. See **rester** for the other forms in A, C, and D.

4. C Review **pouvoir** for the forms in A, B, C, and D.

5. A Review **souhaiter** for the forms in A, B, C, and D.

Test 6

Note: In this test, the verb form you are given in each sentence is the imperative (command) mood. Review the *impératif* on pages 20 and 21. The forms of the imperative are given near the bottom of each page among the 501 verbs fully conjugated in all the tenses in this book. They are the *tu*, *nous*, and *vous* forms; for example: **donne!**/give! (*tu* understood), **donnons!**/let's give! (*nous* understood), **donnez!**/give! (*vous* understood). You have to look at the ending of the verb form to see if the subject understood is 2d person sing. (*tu*), 1st person pl. (*nous*), or 2d person pl., polite sing. (*vous*).

In the imperative, **er** verbs, like **donner**, drop the **s** in the 2d person sing. (*tu* form) of the present indicative, for example: **Marie, donne-moi le chocolat!**/Marie, give me the chocolate! But the **s** remains if the word that follows is **en** or **y** to facilitate a liaison in pronunciation, making the **s** sound as **z**, for example: **Robert, donnes-en aux enfants!**/ Robert, give some to the children! If you need to improve your pronunciation of French—in particular, verb forms—consult Barron's book *Pronounce It Perfectly in French.*

1. **Dites la phrase.** Study the forms of **lire** and **dire**.
2. **Bois le lait.** Study the forms of **prendre** and **boire**.
3. **Partez tout de suite.** Study the forms of **venir** and **partir**.
4. **Ferme la fenêtre.** Study the forms of **ouvrir** and **fermer**.
5. **Prends la valise là-bas.** Study the forms of **mettre** and **prendre**.
6. **Écrivons la lettre.** Study the forms of **lire** and **écrire**.
7. **Lisez le poème.** Study the forms of **apprendre** and **lire**.
8. **Sortons maintenant.** Study the forms of **partir** and **sortir**.
9. **Revenez à l'heure!** Study the forms of **être** (for *soyez*) and **revenir**. Note that in the imperative **être** uses the forms of the present subjunctive. See example (d) at the top of page 21.
10. **Faisons la leçon.** Study the forms of **voir** and **faire**.
11. **Levez-vous, s'il vous plaît.** Study the forms of the reflexive verb **s'asseoir** and **se lever**. Note that when you use a reflexive verb in the imperative, drop the subject pronoun, of course, but keep the reflexive pronoun **nous** or **vous**, placing it after the verb with a hyphen. **Tu** changes to **toi** in the affirmative imperative; for example: **Lève-toi!**/Get up! Under the *Impératif* for these two verbs note where the reflexive pronoun is placed when the imperative is negative.
12. **Refuse l'argent.** Study the forms of **accepter** and **refuser**.
13. **Achète le vélo.** Study the forms of **vendre** and **acheter**. Read the note above for an explanation of when **s** drops or is kept on **er** verbs in the *tu* form of the imperative.
14. **Soyez à l'heure.** Study the forms of **venir** and **être** (for *soyez*). Note that in the imperative **être** uses the forms of the present subjunctive. See example (d) at the top of page 21.
15. **Va dans la maison.** Study the forms of **aller** and **rester**. Note that **s** drops in the 2d person sing. (*tu* form) of the present indicative of **aller** when used in the imperative. But the **s** remains if the word that follows is **y** to facilitate a liaison in pronunciation, making the **s** sound as **z**, for example: **Robert, vas-y!**/ Robert, go to it!
16. **Lève-toi.** Study the forms of **se laver** in the imperative and **se lever**. Read our note of explanation in sentence number 11 above.

17. **Dépêchons-nous.** Study the forms of the imperative of **se cacher** and **se dépêcher**.
18. **Amuse-toi.** Study the forms of the imperative of **s'arrêter** and **s'amuser**. Read the explanation about reflexive verbs in the imperative, affirmative, and negative, above in number 11.
19. **Achète la maison.** Study the forms of the imperative of **vendre** and **acheter**. Review the explanation in number 13 above.
20. **Viens.** Study the imperative of **manger** and **venir**.

Test 7

Note: For all verb forms in this test, review the uses and examples of the future and conditional on pages 12–13. For the formation of the future and conditional of regular verbs, review page 22.

Also, review the future and conditional of each of the verbs given below.

1. **J'irais.** See **aller**.
2. **Je partirais.** See **partir**.
3. **J'aurais.** See **avoir**.
4. **Je serais.** See **être**.
5. **Tu aimerais.** See **aimer**.
6. **Tu ferais.** See **faire**.
7. **Il aurait.** See **avoir**.
8. **Il serait.** See **être**.
9. **Il irait.** See **aller**.
10. **On dirait.** See **dire**.
11. **Vous seriez.** See **être**.
12. **Elle lirait.** See **lire**.
13. **J'ouvrirais.** See **ouvrir**.
14. **Nous saurions.** See **savoir**.
15. **Ils viendraient.** See **venir**.
16. **On boirait.** See **boire**.
17. **Ils courraient.** See **courir**.
18. **Ils liraient.** See **lire**.
19. **Elle mettrait.** See **mettre**.
20. **Il apprendrait.** See **apprendre**.
21. **Je couvrirais.** See **couvrir**.
22. **Il deviendrait.** See **devenir**.
23. **Nous devrions.** See **devoir**.
24. **Vous diriez.** See **dire**.
25. **Vous iriez.** See **aller**.
26. **J'aimerais.** See **aimer**.
27. **Il faudrait.** See **falloir**.
28. **Ils seraient.** See **être**.
29. **Elles feraient.** See **faire**.
30. **On choisirait.** See **choisir**.

Test 8

Note: For the formation of the present indicative tense of regular verbs, review page 22. For the formation of the *passé composé* and other compound tenses, review pages 23 to 25. Note the position of **ne** and **pas** in the following negative sentences.

1. (a) **Non, je ne travaille pas.** (b) **Il ne travaille pas non plus.**
   Review the present indicative of **travailler**.
2. (a) **Non, elle n'étudie pas.** (b) **Ils n'étudient pas non plus.**
   Review the present indicative of **étudier**.
3. (a) **Non, elle ne va pas au match.** (b) **Je ne vais pas au match non plus.**
   Review the present indicative of **aller**.
4. (a) **Non, ils ne crient pas.** (b) **Nous ne crions pas non plus.**
   Review the present indicative of **crier**.
5. (a) **Non, il n'arrive pas.** (b) **Ils n'arrivent pas non plus.**
   Review the present indicative of **arriver**.

6. (a) **Non, je ne suis pas occupé.** (b) **Ils ne sont pas occupés non plus.**
Review the present indicative of **être**. Note the expression **être occupé** (to be busy) under the verb **occuper**. Note also that **occupés** contains **s** to make it masc. pl. because it is an adjective that describes the subject **ils**, which is masc. pl. If the subject were **elles**, the sentence would be **elles ne sont pas occupées non plus.**
7. (a) **Non, je n'ai pas fermé la fenêtre.** (b) **Il n'a pas fermé la fenêtre non plus.**
Review the *passé composé* of **fermer**. Note the position of **ne** and **pas** in a compound tense.
8. (a) **Non, je n'ai pas assisté à la conférence.** (b) **Ils n'ont pas assisté à la conférence non plus.**
Review the *passé composé* of **assister** and note the expression **assister à.** Note also the position of **ne** and **pas** in a compound tense. Also review the use of **assister à**.
9. (a) **Non, il n'est pas allé au supermarché.** (b) **Elle n'est pas allée au supermarché non plus.**
Review the *passé composé* of **aller**. Note the need for the addition of **e** on the past participle **allée**. The fem. sing. agreement must be made on it because **aller** is conjugated with **être** to form a compound tense. The agreement is made with the subject, which is **elle**, fem. sing. Review page 6.
10. (a) **Non, elle n'est pas allée à la piscine.** (b) **Ils ne sont pas allés à la piscine non plus.**
Read the explanation in number 9 above. It's the same idea here.

Test 9

Note: From time to time practice the formation of the seven simple tenses for regular verbs on pages 22 and 23 and the formation of the seven compound tenses on pages 23 to 25.

1. A The subject is **je**; therefore, you need the 1st person sing. of **prier**. Review the forms of **prier** in the present indicative tense and the words and expressions related to that verb.
2. D You need the 1st person pl. of **faire** because the subject is **nous**. The future tense is needed because of the sense of the statement. The other verb forms in A, B, and C would not make any sense here. If you do not recognize those forms, review **faire**.
3. D You need the 1st person sing. of **espérer** because the subject is **je**. The tenses of **espérer** in B and C would make no sense here. In A the infinitive form of the verb cannot be used here because there is a subject. Review **espérer**. If you want to know why the *accent aigu* on **espérer** sometimes changes to *accent grave*, as in **j'espère**, review the section on orthographically changing verbs (those that change in spelling) on pages 32–34, in particular, examples (14) and (15) on page 34.
4. C You need the 3d person sing. because the subject is **le train**, 3d person sing. The future tense is needed because the tenses in A, B, and D would make no sense. A is the *passé composé*. B is the conditional. D is the imperfect indicative. Can you recognize those tenses from the endings of the verb forms? If not, review them on pages 12–13, and under **arriver**. Also, if you are not sure of how they are translated into English, review pages 8 and 9 where you will find English translations of all the tenses using the verb *to go* as an example. Just substitute the verb *to arrive* in place of *to go*.

5. B The only sensible verb tense here is in B: *It seems that it is going to be beautiful weather.* A is the *passé composé* of **faire** but the speakers are not talking about what the weather was like in the past. C is the imperfect indicative of **faire** but the speakers are not talking about what the weather was like at any particular time in the past. D is the present subjunctive of **faire** and there is nothing in the sentence that requires the subjunctive. Review the tenses of **faire** and the expressions regarding weather on the bottom of that page.

6. A The subject is **on**, 3d person sing. The verb form in A is also 3d person sing. As for the tenses of the verb forms in B, C, and D, review the verb **prévoir**.

7. C You cannot use the infinitive form in D because **le train**, 3d person sing., is the subject. As for the tenses of the verb forms in A and B, review the verb **partir**. The speaker supposes that the train *is going to leave* soon.

8. D You need the 1st person sing. of **croire** because the subject is **je**. B is 3d person sing. A is the *passé simple*, which is not used in conversation. C is the imperfect indicative of **croire**, which is a past tense, and the speakers are talking about things happening now. Review the verb forms of **croire**.

Test 10

1. C You need the infinitive form of the reflexive verb **se laver** because the preposition **de** is in front of the blank space where a verb form is required. For that reason, D is not a correct choice because it is not an infinitive. In C the form ***me* laver** (to wash myself) is needed because the subject is **je**. A is not a reflexive verb. B is reflexive but you cannot use **se laver** because the subject is **je**. When you use a reflexive verb, its pronoun (**me, te, se, nous, vous, se**) must agree with the subject; for example: **je me . . . , tu te . . . , il se . . .** and so on. Review the forms of **se laver**. Also, review **avoir besoin de** under **avoir**.

2. D You need the *passé composé* of **entrer** because of the sense of the statement and the use of **a vu** (*passé composé* of **voir**) in the sentence. When Lisa entered the living room, she saw a vase of pretty flowers. In D the past participle **entrée** is fem. sing. because the verb is conjugated with **être** and the subject is fem. sing. Review page 6. In C the past participle **entré** is masc. sing. A is the present tense and B is the future, neither of which makes any sense from the point of view of time because the action is in the past. Review the forms of **entrer**.

3. B The sentence means *If I have the time, I will do the work.* Review the verb tenses in **si** (if) clauses at the top of page 26, example (a). Review the verb **faire** where you will find the *passé composé* in choice A, the future in B, the conditional in C, and the imperfect indicative in D.

4. A The sentence means *If I had the time, I would do the work.* Review the verb tenses in **si** (if) clauses at the top of page 26, example (b). Review the verb **faire** where you will find the conditional in A, the future in B, the conditional perfect in C, and the *passé composé* in D.

5. C The sentence means *If I had had the time, I would have done the work.* Review the verb tenses in **si** (if) clauses at the top of page 26, example (c). Review the verb **faire** where you will find the *passé composé* in A, the future perfect in B, the conditional perfect in C, and the imperfect indicative in D. Also, see page 18, example (b) on the bottom of the page where the uses of the conditional perfect are explained with examples.

6. A This is the conditional of courtesy. See page 13, example (b) on the bottom of the page where the uses of the conditional are explained with examples. Review the verb **aimer** where you will find the conditional in A, the *passé composé* in B, the *passé simple* in C, and the imperfect indicative in D.

7. B At what time *would you be able* to come? The reply to the question contains the same verb (**pouvoir**) in the same tense. Review the English translation of the conditional on page 8. See also the explanation on the bottom of page 13 in note (2) with the example. Study the verb forms of **pouvoir**.

8. B The verb in the **si** (if) clause is imperfect indicative of **être**; for that reason, the verb form in the other clause must be conditional. See the note in example (b) on page 14. See also example (b) at the top of page 26. Review **faire** for the other forms in A, C, and D.

9. B **Je doute** expresses doubt and it requires the subjunctive of **venir** in the clause that follows. Review the subjunctive that begins in the middle of page 26, specifically **douter que** on page 30. Review **venir** for the other forms in A, C, and D.

10. B **Avoir peur** expresses fear and it requires the subjunctive of **être** in the clause that follows. Review the subjunctive that begins in the middle of page 26, specifically **avoir peur que** on page 30, and the last example on the bottom of that page. Review **être** for the other forms in A, C, and D. Review idiomatic expressions with **avoir** under that verb.

11. D **Je regrette** expresses regret and it requires the subjunctive of the verb in the following clause. Review the subjunctive that begins in the middle of page 26, specifically **regretter que** on page 30. Review **être** for the other forms in A, B, and C.

12. A The conjunction **à moins que** (unless) requires the subjunctive of the verb in the clause it introduces. Review the subjunctive that begins in the middle of page 26, specifically **à moins que** listed under certain conjunctions on that page. Review **venir** for the other forms in B, C, and D.

13. B The conjunction **quoique** (although) requires the subjunctive of the verb in the clause it introduces. Review the subjunctive that begins in the middle of page 26, specifically **quoique** listed under certain conjunctions on page 27. Review **être** for the other forms in A, C, and D.

14. B The conjunction **pour que** (in order that, so that) requires the subjunctive of the verb in the clause it introduces. Review the subjunctive that begins in the middle of page 26, specifically **pour que** listed under certain conjunctions on page 27. Review **comprendre** for the other forms in A, C, and D.

15. B The conjunction **dès que** requires the future of the verb in the clause it introduces, provided that the verb in the main clause implies future time. In this sentence, **je partirai** is future. Review the future tense on pages 12–13 and the example in (c). Review **arriver** for the forms in A, B, C, and D.

16. C The impersonal expression **il est urgent que . . .** (it is urgent that . . .) requires the subjunctive of the verb in the clause it introduces. Review the subjunctive that begins in the middle of page 26, specifically **il est urgent que** on page 29. Review **partir** for the forms in A, B, C, and D.

17. D You need the pluperfect indicative tense of **oublier** because this past action occurred *before* the other past action in the sentence (*I remembered that I had forgotten*). Review the explanation and uses of the pluperfect indicative tense on the bottom of page 16 to page 17. Review **oublier** for the forms in A, B, C, and D. Also, review **se rappeler**.

18. C You need the pluperfect indicative tense of **dormir**. Review, again, the explanation and uses of the pluperfect indicative tense on the bottom of page 16 to page 17. Review **dormir**.

19. B You need the *passé composé* of **dormir**. You are saying that you are tired *now* (**maintenant**) because you did not sleep. Review the explanation and uses of the *passé composé* with examples on page 16.

20. A You need the future perfect of **finir** because the verb in the other clause is in the future (**elle arrivera**) and it is introduced by the conjunction **quand** (when). Both actions will take place in the future. The action that will happen in the future *before* another future action is in the future perfect tense. Review the explanation and uses of the future perfect, with examples, on page 18. Review the verb forms of **finir**. If you did not recognize **arrivera** as future, review **arriver**.

Test 11

Note: For all verb forms in this test, review the uses and examples of the present indicative on pages 10 and 11 and the *passé composé* on page 16. For the formation of the present indicative of regular verbs, review page 22. For the formation of the *passé composé*, review the bottom of page 23 and Tense No. 8 at the top of page 24.

For the formation of regular and irregular past participles, see page 3.

Also, review the present indicative and the *passé composé* of the verbs given below.

1. **Elle est allée.**
See **aller**.

2. **Il a eu.**
See **avoir**.

3. **Je me suis assis.**
See **s'asseoir**.

4. **Ils ont eu.**
See **avoir**.

5. **Tu as été.**
See **être**.

6. **Il est allé.**
See **aller**.

7. **Nous sommes allés.**
See **aller**.

8. **Nous avons eu.**
See **avoir**.

9. **J'ai parlé.**
See **parler**.

10. **Elles sont venues.**
See **venir**.

11. **J'ai bu.**
See **boire**.

12. **Ils ont bu.**
See **boire**.

13. **Vous avez bu.**
See **boire**.

14. **J'ai cru.**
See **croire**.

15. **Tu as dit.**
See **dire**.

16. **J'ai pu.**
See **pouvoir**.

17. **Il a fallu.**
See **falloir**.

18. **Vous avez lu.**
See **lire**.

19. **Vous avez dit.**
See **dire**.

20. **Tu as mis.**
See **mettre**.

21. **Elle est née.**
See **naître**.

22. **Elle est morte.**
See **mourir**.

23. **Elle a vendu.**
See **vendre**.

24. **Ils se sont amusés.**
See **s'amuser**.

25. **Elle est entrée.**
See **entrer**.

26. **On a fini.**
See **finir**.

27. **Elles ont couru.**
See **courir**.

28. **Ils ont pris.**
See **prendre**.

29. **On a appris.**
See **apprendre**.

30. **Elles sont arrivées.**
See **arriver**.

Test 12

Note: This test is a good exercise to practice the formation of the seven simple tenses by using the required endings for regular **-er**, **-ir**, and **-re** verbs. The explanations and endings are on pages 22 and 23. For irregular verbs, see the verbs arranged alphabetically at the top of each page among the 501 verbs fully conjugated in all the tenses in this book.

Présent de l'indicatif (Tense No. 1)

1. J'aime.
2. Tu chantes.
3. Il/elle/on étudie.
4. Janine choisit.
5. J'entends.
6. Nous attendons.
7. Vous mangez.
8. Ils/elles vendent.
9. Richard et moi finissons.
10. Marie et Jeanne donnent.

Imparfait de l'indicatif (Tense No. 2)

1. Je parlais.
2. Tu finissais.
3. Il/elle/on vendait.
4. Madeleine était.
5. Il/elle/on avait.
6. Nous venions.
7. Vous faisiez.
8. Ils/elles allaient.
9. Paul et Henri jouaient.
10. Tu donnais.

Passé simple (Tense No. 3)

1. Je parlai.
2. Tu finis.
3. Il/elle/on vendit.
4. Catherine écrivit.
5. Ils/elles allèrent.
6. Nous donnâmes.
7. Vous choisîtes.
8. Ils/elles comprirent.
9. Hélène et Raymond désirèrent.
10. Il/elle/on dansa.

Futur (Tense No. 4)

1. Je mangerai.
2. Tu finiras.
3. Il/elle/on vendra.
4. La femme écrira.
5. J'irai.
6. Nous donnerons.
7. Vous choisirez.
8. Ils/elles comprendront.
9. Les garçons joueront.
10. J'aurai.

Conditionnel (Tense No. 5)

1. J'irais.
2. Tu finirais.
3. Il/elle/on ferait.
4. Je mangerais.
5. Vous pourriez.
6. Nous parlerions.
7. Vous seriez.
8. Ils/elles auraient.
9. Je prendrais.
10. Vous dîneriez.

Présent du subjonctif (Tense No. 6)

1. que je parle
2. que tu donnes
3. qu'il/elle/on ose
4. que je choisisse
5. que tu manges
6. que nous partions
7. que vous vendiez
8. qu'ils/elles prennent
9. que nous finissions
10. qu'il/elle/on ferme

Imparfait du subjonctif (Tense No. 7)

1. que je parlasse
2. que tu donnasses
3. qu'il/elle/on ouvrît
4. que nous partissions
5. que vous voulussiez
6. qu'ils/elles finissent

Test 13

Note: Review the regular and irregular past participiles on page 3.

1 D	O	N	2 N	É	■	3 L	■	4 V
Û	■	■	É	■	5 P	U	■	E
■	■	6 D	■	■	R	■	■	N
7 F	U	I	■	8 R	I	■	9 Û	D
A	■	10 T	U	■	11 S	12 U	■	U
13 L	U	■	■	14 F	■	15 S	U	■
L	■	16 M	■	I	■	É	■	17 É
U	■	O	■	18 N	É	■	■	T
■	19 I	R	■	I	■	20 E	■	É
■	■	21 T	U	■	22 T	U	É	■

Test 14

Note: You must know the verb **avoir** in the seven simple tenses because they are needed to form the seven compound tenses of verbs conjugated with **avoir**. If you did not do well on this test, study them and write them for practice until you are sure that you know them. Review the seven compound tenses of a verb conjugated with **avoir**, for example, **parler**. If you drop the past participle **parlé**, you will see that what is left is the verb **avoir** in the seven simple tenses.

1. Présent de l'indicatif
(Tense No. 1)

j'ai	**nous avons**
tu as	**vous avez**
il/elle/on a	**ils/elles ont**

2. Imparfait de l'indicatif
(Tense No. 2)

j'avais	**nous avions**
tu avais	**vous aviez**
il/elle/on avait	**ils/elles avaient**

3. Passé simple
(Tense No. 3)

j'eus	**nous eûmes**
tu eus	**vous eûtes**
il/elle/on eut	**ils/elles eurent**

4. Futur
(Tense No. 4)

j'aurai	**nous aurons**
tu auras	**vous aurez**
il/elle/on aura	**ils/elles auront**

5. Conditionnel
(Tense No. 5)

j'aurais	**nous aurions**
tu aurais	**vous auriez**
il/elle/on aurait	**ils/elles auraient**

6. Présent du subjonctif
(Tense No. 6)

que j'aie	**que nous ayons**
que tu aies	**que vous ayez**
qu'il/elle/on ait	**qu'ils/elles aient**

7. Imparfait du subjonctif
(Tense No. 7)

que j'eusse	**que nous eussions**
que tu eusses	**que vous eussiez**
qu'il/elle/on eût	**qu'ils/elles eussent**

Test 15

Note: You must know the verb **être** in the seven simple tenses because they are needed to form the seven compound tenses of verbs conjugated with **être**. If you did not do well on this test, study them and write them for practice until you are sure that you know them. Review the seven compound tenses of a verb conjugated with **être**, for example, **aller**. If you drop the past participle **allé**, you will see that what is left is the verb **être** in the seven simple tenses.

1. Présent de l'indicatif
(Tense No. 1)

je suis	**nous sommes**
tu es	**vous êtes**
il/elle/on est	**ils/elles sont**

2. Imparfait de l'indicatif
(Tense No. 2)

j'étais	**nous étions**
tu étais	**vous étiez**
il/elle/on était	**ils/elles étaient**

3. Passé simple
(Tense No. 3)

je fus	**nous fûmes**
tu fus	**vous fûtes**
il/elle/on fut	**ils/elles furent**

4. Futur
(Tense No. 4)

je serai	**nous serons**
tu seras	**vous serez**
il/elle/on sera	**ils/elles seront**

5. Conditionnel
(Tense No. 5)

je serais	**nous serions**
tu serais	**vous seriez**
il/elle/on serait	**ils/elles seraient**

6. Présent du subjonctif
(Tense No. 6)

que je sois	**que nous soyons**
que tu sois	**que vous soyez**
qu'il/elle/on soit	**qu'ils/elles soient**

7. Imparfait du subjonctif
(Tense No. 7)

que je fusse	**que nous fussions**
que tu fusses	**que vous fussiez**
qu'il/elle/on fût	**qu'ils/elles fussent**

Test 16

Note: This test is another example to show that it is very important for you to know the present indicative of **avoir** and **être** so that you can form the *passé composé*. It also shows that you must know the imperfect indicative of **avoir** and **être** so that you can form the pluperfect indicative (*le plus-que-parfait de l'indicatif*). For the English translations of both these tenses, review the *passé composé* and the *plus-que-parfait de l'indicatif* on pages 16–17, where you will find explanations and examples in French and English.

Review the *passé composé* and the *plus-que-parfait de l'indicatif* of the verbs given below.

1. **Elle était allée.**
   See **aller**.
2. **Il avait eu.**
   See **avoir**.
3. **Je m'étais assis.**
   See **s'asseoir**.
4. **Ils avaient eu.**
   See **avoir**.
5. **Tu avais été.**
   See **être**.
6. **Il était allé.**
   See **aller**.
7. **Nous étions allés.**
   See **aller**.
8. **Nous avions eu.**
   See **avoir**.
9. **J'avais parlé.**
   See **parler**.
10. **Elle était venue.**
    See **venir**.
11. **J'avais bu.**
    See **boire**.
12. **Ils s'étaient tus.**
    See **se taire**.
13. **J'avais fait.**
    See **faire**.
14. **Tu avais dû.**
    See **devoir**.
15. **Vous aviez dit.**
    See **dire**.
16. **J'avais pu.**
    See **pouvoir**.
17. **Il avait fallu.**
    See **falloir**.
18. **Vous aviez lu.**
    See **lire**.
19. **Vous aviez dit.**
    See **dire**.
20. **Tu avais mis.**
    See **mettre**.
21. **Elle était née.**
    See **naître**.
22. **Elle était morte.**
    See **mourir**.
23. **Elle s'était lavée.**
    See **se laver**.
24. **Elles s'étaient lavées.**
    See **se laver**.
25. **J'étais entré.**
    See **entrer**.
26. **On avait parlé.**
    See **parler**.
27. **Ils avaient couru.**
    See **courir**.
28. **Ils avaient pris.**
    See **prendre**.
29. **On avait dit.**
    See **dire**.
30. **J'avais compris.**
    See **comprendre**.

Test 17

1. B **Partir** is conjugated with **être** to form a compound tense, so C and D are not appropriate choices because they are forms of **avoir**. You need the present subjunctive of **être** in B because of the impersonal expression **il est possible que** in the beginning of the sentence. Review the section on the uses of the subjunctive that begins in the middle of page 26, in particular, **il est possible que** on page 29. Review also **partir** in the *passé du subjonctif* (Tense No. 13). Refresh your memory by reading about the *passé du subjonctif* with explanations and examples in French and English on page 19.
2. C **Faire** is conjugated with **avoir** to form a compound tense; so B and D are not appropriate choices because they are forms of **être**. You need the present subjunctive of **avoir** in C because the verb in the main clause is **douter**. Review the section on the uses of the subjunctive that begins in the middle of page 26, in particular, **douter que** on page 30. Review also **faire** in the *passé du subjonctif* (Tense No. 13). Refresh your memory by reading about the *passé du subjonctif* with explanations and examples in French and English on page 19.

3. C In front of the blank space there is a verb form (**je ne peux pas**/I can't). That is why you need the infinitive form in C (*I am not able to go out*). Review **pouvoir** + inf. in the section on *Verbs with prepositions* in the Appendixes. Review the other forms of **sortir** in A, B, and D. As for **il fait un temps affreux**, review *Verbs used in weather expressions* in the Appendixes, specifically (b), on page 688.

4. B You need the present participle **entrant** because it is preceded by **en**. Josephine fell *while entering* (***en entrant***) the kitchen. Review regular and irregular present participles on page 3. Review the other forms of **entrer** in A, C, and D.

5. B Simone wiped the table. You need the past participle **essuyé** to complete the *passé composé*. There is no need for the fem. agreement in C because there is no fem. sing. direct object that *precedes* the verb. A is the infinitive form. D is the present participle. Review **essuyer**.

6. B To complete the *passé composé* you need **mise**, which is fem. sing. because the reflexive pronoun **s'** (**se**/herself) serves as the preceding direct object pronoun and it refers to **Françoise**, the subject, which is fem. sing. Review **se mettre à** + inf. in the section on *Verbs with prepositions* in the Appendixes. Review the forms of **se mettre** and the examples on the bottom of that page.

7. D The subject, **les enfants**, is 3d person pl. The only verb form that is also 3d person pl. among the choices is in D. Review the forms of **vouloir**.

8. C To complete the *passé composé* you need **achetées**, which is fem. pl. because the relative pronoun **que** (which or that) refers to the preceding direct object, **les fleurs**, which is fem. pl. The past participle in A is masc. sing. In B it is masc. pl. The infinitive in D cannot be used because you must complete the *passé composé*. Review **acheter** and the examples on the bottom of that page.

9. A The verb form in the clause beginning with **quand** is in the *passé antérieur* (past anterior), which is used in literary style. Review the explanation and examples of that tense on page 17. Since that tense is used in the subordinate clause, you need to use the *passé simple* in the main clause, which is in choice A. You need the 3d person sing. (**partit**) because the subject (**il**) is 3d person sing. Review the uses and explanation of the *passé simple* on page 12 and the examples in French and English. Also, review the *passé antérieur* (Tense No. 10) of **manger** and the *passé simple* (Tense No. 3) of **partir** as well as the other forms in the choices. Remember that the *passé simple* and the *passé antérieur* are literary tenses. They are not normally used in conversational French. These two tenses are occasionally used in these tests so you can become aware of them when reading French literature.

10. B To complete the *conditionnel passé* (Tense No. 12) of **faire**, you need the conditional (Tense No. 5) of **avoir**, which is **aurais**, 1st person sing., since the subject **je** is 1st person sing. As for **j'aurais fait** (I would have done), review the uses and explanation of the *conditionnel passé* on page 18 and the examples in French and English, as well as Tense No. 12 of **faire**. As for **j'avais eu** (I had had) review the *plus-que-parfait de l'indicatif* (Tense No. 9) on pages 16–17, and under the verb **avoir**. Also, review **si** (if) clauses at the top of page 26.

Test 18

Note: Review the regular and irregular present participles on page 3.

C	H	A	N	T	A	N	T	A	T
H	F	Y	T	N	V	E	A	P	N
O	A	A	N	A	E	F	V	R	A
I	I	N	A	N	A	I	E	E	Y
S	S	T	Y	E	N	N	N	N	O
I	A	A	O	T	T	I	D	A	V
S	N	N	R	D	I	S	A	N	T
S	T	T	C	T	É	S	N	T	N
A	L	L	A	N	T	A	T	O	A
N	A	I	S	S	A	N	T	S	N
T	N	O	S	A	N	T	F	A	E
L	I	S	A	N	T	T	A	N	V

Test 19

Note: From time to time practice the formation of the seven simple tenses for regular verbs on pages 22 and 23 and the formation of the seven compound tenses on pages 23 to 25.

1. A The infinitive form is needed because the blank space is preceded by a verb form and a subject (**Je désire**). Review **désirer** + inf. in the section on *Verbs with prepositions* in the Appendixes. In B, **loué** is a masc. sing. past participle. In C, **louée** is a fem. sing. past participle. There is no need for a past participle here because there is no helping verb in the sentence to require the completion of a compound tense. In D, **louant** is a present participle and there is no need for that because it would make no sense. Review **louer**.

2. B You need the present indicative tense (**C'est**/It is) because the conversation is taking place right now. Review the other forms of **être** in A, C, and D.

3. B By now we hope that you are able to recognize the ending of a verb form that agrees with the subject in person (1st, 2d, or 3d) and number (sing. or pl.). For example: **je prends**, **tu prends**, **il prend**, and so forth. There is nothing in the sentence to require the present subjunctive **prenne**. Review the verb forms and tenses of **prendre**.

4. D Same here. The ending of a verb form agrees with the subject in person and number. See number 3 above. There is nothing in the sentence to require the present subjunctive **croie**. Review the verb forms and tenses of **croire**.

5. C The clerk at the hotel desk started the conversation by using the polite **vous** form while talking to you. That is why you need the **vous** form, **montrez**, in C. The clerk also tells you **"Signez"** in the same statement. You are dealing with the imperative (command) because he is telling you to do something. In the imperative the subject is not stated. Review the imperative on pages 20 and 21. In B the infinitive of the verb form **montez** is **monter**/to go up. Review the forms of **montrer**.

Test 20

Note: Review page 6. Review regular and irregular past participles on page 3. Study the formation and uses of the *passé composé* with examples in French and English on page 16. Also, review the *passé composé* of the verbs given after each answer.

1. **Richard a écrit la leçon.** Review **apprendre** and **écrire**.
2. **Elle s'est levée.** Review **s'asseoir** and **se lever**.
3. **J'ai lu la lettre.** Review **écrire** and **lire**.
4. **Elle a ouvert la fenêtre.** Review **fermer** and **ouvrir**.
5. **Hélène est morte.** Review **arriver** and **mourir**.
6. **Avez-vous offert un cadeau?** Review **acheter** and **offrir**.
7. **Marguerite est venue.** Review **sortir** and **venir**.
8. **Nous avons cru l'histoire.** Review **écouter** and **croire**.
9. **Ils ont vu Paris.** Review **visiter** and **voir**.
10. **Les enfants ont ri.** Review **pleurer** and **rire**.
11. **As-tu pris les frites?** Review **commander** and **prendre**.
12. **Ils sont restés à Paris.** Review **aller** and **rester**.
13. **L'étudiant n'a pas su la réponse.** Review **comprendre** and **savoir**.
14. **L'enfant a eu un bon repas.** Review **manger** and **avoir**.
15. **J'ai reçu la lettre.** Review **envoyer** and **recevoir**.
16. **Avez-vous été en France?** Review **voyager** and **être**.
17. **A-t-il couvert la boîte?** Review **ouvrir** and **couvrir**.
18. **Les enfants se sont tus.** Review **se laver** and **se taire**.
19. **Louise a voulu venir chez moi.** Review **désirer** and **vouloir**.
20. **Qui a fait le bruit?** Review **entendre** and **faire**.

Test 21

Note: Review the two-page spread on pages 8 and 9 to be sure you can translate into English the seven simple tenses, the seven compound tenses, and the imperative. The model verb on those two pages is *to go* (*aller*). Keep those two pages open flat and flip back and forth to **aller**, where you see all the forms in all the tenses of **aller**. Compare the forms in English and French. As a guide, follow the tense No. and the name of the tense in both languages as you make your comparison. For practice, you can apply this procedure to other verbs by merely substituting an English verb for a French one, e.g., *to drink* (*boire*).

The asterisks in front of each of the English verb forms below designate the following:

*The French verb forms in Tense No. 3 (*le passé simple*) are used in literary style, formal writing. In French conversation and informal writing use the *passé composé* (Tense No. 8) instead of this tense.

**The French verb forms in Tense No. 7 (*l'imparfait du subjonctif*) are used in literary style, formal writing. In French conversation and informal writing use the *présent du subjonctif* (Tense No. 6) instead of this tense.

***The French verb forms in Tense No. 10 (*le passé antérieur*) are used in literary style, formal writing. In French conversation and informal writing, use *le plus-que-parfait de l'indicatif* (Tense No. 9) instead of this tense.

****The French verb forms in Tense No. 14 (*le plus-que-parfait du subjonctif*) are used in literary style, formal writing. In French conversation and informal writing, use *le passé du subjonctif* (Tense No. 13) instead of this tense.

1. we go, we do go, we are going
2. you were going, you went, you used to go
***3.** he went, he did go
4. we shall go, we will go
5. you would go
6. that I may go
****7.** that I might go
8. she has gone, she went, she did go
9. they had gone
*****10.** we had gone
11. you will have gone
12. you would have gone
13. that he may have gone
******14.** that she might have gone
15. I know, I do know
***16.** he was
17. she will have
18. we would have
19. that I may be
***20.** he had
21. I have had, I had, I did have
22. I put, I have put, I did put
23. we will do, we will make
24. I would have come
25. Go away!
26. You have sold, you sold, you did sell
27. We will have finished
28. You had drunk
29. She has gone up, she went up, she did go up
30. We have stayed, we stayed, we did stay

Test 22

Note: Verify the verb forms in the present indicative tense by looking up the verbs in this test on the pages where they appear among the 501 verbs in this book.

A	I	M	E	B	A	L	I	T	A
C	D	A	L	O	S	E	T	I	D
O	O	E	F	I	O	A	E	G	I
U	I	E	A	A	L	L	O	N	S
R	S	V	S	I	O	U	E	A	U
S	A	I	R	E	U	E	T	E	S
I	L	N	A	P	S	U	V	L	O
A	E	I	P	E	U	V	E	N	T
E	O	N	T	N	E	D	N	E	V
L	U	I	A	L	L	E	Z	O	N
F	A	T	E	Z	V	A	V	A	I
F	I	N	I	S	S	O	N	S	S

Test 23

Note: In Test 21 you translated verb forms in a variety of tenses from French to English. In this test you are translating English verb forms in a variety of tenses back into French.

1. Nous allons
2. Tu allais
3. Il alla
4. Nous irons
5. Vous iriez
6. Que j'aille
7. Que j'allasse
8. Elle est allée
9. Elles étaient allées
10. Nous fûmes allés
11. Tu seras allé
12. Vous seriez allé
13. Qu'il soit allé
14. Qu'elle fût allée
15. Je sais
16. Il fut
17. Elle aura
18. Nous aurions
19. Que je sois
20. Il eut
21. J'ai eu
22. J'ai mis
23. Nous ferons
24. Je serais venu
25. Allez-vous-en!
26. Vous avez vendu
27. Nous aurons fini
28. Tu avais bu
29. Elle est montée
30. Nous sommes restés

Test 24

Note: This is a repeat of Test 14 because you must know thoroughly the verb forms of **avoir** in the seven simple tenses. They are needed to form the seven compound tenses. Go to Test 14 in this answers section and correct your work. Also, review the verb **avoir** where you will find all the forms. Review again the formation of the seven compound tenses on pages 23 to 25.

Test 25

Note: This is a repeat of Test 15 because you must know thoroughly the verb forms of **être** in the seven simple tenses. They are needed to form the seven compound tenses. Go to Test 15 in this answers section and correct your work. Also, review the verb **être** where you will find all the forms. Review again the formation of the seven compound tenses on pages 23 to 25.

Test 26

Note: Verify the verb forms in the *passé composé* by looking up the verbs in this test on the pages where they appear among the 501 verbs in this book.

1. (a) **voir**
   (b) **présent de l'indicatif**
   (c) 1st pers., sing.
2. (a) **être**
   (b) **présent de l'indicatif**
   (c) 1st pers., sing.
3. (a) **promettre**
   (b) **plus-que-parfait de l'indicatif**
   (c) 2d pers., pl.
4. (a) **laisser**
   (b) **passé composé**
   (c) 1st pers., sing.
5. (a) **laisser**
   (b) **présent de l'indicatif**
   (c) 2d pers., pl.
6. (a) **dire**
   (b) **plus-que-parfait de l'indicatif**
   (c) 3d pers., sing.
7. (a) **être**
   (b) **imparfait de l'indicatif**
   (c) 2d pers., pl.
8. (a) **croire**
   (b) **conditionnel**
   (c) 1st pers., sing.
9. (a) **avoir**
   (b) **présent de l'indicatif**
   (c) 2d pers., pl.
10. (a) **attendre**
    (b) **imparfait de l'indicatif**
    (c) 1st pers., sing.
11. (a) **voir**
    (b) **présent de l'indicatif**
    (c) 1st pers., sing.
12. (a) **avoir**
    (b) **présent de l'indicatif**
    (c) 2d pers., pl.
13. (a) **avoir**
    (b) **présent de l'indicatif**
    (c) 2d pers., pl.
14. (a) **se flatter**
    (b) **présent de l'indicatif**
    (c) 1st pers., sing.
15. (a) **venir**
    (b) **conditionnel passé**
    (c) 2d pers., pl.
16. (a) **être**
    (b) **présent de l'indicatif**
    (c) 2d pers., pl.
17. (a) **tirer**
    (b) **impératif**
    (c) 2d pers., pl.
18. (a) **prier**
    (b) **présent de l'indicatif**
    (c) 1st pers., sing.

Essential 55 verb list

Beginning students should pay careful attention to the verbs in this list. We have chosen them because they represent important spelling changes and popular usage. If you study these key verbs you will be able to conjugate just about any verb you come across and express yourself in correct idiomatic French.

acheter
aimer
aller/s'en aller
(Verb Pair)
apprendre
attendre
avoir
boire
chanter
choisir
commencer
connaître
courir
couvrir
se débrouiller
devoir
dire
donner
dormir
écrire
entendre
entrer
envoyer
éteindre
être
étudier
faire
finir
garder
jouer
laver/se laver
(Verb Pair)
se lever
lire
manger
mettre/se mettre
(Verb Pair)
monter
parler
partir
payer
perdre
pouvoir
prendre
rendre
rentrer
savoir
sentir
sortir
tenir
tomber
vendre
venir
voir
vouloir

Subject Pronouns

A. The subject pronouns for all verb forms on the following pages have been omitted in order to emphasize the verb forms, which is what this book is all about.

B. The subject pronouns that have been omitted are, as you know, as follows:

singular	***plural***
je ***or*** j'	nous
tu	vous
il, elle, on	ils, elles

C. You realize, of course, that when you use a verb form in the Imperative (Command) you do not use the subject pronoun with it, as is also done in English. Example: **Parlez!** ***Speak!*** If you use a reflexive verb in the Imperative, drop the subject pronoun but keep the reflexive pronoun. Example: **Lavez-vous!** ***Wash yourself!***

Abbreviations

adj. adjectif, *adjective*
adv. adverbe, *adverb*
ant. antérieur, *anterior*
art. article
comp. computer
cond. conditionnel, *conditional*
def. défini, *definite*
dir. direct
e.g.. for example
f. or *fem.* féminin, *feminine*
fam. familiar
fut. futur, *future*
i.e. that is, that is to say
imp. imparfait, *imperfect*
ind. indicatif, *indicative*
inf. infinitif, *infinitive*
m. or *masc.* masculin, *masculine*
n. nom, *noun*
obj. objet, *object*
p. page
pp. pages
part. participe, *participle*
pl. pluriel, *plural*
plpf. plus-que-parfait, *pluperfect*
pr or *prés.* présent, *present*
prep. préposition, *preposition*
pron. pronom, *pronoun*
qqch quelque chose, *something*
qqn quelqu'un, *someone, somebody*
refl. reflexive
s. or *sing.* singulier, *singular*
subj. subjonctif, *subjunctive*
v. verbe, *verb*

Alphabetical Listing of 501 French Verbs Fully Conjugated in All the Tenses and Moods

Regular **-er** verb

to lower, to reduce, to humiliate, to humble

The Seven Simple Tenses		The Seven Compound Tenses	
Singular	Plural	Singular	Plural
1 présent de l'indicatif		8 passé composé	
abaisse	**abaissons**	**ai abaissé**	**avons abaissé**
abaisses	**abaissez**	**as abaissé**	**avez abaissé**
abaisse	**abaissent**	**a abaissé**	**ont abaissé**
2 imparfait de l'indicatif		9 plus-que-parfait de l'indicatif	
abaissais	**abaissions**	**avais abaissé**	**avions abaissé**
abaissais	**abaissiez**	**avais abaissé**	**aviez abaissé**
abaissait	**abaissaient**	**avait abaissé**	**avaient abaissé**
3 passé simple		10 passé antérieur	
abaissai	**abaissâmes**	**eus abaissé**	**eûmes abaissé**
abaissas	**abaissâtes**	**eus abaissé**	**eûtes abaissé**
abaissa	**abaissèrent**	**eut abaissé**	**eurent abaissé**
4 futur		11 futur antérieur	
abaisserai	**abaisserons**	**aurai abaissé**	**aurons abaissé**
abaisseras	**abaisserez**	**auras abaissé**	**aurez abaissé**
abaissera	**abaisseront**	**aura abaissé**	**auront abaissé**
5 conditionnel		12 conditionnel passé	
abaisserais	**abaisserions**	**aurais abaissé**	**aurions abaissé**
abaisserais	**abaisseriez**	**aurais abaissé**	**auriez abaissé**
abaisserait	**abaisseraient**	**aurait abaissé**	**auraient abaissé**
6 présent du subjonctif		13 passé du subjonctif	
abaisse	**abaissions**	**aie abaissé**	**ayons abaissé**
abaisses	**abaissiez**	**aies abaissé**	**ayez abaissé**
abaisse	**abaissent**	**ait abaissé**	**aient abaissé**
7 imparfait du subjonctif		14 plus-que-parfait du subjonctif	
abaissasse	**abaissassions**	**eusse abaissé**	**eussions abaissé**
abaissasses	**abaissassiez**	**eusses abaissé**	**eussiez abaissé**
abaissât	**abaissassent**	**eût abaissé**	**eussent abaissé**

Impératif
abaisse
abaissons
abaissez

Words and expressions related to this verb

abaisser le store to pull down the (venetian) blind, shade
abaisser les yeux to cast one's eyes down, to look down
un abaissement abasement, lowering
abaisser qqn to humiliate someone
abaisser la valeur de qqch to bring down the value of something
un abaisse-langue tongue depressor
un rabais reduction
vendre au rabais to sell at a discount
Il est important d'abaisser votre taux de cholestérol. It's important to lower your cholesterol level.

See also **s'abaisser** and **baisser.**

The subject pronouns are found on page 103.

s'abaisser (2) — Part. pr. s'abaissant — Part. passé abaissé

to humble oneself, to lower oneself, to condescend, to slope

Reflexive regular **-er** verb

The Seven Simple Tenses		The Seven Compound Tenses	
Singular	Plural	Singular	Plural
1 présent de l'indicatif		8 passé composé	
m'abaisse	**nous abaissons**	**me suis abaissé(e)**	**nous sommes abaissé(e)s**
t'abaisses	**vous abaissez**	**t'es abaissé(e)**	**vous êtes abaissé(e)(s)**
s'abaisse	**s'abaissent**	**s'est abaissé(e)**	**se sont abaissé(e)s**
2 imparfait de l'indicatif		9 plus-que-parfait de l'indicatif	
m'abaissais	**nous abaissions**	**m'étais abaissé(e)**	**nous étions abaissé(e)s**
t'abaissais	**vous abaissiez**	**t'étais abaissé(e)**	**vous étiez abaissé(e)(s)**
s'abaissait	**s'abaissaient**	**s'était abaissé(e)**	**s'étaient abaissé(e)s**
3 passé simple		10 passé antérieur	
m'abaissai	**nous abaissâmes**	**me fus abaissé(e)**	**nous fûmes abaissé(e)s**
t'abaissas	**vous abaissâtes**	**te fus abaissé(e)**	**vous fûtes abaissé(e)(s)**
s'abaissa	**s'abaissèrent**	**se fut abaissé(e)**	**se furent abaissé(e)s**
4 futur		11 futur antérieur	
m'abaisserai	**nous abaisserons**	**me serai abaissé(e)**	**nous serons abaissé(e)s**
t'abaisseras	**vous abaisserez**	**te seras abaissé(e)**	**vous serez abaissé(e)(s)**
s'abaissera	**s'abaisseront**	**se sera abaissé(e)**	**se seront abaissé(e)s**
5 conditionnel		12 conditionnel passé	
m'abaisserais	**nous abaisserions**	**me serais abaissé(e)**	**nous serions abaissé(e)s**
t'abaisserais	**vous abaisseriez**	**te serais abaissé(e)**	**vous seriez abaissé(e)(s)**
s'abaisserait	**s'abaisseraient**	**se serait abaissé(e)**	**se seraient abaissé(e)s**
6 présent du subjonctif		13 passé du subjonctif	
m'abaisse	**nous abaissions**	**me sois abaissé(e)**	**nous soyons abaissé(e)s**
t'abaisses	**vous abaissiez**	**te sois abaissé(e)**	**vous soyez abaissé(e)(s)**
s'abaisse	**s'abaissent**	**se soit abaissé(e)**	**se soient abaissé(e)s**
7 imparfait du subjonctif		14 plus-que-parfait du subjonctif	
m'abaissasse	**nous abaissassions**	**me fusse abaissé(e)**	**nous fussions abaissé(e)s**
t'abaissasses	**vous abaissassiez**	**te fusses abaissé(e)**	**vous fussiez abaissé(e)(s)**
s'abaissât	**s'abaissassent**	**se fût abaissé(e)**	**se fussent abaissé(e)s**

Impératif
abaisse-toi; ne t'abaisse pas
abaissons-nous; ne nous abaissons pas
abaissez-vous; ne vous abaissez pas

Words and expressions related to this verb
s'abaisser to decline, to go down
s'abaisser à to stoop to
s'abaisser devant qqn to humble oneself before someone
Le taux de chômage s'est abaissé. The unemployment rate declined.
Car quiconque s'élève sera abaissé, et celui qui s'abaisse sera élevé. For whoever exalts himself will be humbled, and he who humbles himself will be exalted. (Luke 14:11)

See also **abaisser** and **baisser.**

Regular **-ir** verb

to daze, to deafen, to stun, to bewilder, to stupefy

The Seven Simple Tenses		The Seven Compound Tenses	
Singular	Plural	Singular	Plural
1 présent de l'indicatif		8 passé composé	
abasourdis	**abasourdissons**	**ai abasourdi**	**avons abasourdi**
abasourdis	**abasourdissez**	**as abasourdi**	**avez abasourdi**
abasourdit	**abasourdissent**	**a abasourdi**	**ont abasourdi**
2 imparfait de l'indicatif		9 plus-que-parfait de l'indicatif	
abasourdissais	**abasourdissions**	**avais abasourdi**	**avions abasourdi**
abasourdissais	**abasourdissiez**	**avais abasourdi**	**aviez abasourdi**
abasourdissait	**abasourdissaient**	**avait abasourdi**	**avaient abasourdi**
3 passé simple		10 passé antérieur	
abasourdis	**abasourdîmes**	**eus abasourdi**	**eûmes abasourdi**
abasourdis	**abasourdîtes**	**eus abasourdi**	**eûtes abasourdi**
abasourdit	**abasourdirent**	**eut abasourdi**	**eurent abasourdi**
4 futur		11 futur antérieur	
abasourdirai	**abasourdirons**	**aurai abasourdi**	**aurons abasourdi**
abasourdiras	**abasourdirez**	**auras abasourdi**	**aurez abasourdi**
abasourdira	**abasourdiront**	**aura abasourdi**	**auront abasourdi**
5 conditionnel		12 conditionnel passé	
abasourdirais	**abasourdirions**	**aurais abasourdi**	**aurions abasourdi**
abasourdirais	**abasourdiriez**	**aurais abasourdi**	**auriez abasourdi**
abasourdirait	**abasourdiraient**	**aurait abasourdi**	**auraient abasourdi**
6 présent du subjonctif		13 passé du subjonctif	
abasourdisse	**abasourdissions**	**aie abasourdi**	**ayons abasourdi**
abasourdisses	**abasourdissiez**	**aies abasourdi**	**ayez abasourdi**
abasourdisse	**abasourdissent**	**ait abasourdi**	**aient abasourdi**
7 imparfait du subjonctif		14 plus-que-parfait du subjonctif	
abasourdisse	**abasourdissions**	**eusse abasourdi**	**eussions abasourdi**
abasourdisses	**abasourdissiez**	**eusses abasourdi**	**eussiez abasourdi**
abasourdît	**abasourdissent**	**eût abasourdi**	**eussent abasourdi**

Impératif
abasourdis
abasourdissons
abasourdissez

Words and expressions related to this verb

assourdir to deafen, to deaden a sound, to muffle
s'assourdir to soften the sound of a consonant, to unvoice a consonant
abasourdissant, abasourdissante astounding, amazing
sourd, sourde deaf
devenir sourd to become deaf
faire la sourde oreille to turn a deaf ear, not to listen
être sourd à to be deaf to
la surdité deafness
un abasourdissement amazement, astonishment, bewilderment
Ce que j'ai vu à la télé m'a abasourdi. I was stunned by what I saw on TV.

The *s* in **abasourdir** is pronounced as if it were written *z*.

The subject pronouns are found on page 103.

abattre (4) — Part. pr. **abattant** — Part. passé **abattu**

to dishearten, to strike down, to cut down, to knock down, to slaughter

Irregular verb in 1s, 2s, 3s present indicative

The Seven Simple Tenses		The Seven Compound Tenses	
Singular	Plural	Singular	Plural
1 présent de l'indicatif		8 passé composé	
abats	**abattons**	**ai abattu**	**avons abattu**
abats	**abattez**	**as abattu**	**avez abattu**
abat	**abattent**	**a abattu**	**ont abattu**
2 imparfait de l'indicatif		9 plus-que-parfait de l'indicatif	
abattais	**abattions**	**avais abattu**	**avions abattu**
abattais	**abattiez**	**avais abattu**	**aviez abattu**
abattait	**abattaient**	**avait abattu**	**avaient abattu**
3 passé simple		10 passé antérieur	
abattis	**abattîmes**	**eus abattu**	**eûmes abattu**
abattis	**abattîtes**	**eus abattu**	**eûtes abattu**
abattit	**abattirent**	**eut abattu**	**eurent abattu**
4 futur		11 futur antérieur	
abattrai	**abattrons**	**aurai abattu**	**aurons abattu**
abattras	**abattrez**	**auras abattu**	**aurez abattu**
abattra	**abattront**	**aura abattu**	**auront abattu**
5 conditionnel		12 conditionnel passé	
abattrais	**abattrions**	**aurais abattu**	**aurions abattu**
abattrais	**abattriez**	**aurais abattu**	**auriez abattu**
abattrait	**abattraient**	**aurait abattu**	**auraient abattu**
6 présent du subjonctif		13 passé du subjonctif	
abatte	**abattions**	**aie abattu**	**ayons abattu**
abattes	**abattiez**	**aies abattu**	**ayez abattu**
abatte	**abattent**	**ait abattu**	**aient abattu**
7 imparfait du subjonctif		14 plus-que-parfait du subjonctif	
abattisse	**abattissions**	**eusse abattu**	**eussions abattu**
abattisses	**abattissiez**	**eusses abattu**	**eussiez abattu**
abattît	**abattissent**	**eût abattu**	**eussent abattu**

Impératif
abats
abattons
abattez

Words and expressions related to this verb

l'abattage *m.* slaughtering of animals
un abattoir slaughterhouse
rabattre to pull down, to turn down, to knock down, to beat down
un rabat-joie killjoy, "wet blanket"; (**des rabat-joie**)
un abatteur slaughterer of animals
à bas! down with! **à bas les devoirs!** down with homework!
un abat-jour lampshade
un abat-son louver
Le gangster fut abattu dans la rue. The gangster was struck down (killed) in the street.

See also **battre**, **se battre**, and **combattre**.

Regular **-ir** verb

to abolish, to do away with

The Seven Simple Tenses		The Seven Compound Tenses	
Singular	Plural	Singular	Plural
1 présent de l'indicatif		8 passé composé	
abolis	**abolissons**	**ai aboli**	**avons aboli**
abolis	**abolissez**	**as aboli**	**avez aboli**
abolit	**abolissent**	**a aboli**	**ont aboli**
2 imparfait de l'indicatif		9 plus-que-parfait de l'indicatif	
abolissais	**abolissions**	**avais aboli**	**avions aboli**
abolissais	**abolissiez**	**avais aboli**	**aviez aboli**
abolissait	**abolissaient**	**avait aboli**	**avaient aboli**
3 passé simple		10 passé antérieur	
abolis	**abolîmes**	**eus aboli**	**eûmes aboli**
abolis	**abolîtes**	**eus aboli**	**eûtes aboli**
abolit	**abolirent**	**eut aboli**	**eurent aboli**
4 futur		11 futur antérieur	
abolirai	**abolirons**	**aurai aboli**	**aurons aboli**
aboliras	**abolirez**	**auras aboli**	**aurez aboli**
abolira	**aboliront**	**aura aboli**	**auront aboli**
5 conditionnel		12 conditionnel passé	
abolirais	**abolirions**	**aurais aboli**	**aurions aboli**
abolirais	**aboliriez**	**aurais aboli**	**auriez aboli**
abolirait	**aboliraient**	**aurait aboli**	**auraient aboli**
6 présent du subjonctif		13 passé du subjonctif	
abolisse	**abolissions**	**aie aboli**	**ayons aboli**
abolisses	**abolissiez**	**aies aboli**	**ayez aboli**
abolisse	**abolissent**	**ait aboli**	**aient aboli**
7 imparfait du subjonctif		14 plus-que-parfait du subjonctif	
abolisse	**abolissions**	**eusse aboli**	**eussions aboli**
abolisses	**abolissiez**	**eusses aboli**	**eussiez aboli**
abolît	**abolissent**	**eût aboli**	**eussent aboli**

Impératif
abolis
abolissons
abolissez

Sentences using this verb and words related to this verb

Le législateur a soumis un projet de loi abolissant la peine de mort.
The legislator submitted a bill abolishing the death penalty.

l'abolition *f.* abolition

l'abolitionnisme *m.* abolitionism

abolitionniste abolitionist

Les abolitionnistes ont réussi à éliminer l'esclavage.
The abolitionists succeeded in eliminating slavery.

The subject pronouns are found on page 103.

to absolve

Irregular verb *Tense Nos. 3 and 7 of this verb are rarely used.

The Seven Simple Tenses		The Seven Compound Tenses	
Singular	Plural	Singular	Plural
1 présent de l'indicatif		8 passé composé	
absous	**absolvons**	**ai absous**	**avons absous**
absous	**absolvez**	**as absous**	**avez absous**
absout	**absolvent**	**a absous**	**ont absous**
2 imparfait de l'indicatif		9 plus-que-parfait de l'indicatif	
absolvais	**absolvions**	**avais absous**	**avions absous**
absolvais	**absolviez**	**avais absous**	**aviez absous**
absolvait	**absolvaient**	**avait absous**	**avaient absous**
*3 passé simple		10 passé antérieur	
absolus	**absolûmes**	**eus absous**	**eûmes absous**
absolus	**absolûtes**	**eus absous**	**eûtes absous**
absolut	**absolurent**	**eut absous**	**eurent absous**
4 futur		11 futur antérieur	
absoudrai	**absoudrons**	**aurai absous**	**aurons absous**
absoudras	**absoudrez**	**auras absous**	**aurez absous**
absoudra	**absoudront**	**aura absous**	**auront absous**
5 conditionnel		12 conditionnel passé	
absoudrais	**absoudrions**	**aurais absous**	**aurions absous**
absoudrais	**absoudriez**	**aurais absous**	**auriez absous**
absoudrait	**absoudraient**	**aurait absous**	**auraient absous**
6 présent du subjonctif		13 passé du subjonctif	
absolve	**absolvions**	**aie absous**	**ayons absous**
absolves	**absolviez**	**aies absous**	**ayez absous**
absolve	**absolvent**	**ait absous**	**aient absous**
*7 imparfait du subjonctif		14 plus-que-parfait du subjonctif	
absolusse	**absolussions**	**eusse absous**	**eussions absous**
absolusses	**absolussiez**	**eusses absous**	**eussiez absous**
absolût	**absolussent**	**eût absous**	**eussent absous**

Impératif
absous
absolvons
absolvez

Words and expressions related to this verb

une absolution absolution (of a sin)
donner l'absolution à un pécheur to absolve a sinner (of his sins)
une absoute recitation of prayers for the dead
absolument absolutely; **Je le veux absolument.** I really insist upon it.
une confiance absolue complete confidence
un refus absolu absolute (flat) refusal
absolument pas! certainly not!
absolument rien! absolutely nothing!

The *b* in **absoudre** is pronounced as if it were written *p*. See also **résoudre**.

Get acquainted with what preposition goes with what verb. See *Verbs with prepositions* in the Appendixes.

Reflexive irregular verb

to abstain

The Seven Simple Tenses		The Seven Compound Tenses	
Singular	Plural	Singular	Plural
1 présent de l'indicatif		8 passé composé	
m'abstiens	**nous abstenons**	**me suis abstenu(e)**	**nous sommes abstenu(e)s**
t'abstiens	**vous abstenez**	**t'es abstenu(e)**	**vous êtes abstenu(e)(s)**
s'abstient	**s'abstiennent**	**s'est abstenu(e)**	**se sont abstenu(e)s**
2 imparfait de l'indicatif		9 plus-que-parfait de l'indicatif	
m'abstenais	**nous abstenions**	**m'étais abstenu(e)**	**nous étions abstenu(e)s**
t'abstenais	**vous absteniez**	**t'étais abstenu(e)**	**vous étiez abstenu(e)(s)**
s'abstenait	**s'abstenaient**	**s'était abstenu(e)**	**s'étaient abstenu(e)s**
3 passé simple		10 passé antérieur	
m'abstins	**nous abstînmes**	**me fus abstenu(e)**	**nous fûmes abstenu(e)s**
t'abstins	**vous abstîntes**	**te fus abstenu(e)**	**vous fûtes abstenu(e)(s)**
s'abstint	**s'abstinrent**	**se fut abstenu(e)**	**se furent abstenu(e)s**
4 futur		11 futur antérieur	
m'abstiendrai	**nous abstiendrons**	**me serai abstenu(e)**	**nous serons abstenu(e)s**
t'abstiendras	**vous abstiendrez**	**te seras abstenu(e)**	**vous serez abstenu(e)(s)**
s'abstiendra	**s'abstiendront**	**se sera abstenu(e)**	**se seront abstenu(e)s**
5 conditionnel		12 conditionnel passé	
m'abstiendrais	**nous abstiendrions**	**me serais abstenu(e)**	**nous serions abstenu(e)s**
t'abstiendrais	**vous abstiendriez**	**te serais abstenu(e)**	**vous seriez abstenu(e)(s)**
s'abstiendrait	**s'abstiendraient**	**se serait abstenu(e)**	**se seraient absttenu(e)s**
6 présent du subjonctif		13 passé du subjonctif	
m'abstienne	**nous abstenions**	**me sois abstenu(e)**	**nous soyons abstenu(e)s**
t'abstiennes	**vous absteniez**	**te sois abstenu(e)**	**vous soyez abstenu(e)(s)**
s'abstienne	**s'abstiennent**	**se soit abstenu(e)**	**se soient abstenu(e)s**
7 imparfait du subjonctif		14 plus-que-parfait du subjonctif	
m'abstinsse	**nous abstinssions**	**me fusse abstenu(e)**	**nous fussions abstenu(e)s**
t'abstinsses	**vous abstinssiez**	**te fusses abstenu(e)**	**vous fussiez abstenu(e)(s)**
s'abstînt	**s'abstinssent**	**se fût abstenu(e)**	**se fussent abstenu(e)s**

Impératif
abstiens-toi; ne t'abstiens pas
abstenons-nous; ne nous abstenons pas
abstenez-vous; ne vous abstenez pas

Words and expressions related to this verb

s'abstenir de to abstain from, to refrain from
l'abstinence *f.* abstinence
l'abstention *f.* abstention
abstinent, abstinente abstinent
faire abstinence de to abstain from
un abstentionniste abstentionist
s'abstenir de faire to refrain from doing
Je m'abstiens de fumer dans la bibliothèque.
I refrain from smoking in the library.

The *b* in **s'abstenir** is pronounced as if it were written *p*.

How are you doing? Find out with the verb drills and tests with answers explained on pages 50–101.

The subject pronouns are found on page 103.

accepter (8)

Part. pr. **acceptant** Part. passé **accepté**

to accept

Regular **-er** verb

The Seven Simple Tenses		The Seven Compound Tenses	
Singular	Plural	Singular	Plural
1 présent de l'indicatif		8 passé composé	
accepte	**acceptons**	**ai accepté**	**avons accepté**
acceptes	**acceptez**	**as accepté**	**avez accepté**
accepte	**acceptent**	**a accepté**	**ont accepté**
2 imparfait de l'indicatif		9 plus-que-parfait de l'indicatif	
acceptais	**acceptions**	**avais accepté**	**avions accepté**
acceptais	**acceptiez**	**avais accepté**	**aviez accepté**
acceptait	**acceptaient**	**avait accepté**	**avaient accepté**
3 passé simple		10 passé antérieur	
acceptai	**acceptâmes**	**eus accepté**	**eûmes accepté**
acceptas	**acceptâtes**	**eus accepté**	**eûtes accepté**
accepta	**acceptèrent**	**eut accepté**	**eurent accepté**
4 futur		11 futur antérieur	
accepterai	**accepterons**	**aurai accepté**	**aurons accepté**
accepteras	**accepterez**	**auras accepté**	**aurez accepté**
acceptera	**accepteront**	**aura accepté**	**auront accepté**
5 conditionnel		12 conditionnel passé	
accepterais	**accepterions**	**aurais accepté**	**aurions accepté**
accepterais	**accepteriez**	**aurais accepté**	**auriez accepté**
accepterait	**accepteraient**	**aurait accepté**	**auraient accepté**
6 présent du subjonctif		13 passé du subjonctif	
accepte	**acceptions**	**aie accepté**	**ayons accepté**
acceptes	**acceptiez**	**aies accepté**	**ayez accepté**
accepte	**acceptent**	**ait accepté**	**aient accepté**
7 imparfait du subjonctif		14 plus-que-parfait du subjonctif	
acceptasse	**acceptassions**	**eusse accepté**	**eussions accepté**
acceptasses	**acceptassiez**	**eusses accepté**	**eussiez accepté**
acceptât	**acceptassent**	**eût accepté**	**eussent accepté**

Impératif
accepte
acceptons
acceptez

Words and expressions related to this verb

acceptable acceptable, satisfactory
une acceptation acceptance
accepter une invitation to accept an invitation
l'acception *f.* sense, meaning
accepter de fair qqch to agree to do something

Michel a accepté de travailler dimanche prochain. Michael agreed to work next Sunday.
Acceptez-vous les cartes bancaires? Do you accept credit cards?

Regular **-er** verb

to acclaim, to applaud, to cheer

The Seven Simple Tenses		The Seven Compound Tenses	
Singular	Plural	Singular	Plural
1 présent de l'indicatif		8 passé composé	
acclame	**acclamons**	**ai acclamé**	**avons acclamé**
acclames	**acclamez**	**as acclamé**	**avez acclamé**
acclame	**acclament**	**a acclamé**	**ont acclamé**
2 imparfait de l'indicatif		9 plus-que-parfait de l'indicatif	
acclamais	**acclamions**	**avais acclamé**	**avions acclamé**
acclamais	**acclamiez**	**avais acclamé**	**aviez acclamé**
acclamait	**acclamaient**	**avait acclamé**	**avaient acclamé**
3 passé simple		10 passé antérieur	
acclamai	**acclamâmes**	**eus acclamé**	**eûmes acclamé**
acclamas	**acclamâtes**	**eus acclamé**	**eûtes acclamé**
acclama	**acclamèrent**	**eut acclamé**	**eurent acclamé**
4 futur		11 futur antérieur	
acclamerai	**acclamerons**	**aurai acclamé**	**aurons acclamé**
acclameras	**acclamerez**	**auras acclamé**	**aurez acclamé**
acclamera	**acclameront**	**aura acclamé**	**auront acclamé**
5 conditionnel		12 conditionnel passé	
acclamerais	**acclamerions**	**aurais acclamé**	**aurions acclamé**
acclamerais	**acclameriez**	**aurais acclamé**	**auriez acclamé**
acclamerait	**acclameraient**	**aurait acclamé**	**auraient acclamé**
6 présent du subjonctif		13 passé du subjonctif	
acclame	**acclamions**	**aie acclamé**	**ayons acclamé**
acclames	**acclamiez**	**aies acclamé**	**ayez acclamé**
acclame	**acclament**	**ait acclamé**	**aient acclamé**
7 imparfait du subjonctif		14 plus-que-parfait du subjonctif	
acclamasse	**acclamassions**	**eusse acclamé**	**eussions acclamé**
acclamasses	**acclamassiez**	**eusses acclamé**	**eussiez acclamé**
acclamât	**acclamassent**	**eût acclamé**	**eussent acclamé**

Impératif
acclame
acclamons
acclamez

Words and expressions related to this verb

l'acclamation *f.* acclamation, cheering
nommer par acclamation to name by acclamation
réclamer to demand, to ask for
une réclame advertisement, commercial
élire par acclamation to elect by acclamation
se faire acclamer to be cheered, hailed
une réclamation complaint
Jean-Claude a été acclamé pour tout ce qu'il avait fait pour l'équipe. Jean-Claude was cheered for all that he had done for the team.

It's important that you be familiar with the subjunctive. See pages 26–31.

accompagner (10) Part. pr. accompagnant Part. passé accompagné

to accompany

Regular **-er** verb

The Seven Simple Tenses		The Seven Compound Tenses	
Singular	Plural	Singular	Plural
1 présent de l'indicatif		8 passé composé	
accompagne	**accompagnons**	**ai accompagné**	**avons accompagné**
accompagnes	**accompagnez**	**as accompagné**	**avez accompagné**
accompagne	**accompagnent**	**a accompagné**	**ont accompagné**
2 imparfait de l'indicatif		9 plus-que-parfait de l'indicatif	
accompagnais	**accompagnions**	**avais accompagné**	**avions accompagné**
accompagnais	**accompagniez**	**avais accompagné**	**aviez accompagné**
accompagnait	**accompagnaient**	**avait accompagné**	**avaient accompagné**
3 passé simple		10 passé antérieur	
accompagnai	**accompagnâmes**	**eus accompagné**	**eûmes accompagné**
accompagnas	**accompagnâtes**	**eus accompagné**	**eûtes accompagné**
accompagna	**accompagnèrent**	**eut accompagné**	**eurent accompagné**
4 futur		11 futur antérieur	
accompagnerai	**accompagnerons**	**aurai accompagné**	**aurons accompagné**
accompagneras	**accompagnerez**	**auras accompagné**	**aurez accompagné**
accompagnera	**accompagneront**	**aura accompagné**	**auront accompagné**
5 conditionnel		12 conditionnel passé	
accompagnerais	**accompagnerions**	**aurais accompagné**	**aurions accompagné**
accompagnerais	**accompagneriez**	**aurais accompagné**	**auriez accompagné**
accompagnerait	**accompagneraient**	**aurait accompagné**	**auraient accompagné**
6 présent du subjonctif		13 passé du subjonctif	
accompagne	**accompagnions**	**aie accompagné**	**ayons accompagné**
accompagnes	**accompagniez**	**aies accompagné**	**ayez accompagné**
accompagne	**accompagnent**	**ait accompagné**	**aient accompagné**
7 imparfait du subjonctif		14 plus-que-parfait du subjonctif	
accompagnasse	**accompagnassions**	**eusse accompagné**	**eussions accompagné**
accompagnasses	**accompagnassiez**	**eusses accompagné**	**eussiez accompagné**
accompagnât	**accompagnassent**	**eût accompagné**	**eussent accompagné**

Impératif
accompagne
accompagnons
accompagnez

Words and expressions related to this verb

une compagnie company, theatrical troupe

raccompagner quelqu'un to see someone out, see someone off

un animal de compagnie (animal domestique) a pet

Il vaut mieux être seul qu'en mauvaise compagnie! It's better to be alone than in bad company!

s'accompagner de to be accompanied by

un accompagnement accompanying, accompaniment (music)

un accompagnateur, une accompagnatrice accompanist (music)

un compagnon, une compagne companion

Get acquainted with what preposition goes with what verb. See *Verbs with prepositions* in the Appendixes.

Regular **-er** verb

to accord, to grant, to reconcile, to admit

The Seven Simple Tenses		The Seven Compound Tenses	
Singular	Plural	Singular	Plural
1 présent de l'indicatif		8 passé composé	
accorde	**accordons**	**ai accordé**	**avons accordé**
accordes	**accordez**	**as accordé**	**avez accordé**
accorde	**accordent**	**a accordé**	**ont accordé**
2 imparfait de l'indicatif		9 plus-que-parfait de l'indicatif	
accordais	**accordions**	**avais accordé**	**avions accordé**
accordais	**accordiez**	**avais accordé**	**aviez accordé**
accordait	**accordaient**	**avait accordé**	**avaient accordé**
3 passé simple		10 passé antérieur	
accordai	**accordâmes**	**eus accordé**	**eûmes accordé**
accordas	**accordâtes**	**eus accordé**	**eûtes accordé**
accorda	**accordèrent**	**eut accordé**	**eurent accordé**
4 futur		11 futur antérieur	
accorderai	**accorderons**	**aurai accordé**	**aurons accordé**
accorderas	**accorderez**	**auras accordé**	**aurez accordé**
accordera	**accorderont**	**aura accordé**	**auront accordé**
5 conditionnel		12 conditionnel passé	
accorderais	**accorderions**	**aurais accordé**	**aurions accordé**
accorderais	**accorderiez**	**aurais accordé**	**auriez accordé**
accorderait	**accorderaient**	**aurait accordé**	**auraient accordé**
6 présent du subjonctif		13 passé du subjonctif	
accorde	**accordions**	**aie accordé**	**ayons accordé**
accordes	**accordiez**	**aies accordé**	**ayez accordé**
accorde	**accordent**	**ait accordé**	**aient accordé**
7 imparfait du subjonctif		14 plus-que-parfait du subjonctif	
accordasse	**accordassions**	**eusse accordé**	**eussions accordé**
accordasses	**accordassiez**	**eusses accordé**	**eussiez accordé**
accordât	**accordassent**	**eût accordé**	**eussent accordé**

Impératif
accorde
accordons
accordez

Words and expressions related to this verb

un accord agreement, consent
d'accord agreed, okay
mettre d'accord to reconcile
se mettre d'accord to come to an agreement
l'accord entre le sujet et le verbe subject-verb agreement
une concordance similarity, concordance
un accordage tuning (music)
un accordéon accordion (music)
un, une accordéoniste accordionist
s'accorder to be on good terms; to come to terms, to agree
cordialement cordially, heartily
donner son accord to agree, consent
Le verbe s'accorde en personne et en nombre avec le sujet. The verb agrees in person and number with the subject.

The subject pronouns are found on page 103.

accourir (12) — Part. pr. accourant — Part. passé accouru

to run to, to run up to, to come (go) running to — Irregular verb

This verb is conjugated with either **avoir** or **être** to form the compound tenses.

The Seven Simple Tenses		The Seven Compound Tenses	
Singular	Plural	Singular	Plural
1 présent de l'indicatif		8 passé composé	
accours	**accourons**	**ai accouru**	**avons accouru**
accours	**accourez**	**as accouru**	**avez accouru**
accourt	**accourent**	**a accouru**	**ont accouru**
2 imparfait de l'indicatif		9 plus-que-parfait de l'indicatif	
accourais	**accourions**	**avais accouru**	**avions accouru**
accourais	**accouriez**	**avais accouru**	**aviez accouru**
accourait	**accouraient**	**avait accouru**	**avaient accouru**
3 passé simple		10 passé antérieur	
accourus	**accourûmes**	**eus accouru**	**eûmes accouru**
accourus	**accourûtes**	**eus accouru**	**eûtes accouru**
accourut	**accoururent**	**eut accouru**	**eurent accouru**
4 futur		11 futur antérieur	
accourrai	**accourrons**	**aurai accouru**	**aurons accouru**
accourras	**accourrez**	**auras accouru**	**aurez accouru**
accourra	**accourront**	**aura accouru**	**auront accouru**
5 conditionnel		12 conditionnel passé	
accourrais	**accourrions**	**aurais accouru**	**aurions accouru**
accourrais	**accourriez**	**aurais accouru**	**auriez accouru**
accourrait	**accourraient**	**aurait accouru**	**auraient accouru**
6 présent du subjonctif		13 passé du subjonctif	
accoure	**accourions**	**aie accouru**	**ayons accouru**
accoures	**accouriez**	**aies accouru**	**ayez accouru**
accoure	**accourent**	**ait accouru**	**aient accouru**
7 imparfait du subjonctif		14 plus-que-parfait du subjonctif	
accourusse	**accourussions**	**eusse accouru**	**eussions accouru**
accourusses	**accourussiez**	**eusses accouru**	**eussiez accouru**
accourût	**accourussent**	**eût accouru**	**eussent accouru**

Impératif
accours
accourons
accourez

Words and expressions related to this verb

accourir vers qqn to go (come) running toward someone

J'ai accouru vers la pauvre vieille dame pour l'aider à se relever. I went running up to the poor old lady to help her get on her feet.

courir to run

concourir to compete

encourir to incur

secourir to aid, help

la course et la marche running and walking

la course au pouvoir the race for power

Le bon Samaritain a accouru pour aider les victimes de l'accident. The good Samaritan ran to help the accident victims.

See also **courir**.

Regular **-er** verb

to hang (up), to hook (on a hanger, nail, *e.g.*, a coat)

The Seven Simple Tenses		The Seven Compound Tenses	
Singular	Plural	Singular	Plural
1 présent de l'indicatif		8 passé composé	
accroche	**accrochons**	**ai accroché**	**avons accroché**
accroches	**accrochez**	**as accroché**	**avez accroché**
accroche	**accrochent**	**a accroché**	**ont accroché**
2 imparfait de l'indicatif		9 plus-que-parfait de l'indicatif	
accrochais	**accrochions**	**avais accroché**	**avions accroché**
accrochais	**accrochiez**	**avais accroché**	**aviez accroché**
accrochait	**accrochaient**	**avait accroché**	**avaient accroché**
3 passé simple		10 passé antérieur	
accrochai	**accrochâmes**	**eus accroché**	**eûmes accroché**
accrochas	**accrochâtes**	**eus accroché**	**eûtes accroché**
accrocha	**accrochèrent**	**eut accroché**	**eurent accroché**
4 futur		11 futur antérieur	
accrocherai	**accrocherons**	**aurai accroché**	**aurons accroché**
accrocheras	**accrocherez**	**auras accroché**	**aurez accroché**
accrochera	**accrocheront**	**aura accroché**	**auront accroché**
5 conditionnel		12 conditionnel passé	
accrocherais	**accrocherions**	**aurais accroché**	**aurions accroché**
accrocherais	**accrocheriez**	**aurais accroché**	**auriez accroché**
accrocherait	**accrocheraient**	**aurait accroché**	**auraient accroché**
6 présent du subjonctif		13 passé du subjonctif	
accroche	**accrochions**	**aie accroché**	**ayons accroché**
accroches	**accrochiez**	**aies accroché**	**ayez accroché**
accroche	**accrochent**	**ait accroché**	**aient accroché**
7 imparfait du subjonctif		14 plus-que-parfait du subjonctif	
accrochasse	**accrochassions**	**eusse accroché**	**eussions accroché**
accrochasses	**accrochassiez**	**eusses accroché**	**eussiez accroché**
accrochât	**accrochassent**	**eût accroché**	**eussent accroché**

Impératif
accroche
accrochons
accrochez

Words and expressions related to this verb

accrocher son manteau to hang up one's coat

un accrocheur, une accrocheuse leech (a person who clings, "hangs on" to another person, and is difficult to shake off)

un accroche-plat plate hanger

un accroche-coeur curl of hair against the temple of one's head (kiss curl); **des accroche-coeurs**

Accroche-toi! Hang on! Hang in there!

décrocher to unhook, to pick up the receiver of a telephone; **raccrocher** to hang up

décrocher une bonne place to land a soft job

le décrochage unhooking

un crochet hook, hanger

crocheter to hook in, to pick a lock

faire du crochet to crochet

Félicité a accroché le chapeau au miroir. Felicity hung the hat on the mirror.

The subject pronouns are found on page 103.

accroître (14) — Part. pr. accroissant — Part. passé accru

to increase, to make greater, to enlarge

Irregular verb

The Seven Simple Tenses		The Seven Compound Tenses	
Singular	Plural	Singular	Plural
1 présent de l'indicatif		8 passé composé	
accrois	**accroissons**	**ai accru**	**avons accru**
accrois	**accroissez**	**as accru**	**avez accru**
accroît	**accroissent**	**a accru**	**ont accru**
2 imparfait de l'indicatif		9 plus-que-parfait de l'indicatif	
accroissais	**accroissions**	**avais accru**	**avions accru**
accroissais	**accroissiez**	**avais accru**	**aviez accru**
accroissait	**accroissaient**	**avait accru**	**avaient accru**
3 passé simple		10 passé antérieur	
accrus	**accrûmes**	**eus accru**	**eûmes accru**
accrus	**accrûtes**	**eus accru**	**eûtes accru**
accrut	**accrurent**	**eut accru**	**eurent accru**
4 futur		11 futur antérieur	
accroîtrai	**accroîtrons**	**aurai accru**	**aurons accru**
accroîtras	**accroîtrez**	**auras accru**	**aurez accru**
accroîtra	**accroîtront**	**aura accru**	**auront accru**
5 conditionnel		12 conditionnel passé	
accroîtrais	**accroîtrions**	**aurais accru**	**aurions accru**
accroîtrais	**accroîtriez**	**aurais accru**	**auriez accru**
accroîtrait	**accroîtraient**	**aurait accru**	**auraient accru**
6 présent du subjonctif		13 passé du subjonctif	
accroisse	**accroissions**	**aie accru**	**ayons accru**
accroisses	**accroissiez**	**aies accru**	**ayez accru**
accroisse	**accroissent**	**ait accru**	**aient accru**
7 imparfait du subjonctif		14 plus-que-parfait du subjonctif	
accrusse	**accrussions**	**eusse accru**	**eussions accru**
accrusses	**accrussiez**	**eusses accru**	**eussiez accru**
accrût	**accrussent**	**eût accru**	**eussent accru**

Impératif
accrois
accroissons
accroissez

Words related to this verb
un accroissement growth, increase, accumulation, accretion
une accrue increase, accretion
s'accroître to accrue, to increase
accroître son pouvoir to increase one's power
accroître sa production to increase one's production
Note: **Accroître** is not conjugated exactly like **croître**. In many of the simple tenses **croître** has an added circumflex accent to distinguish it from **croire** (to believe): **je croîs (croître), je crois (croire)**.

See also **croître** and **décroître.**

Irregular verb

to greet, welcome

The Seven Simple Tenses		The Seven Compound Tenses	
Singular	Plural	Singular	Plural
1 présent de l'indicatif		8 passé composé	
accueille	**accueillons**	**ai accueilli**	**avons accueilli**
accueilles	**accueillez**	**as accueilli**	**avez accueilli**
accueille	**accueillent**	**a accueilli**	**ont accueilli**
2 imparfait de l'indicatif		9 plus-que-parfait de l'indicatif	
accueillais	**accueillions**	**avais accueilli**	**avions accueilli**
accueillais	**accueilliez**	**avais accueilli**	**aviez accueilli**
accueillait	**accueillaient**	**avait accueilli**	**avaient accueilli**
3 passé simple		10 passé antérieur	
accueillis	**accueillîmes**	**eus accueilli**	**eûmes accueilli**
accueillis	**accueillîtes**	**eus accueilli**	**eûtes accueilli**
accueillit	**accueillirent**	**eut accueilli**	**eurent accueilli**
4 futur		11 futur antérieur	
accueillerai	**accueillerons**	**aurai accueilli**	**aurons accueilli**
accueilleras	**accueillerez**	**auras accueilli**	**aurez accueilli**
accueillera	**accueilleront**	**aura accueilli**	**auront accueilli**
5 conditionnel		12 conditionnel passé	
accueillerais	**accueillerions**	**aurais accueilli**	**aurions accueilli**
accueillerais	**accueilleriez**	**aurais accueilli**	**auriez accueilli**
accueillerait	**accueilleraient**	**aurait accueilli**	**auraient accueilli**
6 présent du subjonctif		13 passé du subjonctif	
accueille	**accueillions**	**aie accueilli**	**ayons accueilli**
accueilles	**accueilliez**	**aies accueilli**	**ayez accueilli**
accueille	**accueillent**	**ait accueilli**	**aient accueilli**
7 imparfait du subjonctif		14 plus-que-parfait du subjonctif	
accueillisse	**accueillissions**	**eusse accueilli**	**eussions accueilli**
accueillisses	**accueillissiez**	**eusses accueilli**	**eussiez accueilli**
accueillît	**accueillissent**	**eût accueilli**	**eussent accueilli**

Impératif
accueille
accueillons
accueillez

Words and expressions related to this verb

accueillir chaleureusement to give a warm welcome
accueillir froidement to give a cool reception
faire bon accueil to give a warm welcome
l'accueil *m.*/**le bureau d'accueil** reception desk
un accueil welcome, reception;
un accueil chaleureux warm welcome
accueillant, accueillante hospitable;
l'accueil des touristes accommodating the tourists
Avez-vous jamais été accueilli aimablement? Have you ever been welcomed kindly?

For other words and expressions related to this verb, see **cueillir**.

Grammar putting you in a tense mood? Review the definitions of basic grammatical terms with examples on pages 35–49.

The subject pronouns are found on page 103.

accuser (16) — Part. pr. accusant — Part. passé accusé

to accuse

Regular **-er** verb

The Seven Simple Tenses		The Seven Compound Tenses	
Singular	Plural	Singular	Plural
1 présent de l'indicatif		8 passé composé	
accuse	**accusons**	**ai accusé**	**avons accusé**
accuses	**accusez**	**as accusé**	**avez accusé**
accuse	**accusent**	**a accusé**	**ont accusé**
2 imparfait de l'indicatif		9 plus-que-parfait de l'indicatif	
accusais	**accusions**	**avais accusé**	**avions accusé**
accusais	**accusiez**	**avais accusé**	**aviez accusé**
accusait	**accusaient**	**avait accusé**	**avaient accusé**
3 passé simple		10 passé antérieur	
accusai	**accusâmes**	**eus accusé**	**eûmes accusé**
accusas	**accusâtes**	**eus accusé**	**eûtes accusé**
accusa	**accusèrent**	**eut accusé**	**eurent accusé**
4 futur		11 futur antérieur	
accuserai	**accuserons**	**aurai accusé**	**aurons accusé**
accuseras	**accuserez**	**auras accusé**	**aurez accusé**
accusera	**accuseront**	**aura accusé**	**auront accusé**
5 conditionnel		12 conditionnel passé	
accuserais	**accuserions**	**aurais accusé**	**aurions accusé**
accuserais	**accuseriez**	**aurais accusé**	**auriez accusé**
accuserait	**accuseraient**	**aurait accusé**	**auraient accusé**
6 présent du subjonctif		13 passé du subjonctif	
accuse	**accusions**	**aie accusé**	**ayons accusé**
accuses	**accusiez**	**aies accusé**	**ayez accusé**
accuse	**accusent**	**ait accusé**	**aient accusé**
7 imparfait du subjonctif		14 plus-que-parfait du subjonctif	
accusasse	**accusassions**	**eusse accusé**	**eussions accusé**
accusasses	**accusassiez**	**eusses accusé**	**eussiez accusé**
accusât	**accusassent**	**eût accusé**	**eussent accusé**

Impératif
accuse
accusons
accusez

Words and expressions related to this verb

accuser réception de qqch to acknowledge receipt of something
une accusation accusation, charge, indictment
porter une accusation contre to bring charges against
un accusateur, une accusatrice accuser; **l'accusateur public** public prosecutor
s'accuser de to accuse oneself of
un accusé de réception acknowledgment/confirmation of receipt

Proverb: **Qui s'excuse, s'accuse.** A guilty conscience needs no accuser.

Don't forget to check the list of 2,600 additional verbs keyed to the 501 model verbs. It's in the Appendixes!

to buy, to purchase

Regular **-er** verb endings; spelling change:
e changes to **è** before syllable with mute **e**

The Seven Simple Tenses

Singular	Plural
1 présent de l'indicatif	
achète	**achetons**
achètes	**achetez**
achète	**achètent**
2 imparfait de l'indicatif	
achetais	**achetions**
achetais	**achetiez**
achetait	**achetaient**
3 passé simple	
achetai	**achetâmes**
achetas	**achetâtes**
acheta	**achetèrent**
4 futur	
achèterai	**achèterons**
achèteras	**achèterez**
achètera	**achèteront**
5 conditionnel	
achèterais	**achèterions**
achèterais	**achèteriez**
achèterait	**achèteraient**
6 présent du subjonctif	
achète	**achetions**
achètes	**achetiez**
achète	**achètent**
7 imparfait du subjonctif	
achetasse	**achetassions**
achetasses	**achetassiez**
achetât	**achetassent**

The Seven Compound Tenses

Singular	Plural
8 passé composé	
ai acheté	**avons acheté**
as acheté	**avez acheté**
a acheté	**ont acheté**
9 plus-que-parfait de l'indicatif	
avais acheté	**avions acheté**
avais acheté	**aviez acheté**
avait acheté	**avaient acheté**
10 passé antérieur	
eus acheté	**eûmes acheté**
eus acheté	**eûtes acheté**
eut acheté	**eurent acheté**
11 futur antérieur	
aurai acheté	**aurons acheté**
auras acheté	**aurez acheté**
aura acheté	**auront acheté**
12 conditionnel passé	
aurais acheté	**aurions acheté**
aurais acheté	**auriez acheté**
aurait acheté	**auraient acheté**
13 passé du subjonctif	
aie acheté	**ayons acheté**
aies acheté	**ayez acheté**
ait acheté	**aient acheté**
14 plus-que-parfait du subjonctif	
eusse acheté	**eussions acheté**
eusses acheté	**eussiez acheté**
eût acheté	**eussent acheté**

Impératif
achète
achetons
achetez

The subject pronouns are found on page 103.

AN ESSENTIAL 55 VERB

Acheter

Acheter is an essential verb for beginning students because it is useful in many situations and in a number of idiomatic expressions.

Sentences using acheter

Je voudrais acheter des aspirines et des pastilles contre la toux. I would like to buy some aspirin and some cough drops.

J'aimerais acheter quelques pâtisseries. I would like to buy some pastries.

J'achète ce journal et ce magazine. I'm buying this newspaper and this magazine.

Ce vélo? Je l'ai acheté à Michel. This bike? I bought it from Michael.

L'amitié ne s'achète pas. Friendship cannot be bought.

Achetons une nouvelle voiture! Let's buy a new car!

Achetez deux et recevez-en un troisième gratuitement! Buy two and get the third one free!

Le criminel s'est racheté en aidant les pauvres. The criminal redeemed himself by helping the poor.

Il y a plus d'acheteurs que de connaisseurs. There are more buyers than connoisseurs.

Words and expressions related to this verb

un achat **purchase**

faire un achat **to make a purchase**

un achat en ligne **on-line purchase**

un achat électronique **electronic purchase (Internet)**

acheter qqch à qqn **to buy something from someone**

acheter comptant **to buy for cash**

acheter à crédit **to buy on credit**

un acheteur, une acheteuse **buyer, purchaser**

achetable **purchasable**

Acheter has a tricky spelling change before a syllable with a mute **e**. If you can conjugate **acheter** you can also conjugate the following verbs.

corseter **to corset, constrict**

fureter **to ferret out, pry into, snoop, search**

haleter (aspirate h) **to pant, gasp**

racheter **to buy more, buy back, ransom, redeem, atone**

se racheter **to redeem oneself (helping verb être)**

Regular **-er** verb endings; spelling change: **e** changes to **è** before syllable with mute **e**

to achieve, to finish, to complete, to end

The Seven Simple Tenses		The Seven Compound Tenses	
Singular	Plural	Singular	Plural
1 présent de l'indicatif		8 passé composé	
achève	**achevons**	**ai achevé**	**avons achevé**
achèves	**achevez**	**as achevé**	**avez achevé**
achève	**achèvent**	**a achevé**	**ont achevé**
2 imparfait de l'indicatif		9 plus-que-parfait de l'indicatif	
achevais	**achevions**	**avais achevé**	**avions achevé**
achevais	**acheviez**	**avais achevé**	**aviez achevé**
achevait	**achevaient**	**avait achevé**	**avaient achevé**
3 passé simple		10 passé antérieur	
achevai	**achevâmes**	**eus achevé**	**eûmes achevé**
achevas	**achevâtes**	**eus achevé**	**eûtes achevé**
acheva	**achevèrent**	**eut achevé**	**eurent achevé**
4 futur		11 futur antérieur	
achèverai	**achèverons**	**aurai achevé**	**aurons achevé**
achèveras	**achèverez**	**auras achevé**	**aurez achevé**
achèvera	**achèveront**	**aura achevé**	**auront achevé**
5 conditionnel		12 conditionnel passé	
achèverais	**achèverions**	**aurais achevé**	**aurions achevé**
achèverais	**achèveriez**	**aurais achevé**	**auriez achevé**
achèverait	**achèveraient**	**aurait achevé**	**auraient achevé**
6 présent du subjonctif		13 passé du subjonctif	
achève	**achevions**	**aie achevé**	**ayons achevé**
achèves	**acheviez**	**aies achevé**	**ayez achevé**
achève	**achèvent**	**ait achevé**	**aient achevé**
7 imparfait du subjonctif		14 plus-que-parfait du subjonctif	
achevasse	**achevassions**	**eusse achevé**	**eussions achevé**
achevasses	**achevassiez**	**eusses achevé**	**eussiez achevé**
achevât	**achevassent**	**eût achevé**	**eussent achevé**

Impératif
achève
achevons
achevez

Words and expressions related to this verb
achever de faire qqch to finish doing something
s'achever to come to an end, to close, to be fulfilled
un idiot achevé, une idiote achevée a complete idiot
un achèvement completion, end, conclusion; **l'achèvement du travail** completion of the work
Pierre a commencé son roman en 1980, et il l'a achevé vingt ans plus tard. Peter started his novel in 1980, and he finished it twenty years later.

The subject pronouns are found on page 103.

to acquire, to obtain

Irregular verb

The Seven Simple Tenses		The Seven Compound Tenses	
Singular	Plural	Singular	Plural
1 présent de l'indicatif		8 passé composé	
acquiers	**acquérons**	**ai acquis**	**avons acquis**
acquiers	**acquérez**	**as acquis**	**avez acquis**
acquiert	**acquièrent**	**a acquis**	**ont acquis**
2 imparfait de l'indicatif		9 plus-que-parfait de l'indicatif	
acquérais	**acquérions**	**avais acquis**	**avions acquis**
acquérais	**acquériez**	**avais acquis**	**aviez acquis**
acquérait	**acquéraient**	**avait acquis**	**avaient acquis**
3 passé simple		10 passé antérieur	
acquis	**acquîmes**	**eus acquis**	**eûmes acquis**
acquis	**acquîtes**	**eus acquis**	**eûtes acquis**
acquit	**acquirent**	**eut acquis**	**eurent acquis**
4 futur		11 futur antérieur	
acquerrai	**acquerrons**	**aurai acquis**	**aurons acquis**
acquerras	**acquerrez**	**auras acquis**	**aurez acquis**
acquerra	**acquerront**	**aura acquis**	**auront acquis**
5 conditionnel		12 conditionnel passé	
acquerrais	**acquerrions**	**aurais acquis**	**aurions acquis**
acquerrais	**acquerriez**	**aurais acquis**	**auriez acquis**
acquerrait	**acquerraient**	**aurait acquis**	**auraient acquis**
6 présent du subjonctif		13 passé du subjonctif	
acquière	**acquérions**	**aie acquis**	**ayons acquis**
acquières	**acquériez**	**aies acquis**	**ayez acquis**
acquière	**acquièrent**	**ait acquis**	**aient acquis**
7 imparfait du subjonctif		14 plus-que-parfait du subjonctif	
acquisse	**acquissions**	**eusse acquis**	**eussions acquis**
acquisses	**acquissiez**	**eusses acquis**	**eussiez acquis**
acquît	**acquissent**	**eût acquis**	**eussent acquis**

Impératif
acquiers
acquérons
acquérez

Words and expressions related to this verb
s'acquérir to accrue; to improve; to be gained or obtained
une acquisition acquisition, purchase; **faire l'acquisition de** to acquire
un acquit receipt; release
acquis, acquise acquired
conquérir to conquer
tenir quelque chose pour acquis to take something for granted
Il ne faut rien prendre/tenir pour acquis. One must not take anything for granted.

Get acquainted with what preposition goes with what verb. See *Verbs with prepositions* in the Appendixes.

Irregular verb

to admit

The Seven Simple Tenses		The Seven Compound Tenses	
Singular	Plural	Singular	Plural
1 présent de l'indicatif		8 passé composé	
admets	**admettons**	**ai admis**	**avons admis**
admets	**admettez**	**as admis**	**avez admis**
admet	**admettent**	**a admis**	**ont admis**
2 imparfait de l'indicatif		9 plus-que-parfait de l'indicatif	
admettais	**admettions**	**avais admis**	**avions admis**
admettais	**admettiez**	**avais admis**	**aviez admis**
admettait	**admettaient**	**avait admis**	**avaient admis**
3 passé simple		10 passé antérieur	
admis	**admîmes**	**eus admis**	**eûmes admis**
admis	**admîtes**	**eus admis**	**eûtes admis**
admit	**admirent**	**eut admis**	**eurent admis**
4 futur		11 futur antérieur	
admettrai	**admettrons**	**aurai admis**	**aurons admis**
admettras	**admettrez**	**auras admis**	**aurez admis**
admettra	**admettront**	**aura admis**	**auront admis**
5 conditionnel		12 conditionnel passé	
admettrais	**admettrions**	**aurais admis**	**aurions admis**
admettrais	**admettriez**	**aurais admis**	**auriez admis**
admettrait	**admettraient**	**aurait admis**	**auraient admis**
6 présent du subjonctif		13 passé du subjonctif	
admette	**admettions**	**aie admis**	**ayons admis**
admettes	**admettiez**	**aies admis**	**ayez admis**
admette	**admettent**	**ait admis**	**aient admis**
7 imparfait du subjonctif		14 plus-que-parfait du subjonctif	
admisse	**admissions**	**eusse admis**	**eussions admis**
admisses	**admissiez**	**eusses admis**	**eussiez admis**
admît	**admissent**	**eût admis**	**eussent admis**

Impératif
admets
admettons
admettez

Words and expressions related to this verb
admis, admise admitted, accepted
une admission admission, admittance
l'admissibilité *f.* acceptability
se faire admettre dans un club to be admitted to a club
admissible acceptable
C'est une idée folle, je l'admets. It's a crazy idea, I admit it.

See also **commettre, mettre, permettre, promettre, remettre,** and **soumettre.**

to admire

Regular **-er** verb

The Seven Simple Tenses		The Seven Compound Tenses	
Singular	Plural	Singular	Plural
1 présent de l'indicatif		8 passé composé	
admire	**admirons**	**ai admiré**	**avons admiré**
admires	**admirez**	**as admiré**	**avez admiré**
admire	**admirent**	**a admiré**	**ont admiré**
2 imparfait de l'indicatif		9 plus-que-parfait de l'indicatif	
admirais	**admirions**	**avais admiré**	**avions admiré**
admirais	**admiriez**	**avais admiré**	**aviez admiré**
admirait	**admiraient**	**avait admiré**	**avaient admiré**
3 passé simple		10 passé antérieur	
admirai	**admirâmes**	**eus admiré**	**eûmes admiré**
admiras	**admirâtes**	**eus admiré**	**eûtes admiré**
admira	**admirèrent**	**eut admiré**	**eurent admiré**
4 futur		11 futur antérieur	
admirerai	**admirerons**	**aurai admiré**	**aurons admiré**
admireras	**admirerez**	**auras admiré**	**aurez admiré**
admirera	**admireront**	**aura admiré**	**auront admiré**
5 conditionnel		12 conditionnel passé	
admirerais	**admirerions**	**aurais admiré**	**aurions admiré**
admirerais	**admireriez**	**aurais admiré**	**auriez admiré**
admirerait	**admireraient**	**aurait admiré**	**auraient admiré**
6 présent du subjonctif		13 passé du subjonctif	
admire	**admirions**	**aie admiré**	**ayons admiré**
admires	**admiriez**	**aies admiré**	**ayez admiré**
admire	**admirent**	**ait admiré**	**aient admiré**
7 imparfait du subjonctif		14 plus-que-parfait du subjonctif	
admirasse	**admirassions**	**eusse admiré**	**eussions admiré**
admirasses	**admirassiez**	**eusses admiré**	**eussiez admiré**
admirât	**admirassent**	**eût admiré**	**eussent admiré**

Impératif
admire
admirons
admirez

Words and expressions related to this verb

une admiration admiration, wonder
admirativement admiringly
admiratif, admirative admiring
un admirateur, une admiratrice admirer
un mirage mirage, illusion
un miroir mirror
remplir quelqu'un d'admiration to fill someone with admiration
être admirable de courage to show great courage
admirablement admirably, wonderfully
être en admiration devant to be filled with admiration for

See also **mirer.**

Regular **-er** verb

to worship, to adore

The Seven Simple Tenses		The Seven Compound Tenses	
Singular	Plural	Singular	Plural
1 présent de l'indicatif		8 passé composé	
adore	**adorons**	**ai adoré**	**avons adoré**
adores	**adorez**	**as adoré**	**avez adoré**
adore	**adorent**	**a adoré**	**ont adoré**
2 imparfait de l'indicatif		9 plus-que-parfait de l'indicatif	
adorais	**adorions**	**avais adoré**	**avions adoré**
adorais	**adoriez**	**avais adoré**	**aviez adoré**
adorait	**adoraient**	**avait adoré**	**avaient adoré**
3 passé simple		10 passé antérieur	
adorai	**adorâmes**	**eus adoré**	**eûmes adoré**
adoras	**adorâtes**	**eus adoré**	**eûtes adoré**
adora	**adorèrent**	**eut adoré**	**eurent adoré**
4 futur		11 futur antérieur	
adorerai	**adorerons**	**aurai adoré**	**aurons adoré**
adoreras	**adorerez**	**auras adoré**	**aurez adoré**
adorera	**adoreront**	**aura adoré**	**auront adoré**
5 conditionnel		12 conditionnel passé	
adorerais	**adorerions**	**aurais adoré**	**aurions adoré**
adorerais	**adoreriez**	**aurais adoré**	**auriez adoré**
adorerait	**adoreraient**	**aurait adoré**	**auraient adoré**
6 présent du subjonctif		13 passé du subjonctif	
adore	**adorions**	**aie adoré**	**ayons adoré**
adores	**adoriez**	**aies adoré**	**ayez adoré**
adore	**adorent**	**ait adoré**	**aient adoré**
7 imparfait du subjonctif		14 plus-que-parfait du subjonctif	
adorasse	**adorassions**	**eusse adoré**	**eussions adoré**
adorasses	**adorassiez**	**eusses adoré**	**eussiez adoré**
adorât	**adorassent**	**eût adoré**	**eussent adoré**

Impératif
adore
adorons
adorez

Sentences using this verb and words related to it

Laure adore sa nièce. Laura adores her niece.

Madeleine est une fille adorable. Elle adore écouter la musique québécoise. Madeleine is an adorable girl. She adores listening to Québécois music.

une adoration adoration, worship
adorablement adorably
un adorateur, une adoratrice adorer, worshipper
adorable adorable, charming, delightful
un village adorable delightful village
une robe adorable lovely dress

The subject pronouns are found on page 103.

adresser (23) Part. pr. **adressant** Part. passé **adressé**

to address

Regular **-er** verb

The Seven Simple Tenses		The Seven Compound Tenses	
Singular	Plural	Singular	Plural
1 présent de l'indicatif		8 passé composé	
adresse	**adressons**	**ai adressé**	**avons adressé**
adresses	**adressez**	**as adressé**	**avez adressé**
adresse	**adressent**	**a adressé**	**ont adressé**
2 imparfait de l'indicatif		9 plus-que-parfait de l'indicatif	
adressais	**adressions**	**avais adressé**	**avions adressé**
adressais	**adressiez**	**avais adressé**	**aviez adressé**
adressait	**adressaient**	**avait adressé**	**avaient adressé**
3 passé simple		10 passé antérieur	
adressai	**adressâmes**	**eus adressé**	**eûmes adressé**
adressas	**adressâtes**	**eus adressé**	**eûtes adressé**
adressa	**adressèrent**	**eut adressé**	**eurent adressé**
4 futur		11 futur antérieur	
adresserai	**adresserons**	**aurai adressé**	**aurons adressé**
adresseras	**adresserez**	**auras adressé**	**aurez adressé**
adressera	**adresseront**	**aura adressé**	**auront adressé**
5 conditionnel		12 conditionnel passé	
adresserais	**adresserions**	**aurais adressé**	**aurions adressé**
adresserais	**adresseriez**	**aurais adressé**	**auriez adressé**
adresserait	**adresseraient**	**aurait adressé**	**auraient adressé**
6 présent du subjonctif		13 passé du subjonctif	
adresse	**adressions**	**aie adressé**	**ayons adressé**
adresses	**adressiez**	**aies adressé**	**ayez adressé**
adresse	**adressent**	**ait adressé**	**aient adressé**
7 imparfait du subjonctif		14 plus-que-parfait du subjonctif	
adressasse	**adressassions**	**eusse adressé**	**eussions adressé**
adressasses	**adressassiez**	**eusses adressé**	**eussiez adressé**
adressât	**adressassent**	**eût adressé**	**eussent adressé**

Impératif
adresse
adressons
adressez

Words and expressions related to this verb

une adresse address; skill, adroitness
adresser qqn à to refer someone to
adresser la parole à to direct your words to, to speak to
s'adresser à to apply to, to talk to
un tour d'adresse feat of skill
avec adresse skillfully
dresser to tame, to erect
redresser to straighten up
une adresse électronique e-mail address
Pour d'autres renseignements, adressez-vous au service à la clientèle. For more information, talk to customer service.

Regular **-er** verb endings; spelling change:
c changes to **ç** before **a** or **o** to keep **s** sound

to annoy, to irritate, to pester, to vex

The Seven Simple Tenses		The Seven Compound Tenses	
Singular	Plural	Singular	Plural
1 présent de l'indicatif		8 passé composé	
agace	**agaçons**	**ai agacé**	**avons agacé**
agaces	**agacez**	**as agacé**	**avez agacé**
agace	**agacent**	**a agacé**	**ont agacé**
2 imparfait de l'indicatif		9 plus-que-parfait de l'indicatif	
agaçais	**agacions**	**avais agacé**	**avions agacé**
agaçais	**agaciez**	**avais agacé**	**aviez agacé**
agaçait	**agaçaient**	**avait agacé**	**avaient agacé**
3 passé simple		10 passé antérieur	
agaçai	**agaçâmes**	**eus agacé**	**eûmes agacé**
agaças	**agaçâtes**	**eus agacé**	**eûtes agacé**
agaça	**agacèrent**	**eut agacé**	**eurent agacé**
4 futur		11 futur antérieur	
agacerai	**agacerons**	**aurai agacé**	**aurons agacé**
agaceras	**agacerez**	**auras agacé**	**aurez agacé**
agacera	**agaceront**	**aura agacé**	**auront agacé**
5 conditionnel		12 conditionnel passé	
agacerais	**agacerions**	**aurais agacé**	**aurions agacé**
agacerais	**agaceriez**	**aurais agacé**	**auriez agacé**
agacerait	**agaceraient**	**aurait agacé**	**auraient agacé**
6 présent du subjonctif		13 passé du subjonctif	
agace	**agacions**	**aie agacé**	**ayons agacé**
agaces	**agaciez**	**aies agacé**	**ayez agacé**
agace	**agacent**	**ait agacé**	**aient agacé**
7 imparfait du subjonctif		14 plus-que-parfait du subjonctif	
agaçasse	**agaçassions**	**eusse agacé**	**eussions agacé**
agaçasses	**agaçassiez**	**eusses agacé**	**eussiez agacé**
agaçât	**agaçassent**	**eût agacé**	**eussent agacé**

Impératif
agace
agaçons
agacez

Words and expressions related to this verb
un agacement irritation
Cela est agaçant! That's irritating!
agacer les nerfs de qqn to get on someone's nerves
s'agacer to get annoyed, irritated
Cela m'agace! It's getting on my nerves!
Tu m'agaces! You're getting on my nerves!

Don't forget to check the list of 2,600 additional verbs keyed to the 501 model verbs.

The subject pronouns are found on page 103.

agir (25)

Part. pr. **agissant** Part. passé **agi**

to act, to behave, to take effect

Regular **-ir** verb

The Seven Simple Tenses		The Seven Compound Tenses	
Singular	Plural	Singular	Plural
1 présent de l'indicatif		8 passé composé	
agis	**agissons**	**ai agi**	**avons agi**
agis	**agissez**	**as agi**	**avez agi**
agit	**agissent**	**a agi**	**ont agi**
2 imparfait de l'indicatif		9 plus-que-parfait de l'indicatif	
agissais	**agissions**	**avais agi**	**avions agi**
agissais	**agissiez**	**avais agi**	**aviez agi**
agissait	**agissaient**	**avait agi**	**avaient agi**
3 passé simple		10 passé antérieur	
agis	**agîmes**	**eus agi**	**eûmes agi**
agis	**agîtes**	**eus agi**	**eûtes agi**
agit	**agirent**	**eut agi**	**eurent agi**
4 futur		11 futur antérieur	
agirai	**agirons**	**aurai agi**	**aurons agi**
agiras	**agirez**	**auras agi**	**aurez agi**
agira	**agiront**	**aura agi**	**auront agi**
5 conditionnel		12 conditionnel passé	
agirais	**agirions**	**aurais agi**	**aurions agi**
agirais	**agiriez**	**aurais agi**	**auriez agi**
agirait	**agiraient**	**aurait agi**	**auraient agi**
6 présent du subjonctif		13 passé du subjonctif	
agisse	**agissions**	**aie agi**	**ayons agi**
agisses	**agissiez**	**aies agi**	**ayez agi**
agisse	**agissent**	**ait agi**	**aient agi**
7 imparfait du subjonctif		14 plus-que-parfait du subjonctif	
agisse	**agissions**	**eusse agi**	**eussions agi**
agisses	**agissiez**	**eusses agi**	**eussiez agi**
agît	**agissent**	**eût agi**	**eussent agi**

Impératif
agis
agissons
agissez

Words and expressions related to this verb

faire agir to set in motion, to call into action
bien agir to behave well; **mal agir** to behave badly
agir sur to bear upon, to influence, to act upon
agir contre to sue, to take action against
faire agir la loi to put the law into effect
un agitateur, une agitatrice agitator
agiter to rouse, to stir up; to agitate, to shake
réagir to react
agir à la légère to act thoughtlessly

See also **s'agir** in the *Defective and impersonal verb* section.

Get acquainted with what preposition goes with what verb. See *Verbs with prepositions* in the Appendixes.

Regular **-er** verb

to aid, to help, to assist

The Seven Simple Tenses		The Seven Compound Tenses	
Singular	Plural	Singular	Plural
1 présent de l'indicatif		8 passé composé	
aide	**aidons**	**ai aidé**	**avons aidé**
aides	**aidez**	**as aidé**	**avez aidé**
aide	**aident**	**a aidé**	**ont aidé**
2 imparfait de l'indicatif		9 plus-que-parfait de l'indicatif	
aidais	**aidions**	**avais aidé**	**avions aidé**
aidais	**aidiez**	**avais aidé**	**aviez aidé**
aidait	**aidaient**	**avait aidé**	**avaient aidé**
3 passé simple		10 passé antérieur	
aidai	**aidâmes**	**eus aidé**	**eûmes aidé**
aidas	**aidâtes**	**eus aidé**	**eûtes aidé**
aida	**aidèrent**	**eut aidé**	**eurent aidé**
4 futur		11 futur antérieur	
aiderai	**aiderons**	**aurai aidé**	**aurons aidé**
aideras	**aiderez**	**auras aidé**	**aurez aidé**
aidera	**aideront**	**aura aidé**	**auront aidé**
5 conditionnel		12 conditionnel passé	
aiderais	**aiderions**	**aurais aidé**	**aurions aidé**
aiderais	**aideriez**	**aurais aidé**	**auriez aidé**
aiderait	**aideraient**	**aurait aidé**	**auraient aidé**
6 présent du subjonctif		13 passé du subjonctif	
aide	**aidions**	**aie aidé**	**ayons aidé**
aides	**aidiez**	**aies aidé**	**ayez aidé**
aide	**aident**	**ait aidé**	**aient aidé**
7 imparfait du subjonctif		14 plus-que-parfait du subjonctif	
aidasse	**aidassions**	**eusse aidé**	**eussions aidé**
aidasses	**aidassiez**	**eusses aidé**	**eussiez aidé**
aidât	**aidassent**	**eût aidé**	**eussent aidé**

Impératif
aide
aidons
aidez

Sentences using this verb and words related to it

Tous les soirs Daniel aide Matthieu, son petit frère, à faire sa leçon de mathématiques. Every evening Daniel helps his little brother Matthew do his math lesson.

Ce soir, Matthieu lui demande: This evening, Matthew asks him:

—**Après cette leçon, veux-tu m'aider à écrire une composition?** After this lesson, would you like to help me write a composition?

—**Aide-toi et le ciel t'aidera, lui répond Daniel.** Heaven helps those who help themselves, answers Daniel.

aider qqn à faire qqch to help someone do something

s'aider to help oneself; to help each other

une aide aid, assistance, help; **à l'aide de** with the help of

un aide-mémoire handbook, memory aid

À l'aide tout de suite! Get help right away!

Je peux vous aider? May I help you?

s'entraider to help each other

Note that **se servir** should be used when speaking of food or drink: **Sers-toi!** (Help yourself!) **Servez-vous!** (Help yourself/yourselves!) See also **servir** and **se servir**.

The subject pronouns are found on page 103.

aimer (27) Part. pr. **aimant** Part. passé **aimé**

to love, to like

Regular **-er** verb

The Seven Simple Tenses		The Seven Compound Tenses	
Singular	Plural	Singular	Plural
1 présent de l'indicatif		8 passé composé	
aime	**aimons**	**ai aimé**	**avons aimé**
aimes	**aimez**	**as aimé**	**avez aimé**
aime	**aiment**	**a aimé**	**ont aimé**
2 imparfait de l'indicatif		9 plus-que-parfait de l'indicatif	
aimais	**aimions**	**avais aimé**	**avions aimé**
aimais	**aimiez**	**avais aimé**	**aviez aimé**
aimait	**aimaient**	**avait aimé**	**avaient aimé**
3 passé simple		10 passé antérieur	
aimai	**aimâmes**	**eus aimé**	**eûmes aimé**
aimas	**aimâtes**	**eus aimé**	**eûtes aimé**
aima	**aimèrent**	**eut aimé**	**eurent aimé**
4 futur		11 futur antérieur	
aimerai	**aimerons**	**aurai aimé**	**aurons aimé**
aimeras	**aimerez**	**auras aimé**	**aurez aimé**
aimera	**aimeront**	**aura aimé**	**auront aimé**
5 conditionnel		12 conditionnel passé	
aimerais	**aimerions**	**aurais aimé**	**aurions aimé**
aimerais	**aimeriez**	**aurais aimé**	**auriez aimé**
aimerait	**aimeraient**	**aurait aimé**	**auraient aimé**
6 présent du subjonctif		13 passé du subjonctif	
aime	**aimions**	**aie aimé**	**ayons aimé**
aimes	**aimiez**	**aies aimé**	**ayez aimé**
aime	**aiment**	**ait aimé**	**aient aimé**
7 imparfait du subjonctif		14 plus-que-parfait du subjonctif	
aimasse	**aimassions**	**eusse aimé**	**eussions aimé**
aimasses	**aimassiez**	**eusses aimé**	**eussiez aimé**
aimât	**aimassent**	**eût aimé**	**eussent aimé**

Impératif
aime
aimons
aimez

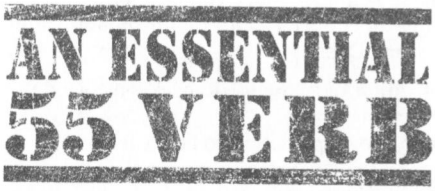

AN ESSENTIAL 55 VERB

Aimer A

Aimer is a very useful verb. It has often been thought of as the model of a regular **-er** verb.

Sentences using aimer and related words

Greg aime faire du vélo. Greg loves to bike.

Est-ce que David aime les cigarettes? Does David like cigarettes?

Je n'aime pas les ascenseurs! Je préfère monter l'escalier. I don't like elevators! I prefer to walk up the stairs.

Vous êtes bien aimable. You are very kind.

J'aimerais acheter quelques pâtisseries. I would like to buy some pastries.

Moi, je n'aime pas le poulet. Je préfère un steak bien cuit. As for me, I don't like chicken. I prefer a steak well-done.

Veuillez avoir l'amabilité de . . . Please be so kind as to . . .

Je t'aimais, je t'aime et je t'aimerai. I loved you, I love you and I will love you. (Francis Cabrel, French singer)

Required sentence
J'aime le français. I love French.

Words and expressions related to this verb

amour *m.* **love**

une chanson d'amour love song (song of love)

aimer bien qqn to like somebody

aimer (à) faire qqch to enjoy doing something

aimer mieux to prefer, to like better

s'entr'aimer to love each other

l'amabilité *f.* **kindness**

aimable friendly, amiable, pleasant

un amant, une amante lover

amoureux, amoureuse de in love with

tomber amoureux, amoureuse to fall in love

Proverb

Choisissez un travail que vous aimez et vous n'aurez pas à travailler un seul jour de votre vie. Choose a job you love and you will never have to work a day in your life. (Confucius)

The subject pronouns are found on page 103.

ajouter (28)

Part. pr. **ajoutant** Part. passé **ajouté**

to add

Regular **-er** verb

The Seven Simple Tenses		The Seven Compound Tenses	
Singular	Plural	Singular	Plural
1 présent de l'indicatif		8 passé composé	
ajoute	**ajoutons**	**ai ajouté**	**avons ajouté**
ajoutes	**ajoutez**	**as ajouté**	**avez ajouté**
ajoute	**ajoutent**	**a ajouté**	**ont ajouté**
2 imparfait de l'indicatif		9 plus-que-parfait de l'indicatif	
ajoutais	**ajoutions**	**avais ajouté**	**avions ajouté**
ajoutais	**ajoutiez**	**avais ajouté**	**aviez ajouté**
ajoutait	**ajoutaient**	**avait ajouté**	**avaient ajouté**
3 passé simple		10 passé antérieur	
ajoutai	**ajoutâmes**	**eus ajouté**	**eûmes ajouté**
ajoutas	**ajoutâtes**	**eus ajouté**	**eûtes ajouté**
ajouta	**ajoutèrent**	**eut ajouté**	**eurent ajouté**
4 futur		11 futur antérieur	
ajouterai	**ajouterons**	**aurai ajouté**	**aurons ajouté**
ajouteras	**ajouterez**	**auras ajouté**	**aurez ajouté**
ajoutera	**ajouteront**	**aura ajouté**	**auront ajouté**
5 conditionnel		12 conditionnel passé	
ajouterais	**ajouterions**	**aurais ajouté**	**aurions ajouté**
ajouterais	**ajouteriez**	**aurais ajouté**	**auriez ajouté**
ajouterait	**ajouteraient**	**aurait ajouté**	**auraient ajouté**
6 présent du subjonctif		13 passé du subjonctif	
ajoute	**ajoutions**	**aie ajouté**	**ayons ajouté**
ajoutes	**ajoutiez**	**aies ajouté**	**ayez ajouté**
ajoute	**ajoutent**	**ait ajouté**	**aient ajouté**
7 imparfait du subjonctif		14 plus-que-parfait du subjonctif	
ajoutasse	**ajoutassions**	**eusse ajouté**	**eussions ajouté**
ajoutasses	**ajoutassiez**	**eusses ajouté**	**eussiez ajouté**
ajoutât	**ajoutassent**	**eût ajouté**	**eussent ajouté**

Impératif
ajoute
ajoutons
ajoutez

Sentences using this verb and words related to it

Une gousse d'ail ajoute du goût à votre ragoût. A clove of garlic adds flavor to your ragout.

un ajout addition (of words in a manuscript or page proofs)
ajouter foi à to add credence to, to give credence to
jouter to tilt, to joust; to dispute, to fight
une joute contest, tournament
rajouter to add more
un rajout an addition

Don't forget to check the list of 2,600 additional verbs keyed to the 501 model verbs. It's in the Appendixes!

Irregular verb

to go

The Seven Simple Tenses		The Seven Compound Tenses	
Singular	Plural	Singular	Plural
1 présent de l'indicatif		8 passé composé	
vais	**allons**	**suis allé(e)**	**sommes allé(e)s**
vas	**allez**	**es allé(e)**	**êtes allé(e)(s)**
va	**vont**	**est allé(e)**	**sont allé(e)s**
2 imparfait de l'indicatif		9 plus-que-parfait de l'indicatif	
allais	**allions**	**étais allé(e)**	**étions allé(e)s**
allais	**alliez**	**étais allé(e)**	**étiez allé(e)(s)**
allait	**allaient**	**était allé(e)**	**étaient allé(e)s**
3 passé simple		10 passé antérieur	
allai	**allâmes**	**fus allé(e)**	**fûmes allé(e)s**
allas	**allâtes**	**fus allé(e)**	**fûtes allé(e)(s)**
alla	**allèrent**	**fut allé(e)**	**furent allé(e)s**
4 futur		11 futur antérieur	
irai	**irons**	**serai allé(e)**	**serons allé(e)s**
iras	**irez**	**seras allé(e)**	**serez allé(e)(s)**
ira	**iront**	**sera allé(e)**	**seront allé(e)s**
5 conditionnel		12 conditionnel passé	
irais	**irions**	**serais allé(e)**	**serions allé(e)s**
irais	**iriez**	**serais allé(e)**	**seriez allé(e)(s)**
irait	**iraient**	**serait allé(e)**	**seraient allé(e)s**
6 présent du subjonctif		13 passé du subjonctif	
aille	**allions**	**sois allé(e)**	**soyons allé(e)s**
ailles	**alliez**	**sois allé(e)**	**soyez allé(e)(s)**
aille	**aillent**	**soit allé(e)**	**soient allé(e)s**
7 imparfait du subjonctif		14 plus-que-parfait du subjonctif	
allasse	**allassions**	**fusse allé(e)**	**fussions allé(e)s**
allasses	**allassiez**	**fusses allé(e)**	**fussiez allé(e)(s)**
allât	**allassent**	**fût allé(e)**	**fussent allé(e)s**

Impératif
va
allons
allez

Can't recognize an irregular verb form? Check out the index of common irregular French verb forms in the Appendixes.

The subject pronouns are found on page 103.

AN ESSENTIAL 55 VERB

Aller and s'en aller

Aller and **s'en aller** are an essential pair of verbs for beginning students. They are used in many everyday situations and common idiomatic expressions.

Sentences using aller and related words

Comment allez-vous? How are you?

Je vais bien, merci. I'm fine, thank you.

Je vais mal. I'm not well.

Je vais mieux maintenant. I'm feeling better now.

Ça va? Is everything O.K.?

Oui, ça va! Yes, everything's O.K.!

Ça va sans dire. That goes without saying.

Allez-y! (polite) Vas-y! (familiar) Go ahead!

Allons donc! Come on, now! Nonsense!

S'il te plaît, pourrais-tu aller chercher Madeleine à l'école? Could you please go get Madeleine at school?

Est-ce que je vais tout droit pour arriver au Château Frontenac? Do I go straight ahead to arrive at the Château Frontenac?

The verb **s'en aller** has the following idiomatic meaning: to move away (from one residence to another), to die, to pass away, to steal away.

Monsieur et Madame Moreau n'habitent plus ici. Ils s'en sont allés. Je crois qu'ils sont maintenant à Bordeaux. Mr. and Mrs. Moreau don't live here anymore. They went away. I believe that they are in Bordeaux now.

Madame Morel est gravement malade; elle s'en va. Mrs. Morel is gravely ill; she's dying.

Le cambrioleur s'en est allé furtivement avec l'argent et les bijoux. The burglar went away stealthily with the money and the jewelry.

Idiomatic expressions related to these verbs

aller à la chasse **to go hunting**
aller à la pêche **to go fishing**
aller à la rencontre de quelqu'un **to go to meet someone**
aller au-devant de quelqu'un **to go to meet someone**
aller à pied **to walk, to go on foot**
aller à quelqu'un **to be becoming, to fit, to suit someone**
aller au fond des choses **to get to the bottom of things**
aller aux urnes **to vote**
aller avec quelque chose **to match something**
aller chercher **to go get**
aller de pair avec . . . **to go hand in hand with . . .**
aller de soi **to go without saying, to be obvious**
aller en voiture **to ride in a car**
aller sans dire **to go without saying**
aller tout droit **to go straight ahead**

Aller is often used to express the future (instead of Tense No. 4):

Nous allons dîner en ville. We are going to have dinner downtown.

Je vais partir demain soir. I'm going to leave tomorrow evening.

Words and expressions using *aller*

un billet aller-retour **a round-trip ticket**
aller-retour **round-trip**
aller simple **one-way**

Reflexive irregular verb

to go away

The Seven Simple Tenses		The Seven Compound Tenses	
Singular	Plural	Singular	Plural
1 présent de l'indicatif		8 passé composé	
m'en vais	**nous en allons**	**m'en suis allé(e)**	**nous en sommes allé(e)s**
t'en vas	**vous en allez**	**t'en es allé(e)**	**vous en êtes allé(e)(s)**
s'en va	**s'en vont**	**s'en est allé(e)**	**s'en sont allé(e)s**
2 imparfait de l'indicatif		9 plus-que-parfait de l'indicatif	
m'en allais	**nous en allions**	**m'en étais allé(e)**	**nous en étions allé(e)s**
t'en allais	**vous en alliez**	**t'en étais allé(e)**	**vous en étiez allé(e)(s)**
s'en allait	**s'en allaient**	**s'en était allé(e)**	**s'en étaient allé(e)s**
3 passé simple		10 passé antérieur	
m'en allai	**nous en allâmes**	**m'en fus allé(e)**	**nous en fûmes allé(e)s**
t'en allas	**vous en allâtes**	**t'en fus allé(e)**	**vous en fûtes allé(e)(s)**
s'en alla	**s'en allèrent**	**s'en fut allé(e)**	**s'en furent allé(e)s**
4 futur		11 futur antérieur	
m'en irai	**nous en irons**	**m'en serai allé(e)**	**nous en serons allé(e)s**
t'en iras	**vous en irez**	**t'en seras allé(e)**	**vous en serez allé(e)(s)**
s'en ira	**s'en iront**	**s'en sera allé(e)**	**s'en seront allé(e)s**
5 conditionnel		12 conditionnel passé	
m'en irais	**nous en irions**	**m'en serais allé(e)**	**nous en serions allé(e)s**
t'en irais	**vous en iriez**	**t'en serais allé(e)**	**vous en seriez allé(e)(s)**
s'en irait	**s'en iraient**	**s'en serait allé(e)**	**s'en seraient allé(e)s**
6 présent du subjonctif		13 passé du subjonctif	
m'en aille	**nous en allions**	**m'en sois allé(e)**	**nous en soyons allé(e)s**
t'en ailles	**vous en alliez**	**t'en sois allé(e)**	**vous en soyez allé(e)(s)**
s'en aille	**s'en aillent**	**s'en soit allé(e)**	**s'en soient allé(e)s**
7 imparfait du subjonctif		14 plus-que-parfait du subjonctif	
m'en allasse	**nous en allassions**	**m'en fusse allé(e)**	**nous en fussions allé(e)s**
t'en allasses	**vous en allassiez**	**t'en fusses allé(e)**	**vous en fussiez allé(e)(s)**
s'en allât	**s'en allassent**	**s'en fût allé(e)**	**s'en fussent allé(e)s**

Impératif
va-t'en; ne t'en va pas
allons-nous-en; ne nous en allons pas
allez-vous-en; ne vous en allez pas

The subject pronouns are found on page 103.

amener (31) — Part. pr. amenant — Part. passé amené

to bring, to lead

Regular **-er** verb endings; spelling change: **e** changes to **è** before syllable with mute **e**

The Seven Simple Tenses		The Seven Compound Tenses	
Singular	Plural	Singular	Plural
1 présent de l'indicatif		8 passé composé	
amène	**amenons**	**ai amené**	**avons amené**
amènes	**amenez**	**as amené**	**avez amené**
amène	**amènent**	**a amené**	**ont amené**
2 imparfait de l'indicatif		9 plus-que-parfait de l'indicatif	
amenais	**amenions**	**avais amené**	**avions amené**
amenais	**ameniez**	**avais amené**	**aviez amené**
amenait	**amenaient**	**avait amené**	**avaient amené**
3 passé simple		10 passé antérieur	
amenai	**amenâmes**	**eus amené**	**eûmes amené**
amenas	**amenâtes**	**eus amené**	**eûtes amené**
amena	**amenèrent**	**eut amené**	**eurent amené**
4 futur		11 futur antérieur	
amènerai	**amènerons**	**aurai amené**	**aurons amené**
amèneras	**amènerez**	**auras amené**	**aurez amené**
amènera	**amèneront**	**aura amené**	**auront amené**
5 conditionnel		12 conditionnel passé	
amènerais	**amènerions**	**aurais amené**	**aurions amené**
amènerais	**amèneriez**	**aurais amené**	**auriez amené**
amènerait	**amèneraient**	**aurait amené**	**auraient amené**
6 présent du subjonctif		13 passé du subjonctif	
amène	**amenions**	**aie amené**	**ayons amené**
amènes	**ameniez**	**aies amené**	**ayez amené**
amène	**amènent**	**ait amené**	**aient amené**
7 imparfait du subjonctif		14 plus-que-parfait du subjonctif	
amenasse	**amenassions**	**eusse amené**	**eussions amené**
amenasses	**amenassiez**	**eusses amené**	**eussiez amené**
amenât	**amenassent**	**eût amené**	**eussent amené**

Impératif
amène
amenons
amenez

Sentences using this verb and words related to it

Aujourd'hui ma mère a amené ma petite soeur chez le dentiste. Quand elles sont entrées chez lui, le dentiste leur a demandé:—Quel bon vent vous amène ici?

amener une conversation to direct, lead a conversation

amène pleasant, agreeable

des propos peu amènes unkind words

un exemple bien amené well-introduced example

See also **emmener** and **mener.**

How are you doing? Find out with the verb drills and tests with answers explained on pages 50–101.

Regular **-er** verb

to amuse, to entertain

The Seven Simple Tenses		The Seven Compound Tenses	
Singular	Plural	Singular	Plural
1 présent de l'indicatif		8 passé composé	
amuse	**amusons**	**ai amusé**	**avons amusé**
amuses	**amusez**	**as amusé**	**avez amusé**
amuse	**amusent**	**a amusé**	**ont amusé**
2 imparfait de l'indicatif		9 plus-que-parfait de l'indicatif	
amusais	**amusions**	**avais amusé**	**avions amusé**
amusais	**amusiez**	**avais amusé**	**aviez amusé**
amusait	**amusaient**	**avait amusé**	**avaient amusé**
3 passé simple		10 passé antérieur	
amusai	**amusâmes**	**eus amusé**	**eûmes amusé**
amusas	**amusâtes**	**eus amusé**	**eûtes amusé**
amusa	**amusèrent**	**eut amusé**	**eurent amusé**
4 futur		11 futur antérieur	
amuserai	**amuserons**	**aurai amusé**	**aurons amusé**
amuseras	**amuserez**	**auras amusé**	**aurez amusé**
amusera	**amuseront**	**aura amusé**	**auront amusé**
5 conditionnel		12 conditionnel passé	
amuserais	**amuserions**	**aurais amusé**	**aurions amusé**
amuserais	**amuseriez**	**aurais amusé**	**auriez amusé**
amuserait	**amuseraient**	**aurait amusé**	**auraient amusé**
6 présent du subjonctif		13 passé du subjonctif	
amuse	**amusions**	**aie amusé**	**ayons amusé**
amuses	**amusiez**	**aies amusé**	**ayez amusé**
amuse	**amusent**	**ait amusé**	**aient amusé**
7 imparfait du subjonctif		14 plus-que-parfait du subjonctif	
amusasse	**amusassions**	**eusse amusé**	**eussions amusé**
amusasses	**amusassiez**	**eusses amusé**	**eussiez amusé**
amusât	**amusassent**	**eût amusé**	**eussent amusé**

Impératif
amuse
amusons
amusez

Sentences using this verb and words related to it

Cet acteur sait bien jouer son rôle. Il amuse les spectateurs. C'est un comédien accompli. Il est amusant, n'est-ce pas?

amusant, amusante amusing
un amuseur amuser, entertainer
un amuse-gueule, un amuse-bouche tidbit, titbit, snack
une amusette diversion, pastime, idle pleasure
un amusement amusement, entertainment
Tes remarques ne m'amusent pas. Your remarks don't amuse me.
C'est pour l'amusement des enfants. It's for the children's entertainment.
le museau muzzle, snout

See also **s'amuser**.

s'amuser (33) — Part. pr. s'amusant — Part. Passé amusé(e)(s)

to have a good time, to amuse oneself, to enjoy oneself

Reflexive regular **-er** verb

The Seven Simple Tenses		The Seven Compound Tenses	
Singular	Plural	Singular	Plural
1 présent de l'indicatif		8 passé composé	
m'amuse	**nous amusons**	**me suis amusé(e)**	**nous sommes amusé(e)s**
t'amuses	**vous amusez**	**t'es amusé(e)**	**vous êtes amusé(e)(s)**
s'amuse	**s'amusent**	**s'est amusé(e)**	**se sont amusé(e)s**
2 imparfait de l'indicatif		9 plus-que-parfait de l'indicatif	
m'amusais	**nous amusions**	**m'étais amusé(e)**	**nous étions amusé(e)s**
t'amusais	**vous amusiez**	**t'étais amusé(e)**	**vous étiez amusé(e)(s)**
s'amusait	**s'amusaient**	**s'était amusé(e)**	**s'étaient amusé(e)s**
3 passé simple		10 passé antérieur	
m'amusai	**nous amusâmes**	**me fus amusé(e)**	**nous fûmes amusé(e)s**
t'amusas	**vous amusâtes**	**te fus amusé(e)**	**vous fûtes amusé(e)(s)**
s'amusa	**s'amusèrent**	**se fut amusé(e)**	**se furent amusé(e)s**
4 futur		11 futur antérieur	
m'amuserai	**nous amuserons**	**me serai amusé(e)**	**nous serons amusé(e)s**
t'amuseras	**vous amuserez**	**te seras amusé(e)**	**vous serez amusé(e)(s)**
s'amusera	**s'amuseront**	**se sera amusé(e)**	**se seront amusé(e)s**
5 conditionnel		12 conditionnel passé	
m'amuserais	**nous amuserions**	**me serais amusé(e)**	**nous serions amusé(e)s**
t'amuserais	**vous amuseriez**	**te serais amusé(e)**	**vous seriez amusé(e)(s)**
s'amuserait	**s'amuseraient**	**se serait amusé(e)**	**se seraient amusé(e)s**
6 présent du subjonctif		13 passé du subjonctif	
m'amuse	**nous amusions**	**me sois amusé(e)**	**nous soyons amusé(e)s**
t'amuses	**vous amusiez**	**te sois amusé(e)**	**vous soyez amusé(e)(s)**
s'amuse	**s'amusent**	**se soit amusé(e)**	**se soient amusé(e)s**
7 imparfait du subjonctif		14 plus-que-parfait du subjonctif	
m'amusasse	**nous amusassions**	**me fusse amusé(e)**	**nous fussions amusé(e)s**
t'amusasses	**vous amusassiez**	**te fusses amusé(e)**	**vous fussiez amusé(e)(s)**
s'amusât	**s'amusassent**	**se fût amusé(e)**	**se fussent amusé(e)s**

Impératif
amuse-toi; ne t'amuse pas
amusons-nous; ne nous amusons pas
amusez-vous; ne vous amusez pas

Sentences using this verb and words related to it

Il y a des élèves qui s'amusent à mettre le professeur en colère. Est-ce que vous vous amusez dans la classe de français? Moi, je m'amuse beaucoup dans cette classe.

Hier soir je suis allé au cinéma et j'ai vu un film très amusant. Je me suis bien amusé. Mon amie, Françoise, s'est bien amusée aussi.

Que faites-vous pour vous amuser?

Amuse-toi bien! Have a great time!
s'amuser à + inf. to enjoy oneself + pres. part.
s'amuser de to make fun of
s'amuser avec to play with

See also **amuser.**

Regular **-er** verb endings; spelling change: **c** changes to **ç** before **a** or **o** to keep **s** sound

to announce

The Seven Simple Tenses		The Seven Compound Tenses	
Singular	Plural	Singular	Plural
1 présent de l'indicatif		8 passé composé	
annonce	**annonçons**	**ai annoncé**	**avons annoncé**
annonces	**annoncez**	**as annoncé**	**avez annoncé**
annonce	**annoncent**	**a annoncé**	**ont annoncé**
2 imparfait de l'indicatif		9 plus-que-parfait de l'indicatif	
annonçais	**annoncions**	**avais annoncé**	**avions annoncé**
annonçais	**annonciez**	**avais annoncé**	**aviez annoncé**
annonçait	**annonçaient**	**avait annoncé**	**avaient annoncé**
3 passé simple		10 passé antérieur	
annonçai	**annonçâmes**	**eus annoncé**	**eûmes annoncé**
annonças	**annonçâtes**	**eus annoncé**	**eûtes annoncé**
annonça	**annoncèrent**	**eut annoncé**	**eurent annoncé**
4 futur		11 futur antérieur	
annoncerai	**annoncerons**	**aurai annoncé**	**aurons annoncé**
annonceras	**annoncerez**	**auras annoncé**	**aurez annoncé**
annoncera	**annonceront**	**aura annoncé**	**auront annoncé**
5 conditionnel		12 conditionnel passé	
annoncerais	**annoncerions**	**aurais annoncé**	**aurions annoncé**
annoncerais	**annonceriez**	**aurais annoncé**	**auriez annoncé**
annoncerait	**annonceraient**	**aurait annoncé**	**auraient annoncé**
6 présent du subjonctif		13 passé du subjonctif	
annonce	**annoncions**	**aie annoncé**	**ayons annoncé**
annonces	**annonciez**	**aies annoncé**	**ayez annoncé**
annonce	**annoncent**	**ait annoncé**	**aient annoncé**
7 imparfait du subjonctif		14 plus-que-parfait du subjonctif	
annonçasse	**annonçassions**	**eusse annoncé**	**eussions annoncé**
annonçasses	**annonçassiez**	**eusses annoncé**	**eussiez annoncé**
annonçât	**annonçassent**	**eût annoncé**	**eussent annoncé**

Impératif
annonce
annonçons
annoncez

Words and expressions related to this verb

une annonce announcement, notification
demander par annonce to advertise for
un annonceur advertiser, announcer, speaker
un annoncier, une annoncière advertising manager
s'annoncer bien to look promising; **Cela s'annonce bien** That looks promising
les petites annonces d'un journal newspaper classified advertisements
s'annoncer to announce (introduce) oneself

See also **prononcer.**

Note that **annoncer** can also mean to predict (weather, event): **J'ai amené mon parapluie parce qu'ils avaient annoncé de la pluie.** I brought my umbrella because rain had been predicted.

apercevoir (35) — Part. pr. apercevant — Part. passé aperçu

to perceive

Irregular verb with spelling change: **c** changes to **ç** before **o** or **u** to keep **s** sound

The Seven Simple Tenses		The Seven Compound Tenses	
Singular	Plural	Singular	Plural
1 présent de l'indicatif		8 passé composé	
aperçois	**apercevons**	**ai aperçu**	**avons aperçu**
aperçois	**apercevez**	**as aperçu**	**avez aperçu**
aperçoit	**aperçoivent**	**a aperçu**	**ont aperçu**
2 imparfait de l'indicatif		9 plus-que-parfait de l'indicatif	
apercevais	**apercevions**	**avais aperçu**	**avions aperçu**
apercevais	**aperceviez**	**avais aperçu**	**aviez aperçu**
apercevait	**apercevaient**	**avait aperçu**	**avaient aperçu**
3 passé simple		10 passé antérieur	
aperçus	**aperçûmes**	**eus aperçu**	**eûmes aperçu**
aperçus	**aperçûtes**	**eus aperçu**	**eûtes aperçu**
aperçut	**aperçurent**	**eut aperçu**	**eurent aperçu**
4 futur		11 futur antérieur	
apercevrai	**apercevrons**	**aurai aperçu**	**aurons aperçu**
apercevras	**apercevrez**	**auras aperçu**	**aurez aperçu**
apercevra	**apercevront**	**aura aperçu**	**auront aperçu**
5 conditionnel		12 conditionnel passé	
apercevrais	**apercevrions**	**aurais aperçu**	**aurions aperçu**
apercevrais	**apercevriez**	**aurais aperçu**	**auriez aperçu**
apercevrait	**apercevraient**	**aurait aperçu**	**auraient aperçu**
6 présent du subjonctif		13 passé du subjonctif	
aperçoive	**apercevions**	**aie aperçu**	**ayons aperçu**
aperçoives	**aperceviez**	**aies aperçu**	**ayez aperçu**
aperçoive	**aperçoivent**	**ait aperçu**	**aient aperçu**
7 imparfait du subjonctif		14 plus-que-parfait du subjonctif	
aperçusse	**aperçussions**	**eusse aperçu**	**eussions aperçu**
aperçusses	**aperçussiez**	**eusse aperçu**	**eussiez aperçu**
aperçût	**aperçussent**	**eût aperçu**	**eussent aperçu**

Impératif
aperçois
apercevons
apercevez

Words and expressions related to this verb

sans s'en apercevoir without taking any notice (of it)
la perception perception, collection (tax)
perceptiblement perceptibly
à peine perceptible scarcely perceptible
un aperçu glimpse, glance, outline
s'apercevoir de to become aware of, to notice
la perceptibilité perceptibility
perceptif, perceptive perceptive
entr'apercevoir to glimpse
percevoir to perceive, to sense

Don't forget to check the list of 2,600 additional verbs keyed to the 501 model verbs. It's in the Appendixes!

Irregular verb

to appear

The Seven Simple Tenses		The Seven Compound Tenses	
Singular	Plural	Singular	Plural
1 présent de l'indicatif		8 passé composé	
apparais	**apparaissons**	**ai apparu**	**avons apparu**
apparais	**apparaissez**	**as apparu**	**avez apparu**
apparaît	**apparaissent**	**a apparu**	**ont apparu**
2 imparfait de l'indicatif		9 plus-que-parfait de l'indicatif	
apparaissais	**apparaissions**	**avais apparu**	**avions apparu**
apparaissais	**apparaissiez**	**avais apparu**	**aviez apparu**
apparaissait	**apparaissaient**	**avait apparu**	**avaient apparu**
3 passé simple		10 passé antérieur	
apparus	**apparûmes**	**eus apparu**	**eûmes apparu**
apparus	**apparûtes**	**eus apparu**	**eûtes apparu**
apparut	**apparurent**	**eut apparu**	**eurent apparu**
4 futur		11 futur antérieur	
apparaîtrai	**apparaîtrons**	**aurai apparu**	**aurons apparu**
apparaîtras	**apparaîtrez**	**auras apparu**	**aurez apparu**
apparaîtra	**apparaîtront**	**aura apparu**	**auront apparu**
5 conditionnel		12 conditionnel passé	
apparaîtrais	**apparaîtrions**	**aurais apparu**	**aurions apparu**
apparaîtrais	**apparaîtriez**	**aurais apparu**	**auriez apparu**
apparaîtrait	**apparaîtraient**	**aurait apparu**	**auraient apparu**
6 présent du subjonctif		13 passé du subjonctif	
apparaisse	**apparaissions**	**aie apparu**	**ayons apparu**
apparaisses	**apparaissiez**	**aies apparu**	**ayez apparu**
apparaisse	**apparaissent**	**ait apparu**	**aient apparu**
7 imparfait du subjonctif		14 plus-que-parfait du subjonctif	
apparusse	**apparussions**	**eusse apparu**	**eussions apparu**
apparusses	**apparussiez**	**eusses apparu**	**eussiez apparu**
apparût	**apparussent**	**eût apparu**	**eussent apparu**

Impératif
apparais
apparaissons
apparaissez

Words and expressions related to this verb

apparemment	apparently	**une apparition**	apparition
apparent, apparente	apparent	**une apparence**	appearance

This verb can be conjugated with ***avoir*** **or** ***être*** to form the seven compound tenses (Nos. 8 to 14) above. The seven simple tense forms (1 to 7) remain as they are above. The past participle remains ***apparu***. Just use the appropriate forms of ***être*** as the auxiliary instead of ***avoir*** and make the required agreements in gender (masc. or fem.) and number (s. or pl.) as you would when you conjugate the verb ***aller***. Example, Tense No. 8: elle a apparu *or* elle est apparue. Summary: this verb is conjugated with ***avoir*** when it expresses an action; it is conjugated with ***être*** when it expresses the state resulting from the accomplished action.

See also **paraître**, **disparaître**, and **reparaître.**

Grammar putting you in a tense mood? Review the definitions of basic grammatical terms with examples on pages 35–49.

appartenir (37) Part. pr. **appartenant** Part. passé **appartenu**

to belong, to pertain

Irregular verb

The Seven Simple Tenses		The Seven Compound Tenses	
Singular	Plural	Singular	Plural
1 présent de l'indicatif		8 passé composé	
appartiens	**appartenons**	**ai appartenu**	**avons appartenu**
appartiens	**appartenez**	**as appartenu**	**avez appartenu**
appartient	**appartiennent**	**a appartenu**	**ont appartenu**
2 imparfait de l'indicatif		9 plus-que-parfait de l'indicatif	
appartenais	**appartenions**	**avais appartenu**	**avions appartenu**
appartenais	**apparteniez**	**avais appartenu**	**aviez appartenu**
appartenait	**appartenaient**	**avait appartenu**	**avaient appartenu**
3 passé simple		10 passé antérieur	
appartins	**appartînmes**	**eus appartenu**	**eûmes appartenu**
appartins	**appartîntes**	**eus appartenu**	**eûtes appartenu**
appartint	**appartinrent**	**eut appartenu**	**eurent appartenu**
4 futur		11 futur antérieur	
appartiendrai	**appartiendrons**	**aurai appartenu**	**aurons appartenu**
appartiendras	**appartiendrez**	**auras appartenu**	**aurez appartenu**
appartiendra	**appartiendront**	**aura appartenu**	**auront appartenu**
5 conditionnel		12 conditionnel passé	
appartiendrais	**appartiendrions**	**aurais appartenu**	**aurions appartenu**
appartiendrais	**appartiendriez**	**aurais appartenu**	**auriez appartenu**
appartiendrait	**appartiendraient**	**aurait appartenu**	**auraient appartenu**
6 présent du subjonctif		13 passé du subjonctif	
appartienne	**appartenions**	**aie appartenu**	**ayons appartenu**
appartiennes	**apparteniez**	**aies appartenu**	**ayez appartenu**
appartienne	**appartiennent**	**ait appartenu**	**aient appartenu**
7 imparfait du subjonctif		14 plus-que-parfait du subjonctif	
appartinsse	**appartinssions**	**eusse appartenu**	**eussions appartenu**
appartinsses	**appartinssiez**	**eusses appartenu**	**eussiez appartenu**
appartînt	**appartinssent**	**eût appartenu**	**eussent appartenu**

Impératif
appartiens
appartenons
appartenez

Words and expressions related to this verb

appartenir à to belong to, to pertain to, to appertain to

Il appartient que . . . It is fitting that . . .

appartenir à qqn de + inf. to behoove someone to; **Il lui appartient de dire la vérité.**

une appartenance appurtenance; **appartenant, appartenante** appertaining, belonging

un sentiment d'appartenance feeling of belonging

A TOUS CEUX QU'IL APPARTIENDRA TO WHOM IT MAY CONCERN

s'appartenir to be independent

appartenir à qqn de faire qqch to be up to someone to do something

Get acquainted with what preposition goes with what verb. See *Verbs with prepositions* in the Appendixes.

Regular **-er** verb endings; spelling change: **l** becomes **ll** before syllable with a mute **e**

to call, to name, to appeal

The Seven Simple Tenses		The Seven Compound Tenses	
Singular	Plural	Singular	Plural
1 présent de l'indicatif		8 passé composé	
appelle	**appelons**	**ai appelé**	**avons appelé**
appelles	**appelez**	**as appelé**	**avez appelé**
appelle	**appellent**	**a appelé**	**ont appelé**
2 imparfait de l'indicatif		9 plus-que-parfait de l'indicatif	
appelais	**appelions**	**avais appelé**	**avions appelé**
appelais	**appeliez**	**avais appelé**	**aviez appelé**
appelait	**appelaient**	**avait appelé**	**avaient appelé**
3 passé simple		10 passé antérieur	
appelai	**appelâmes**	**eus appelé**	**eûmes appelé**
appelas	**appelâtes**	**eus appelé**	**eûtes appelé**
appela	**appelèrent**	**eut appelé**	**eurent appelé**
4 futur		11 futur antérieur	
appellerai	**appellerons**	**aurai appelé**	**aurons appelé**
appelleras	**appellerez**	**auras appelé**	**aurez appelé**
appellera	**appelleront**	**aura appelé**	**auront appelé**
5 conditionnel		12 conditionnel passé	
appellerais	**appellerions**	**aurais appelé**	**aurions appelé**
appellerais	**appelleriez**	**aurais appelé**	**auriez appelé**
appellerait	**appelleraient**	**aurait appelé**	**auraient appelé**
6 présent du subjonctif		13 passé du subjonctif	
appelle	**appelions**	**aie appelé**	**ayons appelé**
appelles	**appeliez**	**aies appelé**	**ayez appelé**
appelle	**appellent**	**ait appelé**	**aient appelé**
7 imparfait du subjonctif		14 plus-que-parfait du subjonctif	
appelasse	**appelassions**	**eusse appelé**	**eussions appelé**
appelasses	**appelassiez**	**eusses appelé**	**eussiez appelé**
appelât	**appelassent**	**eût appelé**	**eussent appelé**

Impératif
appelle
appelons
appelez

Sentences using this verb and words related to it

Madame Dubois va appeler le médecin parce qu'elle ne va pas bien aujourd'hui.
—As-tu appelé le docteur, chérie? lui demande son mari.
—Non, mon chéri—répond sa femme. Je souffre. Veux-tu l'appeler, s'il te plaît?

une appellation appellation; **un appel** appeal, call
en appeler à qqn to appeal to someone
rappeler to call back, to remind, to recall
appellation contrôlée French government approval of the quality of a wine or cheese
un appel call; **appel téléphonique** telephone call; **faire l'appel** to call the roll
faire un appel de phares to flash the high beams (of a vehicle)
être appelé à qqch to be destined for something, to have a calling (vocation, career)
Appelez un taxi, s'il vous plaît. Please call a taxi.

See also **s'appeler**.

s'appeler (39)

Part. pr. **s'appelant** Part. passé **appelé(e)(s)**

to be named, to call oneself

Reflexive verb; regular **-er** verb endings; spelling change: **l** becomes **ll** before syllable with a mute **e**

The Seven Simple Tenses		The Seven Compound Tenses	
Singular	Plural	Singular	Plural
1 présent de l'indicatif		8 passé composé	
m'appelle	**nous appelons**	**me suis appelé(e)**	**nous sommes appelé(e)s**
t'appelles	**vous appelez**	**t'es appelé(e)**	**vous êtes appelé(e)(s)**
s'appelle	**s'appellent**	**s'est appelé(e)**	**se sont appelé(e)s**
2 imparfait de l'indicatif		9 plus-que-parfait de l'indicatif	
m'appelais	**nous appelions**	**m'étais appelé(e)**	**nous étions appelé(e)s**
t'appelais	**vous appeliez**	**t'étais appelé(e)**	**vous étiez appelé(e)(s)**
s'appelait	**s'appelaient**	**s'était appelé(e)**	**s'étaient appelé(e)s**
3 passé simple		10 passé antérieur	
m'appelai	**nous appelâmes**	**me fus appelé(e)**	**nous fûmes appelé(e)s**
t'appelas	**vous appelâtes**	**te fus appelé(e)**	**vous fûtes appelé(e)(s)**
s'appela	**s'appelèrent**	**se fut appelé(e)**	**se furent appelé(e)s**
4 futur		11 futur antérieur	
m'appellerai	**nous appellerons**	**me serai appelé(e)**	**nous serons appelé(e)s**
t'appelleras	**vous appellerez**	**te seras appelé(e)**	**vous serez appelé(e)(s)**
s'appellera	**s'appelleront**	**se sera appelé(e)**	**se seront appelé(e)s**
5 conditionnel		12 conditionnel passé	
m'appellerais	**nous appellerions**	**me serais appelé(e)**	**nous serions appelé(e)s**
t'appellerais	**vous appelleriez**	**te serais appelé(e)**	**vous seriez appelé(e)(s)**
s'appellerait	**s'appelleraient**	**se serait appelé(e)**	**se seraient appelé(e)s**
6 présent du subjonctif		13 passé du subjonctif	
m'appelle	**nous appelions**	**me sois appelé(e)**	**nous soyons appelé(e)s**
t'appelles	**vous appeliez**	**te sois appelé(e)**	**vous soyez appelé(e)(s)**
s'appelle	**s'appellent**	**se soit appelé(e)**	**se soient appelé(e)s**
7 imparfait du subjonctif		14 plus-que-parfait du subjonctif	
m'appelasse	**nous appelassions**	**me fusse appelé(e)**	**nous fussions appelé(e)s**
t'appelasses	**vous appelassiez**	**te fusses appelé(e)**	**vous fussiez appelé(e)(s)**
s'appelât	**s'appelassent**	**se fût appelé(e)**	**se fussent appelé(e)s**

Impératif
appelle-toi; ne t'appelle pas
appelons-nous; ne nous appelons pas
appelez-vous; ne vous appelez pas

Sentences using this verb and words related to it

—Bonjour, mon enfant. Comment t'appelles-tu?
—Je m'appelle Henri.
—As-tu des frères et des soeurs?
—Oui, j'ai deux frères et trois soeurs. Ils s'appellent Joseph, Bernard, Thérèse, Paulette, et Andrée.

Permettez-moi de me présenter. Je m'appelle . . . Please allow me to introduce myself. My name is . . .

For other words and expressions related to this verb, see **appeler, rappeler,** and **se rappeler.**

Don't miss orthographically changing verbs on pages 32–34.

The Seven Simple Tenses		The Seven Compound Tenses	
Singular	Plural	Singular	Plural
1 présent de l'indicatif		8 passé composé	
apporte	**apportons**	**ai apporté**	**avons apporté**
apportes	**apportez**	**as apporté**	**avez apporté**
apporte	**apportent**	**a apporté**	**ont apporté**
2 imparfait de l'indicatif		9 plus-que-parfait de l'indicatif	
apportais	**apportions**	**avais apporté**	**avions apporté**
apportais	**apportiez**	**avais apporté**	**aviez apporté**
apportait	**apportaient**	**avait apporté**	**avaient apporté**
3 passé simple		10 passé antérieur	
apportai	**apportâmes**	**eus apporté**	**eûmes apporté**
apportas	**apportâtes**	**eus apporté**	**eûtes apporté**
apporta	**apportèrent**	**eut apporté**	**eurent apporté**
4 futur		11 futur antérieur	
apporterai	**apporterons**	**aurai apporté**	**aurons apporté**
apporteras	**apporterez**	**auras apporté**	**aurez apporté**
apportera	**apporteront**	**aura apporté**	**auront apporté**
5 conditionnel		12 conditionnel passé	
apporterais	**apporterions**	**aurais apporté**	**aurions apporté**
apporterais	**apporteriez**	**aurais apporté**	**auriez apporté**
apporterait	**apporteraient**	**aurait apporté**	**auraient apporté**
6 présent du subjonctif		13 passé du subjonctif	
apporte	**apportions**	**aie apporté**	**ayons apporté**
apportes	**apportiez**	**aies apporté**	**ayez apporté**
apporte	**apportent**	**ait apporté**	**aient apporté**
7 imparfait du subjonctif		14 plus-que-parfait du subjonctif	
apportasse	**apportassions**	**eusse apporté**	**eussions apporté**
apportasses	**apportassiez**	**eusses apporté**	**eussiez apporté**
apportât	**apportassent**	**eût apporté**	**eussent apporté**

Impératif
apporte
apportons
apportez

Sentences using this verb and words related to it

Hier soir, j'ai dîné dans un restaurant français. Quand le garçon m'a apporté mon repas, je lui ai dit:—Apportez-moi du pain, aussi, s'il vous plaît et n'oubliez pas de m'apporter un verre de vin rouge.

—Tout de suite, monsieur—il m'a répondu. Voulez-vous que je vous apporte l'addition maintenant ou après le dîner? Aimez-vous la salade que je vous ai apportée?

un apport something brought; **un apport dotal** wife's dowry
un apporteur a person who brings something (usually news); **un apporteur de bonnes nouvelles** bearer of good news

See also **porter** and **supporter.**

The subject pronouns are found on page 103.

apprécier (41) — Part. pr. appréciant — Part. passé apprécié

to appreciate

Regular **-er** verb

The Seven Simple Tenses

Singular	Plural
1 présent de l'indicatif	
apprécie	**apprécions**
apprécies	**appréciez**
apprécie	**apprécient**
2 imparfait de l'indicatif	
appréciais	**appréciions**
appréciais	**appréciiez**
appréciait	**appréciaient**
3 passé simple	
appréciai	**appréciâmes**
apprécias	**appréciâtes**
apprécia	**apprécièrent**
4 futur	
apprécierai	**apprécierons**
apprécieras	**apprécierez**
appréciera	**apprécieront**
5 conditionnel	
apprécierais	**apprécierions**
apprécierais	**apprécieriez**
apprécierait	**apprécieraient**
6 présent du subjonctif	
apprécie	**appréciions**
apprécies	**appréciiez**
apprécie	**apprécient**
7 imparfait du subjonctif	
appréciasse	**appréciassions**
appréciasses	**appréciassiez**
appréciât	**appréciassent**

The Seven Compound Tenses

Singular	Plural
8 passé composé	
ai apprécié	**avons apprécié**
as apprécié	**avez apprécié**
a apprécié	**ont apprécié**
9 plus-que-parfait de l'indicatif	
avais apprécié	**avions apprécié**
avais apprécié	**aviez apprécié**
avait apprécié	**avaient apprécié**
10 passé antérieur	
eus apprécié	**eûmes apprécié**
eus apprécié	**eûtes apprécié**
eut apprécié	**eurent apprécié**
11 futur antérieur	
aurai apprécié	**aurons apprécié**
auras apprécié	**aurez apprécié**
aura apprécié	**auront apprécié**
12 conditionnel passé	
aurais apprécié	**aurions apprécié**
aurais apprécié	**auriez apprécié**
aurait apprécié	**auraient apprécié**
13 passé du subjonctif	
aie apprécié	**ayons apprécié**
aies apprécié	**ayez apprécié**
ait apprécié	**aient apprécié**
14 plus-que-parfait du subjonctif	
eusse apprécié	**eussions apprécié**
eusses apprécié	**eussiez apprécié**
eût apprécié	**eussent apprécié**

Impératif
apprécie
apprécions
appréciez

Sentences using this verb and words related to it

Simon n'apprécie pas le goût de ce fromage.
Simon does not appreciate (like) the taste of this cheese.

Il n'y a pas de différence appréciable entre ces deux ordinateurs.
There isn't an appreciable difference between these two computers.

Words and expressions related to this verb

appréciable appreciable
appréciation *f.* appreciation, assessment
déprécier to depreciate
dépréciation depreciation

Note: To say that you are grateful, use the adjective **reconnaissant/reconnaissante. Merci de m'avoir aidé. J'en suis très reconnaissant.** Thank you for helping me. I'm very grateful for it. (I appreciate it.)

Irregular verb

to learn

The Seven Simple Tenses		The Seven Compound Tenses	
Singular	Plural	Singular	Plural
1 présent de l'indicatif		8 passé composé	
apprends	**apprenons**	**ai appris**	**avons appris**
apprends	**apprenez**	**as appris**	**avez appris**
apprend	**apprennent**	**a appris**	**ont appris**
2 imparfait de l'indicatif		9 plus-que-parfait de l'indicatif	
apprenais	**apprenions**	**avais appris**	**avions appris**
apprenais	**appreniez**	**avais appris**	**aviez appris**
apprenait	**apprenaient**	**avait appris**	**avaient appris**
3 passé simple		10 passé antérieur	
appris	**apprîmes**	**eus appris**	**eûmes appris**
appris	**apprîtes**	**eus appris**	**eûtes appris**
apprit	**apprirent**	**eut appris**	**eurent appris**
4 futur		11 futur antérieur	
apprendrai	**apprendrons**	**aurai appris**	**aurons appris**
apprendras	**apprendrez**	**auras appris**	**aurez appris**
apprendra	**apprendront**	**aura appris**	**auront appris**
5 conditionnel		12 conditionnel passé	
apprendrais	**apprendrions**	**aurais appris**	**aurions appris**
apprendrais	**apprendriez**	**aurais appris**	**auriez appris**
apprendrait	**apprendraient**	**aurait appris**	**auraient appris**
6 présent du subjonctif		13 passé du subjonctif	
apprenne	**apprenions**	**aie appris**	**ayons appris**
apprennes	**appreniez**	**aies appris**	**ayez appris**
apprenne	**apprennent**	**ait appris**	**aient appris**
7 imparfait du subjonctif		14 plus-que-parfait du subjonctif	
apprisse	**apprissions**	**eusse appris**	**eussions appris**
apprisses	**apprissiez**	**eusses appris**	**eussiez appris**
apprît	**apprissent**	**eût appris**	**eussent appris**

Impératif
apprends
apprenons
apprenez

The subject pronouns are found on page 103.

AN ESSENTIAL 55 VERB

Apprendre

Apprendre is an important verb for beginning students because it is used in many everyday situations and idiomatic expressions. **Apprendre** is also useful for talking about school.

Sentences using apprendre and related words

J'aime bien ce poème de Verlaine. Je l'ai appris par coeur. I like this poem by Verlaine. I learned it by heart (memorized it).

À l'école j'apprends à lire en français. In school I am learning to read in French.

Tu apprends à écrire et à parler? Formidable! You're learning to write and speak? Wonderful!

Demain nous apprendrons la conjugaison du verbe *apprendre*. Tomorrow we will learn the conjugation of the verb *apprendre*.

François m'a appris à réparer ma voiture. Francis taught me to fix my car.

Sais-tu que Roland est malade? Je l'ai appris ce matin. Did you know that Roland is sick? I found out this morning.

Enseigner, c'est apprendre deux fois. To teach is to learn two times. (Joseph Joubert)

Words and expressions related to this verb

apprendre par coeur **to learn by heart, memorize**

apprendre à qqn à faire qqch **to teach somebody to do something**

apprendre qqch à qqn **to inform someone of something; to teach someone something**

apprendre à faire qqch **to learn to do something**

un apprentissage **apprenticeship, learning**

un apprenti, une apprentie **apprentice**

See also **comprendre**, **entreprendre**, **se méprendre**, **prendre**, **reprendre**, and **surprendre**.

Proverb

Sage et prudent celui qui apprend aux dépens d'autrui. He who learns at someone else's expense is both wise and prudent.

Regular **-er** verb

to approach, to come near, to bring near

The Seven Simple Tenses		The Seven Compound Tenses	
Singular	Plural	Singular	Plural
1 présent de l'indicatif		8 passé composé	
approche	**approchons**	**ai approché**	**avons approché**
approches	**approchez**	**as approché**	**avez approché**
approche	**approchent**	**a approché**	**ont approché**
2 imparfait de l'indicatif		9 plus-que-parfait de l'indicatif	
approchais	**approchions**	**avais approché**	**avions approché**
approchais	**approchiez**	**avais approché**	**aviez approché**
approchait	**approchaient**	**avait approché**	**avaient approché**
3 passé simple		10 passé antérieur	
approchai	**approchâmes**	**eus approché**	**eûmes approché**
approchas	**approchâtes**	**eus approché**	**eûtes approché**
approcha	**approchèrent**	**eut approché**	**eurent approché**
4 futur		11 futur antérieur	
approcherai	**approcherons**	**aurai approché**	**aurons approché**
approcheras	**approcherez**	**auras approché**	**aurez approché**
approchera	**approcheront**	**aura approché**	**auront approché**
5 conditionnel		12 conditionnel passé	
approcherais	**approcherions**	**aurais approché**	**aurions approché**
approcherais	**approcheriez**	**aurais approché**	**auriez approché**
approcherait	**approcheraient**	**aurait approché**	**auraient approché**
6 présent du subjonctif		13 passé du subjonctif	
approche	**approchions**	**aie approché**	**ayons approché**
approches	**approchiez**	**aies approché**	**ayez approché**
approche	**approchent**	**ait approché**	**aient approché**
7 imparfait du subjonctif		14 plus-que-parfait du subjonctif	
approchasse	**approchassions**	**eusse approché**	**eussions approché**
approchasses	**approchassiez**	**eusses approché**	**eussiez approché**
approchât	**approchassent**	**eût approché**	**eussent approché**

Impératif
approche
approchons
approchez

Words and expressions related to this verb
s'approcher de qqn ou qqch to approach someone or something
se rapprocher de to come closer to
rapprocher to bring closer, nearer
reprocher qqch à qqn to reproach someone with something; **un reproche** reproach; **faire des reproches à** to reproach; **sans reproche** without blame, blameless
proche close, near; **la pharmacie la plus proche** the nearest pharmacy
prochain, prochaine next; **la semaine prochaine** next week; **la prochaine fois** the next time

Don't forget to check the list of 2,600 additional verbs keyed to the 501 model verbs. It's in the Appendixes!

approuver (44) — Part. pr. approuvant — Part. passé approuvé

to approve (of)

Regular **-er** verb

The Seven Simple Tenses		The Seven Compound Tenses	
Singular	Plural	Singular	Plural
1 présent de l'indicatif		8 passé composé	
approuve	**approuvons**	**ai approuvé**	**avons approuvé**
approuves	**approuvez**	**as approuvé**	**avez approuvé**
approuve	**approuvent**	**a approuvé**	**ont approuvé**
2 imparfait de l'indicatif		9 plus-que-parfait de l'indicatif	
approuvais	**approuvions**	**avais approuvé**	**avions approuvé**
approuvais	**approuviez**	**avais approuvé**	**aviez approuvé**
approuvait	**approuvaient**	**avait approuvé**	**avaient approuvé**
3 passé simple		10 passé antérieur	
approuvai	**approuvâmes**	**eus approuvé**	**eûmes approuvé**
approuvas	**approuvâtes**	**eus approuvé**	**eûtes approuvé**
approuva	**approuvèrent**	**eut approuvé**	**eurent approuvé**
4 futur		11 futur antérieur	
approuverai	**approuverons**	**aurai approuvé**	**aurons approuvé**
approuveras	**approuverez**	**auras approuvé**	**aurez approuvé**
approuvera	**approuveront**	**aura approuvé**	**auront approuvé**
5 conditionnel		12 conditionnel passé	
approuverais	**approuverions**	**aurais approuvé**	**aurions approuvé**
approuverais	**approuveriez**	**aurais approuvé**	**auriez approuvé**
approuverait	**approuveraient**	**aurait approuvé**	**auraient approuvé**
6 présent du subjonctif		13 passé du subjonctif	
approuve	**approuvions**	**aie approuvé**	**ayons approuvé**
approuves	**approuviez**	**aies approuvé**	**ayez approuvé**
approuve	**approuvent**	**ait approuvé**	**aient approuvé**
7 imparfait du subjonctif		14 plus-que-parfait du subjonctif	
approuvasse	**approuvassions**	**eusse approuvé**	**eussions approuvé**
approuvasses	**approuvassiez**	**eusses approuvé**	**eussiez approuvé**
approuvât	**approuvassent**	**eût approuvé**	**eussent approuvé**

Impératif
approuve
approuvons
approuvez

Words and expressions related to this verb

approuver qqn de faire qqch to approve of someone's doing something
acheter à condition to buy on approval
avec approbation approvingly
la désapprobation disapproval, disapprobation
J'approuve votre décision de continuer l'étude de la langue française.
l'approbation *f.* approval
un approbateur, une approbatrice approver
désapprouver to disapprove, to disapprove of

See also **éprouver** and **prouver.**

Soak up some verbs used in weather expressions. There's a list in the Appendixes!

Regular **-er** verb

to pull up, to pull out, to uproot

The Seven Simple Tenses		The Seven Compound Tenses	
Singular	Plural	Singular	Plural
1 présent de l'indicatif		8 passé composé	
arrache	**arrachons**	**ai arraché**	**avons arraché**
arraches	**arrachez**	**as arraché**	**avez arraché**
arrache	**arrachent**	**a arraché**	**ont arraché**
2 imparfait de l'indicatif		9 plus-que-parfait de l'indicatif	
arrachais	**arrachions**	**avais arraché**	**avions arraché**
arrachais	**arrachiez**	**avais arraché**	**aviez arraché**
arrachait	**arrachaient**	**avait arraché**	**avaient arraché**
3 passé simple		10 passé antérieur	
arrachai	**arrachâmes**	**eus arraché**	**eûmes arraché**
arrachas	**arrachâtes**	**eus arraché**	**eûtes arraché**
arracha	**arrachèrent**	**eut arraché**	**eurent arraché**
4 futur		11 futur antérieur	
arracherai	**arracherons**	**aurai arraché**	**aurons arraché**
arracheras	**arracherez**	**auras arraché**	**aurez arraché**
arrachera	**arracheront**	**aura arraché**	**auront arraché**
5 conditionnel		12 conditionnel passé	
arracherais	**arracherions**	**aurais arraché**	**aurions arraché**
arracherais	**arracheriez**	**aurais arraché**	**auriez arraché**
arracherait	**arracheraient**	**aurait arraché**	**auraient arraché**
6 présent du subjonctif		13 passé du subjonctif	
arrache	**arrachions**	**aie arraché**	**ayons arraché**
arraches	**arrachiez**	**aies arraché**	**ayez arraché**
arrache	**arrachent**	**ait arraché**	**aient arraché**
7 imparfait du subjonctif		14 plus-que-parfait du subjonctif	
arrachasse	**arrachassions**	**eusse arraché**	**eussions arraché**
arrachasses	**arrachassiez**	**eusses arraché**	**eussiez arraché**
arrachât	**arrachassent**	**eût arraché**	**eussent arraché**

Impératif
arrache
arrachons
arrachez

Common idiomatic expressions using this verb and words related to it
arracher qqch des mains de qqn to grab something out of someone's hands
faire qqch d'arrache-pied to do something without interruption
s'arracher à to tear oneself away from
un arrache-clou nail puller (extractor) **(des arrache-clous)**
s'arracher les yeux to have a violent quarrel (to scratch each other's eyes out)
d'arrache-pied relentlessly

How are you doing? Find out with the verb drills and tests with answers explained on pages 50–101.

arranger (46) — Part. pr. arrangeant — Part. passé arrangé

to arrange

Regular **-er** verb endings; spelling change: retain the **ge** before **a** or **o** to keep the soft **g** sound of the verb

The Seven Simple Tenses		The Seven Compound Tenses	
Singular	Plural	Singular	Plural
1 présent de l'indicatif		8 passé composé	
arrange	**arrangeons**	**ai arrangé**	**avons arrangé**
arranges	**arrangez**	**as arrangé**	**avez arrangé**
arrange	**arrangent**	**a arrangé**	**ont arrangé**
2 imparfait de l'indicatif		9 plus-que-parfait de l'indicatif	
arrangeais	**arrangions**	**avais arrangé**	**avions arrangé**
arrangeais	**arrangiez**	**avais arrangé**	**aviez arrangé**
arrangeait	**arrangeaient**	**avait arrangé**	**avaient arrangé**
3 passé simple		10 passé antérieur	
arrangeai	**arrangeâmes**	**eus arrangé**	**eûmes arrangé**
arrangeas	**arrangeâtes**	**eus arrangé**	**eûtes arrangé**
arrangea	**arrangèrent**	**eut arrangé**	**eurent arrangé**
4 futur		11 futur antérieur	
arrangerai	**arrangerons**	**aurai arrangé**	**aurons arrangé**
arrangeras	**arrangerez**	**auras arrangé**	**aurez arrangé**
arrangera	**arrangeront**	**aura arrangé**	**auront arrangé**
5 conditionnel		12 conditionnel passé	
arrangerais	**arrangerions**	**aurais arrangé**	**aurions arrangé**
arrangerais	**arrangeriez**	**aurais arrangé**	**auriez arrangé**
arrangerait	**arrangeraient**	**aurait arrangé**	**auraient arrangé**
6 présent du subjonctif		13 passé du subjonctif	
arrange	**arrangions**	**aie arrangé**	**ayons arrangé**
arranges	**arrangiez**	**aies arrangé**	**ayez arrangé**
arrange	**arrangent**	**ait arrangé**	**aient arrangé**
7 imparfait du subjonctif		14 plus-que-parfait du subjonctif	
arrangeasse	**arrangeassions**	**eusse arrangé**	**eussions arrangé**
arrangeasses	**arrangeassiez**	**eusses arrangé**	**eussiez arrangé**
arrangeât	**arrangeassent**	**eût arrangé**	**eussent arrangé**

Impératif
arrange
arrangeons
arrangez

Sentences using this verb and words related to it

J'aime beaucoup un joli arrangement de fleurs. Aimez-vous les fleurs que j'ai arrangées dans ce vase? Les Japonais savent bien arranger les fleurs. Quand mon père apporte des fleurs à ma mère, nous les arrangeons dans un joli vase.

arranger qqch to arrange, contrive something
arranger l'affaire to straighten out a matter
s'arranger to come to an agreement

arranger qqn to accommodate, suit someone; **Ça m'arrange bien** That suits me fine; **Ça s'arrangera** It will turn out all right.

Regular **-er** verb

to arrest, to stop (someone or something), to halt

The Seven Simple Tenses		The Seven Compound Tenses	
Singular	Plural	Singular	Plural
1 présent de l'indicatif		8 passé composé	
arrête	**arrêtons**	**ai arrêté**	**avons arrêté**
arrêtes	**arrêtez**	**as arrêté**	**avez arrêté**
arrête	**arrêtent**	**a arrêté**	**ont arrêté**
2 imparfait de l'indicatif		9 plus-que-parfait de l'indicatif	
arrêtais	**arrêtions**	**avais arrêté**	**avions arrêté**
arrêtais	**arrêtiez**	**avais arrêté**	**aviez arrêté**
arrêtait	**arrêtaient**	**avait arrêté**	**avaient arrêté**
3 passé simple		10 passé antérieur	
arrêtai	**arrêtâmes**	**eus arrêté**	**eûmes arrêté**
arrêtas	**arrêtâtes**	**eus arrêté**	**eûtes arrêté**
arrêta	**arrêtèrent**	**eut arrêté**	**eurent arrêté**
4 futur		11 futur antérieur	
arrêterai	**arrêterons**	**aurai arrêté**	**aurons arrêté**
arrêteras	**arrêterez**	**auras arrêté**	**aurez arrêté**
arrêtera	**arrêteront**	**aura arrêté**	**auront arrêté**
5 conditionnel		12 conditionnel passé	
arrêterais	**arrêterions**	**aurais arrêté**	**aurions arrêté**
arrêterais	**arrêteriez**	**aurais arrêté**	**auriez arrêté**
arrêterait	**arrêteraient**	**aurait arrêté**	**auraient arrêté**
6 présent du subjonctif		13 passé du subjonctif	
arrête	**arrêtions**	**aie arrêté**	**ayons arrêté**
arrêtes	**arrêtiez**	**aies arrêté**	**ayez arrêté**
arrête	**arrêtent**	**ait arrêté**	**aient arrêté**
7 imparfait du subjonctif		14 plus-que-parfait du subjonctif	
arrêtasse	**arrêtassions**	**eusse arrêté**	**eussions arrêté**
arrêtasses	**arrêtassiez**	**eusses arrêté**	**eussiez arrêté**
arrêtât	**arrêtassent**	**eût arrêté**	**eussent arrêté**

Impératif
arrête
arrêtons
arrêtez

Sentences using this verb and words related to it

L'agent de police a arrêté les voitures pour laisser les piétons traverser la rue. Il a crié:— Arrêtez! Arrêtez! The police officer stopped the cars to let the pedestrians cross the street. He shouted: Stop! Stop!

Arrêtez-la/le/les! Stop her/him/them!

un arrêt halt, stop, arrest; **sans arrêt** continually
arrêt d'autobus bus stop
un arrêté ministériel decree
arrêter qqn de faire qqch to stop someone from doing something
une arrestation arrest, apprehension; **être en état d'arrestation** to be under arrest
arrêter un jour to set a date; **arrêter un marché** to make a deal

See also **s'arrêter.**

The subject pronouns are found on page 103.

s'arrêter (48) Part. pr. s'arrêtant Part. passé arrêté(e)(s)

to stop (oneself, itself), to pause

Reflexive regular **-er** verb

The Seven Simple Tenses		The Seven Compound Tenses	
Singular	Plural	Singular	Plural
1 présent de l'indicatif		8 passé composé	
m'arrête	**nous arrêtons**	**me suis arrêté(e)**	**nous sommes arrêté(e)s**
t'arrêtes	**vous arrêtez**	**t'es arrêté(e)**	**vous êtes arrêté(e)(s)**
s'arrête	**s'arrêtent**	**s'est arrêté(e)**	**se sont arrêté(e)s**
2 imparfait de l'indicatif		9 plus-que-parfait de l'indicatif	
m'arrêtais	**nous arrêtions**	**m'étais arrêté(e)**	**nous étions arrêté(e)s**
t'arrêtais	**vous arrêtiez**	**t'étais arrêté(e)**	**vous étiez arrêté(e)(s)**
s'arrêtait	**s'arrêtaient**	**s'était arrêté(e)**	**s'étaient arrêté(e)s**
3 passé simple		10 passé antérieur	
m'arrêtai	**nous arrêtâmes**	**me fus arrêté(e)**	**nous fûmes arrêté(e)s**
t'arrêtas	**vous arrêtâtes**	**te fus arrêté(e)**	**vous fûtes arrêté(e)(s)**
s'arrêta	**s'arrêtèrent**	**se fut arrêté(e)**	**se furent arrêté(e)s**
4 futur		11 futur antérieur	
m'arrêterai	**nous arrêterons**	**me serai arrêté(e)**	**nous serons arrêté(e)s**
t'arrêteras	**vous arrêterez**	**te seras arrêté(e)**	**vous serez arrêté(e)(s)**
s'arrêtera	**s'arrêteront**	**se sera arrêté(e)**	**se seront arrêté(e)s**
5 conditionnel		12 conditionnel passé	
m'arrêterais	**nous arrêterions**	**me serais arrêté(e)**	**nous serions arrêté(e)s**
t'arrêterais	**vous arrêteriez**	**te serais arrêté(e)**	**vous seriez arrêté(e)(s)**
s'arrêterait	**s'arrêteraient**	**se serait arrêté(e)**	**se seraient arrêté(e)s**
6 présent du subjonctif		13 passé du subjonctif	
m'arrête	**nous arrêtions**	**me sois arrêté(e)**	**nous soyons arrêté(e)s**
t'arrêtes	**vous arrêtiez**	**te sois arrêté(e)**	**vous soyez arrêté(e)(s)**
s'arrête	**s'arrêtent**	**se soit arrêté(e)**	**se soient arrêté(e)s**
7 imparfait du subjonctif		14 plus-que-parfait du subjonctif	
m'arrêtasse	**nous arrêtassions**	**me fusse arrêté(e)**	**nous fussions arrêté(e)s**
t'arrêtasses	**vous arrêtassiez**	**te fusses arrêté(e)**	**vous fussiez arrêté(e)(s)**
s'arrêtât	**s'arrêtassent**	**se fût arrêté(e)**	**se fussent arrêté(e)s**

Impératif
arrête-toi; ne t'arrête pas
arrêtons-nous; ne nous arrêtons pas
arrêtez-vous; ne vous arrêtez pas

Sentences using this verb and words related to it

Madame Dumont s'est arrêtée devant une pâtisserie pour acheter une belle tarte aux cerises. Deux autres dames se sont arrêtées derrière elle et les trois sont entrées dans le magasin.

s'arrêter de faire qqch to desist from doing something

s'arrêter de fumer to stop smoking

sans s'arrêter without stopping

Madame Martin s'est arrêtée pour se reposer. Mrs. Martin stopped to rest.

See also **arrêter.**

Don't forget to use the English-French verb index. It's in the Appendixes.

Regular **-er** verb

to arrive, to happen

The Seven Simple Tenses		The Seven Compound Tenses	
Singular	Plural	Singular	Plural
1 présent de l'indicatif		8 passé composé	
arrive	**arrivons**	**suis arrivé(e)**	**sommes arrivé(e)s**
arrives	**arrivez**	**es arrivé(e)**	**êtes arrivé(e)(s)**
arrive	**arrivent**	**est arrivé(e)**	**sont arrivé(e)s**
2 imparfait de l'indicatif		9 plus-que-parfait de l'indicatif	
arrivais	**arrivions**	**étais arrivé(e)**	**étions arrivé(e)s**
arrivais	**arriviez**	**étais arrivé(e)**	**étiez arrivé(e)(s)**
arrivait	**arrivaient**	**était arrivé(e)**	**étaient arrivé(e)s**
3 passé simple		10 passé antérieur	
arrivai	**arrivâmes**	**fus arrivé(e)**	**fûmes arrivé(e)s**
arrivas	**arrivâtes**	**fus arrivé(e)**	**fûtes arrivé(e)(s)**
arriva	**arrivèrent**	**fut arrivé(e)**	**furent arrivé(e)s**
4 futur		11 futur antérieur	
arriverai	**arriverons**	**serai arrivé(e)**	**serons arrivé(e)s**
arriveras	**arriverez**	**seras arrivé(e)**	**serez arrivé(e)(s)**
arrivera	**arriveront**	**sera arrivé(e)**	**seront arrivé(e)s**
5 conditionnel		12 conditionnel passé	
arriverais	**arriverions**	**serais arrivé(e)**	**serions arrivé(e)s**
arriverais	**arriveriez**	**serais arrivé(e)**	**seriez arrivé(e)(s)**
arriverait	**arriveraient**	**serait arrivé(e)**	**seraient arrivé(e)s**
6 présent du subjonctif		13 passé du subjonctif	
arrive	**arrivions**	**sois arrivé(e)**	**soyons arrivé(e)s**
arrives	**arriviez**	**sois arrivé(e)**	**soyez arrivé(e)(s)**
arrive	**arrivent**	**soit arrivé(e)**	**soient arrivé(e)s**
7 imparfait du subjonctif		14 plus-que-parfait du subjonctif	
arrivasse	**arrivassions**	**fusse arrivé(e)**	**fussions arrivé(e)s**
arrivasses	**arrivassiez**	**fusses arrivé(e)**	**fussiez arrivé(e)(s)**
arrivât	**arrivassent**	**fût arrivé(e)**	**fussent arrivé(e)s**

Impératif
arrive
arrivons
arrivez

Sentences using this verb and words related to it

À quelle heure est-ce que l'avion arrive à Paris? At what time does the plane arrive in Paris?
Le train pour Québec arrivera à 15h22. The train to Québec will arrive at 3:22 P.M.
Qu'est-ce qui arrive? What's happening? What's going on?
Qu'est-ce qui est arrivé? What happened?
Quoi qu'il arrive . . . Come what may . . .

arriver à faire qqch to succeed in + pres. part.; to manage to do something
arriver à to happen to; **Cela n'arrive qu'à moi!** It's just my luck! That would happen to me!
J'arrive! I'm coming!

The subject pronouns are found on page 103.

to attack, to beset, to assail

Irregular verb

The Seven Simple Tenses		The Seven Compound Tenses	
Singular	Plural	Singular	Plural
1 présent de l'indicatif		8 passé composé	
assaille	**assaillons**	**ai assailli**	**avons assailli**
assailles	**assaillez**	**as assailli**	**avez assailli**
assaille	**assaillent**	**a assailli**	**ont assailli**
2 imparfait de l'indicatif		9 plus-que-parfait de l'indicatif	
assaillais	**assaillions**	**avais assailli**	**avions assailli**
assaillais	**assailliez**	**avais assailli**	**aviez assailli**
assaillait	**assaillaient**	**avait assailli**	**avaient assailli**
3 passé simple		10 passé antérieur	
assaillis	**assaillîmes**	**eus assailli**	**eûmes assailli**
assaillis	**assaillîtes**	**eus assailli**	**eûtes assailli**
assaillit	**assaillirent**	**eut assailli**	**eurent assailli**
4 futur		11 futur antérieur	
assaillirai	**assaillirons**	**aurai assailli**	**aurons assailli**
assailliras	**assaillirez**	**auras assailli**	**aurez assailli**
assaillira	**assailliront**	**aura assailli**	**auront assailli**
5 conditionnel		12 conditionnel passé	
assaillirais	**assaillirions**	**aurais assailli**	**aurions assailli**
assaillirais	**assailliriez**	**aurais assailli**	**auriez assailli**
assaillirait	**assailliraient**	**aurait assailli**	**auraient assailli**
6 présent du subjonctif		13 passé du subjonctif	
assaille	**assaillions**	**aie assailli**	**ayons assailli**
assailles	**assailliez**	**aies assailli**	**ayez assailli**
assaille	**assaillent**	**ait assailli**	**aient assailli**
7 imparfait du subjonctif		14 plus-que-parfait du subjonctif	
assaillisse	**assaillissions**	**eusse assailli**	**eussions assailli**
assaillisses	**assaillissiez**	**eusses assailli**	**eussiez assailli**
assaillît	**assaillissent**	**eût assailli**	**eussent assailli**

Impératif
assaille
assaillons
assaillez

Sentences using this verb and words related to it

Leurs ennemis les ont assaillis pendant la nuit. Their enemies attacked them during the night.
Le coup de tonnerre m'a fait tressaillir. The thunderclap made me jump.

Words and expressions related to this verb

un assaillant, une assaillante assailant
saillir to project (conj. like **assaillir**, 3d person and infinitive); to mate (conj. like **finir**, 3d person and present participle)
saillant, saillante protruding, prominent
une saillie projection, ledge
tressaillir to jump, flinch

Don't forget to check the list of 2,600 additional verbs keyed to the 501 model verbs. It's in the Appendixes!

Reflexive irregular verb

to sit down

The Seven Simple Tenses		The Seven Compound Tenses	
Singular	Plural	Singular	Plural
1 présent de l'indicatif		8 passé composé	
m'assieds	**nous asseyons**	**me suis assis(e)**	**nous sommes assis(es)**
t'assieds	**vous asseyez**	**t'es assis(e)**	**vous êtes assis(e)(es)**
s'assied	**s'asseyent**	**s'est assis(e)**	**se sont assis(es)**
2 imparfait de l'indicatif		9 plus-que-parfait de l'indicatif	
m'asseyais	**nous asseyions**	**m'étais assis(e)**	**nous étions assis(es)**
t'asseyais	**vous asseyiez**	**t'étais assis(e)**	**vous étiez assis(e)(es)**
s'asseyait	**s'asseyaient**	**s'était assis(e)**	**s'étaient assis(es)**
3 passé simple		10 passé antérieur	
m'assis	**nous assîmes**	**me fus assis(e)**	**nous fûmes assis(es)**
t'assis	**vous assîtes**	**te fus assis(e)**	**vous fûtes assis(e)(es)**
s'assit	**s'assirent**	**se fut assis(e)**	**se furent assis(es)**
4 futur		11 futur antérieur	
m'assiérai	**nous assiérons**	**me serai assis(e)**	**nous serons assis(es)**
t'assiéras	**vous assiérez**	**te seras assis(e)**	**vous serez assis(e)(es)**
s'assiéra	**s'assiéront**	**se sera assis(e)**	**se seront assis(es)**
5 conditionnel		12 conditionnel passé	
m'assiérais	**nous assiérions**	**me serais assis(e)**	**nous serions assis(es)**
t'assiérais	**vous assiériez**	**te serais assis(e)**	**vous seriez assis(e)(es)**
s'assiérait	**s'assiéraient**	**se serait assis(e)**	**se seraient assis(es)**
6 présent du subjonctif		13 passé du subjonctif	
m'asseye	**nous asseyions**	**me sois assis(e)**	**nous soyons assis(es)**
t'asseyes	**vous asseyiez**	**te sois assis(e)**	**vous soyez assis(e)(es)**
s'asseye	**s'asseyent**	**se soit assis(e)**	**se soient assis(es)**
7 imparfait du subjonctif		14 plus-que-parfait du subjonctif	
m'assisse	**nous assissions**	**me fusse assis(e)**	**nous fussions assis(es)**
t'assisses	**vous assissiez**	**te fusses assis(e)**	**vous fussiez assis(e)(es)**
s'assît	**s'assissent**	**se fût assis(e)**	**se fussent assis(es)**

Impératif
assieds-toi; ne t'assieds pas
asseyons-nous; ne nous asseyons pas
asseyez-vous; ne vous asseyez pas

Common idiomatic expressions using this verb and words related to it

Quand je voyage en train, je m'assieds toujours près d'une fenêtre si c'est possible.
Une fois, pendant un voyage, une belle jeune fille s'est approchée de moi et m'a demandé:
—Puis-je m'asseoir ici? Est-ce que cette place est libre?
—Certainement, j'ai répondu—asseyez-vous, je vous en prie.
Elle s'est assise auprès de moi et nous nous sommes bien amusés à raconter des histoires drôles.

asseoir qqn to seat someone
rasseoir to seat again, to reseat; **se rasseoir** to sit down again
s'asseoir à califourchon to sit astride

See also **seoir.**

The subject pronouns are found on page 103.

to besiege, to lay siege to

Regular **-er** verb endings; spelling changes: retain the **ge** before **a** or **o** to keep the soft **g** sound of the verb; **e** changes to **è** before syllable with mute **e**

The Seven Simple Tenses		The Seven Compound Tenses	
Singular	Plural	Singular	Plural
1 présent de l'indicatif		8 passé composé	
assiège	**assiégeons**	**ai assiégé**	**avons assiégé**
assièges	**assiégez**	**as assiégé**	**avez assiégé**
assiège	**assiègent**	**a assiégé**	**ont assiégé**
2 imparfait de l'indicatif		9 plus-que-parfait de l'indicatif	
assiégeais	**assiégions**	**avais assiégé**	**avions assiégé**
assiégeais	**assiégiez**	**avais assiégé**	**aviez assiégé**
assiégeait	**assiégeaient**	**avait assiégé**	**avaient assiégé**
3 passé simple		10 passé antérieur	
assiégeai	**assiégeâmes**	**eus assiégé**	**eûmes assiégé**
assiégeas	**assiégeâtes**	**eus assiégé**	**eûtes assiégé**
assiégea	**assiégèrent**	**eut assiégé**	**eurent assiégé**
4 futur		11 futur antérieur	
assiégerai	**assiégerons**	**aurai assiégé**	**aurons assiégé**
assiégeras	**assiégerez**	**auras assiégé**	**aurez assiégé**
assiégera	**assiégeront**	**aura assiégé**	**auront assiégé**
5 conditionnel		12 conditionnel passé	
assiégerais	**assiégerions**	**aurais assiégé**	**aurions assiégé**
assiégerais	**assiégeriez**	**aurais assiégé**	**auriez assiégé**
assiégerait	**assiégeraient**	**aurait assiégé**	**auraient assiégé**
6 présent du subjonctif		13 passé du subjonctif	
assiège	**assiégions**	**aie assiégé**	**ayons assiégé**
assièges	**assiégiez**	**aies assiégé**	**ayez assiégé**
assiège	**assiègent**	**ait assiégé**	**aient assiégé**
7 imparfait du subjonctif		14 plus-que-parfait du subjonctif	
assiégeasse	**assiégeassions**	**eusse assiégé**	**eussions assiégé**
assiégeasses	**assiégeassiez**	**eusses assiégé**	**eussiez assiégé**
assiégeât	**assiégeassent**	**eût assiégé**	**eussent assiégé**

Impératif
assiège
assiégeons
assiégez

Words and expressions related to this verb

assiégeant, assiégeante *adj.* besieging
le siège seat, siege
siéger to sit (committee, government)
Les barbares nous assiègent. Ils sont aux portes de la ville. The barbarians are laying siege to us. They are at the gates of the city.

If you can conjugate **assiéger** you can also conjugate:

abréger to shorten
agréger to agglomerate
alléger to lighten
piéger to trap

Regular **-er** verb

to assist (at), to be present (at), to attend

The Seven Simple Tenses		The Seven Compound Tenses	
Singular	Plural	Singular	Plural
1 présent de l'indicatif		8 passé composé	
assiste	**assistons**	**ai assisté**	**avons assisté**
assistes	**assistez**	**as assisté**	**avez assisté**
assiste	**assistent**	**a assisté**	**ont assisté**
2 imparfait de l'indicatif		9 plus-que-parfait de l'indicatif	
assistais	**assistions**	**avais assisté**	**avions assisté**
assistais	**assistiez**	**avais assisté**	**aviez assisté**
assistait	**assistaient**	**avait assisté**	**avaient assisté**
3 passé simple		10 passé antérieur	
assistai	**assistâmes**	**eus assisté**	**eûmes assisté**
assistas	**assistâtes**	**eus assisté**	**eûtes assisté**
assista	**assistèrent**	**eut assisté**	**eurent assisté**
4 futur		11 futur antérieur	
assisterai	**assisterons**	**aurai assisté**	**aurons assisté**
assisteras	**assisterez**	**auras assisté**	**aurez assisté**
assistera	**assisteront**	**aura assisté**	**auront assisté**
5 conditionnel		12 conditionnel passé	
assisterais	**assisterions**	**aurais assisté**	**aurions assisté**
assisterais	**assisteriez**	**aurais assisté**	**auriez assisté**
assisterait	**assisteraient**	**aurait assisté**	**auraient assisté**
6 présent du subjonctif		13 passé du subjonctif	
assiste	**assistions**	**aie assisté**	**ayons assisté**
assistes	**assistiez**	**aies assisté**	**ayez assisté**
assiste	**assistent**	**ait assisté**	**aient assisté**
7 imparfait du subjonctif		14 plus-que-parfait du subjonctif	
assistasse	**assistassions**	**eusse assisté**	**eussions assisté**
assistasses	**assistassiez**	**eusses assisté**	**eussiez assisté**
assistât	**assistassent**	**eût assisté**	**eussent assisté**

Impératif
assiste
assistons
assistez

Sentences using this verb

Lundi prochain, j'assisterai à une conférence de presse. Next Monday, I will attend a press conference.

L'année dernière j'ai assisté à la même conférence de presse et il y avait beaucoup de monde. Last year I attended the same press conference and there were a lot of people.

Words and expressions using this verb

assistance *f.* assistance, help; attendance; audience
assister à to be present at, to attend
les services de l'Assistance publique health and social security services
les assistants those present; spectators

The subject pronouns are found on page 103.

assurer (54) — Part. pr. assurant — Part. passé assuré

to assure, to ensure, to insure, to guarantee

Regular **-er** verb

The Seven Simple Tenses		The Seven Compound Tenses	
Singular	Plural	Singular	Plural
1 présent de l'indicatif		8 passé composé	
assure	**assurons**	**ai assuré**	**avons assuré**
assures	**assurez**	**as assuré**	**avez assuré**
assure	**assurent**	**a assuré**	**ont assuré**
2 imparfait de l'indicatif		9 plus-que-parfait de l'indicatif	
assurais	**assurions**	**avais assuré**	**avions assuré**
assurais	**assuriez**	**avais assuré**	**aviez assuré**
assurait	**assuraient**	**avait assuré**	**avaient assuré**
3 passé simple		10 passé antérieur	
assurai	**assurâmes**	**eus assuré**	**eûmes assuré**
assuras	**assurâtes**	**eus assuré**	**eûtes assuré**
assura	**assurèrent**	**eut assuré**	**eurent assuré**
4 futur		11 futur antérieur	
assurerai	**assurerons**	**aurai assuré**	**aurons assuré**
assureras	**assurerez**	**auras assuré**	**aurez assuré**
assurera	**assureront**	**aura assuré**	**auront assuré**
5 conditionnel		12 conditionnel passé	
assurerais	**assurerions**	**aurais assuré**	**aurions assuré**
assurerais	**assureriez**	**aurais assuré**	**auriez assuré**
assurerait	**assureraient**	**aurait assuré**	**auraient assuré**
6 présent du subjonctif		13 passé du subjonctif	
assure	**assurions**	**aie assuré**	**ayons assuré**
assures	**assuriez**	**aies assuré**	**ayez assuré**
assure	**assurent**	**ait assuré**	**aient assuré**
7 imparfait du subjonctif		14 plus-que-parfait du subjonctif	
assurasse	**assurassions**	**eusse assuré**	**eussions assuré**
assurasses	**assurassiez**	**eusses assuré**	**eussiez assuré**
assurât	**assurassent**	**eût assuré**	**eussent assuré**

Impératif
assure
assurons
assurez

Words and expressions related to this verb
assurer qqn de qqch to assure someone of something; **sûr, sûre** sure
assurable insurable, assurable; **sûrement** surely; **sûrement pas** certainly not
rassurer to reassure; **la sûreté** safety
se rassurer to be reassured
assuré, assurée certain

See also **s'assurer.**

How are you doing? Find out with the verb drills and tests with answers explained on pages 50–101.

Reflexive regular **-er** verb

to make sure, to assure oneself, to insure oneself

The Seven Simple Tenses		The Seven Compound Tenses	
Singular	Plural	Singular	Plural
1 présent de l'indicatif		8 passé composé	
m'assure	**nous assurons**	**me suis assuré(e)**	**nous sommes assuré(e)s**
t'assures	**vous assurez**	**t'es assuré(e)**	**vous êtes assuré(e)(s)**
s'assure	**s'assurent**	**s'est assuré(e)**	**se sont assuré(e)s**
2 imparfait de l'indicatif		9 plus-que-parfait de l'indicatif	
m'assurais	**nous assurions**	**m'étais assuré(e)**	**nous étions assuré(e)s**
t'assurais	**vous assuriez**	**t'étais assuré(e)**	**vous étiez assuré(e)(s)**
s'assurait	**s'assuraient**	**s'était assuré(e)**	**s'étaient assuré(e)s**
3 passé simple		10 passé antérieur	
m'assurai	**nous assurâmes**	**me fus assuré(e)**	**nous fûmes assuré(e)s**
t'assuras	**vous assurâtes**	**te fus assuré(e)**	**vous fûtes assuré(e)(s)**
s'assura	**s'assurèrent**	**se fut assuré(e)**	**se furent assuré(e)s**
4 futur		11 futur antérieur	
m'assurerai	**nous assurerons**	**me serai assuré(e)**	**nous serons assuré(e)s**
t'assureras	**vous assurerez**	**te seras assuré(e)**	**vous serez assuré(e)(s)**
s'assurera	**s'assureront**	**se sera assuré(e)**	**se seront assuré(e)s**
5 conditionnel		12 conditionnel passé	
m'assurerais	**nous assurerions**	**me serais assuré(e)**	**nous serions assuré(e)s**
t'assurerais	**vous assureriez**	**te serais assuré(e)**	**vous seriez assuré(e)(s)**
s'assurerait	**s'assureraient**	**se serait assuré(e)**	**se seraient assuré(e)s**
6 présent du subjonctif		13 passé du subjonctif	
m'assure	**nous assurions**	**me sois assuré(e)**	**nous soyons assuré(e)s**
t'assures	**vous assuriez**	**te sois assuré(e)**	**vous soyez assuré(e)(s)**
s'assure	**s'assurent**	**se soit assuré(e)**	**se soient assuré(e)s**
7 imparfait du subjonctif		14 plus-que-parfait du subjonctif	
m'assurasse	**nous assurassions**	**me fusse assuré(e)**	**nous fussions assuré(e)s**
t'assurasses	**vous assurassiez**	**te fusses assuré(e)**	**vous fussiez assuré(e)(s)**
s'assurât	**s'assurassent**	**se fût assuré(e)**	**se fussent assuré(e)s**

Impératif
assure-toi; ne t'assure pas
assurons-nous; ne nous assurons pas
assurez-vous; ne vous assurez pas

Sentences using this verb and words related to it

Pour s'assurer que la porte était bien fermée, Madame Lafontaine l'a fermée à clef. Puis elle a fermé toutes les fenêtres pour avoir de l'assurance et un sentiment de sécurité.

Assurément, elle a raison. Il y a des cambrioleurs dans le voisinage.

assurément assuredly
assurance *f.* assurance, insurance
un assureur insurer
s'assurer de la protection de qqn to secure someone's protection
l'assurance-vie *f.* life insurance, life assurance
l'assurance automobile *f.* car insurance

See also **assurer.**

to attain

Irregular verb

The Seven Simple Tenses		The Seven Compound Tenses	
Singular	Plural	Singular	Plural
1 présent de l'indicatif		8 passé composé	
atteins	**atteignons**	**ai atteint**	**avons atteint**
atteins	**atteignez**	**as atteint**	**avez atteint**
atteint	**atteignent**	**a atteint**	**ont atteint**
2 imparfait de l'indicatif		9 plus-que-parfait de l'indicatif	
atteignais	**atteignions**	**avais atteint**	**avions atteint**
atteignais	**atteigniez**	**avais atteint**	**aviez atteint**
atteignait	**atteignaient**	**avait atteint**	**avaient atteint**
3 passé simple		10 passé antérieur	
atteignis	**atteignîmes**	**eus atteint**	**eûmes atteint**
atteignis	**atteignîtes**	**eus atteint**	**eûtes atteint**
atteignit	**atteignirent**	**eut atteint**	**eurent atteint**
4 futur		11 futur antérieur	
atteindrai	**atteindrons**	**aurai atteint**	**aurons atteint**
atteindras	**atteindrez**	**auras atteint**	**aurez atteint**
atteindra	**atteindront**	**aura atteint**	**auront atteint**
5 conditionnel		12 conditionnel passé	
atteindrais	**atteindrions**	**aurais atteint**	**aurions atteint**
atteindrais	**atteindriez**	**aurais atteint**	**auriez atteint**
atteindrait	**atteindraient**	**aurait atteint**	**auraient atteint**
6 présent du subjonctif		13 passé du subjonctif	
atteigne	**atteignions**	**aie atteint**	**ayons atteint**
atteignes	**atteigniez**	**aies atteint**	**ayez atteint**
atteigne	**atteignent**	**ait atteint**	**aient atteint**
7 imparfait du subjonctif		14 plus-que-parfait du subjonctif	
atteignisse	**atteignissions**	**eusse atteint**	**eussions atteint**
atteignisses	**atteignissiez**	**eusses atteint**	**eussiez atteint**
atteignît	**atteignissent**	**eût atteint**	**eussent atteint**

Impératif
atteins
atteignons
atteignez

Words and expressions related to this verb
atteindre le but/la cible to hit the target
atteindre à to reach
une atteinte reach; attack
hors d'atteinte beyond reach
être atteint (atteinte) de to suffer from

Don't forget to check the list of 2,600 additional verbs keyed to the 501 model verbs. It's in the Appendixes!

Regular **-re** verb

to wait, to wait for, to expect

The Seven Simple Tenses		The Seven Compound Tenses	
Singular	Plural	Singular	Plural
1 présent de l'indicatif		8 passé composé	
attends	**attendons**	**ai attendu**	**avons attendu**
attends	**attendez**	**as attendu**	**avez attendu**
attend	**attendent**	**a attendu**	**ont attendu**
2 imparfait de l'indicatif		9 plus-que-parfait de l'indicatif	
attendais	**attendions**	**avais attendu**	**avions attendu**
attendais	**attendiez**	**avais attendu**	**aviez attendu**
attendait	**attendaient**	**avait attendu**	**avaient attendu**
3 passé simple		10 passé antérieur	
attendis	**attendîmes**	**eus attendu**	**eûmes attendu**
attendis	**attendîtes**	**eus attendu**	**eûtes attendu**
attendit	**attendirent**	**eut attendu**	**eurent attendu**
4 futur		11 futur antérieur	
attendrai	**attendrons**	**aurai attendu**	**aurons attendu**
attendras	**attendrez**	**auras attendu**	**aurez attendu**
attendra	**attendront**	**aura attendu**	**auront attendu**
5 conditionnel		12 conditionnel passé	
attendrais	**attendrions**	**aurais attendu**	**aurions attendu**
attendrais	**attendriez**	**aurais attendu**	**auriez attendu**
attendrait	**attendraient**	**aurait attendu**	**auraient attendu**
6 présent du subjonctif		13 passé du subjonctif	
attende	**attendions**	**aie attendu**	**ayons attendu**
attendes	**attendiez**	**aies attendu**	**ayez attendu**
attende	**attendent**	**ait attendu**	**aient attendu**
7 imparfait du subjonctif		14 plus-que-parfait du subjonctif	
attendisse	**attendissions**	**eusse attendu**	**eussions attendu**
attendisses	**attendissiez**	**eusses attendu**	**eussiez attendu**
attendît	**attendissent**	**eût attendu**	**eussent attendu**

Impératif
attends
attendons
attendez

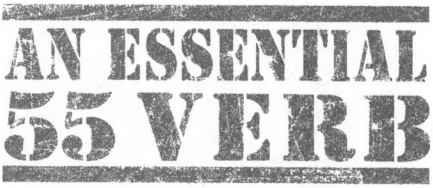

The subject pronouns are found on page 103.

AN ESSENTIAL 55 VERB

Attendre

Attendre is a regular **-re** verb that is used in many everyday situations and expressions.

Sentences using attendre and related words

J'attends l'autobus depuis vingt minutes! I have been waiting for the bus for twenty minutes!

Hier, j'ai attendu dix minutes. Yesterday, I waited for ten minutes.

Quand le bus arrivera, je m'attendrai à trouver une place libre. When the bus arrives, I will expect to find an empty seat.

Georges ne s'attendait pas à gagner. George wasn't expecting to win.

Cela peut attendre! It can wait!

Sa réaction était complètement inattendu. His reaction was completely unexpected.

M. Godot n'est pas encore arrivé. En attendant, prenons un café. Mr. Godot hasn't arrived yet. In the meantime, let's have a coffee.

Manon a manqué le bus. Il faut qu'elle attende le prochain. Manon missed the bus. She has to wait for the next one.

Bob et Katie attendent un enfant. Bob and Katie are expecting a child.

Words and expressions related to this verb

l'attente *f.* **wait, waiting**

une salle d'attente **waiting room**

faire attendre qqch à qqn **to make someone wait for something; to keep someone waiting for something**

en attendant **meanwhile, in the meantime**

s'attendre à **to expect**

inattendu, inattendue *adj.* **unexpected**

If you can conjugate **attendre** you can also conjugate the following verbs:

détendre **to relax, loosen**

se détendre **to relax (use être for auxiliary)**

distendre **to stretch**

entendre **to hear**

étendre **to spread**

prétendre **to claim**

retendre **to retighten**

sous-tendre **to underlie, subtend**

tendre **to tighten, offer**

Regular **-er** verb

to attract, to allure

The Seven Simple Tenses		The Seven Compound Tenses	
Singular	Plural	Singular	Plural
1 présent de l'indicatif		8 passé composé	
attire	**attirons**	**ai attiré**	**avons attiré**
attires	**attirez**	**as attiré**	**avez attiré**
attire	**attirent**	**a attiré**	**ont attiré**
2 imparfait de l'indicatif		9 plus-que-parfait de l'indicatif	
attirais	**attirions**	**avais attiré**	**avions attiré**
attirais	**attiriez**	**avais attiré**	**aviez attiré**
attirait	**attiraient**	**avait attiré**	**avaient attiré**
3 passé simple		10 passé antérieur	
attirai	**attirâmes**	**eus attiré**	**eûmes attiré**
attiras	**attirâtes**	**eus attiré**	**eûtes attiré**
attira	**attirèrent**	**eut attiré**	**eurent attiré**
4 futur		11 futur antérieur	
attirerai	**attirerons**	**aurai attiré**	**aurons attiré**
attireras	**attirerez**	**auras attiré**	**aurez attiré**
attirera	**attireront**	**aura attiré**	**auront attiré**
5 conditionnel		12 conditionnel passé	
attirerais	**attirerions**	**aurais attiré**	**aurions attiré**
attirerais	**attireriez**	**aurais attiré**	**auriez attiré**
attirerait	**attireraient**	**aurait attiré**	**auraient attiré**
6 présent du subjonctif		13 passé du subjonctif	
attire	**attirions**	**aie attiré**	**ayons attiré**
attires	**attiriez**	**aies attiré**	**ayez attiré**
attire	**attirent**	**ait attiré**	**aient attiré**
7 imparfait du subjonctif		14 plus-que-parfait du subjonctif	
attirasse	**attirassions**	**eusse attiré**	**eussions attiré**
attirasses	**attirassiez**	**eusses attiré**	**eussiez attiré**
attirât	**attirassent**	**eût attiré**	**eussent attiré**

Impératif
attire
attirons
attirez

Common idiomatic expressions using this verb and words related to it

attirant, attirante attractive
le tirage drawing, pulling; printing of a publication
premier tirage first printing
à gros tirage large number of copies printed
une attraction attraction
tirer to pull
un tirage limité limited number of copies
les attraits *m.* charms, beauty
Do not confuse **un tirage** with **un triage**, which means sorting, selecting.

See also **retirer, se retirer,** and **tirer.**

Use the guide to French pronunciation. It's in the Appendixes.

attraper (59) — Part. pr. **attrapant** — Part. passé **attrapé**

to catch

Regular **-er** verb

The Seven Simple Tenses		The Seven Compound Tenses	
Singular	Plural	Singular	Plural
1 présent de l'indicatif		8 passé composé	
attrape	**attrapons**	**ai attrapé**	**avons attrapé**
attrapes	**attrapez**	**as attrapé**	**avez attrapé**
attrape	**attrapent**	**a attrapé**	**ont attrapé**
2 imparfait de l'indicatif		9 plus-que-parfait de l'indicatif	
attrapais	**attrapions**	**avais attrapé**	**avions attrapé**
attrapais	**attrapiez**	**avais attrapé**	**aviez attrapé**
attrapait	**attrapaient**	**avait attrapé**	**avaient attrapé**
3 passé simple		10 passé antérieur	
attrapai	**attrapâmes**	**eus attrapé**	**eûmes attrapé**
attrapas	**attrapâtes**	**eus attrapé**	**eûtes attrapé**
attrapa	**attrapèrent**	**eut attrapé**	**eurent attrapé**
4 futur		11 futur antérieur	
attraperai	**attraperons**	**aurai attrapé**	**aurons attrapé**
attraperas	**attraperez**	**auras attrapé**	**aurez attrapé**
attrapera	**attraperont**	**aura attrapé**	**auront attrapé**
5 conditionnel		12 conditionnel passé	
attraperais	**attraperions**	**aurais attrapé**	**aurions attrapé**
attraperais	**attraperiez**	**aurais attrapé**	**auriez attrapé**
attraperait	**attraperaient**	**aurait attrapé**	**auraient attrapé**
6 présent du subjonctif		13 passé du subjonctif	
attrape	**attrapions**	**aie attrapé**	**ayons attrapé**
attrapes	**attrapiez**	**aies attrapé**	**ayez attrapé**
attrape	**attrapent**	**ait attrapé**	**aient attrapé**
7 imparfait du subjonctif		14 plus-que-parfait du subjonctif	
attrapasse	**attrapassions**	**eusse attrapé**	**eussions attrapé**
attrapasses	**attrapassiez**	**eusses attrapé**	**eussiez attrapé**
attrapât	**attrapassent**	**eût attrapé**	**eussent attrapé**

Impératif
attrape
attrapons
attrapez

Common idiomatic expressions using this verb

—Si tu ne veux pas attraper un rhume, mets ton manteau parce qu'il fait froid dehors. If you don't want to catch cold, put on your coat because it's cold outside.

—Je n'ai pas le temps maintenant, maman—je dois attraper l'autobus. I don't have the time right now, Mom—I have to catch the bus.

attraper un rhume to catch cold
attraper qqn à qqch to catch someone at something (to surprise)
s'attraper to be catching, infectious
une attrape trick
un attrape-mouche flypaper (sticky paper to catch flies), fly trap
une trappe trap

Get acquainted with what preposition goes with what verb. See *Verbs with prepositions* in the Appendixes.

Regular **-er** verb

to augment, to increase

The Seven Simple Tenses		The Seven Compound Tenses	
Singular	Plural	Singular	Plural
1 présent de l'indicatif		8 passé composé	
augmente	**augmentons**	**ai augmenté**	**avons augmenté**
augmentes	**augmentez**	**as augmenté**	**avez augmenté**
augmente	**augmentent**	**a augmenté**	**ont augmenté**
2 imparfait de l'indicatif		9 plus-que-parfait de l'indicatif	
augmentais	**augmentions**	**avais augmenté**	**avions augmenté**
augmentais	**augmentiez**	**avais augmenté**	**aviez augmenté**
augmentait	**augmentaient**	**avait augmenté**	**avaient augmenté**
3 passé simple		10 passé antérieur	
augmentai	**augmentâmes**	**eus augmenté**	**eûmes augmenté**
augmentas	**augmentâtes**	**eus augmenté**	**eûtes augmenté**
augmenta	**augmentèrent**	**eut augmenté**	**eurent augmenté**
4 futur		11 futur antérieur	
augmenterai	**augmenterons**	**aurai augmenté**	**aurons augmenté**
augmenteras	**augmenterez**	**auras augmenté**	**aurez augmenté**
augmentera	**augmenteront**	**aura augmenté**	**auront augmenté**
5 conditionnel		12 conditionnel passé	
augmenterais	**augmenterions**	**aurais augmenté**	**aurions augmenté**
augmenterais	**augmenteriez**	**aurais augmenté**	**auriez augmenté**
augmenterait	**augmenteraient**	**aurait augmenté**	**auraient augmenté**
6 présent du subjonctif		13 passé du subjonctif	
augmente	**augmentions**	**aie augmenté**	**ayons augmenté**
augmentes	**augmentiez**	**aies augmenté**	**ayez augmenté**
augmente	**augmentent**	**ait augmenté**	**aient augmenté**
7 imparfait du subjonctif		14 plus-que-parfait du subjonctif	
augmentasse	**augmentassions**	**eusse augmenté**	**eussions augmenté**
augmentasses	**augmentassiez**	**eusses augmenté**	**eussiez augmenté**
augmentât	**augmentassent**	**eût augmenté**	**eussent augmenté**

Impératif
augmente
augmentons
augmentez

Words and expressions related to this verb
augmentation *f.* increase, augmentation; **augmentation de salaire** increase in salary
l'augmentation de la mémoire vive RAM increase (computer)
une augmentation des impôts tax increase
augmenter une douleur to aggravate a pain
augmenter les prix to increase prices

Grammar putting you in a tense mood? Review the definitions of basic grammatical terms with examples on pages 35–49.

avancer (61)

Part. pr. **avançant** Part. passé **avancé**

to advance, to go forward

Regular **-er** verb endings; spelling change: **c** changes to **ç** before **a** or **o** to keep **s** sound

The Seven Simple Tenses		The Seven Compound Tenses	
Singular	Plural	Singular	Plural
1 présent de l'indicatif		8 passé composé	
avance	**avançons**	**ai avancé**	**avons avancé**
avances	**avancez**	**as avancé**	**avez avancé**
avance	**avancent**	**a avancé**	**ont avancé**
2 imparfait de l'indicatif		9 plus-que-parfait de l'indicatif	
avançais	**avancions**	**avais avancé**	**avions avancé**
avançais	**avanciez**	**avais avancé**	**aviez avancé**
avançait	**avançaient**	**avait avancé**	**avaient avancé**
3 passé simple		10 passé antérieur	
avançai	**avançâmes**	**eus avancé**	**eûmes avancé**
avanças	**avançâtes**	**eus avancé**	**eûtes avancé**
avança	**avancèrent**	**eut avancé**	**eurent avancé**
4 futur		11 futur antérieur	
avancerai	**avancerons**	**aurai avancé**	**aurons avancé**
avanceras	**avancerez**	**auras avancé**	**aurez avancé**
avancera	**avanceront**	**aura avancé**	**auront avancé**
5 conditionnel		12 conditionnel passé	
avancerais	**avancerions**	**aurais avancé**	**aurions avancé**
avancerais	**avanceriez**	**aurais avancé**	**auriez avancé**
avancerait	**avanceraient**	**aurait avancé**	**auraient avancé**
6 présent du subjonctif		13 passé du subjonctif	
avance	**avancions**	**aie avancé**	**ayons avancé**
avances	**avanciez**	**aies avancé**	**ayez avancé**
avance	**avancent**	**ait avancé**	**aient avancé**
7 imparfait du subjonctif		14 plus-que-parfait du subjonctif	
avançasse	**avançassions**	**eusse avancé**	**eussions avancé**
avançasses	**avançassiez**	**eusses avancé**	**eussiez avancé**
avançât	**avançassent**	**eût avancé**	**eussent avancé**

Impératif
avance
avançons
avancez

Sentences using this verb and words related to it

Le docteur a dit au petit garçon:—Ouvre la bouche et avance la langue.
Le garçon n'a pas ouvert la bouche et il n'a pas avancé la langue.
Le docteur a insisté:—Ouvrons la bouche et avançons la langue!

une avance advance; **faire des avances à qqn** to make advances to somebody
à l'avance, d'avance in advance, beforehand
arriver en avance to arrive early
s'avancer to advance (oneself)
l'avant *m.* front
Ta montre avance. Your watch is fast.
avancer une théorie to promote a theory
Comment avance le travail? How is the work coming along?
en avant ahead, in front
devancer to arrive ahead

The Seven Simple Tenses		The Seven Compound Tenses	
Singular	Plural	Singular	Plural
1 présent de l'indicatif		8 passé composé	
ai	**avons**	**ai eu**	**avons eu**
as	**avez**	**as eu**	**avez eu**
a	**ont**	**a eu**	**ont eu**
2 imparfait de l'indicatif		9 plus-que-parfait de l'indicatif	
avais	**avions**	**avais eu**	**avions eu**
avais	**aviez**	**avais eu**	**aviez eu**
avait	**avaient**	**avait eu**	**avaient eu**
3 passé simple		10 passé antérieur	
eus	**eûmes**	**eus eu**	**eûmes eu**
eus	**eûtes**	**eus eu**	**eûtes eu**
eut	**eurent**	**eut eu**	**eurent eu**
4 futur		11 futur antérieur	
aurai	**aurons**	**aurai eu**	**aurons eu**
auras	**aurez**	**auras eu**	**aurez eu**
aura	**auront**	**aura eu**	**auront eu**
5 conditionnel		12 conditionnel passé	
aurais	**aurions**	**aurais eu**	**aurions eu**
aurais	**auriez**	**aurais eu**	**auriez eu**
aurait	**auraient**	**aurait eu**	**auraient eu**
6 présent du subjonctif		13 passé du subjonctif	
aie	**ayons**	**aie eu**	**ayons eu**
aies	**ayez**	**aies eu**	**ayez eu**
ait	**aient**	**ait eu**	**aient eu**
7 imparfait du subjonctif		14 plus-que-parfait du subjonctif	
eusse	**eussions**	**eusse eu**	**eussions eu**
eusses	**eussiez**	**eusses eu**	**eussiez eu**
eût	**eussent**	**eût eu**	**eussent eu**

Impératif
aie
ayons
ayez

The subject pronouns are found on page 103.

AN ESSENTIAL 55 VERB

Avoir

Avoir is a very important verb. First of all, it is used as the auxiliary for the compound tenses of most French verbs. So, if you can conjugate **avoir** in the seven simple tenses (1–7) all you need is a verb's past participle and you can create the seven compound tenses (8–14). Secondly, **avoir** is used in a vast number of idiomatic expressions. That's why **avoir** gets an extra page of examples!

Avoir is used in a great number of idiomatic expressions. Here are a few of the more useful ones with sample sentences:

Avoir by itself can mean to have something the matter.
Qu'est-ce que vous avez? What's the matter with you?
Qu'est-ce qu'il y a? What's the matter?

avoir . . . ans to be . . . years old
Quel âge avez-vous? How old are you?
J'ai seize ans. I'm sixteen.

avoir à + inf. to have to, to be obliged to + inf.
J'ai quelque chose à vous dire. I have something to tell you.

avoir beau + inf. to be useless + inf., to do something in vain
Vous avez beau parler; je ne vous écoute pas. You're talking in vain (uselessly); I'm not listening to you.

avoir besoin de to need, to have need of
Vous avez l'air fatigué; vous avez besoin de repos. You look tired; you need some rest.

avoir bonne mine to look well, to look good (persons)
Joseph a bonne mine aujourd'hui, ne trouvez-vous pas? Joseph looks good today, don't you think so?

avoir chaud to be (feel) warm (persons)
J'ai chaud; ouvrez la fenêtre, s'il vous plaît. I feel warm; open the window, please.

avoir congé to have a day off, a holiday from work or school
Demain nous avons congé et nous allons à la plage. Tomorrow we have the day off and we're going to the beach.

avoir de la chance to be lucky
Tu as trouvé une pièce de monnaie?! Tu as de la chance! You found a coin?! You're lucky!

avoir de quoi + inf. to have the material, means, enough + inf.
As-tu de quoi manger? Have you something (enough) to eat?

avoir envie de to feel like, to have a desire to
Madame Loisel a toujours envie de danser. Mrs. Loisel always feels like dancing.

avoir faim to be hungry
As-tu faim, Anne? Bon, alors je vais te donner à manger. Are you hungry, Anne? Good, then I'm going to give you something to eat.

avoir froid to be (feel) cold (persons)
J'ai froid; fermez la fenêtre, s'il vous plaît. I feel cold; close the window, please.

avoir l'air + adj. to seem, to appear, to look + adj.
Vous avez l'air malade; asseyez-vous. You look sick; sit down.

Expressions using *avoir*

Qui ne risque rien n'a rien.
Nothing ventured, nothing gained.

Les murs ont des oreilles.
The walls have ears.

avoir l'air de + inf. to appear + inf.
Vous avez l'air d'être malade; couchez-vous. You appear to be sick; lie down.

avoir l'habitude de + inf. to be accustomed to, to be in the habit of
J'ai l'habitude de faire mes devoirs avant le dîner. I'm in the habit of doing my homework before dinner.

avoir lieu to take place
Le match aura lieu demain. The game will take place tomorrow.

avoir mal to feel sick
Qu'est-ce que tu as, Robert? What's the matter, Robert?
J'ai mal. I feel sick.

avoir mal à + (place where it hurts) to have a pain or ache in . . .
J'ai mal à la jambe. My leg hurts.
J'ai mal à la tête. I have a headache.

avoir mauvaise mine to look ill, not to look well
Qu'est-ce que tu as, Janine? What's the matter, Janine?
Tu as mauvaise mine. You don't look well.

avoir qqn to get the better of someone
Je t'ai eu! I got you!

en avoir marre to be fed up, to be bored stiff, to be sick and tired of something
J'en ai marre! I'm fed up! I've had it!

en avoir par-dessus la tête to have enough of it, to be sick and tired of it, to have it up to here
J'en ai par-dessus la tête! I've had it up to here!

il y a + length of time ago
Madame Duclos est partie il y a un mois. Mrs. Duclos left a month ago.
Il y a dix minutes que j'attends l'autobus. I have been waiting for the bus for ten minutes.
Il n'y a pas de quoi. You're welcome.

n'avoir qu'à + inf. to have only + inf.
Tu n'as qu'à appuyer sur le bouton et la machine se met en marche. All you have to do is press the button and the machine starts itself.

More idiomatic expressions using avoir

avoir affaire à quelqu'un to deal with someone
avoir des nouvelles to receive news, to hear (from someone)
avoir droit à to be entitled to
avoir du savoir-faire to have tact
avoir du savoir-vivre to have good manners, etiquette
avoir hâte to be in a hurry
avoir hâte de faire qqch to be anxious to do something, to look forward to doing something
avoir honte to be (feel) ashamed
avoir l'idée de + inf. to have a notion + inf.
avoir l'impression to be under the impression
avoir l'intention de to intend + inf.
avoir l'occasion de + inf. to have the opportunity + inf.
avoir l'occasion de faire qqch to have the opportunity to do something
avoir la bonté de + inf. to have the kindness + inf.
avoir la langue bien pendue to have the gift of gab
avoir la parole to have the floor (to speak)
avoir le cafard to feel downhearted (downcast), to have the blues
avoir le coeur gros to be heartbroken
avoir le droit de faire qqch to be entitled (have the right) to do something
avoir le temps de + inf. to have (the) time + inf.
avoir mal au coeur to feel nauseous
avoir peine à + inf. to have difficulty in + pres. part.
avoir peur de to be afraid of
avoir raison to be right (persons)
avoir rendez-vous avec qqn to have a date (appointment) with someone
avoir soif to be thirsty
avoir sommeil to be (feel) sleepy
avoir son mot à dire to have one's way
avoir tendance à faire qqch to tend to do something
avoir tort to be wrong (persons)
avoir trait à qqch to have to do with something
avoir une faim de loup to be starving
en avoir assez to have enough of it
il y a . . . there is . . ., there are . . .
il y avait . . . there was . . ., there were . . .
il y a eu . . . there was . . ., there were . . .
il y aura . . . there will be . . .
il y aurait . . . there would be . . .
Il y a lieu de croire que . . . There is reason to believe that . . .

The subject pronouns are found on page 103.

baisser (63)

Part. pr. **baissant** Part. passé **baissé**

to lower, to sink

Regular **-er** verb

The Seven Simple Tenses		The Seven Compound Tenses	
Singular	Plural	Singular	Plural
1 présent de l'indicatif		8 passé composé	
baisse	**baissons**	**ai baissé**	**avons baissé**
baisses	**baissez**	**as baissé**	**avez baissé**
baisse	**baissent**	**a baissé**	**ont baissé**
2 imparfait de l'indicatif		9 plus-que-parfait de l'indicatif	
baissais	**baissions**	**avais baissé**	**avions baissé**
baissais	**baissiez**	**avais baissé**	**aviez baissé**
baissait	**baissaient**	**avait baissé**	**avaient baissé**
3 passé simple		10 passé antérieur	
baissai	**baissâmes**	**eus baissé**	**eûmes baissé**
baissas	**baissâtes**	**eus baissé**	**eûtes baissé**
baissa	**baissèrent**	**eut baissé**	**eurent baissé**
4 futur		11 futur antérieur	
baisserai	**baisserons**	**aurai baissé**	**aurons baissé**
baisseras	**baisserez**	**auras baissé**	**aurez baissé**
baissera	**baisseront**	**aura baissé**	**auront baissé**
5 conditionnel		12 conditionnel passé	
baisserais	**baisserions**	**aurais baissé**	**aurions baissé**
baisserais	**baisseriez**	**aurais baissé**	**auriez baissé**
baisserait	**baisseraient**	**aurait baissé**	**auraient baissé**
6 présent du subjonctif		13 passé du subjonctif	
baisse	**baissions**	**aie baissé**	**ayons baissé**
baisses	**baissiez**	**aies baissé**	**ayez baissé**
baisse	**baissent**	**ait baissé**	**aient baissé**
7 imparfait du subjonctif		14 plus-que-parfait du subjonctif	
baissasse	**baissassions**	**eusse baissé**	**eussions baissé**
baissasses	**baissassiez**	**eusses baissé**	**eussiez baissé**
baissât	**baissassent**	**eût baissé**	**eussent baissé**

Impératif
baisse
baissons
baissez

Common idiomatic expressions using this verb

baisser la voix to lower one's voice

baisser les yeux to look down, cast one's eyes down

baisser les bras to admit defeat, to give in

se jeter tête baissée dans qqch to do something blindly, headlong

se baisser to bend (stoop) down

rabaisser to depreciate, to humble, to lower

un rabais discount

See also **abaisser** and **s'abaisser.**

Don't forget to use the English-French verb index. It's in the Appendixes.

Regular **-er** verb endings; spelling change: **c** changes to **ç** before **a** or **o** to keep **s** sound

to balance, to sway, to swing, to weigh, to throw away

The Seven Simple Tenses		The Seven Compound Tenses	
Singular	Plural	Singular	Plural
1 présent de l'indicatif		8 passé composé	
balance	**balançons**	**ai balancé**	**avons balancé**
balances	**balancez**	**as balancé**	**avez balancé**
balance	**balancent**	**a balancé**	**ont balancé**
2 imparfait de l'indicatif		9 plus-que-parfait de l'indicatif	
balançais	**balancions**	**avais balancé**	**avions balancé**
balançais	**balanciez**	**avais balancé**	**aviez balancé**
balançait	**balançaient**	**avait balancé**	**avaient balancé**
3 passé simple		10 passé antérieur	
balançai	**balançâmes**	**eus balancé**	**eûmes balancé**
balanças	**balançâtes**	**eus balancé**	**eûtes balancé**
balança	**balancèrent**	**eut balancé**	**eurent balancé**
4 futur		11 futur antérieur	
balancerai	**balancerons**	**aurai balancé**	**aurons balancé**
balanceras	**balancerez**	**auras balancé**	**aurez balancé**
balancera	**balanceront**	**aura balancé**	**auront balancé**
5 conditionnel		12 conditionnel passé	
balancerais	**balancerions**	**aurais balancé**	**aurions balancé**
balancerais	**balanceriez**	**aurais balancé**	**auriez balancé**
balancerait	**balanceraient**	**aurait balancé**	**auraient balancé**
6 présent du subjonctif		13 passé du subjonctif	
balance	**balancions**	**aie balancé**	**ayons balancé**
balances	**balanciez**	**aies balancé**	**ayez balancé**
balance	**balancent**	**ait balancé**	**aient balancé**
7 imparfait du subjonctif		14 plus-que-parfait du subjonctif	
balançasse	**balançassions**	**eusse balancé**	**eussions balancé**
balançasses	**balançassiez**	**eusses balancé**	**eussiez balancé**
balançât	**balançassent**	**eût balancé**	**eussent balancé**

Impératif
balance
balançons
balancez

Words and expressions related to this verb

une balançoire see-saw, swing
une balance weight scale
la balance des pouvoirs the balance of powers
le balancement balancing, rocking

Il a balancé la bouteille par la vitre de l'auto. He tossed the bottle out of the car window.
faire pencher la balance to favor someone
balancer le pour et le contre to weigh the pros and cons

Don't forget to use the English-French verb index. It's in the Appendixes!

balayer (65) — Part. pr. balayant — Part. passé balayé

to sweep

Regular **-er** verb endings; spelling change: **-ayer** verbs may change **y** to **i** in front of a mute **e** or may keep **y**

The Seven Simple Tenses		The Seven Compound Tenses	
Singular	Plural	Singular	Plural
1 présent de l'indicatif		8 passé composé	
balaye	**balayons**	**ai balayé**	**avons balayé**
balayes	**balayez**	**as balayé**	**avez balayé**
balaye	**balayent**	**a balayé**	**ont balayé**
2 imparfait de l'indicatif		9 plus-que-parfait de l'indicatif	
balayais	**balayions**	**avais balayé**	**avions balayé**
balayais	**balayiez**	**avais balayé**	**aviez balayé**
balayait	**balayaient**	**avait balayé**	**avaient balayé**
3 passé simple		10 passé antérieur	
balayai	**balayâmes**	**eus balayé**	**eûmes balayé**
balayas	**balayâtes**	**eus balayé**	**eûtes balayé**
balaya	**balayèrent**	**eut balayé**	**eurent balayé**
4 futur		11 futur antérieur	
balayerai	**balayerons**	**aurai balayé**	**aurons balayé**
balayeras	**balayerez**	**auras balayé**	**aurez balayé**
balayera	**balayeront**	**aura balayé**	**auront balayé**
5 conditionnel		12 conditionnel passé	
balayerais	**balayerions**	**aurais balayé**	**aurions balayé**
balayerais	**balayeriez**	**aurais balayé**	**auriez balayé**
balayerait	**balayeraient**	**aurait balayé**	**auraient balayé**
6 présent du subjonctif		13 passé du subjonctif	
balaye	**balayions**	**aie balayé**	**ayons balayé**
balayes	**balayiez**	**aies balayé**	**ayez balayé**
balaye	**balayent**	**ait balayé**	**aient balayé**
7 imparfait du subjonctif		14 plus-que-parfait du subjonctif	
balayasse	**balayassions**	**eusse balayé**	**eussions balayé**
balayasses	**balayassiez**	**eusses balayé**	**eussiez balayé**
balayât	**balayassent**	**eût balayé**	**eussent balayé**

Impératif
balaye
balayons
balayez

Sentences using this verb and words related to it

—Marie, as-tu balayé ta chambre?
—Non, maman.
—Et pourquoi pas?
—Parce que je n'ai pas de balai, je n'ai pas de balayette, et je ne suis pas balayeuse. Voilà pourquoi!
—Quelle fille!

un balai broom; **une balayette** small brush, whiskbroom; **un balayeur, une balayeuse** sweeper
un balai d'essuie-glace windshield wiper blade

Regular **-ir** verb

to build, to construct

The Seven Simple Tenses		The Seven Compound Tenses	
Singular	Plural	Singular	Plural
1 présent de l'indicatif		8 passé composé	
bâtis	**bâtissons**	**ai bâti**	**avons bâti**
bâtis	**bâtissez**	**as bâti**	**avez bâti**
bâtit	**bâtissent**	**a bâti**	**ont bâti**
2 imparfait de l'indicatif		9 plus-que-parfait de l'indicatif	
bâtissais	**bâtissions**	**avais bâti**	**avions bâti**
bâtissais	**bâtissiez**	**avais bâti**	**aviez bâti**
bâtissait	**bâtissaient**	**avait bâti**	**avaient bâti**
3 passé simple		10 passé antérieur	
bâtis	**bâtîmes**	**eus bâti**	**eûmes bâti**
bâtis	**bâtîtes**	**eus bâti**	**eûtes bâti**
bâtit	**bâtirent**	**eut bâti**	**eurent bâti**
4 futur		11 futur antérieur	
bâtirai	**bâtirons**	**aurai bâti**	**aurons bâti**
bâtiras	**bâtirez**	**auras bâti**	**aurez bâti**
bâtira	**bâtiront**	**aura bâti**	**auront bâti**
5 conditionnel		12 conditionnel passé	
bâtirais	**bâtirions**	**aurais bâti**	**aurions bâti**
bâtirais	**bâtiriez**	**aurais bâti**	**auriez bâti**
bâtirait	**bâtiraient**	**aurait bâti**	**auraient bâti**
6 présent du subjonctif		13 passé du subjonctif	
bâtisse	**bâtissions**	**aie bâti**	**ayons bâti**
bâtisses	**bâtissiez**	**aies bâti**	**ayez bâti**
bâtisse	**bâtissent**	**ait bâti**	**aient bâti**
7 imparfait du subjonctif		14 plus-que-parfait du subjonctif	
bâtisse	**bâtissions**	**eusse bâti**	**eussions bâti**
bâtisses	**bâtissiez**	**eusses bâti**	**eussiez bâti**
bâtît	**bâtissent**	**eût bâti**	**eussent bâti**

Impératif
bâtis
bâtissons
bâtissez

Words and expressions related to this verb
un bâtiment building, edifice, ship; **un bâtisseur** builder
bâtir to baste (sewing term; when basting food, use **arroser**); **du fil à bâtir** basting thread
un bâtiment de guerre warship
rebâtir to rebuild
bâtir des châteaux en Espagne to build castles in the air
bâtir sur le sable to build on sand
bien bâti, bien bâtie well built
Sergio est bien bâti parce qu'il est culturiste. Sergio is well built because he is a bodybuilder.

The subject pronouns are found on page 103.

battre (67)

Part. pr. **battant** Part. passé **battu**

to beat, to hit, to strike

Irregular verb in 1s, 2s, 3s present indicative

The Seven Simple Tenses		The Seven Compound Tenses	
Singular	Plural	Singular	Plural
1 présent de l'indicatif		8 passé composé	
bats	**battons**	**ai battu**	**avons battu**
bats	**battez**	**as battu**	**avez battu**
bat	**battent**	**a battu**	**ont battu**
2 imparfait de l'indicatif		9 plus-que-parfait de l'indicatif	
battais	**battions**	**avais battu**	**avions battu**
battais	**battiez**	**avais battu**	**aviez battu**
battait	**battaient**	**avait battu**	**avaient battu**
3 passé simple		10 passé antérieur	
battis	**battîmes**	**eus battu**	**eûmes battu**
battis	**battîtes**	**eus battu**	**eûtes battu**
battit	**battirent**	**eut battu**	**eurent battu**
4 futur		11 futur antérieur	
battrai	**battrons**	**aurai battu**	**aurons battu**
battras	**battrez**	**auras battu**	**aurez battu**
battra	**battront**	**aura battu**	**auront battu**
5 conditionnel		12 conditionnel passé	
battrais	**battrions**	**aurais battu**	**aurions battu**
battrais	**battriez**	**aurais battu**	**auriez battu**
battrait	**battraient**	**aurait battu**	**auraient battu**
6 présent du subjonctif		13 passé du subjonctif	
batte	**battions**	**aie battu**	**ayons battu**
battes	**battiez**	**aies battu**	**ayez battu**
batte	**battent**	**ait battu**	**aient battu**
7 imparfait du subjonctif		14 plus-que-parfait du subjonctif	
battisse	**battissions**	**eusse battu**	**eussions battu**
battisses	**battissiez**	**eusses battu**	**eussiez battu**
battît	**battissent**	**eût battu**	**eussent battu**

Impératif
bats
battons
battez

Sentences using this verb and words related to it

Il faut battre le fer quand il est chaud. You have to strike while the iron is hot.

battre des mains to clap, to applaud
battre la campagne to scour the countryside
le battant leaf, flap (of a table)
une porte à deux battants double door
une batte bat, beater
le battement banging (of a door); throbbing, flutter, beating
un batteur whisk, beater
le battage beating

See also **abattre, se battre,** and **combattre.**

Review the Subjunctive clearly and simply on pages 26–31.

Reflexive irregular verb in 1s, 2s, 3s present indicative

to fight

The Seven Simple Tenses		The Seven Compound Tenses	
Singular	Plural	Singular	Plural
1 présent de l'indicatif		8 passé composé	
me bats	**nous battons**	**me suis battu(e)**	**nous sommes battu(e)s**
te bats	**vous battez**	**t'es battu(e)**	**vous êtes battu(e)(s)**
se bat	**se battent**	**s'est battu(e)**	**se sont battu(e)s**
2 imparfait de l'indicatif		9 plus-que-parfait de l'indicatif	
me battais	**nous battions**	**m'étais battu(e)**	**nous étions battu(e)s**
te battais	**vous battiez**	**t'étais battu(e)**	**vous étiez battu(e)(s)**
se battait	**se battaient**	**s'était battu(e)**	**s'étaient battu(e)s**
3 passé simple		10 passé antérieur	
me battis	**nous battîmes**	**me fus battu(e)**	**nous fûmes battu(e)s**
te battis	**vous battîtes**	**te fus battu(e)**	**vous fûtes battu(e)(s)**
se battit	**se battirent**	**se fut battu(e)**	**se furent battu(e)s**
4 futur		11 futur antérieur	
me battrai	**nous battrons**	**me serai battu(e)**	**nous serons battu(e)s**
te battras	**vous battrez**	**te seras battu(e)**	**vous serez battu(e)(s)**
se battra	**se battront**	**se sera battu(e)**	**se seront battu(e)s**
5 conditionnel		12 conditionnel passé	
me battrais	**nous battrions**	**me serais battu(e)**	**nous serions battu(e)s**
te battrais	**vous battriez**	**te serais battu(e)**	**vous seriez battu(e)(s)**
se battrait	**se battraient**	**se serait battu(e)**	**se seraient battu(e)s**
6 présent du subjonctif		13 passé du subjonctif	
me batte	**nous battions**	**me sois battu(e)**	**nous soyons battu(e)s**
te battes	**vous battiez**	**te sois battu(e)**	**vous soyez battu(e)(s)**
se batte	**se battent**	**se soit battu(e)**	**se soient battu(e)s**
7 imparfait du subjonctif		14 plus-que-parfait du subjonctif	
me battisse	**nous battissions**	**me fusse battu(e)**	**nous fussions battu(e)s**
te battisses	**vous battissiez**	**te fusses battu(e)**	**vous fussiez battu(e)(s)**
se battît	**se battissent**	**se fût battu(e)**	**se fussent battu(e)s**

Impératif
bats-toi; ne te bats pas
battons-nous; ne nous battons pas
battez-vous; ne vous battez pas

Sentences using this verb and words related to it

Ecoutez! Nos voisins commencent à se battre. Ils se battent toujours. La dernière fois ils se sont battus à coups de poings. Il y a toujours un grand combat chez eux.

For other words and expressions related to this verb, see **abattre, battre,** and **combattre.**

Don't forget to check the list of 2,600 additional verbs keyed to the 501 model verbs. It's in the Appendixes!

bavarder (69) — Part. pr. bavardant — Part. passé bavardé

to chat, to chatter, to babble, to gossip

Regular **-er** verb

The Seven Simple Tenses		The Seven Compound Tenses	
Singular	Plural	Singular	Plural
1 présent de l'indicatif		8 passé composé	
bavarde	**bavardons**	**ai bavardé**	**avons bavardé**
bavardes	**bavardez**	**as bavardé**	**avez bavardé**
bavarde	**bavardent**	**a bavardé**	**ont bavardé**
2 imparfait de l'indicatif		9 plus-que-parfait de l'indicatif	
bavardais	**bavardions**	**avais bavardé**	**avions bavardé**
bavardais	**bavardiez**	**avais bavardé**	**aviez bavardé**
bavardait	**bavardaient**	**avait bavardé**	**avaient bavardé**
3 passé simple		10 passé antérieur	
bavardai	**bavardâmes**	**eus bavardé**	**eûmes bavardé**
bavardas	**bavardâtes**	**eus bavardé**	**eûtes bavardé**
bavarda	**bavardèrent**	**eut bavardé**	**eurent bavardé**
4 futur		11 futur antérieur	
bavarderai	**bavarderons**	**aurai bavardé**	**aurons bavardé**
bavarderas	**bavarderez**	**auras bavardé**	**aurez bavardé**
bavardera	**bavarderont**	**aura bavardé**	**auront bavardé**
5 conditionnel		12 conditionnel passé	
bavarderais	**bavarderions**	**aurais bavardé**	**aurions bavardé**
bavarderais	**bavarderiez**	**aurais bavardé**	**auriez bavardé**
bavarderait	**bavarderaient**	**aurait bavardé**	**auraient bavardé**
6 présent du subjonctif		13 passé du subjonctif	
bavarde	**bavardions**	**aie bavardé**	**ayons bavardé**
bavardes	**bavardiez**	**aies bavardé**	**ayez bavardé**
bavarde	**bavardent**	**ait bavardé**	**aient bavardé**
7 imparfait du subjonctif		14 plus-que-parfait du subjonctif	
bavardasse	**bavardassions**	**eusse bavardé**	**eussions bavardé**
bavardasses	**bavardassiez**	**eusses bavardé**	**eussiez bavardé**
bavardât	**bavardassent**	**eût bavardé**	**eussent bavardé**

Impératif
bavarde
bavardons
bavardez

Sentences using this verb and words related to it

Aimez-vous les personnes qui bavardent tout le temps? Je connais un homme qui est bavard. Sa femme est bavarde aussi. Elle aime à parler avec abondance. Moi, je n'aime pas le bavardage. Je ne bavarde pas parce que je n'aime pas perdre mon temps.

le bavardage chitchat, chattering, talkativeness
bavard, bavarde talkative, loquacious, garrulous
perdre son temps à bavarder to waste one's time babbling
la bave drool, dribble
baver to drool
le clavardage chat (Internet); combination of **le clavier** (keyboard) and **le bavardage**
clavarder to chat (Internet)

Regular **-ir** verb

to bless, to consecrate

The Seven Simple Tenses		The Seven Compound Tenses	
Singular	Plural	Singular	Plural
1 présent de l'indicatif		8 passé composé	
bénis	**bénissons**	**ai béni**	**avons béni**
bénis	**bénissez**	**as béni**	**avez béni**
bénit	**bénissent**	**a béni**	**ont béni**
2 imparfait de l'indicatif		9 plus-que-parfait de l'indicatif	
bénissais	**bénissions**	**avais béni**	**avions béni**
bénissais	**bénissiez**	**avais béni**	**aviez béni**
bénissait	**bénissaient**	**avait béni**	**avaient béni**
3 passé simple		10 passé antérieur	
bénis	**bénîmes**	**eus béni**	**eûmes béni**
bénis	**bénîtes**	**eus béni**	**eûtes béni**
bénit	**bénirent**	**eut béni**	**eurent béni**
4 futur		11 futur antérieur	
bénirai	**bénirons**	**aurai béni**	**aurons béni**
béniras	**bénirez**	**auras béni**	**aurez béni**
bénira	**béniront**	**aura béni**	**auront béni**
5 conditionnel		12 conditionnel passé	
bénirais	**bénirions**	**aurais béni**	**aurions béni**
bénirais	**béniriez**	**aurais béni**	**auriez béni**
bénirait	**béniraient**	**aurait béni**	**auraient béni**
6 présent du subjonctif		13 passé du subjonctif	
bénisse	**bénissions**	**aie béni**	**ayons béni**
bénisses	**bénissiez**	**aies béni**	**ayez béni**
bénisse	**bénissent**	**ait béni**	**aient béni**
7 imparfait du subjonctif		14 plus-que-parfait du subjonctif	
bénisse	**bénissions**	**eusse béni**	**eussions béni**
bénisses	**bénissiez**	**eusses béni**	**eussiez béni**
bénît	**bénissent**	**eût béni**	**eussent béni**

Impératif
bénis
bénissons
bénissez

Words and expressions related to this verb
de l'eau bénite holy (blessed) water; **du pain bénit** holy (blessed) bread
le bénitier holy water font
une bénédiction blessing
dire le bénédicité to say grace (before a meal)

Do not confuse **bénir** with **blesser**, which means *to wound.*

Don't forget to study the section on defective and impersonal verbs. It's right after this main list.

blâmer (71) — Part. pr. blâmant — Part. passé blâmé

to blame

Regular **-er** verb

The Seven Simple Tenses		The Seven Compound Tenses	
Singular	Plural	Singular	Plural
1 présent de l'indicatif		8 passé composé	
blâme	**blâmons**	**ai blâmé**	**avons blâmé**
blâmes	**blâmez**	**as blâmé**	**avez blâmé**
blâme	**blâment**	**a blâmé**	**ont blâmé**
2 imparfait de l'indicatif		9 plus-que-parfait de l'indicatif	
blâmais	**blâmions**	**avais blâmé**	**avions blâmé**
blâmais	**blâmiez**	**avais blâmé**	**aviez blâmé**
blâmait	**blâmaient**	**avait blâmé**	**avaient blâmé**
3 passé simple		10 passé antérieur	
blâmai	**blâmâmes**	**eus blâmé**	**eûmes blâmé**
blâmas	**blâmâtes**	**eus blâmé**	**eûtes blâmé**
blâma	**blâmèrent**	**eut blâmé**	**eurent blâmé**
4 futur		11 futur antérieur	
blâmerai	**blâmerons**	**aurai blâmé**	**aurons blâmé**
blâmeras	**blâmerez**	**auras blâmé**	**aurez blâmé**
blâmera	**blâmeront**	**aura blâmé**	**auront blâmé**
5 conditionnel		12 conditionnel passé	
blâmerais	**blâmerions**	**aurais blâmé**	**aurions blâmé**
blâmerais	**blâmeriez**	**aurais blâmé**	**auriez blâmé**
blâmerait	**blâmeraient**	**aurait blâmé**	**auraient blâmé**
6 présent du subjonctif		13 passé du subjonctif	
blâme	**blâmions**	**aie blâmé**	**ayons blâmé**
blâmes	**blâmiez**	**aies blâmé**	**ayez blâmé**
blâme	**blâment**	**ait blâmé**	**aient blâmé**
7 imparfait du subjonctif		14 plus-que-parfait du subjonctif	
blâmasse	**blâmassions**	**eusse blâmé**	**eussions blâmé**
blâmasses	**blâmassiez**	**eusses blâmé**	**eussiez blâmé**
blâmât	**blâmassent**	**eût blâmé**	**eussent blâmé**

Impératif
blâme
blâmons
blâmez

Words and expressions related to this verb

être blâmé (blâmée) to be blamed
le blâme blame
blasphémer to blaspheme
se blâmer to blame oneself
blâmable blameworthy, blamable
le blasphème blasphemy

Don't forget to use the English-French verb index. It's in the Appendixes.

Regular **-ir** verb

to whiten, to launder, to exonerate

The Seven Simple Tenses		The Seven Compound Tenses	
Singular	Plural	Singular	Plural
1 présent de l'indicatif		8 passé composé	
blanchis	**blanchissons**	**ai blanchi**	**avons blanchi**
blanchis	**blanchissez**	**as blanchi**	**avez blanchi**
blanchit	**blanchissent**	**a blanchi**	**ont blanchi**
2 imparfait de l'indicatif		9 plus-que-parfait de l'indicatif	
blanchissais	**blanchissions**	**avais blanchi**	**avions blanchi**
blanchissais	**blanchissiez**	**avais blanchi**	**aviez blanchi**
blanchissait	**blanchissaient**	**avait blanchi**	**avaient blanchi**
3 passé simple		10 passé antérieur	
blanchis	**blanchîmes**	**eus blanchi**	**eûmes blanchi**
blanchis	**blanchîtes**	**eus blanchi**	**eûtes blanchi**
blanchit	**blanchirent**	**eut blanchi**	**eurent blanchi**
4 futur		11 futur antérieur	
blanchirai	**blanchirons**	**aurai blanchi**	**aurons blanchi**
blanchiras	**blanchirez**	**auras blanchi**	**aurez blanchi**
blanchira	**blanchiront**	**aura blanchi**	**auront blanchi**
5 conditionnel		12 conditionnel passé	
blanchirais	**blanchirions**	**aurais blanchi**	**aurions blanchi**
blanchirais	**blanchiriez**	**aurais blanchi**	**auriez blanchi**
blanchirait	**blanchiraient**	**aurait blanchi**	**auraient blanchi**
6 présent du subjonctif		13 passé du subjonctif	
blanchisse	**blanchissions**	**aie blanchi**	**ayons blanchi**
blanchisses	**blanchissiez**	**aies blanchi**	**ayez blanchi**
blanchisse	**blanchissent**	**ait blanchi**	**aient blanchi**
7 imparfait du subjonctif		14 plus-que-parfait du subjonctif	
blanchisse	**blanchissions**	**eusse blanchi**	**eussions blanchi**
blanchisses	**blanchissiez**	**eusses blanchi**	**eussiez blanchi**
blanchît	**blanchissent**	**eût blanchi**	**eussent blanchi**

Impératif
blanchis
blanchissons
blanchissez

Common idiomatic expressions using this verb and words related to it

le blanc white
le blanc d'oeil the white of the eye
la bille blanche white billiard ball
du vin blanc white wine
la blanchisserie laundry (store where clothes are washed)
carte blanche unlimited privileges and authority
blanc comme neige as white as snow
Blanche-Neige Snow White
un chèque en blanc blank check
un verre de blanc a glass of white wine
le blanchissage washing
Le maire a été blanchi des accusations de corruption. The mayor was cleared of the charges of corruption.

The subject pronouns are found on page 103.

blesser (73) — Part. pr. **blessant** — Part. passé **blessé**

to harm, to hurt, to injure, to wound, to offend

Regular **-er** verb

The Seven Simple Tenses		The Seven Compound Tenses	
Singular	Plural	Singular	Plural
1 présent de l'indicatif		8 passé composé	
blesse	**blessons**	**ai blessé**	**avons blessé**
blesses	**blessez**	**as blessé**	**avez blessé**
blesse	**blessent**	**a blessé**	**ont blessé**
2 imparfait de l'indicatif		9 plus-que-parfait de l'indicatif	
blessais	**blessions**	**avais blessé**	**avions blessé**
blessais	**blessiez**	**avais blessé**	**aviez blessé**
blessait	**blessaient**	**avait blessé**	**avaient blessé**
3 passé simple		10 passé antérieur	
blessai	**blessâmes**	**eus blessé**	**eûmes blessé**
blessas	**blessâtes**	**eus blessé**	**eûtes blessé**
blessa	**blessèrent**	**eut blessé**	**eurent blessé**
4 futur		11 futur antérieur	
blesserai	**blesserons**	**aurai blessé**	**aurons blessé**
blesseras	**blesserez**	**auras blessé**	**aurez blessé**
blessera	**blesseront**	**aura blessé**	**auront blessé**
5 conditionnel		12 conditionnel passé	
blesserais	**blesserions**	**aurais blessé**	**aurions blessé**
blesserais	**blesseriez**	**aurais blessé**	**auriez blessé**
blesserait	**blesseraient**	**aurait blessé**	**auraient blessé**
6 présent du subjonctif		13 passé du subjonctif	
blesse	**blessions**	**aie blessé**	**ayons blessé**
blesses	**blessiez**	**aies blessé**	**ayez blessé**
blesse	**blessent**	**ait blessé**	**aient blessé**
7 imparfait du subjonctif		14 plus-que-parfait du subjonctif	
blessasse	**blessassions**	**eusse blessé**	**eussions blessé**
blessasses	**blessassiez**	**eusses blessé**	**eussiez blessé**
blessât	**blessassent**	**eût blessé**	**eussent blessé**

Impératif
blesse
blessons
blessez

Sentences using this verb and words related to it

Ma soeur est tombée sur un rocher qui l'a blessée au visage. Ce fut* une blessure grave.

blesser à mort to wound mortally
une blessure wound, injury
une parole blessante a cutting word
être blessé à la jambe (au bras) to be injured in the leg (in the arm)

See also **se blesser.**

*The verb form **fut** is the **passé simple** of **être.**

Do not confuse **blesser** with **bénir,** which means *to bless.*

Reflexive regular **-er** verb

to hurt oneself, to injure oneself, to wound oneself

The Seven Simple Tenses		The Seven Compound Tenses	
Singular	Plural	Singular	Plural
1 présent de l'indicatif		8 passé composé	
me blesse	**nous blessons**	**me suis blessé(e)**	**nous sommes blessé(e)s**
te blesses	**vous blessez**	**t'es blessé(e)**	**vous êtes blessé(e)(s)**
se blesse	**se blessent**	**s'est blessé(e)**	**se sont blessé(e)s**
2 imparfait de l'indicatif		9 plus-que-parfait de l'indicatif	
me blessais	**nous blessions**	**m'étais blessé(e)**	**nous étions blessé(e)s**
te blessais	**vous blessiez**	**t'étais blessé(e)**	**vous étiez blessé(e)(s)**
se blessait	**se blessaient**	**s'était blessé(e)**	**s'étaient blessé(e)s**
3 passé simple		10 passé antérieur	
me blessai	**nous blessâmes**	**me fus blessé(e)**	**nous fûmes blessé(e)s**
te blessas	**vous blessâtes**	**te fus blessé(e)**	**vous fûtes blessé(e)(s)**
se blessa	**se blessèrent**	**se fut blessé(e)**	**se furent blessé(e)s**
4 futur		11 futur antérieur	
me blesserai	**nous blesserons**	**me serai blessé(e)**	**nous serons blessé(e)s**
te blesseras	**vous blesserez**	**te seras blessé(e)**	**vous serez blessé(e)(s)**
se blessera	**se blesseront**	**se sera blessé(e)**	**se seront blessé(e)s**
5 conditionnel		12 conditionnel passé	
me blesserais	**nous blesserions**	**me serais blessé(e)**	**nous serions blessé(e)s**
te blesserais	**vous blesseriez**	**te serais blessé(e)**	**vous seriez blessé(e)(s)**
se blesserait	**se blesseraient**	**se serait blessé(e)**	**se seraient blessé(e)s**
6 présent du subjonctif		13 passé du subjonctif	
me blesse	**nous blessions**	**me sois blessé(e)**	**nous soyons blessé(e)s**
te blesses	**vous blessiez**	**te sois blessé(e)**	**vous soyez blessé(e)(s)**
se blesse	**se blessent**	**se soit blessé(e)**	**se soient blessé(e)s**
7 imparfait du subjonctif		14 plus-que-parfait du subjonctif	
me blessasse	**nous blessassions**	**me fusse blessé(e)**	**nous fussions blessé(e)s**
te blessasses	**vous blessassiez**	**te fusses blessé(e)**	**vous fussiez blessé(e)(s)**
se blessât	**se blessassent**	**se fût blessé(e)**	**se fussent blessé(e)s**

Impératif
blesse-toi; ne te blesse pas
blessons-nous; ne nous blessons pas
blessez-vous; ne vous blessez pas

Sentences using this verb and words related to it

Madame Leblanc est tombée dans la rue et elle s'est blessée au genou. Ce fut* une blessure légère, heureusement.

se blesser de to take offense at

se blesser pour un rien to be easily offended

For other words and expressions related to this verb, see **blesser**.

*The verb form **fut** is the **passé simple** of **être.**

Do not confuse **blesser** and **se blesser** with **bénir,** which means *to bless.*

boire (75)

Part. pr. **buvant** Part. passé **bu**

to drink

Irregular verb

The Seven Simple Tenses		The Seven Compound Tenses	
Singular	Plural	Singular	Plural
1 présent de l'indicatif		8 passé composé	
bois	**buvons**	**ai bu**	**avons bu**
bois	**buvez**	**as bu**	**avez bu**
boit	**boivent**	**a bu**	**ont bu**
2 imparfait de l'indicatif		9 plus-que-parfait de l'indicatif	
buvais	**buvions**	**avais bu**	**avions bu**
buvais	**buviez**	**avais bu**	**aviez bu**
buvait	**buvaient**	**avait bu**	**avaient bu**
3 passé simple		10 passé antérieur	
bus	**bûmes**	**eus bu**	**eûmes bu**
bus	**bûtes**	**eus bu**	**eûtes bu**
but	**burent**	**eut bu**	**eurent bu**
4 futur		11 futur antérieur	
boirai	**boirons**	**aurai bu**	**aurons bu**
boiras	**boirez**	**auras bu**	**aurez bu**
boira	**boiront**	**aura bu**	**auront bu**
5 conditionnel		12 conditionnel passé	
boirais	**boirions**	**aurais bu**	**aurions bu**
boirais	**boiriez**	**aurais bu**	**auriez bu**
boirait	**boiraient**	**aurait bu**	**auraient bu**
6 présent du subjonctif		13 passé du subjonctif	
boive	**buvions**	**aie bu**	**ayons bu**
boives	**buviez**	**aies bu**	**ayez bu**
boive	**boivent**	**ait bu**	**aient bu**
7 imparfait du subjonctif		14 plus-que-parfait du subjonctif	
busse	**bussions**	**eusse bu**	**eussions bu**
busses	**bussiez**	**eusses bu**	**eussiez bu**
bût	**bussent**	**eût bu**	**eussent bu**

Impératif
bois
buvons
buvez

AN ESSENTIAL 55 VERB

Boire

B

Boire is a very useful verb for a beginning French student. Pay attention to its irregular conjugation pattern.

Sentences using boire and related words

Boire un petit coup, c'est agréable! It's pleasant to have a little drink. (French song)

Il pleut à boire debout! It's raining hard! (It's raining so hard you could drink standing up.)

—René, as-tu bu ton lait?
—Non, maman, je ne l'ai pas bu.
—Bois-le tout de suite, je te dis.
—Tous les jours je bois du lait. N'y a-t-il pas d'autres boissons dans la maison?
—Si, il y a d'autres boissons dans la maison mais les bons garçons comme toi boivent du lait.

(Note that **si** is used instead of **oui** for *yes* in answer to a question in the negative.)

—René, did you drink your milk?
—No, Mother, I didn't drink it.
—I'm telling you: drink it right away.
—I drink milk every day. Aren't there other drinks in the house?
—Yes, there are other drinks in the house, but good boys like you drink milk.

Words and expressions related to this verb

boire à la santé de qqn **to drink to someone's health**

boire à la bouteille **to drink right out of the bottle**

boire à sa soif **to drink to one's heart's content**

boire comme un trou **to drink too much (alcohol)**

un buveur, une buveuse **drinker**

une buvette **bar**

un buvard **ink blotter**

boire un coup **to have a drink**

une boisson **drink**

une boisson gazeuse **carbonated drink**

un breuvage **beverage**

The subject pronouns are found on page 103.

bouger (76) — Part. pr. **bougeant** — Part. passé **bougé**

to budge, to move

Regular **-er** verb endings; spelling change: retain the **ge** before **a** or **o** to keep the soft **g** sound of the verb

The Seven Simple Tenses		The Seven Compound Tenses	
Singular	Plural	Singular	Plural
1 présent de l'indicatif		8 passé composé	
bouge	**bougeons**	**ai bougé**	**avons bougé**
bouges	**bougez**	**as bougé**	**avez bougé**
bouge	**bougent**	**a bougé**	**ont bougé**
2 imparfait de l'indicatif		9 plus-que-parfait de l'indicatif	
bougeais	**bougions**	**avais bougé**	**avions bougé**
bougeais	**bougiez**	**avais bougé**	**aviez bougé**
bougeait	**bougeaient**	**avait bougé**	**avaient bougé**
3 passé simple		10 passé antérieur	
bougeai	**bougeâmes**	**eus bougé**	**eûmes bougé**
bougeas	**bougeâtes**	**eus bougé**	**eûtes bougé**
bougea	**bougèrent**	**eut bougé**	**eurent bougé**
4 futur		11 futur antérieur	
bougerai	**bougerons**	**aurai bougé**	**aurons bougé**
bougeras	**bougerez**	**auras bougé**	**aurez bougé**
bougera	**bougeront**	**aura bougé**	**auront bougé**
5 conditionnel		12 conditionnel passé	
bougerais	**bougerions**	**aurais bougé**	**aurions bougé**
bougerais	**bougeriez**	**aurais bougé**	**auriez bougé**
bougerait	**bougeraient**	**aurait bougé**	**auraient bougé**
6 présent du subjonctif		13 passé du subjonctif	
bouge	**bougions**	**aie bougé**	**ayons bougé**
bouges	**bougiez**	**aies bougé**	**ayez bougé**
bouge	**bougent**	**ait bougé**	**aient bougé**
7 imparfait du subjonctif		14 plus-que-parfait du subjonctif	
bougeasse	**bougeassions**	**eusse bougé**	**eussions bougé**
bougeasses	**bougeassiez**	**eusses bougé**	**eussiez bougé**
bougeât	**bougeassent**	**eût bougé**	**eussent bougé**

Impératif
bouge
bougeons
bougez

Words and expressions related to this verb

avoir la bougeotte to be on the move; to be restless, to move about restlessly; to be fidgety
La terre a bougé. The ground shook.

ne pas bouger not to make a move; **Personne n'a bougé.** Nobody moved.

Get acquainted with what preposition goes with what verb. See *Verbs with prepositions* in the Appendixes.

Don't miss orthographically changing verbs on pages 32–34.

Irregular verb

to boil

The Seven Simple Tenses		The Seven Compound Tenses	
Singular	Plural	Singular	Plural
1 présent de l'indicatif		8 passé composé	
bous	**bouillons**	**ai bouilli**	**avons bouilli**
bous	**bouillez**	**as bouilli**	**avez bouilli**
bout	**bouillent**	**a bouilli**	**ont bouilli**
2 imparfait de l'indicatif		9 plus-que-parfait de l'indicatif	
bouillais	**bouillions**	**avais bouilli**	**avions bouilli**
bouillais	**bouilliez**	**avais bouilli**	**aviez bouilli**
bouillait	**bouillaient**	**avait bouilli**	**avaient bouilli**
3 passé simple		10 passé antérieur	
bouillis	**bouillîmes**	**eus bouilli**	**eûmes bouilli**
bouillis	**bouillîtes**	**eus bouilli**	**eûtes bouilli**
bouillit	**bouillirent**	**eut bouilli**	**eurent bouilli**
4 futur		11 futur antérieur	
bouillirai	**bouillirons**	**aurai bouilli**	**aurons bouilli**
bouilliras	**bouillirez**	**auras bouilli**	**aurez bouilli**
bouillira	**bouilliront**	**aura bouilli**	**auront bouilli**
5 conditionnel		12 conditionnel passé	
bouillirais	**bouillirions**	**aurais bouilli**	**aurions bouilli**
bouillirais	**bouilliriez**	**aurais bouilli**	**auriez bouilli**
bouillirait	**bouilliraient**	**aurait bouilli**	**auraient bouilli**
6 présent du subjonctif		13 passé du subjonctif	
bouille	**bouillions**	**aie bouilli**	**ayons bouilli**
bouilles	**bouilliez**	**aies bouilli**	**ayez bouilli**
bouille	**bouillent**	**ait bouilli**	**aient bouilli**
7 imparfait du subjonctif		14 plus-que-parfait du subjonctif	
bouillisse	**bouillissions**	**eusse bouilli**	**eussions bouilli**
bouillisses	**bouillissiez**	**eusses bouilli**	**eussiez bouilli**
bouillît	**bouillissent**	**eût bouilli**	**eussent bouilli**

Impératif
bous
bouillons
bouillez

Words and expressions related to this verb

faire bouillir to boil
le bouillon broth; bubble
une bulle *(ewn bewl)* bubble, blister
faire des bulles to blow bubbles
la bouillabaisse fish soup (chowder)
le bouillonnement bubbling, boiling
faire donner un bouillon to bring to boil
une bulle de savon soap bubble
une bouilloire kettle
réduire en bouillie to beat to a pulp
la bouillie baby food, cereal, porridge
manger de la bouillie to speak badly, mumble

Use the guide to French pronunciation. It's in the Appendixes.

See the summary of sequence of tenses with **si** (*if*) clauses on page 26.

brancher (78) — Part. pr. branchant — Part. passé branché

to plug in, to connect

Regular **-er** verb

The Seven Simple Tenses		The Seven Compound Tenses	
Singular	Plural	Singular	Plural
1 présent de l'indicatif		8 passé composé	
branche	**branchons**	**ai branché**	**avons branché**
branches	**branchez**	**as branché**	**avez branché**
branche	**branchent**	**a branché**	**ont branché**
2 imparfait de l'indicatif		9 plus-que-parfait de l'indicatif	
branchais	**branchions**	**avais branché**	**avions branché**
branchais	**branchiez**	**avais branché**	**aviez branché**
branchait	**branchaient**	**avait branché**	**avaient branché**
3 passé simple		10 passé antérieur	
branchai	**branchâmes**	**eus branché**	**eûmes branché**
branchas	**branchâtes**	**eus branché**	**eûtes branché**
brancha	**branchèrent**	**eut branché**	**eurent branché**
4 futur		11 futur antérieur	
brancherai	**brancherons**	**aurai branché**	**aurons branché**
brancheras	**brancherez**	**auras branché**	**aurez branché**
branchera	**brancheront**	**aura branché**	**auront branché**
5 conditionnel		12 conditionnel passé	
brancherais	**brancherions**	**aurais branché**	**aurions branché**
brancherais	**brancheriez**	**aurais branché**	**auriez branché**
brancherait	**brancheraient**	**aurait branché**	**auraient branché**
6 présent du subjonctif		13 passé du subjonctif	
branche	**branchions**	**aie branché**	**ayons branché**
branches	**branchiez**	**aies branché**	**ayez branché**
branche	**branchent**	**ait branché**	**aient branché**
7 imparfait du subjonctif		14 plus-que-parfait du subjonctif	
branchasse	**branchassions**	**eusse branché**	**eussions branché**
branchasses	**branchassiez**	**eusses branché**	**eussiez branché**
branchât	**branchassent**	**eût branché**	**eussent branché**

Impératif
branche
branchons
branchez

Sentences using this verb and words related to it

Pierre est branché sur le jardinage. Pierre is into gardening.

Branche ton modem sur le bon port de ton ordinateur. Plug your modem into the correct port on your computer.

Words and expressions related to this verb

débrancher to unplug, disconnect

une branche branch

ma vieille branche my old friend

Don't forget to study the section on defective and impersonal verbs. It's right after this main list.

Regular **-er** verb

to brush

The Seven Simple Tenses		The Seven Compound Tenses	
Singular	Plural	Singular	Plural
1 présent de l'indicatif		8 passé composé	
brosse	**brossons**	**ai brossé**	**avons brossé**
brosses	**brossez**	**as brossé**	**avez brossé**
brosse	**brossent**	**a brossé**	**ont brossé**
2 imparfait de l'indicatif		9 plus-que-parfait de l'indicatif	
brossais	**brossions**	**avais brossé**	**avions brossé**
brossais	**brossiez**	**avais brossé**	**aviez brossé**
brossait	**brossaient**	**avait brossé**	**avaient brossé**
3 passé simple		10 passé antérieur	
brossai	**brossâmes**	**eus brossé**	**eûmes brossé**
brossas	**brossâtes**	**eus brossé**	**eûtes brossé**
brossa	**brossèrent**	**eut brossé**	**eurent brossé**
4 futur		11 futur antérieur	
brosserai	**brosserons**	**aurai brossé**	**aurons brossé**
brosseras	**brosserez**	**auras brossé**	**aurez brossé**
brossera	**brosseront**	**aura brossé**	**auront brossé**
5 conditionnel		12 conditionnel passé	
brosserais	**brosserions**	**aurais brossé**	**aurions brossé**
brosserais	**brosseriez**	**aurais brossé**	**auriez brossé**
brosserait	**brosseraient**	**aurait brossé**	**auraient brossé**
6 présent du subjonctif		13 passé du subjonctif	
brosse	**brossions**	**aie brossé**	**ayons brossé**
brosses	**brossiez**	**aies brossé**	**ayez brossé**
brosse	**brossent**	**ait brossé**	**aient brossé**
7 imparfait du subjonctif		14 plus-que-parfait du subjonctif	
brossasse	**brossassions**	**eusse brossé**	**eussions brossé**
brossasses	**brossassiez**	**eusses brossé**	**eussiez brossé**
brossât	**brossassent**	**eût brossé**	**eussent brossé**

Impératif
brosse
brossons
brossez

Sentences using this verb and words related to it

—Henriette, as-tu brossé tes souliers?
—Non, maman, je ne les ai pas brossés.
—Et pourquoi pas, ma petite?
—Parce que je n'ai pas de brosse.

une brosse brush; **brosse à chaussures** shoebrush; **brosse à dents** toothbrush; **brosse à ongles** nailbrush
donner un coup de brosse to brush
le brossage brushing

See also **se brosser.**

If you don't know the French verb for an English verb you have in mind, try the index in the Appendixes.

se brosser (80) — Part. pr. se brossant — Part. passé brossé(e)(s)

to brush oneself

Reflexive regular **-er** verb

The Seven Simple Tenses		The Seven Compound Tenses	
Singular	Plural	Singular	Plural
1 présent de l'indicatif		8 passé composé	
me brosse	**nous brossons**	**me suis brossé(e)**	**nous sommes brossé(e)s**
te brosses	**vous brossez**	**t'es brossé(e)**	**vous êtes brossé(e)(s)**
se brosse	**se brossent**	**s'est brossé(e)**	**se sont brossé(e)s**
2 imparfait de l'indicatif		9 plus-que-parfait de l'indicatif	
me brossais	**nous brossions**	**m'étais brossé(e)**	**nous étions brossé(e)s**
te brossais	**vous brossiez**	**t'étais brossé(e)**	**vous étiez brossé(e)(s)**
se brossait	**se brossaient**	**s'était brossé(e)**	**s'étaient brossé(e)s**
3 passé simple		10 passé antérieur	
me brossai	**nous brossâmes**	**me fus brossé(e)**	**nous fûmes brossé(e)s**
te brossas	**vous brossâtes**	**te fus brossé(e)**	**vous fûtes brossé(e)(s)**
se brossa	**se brossèrent**	**se fut brossé(e)**	**se furent brossé(e)s**
4 futur		11 futur antérieur	
me brosserai	**nous brosserons**	**me serai brossé(e)**	**nous serons brossé(e)s**
te brosseras	**vous brosserez**	**te seras brossé(e)**	**vous serez brossé(e)(s)**
se brossera	**se brosseront**	**se sera brossé(e)**	**se seront brossé(e)s**
5 conditionnel		12 conditionnel passé	
me brosserais	**nous brosserions**	**me serais brossé(e)**	**nous serions brossé(e)s**
te brosserais	**vous brosseriez**	**te serais brossé(e)**	**vous seriez brossé(e)(s)**
se brosserait	**se brosseraient**	**se serait brossé(e)**	**se seraient brossé(e)s**
6 présent du subjonctif		13 passé du subjonctif	
me brosse	**nous brossions**	**me sois brossé(e)**	**nous soyons brossé(e)s**
te brosses	**vous brossiez**	**te sois brossé(e)**	**vous soyez brossé(e)(s)**
se brosse	**se brossent**	**se soit brossé(e)**	**se soient brossé(e)s**
7 imparfait du subjonctif		14 plus-que-parfait du subjonctif	
me brossasse	**nous brossassions**	**me fusse brossé(e)**	**nous fussions brossé(e)s**
te brossasses	**vous brossassiez**	**te fusses brossé(e)**	**vous fussiez brossé(e)(s)**
se brossât	**se brossassent**	**se fût brossé(e)**	**se fussent brossé(e)s**

Impératif
brosse-toi; ne te brosse pas
brossons-nous; ne nous brossons pas
brossez-vous; ne vous brossez pas

Sentences using this verb and words related to it

—Tina Marie, est-ce que tu t'es brossée?
—Non, maman, je ne me suis pas brossée.
—Et pourquoi pas? Brosse-toi vite!
—Parce que je n'ai pas de brosse à habits, je n'ai pas de brosse à cheveux, je n'ai pas de brosse à chaussures. Je n'ai aucune brosse. Je n'ai pas de brosse à dents, non plus.
—Quelle fille!

se brosser les dents, les cheveux, etc. to brush one's teeth, hair, etc.

For other words and expressions related to this verb, see **brosser.**

If you want to see a sample English verb fully conjugated in all the tenses, check out pages 8 and 9.

Regular **-er** verb

to burn

The Seven Simple Tenses		The Seven Compound Tenses	
Singular	Plural	Singular	Plural
1 présent de l'indicatif		8 passé composé	
brûle	**brûlons**	**ai brûlé**	**avons brûlé**
brûles	**brûlez**	**as brûlé**	**avez brûlé**
brûle	**brûlent**	**a brûlé**	**ont brûlé**
2 imparfait de l'indicatif		9 plus-que-parfait de l'indicatif	
brûlais	**brûlions**	**avais brûlé**	**avions brûlé**
brûlais	**brûliez**	**avais brûlé**	**aviez brûlé**
brûlait	**brûlaient**	**avait brûlé**	**avaient brûlé**
3 passé simple		10 passé antérieur	
brûlai	**brûlâmes**	**eus brûlé**	**eûmes brûlé**
brûlas	**brûlâtes**	**eus brûlé**	**eûtes brûlé**
brûla	**brûlèrent**	**eut brûlé**	**eurent brûlé**
4 futur		11 futur antérieur	
brûlerai	**brûlerons**	**aurai brûlé**	**aurons brûlé**
brûleras	**brûlerez**	**auras brûlé**	**aurez brûlé**
brûlera	**brûleront**	**aura brûlé**	**auront brûlé**
5 conditionnel		12 conditionnel passé	
brûlerais	**brûlerions**	**aurais brûlé**	**aurions brûlé**
brûlerais	**brûleriez**	**aurais brûlé**	**auriez brûlé**
brûlerait	**brûleraient**	**aurait brûlé**	**auraient brûlé**
6 présent du subjonctif		13 passé du subjonctif	
brûle	**brûlions**	**aie brûlé**	**ayons brûlé**
brûles	**brûliez**	**aies brûlé**	**ayez brûlé**
brûle	**brûlent**	**ait brûlé**	**aient brûlé**
7 imparfait du subjonctif		14 plus-que-parfait du subjonctif	
brûlasse	**brûlassions**	**eusse brûlé**	**eussions brûlé**
brûlasses	**brûlassiez**	**eusses brûlé**	**eussiez brûlé**
brûlât	**brûlassent**	**eût brûlé**	**eussent brûlé**

Impératif
brûle
brûlons
brûlez

Sentences using this verb and words related to it

—Joséphine, avez-vous brûlé les vieux papiers que je vous ai donnés?
—Oui, madame, et je me suis brûlée. J'ai une brûlure aux doigts.

une brûlure burn
un brûleur burner, roaster
brûler d'amour to be madly in love
brûler de faire qqch to be eager to do something
brûler un feu rouge to pass through a red traffic light
une crème brûlée a crème brûlée (dessert)

It's important that you be familiar with the Subjunctive. See pages 26–31.

cacher (82) — Part. pr. **cachant** — Part. passé **caché**

to hide

Regular **-er** verb

The Seven Simple Tenses		The Seven Compound Tenses	
Singular	Plural	Singular	Plural
1 présent de l'indicatif		8 passé composé	
cache	**cachons**	**ai caché**	**avons caché**
caches	**cachez**	**as caché**	**avez caché**
cache	**cachent**	**a caché**	**ont caché**
2 imparfait de l'indicatif		9 plus-que-parfait de l'indicatif	
cachais	**cachions**	**avais caché**	**avions caché**
cachais	**cachiez**	**avais caché**	**aviez caché**
cachait	**cachaient**	**avait caché**	**avaient caché**
3 passé simple		10 passé antérieur	
cachai	**cachâmes**	**eus caché**	**eûmes caché**
cachas	**cachâtes**	**eus caché**	**eûtes caché**
cacha	**cachèrent**	**eut caché**	**eurent caché**
4 futur		11 futur antérieur	
cacherai	**cacherons**	**aurai caché**	**aurons caché**
cacheras	**cacherez**	**auras caché**	**aurez caché**
cachera	**cacheront**	**aura caché**	**auront caché**
5 conditionnel		12 conditionnel passé	
cacherais	**cacherions**	**aurais caché**	**aurions caché**
cacherais	**cacheriez**	**aurais caché**	**auriez caché**
cacherait	**cacheraient**	**aurait caché**	**auraient caché**
6 présent du subjonctif		13 passé du subjonctif	
cache	**cachions**	**aie caché**	**ayons caché**
caches	**cachiez**	**aies caché**	**ayez caché**
cache	**cachent**	**ait caché**	**aient caché**
7 imparfait du subjonctif		14 plus-que-parfait du subjonctif	
cachasse	**cachassions**	**eusse caché**	**eussions caché**
cachasses	**cachassiez**	**eusses caché**	**eussiez caché**
cachât	**cachassent**	**eût caché**	**eussent caché**

Impératif
cache
cachons
cachez

Sentences using this verb and words related to it

—Pierre, qu'est-ce que tu as caché derrière toi?
—Rien, papa.
—Ne me dis pas ça. Tu caches quelque chose.
—Voilà, papa, c'est un petit chat que j'ai trouvé dans le parc.

une cache, une cachette hiding place
la cache cache (computer)
un cachet seal, mark
un cachetage sealing
cacheter to seal up

See also **se cacher.**

le cache-cache hide-and-seek
le vin cacheté vintage wine
cacher qqch à qqn to hide something from someone
un cache-nez muffler
en cachette in secret

Reflexive regular **-er** verb

to hide oneself

The Seven Simple Tenses		The Seven Compound Tenses	
Singular	Plural	Singular	Plural
1 présent de l'indicatif		8 passé composé	
me cache	**nous cachons**	**me suis caché(e)**	**nous sommes caché(e)s**
te caches	**vous cachez**	**t'es caché(e)**	**vous êtes caché(e)(s)**
se cache	**se cachent**	**s'est caché(e)**	**se sont caché(e)s**
2 imparfait de l'indicatif		9 plus-que-parfait de l'indicatif	
me cachais	**nous cachions**	**m'étais caché(e)**	**nous étions caché(e)s**
te cachais	**vous cachiez**	**t'étais caché(e)**	**vous étiez caché(e)(s)**
se cachait	**se cachaient**	**s'était caché(e)**	**s'étaient caché(e)s**
3 passé simple		10 passé antérieur	
me cachai	**nous cachâmes**	**me fus caché(e)**	**nous fûmes caché(e)s**
te cachas	**vous cachâtes**	**te fus caché(e)**	**vous fûtes caché(e)(s)**
se cacha	**se cachèrent**	**se fut caché(e)**	**se furent caché(e)s**
4 futur		11 futur antérieur	
me cacherai	**nous cacherons**	**me serai caché(e)**	**nous serons caché(e)s**
te cacheras	**vous cacherez**	**te seras caché(e)**	**vous serez caché(e)(s)**
se cachera	**se cacheront**	**se sera caché(e)**	**se seront caché(e)s**
5 conditionnel		12 conditionnel passé	
me cacherais	**nous cacherions**	**me serais caché(e)**	**nous serions caché(e)s**
te cacherais	**vous cacheriez**	**te serais caché(e)**	**vous seriez caché(e)(s)**
se cacherait	**se cacheraient**	**se serait caché(e)**	**se seraient caché(e)s**
6 présent du subjonctif		13 passé du subjonctif	
me cache	**nous cachions**	**me sois caché(e)**	**nous soyons caché(e)s**
te caches	**vous cachiez**	**te sois caché(e)**	**vous soyez caché(e)(s)**
se cache	**se cachent**	**se soit caché(e)**	**se soient caché(e)s**
7 imparfait du subjonctif		14 plus-que-parfait du subjonctif	
me cachasse	**nous cachassions**	**me fusse caché(e)**	**nous fussions caché(e)s**
te cachasses	**vous cachassiez**	**te fusses caché(e)**	**vous fussiez caché(e)(s)**
se cachât	**se cachassent**	**se fût caché(e)**	**se fussent caché(e)s**

Impératif
cache-toi; ne te cache pas
cachons-nous; ne nous cachons pas
cachez-vous; ne vous cachez pas

Sentences using this verb and words related to it

J'ai un petit chien que j'appelle Coco. Quelquefois je ne peux pas le trouver parce qu'il se cache sous mon lit ou derrière l'arbre dans le jardin. La semaine dernière il s'est caché sous le chapeau de mon père. Il aime jouer à cache-cache. Il est très intelligent.

une cache, une cachette hiding place
un cachet seal, mark
un cachetage sealing
se cacher de qqn to hide from someone
cacheter to seal up
le cache-cache hide-and-seek
le vin cacheté vintage wine
un cachot cell, prison; dungeon
en cachette de qqn behind someone's back

See also **cacher.**

to break

Regular **-er** verb

The Seven Simple Tenses		The Seven Compound Tenses	
Singular	Plural	Singular	Plural
1 présent de l'indicatif		8 passé composé	
casse	**cassons**	**ai cassé**	**avons cassé**
casses	**cassez**	**as cassé**	**avez cassé**
casse	**cassent**	**a cassé**	**ont cassé**
2 imparfait de l'indicatif		9 plus-que-parfait de l'indicatif	
cassais	**cassions**	**avais cassé**	**avions cassé**
cassais	**cassiez**	**avais cassé**	**aviez cassé**
cassait	**cassaient**	**avait cassé**	**avaient cassé**
3 passé simple		10 passé antérieur	
cassai	**cassâmes**	**eus cassé**	**eûmes cassé**
cassas	**cassâtes**	**eus cassé**	**eûtes cassé**
cassa	**cassèrent**	**eut cassé**	**eurent cassé**
4 futur		11 futur antérieur	
casserai	**casserons**	**aurai cassé**	**aurons cassé**
casseras	**casserez**	**auras cassé**	**aurez cassé**
cassera	**casseront**	**aura cassé**	**auront cassé**
5 conditionnel		12 conditionnel passé	
casserais	**casserions**	**aurais cassé**	**aurions cassé**
casserais	**casseriez**	**aurais cassé**	**auriez cassé**
casserait	**casseraient**	**aurait cassé**	**auraient cassé**
6 présent du subjonctif		13 passé du subjonctif	
casse	**cassions**	**aie cassé**	**ayons cassé**
casses	**cassiez**	**aies cassé**	**ayez cassé**
casse	**cassent**	**ait cassé**	**aient cassé**
7 imparfait du subjonctif		14 plus-que-parfait du subjonctif	
cassasse	**cassassions**	**eusse cassé**	**eussions cassé**
cassasses	**cassassiez**	**eusses cassé**	**eussiez cassé**
cassât	**cassassent**	**eût cassé**	**eussent cassé**

Impératif
casse
cassons
cassez

Sentences using this verb and words related to it

—Jean, c'est toi qui as cassé mon joli vase? John, is it you who broke my pretty vase?
—Non, maman, c'est Mathilde. No, Mother, it was Mathilda.
—Mathilde, c'est toi qui as cassé mon joli vase? Mathilda, is it you who broke my pretty vase?
—Non, maman, c'est Jean. No, Mother, it was John.
—Quels enfants! What children!

une casse breakage, damage
un casse-croûte snack
un casse-noisettes, un casse-noix nutcracker
casser la croûte to have a snack
un casse-pieds a bore, a pain in the neck
un cassement de tête puzzle, worry

See also **se casser.**

un casse-tête puzzle
concasser to crush (cereal, sugar lumps, stones)
casser la tête à qqn to pester someone
casser les oreilles à qqn to bore someone stiff (by talking too much)
casser les pieds à qqn to be a pain in the neck to someone

Reflexive regular **-er** verb

to break (a part of one's body, *e.g.*, leg, arm, nose)

The Seven Simple Tenses		The Seven Compound Tenses	
Singular	Plural	Singular	Plural
1 présent de l'indicatif		8 passé composé	
me casse	**nous cassons**	**me suis cassé(e)**	**nous sommes cassé(e)s**
te casses	**vous cassez**	**t'es cassé(e)**	**vous êtes cassé(e)(s)**
se casse	**se cassent**	**s'est cassé(e)**	**se sont cassé(e)s**
2 imparfait de l'indicatif		9 plus-que-parfait de l'indicatif	
me cassais	**nous cassions**	**m'étais cassé(e)**	**nous étions cassé(e)s**
te cassais	**vous cassiez**	**t'étais cassé(e)**	**vous étiez cassé(e)(s)**
se cassait	**se cassaient**	**s'était cassé(e)**	**s'étaient cassé(e)s**
3 passé simple		10 passé antérieur	
me cassai	**nous cassâmes**	**me fus cassé(e)**	**nous fûmes cassé(e)s**
te cassas	**vous cassâtes**	**te fus cassé(e)**	**vous fûtes cassé(e)(s)**
se cassa	**se cassèrent**	**se fut cassé(e)**	**se furent cassé(e)s**
4 futur		11 futur antérieur	
me casserai	**nous casserons**	**me serai cassé(e)**	**nous serons cassé(e)s**
te casseras	**vous casserez**	**te seras cassé(e)**	**vous serez cassé(e)(s)**
se cassera	**se casseront**	**se sera cassé(e)**	**se seront cassé(e)s**
5 conditionnel		12 conditionnel passé	
me casserais	**nous casserions**	**me serais cassé(e)**	**nous serions cassé(e)s**
te casserais	**vous casseriez**	**te serais cassé(e)**	**vous seriez cassé(e)(s)**
se casserait	**se casseraient**	**se serait cassé(e)**	**se seraient cassé(e)s**
6 présent du subjonctif		13 passé du subjonctif	
me casse	**nous cassions**	**me sois cassé(e)**	**nous soyons cassé(e)s**
te casses	**vous cassiez**	**te sois cassé(e)**	**vous soyez cassé(e)(s)**
se casse	**se cassent**	**se soit cassé(e)**	**se soient cassé(e)s**
7 imparfait du subjonctif		14 plus-que-parfait du subjonctif	
me cassasse	**nous cassassions**	**me fusse cassé(e)**	**nous fussions cassé(e)s**
te cassasses	**vous cassassiez**	**te fusses cassé(e)**	**vous fussiez cassé(e)(s)**
se cassât	**se cassassent**	**se fût cassé(e)**	**se fussent cassé(e)s**

Impératif
casse-toi . . . ; ne te casse pas . . .
cassons-nous . . . ; ne nous cassons pas . . .
cassez-vous . . . ; ne vous cassez pas . . .

Sentences using this verb and words related do it

Pendant les vacances d'hiver, nous sommes allés faire du ski dans les montagnes. Mon père s'est cassé le bras, ma mère s'est cassé la jambe, et moi, je me suis cassé le pied. During winter vacation we went skiing in the mountains. My father broke his arm, my mother broke her leg, and I broke my foot.

se casser la tête to rack one's brains
se casser le nez to find nobody answering the door
casser la tête à qqn to annoy someone; **un casse-cou** daredevil, reckless person

See also **casser.**

How are you doing? Find out with the verb drills and tests with answers explained on pages 50–101.

causer (86) — Part. pr. causant — Part. passé causé

to cause, to chat

Regular **-er** verb

The Seven Simple Tenses		The Seven Compound Tenses	
Singular	Plural	Singular	Plural
1 présent de l'indicatif		8 passé composé	
cause	**causons**	**ai causé**	**avons causé**
causes	**causez**	**as causé**	**avez causé**
cause	**causent**	**a causé**	**ont causé**
2 imparfait de l'indicatif		9 plus-que-parfait de l'indicatif	
causais	**causions**	**avais causé**	**avions causé**
causais	**causiez**	**avais causé**	**aviez causé**
causait	**causaient**	**avait causé**	**avaient causé**
3 passé simple		10 passé antérieur	
causai	**causâmes**	**eus causé**	**eûmes causé**
causas	**causâtes**	**eus causé**	**eûtes causé**
causa	**causèrent**	**eut causé**	**eurent causé**
4 futur		11 futur antérieur	
causerai	**causerons**	**aurai causé**	**aurons causé**
causeras	**causerez**	**auras causé**	**aurez causé**
causera	**causeront**	**aura causé**	**auront causé**
5 conditionnel		12 conditionnel passé	
causerais	**causerions**	**aurais causé**	**aurions causé**
causerais	**causeriez**	**aurais causé**	**auriez causé**
causerait	**causeraient**	**aurait causé**	**auraient causé**
6 présent du subjonctif		13 passé du subjonctif	
cause	**causions**	**aie causé**	**ayons causé**
causes	**causiez**	**aies causé**	**ayez causé**
cause	**causent**	**ait causé**	**aient causé**
7 imparfait du subjonctif		14 plus-que-parfait du subjonctif	
causasse	**causassions**	**eusse causé**	**eussions causé**
causasses	**causassiez**	**eusses causé**	**eussiez causé**
causât	**causassent**	**eût causé**	**eussent causé**

Impératif
cause
causons
causez

Sentences using this verb and words related to it

Quand je voyage, j'aime beaucoup causer avec les passagers. Est-ce que vous causez avec vos voisins dans la salle de classe? En français, bien sûr! Je connais un garçon qui n'est pas très causant.

causant, causante talkative
causatif, causative causative
une cause cause, reason
causer de la pluie et du beau temps to chat about the weather
une causette chat
une cause célèbre famous trial
une causerie chat, informal talk
causeur, causeuse talkative
une causeuse love seat
causer de la peine à qqn to hurt someone

Don't forget to use the English-French verb index. It's in the Appendixes.

Regular **-er** verb endings; spelling change: **é** changes to **è** before syllable with mute **e**

to yield, to cede

The Seven Simple Tenses		The Seven Compound Tenses	
Singular	Plural	Singular	Plural
1 présent de l'indicatif		8 passé composé	
cède	**cédons**	**ai cédé**	**avons cédé**
cèdes	**cédez**	**as cédé**	**avez cédé**
cède	**cèdent**	**a cédé**	**ont cédé**
2 imparfait de l'indicatif		9 plus-que-parfait de l'indicatif	
cédais	**cédions**	**avais cédé**	**avions cédé**
cédais	**cédiez**	**avais cédé**	**aviez cédé**
cédait	**cédaient**	**avait cédé**	**avaient cédé**
3 passé simple		10 passé antérieur	
cédai	**cédâmes**	**eus cédé**	**eûmes cédé**
cédas	**cédâtes**	**eus cédé**	**eûtes cédé**
céda	**cédèrent**	**eut cédé**	**eurent cédé**
4 futur		11 futur antérieur	
céderai	**céderons**	**aurai cédé**	**aurons cédé**
céderas	**céderez**	**auras cédé**	**aurez cédé**
cédera	**céderont**	**aura cédé**	**auront cédé**
5 conditionnel		12 conditionnel passé	
céderais	**céderions**	**aurais cédé**	**aurions cédé**
céderais	**céderiez**	**aurais cédé**	**auriez cédé**
céderait	**céderaient**	**aurait cédé**	**auraient cédé**
6 présent du subjonctif		13 passé du subjonctif	
cède	**cédions**	**aie cédé**	**ayons cédé**
cèdes	**cédiez**	**aies cédé**	**ayez cédé**
cède	**cèdent**	**ait cédé**	**aient cédé**
7 imparfait du subjonctif		14 plus-que-parfait du subjonctif	
cédasse	**cédassions**	**eusse cédé**	**eussions cédé**
cédasses	**cédassiez**	**eusses cédé**	**eussiez cédé**
cédât	**cédassent**	**eût cédé**	**eussent cédé**

Impératif
cède
cédons
cédez

Sentences using this verb and words related to it

Hier soir j'ai pris l'autobus pour rentrer chez moi. J'ai pris la dernière place libre. Après quelques minutes, une vieille dame est entrée dans l'autobus et j'ai cédé ma place à cette aimable personne.

céder à to give up, give in, yield to
accéder à to accede to, to comply with
concéder à to concede to, to grant
décéder to pass away
céder le pas à qqn to give way to someone
céder qqch à qqn to let somebody have something

NOTE: The Académie française now allows the accent grave (`) in the future (*e.g.*, **je cèderai**) and conditional (*e.g.*, **je cèderais**) of this verb.

to cease

Regular **-er** verb

The Seven Simple Tenses		The Seven Compound Tenses	
Singular	Plural	Singular	Plural
1 présent de l'indicatif		8 passé composé	
cesse	**cessons**	**ai cessé**	**avons cessé**
cesses	**cessez**	**as cessé**	**avez cessé**
cesse	**cessent**	**a cessé**	**ont cessé**
2 imparfait de l'indicatif		9 plus-que-parfait de l'indicatif	
cessais	**cessions**	**avais cessé**	**avions cessé**
cessais	**cessiez**	**avais cessé**	**aviez cessé**
cessait	**cessaient**	**avait cessé**	**avaient cessé**
3 passé simple		10 passé antérieur	
cessai	**cessâmes**	**eus cessé**	**eûmes cessé**
cessas	**cessâtes**	**eus cessé**	**eûtes cessé**
cessa	**cessèrent**	**eut cessé**	**eurent cessé**
4 futur		11 futur antérieur	
cesserai	**cesserons**	**aurai cessé**	**aurons cessé**
cesseras	**cesserez**	**auras cessé**	**aurez cessé**
cessera	**cesseront**	**aura cessé**	**auront cessé**
5 conditionnel		12 conditionnel passé	
cesserais	**cesserions**	**aurais cessé**	**aurions cessé**
cesserais	**cesseriez**	**aurais cessé**	**auriez cessé**
cesserait	**cesseraient**	**aurait cessé**	**auraient cessé**
6 présent du subjonctif		13 passé du subjonctif	
cesse	**cessions**	**aie cessé**	**ayons cessé**
cesses	**cessiez**	**aies cessé**	**ayez cessé**
cesse	**cessent**	**ait cessé**	**aient cessé**
7 imparfait du subjonctif		14 plus-que-parfait du subjonctif	
cessasse	**cessassions**	**eusse cessé**	**eussions cessé**
cessasses	**cessassiez**	**eusses cessé**	**eussiez cessé**
cessât	**cessassent**	**eût cessé**	**eussent cessé**

Impératif
cesse
cessons
cessez

Sentences using this verb and words related to it

Proverb: **Quand le sage est en colère, il cesse d'être sage.** When the wise man is angry, he stops being wise.

une cesse cease, ceasing; **cesser de faire qqch** to stop doing something
sans cesse constantly
incessant incessant, ceaseless
cesser de se voir to stop seeing each other; **Il n'a pas cessé de neiger depuis hier.** It has not stopped snowing since yesterday.
cesser le feu to cease fire; **un cessez-le-feu** cease-fire

For **je me tais,** see **se taire**. See also **bavarder.**

to change

Regular **-er** verb endings; spelling change: retain the **ge** before **a** or **o** to keep the soft **g** sound of the verb

The Seven Simple Tenses		The Seven Compound Tenses	
Singular	Plural	Singular	Plural
1 présent de l'indicatif		8 passé composé	
change	**changeons**	**ai changé**	**avons changé**
changes	**changez**	**as changé**	**avez changé**
change	**changent**	**a changé**	**ont changé**
2 imparfait de l'indicatif		9 plus-que-parfait de l'indicatif	
changeais	**changions**	**avais changé**	**avions changé**
changeais	**changiez**	**avais changé**	**aviez changé**
changeait	**changeaient**	**avait changé**	**avaient changé**
3 passé simple		10 passé antérieur	
changeai	**changeâmes**	**eus changé**	**eûmes changé**
changeas	**changeâtes**	**eus changé**	**eûtes changé**
changea	**changèrent**	**eut changé**	**eurent changé**
4 futur		11 futur antérieur	
changerai	**changerons**	**aurai changé**	**aurons changé**
changeras	**changerez**	**auras changé**	**aurez changé**
changera	**changeront**	**aura changé**	**auront changé**
5 conditionnel		12 conditionnel passé	
changerais	**changerions**	**aurais changé**	**aurions changé**
changerais	**changeriez**	**aurais changé**	**auriez changé**
changerait	**changeraient**	**aurait changé**	**auraient changé**
6 présent du subjonctif		13 passé du subjonctif	
change	**changions**	**aie changé**	**ayons changé**
changes	**changiez**	**aies changé**	**ayez changé**
change	**changent**	**ait changé**	**aient changé**
7 imparfait du subjonctif		14 plus-que-parfait du subjonctif	
changeasse	**changeassions**	**eusse changé**	**eussions changé**
changeasses	**changeassiez**	**eusses changé**	**eussiez changé**
changeât	**changeassent**	**eût changé**	**eussent changé**

Impératif
change
changeons
changez

Common idiomatic expressions using this verb

Je vais changer de vêtements maintenant parce que je prends le train pour Paris, et là, je vais changer de train pour aller à Marseille.

changer d'avis to change one's mind
changer de route to take another road
un changement soudain a sudden change
une pièce/un pneu de rechange spare part/tire
échanger to exchange
Plus ça change, plus c'est la même chose. The more things change, the more they remain the same.
changer de train to change trains
changer de vêtements to change clothes
changer de l'argent to exchange some money
le bureau de change money exchange desk (office)
Je désire changer de l'argent. I would like to exchange some money.

The subject pronouns are found on page 103.

chanter (90)

Part. pr. **chantant** Part. passé **chanté**

to sing

Regular **-er** verb

The Seven Simple Tenses		The Seven Compound Tenses	
Singular	Plural	Singular	Plural
1 présent de l'indicatif		8 passé composé	
chante	**chantons**	**ai chanté**	**avons chanté**
chantes	**chantez**	**as chanté**	**avez chanté**
chante	**chantent**	**a chanté**	**ont chanté**
2 imparfait de l'indicatif		9 plus-que-parfait de l'indicatif	
chantais	**chantions**	**avais chanté**	**avions chanté**
chantais	**chantiez**	**avais chanté**	**aviez chanté**
chantait	**chantaient**	**avait chanté**	**avaient chanté**
3 passé simple		10 passé antérieur	
chantai	**chantâmes**	**eus chanté**	**eûmes chanté**
chantas	**chantâtes**	**eus chanté**	**eûtes chanté**
chanta	**chantèrent**	**eut chanté**	**eurent chanté**
4 futur		11 futur antérieur	
chanterai	**chanterons**	**aurai chanté**	**aurons chanté**
chanteras	**chanterez**	**auras chanté**	**aurez chanté**
chantera	**chanteront**	**aura chanté**	**auront chanté**
5 conditionnel		12 conditionnel passé	
chanterais	**chanterions**	**aurais chanté**	**aurions chanté**
chanterais	**chanteriez**	**aurais chanté**	**auriez chanté**
chanterait	**chanteraient**	**aurait chanté**	**auraient chanté**
6 présent du subjonctif		13 passé du subjonctif	
chante	**chantions**	**aie chanté**	**ayons chanté**
chantes	**chantiez**	**aies chanté**	**ayez chanté**
chante	**chantent**	**ait chanté**	**aient chanté**
7 imparfait du subjonctif		14 plus-que-parfait du subjonctif	
chantasse	**chantassions**	**eusse chanté**	**eussions chanté**
chantasses	**chantassiez**	**eusses chanté**	**eussiez chanté**
chantât	**chantassent**	**eût chanté**	**eussent chanté**

Impératif
chante
chantons
chantez

AN ESSENTIAL 55 VERB

Chanter

C

Chanter is a regular **-er** verb that is used in many common expressions and situations. If you can conjugate **chanter**, you can conjugate any regular **-er** verb.

Sentences using chanter and words related to it

Madame Chanteclaire aime bien chanter en jouant du piano. Mrs. Chanteclaire likes to sing while playing the piano.

Marie donne des leçons de chant. Mary gives singing lessons.

C'est une autre chanson! That's another story!

Mais qu'est-ce que vous chantez là? What are you talking about?

Demain, je vais me lever au chant du coq pour attraper le bus. Tomorrow I'm going to get up at the crack of dawn to catch the bus.

Claire a étudié l'ancien français pour lire les chansons de geste. Claire studied Old French in order to read epic poems.

Proverbs

C'est la poule qui chante qui a fait l'oeuf. **It's the hen who sings who made (laid) the egg.**

Vous chantiez? j'en suis fort aise: Eh bien! dansez maintenant. **You were singing? I'm very delighted about it. Well! Now dance. (La Fontaine, *La Cigale et la Fourmi*)**

Words and expressions related to this verb

une chanson **song**

une chanson d'amour **love song**

une chanson de geste **epic poem**

chansons! **nonsense! fiddlesticks!**

Si ça vous chante . . . **If you are in the mood for it . . .**

Ça ne me chante pas. **I'm not in the mood.**

un chant **carol, chant, singing**

le chantage **blackmail**

faire chanter qqn **to blackmail someone**

un chanteur, une chanteuse **singer**

chanter ô ma belle **to cry out in pain (Antilles)**

enchanter **to enchant**

Enchanté! **Pleased to meet you!**

au chant du coq **at the crack of dawn (when the rooster crows)**

Don't forget to check the list of 2,600 additional verbs keyed to the 501 model verbs. It's in the Appendixes!

The subject pronouns are found on page 103.

charger (91) — Part. pr. chargeant — Part. passé chargé

to burden, to charge, to load

Regular **-er** verb endings; spelling change: retain the **ge** before **a** or **o** to keep the soft **g** sound of the verb

The Seven Simple Tenses

Singular	Plural
1 présent de l'indicatif	
charge	**chargeons**
charges	**chargez**
charge	**chargent**
2 imparfait de l'indicatif	
chargeais	**chargions**
chargeais	**chargiez**
chargeait	**chargeaient**
3 passé simple	
chargeai	**chargeâmes**
chargeas	**chargeâtes**
chargea	**chargèrent**
4 futur	
chargerai	**chargerons**
chargeras	**chargerez**
chargera	**chargeront**
5 conditionnel	
chargerais	**chargerions**
chargerais	**chargeriez**
chargerait	**chargeraient**
6 présent du subjonctif	
charge	**chargions**
charges	**chargiez**
charge	**chargent**
7 imparfait du subjonctif	
chargeasse	**chargeassions**
chargeasses	**chargeassiez**
chargeât	**chargeassent**

The Seven Compound Tenses

Singular	Plural
8 passé composé	
ai chargé	**avons chargé**
as chargé	**avez chargé**
a chargé	**ont chargé**
9 plus-que-parfait de l'indicatif	
avais chargé	**avions chargé**
avais chargé	**aviez chargé**
avait chargé	**avaient chargé**
10 passé antérieur	
eus chargé	**eûmes chargé**
eus chargé	**eûtes chargé**
eut chargé	**eurent chargé**
11 futur antérieur	
aurai chargé	**aurons chargé**
auras chargé	**aurez chargé**
aura chargé	**auront chargé**
12 conditionnel passé	
aurais chargé	**aurions chargé**
aurais chargé	**auriez chargé**
aurait chargé	**auraient chargé**
13 passé du subjonctif	
aie chargé	**ayons chargé**
aies chargé	**ayez chargé**
ait chargé	**aient chargé**
14 plus-que-parfait du subjonctif	
eusse chargé	**eussions chargé**
eusses chargé	**eussiez chargé**
eût chargé	**eussent chargé**

Impératif
charge
chargeons
chargez

Common idiomatic expressions using this verb

Je connais une dame qui charge son mari de paquets chaque fois qu'ils vont faire des emplettes. Une fois quand je les ai vus en ville, il a chargé sa femme de malédictions.

une charge a load, burden
chargé d'impôts heavily taxed
un chargé d'affaires envoy
Je m'en charge. I'll take care of it.
télécharger to download (computer)
charger de malédictions to curse
charger de louanges to overwhelm with praises
un chargeur de batterie battery charger
décharger to unload

Grammar putting you in a tense mood? Review the definitions of basic grammatical terms with examples on pages 35–49.

Regular **-er** verb

to hunt, to pursue, to chase, to drive out

The Seven Simple Tenses		The Seven Compound Tenses	
Singular	Plural	Singular	Plural
1 présent de l'indicatif		8 passé composé	
chasse	**chassons**	**ai chassé**	**avons chassé**
chasses	**chassez**	**as chassé**	**avez chassé**
chasse	**chassent**	**a chassé**	**ont chassé**
2 imparfait de l'indicatif		9 plus-que-parfait de l'indicatif	
chassais	**chassions**	**avais chassé**	**avions chassé**
chassais	**chassiez**	**avais chassé**	**aviez chassé**
chassait	**chassaient**	**avait chassé**	**avaient chassé**
3 passé simple		10 passé antérieur	
chassai	**chassâmes**	**eus chassé**	**eûmes chassé**
chassas	**chassâtes**	**eus chassé**	**eûtes chassé**
chassa	**chassèrent**	**eut chassé**	**eurent chassé**
4 futur		11 futur antérieur	
chasserai	**chasserons**	**aurai chassé**	**aurons chassé**
chasseras	**chasserez**	**auras chassé**	**aurez chassé**
chassera	**chasseront**	**aura chassé**	**auront chassé**
5 conditionnel		12 conditionnel passé	
chasserais	**chasserions**	**aurais chassé**	**aurions chassé**
chasserais	**chasseriez**	**aurais chassé**	**auriez chassé**
chasserait	**chasseraient**	**aurait chassé**	**auraient chassé**
6 présent du subjonctif		13 passé du subjonctif	
chasse	**chassions**	**aie chassé**	**ayons chassé**
chasses	**chassiez**	**aies chassé**	**ayez chassé**
chasse	**chassent**	**ait chassé**	**aient chassé**
7 imparfait du subjonctif		14 plus-que-parfait du subjonctif	
chassasse	**chassassions**	**eusse chassé**	**eussions chassé**
chassasses	**chassassiez**	**eusses chassé**	**eussiez chassé**
chassât	**chassassent**	**eût chassé**	**eussent chassé**

Impératif
chasse
chassons
chassez

Words and expressions related to this verb
pourchasser to chase, pursue
un chasse-neige snowplow
un chasse-mouches fly swatter
tirer la chasse d'eau to flush the toilet

Proverb:
Je chasse toujours les arcs-en-ciel. I'm always chasing rainbows.

Pronounce out loud this tongue twister as fast as you can: **Le chasseur, sachant* chasser sans son chien, chassera.** (The hunter, knowing how to hunt without his dog, will hunt.)
***Sachant** is the pres. part. of **savoir**.

chercher (93) — Part. pr. **cherchant** — Part. passé **cherché**

to look for, to search, to seek

Regular **-er** verb

The Seven Simple Tenses

Singular	Plural
1 présent de l'indicatif	
cherche	**cherchons**
cherches	**cherchez**
cherche	**cherchent**
2 imparfait de l'indicatif	
cherchais	**cherchions**
cherchais	**cherchiez**
cherchait	**cherchaient**
3 passé simple	
cherchai	**cherchâmes**
cherchas	**cherchâtes**
chercha	**cherchèrent**
4 futur	
chercherai	**chercherons**
chercheras	**chercherez**
cherchera	**chercheront**
5 conditionnel	
chercherais	**chercherions**
chercherais	**chercheriez**
chercherait	**chercheraient**
6 présent du subjonctif	
cherche	**cherchions**
cherches	**cherchiez**
cherche	**cherchent**
7 imparfait du subjonctif	
cherchasse	**cherchassions**
cherchasses	**cherchassiez**
cherchât	**cherchassent**

The Seven Compound Tenses

Singular	Plural
8 passé composé	
ai cherché	**avons cherché**
as cherché	**avez cherché**
a cherché	**ont cherché**
9 plus-que-parfait de l'indicatif	
avais cherché	**avions cherché**
avais cherché	**aviez cherché**
avait cherché	**avaient cherché**
10 passé antérieur	
eus cherché	**eûmes cherché**
eus cherché	**eûtes cherché**
eut cherché	**eurent cherché**
11 futur antérieur	
aurai cherché	**aurons cherché**
auras cherché	**aurez cherché**
aura cherché	**auront cherché**
12 conditionnel passé	
aurais cherché	**aurions cherché**
aurais cherché	**auriez cherché**
aurait cherché	**auraient cherché**
13 passé du subjonctif	
aie cherché	**ayons cherché**
aies cherché	**ayez cherché**
ait cherché	**aient cherché**
14 plus-que-parfait du subjonctif	
eusse cherché	**eussions cherché**
eusses cherché	**eussiez cherché**
eût cherché	**eussent cherché**

Impératif
cherche
cherchons
cherchez

Sentences using this verb and words related to it

—Monsieur, monsieur, j'ai perdu mon livre de français. J'ai cherché partout et je n'arrive pas à le trouver.

—Continue à chercher parce que demain je donnerai un examen.

se chercher to look for one another
chercheur seeker, investigator, researcher
aller chercher to go and get
chercher à to attempt to, try to
aller chercher qqn ou qqch to go get someone or something
rechercher to investigate, to seek, to look for again
faire des travaux de recherches to carry out research work
envoyer chercher to send for
un moteur de recherche search engine (Internet)
Je vais envoyer chercher le médecin. I am going to send for the doctor.

Regular **-ir** verb

to cherish

The Seven Simple Tenses		The Seven Compound Tenses	
Singular	Plural	Singular	Plural
1 présent de l'indicatif		8 passé composé	
chéris	**chérissons**	**ai chéri**	**avons chéri**
chéris	**chérissez**	**as chéri**	**avez chéri**
chérit	**chérissent**	**a chéri**	**ont chéri**
2 imparfait de l'indicatif		9 plus-que-parfait de l'indicatif	
chérissais	**chérissions**	**avais chéri**	**avions chéri**
chérissais	**chérissiez**	**avais chéri**	**aviez chéri**
chérissait	**chérissaient**	**avait chéri**	**avaient chéri**
3 passé simple		10 passé antérieur	
chéris	**chérîmes**	**eus chéri**	**eûmes chéri**
chéris	**chérîtes**	**eus chéri**	**eûtes chéri**
chérit	**chérirent**	**eut chéri**	**eurent chéri**
4 futur		11 futur antérieur	
chérirai	**chérirons**	**aurai chéri**	**aurons chéri**
chériras	**chérirez**	**auras chéri**	**aurez chéri**
chérira	**chériront**	**aura chéri**	**auront chéri**
5 conditionnel		12 conditionnel passé	
chérirais	**chéririons**	**aurais chéri**	**aurions chéri**
chérirais	**chéririez**	**aurais chéri**	**auriez chéri**
chérirait	**chériraient**	**aurait chéri**	**auraient chéri**
6 présent du subjonctif		13 passé du subjonctif	
chérisse	**chérissions**	**aie chéri**	**ayons chéri**
chérisses	**chérissiez**	**aies chéri**	**ayez chéri**
chérisse	**chérissent**	**ait chéri**	**aient chéri**
7 imparfait du subjonctif		14 plus-que-parfait du subjonctif	
chérisse	**chérissions**	**eusse chéri**	**eussions chéri**
chérisses	**chérissiez**	**eusses chéri**	**eussiez chéri**
chérît	**chérissent**	**eût chéri**	**eussent chéri**

Impératif
chéris
chérissons
chérissez

Words and expressions related to this verb

cher, chère dear; expensive
Ça coûte cher! That costs a lot!
chéri, chérie darling, dear
chèrement dearly
renchérir to go up in cost, to make a higher bid
acheter cher to buy at a high price
vendre cher to sell at a high price
Vous me le paierez cher! You will pay dearly for it!
un renchérissement increase

Don't forget to study the section on defective and impersonal verbs. It's right after this main list.

choisir (95) Part. pr. **choisissant** Part. passé **choisi**

to choose, to select, to pick

Regular **-ir** verb

The Seven Simple Tenses		The Seven Compound Tenses	
Singular	Plural	Singular	Plural
1 présent de l'indicatif		8 passé composé	
choisis	**choisissons**	**ai choisi**	**avons choisi**
choisis	**choisissez**	**as choisi**	**avez choisi**
choisit	**choisissent**	**a choisi**	**ont choisi**
2 imparfait de l'indicatif		9 plus-que-parfait de l'indicatif	
choisissais	**choisissions**	**avais choisi**	**avions choisi**
choisissais	**choisissiez**	**avais choisi**	**aviez choisi**
choisissait	**choisissaient**	**avait choisi**	**avaient choisi**
3 passé simple		10 passé antérieur	
choisis	**choisîmes**	**eus choisi**	**eûmes choisi**
choisis	**choisîtes**	**eus choisi**	**eûtes choisi**
choisit	**choisirent**	**eut choisi**	**eurent choisi**
4 futur		11 futur antérieur	
choisirai	**choisirons**	**aurai choisi**	**aurons choisi**
choisiras	**choisirez**	**auras choisi**	**aurez choisi**
choisira	**choisiront**	**aura choisi**	**auront choisi**
5 conditionnel		12 conditionnel passé	
choisirais	**choisirions**	**aurais choisi**	**aurions choisi**
choisirais	**choisiriez**	**aurais choisi**	**auriez choisi**
choisirait	**choisiraient**	**aurait choisi**	**auraient choisi**
6 présent du subjonctif		13 passé du subjonctif	
choisisse	**choisissions**	**aie choisi**	**ayons choisi**
choisisses	**choisissiez**	**aies choisi**	**ayez choisi**
choisisse	**choisissent**	**ait choisi**	**aient choisi**
7 imparfait du subjonctif		14 plus-que-parfait du subjonctif	
choisisse	**choisissions**	**eusse choisi**	**eussions choisi**
choisisses	**choisissiez**	**eusses choisi**	**eussiez choisi**
choisît	**choisissent**	**eût choisi**	**eussent choisi**

Impératif
choisis
choisissons
choisissez

AN ESSENTIAL 55 VERB

Choisir

C

We have chosen **choisir** as a key verb because it is a regular **-ir** verb and because **choisir** is used in numerous everyday situations and idiomatic expressions.

Sentences using choisir and related words

Au restaurant français j'ai choisi la crêpe Suzette et Raymond a choisi le filet mignon. Joseph a choisi d'aller au fast-food quand il a vu les prix. At the French restaurant I chose the crêpe suzette and Raymond chose the filet mignon. Joseph chose to go to the fast food restaurant when he saw the prices.

Il n'y a pas grand choix.
There's not much choice.

Choisissez bien vos amis.
Choose your friends well.

Words and expressions related to this verb

un choix **choice**

faire un bon choix **to make a good choice**

faire un mauvais choix **to make a bad choice**

faire choix de **to make choice of**

l'embarras du choix **too much to choose from**

savoir choisir ses amis **to know how to choose one's friends**

au choix **optional, elective**

If you can conjugate **choisir** you can also conjugate the following verbs (and many others):

adoucir **to reduce, soften, mellow**

grossir **to gain weight, grow larger**

moisir **to get moldy**

radoucir **to soften**

réussir **to succeed**

Proverb

Choisissez un travail que vous aimez et vous n'aurez pas à travailler un seul jour de votre vie. Choose a job you love and you will never have to work a day in your life. (Confucius)

Don't forget to check the list of 2,600 additional verbs keyed to the 501 model verbs. It's in the Appendixes!

The subject pronouns are found on page 103.

chuchoter (96) — Part. pr. chuchotant — Part. passé chuchoté

to whisper

Regular **-er** verb

The Seven Simple Tenses		The Seven Compound Tenses	
Singular	Plural	Singular	Plural
1 présent de l'indicatif		8 passé composé	
chuchote	**chuchotons**	**ai chuchoté**	**avons chuchoté**
chuchotes	**chuchotez**	**as chuchoté**	**avez chuchoté**
chuchote	**chuchotent**	**a chuchoté**	**ont chuchoté**
2 imparfait de l'indicatif		9 plus-que-parfait de l'indicatif	
chuchotais	**chuchotions**	**avais chuchoté**	**avions chuchoté**
chuchotais	**chuchotiez**	**avais chuchoté**	**aviez chuchoté**
chuchotait	**chuchotaient**	**avait chuchoté**	**avaient chuchoté**
3 passé simple		10 passé antérieur	
chuchotai	**chuchotâmes**	**eus chuchoté**	**eûmes chuchoté**
chuchotas	**chuchotâtes**	**eus chuchoté**	**eûtes chuchoté**
chuchota	**chuchotèrent**	**eut chuchoté**	**eurent chuchoté**
4 futur		11 futur antérieur	
chuchoterai	**chuchoterons**	**aurai chuchoté**	**aurons chuchoté**
chuchoteras	**chuchoterez**	**auras chuchoté**	**aurez chuchoté**
chuchotera	**chuchoteront**	**aura chuchoté**	**auront chuchoté**
5 conditionnel		12 conditionnel passé	
chuchoterais	**chuchoterions**	**aurais chuchoté**	**aurions chuchoté**
chuchoterais	**chuchoteriez**	**aurais chuchoté**	**auriez chuchoté**
chuchoterait	**chuchoteraient**	**aurait chuchoté**	**auraient chuchoté**
6 présent du subjonctif		13 passé du subjonctif	
chuchote	**chuchotions**	**aie chuchoté**	**ayons chuchoté**
chuchotes	**chuchotiez**	**aies chuchoté**	**ayez chuchoté**
chuchote	**chuchotent**	**ait chuchoté**	**aient chuchoté**
7 imparfait du subjonctif		14 plus-que-parfait du subjonctif	
chuchotasse	**chuchotassions**	**eusse chuchoté**	**eussions chuchoté**
chuchotasses	**chuchotassiez**	**eusses chuchoté**	**eussiez chuchoté**
chuchotât	**chuchotassent**	**eût chuchoté**	**eussent chuchoté**

Impératif
chuchote
chuchotons
chuchotez

Common idiomatic expressions using this verb and words related to it

un chuchoteur, une chuchoteuse whisperer
chuchoter à l'oreille de qqn to whisper in someone's ear
souffler to prompt (in a stage whisper)
le chuchotement whispering
une chuchoterie a conversation in whispering tones so that others may not hear

Get acquainted with what preposition goes with what verb. See *Verbs with prepositions* in the Appendixes.

Irregular verb in 1s, 2s, 3s present indicative

to combat, to fight

The Seven Simple Tenses		The Seven Compound Tenses	
Singular	Plural	Singular	Plural
1 présent de l'indicatif		8 passé composé	
combats	**combattons**	**ai combattu**	**avons combattu**
combats	**combattez**	**as combattu**	**avez combattu**
combat	**combattent**	**a combattu**	**ont combattu**
2 imparfait de l'indicatif		9 plus-que-parfait de l'indicatif	
combattais	**combattions**	**avais combattu**	**avions combattu**
combattais	**combattiez**	**avais combattu**	**aviez combattu**
combattait	**combattaient**	**avait combattu**	**avaient combattu**
3 passé simple		10 passé antérieur	
combattis	**combattîmes**	**eus combattu**	**eûmes combattu**
combattis	**combattîtes**	**eus combattu**	**eûtes combattu**
combattit	**combattirent**	**eut combattu**	**eurent combattu**
4 futur		11 futur antérieur	
combattrai	**combattrons**	**aurai combattu**	**aurons combattu**
combattras	**combattrez**	**auras combattu**	**aurez combattu**
combattra	**combattront**	**aura combattu**	**auront combattu**
5 conditionnel		12 conditionnel passé	
combattrais	**combattrions**	**aurais combattu**	**aurions combattu**
combattrais	**combattriez**	**aurais combattu**	**auriez combattu**
combattrait	**combattraient**	**aurait combattu**	**auraient combattu**
6 présent du subjonctif		13 passé du subjonctif	
combatte	**combattions**	**aie combattu**	**ayons combattu**
combattes	**combattiez**	**aies combattu**	**ayez combattu**
combatte	**combattent**	**ait combattu**	**aient combattu**
7 imparfait du subjonctif		14 plus-que-parfait du subjonctif	
combattisse	**combattissions**	**eusse combattu**	**eussions combattu**
combattisses	**combattissiez**	**eusses combattu**	**eussiez combattu**
combattît	**combattissent**	**eût combattu**	**eussent combattu**

Impératif
combats
combattons
combattez

Words and expressions related to this verb

un combat fight, struggle
hors de combat out of the fight
combattant, combattante fighting
un non-combattant, une non-combattante noncombatant
un combat aérien aerial combat
combatif, combative pugnacious, aggressive

For other words and expressions related to this verb, see **abattre**, **battre**, and **se battre.**

Don't forget to study the section on defective and impersonal verbs. It's right after this main list.

commander (98) Part. pr. commandant Part. passé commandé

to command, to order

Regular **-er** verb

The Seven Simple Tenses		The Seven Compound Tenses	
Singular	Plural	Singular	Plural
1 présent de l'indicatif		8 passé composé	
commande	**commandons**	**ai commandé**	**avons commandé**
commandes	**commandez**	**as commandé**	**avez commandé**
commande	**commandent**	**a commandé**	**ont commandé**
2 imparfait de l'indicatif		9 plus-que-parfait de l'indicatif	
commandais	**commandions**	**avais commandé**	**avions commandé**
commandais	**commandiez**	**avais commandé**	**aviez commandé**
commandait	**commandaient**	**avait commandé**	**avaient commandé**
3 passé simple		10 passé antérieur	
commandai	**commandâmes**	**eus commandé**	**eûmes commandé**
commandas	**commandâtes**	**eus commandé**	**eûtes commandé**
commanda	**commandèrent**	**eut commandé**	**eurent commandé**
4 futur		11 futur antérieur	
commanderai	**commanderons**	**aurai commandé**	**aurons commandé**
commanderas	**commanderez**	**auras commandé**	**aurez commandé**
commandera	**commanderont**	**aura commandé**	**auront commandé**
5 conditionnel		12 conditionnel passé	
commanderais	**commanderions**	**aurais commandé**	**aurions commandé**
commanderais	**commanderiez**	**aurais commandé**	**auriez commandé**
commanderait	**commanderaient**	**aurait commandé**	**auraient commandé**
6 présent du subjonctif		13 passé du subjonctif	
commande	**commandions**	**aie commandé**	**ayons commandé**
commandes	**commandiez**	**aies commandé**	**ayez commandé**
commande	**commandent**	**ait commandé**	**aient commandé**
7 imparfait du subjonctif		14 plus-que-parfait du subjonctif	
commandasse	**commandassions**	**eusse commandé**	**eussions commandé**
commandasses	**commandassiez**	**eusses commandé**	**eussiez commandé**
commandât	**commandassent**	**eût commandé**	**eussent commandé**

Impératif
commande
commandons
commandez

Common idiomatic expressions using this verb

Hier soir mes amis et moi avons dîné dans un restaurant chinois. Nous avons commandé beaucoup de choses intéressantes.

un commandant commanding officer
une commande an order
commander à qqn de faire qqch to order someone to do something
recommander to recommend; **recommander à qqn de faire qqch** to advise someone to do something
décommander un rendez-vous to cancel a date, an appointment

Try the verb drills and verb tests with answers explained on pages 50–101.

Regular **-er** verb endings; spelling change:
c changes to **ç** before **a** or **o** to keep **s** sound

to begin, to start, to commence

The Seven Simple Tenses		The Seven Compound Tenses	
Singular	Plural	Singular	Plural
1 présent de l'indicatif		8 passé composé	
commence	**commençons**	**ai commencé**	**avons commencé**
commences	**commencez**	**as commencé**	**avez commencé**
commence	**commencent**	**a commencé**	**ont commencé**
2 imparfait de l'indicatif		9 plus-que-parfait de l'indicatif	
commençais	**commencions**	**avais commencé**	**avions commencé**
commençais	**commenciez**	**avais commencé**	**aviez commencé**
commençait	**commençaient**	**avait commencé**	**avaient commencé**
3 passé simple		10 passé antérieur	
commençai	**commençâmes**	**eus commencé**	**eûmes commencé**
commença	**commençâtes**	**eus commencé**	**eûtes commencé**
commença	**commencèrent**	**eut commencé**	**eurent commencé**
4 futur		11 futur antérieur	
commencerai	**commencerons**	**aurai commencé**	**aurons commencé**
commenceras	**commencerez**	**auras commencé**	**aurez commencé**
commencera	**commenceront**	**aura commencé**	**auront commencé**
5 conditionnel		12 conditionnel passé	
commencerais	**commencerions**	**aurais commencé**	**aurions commencé**
commencerais	**commenceriez**	**aurais commencé**	**auriez commencé**
commencerait	**commenceraient**	**aurait commencé**	**auraient commencé**
6 présent du subjonctif		13 passé du subjonctif	
commence	**commencions**	**aie commencé**	**ayons commencé**
commences	**commenciez**	**aies commencé**	**ayez commencé**
commence	**commencent**	**ait commencé**	**aient commencé**
7 imparfait du subjonctif		14 plus-que-parfait du subjonctif	
commençasse	**commençassions**	**eusse commencé**	**eussions commencé**
commençasses	**commençassiez**	**eusses commencé**	**eussiez commencé**
commençât	**commençassent**	**eût commencé**	**eussent commencé**

Impératif
commence
commençons
commencez

Get acquainted with what preposition goes with what verb. See *Verbs with prepositions* in the Appendixes.

The subject pronouns are found on page 103.

AN ESSENTIAL 55 VERB

Commencer

Commencer is an essential verb for beginning students because of its spelling change and because it is used in a number of everyday situations.

Sentences using commencer and related words

Dépêche-toi! Le film commence à midi! Hurry up! The movie starts at noon!

Nous commençons à nous inquiéter parce que Marie-Ève n'est pas encore revenue. We are beginning to worry because Marie-Eve hasn't come back yet.

Commençons au commencement. Let's begin at the beginning.

—Alexandre, as-tu commencé tes devoirs pour la classe de français?
—Non, maman, pas encore. Je vais faire une promenade maintenant.
—Tu ne vas pas faire une promenade parce qu'il commence à pleuvoir. Commence à faire tes devoirs tout de suite!

—Alexander, have you begun your homework for French class?
—No, Mother, not yet. I'm going to take a walk now.
—You are not going to take a walk because it is beginning to rain. Start to do your homework immediately!

Words and expressions related to this verb

commencer à + inf. to begin + inf.

le commencement the beginning

au commencement in the beginning

du commencement à la fin from beginning to end

pour commencer to begin with

commencer par to begin by

recommencer à to begin again + inf.

un recommencement a new start

The **c** before the **-er** ending in **commencer** takes a cedilla before the letters **a** and **o**. This is done to retain the sound of **s** in **-cer**. Otherwise, **c** before **a** would sound like **k** as in **camion** (truck) and **coûter** (to cost). If you can conjugate **commencer** you can also conjugate:

annoncer to announce
balancer to balance
cadencer to give rhythm, cadence
concurrencer to compete
dénoncer to denounce
financer to finance
lancer to throw
prononcer to pronounce
recommencer to begin again

Irregular verb

to commit

The Seven Simple Tenses		The Seven Compound Tenses	
Singular	Plural	Singular	Plural
1 présent de l'indicatif		8 passé composé	
commets	**commettons**	**ai commis**	**avons commis**
commets	**commettez**	**as commis**	**avez commis**
commet	**commettent**	**a commis**	**ont commis**
2 imparfait de l'indicatif		9 plus-que-parfait de l'indicatif	
commettais	**commettions**	**avais commis**	**avions commis**
commettais	**commettiez**	**avais commis**	**aviez commis**
commettait	**commettaient**	**avait commis**	**avaient commis**
3 passé simple		10 passé antérieur	
commis	**commîmes**	**eus commis**	**eûmes commis**
commis	**commîtes**	**eus commis**	**eûtes commis**
commit	**commirent**	**eut commis**	**eurent commis**
4 futur		11 futur antérieur	
commettrai	**commettrons**	**aurai commis**	**aurons commis**
commettras	**commettrez**	**auras commis**	**aurez commis**
commettra	**commettront**	**aura commis**	**auront commis**
5 conditionnel		12 conditionnel passé	
commettrais	**commettrions**	**aurais commis**	**aurions commis**
commettrais	**commettriez**	**aurais commis**	**auriez commis**
commettrait	**commettraient**	**aurait commis**	**auraient commis**
6 présent du subjonctif		13 passé du subjonctif	
commette	**commettions**	**aie commis**	**ayons commis**
commettes	**commettiez**	**aies commis**	**ayez commis**
commette	**commettent**	**ait commis**	**aient commis**
7 imparfait du subjonctif		14 plus-que-parfait du subjonctif	
commisse	**commissions**	**eusse commis**	**eussions commis**
commisses	**commissiez**	**eusses commis**	**eussiez commis**
commît	**commissent**	**eût commis**	**eussent commis**

Impératif
commets
commettons
commettez

Words and expressions related to this verb

commettre un péché to commit a sin
être commis à to be committed to
commis aux soins de to be placed under the care of
se commettre to commit oneself
commettre qqch à qqn to entrust something to someone
commettre qqn à qqn to entrust someone to someone, to place someone under someone's care

See also **mettre, permettre, promettre, remettre, soumettre,** and **transmettre.**

Soak up some verbs used in weather expressions. There's a list in the Appendixes!

comparer (101) Part. pr. **comparant** Part. passé **comparé**

to compare

Regular **-er** verb

The Seven Simple Tenses		The Seven Compound Tenses	
Singular	Plural	Singular	Plural
1 présent de l'indicatif		8 passé composé	
compare	**comparons**	**ai comparé**	**avons comparé**
compares	**comparez**	**as comparé**	**avez comparé**
compare	**comparent**	**a comparé**	**ont comparé**
2 imparfait de l'indicatif		9 plus-que-parfait de l'indicatif	
comparais	**comparions**	**avais comparé**	**avions comparé**
comparais	**compariez**	**avais comparé**	**aviez comparé**
comparait	**comparaient**	**avait comparé**	**avaient comparé**
3 passé simple		10 passé antérieur	
comparai	**comparâmes**	**eus comparé**	**eûmes comparé**
comparas	**comparâtes**	**eus comparé**	**eûtes comparé**
compara	**comparèrent**	**eut comparé**	**eurent comparé**
4 futur		11 futur antérieur	
comparerai	**comparerons**	**aurai comparé**	**aurons comparé**
compareras	**comparerez**	**auras comparé**	**aurez comparé**
comparera	**compareront**	**aura comparé**	**auront comparé**
5 conditionnel		12 conditionnel passé	
comparerais	**comparerions**	**aurais comparé**	**aurions comparé**
comparerais	**compareriez**	**aurais comparé**	**auriez comparé**
comparerait	**compareraient**	**aurait comparé**	**auraient comparé**
6 présent du subjonctif		13 passé du subjonctif	
compare	**comparions**	**aie comparé**	**ayons comparé**
compares	**compariez**	**aies comparé**	**ayez comparé**
compare	**comparent**	**ait comparé**	**aient comparé**
7 imparfait du subjonctif		14 plus-que-parfait du subjonctif	
comparasse	**comparassions**	**eusse comparé**	**eussions comparé**
comparasses	**comparassiez**	**eusses comparé**	**eussiez comparé**
comparât	**comparassent**	**eût comparé**	**eussent comparé**

Impératif
compare
comparons
comparez

Words and expressions related to this verb

comparer à to compare to (when some equality exists between the two compared)
comparer avec to compare with (when one is considered to be of a higher degree than the rest)
sans comparaison without comparison
une comparaison comparison
comparativement comparatively
comparatif, comparative comparative
par comparaison avec comparatively to
comparable à comparable to
en comparaison de in comparison with

For an explanation of meanings and uses of French and English verb tenses and moods, see pages 10–21.

Irregular verb

to understand, to include

The Seven Simple Tenses		The Seven Compound Tenses	
Singular	Plural	Singular	Plural
1 présent de l'indicatif		8 passé composé	
comprends	**comprenons**	**ai compris**	**avons compris**
comprends	**comprenez**	**as compris**	**avez compris**
comprend	**comprennent**	**a compris**	**ont compris**
2 imparfait de l'indicatif		9 plus-que-parfait de l'indicatif	
comprenais	**comprenions**	**avais compris**	**avions compris**
comprenais	**compreniez**	**avais compris**	**aviez compris**
comprenait	**comprenaient**	**avait compris**	**avaient compris**
3 passé simple		10 passé antérieur	
compris	**comprîmes**	**eus compris**	**eûmes compris**
compris	**comprîtes**	**eus compris**	**eûtes compris**
comprit	**comprirent**	**eut compris**	**eurent compris**
4 futur		11 futur antérieur	
comprendrai	**comprendrons**	**aurai compris**	**aurons compris**
comprendras	**comprendrez**	**auras compris**	**aurez compris**
comprendra	**comprendront**	**aura compris**	**auront compris**
5 conditionnel		12 conditionnel passé	
comprendrais	**comprendrions**	**aurais compris**	**aurions compris**
comprendrais	**comprendriez**	**aurais compris**	**auriez compris**
comprendrait	**comprendraient**	**aurait compris**	**auraient compris**
6 présent du subjonctif		13 passé du subjonctif	
comprenne	**comprenions**	**aie compris**	**ayons compris**
comprennes	**compreniez**	**aies compris**	**ayez compris**
comprenne	**comprennent**	**ait compris**	**aient compris**
7 imparfait du subjonctif		14 plus-que-parfait du subjonctif	
comprisse	**comprissions**	**eusse compris**	**eussions compris**
comprisses	**comprissiez**	**eusses compris**	**eussiez compris**
comprît	**comprissent**	**eût compris**	**eussent compris**

Impératif
comprends
comprenons
comprenez

Sentences using this verb and expressions related to it

Je ne comprends jamais le prof de biologie. Je n'ai pas compris la leçon d'hier, je ne comprends pas la leçon d'aujourd'hui, et je ne comprendrai jamais rien.

faire comprendre à qqn que . . . to make it clear to someone that . . .
la compréhension comprehension, understanding
Ça se comprend. Of course; That is understood.
y compris included, including
y compris la taxe tax included
service compris, y compris le service service included (no tip necessary)
Est-ce que le service est compris? Is the service (tip) included?
compréhensif, compréhensive *adj.* understanding

See also **apprendre, entreprendre, se méprendre, prendre, reprendre,** and **surprendre.**

The subject pronouns are found on page 103.

compter (103) — Part. pr. comptant — Part. passé compté

to count, to intend, to expect to

Regular **-er** verb

The Seven Simple Tenses		The Seven Compound Tenses	
Singular	Plural	Singular	Plural
1 présent de l'indicatif		8 passé composé	
compte	**comptons**	**ai compté**	**avons compté**
comptes	**comptez**	**as compté**	**avez compté**
compte	**comptent**	**a compté**	**ont compté**
2 imparfait de l'indicatif		9 plus-que-parfait de l'indicatif	
comptais	**comptions**	**avais compté**	**avions compté**
comptais	**comptiez**	**avais compté**	**aviez compté**
comptait	**comptaient**	**avait compté**	**avaient compté**
3 passé simple		10 passé antérieur	
comptai	**comptâmes**	**eus compté**	**eûmes compté**
comptas	**comptâtes**	**eus compté**	**eûtes compté**
compta	**comptèrent**	**eut compté**	**eurent compté**
4 futur		11 futur antérieur	
compterai	**compterons**	**aurai compté**	**aurons compté**
compteras	**compterez**	**auras compté**	**aurez compté**
comptera	**compteront**	**aura compté**	**auront compté**
5 conditionnel		12 conditionnel passé	
compterais	**compterions**	**aurais compté**	**aurions compté**
compterais	**compteriez**	**aurais compté**	**auriez compté**
compterait	**compteraient**	**aurait compté**	**auraient compté**
6 présent du subjonctif		13 passé du subjonctif	
compte	**comptions**	**aie compté**	**ayons compté**
comptes	**comptiez**	**aies compté**	**ayez compté**
compte	**comptent**	**ait compté**	**aient compté**
7 imparfait du subjonctif		14 plus-que-parfait du subjonctif	
comptasse	**comptassions**	**eusse compté**	**eussions compté**
comptasses	**comptassiez**	**eusses compté**	**eussiez compté**
comptât	**comptassent**	**eût compté**	**eussent compté**

Impératif
compte
comptons
comptez

Common idiomatic expressions using this verb

Je compte aller en France l'été prochain avec ma femme pour voir nos amis français.

la comptabilité bookkeeping, accounting
comptable accountable
le comptage counting
payer comptant to pay cash
compter faire qqch to expect to do something
compter sur to count (rely) on; **Puis-je y compter?** Can I depend on it?
escompter to discount; **un escompte** a discount
donner sans compter to give generously
sans compter . . . to say nothing of . . .
le comptoir counter (in a store)

Irregular verb with spelling change:
c changes to **ç** before **o** or **u** to keep **s** sound

to conceive

The Seven Simple Tenses		The Seven Compound Tenses	
Singular	Plural	Singular	Plural
1 présent de l'indicatif		8 passé composé	
conçois	**concevons**	**ai conçu**	**avons conçu**
conçois	**concevez**	**as conçu**	**avez conçu**
conçoit	**conçoivent**	**a conçu**	**ont conçu**
2 imparfait de l'indicatif		9 plus-que-parfait de l'indicatif	
concevais	**concevions**	**avais conçu**	**avions conçu**
concevais	**conceviez**	**avais conçu**	**aviez conçu**
concevait	**concevaient**	**avait conçu**	**avaient conçu**
3 passé simple		10 passé antérieur	
conçus	**conçûmes**	**eus conçu**	**eûmes conçu**
conçus	**conçûtes**	**eus conçu**	**eûtes conçu**
conçut	**conçurent**	**eut conçu**	**eurent conçu**
4 futur		11 futur antérieur	
concevrai	**concevrons**	**aurai conçu**	**aurons conçu**
concevras	**concevrez**	**auras conçu**	**aurez conçu**
concevra	**concevront**	**aura conçu**	**auront conçu**
5 conditionnel		12 conditionnel passé	
concevrais	**concevrions**	**aurais conçu**	**aurions conçu**
concevrais	**concevriez**	**aurais conçu**	**auriez conçu**
concevrait	**concevraient**	**aurait conçu**	**auraient conçu**
6 présent du subjonctif		13 passé du subjonctif	
conçoive	**concevions**	**aie conçu**	**ayons conçu**
conçoives	**conceviez**	**aies conçu**	**ayez conçu**
conçoive	**conçoivent**	**ait conçu**	**aient conçu**
7 imparfait du subjonctif		14 plus-que-parfait du subjonctif	
conçusse	**conçussions**	**eusse conçu**	**eussions conçu**
conçusses	**conçussiez**	**eusses conçu**	**eussiez conçu**
conçût	**conçussent**	**eût conçu**	**eussent conçu**

Impératif
conçois
concevons
concevez

Words and expressions related to this verb

concevoir des idées to form ideas
concevable conceivable
une conception concept, idea
un concepteur, une conceptrice designer
ainsi conçu written as follows
Je ne peux même pas concevoir . . . I just can't even imagine . . .

Don't forget to use the English-French verb index. It's in the Appendixes.

to conclude

Irregular verb

The Seven Simple Tenses		The Seven Compound Tenses	
Singular	Plural	Singular	Plural
1 présent de l'indicatif		8 passé composé	
conclus	**concluons**	**ai conclu**	**avons conclu**
conclus	**concluez**	**as conclu**	**avez conclu**
conclut	**concluent**	**a conclu**	**ont conclu**
2 imparfait de l'indicatif		9 plus-que-parfait de l'indicatif	
concluais	**concluions**	**avais conclu**	**avions conclu**
concluais	**concluiez**	**avais conclu**	**aviez conclu**
concluait	**concluaient**	**avait conclu**	**avaient conclu**
3 passé simple		10 passé antérieur	
conclus	**conclûmes**	**eus conclu**	**eûmes conclu**
conclus	**conclûtes**	**eus conclu**	**eûtes conclu**
conclut	**conclurent**	**eut conclu**	**eurent conclu**
4 futur		11 futur antérieur	
conclurai	**conclurons**	**aurai conclu**	**aurons conclu**
concluras	**conclurez**	**auras conclu**	**aurez conclu**
conclura	**concluront**	**aura conclu**	**auront conclu**
5 conditionnel		12 conditionnel passé	
conclurais	**conclurions**	**aurais conclu**	**aurions conclu**
conclurais	**concluriez**	**aurais conclu**	**auriez conclu**
conclurait	**concluraient**	**aurait conclu**	**auraient conclu**
6 présent du subjonctif		13 passé du subjonctif	
conclue	**concluions**	**aie conclu**	**ayons conclu**
conclues	**concluiez**	**aies conclu**	**ayez conclu**
conclue	**concluent**	**ait conclu**	**aient conclu**
7 imparfait du subjonctif		14 plus-que-parfait du subjonctif	
conclusse	**conclussions**	**eusse conclu**	**eussions conclu**
conclusses	**conclussiez**	**eusses conclu**	**eussiez conclu**
conclût	**conclussent**	**eût conclu**	**eussent conclu**

Impératif
conclus
concluons
concluez

Words and expressions related to this verb

la conclusion conclusion
en conclusion in conclusion
exclure to exclude
exclu, exclue excluded
un film en exclusivité a first-run motion picture

See also **inclure.**

inclure to enclose, to include (**part. passé: inclus, incluse**); **une photo ci-incluse** a photo enclosed herewith; **jusqu'à la page 100 incluse** up to and including page 100

Soak up some verbs used in weather expressions. There's a list in the Appendixes.

Irregular verb

to lead, to drive, to conduct, to manage

The Seven Simple Tenses		The Seven Compound Tenses	
Singular	Plural	Singular	Plural
1 présent de l'indicatif		8 passé composé	
conduis	**conduisons**	**ai conduit**	**avons conduit**
conduis	**conduisez**	**as conduit**	**avez conduit**
conduit	**conduisent**	**a conduit**	**ont conduit**
2 imparfait de l'indicatif		9 plus-que-parfait de l'indicatif	
conduisais	**conduisions**	**avais conduit**	**avions conduit**
conduisais	**conduisiez**	**avais conduit**	**aviez conduit**
conduisait	**conduisaient**	**avait conduit**	**avaient conduit**
3 passé simple		10 passé antérieur	
conduisis	**conduisîmes**	**eus conduit**	**eûmes conduit**
conduisis	**conduisîtes**	**eus conduit**	**eûtes conduit**
conduisit	**conduisirent**	**eut conduit**	**eurent conduit**
4 futur		11 futur antérieur	
conduirai	**conduirons**	**aurai conduit**	**aurons conduit**
conduiras	**conduirez**	**auras conduit**	**aurez conduit**
conduira	**conduiront**	**aura conduit**	**auront conduit**
5 conditionnel		12 conditionnel passé	
conduirais	**conduirions**	**aurais conduit**	**aurions conduit**
conduirais	**conduiriez**	**aurais conduit**	**auriez conduit**
conduirait	**conduiraient**	**aurait conduit**	**auraient conduit**
6 présent du subjonctif		13 passé du subjonctif	
conduise	**conduisions**	**aie conduit**	**ayons conduit**
conduises	**conduisiez**	**aies conduit**	**ayez conduit**
conduise	**conduisent**	**ait conduit**	**aient conduit**
7 imparfait du subjonctif		14 plus-que-parfait du subjonctif	
conduisisse	**conduisissions**	**eusse conduit**	**eussions conduit**
conduisisses	**conduisissiez**	**eusses conduit**	**eussiez conduit**
conduisît	**conduisissent**	**eût conduit**	**eussent conduit**

Impératif
conduis
conduisons
conduisez

Sentences using this verb and words related to it

—Savez-vous conduire?

—Oui, je sais conduire. Je conduis une voiture, je dirige un orchestre, et hier j'ai conduit quelqu'un à la gare. Attendez, je vais vous conduire à la porte.

—Merci, vous êtes très aimable.

un conducteur, une conductrice driver
la conduite conduct, behavior
induire to induce
induire en to lead into
conduire une voiture to drive a car
se conduire to conduct (behave) oneself
un permis de conduire driver's license
enduire to coat, spread

See also **déduire, introduire, produire, réduire, reproduire, séduire,** and **traduire.**

The subject pronouns are found on page 103.

connaître (107) Part. pr. **connaissant** Part. passé **connu**

to know, to be acquainted with, to make the acquaintance of

Irregular verb

The Seven Simple Tenses		The Seven Compound Tenses	
Singular	Plural	Singular	Plural
1 présent de l'indicatif		8 passé composé	
connais	**connaissons**	**ai connu**	**avons connu**
connais	**connaissez**	**as connu**	**avez connu**
connaît	**connaissent**	**a connu**	**ont connu**
2 imparfait de l'indicatif		9 plus-que-parfait de l'indicatif	
connaissais	**connaissions**	**avais connu**	**avions connu**
connaissais	**connaissiez**	**avais connu**	**aviez connu**
connaissait	**connaissaient**	**avait connu**	**avaient connu**
3 passé simple		10 passé antérieur	
connus	**connûmes**	**eus connu**	**eûmes connu**
connus	**connûtes**	**eus connu**	**eûtes connu**
connut	**connurent**	**eut connu**	**eurent connu**
4 futur		11 futur antérieur	
connaîtrai	**connaîtrons**	**aurai connu**	**aurons connu**
connaîtras	**connaîtrez**	**auras connu**	**aurez connu**
connaîtra	**connaîtront**	**aura connu**	**auront connu**
5 conditionnel		12 conditionnel passé	
connaîtrais	**connaîtrions**	**aurais connu**	**aurions connu**
connaîtrais	**connaîtriez**	**aurais connu**	**auriez connu**
connaîtrait	**connaîtraient**	**aurait connu**	**auraient connu**
6 présent du subjonctif		13 passé du subjonctif	
connaisse	**connaissions**	**aie connu**	**ayons connu**
connaisses	**connaissiez**	**aies connu**	**ayez connu**
connaisse	**connaissent**	**ait connu**	**aient connu**
7 imparfait du subjonctif		14 plus-que-parfait du subjonctif	
connusse	**connussions**	**eusse connu**	**eussions connu**
connusses	**connussiez**	**eusses connu**	**eussiez connu**
connût	**connussent**	**eût connu**	**eussent connu**

Impératif
connais
connaissons
connaissez

AN ESSENTIAL 55 VERB

Connaître

C

Connaître is an important verb to know. It is used in a number of expressions and in many everyday situations.

Sample sentences using connaître

—Connaissez-vous quelqu'un qui puisse m'aider?
—Je suis touriste et je ne connais pas cette ville.
—Non, je ne connais personne. Je suis touriste aussi.
—Voulez-vous aller prendre un café? Nous pouvons faire connaissance.
—Pas du tout! Je ne vous connais pas!

—Do you know someone who can help me?
—I am a tourist and I don't know this city.
—No, I don't know anyone. I'm a tourist too.
—Would you like to go have a coffee? We could get acquainted.
—Not at all! I don't know you!

À ma connaissance, il est impossible de dépasser la vitesse de la lumière. As far as I know, it is impossible to go beyond the speed of light.

Michel et Dorothea sont de vrais connaisseurs en vin. Michael and Dorothy are real wine connoisseurs.

Il a connu beaucoup de difficultés pendant son adolescence. He experienced many difficulties (problems) during his adolescence.

Ce film a connu un grand succès en Europe. This movie was very successful (well received) in Europe.

Ça me connaît! I know that well!/I know about that! (Note: This is a rare construction.)

Mon père a connu ma mère à New York. My father met my mother in New York.

Words and expressions related to this verb

la connaissance **knowledge, understanding, acquaintance**

à ma connaissance **as far as I know**

connaisseur, connaisseuse *adj.* **expert**

un connaisseur, une connaisseuse **connoisseur**

se connaître **to know each other, to know oneself**

faire connaissance **to get acquainted**

avoir des connaissances en **to be knowledgeable in**

The subject pronouns are found on page 103.

conquérir (108) — Part. pr. conquérant — Part. passé conquis

to conquer

Irregular verb

The Seven Simple Tenses		The Seven Compound Tenses	
Singular	Plural	Singular	Plural
1 présent de l'indicatif		8 passé composé	
conquiers	**conquérons**	**ai conquis**	**avons conquis**
conquiers	**conquérez**	**as conquis**	**avez conquis**
conquiert	**conquièrent**	**a conquis**	**ont conquis**
2 imparfait de l'indicatif		9 plus-que-parfait de l'indicatif	
conquérais	**conquérions**	**avais conquis**	**avions conquis**
conquérais	**conquériez**	**avais conquis**	**aviez conquis**
conquérait	**conquéraient**	**avait conquis**	**avaient conquis**
3 passé simple		10 passé antérieur	
conquis	**conquîmes**	**eus conquis**	**eûmes conquis**
conquis	**conquîtes**	**eus conquis**	**eûtes conquis**
conquit	**conquirent**	**eut conquis**	**eurent conquis**
4 futur		11 futur antérieur	
conquerrai	**conquerrons**	**aurai conquis**	**aurons conquis**
conquerras	**conquerrez**	**auras conquis**	**aurez conquis**
conquerra	**conquerront**	**aura conquis**	**auront conquis**
5 conditionnel		12 conditionnel passé	
conquerrais	**conquerrions**	**aurais conquis**	**aurions conquis**
conquerrais	**conquerriez**	**aurais conquis**	**auriez conquis**
conquerrait	**conquerraient**	**aurait conquis**	**auraient conquis**
6 présent du subjonctif		13 passé du subjonctif	
conquière	**conquérions**	**aie conquis**	**ayons conquis**
conquières	**conquériez**	**aies conquis**	**ayez conquis**
conquière	**conquièrent**	**ait conquis**	**aient conquis**
7 imparfait du subjonctif		14 plus-que-parfait du subjonctif	
conquisse	**conquissions**	**eusse conquis**	**eussions conquis**
conquisses	**conquissiez**	**eusses conquis**	**eussiez conquis**
conquît	**conquissent**	**eût conquis**	**eussent conquis**

Impératif
conquiers
conquérons
conquérez

Words and expressions related to this verb
conquérir l'affection de qqn to win someone's affection
conquérir une femme to win over a woman; **conquérir un homme** to win over a man
la conquête conquest; **la conquête du pouvoir** conquest of power
avoir un air conquérant to seem pretentious
Guillaume le Conquérant William the Conqueror

Conquer your fear of the Subjunctive. See pages 26–31.

Regular **-er** verb

to advise, to counsel, to recommend

The Seven Simple Tenses		The Seven Compound Tenses	
Singular	Plural	Singular	Plural
1 présent de l'indicatif		8 passé composé	
conseille	**conseillons**	**ai conseillé**	**avons conseillé**
conseilles	**conseillez**	**as conseillé**	**avez conseillé**
conseille	**conseillent**	**a conseillé**	**ont conseillé**
2 imparfait de l'indicatif		9 plus-que-parfait de l'indicatif	
conseillais	**conseillions**	**avais conseillé**	**avions conseillé**
conseillais	**conseilliez**	**avais conseillé**	**aviez conseillé**
conseillait	**conseillaient**	**avait conseillé**	**avaient conseillé**
3 passé simple		10 passé antérieur	
conseillai	**conseillâmes**	**eus conseillé**	**eûmes conseillé**
conseillas	**conseillâtes**	**eus conseillé**	**eûtes conseillé**
conseilla	**conseillèrent**	**eut conseillé**	**eurent conseillé**
4 futur		11 futur antérieur	
conseillerai	**conseillerons**	**aurai conseillé**	**aurons conseillé**
conseilleras	**conseillerez**	**auras conseillé**	**aurez conseillé**
conseillera	**conseilleront**	**aura conseillé**	**auront conseillé**
5 conditionnel		12 conditionnel passé	
conseillerais	**conseillerions**	**aurais conseillé**	**aurions conseillé**
conseillerais	**conseilleriez**	**aurais conseillé**	**auriez conseillé**
conseillerait	**conseilleraient**	**aurait conseillé**	**auraient conseillé**
6 présent du subjonctif		13 passé du subjonctif	
conseille	**conseillions**	**aie conseillé**	**ayons conseillé**
conseilles	**conseilliez**	**aies conseillé**	**ayez conseillé**
conseille	**conseillent**	**ait conseillé**	**aient conseillé**
7 imparfait du subjonctif		14 plus-que-parfait du subjonctif	
conseillasse	**conseillassions**	**eusse conseillé**	**eussions conseillé**
conseillasses	**conseillassiez**	**eusses conseillé**	**eussiez conseillé**
conseillât	**conseillassent**	**eût conseillé**	**eussent conseillé**

Impératif
conseille
conseillons
conseillez

Words and expressions related to this verb
conseiller qqch à qqn to recommend something to someone
conseiller à qqn de faire qqch to advise someone to do something
un conseiller (un conseilleur), une conseillère (une conseilleuse) counselor, adviser
un conseil counsel, advice; **sur le conseil de** on the advice of
déconseiller to advise, warn against; **déconseiller qqch à qqn** to advise someone against something

We recommend that you try the verb drills and tests with answers explained on pages 50–101.

consentir (110) — Part. pr consentant — Part. passé consenti

to consent, to agree

Irregular verb

The Seven Simple Tenses		The Seven Compound Tenses	
Singular	Plural	Singular	Plural
1 présent de l'indicatif		8 passé composé	
consens	**consentons**	**ai consenti**	**avons consenti**
consens	**consentez**	**as consenti**	**avez consenti**
consent	**consentent**	**a consenti**	**ont consenti**
2 imparfait de l'indicatif		9 plus-que-parfait de l'indicatif	
consentais	**consentions**	**avais consenti**	**avions consenti**
consentais	**consentiez**	**avais consenti**	**aviez consenti**
consentait	**consentaient**	**avait consenti**	**avaient consenti**
3 passé simple		10 passé antérieur	
consentis	**consentîmes**	**eus consenti**	**eûmes consenti**
consentis	**consentîtes**	**eus consenti**	**eûtes consenti**
consentit	**consentirent**	**eut consenti**	**eurent consenti**
4 futur		11 futur antérieur	
consentirai	**consentirons**	**aurai consenti**	**aurons consenti**
consentiras	**consentirez**	**auras consenti**	**aurez consenti**
consentira	**consentiront**	**aura consenti**	**auront consenti**
5 conditionnel		12 conditionnel passé	
consentirais	**consentirions**	**aurais consenti**	**aurions consenti**
consentirais	**consentiriez**	**aurais consenti**	**auriez consenti**
consentirait	**consentiraient**	**aurait consenti**	**auraient consenti**
6 présent du subjonctif		13 passé du subjonctif	
consente	**consentions**	**aie consenti**	**ayons consenti**
consentes	**consentiez**	**aies consenti**	**ayez consenti**
consente	**consentent**	**ait consenti**	**aient consenti**
7 imparfait du subjonctif		14 plus-que-parfait du subjonctif	
consentisse	**consentissions**	**eusse consenti**	**eussions consenti**
consentisses	**consentissiez**	**eusses consenti**	**eussiez consenti**
consentît	**consentissent**	**eût consenti**	**eussent consenti**

Impératif
consens
consentons
consentez

Words and expressions related to this verb

consentir à faire qqch to agree to do something
le consentement consent, approval
consentant, consentante agreeable, willing
consentir à qqch to consent to something
consentir au mariage to consent to marriage
donner son consentement to give one's consent, agreement

See also **sentir.**

Grammar putting you in a tense mood? Review the definitions of basic grammatical terms on pages 35–49.

Irregular verb

to construct, to build

The Seven Simple Tenses		The Seven Compound Tenses	
Singular	Plural	Singular	Plural
1 présent de l'indicatif		8 passé composé	
construis	**construisons**	**ai construit**	**avons construit**
construis	**construisez**	**as construit**	**avez construit**
construit	**construisent**	**a construit**	**ont construit**
2 imparfait de l'indicatif		9 plus-que-parfait de l'indicatif	
construisais	**construisions**	**avais construit**	**avions construit**
construisais	**construisiez**	**avais construit**	**aviez construit**
construisait	**construisaient**	**avait construit**	**avaient construit**
3 passé simple		10 passé antérieur	
construisis	**construisîmes**	**eus construit**	**eûmes construit**
construisis	**construisîtes**	**eus construit**	**eûtes construit**
construisit	**construisirent**	**eut construit**	**eurent construit**
4 futur		11 futur antérieur	
construirai	**construirons**	**aurai construit**	**aurons construit**
construiras	**construirez**	**auras construit**	**aurez construit**
construira	**construiront**	**aura construit**	**auront construit**
5 conditionnel		12 conditionnel passé	
construirais	**construirions**	**aurais construit**	**aurions construit**
construirais	**construiriez**	**aurais construit**	**auriez construit**
construirait	**construiraient**	**aurait construit**	**auraient construit**
6 présent du subjonctif		13 passé du subjonctif	
construise	**construisions**	**aie construit**	**ayons construit**
construises	**construisiez**	**aies construit**	**ayez construit**
construise	**construisent**	**ait construit**	**aient construit**
7 imparfait du subjonctif		14 plus-que-parfait du subjonctif	
construisisse	**construisissions**	**eusse construit**	**eussions construit**
construisisses	**construisissiez**	**eusses construit**	**eussiez construit**
construisît	**construisissent**	**eût construit**	**eussent construit**

Impératif
construis
construisons
construisez

Sentences using this verb and words related to it

—Je vois que vous êtes en train de construire quelque chose. Qu'est-ce que vous construisez?

—Je construis une tour comme la Tour Eiffel. Aimez-vous ce bateau que j'ai construit?

un constructeur a manufacturer, builder, constructor
une construction construction, building
reconstruire to reconstruct, to rebuild; **en construction** under construction

For an explanation of meanings and uses of French and English verb tenses and moods, see pages 10–21.

contenir (112) — Part. pr. contenant — Part. passé contenu

to contain

Irregular verb

The Seven Simple Tenses		The Seven Compound Tenses	
Singular	Plural	Singular	Plural
1 présent de l'indicatif		8 passé composé	
contiens	**contenons**	**ai contenu**	**avons contenu**
contiens	**contenez**	**as contenu**	**avez contenu**
contient	**contiennent**	**a contenu**	**ont contenu**
2 imparfait de l'indicatif		9 plus-que-parfait de l'indicatif	
contenais	**contenions**	**avais contenu**	**avions contenu**
contenais	**conteniez**	**avais contenu**	**aviez contenu**
contenait	**contenaient**	**avait contenu**	**avaient contenu**
3 passé simple		10 passé antérieur	
contins	**contînmes**	**eus contenu**	**eûmes contenu**
contins	**contîntes**	**eus contenu**	**eûtes contenu**
continT	**continrent**	**eut contenu**	**eurent contenu**
4 futur		11 futur antérieur	
contiendrai	**contiendrons**	**aurai contenu**	**aurons contenu**
contiendras	**contiendrez**	**auras contenu**	**aurez contenu**
contiendra	**contiendront**	**aura contenu**	**auront contenu**
5 conditionnel		12 conditionnel passé	
contiendrais	**contiendrions**	**aurais contenu**	**aurions contenu**
contiendrais	**contiendriez**	**aurais contenu**	**auriez contenu**
contiendrait	**contiendraient**	**aurait contenu**	**auraient contenu**
6 présent du subjonctif		13 passé du subjonctif	
contienne	**contenions**	**aie contenu**	**ayons contenu**
contiennes	**conteniez**	**aies contenu**	**ayez contenu**
contienne	**contiennent**	**ait contenu**	**aient contenu**
7 imparfait du subjonctif		14 plus-que-parfait du subjonctif	
continsse	**continssions**	**eusse contenu**	**eussions contenu**
continsses	**continssiez**	**eusses contenu**	**eussiez contenu**
contînt	**continssent**	**eût contenu**	**eussent contenu**

Impératif
contiens
contenons
contenez

Common idiomatic expressions using this verb and words related to it

contenir ses émotions to contain (dominate) one's emotions
être content (contente) to be content, satisfied
être content (contente) des autres to be content (satisfied) with others
se contenir to contain oneself, to dominate (control) oneself
un contenant container
le contenu contents
être content (contente) de soi to be self-satisfied
avoir l'air content to seem pleased

See also **obtenir, retenir,** and **tenir.**

Don't forget to check the list of 2,600 additional verbs keyed to the 501 model verbs. It's in the Appendixes!

Regular **-er** verb

to relate, to narrate

The Seven Simple Tenses		The Seven Compound Tenses	
Singular	Plural	Singular	Plural
1 présent de l'indicatif		8 passé composé	
conte	**contons**	**ai conté**	**avons conté**
contes	**contez**	**as conté**	**avez conté**
conte	**content**	**a conté**	**ont conté**
2 imparfait de l'indicatif		9 plus-que-parfait de l'indicatif	
contais	**contions**	**avais conté**	**avions conté**
contais	**contiez**	**avais conté**	**aviez conté**
contait	**contaient**	**avait conté**	**avaient conté**
3 passé simple		10 passé antérieur	
contai	**contâmes**	**eus conté**	**eûmes conté**
contas	**contâtes**	**eus conté**	**eûtes conté**
conta	**contèrent**	**eut conté**	**eurent conté**
4 futur		11 futur antérieur	
conterai	**conterons**	**aurai conté**	**aurons conté**
conteras	**conterez**	**auras conté**	**aurez conté**
contera	**conteront**	**aura conté**	**auront conté**
5 conditionnel		12 conditionnel passé	
conterais	**conterions**	**aurais conté**	**aurions conté**
conterais	**conteriez**	**aurais conté**	**auriez conté**
conterait	**conteraient**	**aurait conté**	**auraient conté**
6 présent du subjonctif		13 passé du subjonctif	
conte	**contions**	**aie conté**	**ayons conté**
contes	**contiez**	**aies conté**	**ayez conté**
conte	**content**	**ait conté**	**aient conté**
7 imparfait du subjonctif		14 plus-que-parfait du subjonctif	
contasse	**contassions**	**eusse conté**	**eussions conté**
contasses	**contassiez**	**eusses conté**	**eussiez conté**
contât	**contassent**	**eût conté**	**eussent conté**

Impératif
conte
contons
contez

Sentences using this verb and words related to it

Notre professeur de français nous conte toujours des histoires intéressantes. Son conte favori est *Un coeur simple* **de Flaubert.**

un conte a story, tale
un conte de fées fairy tale
un conte à dormir debout cock-and-bull story
un conteur, une conteuse writer of short stories
Contez-moi vos malheurs. Tell me about your troubles.

See also **raconter.**

Use the guide to French pronunciation. It's in the Appendixes.

continuer (114) — Part. pr. continuant — Part. passé continué

to continue

Regular **-er** verb

The Seven Simple Tenses		The Seven Compound Tenses	
Singular	Plural	Singular	Plural
1 présent de l'indicatif		8 passé composé	
continue	**continuons**	**ai continué**	**avons continué**
continues	**continuez**	**as continué**	**avez continué**
continue	**continuent**	**a continué**	**ont continué**
2 imparfait de l'indicatif		9 plus-que-parfait de l'indicatif	
continuais	**continuions**	**avais continué**	**avions continué**
continuais	**continuiez**	**avais continué**	**aviez continué**
continuait	**continuaient**	**avait continué**	**avaient continué**
3 passé simple		10 passé antérieur	
continuai	**continuâmes**	**eus continué**	**eûmes continué**
continuas	**continuâtes**	**eus continué**	**eûtes continué**
continua	**continuèrent**	**eut continué**	**eurent continué**
4 futur		11 futur antérieur	
continuerai	**continuerons**	**aurai continué**	**aurons continué**
continueras	**continuerez**	**auras continué**	**aurez continué**
continuera	**continueront**	**aura continué**	**auront continué**
5 conditionnel		12 conditionnel passé	
continuerais	**continuerions**	**aurais continué**	**aurions continué**
continuerais	**continueriez**	**aurais continué**	**auriez continué**
continuerait	**continueraient**	**aurait continué**	**auraient continué**
6 présent du subjonctif		13 passé du subjonctif	
continue	**continuions**	**aie continué**	**ayons continué**
continues	**continuiez**	**aies continué**	**ayez continué**
continue	**continuent**	**ait continué**	**aient continué**
7 imparfait du subjonctif		14 plus-que-parfait du subjonctif	
continuasse	**continuassions**	**eusse continué**	**eussions continué**
continuasses	**continuassiez**	**eusses continué**	**eussiez continué**
continuât	**continuassent**	**eût continué**	**eussent continué**

Impératif
continue
continuons
continuez

Sentences using this verb and words related to it

—Allez-vous continuer à étudier le français l'année prochaine?
—Certainement. Je compte étudier cette belle langue continuellement.

la continuation continuation
continuel, continuelle continual
continuellement continually
continuer à + inf. to continue + inf.
continuer de + inf. to continue (persist) in; **Cet ivrogne continue de boire.** This drunkard persists in drinking (habit).

Get acquainted with what preposition goes with what verb. See *Verbs with prepositions* in the Appendixes.

Irregular verb

to constrain, to restrain, to compel

The Seven Simple Tenses		The Seven Compound Tenses	
Singular	Plural	Singular	Plural
1 présent de l'indicatif		8 passé composé	
contrains	**contraignons**	**ai contraint**	**avons contraint**
contrains	**contraignez**	**as contraint**	**avez contraint**
contraint	**contraignent**	**a contraint**	**ont contraint**
2 imparfait de l'indicatif		9 plus-que-parfait de l'indicatif	
contraignais	**contraignions**	**avais contraint**	**avions contraint**
contraignais	**contraigniez**	**avais contraint**	**aviez contraint**
contraignait	**contraignaient**	**avait contraint**	**avaient contraint**
3 passé simple		10 passé antérieur	
contraignis	**contraignîmes**	**eus contraint**	**eûmes contraint**
contraignis	**contraignîtes**	**eus contraint**	**eûtes contraint**
contraignit	**contraignirent**	**eut contraint**	**eurent contraint**
4 futur		11 futur antérieur	
contraindrai	**contraindrons**	**aurai contraint**	**aurons contraint**
contraindras	**contraindrez**	**auras contraint**	**aurez contraint**
contraindra	**contraindront**	**aura contraint**	**auront contraint**
5 conditionnel		12 conditionnel passé	
contraindrais	**contraindrions**	**aurais contraint**	**aurions contraint**
contraindrais	**contraindriez**	**aurais contraint**	**auriez contraint**
contraindrait	**contraindraient**	**aurait contraint**	**auraient contraint**
6 présent du subjonctif		13 passé du subjonctif	
contraigne	**contraignions**	**aie contraint**	**ayons contraint**
contraignes	**contraigniez**	**aies contraint**	**ayez contraint**
contraigne	**contraignent**	**ait contraint**	**aient contraint**
7 imparfait du subjonctif		14 plus-que-parfait du subjonctif	
contraignisse	**contraignissions**	**eusse contraint**	**eussions contraint**
contraignisses	**contraignissiez**	**eusses contraint**	**eussiez contraint**
contraignît	**contraignissent**	**eût contraint**	**eussent contraint**

Impératif
contrains
contraignons
contraignez

Words and expressions related to this verb

se contraindre à faire qqch to constrain oneself from doing something
avoir l'air contraint to have a constrained expression (on one's face)
parler sans contrainte to speak freely
contraint, contrainte constrained, forced
être contraint (contrainte) à faire qqch to be constrained to doing something
la contrainte constraint
tenir qqn dans la contrainte to hold someone in constraint

Check out the principal parts of some important French verbs on page 7.

contredire (116) — Part. pr. contredisant — Part. passé contredit

to contradict

Irregular verb

The Seven Simple Tenses		The Seven Compound Tenses	
Singular	Plural	Singular	Plural
1 présent de l'indicatif		8 passé composé	
contredis	**contredisons**	**ai contredit**	**avons contredit**
contredis	**contredisez**	**as contredit**	**avez contredit**
contredit	**contredisent**	**a contredit**	**ont contredit**
2 imparfait de l'indicatif		9 plus-que-parfait de l'indicatif	
contredisais	**contredisions**	**avais contredit**	**avions contredit**
contredisais	**contredisiez**	**avais contredit**	**aviez contredit**
contredisait	**contredisaient**	**avait contredit**	**avaient contredit**
3 passé simple		10 passé antérieur	
contredis	**contredîmes**	**eus contredit**	**eûmes contredit**
contredis	**contredîtes**	**eus contredit**	**eûtes contredit**
contredit	**contredirent**	**eut contredit**	**eurent contredit**
4 futur		11 futur antérieur	
contredirai	**contredirons**	**aurai contredit**	**aurons contredit**
contrediras	**contredirez**	**auras contredit**	**aurez contredit**
contredira	**contrediront**	**aura contredit**	**auront contredit**
5 conditionnel		12 conditionnel passé	
contredirais	**contredirions**	**aurais contredit**	**aurions contredit**
contredirais	**contrediriez**	**aurais contredit**	**auriez contredit**
contredirait	**contrediraient**	**aurait contredit**	**auraient contredit**
6 présent du subjonctif		13 passé du subjonctif	
contredise	**contredisions**	**aie contredit**	**ayons contredit**
contredises	**contredisiez**	**aies contredit**	**ayez contredit**
contredise	**contredisent**	**ait contredit**	**aient contredit**
7 imparfait du subjonctif		14 plus-que-parfait du subjonctif	
contredisse	**contredissions**	**eusse contredit**	**eussions contredit**
contredisses	**contredissiez**	**eusses contredit**	**eussiez contredit**
contredît	**contredissent**	**eût contredit**	**eussent contredit**

Impératif
contredis
contredisons
contredisez

Words and expressions related to this verb

se contredire to contradict oneself, to contradict each other (one another)
un contredit contradiction; **sans contredit** unquestionably
une contradiction contradiction
contradictoire contradictory
contradicteur, contradictrice contradictor
contradictoirement contradictorily
en contradiction avec inconsistent with

See also **dire, interdire, maudire, médire,** and **prédire.**

It's important that you be familiar with the Subjunctive. See pages 26–31.

Irregular verb

to convince

The Seven Simple Tenses		The Seven Compound Tenses	
Singular	Plural	Singular	Plural
1 présent de l'indicatif		8 passé composé	
convaincs	**convainquons**	**ai convaincu**	**avons convaincu**
convaincs	**convainquez**	**as convaincu**	**avez convaincu**
convainc	**convainquent**	**a convaincu**	**ont convaincu**
2 imparfait de l'indicatif		9 plus-que-parfait de l'indicatif	
convainquais	**convainquions**	**avais convaincu**	**avions convaincu**
convainquais	**convainquiez**	**avais convaincu**	**aviez convaincu**
convainquait	**convainquaient**	**avait convaincu**	**avaient convaincu**
3 passé simple		10 passé antérieur	
convainquis	**convainquîmes**	**eus convaincu**	**eûmes convaincu**
convainquis	**convainquîtes**	**eus convaincu**	**eûtes convaincu**
convainquit	**convainquirent**	**eut convaincu**	**eurent convaincu**
4 futur		11 futur antérieur	
convaincrai	**convaincrons**	**aurai convaincu**	**aurons convaincu**
convaincras	**convaincrez**	**auras convaincu**	**aurez convaincu**
convaincra	**convaincront**	**aura convaincu**	**auront convaincu**
5 conditionnel		12 conditionnel passé	
convaincrais	**convaincrions**	**aurais convaincu**	**aurions convaincu**
convaincrais	**convaincriez**	**aurais convaincu**	**auriez convaincu**
convaincrait	**convaincraient**	**aurait convaincu**	**auraient convaincu**
6 présent du subjonctif		13 passé du subjonctif	
convainque	**convainquions**	**aie convaincu**	**ayons convaincu**
convainques	**convainquiez**	**aies convaincu**	**ayez convaincu**
convainque	**convainquent**	**ait convaincu**	**aient convaincu**
7 imparfait du subjonctif		14 plus-que-parfait du subjonctif	
convainquisse	**convainquissions**	**eusse convaincu**	**eussions convaincu**
convainquisses	**convainquissiez**	**eusses convaincu**	**eussiez convaincu**
convainquît	**convainquissent**	**eût convaincu**	**eussent convaincu**

Impératif
convaincs
convainquons
convainquez

Words and expressions related to this verb

convaincre qqn de qqch to convince (persuade) someone of something

se laisser convaincre to allow oneself to be persuaded

d'un ton convaincu in a convincing tone

convaincant, convaincante convincing

se convaincre to convince oneself, to realize

See also **vaincre.**

How are you doing? Find out with the verb drills and tests with answers explained on pages 50–101.

convenir (118) Part. pr. convenant Part. passé convenu

to suit, to be suitable, to be appropriate, to agree, to acknowledge

Irregular verb

The Seven Simple Tenses		The Seven Compound Tenses	
Singular	Plural	Singular	Plural
1 présent de l'indicatif		8 passé composé	
conviens	**convenons**	**ai convenu**	**avons convenu**
conviens	**convenez**	**as convenu**	**avez convenu**
convient	**conviennent**	**a convenu**	**ont convenu**
2 imparfait de l'indicatif		9 plus-que-parfait de l'indicatif	
convenais	**convenions**	**avais convenu**	**avions convenu**
convenais	**conveniez**	**avais convenu**	**aviez convenu**
convenait	**convenaient**	**avait convenu**	**avaient convenu**
3 passé simple		10 passé antérieur	
convins	**convînmes**	**eus convenu**	**eûmes convenu**
convins	**convîntes**	**eus convenu**	**eûtes convenu**
convint	**convinrent**	**eut convenu**	**eurent convenu**
4 futur		11 futur antérieur	
conviendrai	**conviendrons**	**aurai convenu**	**aurons convenu**
conviendras	**conviendrez**	**auras convenu**	**aurez convenu**
conviendra	**conviendront**	**aura convenu**	**auront convenu**
5 conditionnel		12 conditionnel passé	
conviendrais	**conviendrions**	**aurais convenu**	**aurions convenu**
conviendrais	**conviendriez**	**aurais convenu**	**auriez convenu**
conviendrait	**conviendraient**	**aurait convenu**	**auraient convenu**
6 présent du subjonctif		13 passé du subjonctif	
convienne	**convenions**	**aie convenu**	**ayons convenu**
conviennes	**conveniez**	**aies convenu**	**ayez convenu**
convienne	**conviennent**	**ait convenu**	**aient convenu**
7 imparfait du subjonctif		14 plus-que-parfait du subjonctif	
convinsse	**convinssions**	**eusse convenu**	**eussions convenu**
convinsses	**convinssiez**	**eusses convenu**	**eussiez convenu**
convînt	**convinssent**	**eût convenu**	**eussent convenu**

Impératif
conviens
convenons
convenez

Common idiomatic expressions using this verb

convenir à to please, to suit (conjugated with **avoir**); **Cela lui a convenu.** That suited him.

convenir de qqch to agree on something (conjugated with **être**); **Ils sont convenus d'aller au cinéma.** They agreed to go to the movies.

J'en conviens. I agree to it.

Ce n'est pas convenable. That's not appropriate.

Faites ce qui convient. Do what is suitable.

convenir de faire qqch to agree to do something; **Mon père et moi, nous avons convenu de venir chez vous à 8 h. du soir.** My father and I agreed to come to your place at 8 in the evening.

Il faut convenir que vous avez raison. Admittedly, you are right (One must admit that you are right).

Cela ne me convient pas. That does not suit me.

See also **devenir, prévenir, revenir, se souvenir,** and **venir.**

to correct

Regular **-er** verb endings; spelling change: retain the **ge** before **a** or **o** to keep the soft **g** sound of the verb

The Seven Simple Tenses		The Seven Compound Tenses	
Singular	Plural	Singular	Plural
1 présent de l'indicatif		8 passé composé	
corrige	**corrigeons**	**ai corrigé**	**avons corrigé**
corriges	**corrigez**	**as corrigé**	**avez corrigé**
corrige	**corrigent**	**a corrigé**	**ont corrigé**
2 imparfait de l'indicatif		9 plus-que-parfait de l'indicatif	
corrigeais	**corrigions**	**avais corrigé**	**avions corrigé**
corrigeais	**corrigiez**	**avais corrigé**	**aviez corrigé**
corrigeait	**corrigeaient**	**avait corrigé**	**avaient corrigé**
3 passé simple		10 passé antérieur	
corrigeai	**corrigeâmes**	**eus corrigé**	**eûmes corrigé**
corrigeas	**corrigeâtes**	**eus corrigé**	**eûtes corrigé**
corrigea	**corrigèrent**	**eut corrigé**	**eurent corrigé**
4 futur		11 futur antérieur	
corrigerai	**corrigerons**	**aurai corrigé**	**aurons corrigé**
corrigeras	**corrigerez**	**auras corrigé**	**aurez corrigé**
corrigera	**corrigeront**	**aura corrigé**	**auront corrigé**
5 conditionnel		12 conditionnel passé	
corrigerais	**corrigerions**	**aurais corrigé**	**aurions corrigé**
corrigerais	**corrigeriez**	**aurais corrigé**	**auriez corrigé**
corrigerait	**corrigeraient**	**aurait corrigé**	**auraient corrigé**
6 présent du subjonctif		13 passé du subjonctif	
corrige	**corrigions**	**aie corrigé**	**ayons corrigé**
corriges	**corrigiez**	**aies corrigé**	**ayez corrigé**
corrige	**corrigent**	**ait corrigé**	**aient corrigé**
7 imparfait du subjonctif		14 plus-que-parfait du subjonctif	
corrigeasse	**corrigeassions**	**eusse corrigé**	**eussions corrigé**
corrigeasses	**corrigeassiez**	**eusses corrigé**	**eussiez corrigé**
corrigeât	**corrigeassent**	**eût corrigé**	**eussent corrigé**

Impératif
corrige
corrigeons
corrigez

Sentences using this verb and words related to it

Dans la classe de français nous corrigeons toujours nos devoirs en classe. Le (La) prof de français écrit les corrections au tableau.

une correction correction; **la correction** accuracy, correctness; **recorriger** to correct again

corriger qqn de to correct someone of

se corriger de to correct one's ways

corrigible corrigible; **incorrigible** incorrigible

incorrectement inaccurately, incorrectly

la correction automatique automatic correction (comp.)

un correcteur, une correctrice proofreader

corrompre (120) Part. pr. corrompant Part. passé corrompu

to corrupt

Regular **-re** verb endings; spelling change: 3rd person sing. of Tense No. 1 adds **t**

The Seven Simple Tenses		The Seven Compound Tenses	
Singular	Plural	Singular	Plural
1 présent de l'indicatif		8 passé composé	
corromps	**corrompons**	**ai corrompu**	**avons corrompu**
corromps	**corrompez**	**as corrompu**	**avez corrompu**
corrompt	**corrompent**	**a corrompu**	**ont corrompu**
2 imparfait de l'indicatif		9 plus-que-parfait de l'indicatif	
corrompais	**corrompions**	**avais corrompu**	**avions corrompu**
corrompais	**corrompiez**	**avais corrompu**	**aviez corrompu**
corrompait	**corrompaient**	**avait corrompu**	**avaient corrompu**
3 passé simple		10 passé antérieur	
corrompis	**corrompîmes**	**eus corrompu**	**eûmes corrompu**
corrompis	**corrompîtes**	**eus corrompu**	**eûtes corrompu**
corrompit	**corrompirent**	**eut corrompu**	**eurent corrompu**
4 futur		11 futur antérieur	
corromprai	**corromprons**	**aurai corrompu**	**aurons corrompu**
corrompras	**corromprez**	**auras corrompu**	**aurez corrompu**
corrompra	**corrompront**	**aura corrompu**	**auront corrompu**
5 conditionnel		12 conditionnel passé	
corromprais	**corromprions**	**aurais corrompu**	**aurions corrompu**
corromprais	**corrompriez**	**aurais corrompu**	**auriez corrompu**
corromprait	**corrompraient**	**aurait corrompu**	**auraient corrompu**
6 présent du subjonctif		13 passé du subjonctif	
corrompe	**corrompions**	**aie corrompu**	**ayons corrompu**
corrompes	**corrompiez**	**aies corrompu**	**ayez corrompu**
corrompe	**corrompent**	**ait corrompu**	**aient corrompu**
7 imparfait du subjonctif		14 plus-que-parfait du subjonctif	
corrompisse	**corrompissions**	**eusse corrompu**	**eussions corrompu**
corrompisses	**corrompissiez**	**eusses corrompu**	**eussiez corrompu**
corrompît	**corrompissent**	**eût corrompu**	**eussent corrompu**

Impératif
corromps
corrompons
corrompez

Sentences using this verb and words related to it

corrompre qqch to corrupt something; **Je connais un élève qui corrompt la prononciation de la langue française.** I know a student who corrupts the pronunciation of the French language.

corruptible corruptible

se laisser corrompre to allow oneself to be corrupted

corrompre qqn to corrupt someone; **Les spectacles ignobles à la télévision corrompent la jeunesse de ce pays.** The disgraceful shows on television corrupt the youth of this country.

la corruption corruption

un corrupteur, une corruptrice corrupter

See also **interrompre** and **rompre.**

Can't recognize an irregular verb form? Check out the index of common irregular French verb forms, in the Appendixes.

Regular **-er** verb

to put to bed, to lay, to flatten

The Seven Simple Tenses		The Seven Compound Tenses	
Singular	Plural	Singular	Plural
1 présent de l'indicatif		8 passé composé	
couche	**couchons**	**ai couché**	**avons couché**
couches	**couchez**	**as couché**	**avez couché**
couche	**couchent**	**a couché**	**ont couché**
2 imparfait de l'indicatif		9 plus-que-parfait de l'indicatif	
couchais	**couchions**	**avais couché**	**avions couché**
couchais	**couchiez**	**avais couché**	**aviez couché**
couchait	**couchaient**	**avait couché**	**avaient couché**
3 passé simple		10 passé antérieur	
couchai	**couchâmes**	**eus couché**	**eûmes couché**
couchas	**couchâtes**	**eus couché**	**eûtes couché**
coucha	**couchèrent**	**eut couché**	**eurent couché**
4 futur		11 futur antérieur	
coucherai	**coucherons**	**aurai couché**	**aurons couché**
coucheras	**coucherez**	**auras couché**	**aurez couché**
couchera	**coucheront**	**aura couché**	**auront couché**
5 conditionnel		12 conditionnel passé	
coucherais	**coucherions**	**aurais couché**	**aurions couché**
coucherais	**coucheriez**	**aurais couché**	**auriez couché**
coucherait	**coucheraient**	**aurait couché**	**auraient couché**
6 présent du subjonctif		13 passé du subjonctif	
couche	**couchions**	**aie couché**	**ayons couché**
couches	**couchiez**	**aies couché**	**ayez couché**
couche	**couchent**	**ait couché**	**aient couché**
7 imparfait du subjonctif		14 plus-que-parfait du subjonctif	
couchasse	**couchassions**	**eusse couché**	**eussions couché**
couchasses	**couchassiez**	**eusses couché**	**eussiez couché**
couchât	**couchassent**	**eût couché**	**eussent couché**

Impératif
couche
couchons
couchez

Words and expressions related to this verb

C'est l'heure du coucher. It's time for bed.
le coucher et la nourriture bed and board
au coucher du soleil at sunset
découcher to sleep somewhere other than in one's own bed
coucher à l'hôtel to sleep in a hotel
accoucher de to give birth to a child; **Elle a accouché d'une fille.** She has given birth to a girl.
recoucher to put back to bed
Ils couchent ensemble. They sleep together.

See also **se coucher.**

Can't find the verb you're looking for? Check the back pages of this book for a list of over 2,600 additional verbs!

se coucher (122) — Part. pr. se couchant — Part. passé couché(e)(s)

to go to bed, to lie down

Reflexive regular **-er** verb

The Seven Simple Tenses

Singular	Plural
1 présent de l'indicatif	
me couche	**nous couchons**
te couches	**vous couchez**
se couche	**se couchent**
2 imparfait de l'indicatif	
me couchais	**nous couchions**
te couchais	**vous couchiez**
se couchait	**se couchaient**
3 passé simple	
me couchai	**nous couchâmes**
te couchas	**vous couchâtes**
se coucha	**se couchèrent**
4 futur	
me coucherai	**nous coucherons**
te coucheras	**vous coucherez**
se couchera	**se coucheront**
5 conditionnel	
me coucherais	**nous coucherions**
te coucherais	**vous coucheriez**
se coucherait	**se coucheraient**
6 présent du subjonctif	
me couche	**nous couchions**
te couches	**vous couchiez**
se couche	**se couchent**
7 imparfait du subjonctif	
me couchasse	**nous couchassions**
te couchasses	**vous couchassiez**
se couchât	**se couchassent**

The Seven Compound Tenses

Singular	Plural
8 passé composé	
me suis couché(e)	**nous sommes couché(e)s**
t'es couché(e)	**vous êtes couché(e)(s)**
s'est couché(e)	**se sont couché(e)s**
9 plus-que-parfait de l'indicatif	
m'étais couché(e)	**nous étions couché(e)s**
t'étais couché(e)	**vous étiez couché(e)(s)**
s'était couché(e)	**s'étaient couché(e)s**
10 passé antérieur	
me fus couché(e)	**nous fûmes couché(e)s**
te fus couché(e)	**vous fûtes couché(e)(s)**
se fut couché(e)	**se furent couché(e)s**
11 futur antérieur	
me serai couché(e)	**nous serons couché(e)s**
te seras couché(e)	**vous serez couché(e)(s)**
se sera couché(e)	**se seront couché(e)s**
12 conditionnel passé	
me serais couché(e)	**nous serions couché(e)s**
te serais couché(e)	**vous seriez couché(e)(s)**
se serait couché(e)	**se seraient couché(e)s**
13 passé du subjonctif	
me sois couché(e)	**nous soyons couché(e)s**
te sois couché(e)	**vous soyez couché(e)(s)**
se soit couché(e)	**se soient couché(e)s**
14 plus-que-parfait du subjonctif	
me fusse couché(e)	**nous fussions couché(e)s**
te fusses couché(e)	**vous fussiez couché(e)(s)**
se fût couché(e)	**se fussent couché(e)s**

Impératif

couche-toi; ne te couche pas
couchons-nous; ne nous couchons pas
couchez-vous; ne vous couchez pas

Sentences using this verb and words related to it

—Couche-toi, Hélène! Il est minuit. Hier soir tu t'es couchée tard.
—Donne-moi ma poupée pour coucher ensemble.

le coucher du soleil sunset
une couche a layer
une couchette bunk, cot
Le soleil se couche. The sun is setting.
se recoucher to go back to bed
se coucher tôt to go to bed early
Comme on fait son lit on se couche! You've made your bed; now lie in it!
un sac de couchage sleeping bag
un couche-tard night owl

See also **coucher.**

Irregular verb

to sew, to stitch

The Seven Simple Tenses		The Seven Compound Tenses	
Singular	Plural	Singular	Plural
1 présent de l'indicatif		8 passé composé	
couds	**cousons**	**ai cousu**	**avons cousu**
couds	**cousez**	**as cousu**	**avez cousu**
coud	**cousent**	**a cousu**	**ont cousu**
2 imparfait de l'indicatif		9 plus-que-parfait de l'indicatif	
cousais	**cousions**	**avais cousu**	**avions cousu**
cousais	**cousiez**	**avais cousu**	**aviez cousu**
cousait	**cousaient**	**avait cousu**	**avaient cousu**
3 passé simple		10 passé antérieur	
cousis	**cousîmes**	**eus cousu**	**eûmes cousu**
cousis	**cousîtes**	**eus cousu**	**eûtes cousu**
cousit	**cousirent**	**eut cousu**	**eurent cousu**
4 futur		11 futur antérieur	
coudrai	**coudrons**	**aurai cousu**	**aurons cousu**
coudras	**coudrez**	**auras cousu**	**aurez cousu**
coudra	**coudront**	**aura cousu**	**auront cousu**
5 conditionnel		12 conditionnel passé	
coudrais	**coudrions**	**aurais cousu**	**aurions cousu**
coudrais	**coudriez**	**aurais cousu**	**auriez cousu**
coudrait	**coudraient**	**aurait cousu**	**auraient cousu**
6 présent du subjonctif		13 passé du subjonctif	
couse	**cousions**	**aie cousu**	**ayons cousu**
couses	**cousiez**	**aies cousu**	**ayez cousu**
couse	**cousent**	**ait cousu**	**aient cousu**
7 imparfait du subjonctif		14 plus-que-parfait du subjonctif	
cousisse	**cousissions**	**eusse cousu**	**eussions cousu**
cousisses	**cousissiez**	**eusses cousu**	**eussiez cousu**
cousît	**cousissent**	**eût cousu**	**eussent cousu**

Impératif
couds
cousons
cousez

Words and expressions related to this verb

recoudre to sew again, to sew up
la couture sewing; dressmaking
la couture à la machine machine sewing
découdre to unstitch, to rip up some sewing
une machine à coudre sewing machine
un couturier, une couturière fashion designer
la haute couture high fashion
décousu, décousue unstitched, unsewn; incoherent **Mon professeur d'algèbre explique les leçons d'une manière décousue.**

Don't forget to study the section on defective and impersonal verbs. It's right after this main list.

The subject pronouns are found on page 103.

couper (124) — Part. pr. coupant — Part. passé coupé

to cut, to switch off

Regular **-er** verb

The Seven Simple Tenses		The Seven Compound Tenses	
Singular	Plural	Singular	Plural
1 présent de l'indicatif		8 passé composé	
coupe	**coupons**	**ai coupé**	**avons coupé**
coupes	**coupez**	**as coupé**	**avez coupé**
coupe	**coupent**	**a coupé**	**ont coupé**
2 imparfait de l'indicatif		9 plus-que-parfait de l'indicatif	
coupais	**coupions**	**avais coupé**	**avions coupé**
coupais	**coupiez**	**avais coupé**	**aviez coupé**
coupait	**coupaient**	**avait coupé**	**avaient coupé**
3 passé simple		10 passé antérieur	
coupai	**coupâmes**	**eus coupé**	**eûmes coupé**
coupas	**coupâtes**	**eus coupé**	**eûtes coupé**
coupa	**coupèrent**	**eut coupé**	**eurent coupé**
4 futur		11 futur antérieur	
couperai	**couperons**	**aurai coupé**	**aurons coupé**
couperas	**couperez**	**auras coupé**	**aurez coupé**
coupera	**couperont**	**aura coupé**	**auront coupé**
5 conditionnel		12 conditionnel passé	
couperais	**couperions**	**aurais coupé**	**aurions coupé**
couperais	**couperiez**	**aurais coupé**	**auriez coupé**
couperait	**couperaient**	**aurait coupé**	**auraient coupé**
6 présent du subjonctif		13 passé du subjonctif	
coupe	**coupions**	**aie coupé**	**ayons coupé**
coupes	**coupiez**	**aies coupé**	**ayez coupé**
coupe	**coupent**	**ait coupé**	**aient coupé**
7 imparfait du subjonctif		14 plus-que-parfait du subjonctif	
coupasse	**coupassions**	**eusse coupé**	**eussions coupé**
coupasses	**coupassiez**	**eusses coupé**	**eussiez coupé**
coupât	**coupassent**	**eût coupé**	**eussent coupé**

Impératif
coupe
coupons
coupez

Common idiomatic expressions using this verb

Ce morceau de pain est trop grand. Je vais le couper en deux.

un coupon coupon
une coupure cut, gash, crack
couper les cheveux en quatre to split hairs
se faire couper les cheveux to have one's hair cut
Aïe! Je me suis coupé le doigt! Ouch! I cut my finger!
découper to cut out
entrecouper to interrupt
couper la fièvre to reduce the fever
une coupe (de cheveux) haircut
une coupe croisée crosscut

How are you doing? Find out with the verb drills and tests with answers explained on pages 50–101.

Irregular verb

to run, to race

The Seven Simple Tenses		The Seven Compound Tenses	
Singular	Plural	Singular	Plural
1 présent de l'indicatif		8 passé composé	
cours	**courons**	**ai couru**	**avons couru**
cours	**courez**	**as couru**	**avez couru**
court	**courent**	**a couru**	**ont couru**
2 imparfait de l'indicatif		9 plus-que-parfait de l'indicatif	
courais	**courions**	**avais couru**	**avions couru**
courais	**couriez**	**avais couru**	**aviez couru**
courait	**couraient**	**avait couru**	**avaient couru**
3 passé simple		10 passé antérieur	
courus	**courûmes**	**eus couru**	**eûmes couru**
courus	**courûtes**	**eus couru**	**eûtes couru**
courut	**coururent**	**eut couru**	**eurent couru**
4 futur		11 futur antérieur	
courrai	**courrons**	**aurai couru**	**aurons couru**
courras	**courrez**	**auras couru**	**aurez couru**
courra	**courront**	**aura couru**	**auront couru**
5 conditionnel		12 conditionnel passé	
courrais	**courrions**	**aurais couru**	**aurions couru**
courrais	**courriez**	**aurais couru**	**auriez couru**
courrait	**courraient**	**aurait couru**	**auraient couru**
6 présent du subjonctif		13 passé du subjonctif	
coure	**courions**	**aie couru**	**ayons couru**
coures	**couriez**	**aies couru**	**ayez couru**
coure	**courent**	**ait couru**	**aient couru**
7 imparfait du subjonctif		14 plus-que-parfait du subjonctif	
courusse	**courussions**	**eusse couru**	**eussions couru**
courusses	**courussiez**	**eusses couru**	**eussiez couru**
courût	**courussent**	**eût couru**	**eussent couru**

Impératif
cours
courons
courez

AN ESSENTIAL 55 VERB

Courir

Courir is an important verb for a beginning student because, even though it is considered to be an irregular verb, there are several verbs that are conjugated like it.

Sentences using courir

Les enfants sont toujours prêts à courir. Children are always ready to run.

Quand on est jeune, on court sans se fatiguer. When you're young (one is young), you run (one runs) without getting tired.

Michel a couru de la maison jusqu'à l'école. Michael ran from home to school.

Si tu cours dans la maison tu cours le risque de te faire mal. If you run in the house you run the risk of hurting yourself.

Rien ne sert de courir; il faut partir à point. (La Fontaine, *Le Lièvre et la Tortue*) It's no use running; you have to leave at the right moment. (La Fontaine, *The Tortoise and the Hare*)

Le facteur est arrivé en courant pour nous livrer notre courrier, mais le courrier électronique est toujours plus rapide. The mail carrier arrived in a hurry to deliver our mail to us, but e-mail is still faster.

If you can conjugate **courir** you can also conjugate these verbs:

accourir **to come running**

concourir **to compete**

discourir **to discourse, talk at length**

encourir **to incur**

parcourir **to go through, to travel through, to cover (distance), to skim (reading)**

recourir **to run again**

secourir **to help**

Words and expressions related to this verb

un coureur, une coureuse **runner**

faire courir un bruit **to spread a rumor**

courir une course **to run a race**

courir le monde **to roam all over the world**

recourir à qqn **to turn to someone (for help)**

recourir à qqch **to resort to something**

accourir vers **to come running toward**

courir les rues **to run about the streets**

par le temps qui court **these days, nowadays**

faire les courses **to do the shopping**

un cheval de course **racehorse**

le courrier **mail, messenger, courier**

le courriel, le courrier électronique **e-mail, electronic mail**

courir le risque, courir un risque **to run the risk, to run a risk, to risk**

Cela/Ça court les rues. **That's common/dull.**

Cela/Ça ne court pas les rues. **That's unusual/uncommon.**

Irregular verb

to cover

The Seven Simple Tenses		The Seven Compound Tenses	
Singular	Plural	Singular	Plural
1 présent de l'indicatif		8 passé composé	
couvre	**couvrons**	**ai couvert**	**avons couvert**
couvres	**couvrez**	**as couvert**	**avez couvert**
couvre	**couvrent**	**a couvert**	**ont couvert**
2 imparfait de l'indicatif		9 plus-que-parfait de l'indicatif	
couvrais	**couvrions**	**avais couvert**	**avions couvert**
couvrais	**couvriez**	**avais couvert**	**aviez couvert**
couvrait	**couvraient**	**avait couvert**	**avaient couvert**
3 passé simple		10 passé antérieur	
couvris	**couvrîmes**	**eus couvert**	**eûmes couvert**
couvris	**couvrîtes**	**eus couvert**	**eûtes couvert**
couvrit	**couvrirent**	**eut couvert**	**eurent couvert**
4 futur		11 futur antérieur	
couvrirai	**couvrirons**	**aurai couvert**	**aurons couvert**
couvriras	**couvrirez**	**auras couvert**	**aurez couvert**
couvrira	**couvriront**	**aura couvert**	**auront couvert**
5 conditionnel		12 conditionnel passé	
couvrirais	**couvririons**	**aurais couvert**	**aurions couvert**
couvrirais	**couvririez**	**aurais couvert**	**auriez couvert**
couvrirait	**couvriraient**	**aurait couvert**	**auraient couvert**
6 présent du subjonctif		13 passé du subjonctif	
couvre	**couvrions**	**aie couvert**	**ayons couvert**
couvres	**couvriez**	**aies couvert**	**ayez couvert**
couvre	**couvrent**	**ait couvert**	**aient couvert**
7 imparfait du subjonctif		14 plus-que-parfait du subjonctif	
couvrisse	**couvrissions**	**eusse couvert**	**eussions couvert**
couvrisses	**couvrissiez**	**eusses couvert**	**eussiez couvert**
couvrît	**couvrissent**	**eût couvert**	**eussent couvert**

Impératif
couvre
couvrons
couvrez

AN ESSENTIAL 55 VERB

Couvrir

Couvrir is an important verb for you to study because, even though it is considered to be irregular, there are many verbs that are conjugated in the same way. Pay special attention to the past participle, which ends in **-ert**.

Sentences using couvrir and related words

Le temps se couvre aujourd'hui. It's getting overcast today.

Le ciel est couvert aujourd'hui. The sky is overcast today.

Avant de quitter la maison, Madame Champlain a couvert le lit d'un couvre-lit. Before leaving the house, Mrs. Champlain covered the bed with a bedspread.

Dans ce cours nous couvrirons l'histoire du monde, de l'an mil jusqu'à présent. In this course we will cover the history of the world, from the year one thousand to the present.

Couvre-toi. Il pleut aujourd'hui. Put on your hat. It's raining today.

À cause des émeutes la police a imposé un couvre-feu. Because of the riots the police imposed a curfew.

J'ai couvert la marmite pour laisser le ragoût mijoter. I covered the cooking pot to let the stew simmer.

N'oublie pas de mettre le couvert. Don't forget to set the table.

Words and expressions related to this verb

le couvre-feu **curfew**

un couvre-lit **bedspread**

une couverture **blanket**

un couvert **place setting (spoon, knife, fork, etc.)**

acheter des couverts **to buy cutlery**

se couvrir **to cover oneself, to put on one's hat**

If you can conjugate **couvrir** you can also conjugate these verbs:

découvrir **to discover, to disclose, to uncover**

entrouvrir **to open halfway**

ouvrir **to open**

recouvrir **to cover, to cover again**

rouvrir **to reopen, to open again**

Irregular verb

to fear, to be afraid

The Seven Simple Tenses		The Seven Compound Tenses	
Singular	Plural	Singular	Plural
1 présent de l'indicatif		8 passé composé	
crains	**craignons**	**ai craint**	**avons craint**
crains	**craignez**	**as craint**	**avez craint**
craint	**craignent**	**a craint**	**ont craint**
2 imparfait de l'indicatif		9 plus-que-parfait de l'indicatif	
craignais	**craignions**	**avais craint**	**avions craint**
craignais	**craigniez**	**avais craint**	**aviez craint**
craignait	**craignaient**	**avait craint**	**avaient craint**
3 passé simple		10 passé antérieur	
craignis	**craignîmes**	**eus craint**	**eûmes craint**
craignis	**craignîtes**	**eus craint**	**eûtes craint**
craignit	**craignirent**	**eut craint**	**eurent craint**
4 futur		11 futur antérieur	
craindrai	**craindrons**	**aurai craint**	**aurons craint**
craindras	**craindrez**	**auras craint**	**aurez craint**
craindra	**craindront**	**aura craint**	**auront craint**
5 conditionnel		12 conditionnel passé	
craindrais	**craindrions**	**aurais craint**	**aurions craint**
craindrais	**craindriez**	**aurais craint**	**auriez craint**
craindrait	**craindraient**	**aurait craint**	**auraient craint**
6 présent du subjonctif		13 passé du subjonctif	
craigne	**craignions**	**aie craint**	**ayons craint**
craignes	**craigniez**	**aies craint**	**ayez craint**
craigne	**craignent**	**ait craint**	**aient craint**
7 imparfait du subjonctif		14 plus-que-parfait du subjonctif	
craignisse	**craignissions**	**eusse craint**	**eussions craint**
craignisses	**craignissiez**	**eusses craint**	**eussiez craint**
craignît	**craignissent**	**eût craint**	**eussent craint**

Impératif
crains
craignons
craignez

Sentences using this verb and words related to it

Le petit garçon craint de traverser le parc pendant la nuit. Il a raison parce que c'est dangereux. Il a des craintes.

une crainte fear, dread
craindre pour sa vie to be in fear of one's life
sans crainte fearless
craintif, craintive fearful
craintivement fearfully
avec crainte fearfully
de crainte que + subj. for fear that, for fear of
Kevin a mis ses lunettes de soleil, de crainte qu'on ne le reconnaisse. Kevin put on his sunglasses, for fear that someone might recognize him.

Use the guide to French pronunciation. It's in the Appendixes.

to create

Regular **-er** verb

The Seven Simple Tenses		The Seven Compound Tenses	
Singular	Plural	Singular	Plural
1 présent de l'indicatif		8 passé composé	
crée	**créons**	**ai créé**	**avons créé**
crées	**créez**	**as créé**	**avez créé**
crée	**créent**	**a créé**	**ont créé**
2 imparfait de l'indicatif		9 plus-que-parfait de l'indicatif	
créais	**créions**	**avais créé**	**avions créé**
créais	**créiez**	**avais créé**	**aviez créé**
créait	**créaient**	**avait créé**	**avaient créé**
3 passé simple		10 passé antérieur	
créai	**créâmes**	**eus créé**	**eûmes créé**
créas	**créâtes**	**eus créé**	**eûtes créé**
créa	**créèrent**	**eut créé**	**eurent créé**
4 futur		11 futur antérieur	
créerai	**créerons**	**aurai créé**	**aurons créé**
créeras	**créerez**	**auras créé**	**aurez créé**
créera	**créeront**	**aura créé**	**auront créé**
5 conditionnel		12 conditionnel passé	
créerais	**créerions**	**aurais créé**	**aurions créé**
créerais	**créeriez**	**aurais créé**	**auriez créé**
créerait	**créeraient**	**aurait créé**	**auraient créé**
6 présent du subjonctif		13 passé du subjonctif	
crée	**créions**	**aie créé**	**ayons créé**
crées	**créiez**	**aies créé**	**ayez créé**
crée	**créent**	**ait créé**	**aient créé**
7 imparfait du subjonctif		14 plus-que-parfait du subjonctif	
créasse	**créassions**	**eusse créé**	**eussions créé**
créasses	**créassiez**	**eusses créé**	**eussiez créé**
créât	**créassent**	**eût créé**	**eussent créé**

Impératif
crée
créons
créez

Sentences using this verb and words related to it

Madame Imbert, professeur de mathématiques, est une drôle de créature. Tout ce qu'elle fait manque d'originalité. Quelle misérable créature!

drôle de créature funny, queer person
la création creation; **depuis la création du monde** since the creation of the world
la créativité creativity; **la récréation** recreation
une créature creature
recréer to create again; **récréer** to enliven
un créateur, une créatrice creator

Don't forget to use the English-French verb index. It's in the Appendixes.

Regular **-er** verb

to shout, to cry out

The Seven Simple Tenses		The Seven Compound Tenses	
Singular	Plural	Singular	Plural
1 présent de l'indicatif		8 passé composé	
crie	**crions**	**ai crié**	**avons crié**
cries	**criez**	**as crié**	**avez crié**
crie	**crient**	**a crié**	**ont crié**
2 imparfait de l'indicatif		9 plus-que-parfait de l'indicatif	
criais	**criions**	**avais crié**	**avions crié**
criais	**criiez**	**avais crié**	**aviez crié**
criait	**criaient**	**avait crié**	**avaient crié**
3 passé simple		10 passé antérieur	
criai	**criâmes**	**eus crié**	**eûmes crié**
crias	**criâtes**	**eus crié**	**eûtes crié**
cria	**crièrent**	**eut crié**	**eurent crié**
4 futur		11 futur antérieur	
crierai	**crierons**	**aurai crié**	**aurons crié**
crieras	**crierez**	**auras crié**	**aurez crié**
criera	**crieront**	**aura crié**	**auront crié**
5 conditionnel		12 conditionnel passé	
crierais	**crierions**	**aurais crié**	**aurions crié**
crierais	**crieriez**	**aurais crié**	**auriez crié**
crierait	**crieraient**	**aurait crié**	**auraient crié**
6 présent du subjonctif		13 passé du subjonctif	
crie	**criions**	**aie crié**	**ayons crié**
cries	**criiez**	**aies crié**	**ayez crié**
crie	**crient**	**ait crié**	**aient crié**
7 imparfait du subjonctif		14 plus-que-parfait du subjonctif	
criasse	**criassions**	**eusse crié**	**eussions crié**
criasses	**criassiez**	**eusses crié**	**eussiez crié**
criât	**criassent**	**eût crié**	**eussent crié**

Impératif
crie
crions
criez

Words and expressions related to this verb

un cri a shout, a cry
pousser un cri to utter a cry
crier à tue-tête to shout one's head off
un crieur hawker
un crieur de journaux newsboy
décrier to decry, criticize
un criailleur, une criailleuse nagger
un criard, une criarde someone who constantly shouts, nags, scolds; screecher
un portrait criant de vérité a portrait strikingly true to life

Pour attraper l'autobus qui était en train de partir, Monsieur Duval a crié à tue-tête.
To catch the bus that was about to leave, Mr. Duval shouted at the top of his voice.

The subject pronouns are found on page 103.

to believe

Irregular verb

The Seven Simple Tenses		The Seven Compound Tenses	
Singular	Plural	Singular	Plural
1 présent de l'indicatif		8 passé composé	
crois	**croyons**	**ai cru**	**avons cru**
crois	**croyez**	**as cru**	**avez cru**
croit	**croient**	**a cru**	**ont cru**
2 imparfait de l'indicatif		9 plus-que-parfait de l'indicatif	
croyais	**croyions**	**avais cru**	**avions cru**
croyais	**croyiez**	**avais cru**	**aviez cru**
croyait	**croyaient**	**avait cru**	**avaient cru**
3 passé simple		10 passé antérieur	
crus	**crûmes**	**eus cru**	**eûmes cru**
crus	**crûtes**	**eus cru**	**eûtes cru**
crut	**crurent**	**eut cru**	**eurent cru**
4 futur		11 futur antérieur	
croirai	**croirons**	**aurai cru**	**aurons cru**
croiras	**croirez**	**auras cru**	**aurez cru**
croira	**croiront**	**aura cru**	**auront cru**
5 conditionnel		12 conditionnel passé	
croirais	**croirions**	**aurais cru**	**aurions cru**
croirais	**croiriez**	**aurais cru**	**auriez cru**
croirait	**croiraient**	**aurait cru**	**auraient cru**
6 présent du subjonctif		13 passé du subjonctif	
croie	**croyions**	**aie cru**	**ayons cru**
croies	**croyiez**	**aies cru**	**ayez cru**
croie	**croient**	**ait cru**	**aient cru**
7 imparfait du subjonctif		14 plus-que-parfait du subjonctif	
crusse	**crussions**	**eusse cru**	**eussions cru**
crusses	**crussiez**	**eusses cru**	**eussiez cru**
crût	**crussent**	**eût cru**	**eussent cru**

Impératif
crois
croyons
croyez

Sentences using this verb and words related to it

Est-ce que vous croyez tout ce que vous entendez? Avez-vous cru l'histoire que je vous ai racontée?

Croyez-m'en! Take my word for it!
se croire to think oneself; to consider oneself
Paul se croit beau. Paul thinks himself handsome.
croyable believable
incroyable unbelievable
croire à qqch to believe in something
croire en qqn to believe in someone
croire en Dieu to believe in God
Je crois que oui. I think so.
Je crois que non. I don't think so.

Get acquainted with what preposition goes with what verb. See *Verbs with prepositions* in the Appendixes.

Irregular verb

to grow, to increase

The Seven Simple Tenses		The Seven Compound Tenses	
Singular	Plural	Singular	Plural
1 présent de l'indicatif		8 passé composé	
croîs	**croissons**	**ai crû**	**avons crû**
croîs	**croissez**	**as crû**	**avez crû**
croît	**croissent**	**a crû**	**ont crû**
2 imparfait de l'indicatif		9 plus-que-parfait de l'indicatif	
croissais	**croissions**	**avais crû**	**avions crû**
croissais	**croissiez**	**avais crû**	**aviez crû**
croissait	**croissaient**	**avait crû**	**avaient crû**
3 passé simple		10 passé antérieur	
crûs	**crûmes**	**eus crû**	**eûmes crû**
crûs	**crûtes**	**eus crû**	**eûtes crû**
crût	**crûrent**	**eut crû**	**eurent crû**
4 futur		11 futur antérieur	
croîtrai	**croîtrons**	**aurai crû**	**aurons crû**
croîtras	**croîtrez**	**auras crû**	**aurez crû**
croîtra	**croîtront**	**aura crû**	**auront crû**
5 conditionnel		12 conditionnel passé	
croîtrais	**croîtrions**	**aurais crû**	**aurions crû**
croîtrais	**croîtriez**	**aurais crû**	**auriez crû**
croîtrait	**croîtraient**	**aurait crû**	**auraient crû**
6 présent du subjonctif		13 passé du subjonctif	
croisse	**croissions**	**aie crû**	**ayons crû**
croisses	**croissiez**	**aies crû**	**ayez crû**
croisse	**croissent**	**ait crû**	**aient crû**
7 imparfait du subjonctif		14 plus-que-parfait du subjonctif	
crûsse	**crûssions**	**eusse crû**	**eussions crû**
crûsses	**crûssiez**	**eusses crû**	**eussiez crû**
crût	**crûssent**	**eût crû**	**eussent crû**

Impératif
croîs
croissons
croissez

Words and expressions related to this verb

un croissant crescent (shape of moon); name of a pastry in crescent shape: **Au petit déjeuner, les Français aiment prendre un café et un croissant.** / For breakfast, French people like to have coffee and a croissant (crescent shaped roll).

la croissance growth; **un accroissement** increase

crescendo crescendo (progressive increase in intensity of sound in music; an Italian word related to **croître**).

Note: In many of the simple tenses **croître** has an added circumflex accent to distinguish it from **croire** (to believe): **je croîs (croître), je crois (croire).**

See also **accroître** and **décroître.**

cueillir (132) — Part. pr. **cueillant** — Part. passé **cueilli**

to gather, to pick

Irregular verb

The Seven Simple Tenses		The Seven Compound Tenses	
Singular	Plural	Singular	Plural
1 présent de l'indicatif		8 passé composé	
cueille	**cueillons**	**ai cueilli**	**avons cueilli**
cueilles	**cueillez**	**as cueilli**	**avez cueilli**
cueille	**cueillent**	**a cueilli**	**ont cueilli**
2 imparfait de l'indicatif		9 plus-que-parfait de l'indicatif	
cueillais	**cueillions**	**avais cueilli**	**avions cueilli**
cueillais	**cueilliez**	**avais cueilli**	**aviez cueilli**
cueillait	**cueillaient**	**avait cueilli**	**avaient cueilli**
3 passé simple		10 passé antérieur	
cueillis	**cueillîmes**	**eus cueilli**	**eûmes cueilli**
cueillis	**cueillîtes**	**eus cueilli**	**eûtes cueilli**
cueillit	**cueillirent**	**eut cueilli**	**eurent cueilli**
4 futur		11 futur antérieur	
cueillerai	**cueillerons**	**aurai cueilli**	**aurons cueilli**
cueilleras	**cueillerez**	**auras cueilli**	**aurez cueilli**
cueillera	**cueilleront**	**aura cueilli**	**auront ceuilli**
5 conditionnel		12 conditionnel passé	
cueillerais	**cueillerions**	**aurais cueilli**	**aurions cueilli**
cueillerais	**cueilleriez**	**aurais cueilli**	**auriez cueilli**
cueillerait	**cueilleraient**	**aurait cueilli**	**auraient cueilli**
6 présent du subjonctif		13 passé du subjonctif	
cueille	**cueillions**	**aie cueilli**	**ayons cueilli**
cueilles	**cueilliez**	**aies cueilli**	**ayez cueilli**
cueille	**cueillent**	**ait cueilli**	**aient cueilli**
7 imparfait du subjonctif		14 plus-que-parfait du subjonctif	
cueillisse	**cueillissions**	**eusse cueilli**	**eussions cueilli**
cueillisses	**cueillissiez**	**eusses cueilli**	**eussiez cueilli**
cueillît	**cueillissent**	**eût cueilli**	**eussent cueilli**

Impératif
cueille
cueillons
cueillez

Sentences using this verb and words related to it

Je vois que tu cueilles des fleurs. As-tu cueilli toutes les fleurs qui sont dans ce vase?

un cueilleur, une cueilleuse gatherer, picker
la cueillaison, la cueillette gathering, picking
un cueilloir basket for picking fruit; instrument for picking fruit on high branches

Cueillez, cueillez votre jeunesse. (Ronsard: Make the most of your youth.) Seize the day. (Horace: *Carpe diem*)

For other words related to this verb, see **accueillir** and **recueillir.**

Grammar putting you in a tense mood? Review the definitions of basic grammatical terms with examples on pages 35–49.

Irregular verb

to cook

The Seven Simple Tenses		The Seven Compound Tenses	
Singular	Plural	Singular	Plural
1 présent de l'indicatif		8 passé composé	
cuis	**cuisons**	**ai cuit**	**avons cuit**
cuis	**cuisez**	**as cuit**	**avez cuit**
cuit	**cuisent**	**a cuit**	**ont cuit**
2 imparfait de l'indicatif		9 plus-que-parfait de l'indicatif	
cuisais	**cuisions**	**avais cuit**	**avions cuit**
cuisais	**cuisiez**	**avais cuit**	**aviez cuit**
cuisait	**cuisaient**	**avait cuit**	**avaient cuit**
3 passé simple		10 passé antérieur	
cuisis	**cuisîmes**	**eus cuit**	**eûmes cuit**
cuisis	**cuisîtes**	**eus cuit**	**eûtes cuit**
cuisit	**cuisirent**	**eut cuit**	**eurent cuit**
4 futur		11 futur antérieur	
cuirai	**cuirons**	**aurai cuit**	**aurons cuit**
cuiras	**cuirez**	**auras cuit**	**aurez cuit**
cuira	**cuiront**	**aura cuit**	**auront cuit**
5 conditionnel		12 conditionnel passé	
cuirais	**cuirions**	**aurais cuit**	**aurions cuit**
cuirais	**cuiriez**	**aurais cuit**	**auriez cuit**
cuirait	**cuiraient**	**aurait cuit**	**auraient cuit**
6 présent du subjonctif		13 passé du subjonctif	
cuise	**cuisions**	**aie cuit**	**ayons cuit**
cuises	**cuisiez**	**aies cuit**	**ayez cuit**
cuise	**cuisent**	**ait cuit**	**aient cuit**
7 imparfait du subjonctif		14 plus-que-parfait du subjonctif	
cuisisse	**cuisissions**	**eusse cuit**	**eussions cuit**
cuisisses	**cuisissiez**	**eusses cuit**	**eussiez cuit**
cuisît	**cuisissent**	**eût cuit**	**eussent cuit**

Impératif
cuis
cuisons
cuisez

Sentences using this verb and words related to it

Qui a cuit ce morceau de viande? C'est dégoûtant! Il est trop cuit. Ne savez-vous pas faire cuire un bon morceau de viande? Vous n'êtes pas bon cuisinier.

Moi, je n'aime pas le poulet. Je préfère un steak bien cuit. As for me, I don't like chicken. I prefer a steak well-done.

la cuisine kitchen
cuisinier, cuisinière cook
faire cuire à la poêle to pan fry
Il est cuit. He's done for; His goose is cooked.
une cuisinière kitchen range (stove)
un cuiseur pressure cooker
trop cuit overcooked, overdone
la cuisson cooking (time)
bien cuit well done

The subject pronouns are found on page 103.

danser (134) — Part. pr. dansant — Part. passé dansé

to dance

Regular **-er** verb

The Seven Simple Tenses		The Seven Compound Tenses	
Singular	Plural	Singular	Plural
1 présent de l'indicatif		8 passé composé	
danse	**dansons**	**ai dansé**	**avons dansé**
danses	**dansez**	**as dansé**	**avez dansé**
danse	**dansent**	**a dansé**	**ont dansé**
2 imparfait de l'indicatif		9 plus-que-parfait de l'indicatif	
dansais	**dansions**	**avais dansé**	**avions dansé**
dansais	**dansiez**	**avais dansé**	**aviez dansé**
dansait	**dansaient**	**avait dansé**	**avaient dansé**
3 passé simple		10 passé antérieur	
dansai	**dansâmes**	**eus dansé**	**eûmes dansé**
dansas	**dansâtes**	**eus dansé**	**eûtes dansé**
dansa	**dansèrent**	**eut dansé**	**eurent dansé**
4 futur		11 futur antérieur	
danserai	**danserons**	**aurai dansé**	**aurons dansé**
denseras	**danserez**	**auras dansé**	**aurez dansé**
dansera	**danseront**	**aura dansé**	**auront dansé**
5 conditionnel		12 conditionnel passé	
danserais	**danserions**	**aurais dansé**	**aurions dansé**
danserais	**danseriez**	**aurais dansé**	**auriez dansé**
danserait	**danseraient**	**aurait dansé**	**auraient dansé**
6 présent du subjonctif		13 passé du subjonctif	
danse	**dansions**	**aie dansé**	**ayons dansé**
danses	**dansiez**	**aies dansé**	**ayez dansé**
danse	**dansent**	**ait dansé**	**aient dansé**
7 imparfait du subjonctif		14 plus-que-parfait du subjonctif	
dansasse	**dansassions**	**eusse dansé**	**eussions dansé**
dansasses	**dansassiez**	**eusses dansé**	**eussiez dansé**
dansât	**dansassent**	**eût dansé**	**eussent dansé**

Impératif
danse
dansons
dansez

Sentences using this verb and words related to it

René: Veux-tu danser avec moi?
Renée: Je ne sais pas danser.
René: Je suis bon danseur. Je vais t'apprendre à danser. Viens! Dansons!

danser de joie to dance for joy
une soirée dansante evening dancing party
un thé dansant dancing at teatime (usually 5 o'clock); tea dance
Le chat parti, les souris dansent. When the cat's away the mice will play.
un danseur, une danseuse dancer
une danse dance; **un bal** ball (dance)
danseur, danseuse de claquettes tap dancer
la danse macabre dance of death

Don't forget to study the section on defective and impersonal verbs. It's right after this main list.

Reflexive regular **-er** verb

to manage, to improvise, to get by

The Seven Simple Tenses

Singular	Plural
1 présent de l'indicatif	
me débrouille	**nous débrouillons**
te débrouilles	**vous débrouillez**
se débrouille	**se débrouillent**
2 imparfait de l'indicatif	
me débrouillais	**nous débrouillions**
te débrouillais	**vous débrouilliez**
se débrouillait	**se débrouillaient**
3 passé simple	
me débrouillai	**nous débrouillâmes**
te débrouillas	**vous débrouillâtes**
se débrouilla	**se débrouillèrent**
4 futur	
me débrouillerai	**nous débrouillerons**
te débrouilleras	**vous débrouillerez**
se débrouillera	**se débrouilleront**
5 conditionnel	
me débrouillerais	**nous débrouillerions**
te débrouillerais	**vous débrouilleriez**
se débrouillerait	**se débrouilleraient**
6 présent du subjonctif	
me débrouille	**nous débrouillions**
te débrouilles	**vous débrouilliez**
se débrouille	**se débrouillent**
7 imparfait du subjonctif	
me débrouillasse	**nous débrouillassions**
te débrouillasses	**vous débrouillassiez**
se débrouillât	**se débrouillassent**

The Seven Compound Tenses

Singular	Plural
8 passé composé	
me suis débrouillé(e)	**nous sommes débrouillé(e)s**
t'es débrouillé(e)	**vous êtes débrouillé(e)(s)**
s'est débrouillé(e)	**se sont débrouillé(e)s**
9 plus-que-parfait de l'indicatif	
m'étais débrouillé(e)	**nous étions débrouillé(e)s**
t'étais débrouillé(e)	**vous étiez débrouillé(e)(s)**
s'était débrouillé(e)	**s'étaient débrouillé(e)s**
10 passé antérieur	
me fus débrouillé(e)	**nous fûmes débrouillé(e)s**
te fus débrouillé(e)	**vous fûtes débrouillé(e)(s)**
se fut débrouillé(e)	**se furent débrouillé(e)s**
11 futur antérieur	
me serai débrouillé(e)	**nous serons débrouillé(e)s**
te seras débrouillé(e)	**vous serez débrouillé(e)(s)**
se sera débrouillé(e)	**se seront débrouillé(e)s**
12 conditionnel passé	
me serais débrouillé(e)	**nous serions débrouillé(e)s**
te serais débrouillé(e)	**vous seriez débrouillé(e)(s)**
se serait débrouillé(e)	**se seraient débrouillé(e)s**
13 passé du subjonctif	
me sois débrouillé(e)	**nous soyons débrouillé(e)s**
te sois débrouillé(e)	**vous soyez débrouillé(e)(s)**
se soit débrouillé(e)	**se soient débrouillé(e)s**
14 plus-que-parfait du subjonctif	
me fusse débrouillé(e)	**nous fussions débrouillé(e)s**
te fusses débrouillé(e)	**vous fussiez débrouillé(e)(s)**
se fût débrouillé(e)	**se fussent débrouillé(e)s**

Impératif

débrouille-toi; ne te débrouille pas
débrouillons-nous; ne nous débrouillons pas
débrouillez-vous; ne vous débrouillez pas

AN ESSENTIAL 55 VERB

Se débrouiller

Se débrouiller is an essential verb because it is used in many everyday expressions and situations. The "**Système D**" has long been an important part of French culture and it is known throughout the francophone world.

Sentences using se débrouiller

Jean-Claude est très débrouillard. Jean-Claude is very resourceful.

Je ne parle pas japonais, mais je me débrouille. I don't know Japanese, but I get by.

C'est ton problème. Débrouille-toi! It's your problem. Straighten it out yourself!

Mon oncle a acheté les billets, grâce au Système D. My uncle bought the tickets, thanks to his ability to work around the system.

Laisse-le se débrouiller tout seul. Let him manage alone.

Words and expressions related to this verb

brouiller **to mix up, confuse, cloud, scramble (eggs)**

le brouillard **fog, mist**

débrouiller **to disentangle**

embrouiller **to tangle, complicate**

débrouillard **resourceful**

un débrouillard, une débrouillarde **a resourceful person**

le système D (le système des débrouillards) **resourcefulness, ability to work around the system**

la débrouillardise **resourcefulness**

le débrouillage **untangling**

Can't find the verb you're looking for? Check the back pages of this book for a list of over 2,600 additional verbs!

Irregular verb; spelling change: **c** changes to **ç** before **o** or **u** to keep **s** sound

to deceive, to disappoint

The Seven Simple Tenses		The Seven Compound Tenses	
Singular	Plural	Singular	Plural
1 présent de l'indicatif		8 passé composé	
déçois	**décevons**	**ai déçu**	**avons déçu**
déçois	**décevez**	**as déçu**	**avez déçu**
déçoit	**déçoivent**	**a déçu**	**ont déçu**
2 imparfait de l'indicatif		9 plus-que-parfait de l'indicatif	
décevais	**décevions**	**avais déçu**	**avions déçu**
décevais	**déceviez**	**avais déçu**	**aviez déçu**
décevait	**décevaient**	**avait déçu**	**avaient déçu**
3 passé simple		10 passé antérieur	
déçus	**déçûmes**	**eus déçu**	**eûmes déçu**
déçus	**déçûtes**	**eus déçu**	**eûtes déçu**
déçut	**déçurent**	**eut déçu**	**eurent déçu**
4 futur		11 futur antérieur	
décevrai	**décevrons**	**aurai déçu**	**aurons déçu**
décevras	**décevrez**	**auras déçu**	**aurez déçu**
décevra	**décevront**	**aura déçu**	**auront déçu**
5 conditionnel		12 conditionnel passé	
décevrais	**décevrions**	**aurais déçu**	**aurions déçu**
décevrais	**décevriez**	**aurais déçu**	**auriez déçu**
décevrait	**décevraient**	**aurait déçu**	**auraient déçu**
6 présent du subjonctif		13 passé du subjonctif	
déçoive	**décevions**	**aie déçu**	**ayons déçu**
déçoives	**déceviez**	**aies déçu**	**ayez déçu**
déçoive	**déçoivent**	**ait déçu**	**aient déçu**
7 imparfait du subjonctif		14 plus-que-parfait du subjonctif	
déçusse	**déçussions**	**eusse déçu**	**eussions déçu**
déçusses	**déçussiez**	**eusses déçu**	**eussiez déçu**
déçût	**déçussent**	**eût déçu**	**eussent déçu**

Impératif
déçois
décevons
décevez

Words and expressions related to this verb

décevoir la confiance de qqn to deceive someone's confidence (trust)
décevant, décevante disappointing, deceptive
être déçu to be disappointed
décevoir les espoirs de qqn to disappoint someone's hopes
la déception disappointment; **la tromperie** deceit
Vous m'avez déçu. You have disappointed me.
Quelle déception! What a disappointment!

déchirer (137) — Part. pr. déchirant — Part. passé déchiré

to rip, to tear, to rend

Regular **-er** verb

The Seven Simple Tenses		The Seven Compound Tenses	
Singular	Plural	Singular	Plural
1 présent de l'indicatif		8 passé composé	
déchire	**déchirons**	**ai déchiré**	**avons déchiré**
déchires	**déchirez**	**as déchiré**	**avez déchiré**
déchire	**déchirent**	**a déchiré**	**ont déchiré**
2 imparfait de l'indicatif		9 plus-que-parfait de l'indicatif	
déchirais	**déchirions**	**avais déchiré**	**avions déchiré**
déchirais	**déchiriez**	**avais déchiré**	**aviez déchiré**
déchirait	**déchiraient**	**avait déchiré**	**avaient déchiré**
3 passé simple		10 passé antérieur	
déchirai	**déchirâmes**	**eus déchiré**	**eûmes déchiré**
déchiras	**déchirâtes**	**eus déchiré**	**eûtes déchiré**
déchira	**déchirèrent**	**eut déchiré**	**eurent déchiré**
4 futur		11 futur antérieur	
déchirerai	**déchirerons**	**aurai déchiré**	**aurons déchiré**
déchireras	**déchirerez**	**auras déchiré**	**aurez déchiré**
déchirera	**déchireront**	**aura déchiré**	**auront déchiré**
5 conditionnel		12 conditionnel passé	
déchirerais	**déchirerions**	**aurais déchiré**	**aurions déchiré**
déchirerais	**déchireriez**	**aurais déchiré**	**auriez déchiré**
déchirerait	**déchireraient**	**aurait déchiré**	**auraient déchiré**
6 présent du subjonctif		13 passé du subjonctif	
déchire	**déchirions**	**aie déchiré**	**ayons déchiré**
déchires	**déchiriez**	**aies déchiré**	**ayez déchiré**
déchire	**déchirent**	**ait déchiré**	**aient déchiré**
7 imparfait du subjonctif		14 plus-que-parfait du subjonctif	
déchirasse	**déchirassions**	**eusse déchiré**	**eussions déchiré**
déchirasses	**déchirassiez**	**eusses déchiré**	**eussiez déchiré**
déchirât	**déchirassent**	**eût déchiré**	**eussent déchiré**

Impératif
déchire
déchirons
déchirez

Words and expressions related to this verb

déchirer qqn à belles dents to tear someone apart
déchirer le voile to discover the truth
une déchirure laceration, tear
une déchiqueteuse de papier paper shredder
déchirer en lambeaux to tear into shreds
se déchirer to tear each other apart
un déchirement tearing; **un déchirement du coeur** heartbreak
déchiqueter to cut to pieces

Grammar putting you in a tense mood? Review the definitions of basic grammatical terms with examples on pages 35–49.

The Seven Simple Tenses		The Seven Compound Tenses	
Singular	Plural	Singular	Plural
1 présent de l'indicatif		8 passé composé	
décide	**décidons**	**ai décidé**	**avons décidé**
décides	**décidez**	**as décidé**	**avez décidé**
décide	**décident**	**a décidé**	**ont décidé**
2 imparfait de l'indicatif		9 plus-que-parfait de l'indicatif	
décidais	**décidions**	**avais décidé**	**avions décidé**
décidais	**décidiez**	**avais décidé**	**aviez décidé**
décidait	**décidaient**	**avait décidé**	**avaient décidé**
3 passé simple		10 passé antérieur	
décidai	**décidâmes**	**eus décidé**	**eûmes décidé**
décidas	**décidâtes**	**eus décidé**	**eûtes décidé**
décida	**décidèrent**	**eut décidé**	**eurent décidé**
4 futur		11 futur antérieur	
déciderai	**déciderons**	**aurai décidé**	**aurons décidé**
décideras	**déciderez**	**auras décidé**	**aurez décidé**
décidera	**décideront**	**aura décidé**	**auront décidé**
5 conditionnel		12 conditionnel passé	
déciderais	**déciderions**	**aurais décidé**	**aurions décidé**
déciderais	**décideriez**	**aurais décidé**	**auriez décidé**
déciderait	**décideraient**	**aurait décidé**	**auraient décidé**
6 présent du subjonctif		13 passé du subjonctif	
décide	**décidions**	**aie décidé**	**ayons décidé**
décides	**décidiez**	**aies décidé**	**ayez décidé**
décide	**décident**	**ait décidé**	**aient décidé**
7 imparfait du subjonctif		14 plus-que-parfait du subjonctif	
décidasse	**décidassions**	**eusse décidé**	**eussions décidé**
décidasses	**décidassiez**	**eusses décidé**	**eussiez décidé**
décidât	**décidassent**	**eût décidé**	**eussent décidé**

Impératif
décide
décidons
décidez

Words and expressions related to this verb
une décision decision; **prendre une décision** to make (come to) a decision
décidément decidedly
décider de faire qqch to decide to do something; **J'ai décidé de partir.** I decided to leave.
se décider à faire qqch to make up one's mind, to resolve to do something; **Le docteur Malaise s'est décidé à faire l'opération.**
Décidez-vous! Make up your mind!

Get acquainted with what preposition goes with what verb. See *Verbs with prepositions* in the Appendixes.

découvrir (139) Part. pr. découvrant Part. passé découvert

discover, to uncover

Irregular verb

The Seven Simple Tenses		The Seven Compound Tenses	
Singular	Plural	Singular	Plural
1 présent de l'indicatif		8 passé composé	
découvre	**découvrons**	**ai découvert**	**avons découvert**
découvres	**découvrez**	**as découvert**	**avez découvert**
découvre	**découvrent**	**a découvert**	**ont découvert**
2 imparfait de l'indicatif		9 plus-que-parfait de l'indicatif	
découvrais	**découvrions**	**avais découvert**	**avions découvert**
découvrais	**découvriez**	**avais découvert**	**aviez découvert**
découvrait	**découvraient**	**avait découvert**	**avaient découvert**
3 passé simple		10 passé antérieur	
découvris	**découvrîmes**	**eus découvert**	**eûmes découvert**
découvris	**découvrîtes**	**eus découvert**	**eûtes découvert**
découvrit	**découvrirent**	**eut découvert**	**eurent découvert**
4 futur		11 futur antérieur	
découvrirai	**découvrirons**	**aurai découvert**	**aurons découvert**
découvriras	**découvrirez**	**auras découvert**	**aurez découvert**
découvrira	**découvriront**	**aura découvert**	**auront découvert**
5 conditionnel		12 conditionnel passé	
découvrirais	**découvririons**	**aurais découvert**	**aurions découvert**
découvrirais	**découvririez**	**aurais découvert**	**auriez découvert**
découvrirait	**découvriraient**	**aurait découvert**	**auraient découvert**
6 présent du subjonctif		13 passé du subjonctif	
découvre	**découvrions**	**aie découvert**	**ayons découvert**
découvres	**découvriez**	**aies découvert**	**ayez découvert**
découvre	**découvrent**	**ait découvert**	**aient découvert**
7 imparfait du subjonctif		14 plus-que-parfait du subjonctif	
découvrisse	**découvrissions**	**eusse découvert**	**eussions découvert**
découvrisses	**découvrissiez**	**eusses découvert**	**eussiez découvert**
découvrît	**découvrissent**	**eût découvert**	**eussent découvert**

Impératif
découvre
découvrons
découvrez

Sentences using this verb and words related to it

Ce matin j'ai couvert ce panier de fruits et maintenant il est découvert. Qui l'a découvert?

un découvreur discoverer
une découverte a discovery, invention
un découvert overdraft
se découvrir to take off one's clothes; to take off one's hat
aller à la découverte to explore
Découvrir saint Pierre pour couvrir saint Paul. To rob Peter to pay Paul.

See also **couvrir.**

Can't find the verb you're looking for? Check the back pages of this book for a list of over 2,600 additional verbs!

Irregular verb

to describe

The Seven Simple Tenses		The Seven Compound Tenses	
Singular	Plural	Singular	Plural
1 présent de l'indicatif		8 passé composé	
décris	**décrivons**	**ai décrit**	**avons décrit**
décris	**décrivez**	**as décrit**	**avez décrit**
décrit	**décrivent**	**a décrit**	**ont décrit**
2 imparfait de l'indicatif		9 plus-que-parfait de l'indicatif	
décrivais	**décrivions**	**avais décrit**	**avions décrit**
décrivais	**décriviez**	**avais décrit**	**aviez décrit**
décrivait	**décrivaient**	**avait décrit**	**avaient décrit**
3 passé simple		10 passé antérieur	
décrivis	**décrivîmes**	**eus décrit**	**eûmes décrit**
décrivis	**décrivîtes**	**eus décrit**	**eûtes décrit**
décrivit	**décrivirent**	**eut décrit**	**eurent décrit**
4 futur		11 futur antérieur	
décrirai	**décrirons**	**aurai décrit**	**aurons décrit**
décriras	**décrirez**	**auras décrit**	**aurez décrit**
décrira	**décriront**	**aura décrit**	**auront décrit**
5 conditionnel		12 conditionnel passé	
décrirais	**décririons**	**aurais décrit**	**aurions décrit**
décrirais	**décririez**	**aurais décrit**	**auriez décrit**
décrirait	**décriraient**	**aurait décrit**	**auraient décrit**
6 présent du subjonctif		13 passé du subjonctif	
décrive	**décrivions**	**aie décrit**	**ayons décrit**
décrives	**décriviez**	**aies décrit**	**ayez décrit**
décrive	**décrivent**	**ait décrit**	**aient décrit**
7 imparfait du subjonctif		14 plus-que-parfait du subjonctif	
décrivisse	**décrivissions**	**eusse décrit**	**eussions décrit**
décrivisses	**décrivissiez**	**eusses décrit**	**eussiez décrit**
décrivît	**décrivissent**	**eût décrit**	**eussent décrit**

Impératif
décris
décrivons
décrivez

Sentences using this verb and words related to it

Quel beau paysage! Je le décrirai dans une lettre à mon ami. Je ferai une description en détail.

une description description
indescriptible indescribable
écrire to write
proscrire to proscribe
prescrire to prescribe, stipulate
une prescription prescription (medical prescription: **une ordonnance**)

See also **écrire.**

How are you doing? Find out with the verb drills and tests with answers explained on pages 50–101.

to decrease, to diminish

Irregular verb

The Seven Simple Tenses		The Seven Compound Tenses	
Singular	Plural	Singular	Plural
1 présent de l'indicatif		8 passé composé	
décrois	**décroissons**	**ai décru**	**avons décru**
décrois	**décroissez**	**as décru**	**avez décru**
décroît	**décroissent**	**a décru**	**ont décru**
2 imparfait de l'indicatif		9 plus-que-parfait de l'indicatif	
décroissais	**décroissions**	**avais décru**	**avions décru**
décroissais	**décroissiez**	**avais décru**	**aviez décru**
décroissait	**décroissaient**	**avait décru**	**avaient décru**
3 passé simple		10 passé antérieur	
décrus	**décrûmes**	**eus décru**	**eûmes décru**
décrus	**décrûtes**	**eus décru**	**eûtes décru**
décrut	**décrurent**	**eut décru**	**eurent décru**
4 futur		11 futur antérieur	
décroîtrai	**décroîtrons**	**aurai décru**	**aurons décru**
décroîtras	**décroîtrez**	**auras décru**	**aurez décru**
décroîtra	**décroîtront**	**aura décru**	**auront décru**
5 conditionnel		12 conditionnel passé	
décroîtrais	**décroîtrions**	**aurais décru**	**aurions décru**
décroîtrais	**décroîtriez**	**aurais décru**	**auriez décru**
décroîtrait	**décroîtraient**	**aurait décru**	**auraient décru**
6 présent du subjonctif		13 passé du subjonctif	
décroisse	**décroissions**	**aie décru**	**ayons décru**
décroisses	**décroissiez**	**aies décru**	**ayez décru**
décroisse	**décroissent**	**ait décru**	**aient décru**
7 imparfait du subjonctif		14 plus-que-parfait du subjonctif	
décrusse	**décrussions**	**eusse décru**	**eussions décru**
décrusses	**décrussiez**	**eusses décru**	**eussiez décru**
décrût	**décrussent**	**eût décru**	**eussent décru**

Impératif
décrois
décroissons
décroissez

Words and expressions related to this verb
le décroît de la lune waning of the moon
la décroissance decrease
être en décroissance to be diminishing
une décrue decrease (water level)
décroissant, décroissante decreasing, diminishing
un croissant crescent shaped roll; crescent (of the moon)
la croissance increase, growth
croître to grow, to increase

Note: **Décroître** is not conjugated exactly like **croître**. In many of the simple tenses **croître** has an added circumflex accent to distinguish it from **croire** (to believe): **je croîs (croître), je crois (croire).**

See also **accroître** and **croître.**

Irregular verb

to deduce, to infer, to deduct

The Seven Simple Tenses		The Seven Compound Tenses	
Singular	Plural	Singular	Plural
1 présent de l'indicatif		8 passé composé	
déduis	**déduisons**	**ai déduit**	**avons déduit**
déduis	**déduisez**	**as déduit**	**avez déduit**
déduit	**déduisent**	**a déduit**	**ont déduit**
2 imparfait de l'indicatif		9 plus-que-parfait de l'indicatif	
déduisais	**déduisions**	**avais déduit**	**avions déduit**
déduisais	**déduisiez**	**avais déduit**	**aviez déduit**
déduisait	**déduisaient**	**avait déduit**	**avaient déduit**
3 passé simple		10 passé antérieur	
déduisis	**déduisîmes**	**eus déduit**	**eûmes déduit**
déduisis	**déduisîtes**	**eus déduit**	**eûtes déduit**
déduisit	**déduisirent**	**eut déduit**	**eurent déduit**
4 futur		11 futur antérieur	
déduirai	**déduirons**	**aurai déduit**	**aurons déduit**
déduiras	**déduirez**	**auras déduit**	**aurez déduit**
déduira	**déduiront**	**aura déduit**	**auront déduit**
5 conditionnel		12 conditionnel passé	
déduirais	**déduirions**	**aurais déduit**	**aurions déduit**
déduirais	**déduiriez**	**aurais déduit**	**auriez déduit**
déduirait	**déduiraient**	**aurait déduit**	**auraient déduit**
6 présent du subjonctif		13 passé du subjonctif	
déduise	**déduisions**	**aie déduit**	**ayons déduit**
déduises	**déduisiez**	**aies déduit**	**ayez déduit**
déduise	**déduisent**	**ait déduit**	**aient déduit**
7 imparfait du subjonctif		14 plus-que-parfait du subjonctif	
déduisisse	**déduisissions**	**eusse déduit**	**eussions déduit**
déduisisses	**déduisissiez**	**eusses déduit**	**eussiez déduit**
déduisît	**déduisissent**	**eût déduit**	**eussent déduit**

Impératif
déduis
déduisons
déduisez

Words and expressions related to this verb

une déduction deduction, inference; allowance
déductif, déductive deductive
se déduire to be deduced
une réduction reduction
réduire to reduce
à prix réduit at a reduced price
déductible deductible

See also **conduire**, **introduire**, **produire**, **réduire**, **reproduire**, **séduire**, and **traduire.**

It's important that you be familiar with the Subjunctive. See pages 26–31.

to undo, to untie

Irregular verb

The Seven Simple Tenses		The Seven Compound Tenses	
Singular	Plural	Singular	Plural
1 présent de l'indicatif		8 passé composé	
défais	**défaisons**	**ai défait**	**avons défait**
défais	**défaites**	**as défait**	**avez défait**
défait	**défont**	**a défait**	**ont défait**
2 imparfait de l'indicatif		9 plus-que-parfait de l'indicatif	
défaisais	**défaisions**	**avais défait**	**avions défait**
défaisais	**défaisiez**	**avais défait**	**aviez défait**
défaisait	**défaisaient**	**avait défait**	**avaient défait**
3 passé simple		10 passé antérieur	
défis	**défîmes**	**eus défait**	**eûmes défait**
défis	**défîtes**	**eus défait**	**eûtes défait**
défit	**défirent**	**eut défait**	**eurent défait**
4 futur		11 futur antérieur	
déferai	**déferons**	**aurai défait**	**aurons défait**
déferas	**déferez**	**auras défait**	**aurez défait**
défera	**déferont**	**aura défait**	**auront défait**
5 conditionnel		12 conditionnel passé	
déferais	**déferions**	**aurais défait**	**aurions défait**
déferais	**déferiez**	**aurais défait**	**auriez défait**
déferait	**déferaient**	**aurait défait**	**auraient défait**
6 présent du subjonctif		13 passé du subjonctif	
défasse	**défassions**	**aie défait**	**ayons défait**
défasses	**défassiez**	**aies défait**	**ayez défait**
défasse	**défassent**	**ait défait**	**aient défait**
7 imparfait du subjonctif		14 plus-que-parfait du subjonctif	
défisse	**défissions**	**eusse défait**	**eussions défait**
défisses	**défissiez**	**eusses défait**	**eussiez défait**
défît	**défissent**	**eût défait**	**eussent défait**

Impératif
défais
défaisons
défaites

Common idiomatic expressions using this verb and words related to it

défaire un lit to strip a bed
défaire une malle, une valise, etc. to unpack a trunk, suitcase, etc.
une défaite (military) defeat
avoir le visage défait to look pale
défaire les boutons to unbutton, to undo the buttons
défaire la table to clear the table
se défaire de qqch to rid oneself of something
se défaire d'une habitude to break a habit
le défaitisme defeatism
des cheveux défaits dishevelled hair

See also **faire** and **satisfaire.**

Regular **-re** verb

to defend, to forbid, to prohibit

The Seven Simple Tenses		The Seven Compound Tenses	
Singular	Plural	Singular	Plural
1 présent de l'indicatif		8 passé composé	
défends	**défendons**	**ai défendu**	**avons défendu**
défends	**défendez**	**as défendu**	**avez défendu**
défend	**défendent**	**a défendu**	**ont défendu**
2 imparfait de l'indicatif		9 plus-que-parfait de l'indicatif	
défendais	**défendions**	**avais défendu**	**avions défendu**
défendais	**défendiez**	**avais défendu**	**aviez défendu**
défendait	**défendaient**	**avait défendu**	**avaient défendu**
3 passé simple		10 passé antérieur	
défendis	**défendîmes**	**eus défendu**	**eûmes défendu**
défendis	**défendîtes**	**eus défendu**	**eûtes défendu**
défendit	**défendirent**	**eut défendu**	**eurent défendu**
4 futur		11 futur antérieur	
défendrai	**défendrons**	**aurai défendu**	**aurons défendu**
défendras	**défendrez**	**auras défendu**	**aurez défendu**
défendra	**défendront**	**aura défendu**	**auront défendu**
5 conditionnel		12 conditionnel passé	
défendrais	**défendrions**	**aurais défendu**	**aurions défendu**
défendrais	**défendriez**	**aurais défendu**	**auriez défendu**
défendrait	**défendraient**	**aurait défendu**	**auraient défendu**
6 présent du subjonctif		13 passé du subjonctif	
défende	**défendions**	**aie défendu**	**ayons défendu**
défendes	**défendiez**	**aies défendu**	**ayez défendu**
défende	**défendent**	**ait défendu**	**aient défendu**
7 imparfait du subjonctif		14 plus-que-parfait du subjonctif	
défendisse	**défendissions**	**eusse défendu**	**eussions défendu**
défendisses	**défendissiez**	**eusses défendu**	**eussiez défendu**
défendît	**défendissent**	**eût défendu**	**eussent défendu**

Impératif
défends
défendons
défendez

Sentences using this verb and words related to it

Le père: Je te défends de fumer. C'est une mauvaise habitude.
Le fils: Alors, pourquoi fumes-tu, papa?

une défense defense
Défense de . . . No . . . Allowed
Défense d'afficher Post No Bills (signs)
Défense d"entrer Keep Out/No Entry
Défense de fumer No Smoking
défendable justifiable
défendre qqch à qqn to forbid someone something
se défendre to defend oneself
défensif, défensive defensive
défensivement defensively
se défendre d'avoir fait qqch to deny having done something

The subject pronouns are found on page 103.

dégager (145) — Part. pr. dégageant — Part. passé dégagé

to free, to clear (out), to remove, to give off, to emit

Regular **-er** verb endings; spelling change: retain the **ge** before **a** or **o** to keep the soft **g** sound of the verb

The Seven Simple Tenses		The Seven Compound Tenses	
Singular	Plural	Singular	Plural
1 présent de l'indicatif		8 passé composé	
dégage	**dégageons**	**ai dégagé**	**avons dégagé**
dégages	**dégagez**	**as dégagé**	**avez dégagé**
dégage	**dégagent**	**a dégagé**	**ont dégagé**
2 imparfait de l'indicatif		9 plus-que-parfait de l'indicatif	
dégageais	**dégagions**	**avais dégagé**	**avions dégagé**
dégageais	**dégagiez**	**avais dégagé**	**aviez dégagé**
dégageait	**dégageaient**	**avait dégagé**	**avaient dégagé**
3 passé simple		10 passé antérieur	
dégageai	**dégageâmes**	**eus dégagé**	**eûmes dégagé**
dégageas	**dégageâtes**	**eus dégagé**	**eûtes dégagé**
dégagea	**dégagèrent**	**eut dégagé**	**eurent dégagé**
4 futur		11 futur antérieur	
dégagerai	**dégagerons**	**aurai dégagé**	**aurons dégagé**
dégageras	**dégagerez**	**auras dégagé**	**aurez dégagé**
dégagera	**dégageront**	**aura dégagé**	**auront dégagé**
5 conditionnel		12 conditionnel passé	
dégagerais	**dégagerions**	**aurais dégagé**	**aurions dégagé**
dégagerais	**dégageriez**	**aurais dégagé**	**auriez dégagé**
dégagerait	**dégageraient**	**aurait dégagé**	**auraient dégagé**
6 présent du subjonctif		13 passé du subjonctif	
dégage	**dégagions**	**aie dégagé**	**ayons dégagé**
dégages	**dégagiez**	**aies dégagé**	**ayez dégagé**
dégage	**dégagent**	**ait dégagé**	**aient dégagé**
7 imparfait du subjonctif		14 plus-que-parfait du subjonctif	
dégageasse	**dégageassions**	**eusse dégagé**	**eussions dégagé**
dégageasses	**dégageassiez**	**eusses dégagé**	**eussiez dégagé**
dégageât	**dégageassent**	**eût dégagé**	**eussent dégagé**

Impératif
dégage
dégageons
dégagez

Sentences using this verb and words related to it

Paul m'a répondu d'un ton dégagé. Paul answered me casually.

Dégage! Go away! Take off!

Nous ne pouvons pas partir; ils n'ont pas encore dégagé la route. We can't leave; they haven't cleared the road yet.

Stéphane, il y a une odeur désagréable qui se dégage de ta chambre. Steven, there's an unpleasant odor emanating from your room.

On annonce un ciel dégagé cet après-midi. They're predicting a clear sky this afternoon.

Words and expressions related to this verb

d'un air dégagé, d'un ton dégagé *adv.* casually
engager to commit, to begin, to hire, to insert
s'engager to begin, to commit
le dégagement release, clearing (out)

Don't forget to study the section on defective and impersonal verbs. It's right after this main list.

Regular **-er** verb

to lunch, to have lunch, breakfast

The Seven Simple Tenses		The Seven Compound Tenses	
Singular	Plural	Singular	Plural
1 présent de l'indicatif		8 passé composé	
déjeune	**déjeunons**	**ai déjeuné**	**avons déjeuné**
déjeunes	**déjeunez**	**as déjeuné**	**avez déjeuné**
déjeune	**déjeunent**	**a déjeuné**	**ont déjeuné**
2 imparfait de l'indicatif		9 plus-que-parfait de l'indicatif	
déjeunais	**déjeunions**	**avais déjeuné**	**avions déjeuné**
déjeunais	**déjeuniez**	**avais déjeuné**	**aviez déjeuné**
déjeunait	**déjeunaient**	**avait déjeuné**	**avaient déjeuné**
3 passé simple		10 passé antérieur	
déjeunai	**déjeunâmes**	**eus déjeuné**	**eûmes déjeuné**
déjeunas	**déjeunâtes**	**eus déjeuné**	**eûtes déjeuné**
déjeuna	**déjeunèrent**	**eut déjeuné**	**eurent déjeuné**
4 futur		11 futur antérieur	
déjeunerai	**déjeunerons**	**aurai déjeuné**	**aurons déjeuné**
déjeuneras	**déjeunerez**	**auras déjeuné**	**aurez déjeuné**
déjeunera	**déjeuneront**	**aura déjeuné**	**auront déjeuné**
5 conditionnel		12 conditionnel passé	
déjeunerais	**déjeunerions**	**aurais déjeuné**	**aurions déjeuné**
déjeunerais	**déjeuneriez**	**aurais déjeuné**	**auriez déjeuné**
déjeunerait	**déjeuneraient**	**aurait déjeuné**	**auraient déjeuné**
6 présent du subjonctif		13 passé du subjonctif	
déjeune	**déjeunions**	**aie déjeuné**	**ayons déjeuné**
déjeunes	**déjeuniez**	**aies déjeuné**	**ayez déjeuné**
déjeune	**déjeunent**	**ait déjeuné**	**aient déjeuné**
7 imparfait du subjonctif		14 plus-que-parfait du subjonctif	
déjeunasse	**déjeunassions**	**eusse déjeuné**	**eussions déjeuné**
déjeunasses	**déjeunassiez**	**eusses déjeuné**	**eussiez déjeuné**
déjeunât	**déjeunassent**	**eût déjeuné**	**eussent déjeuné**

Impératif
déjeune
déjeunons
déjeunez

Sentences using this verb and words related to it

Tous les matins je me lève et je prends mon petit déjeuner à sept heures et demie. A midi je déjeune avec mes camarades à l'école. Avec qui déjeunez-vous?

le déjeuner lunch
le petit déjeuner breakfast
jeûner to fast
le jeûne fast, fasting
rompre le jeûne to break one's fast
un jour de jeûne a day of fasting
le déjeuner sur l'herbe picnic lunch (on the grass)

NOTE: The French tend to say **le petit déjeuner** (breakfast), **le déjeuner** (lunch), and **le dîner** (evening meal) or **le souper** (late evening snack). However, in some French-speaking regions, the meals one eats during the day are **le déjeuner** (breakfast), **le dîner** (lunch), and **le souper** (supper).

demander (147) Part. pr. demandant Part. passé demandé

to ask (for), to request

Regular **-er** verb

The Seven Simple Tenses		The Seven Compound Tenses	
Singular	Plural	Singular	Plural
1 présent de l'indicatif		8 passé composé	
demande	**demandons**	**ai demandé**	**avons demandé**
demandes	**demandez**	**as demandé**	**avez demandé**
demande	**demandent**	**a demandé**	**ont demandé**
2 imparfait de l'indicatif		9 plus-que-parfait de l'indicatif	
demandais	**demandions**	**avais demandé**	**avions demandé**
demandais	**demandiez**	**avais demandé**	**aviez demandé**
demandait	**demandaient**	**avait demandé**	**avaient demandé**
3 passé simple		10 passé antérieur	
demandai	**demandâmes**	**eus demandé**	**eûmes demandé**
demandas	**demandâtes**	**eus demandé**	**eûtes demandé**
demanda	**demandèrent**	**eut demandé**	**eurent demandé**
4 futur		11 futur antérieur	
demanderai	**demanderons**	**aurai demandé**	**aurons demandé**
demanderas	**demanderez**	**auras demandé**	**aurez demandé**
demandera	**demanderont**	**aura demandé**	**auront demandé**
5 conditionnel		12 conditionnel passé	
demanderais	**demanderions**	**aurais demandé**	**aurions demandé**
demanderais	**demanderiez**	**aurais demandé**	**auriez demandé**
demanderait	**demanderaient**	**aurait demandé**	**auraient demandé**
6 présent du subjonctif		13 passé du subjonctif	
demande	**demandions**	**aie demandé**	**ayons demandé**
demandes	**demandiez**	**aies demandé**	**ayez demandé**
demande	**demandent**	**ait demandé**	**aient demandé**
7 imparfait du subjonctif		14 plus-que-parfait du subjonctif	
demandasse	**demandassions**	**eusse demandé**	**eussions demandé**
demandasses	**demandassiez**	**eusses demandé**	**eussiez demandé**
demandât	**demandassent**	**eût demandé**	**eussent demandé**

Impératif
demande
demandons
demandez

Sentences using this verb and words related to it

J'ai demandé à une passante où s'arrête l'autobus. Elle m'a répondu:—Je ne sais pas, monsieur. Demandez à l'agent de police. I asked a passerby where the bus stops. She answered me:—I don't know, Sir. Ask the police officer.

une demande a request
sur demande on request, on application
faire une demande de to apply for
Si votre fils demande un morceau de pain, lui donnerez-vous une pierre? If your son asks for a piece of bread, will you give him a stone? (Matthew 7:9) See "if" clauses, top of page 26.

se demander to wonder
mander to send word by letter
un mandat mandate; **un mandat-lettre** letter money order; **un mandat-poste** postal money order
une demande d'emploi job application

Regular **-er** verb

to reside, to live, to remain, to stay

The Seven Simple Tenses		The Seven Compound Tenses	
Singular	Plural	Singular	Plural
1 présent de l'indicatif		8 passé composé	
demeure	**demeurons**	**ai demeuré**	**avons demeuré**
demeures	**demeurez**	**as demeuré**	**avez demeuré**
demeure	**demeurent**	**a demeuré**	**ont demeuré**
2 imparfait de l'indicatif		9 plus-que-parfait de l'indicatif	
demeurais	**demeurions**	**avais demeuré**	**avions demeuré**
demeurais	**demeuriez**	**avais demeuré**	**aviez demeuré**
demeurait	**demeuraient**	**avait demeuré**	**avaient demeuré**
3 passé simple		10 passé antérieur	
demeurai	**demeurâmes**	**eus demeuré**	**eûmes demeuré**
demeuras	**demeurâtes**	**eus demeuré**	**eûtes demeuré**
demeura	**demeurèrent**	**eut demeuré**	**eurent demeuré**
4 futur		11 futur antérieur	
demeurerai	**demeurerons**	**aurai demeuré**	**aurons demeuré**
demeureras	**demeurerez**	**auras demeuré**	**aurez demeuré**
demeurera	**demeureront**	**aura demeuré**	**auront demeuré**
5 conditionnel		12 conditionnel passé	
demeurerais	**demeurerions**	**aurais demeuré**	**aurions demeuré**
demeurerais	**demeureriez**	**aurais demeuré**	**auriez demeuré**
demeurerait	**demeureraient**	**aurait demeuré**	**auraient demeuré**
6 présent du subjonctif		13 passé du subjonctif	
demeure	**demeurions**	**aie demeuré**	**ayons demeuré**
demeures	**demeuriez**	**aies demeuré**	**ayez demeuré**
demeure	**demeurent**	**ait demeuré**	**aient demeuré**
7 imparfait du subjonctif		14 plus-que-parfait du subjonctif	
demeurasse	**demeurassions**	**eusse demeuré**	**eussions demeuré**
demeurasses	**demeurassiez**	**eusses demeuré**	**eussiez demeuré**
demeurât	**demeurassent**	**eût demeuré**	**eussent demeuré**

Impératif
demeure
demeurons
demeurez

Sentences using this verb and words related to it
—**Où demeurez-vous?**
—**Je demeure dans un appartement, rue des Jardins.**

une demeure dwelling, residence
au demeurant incidentally
demeurer couché to stay in bed
demeurer court to stop short
demeurer à un hôtel to stay at a hotel
une mise en demeure injunction
demeurer fidèle to remain faithful

When **demeurer** means "to remain" or "to stay" the auxiliary is **être**.
Marcel est demeuré muet devant les accusations. Marcel remained silent in the face of the charges.

The subject pronouns are found on page 103.

démolir (149) — Part. pr. démolissant — Part. passé démoli

to demolish

Regular -ir verb

The Seven Simple Tenses		The Seven Compound Tenses	
Singular	Plural	Singular	Plural
1 présent de l'indicatif		8 passé composé	
démolis	**démolissons**	**ai démoli**	**avons démoli**
démolis	**démolissez**	**as démoli**	**avez démoli**
démolit	**démolissent**	**a démoli**	**ont démoli**
2 imparfait de l'indicatif		9 plus-que-parfait de l'indicatif	
démolissais	**démolissions**	**avais démoli**	**avions démoli**
démolissais	**démolissiez**	**avais démoli**	**aviez démoli**
démolissait	**démolissaient**	**avait démoli**	**avaient démoli**
3 passé simple		10 passé antérieur	
démolis	**démolîmes**	**eus démoli**	**eûmes démoli**
démolis	**démolîtes**	**eus démoli**	**eûtes démoli**
démolit	**démolirent**	**eut démoli**	**eurent démoli**
4 futur		11 futur antérieur	
démolirai	**démolirons**	**aurai démoli**	**aurons démoli**
démoliras	**démolirez**	**auras démoli**	**aurez démoli**
démolira	**démoliront**	**aura démoli**	**auront démoli**
5 conditionnel		12 conditionnel passé	
démolirais	**démolirions**	**aurais démoli**	**aurions démoli**
démolirais	**démoliriez**	**aurais démoli**	**auriez démoli**
démolirait	**démoliraient**	**aurait démoli**	**auraient démoli**
6 présent du subjonctif		13 passé du subjonctif	
démolisse	**démolissions**	**aie démoli**	**ayons démoli**
démolisses	**démolissiez**	**aies démoli**	**ayez démoli**
démolisse	**démolissent**	**ait démoli**	**aient démoli**
7 imparfait du subjonctif		14 plus-que-parfait du subjonctif	
démolisse	**démolissions**	**eusse démoli**	**eussions démoli**
démolisses	**démolissiez**	**eusses démoli**	**eussiez démoli**
démolît	**démolissent**	**eût démoli**	**eussent démoli**

Impératif
démolis
démolissons
démolissez

Words and expressions related to this verb

une démolition demolition
un démolisseur, une démolisseuse demolisher
se démolir to fall apart, to fall to pieces
démolir l'estomac to ruin one's stomach

Grammar putting you in a tense mood? Review the definitions of basic grammatical terms with examples on pages 35–49.

Regular **-er** verb

to pass, to go past, to go beyond, to exceed

The Seven Simple Tenses		The Seven Compound Tenses	
Singular	Plural	Singular	Plural
1 présent de l'indicatif		8 passé composé	
dépasse	**dépassons**	**ai dépassé**	**avons dépassé**
dépasses	**dépassez**	**as dépassé**	**avez dépassé**
dépasse	**dépassent**	**a dépassé**	**ont dépassé**
2 imparfait de l'indicatif		9 plus-que-parfait de l'indicatif	
dépassais	**dépassions**	**avais dépassé**	**avions dépassé**
dépassais	**dépassiez**	**avais dépassé**	**aviez dépassé**
dépassait	**dépassaient**	**avait dépassé**	**avaient dépassé**
3 passé simple		10 passé antérieur	
dépassai	**dépassâmes**	**eus dépassé**	**eûmes dépassé**
dépassas	**dépassâtes**	**eus dépassé**	**eûtes dépassé**
dépassa	**dépassèrent**	**eut dépassé**	**eurent dépassé**
4 futur		11 futur antérieur	
dépasserai	**dépasserons**	**aurai dépassé**	**aurons dépassé**
dépasseras	**dépasserez**	**auras dépassé**	**aurez dépassé**
dépassera	**dépasseront**	**aura dépassé**	**auront dépassé**
5 conditionnel		12 conditionnel passé	
dépasserais	**dépasserions**	**aurais dépassé**	**aurions dépassé**
dépasserais	**dépasseriez**	**aurais dépassé**	**auriez dépassé**
dépasserait	**dépasseraient**	**aurait dépassé**	**auraient dépassé**
6 présent du subjonctif		13 passé du subjonctif	
dépasse	**dépassions**	**aie dépassé**	**ayons dépassé**
dépasses	**dépassiez**	**aies dépassé**	**ayez dépassé**
dépasse	**dépassent**	**ait dépassé**	**aient dépassé**
7 imparfait du subjonctif		14 plus-que-parfait du subjonctif	
dépassasse	**dépassassions**	**eusse dépassé**	**eussions dépassé**
dépassasses	**dépassassiez**	**eusses dépassé**	**eussiez dépassé**
dépassât	**dépassassent**	**eût dépassé**	**eussent dépassé**

Impératif
dépasse
dépassons
dépassez

Words and expressions related to this verb

le dépassement passing, exceeding
dépassé, dépassée outdated
se dépasser to outdo oneself
passer to pass, to spend (time)
passable passable, adequate
une passoire colander

Fais attention! Tu dépasses la limite de vitesse! Watch out! You're going over the speed limit!

Can't find the verb you're looking for? Check the back pages of this book for a list of over 2,600 additional verbs!

se dépêcher (151) Part. pr. se dépêchant Part. passé dépêché(e)(s)

to hurry, to hasten

Reflexive regular **-er** verb

The Seven Simple Tenses		The Seven Compound Tenses	
Singular	Plural	Singular	Plural
1 présent de l'indicatif		8 passé composé	
me dépêche	**nous dépêchons**	**me suis dépêché(e)**	**nous sommes dépêché(e)s**
te dépêches	**vous dépêchez**	**t'es dépêché(e)**	**vous êtes dépêché(e)(s)**
se dépêche	**se dépêchent**	**s'est dépêché(e)**	**se sont dépêché(e)s**
2 imparfait de l'indicatif		9 plus-que-parfait de l'indicatif	
me dépêchais	**nous dépêchions**	**m'étais dépêché(e)**	**nous étions dépêché(e)s**
te dépêchais	**vous dépêchiez**	**t'étais dépêché(e)**	**vous étiez dépêché(e)(s)**
se dépêchait	**se dépêchaient**	**s'était dépêché(e)**	**s'étaient dépêché(e)s**
3 passé simple		10 passé antérieur	
me dépêchai	**nous dépêchâmes**	**me fus dépêché(e)**	**nous fûmes dépêché(e)s**
te dépêchas	**vous dépêchâtes**	**te fus dépêché(e)**	**vous fûtes dépêché(e)(s)**
se dépêcha	**se dépêchèrent**	**se fut dépêché(e)**	**se furent dépêché(e)s**
4 futur		11 futur antérieur	
me dépêcherai	**nous dépêcherons**	**me serai dépêché(e)**	**nous serons dépêché(e)s**
te dépêcheras	**vous dépêcherez**	**te seras dépêché(e)**	**vous serez dépêché(e)(s)**
se dépêchera	**se dépêcheront**	**se sera dépêché(e)**	**se seront dépêché(e)s**
5 conditionnel		12 conditionnel passé	
me dépêcherais	**nous dépêcherions**	**me serais dépêché(e)**	**nous serions dépêché(e)s**
te dépêcherais	**vous dépêcheriez**	**te serais dépêché(e)**	**vous seriez dépêché(e)(s)**
se dépêcherait	**se dépêcheraient**	**se serait dépêché(e)**	**se seraient dépêché(e)s**
6 présent du subjonctif		13 passé du subjonctif	
me dépêche	**nous dépêchions**	**me sois dépêché(e)**	**nous soyons dépêché(e)s**
te dépêches	**vous dépêchiez**	**te sois dépêché(e)**	**vous soyez dépêché(e)(s)**
se dépêche	**se dépêchent**	**se soit dépêché(e)**	**se soient dépêché(e)s**
7 imparfait du subjonctif		14 plus-que-parfait du subjonctif	
me dépêchasse	**nous dépêchassions**	**me fusse dépêché(e)**	**nous fussions dépêché(e)s**
te dépêchasses	**vous dépêchassiez**	**te fusses dépêché(e)**	**vous fussiez dépêché(e)(s)**
se dépêchât	**se dépêchassent**	**se fût dépêché(e)**	**se fussent dépêché(e)s**

Impératif
dépêche-toi; ne te dépêche pas
dépêchons-nous; ne nous dépêchons pas
dépêchez-vous; ne vous dépêchez pas

Sentences using this verb and words related to it

En me dépêchant pour attraper l'autobus, je suis tombé et je me suis fait mal au genou.
Je me dépêchais de venir chez vous pour vous dire quelque chose de très important.

une dépêche a telegram, a dispatch
dépêcher to dispatch
faire les courses en se dépêchant to do the shopping hurriedly

See also **empêcher.**

Don't forget to study the section on defective and impersonal verbs. It's right after this main list.

Irregular verb

to depict, to describe, to portray

The Seven Simple Tenses		The Seven Compound Tenses	
Singular	Plural	Singular	Plural
1 présent de l'indicatif		8 passé composé	
dépeins	**dépeignons**	**ai dépeint**	**avons dépeint**
dépeins	**dépeignez**	**as dépeint**	**avez dépeint**
dépeint	**dépeignent**	**a dépeint**	**ont dépeint**
2 imparfait de l'indicatif		9 plus-que-parfait de l'indicatif	
dépeignais	**dépeignions**	**avais dépeint**	**avions dépeint**
dépeignais	**dépeigniez**	**avais dépeint**	**aviez dépeint**
dépeignait	**dépeignaient**	**avait dépeint**	**avaient dépeint**
3 passé simple		10 passé antérieur	
dépeignis	**dépeignîmes**	**eus dépeint**	**eûmes dépeint**
dépeignis	**dépeignîtes**	**eus dépeint**	**eûtes dépeint**
dépeignit	**dépeignirent**	**eut dépeint**	**eurent dépeint**
4 futur		11 futur antérieur	
dépeindrai	**dépeindrons**	**aurai dépeint**	**aurons dépeint**
dépeindras	**dépeindrez**	**auras dépeint**	**aurez dépeint**
dépeindra	**dépeindront**	**aura dépeint**	**auront dépeint**
5 conditionnel		12 conditionnel passé	
dépeindrais	**dépeindrions**	**aurais dépeint**	**aurions dépeint**
dépeindrais	**dépeindriez**	**aurais dépeint**	**auriez dépeint**
dépeindrait	**dépeindraient**	**aurait dépeint**	**auraient dépeint**
6 présent du subjonctif		13 passé du subjonctif	
dépeigne	**dépeignions**	**aie dépeint**	**ayons dépeint**
dépeignes	**dépeigniez**	**aies dépeint**	**ayez dépeint**
dépeigne	**dépeignent**	**ait dépeint**	**aient dépeint**
7 imparfait du subjonctif		14 plus-que-parfait du subjonctif	
dépeignisse	**dépeignissions**	**eusse dépeint**	**eussions dépeint**
dépeignisses	**dépeignissiez**	**eusses dépeint**	**eussiez dépeint**
dépeignît	**dépeignissent**	**eût dépeint**	**eussent dépeint**

Impératif
dépeins
dépeignons
dépeignez

Words and expressions related to this verb

dépeindre une scène to depict a scene
peindre to paint
une peinture à l'huile oil painting
la peinture painting
peinturer to daub
un peintre painter; **une femme peintre** woman artist
repeindre to repaint

For other words and expressions related to this verb, see **peindre.**

Soak up some verbs used in weather expressions. There's a list in the Appendixes!

dépendre (153) — Part. pr. dépendant — Part. passé dépendu

to depend (on), to be dependent (on), to take down (something that is hanging)

Regular **-re** verb

The Seven Simple Tenses		The Seven Compound Tenses	
Singular	Plural	Singular	Plural
1 présent de l'indicatif		8 passé composé	
dépends	**dépendons**	**ai dépendu**	**avons dépendu**
dépends	**dépendez**	**as dépendu**	**avez dépendu**
dépend	**dépendent**	**a dépendu**	**ont dépendu**
2 imparfait de l'indicatif		9 plus-que-parfait de l'indicatif	
dépendais	**dépendions**	**avais dépendu**	**avions dépendu**
dépendais	**dépendiez**	**avais dépendu**	**aviez dépendu**
dépendait	**dépendaient**	**avait dépendu**	**avaient dépendu**
3 passé simple		10 passé antérieur	
dépendis	**dépendîmes**	**eus dépendu**	**eûmes dépendu**
dépendis	**dépendîtes**	**eus dépendu**	**eûtes dépendu**
dépendit	**dépendirent**	**eut dépendu**	**eurent dépendu**
4 futur		11 futur antérieur	
dépendrai	**dépendrons**	**aurai dépendu**	**aurons dépendu**
dépendras	**dépendrez**	**auras dépendu**	**aurez dépendu**
dépendra	**dépendront**	**aura dépendu**	**auront dépendu**
5 conditionnel		12 conditionnel passé	
dépendrais	**dépendrions**	**aurais dépendu**	**aurions dépendu**
dépendrais	**dépendriez**	**aurais dépendu**	**auriez dépendu**
dépendrait	**dépendraient**	**aurait dépendu**	**auraient dépendu**
6 présent du subjonctif		13 passé du subjonctif	
dépende	**dépendions**	**aie dépendu**	**ayons dépendu**
dépendes	**dépendiez**	**aies dépendu**	**ayez dépendu**
dépende	**dépendent**	**ait dépendu**	**aient dépendu**
7 imparfait du subjonctif		14 plus-que-parfait du subjonctif	
dépendisse	**dépendissions**	**eusse dépendu**	**eussions dépendu**
dépendisses	**dépendissiez**	**eusses dépendu**	**eussiez dépendu**
dépendît	**dépendissent**	**eût dépendu**	**eussent dépendu**

Impératif
dépends
dépendons
dépendez

Common idiomatic expressions using this verb and words related to it

dépendre de to depend on, to be dependent on
la dépendance dependence
l'indépendance independence
être sous la dépendance de to be dependent on
Il dépend de vous de + inf. It depends on you + inf.
indépendamment de independently of
dépendant de depending on, subject to
indépendant, indépendante independent
Cela dépend! That depends!

See also **pendre** (to hang).

Get acquainted with what preposition goes with what verb. See *Verbs with prepositions* in the Appendixes.

The Seven Simple Tenses		The Seven Compound Tenses	
Singular	Plural	Singular	Plural
1 présent de l'indicatif		8 passé composé	
dépense	**dépensons**	**ai dépensé**	**avons dépensé**
dépenses	**dépensez**	**as dépensé**	**avez dépensé**
dépense	**dépensent**	**a dépensé**	**ont dépensé**
2 imparfait de l'indicatif		9 plus-que-parfait de l'indicatif	
dépensais	**dépensions**	**avais dépensé**	**avions dépensé**
dépensais	**dépensiez**	**avais dépensé**	**aviez dépensé**
dépensait	**dépensaient**	**avait dépensé**	**avaient dépensé**
3 passé simple		10 passé antérieur	
dépensai	**dépensâmes**	**eus dépensé**	**eûmes dépensé**
dépensas	**dépensâtes**	**eus dépensé**	**eûtes dépensé**
dépensa	**dépensèrent**	**eut dépensé**	**eurent dépensé**
4 futur		11 futur antérieur	
dépenserai	**dépenserons**	**aurai dépensé**	**aurons dépensé**
dépenseras	**dépenserez**	**auras dépensé**	**aurez dépensé**
dépensera	**dépenseront**	**aura dépensé**	**auront dépensé**
5 conditionnel		12 conditionnel passé	
dépenserais	**dépenserions**	**aurais dépensé**	**aurions dépensé**
dépenserais	**dépenseriez**	**aurais dépensé**	**auriez dépensé**
dépenserait	**dépenseraient**	**aurait dépensé**	**auraient dépensé**
6 présent du subjonctif		13 passé du subjonctif	
dépense	**dépensions**	**aie dépensé**	**ayons dépensé**
dépenses	**dépensiez**	**aies dépensé**	**ayez dépensé**
dépense	**dépensent**	**ait dépensé**	**aient dépensé**
7 imparfait du subjonctif		14 plus-que-parfait du subjonctif	
dépensasse	**dépensassions**	**eusse dépensé**	**eussions dépensé**
dépensasses	**dépensassiez**	**eusses dépensé**	**eussiez dépensé**
dépensât	**dépensassent**	**eût dépensé**	**eussent dépensé**

Impératif
dépense
dépensons
dépensez

Sentences using this verb and words related to it

Mon père m'a dit que je dépense sottement. Je lui ai répondu que je n'ai rien dépensé cette semaine.

dépensier, dépensière extravagant, unthrifty, spendthrift
dépenser sottement to spend money foolishly
aux dépens de quelqu'un at someone's expense
les dépenses du ménage household expenses

How are you doing? Find out with the verb drills and tests with answers explained on pages 50–101.

déplaire (155) — Part. pr. déplaisant — Part. passé déplu

to displease

Irregular verb

The Seven Simple Tenses		The Seven Compound Tenses	
Singular	Plural	Singular	Plural
1 présent de l'indicatif		8 passé composé	
déplais	**déplaisons**	**ai déplu**	**avons déplu**
déplais	**déplaisez**	**as déplu**	**avez déplu**
déplaît	**déplaisent**	**a déplu**	**ont déplu**
2 imparfait de l'indicatif		9 plus-que-parfait de l'indicatif	
déplaisais	**déplaisions**	**avais déplu**	**avions déplu**
déplaisais	**déplaisiez**	**avais déplu**	**aviez déplu**
déplaisait	**déplaisaient**	**avait déplu**	**avaient déplu**
3 passé simple		10 passé antérieur	
déplus	**déplûmes**	**eus déplu**	**eûmes déplu**
déplus	**déplûtes**	**eus déplu**	**eûtes déplu**
déplut	**déplurent**	**eut déplu**	**eurent déplu**
4 futur		11 futur antérieur	
déplairai	**déplairons**	**aurai déplu**	**aurons déplu**
déplairas	**déplairez**	**auras déplu**	**aurez déplu**
déplaira	**déplairont**	**aura déplu**	**auront déplu**
5 conditionnel		12 conditionnel passé	
déplairais	**déplairions**	**aurais déplu**	**aurions déplu**
déplairais	**déplairiez**	**aurais déplu**	**auriez déplu**
déplairait	**déplairaient**	**aurait déplu**	**auraient déplu**
6 présent du subjonctif		13 passé du subjonctif	
déplaise	**déplaisions**	**aie déplu**	**ayons déplu**
déplaises	**déplaisiez**	**aies déplu**	**ayez déplu**
déplaise	**déplaisent**	**ait déplu**	**aient déplu**
7 imparfait du subjonctif		14 plus-que-parfait du subjonctif	
déplusse	**déplussions**	**eusse déplu**	**eussions déplu**
déplusses	**déplussiez**	**eusses déplu**	**eussiez déplu**
déplût	**déplussent**	**eût déplu**	**eussent déplu**

Impératif
déplais
déplaisons
déplaisez

Common idiomatic expressions using this verb

Cela me déplaît I don't like that.
Il me déplaît de + inf. I don't like + inf.
Plaise à Dieu . . . May God grant that . . .
le plaisir pleasure
le déplaisir displeasure
plaire à qqn to please someone
A Dieu ne plaise! God forbid!
Plaît-il? Pardon me? I beg your pardon? What did you say?
déplaisant, déplaisante displeasing, offensive
déplaire à qqn to displease someone

See also **plaire.**

Use the guide to French pronunciation. It's in the Appendixes.

Regular **-er** verb endings; spelling change: retain the **ge** before **a** or **o** to keep the soft **g** sound of the verb

to disturb, to derange

The Seven Simple Tenses		The Seven Compound Tenses	
Singular	Plural	Singular	Plural
1 présent de l'indicatif		8 passé composé	
dérange	**dérangeons**	**ai dérangé**	**avons dérangé**
déranges	**dérangez**	**as dérangé**	**avez dérangé**
dérange	**dérangent**	**a dérangé**	**ont dérangé**
2 imparfait de l'indicatif		9 plus-que-parfait de l'indicatif	
dérangeais	**dérangions**	**avais dérangé**	**avions dérangé**
dérangeais	**dérangiez**	**avais dérangé**	**aviez dérangé**
dérangeait	**dérangeaient**	**avait dérangé**	**avaient dérangé**
3 passé simple		10 passé antérieur	
dérangeai	**dérangeâmes**	**eus dérangé**	**eûmes dérangé**
dérangeas	**dérangeâtes**	**eus dérangé**	**eûtes dérangé**
dérangea	**dérangèrent**	**eut dérangé**	**eurent dérangé**
4 futur		11 futur antérieur	
dérangerai	**dérangerons**	**aurai dérangé**	**aurons dérangé**
dérangeras	**dérangerez**	**auras dérangé**	**aurez dérangé**
dérangera	**dérangeront**	**aura dérangé**	**auront dérangé**
5 conditionnel		12 conditionnel passé	
dérangerais	**dérangerions**	**aurais dérangé**	**aurions dérangé**
dérangerais	**dérangeriez**	**aurais dérangé**	**auriez dérangé**
dérangerait	**dérangeraient**	**aurait dérangé**	**auraient dérangé**
6 présent du subjonctif		13 passé du subjonctif	
dérange	**dérangions**	**aie dérangé**	**ayons dérangé**
déranges	**dérangiez**	**aies dérangé**	**ayez dérangé**
dérange	**dérangent**	**ait dérangé**	**aient dérangé**
7 imparfait du subjonctif		14 plus-que-parfait du subjonctif	
dérangeasse	**dérangeassions**	**eusse dérangé**	**eussions dérangé**
dérangeasses	**dérangeassiez**	**eusses dérangé**	**eussiez dérangé**
dérangeât	**dérangeassent**	**eût dérangé**	**eussent dérangé**

Impératif
dérange
dérangeons
dérangez

Sentences using this verb and words related to it

Le professeur: Entrez!

L'élève: Excusez-moi, monsieur. Est-ce que je vous dérange?

Le professeur: Non, tu ne me déranges pas. Qu'est-ce que tu veux?

L'élève: Je veux savoir si nous avons un jour de congé demain.

NE PAS DÉRANGER DO NOT DISTURB

dérangé, dérangée upset, out of order, broken down

une personne dérangée a deranged person

un dérangement disarrangement, disorder, inconvenience

se déranger to inconvenience oneself

Je vous en prie, ne vous dérangez pas! I beg you (please), don't disturb yourself!

descendre (157) Part. pr. descendant Part. passé descendu(e)(s)

to go down, to descend, to take down, to bring down

Regular **-re** verb

The Seven Simple Tenses		The Seven Compound Tenses	
Singular	Plural	Singular	Plural
1 présent de l'indicatif		8 passé composé	
descends	**descendons**	**suis descendu(e)**	**sommes descendu(e)s**
descends	**descendez**	**es descendu(e)**	**êtes descendu(e)(s)**
descend	**descendent**	**est descendu(e)**	**sont descendu(e)s**
2 imparfait de l'indicatif		9 plus-que-parfait de l'indicatif	
descendais	**descendions**	**étais descendu(e)**	**étions descendu(e)s**
descendais	**descendiez**	**étais descendu(e)**	**étiez descendu(e)(s)**
descendait	**descendaient**	**était descendu(e)**	**étaient descendu(e)s**
3 passé simple		10 passé antérieur	
descendis	**descendîmes**	**fus descendu(e)**	**fûmes descendu(e)s**
descendis	**descendîtes**	**fus descendu(e)**	**fûtes descendu(e)(s)**
descendit	**descendirent**	**fut descendu(e)**	**furent descendu(e)s**
4 futur		11 futur antérieur	
descendrai	**descendrons**	**serai descendu(e)**	**serons descendu(e)s**
descendras	**descendrez**	**seras descendu(e)**	**serez descendu(e)(s)**
descendra	**descendront**	**sera descendu(e)**	**seront descendu(e)s**
5 conditionnel		12 conditionnel passé	
descendrais	**descendrions**	**serais descendu(e)**	**serions descendu(e)s**
descendrais	**descendriez**	**serais descendu(e)**	**seriez descendu(e)(s)**
descendrait	**descendraient**	**serait descendu(e)**	**seraient descendu(e)s**
6 présent du subjonctif		13 passé du subjonctif	
descende	**descendions**	**sois descendu(e)**	**soyons descendu(e)s**
descendes	**descendiez**	**sois descendu(e)**	**soyez descendu(e)(s)**
descende	**descendent**	**soit descendu(e)**	**soient descendu(e)s**
7 imparfait du subjonctif		14 plus-que-parfait du subjonctif	
descendisse	**descendissions**	**fusse descendu(e)**	**fussions descendu(e)s**
descendisses	**descendissiez**	**fusses descendu(e)**	**fussiez descendu(e)(s)**
descendît	**descendissent**	**fût descendu(e)**	**fussent descendu(e)s**

Impératif
descends
descendons
descendez

Words and expressions related to this verb
descendre à un hôtel to stop (stay over) at a hotel
descendre le store to pull down the window shade
une descente slope
Aidez-moi à descendre mes bagages, s'il vous plaît. Please help me bring down my luggage.

See also the verb **monter.**

This verb is conjugated with *avoir* when it has a direct object.
Examples: **J'ai descendu l'escalier** I went down the stairs.
J'ai descendu les valises I brought down the suitcases.
BUT: **Elle est descendue vite** She came down quickly.

The Seven Simple Tenses

Singular	Plural
1 présent de l'indicatif	
désire	**désirons**
désires	**désirez**
désire	**désirent**
2 imparfait de l'indicatif	
désirais	**désirions**
désirais	**désiriez**
désirait	**désiraient**
3 passé simple	
désirai	**désirâmes**
désiras	**désirâtes**
désira	**désirèrent**
4 futur	
désirerai	**désirerons**
désireras	**désirerez**
désirera	**désireront**
5 conditionnel	
désirerais	**désirerions**
désirerais	**désireriez**
désirerait	**désireraient**
6 présent du subjonctif	
désire	**désirions**
désires	**désiriez**
désire	**désirent**
7 imparfait du subjonctif	
désirasse	**désirassions**
désirasses	**désirassiez**
désirât	**désirassent**

The Seven Compound Tenses

Singular	Plural
8 passé composé	
ai désiré	**avons désiré**
as désiré	**avez désiré**
a désiré	**ont désiré**
9 plus-que-parfait de l'indicatif	
avais désiré	**avions désiré**
avais désiré	**aviez désiré**
avait désiré	**avaient désiré**
10 passé antérieur	
eus désiré	**eûmes désiré**
eus désiré	**eûtes désiré**
eut désiré	**eurent désiré**
11 futur antérieur	
aurai désiré	**aurons désiré**
auras désiré	**aurez désiré**
aura désiré	**auront désiré**
12 conditionnel passé	
aurais désiré	**aurions désiré**
aurais désiré	**auriez désiré**
aurait désiré	**auraient désiré**
13 passé du subjonctif	
aie désiré	**ayons désiré**
aies désiré	**ayez désiré**
ait désiré	**aient désiré**
14 plus-que-parfait du subjonctif	
eusse désiré	**eussions désiré**
eusses désiré	**eussiez désiré**
eût désiré	**eussent désiré**

Impératif
désire
désirons
désirez

Sentences using this verb and words related to it

La vendeuse: **Bonjour, monsieur. Vous désirez?**
Le client: **Je désire acheter une cravate.**
La vendeuse: **Bien, monsieur. Vous pouvez choisir. Voici toutes nos cravates.**
un désir desire, wish; **la désirabilité** desirability
désirable desirable; **désireux, désireuse** desirous
indésirable undesirable
un désir de plaire a desire to please
laisser à désirer to leave much to be desired; **le désir de faire qqch** the desire to do something
Je désire changer de l'argent. I would like to exchange some money.
Combien désirez-vous changer? How much do you want to exchange?

dessiner (159) — Part. pr. dessinant — Part. passé dessiné

to draw, to sketch

Regular **-er** verb

The Seven Simple Tenses		The Seven Compound Tenses	
Singular	Plural	Singular	Plural
1 présent de l'indicatif		8 passé composé	
dessine	**dessinons**	**ai dessiné**	**avons dessiné**
dessines	**dessinez**	**as dessiné**	**avez dessiné**
dessine	**dessinent**	**a dessiné**	**ont dessiné**
2 imparfait de l'indicatif		9 plus-que-parfait de l'indicatif	
dessinais	**dessinions**	**avais dessiné**	**avions dessiné**
dessinais	**dessiniez**	**avais dessiné**	**aviez dessiné**
dessinait	**dessinaient**	**avait dessiné**	**avaient dessiné**
3 passé simple		10 passé antérieur	
dessinai	**dessinâmes**	**eus dessiné**	**eûmes dessiné**
dessinas	**dessinâtes**	**eus dessiné**	**eûtes dessiné**
dessina	**dessinèrent**	**eut dessiné**	**eurent dessiné**
4 futur		11 futur antérieur	
dessinerai	**dessinerons**	**aurai dessiné**	**aurons dessiné**
dessineras	**dessinerez**	**auras dessiné**	**aurez dessiné**
dessinera	**dessineront**	**aura dessiné**	**auront dessiné**
5 conditionnel		12 conditionnel passé	
dessinerais	**dessinerions**	**aurais dessiné**	**aurions dessiné**
dessinerais	**dessineriez**	**aurais dessiné**	**auriez dessiné**
dessinerait	**dessineraient**	**aurait dessiné**	**auraient dessiné**
6 présent du subjonctif		13 passé du subjonctif	
dessine	**dessinions**	**aie dessiné**	**ayons dessiné**
dessines	**dessiniez**	**aies dessiné**	**ayez dessiné**
dessine	**dessinent**	**ait dessiné**	**aient dessiné**
7 imparfait du subjonctif		14 plus-que-parfait du subjonctif	
dessinasse	**dessinassions**	**eusse dessiné**	**eussions dessiné**
dessinasses	**dessinassiez**	**eusses dessiné**	**eussiez dessiné**
dessinât	**dessinassent**	**eût dessiné**	**eussent dessiné**

Impératif
dessine
dessinons
dessinez

Words and expressions related to this verb

dessiner au crayon to draw with a pencil
un dessinateur, une dessinatrice sketcher; **— de journal** cartoonist; **— de modes** dress designer; **— de dessins animés** cartoonist
une bande dessinée comic strip
un dessin animé cartoon
dessiner très vite to do a quick sketch
se dessiner to take shape, to stand out
un dessin drawing, sketch
un dessin à la plume pen and ink sketch
le dessin assisté par ordinateur CAD (computer-aided design)

Do not confuse **un dessin** (sketch, drawing) with **un dessein** (plan, project, purpose).

Regular **-er** verb

to detest, to dislike, to hate

The Seven Simple Tenses		The Seven Compound Tenses	
Singular	Plural	Singular	Plural
1 présent de l'indicatif		8 passé composé	
déteste	**détestons**	**ai détesté**	**avons détesté**
détestes	**détestez**	**as détesté**	**avez détesté**
déteste	**détestent**	**a détesté**	**ont détesté**
2 imparfait de l'indicatif		9 plus-que-parfait de l'indicatif	
détestais	**détestions**	**avais détesté**	**avions détesté**
détestais	**détestiez**	**avais détesté**	**aviez détesté**
détestait	**détestaient**	**avait détesté**	**avaient détesté**
3 passé simple		10 passé antérieur	
détestai	**détestâmes**	**eus détesté**	**eûmes détesté**
détestas	**détestâtes**	**eus détesté**	**eûtes détesté**
détesta	**détestèrent**	**eut détesté**	**eurent détesté**
4 futur		11 futur antérieur	
détesterai	**détesterons**	**aurai détesté**	**aurons détesté**
détesteras	**détesterez**	**auras détesté**	**aurez détesté**
détestera	**détesteront**	**aura détesté**	**auront détesté**
5 conditionnel		12 conditionnel passé	
détesterais	**détesterions**	**aurais détesté**	**aurions détesté**
détesterais	**détesteriez**	**aurais détesté**	**auriez détesté**
détesterait	**détesteraient**	**aurait détesté**	**auraient détesté**
6 présent du subjonctif		13 passé du subjonctif	
déteste	**détestions**	**aie détesté**	**ayons détesté**
détestes	**détestiez**	**aies détesté**	**ayez détesté**
déteste	**détestent**	**ait détesté**	**aient détesté**
7 imparfait du subjonctif		14 plus-que-parfait du subjonctif	
détestasse	**détestassions**	**eusse détesté**	**eussions détesté**
détestasses	**détestassiez**	**eusses détesté**	**eussiez détesté**
détestât	**détestassent**	**eût détesté**	**eussent détesté**

Impératif
déteste
détestons
détestez

Sentences using this verb and words related to it

Je déteste la médiocrité, je déteste le mensonge, et je déteste la calomnie. Ce sont des choses détestables.

détestable loathsome, hateful, dreadful
détestablement detestably

How are you doing? Find out with the verb drills and tests with answers explained on pages 50–101.

détourner (161) Part. pr. détournant Part. passé détourné

to turn aside, to turn away, to divert

Regular **-er** verb

The Seven Simple Tenses		The Seven Compound Tenses	
Singular	Plural	Singular	Plural
1 présent de l'indicatif		8 passé composé	
détourne	**détournons**	**ai détourné**	**avons détourné**
détournes	**détournez**	**as détourné**	**avez détourné**
détourne	**détournent**	**a détourné**	**ont détourné**
2 imparfait de l'indicatif		9 plus-que-parfait de l'indicatif	
détournais	**détournions**	**avais détourné**	**avions détourné**
détournais	**détourniez**	**avais détourné**	**aviez détourné**
détournait	**détournaient**	**avait détourné**	**avaient détourné**
3 passé simple		10 passé antérieur	
détournai	**détournâmes**	**eus détourné**	**eûmes détourné**
détournas	**détournâtes**	**eus détourné**	**eûtes détourné**
détourna	**détournèrent**	**eut détourné**	**eurent détourné**
4 futur		11 futur antérieur	
détournerai	**détournerons**	**aurai détourné**	**aurons détourné**
détourneras	**détournerez**	**auras détourné**	**aurez détourné**
détournera	**détourneront**	**aura détourné**	**auront détourné**
5 conditionnel		12 conditionnel passé	
détournerais	**détournerions**	**aurais détourné**	**aurions détourné**
détournerais	**détourneriez**	**aurais détourné**	**auriez détourné**
détournerait	**détourneraient**	**aurait détourné**	**auraient détourné**
6 présent du subjonctif		13 passé du subjonctif	
détourne	**détournions**	**aie détourné**	**ayons détourné**
détournes	**détourniez**	**aies détourné**	**ayez détourné**
détourne	**détournent**	**ait détourné**	**aient détourné**
7 imparfait du subjonctif		14 plus-que-parfait du subjonctif	
détournasse	**détournassions**	**eusse détourné**	**eussions détourné**
détournasses	**détournassiez**	**eusses détourné**	**eussiez détourné**
détournât	**détournassent**	**eût détourné**	**eussent détourné**

Impératif
détourne
détournons
détournez

Words and expressions related to this verb

détourner les yeux to look away
détourner qqn de faire qqch to discourage someone from doing something
un chemin détourné side road
se détourner de to turn oneself away from
un détour detour; **faire un détour** to make a detour
tourner to turn

See also **retourner** and **tourner**.

Can't find the verb you're looking for? Check the back pages of this book for a list of over 2,600 additional verbs!

Irregular verb

to destroy

The Seven Simple Tenses		The Seven Compound Tenses	
Singular	Plural	Singular	Plural
1 présent de l'indicatif		8 passé composé	
détruis	**détruisons**	**ai détruit**	**avons détruit**
détruis	**détruisez**	**as détruit**	**avez détruit**
détruit	**détruisent**	**a détruit**	**ont détruit**
2 imparfait de l'indicatif		9 plus-que-parfait de l'indicatif	
détruisais	**détruisions**	**avais détruit**	**avions détruit**
détruisais	**détruisiez**	**avais détruit**	**aviez détruit**
détruisait	**détruisaient**	**avait détruit**	**avaient détruit**
3 passé simple		10 passé antérieur	
détruisis	**détruisîmes**	**eus détruit**	**eûmes détruit**
détruisis	**détruisîtes**	**eus détruit**	**eûtes détruit**
détruisit	**détruisirent**	**eut détruit**	**eurent détruit**
4 futur		11 futur antérieur	
détruirai	**détruirons**	**aurai détruit**	**aurons détruit**
détruiras	**détruirez**	**auras détruit**	**aurez détruit**
détruira	**détruiront**	**aura détruit**	**auront détruit**
5 conditionnel		12 conditionnel passé	
détruirais	**détruirions**	**aurais détruit**	**aurions détruit**
détruirais	**détruiriez**	**aurais détruit**	**auriez détruit**
détruirait	**détruiraient**	**aurait détruit**	**auraient détruit**
6 présent du subjonctif		13 passé du subjonctif	
détruise	**détruisions**	**aie détruit**	**ayons détruit**
détruises	**détruisiez**	**aies détruit**	**ayez détruit**
détruise	**détruisent**	**ait détruit**	**aient détruit**
7 imparfait du subjonctif		14 plus-que-parfait du subjonctif	
détruisisse	**détruisissions**	**eusse détruit**	**eussions détruit**
détruisisses	**détruisissiez**	**eusses détruit**	**eussiez détruit**
détruisît	**détruisissent**	**eût détruit**	**eussent détruit**

Impératif
détruis
détruisons
détruisez

Words related to this verb

la destruction destruction
destructif, destructive destructive
destructeur, destructrice *adj.* destructive; *n.* destroyer
la destructivité destructiveness
destructible destructible

se détruire to destroy (to do away with) oneself
Les drogues ont détruit sa vie. Drugs destroyed his/her life.

It's important that you be familiar with the Subjunctive. See pages 26–31.

développer (163) Part. pr. développant Part. passé développé

to develop, to spread out

Regular **-er** verb

The Seven Simple Tenses		The Seven Compound Tenses	
Singular	Plural	Singular	Plural
1 présent de l'indicatif		8 passé composé	
développe	**développons**	**ai développé**	**avons développé**
développes	**développez**	**as développé**	**avez développé**
développe	**développent**	**a développé**	**ont développé**
2 imparfait de l'indicatif		9 plus-que-parfait de l'indicatif	
développais	**développions**	**avais développé**	**avions développé**
développais	**développiez**	**avais développé**	**aviez développé**
développait	**développaient**	**avait développé**	**avaient développé**
3 passé simple		10 passé antérieur	
développai	**développâmes**	**eus développé**	**eûmes développé**
développas	**développâtes**	**eus développé**	**eûtes développé**
développa	**développèrent**	**eut développé**	**eurent développé**
4 futur		11 futur antérieur	
développerai	**développerons**	**aurai développé**	**aurons développé**
développeras	**développerez**	**auras développé**	**aurez développé**
développera	**développeront**	**aura développé**	**auront développé**
5 conditionnel		12 conditionnel passé	
développerais	**développerions**	**aurais développé**	**aurions développé**
développerais	**développeriez**	**aurais développé**	**auriez développé**
développerait	**développeraient**	**aurait développé**	**auraient développé**
6 présent du subjonctif		13 passé du subjonctif	
développe	**développions**	**aie développé**	**ayons développé**
développes	**développiez**	**aies développé**	**ayez développé**
développe	**développent**	**ait développé**	**aient développé**
7 imparfait du subjonctif		14 plus-que-parfait du subjonctif	
développasse	**développassions**	**eusse développé**	**eussions développé**
développasses	**développassiez**	**eusses développé**	**eussiez développé**
développât	**développassent**	**eût développé**	**eussent développé**

Impératif
développe
développons
développez

Words related to this verb
un développement development
un enveloppement envelopment, wrapping up; **enveloppement sinapisé** mustard poultice
envelopper to envelop, to wrap up
une enveloppe envelope
développer une pellicule to develop film

Don't forget to use the English-French verb index. It's in the Appendixes.

Irregular verb

to become

The Seven Simple Tenses		The Seven Compound Tenses	
Singular	Plural	Singular	Plural
1 présent de l'indicatif		8 passé composé	
deviens	**devenons**	**suis devenu(e)**	**sommes devenu(e)s**
deviens	**devenez**	**es devenu(e)**	**êtes devenu(e)(s)**
devient	**deviennent**	**est devenu(e)**	**sont devenu(e)s**
2 imparfait de l'indicatif		9 plus-que-parfait de l'indicatif	
devenais	**devenions**	**étais devenu(e)**	**étions devenu(e)s**
devenais	**deveniez**	**étais devenu(e)**	**étiez devenu(e)(s)**
devenait	**devenaient**	**était devenu(e)**	**étaient devenu(e)s**
3 passé simple		10 passé antérieur	
devins	**devînmes**	**fus devenu(e)**	**fûmes devenu(e)s**
devins	**devîntes**	**fus devenu(e)**	**fûtes devenu(e)(s)**
devint	**devinrent**	**fut devenu(e)**	**furent devenu(e)s**
4 futur		11 futur antérieur	
deviendrai	**deviendrons**	**serai devenu(e)**	**serons devenu(e)s**
deviendras	**deviendrez**	**seras devenu(e)**	**serez devenu(e)(s)**
deviendra	**deviendront**	**sera devenu(e)**	**seront devenu(e)s**
5 conditionnel		12 conditionnel passé	
deviendrais	**deviendrions**	**serais devenu(e)**	**serions devenu(e)s**
deviendrais	**deviendriez**	**serais devenu(e)**	**seriez devenu(e)(s)**
deviendrait	**deviendraient**	**serait devenu(e)**	**seraient devenu(e)s**
6 présent du subjonctif		13 passé du subjonctif	
devienne	**devenions**	**sois devenu(e)**	**soyons devenu(e)s**
deviennes	**deveniez**	**sois devenu(e)**	**soyez devenu(e)(s)**
devienne	**deviennent**	**soit devenu(e)**	**soient devenu(e)s**
7 imparfait du subjonctif		14 plus-que-parfait du subjonctif	
devinsse	**devinssions**	**fusse devenu(e)**	**fussions devenu(e)s**
devinsses	**devinssiez**	**fusses devenu(e)**	**fussiez devenu(e)(s)**
devînt	**devinssent**	**fût devenu(e)**	**fussent devenu(e)s**

Impératif
deviens
devenons
devenez

Common idiomatic expressions using this verb

J'ai entendu dire que Claudette est devenue docteur. Et vous, qu'est-ce que vous voulez devenir?

devenir fou, devenir folle to go mad, crazy; **devenir vieux/grand** to grow old/tall
Qu'est devenue votre soeur? What has become of your sister?

See also **convenir, prévenir, revenir, se souvenir,** and **venir.**

Don't forget to study the section on defective and impersonal verbs. It's right after this main list.

devoir (165) Part. pr. **devant** Part. passé **dû (due)**

to have to, must, ought, owe, should

Irregular verb

The Seven Simple Tenses		The Seven Compound Tenses	
Singular	Plural	Singular	Plural
1 présent de l'indicatif		8 passé composé	
dois	**devons**	**ai dû**	**avons dû**
dois	**devez**	**as dû**	**avez dû**
doit	**doivent**	**a dû**	**ont dû**
2 imparfait de l'indicatif		9 plus-que-parfait de l'indicatif	
devais	**devions**	**avais dû**	**avions dû**
devais	**deviez**	**avais dû**	**aviez dû**
devait	**devaient**	**avait dû**	**avaient dû**
3 passé simple		10 passé antérieur	
dus	**dûmes**	**eus dû**	**eûmes dû**
dus	**dûtes**	**eus dû**	**eûtes dû**
dut	**durent**	**eut dû**	**eurent dû**
4 futur		11 futur antérieur	
devrai	**devrons**	**aurai dû**	**aurons dû**
devras	**devrez**	**auras dû**	**aurez dû**
devra	**devront**	**aura dû**	**auront dû**
5 conditionnel		12 conditionnel passé	
devrais	**devrions**	**aurais dû**	**aurions dû**
devrais	**devriez**	**aurais dû**	**auriez dû**
devrait	**devraient**	**aurait dû**	**auraient dû**
6 présent du subjonctif		13 passé du subjonctif	
doive	**devions**	**aie dû**	**ayons dû**
doives	**deviez**	**aies dû**	**ayez dû**
doive	**doivent**	**ait dû**	**aient dû**
7 imparfait du subjonctif		14 plus-que-parfait du subjonctif	
dusse	**dussions**	**eusse dû**	**eussions dû**
dusses	**dussiez**	**eusses dû**	**eussiez dû**
dût	**dussent**	**eût dû**	**eussent dû**

Impératif
dois
devons
devez

AN ESSENTIAL 55 VERB

Devoir

Devoir is a verb that you ought to know. It is useful in numerous everyday situations.

D

Sentences using devoir and words related to it

Cette grosse somme d'argent est due lundi. This large amount of money is due Monday.

Combien je vous dois? How much do I owe you?

Vous me devez cent euros. You owe me 100 euros.

J'ai dû attendre deux heures! I had to wait two hours!

Avant quelle heure dois-je quitter la chambre? Before what time must I leave (check out of) the room?

Hier soir, je suis allé au cinéma avec mes amis. Vous auriez dû venir avec nous. Le film était excellent. Yesterday evening I went to the movies with my friends. You should have come with us. The film was excellent.

—Où sont tes devoirs, Robert?
—Un lézard a mangé mes devoirs!
—Tu dois arrêter de dire des bêtises, Robert!

—Where is your homework, Robert?
—A lizard ate my homework!
—You should stop talking nonsense, Robert!

Words and expressions related to this verb

le devoir **duty, obligation**

les devoirs **homework**

faire ses devoirs **to do one's homework**

Don't forget to check the list of 2,600 additional verbs keyed to the 501 model verbs. It's in the Appendixes!

The subject pronouns are found on page 103.

diminuer (166) — Part. pr. **diminuant** — Part. passé **diminué**

to diminish, to decrease, to lessen

Regular **-er** verb

The Seven Simple Tenses		The Seven Compound Tenses	
Singular	Plural	Singular	Plural
1 présent de l'indicatif		8 passé composé	
diminue	**diminuons**	**ai diminué**	**avons diminué**
diminues	**diminuez**	**as diminué**	**avez diminué**
diminue	**diminuent**	**a diminué**	**ont diminué**
2 imparfait de l'indicatif		9 plus-que-parfait de l'indicatif	
diminuais	**diminuions**	**avais diminué**	**avions diminué**
diminuais	**diminuiez**	**avais diminué**	**aviez diminué**
diminuait	**diminuaient**	**avait diminué**	**avaient diminué**
3 passé simple		10 passé antérieur	
diminuai	**diminuâmes**	**eus diminué**	**eûmes diminué**
diminuas	**diminuâtes**	**eus diminué**	**eûtes diminué**
diminua	**diminuèrent**	**eut diminué**	**eurent diminué**
4 futur		11 futur antérieur	
diminuerai	**diminuerons**	**aurai diminué**	**aurons diminué**
diminueras	**diminuerez**	**auras diminué**	**aurez diminué**
diminuera	**diminueront**	**aura diminué**	**auront diminué**
5 conditionnel		12 conditionnel passé	
diminuerais	**diminuerions**	**aurais diminué**	**aurions diminué**
diminuerais	**diminueriez**	**aurais diminué**	**auriez diminué**
diminuerait	**diminueraient**	**aurait diminué**	**auraient diminué**
6 présent du subjonctif		13 passé du subjonctif	
diminue	**diminuions**	**aie diminué**	**ayons diminué**
diminues	**diminuiez**	**aies diminué**	**ayez diminué**
diminue	**diminuent**	**ait diminué**	**aient diminué**
7 imparfait du subjonctif		14 plus-que-parfait du subjonctif	
diminuasse	**diminuassions**	**eusse diminué**	**eussions diminué**
diminuasses	**diminuassiez**	**eusses diminué**	**eussiez diminué**
diminuât	**diminuassent**	**eût diminué**	**eussent diminué**

Impératif
diminue
diminuons
diminuez

Words and expressions related to this verb

une diminution decrease, diminution, reduction

Le prix du café n'a pas diminué. The price of coffee has not gone down.

Votre travail a diminué de moitié. Your work has decreased by half.

diminutif, diminutive diminutive

faire diminuer to lower, to decrease

la diminution d'un prix lowering of a price

se diminuer to lower oneself

Don't forget to study the section on defective and impersonal verbs. It's right after this main list.

Regular **-er** verb

to dine, to have dinner

The Seven Simple Tenses		The Seven Compound Tenses	
Singular	Plural	Singular	Plural
1 présent de l'indicatif		8 passé composé	
dîne	**dînons**	**ai dîné**	**avons dîné**
dînes	**dînez**	**as dîné**	**avez dîné**
dîne	**dînent**	**a dîné**	**ont dîné**
2 imparfait de l'indicatif		9 plus-que-parfait de l'indicatif	
dînais	**dînions**	**avais dîné**	**avions dîné**
dînais	**dîniez**	**avais dîné**	**aviez dîné**
dînait	**dînaient**	**avait dîné**	**avaient dîné**
3 passé simple		10 passé antérieur	
dînai	**dînâmes**	**eus dîné**	**eûmes dîné**
dînas	**dînâtes**	**eus dîné**	**eûtes dîné**
dîna	**dînèrent**	**eut dîné**	**eurent dîné**
4 futur		11 futur antérieur	
dînerai	**dînerons**	**aurai dîné**	**aurons dîné**
dîneras	**dînerez**	**auras dîné**	**aurez dîné**
dînera	**dîneront**	**aura dîné**	**auront dîné**
5 conditionnel		12 conditionnel passé	
dînerais	**dînerions**	**aurais dîné**	**aurions dîné**
dînerais	**dîneriez**	**aurais dîné**	**auriez dîné**
dînerait	**dîneraient**	**aurait dîné**	**auraient dîné**
6 présent du subjonctif		13 passé du subjonctif	
dîne	**dînions**	**aie dîné**	**ayons dîné**
dînes	**dîniez**	**aies dîné**	**ayez dîné**
dîne	**dînent**	**ait dîné**	**aient dîné**
7 imparfait du subjonctif		14 plus-que-parfait du subjonctif	
dînasse	**dînassions**	**eusse dîné**	**eussions dîné**
dînasses	**dînassiez**	**eusses dîné**	**eussiez dîné**
dînât	**dînassent**	**eût dîné**	**eussent dîné**

Impératif
dîne
dînons
dînez

Common idiomatic expressions using this verb

Lundi j'ai dîné chez des amis. Mardi tu as dîné chez moi. Mercredi nous avons dîné chez Pierre. J'aurais dû dîner seul.

le dîner dinner
une dînette child's tea party
l'heure du dîner dinner time
j'aurais dû I should have
un dîneur diner
donner un dîner to give a dinner
dîner en ville to dine out
J'aurais dû dîner. I should have had dinner.

Try reading aloud this play on sounds (the letter **d**) as fast as you can:
Denis a dîné du dos d'un dindon dodu.
Dennis dined on (ate) the back of a plump turkey.

dire (168)

Part. pr. **disant** Part. passé **dit**

to say, to tell

Irregular verb

The Seven Simple Tenses		The Seven Compound Tenses	
Singular	Plural	Singular	Plural
1 présent de l'indicatif		8 passé composé	
dis	**disons**	**ai dit**	**avons dit**
dis	**dites**	**as dit**	**avez dit**
dit	**disent**	**a dit**	**ont dit**
2 imparfait de l'indicatif		9 plus-que-parfait de l'indicatif	
disais	**disions**	**avais dit**	**avions dit**
disais	**disiez**	**avais dit**	**aviez dit**
disait	**disaient**	**avait dit**	**avaient dit**
3 passé simple		10 passé antérieur	
dis	**dîmes**	**eus dit**	**eûmes dit**
dis	**dîtes**	**eus dit**	**eûtes dit**
dit	**dirent**	**eut dit**	**eurent dit**
4 futur		11 futur antérieur	
dirai	**dirons**	**aurai dit**	**aurons dit**
diras	**direz**	**auras dit**	**aurez dit**
dira	**diront**	**aura dit**	**auront dit**
5 conditionnel		12 conditionnel passé	
dirais	**dirions**	**aurais dit**	**aurions dit**
dirais	**diriez**	**aurais dit**	**auriez dit**
dirait	**diraient**	**aurait dit**	**auraient dit**
6 présent du subjonctif		13 passé du subjonctif	
dise	**disions**	**aie dit**	**ayons dit**
dises	**disiez**	**aies dit**	**ayez dit**
dise	**disent**	**ait dit**	**aient dit**
7 imparfait du subjonctif		14 plus-que-parfait du subjonctif	
disse	**dissions**	**eusse dit**	**eussions dit**
disses	**dissiez**	**eusses dit**	**eussiez dit**
dît	**dissent**	**eût dit**	**eussent dit**

Impératif
dis
disons
dites

See also **contredire, interdire, maudire, médire, prédire,** and note the different *vous* form in the *présent de l'indicatif* and the *impératif.*

AN ESSENTIAL 55 VERB

Dire

Dire is an important verb for a beginning student because it is useful in many idiomatic expressions and situations and because there are many verbs conjugated like it.

Sentences using dire

J'entends dire que Tina s'est mariée avec Alexandre. I hear that Tina married Alexander.

Qu'est-ce que vous avez dit? What did you say?

Dites-moi comment ouvrir cette porte, s'il vous plaît. Please tell me how to open this door.

Qui l'aurait dit? Who would have thought so?

Que veut dire ce mot? What does this word mean?

Cela va sans dire. That goes without saying.

Cela me dit qqch. That rings a bell.

Words and expressions related to this verb

à ce qu'on dit . . . **according to what they say . . .**

à vrai dire **to tell the truth**

aussitôt dit, aussitôt fait **no sooner said than done**

avoir son mot à dire **to have one's say (in something)**

c'est-à-dire **that is, that is to say**

dire du bien de **to speak well of**

dire du mal de **to speak ill of**

Dis donc . . . **Say now . . .; Hey . . .**

entendre dire que **to hear it said that, to hear tell that**

soi-disant **so-called**

vouloir dire **to mean**

If you can conjugate **dire** you can also conjugate the following verbs:

contredire **to contradict**

se dédire **to retract, to go back on one's word (être for compound tenses)**

interdire **to forbid**

maudire **to curse**

médire de **to speak ill (badly) of**

prédire **to predict**

redire **to repeat, to say again**

Proverbs

Dis-moi ce que tu manges, je te dirai ce que tu es. (Brillat-Savarin) **Tell me what you eat and I will tell you what you are.**

Bien faire et laisser dire. **Do your work well and never mind the critics.**

Qui ne dit mot consent. **If you don't speak up you agree.**

The subject pronouns are found on page 103.

discuter (169) — Part. pr. discutant — Part. passé discuté

to discuss, to argue

Regular **-er** verb

The Seven Simple Tenses		The Seven Compound Tenses	
Singular	Plural	Singular	Plural
1 présent de l'indicatif		8 passé composé	
discute	**discutons**	**ai discuté**	**avons discuté**
discutes	**discutez**	**as discuté**	**avez discuté**
discute	**discutent**	**a discuté**	**ont discuté**
2 imparfait de l'indicatif		9 plus-que-parfait de l'indicatif	
discutais	**discutions**	**avais discuté**	**avions discuté**
discutais	**discutiez**	**avais discuté**	**aviez discuté**
discutait	**discutaient**	**avait discuté**	**avaient discuté**
3 passé simple		10 passé antérieur	
discutai	**discutâmes**	**eus discuté**	**eûmes discuté**
discutas	**discutâtes**	**eus discuté**	**eûtes discuté**
discuta	**discutèrent**	**eut discuté**	**eurent discuté**
4 futur		11 futur antérieur	
discuterai	**discuterons**	**aurai discuté**	**aurons discuté**
discuteras	**discuterez**	**auras discuté**	**aurez discuté**
discutera	**discuteront**	**aura discuté**	**auront discuté**
5 conditionnel		12 conditionnel passé	
discuterais	**discuterions**	**aurais discuté**	**aurions discuté**
discuterais	**discuteriez**	**aurais discuté**	**auriez discuté**
discuterait	**discuteraient**	**aurait discuté**	**auraient discuté**
6 présent du subjonctif		13 passé du subjonctif	
discute	**discutions**	**aie discuté**	**ayons discuté**
discutes	**discutiez**	**aies discuté**	**ayez discuté**
discute	**discutent**	**ait discuté**	**aient discuté**
7 imparfait du subjonctif		14 plus-que-parfait du subjonctif	
discutasse	**discutassions**	**eusse discuté**	**eussions discuté**
discutasses	**discutassiez**	**eusses discuté**	**eussiez discuté**
discutât	**discutassent**	**eût discuté**	**eussent discuté**

Impératif
discute
discutons
discutez

Words and expressions related to this verb
une discussion discussion
discutable disputable, questionable
discuter avec to argue with; **discuter de** to argue about
un groupe de discussion newsgroup (Internet)

Get acquainted with what preposition goes with what verb. See *Verbs with prepositions* in the Appendixes.

Irregular verb

to disappear

The Seven Simple Tenses		The Seven Compound Tenses	
Singular	Plural	Singular	Plural
1 présent de l'indicatif		8 passé composé	
disparais	**disparaissons**	**ai disparu**	**avons disparu**
disparais	**disparaissez**	**as disparu**	**avez disparu**
disparaît	**disparaissent**	**a disparu**	**ont disparu**
2 imparfait de l'indicatif		9 plus-que-parfait de l'indicatif	
disparaissais	**disparaissions**	**avais disparu**	**avions disparu**
disparaissais	**disparaissiez**	**avais disparu**	**aviez disparu**
disparaissait	**disparaissaient**	**avait disparu**	**avaient disparu**
3 passé simple		10 passé antérieur	
disparus	**disparûmes**	**eus disparu**	**eûmes disparu**
disparus	**disparûtes**	**eus disparu**	**eûtes disparu**
disparut	**disparurent**	**eut disparu**	**eurent disparu**
4 futur		11 futur antérieur	
disparaîtrai	**disparaîtrons**	**aurai disparu**	**aurons disparu**
disparaîtras	**disparaîtrez**	**auras disparu**	**aurez disparu**
disparaîtra	**disparaîtront**	**aura disparu**	**auront disparu**
5 conditionnel		12 conditionnel passé	
disparaîtrais	**disparaîtrions**	**aurais disparu**	**aurions disparu**
disparaîtrais	**disparaîtriez**	**aurais disparu**	**auriez disparu**
disparaîtrait	**disparaîtraient**	**aurait disparu**	**auraient disparu**
6 présent du subjonctif		13 passé du subjonctif	
disparaisse	**disparaissions**	**aie disparu**	**ayons disparu**
disparaisses	**disparaissiez**	**aies disparu**	**ayez disparu**
disparaisse	**disparaissent**	**ait disparu**	**aient disparu**
7 imparfait du subjonctif		14 plus-que-parfait du subjonctif	
disparusse	**disparussions**	**eusse disparu**	**eussions disparu**
disparusses	**disparussiez**	**eusses disparu**	**eussiez disparu**
disparût	**disparussent**	**eût disparu**	**eussent disparu**

Impératif
disparais
disparaissons
disparaissez

Words and expressions related to this verb

faire disparaître aux regards to hide from sight

notre cher ami disparu (notre chère amie disparue) our dear departed friend

la disparition disappearance, disappearing

disparu, disparue en mer lost at sea

être porté disparu to be declared missing

un disparu missing person

See also **apparaître, paraître,** and **reparaître.**

Grammar putting you in a tense mood? Review the definitions of basic grammatical terms with examples on pages 35–49.

donner (171) — Part. pr. donnant — Part. passé donné

to give

Regular **-er** verb

The Seven Simple Tenses		The Seven Compound Tenses	
Singular	Plural	Singular	Plural
1 présent de l'indicatif		8 passé composé	
donne	**donnons**	**ai donné**	**avons donné**
donnes	**donnez**	**as donné**	**avez donné**
donne	**donnent**	**a donné**	**ont donné**
2 imparfait de l'indicatif		9 plus-que-parfait de l'indicatif	
donnais	**donnions**	**avais donné**	**avions donné**
donnais	**donniez**	**avais donné**	**aviez donné**
donnait	**donnaient**	**avait donné**	**avaient donné**
3 passé simple		10 passé antérieur	
donnai	**donnâmes**	**eus donné**	**eûmes donné**
donnas	**donnâtes**	**eus donné**	**eûtes donné**
donna	**donnèrent**	**eut donné**	**eurent donné**
4 futur		11 futur antérieur	
donnerai	**donnerons**	**aurai donné**	**aurons donné**
donneras	**donnerez**	**auras donné**	**aurez donné**
donnera	**donneront**	**aura donné**	**auront donné**
5 conditionnel		12 conditionnel passé	
donnerais	**donnerions**	**aurais donné**	**aurions donné**
donnerais	**donneriez**	**aurais donné**	**auriez donné**
donnerait	**donneraient**	**aurait donné**	**auraient donné**
6 présent du subjonctif		13 passé du subjonctif	
donne	**donnions**	**aie donné**	**ayons donné**
donnes	**donniez**	**aies donné**	**ayez donné**
donne	**donnent**	**ait donné**	**aient donné**
7 imparfait du subjonctif		14 plus-que-parfait du subjonctif	
donnasse	**donnassions**	**eusse donné**	**eussions donné**
donnasses	**donnassiez**	**eusses donné**	**eussiez donné**
donnât	**donnassent**	**eût donné**	**eussent donné**

Impératif
donne
donnons
donnez

AN ESSENTIAL 55 VERB

Donner

Donner is an important verb for you to know because it is used in many everyday situations and idiomatic expressions. It is a regular **-er** verb.

Sentences using donner

La salle à manger donne sur le jardin. The dining room looks out on (faces) the garden.

Donnez-moi, s'il vous plaît, cet éclair et deux beignets aux pommes. Please give me this eclair and two apple fritters.

J'aimerais une chambre qui donne sur la rue. I would like a room that looks out on the street.

Proverbs and expressions

Il y a plus de bonheur à donner qu'à recevoir. It is better to give than to receive.

Ce qui est donné est donné. What is given is given. (Never take back what you have given.)

La façon de donner vaut mieux que ce qu'on donne. (Corneille) The way you give is worth more than what you give.

Words and expressions related to this verb

donner rendez-vous à qqn to make an appointment (a date) with someone

donner sur to look out on

donner à boire à qqn to give someone something to drink

donner à manger à qqn to give someone something to eat

donner congé à to grant leave to

donner du chagrin à qqn to give someone grief

donner un cours to give a course, to lecture

une base de données database (computer)

If you can conjugate **donner** you can also conjugate the following verbs (and any regular **-er** verb):

abandonner to abandon

amidonner to starch

se désabonner to cancel a subscription (helping verb être)

ordonner to order, to prescribe

pardonner to pardon, to forgive

randonner to hike

rognonner to grumble

ronronner to purr

Can't find the verb you're looking for? Check the back pages of this book for a list of over 2,600 additional verbs!

The subject pronouns are found on page 103.

dormir (172) Part. pr. **dormant** Part. passé **dormi**

to sleep

Irregular verb

The Seven Simple Tenses		The Seven Compound Tenses	
Singular	Plural	Singular	Plural
1 présent de l'indicatif		8 passé composé	
dors	**dormons**	**ai dormi**	**avons dormi**
dors	**dormez**	**as dormi**	**avez dormi**
dort	**dorment**	**a dormi**	**ont dormi**
2 imparfait de l'indicatif		9 plus-que-parfait de l'indicatif	
dormais	**dormions**	**avais dormi**	**avions dormi**
dormais	**dormiez**	**avais dormi**	**aviez dormi**
dormait	**dormaient**	**avait dormi**	**avaient dormi**
3 passé simple		10 passé antérieur	
dormis	**dormîmes**	**eus dormi**	**eûmes dormi**
dormis	**dormîtes**	**eus dormi**	**eûtes dormi**
dormit	**dormirent**	**eut dormi**	**eurent dormi**
4 futur		11 futur antérieur	
dormirai	**dormirons**	**aurai dormi**	**aurons dormi**
dormiras	**dormirez**	**auras dormi**	**aurez dormi**
dormira	**dormiront**	**aura dormi**	**auront dormi**
5 conditionnel		12 conditionnel passé	
dormirais	**dormirions**	**aurais dormi**	**aurions dormi**
dormirais	**dormiriez**	**aurais dormi**	**auriez dormi**
dormirait	**dormiraient**	**aurait dormi**	**auraient dormi**
6 présent du subjonctif		13 passé du subjonctif	
dorme	**dormions**	**aie dormi**	**ayons dormi**
dormes	**dormiez**	**aies dormi**	**ayez dormi**
dorme	**dorment**	**ait dormi**	**aient dormi**
7 imparfait du subjonctif		14 plus-que-parfait du subjonctif	
dormisse	**dormissions**	**eusse dormi**	**eussions dormi**
dormisses	**dormissiez**	**eusses dormi**	**eussiez dormi**
dormît	**dormissent**	**eût dormi**	**eussent dormi**

Impératif
dors
dormons
dormez

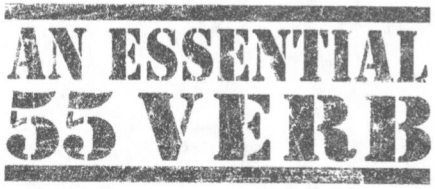

AN ESSENTIAL 55 VERB

Dormir

Dormir is an important verb for you to know because, although it is irregular, several verbs are conjugated like it. **Dormir** is also used in many idiomatic expressions and situations.

Sentences using dormir

As-tu bien dormi, chéri? Did you sleep well, darling?

J'ai acheté des bouche-oreilles et maintenant je dors comme une bûche. I bought some earplugs and now I sleep like a log.

La semaine prochaine nous allons faire du camping. J'aime bien dormir à la belle étoile. Next week we are going camping. I like to sleep outdoors.

Madeleine s'est endormie à une heure du matin. Madeleine fell asleep at one o'clock in the morning.

Proverb

Bon dîneur, mauvais dormeur. **If you eat too much you won't sleep well.**

Words and expressions related to this verb

dormir toute la nuit **to sleep through the night**

parler en dormant **to talk in one's sleep**

empêcher de dormir **to keep from sleeping**

la dormition **dormition (falling asleep)**

le dortoir **dormitory**

dormir à la belle étoile **to sleep outdoors**

dormir sur les deux oreilles **to sleep soundly**

dormir comme une bûche **to sleep like a log**

avoir envie de dormir **to feel like sleeping**

un conte à dormir debout **a cock-and-bull story**

If you can conjugate **dormir** you can also conjugate:

endormir **to put to sleep**

s'endormir **to fall asleep (helping verb être)**

redormir **to sleep again, to sleep a little more**

rendormir **to put to sleep again**

se rendormir **to fall asleep again (helping verb être)**

The subject pronouns are found on page 103.

to doubt

Regular **-er** verb

The Seven Simple Tenses		The Seven Compound Tenses	
Singular	Plural	Singular	Plural
1 présent de l'indicatif		8 passé composé	
doute	**doutons**	**ai douté**	**avons douté**
doutes	**doutez**	**as douté**	**avez douté**
doute	**doutent**	**a douté**	**ont douté**
2 imparfait de l'indicatif		9 plus-que-parfait de l'indicatif	
doutais	**doutions**	**avais douté**	**avions douté**
doutais	**doutiez**	**avais douté**	**aviez douté**
doutait	**doutaient**	**avait douté**	**avaient douté**
3 passé simple		10 passé antérieur	
doutai	**doutâmes**	**eus douté**	**eûmes douté**
doutas	**doutâtes**	**eus douté**	**eûtes douté**
douta	**doutèrent**	**eut douté**	**eurent douté**
4 futur		11 futur antérieur	
douterai	**douterons**	**aurai douté**	**aurons douté**
douteras	**douterez**	**auras douté**	**aurez douté**
doutera	**douteront**	**aura douté**	**auront douté**
5 conditionnel		12 conditionnel passé	
douterais	**douterions**	**aurais douté**	**aurions douté**
douterais	**douteriez**	**aurais douté**	**auriez douté**
douterait	**douteraient**	**aurait douté**	**auraient douté**
6 présent du subjonctif		13 passé du subjonctif	
doute	**doutions**	**aie douté**	**ayons douté**
doutes	**doutiez**	**aies douté**	**ayez douté**
doute	**doutent**	**ait douté**	**aient douté**
7 imparfait du subjonctif		14 plus-que-parfait du subjonctif	
doutasse	**doutassions**	**eusse douté**	**eussions douté**
doutasses	**doutassiez**	**eusses douté**	**eussiez douté**
doutât	**doutassent**	**eût douté**	**eussent douté**

Impératif
doute
doutons
doutez

Common idiomatic expressions using this verb

Je doute que cet homme soit coupable. Il n'y a pas de doute qu'il est innocent.

le doute doubt
sans doute no doubt
sans aucun doute undoubtedly
d'un air de doute dubiously
redouter to dread, to fear
ne douter de rien to doubt nothing, to be too credulous
ne se douter de rien to suspect nothing
se douter de to suspect
douteux, douteuse doubtful

It's important that you be familiar with the Subjunctive. See pages 26–31.

The Seven Simple Tenses		The Seven Compound Tenses	
Singular	Plural	Singular	Plural
1 présent de l'indicatif		8 passé composé	
échappe	**échappons**	**ai échappé**	**avons échappé**
échappes	**échappez**	**as échappé**	**avez échappé**
échappe	**échappent**	**a échappé**	**ont échappé**
2 imparfait de l'indicatif		9 plus-que-parfait de l'indicatif	
échappais	**échappions**	**avais échappé**	**avions échappé**
échappais	**échappiez**	**avais échappé**	**aviez échappé**
échappait	**échappaient**	**avait échappé**	**avaient échappé**
3 passé simple		10 passé antérieur	
échappai	**échappâmes**	**eus échappé**	**eûmes échappé**
échappas	**échappâtes**	**eus échappé**	**eûtes échappé**
échappa	**échappèrent**	**eut échappé**	**eurent échappé**
4 futur		11 futur antérieur	
échapperai	**échapperons**	**aurai échappé**	**aurons échappé**
échapperas	**échapperez**	**auras échappé**	**aurez échappé**
échappera	**échapperont**	**aura échappé**	**auront échappé**
5 conditionnel		12 conditionnel passé	
échapperais	**échapperions**	**aurais échappé**	**aurions échappé**
échapperais	**échapperiez**	**aurais échappé**	**auriez échappé**
échapperait	**échapperaient**	**aurait échappé**	**auraient échappé**
6 présent du subjonctif		13 passé du subjonctif	
échappe	**échappions**	**aie échappé**	**ayons échappé**
échappes	**échappiez**	**aies échappé**	**ayez échappé**
échappe	**échappent**	**ait échappé**	**aient échappé**
7 imparfait du subjonctif		14 plus-que-parfait du subjonctif	
échappasse	**échappassions**	**eusse échappé**	**eussions échappé**
échappasses	**échappassiez**	**eusses échappé**	**eussiez échappé**
échappât	**échappassent**	**eût échappé**	**eussent échappé**

Impératif
échappe
échappons
échappez

Words and expressions related to this verb
échapper à to avoid; **échapper de** to escape from
l'échapper belle to have a narrow escape; **Je l'ai échappé belle.** I had a narrow escape.
Cela m'a échappé. I did not notice it.
Cela m'est échappé. It slipped my mind (I forgot it).
laisser échapper to let slip, to overlook
s'échapper de to escape from
une échappée de lumière a glimmer of light
l'échappement *m.* exhaust
le pot d'échappement muffler (auto)

Check out the principal parts of some important French verbs on page 7.

échouer (175) — Part. pr. échouant — Part. passé échoué

to fail, to run aground

Regular **-er** verb

The Seven Simple Tenses		The Seven Compound Tenses	
Singular	Plural	Singular	Plural
1 présent de l'indicatif		8 passé composé	
échoue	**échouons**	**ai échoué**	**avons échoué**
échoues	**échouez**	**as échoué**	**avez échoué**
échoue	**échouent**	**a échoué**	**ont échoué**
2 imparfait de l'indicatif		9 plus-que-parfait de l'indicatif	
échouais	**échouions**	**avais échoué**	**avions échoué**
échouais	**échouiez**	**avais échoué**	**aviez échoué**
échouait	**échouaient**	**avait échoué**	**avaient échoué**
3 passé simple		10 passé antérieur	
échouai	**échouâmes**	**eus échoué**	**eûmes échoué**
échouas	**échouâtes**	**eus échoué**	**eûtes échoué**
échoua	**échouèrent**	**eut échoué**	**eurent échoué**
4 futur		11 futur antérieur	
échouerai	**échouerons**	**aurai échoué**	**aurons échoué**
échoueras	**échouerez**	**auras échoué**	**aurez échoué**
échouera	**échoueront**	**aura échoué**	**auront échoué**
5 conditionnel		12 conditionnel passé	
échouerais	**échouerions**	**aurais échoué**	**aurions échoué**
échouerais	**échoueriez**	**aurais échoué**	**auriez échoué**
échouerait	**échoueraient**	**aurait échoué**	**auraient échoué**
6 présent du subjonctif		13 passé du subjonctif	
échoue	**échouions**	**aie échoué**	**ayons échoué**
échoues	**échouiez**	**aies échoué**	**ayez échoué**
échoue	**échouent**	**ait échoué**	**aient échoué**
7 imparfait du subjonctif		14 plus-que-parfait du subjonctif	
échouasse	**échouassions**	**eusse échoué**	**eussions échoué**
échouasses	**échouassiez**	**eusses échoué**	**eussiez échoué**
échouât	**échouassent**	**eût échoué**	**eussent échoué**

Impératif
échoue
échouons
échouez

Common idiomatic expressions using this verb
échouer à qqch to fail (flunk) at something
échouer à un examen to flunk an exam
échouer to touch bottom (accidentally), to fail
Tous mes espoirs ont échoué. All my hopes have touched bottom (have failed).
Le bateau a échoué sur un banc de sable. The ship ran aground on a shoal.

Can't find the verb you're looking for? Check the back pages of this book for a list of over 2,600 additional verbs!

The Seven Simple Tenses		The Seven Compound Tenses	
Singular	Plural	Singular	Plural
1 présent de l'indicatif		8 passé composé	
écoute	**écoutons**	**ai écouté**	**avons écouté**
écoutes	**écoutez**	**as écouté**	**avez écouté**
écoute	**écoutent**	**a écouté**	**ont écouté**
2 imparfait de l'indicatif		9 plus-que-parfait de l'indicatif	
écoutais	**écoutions**	**avais écouté**	**avions écouté**
écoutais	**écoutiez**	**avais écouté**	**aviez écouté**
écoutait	**écoutaient**	**avait écouté**	**avaient écouté**
3 passé simple		10 passé antérieur	
écoutai	**écoutâmes**	**eus écouté**	**eûmes écouté**
écoutas	**écoutâtes**	**eus écouté**	**eûtes écouté**
écouta	**écoutèrent**	**eut écouté**	**eurent écouté**
4 futur		11 futur antérieur	
écouterai	**écouterons**	**aurai écouté**	**aurons écouté**
écouteras	**écouterez**	**auras écouté**	**aurez écouté**
écoutera	**écouteront**	**aura écouté**	**auront écouté**
5 conditionnel		12 conditionnel passé	
écouterais	**écouterions**	**aurais écouté**	**aurions écouté**
écouterais	**écouteriez**	**aurais écouté**	**auriez écouté**
écouterait	**écouteraient**	**aurait écouté**	**auraient écouté**
6 présent du subjonctif		13 passé du subjonctif	
écoute	**écoutions**	**aie écouté**	**ayons écouté**
écoutes	**écoutiez**	**aies écouté**	**ayez écouté**
écoute	**écoutent**	**ait écouté**	**aient écouté**
7 imparfait du subjonctif		14 plus-que-parfait du subjonctif	
écoutasse	**écoutassions**	**eusse écouté**	**eussions écouté**
écoutasses	**écoutassiez**	**eusses écouté**	**eussiez écouté**
écoutât	**écoutassent**	**eût écouté**	**eussent écouté**

Impératif
écoute
écoutons
écoutez

Common idiomatic expressions using this verb and words related to it
Ecoutez-vous le professeur quand il explique la leçon? L'avez-vous écouté ce matin en classe?

aimer à s'écouter parler to love to hear one's own voice
un écouteur telephone receiver (earpiece)
être à l'écoute to be listening in
être aux écoutes to be on the watch, to eavesdrop
n'écouter personne not to heed anyone
savoir écouter to be a good listener
écouter aux portes to eavesdrop, to listen secretly
Ecoutez-moi. Listen to me.
Je vous écoute. I'm listening to you.
Parlez donc! Speak up!

Don't forget to study the section on defective and impersonal verbs. It's right after this main list.

to write

Irregular verb

The Seven Simple Tenses		The Seven Compound Tenses	
Singular	Plural	Singular	Plural
1 présent de l'indicatif		8 passé composé	
écris	**écrivons**	**ai écrit**	**avons écrit**
écris	**écrivez**	**as écrit**	**avez écrit**
écrit	**écrivent**	**a écrit**	**ont écrit**
2 imparfait de l'indicatif		9 plus-que-parfait de l'indicatif	
écrivais	**écrivions**	**avais écrit**	**avions écrit**
écrivais	**écriviez**	**avais écrit**	**aviez écrit**
écrivait	**écrivaient**	**avait écrit**	**avaient écrit**
3 passé simple		10 passé antérieur	
écrivis	**écrivîmes**	**eus écrit**	**eûmes écrit**
écrivis	**écrivîtes**	**eus écrit**	**eûtes écrit**
écrivit	**écrivirent**	**eut écrit**	**eurent écrit**
4 futur		11 futur antérieur	
écrirai	**écrirons**	**aurai écrit**	**aurons écrit**
écriras	**écrirez**	**auras écrit**	**aurez écrit**
écrira	**écriront**	**aura écrit**	**auront écrit**
5 conditionnel		12 conditionnel passé	
écrirais	**écririons**	**aurais écrit**	**aurions écrit**
écrirais	**écririez**	**aurais écrit**	**auriez écrit**
écrirait	**écriraient**	**aurait écrit**	**auraient écrit**
6 présent du subjonctif		13 passé du subjonctif	
écrive	**écrivions**	**aie écrit**	**ayons écrit**
écrives	**écriviez**	**aies écrit**	**ayez écrit**
écrive	**écrivent**	**ait écrit**	**aient écrit**
7 imparfait du subjonctif		14 plus-que-parfait du subjonctif	
écrivisse	**écrivissions**	**eusse écrit**	**eussions écrit**
écrivisses	**écrivissiez**	**eusses écrit**	**eussiez écrit**
écrivît	**écrivissent**	**eût écrit**	**eussent écrit**

Impératif
écris
écrivons
écrivez

AN ESSENTIAL 55 VERB

Écrire

Écrire is a very useful verb for a beginning French student. There are several verbs that are conjugated like **écrire**.

Sentences using écrire

Jean: **As-tu écrit ta composition pour la classe de français?**
Jeanne: **Non, je ne l'ai pas écrite.**
Jean: **Écris-la tout de suite!**

John: Did you write your composition for French class?
Jean: No, I didn't write it.
John: Write it right away!

J'ai oublié mon stylo. Pourrais-tu me prêter de quoi écrire? I forgot my pen. Could you lend me something to write with?

C'est un nom bizarre. Comment est-ce que cela s'écrit? That's a strange name. How is it written?

Avant donc d'écrire, apprenez à penser. (Boileau) Before writing, learn to think.

Words and expressions related to this verb

un écrivain **writer**

une femme écrivain **female writer; une écrivaine (Québec) female writer**

écriture *f.* **handwriting, writing**

par écrit **in writing**

écrivasser **to write badly**

une machine à écrire **a typewriter**

de quoi écrire **something to write with**

écrire un petit mot à qqn **to write a note to someone**

If you can conjugate **écrire** you can also conjugate these verbs:

circonscrire **to limit, circumscribe**

décrire **to describe**

inscrire **to inscribe, write down**

préscrire **to prescribe**

proscrire **to proscribe, ban, outlaw**

récrire, réécrire **to rewrite**

retranscrire **to retranscribe**

souscrire à **to subscribe to**

transcrire **to transcribe**

The subject pronouns are found on page 103.

effrayer (178) — Part. pr. effrayant — Part. passé effrayé

to frighten

Regular **-er** verb endings; spelling change: **-ayer** verbs may change **y** to **i** in front of a mute **e** or may keep **y**

The Seven Simple Tenses		The Seven Compound Tenses	
Singular	Plural	Singular	Plural
1 présent de l'indicatif		8 passé composé	
effraye	**effrayons**	**ai effrayé**	**avons effrayé**
effrayes	**effrayez**	**as effrayé**	**avez effrayé**
effraye	**effrayent**	**a effrayé**	**ont effrayé**
2 imparfait de l'indicatif		9 plus-que-parfait de l'indicatif	
effrayais	**effrayions**	**avais effrayé**	**avions effrayé**
effrayais	**effrayiez**	**avais effrayé**	**aviez effrayé**
effrayait	**effrayaient**	**avait effrayé**	**avaient effrayé**
3 passé simple		10 passé antérieur	
effrayai	**effrayâmes**	**eus effrayé**	**eûmes effrayé**
effrayas	**effrayâtes**	**eus effrayé**	**eûtes effrayé**
effraya	**effrayèrent**	**eut effrayé**	**eurent effrayé**
4 futur		11 futur antérieur	
effrayerai	**effrayerons**	**aurai effrayé**	**aurons effrayé**
effrayeras	**effrayerez**	**auras effrayé**	**aurez effrayé**
effrayera	**effrayeront**	**aura effrayé**	**auront effrayé**
5 conditionnel		12 conditionnel passé	
effrayerais	**effrayerions**	**aurais effrayé**	**aurions effrayé**
effrayerais	**effrayeriez**	**aurais effrayé**	**auriez effrayé**
effrayerait	**effrayeraient**	**aurait effrayé**	**auraient effrayé**
6 présent du subjonctif		13 passé du subjonctif	
effraye	**effrayions**	**aie effrayé**	**ayons effrayé**
effrayes	**effrayiez**	**aies effrayé**	**ayez effrayé**
effraye	**effrayent**	**ait effrayé**	**aient effrayé**
7 imparfait du subjonctif		14 plus-que-parfait du subjonctif	
effrayasse	**effrayassions**	**eusse effrayé**	**eussions effrayé**
effrayasses	**effrayassiez**	**eusses effrayé**	**eussiez effrayé**
effrayât	**effrayassent**	**eût effrayé**	**eussent effrayé**

Impératif
effraye
effrayons
effrayez

Sentences using this verb and words related to it

Le tigre a effrayé l'enfant. L'enfant a effrayé le singe. Le singe effraiera le bébé. C'est effrayant!

effrayant, effrayante frightful, awful
effrayé, effrayée frightened
l'effroi *m.* fright, terror
effroyable dreadful, fearful
effroyablement dreadfully, fearfully

Don't forget to check the list of 2,600 additional verbs keyed to the 501 model verbs. It's in the Appendixes!

Regular **-er** verb endings; spelling change: **-ayer** verbs may change **y** to **i** in front of a mute **e** or may keep **y**

to amuse, to cheer up, to enliven, to entertain

The Seven Simple Tenses		The Seven Compound Tenses	
Singular	Plural	Singular	Plural
1 présent de l'indicatif		8 passé composé	
égaye	**égayons**	**ai égayé**	**avons égayé**
égayes	**égayez**	**as égayé**	**avez égayé**
égaye	**égayent**	**a égayé**	**ont égayé**
2 imparfait de l'indicatif		9 plus-que-parfait de l'indicatif	
égayais	**égayions**	**avais égayé**	**avions égayé**
égayais	**égayiez**	**avais égayé**	**aviez égayé**
égayait	**égayaient**	**avait égayé**	**avaient égayé**
3 passé simple		10 passé antérieur	
égayai	**égayâmes**	**eus égayé**	**eûmes égayé**
égayas	**égayâtes**	**eus égayé**	**eûtes égayé**
égaya	**égayèrent**	**eut égayé**	**eurent égayé**
4 futur		11 futur antérieur	
égayerai	**égayerons**	**aurai égayé**	**aurons égayé**
égayeras	**égayerez**	**auras égayé**	**aurez égayé**
égayera	**égayeront**	**aura égayé**	**auront égayé**
5 conditionnel		12 conditionnel passé	
égayerais	**égayerions**	**aurais égayé**	**aurions égayé**
égayerais	**égayeriez**	**aurais égayé**	**auriez égayé**
égayerait	**égayeraient**	**aurait égayé**	**auraient égayé**
6 présent du subjonctif		13 passé du subjonctif	
égaye	**égayions**	**aie égayé**	**ayons égayé**
égayes	**égayiez**	**aies égayé**	**ayez égayé**
égaye	**égayent**	**ait égayé**	**aient égayé**
7 imparfait du subjonctif		14 plus-que-parfait du subjonctif	
égayasse	**égayassions**	**eusse égayé**	**eussions égayé**
égayasses	**égayassiez**	**eusses égayé**	**eussiez égayé**
égayât	**égayassent**	**eût égayé**	**eussent égayé**

Impératif
égaye
égayons
égayez

Words related to this verb

égayant, égayante lively
un égaiement amusement
s'égayer aux dépens de to amuse oneself at someone's expense
gai, gaie gay, cheerful, merry
gaiement gaily, cheerfully

Grammar putting you in a tense mood? Review the definitions of basic grammatical terms on pages 35–49.

élever (180) — Part. pr. **élevant** — Part. passé **élevé**

to raise, to rear, to bring up

Regular **-er** verb endings; spelling change: **e** changes to **è** before syllable with mute **e**

The Seven Simple Tenses		The Seven Compound Tenses	
Singular	Plural	Singular	Plural
1 présent de l'indicatif		8 passé composé	
élève	**élevons**	**ai élevé**	**avons élevé**
élèves	**élevez**	**as élevé**	**avez élevé**
élève	**élèvent**	**a élevé**	**ont élevé**
2 imparfait de l'indicatif		9 plus-que-parfait de l'indicatif	
élevais	**élevions**	**avais élevé**	**avions élevé**
élevais	**éleviez**	**avais élevé**	**aviez élevé**
élevait	**élevaient**	**avait élevé**	**avaient élevé**
3 passé simple		10 passé antérieur	
élevai	**élevâmes**	**eus élevé**	**eûmes élevé**
élevas	**élevâtes**	**eus élevé**	**eûtes élevé**
éleva	**élevèrent**	**eut élevé**	**eurent élevé**
4 futur		11 futur antérieur	
élèverai	**élèverons**	**aurai élevé**	**aurons élevé**
élèveras	**élèverez**	**auras élevé**	**aurez élevé**
élèvera	**élèveront**	**aura élevé**	**auront élevé**
5 conditionnel		12 conditionnel passé	
élèverais	**élèverions**	**aurais élevé**	**aurions élevé**
élèverais	**élèveriez**	**aurais élevé**	**auriez élevé**
élèverait	**élèveraient**	**aurait élevé**	**auraient élevé**
6 présent du subjonctif		13 passé du subjonctif	
élève	**élevions**	**aie élevé**	**ayons élevé**
élèves	**éleviez**	**aies élevé**	**ayez élevé**
élève	**élèvent**	**ait élevé**	**aient élevé**
7 imparfait du subjonctif		14 plus-que-parfait du subjonctif	
élevasse	**élevassions**	**eusse élevé**	**eussions élevé**
élevasses	**élevassiez**	**eusses élevé**	**eussiez élevé**
élevât	**élevassent**	**eût élevé**	**eussent élevé**

Impératif
élève
élevons
élevez

Words and expressions related to this verb

un, une élève pupil, student; **un, une élève professeur** student teacher

élevage *m.* breeding, rearing; **occuper une position élevée** to hold a high position

élévation *f.* elevation, raising; **La musique élève l'âme.** Music uplifts the soul.

bien élevé well-bred, well brought up

mal élevé ill-bred, badly brought up

Car quiconque s'élève sera abaissé, et celui qui s'abaisse sera élevé. For whoever exalts himself will be humbled, and he who humbles himself will be exalted. (Luke 14:11)

See also **enlever** and **lever.**

Irregular verb

to elect, to choose

The Seven Simple Tenses		The Seven Compound Tenses	
Singular	Plural	Singular	Plural
1 présent de l'indicatif		8 passé composé	
élis	**élisons**	**ai élu**	**avons élu**
élis	**élisez**	**as élu**	**avez élu**
élit	**élisent**	**a élu**	**ont élu**
2 imparfait de l'indicatif		9 plus-que-parfait de l'indicatif	
élisais	**élisions**	**avais élu**	**avions élu**
élisais	**élisiez**	**avais élu**	**aviez élu**
élisait	**élisaient**	**avait élu**	**avaient élu**
3 passé simple		10 passé antérieur	
élus	**élûmes**	**eus élu**	**eûmes élu**
élus	**élûtes**	**eus élu**	**eûtes élu**
élut	**élurent**	**eut élu**	**eurent élu**
4 futur		11 futur antérieur	
élirai	**élirons**	**aurai élu**	**aurons élu**
éliras	**élirez**	**auras élu**	**aurez élu**
élira	**éliront**	**aura élu**	**auront élu**
5 conditionnel		12 conditionnel passé	
élirais	**élirions**	**aurais élu**	**aurions élu**
élirais	**éliriez**	**aurais élu**	**auriez élu**
élirait	**éliraient**	**aurait élu**	**auraient élu**
6 présent du subjonctif		13 passé du subjonctif	
élise	**élisions**	**aie élu**	**ayons élu**
élises	**élisiez**	**aies élu**	**ayez élu**
élise	**élisent**	**ait élu**	**aient élu**
7 imparfait du subjonctif		14 plus-que-parfait du subjonctif	
élusse	**élussions**	**eusse élu**	**eussions élu**
élusses	**élussiez**	**eusses élu**	**eussiez élu**
élût	**élussent**	**eût élu**	**eussent élu**

Impératif
élis
élisons
élisez

Words and expressions related to this verb

Car il y a beaucoup d'appelés mais peu d'élus. For many are called but few are chosen. (Matthew 22:14)
une élection election, choice
le jour des élections election day
électif, élective elective
un électeur, une électrice voter
se rendre aux urnes to vote, go to the polls

Don't forget to use the English-French verb index. It's in the Appendixes.

s'éloigner (182) Part. pr. s'éloignant Part. passé éloigné

to move away, to go away, to withdraw, to step back, to keep back, to keep away

Reflexive regular **-er** verb

The Seven Simple Tenses		The Seven Compound Tenses	
Singular	Plural	Singular	Plural
1 présent de l'indicatif		8 passé composé	
m'éloigne	**nous éloignons**	**me suis éloigné(e)**	**nous sommes éloigné(e)s**
t'éloignes	**vous éloignez**	**t'es éloigné(e)**	**vous êtes éloigné(e)(s)**
s'éloigne	**s'éloignent**	**s'est éloigné(e)**	**se sont éloigné(e)s**
2 imparfait de l'indicatif		9 plus-que-parfait de l'indicatif	
m'éloignais	**nous éloignions**	**m'étais éloigné(e)**	**nous étions éloigné(e)s**
t'éloignais	**vous éloigniez**	**t'étais éloigné(e)**	**vous étiez éloigné(e)(s)**
s'éloignait	**s'éloignaient**	**s'était éloigné(e)**	**s'étaient éloigné(e)s**
3 passé simple		10 passé antérieur	
m'éloignai	**nous éloignâmes**	**me fus éloigné(e)**	**nous fûmes éloigné(e)s**
t'éloignas	**vous éloignâtes**	**te fus éloigné(e)**	**vous fûtes éloigné(e)(s)**
s'éloigna	**s'éloignèrent**	**se fut éloigné(e)**	**se furent éloigné(e)s**
4 futur		11 futur antérieur	
m'éloignerai	**nous éloignerons**	**me serai éloigné(e)**	**nous serons éloigné(e)s**
t'éloigneras	**vous éloignerez**	**te seras éloigné(e)**	**vous serez éloigné(e)(s)**
s'éloignera	**s'éloigneront**	**se sera éloigné(e)**	**se seront éloigné(e)s**
5 conditionnel		12 conditionnel passé	
m'éloignerais	**nous éloignerions**	**me serais éloigné(e)**	**nous serions éloigné(e)s**
t'éloignerais	**vous éloigneriez**	**te serais éloigné(e)**	**vous seriez éloigné(e)(s)**
s'éloignerait	**s'éloigneraient**	**se serait éloigné(e)**	**se seraient éloigné(e)s**
6 présent du subjonctif		13 passé du subjonctif	
m'éloigne	**nous éloignions**	**me sois éloigné(e)**	**nous soyons éloigné(e)s**
t'éloignes	**vous éloigniez**	**te sois éloigné(e)**	**vous soyez éloigné(e)(s)**
s'éloigne	**s'éloignent**	**se soit éloigné(e)**	**se soient éloigné(e)s**
7 imparfait du subjonctif		14 plus-que-parfait du subjonctif	
m'éloignasse	**nous éloignassions**	**me fusse éloigné(e)**	**nous fussions éloigné(e)s**
t'éloignasses	**vous éloignassiez**	**te fusses éloigné(e)**	**vous fussiez éloigné(e)(s)**
s'éloignât	**s'éloignassent**	**se fût éloigné(e)**	**se fussent éloigné(e)s**

Impératif
éloigne-toi; ne t'éloigne pas
éloignons-nous; ne nous éloignons pas
éloignez-vous; ne vous éloignez pas

Words and expressions related to this verb
éloigner de to keep away from, to keep at a distance
s'éloigner de to keep one's distance from, to move away from
s'éloigner en courant to run away, to move away while running
loin far; **lointain, lointaine** distant
loin de là, loin de ça far from it
Loin des yeux, loin du coeur. Out of sight, out of mind.
Eloignez-vous, s'il vous plaît! Stay back! Keep your distance, please!
l'éloignement *m.* distance

Regular **-er** verb

to kiss, to embrace

The Seven Simple Tenses		The Seven Compound Tenses	
Singular	Plural	Singular	Plural
1 présent de l'indicatif		8 passé composé	
embrasse	**embrassons**	**ai embrassé**	**avons embrassé**
embrasses	**embrassez**	**as embrassé**	**avez embrassé**
embrasse	**embrassent**	**a embrassé**	**ont embrassé**
2 imparfait de l'indicatif		9 plus-que-parfait de l'indicatif	
embrassais	**embrassions**	**avais embrassé**	**avions embrassé**
embrassais	**embrassiez**	**avais embrassé**	**aviez embrassé**
embrassait	**embrassaient**	**avait embrassé**	**avaient embrassé**
3 passé simple		10 passé antérieur	
embrassai	**embrassâmes**	**eus embrassé**	**eûmes embrassé**
embrassas	**embrassâtes**	**eus embrassé**	**eûtes embrassé**
embrassa	**embrassèrent**	**eut embrassé**	**eurent embrassé**
4 futur		11 futur antérieur	
embrasserai	**embrasserons**	**aurai embrassé**	**aurons embrassé**
embrasseras	**embrasserez**	**auras embrassé**	**aurez embrassé**
embrassera	**embrasseront**	**aura embrassé**	**auront embrassé**
5 conditionnel		12 conditionnel passé	
embrasserais	**embrasserions**	**aurais embrassé**	**aurions embrassé**
embrasserais	**embrasseriez**	**aurais embrassé**	**auriez embrassé**
embrasserait	**embrasseraient**	**aurait embrassé**	**auraient embrassé**
6 présent du subjonctif		13 passé du subjonctif	
embrasse	**embrassions**	**aie embrassé**	**ayons embrassé**
embrasses	**embrassiez**	**aies embrassé**	**ayez embrassé**
embrasse	**embrassent**	**ait embrassé**	**aient embrassé**
7 imparfait du subjonctif		14 plus-que-parfait du subjonctif	
embrassasse	**embrassassions**	**eusse embrassé**	**eussions embrassé**
embrassasses	**embrassassiez**	**eusses embrassé**	**eussiez embrassé**
embrassât	**embrassassent**	**eût embrassé**	**eussent embrassé**

Impératif
embrasse
embrassons
embrassez

Sentences using this verb and words related to it
—Embrasse-moi. Je t'aime. Ne me quitte pas.
—Je t'embrasse. Je t'aime aussi. Je ne te quitte pas. Embrassons-nous.

le bras arm
un embrassement embracement, embrace
s'embrasser to embrace each other, to hug each other
embrasseur, embrasseuse a person who likes to kiss a lot

How are you doing? Find out with the verb drills and tests with answers explained on pages 50–101.

emmener (184)

Part. pr. **emmenant** Part. passé **emmené**

to lead, to lead away, to take away (persons)

Regular **-er** verb endings; spelling change: **e** changes to **è** before syllable with mute **e**

The Seven Simple Tenses		The Seven Compound Tenses	
Singular	Plural	Singular	Plural
1 présent de l'indicatif		8 passé composé	
emmène	**emmenons**	**ai emmené**	**avons emmené**
emmènes	**emmenez**	**as emmené**	**avez emmené**
emmène	**emmènent**	**a emmené**	**ont emmené**
2 imparfait de l'indicatif		9 plus-que-parfait de l'indicatif	
emmenais	**emmenions**	**avais emmené**	**avions emmené**
emmenais	**emmeniez**	**avais emmené**	**aviez emmené**
emmenait	**emmenaient**	**avait emmené**	**avaient emmené**
3 passé simple		10 passé antérieur	
emmenai	**emmenâmes**	**eus emmené**	**eûmes emmené**
emmenas	**emmenâtes**	**eus emmené**	**eûtes emmené**
emmena	**emmenèrent**	**eut emmené**	**eurent emmené**
4 futur		11 futur antérieur	
emmènerai	**emmènerons**	**aurai emmené**	**aurons emmené**
emmèneras	**emmènerez**	**auras emmené**	**aurez emmené**
emmènera	**emmèneront**	**aura emmené**	**auront emmené**
5 conditionnel		12 conditionnel passé	
emmènerais	**emmènerions**	**aurais emmené**	**aurions emmené**
emmènerais	**emmèneriez**	**aurais emmené**	**auriez emmené**
emmènerait	**emmèneraient**	**aurait emmené**	**auraient emmené**
6 présent du subjonctif		13 passé du subjonctif	
emmène	**emmenions**	**aie emmené**	**ayons emmené**
emmènes	**emmeniez**	**aies emmené**	**ayez emmené**
emmène	**emmènent**	**ait emmené**	**aient emmené**
7 imparfait du subjonctif		14 plus-que-parfait du subjonctif	
emmenasse	**emmenassions**	**eusse emmené**	**eussions emmené**
emmenasses	**emmenassiez**	**eusses emmené**	**eussiez emmené**
emmenât	**emmenassent**	**eût emmené**	**eussent emmené**

Impératif
emmène
emmenons
emmenez

Sentences using this verb and words related to it

Quand j'emmène une personne d'un lieu dans un autre, je mène cette personne avec moi. Mon père nous emmènera au cinéma lundi prochain. Samedi dernier il nous a emmenés au théâtre.

Le train m'a emmené à Paris. The train took me to Paris.
Un agent de police a emmené l'assassin. A policeman took away the assassin.

See also **mener** and **amener.**

Can't find the verb you're looking for? Check the back pages of this book for a list of over 2,600 additional verbs!

Irregular verb

to move, to touch, to excite, to arouse

The Seven Simple Tenses		The Seven Compound Tenses	
Singular	Plural	Singular	Plural
1 présent de l'indicatif		8 passé composé	
émeus	**émouvons**	**ai ému**	**avons ému**
émeus	**émouvez**	**as ému**	**avez ému**
émeut	**émeuvent**	**a ému**	**ont ému**
2 imparfait de l'indicatif		9 plus-que-parfait de l'indicatif	
émouvais	**émouvions**	**avais ému**	**avions ému**
émouvais	**émouviez**	**avais ému**	**aviez ému**
émouvait	**émouvaient**	**avait ému**	**avaient ému**
3 passé simple		10 passé antérieur	
émus	**émûmes**	**eus ému**	**eûmes ému**
émus	**émûtes**	**eus ému**	**eûtes ému**
émut	**émurent**	**eut ému**	**eurent ému**
4 futur		11 futur antérieur	
émouvrai	**émouvrons**	**aurai ému**	**aurons ému**
émouvras	**émouvrez**	**auras ému**	**aurez ému**
émouvra	**émouvront**	**aura ému**	**auront ému**
5 conditionnel		12 conditionnel passé	
émouvrais	**émouvrions**	**aurais ému**	**aurions ému**
émouvrais	**émouvriez**	**aurais ému**	**auriez ému**
émouvrait	**émouvraient**	**aurait ému**	**auraient ému**
6 présent du subjonctif		13 passé du subjonctif	
émeuve	**émouvions**	**aie ému**	**ayons ému**
émeuves	**émouviez**	**aies ému**	**ayez ému**
émeuve	**émeuvent**	**ait ému**	**aient ému**
7 imparfait du subjonctif		14 plus-que-parfait du subjonctif	
émusse	**émussions**	**eusse ému**	**eussions ému**
émusses	**émussiez**	**eusses ému**	**eussiez ému**
émût	**émussent**	**eût ému**	**eussent ému**

Impératif
émeus
émouvons
émouvez

Words and expressions related to this verb

s'émouvoir de to be moved (touched) by
une émeute insurrection, insurgency
un émeutier, une émeutière insurrectionist, insurgent, rioter
être ému(e) to be moved
émouvant, émouvante moving, touching
fort émouvant thrilling
émouvoir la pitié de qqn to move someone to pity
l'émotion *f.* feeling

Don't forget to check the list of 2,600 additional verbs keyed to the 501 model verbs. It's in the Appendixes!

empêcher (186) — Part. pr. empêchant — Part. passé empêché

to hinder, to prevent

Regular **-er** verb

The Seven Simple Tenses		The Seven Compound Tenses	
Singular	Plural	Singular	Plural
1 présent de l'indicatif		8 passé composé	
empêche	**empêchons**	**ai empêché**	**avons empêché**
empêches	**empêchez**	**as empêché**	**avez empêché**
empêche	**empêchent**	**a empêché**	**ont empêché**
2 imparfait de l'indicatif		9 plus-que-parfait de l'indicatif	
empêchais	**empêchions**	**avais empêché**	**avions empêché**
empêchais	**empêchiez**	**avais empêché**	**aviez empêché**
empêchait	**empêchaient**	**avait empêché**	**avaient empêché**
3 passé simple		10 passé antérieur	
empêchai	**empêchâmes**	**eus empêché**	**eûmes empêché**
empêchas	**empêchâtes**	**eus empêché**	**eûtes empêché**
empêcha	**empêchèrent**	**eut empêché**	**eurent empêché**
4 futur		11 futur antérieur	
empêcherai	**empêcherons**	**aurai empêché**	**aurons empêché**
empêcheras	**empêcherez**	**auras empêché**	**aurez empêché**
empêchera	**empêcheront**	**aura empêché**	**auront empêché**
5 conditionnel		12 conditionnel passé	
empêcherais	**empêcherions**	**aurais empêché**	**aurions empêché**
empêcherais	**empêcheriez**	**aurais empêché**	**auriez empêché**
empêcherait	**empêcheraient**	**aurait empêché**	**auraient empêché**
6 présent du subjonctif		13 passé du subjonctif	
empêche	**empêchions**	**aie empêché**	**ayons empêché**
empêches	**empêchiez**	**aies empêché**	**ayez empêché**
empêche	**empêchent**	**ait empêché**	**aient empêché**
7 imparfait du subjonctif		14 plus-que-parfait du subjonctif	
empêchasse	**empêchassions**	**eusse empêché**	**eussions empêché**
empêchasses	**empêchassiez**	**eusses empêché**	**eussiez empêché**
empêchât	**empêchassent**	**eût empêché**	**eussent empêché**

Impératif
empêche
empêchons
empêchez

Sentences using this verb and words related to it

Georgette a empêché son frère de finir ses devoirs parce qu'elle jouait des disques en même temps. Le bruit était un vrai empêchement.

un empêchement impediment, hindrance
en cas d'empêchement in case of prevention
empêcher qqn de faire qqch to prevent someone from doing something
empêcher d'entrer to keep from entering
s'empêcher de faire qqch to refrain from doing something
Je n'ai pas pu m'empêcher de rire. I couldn't help laughing.

See also **dépêcher.**

Get acquainted with what preposition (if any) goes with what verb. There's a list in the Appendixes.

Regular **-er** verb endings; spelling change: **-oyer** verbs must change **y** to **i** in front of a mute **e**

to use, to employ

The Seven Simple Tenses		The Seven Compound Tenses	
Singular	Plural	Singular	Plural
1 présent de l'indicatif		8 passé composé	
emploie	**employons**	**ai employé**	**avons employé**
emploies	**employez**	**as employé**	**avez employé**
emploie	**emploient**	**a employé**	**ont employé**
2 imparfait de l'indicatif		9 plus-que-parfait de l'indicatif	
employais	**employions**	**avais employé**	**avions employé**
employais	**employiez**	**avais employé**	**aviez employé**
employait	**employaient**	**avait employé**	**avaient employé**
3 passé simple		10 passé antérieur	
employai	**employâmes**	**eus employé**	**eûmes employé**
employas	**employâtes**	**eus employé**	**eûtes employé**
employa	**employèrent**	**eut employé**	**eurent employé**
4 futur		11 futur antérieur	
emploierai	**emploierons**	**aurai employé**	**aurons employé**
emploieras	**emploierez**	**auras employé**	**aurez employé**
emploiera	**emploieront**	**aura employé**	**auront employé**
5 conditionnel		12 conditionnel passé	
emploierais	**emploierions**	**aurais employé**	**aurions employé**
emploierais	**emploieriez**	**aurais employé**	**auriez employé**
emploierait	**emploieraient**	**aurait employé**	**auraient employé**
6 présent du subjonctif		13 passé du subjonctif	
emploie	**employions**	**aie employé**	**ayons employé**
emploies	**employiez**	**aies employé**	**ayez employé**
emploie	**emploient**	**ait employé**	**aient employé**
7 imparfait du subjonctif		14 plus-que-parfait du subjonctif	
employasse	**employassions**	**eusse employé**	**eussions employé**
employasses	**employassiez**	**eusses employé**	**eussiez employé**
employât	**employassent**	**eût employé**	**eussent employé**

Impératif
emploie
employons
employez

Words and expressions related to this verb

un employé, une employée employee
un employeur, une employeuse employer
sans emploi jobless
un emploi employment
une demande d'emploi job application
s'employer à faire qqch to occupy oneself doing something
employer son temps to spend one's time
un emploi nouveau a new use

It's important that you use the Subjunctive correctly. See pages 26–31.

emprunter (188) — Part. pr. empruntant — Part. passé emprunté

to borrow

Regular **-er** verb

The Seven Simple Tenses		The Seven Compound Tenses	
Singular	Plural	Singular	Plural
1 présent de l'indicatif		8 passé composé	
emprunte	**empruntons**	**ai emprunté**	**avons emprunté**
empruntes	**empruntez**	**as emprunté**	**avez emprunté**
emprunte	**empruntent**	**a emprunté**	**ont emprunté**
2 imparfait de l'indicatif		9 plus-que-parfait de l'indicatif	
empruntais	**empruntions**	**avais emprunté**	**avions emprunté**
empruntais	**empruntiez**	**avais emprunté**	**aviez emprunté**
empruntait	**empruntaient**	**avait emprunté**	**avaient emprunté**
3 passé simple		10 passé antérieur	
empruntai	**empruntâmes**	**eus emprunté**	**eûmes emprunté**
empruntas	**empruntâtes**	**eus emprunté**	**eûtes emprunté**
emprunta	**empruntèrent**	**eut emprunté**	**eurent emprunté**
4 futur		11 futur antérieur	
emprunterai	**emprunterons**	**aurai emprunté**	**aurons emprunté**
emprunteras	**emprunterez**	**auras emprunté**	**aurez emprunté**
empruntera	**emprunteront**	**aura emprunté**	**auront emprunté**
5 conditionnel		12 conditionnel passé	
emprunterais	**emprunterions**	**aurais emprunté**	**aurions emprunté**
emprunterais	**emprunteriez**	**aurais emprunté**	**auriez emprunté**
emprunterait	**emprunteraient**	**aurait emprunté**	**auraient emprunté**
6 présent du subjonctif		13 passé du subjonctif	
emprunte	**empruntions**	**aie emprunté**	**ayons emprunté**
empruntes	**empruntiez**	**aies emprunté**	**ayez emprunté**
emprunte	**empruntent**	**ait emprunté**	**aient emprunté**
7 imparfait du subjonctif		14 plus-que-parfait du subjonctif	
empruntasse	**empruntassions**	**eusse emprunté**	**eussions emprunté**
empruntasses	**empruntassiez**	**eusses emprunté**	**eussiez emprunté**
empruntât	**empruntassent**	**eût emprunté**	**eussent emprunté**

Impératif
emprunte
empruntons
empruntez

Words related to this verb

emprunteur, emprunteuse a person who makes a habit of borrowing

un emprunt loan, borrowing

emprunter quelque chose à quelqu'un to borrow something from someone

Monsieur Leblanc a emprunté de l'argent à mon père. Mr. Leblanc borrowed some money from my father.

faire un emprunt pour payer ses dettes de jeu to take out a loan to pay one's gambling debts

Don't confuse **emprunter** with **prêter** (*to lend*).

Regular **-er** verb endings; spelling change: retain the **ge** before **a** or **o** to keep the soft **g** sound of the verb

to encourage

The Seven Simple Tenses		The Seven Compound Tenses	
Singular	Plural	Singular	Plural
1 présent de l'indicatif		8 passé composé	
encourage	**encourageons**	**ai encouragé**	**avons encouragé**
encourages	**encouragez**	**as encouragé**	**avez encouragé**
encourage	**encouragent**	**a encouragé**	**ont encouragé**
2 imparfait de l'indicatif		9 plus-que-parfait de l'indicatif	
encourageais	**encouragions**	**avais encouragé**	**avions encouragé**
encourageais	**encouragiez**	**avais encouragé**	**aviez encouragé**
encourageait	**encourageaient**	**avait encouragé**	**avaient encouragé**
3 passé simple		10 passé antérieur	
encourageai	**encourageâmes**	**eus encouragé**	**eûmes encouragé**
encourageas	**encourageâtes**	**eus encouragé**	**eûtes encouragé**
encouragea	**encouragèrent**	**eut encouragé**	**eurent encouragé**
4 futur		11 futur antérieur	
encouragerai	**encouragerons**	**aurai encouragé**	**aurons encouragé**
encourageras	**encouragerez**	**auras encouragé**	**aurez encouragé**
encouragera	**encourageront**	**aura encouragé**	**auront encouragé**
5 conditionnel		12 conditionnel passé	
encouragerais	**encouragerions**	**aurais encouragé**	**aurions encouragé**
encouragerais	**encourageriez**	**aurais encouragé**	**auriez encouragé**
encouragerait	**encourageraient**	**aurait encouragé**	**auraient encouragé**
6 présent du subjonctif		13 passé du subjonctif	
encourage	**encouragions**	**aie encouragé**	**ayons encouragé**
encourages	**encouragiez**	**aies encouragé**	**ayez encouragé**
encourage	**encouragent**	**ait encouragé**	**aient encouragé**
7 imparfait du subjonctif		14 plus-que-parfait du subjonctif	
encourageasse	**encourageassions**	**eusse encouragé**	**eussions encouragé**
encourageasses	**encourageassiez**	**eusses encouragé**	**eussiez encouragé**
encourageât	**encourageassent**	**eût encouragé**	**eussent encouragé**

Impératif
encourage
encourageons
encouragez

Words and expressions related to this verb

encourager qqn à faire qqch to encourage someone to do something
encourageant, encourageante encouraging; **des paroles encourageantes** encouraging words
Bon courage! Good luck! (Take heart!)
l'encouragement *m.* encouragement
le découragement discouragement
le courage courage
décourager to discourage
se décourager to become discouraged

Don't forget to study the section on defective and impersonal verbs. It's right after this main list.

s'enfuir (190) — Part. pr. s'enfuyant — Part. passé enfui

to run away, to slip away,
to escape, to flee, to fly away

Reflexive irregular verb

The Seven Simple Tenses		The Seven Compound Tenses	
Singular	Plural	Singular	Plural
1 présent de l'indicatif		8 passé composé	
m'enfuis	**nous enfuyons**	**me suis enfui(e)**	**nous sommes enfui(e)s**
t'enfuis	**vous enfuyez**	**t'es enfui(e)**	**vous êtes enfui(e)(s)**
s'enfuit	**s'enfuient**	**s'est enfui(e)**	**se sont enfui(e)s**
2 imparfait de l'indicatif		9 plus-que-parfait de l'indicatif	
m'enfuyais	**nous enfuyions**	**m'étais enfui(e)**	**nous étions enfui(e)s**
t'enfuyais	**vous enfuyiez**	**t'étais enfui(e)**	**vous étiez enfui(e)(s)**
s'enfuyait	**s'enfuyaient**	**s'était enfui(e)**	**s'étaient enfui(e)s**
3 passé simple		10 passé antérieur	
m'enfuis	**nous enfuîmes**	**me fus enfui(e)**	**nous fûmes enfui(e)s**
t'enfuis	**vous enfuîtes**	**te fus enfui(e)**	**vous fûtes enfui(e)(s)**
s'enfuit	**s'enfuirent**	**se fut enfui(e)**	**se furent enfui(e)s**
4 futur		11 futur antérieur	
m'enfuirai	**nous enfuirons**	**me serai enfui(e)**	**nous serons enfui(e)s**
t'enfuiras	**vous enfuirez**	**te seras enfui(e)**	**vous serez enfui(e)(s)**
s'enfuira	**s'enfuiront**	**se sera enfui(e)**	**se seront enfui(e)s**
5 conditionnel		12 conditionnel passé	
m'enfuirais	**nous enfuirions**	**me serais enfui(e)**	**nous serions enfui(e)s**
t'enfuirais	**vous enfuiriez**	**te serais enfui(e)**	**vous seriez enfui(e)(s)**
s'enfuirait	**s'enfuiraient**	**se serait enfui(e)**	**se seraient enfui(e)s**
6 présent du subjonctif		13 passé du subjonctif	
m'enfuie	**nous enfuyions**	**me sois enfui(e)**	**nous soyons enfui(e)s**
t'enfuies	**vous enfuyiez**	**te sois enfui(e)**	**vous soyez enfui(e)(s)**
s'enfuie	**s'enfuient**	**se soit enfui(e)**	**se soient enfui(e)s**
7 imparfait du subjonctif		14 plus-que-parfait du subjonctif	
m'enfuisse	**nous enfuissions**	**me fusse enfui(e)**	**nous fussions enfui(e)s**
t'enfuisses	**vous enfuissiez**	**te fusses enfui(e)**	**vous fussiez enfui(e)(s)**
s'enfuît	**s'enfuissent**	**se fût enfui(e)**	**se fussent enfui(e)s**

Impératif
enfuis-toi; ne t'enfuis pas
enfuyons-nous; ne nous enfuyons pas
enfuyez-vous; ne vous enfuyez pas

Common idiomatic expressions using this verb and words related to it

s'enfuir d'un endroit to flee from a place
prendre la fuite to take to flight
laid à faire fuir ugly enough to make you run off
fuir to flee
faire fuir to put to flight
la fuite flight
fuir devant un danger to run away from danger
Le temps fuit. Time flies.

See also **fuir.**

Can't find the verb you're looking for? Check the back pages of this book for a list of over 2,600 additional verbs!

Regular **-er** verb endings; spelling change: **e** changes to **è** before syllable with mute **e**

to carry away, to take away, to remove

The Seven Simple Tenses		The Seven Compound Tenses	
Singular	Plural	Singular	Plural
1 présent de l'indicatif		8 passé composé	
enlève	**enlevons**	**ai enlevé**	**avons enlevé**
enlèves	**enlevez**	**as enlevé**	**avez enlevé**
enlève	**enlèvent**	**a enlevé**	**ont enlevé**
2 imparfait de l'indicatif		9 plus-que-parfait de l'indicatif	
enlevais	**enlevions**	**avais enlevé**	**avons enlevé**
enlevais	**enleviez**	**avais enlevé**	**aviez enlevé**
enlevait	**enlevaient**	**avait enlevé**	**avaient enlevé**
3 passé simple		10 passé antérieur	
enlevai	**enlevâmes**	**eus enlevé**	**eûmes enlevé**
enlevas	**enlevâtes**	**eus enlevé**	**eûtes enlevé**
enleva	**enlevèrent**	**eut enlevé**	**eurent enlevé**
4 futur		11 futur antérieur	
enlèverai	**enlèverons**	**aurai enlevé**	**aurons enlevé**
enlèveras	**enlèverez**	**auras enlevé**	**aurez enlevé**
enlèvera	**enlèveront**	**aura enlevé**	**auront enlevé**
5 conditionnel		12 conditionnel passé	
enlèverais	**enlèverions**	**aurais enlevé**	**aurions enlevé**
enlèverais	**enlèveriez**	**aurais enlevé**	**auriez enlevé**
enlèverait	**enlèveraient**	**aurait enlevé**	**auraient enlevé**
6 présent du subjonctif		13 passé du subjonctif	
enlève	**enlevions**	**aie enlevé**	**ayons enlevé**
enlèves	**enleviez**	**aies enlevé**	**ayez enlevé**
enlève	**enlèvent**	**ait enlevé**	**aient enlevé**
7 imparfait du subjonctif		14 plus-que-parfait du subjonctif	
enlevasse	**enlevassions**	**eusse enlevé**	**eussions enlevé**
enlevasses	**enlevassiez**	**eusses enlevé**	**eussiez enlevé**
enlevât	**enlevassent**	**eût enlevé**	**eussent enlevé**

Impératif
enlève
enlevons
enlevez

Sentences using this verb and words related to it

Madame Dubac est entrée dans sa maison. Elle a enlevé son chapeau, son manteau et ses gants. Puis, elle est allée directement au salon pour enlever une chaise et la mettre dans la salle à manger. Après cela, elle a enlevé les ordures.

enlever les ordures to take the garbage out
un enlèvement lifting, carrying off, removal
enlèvement d'un enfant baby snatching, kidnapping
un enlevage spurt (sports)

See also **élever** and **lever.**

Don't miss orthographically changing verbs on pages 32–34.

ennuyer (192)

Part. pr. **ennuyant** Part. passé **ennuyé**

to bore, to annoy, to weary

Regular **-er** verb endings; spelling change: **-uyer** verbs must change **y** to **i** in front of mute **e**

The Seven Simple Tenses		The Seven Compound Tenses	
Singular	Plural	Singular	Plural
1 présent de l'indicatif		8 passé composé	
ennuie	**ennuyons**	**ai ennuyé**	**avons ennuyé**
ennuies	**ennuyez**	**as ennuyé**	**avez ennuyé**
ennuie	**ennuient**	**a ennuyé**	**ont ennuyé**
2 imparfait de l'indicatif		9 plus-que-parfait de l'indicatif	
ennuyais	**ennuyions**	**avais ennuyé**	**avions ennuyé**
ennuyais	**ennuyiez**	**avais ennuyé**	**aviez ennuyé**
ennuyait	**ennuyaient**	**avait ennuyé**	**avaient ennuyé**
3 passé simple		10 passé antérieur	
ennuyai	**ennuyâmes**	**eus ennuyé**	**eûmes ennuyé**
ennuyas	**ennuyâtes**	**eus ennuyé**	**eûtes ennuyé**
ennuya	**ennuyèrent**	**eut ennuyé**	**eurent ennuyé**
4 futur		11 futur antérieur	
ennuierai	**ennuierons**	**aurai ennuyé**	**aurons ennuyé**
ennuieras	**ennuierez**	**auras ennuyé**	**aurez ennuyé**
ennuiera	**ennuieront**	**aura ennuyé**	**auront ennuyé**
5 conditionnel		12 conditionnel passé	
ennuierais	**ennuierions**	**aurais ennuyé**	**aurions ennuyé**
ennuierais	**ennuieriez**	**aurais ennuyé**	**auriez ennuyé**
ennuierait	**ennuieraient**	**aurait ennuyé**	**auraient ennuyé**
6 présent du subjonctif		13 passé du subjonctif	
ennuie	**ennuyions**	**aie ennuyé**	**ayons ennuyé**
ennuies	**ennuyiez**	**aies ennuyé**	**ayez ennuyé**
ennuie	**ennuient**	**ait ennuyé**	**aient ennuyé**
7 imparfait du subjonctif		14 plus-que-parfait du subjonctif	
ennuyasse	**ennuyassions**	**eusse ennuyé**	**eussions ennuyé**
ennuyasses	**ennuyassiez**	**eusses ennuyé**	**eussiez ennuyé**
ennuyât	**ennuyassent**	**eût ennuyé**	**eussent ennuyé**

Impératif
ennuie
ennuyons
ennuyez

Sentences using this verb and words related to it

—**Est-ce que je vous ennuie?** — Am I boring you?
—**Oui, vous m'ennuyez. Allez-vous-en!** — Yes, you're boring me. Go away!

un ennui weariness, boredom, ennui
des ennuis worries, troubles
ennuyeux, ennuyeuse boring
s'ennuyer de quelqu'un to miss someone
mourir d'ennui to be bored to tears
s'ennuyer to become bored, to get bored
Quel ennui! What a nuisance!

Reflexive verb; regular **-er** verb endings; spelling change: **-uyer** verbs must change **y** to **i** in front of mute **e**

to be bored

The Seven Simple Tenses		The Seven Compound Tenses	
Singular	Plural	Singular	Plural
1 présent de l'indicatif		8 passé composé	
m'ennuie	**nous ennuyons**	**me suis ennuyé(e)**	**nous sommes ennuyé(e)s**
t'ennuies	**vous ennuyez**	**t'es ennuyé(e)**	**vous êtes ennuyé(e)(s)**
s'ennuie	**se ennuient**	**s'est ennuyé(e)**	**se sont ennuyé(e)s**
2 imparfait de l'indicatif		9 plus-que-parfait de l'indicatif	
m'ennuyais	**nous ennuyions**	**m'étais ennuyé(e)**	**nous étions ennuyé(e)s**
t'ennuyais	**vous ennuyiez**	**t'étais ennuyé(e)**	**vous étiez ennuyé(e)(s)**
s'ennuyait	**s'ennuyaient**	**s'était ennuyé(e)**	**s'étaient ennuyé(e)s**
3 passé simple		10 passé antérieur	
m'ennuyai	**nous ennuyâmes**	**me fus ennuyé(e)**	**nous fûmes ennuyé(e)s**
t'ennuyas	**vous ennuyâtes**	**te fus ennuyé(e)**	**vous fûtes ennuyé(e)(s)**
s'ennuya	**s'ennuyèrent**	**se fut ennuyé(e)**	**se furent ennuyé(e)s**
4 futur		11 futur antérieur	
m'ennuierai	**nous ennuierons**	**me serai ennuyé(e)**	**nous serons ennuyé(e)s**
t'ennuieras	**vous ennuierez**	**te seras ennuyé(e)**	**vous serez ennuyé(e)(s)**
s'ennuiera	**s'ennuieront**	**se sera ennuyé(e)**	**se seront ennuyé(e)s**
5 conditionnel		12 conditionnel passé	
m'ennuierais	**nous ennuierions**	**me serais ennuyé(e)**	**nous serions ennuyé(e)s**
t'ennuierais	**vous ennuieriez**	**te serais ennuyé(e)**	**vous seriez ennuyé(e)(s)**
s'ennuierait	**s'ennuieraient**	**se serait ennuyé(e)**	**se seraient ennuyé(e)s**
6 présent du subjonctif		13 passé du subjonctif	
m'ennuie	**nous ennuyions**	**me sois ennuyé(e)**	**nous soyons ennuyé(e)s**
t'ennuies	**vous ennuyiez**	**te sois ennuyé(e)**	**vous soyez ennuyé(e)(s)**
s'ennuie	**s'ennuient**	**se soit ennuyé(e)**	**se soient ennuyé(e)s**
7 imparfait du subjonctif		14 plus-que-parfait du subjonctif	
m'ennuyasse	**nous ennuyassions**	**me fusse ennuyé(e)**	**nous fussions ennuyé(e)s**
t'ennuyasses	**vous ennuyassiez**	**te fusses ennuyé(e)**	**vous fussiez ennuyé(e)(s)**
s'ennuyât	**s'ennuyassent**	**se fût ennuyé(e)**	**se fussent ennuyé(e)s**

Impératif
ennuie-toi; ne t'ennuie pas
ennuyons-nous; ne nous ennuyons pas
ennuyez-vous; ne vous ennuyez pas

Sentences using this verb and words related to it

Quelle barbe! On s'ennuie à 100 sous de l'heure dans cette classe! How boring! We're really bored in this class!

Je m'ennuie de toi. I miss you.

Proverb

Un ennui ne vient jamais seul. (Similar to: **Jamais deux sans trois.**) Bad luck comes in threes.

Words and expressions related to this verb

s'ennuyer de qqn to miss someone

l'ennui *m.* boredom, trouble

s'ennuyer à 100 sous de l'heure to be very bored (Literally, to be bored at 100 cents per hour. One hundred sous used to make up five **francs**; **un franc** was the former monetary unit in France, replaced by **un euro**.)

ennuyeux, ennuyeuse *adj.* boring

enseigner (194) — Part. pr. enseignant — Part. passé enseigné

to teach

Regular **-er** verb

The Seven Simple Tenses		The Seven Compound Tenses	
Singular	Plural	Singular	Plural
1 présent de l'indicatif		8 passé composé	
enseigne	**enseignons**	**ai enseigné**	**avons enseigné**
enseignes	**enseignez**	**as enseigné**	**avez enseigné**
enseigne	**enseignent**	**a enseigné**	**ont enseigné**
2 imparfait de l'indicatif		9 plus-que-parfait de l'indicatif	
enseignais	**enseignions**	**avais enseigné**	**avions enseigné**
enseignais	**enseigniez**	**avais enseigné**	**aviez enseigné**
enseignait	**enseignaient**	**avait enseigné**	**avaient enseigné**
3 passé simple		10 passé antérieur	
enseignai	**enseignâmes**	**eus enseigné**	**eûmes enseigné**
enseignas	**enseignâtes**	**eus enseigné**	**eûtes enseigné**
enseigna	**enseignèrent**	**eut enseigné**	**eurent enseigné**
4 futur		11 futur antérieur	
enseignerai	**enseignerons**	**aurai enseigné**	**aurons enseigné**
enseigneras	**enseignerez**	**auras enseigné**	**aurez enseigné**
enseignera	**enseigneront**	**aura enseigné**	**auront enseigné**
5 conditionnel		12 conditionnel passé	
enseignerais	**enseignerions**	**aurais enseigné**	**aurions enseigné**
enseignerais	**enseigneriez**	**aurais enseigné**	**auriez enseigné**
enseignerait	**enseigneraient**	**aurait enseigné**	**auraient enseigné**
6 présent du subjonctif		13 passé du subjonctif	
enseigne	**enseignions**	**aie enseigné**	**ayons enseigné**
enseignes	**enseigniez**	**aies enseigné**	**ayez enseigné**
enseigne	**enseignent**	**ait enseigné**	**aient enseigné**
7 imparfait du subjonctif		14 plus-que-parfait du subjonctif	
enseignasse	**enseignassions**	**eusse enseigné**	**eussions enseigné**
enseignasses	**enseignassiez**	**eusses enseigné**	**eussiez enseigné**
enseignât	**enseignassent**	**eût enseigné**	**eussent enseigné**

Impératif
enseigne
enseignons
enseignez

Sentences using this verb and words and expressions related to it

J'enseigne aux élèves à lire en français. L'enseignement est une belle profession.

enseigner quelque chose à quelqu'un to teach something to someone

une enseigne sign; **une enseigne lumineuse** neon sign

les enseignements du Christ/de Moïse/de Mahomet/du Bouddha the teachings of Christ/of Moses/of Mohammed/of Buddha

l'enseignement *m.* teaching

l'enseignement à distance distance education

renseigner qqn de qqch to inform someone about something

se renseigner to get information, to inquire

un renseignement, des renseignements information

Regular **-re** verb

to hear, to understand

The Seven Simple Tenses		The Seven Compound Tenses	
Singular	Plural	Singular	Plural
1 présent de l'indicatif		8 passé composé	
entends	**entendons**	**ai entendu**	**avons entendu**
entends	**entendez**	**as entendu**	**avez entendu**
entend	**entendent**	**a entendu**	**ont entendu**
2 imparfait de l'indicatif		9 plus-que-parfait de l'indicatif	
entendais	**entendions**	**avais entendu**	**avions entendu**
entendais	**entendiez**	**avais entendu**	**aviez entendu**
entendait	**entendaient**	**avait entendu**	**avaient entendu**
3 passé simple		10 passé antérieur	
entendis	**entendîmes**	**eus entendu**	**eûmes entendu**
entendis	**entendîtes**	**eus entendu**	**eûtes entendu**
entendit	**entendirent**	**eut entendu**	**eurent entendu**
4 futur		11 futur antérieur	
entendrai	**entendrons**	**aurai entendu**	**aurons entendu**
entendras	**entendrez**	**auras entendu**	**aurez entendu**
entendra	**entendront**	**aura entendu**	**auront entendu**
5 conditionnel		12 conditionnel passé	
entendrais	**entendrions**	**aurais entendu**	**aurions entendu**
entendrais	**entendriez**	**aurais entendu**	**auriez entendu**
entendrait	**entendraient**	**aurait entendu**	**auraient entendu**
6 présent du subjonctif		13 passé du subjonctif	
entende	**entendions**	**aie entendu**	**ayons entendu**
entendes	**entendiez**	**aies entendu**	**ayez entendu**
entende	**entendent**	**ait entendu**	**aient entendu**
7 imparfait du subjonctif		14 plus-que-parfait du subjonctif	
entendisse	**entendissions**	**eusse entendu**	**eussions entendu**
entendisses	**entendissiez**	**eusses entendu**	**eussiez entendu**
entendît	**entendissent**	**eût entendu**	**eussent entendu**

Impératif
entends
entendons
entendez

AN ESSENTIAL 55 VERB

Entendre

Entendre is a very useful verb for a beginning French student. **Entendre** is a regular **-re** verb so many verbs are conjugated like it.

Sentences using entendre

—As-tu entendu quelque chose?
—Non, chéri, je n'ai rien entendu.
—J'ai entendu un bruit . . . de la cuisine . . . silence . . . je l'entends encore. C'est un cambrioleur!
—Non, chéri, c'est notre chien que tu entends.

—Did you hear something?
—No, dear, I didn't hear anything.
—I heard a noise . . . from the kitchen . . . quiet . . . I still hear it. It's a burglar!
—No, dear, it's our dog that you hear.

C'est entendu! It's understood! Agreed!

Je m'entends bien avec ma soeur. I get along well with my sister.

J'ai entendu dire qu'on mange bien dans ce restaurant. I've heard that a person can have a good meal in this restaurant.

Qu'entendez-vous par là?! What do you mean by that?!

J'ai entendu parler d'un grand changement dans l'administration de cette école. I've heard about a big change in the administration of this school.

Je ne peux pas vous entendre. Parlez plus fort, s'il vous plaît. I can't hear you. Please speak more loudly.

Words and expressions related to this verb

un entendement **understanding**

une entente **understanding**

une mésentente **disagreement**

malentendant, malentendante **hard of hearing**

bien entendu **of course**

laisser entendre **to hint**

entendre raison **to listen to reason**

ne pas entendre malice **not to mean any harm**

entendre parler de **to hear about, to hear of**

un sous-entendu **innuendo**

If you can conjugate **entendre** you can also conjugate these verbs:

s'entendre avec qqn **to get along with someone, to understand each other**

s'entendre à merveille **to get along with each other marvelously**

sous-entendre **to imply**

Regular **-er** verb

to bury

The Seven Simple Tenses		The Seven Compound Tenses	
Singular	Plural	Singular	Plural
1 présent de l'indicatif		8 passé composé	
enterre	**enterrons**	**ai enterré**	**avons enterré**
enterres	**enterrez**	**as enterré**	**avez enterré**
enterre	**enterrent**	**a enterré**	**ont enterré**
2 imparfait de l'indicatif		9 plus-que-parfait de l'indicatif	
enterrais	**enterrions**	**avais enterré**	**avions enterré**
enterrais	**enterriez**	**avais enterré**	**aviez enterré**
enterrait	**enterraient**	**avait enterré**	**avaient enterré**
3 passé simple		10 passé antérieur	
enterrai	**enterrâmes**	**eus enterré**	**eûmes enterré**
enterras	**enterrâtes**	**eus enterré**	**eûtes enterré**
enterra	**enterrèrent**	**eut enterré**	**eurent enterré**
4 futur		11 futur antérieur	
enterrerai	**enterrerons**	**aurai enterré**	**aurons enterré**
enterreras	**enterrerez**	**auras enterré**	**aurez enterré**
enterrera	**enterreront**	**aura enterré**	**auront enterré**
5 conditionnel		12 conditionnel passé	
enterrerais	**enterrerions**	**aurais enterré**	**aurions enterré**
enterrerais	**enterreriez**	**aurais enterré**	**auriez enterré**
enterrerait	**enterreraient**	**aurait enterré**	**auraient enterré**
6 présent du subjonctif		13 passé du subjonctif	
enterre	**enterrions**	**aie enterré**	**ayons enterré**
enterres	**enterriez**	**aies enterré**	**ayez enterré**
enterre	**enterrent**	**ait enterré**	**aient enterré**
7 imparfait du subjonctif		14 plus-que-parfait du subjonctif	
enterrasse	**enterrassions**	**eusse enterré**	**eussions enterré**
enterrasses	**enterrassiez**	**eusses enterré**	**eussiez enterré**
enterrât	**enterrassent**	**eût enterré**	**eussent enterré**

Impératif
enterre
enterrons
enterrez

Words and expressions related to this verb

enterrer un cadavre to bury a corpse
s'enterrer to bury oneself
enterrer une affaire to abandon a matter
enterrer sa vie de garçon to hold a bachelor's party (for a man about to be married)
la terre earth, soil
enterrer une chose to bury something, to forget about something, to shelve something
un enterrement burial, interment
s'enterrer dans un endroit to bury oneself in a place, to isolate oneself from the rest of the world

Soak up some verbs used in weather expressions. There's a list in the Appendixes!

The subject pronouns are found on page 103.

entreprendre (197) Part. pr. entreprenant Part. passé entrepris

to undertake, to engage upon

Irregular verb

The Seven Simple Tenses		The Seven Compound Tenses	
Singular	Plural	Singular	Plural
1 présent de l'indicatif		8 passé composé	
entreprends	**entreprenons**	**ai entrepris**	**avons entrepris**
entreprends	**entreprenez**	**as entrepris**	**avez entrepris**
entreprend	**entreprennent**	**a entrepris**	**ont entrepris**
2 imparfait de l'indicatif		9 plus-que-parfait de l'indicatif	
entreprenais	**entreprenions**	**avais entrepris**	**avions entrepris**
entreprenais	**entrepreniez**	**avais entrepris**	**aviez entrepris**
entreprenait	**entreprenaient**	**avait entrepris**	**avaient entrepris**
3 passé simple		10 passé antérieur	
entrepris	**entreprîmes**	**eus entrepris**	**eûmes entrepris**
entrepris	**entreprîtes**	**eus entrepris**	**eûtes entrepris**
entreprit	**entreprirent**	**eut entrepris**	**eurent entrepris**
4 futur		11 futur antérieur	
entreprendrai	**entreprendrons**	**aurai entrepris**	**aurons entrepris**
entreprendras	**entreprendrez**	**auras entrepris**	**aurez entrepris**
entreprendra	**entreprendront**	**aura entrepris**	**auront entrepris**
5 conditionnel		12 conditionnel passé	
entreprendrais	**entreprendrions**	**aurais entrepris**	**aurions entrepris**
entreprendrais	**entreprendriez**	**aurais entrepris**	**auriez entrepris**
entreprendrait	**entreprendraient**	**aurait entrepris**	**auraient entrepris**
6 présent du subjonctif		13 passé du subjonctif	
entreprenne	**entreprenions**	**aie entrepris**	**ayons entrepris**
entreprennes	**entrepreniez**	**aies entrepris**	**ayez entrepris**
entreprenne	**entreprennent**	**ait entrepris**	**aient entrepris**
7 imparfait du subjonctif		14 plus-que-parfait du subjonctif	
entreprisse	**entreprissions**	**eusse entrepris**	**eussions entrepris**
entreprisses	**entreprissiez**	**eusses entrepris**	**eussiez entrepris**
entreprît	**entreprissent**	**eût entrepris**	**eussent entrepris**

Impératif
entreprends
entreprenons
entreprenez

Words and expressions related to this verb

entreprendre de faire qqch to undertake to do something

avoir un esprit entreprenant to be bold, daring, enterprising

une entreprise enterprise; **une entreprise rémunératrice** profitable enterprise

entreprenant, entreprenante enterprising

un entrepreneur, une entrepreneuse contractor

une entreprise de déménagement moving company

See also **apprendre, comprendre, se méprendre, prendre, reprendre,** and **surprendre.**

Don't forget to use the English-French verb index. It's in the Appendixes.

Regular **-er** verb

to enter, to come in, to go in

The Seven Simple Tenses		The Seven Compound Tenses	
Singular	Plural	Singular	Plural
1 présent de l'indicatif		8 passé composé	
entre	**entrons**	**suis entré(e)**	**sommes entré(e)s**
entres	**entrez**	**es entré(e)**	**êtes entré(e)(s)**
entre	**entrent**	**est entré(e)**	**sont entré(e)s**
2 imparfait de l'indicatif		9 plus-que-parfait de l'indicatif	
entrais	**entrions**	**étais entré(e)**	**étions entré(e)s**
entrais	**entriez**	**étais entré(e)**	**étiez entré(e)(s)**
entrait	**entraient**	**était entré(e)**	**étaient entré(e)s**
3 passé simple		10 passé antérieur	
entrai	**entrâmes**	**fus entré(e)**	**fûmes entré(e)s**
entras	**entrâtes**	**fus entré(e)**	**fûtes entré(e)(s)**
entra	**entrèrent**	**fut entré(e)**	**furent entré(e)s**
4 futur		11 futur antérieur	
entrerai	**entrerons**	**serai entré(e)**	**serons entré(e)s**
entreras	**entrerez**	**seras entré(e)**	**serez entré(e)(s)**
entrera	**entreront**	**sera entré(e)**	**seront entré(e)s**
5 conditionnel		12 conditionnel passé	
entrerais	**entrerions**	**serais entré(e)**	**serions entré(e)s**
entrerais	**entreriez**	**serais entré(e)**	**seriez entré(e)(s)**
entrerait	**entreraient**	**serait entré(e)**	**seraient entré(e)s**
6 présent du subjonctif		13 passé du subjonctif	
entre	**entrions**	**sois entré(e)**	**soyons entré(e)s**
entres	**entriez**	**sois entré(e)**	**soyez entré(e)(s)**
entre	**entrent**	**soit entré(e)**	**soient entré(e)s**
7 imparfait du subjonctif		14 plus-que-parfait du subjonctif	
entrasse	**entrassions**	**fusse entré(e)**	**fussions entré(e)s**
entrasses	**entrassiez**	**fusses entré(e)**	**fussiez entré(e)(s)**
entrât	**entrassent**	**fût entré(e)**	**fussent entré(e)s**

Impératif
entre
entrons
entrez

AN ESSENTIAL 55 VERB

Entrer

Entrer is an essential verb for a beginning student of French. Pay attention to the choice of helping verb when you use **entrer** in the compound tenses. It is usually conjugated with *être*, unless there is a direct object. In that case, you should use *avoir*, as noted below.

Sentences using entrer

Le cambrioleur est entré par la fenêtre.
The burglar entered through the window.

Entrez donc!
Do come in!

Entrons voir.
Let's go in and see.

This verb is conjugated with *avoir* when it has a direct object.

Example:
Ma mère a entré la clé dans la serrure pour ouvrir la porte.
My mother put the key in the lock to open the door.

BUT:
Ma mère est entrée dans la maison.
My mother went in the house.

Words and expressions related to this verb

l'entrée *f.* **entrance**

entrée interdite **no entry**

l'entrée *f.* **des données** **data input, data entry**

entrer par la fenêtre **to enter through the window**

entrer dans + noun **to enter (into) + noun**

entrer dans le décor **to drive off the road and have an accident (le décor/scenery)**

une entrée gratuite **free admission**

entrer des données **to enter/input data (computer)**

faire entrer qqn **to show somebody in**

entrer comme dans un moulin **to have free access**

entrer dans le vif du sujet **to get to the heart of the matter**

entrer dans une famille **to marry into a family**

entrer dans les détails **to go into the details**

Can't find the verb you're looking for? Check the back pages of this book for a list of over 2,600 additional verbs!

Reflexive regular **-er** verb

to fly off, to fly away, to take flight, to take wing (birds), to take off (airplane)

The Seven Simple Tenses		The Seven Compound Tenses	
Singular	Plural	Singular	Plural
1 présent de l'indicatif		8 passé composé	
m'envole	**nous envolons**	**me suis envolé(e)**	**nous sommes envolé(e)s**
t'envoles	**vous envolez**	**t'es envolé(e)**	**vous êtes envolé(e)(s)**
s'envole	**s'envolent**	**s'est envolé(e)**	**se sont envolé(e)s**
2 imparfait de l'indicatif		9 plus-que-parfait de l'indicatif	
m'envolais	**nous envolions**	**m'étais envolé(e)**	**nous étions envolé(e)s**
t'envolais	**vous envoliez**	**t'étais envolé(e)**	**vous étiez envolé(e)(s)**
s'envolait	**s'envolaient**	**s'était envolé(e)**	**s'étaient envolé(e)s**
3 passé simple		10 passé antérieur	
m'envolai	**nous envolâmes**	**me fus envolé(e)**	**nous fûmes envolé(e)s**
t'envolas	**vous envolâtes**	**te fus envolé(e)**	**vous fûtes envolé(e)(s)**
s'envola	**s'envolèrent**	**se fut envolé(e)**	**se furent envolé(e)s**
4 futur		11 futur antérieur	
m'envolerai	**nous envolerons**	**me serai envolé(e)**	**nous serons envolé(e)s**
t'envoleras	**vous envolerez**	**te seras envolé(e)**	**vous serez envolé(e)(s)**
s'envolera	**s'envoleront**	**se sera envolé(e)**	**se seront envolé(e)s**
5 conditionnel		12 conditionnel passé	
m'envolerais	**nous envolerions**	**me serais envolé(e)**	**nous serions envolé(e)s**
t'envolerais	**vous envoleriez**	**te serais envolé(e)**	**vous seriez envolé(e)(s)**
s'envolerait	**s'envoleraient**	**se serait envolé(e)**	**se seraient envolé(e)s**
6 présent du subjonctif		13 passé du subjonctif	
m'envole	**nous envolions**	**me sois envolé(e)**	**nous soyons envolé(e)s**
t'envoles	**vous envoliez**	**te sois envolé(e)**	**vous soyez envolé(e)(s)**
s'envole	**s'envolent**	**se soit envolé(e)**	**se soient envolé(e)s**
7 imparfait du subjonctif		14 plus-que-parfait du subjonctif	
m'envolasse	**nous envolassions**	**me fusse envolé(e)**	**nous fussions envolé(e)s**
t'envolasses	**vous envolassiez**	**te fusses envolé(e)**	**vous fussiez envolé(e)(s)**
s'envolât	**s'envolassent**	**se fût envolé(e)**	**se fussent envolé(e)s**

Impératif
envole-toi; ne t'envole pas
envolons-nous; ne nous envolons pas
envolez-vous; ne vous envolez pas

Words and expressions related to this verb

une envolée flying off
un envol flight of a bird; take-off of an airplane
voler to fly, to steal
le vol flight, theft
Les paroles s'envolent. Spoken words fly away.

See also **voler.**

Don't forget to check the list of 2,600 additional verbs keyed to the 501 model verbs. It's in the Appendixes!

envoyer (200) — Part. pr. envoyant — Part. passé envoyé

to send

Regular **-er** verb endings; spelling change: **-oyer** verbs must change **y** to **i** in front of a mute **e**, future and conditional stem is **enverr-**

The Seven Simple Tenses		The Seven Compound Tenses	
Singular	Plural	Singular	Plural
1 présent de l'indicatif		8 passé composé	
envoie	**envoyons**	**ai envoyé**	**avons envoyé**
envoies	**envoyez**	**as envoyé**	**avez envoyé**
envoie	**envoient**	**a envoyé**	**ont envoyé**
2 imparfait de l'indicatif		9 plus-que-parfait de l'indicatif	
envoyais	**envoyions**	**avais envoyé**	**avions envoyé**
envoyais	**envoyiez**	**avais envoyé**	**aviez envoyé**
envoyait	**envoyaient**	**avait envoyé**	**avaient envoyé**
3 passé simple		10 passé antérieur	
envoyai	**envoyâmes**	**eus envoyé**	**eûmes envoyé**
envoyas	**envoyâtes**	**eus envoyé**	**eûtes envoyé**
envoya	**envoyèrent**	**eut envoyé**	**eurent envoyé**
4 futur		11 futur antérieur	
enverrai	**enverrons**	**aurai envoyé**	**aurons envoyé**
enverras	**enverrez**	**auras envoyé**	**aurez envoyé**
enverra	**enverront**	**aura envoyé**	**auront envoyé**
5 conditionnel		12 conditionnel passé	
enverrais	**enverrions**	**aurais envoyé**	**aurions envoyé**
enverrais	**enverriez**	**aurais envoyé**	**auriez envoyé**
enverrait	**enverraient**	**aurait envoyé**	**auraient envoyé**
6 présent du subjonctif		13 passé du subjonctif	
envoie	**envoyions**	**aie envoyé**	**ayons envoyé**
envoies	**envoyiez**	**aies envoyé**	**ayez envoyé**
envoie	**envoient**	**ait envoyé**	**aient envoyé**
7 imparfait du subjonctif		14 plus-que-parfait du subjonctif	
envoyasse	**envoyassions**	**eusse envoyé**	**eussions envoyé**
envoyasses	**envoyassiez**	**eusses envoyé**	**eussiez envoyé**
envoyât	**envoyassent**	**eût envoyé**	**eussent envoyé**

Impératif
envoie
envoyons
envoyez

AN ESSENTIAL 55 VERB

Envoyer

Envoyer is an important verb because it has an interesting spelling change and because it is very useful for a beginning French student.

Sentences using envoyer and related words and expressions

Hier j'ai envoyé une lettre à des amis en France. Yesterday I sent a letter to some friends in France.

Demain j'enverrai une lettre à mes amis au Canada. Tomorrow I will send a letter to my friends in Canada.

J'enverrais une lettre en Italie mais je ne connais personne dans ce pays. I would send a letter to Italy but I don't know anyone in that country.

Mon père a envoyé chercher le docteur parce que mon petit frère est malade. My father sent for the doctor because my little brother is sick.

Où est-ce que je peux envoyer un courriel/un courrier électronique? Where can I send an e-mail?

Marc a été renvoyé de l'école. Mark was kicked out of school.

Words and expressions related to this verb

envoyer chercher **to send for**

un envoi **envoi (poetry), sending**

envoyer promener qqn **to send someone packing**

envoyeur, envoyeuse **sender**

un envoyé, une envoyée **envoy, messenger**

le renvoi **return, call forwarding**

renvoyer **to send away (back), to discharge someone, to sack someone**

Don't forget to study the section on defective and impersonal verbs. It's right after this main list.

The subject pronouns are found on page 103.

épouser (201)

Part. pr. **épousant** Part. passé **épousé**

to marry, to wed

Regular **-er** verb

The Seven Simple Tenses		The Seven Compound Tenses	
Singular	Plural	Singular	Plural
1 présent de l'indicatif		8 passé composé	
épouse	**épousons**	**ai épousé**	**avons épousé**
épouses	**épousez**	**as épousé**	**avez épousé**
épouse	**épousent**	**a épousé**	**ont épousé**
2 imparfait de l'indicatif		9 plus-que-parfait de l'indicatif	
épousais	**épousions**	**avais épousé**	**avions épousé**
épousais	**épousiez**	**avais épousé**	**aviez épousé**
épousait	**épousaient**	**avait épousé**	**avaient épousé**
3 passé simple		10 passé antérieur	
épousai	**épousâmes**	**eus épousé**	**eûmes épousé**
épousas	**épousâtes**	**eus épousé**	**eûtes épousé**
épousa	**épousèrent**	**eut épousé**	**eurent épousé**
4 futur		11 futur antérieur	
épouserai	**épouserons**	**aurai épousé**	**aurons épousé**
épouseras	**épouserez**	**auras épousé**	**aurez épousé**
épousera	**épouseront**	**aura épousé**	**auront épousé**
5 conditionnel		12 conditionnel passé	
épouserais	**épouserions**	**aurais épousé**	**aurions épousé**
épouserais	**épouseriez**	**aurais épousé**	**auriez épousé**
épouserait	**épouseraient**	**aurait épousé**	**auraient épousé**
6 présent du subjonctif		13 passé du subjonctif	
épouse	**épousions**	**aie épousé**	**ayons épousé**
épouses	**épousiez**	**aies épousé**	**ayez épousé**
épouse	**épousent**	**ait épousé**	**aient épousé**
7 imparfait du subjonctif		14 plus-que-parfait du subjonctif	
épousasse	**épousassions**	**eusse épousé**	**eussions épousé**
épousasses	**épousassiez**	**eusses épousé**	**eussiez épousé**
épousât	**épousassent**	**eût épousé**	**eussent épousé**

Impératif
épouse
épousons
épousez

Sentences using this verb and words related to it

J'ai trois frères. Le premier a épousé une jolie jeune fille française. Le deuxième a épousé une belle jeune fille italienne, et le troisième a épousé une jolie fille espagnole. Elles sont très intelligentes.

un époux husband, spouse
une épouse wife, spouse
les nouveaux mariés the newlyweds
épouser une grosse fortune to marry into money
se marier avec quelqu'un to get married to someone

Can't remember the French verb you need? Check the back pages of this book for the English-French verb index!

Regular **-er** verb

to try, to test, to put to the test, to feel, to experience

The Seven Simple Tenses		The Seven Compound Tenses	
Singular	Plural	Singular	Plural
1 présent de l'indicatif		8 passé composé	
éprouve	**éprouvons**	**ai éprouvé**	**avons éprouvé**
éprouves	**éprouvez**	**as éprouvé**	**avez éprouvé**
éprouve	**éprouvent**	**a éprouvé**	**ont éprouvé**
2 imparfait de l'indicatif		9 plus-que-parfait de l'indicatif	
éprouvais	**éprouvions**	**avais éprouvé**	**avions éprouvé**
éprouvais	**éprouviez**	**avais éprouvé**	**aviez éprouvé**
éprouvait	**éprouvaient**	**avait éprouvé**	**avaient éprouvé**
3 passé simple		10 passé antérieur	
éprouvai	**éprouvâmes**	**eus éprouvé**	**eûmes éprouvé**
éprouvas	**éprouvâtes**	**eus éprouvé**	**eûtes éprouvé**
éprouva	**éprouvèrent**	**eut éprouvé**	**eurent éprouvé**
4 futur		11 futur antérieur	
éprouverai	**éprouverons**	**aurai éprouvé**	**aurons éprouvé**
éprouveras	**éprouverez**	**auras éprouvé**	**aurez éprouvé**
éprouvera	**éprouveront**	**aura éprouvé**	**auront éprouvé**
5 conditionnel		12 conditionnel passé	
éprouverais	**éprouverions**	**aurais éprouvé**	**aurions éprouvé**
éprouverais	**éprouveriez**	**aurais éprouvé**	**auriez éprouvé**
éprouverait	**éprouveraient**	**aurait éprouvé**	**auraient éprouvé**
6 présent du subjonctif		13 passé du subjonctif	
éprouve	**éprouvions**	**aie éprouvé**	**ayons éprouvé**
éprouves	**éprouviez**	**aies éprouvé**	**ayez éprouvé**
éprouve	**éprouvent**	**ait éprouvé**	**aient éprouvé**
7 imparfait du subjonctif		14 plus-que-parfait du subjonctif	
éprouvasse	**éprouvassions**	**eusse éprouvé**	**eussions éprouvé**
éprouvasses	**éprouvassiez**	**eusses éprouvé**	**eussiez éprouvé**
éprouvât	**éprouvassent**	**eût éprouvé**	**eussent éprouvé**

Impératif
éprouve
éprouvons
éprouvez

Common idiomatic expressions using this verb and words related to it

éprouver des doutes to have doubts, to feel doubtful
éprouver qqn to put someone to the test
mettre qqn à l'épreuve to put someone to the test
éprouver un regret to feel a regret
éprouver de la sympathie pour qqn to feel sympathy for someone
mettre à l'épreuve to put to the test
une épreuve test, proof, page proof
une épreuve écrite written test
une épreuve orale oral test
éprouver de la honte to experience shame

How are you doing? Find out with the verb drills and tests with answers explained on pages 50–101.

espérer (203)

Part. pr. **espérant** Part. passé **espéré**

to hope

Regular **-er** verb endings; spelling change: **é** changes to **è** before syllable with mute **e**

The Seven Simple Tenses		The Seven Compound Tenses	
Singular	Plural	Singular	Plural
1 présent de l'indicatif		8 passé composé	
espère	**espérons**	**ai espéré**	**avons espéré**
espères	**espérez**	**as espéré**	**avez espéré**
espère	**espèrent**	**a espéré**	**ont espéré**
2 imparfait de l'indicatif		9 plus-que-parfait de l'indicatif	
espérais	**espérions**	**avais espéré**	**avions espéré**
espérais	**espériez**	**avais espéré**	**aviez espéré**
espérait	**espéraient**	**avait espéré**	**avaient espéré**
3 passé simple		10 passé antérieur	
espérai	**espérâmes**	**eus espéré**	**eûmes espéré**
espéras	**espérâtes**	**eus espéré**	**eûtes espéré**
espéra	**espérèrent**	**eut espéré**	**eurent espéré**
4 futur		11 futur antérieur	
espérerai	**espérerons**	**aurai espéré**	**aurons espéré**
espéreras	**espérerez**	**auras espéré**	**aurez espéré**
espérera	**espéreront**	**aura espéré**	**auront espéré**
5 conditionnel		12 conditionnel passé	
espérerais	**espérerions**	**aurais espéré**	**aurions espéré**
espérerais	**espéreriez**	**aurais espéré**	**auriez espéré**
espérerait	**espéreraient**	**aurait espéré**	**auraient espéré**
6 présent du subjonctif		13 passé du subjonctif	
espère	**espérions**	**aie espéré**	**ayons espéré**
espères	**espériez**	**aies espéré**	**ayez espéré**
espère	**espèrent**	**ait espéré**	**aient espéré**
7 imparfait du subjonctif		14 plus-que-parfait du subjonctif	
espérasse	**espérassions**	**eusse espéré**	**eussions espéré**
espérasses	**espérassiez**	**eusses espéré**	**eussiez espéré**
espérât	**espérassent**	**eût espéré**	**eussent espéré**

Impératif
espère
espérons
espérez

Sentences using this verb and words and expressions related to it

J'espère que Paul viendra mais je n'espère pas que son frère vienne.

l'espérance *f.* hope, expectation
plein d'espérance hopeful, full of hope
l'espoir *m.* hope
avoir bon espoir de réussir to have good hopes of succeeding
désespérer de to despair of; **se désespérer** to be in despair
le désespoir despair; **un désespoir d'amour** disappointed love

Don't forget to check the list of 2,600 additional verbs keyed to the 501 model verbs. It's in the Appendixes!

Regular **-er** verb endings; spelling change: **-ayer** verbs may change **y** to **i** in front of a mute **e** or may keep **y**

to try, to try on

The Seven Simple Tenses		The Seven Compound Tenses	
Singular	Plural	Singular	Plural
1 présent de l'indicatif		8 passé composé	
essaye	**essayons**	**ai essayé**	**avons essayé**
essayes	**essayez**	**as essayé**	**avez essayé**
essaye	**essayent**	**a essayé**	**ont essayé**
2 imparfait de l'indicatif		9 plus-que-parfait de l'indicatif	
essayais	**essayions**	**avais essayé**	**avions essayé**
essayais	**essayiez**	**avais essayé**	**aviez essayé**
essayait	**essayaient**	**avait essayé**	**avaient essayé**
3 passé simple		10 passé antérieur	
essayai	**essayâmes**	**eus essayé**	**eûmes essayé**
essayas	**essayâtes**	**eus essayé**	**eûtes essayé**
essaya	**essayèrent**	**eut essayé**	**eurent essayé**
4 futur		11 futur antérieur	
essayerai	**essayerons**	**aurai essayé**	**aurons essayé**
essayeras	**essayerez**	**auras essayé**	**aurez essayé**
essayera	**essayeront**	**aura essayé**	**auront essayé**
5 conditionnel		12 conditionnel passé	
essayerais	**essayerions**	**aurais essayé**	**aurions essayé**
essayerais	**essayeriez**	**aurais essayé**	**auriez essayé**
essayerait	**essayeraient**	**aurait essayé**	**auraient essayé**
6 présent du subjonctif		13 passé du subjonctif	
essaye	**essayions**	**aie essayé**	**ayons essayé**
essayes	**essayiez**	**aies essayé**	**ayez essayé**
essaye	**essayent**	**ait essayé**	**aient essayé**
7 imparfait du subjonctif		14 plus-que-parfait du subjonctif	
essayasse	**essayassions**	**eusse essayé**	**eussions essayé**
essayasses	**essayassiez**	**eusses essayé**	**eussiez essayé**
essayât	**essayassent**	**eût essayé**	**eussent essayé**

Impératif
essaye
essayons
essayez

Sentences using this verb and words related to it

Marcel a essayé d'écrire un essai sur la vie des animaux sauvages mais il n'a pas pu réussir à écrire une seule phrase. Alors, il est allé dans la chambre de son grand frère pour travailler avec lui.

Puis-je essayer cette robe? May I try on this dress?

un essai essay
essayiste essayist
essayer de faire qqch to try to do something
une salle/un salon d'essayage fitting room
essayeur, essayeuse fitter (clothing)
essayage *m.* fitting (clothing)

essuyer (205)

Part. pr. **essuyant** Part. passé **essuyé**

to wipe

Regular **-er** verb endings; spelling change: **-uyer** verbs must change **y** to **i** in front of a mute **e**

The Seven Simple Tenses		The Seven Compound Tenses	
Singular	Plural	Singular	Plural
1 présent de l'indicatif		8 passé composé	
essuie	**essuyons**	**ai essuyé**	**avons essuyé**
essuies	**essuyez**	**as essuyé**	**avez essuyé**
essuie	**essuient**	**a essuyé**	**ont essuyé**
2 imparfait de l'indicatif		9 plus-que-parfait de l'indicatif	
essuyais	**essuyions**	**avais essuyé**	**avions essuyé**
essuyais	**essuyiez**	**avais essuyé**	**aviez essuyé**
essuyait	**essuyaient**	**avait essuyé**	**avaient essuyé**
3 passé simple		10 passé antérieur	
essuyai	**essuyâmes**	**eus essuyé**	**eûmes essuyé**
essuyas	**essuyâtes**	**eus essuyé**	**eûtes essuyé**
essuya	**essuyèrent**	**eut essuyé**	**eurent essuyé**
4 futur		11 futur antérieur	
essuierai	**essuierons**	**aurai essuyé**	**aurons essuyé**
essuieras	**essuierez**	**auras essuyé**	**aurez essuyé**
essuiera	**essuieront**	**aura essuyé**	**auront essuyé**
5 conditionnel		12 conditionnel passé	
essuierais	**essuierions**	**aurais essuyé**	**aurions essuyé**
essuierais	**essuieriez**	**aurais essuyé**	**auriez essuyé**
essuierait	**essuieraient**	**aurait essuyé**	**auraient essuyé**
6 présent du subjonctif		13 passé du subjonctif	
essuie	**essuyions**	**aie essuyé**	**ayons essuyé**
essuies	**essuyiez**	**aies essuyé**	**ayez essuyé**
essuie	**essuient**	**ait essuyé**	**aient essuyé**
7 imparfait du subjonctif		14 plus-que-parfait du subjonctif	
essuyasse	**essuyassions**	**eusse essuyé**	**eussions essuyé**
essuyasses	**essuyassiez**	**eusses essuyé**	**eussiez essuyé**
essuyât	**essuyassent**	**eût essuyé**	**eussent essuyé**

Impératif
essuie
essuyons
essuyez

Words and expressions related to this verb

un essuie-mains hand towel
un essuie-glace windshield wiper
l'essuyage *m.* wiping
un essuie-verres glass cloth
s'essuyer to wipe oneself
s'essuyer le front to wipe one's brow

S'il vous plaît, essuyez vos pieds avant d'entrer. Please wipe your feet before entering.
Notre équipe a essuyé une défaite dans le championnat. Our team suffered a defeat in the championship. (Note: This does not mean "wiped defeat.")

Soak up some verbs used in weather expressions. There's a list in the Appendixes!

Regular **-ir** verb

to establish, to set up, to draw up

The Seven Simple Tenses		The Seven Compound Tenses	
Singular	Plural	Singular	Plural
1 présent de l'indicatif		8 passé composé	
établis	**établissons**	**ai établi**	**avons établi**
établis	**établissez**	**as établi**	**avez établi**
établit	**établissent**	**a établi**	**ont établi**
2 imparfait de l'indicatif		9 plus-que-parfait de l'indicatif	
établissais	**établissions**	**avais établi**	**avions établi**
établissais	**établissiez**	**avais établi**	**aviez établi**
établissait	**établissaient**	**avait établi**	**avaient établi**
3 passé simple		10 passé antérieur	
établis	**établîmes**	**eus établi**	**eûmes établi**
établis	**établîtes**	**eus établi**	**eûtes établi**
établit	**établirent**	**eut établi**	**eurent établi**
4 futur		11 futur antérieur	
établirai	**établirons**	**aurai établi**	**aurons établi**
établiras	**établirez**	**auras établi**	**aurez établi**
établira	**établiront**	**aura établi**	**auront établi**
5 conditionnel		12 conditionnel passé	
établirais	**établirions**	**aurais établi**	**aurions établi**
établirais	**établiriez**	**aurais établi**	**auriez établi**
établirait	**établiraient**	**aurait établi**	**auraient établi**
6 présent du subjonctif		13 passé du subjonctif	
établisse	**établissions**	**aie établi**	**ayons établi**
établisses	**établissiez**	**aies établi**	**ayez établi**
établisse	**établissent**	**ait établi**	**aient établi**
7 imparfait du subjonctif		14 plus-que-parfait du subjonctif	
établisse	**établissions**	**eusse établi**	**eussions établi**
établisses	**établissiez**	**eusses établi**	**eussiez établi**
établît	**établissent**	**eût établi**	**eussent établi**

Impératif
établis
établissons
établissez

Words related to this verb
rétablir to reestablish, to restore
s'établir to settle down, to start a business
se rétablir to recover one's health
un établissement establishment
Bon rétablissement! Get well soon!

Grammar putting you in a tense mood? Review the definitions of basic grammatical terms with examples on pages 35–49.

éteindre (207) — Part. pr. éteignant — Part. passé éteint

to extinguish, to shut down (computer), to turn off

Irregular verb

The Seven Simple Tenses		The Seven Compound Tenses	
Singular	Plural	Singular	Plural
1 présent de l'indicatif		8 passé composé	
éteins	**éteignons**	**ai éteint**	**avons éteint**
éteins	**éteignez**	**as éteint**	**avez éteint**
éteint	**éteignent**	**a éteint**	**ont éteint**
2 imparfait de l'indicatif		9 plus-que-parfait de l'indicatif	
éteignais	**éteignions**	**avais éteint**	**avions éteint**
éteignais	**éteigniez**	**avais éteint**	**aviez éteint**
éteignait	**éteignaient**	**avait éteint**	**avaient éteint**
3 passé simple		10 passé antérieur	
éteignis	**éteignîmes**	**eus éteint**	**eûmes éteint**
éteignis	**éteignîtes**	**eus éteint**	**eûtes éteint**
éteignit	**éteignirent**	**eut éteint**	**eurent éteint**
4 futur		11 futur antérieur	
éteindrai	**éteindrons**	**aurai éteint**	**aurons éteint**
éteindras	**éteindrez**	**auras éteint**	**aurez éteint**
éteindra	**éteindront**	**aura éteint**	**auront éteint**
5 conditionnel		12 conditionnel passé	
éteindrais	**éteindrions**	**aurais éteint**	**aurions éteint**
éteindrais	**éteindriez**	**aurais éteint**	**auriez éteint**
éteindrait	**éteindraient**	**aurait éteint**	**auraient éteint**
6 présent du subjonctif		13 passé du subjonctif	
éteigne	**éteignions**	**aie éteint**	**ayons éteint**
éteignes	**éteigniez**	**aies éteint**	**ayez éteint**
éteigne	**éteignent**	**ait éteint**	**aient éteint**
7 imparfait du subjonctif		14 plus-que-parfait du subjonctif	
éteignisse	**éteignissions**	**eusse éteint**	**eussions éteint**
éteignisses	**éteignissiez**	**eusses éteint**	**eussiez éteint**
éteignît	**éteignissent**	**eût éteint**	**eussent éteint**

Impératif
éteins
éteignons
éteignez

AN ESSENTIAL 55 VERB

Éteindre

Éteindre is an important verb for you to know because, although it is irregular, there are a number of verbs that are conjugated like it. Pay attention to the past participle.

Sentences using éteindre

J'éteins la lumière. Bonne nuit! I'm turning out the light. Good night!

N'oublie pas d'enregistrer (sauver) le document que tu as créé avant d'éteindre ton ordinateur. Don't forget to save the document you created before shutting down your computer.

Julie est triste parce que sa tante s'est éteinte hier. Julie is sad because her aunt passed away yesterday.

On pourra m'ôter cette vie, mais on n'éteindra pas mon chant. (Aragon) You can take this life from me, but you will not kill my song.

Les pompiers ont éteint l'incendie après une lutte de trois heures. The firemen put out the fire after a three-hour struggle.

Words and expressions related to this verb

éteint, éteinte **extinct, extinguished**

un éteignoir **snuffer, extinguisher**

s'éteindre **to flicker out, to die out, to die**

éteindre le feu **to put out the fire**

éteindre la lumière **to turn off the light**

un extincteur **fire extinguisher**

Arriver pour éteindre les cierges. **To arrive in time to put out the altar candles. (To arrive too late. To arrive after the church service.)**

If you can conjugate **éteindre** you can also conjugate the following verbs:

étreindre **to hug**

restreindre **to restrict**

déteindre **to rub off, lose color**

reteindre **to dye again**

The subject pronouns are found on page 103.

s'étendre (208) Part. pr. s'étendant Part. passé étendu(e)(s)

to stretch oneself, to stretch out, to lie down

Reflexive regular **-re** verb

The Seven Simple Tenses

Singular	Plural
1 présent de l'indicatif	
m'étends	**nous étendons**
t'étends	**vous étendez**
s'étend	**s'étendent**
2 imparfait de l'indicatif	
m'étendais	**nous étendions**
t'étendais	**vous étendiez**
s'étendait	**s'étendaient**
3 passé simple	
m'étendis	**nous étendîmes**
t'étendis	**vous étendîtes**
s'étendit	**s'étendirent**
4 futur	
m'étendrai	**nous étendrons**
t'étendras	**vous étendrez**
s'étendra	**s'étendront**
5 conditionnel	
m'étendrais	**nous étendrions**
t'étendrais	**vous étendriez**
s'étendrait	**s'étendraient**
6 présent du subjonctif	
m'étende	**nous étendions**
t'étendes	**vous étendiez**
s'étende	**s'étendent**
7 imparfait du subjonctif	
m'étendisse	**nous étendissions**
t'étendisses	**vous étendissiez**
s'étendît	**s'étendissent**

The Seven Compound Tenses

Singular	Plural
8 passé composé	
me suis étendu(e)	**nous sommes étendu(e)s**
t'es étendu(e)	**vous êtes étendu(e)(s)**
s'est étendu(e)	**se sont étendu(e)s**
9 plus-que-parfait de l'indicatif	
m'étais étendu(e)	**nous étions étendu(e)s**
t'étais étendu(e)	**vous étiez étendu(e)(s)**
s'était étendu(e)	**s'étaient étendu(e)s**
10 passé antérieur	
me fus étendu(e)	**nous fûmes étendu(e)s**
te fus étendu(e)	**vous fûtes étendu(e)(s)**
se fut étendu(e)	**se furent étendu(e)s**
11 futur antérieur	
me serai étendu(e)	**nous serons étendu(e)s**
te seras étendu(e)	**vous serez étendu(e)(s)**
se sera étendu(e)	**se seront étendu(e)s**
12 conditionnel passé	
me serais étendu(e)	**nous serions étendu(e)s**
te serais étendu(e)	**vous seriez étendu(e)(s)**
se serait étendu(e)	**se seraient étendu(e)s**
13 passé du subjonctif	
me sois étendu(e)	**nous soyons étendu(e)s**
te sois étendu(e)	**vous soyez étendu(e)(s)**
se soit étendu(e)	**se soient étendu(e)s**
14 plus-que-parfait du subjonctif	
me fusse étendu(e)	**nous fussions étendu(e)s**
te fusses étendu(e)	**vous fussiez étendu(e)(s)**
se fût étendu(e)	**se fussent étendu(e)s**

Impératif

étends-toi; ne t'étends pas
étendons-nous; ne nous étendons pas
étendez-vous; ne vous étendez pas

Sentences using this verb and words and expressions related to it

Ma mère était si fatiguée quand elle est rentrée à la maison après avoir fait du shopping, qu'elle est allée directement au lit et elle s'est étendue.

étendre le linge to hang out the wash
étendre d'eau to water down
s'étendre sur qqch to dwell on something
l'étendue *f.* area, extent
s'étendre to stretch

Regular **-er** verb

to amaze, to astonish, to stun, to surprise

The Seven Simple Tenses		The Seven Compound Tenses	
Singular	Plural	Singular	Plural
1 présent de l'indicatif		8 passé composé	
étonne	**étonnons**	**ai étonné**	**avons étonné**
étonnes	**étonnez**	**as étonné**	**avez étonné**
étonne	**étonnent**	**a étonné**	**ont étonné**
2 imparfait de l'indicatif		9 plus-que-parfait de l'indicatif	
étonnais	**étonnions**	**avais étonné**	**avions étonné**
étonnais	**étonniez**	**avais étonné**	**aviez étonné**
étonnait	**étonnaient**	**avait étonné**	**avaient étonné**
3 passé simple		10 passé antérieur	
étonnai	**étonnâmes**	**eus étonné**	**eûmes étonné**
étonnas	**étonnâtes**	**eus étonné**	**eûtes étonné**
étonna	**étonnèrent**	**eut étonné**	**eurent étonné**
4 futur		11 futur antérieur	
étonnerai	**étonnerons**	**aurai étonné**	**aurons étonné**
étonneras	**étonnerez**	**auras étonné**	**aurez étonné**
étonnera	**étonneront**	**aura étonné**	**auront étonné**
5 conditionnel		12 conditionnel passé	
étonnerais	**étonnerions**	**aurais étonné**	**aurions étonné**
étonnerais	**étonneriez**	**aurais étonné**	**auriez étonné**
étonnerait	**étonneraient**	**aurait étonné**	**auraient étonné**
6 présent du subjonctif		13 passé du subjonctif	
étonne	**étonnions**	**aie étonné**	**ayons étonné**
étonnes	**étonniez**	**aies étonné**	**ayez étonné**
étonne	**étonnent**	**ait étonné**	**aient étonné**
7 imparfait du subjonctif		14 plus-que-parfait du subjonctif	
étonnasse	**étonnassions**	**eusse étonné**	**eussions étonné**
étonnasses	**étonnassiez**	**eusses étonné**	**eussiez étonné**
étonnât	**étonnassent**	**eût étonné**	**eussent étonné**

Impératif
étonne
étonnons
étonnez

Words related to this verb

étonnant, étonnante astonishing
C'est bien étonnant! It's quite astonishing!
l'étonnement *m.* astonishment, amazement
s'étonner de to be astonished at
Cela m'étonne! That astonishes me!
Cela ne m'étonne pas! That does not surprise me!

Don't be caught by surprise. Try the verb drills and tests with answers explained on pages 50–101.

étourdir (210) Part. pr. étourdissant Part. passé étourdi

to daze, to stun, to make dizzy, to deafen, to bewilder

Regular **-ir** verb

The Seven Simple Tenses		The Seven Compound Tenses	
Singular	Plural	Singular	Plural
1 présent de l'indicatif		8 passé composé	
étourdis	**étourdissons**	**ai étourdi**	**avons étourdi**
étourdis	**étourdissez**	**as étourdi**	**avez étourdi**
étourdit	**étourdissent**	**a étourdi**	**ont étourdi**
2 imparfait de l'indicatif		9 plus-que-parfait de l'indicatif	
étourdissais	**étourdissions**	**avais étourdi**	**avions étourdi**
étourdissais	**étourdissiez**	**avais étourdi**	**aviez étourdi**
étourdissait	**étourdissaient**	**avait étourdi**	**avaient étourdi**
3 passé simple		10 passé antérieur	
étourdis	**étourdîmes**	**eus étourdi**	**eûmes étourdi**
étourdis	**étourdîtes**	**eus étourdi**	**eûtes étourdi**
étourdit	**étourdirent**	**eut étourdi**	**eurent étourdi**
4 futur		11 futur antérieur	
étourdirai	**étourdirons**	**aurai étourdi**	**aurons étourdi**
étourdiras	**étourdirez**	**auras étourdi**	**aurez étourdi**
étourdira	**étourdiront**	**aura étourdi**	**auront étourdi**
5 conditionnel		12 conditionnel passé	
étourdirais	**étourdirions**	**aurais étourdi**	**aurions étourdi**
étourdirais	**étourdiriez**	**aurais étourdi**	**auriez étourdi**
étourdirait	**étourdiraient**	**aurait étourdi**	**auraient étourdi**
6 présent du subjonctif		13 passé du subjonctif	
étourdisse	**étourdissions**	**aie étourdi**	**ayons étourdi**
étourdisses	**étourdissiez**	**aies étourdi**	**ayez étourdi**
étourdisse	**étourdissent**	**ait étourdi**	**aient étourdi**
7 imparfait du subjonctif		14 plus-que-parfait du subjonctif	
étourdisse	**étourdissions**	**eusse étourdi**	**eussions étourdi**
étourdisses	**étourdissiez**	**eusses étourdi**	**eussiez étourdi**
étourdît	**étourdissent**	**eût étourdi**	**eussent étourdi**

Impératif
étourdis
étourdissons
étourdissez

Words and expressions related to this verb

s'étourdir to lose one's senses in some kind of outlet
une étourderie thoughtlessness, carelessness
un étourdissement giddiness; temporary loss of one's senses
étourdiment thoughtlessly
étourdi, étourdie thoughtless, giddy
par étourderie by an oversight
étourdissant, étourdissante staggering, deafening

Are you bewildered by the Subjunctive? Read pages 26–31.

Irregular verb

to be

The Seven Simple Tenses		The Seven Compound Tenses	
Singular	Plural	Singular	Plural
1 présent de l'indicatif		8 passé composé	
suis	**sommes**	**ai été**	**avons été**
es	**êtes**	**as été**	**avez été**
est	**sont**	**a été**	**ont été**
2 imparfait de l'indicatif		9 plus-que-parfait de l'indicatif	
étais	**étions**	**avais été**	**avions été**
étais	**étiez**	**avais été**	**aviez été**
était	**étaient**	**avait été**	**avaient été**
3 passé simple		10 passé antérieur	
fus	**fûmes**	**eus été**	**eûmes été**
fus	**fûtes**	**eus été**	**eûtes été**
fut	**furent**	**eut été**	**eurent été**
4 futur		11 futur antérieur	
serai	**serons**	**aurai été**	**aurons été**
seras	**serez**	**auras été**	**aurez été**
sera	**seront**	**aura été**	**auront été**
5 conditionnel		12 conditionnel passé	
serais	**serions**	**aurais été**	**aurions été**
serais	**seriez**	**aurais été**	**auriez été**
serait	**seraient**	**aurait été**	**auraient été**
6 présent du subjonctif		13 passé du subjonctif	
sois	**soyons**	**aie été**	**ayons été**
sois	**soyez**	**aies été**	**ayez été**
soit	**soient**	**ait été**	**aient été**
7 imparfait du subjonctif		14 plus-que-parfait du subjonctif	
fusse	**fussions**	**eusse été**	**eussions été**
fusses	**fussiez**	**eusses été**	**eussiez été**
fût	**fussent**	**eût été**	**eussent été**

Impératif
sois
soyons
soyez

The subject pronouns are found on page 103.

AN ESSENTIAL 55 VERB

Être

Être is an obvious choice to be a key verb. It is used as an auxiliary in compound tenses for a number of verbs (see page 6) and it is used in a seemingly endless list of idiomatic expressions.

Sentences using être

Ma soeur est en train d'écrire un courriel à son petit ami. My sister is busy writing an e-mail to her boyfriend.

Je suis à vous. I am at your service.

Madame Paquet est toujours bien mise. Mrs. Paquet is always well dressed.

Je ne suis pas dans mon assiette aujourd'hui. I'm not feeling up to par (quite myself) today.

À quelle heure ta mère sera-t-elle de retour? At what time will your mother be back?

Ma mère est très malade; elle n'est pas en état de vous parler maintenant. My mother is very sick; she isn't able to talk to you now.

Vous êtes toujours le bienvenu chez nous. You are always welcome in our home.

Dépêchons-nous parce que le train est sur le point de partir. Let's hurry because the train is about to leave.

—Quelle heure est-il? What time is it?
—Il est une heure. It is one o'clock.
—Il est trois heures. It is three o'clock.

Ça y est! That's it!

—À qui est ce livre? Whose book is this?
—Ce livre est à moi. This book is mine.

Madame Beaupuy est au courant de tout. Mrs. Beaupuy is informed on (knows about) everything.

Est-ce que vous êtes bien dans cette chaise? Are you comfortable in this chair?

Ainsi soit-il! So be it!

Words and expressions using this verb

le bien-être **well-being**
être à qqn **to belong to someone**
être à l'heure **to be on time**
être à temps **to be in time**
être au courant de **to be informed about**
être bien **to be comfortable**
être bien aise (de) **to be very glad (to)**
être bien mis (mise) **to be well dressed**
être d'accord avec **to agree with**
être dans son assiette **to feel up to par**
être de bonne (mauvaise) humeur **to be in a good (bad) mood**
être de retour **to be back**
être en (bonne) forme **to be in (good) shape**
être en état de + inf. **to be able + inf.**
être en panne **to be broken down, out of order (machine, auto)**
être pressé, être pressée **to be in a hurry**
être en retard **to be late**
être en train de + inf. **to be in the act of + pres. part., to be in the process of, to be busy + pres. part.**
être en vacances **to be on vacation**
être en vie **to be alive**
être enrhumé **to have a cold**
être hors de soi **to be beside oneself, to be upset**
être le bienvenu (la bienvenue) **to be welcome**
être sur le point de + inf. **to be about + inf.**
être temps de + inf. **to be time to + inf.**
De quelle couleur est (sont) . . .? **What color is (are) . . .?**
Il était une fois . . . **Once upon a time there was . . .**
un être humain **human being**

Regular **-er** verb

to study

The Seven Simple Tenses		The Seven Compound Tenses	
Singular	Plural	Singular	Plural
1 présent de l'indicatif		8 passé composé	
étudie	**étudions**	**ai étudié**	**avons étudié**
étudies	**étudiez**	**as étudié**	**avez étudié**
étudie	**étudient**	**a étudié**	**ont étudié**
2 imparfait de l'indicatif		9 plus-que-parfait de l'indicatif	
étudiais	**étudiions**	**avais étudié**	**avions étudié**
étudiais	**étudiiez**	**avais étudié**	**aviez étudié**
étudiait	**étudiaient**	**avait étudié**	**avaient étudié**
3 passé simple		10 passé antérieur	
étudiai	**étudiâmes**	**eus étudié**	**eûmes étudié**
étudias	**étudiâtes**	**eus étudié**	**eûtes étudié**
étudia	**étudièrent**	**eut étudié**	**eurent étudié**
4 futur		11 futur antérieur	
étudierai	**étudierons**	**aurai étudié**	**aurons étudié**
étudieras	**étudierez**	**auras étudié**	**aurez étudié**
étudiera	**étudieront**	**aura étudié**	**auront étudié**
5 conditionnel		12 conditionnel passé	
étudierais	**étudierions**	**aurais étudié**	**aurions étudié**
étudierais	**étudieriez**	**aurais étudié**	**auriez étudié**
étudierait	**étudieraient**	**aurait étudié**	**auraient étudié**
6 présent du subjonctif		13 passé du subjonctif	
étudie	**étudiions**	**aie étudié**	**ayons étudié**
étudies	**étudiiez**	**aies étudié**	**ayez étudié**
étudie	**étudient**	**ait étudié**	**aient étudié**
7 imparfait du subjonctif		14 plus-que-parfait du subjonctif	
étudiasse	**étudiassions**	**eusse étudié**	**eussions étudié**
étudiasses	**étudiassiez**	**eusses étudié**	**eussiez étudié**
étudiât	**étudiassent**	**eût étudié**	**eussent étudié**

Impératif
étudie
étudions
étudiez

AN ESSENTIAL 55 VERB

Étudier

Étudier is a very useful verb for a beginning French student. As you study this verb, be careful about the **ii** in the **nous** and **vous** forms of the **imparfait** and the **présent du subjonctif**.

Sentences using étudier and related words

Ma tante étudie le piano depuis dix ans. My aunt has been studying piano for ten years.

Le dossier de Monsieur Pompier est à l'étude. Mr. Pompier's file is under study.

Thomas fait ses études à l'Université de Grenoble. Thomas is studying at the University of Grenoble.

—Depuis combien de temps étudiez-vous le français? How long have you been studying French?
—J'étudie le français depuis deux ans. I have been studying French for two years.

Words and expressions using this verb

un étudiant, une étudiante student

l'étude *f.* study

les études *f.* studies

une salle d'études study hall

étudier à fond to study thoroughly

faire ses études to study, to go to school

à l'étude under consideration, under study

s'étudier to analyze oneself

étudier qqch de près to study something closely

s'amuser au lieu d'étudier to have a good time instead of studying

If you can conjugate **étudier** you can also conjugate these verbs:

apprécier to appreciate
balbutier to stammer
certifier to guarantee
clarifier to clarify
classifier to classify
copier to copy
identifier to identify
justifier to justify
planifier to plan
skier to ski

Regular **-er** verb

to evaluate, to appraise, to assess, to estimate

The Seven Simple Tenses		The Seven Compound Tenses	
Singular	Plural	Singular	Plural
1 présent de l'indicatif		8 passé composé	
évalue	**évaluons**	**ai évalué**	**avons évalué**
évalues	**évaluez**	**as évalué**	**avez évalué**
évalue	**évaluent**	**a évalué**	**ont évalué**
2 imparfait de l'indicatif		9 plus-que-parfait de l'indicatif	
évaluais	**évaluions**	**avais évalué**	**avions évalué**
évaluais	**évaluiez**	**avais évalué**	**aviez évalué**
évaluait	**évaluaient**	**avait évalué**	**avaient évalué**
3 passé simple		10 passé antérieur	
évaluai	**évaluâmes**	**eus évalué**	**eûmes évalué**
évaluas	**évaluâtes**	**eus évalué**	**eûtes évalué**
évalua	**évaluèrent**	**eut évalué**	**eurent évalué**
4 futur		11 futur antérieur	
évaluerai	**évaluerons**	**aurai évalué**	**aurons évalué**
évalueras	**évaluerez**	**auras évalué**	**aurez évalué**
évaluera	**évalueront**	**aura évalué**	**auront évalué**
5 conditionnel		12 conditionnel passé	
évaluerais	**évaluerions**	**aurais évalué**	**aurions évalué**
évaluerais	**évalueriez**	**aurais évalué**	**auriez évalué**
évaluerait	**évalueraient**	**aurait évalué**	**auraient évalué**
6 présent du subjonctif		13 passé du subjonctif	
évalue	**évaluions**	**aie évalué**	**ayons évalué**
évalues	**évaluiez**	**aies évalué**	**ayez évalué**
évalue	**évaluent**	**ait évalué**	**aient évalué**
7 imparfait du subjonctif		14 plus-que-parfait du subjonctif	
évaluasse	**évaluassions**	**eusse évalué**	**eussions évalué**
évaluasses	**évaluassiez**	**eusses évalué**	**eussiez évalué**
évaluât	**évaluassent**	**eût évalué**	**eussent évalué**

Impératif
évalue
évaluons
évaluez

Words and expressions related to this verb

une évaluation evaluation, estimate, assessment
de valeur valuable, of value
valable valid
mettre en valeur to emphasize, to enhance
faire évaluer qqch par un expert to have something appraised by an expert
valablement validly
valeureusement valorously
la valeur value, valor

Can't find the verb you're looking for? Check the back pages of this book for a list of over 2,600 additional verbs!

s'évanouir (214) Part. pr. s'évanouissant Part. passé évanoui

to faint, to lose consciousness, to swoon, to vanish

Reflexive regular **-ir** verb

The Seven Simple Tenses		The Seven Compound Tenses	
Singular	Plural	Singular	Plural
1 présent de l'indicatif		8 passé composé	
m'évanouis	**nous évanouissons**	**me suis évanoui(e)**	**nous sommes évanoui(e)s**
t'évanouis	**vous évanouissez**	**t'es évanoui(e)**	**vous êtes évanoui(e)(s)**
s'évanouit	**s'évanouissent**	**s'est évanoui(e)**	**se sont évanoui(e)s**
2 imparfait de l'indicatif		9 plus-que-parfait de l'indicatif	
m'évanouissais	**nous évanouissions**	**m'étais évanoui(e)**	**nous étions évanoui(e)s**
t'évanouissais	**vous évanouissiez**	**t'étais évanoui(e)**	**vous étiez évanoui(e)(s)**
s'évanouissait	**s'évanouissaient**	**s'était évanoui(e)**	**s'étaient évanoui(e)s**
3 passé simple		10 passé antérieur	
m'évanouis	**nous évanouîmes**	**me fus évanoui(e)**	**nous fûmes évanoui(e)s**
t'évanouis	**vous évanouîtes**	**te fus évanoui(e)**	**vous fûtes évanoui(e)(s)**
s'évanouit	**s'évanouirent**	**se fut évanoui(e)**	**se furent évanoui(e)s**
4 futur		11 futur antérieur	
m'évanouirai	**nous évanouirons**	**me serai évanoui(e)**	**nous serons évanoui(e)s**
t'évanouiras	**vous évanouirez**	**te seras évanoui(e)**	**vous serez évanoui(e)(s)**
s'évanouira	**s'évanouiront**	**se sera évanoui(e)**	**se seront évanoui(e)s**
5 conditionnel		12 conditionnel passé	
m'évanouirais	**nous évanouirions**	**me serais évanoui(e)**	**nous serions évanoui(e)s**
t'évanouirais	**vous évanouiriez**	**te serais évanoui(e)**	**vous seriez évanoui(e)(s)**
s'évanouirait	**s'évanouiraient**	**se serait évanoui(e)**	**se seraient évanoui(e)s**
6 présent du subjonctif		13 passé du subjonctif	
m'évanouisse	**nous évanouissions**	**me sois évanoui(e)**	**nous soyons évanoui(e)s**
t'évanouisses	**vous évanouissiez**	**te sois évanoui(e)**	**vous soyez évanoui(e)(s)**
s'évanouisse	**s'évanouissent**	**se soit évanoui(e)**	**se soient évanoui(e)s**
7 imparfait du subjonctif		14 plus-que-parfait du subjonctif	
m'évanouisse	**nous évanouissions**	**me fusse évanoui(e)**	**nous fussions évanoui(e)s**
t'évanouisses	**vous évanouissiez**	**te fusses évanoui(e)**	**vous fussiez évanoui(e)(s)**
s'évanouît	**s'évanouissent**	**se fût évanoui(e)**	**se fussent évanoui(e)s**

Impératif
évanouis-toi; ne t'évanouis pas
évanouissons-nous; ne nous évanouissons pas
évanouissez-vous; ne vous évanouissez pas

Words and expressions related to this verb

un évanouissement faint, fading
un rêve évanoui vanished dream
tomber évanoui, évanouie to faint, to pass out
évanoui, évanouie unconscious, fainted, in a faint; vanished
revenir d'un évanouissement to come out of a faint

Grammar putting you in a tense mood? Review the definitions of basic grammatical terms with examples on pages 35–49.

Regular **-er** verb

to avoid

The Seven Simple Tenses		The Seven Compound Tenses	
Singular	Plural	Singular	Plural
1 présent de l'indicatif		8 passé composé	
évite	**évitons**	**ai évité**	**avons évité**
évites	**évitez**	**as évité**	**avez évité**
évite	**évitent**	**a évité**	**ont évité**
2 imparfait de l'indicatif		9 plus-que-parfait de l'indicatif	
évitais	**évitions**	**avais évité**	**avions évité**
évitais	**évitiez**	**avais évité**	**aviez évité**
évitait	**évitaient**	**avait évité**	**avaient évité**
3 passé simple		10 passé antérieur	
évitai	**évitâmes**	**eus évité**	**eûmes évité**
évitas	**évitâtes**	**eus évité**	**eûtes évité**
évita	**évitèrent**	**eut évité**	**eurent évité**
4 futur		11 futur antérieur	
éviterai	**éviterons**	**aurai évité**	**aurons évité**
éviteras	**éviterez**	**auras évité**	**aurez évité**
évitera	**éviteront**	**aura évité**	**auront évité**
5 conditionnel		12 conditionnel passé	
éviterais	**éviterions**	**aurais évité**	**aurions évité**
éviterais	**éviteriez**	**aurais évité**	**auriez évité**
éviterait	**éviteraient**	**aurait évité**	**auraient évité**
6 présent du subjonctif		13 passé du subjonctif	
évite	**évitions**	**aie évité**	**ayons évité**
évites	**évitiez**	**aies évité**	**ayez évité**
évite	**évitent**	**ait évité**	**aient évité**
7 imparfait du subjonctif		14 plus-que-parfait du subjonctif	
évitasse	**évitassions**	**eusse évité**	**eussions évité**
évitasses	**évitassiez**	**eusses évité**	**eussiez évité**
évitât	**évitassent**	**eût évité**	**eussent évité**

Impératif
évite
évitons
évitez

Words and expressions related to this verb
éviter de faire qqch to avoid doing something
éviter à qqn la peine de faire qqch to spare someone the trouble of doing something
évitable avoidable
inévitable inevitable, unavoidable
inévitablement inevitably, unavoidably

Get acquainted with what preposition goes with what verb. See *Verbs with prepositions* in the Appendixes.

to excuse

Regular **-er** verb

The Seven Simple Tenses		The Seven Compound Tenses	
Singular	Plural	Singular	Plural
1 présent de l'indicatif		8 passé composé	
excuse	**excusons**	**ai excusé**	**avons excusé**
excuses	**excusez**	**as excusé**	**avez excusé**
excuse	**excusent**	**a excusé**	**ont excusé**
2 imparfait de l'indicatif		9 plus-que-parfait de l'indicatif	
excusais	**excusions**	**avais excusé**	**avions excusé**
excusais	**excusiez**	**avais excusé**	**aviez excusé**
excusait	**excusaient**	**avait excusé**	**avaient excusé**
3 passé simple		10 passé antérieur	
excusai	**excusâmes**	**eus excusé**	**eûmes excusé**
excusas	**excusâtes**	**eus excusé**	**eûtes excusé**
excusa	**excusèrent**	**eut excusé**	**eurent excusé**
4 futur		11 futur antérieur	
excuserai	**excuserons**	**aurai excusé**	**aurons excusé**
excuseras	**excuserez**	**auras excusé**	**aurez excusé**
excusera	**excuseront**	**aura excusé**	**auront excusé**
5 conditionnel		12 conditionnel passé	
excuserais	**excuserions**	**aurais excusé**	**aurions excusé**
excuserais	**excuseriez**	**aurais excusé**	**auriez excusé**
excuserait	**excuseraient**	**aurait excusé**	**auraient excusé**
6 présent du subjonctif		13 passé du subjonctif	
excuse	**excusions**	**aie excusé**	**ayons excusé**
excuses	**excusiez**	**aies excusé**	**ayez excusé**
excuse	**excusent**	**ait excusé**	**aient excusé**
7 imparfait du subjonctif		14 plus-que-parfait du subjonctif	
excusasse	**excusassions**	**eusse excusé**	**eussions excusé**
excusasses	**excusassiez**	**eusses excusé**	**eussiez excusé**
excusât	**excusassent**	**eût excusé**	**eussent excusé**

Impératif
excuse
excusons
excusez

Words and expressions related to this verb
excuser de to excuse from (for)
excuser qqn de faire qqch to excuse someone from doing something; to excuse someone's doing something
se faire excuser to ask to be excused
une excuse excuse
faire ses excuses à qqn pour qqch to apologize to someone for something
Mille excuses! Excuse me! (a thousand pardons)

See also **s'excuser.**

Can't remember the French verb you need? Check the back pages of this book for the English-French verb index!

Reflexive regular **-er** verb

to excuse oneself, to apologize

The Seven Simple Tenses		The Seven Compound Tenses	
Singular	Plural	Singular	Plural
1 présent de l'indicatif		8 passé composé	
m'excuse	**nous excusons**	**me suis excusé(e)**	**nous sommes excusé(e)s**
t'excuses	**vous excusez**	**t'es excusé(e)**	**vous êtes excusé(e)(s)**
s'excuse	**s'excusent**	**s'est excusé(e)**	**se sont excusé(e)s**
2 imparfait de l'indicatif		9 plus-que-parfait de l'indicatif	
m'excusais	**nous excusions**	**m'étais excusé(e)**	**nous étions excusé(e)s**
t'excusais	**vous excusiez**	**t'étais excusé(e)**	**vous étiez excusé(e)(s)**
s'excusait	**s'excusaient**	**s'était excusé(e)**	**s'étaient excusé(e)s**
3 passé simple		10 passé antérieur	
m'excusai	**nous excusâmes**	**me fus excusé(e)**	**nous fûmes excusé(e)s**
t'excusas	**vous excusâtes**	**te fus excusé(e)**	**vous fûtes excusé(e)(s)**
s'excusa	**s'excusèrent**	**se fut excusé(e)**	**se furent excusé(e)s**
4 futur		11 futur antérieur	
m'excuserai	**nous excuserons**	**me serai excusé(e)**	**nous serons excusé(e)s**
t'excuseras	**vous excuserez**	**te seras excusé(e)**	**vous serez excusé(e)(s)**
s'excusera	**s'excuseront**	**se sera excusé(e)**	**se seront excusé(e)s**
5 conditionnel		12 conditionnel passé	
m'excuserais	**nous excuserions**	**me serais excusé(e)**	**nous serions excusé(e)s**
t'excuserais	**vous excuseriez**	**te serais excusé(e)**	**vous seriez excusé(e)(s)**
s'excuserait	**s'excuseraient**	**se serait excusé(e)**	**se seraient excusé(e)s**
6 présent du subjonctif		13 passé du subjonctif	
m'excuse	**nous excusions**	**me sois excusé(e)**	**nous soyons excusé(e)s**
t'excuses	**vous excusiez**	**te sois excusé(e)**	**vous soyez excusé(e)(s)**
s'excuse	**s'excusent**	**se soit excusé(e)**	**se soient excusé(e)s**
7 imparfait du subjonctif		14 plus-que-parfait du subjonctif	
m'excusasse	**nous excusassions**	**me fusse excusé(e)**	**nous fussions excusé(e)s**
t'excusasses	**vous excusassiez**	**te fusses excusé(e)**	**vous fussiez excusé(e)(s)**
s'excusât	**s'excusassent**	**se fût excusé(e)**	**se fussent excusé(e)s**

Impératif
excuse-toi; ne t'excuse pas
excusons-nous; ne nous excusons pas
excusez-vous; ne vous excusez pas

Sentences using this verb and words and expressions related to it

L'élève: **Je m'excuse, madame. Excusez-moi. Je m'excuse de vous déranger. Est-ce que vous m'excusez? Est-ce que je vous dérange?**
La maîtresse: **Oui, je t'excuse. Non, tu ne me déranges pas. Que veux-tu?**
L'élève: **Est-ce que je peux quitter la salle de classe pour aller aux toilettes?**
La maîtresse: **Oui, vas-y.**

s'excuser de to apologize for
Veuillez m'excuser. Please (Be good enough to) excuse me.
Qui s'excuse s'accuse. A guilty conscience needs no accuser.

Don't forget to study the section on defective and impersonal verbs. It's right after this main list.

exiger (218) — Part. pr. **exigeant** — Part. passé **exigé**

to demand, to require

Regular **-er** verb endings; spelling change: retain the **ge** before **a** or **o** to keep the soft **g** sound of the verb

The Seven Simple Tenses		The Seven Compound Tenses	
Singular	Plural	Singular	Plural
1 présent de l'indicatif		8 passé composé	
exige	**exigeons**	**ai exigé**	**avons exigé**
exiges	**exigez**	**as exigé**	**avez exigé**
exige	**exigent**	**a exigé**	**ont exigé**
2 imparfait de l'indicatif		9 plus-que-parfait de l'indicatif	
exigeais	**exigions**	**avais exigé**	**avions exigé**
exigeais	**exigiez**	**avais exigé**	**aviez exigé**
exigeait	**exigeaient**	**avait exigé**	**avaient exigé**
3 passé simple		10 passé antérieur	
exigeai	**exigeâmes**	**eus exigé**	**eûmes exigé**
exigeas	**exigeâtes**	**eus exigé**	**eûtes exigé**
exigea	**exigèrent**	**eut exigé**	**eurent exigé**
4 futur		11 futur antérieur	
exigerai	**exigerons**	**aurai exigé**	**aurons exigé**
exigeras	**exigerez**	**auras exigé**	**aurez exigé**
exigera	**exigeront**	**aura exigé**	**auront exigé**
5 conditionnel		12 conditionnel passé	
exigerais	**exigerions**	**aurais exigé**	**aurions exigé**
exigerais	**exigeriez**	**aurais exigé**	**auriez exigé**
exigerait	**exigeraient**	**aurait exigé**	**auraient exigé**
6 présent du subjonctif		13 passé du subjonctif	
exige	**exigions**	**aie exigé**	**ayons exigé**
exiges	**exigiez**	**aies exigé**	**ayez exigé**
exige	**exigent**	**ait exigé**	**aient exigé**
7 imparfait du subjonctif		14 plus-que-parfait du subjonctif	
exigeasse	**exigeassions**	**eusse exigé**	**eussions exigé**
exigeasses	**exigeassiez**	**eusses exigé**	**eussiez exigé**
exigeât	**exigeassent**	**eût exigé**	**eussent exigé**

Impératif
exige
exigeons
exigez

Sentences using this verb and words related to it

La maîtresse de français: **Paul, viens ici. Ta composition est pleine de fautes. J'exige que tu la refasses. Rends-la-moi dans dix minutes.**

L'élève: **Ce n'est pas de ma faute, madame. C'est mon père qui l'a écrite. Dois-je la refaire?**

exigeant, exigeante exacting
l'exigence *f.* exigency
exiger des soins attentifs to demand great care
les exigences requirements

Soak up some verbs used in weather expressions. There's a list in the Appendixes!

Regular **-er** verb

to explain

The Seven Simple Tenses		The Seven Compound Tenses	
Singular	Plural	Singular	Plural
1 présent de l'indicatif		8 passé composé	
explique	**expliquons**	**ai expliqué**	**avons expliqué**
expliques	**expliquez**	**as expliqué**	**avez expliqué**
explique	**expliquent**	**a expliqué**	**ont expliqué**
2 imparfait de l'indicatif		9 plus-que-parfait de l'indicatif	
expliquais	**expliquions**	**avais expliqué**	**avions expliqué**
expliquais	**expliquiez**	**avais expliqué**	**aviez expliqué**
expliquait	**expliquaient**	**avait expliqué**	**avaient expliqué**
3 passé simple		10 passé antérieur	
expliquai	**expliquâmes**	**eus expliqué**	**eûmes expliqué**
expliquas	**expliquâtes**	**eus expliqué**	**eûtes expliqué**
expliqua	**expliquèrent**	**eut expliqué**	**eurent expliqué**
4 futur		11 futur antérieur	
expliquerai	**expliquerons**	**aurai expliqué**	**aurons expliqué**
expliqueras	**expliquerez**	**auras expliqué**	**aurez expliqué**
expliquera	**expliqueront**	**aura expliqué**	**auront expliqué**
5 conditionnel		12 conditionnel passé	
expliquerais	**expliquerions**	**aurais expliqué**	**aurions expliqué**
expliquerais	**expliqueriez**	**aurais expliqué**	**auriez expliqué**
expliquerait	**expliqueraient**	**aurait expliqué**	**auraient expliqué**
6 présent du subjonctif		13 passé du subjonctif	
explique	**expliquions**	**aie expliqué**	**ayons expliqué**
expliques	**expliquiez**	**aies expliqué**	**ayez expliqué**
explique	**expliquent**	**ait expliqué**	**aient expliqué**
7 imparfait du subjonctif		14 plus-que-parfait du subjonctif	
expliquasse	**expliquassions**	**eusse expliqué**	**eussions expliqué**
expliquasses	**expliquassiez**	**eusses expliqué**	**eussiez expliqué**
expliquât	**expliquassent**	**eût expliqué**	**eussent expliqué**

Impératif
explique
expliquons
expliquez

Words related to this verb
explicite explicit
explicitement explicitly
l'explication *f.* explanation
une explication de texte interpretation, critical analysis of a text
explicable explainable
explicatif, explicative explanatory
s'expliciter to be explicit

Note the difference in meaning in the following two sentences. See page 17 (b).

J'ai étudié la leçon que le professeur avait expliquée. I studied the lesson that the teacher had explained.
J'avais étudié la leçon que le professeur a expliquée. I had studied the lesson that the teacher explained.

exprimer (220) — Part. pr. exprimant — Part. passé exprimé

to express

Regular **-er** verb

The Seven Simple Tenses		The Seven Compound Tenses	
Singular	Plural	Singular	Plural
1 présent de l'indicatif		8 passé composé	
exprime	**exprimons**	**ai exprimé**	**avons exprimé**
exprimes	**exprimez**	**as exprimé**	**avez exprimé**
exprime	**expriment**	**a exprimé**	**ont exprimé**
2 imparfait de l'indicatif		9 plus-que-parfait de l'indicatif	
exprimais	**exprimions**	**avais exprimé**	**avions exprimé**
exprimais	**exprimiez**	**avais exprimé**	**aviez exprimé**
exprimait	**exprimaient**	**avait exprimé**	**avaient exprimé**
3 passé simple		10 passé antérieur	
exprimai	**exprimâmes**	**eus exprimé**	**eûmes exprimé**
exprimas	**exprimâtes**	**eus exprimé**	**eûtes exprimé**
exprima	**exprimèrent**	**eut exprimé**	**eurent exprimé**
4 futur		11 futur antérieur	
exprimerai	**exprimerons**	**aurai exprimé**	**aurons exprimé**
exprimeras	**exprimerez**	**auras exprimé**	**aurez exprimé**
exprimera	**exprimeront**	**aura exprimé**	**auront exprimé**
5 conditionnel		12 conditionnel passé	
exprimerais	**exprimerions**	**aurais exprimé**	**aurions exprimé**
exprimerais	**exprimeriez**	**aurais exprimé**	**auriez exprimé**
exprimerait	**exprimeraient**	**aurait exprimé**	**auraient exprimé**
6 présent du subjonctif		13 passé du subjonctif	
exprime	**exprimions**	**aie exprimé**	**ayons exprimé**
exprimes	**exprimiez**	**aies exprimé**	**ayez exprimé**
exprime	**expriment**	**ait exprimé**	**aient exprimé**
7 imparfait du subjonctif		14 plus-que-parfait du subjonctif	
exprimasse	**exprimassions**	**eusse exprimé**	**eussions exprimé**
exprimasses	**exprimassiez**	**eusses exprimé**	**eussiez exprimé**
exprimât	**exprimassent**	**eût exprimé**	**eussent exprimé**

Impératif
exprime
exprimons
exprimez

Words and expressions related to this verb

exprimer ses voeux to express (convey) one's wishes
exprimable expressible
une expression expression; **expression des sentiments** expression of feelings

Closing of letter:

Agréez, Monsieur (Madame), l'expression de mes sentiments distingués Sincerely
s'exprimer to express oneself
s'exprimer par gestes to express oneself with gestures

Can't find the verb you're looking for? Check the back pages of this book for a list of over 2,600 additional verbs!

Reflexive regular **-er** verb

to become angry, to get angry

The Seven Simple Tenses		The Seven Compound Tenses	
Singular	Plural	Singular	Plural
1 présent de l'indicatif		8 passé composé	
me fâche	**nous fâchons**	**me suis fâché(e)**	**nous sommes fâché(e)s**
te fâches	**vous fâchez**	**t'es fâché(e)**	**vous êtes fâché(e)(s)**
se fâche	**se fâchent**	**s'est fâché(e)**	**se sont fâché(e)s**
2 imparfait de l'indicatif		9 plus-que-parfait de l'indicatif	
me fâchais	**nous fâchions**	**m'étais fâché(e)**	**nous étions fâché(e)s**
te fâchais	**vous fâchiez**	**t'étais fâché(e)**	**vous étiez fâché(e)(s)**
se fâchait	**se fâchaient**	**s'était fâché(e)**	**s'étaient fâché(e)s**
3 passé simple		10 passé antérieur	
me fâchai	**nous fâchâmes**	**me fus fâché(e)**	**nous fûmes fâché(e)s**
te fâchas	**vous fâchâtes**	**te fus fâché(e)**	**vous fûtes fâché(e)(s)**
se fâcha	**se fâchèrent**	**se fut fâché(e)**	**se furent fâché(e)s**
4 futur		11 futur antérieur	
me fâcherai	**nous fâcherons**	**me serai fâché(e)**	**nous serons fâché(e)s**
te fâcheras	**vous fâcherez**	**te seras fâché(e)**	**vous serez fâché(e)(s)**
se fâchera	**se fâcheront**	**se sera fâché(e)**	**se seront fâché(e)s**
5 conditionnel		12 conditionnel passé	
me fâcherais	**nous fâcherions**	**me serais fâché(e)**	**nous serions fâché(e)s**
te fâcherais	**vous fâcheriez**	**te serais fâché(e)**	**vous seriez fâché(e)(s)**
se fâcherait	**se fâcheraient**	**se serait fâché(e)**	**se seraient fâché(e)s**
6 présent du subjonctif		13 passé du subjonctif	
me fâche	**nous fâchions**	**me sois fâché(e)**	**nous soyons fâché(e)s**
te fâches	**vous fâchiez**	**te sois fâché(e)**	**vous soyez fâché(e)(s)**
se fâche	**se fâchent**	**se soit fâché(e)**	**se soient fâché(e)s**
7 imparfait du subjonctif		14 plus-que-parfait du subjonctif	
me fâchasse	**nous fâchassions**	**me fusse fâché(e)**	**nous fussions fâché(e)s**
te fâchasses	**vous fâchassiez**	**te fusses fâché(e)**	**vous fussiez fâché(e)(s)**
se fâchât	**se fâchassent**	**se fût fâché(e)**	**se fussent fâché(e)s**

Impératif
fâche-toi; ne te fâche pas
fâchons-nous; ne nous fâchons pas
fâchez-vous; ne vous fâchez pas

Words and expressions related to this verb

fâcher qqn to anger someone, to offend someone
se fâcher contre qqn to become angry at someone
une fâcherie tiff, quarrel
C'est fâcheux! It's a nuisance! It's annoying!
fâcheusement awkwardly, unfortunately
se fâcher tout rouge to turn red with anger

How are you doing? Find out with the verb drills and tests with answers explained on pages 50–101.

faillir (222) — Part. pr. faillant — Part. passé failli

to fail, to almost (do something)

Irregular verb

The Seven Simple Tenses		The Seven Compound Tenses	
Singular	Plural	Singular	Plural
1 présent de l'indicatif		8 passé composé	
faux	**faillons**	**ai failli**	**avons failli**
faux	**faillez**	**as failli**	**avez failli**
faut	**faillent**	**a failli**	**ont failli**
2 imparfait de l'indicatif		9 plus-que-parfait de l'indicatif	
faillais	**faillions**	**avais failli**	**avions failli**
faillais	**failliez**	**avais failli**	**aviez failli**
faillait	**faillaient**	**avait failli**	**avaient failli**
3 passé simple		10 passé antérieur	
faillis	**faillîmes**	**eus failli**	**eûmes failli**
faillis	**faillîtes**	**eus failli**	**eûtes failli**
faillit	**faillirent**	**eut failli**	**eurent failli**
4 futur		11 futur antérieur	
faillirai or faudrai	**faillirons or faudrons**	**aurai failli**	**aurons failli**
failliras or faudras	**faillirez or faudrez**	**auras failli**	**aurez failli**
faillira or faudra	**failliront or faudront**	**aura failli**	**auront failli**
5 conditionnel		12 conditionnel passé	
faillirais or faudrais	**faillirions or faudrions**	**aurais failli**	**aurions failli**
faillirais or faudrais	**failliriez or faudriez**	**aurais failli**	**auriez failli**
faillirait or faudrait	**failliraient or faudraient**	**aurait failli**	**auraient failli**
6 présent du subjonctif		13 passé du subjonctif	
faille	**faillions**	**aie failli**	**ayons failli**
failles	**failliez**	**aies failli**	**ayez failli**
faille	**faillent**	**ait failli**	**aient failli**
7 imparfait du subjonctif		14 plus-que-parfait du subjonctif	
faillisse	**faillissions**	**eusse failli**	**eussions failli**
faillisses	**faillissiez**	**eusses failli**	**eussiez failli**
faillît	**faillissent**	**eût failli**	**eussent failli**

Impératif
[not in use]

Words and expressions related to this verb

la faillite bankruptcy, failure
failli, faillie bankrupt
faillir + inf. to almost do something
J'ai failli tomber. I almost fell.
faire faillite to go bankrupt
défaillir to weaken, to faint
défaillant, défaillante feeble
une défaillance faint (swoon)
être en faillite to be bankrupt

The conjugated forms of this verb are used most of the time in the **passé simple** and compound tenses. The other tenses are rarely used.

Irregular verb

to do, to make

The Seven Simple Tenses		The Seven Compound Tenses	
Singular	Plural	Singular	Plural
1 présent de l'indicatif		8 passé composé	
fais	**faisons**	**ai fait**	**avons fait**
fais	**faites**	**as fait**	**avez fait**
fait	**font**	**a fait**	**ont fait**
2 imparfait de l'indicatif		9 plus-que-parfait de l'indicatif	
faisais	**faisions**	**avais fait**	**avions fait**
faisais	**faisiez**	**avais fait**	**aviez fait**
faisait	**faisaient**	**avait fait**	**avaient fait**
3 passé simple		10 passé antérieur	
fis	**fîmes**	**eus fait**	**eûmes fait**
fis	**fîtes**	**eus fait**	**eûtes fait**
fit	**firent**	**eut fait**	**eurent fait**
4 futur		11 futur antérieur	
ferai	**ferons**	**aurai fait**	**aurons fait**
feras	**ferez**	**auras fait**	**aurez fait**
fera	**feront**	**aura fait**	**auront fait**
5 conditionnel		12 conditionnel passé	
ferais	**ferions**	**aurais fait**	**aurions fait**
ferais	**feriez**	**aurais fait**	**auriez fait**
ferait	**feraient**	**aurait fait**	**auraient fait**
6 présent du subjonctif		13 passé du subjonctif	
fasse	**fassions**	**aie fait**	**ayons fait**
fasses	**fassiez**	**aies fait**	**ayez fait**
fasse	**fassent**	**ait fait**	**aient fait**
7 imparfait du subjonctif		14 plus-que-parfait du subjonctif	
fisse	**fissions**	**eusse fait**	**eussions fait**
fisses	**fissiez**	**eusses fait**	**eussiez fait**
fît	**fissent**	**eût fait**	**eussent fait**

Impératif
fais
faisons
faites

F

AN ESSENTIAL 55 VERB

Faire

Faire is a verb that a beginning French student should find very useful. It is so useful that we have given it an extra page!

Sentences using faire

Cela ne fait rien. That doesn't matter. That makes no difference.

Ma mère a fait faire une jolie robe. My mother had a pretty dress made.

Quel temps fait-il? What's the weather like?

Il fait beau aujourd'hui. The weather's nice today.

Il fait très froid ce matin. It's very cold this morning.

Il a fait très chaud hier. It was very warm yesterday.

Faites comme chez vous! (formal, plural) Make yourself/yourselves at home!

Fais comme chez toi! (informal) Make yourself at home!

Cela lui fera du bien. That will do her (him) some good.

Que faire? What is to be done?

Mon père a fait venir le médecin parce que ma mère est malade. My father had the doctor come because my mother is sick.

Faisons le tour du parc. Let's go around the park.

Ce grand garçon-là a fait mal à mon petit frère. That big boy hurt my little brother.

Je leur ai fait part du mariage de mon fils. I notified them of the marriage of my son.

Faites suivre mes lettres, s'il vous plaît. Forward my letters please.

Ma fille fait ses études à l'Université de Montréal. My daughter is studying at the University of Montreal.

Est-il nécessaire de faire la correspondance? Dans quelle direction? Is it necessary to transfer (change trains)? In what direction?

Proverb

Bien faire et laisser dire. Do your work well and never mind the critics.

Words and expressions related to this verb

aussitôt dit aussitôt fait (aussitôt dit que fait) no sooner said than done

Comment se fait-il . . .? How come . . .?

en faire autant to do the same, to do as much

faire + inf. to have something done

Note: When you use **faire** with another verb, this is the causative **faire** (see page 37). Example: **Mon père fait peindre la maison.** My father is having the house painted. [That is, someone else does the action.]

faire faire to have something made (done)

faire à sa tête to have one's way

faire attention (à) to pay attention (to)

faire beau to be pleasant, nice weather

faire mauvais to be bad weather

faire bon accueil to welcome

faire chaud to be warm (weather)

(Continued on next page)

faire comme chez soi **to make oneself at home**

faire d'une pierre deux coups **to kill two birds with one stone**

faire de l'autostop, faire du pouce **to hitchhike**

faire de la peine à qqn **to hurt someone (morally, emotionally)**

faire de son mieux **to do one's best**

faire des châteaux en Espagne **to build castles in the air**

faire des cours **to give courses, to lecture**

faire des emplettes, faire des courses, faire des achats, faire du shopping **to go shopping**

faire des progrès **to make progress**

faire du bien à qqn **to do good for someone**

faire du ski **to ski**

faire du sport **to play sports**

faire du vélo **to ride a bike**

faire exprès **to do on purpose**

faire face à **to oppose**

faire fi **to scorn**

faire froid **to be cold (weather)**

faire jour **to be daylight**

faire la bête **to act like a fool**

faire la connaissance de qqn **to make the acquaintance of someone, to meet someone for the first time**

faire la cuisine **to do the cooking**

faire la grasse matinée **to sleep late in the morning**

faire la lessive **to do the laundry**

faire la malle **to pack the trunk**

faire la queue **to line up, to get in line, to stand in line, to queue up**

faire la sourde oreille **to turn a deaf ear, to pretend not to hear**

faire la vaisselle **to do (wash) the dishes**

faire le ménage **to do housework**

faire le tour de **to take a stroll, to go around**

faire les bagages **to pack the baggage, luggage**

faire les valises **to pack the suitcases, valises**

faire mal à qqn **to hurt, to harm someone**

faire mon affaire **to suit me, to be just the thing for me**

faire nuit **to be night(time)**

faire part à qqn **to inform someone**

faire part de qqch à qqn **to let someone know about something, to inform, to notify someone of something**

faire partie de **to be a part of**

faire peur à qqn **to frighten someone**

faire plaisir à qqn **to please someone**

faire sa toilette **to wash up**

faire savoir qqch à qqn **to inform someone of something**

faire semblant de + inf. **to pretend + inf.**

faire ses adieux **to say goodbye**

faire ses amitiés à qqn **to give one's regards to someone**

faire ses études à **to study at**

faire son lit **to make one's bed**

faire son possible **to do one's best (utmost)**

faire suivre **to forward mail**

faire un appel (téléphonique) **to make a (telephone) call**

faire un cours **to give a course, to lecture**

faire un tour **to go for a stroll**

faire un voyage **to take a trip**

faire une partie de **to play a game of**

faire une plainte **to make a complaint**

faire une promenade **to take a walk**

faire une promenade en voiture **to go for a drive**

faire une question **to ask (to pose) a question**

faire une réclamation **to make a complaint**

faire une visite **to pay a visit**

faire venir qqn **to have someone come**

faire venir l'eau à la bouche **to make one's mouth water**

The subject pronouns are found on page 103.

feindre (224) Part. pr. feignant Part. passé feint

to feign, to make believe, to pretend, to simulate

Irregular verb

The Seven Simple Tenses		The Seven Compound Tenses	
Singular	Plural	Singular	Plural
1 présent de l'indicatif		8 passé composé	
feins	**feignons**	**ai feint**	**avons feint**
feins	**feignez**	**as feint**	**avez feint**
feint	**feignent**	**a feint**	**ont feint**
2 imparfait de l'indicatif		9 plus-que-parfait de l'indicatif	
feignais	**feignions**	**avais feint**	**avions feint**
feignais	**feigniez**	**avais feint**	**aviez feint**
feignait	**feignaient**	**avait feint**	**avaient feint**
3 passé simple		10 passé antérieur	
feignis	**feignîmes**	**eus feint**	**eûmes feint**
feignis	**feignîtes**	**eus feint**	**eûtes feint**
feignit	**feignirent**	**eut feint**	**eurent feint**
4 futur		11 futur antérieur	
feindrai	**feindrons**	**aurai feint**	**aurons feint**
feindras	**feindrez**	**auras feint**	**aurez feint**
feindra	**feindront**	**aura feint**	**auront feint**
5 conditionnel		12 conditionnel passé	
feindrais	**feindrions**	**aurais feint**	**aurions feint**
feindrais	**feindriez**	**aurais feint**	**auriez feint**
feindrait	**feindraient**	**aurait feint**	**auraient feint**
6 présent du subjonctif		13 passé du subjonctif	
feigne	**feignions**	**aie feint**	**ayons feint**
feignes	**feigniez**	**aies feint**	**ayez feint**
feigne	**feignent**	**ait feint**	**aient feint**
7 imparfait du subjonctif		14 plus-que-parfait du subjonctif	
feignisse	**feignissions**	**eusse feint**	**eussions feint**
feignisses	**feignissiez**	**eusses feint**	**eussiez feint**
feignît	**feignissent**	**eût feint**	**eussent feint**

Impératif
feins
feignons
feignez

Words and expressions related to this verb

feint, feinte feigned, pretended
la feinte pretense, sham
feinter to feint, to fake
feindre la colère to pretend to be angry
feignant, feignante lazy
fainéant, fainéante lazy
sans feinte without pretense
feinter qqn to fool someone
faire une feinte à qqn to fool someone

Can't find the verb you're looking for? Check the back pages of this book for a list of over 2,600 additional verbs!

Regular **-er** verb

to congratulate

The Seven Simple Tenses		The Seven Compound Tenses	
Singular	Plural	Singular	Plural
1 présent de l'indicatif		8 passé composé	
félicite	**félicitons**	**ai félicité**	**avons félicité**
félicites	**félicitez**	**as félicité**	**avez félicité**
félicite	**félicitent**	**a félicité**	**ont félicité**
2 imparfait de l'indicatif		9 plus-que-parfait de l'indicatif	
félicitais	**félicitions**	**avais félicité**	**avions félicité**
félicitais	**félicitiez**	**avais félicité**	**aviez félicité**
félicitait	**félicitaient**	**avait félicité**	**avaient félicité**
3 passé simple		10 passé antérieur	
félicitai	**félicitâmes**	**eus félicité**	**eûmes félicité**
félicitas	**félicitâtes**	**eus félicité**	**eûtes félicité**
félicita	**félicitèrent**	**eut félicité**	**eurent félicité**
4 futur		11 futur antérieur	
féliciterai	**féliciterons**	**aurai félicité**	**aurons félicité**
féliciteras	**féliciterez**	**auras félicité**	**aurez félicité**
félicitera	**féliciteront**	**aura félicité**	**auront félicité**
5 conditionnel		12 conditionnel passé	
féliciterais	**féliciterions**	**aurais félicité**	**aurions félicité**
féliciterais	**féliciteriez**	**aurais félicité**	**auriez félicité**
féliciterait	**féliciteraient**	**aurait félicité**	**auraient félicité**
6 présent du subjonctif		13 passé du subjonctif	
félicite	**félicitions**	**aie félicité**	**ayons félicité**
félicites	**félicitiez**	**aies félicité**	**ayez félicité**
félicite	**félicitent**	**ait félicité**	**aient félicité**
7 imparfait du subjonctif		14 plus-que-parfait du subjonctif	
félicitasse	**félicitassions**	**eusse félicité**	**eussions félicité**
félicitasses	**félicitassiez**	**eusses félicité**	**eussiez félicité**
félicitât	**félicitassent**	**eût félicité**	**eussent félicité**

Impératif
félicite
félicitons
félicitez

Words and expressions related to this verb

féliciter qqn de qqch to congratulate someone for something
Je vous félicite! I congratulate you!
la félicitation congratulation
Félicitations! Congratulations!
se féliciter de qqch to congratulate oneself about something
la félicité bliss, felicity, happiness

Don't forget to study the section on defective and impersonal verbs. It's right after this main list.

fendre (226) — Part. pr. fendant — Part. passé fendu

to split, to crack, to cleave

Regular **-re** verb

The Seven Simple Tenses		The Seven Compound Tenses	
Singular	Plural	Singular	Plural
1 présent de l'indicatif		8 passé composé	
fends	**fendons**	**ai fendu**	**avons fendu**
fends	**fendez**	**as fendu**	**avez fendu**
fend	**fendent**	**a fendu**	**ont fendu**
2 imparfait de l'indicatif		9 plus-que-parfait de l'indicatif	
fendais	**fendions**	**avais fendu**	**avions fendu**
fendais	**fendiez**	**avais fendu**	**aviez fendu**
fendait	**fendaient**	**avait fendu**	**avaient fendu**
3 passé simple		10 passé antérieur	
fendis	**fendîmes**	**eus fendu**	**eûmes fendu**
fendis	**fendîtes**	**eus fendu**	**eûtes fendu**
fendit	**fendirent**	**eut fendu**	**eurent fendu**
4 futur		11 futur antérieur	
fendrai	**fendrons**	**aurai fendu**	**aurons fendu**
fendras	**fendrez**	**auras fendu**	**aurez fendu**
fendra	**fendront**	**aura fendu**	**auront fendu**
5 conditionnel		12 conditionnel passé	
fendrais	**fendrions**	**aurais fendu**	**aurions fendu**
fendrais	**fendriez**	**aurais fendu**	**auriez fendu**
fendrait	**fendraient**	**aurait fendu**	**auraient fendu**
6 présent du subjonctif		13 passé du subjonctif	
fende	**fendions**	**aie fendu**	**ayons fendu**
fendes	**fendiez**	**aies fendu**	**ayez fendu**
fende	**fendent**	**ait fendu**	**aient fendu**
7 imparfait du subjonctif		14 plus-que-parfait du subjonctif	
fendisse	**fendissions**	**eusse fendu**	**eussions fendu**
fendisses	**fendissiez**	**eusses fendu**	**eussiez fendu**
fendît	**fendissent**	**eût fendu**	**eussent fendu**

Impératif
fends
fendons
fendez

Common idiomatic expressions using this verb and words related to it

fendre un mur to make a crack in a wall
une fente crack, split, slot
se fendre de chagrin to feel heartbroken
fendre du bois to split wood
fendre son coeur to break one's heart
un fendoir cleaver
à fendre l'âme enough to break one's spirit, to crush one's heart

Grammar putting you in a tense mood? Review the definitions of basic grammatical terms on pages 35–49.

Regular **-er** verb

to close

The Seven Simple Tenses		The Seven Compound Tenses	
Singular	Plural	Singular	Plural
1 présent de l'indicatif		8 passé composé	
ferme	**fermons**	**ai fermé**	**avons fermé**
fermes	**fermez**	**as fermé**	**avez fermé**
ferme	**ferment**	**a fermé**	**ont fermé**
2 imparfait de l'indicatif		9 plus-que-parfait de l'indicatif	
fermais	**fermions**	**avais fermé**	**avions fermé**
fermais	**fermiez**	**avais fermé**	**aviez fermé**
fermait	**fermaient**	**avait fermé**	**avaient fermé**
3 passé simple		10 passé antérieur	
fermai	**fermâmes**	**eus fermé**	**eûmes fermé**
fermas	**fermâtes**	**eus fermé**	**eûtes fermé**
ferma	**fermèrent**	**eut fermé**	**eurent fermé**
4 futur		11 futur antérieur	
fermerai	**fermerons**	**aurai fermé**	**aurons fermé**
fermeras	**fermerez**	**auras fermé**	**aurez fermé**
fermera	**fermeront**	**aura fermé**	**auront fermé**
5 conditionnel		12 conditionnel passé	
fermerais	**fermerions**	**aurais fermé**	**aurions fermé**
fermerais	**fermeriez**	**aurais fermé**	**auriez fermé**
fermerait	**fermeraient**	**aurait fermé**	**auraient fermé**
6 présent du subjonctif		13 passé du subjonctif	
ferme	**fermions**	**aie fermé**	**ayons fermé**
fermes	**fermiez**	**aies fermé**	**ayez fermé**
ferme	**ferment**	**ait fermé**	**aient fermé**
7 imparfait du subjonctif		14 plus-que-parfait du subjonctif	
fermasse	**fermassions**	**eusse fermé**	**eussions fermé**
fermasses	**fermassiez**	**eusses fermé**	**eussiez fermé**
fermât	**fermassent**	**eût fermé**	**eussent fermé**

Impératif
ferme
fermons
fermez

Sentences using this verb and words and expressions related to it

Je fermais la porte quand j'ai entendu le téléphone sonner. I was closing the door when I heard the phone ring.

Fermez la porte, s'il vous plaît. Please close the door.

enfermer to shut in
fermer à clef to lock
fermer au verrou to bolt
Ferme-la! Shut up! Zip it!
fermer le robinet to turn off the tap
fermer un programme to close a program (computer)
renfermer to enclose
Ça sent le renfermé. It's musty in here.
une fermeture closing, shutting
une fermeture éclair, une fermeture à glissière zipper
l'heure de fermer closing time

se fier (228) — Part. pr. se fiant — Part. passé fié(e)(s)

to depend on, to rely on, to trust in

Reflexive regular **-er** verb

The Seven Simple Tenses		The Seven Compound Tenses	
Singular	Plural	Singular	Plural
1 présent de l'indicatif		8 passé composé	
me fie	**nous fions**	**me suis fié(e)**	**nous sommes fié(e)s**
te fies	**vous fiez**	**t'es fié(e)**	**vous êtes fié(e)(s)**
se fie	**se fient**	**s'est fié(e)**	**se sont fié(e)s**
2 imparfait de l'indicatif		9 plus-que-parfait de l'indicatif	
me fiais	**nous fiions**	**m'étais fié(e)**	**nous étions fié(e)s**
te fiais	**vous fiiez**	**t'étais fié(e)**	**vous étiez fié(e)(s)**
se fiait	**se fiaient**	**s'était fié(e)**	**s'étaient fié(e)s**
3 passé simple		10 passé antérieur	
me fiai	**nous fiâmes**	**me fus fié(e)**	**nous fûmes fié(e)s**
te fias	**vous fiâtes**	**te fus fié(e)**	**vous fûtes fié(e)(s)**
se fia	**se fièrent**	**se fut fié(e)**	**se furent fié(e)s**
4 futur		11 futur antérieur	
me fierai	**nous fierons**	**me serai fié(e)**	**nous serons fié(e)s**
te fieras	**vous fierez**	**te seras fié(e)**	**vous serez fié(e)(s)**
se fiera	**se fieront**	**se sera fié(e)**	**se seront fié(e)s**
5 conditionnel		12 conditionnel passé	
me fierais	**nous fierions**	**me serais fié(e)**	**nous serions fié(e)s**
te fierais	**vous fieriez**	**te serais fié(e)**	**vous seriez fié(e)(s)**
se fierait	**se fieraient**	**se serait fié(e)**	**se seraient fié(e)s**
6 présent du subjonctif		13 passé du subjonctif	
me fie	**nous fiions**	**me sois fié(e)**	**nous soyons fié(e)s**
te fies	**vous fiiez**	**te sois fié(e)**	**vous soyez fié(e)(s)**
se fie	**se fient**	**se soit fié(e)**	**se soient fié(e)s**
7 imparfait du subjonctif		14 plus-que-parfait du subjonctif	
me fiasse	**nous fiassions**	**me fusse fié(e)**	**nous fussions fié(e)s**
te fiasses	**vous fiassiez**	**te fusses fié(e)**	**vous fussiez fié(e)(s)**
se fiât	**se fiassent**	**se fût fié(e)**	**se fussent fié(e)s**

Impératif
fie-toi; ne te fie pas
fions-nous; ne nous fions pas
fiez-vous; ne vous fiez pas

Words and expressions related to this verb

la confiance confidence, trust
avoir confiance en soi to be self-confident
confier à to confide to
se méfier de to mistrust, to distrust, to beware of
fiable reliable, trustworthy
la méfiance mistrust, distrust
se fier à to depend on, to trust in, to rely on
se confier à to trust to, to confide in
Ne vous fiez pas aux apparences. Don't trust appearances.

Get acquainted with what preposition goes with what verb. See *Verbs with prepositions* in the Appendixes.

Regular **-ir** verb

to finish, to end, to terminate, to complete

The Seven Simple Tenses		The Seven Compound Tenses	
Singular	Plural	Singular	Plural
1 présent de l'indicatif		8 passé composé	
finis	**finissons**	**ai fini**	**avons fini**
finis	**finissez**	**as fini**	**avez fini**
finit	**finissent**	**a fini**	**ont fini**
2 imparfait de l'indicatif		9 plus-que-parfait de l'indicatif	
finissais	**finissions**	**avais fini**	**avions fini**
finissais	**finissiez**	**avais fini**	**aviez fini**
finissait	**finissaient**	**avait fini**	**avaient fini**
3 passé simple		10 passé antérieur	
finis	**finîmes**	**eus fini**	**eûmes fini**
finis	**finîtes**	**eus fini**	**eûtes fini**
finit	**finirent**	**eut fini**	**eurent fini**
4 futur		11 futur antérieur	
finirai	**finirons**	**aurai fini**	**aurons fini**
finiras	**finirez**	**auras fini**	**aurez fini**
finira	**finiront**	**aura fini**	**auront fini**
5 conditionnel		12 conditionnel passé	
finirais	**finirions**	**aurais fini**	**aurions fini**
finirais	**finiriez**	**aurais fini**	**auriez fini**
finirait	**finiraient**	**aurait fini**	**auraient fini**
6 présent du subjonctif		13 passé du subjonctif	
finisse	**finissions**	**aie fini**	**ayons fini**
finisses	**finissiez**	**aies fini**	**ayez fini**
finisse	**finissent**	**ait fini**	**aient fini**
7 imparfait du subjonctif		14 plus-que-parfait du subjonctif	
finisse	**finissions**	**eusse fini**	**eussions fini**
finisses	**finissiez**	**eusses fini**	**eussiez fini**
finît	**finissent**	**eût fini**	**eussent fini**

Impératif
finis
finissons
finissez

AN ESSENTIAL 55 VERB

Finir

Finir is a very useful verb because it is a regular **-ir** verb and many **-ir** verbs are conjugated like it. There are also many common words and expressions related to **finir.**

Sentences using finir

J'ai fini de travailler pour aujourd'hui. I have finished working for today.

Louis a fini par épouser une femme plus riche que lui. Louis ended up by marrying a woman richer than he.

Tout est bien qui finit bien. All's well that ends well.

Le psychologue a aidé ce pauvre homme qui voulait mettre fin à ses jours. The psychologist helped this poor man who wanted to put an end to his days.

Finissons-en avec la pauvreté! Let's put an end to poverty!

La fin justifie les moyens. The end justifies the means.

Words and expressions related to this verb

finir de + inf. **to finish + pr. part.**

finir par + inf. **to end up by + pr. part.**

la fin **the end**

la fin de semaine **weekend**

afin de **in order to**

enfin **finally**

finalement **finally**

mettre fin à **to put an end to**

en finir avec qqch **to get something over with**

en finir avec qqn **to be finished/done with someone**

final, finale **final**

la finition **finish (of a piece of work)**

If you can conjugate **finir** you can also conjugate these verbs (and any regular **-ir** verb):

définir **to define**

redéfinir **to redefine**

Regular **-er** verb

to found, to establish, to lay the foundation

The Seven Simple Tenses		The Seven Compound Tenses	
Singular	Plural	Singular	Plural
1 présent de l'indicatif		8 passé composé	
fonde	**fondons**	**ai fondé**	**avons fondé**
fondes	**fondez**	**as fondé**	**avez fondé**
fonde	**fondent**	**a fondé**	**ont fondé**
2 imparfait de l'indicatif		9 plus-que-parfait de l'indicatif	
fondais	**fondions**	**avais fondé**	**avions fondé**
fondais	**fondiez**	**avais fondé**	**aviez fondé**
fondait	**fondaient**	**avait fondé**	**avaient fondé**
3 passé simple		10 passé antérieur	
fondai	**fondâmes**	**eus fondé**	**eûmes fondé**
fondas	**fondâtes**	**eus fondé**	**eûtes fondé**
fonda	**fondèrent**	**eut fondé**	**eurent fondé**
4 futur		11 futur antérieur	
fonderai	**fonderons**	**aurai fondé**	**aurons fondé**
fonderas	**fonderez**	**auras fondé**	**aurez fondé**
fondera	**fonderont**	**aura fondé**	**auront fondé**
5 conditionnel		12 conditionnel passé	
fonderais	**fonderions**	**aurais fondé**	**aurions fondé**
fonderais	**fonderiez**	**aurais fondé**	**auriez fondé**
fonderait	**fonderaient**	**aurait fondé**	**auraient fondé**
6 présent du subjonctif		13 passé du subjonctif	
fonde	**fondions**	**aie fondé**	**ayons fondé**
fondes	**fondiez**	**aies fondé**	**ayez fondé**
fonde	**fondent**	**ait fondé**	**aient fondé**
7 imparfait du subjonctif		14 plus-que-parfait du subjonctif	
fondasse	**fondassions**	**eusse fondé**	**eussions fondé**
fondasses	**fondassiez**	**eusses fondé**	**eussiez fondé**
fondât	**fondassent**	**eût fondé**	**eussent fondé**

Impératif
fonde
fondons
fondez

Common idiomatic expressions using this verb and words related to it

se fonder sur to be based on
un fondateur, une fondatrice founder
le fond bottom; background
à fond thoroughly
du fond du coeur from the bottom of one's heart
de fond en comble from top to bottom (from bottom to top)
le fondement foundation of a building
la fondation foundation, endowment
bien fondé well founded; **mal fondé** ill founded
au fond in the bottom, in the back, in the rear; at bottom, after all
manquer de fond to be shallow

Can't remember the French verb you need? Check the back pages of this book for the English-French verb index!

fondre (231) — Part. pr. fondant — Part. passé fondu

to melt, to dissolve, to mix colors

Regular **-re** verb

The Seven Simple Tenses		The Seven Compound Tenses	
Singular	Plural	Singular	Plural
1 présent de l'indicatif		8 passé composé	
fonds	**fondons**	**ai fondu**	**avons fondu**
fonds	**fondez**	**as fondu**	**avez fondu**
fond	**fondent**	**a fondu**	**ont fondu**
2 imparfait de l'indicatif		9 plus-que-parfait de l'indicatif	
fondais	**fondions**	**avais fondu**	**avions fondu**
fondais	**fondiez**	**avais fondu**	**aviez fondu**
fondait	**fondaient**	**avait fondu**	**avaient fondu**
3 passé simple		10 passé antérieur	
fondis	**fondîmes**	**eus fondu**	**eûmes fondu**
fondis	**fondîtes**	**eus fondu**	**eûtes fondu**
fondit	**fondirent**	**eut fondu**	**eurent fondu**
4 futur		11 futur antérieur	
fondrai	**fondrons**	**aurai fondu**	**aurons fondu**
fondras	**fondrez**	**auras fondu**	**aurez fondu**
fondra	**fondront**	**aura fondu**	**auront fondu**
5 conditionnel		12 conditionnel passé	
fondrais	**fondrions**	**aurais fondu**	**aurions fondu**
fondrais	**fondriez**	**aurais fondu**	**auriez fondu**
fondrait	**fondraient**	**aurait fondu**	**auraient fondu**
6 présent du subjonctif		13 passé du subjonctif	
fonde	**fondions**	**aie fondu**	**ayons fondu**
fondes	**fondiez**	**aies fondu**	**ayez fondu**
fonde	**fondent**	**ait fondu**	**aient fondu**
7 imparfait du subjonctif		14 plus-que-parfait du subjonctif	
fondisse	**fondissions**	**eusse fondu**	**eussions fondu**
fondisses	**fondissiez**	**eusses fondu**	**eussiez fondu**
fondît	**fondissent**	**eût fondu**	**eussent fondu**

Impératif
fonds
fondons
fondez

Words and expressions related to this verb
confondre to confound, to confuse; **se confondre** to merge, to mingle
refondre to recast, to remelt; **se fondre** to melt, to dissolve
la refonte recasting, remelting of metal
du beurre fondu melted butter; **du fromage fondu** melted cheese
fondre en larmes to burst into tears

How are you doing? Find out with the verb drills and tests with answers explained on pages 50–101.

Regular **-er** verb endings; spelling change: **c** changes to **ç** before **a** or **o** to keep **s** sound

to force

The Seven Simple Tenses		The Seven Compound Tenses	
Singular	Plural	Singular	Plural
1 présent de l'indicatif		8 passé composé	
force	**forçons**	**ai forcé**	**avons forcé**
forces	**forcez**	**as forcé**	**avez forcé**
force	**forcent**	**a forcé**	**ont forcé**
2 imparfait de l'indicatif		9 plus-que-parfait de l'indicatif	
forçais	**forcions**	**avais forcé**	**avions forcé**
forçais	**forciez**	**avais forcé**	**aviez forcé**
forçait	**forçaient**	**avait forcé**	**avaient forcé**
3 passé simple		10 passé antérieur	
forçai	**forçâmes**	**eus forcé**	**eûmes forcé**
forças	**forçâtes**	**eus forcé**	**eûtes forcé**
força	**forcèrent**	**eut forcé**	**eurent forcé**
4 futur		11 futur antérieur	
forcerai	**forcerons**	**aurai forcé**	**aurons forcé**
forceras	**forcerez**	**auras forcé**	**aurez forcé**
forcera	**forceront**	**aura forcé**	**auront forcé**
5 conditionnel		12 conditionnel passé	
forcerais	**forcerions**	**aurais forcé**	**aurions forcé**
forcerais	**forceriez**	**aurais forcé**	**auriez forcé**
forcerait	**forceraient**	**aurait forcé**	**auraient forcé**
6 présent du subjonctif		13 passé du subjonctif	
force	**forcions**	**aie forcé**	**ayons forcé**
forces	**forciez**	**aies forcé**	**ayez forcé**
force	**forcent**	**ait forcé**	**aient forcé**
7 imparfait du subjonctif		14 plus-que-parfait du subjonctif	
forçasse	**forçassions**	**eusse forcé**	**eussions forcé**
forçasses	**forçassiez**	**eusses forcé**	**eussiez forcé**
forçât	**forçassent**	**eût forcé**	**eussent forcé**

Impératif
force
forçons
forcez

Words and expressions related to this verb

forcer la porte de qqn to force one's way into someone's house
être forcé de faire qqch to be obliged to do something
se forcer la voix to strain one's voice
à force de by dint of, by means of
A force d'essayer, il a réussi. By dint of trying, he succeeded.
la force strength, force; **avec force** forcefully, with force
forcément necessarily, inevitably
forcer qqn à faire qqch to force someone to do something
un forçat a convict

fouiller (233) — Part. pr. **fouillant** — Part. passé **fouillé**

to dig deeply, to excavate, to go deep into, to search

Regular **-er** verb

The Seven Simple Tenses		The Seven Compound Tenses	
Singular	Plural	Singular	Plural
1 présent de l'indicatif		8 passé composé	
fouille	**fouillons**	**ai fouillé**	**avons fouillé**
fouilles	**fouillez**	**as fouillé**	**avez fouillé**
fouille	**fouillent**	**a fouillé**	**ont fouillé**
2 imparfait de l'indicatif		9 plus-que-parfait de l'indicatif	
fouillais	**fouillions**	**avais fouillé**	**avions fouillé**
fouillais	**fouilliez**	**avais fouillé**	**aviez fouillé**
fouillait	**fouillaient**	**avait fouillé**	**avaient fouillé**
3 passé simple		10 passé antérieur	
fouillai	**fouillâmes**	**eus fouillé**	**eûmes fouillé**
fouillas	**fouillâtes**	**eus fouillé**	**eûtes fouillé**
fouilla	**fouillèrent**	**eut fouillé**	**eurent fouillé**
4 futur		11 futur antérieur	
fouillerai	**fouillerons**	**aurai fouillé**	**aurons fouillé**
fouilleras	**fouillerez**	**auras fouillé**	**aurez fouillé**
fouillera	**fouilleront**	**aura fouillé**	**auront fouillé**
5 conditionnel		12 conditionnel passé	
fouillerais	**fouillerions**	**aurais fouillé**	**aurions fouillé**
fouillerais	**fouilleriez**	**aurais fouillé**	**auriez fouillé**
fouillerait	**fouilleraient**	**aurait fouillé**	**auraient fouillé**
6 présent du subjonctif		13 passé du subjonctif	
fouille	**fouillions**	**aie fouillé**	**ayons fouillé**
fouilles	**fouilliez**	**aies fouillé**	**ayez fouillé**
fouille	**fouillent**	**ait fouillé**	**aient fouillé**
7 imparfait du subjonctif		14 plus-que-parfait du subjonctif	
fouillasse	**fouillassions**	**eusse fouillé**	**eussions fouillé**
fouillasses	**fouillassiez**	**eusses fouillé**	**eussiez fouillé**
fouillât	**fouillassent**	**eût fouillé**	**eussent fouillé**

Impératif
fouille
fouillons
fouillez

Words and expressions related to this verb

fouiller la maision to search the house

fouiller dans les poches to search around (to rummage) in one's pockets

fouiller qqn to frisk (search) someone

la fouille excavation

un fouilleur, une fouilleuse searcher

Don't forget to check the list of 2,600 additional verbs keyed to the 501 model verbs. It's in the Appendixes!

Regular **-ir** verb

to furnish, to supply

The Seven Simple Tenses		The Seven Compound Tenses	
Singular	Plural	Singular	Plural
1 présent de l'indicatif		8 passé composé	
fournis	**fournissons**	**ai fourni**	**avons fourni**
fournis	**fournissez**	**as fourni**	**avez fourni**
fournit	**fournissent**	**a fourni**	**ont fourni**
2 imparfait de l'indicatif		9 plus-que-parfait de l'indicatif	
fournissais	**fournissions**	**avais fourni**	**avions fourni**
fournissais	**fournissiez**	**avais fourni**	**aviez fourni**
fournissait	**fournissaient**	**avait fourni**	**avaient fourni**
3 passé simple		10 passé antérieur	
fournis	**fournîmes**	**eus fourni**	**eûmes fourni**
fournis	**fournîtes**	**eus fourni**	**eûtes fourni**
fournit	**fournirent**	**eut fourni**	**eurent fourni**
4 futur		11 futur antérieur	
fournirai	**fournirons**	**aurai fourni**	**aurons fourni**
fourniras	**fournirez**	**auras fourni**	**aurez fourni**
fournira	**fourniront**	**aura fourni**	**auront fourni**
5 conditionnel		12 conditionnel passé	
fournirais	**fournirions**	**aurais fourni**	**aurions fourni**
fournirais	**fourniriez**	**aurais fourni**	**auriez fourni**
fournirait	**fourniraient**	**aurait fourni**	**auraient fourni**
6 présent du subjonctif		13 passé du subjonctif	
fournisse	**fournissions**	**aie fourni**	**ayons fourni**
fournisses	**fournissiez**	**aies fourni**	**ayez fourni**
fournisse	**fournissent**	**ait fourni**	**aient fourni**
7 imparfait du subjonctif		14 plus-que-parfait du subjonctif	
fournisse	**fournissions**	**eusse fourni**	**eussions fourni**
fournisses	**fournissiez**	**eusses fourni**	**eussiez fourni**
fournît	**fournissent**	**eût fourni**	**eussent fourni**

Impératif
fournis
fournissons
fournissez

Words and expressions related to this verb
fournir qqch à qqn to supply somebody with something
se fournir de to provide oneself with
un fournisseur supplier
fournir à to provide for; **fournir de** to furnish with
la fourniture supplying; **les fournitures** supplies

Don't forget to study the section on defective and impersonal verbs. It's right after this main list.

frapper (235) — Part. pr. frappant — Part. passé frappé

to knock, to hit, to frap, to rap, to strike (hit)

Regular **-er** verb

The Seven Simple Tenses		The Seven Compound Tenses	
Singular	Plural	Singular	Plural
1 présent de l'indicatif		8 passé composé	
frappe	**frappons**	**ai frappé**	**avons frappé**
frappes	**frappez**	**as frappé**	**avez frappé**
frappe	**frappent**	**a frappé**	**ont frappé**
2 imparfait de l'indicatif		9 plus-que-parfait de l'indicatif	
frappais	**frappions**	**avais frappé**	**avions frappé**
frappais	**frappiez**	**avais frappé**	**aviez frappé**
frappait	**frappaient**	**avait frappé**	**avaient frappé**
3 passé simple		10 passé antérieur	
frappai	**frappâmes**	**eus frappé**	**eûmes frappé**
frappas	**frappâtes**	**eus frappé**	**eûtes frappé**
frappa	**frappèrent**	**eut frappé**	**eurent frappé**
4 futur		11 futur antérieur	
frapperai	**frapperons**	**aurai frappé**	**aurons frappé**
frapperas	**frapperez**	**auras frappé**	**aurez frappé**
frappera	**frapperont**	**aura frappé**	**auront frappé**
5 conditionnel		12 conditionnel passé	
frapperais	**frapperions**	**aurais frappé**	**aurions frappé**
frapperais	**frapperiez**	**aurais frappé**	**auriez frappé**
frapperait	**frapperaient**	**aurait frappé**	**auraient frappé**
6 présent du subjonctif		13 passé du subjonctif	
frappe	**frappions**	**aie frappé**	**ayons frappé**
frappes	**frappiez**	**aies frappé**	**ayez frappé**
frappe	**frappent**	**ait frappé**	**aient frappé**
7 imparfait du subjonctif		14 plus-que-parfait du subjonctif	
frappasse	**frappassions**	**eusse frappé**	**eussions frappé**
frappasses	**frappassiez**	**eusses frappé**	**eussiez frappé**
frappât	**frappassent**	**eût frappé**	**eussent frappé**

Impératif
frappe
frappons
frappez

Common idiomatic expressions using this verb and words related to it

se frapper la poitrine to beat one's chest
le frappage striking (medals, coins)
une faute de frappe a typing mistake
frapper à la porte to knock on the door
frapper du pied to stamp one's foot
entrer sans frapper enter without knocking
C'est frappant! It's striking!
frappé (frappée) de stricken with
le frappement beating, striking
frappé à mort mortally wounded
un lait frappé milkshake

It's important that you be familiar with the Subjunctive. See pages 26–31.

Regular **-ir** verb

to shudder, to quiver, to tremble

The Seven Simple Tenses		The Seven Compound Tenses	
Singular	Plural	Singular	Plural
1 présent de l'indicatif		8 passé composé	
frémis	**frémissons**	**ai frémi**	**avons frémi**
frémis	**frémissez**	**as frémi**	**avez frémi**
frémit	**frémissent**	**a frémi**	**ont frémi**
2 imparfait de l'indicatif		9 plus-que-parfait de l'indicatif	
frémissais	**frémissions**	**avais frémi**	**avions frémi**
frémissais	**frémissiez**	**avais frémi**	**aviez frémi**
frémissait	**frémissaient**	**avait frémi**	**avaient frémi**
3 passé simple		10 passé antérieur	
frémis	**frémîmes**	**eus frémi**	**eûmes frémi**
frémis	**frémîtes**	**eus frémi**	**eûtes frémi**
frémit	**frémirent**	**eut frémi**	**eurent frémi**
4 futur		11 futur antérieur	
frémirai	**frémirons**	**aurai frémi**	**aurons frémi**
frémiras	**frémirez**	**auras frémi**	**aurez frémi**
frémira	**frémiront**	**aura frémi**	**auront frémi**
5 conditionnel		12 conditionnel passé	
frémirais	**frémirions**	**aurais frémi**	**aurions frémi**
frémirais	**frémiriez**	**aurais frémi**	**auriez frémi**
frémirait	**frémiraient**	**aurait frémi**	**auraient frémi**
6 présent du subjonctif		13 passé du subjonctif	
frémisse	**frémissions**	**aie frémi**	**ayons frémi**
frémisses	**frémissiez**	**aies frémi**	**ayez frémi**
frémisse	**frémissent**	**ait frémi**	**aient frémi**
7 imparfait du subjonctif		14 plus-que-parfait du subjonctif	
frémisse	**frémissions**	**eusse frémi**	**eussions frémi**
frémisses	**frémissiez**	**eusses frémi**	**eussiez frémi**
frémît	**frémissent**	**eût frémi**	**eussent frémi**

Impératif
frémis
frémissons
frémissez

Words and expressions related to this verb

frémir de colère to shake with anger

le frémissement quivering, rustling, shuddering; **le frémissement des feuilles** rustling of leaves

faire frémir qqn to give someone the shivers

une histoire à faire frémir a horror story, a chiller thriller

frémissant, frémissante rustling, quivering, shuddering

de l'eau frémissante simmering water

Don't forget to use the English-French verb index. It's in the Appendixes.

fuir (237) — Part. pr. fuyant — Part. passé fui

to flee, to fly off, to shun, to leak

Irregular verb

The Seven Simple Tenses		The Seven Compound Tenses	
Singular	Plural	Singular	Plural
1 présent de l'indicatif		8 passé composé	
fuis	**fuyons**	**ai fui**	**avons fui**
fuis	**fuyez**	**as fui**	**avez fui**
fuit	**fuient**	**a fui**	**ont fui**
2 imparfait de l'indicatif		9 plus-que-parfait de l'indicatif	
fuyais	**fuyions**	**avais fui**	**avions fui**
fuyais	**fuyiez**	**avais fui**	**aviez fui**
fuyait	**fuyaient**	**avait fui**	**avaient fui**
3 passé simple		10 passé antérieur	
fuis	**fuîmes**	**eus fui**	**eûmes fui**
fuis	**fuîtes**	**eus fui**	**eûtes fui**
fuit	**fuirent**	**eut fui**	**eurent fui**
4 futur		11 futur antérieur	
fuirai	**fuirons**	**aurai fui**	**aurons fui**
fuiras	**fuirez**	**auras fui**	**aurez fui**
fuira	**fuiront**	**aura fui**	**auront fui**
5 conditionnel		12 conditionnel passé	
fuirais	**fuirions**	**aurais fui**	**aurions fui**
fuirais	**fuiriez**	**aurais fui**	**auriez fui**
fuirait	**fuiraient**	**aurait fui**	**auraient fui**
6 présent du subjonctif		13 passé du subjonctif	
fuie	**fuyions**	**aie fui**	**ayons fui**
fuies	**fuyiez**	**aies fui**	**ayez fui**
fuie	**fuient**	**ait fui**	**aient fui**
7 imparfait du subjonctif		14 plus-que-parfait du subjonctif	
fuisse	**fuissions**	**eusse fui**	**eussions fui**
fuisses	**fuissiez**	**eusses fui**	**eussiez fui**
fuît	**fuissent**	**eût fui**	**eussent fui**

Impératif
fuis
fuyons
fuyez

Common idiomatic expressions using this verb

faire fuir to put to flight
la fuite flight, escape
prendre la fuite to take to flight
une fuite de gaz gas leak
s'enfuir de to flee from, to run away from
fugitif, fugitive fugitive, fleeting, runaway
fugitivement fugitively
une fuite d'huile oil leak
faire une fugue to run away, to elope

See also **s'enfuir.**

Grammar putting you in a tense mood? Review the definitions of basic grammatical terms with examples on pages 35–49.

Regular **-er** verb

to smoke, to steam

The Seven Simple Tenses		The Seven Compound Tenses	
Singular	Plural	Singular	Plural
1 présent de l'indicatif		8 passé composé	
fume	**fumons**	**ai fumé**	**avons fumé**
fumes	**fumez**	**as fumé**	**avez fumé**
fume	**fument**	**a fumé**	**ont fumé**
2 imparfait de l'indicatif		9 plus-que-parfait de l'indicatif	
fumais	**fumions**	**avais fumé**	**avions fumé**
fumais	**fumiez**	**avais fumé**	**aviez fumé**
fumait	**fumaient**	**avait fumé**	**avaient fumé**
3 passé simple		10 passé antérieur	
fumai	**fumâmes**	**eus fumé**	**eûmes fumé**
fumas	**fumâtes**	**eus fumé**	**eûtes fumé**
fuma	**fumèrent**	**eut fumé**	**eurent fumé**
4 futur		11 futur antérieur	
fumerai	**fumerons**	**aurai fumé**	**aurons fumé**
fumeras	**fumerez**	**auras fumé**	**aurez fumé**
fumera	**fumeront**	**aura fumé**	**auront fumé**
5 conditionnel		12 conditionnel passé	
fumerais	**fumerions**	**aurais fumé**	**aurions fumé**
fumerais	**fumeriez**	**aurais fumé**	**auriez fumé**
fumerait	**fumeraient**	**aurait fumé**	**auraient fumé**
6 présent du subjonctif		13 passé du subjonctif	
fume	**fumions**	**aie fumé**	**ayons fumé**
fumes	**fumiez**	**aies fumé**	**ayez fumé**
fume	**fument**	**ait fumé**	**aient fumé**
7 imparfait du subjonctif		14 plus-que-parfait du subjonctif	
fumasse	**fumassions**	**eusse fumé**	**eussions fumé**
fumasses	**fumassiez**	**eusses fumé**	**eussiez fumé**
fumât	**fumassent**	**eût fumé**	**eussent fumé**

Impératif
fume
fumons
fumez

Sentences using this verb and words related to it

Le père: **Je te défends de fumer. C'est une mauvaise habitude.** I forbid you to smoke. It's a bad habit.

Le fils: **Alors, pourquoi fumes-tu, papa?** Then why do you smoke, Dad?

Il n'y a pas de fumée sans feu. Where there's smoke, there's fire.

Défense de fumer No smoking allowed
la fumée smoke
un rideau de fumée smoke screen
parfumer to perfume
non-fumeur nonsmoking
fumeux, fumeuse smoky
un fume-cigare cigar holder
un fume-cigarette cigarette holder
un fumeur, une fumeuse smoker (person who smokes)

The subject pronouns are found on page 103.

gagner (239)

Part. pr. **gagnant** Part. passé **gagné**

to win, to earn, to gain

Regular **-er** verb

The Seven Simple Tenses		The Seven Compound Tenses	
Singular	Plural	Singular	Plural
1 présent de l'indicatif		8 passé composé	
gagne	**gagnons**	**ai gagné**	**avons gagné**
gagnes	**gagnez**	**as gagné**	**avez gagné**
gagne	**gagnent**	**a gagné**	**ont gagné**
2 imparfait de l'indicatif		9 plus-que-parfait de l'indicatif	
gagnais	**gagnions**	**avais gagné**	**avions gagné**
gagnais	**gagniez**	**avais gagné**	**aviez gagné**
gagnait	**gagnaient**	**avait gagné**	**avaient gagné**
3 passé simple		10 passé antérieur	
gagnai	**gagnâmes**	**eus gagné**	**eûmes gagné**
gagnas	**gagnâtes**	**eus gagné**	**eûtes gagné**
gagna	**gagnèrent**	**eut gagné**	**eurent gagné**
4 futur		11 futur antérieur	
gagnerai	**gagnerons**	**aurai gagné**	**aurons gagné**
gagneras	**gagnerez**	**auras gagné**	**aurez gagné**
gagnera	**gagneront**	**aura gagné**	**auront gagné**
5 conditionnel		12 conditionnel passé	
gagnerais	**gagnerions**	**aurais gagné**	**aurions gagné**
gagnerais	**gagneriez**	**aurais gagné**	**auriez gagné**
gagnerait	**gagneraient**	**aurait gagné**	**auraient gagné**
6 présent du subjonctif		13 passé du subjonctif	
gagne	**gagnions**	**aie gagné**	**ayons gagné**
gagnes	**gagniez**	**aies gagné**	**ayez gagné**
gagne	**gagnent**	**ait gagné**	**aient gagné**
7 imparfait du subjonctif		14 plus-que-parfait du subjonctif	
gagnasse	**gagnassions**	**eusse gagné**	**eussions gagné**
gagnasses	**gagnassiez**	**eusses gagné**	**eussiez gagné**
gagnât	**gagnassent**	**eût gagné**	**eussent gagné**

Impératif
gagne
gagnons
gagnez

Common idiomatic expressions using this verb and words related to it

gagner sa vie to earn one's living
gagner du poids to gain weight
gagner de l'argent to earn money
gagnable obtainable
gagner du temps to save time
regagner to regain, to recover, to win back
regagner le temps perdu to make up (to recover) lost time
un gagne-pain a job
un gagnant, une gagnante a winner

How are you doing? Find out with the verb drills and tests with answers explained on pages 50–101.

Regular **-er** verb

to guard, to keep, to retain

The Seven Simple Tenses		The Seven Compound Tenses	
Singular	Plural	Singular	Plural
1 présent de l'indicatif		8 passé composé	
garde	**gardons**	**ai gardé**	**avons gardé**
gardes	**gardez**	**as gardé**	**avez gardé**
garde	**gardent**	**a gardé**	**ont gardé**
2 imparfait de l'indicatif		9 plus-que-parfait de l'indicatif	
gardais	**gardions**	**avais gardé**	**avions gardé**
gardais	**gardiez**	**avais gardé**	**aviez gardé**
gardait	**gardaient**	**avait gardé**	**avaient gardé**
3 passé simple		10 passé antérieur	
gardai	**gardâmes**	**eus gardé**	**eûmes gardé**
gardas	**gardâtes**	**eus gardé**	**eûtes gardé**
garda	**gardèrent**	**eut gardé**	**eurent gardé**
4 futur		11 futur antérieur	
garderai	**garderons**	**aurai gardé**	**aurons gardé**
garderas	**garderez**	**auras gardé**	**aurez gardé**
gardera	**garderont**	**aura gardé**	**auront gardé**
5 conditionnel		12 conditionnel passé	
garderais	**garderions**	**aurais gardé**	**aurions gardé**
garderais	**garderiez**	**aurais gardé**	**auriez gardé**
garderait	**garderaient**	**aurait gardé**	**auraient gardé**
6 présent du subjonctif		13 passé du subjonctif	
garde	**gardions**	**aie gardé**	**ayons gardé**
gardes	**gardiez**	**aies gardé**	**ayez gardé**
garde	**gardent**	**ait gardé**	**aient gardé**
7 imparfait du subjonctif		14 plus-que-parfait du subjonctif	
gardasse	**gardassions**	**eusse gardé**	**eussions gardé**
gardasses	**gardassiez**	**eusses gardé**	**eussiez gardé**
gardât	**gardassent**	**eût gardé**	**eussent gardé**

Impératif
garde
gardons
gardez

AN ESSENTIAL 55 VERB

Garder

Garder is an essential French verb because it is used in many everyday situations and idiomatic expressions.

Sentences using garder

Madame Dupont a mis son enfant chez une gardienne d'enfants parce qu'elle va travailler aujourd'hui. Mrs. Dupont left her child with a babysitter because she is going to work today.

Françoise a besoin d'acheter une nouvelle garde-robe. Françoise needs to buy a new wardrobe.

Garde-à-vous! Attention! (military)

Dieu m'en garde! God forbid!

Raoul garde tout son argent dans son matelas. Ralph keeps all his money in his mattress.

Je garde de très beaux souvenirs de cette ville. I have many beautiful memories of this city.

Words and expressions related to this verb

se garder de tomber **to take care not to fall**

un gardien, une gardienne **guardian**

un gardien de but, une gardienne de but **goalie**

une gardienne d'enfants **babysitter**

la garderie **day care**

une garde-robe **wardrobe (closet)**

un garde-fou **guardrail**

un garde-manger **pantry**

un garde-vue **eyeshade (visor)**

un chien de garde, une chienne de garde **guard dog**

à bien des égards **in many regards/respects**

sans égard pour **without regard for**

If you can conjugate **garder** you can also conjugate the following verbs (along with other regular **-er** verbs):

se garder **to protect oneself (Use être as auxiliary)**

regarder **to look at, to watch, to consider, to regard**

se regarder **to look at oneself, each other (Use être as auxiliary)**

sauvegarder **to protect, to save (computer)**

Regular **-er** verb

to spoil, to damage

The Seven Simple Tenses		The Seven Compound Tenses	
Singular	Plural	Singular	Plural
1 présent de l'indicatif		8 passé composé	
gâte	**gâtons**	**ai gâté**	**avons gâté**
gâtes	**gâtez**	**as gâté**	**avez gâté**
gâte	**gâtent**	**a gâté**	**ont gâté**
2 imparfait de l'indicatif		9 plus-que-parfait de l'indicatif	
gâtais	**gâtions**	**avais gâté**	**avions gâté**
gâtais	**gâtiez**	**avais gâté**	**aviez gâté**
gâtait	**gâtaient**	**avait gâté**	**avaient gâté**
3 passé simple		10 passé antérieur	
gâtai	**gâtâmes**	**eus gâté**	**eûmes gâté**
gâtas	**gâtâtes**	**eus gâté**	**eûtes gâté**
gâta	**gâtèrent**	**eut gâté**	**eurent gâté**
4 futur		11 futur antérieur	
gâterai	**gâterons**	**aurai gâté**	**aurons gâté**
gâteras	**gâterez**	**auras gâté**	**aurez gâté**
gâtera	**gâteront**	**aura gâté**	**auront gâté**
5 conditionnel		12 conditionnel passé	
gâterais	**gâterions**	**aurais gâté**	**aurions gâté**
gâterais	**gâteriez**	**aurais gâté**	**auriez gâté**
gâterait	**gâteraient**	**aurait gâté**	**auraient gâté**
6 présent du subjonctif		13 passé du subjonctif	
gâte	**gâtions**	**aie gâté**	**ayons gâté**
gâtes	**gâtiez**	**aies gâté**	**ayez gâté**
gâte	**gâtent**	**ait gâté**	**aient gâté**
7 imparfait du subjonctif		14 plus-que-parfait du subjonctif	
gâtasse	**gâtassions**	**eusse gâté**	**eussions gâté**
gâtasses	**gâtassiez**	**eusses gâté**	**eussiez gâté**
gâtât	**gâtassent**	**eût gâté**	**eussent gâté**

Impératif
gâte
gâtons
gâtez

Sentences using this verb and words related to it

Marcel est un enfant gâté. Je n'aime pas jouer avec lui. Il gâte tout. Il demande toujours des gâteries.

gâter un enfant to spoil a child
se gâter to pamper oneself
faire des dégâts to cause damage
un enfant gâté a spoiled child
une gâterie a treat

Can't remember the French verb you need? Check the back pages of this book for the English-French verb index!

geler (242) — Part. pr. **gelant** — Part. passé **gelé**

to freeze

Regular **-er** verb endings; spelling change: **e** changes to **è** before syllable with mute **e**

The Seven Simple Tenses		The Seven Compound Tenses	
Singular	Plural	Singular	Plural
1 présent de l'indicatif		8 passé composé	
gèle	**gelons**	**ai gelé**	**avons gelé**
gèles	**gelez**	**as gelé**	**avez gelé**
gèle	**gèlent**	**a gelé**	**ont gelé**
2 imparfait de l'indicatif		9 plus-que-parfait de l'indicatif	
gelais	**gelions**	**avais gelé**	**avions gelé**
gelais	**geliez**	**avais gelé**	**aviez gelé**
gelait	**gelaient**	**avait gelé**	**avaient gelé**
3 passé simple		10 passé antérieur	
gelai	**gelâmes**	**eus gelé**	**eûmes gelé**
gelas	**gelâtes**	**eus gelé**	**eûtes gelé**
gela	**gelèrent**	**eut gelé**	**eurent gelé**
4 futur		11 futur antérieur	
gèlerai	**gèlerons**	**aurai gelé**	**aurons gelé**
gèleras	**gèlerez**	**auras gelé**	**aurez gelé**
gèlera	**gèleront**	**aura gelé**	**auront gelé**
5 conditionnel		12 conditionnel passé	
gèlerais	**gèlerions**	**aurais gelé**	**aurions gelé**
gèlerais	**gèleriez**	**aurais gelé**	**auriez gelé**
gèlerait	**gèleraient**	**aurait gelé**	**auraient gelé**
6 présent du subjonctif		13 passé du subjonctif	
gèle	**gelions**	**aie gelé**	**ayons gelé**
gèles	**geliez**	**aies gelé**	**ayez gelé**
gèle	**gèlent**	**ait gelé**	**aient gelé**
7 imparfait du subjonctif		14 plus-que-parfait du subjonctif	
gelasse	**gelassions**	**eusse gelé**	**eussions gelé**
gelasses	**gelassiez**	**eusses gelé**	**eussiez gelé**
gelât	**gelassent**	**eût gelé**	**eussent gelé**

Impératif
gèle
gelons
gelez

Sentences using this verb and words related to it

Je ne veux pas sortir aujourd'hui parce qu'il gèle. Quand je me suis levé ce matin, j'ai regardé par la fenêtre et j'ai vu de la gelée partout.

Il gèle! It's freezing!
Qu'il gèle! Let it freeze!
le gel frost, freezing
la gelée frost; jello; jelly
congeler to congeal, to freeze
la congélation congelation, freezing, icing
le point de congélation freezing point
à la gelée jellied
le congélateur freezer

Soak up some verbs used in weather expressions. There's a list in the Appendixes!

Regular **-er** verb

to bother, to hamper, to constrict, to embarrass, to hinder, to impede, to inconvenience

The Seven Simple Tenses		The Seven Compound Tenses	
Singular	Plural	Singular	Plural
1 présent de l'indicatif		8 passé composé	
gêne	**gênons**	**ai gêné**	**avons gêné**
gênes	**gênez**	**as gêné**	**avez gêné**
gêne	**gênent**	**a gêné**	**ont gêné**
2 imparfait de l'indicatif		9 plus-que-parfait de l'indicatif	
gênais	**gênions**	**avais gêné**	**avions gêné**
gênais	**gêniez**	**avais gêné**	**aviez gêné**
gênait	**gênaient**	**avait gêné**	**avaient gêné**
3 passé simple		10 passé antérieur	
gênai	**gênâmes**	**eus gêné**	**eûmes gêné**
gênas	**gênâtes**	**eus gêné**	**eûtes gêné**
gêna	**gênèrent**	**eut gêné**	**eurent gêné**
4 futur		11 futur antérieur	
gênerai	**gênerons**	**aurai gêné**	**aurons gêné**
gêneras	**gênerez**	**auras gêné**	**aurez gêné**
gênera	**gêneront**	**aura gêné**	**auront gêné**
5 conditionnel		12 conditionnel passé	
gênerais	**gênerions**	**aurais gêné**	**aurions gêné**
gênerais	**gêneriez**	**aurais gêné**	**auriez gêné**
gênerait	**gêneraient**	**aurait gêné**	**auraient gêné**
6 présent du subjonctif		13 passé du subjonctif	
gêne	**gênions**	**aie gêné**	**ayons gêné**
gênes	**gêniez**	**aies gêné**	**ayez gêné**
gêne	**gênent**	**ait gêné**	**aient gêné**
7 imparfait du subjonctif		14 plus-que-parfait du subjonctif	
gênasse	**gênassions**	**eusse gêné**	**eussions gêné**
gênasses	**gênassiez**	**eusses gêné**	**eussiez gêné**
gênât	**gênassent**	**eût gêné**	**eussent gêné**

Impératif
gêne
gênons
gênez

Words and expressions related to this verb

se gêner to inconvenience oneself
Ne vous gênez pas! Put yourself at ease! Don't trouble yourself!
gêné, gênée bothered, uncomfortable
un gêneur, une gêneuse nuisance (person)
C'est gênant! It's bothersome!
Cela vous gêne? Does that bother you?
la gêne embarrassment, discomfort
sans gêne inconsiderate

Don't forget to check the list of 2,600 additional verbs keyed to the 501 model verbs. It's in the Appendixes!

goûter (244)

Part. pr. **goûtant** Part. passé **goûté**

to taste, to have a snack, to enjoy

Regular **-er** verb

The Seven Simple Tenses		The Seven Compound Tenses	
Singular	Plural	Singular	Plural
1 présent de l'indicatif		8 passé composé	
goûte	**goûtons**	**ai goûté**	**avons goûté**
goûtes	**goûtez**	**as goûté**	**avez goûté**
goûte	**goûtent**	**a goûté**	**ont goûté**
2 imparfait de l'indicatif		9 plus-que-parfait de l'indicatif	
goûtais	**goûtions**	**avais goûté**	**avions goûté**
goûtais	**goûtiez**	**avais goûté**	**aviez goûté**
goûtait	**goûtaient**	**avait goûté**	**avaient goûté**
3 passé simple		10 passé antérieur	
goûtai	**goûtâmes**	**eus goûté**	**eûmes goûté**
goûtas	**goûtâtes**	**eus goûté**	**eûtes goûté**
goûta	**goûtèrent**	**eut goûté**	**eurent goûté**
4 futur		11 futur antérieur	
goûterai	**goûterons**	**aurai goûté**	**aurons goûté**
goûteras	**goûterez**	**auras goûté**	**aurez goûté**
goûtera	**goûteront**	**aura goûté**	**auront goûté**
5 conditionnel		12 conditionnel passé	
goûterais	**goûterions**	**aurais goûté**	**aurions goûté**
goûterais	**goûteriez**	**aurais goûté**	**auriez goûté**
goûterait	**goûteraient**	**aurait goûté**	**auraient goûté**
6 présent du subjonctif		13 passé du subjonctif	
goûte	**goûtions**	**aie goûté**	**ayons goûté**
goûtes	**goûtiez**	**aies goûté**	**ayez goûté**
goûte	**goûtent**	**ait goûté**	**aient goûté**
7 imparfait du subjonctif		14 plus-que-parfait du subjonctif	
goûtasse	**goûtassions**	**eusse goûté**	**eussions goûté**
goûtasses	**goûtassiez**	**eusses goûté**	**eussiez goûté**
goûtât	**goûtassent**	**eût goûté**	**eussent goûté**

Impératif
goûte
goûtons
goûtez

Common idiomatic expressions using this verb

Quand j'arrive chez moi de l'école l'après-midi, j'ai l'habitude de prendre le goûter à quatre heures.

le goûter snack, bite to eat
goûter sur l'herbe to have a picnic
à chacun son goût To each his own
goûter à to drink or eat only a small quantity
le goût taste
de mauvais goût in bad taste
avoir un goût de to taste like
goûter de to eat or drink something for the first time
dégoûter to disgust
C'est dégoûtant! It's disgusting!

Regular **-ir** verb

to grow (up, taller), to increase

The Seven Simple Tenses		The Seven Compound Tenses	
Singular	Plural	Singular	Plural
1 présent de l'indicatif		8 passé composé	
grandis	**grandissons**	**ai grandi**	**avons grandi**
grandis	**grandissez**	**as grandi**	**avez grandi**
grandit	**grandissent**	**a grandi**	**ont grandi**
2 imparfait de l'indicatif		9 plus-que-parfait de l'indicatif	
grandissais	**grandissions**	**avais grandi**	**avions grandi**
grandissais	**grandissiez**	**avais grandi**	**aviez grandi**
grandissait	**grandissaient**	**avait grandi**	**avaient grandi**
3 passé simple		10 passé antérieur	
grandis	**grandîmes**	**eus grandi**	**eûmes grandi**
grandis	**grandîtes**	**eus grandi**	**eûtes grandi**
grandit	**grandirent**	**eut grandi**	**eurent grandi**
4 futur		11 futur antérieur	
grandirai	**grandirons**	**aurai grandi**	**aurons grandi**
grandiras	**grandirez**	**auras grandi**	**aurez grandi**
grandira	**grandiront**	**aura grandi**	**auront grandi**
5 conditionnel		12 conditionnel passé	
grandirais	**grandirions**	**aurais grandi**	**aurions grandi**
grandirais	**grandiriez**	**aurais grandi**	**auriez grandi**
grandirait	**grandiraient**	**aurait grandi**	**auraient grandi**
6 présent du subjonctif		13 passé du subjonctif	
grandisse	**grandissions**	**aie grandi**	**ayons grandi**
grandisses	**grandissiez**	**aies grandi**	**ayez grandi**
grandisse	**grandissent**	**ait grandi**	**aient grandi**
7 imparfait du subjonctif		14 plus-que-parfait du subjonctif	
grandisse	**grandissions**	**eusse grandi**	**eussions grandi**
grandisses	**grandissiez**	**eusses grandi**	**eussiez grandi**
grandît	**grandissent**	**eût grandi**	**eussent grandi**

Impératif
grandis
grandissons
grandissez

Sentences using this verb and words related to it

Voyez-vous comme Joseph et Joséphine ont grandi? C'est incroyable! Quel âge ont-ils maintenant?

le grandissement growth
grandiose grandiose, grand
grand, grande tall
la grandeur size, greatness, grandeur
grandiosement grandiosely
agrandir to expand, to enlarge
un agrandissement enlargement, extension, aggrandizement
un enfant grandi trop vite a lanky child (grew tall too fast)

Can't find the verb you're looking for? Check the back pages of this book for a list of over 2,600 additional verbs!

gratter (246) — Part. pr. grattant — Part. passé gratté

to grate, to scrape, to scratch

Regular **-er** verb

The Seven Simple Tenses		The Seven Compound Tenses	
Singular	Plural	Singular	Plural
1 présent de l'indicatif		8 passé composé	
gratte	**grattons**	**ai gratté**	**avons gratté**
grattes	**grattez**	**as gratté**	**avez gratté**
gratte	**grattent**	**a gratté**	**ont gratté**
2 imparfait de l'indicatif		9 plus-que-parfait de l'indicatif	
grattais	**grattions**	**avais gratté**	**avions gratté**
grattais	**grattiez**	**avais gratté**	**aviez gratté**
grattait	**grattaient**	**avait gratté**	**avaient gratté**
3 passé simple		10 passé antérieur	
grattai	**grattâmes**	**eus gratté**	**eûmes gratté**
grattas	**grattâtes**	**eus gratté**	**eûtes gratté**
gratta	**grattèrent**	**eut gratté**	**eurent gratté**
4 futur		11 futur antérieur	
gratterai	**gratterons**	**aurai gratté**	**aurons gratté**
gratteras	**gratterez**	**auras gratté**	**aurez gratté**
grattera	**gratteront**	**aura gratté**	**auront gratté**
5 conditionnel		12 conditionnel passé	
gratterais	**gratterions**	**aurais gratté**	**aurions gratté**
gratterais	**gratteriez**	**aurais gratté**	**auriez gratté**
gratterait	**gratteraient**	**aurait gratté**	**auraient gratté**
6 présent du subjonctif		13 passé du subjonctif	
gratte	**grattions**	**aie gratté**	**ayons gratté**
grattes	**grattiez**	**aies gratté**	**ayez gratté**
gratte	**grattent**	**ait gratté**	**aient gratté**
7 imparfait du subjonctif		14 plus-que-parfait du subjonctif	
grattasse	**grattassions**	**eusse gratté**	**eussions gratté**
grattasses	**grattassiez**	**eusses gratté**	**eussiez gratté**
grattât	**grattassent**	**eût gratté**	**eussent gratté**

Impératif
gratte
grattons
grattez

Words and expressions related to this verb

le grattement scratching
un gratte-ciel skyscraper (**des gratte-ciel**)
un gratte-dos back scratcher (**des gratte-dos**)
le grattage scratching, scraping
un grattoir scraper, grater
se gratter to scratch oneself

Grammar putting you in a tense mood? Review the definitions of basic grammatical terms with examples on pages 35–49.

Regular **-er** verb

to climb

The Seven Simple Tenses		The Seven Compound Tenses	
Singular	Plural	Singular	Plural
1 présent de l'indicatif		8 passé composé	
grimpe	**grimpons**	**ai grimpé**	**avons grimpé**
grimpes	**grimpez**	**as grimpé**	**avez grimpé**
grimpe	**grimpent**	**a grimpé**	**ont grimpé**
2 imparfait de l'indicatif		9 plus-que-parfait de l'indicatif	
grimpais	**grimpions**	**avais grimpé**	**avions grimpé**
grimpais	**grimpiez**	**avais grimpé**	**aviez grimpé**
grimpait	**grimpaient**	**avait grimpé**	**avaient grimpé**
3 passé simple		10 passé antérieur	
grimpai	**grimpâmes**	**eus grimpé**	**eûmes grimpé**
grimpas	**grimpâtes**	**eus grimpé**	**eûtes grimpé**
grimpa	**grimpèrent**	**eut grimpé**	**eurent grimpé**
4 futur		11 futur antérieur	
grimperai	**grimperons**	**aurai grimpé**	**aurons grimpé**
grimperas	**grimperez**	**auras grimpé**	**aurez grimpé**
grimpera	**grimperont**	**aura grimpé**	**auront grimpé**
5 conditionnel		12 conditionnel passé	
grimperais	**grimperions**	**aurais grimpé**	**aurions grimpé**
grimperais	**grimperiez**	**aurais grimpé**	**auriez grimpé**
grimperait	**grimperaient**	**aurait grimpé**	**auraient grimpé**
6 présent du subjonctif		13 passé du subjonctif	
grimpe	**grimpions**	**aie grimpé**	**ayons grimpé**
grimpes	**grimpiez**	**aies grimpé**	**ayez grimpé**
grimpe	**grimpent**	**ait grimpé**	**aient grimpé**
7 imparfait du subjonctif		14 plus-que-parfait du subjonctif	
grimpasse	**grimpassions**	**eusse grimpé**	**eussions grimpé**
grimpasses	**grimpassiez**	**eusses grimpé**	**eussiez grimpé**
grimpât	**grimpassent**	**eût grimpé**	**eussent grimpé**

Impératif
grimpe
grimpons
grimpez

Words and expressions related to this verb
grimper à l'échelle to climb a ladder
une plante grimpante climbing plant
une grimpée, une grimpette steep climb
un grimpeur, une grimpeuse climber
grimper aux arbres to climb trees

Use the guide to French pronunciation. It's in the Appendixes.

gronder (248) — Part. pr. grondant — Part. passé grondé

to chide, to reprimand, to scold

Regular **-er** verb

The Seven Simple Tenses		The Seven Compound Tenses	
Singular	Plural	Singular	Plural
1 présent de l'indicatif		8 passé composé	
gronde	**grondons**	**ai grondé**	**avons grondé**
grondes	**grondez**	**as grondé**	**avez grondé**
gronde	**grondent**	**a grondé**	**ont grondé**
2 imparfait de l'indicatif		9 plus-que-parfait de l'indicatif	
grondais	**grondions**	**avais grondé**	**avions grondé**
grondais	**grondiez**	**avais grondé**	**aviez grondé**
grondait	**grondaient**	**avait grondé**	**avaient grondé**
3 passé simple		10 passé antérieur	
grondai	**grondâmes**	**eus grondé**	**eûmes grondé**
grondas	**grondâtes**	**eus grondé**	**eûtes grondé**
gronda	**grondèrent**	**eut grondé**	**eurent grondé**
4 futur		11 futur antérieur	
gronderai	**gronderons**	**aurai grondé**	**aurons grondé**
gronderas	**gronderez**	**auras grondé**	**aurez grondé**
grondera	**gronderont**	**aura grondé**	**auront grondé**
5 conditionnel		12 conditionnel passé	
gronderais	**gronderions**	**aurais grondé**	**aurions grondé**
gronderais	**gronderiez**	**aurais grondé**	**auriez grondé**
gronderait	**gronderaient**	**aurait grondé**	**auraient grondé**
6 présent du subjonctif		13 passé du subjonctif	
gronde	**grondions**	**aie grondé**	**ayons grondé**
grondes	**grondiez**	**aies grondé**	**ayez grondé**
gronde	**grondent**	**ait grondé**	**aient grondé**
7 imparfait du subjonctif		14 plus-que-parfait du subjonctif	
grondasse	**grondassions**	**eusse grondé**	**eussions grondé**
grondasses	**grondassiez**	**eusses grondé**	**eussiez grondé**
grondât	**grondassent**	**eût grondé**	**eussent grondé**

Impératif
gronde
grondons
grondez

Sentences using this verb and words related to it

—Victor, pourquoi pleures-tu?

—La maîtresse de mathématiques m'a grondé.

—Pourquoi est-ce qu'elle t'a grondé? Qu'est-ce que tu as fait?

—Ce n'est pas parce que j'ai fait quelque chose. C'est parce que je n'ai rien fait. Je n'ai pas préparé la leçon.

—Alors, tu mérites une gronderie et une réprimande.

—C'est une grondeuse. Elle gronde à chaque instant. C'est une criarde.

une grondeuse a scolder
une criarde a nag, nagger
une gronderie a scolding
à chaque instant constantly

Regular **-ir** verb

to cure, to heal, to remedy, to recover

The Seven Simple Tenses		The Seven Compound Tenses	
Singular	Plural	Singular	Plural
1 présent de l'indicatif		8 passé composé	
guéris	**guérissons**	**ai guéri**	**avons guéri**
guéris	**guérissez**	**as guéri**	**avez guéri**
guérit	**guérissent**	**a guéri**	**ont guéri**
2 imparfait de l'indicatif		9 plus-que-parfait de l'indicatif	
guérissais	**guérissions**	**avais guéri**	**avions guéri**
guérissais	**guérissiez**	**avais guéri**	**aviez guéri**
guérissait	**guérissaient**	**avait guéri**	**avaient guéri**
3 passé simple		10 passé antérieur	
guéris	**guérîmes**	**eus guéri**	**eûmes guéri**
guéris	**guérîtes**	**eus guéri**	**eûtes guéri**
guérit	**guérirent**	**eut guéri**	**eurent guéri**
4 futur		11 futur antérieur	
guérirai	**guérirons**	**aurai guéri**	**aurons guéri**
guériras	**guérirez**	**auras guéri**	**aurez guéri**
guérira	**guériront**	**aura guéri**	**auront guéri**
5 conditionnel		12 conditionnel passé	
guérirais	**guéririons**	**aurais guéri**	**aurions guéri**
guérirais	**guéririez**	**aurais guéri**	**auriez guéri**
guérirait	**guériraient**	**aurait guéri**	**auraient guéri**
6 présent du subjonctif		13 passé du subjonctif	
guérisse	**guérissions**	**aie guéri**	**ayons guéri**
guérisses	**guérissiez**	**aies guéri**	**ayez guéri**
guérisse	**guérissent**	**ait guéri**	**aient guéri**
7 imparfait du subjonctif		14 plus-que-parfait du subjonctif	
guérisse	**guérissions**	**eusse guéri**	**eussions guéri**
guérisses	**guérissiez**	**eusses guéri**	**eussiez guéri**
guérît	**guérissent**	**eût guéri**	**eussent guéri**

Impératif
guéris
guérissons
guérissez

Sentences using this verb and words related to it

Madame Gérard est tombée dans l'escalier la semaine dernière et elle a reçu une blessure au genou. Elle est allée chez le médecin et maintenant elle est guérie.

une guérison healing, cure
guérisseur, guérisseuse healer
guérissable curable
guérir de to recover from, to cure of
la guérison par la foi faith healing

How are you doing? Find out with the verb drills and tests with answers explained on pages 50–101.

s'habiller (250) Part. pr. s'habillant Part. passé habillé(e)(s)

to get dressed, to dress (oneself)

Reflexieve regular **-er** verb

The Seven Simple Tenses		The Seven Compound Tenses	
Singular	Plural	Singular	Plural
1 présent de l'indicatif		8 passé composé	
m'habille	**nous habillons**	**me suis habillé(e)**	**nous sommes habillé(e)s**
t'habilles	**vous habillez**	**t'es habillé(e)**	**vous êtes habillé(e)(s)**
s'habille	**s'habillent**	**s'est habillé(e)**	**se sont habillé(e)s**
2 imparfait de l'indicatif		9 plus-que-parfait de l'indicatif	
m'habillais	**nous habillions**	**m'étais habillé(e)**	**nous étions habillé(e)s**
t'habillais	**vous habilliez**	**t'étais habillé(e)**	**vous étiez habillé(e)(s)**
s'habillait	**s'habillaient**	**s'était habillé(e)**	**s'étaient habillé(e)s**
3 passé simple		10 passé antérieur	
m'habillai	**nous habillâmes**	**me fus habillé(e)**	**nous fûmes habillé(e)s**
t'habillas	**vous habillâtes**	**te fus habillé(e)**	**vous fûtes habillé(e)(s)**
s'habilla	**s'habillèrent**	**se fut habillé(e)**	**se furent habillé(e)s**
4 futur		11 futur antérieur	
m'habillerai	**nous habillerons**	**me serai habillé(e)**	**nous serons habillé(e)s**
t'habilleras	**vous habillerez**	**te seras habillé(e)**	**vous serez habillé(e)(s)**
s'habillera	**s'habilleront**	**se sera habillé(e)**	**se seront habillé(e)s**
5 conditionnel		12 conditionnel passé	
m'habillerais	**nous habillerions**	**me serais habillé(e)**	**nous serions habillé(e)s**
t'habillerais	**vous habilleriez**	**te serais habillé(e)**	**vous seriez habillé(e)(s)**
s'habillerait	**s'habilleraient**	**se serait habillé(e)**	**se seraient habillé(e)s**
6 présent du subjonctif		13 passé du subjonctif	
m'habille	**nous habillions**	**me sois habillé(e)**	**nous soyons habillé(e)s**
t'habilles	**vous habilliez**	**te sois habillé(e)**	**vous soyez habillé(e)(s)**
s'habille	**s'habillent**	**se soit habillé(e)**	**se soient habillé(e)s**
7 imparfait du subjonctif		14 plus-que-parfait du subjonctif	
m'habillasse	**nous habillassions**	**me fusse habillé(e)**	**nous fussions habillé(e)s**
t'habillasses	**vous habillassiez**	**te fusses habillé(e)**	**vous fussiez habillé(e)(s)**
s'habillât	**s'habillassent**	**se fût habillé(e)**	**se fussent habillé(e)s**

Impératif
habille-toi; ne t'habille pas
habillons-nous; ne nous habillons pas
habillez-vous; ne vous habillez pas

Sentences using this verb and words related to it

un habit costume, outfit
les habits clothes
habiller qqn to dress someone
habillement *m.* garment, wearing apparel
L'habit ne fait pas le moine. Clothes don't make the person (the monk).
déshabiller to undress
se déshabiller to undress oneself, to get undressed
habiller de to clothe with
l'habit de gala formal wear
l'habit militaire military dress

See also **vêtir.**

Don't miss the definitions of basic grammatical terms with examples in English and French on pages 35–49.

Regular **-er** verb

to live (in), to dwell (in), to inhabit

The Seven Simple Tenses		The Seven Compound Tenses	
Singular	Plural	Singular	Plural
1 présent de l'indicatif		8 passé composé	
habite	**habitons**	**ai habité**	**avons habité**
habites	**habitez**	**as habité**	**avez habité**
habite	**habitent**	**a habité**	**ont habité**
2 imparfait de l'indicatif		9 plus-que-parfait de l'indicatif	
habitais	**habitions**	**avais habité**	**avions habité**
habitais	**habitiez**	**avais habité**	**aviez habité**
habitait	**habitaient**	**avait habité**	**avaient habité**
3 passé simple		10 passé antérieur	
habitai	**habitâmes**	**eus habité**	**eûmes habité**
habitas	**habitâtes**	**eus habité**	**eûtes habité**
habita	**habitèrent**	**eut habité**	**eurent habité**
4 futur		11 futur antérieur	
habiterai	**habiterons**	**aurai habité**	**aurons habité**
habiteras	**habiterez**	**auras habité**	**aurez habité**
habitera	**habiteront**	**aura habité**	**auront habité**
5 conditionnel		12 conditionnel passé	
habiterais	**habiterions**	**aurais habité**	**aurions habité**
habiterais	**habiteriez**	**aurais habité**	**auriez habité**
habiterait	**habiteraient**	**aurait habité**	**auraient habité**
6 présent du subjonctif		13 passé du subjonctif	
habite	**habitions**	**aie habité**	**ayons habité**
habites	**habitiez**	**aies habité**	**ayez habité**
habite	**habitent**	**ait habité**	**aient habité**
7 imparfait du subjonctif		14 plus-que-parfait du subjonctif	
habitasse	**habitassions**	**eusse habité**	**eussions habité**
habitasses	**habitassiez**	**eusses habité**	**eussiez habité**
habitât	**habitassent**	**eût habité**	**eussent habité**

Impératif
habite
habitons
habitez

Sentences using this verb and words related to it

—Où habitez-vous?
—J'habite 27 rue Duparc dans une petite maison blanche.
—Avec qui habitez-vous?
—J'habite avec mes parents, mes frères, mes soeurs, et mon chien.

une habitation dwelling, residence, abode
un habitat habitat
un habitant inhabitant
H.L.M. (habitation à loyer modéré) lodging at a moderate rental
l' amélioration de l'habitat improvement of living conditions
habiter à la campagne to live in the country
habiter la banlieue to live in the suburbs

Be careful! **Habitable** means *habitable* or *inhabitable*. But **inhabitable** means *uninhabitable*.

The subject pronouns are found on page 103.

to hate

Irregular verb

The Seven Simple Tenses		The Seven Compound Tenses	
Singular	Plural	Singular	Plural
1 présent de l'indicatif		8 passé composé	
hais	**haïssons**	**ai haï**	**avons haï**
hais	**haïssez**	**as haï**	**avez haï**
hait	**haïssent**	**a haï**	**ont haï**
2 imparfait de l'indicatif		9 plus-que-parfait de l'indicatif	
haïssais	**haïssions**	**avais haï**	**avions haï**
haïssais	**haïssiez**	**avais haï**	**aviez haï**
haïssait	**haïssaient**	**avait haï**	**avaient haï**
3 passé simple		10 passé antérieur	
haïs	**haïmes**	**eus haï**	**eûmes haï**
haïs	**haïtes**	**eus haï**	**eûtes haï**
haït	**haïrent**	**eut haï**	**eurent haï**
4 futur		11 futur antérieur	
haïrai	**haïrons**	**aurai haï**	**aurons haï**
haïras	**haïrez**	**auras haï**	**aurez haï**
haïra	**haïront**	**aura haï**	**auront haï**
5 conditionnel		12 conditionnel passé	
haïrais	**haïrions**	**aurais haï**	**aurions haï**
haïrais	**haïriez**	**aurais haï**	**auriez haï**
haïrait	**haïraient**	**aurait haï**	**auraient haï**
6 présent du subjonctif		13 passé du subjonctif	
haïsse	**haïssions**	**aie haï**	**ayons haï**
haïsses	**haïssiez**	**aies haï**	**ayez haï**
haïsse	**haïssent**	**ait haï**	**aient haï**
7 imparfait du subjonctif		14 plus-que-parfait du subjonctif	
haïsse	**haïssions**	**eusse haï**	**eussions haï**
haïsses	**haïssiez**	**eusses haï**	**eussiez haï**
haït	**haïssent**	**eût haï**	**eussent haï**

Impératif
hais
haïssons
haïssez

Sentences using this verb and words related to it

Je hais le mensonge, je hais la médiocrité, et je hais la calomnie. Ces choses sont haïssables. Je hais Marguerite et Jeanne; elles sont haineuses.

haïssable detestable, hateful
la haine hatred, hate
haineux, haineuse hateful, heinous
haïr qqn comme la peste to hate somebody like poison
des haines mesquines petty hatreds

This verb begins with aspirate *h*; make no liaison and use *je* instead of *j'*.

Regular **-er** verb

to hesitate

The Seven Simple Tenses		The Seven Compound Tenses	
Singular	Plural	Singular	Plural
1 présent de l'indicatif		8 passé composé	
hésite	**hésitons**	**ai hésité**	**avons hésité**
hésites	**hésitez**	**as hésité**	**avez hésité**
hésite	**hésitent**	**a hésité**	**ont hésité**
2 imparfait de l'indicatif		9 plus-que-parfait de l'indicatif	
hésitais	**hésitions**	**avais hésité**	**avions hésité**
hésitais	**hésitiez**	**avais hésité**	**aviez hésité**
hésitait	**hésitaient**	**avait hésité**	**avaient hésité**
3 passé simple		10 passé antérieur	
hésitai	**hésitâmes**	**eus hésité**	**eûmes hésité**
hésitas	**hésitâtes**	**eus hésité**	**eûtes hésité**
hésita	**hésitèrent**	**eut hésité**	**eurent hésité**
4 futur		11 futur antérieur	
hésiterai	**hésiterons**	**aurai hésité**	**aurons hésité**
hésiteras	**hésiterez**	**auras hésité**	**aurez hésité**
hésitera	**hésiteront**	**aura hésité**	**auront hésité**
5 conditionnel		12 conditionnel passé	
hésiterais	**hésiterions**	**aurais hésité**	**aurions hésité**
hésiterais	**hésiteriez**	**aurais hésité**	**auriez hésité**
hésiterait	**hésiteraient**	**aurait hésité**	**auraient hésité**
6 présent du subjonctif		13 passé du subjonctif	
hésite	**hésitions**	**aie hésité**	**ayons hésité**
hésites	**hésitiez**	**aies hésité**	**ayez hésité**
hésite	**hésitent**	**ait hésité**	**aient hésité**
7 imparfait du subjonctif		14 plus-que-parfait du subjonctif	
hésitasse	**hésitassions**	**eusse hésité**	**eussions hésité**
hésitasses	**hésitassiez**	**eusses hésité**	**eussiez hésité**
hésitât	**hésitassent**	**eût hésité**	**eussent hésité**

Impératif
hésite
hésitons
hésitez

Words and expressions related to this verb
hésiter à faire qqch to hesitate to do something
une hésitation hesitation
hésitant, hésitante undecided, hesitating
sans hésitation unhesitatingly, without hesitation

Get acquainted with what preposition goes with what verb. See *Verbs with prepositions* in the Appendixes.

imposer (254) — Part. pr. imposant — Part. passé imposé

to impose

Regular **-er** verb

The Seven Simple Tenses		The Seven Compound Tenses	
Singular	Plural	Singular	Plural
1 présent de l'indicatif		8 passé composé	
impose	**imposons**	**ai imposé**	**avons imposé**
imposes	**imposez**	**as imposé**	**avez imposé**
impose	**imposent**	**a imposé**	**ont imposé**
2 imparfait de l'indicatif		9 plus-que-parfait de l'indicatif	
imposais	**imposions**	**avais imposé**	**avions imposé**
imposais	**imposiez**	**avais imposé**	**aviez imposé**
imposait	**imposaient**	**avait imposé**	**avaient imposé**
3 passé simple		10 passé antérieur	
imposai	**imposâmes**	**eus imposé**	**eûmes imposé**
imposas	**imposâtes**	**eus imposé**	**eûtes imposé**
imposa	**imposèrent**	**eut imposé**	**eurent imposé**
4 futur		11 futur antérieur	
imposerai	**imposerons**	**aurai imposé**	**aurons imposé**
imposeras	**imposerez**	**auras imposé**	**aurez imposé**
imposera	**imposeront**	**aura imposé**	**auront imposé**
5 conditionnel		12 conditionnel passé	
imposerais	**imposerions**	**aurais imposé**	**aurions imposé**
imposerais	**imposeriez**	**aurais imposé**	**auriez imposé**
imposerait	**imposeraient**	**aurait imposé**	**auraient imposé**
6 présent du subjonctif		13 passé du subjonctif	
impose	**imposions**	**aie imposé**	**ayons imposé**
imposes	**imposiez**	**aies imposé**	**ayez impoé**
impose	**imposent**	**ait imposé**	**aient imposé**
7 imparfait du subjonctif		14 plus-que-parfait du subjonctif	
imposasse	**imposassions**	**eusse imposé**	**eussions imposé**
imposasses	**imposassiez**	**eusses imposé**	**eussiez imposé**
imposât	**imposassent**	**eût imposé**	**eussent imposé**

Impératif
impose
imposons
imposez

Words and expressions related to this verb

s'imposer to assert oneself
s'imposer à to intrude on
imposable taxable
un impôt tax; **l'impôt sur le revenu** income tax
une imposition imposition
imposant, imposante imposing, impressive
imposer le respect to compel respect
imposer une règle to lay down a rule

Can't remember the French verb you need? Check the back pages of this book for the English-French verb index!

Irregular verb

to include, to enclose

The Seven Simple Tenses		The Seven Compound Tenses	
Singular	Plural	Singular	Plural
1 présent de l'indicatif		8 passé composé	
inclus	**incluons**	**ai inclus**	**avons inclus**
inclus	**incluez**	**as inclus**	**avez inclus**
inclut	**incluent**	**a inclus**	**ont inclus**
2 imparfait de l'indicatif		9 plus-que-parfait de l'indicatif	
incluais	**incluions**	**avais inclus**	**avions inclus**
incluais	**incluiez**	**avais inclus**	**aviez inclus**
incluait	**incluaient**	**avait inclus**	**avaient inclus**
3 passé simple		10 passé antérieur	
inclus	**inclûmes**	**eus inclus**	**eûmes inclus**
inclus	**inclûtes**	**eus inclus**	**eûtes inclus**
inclut	**inclurent**	**eut inclus**	**eurent inclus**
4 futur		11 futur antérieur	
inclurai	**inclurons**	**aurai inclus**	**aurons inclus**
incluras	**inclurez**	**auras inclus**	**aurez inclus**
inclura	**incluront**	**aura inclus**	**auront inclus**
5 conditionnel		12 conditionnel passé	
inclurais	**inclurions**	**aurais inclus**	**aurions inclus**
inclurais	**incluriez**	**aurais inclus**	**auriez inclus**
inclurait	**incluraient**	**aurait inclus**	**auraient inclus**
6 présent du subjonctif		13 passé du subjonctif	
inclue	**incluions**	**aie inclus**	**ayons inclus**
inclues	**incluiez**	**aies inclus**	**ayez inclus**
inclue	**incluent**	**ait inclus**	**aient inclus**
7 imparfait du subjonctif		14 plus-que-parfait du subjonctif	
inclusse	**inclussions**	**eusse inclus**	**eussions inclus**
inclusses	**inclussiez**	**eusses inclus**	**eussiez inclus**
inclût	**inclussent**	**eût inclus**	**eussent inclus**

Impératif
inclus
incluons
incluez

Words and expressions related to this verb

la lettre ci-incluse the letter enclosed herewith
l'argent ci-inclus the money enclosed herewith
une inclusion inclusion
inclusif, inclusive inclusive

See also **conclure.**

inclusivement inclusively
service inclus service included (no tip necessary)
exclure to exclude
exclusivement exclusively
exclusif, exclusive exclusive
une exclusion exclusion
exclu, exclue excluded

Don't forget to study the section on defective and impersonal verbs. It's right after this main list.

indiquer (256) Part. pr. indiquant Part. passé indiqué

to indicate, to point out, to show

Regular **-er** verb

The Seven Simple Tenses		The Seven Compound Tenses	
Singular	Plural	Singular	Plural
1 présent de l'indicatif		8 passé composé	
indique	**indiquons**	**ai indiqué**	**avons indiqué**
indiques	**indiquez**	**as indiqué**	**avez indiqué**
indique	**indiquent**	**a indiqué**	**ont indiqué**
2 imparfait de l'indicatif		9 plus-que-parfait de l'indicatif	
indiquais	**indiquions**	**avais indiqué**	**avions indiqué**
indiquais	**indiquiez**	**avais indiqué**	**aviez indiqué**
indiquait	**indiquaient**	**avait indiqué**	**avaient indiqué**
3 passé simple		10 passé antérieur	
indiquai	**indiquâmes**	**eus indiqué**	**eûmes indiqué**
indiquas	**indiquâtes**	**eus indiqué**	**eûtes indiqué**
indiqua	**indiquèrent**	**eut indiqué**	**eurent indiqué**
4 futur		11 futur antérieur	
indiquerai	**indiquerons**	**aurai indiqué**	**aurons indiqué**
indiqueras	**indiquerez**	**auras indiqué**	**aurez indiqué**
indiquera	**indiqueront**	**aura indiqué**	**auront indiqué**
5 conditionnel		12 conditionnel passé	
indiquerais	**indiquerions**	**aurais indiqué**	**aurions indiqué**
indiquerais	**indiqueriez**	**aurais indiqué**	**auriez indiqué**
indiquerait	**indiqueraient**	**aurait indiqué**	**auraient indiqué**
6 présent du subjonctif		13 passé du subjonctif	
indique	**indiquions**	**aie indiqué**	**ayons indiqué**
indiques	**indiquiez**	**aies indiqué**	**ayez indiqué**
indique	**indiquent**	**ait indiqué**	**aient indiqué**
7 imparfait du subjonctif		14 plus-que-parfait du subjonctif	
indiquasse	**indiquassions**	**eusse indiqué**	**eussions indiqué**
indiquasses	**indiquassiez**	**eusses indiqué**	**eussiez indiqué**
indiquât	**indiquassent**	**eût indiqué**	**eussent indiqué**

Impératif
indique
indiquons
indiquez

Words and expressions related to this verb
indiquer du doigt to point out (with one's finger)
indiquer un bon médecin to recommend a good doctor
une indication indication
indicatif, indicative indicative
un indice index
indicateur, indicatrice indicator
un indicateur de vitesse speedometer

How are you doing? Find out with the verb drills and tests with answers explained on pages 50–101.

Reflexive regular **-er** verb

to find out, to inquire, to make inquiries, to inform oneself

The Seven Simple Tenses		The Seven Compound Tenses	
Singular	Plural	Singular	Plural
1 présent de l'indicatif		8 passé composé	
m'informe	**nous informons**	**me suis informé(e)**	**nous sommes informé(e)s**
t'informes	**vous informez**	**t'es informé(e)**	**vous êtes informé(e)(s)**
s'informe	**s'informent**	**s'est informé(e)**	**se sont informé(e)s**
2 imparfait de l'indicatif		9 plus-que-parfait de l'indicatif	
m'informais	**nous informions**	**m'étais informé(e)**	**nous étions informé(e)s**
t'informais	**vous informiez**	**t'étais informé(e)**	**vous étiez informé(e)(s)**
s'informait	**s'informaient**	**s'était informé(e)**	**s'étaient informé(e)s**
3 passé simple		10 passé antérieur	
m'informai	**nous informâmes**	**me fus informé(e)**	**nous fûmes informé(e)s**
t'informas	**vous informâtes**	**te fus informé(e)**	**vous fûtes informé(e)(s)**
s'informa	**s'informèrent**	**se fut informé(e)**	**se furent informé(e)s**
4 futur		11 futur antérieur	
m'informerai	**nous informerons**	**me serai informé(e)**	**nous serons informé(e)s**
t'informeras	**vous informerez**	**te seras informé(e)**	**vous serez informé(e)(s)**
s'informera	**s'informeront**	**se sera informé(e)**	**se seront informé(e)s**
5 conditionnel		12 conditionnel passé	
m'informerais	**nous informerions**	**me serais informé(e)**	**nous serions informé(e)s**
t'informerais	**vous informeriez**	**te serais informé(e)**	**vous seriez informé(e)(s)**
s'informerait	**s'informeraient**	**se serait informé(e)**	**se seraient informé(e)s**
6 présent du subjonctif		13 passé du subjonctif	
m'informe	**nous informions**	**me sois informé(e)**	**nous soyons informé(e)s**
t'informes	**vous informiez**	**te sois informé(e)**	**vous soyez informé(e)(s)**
s'informe	**s'informent**	**se soit informé(e)**	**se soient informé(e)s**
7 imparfait du subjonctif		14 plus-que-parfait du subjonctif	
m'informasse	**nous informassions**	**me fusse informé(e)**	**nous fussions informé(e)s**
t'informasses	**vous informassiez**	**te fusses informé(e)**	**vous fussiez informé(e)(s)**
s'informât	**s'informassent**	**se fût informé(e)**	**se fussent informé(e)s**

Impératif
informe-toi; ne t'informe pas
informons-nous; ne nous informons pas
informez-vous; ne vous informez pas

Words and expressions related to this verb

informer to inform, to advise
Je vous informe que . . . I am informing you that . . .
les informations *f.* new items, news bulletins
informatif, informative informative
informationnel, informationnelle informational
l'informatique *f.* computer science
s'informer de to inquire about
prendre des informations sur qqn to make inquiries about someone
un informateur, une informatrice informer, informant
une information officielle official investigation
former to form
un informaticien, une informaticienne computer scientist

Don't forget to check the list of 2,600 additional verbs keyed to the 501 model verbs. It's in the Appendixes!

s'inquiéter (258) Part. pr. s'inquiétant Part. passé inquiété(e)(s)

to worry, to be upset

Reflexive regular **-er** verb endings; spelling change: **é** changes to **è** before syllable with mute **e**

The Seven Simple Tenses		The Seven Compound Tenses	
Singular	Plural	Singular	Plural
1 présent de l'indicatif		8 passé composé	
m'inquiète	**nous inquiétons**	**me suis inquiété(e)**	**nous sommes inquiété(e)s**
t'inquiètes	**vous inquiétez**	**t'es inquiété(e)**	**vous êtes inquiété(e)(s)**
s'inquiète	**s'inquiètent**	**s'est inquiété(e)**	**se sont inquiété(e)s**
2 imparfalt de l'indicatif		9 plus-que-parfait de l'indicatif	
m'inquiétais	**nous inquiétions**	**m'étais inquiété(e)**	**nous étions inquiété(e)s**
t'inquiétais	**vous inquiétiez**	**t'étais inquiété(e)**	**vous étiez inquiété(e)(s)**
s'inquiétait	**s'inquiétaient**	**s'était inquiété(e)**	**s'étaient inquiété(e)s**
3 passé simple		10 passé antérieur	
m'inquiétai	**nous inquiétâmes**	**me fus inquiété(e)**	**nous fûmes inquiété(e)s**
t'inquiétas	**vous inquiétâtes**	**te fus inquiété(e)**	**vous fûtes inquiété(e)(s)**
s'inquiéta	**s'inquiétèrent**	**se fut inquiété(e)**	**se furent inquiété(e)s**
4 futur		11 futur antérieur	
m'inquiéterai	**nous inquiéterons**	**me serai inquiété(e)**	**nous serons inquiété(e)s**
t'inquiéteras	**vous inquiéterez**	**te seras inquiété(e)**	**vous serez inquiété(e)(s)**
s'inquiétera	**s'inquiéteront**	**se sera inquiété(e)**	**se seront inquiété(e)s**
5 conditionnel		12 conditionnel passé	
m'inquiéterais	**nous inquiéterions**	**me serais inquiété(e)**	**nous serions inquiété(e)s**
t'inquiéterais	**vous inquiéteriez**	**te serais inquiété(e)**	**vous seriez inquiété(e)(s)**
s'inquiéterait	**s'inquiéteraient**	**se serait inquiété(e)**	**se seraient inquiété(e)s**
6 présent du subjonctif		13 passé du subjonctif	
m'inquiète	**nous inquiétions**	**me sois inquiété(e)**	**nous soyons inquiété(e)s**
t'inquiètes	**vous inquiétiez**	**te sois inquiété(e)**	**vous soyez inquiété(e)(s)**
s'inquiète	**s'inquiètent**	**se soit inquiété(e)**	**se soient inquiété(e)s**
7 imparfait du subjonctif		14 plus-que-parfait du subjonctif	
m'inquiétasse	**nous inquiétassions**	**me fusse inquiété(e)**	**nous fussions inquiété(e)s**
t'inquiétasses	**vous inquiétassiez**	**te fusses inquiété(e)**	**vous fussiez inquiété(e)(s)**
s'inquiétât	**s'inquiétassent**	**se fût inquiété(e)**	**se fussent inquiété(e)s**

Impératif
inquiète-toi; ne t'inquiète pas
inquiétons-nous; ne nous inquiétons pas
inquiétez-vous; ne vous inquiétez pas

Words related to this verb
s'inquiéter de to worry about
inquiéter to trouble, to worry
une inquiétude restlessness, anxiety, uneasiness
inquiétant, inquiétante disturbing, alarming
inquiet, inquiète restless, alarmed, disturbed, worried

Grammar putting you in a tense mood? Review the definitions of basic grammatical terms with examples on pages 35–49.

The Seven Simple Tenses		The Seven Compound Tenses	
Singular	Plural	Singular	Plural
1 présent de l'indicatif		8 passé composé	
insiste	**insistons**	**ai insisté**	**avons insisté**
insistes	**insistez**	**as insisté**	**avez insisté**
insiste	**insistent**	**a insisté**	**ont insisté**
2 imparfait de l'indicatif		9 plus-que-parfait de l'indicatif	
insistais	**insistions**	**avais insisté**	**avions insisté**
insistais	**insistiez**	**avais insisté**	**aviez insisté**
insistait	**insistaient**	**avait insisté**	**avaient insisté**
3 passé simple		10 passé antérieur	
insistai	**insistâmes**	**eus insisté**	**eûmes insisté**
insistas	**insistâtes**	**eus insisté**	**eûtes insisté**
insista	**insistèrent**	**eut insisté**	**eurent insisté**
4 futur		11 futur antérieur	
insisterai	**insisterons**	**aurai insisté**	**aurons insisté**
insisteras	**insisterez**	**auras insisté**	**aurez insisté**
insistera	**insisteront**	**aura insisté**	**auront insisté**
5 conditionnel		12 conditionnel passé	
insisterais	**insisterions**	**aurais insisté**	**aurions insisté**
insisterais	**insisteriez**	**aurais insisté**	**auriez insisté**
insisterait	**insisteraient**	**aurait insisté**	**auraient insisté**
6 présent du subjonctif		13 passé du subjonctif	
insiste	**insistions**	**aie insisté**	**ayons insisté**
insistes	**insistiez**	**aies insisté**	**ayez insisté**
insiste	**insistent**	**ait insisté**	**aient insisté**
7 imparfait du subjonctif		14 plus-que-parfait du subjonctif	
insistasse	**insistassions**	**eusse insisté**	**eussions insisté**
insistasses	**insistassiez**	**eusses insisté**	**eussiez insisté**
insistât	**insistassent**	**eût insisté**	**eussent insisté**

Impératif
insiste
insistons
insistez

Sentences using this verb and words related to it
Madame Albertine, maîtresse de français, insiste beaucoup sur la discipline dans cette école.

insistant, insistante insistent, persistent
l'insistance *f.* insistence
insister sur to insist on
inutile d'insister useless to insist

It's important that you be familiar with the Subjunctive. See pages 26–31.

to instruct

Irregular verb

The Seven Simple Tenses		The Seven Compound Tenses	
Singular	Plural	Singular	Plural
1 présent de l'indicatif		8 passé composé	
instruis	**instruisons**	**ai instruit**	**avons instruit**
instruis	**instruisez**	**as instruit**	**avez instruit**
instruit	**instruisent**	**a instruit**	**ont instruit**
2 imparfait de l'indicatif		9 plus-que-parfait de l'indicatif	
instruisais	**instruisions**	**avais instruit**	**avions instruit**
instruisais	**instruisiez**	**avais instruit**	**aviez instruit**
instruisait	**instruisaient**	**avait instruit**	**avaient instruit**
3 passé simple		10 passé antérieur	
instruisis	**instruisîmes**	**eus instruit**	**eûmes instruit**
instruisis	**instruisîtes**	**eus instruit**	**eûtes instruit**
instruisit	**instruisirent**	**eut instruit**	**eurent instruit**
4 futur		11 futur antérieur	
instruirai	**instruirons**	**aurai instruit**	**aurons instruit**
instruiras	**instruirez**	**auras instruit**	**aurez instruit**
instruira	**instruiront**	**aura instruit**	**auront instruit**
5 conditionnel		12 conditionnel passé	
instruirais	**instruirions**	**aurais instruit**	**aurions instruit**
instruirais	**instruiriez**	**aurais instruit**	**auriez instruit**
instruirait	**instruiraient**	**aurait instruit**	**auraient instruit**
6 présent du subjonctif		13 passé du subjonctif	
instruise	**instruisions**	**aie instruit**	**ayons instruit**
instruises	**instruisiez**	**aies instruit**	**ayez instruit**
instruise	**instruisent**	**ait instruit**	**aient instruit**
7 imparfait du subjonctif		14 plus-que-parfait du subjonctif	
instruisisse	**instruisissions**	**eusse instruit**	**eussions instruit**
instruisisses	**instruisissiez**	**eusses instruit**	**eussiez instruit**
instruisît	**instruisissent**	**eût instruit**	**eussent instruit**

Impératif
instruis
instruisons
instruisez

Words and expressions related to this verb

instruit, instruite educated
instruction *f.* instruction, teaching
sans instruction uneducated
instructeur, instructrice instructor
instructif, instructive instructive
les instructions instructions
s'instruire to teach oneself, to educate oneself
l'instruction publique public education
bien instruit (instruite), fort instruit (instruite) well educated

Get acquainted with what preposition goes with what verb. See *Verbs with prepositions* in the Appendixes.

Irregular verb

to forbid, to prohibit

The Seven Simple Tenses		The Seven Compound Tenses	
Singular	Plural	Singular	Plural
1 présent de l'indicatif		8 passé composé	
interdis	**interdisons**	**ai interdit**	**avons interdit**
interdis	**interdisez**	**as interdit**	**avez interdit**
interdit	**interdisent**	**a interdit**	**ont interdit**
2 imparfait de l'indicatif		9 plus-que-parfait de l'indicatif	
interdisais	**interdisions**	**avais interdit**	**avions interdit**
interdisais	**interdisiez**	**avais interdit**	**aviez interdit**
interdisait	**interdisaient**	**avait interdit**	**avaient interdit**
3 passé simple		10 passé antérieur	
interdis	**interdîmes**	**eus interdit**	**eûmes interdit**
interdis	**interdîtes**	**eus interdit**	**eûtes interdit**
interdit	**interdirent**	**eut interdit**	**eurent interdit**
4 futur		11 futur antérieur	
interdirai	**interdirons**	**aurai interdit**	**aurons interdit**
interdiras	**interdirez**	**auras interdit**	**aurez interdit**
interdira	**interdiront**	**aura interdit**	**auront interdit**
5 conditionnel		12 conditionnel passé	
interdirais	**interdirions**	**aurais interdit**	**aurions interdit**
interdirais	**interdiriez**	**aurais interdit**	**auriez interdit**
interdirait	**interdiraient**	**aurait interdit**	**auraient interdit**
6 présent du subjonctif		13 passé du subjonctif	
interdise	**interdisions**	**aie interdit**	**ayons interdit**
interdises	**interdisiez**	**aies interdit**	**ayez interdit**
interdise	**interdisent**	**ait interdit**	**aient interdit**
7 imparfait du subjonctif		14 plus-que-parfait du subjonctif	
interdisse	**interdissions**	**eusse interdit**	**eussions interdit**
interdisses	**interdissiez**	**eusses interdit**	**eussiez interdit**
interdît	**interdissent**	**eût interdit**	**eussent interdit**

Impératif
interdis
interdisons
interdisez

Sentences using this verb and words and expressions related to it

Je vous interdis de m'interrompre constamment. I forbid you to interrupt me constantly.
Il est interdit de marcher sur l'herbe. Do not walk on the grass.

interdire qqch à qqn to forbid someone something
l'interdit *m.* interdict; *adj.* **les jeux interdits** forbidden games
l'interdiction *f.* interdiction, prohibition
interdire à qqn de faire qqch to forbid someone from doing something
STATIONNEMENT INTERDIT NO PARKING

See also **contredire, dire, maudire, médire,** and **prédire.**

s'intéresser (262) Part. pr. s'intéressant Part. passé intéressé(e)(s)

to be interested in

Reflexive regular **-er** verb

The Seven Simple Tenses		The Seven Compound Tenses	
Singular	Plural	Singular	Plural
1 présent de l'indicatif		8 passé composé	
m'intéresse	**nous intéressons**	**me suis intéressé(e)**	**nous sommes intéressé(e)s**
t'intéresses	**vous intéressez**	**t'es intéressé(e)**	**vous êtes intéressé(e)(s)**
s'intéresse	**s'intéressent**	**s'est intéressé(e)**	**se sont intéressé(e)s**
2 imparfait de l'indicatif		9 plus-que-parfait de l'indicatif	
m'intéressais	**nous intéressions**	**m'étais intéressé(e)**	**nous étions intéressé(e)s**
t'intéressais	**vous intéressiez**	**t'étais intéressé(e)**	**vous étiez intéressé(e)(s)**
s'intéressait	**s'intéressaient**	**s'était intéressé(e)**	**s'étaient intéressé(e)s**
3 passé simple		10 passé antérieur	
m'intéressai	**nous intéressâmes**	**me fus intéressé(e)**	**nous fûmes intéressé(e)s**
t'intéressas	**vous intéressâtes**	**te fus intéressé(e)**	**vous fûtes intéressé(e)(s)**
s'intéressa	**s'intéressèrent**	**se fut intéressé(e)**	**se furent intéressé(e)s**
4 futur		11 futur antérieur	
m'intéresserai	**nous intéresserons**	**me serai intéressé(e)**	**nous serons intéressé(e)s**
t'intéresseras	**vous intéresserez**	**te seras intéressé(e)**	**vous serez intéressé(e)(s)**
s'intéressera	**s'intéresseront**	**se sera intéressé(e)**	**se seront intéressé(e)s**
5 conditionnel		12 conditionnel passé	
m'intéresserais	**nous intéresserions**	**me serais intéressé(e)**	**nous serions intéressé(e)s**
t'intéresserais	**vous intéresseriez**	**te serais intéressé(e)**	**vous seriez intéressé(e)(s)**
s'intéresserait	**s'intéresseraient**	**se serait intéressé(e)**	**se seraient intéressé(e)s**
6 présent du subjonctif		13 passé du subjonctif	
m'intéresse	**nous intéressions**	**me sois intéressé(e)**	**nous soyons intéressé(e)s**
t'intéresses	**vous intéressiez**	**te sois intéressé(e)**	**vous soyez intéressé(e)(s)**
s'intéresse	**s'intéressent**	**se soit intéressé(e)**	**se soient intéressé(e)s**
7 imparfait du subjonctif		14 plus-que-parfait du subjonctif	
m'intéressasse	**nous intéressassions**	**me fusse intéressé(e)**	**nous fussions intéressé(e)s**
t'intéressasses	**vous intéressassiez**	**te fusses intéressé(e)**	**vous fussiez intéressé(e)(s)**
s'intéressât	**s'intéressassent**	**se fût intéressé(e)**	**se fussent intéressé(e)s**

Impératif
intéresse-toi; ne t'intéresse pas
intéressons-nous; ne nous intéressons pas
intéressez-vous; ne vous intéressez pas

Words and expressions related to this verb
s'intéresser à qqch to be interested in something, to concern oneself with
Je m'intéresse aux sports. I am interested in sports.
s'intéresser à qqn to be interested in someone
Janine s'intéresse à lui. Janine is interested in him.
intéresser qqn à qqch to interest someone in something
Je m'intéresse à tout. I am interested in everything.
Cela ne m'intéresse pas du tout. That does not interest me at all.
un intérêt interest
intéressant, intéressante interesting
Rien ne m'intéresse. Nothing interests me.

Regular **-er** verb endings; spelling change: retain the **ge** before **a** or **o** to keep the soft **g** sound of the verb

to interrogate, to question

The Seven Simple Tenses		The Seven Compound Tenses	
Singular	Plural	Singular	Plural
1 présent de l'indicatif		8 passé composé	
interroge	**interrogeons**	**ai interrogé**	**avons interrogé**
interroges	**interrogez**	**as interrogé**	**avez interrogé**
interroge	**interrogent**	**a interrogé**	**ont interrogé**
2 imparfait de l'indicatif		9 plus-que-parfait de l'indicatif	
interrogeais	**interrogions**	**avais interrogé**	**avions interrogé**
interrogeais	**interrogiez**	**avais interrogé**	**aviez interrogé**
interrogeait	**interrogeaient**	**avait interrogé**	**avaient interrogé**
3 passé simple		10 passé antérieur	
interrogeai	**interrogeâmes**	**eus interrogé**	**eûmes interrogé**
interrogeas	**interrogeâtes**	**eus interrogé**	**eûtes interrogé**
interrogea	**interrogèrent**	**eut interrogé**	**eurent interrogé**
4 futur		11 futur antérieur	
interrogerai	**interrogerons**	**aurai interrogé**	**aurons interrogé**
interrogeras	**interrogerez**	**auras interrogé**	**aurez interrogé**
interrogera	**interrogeront**	**aura interrogé**	**auront interrogé**
5 conditionnel		12 conditionnel passé	
interrogerais	**interrogerions**	**aurais interrogé**	**aurions interrogé**
interrogerais	**interrogeriez**	**aurais interrogé**	**auriez interrogé**
interrogerait	**interrogeraient**	**aurait interrogé**	**auraient interrogé**
6 présent du subjonctif		13 passé du subjonctif	
interroge	**interrogions**	**aie interrogé**	**ayons interrogé**
interroges	**interrogiez**	**aies interrogé**	**ayez interrogé**
interroge	**interrogent**	**ait interrogé**	**aient interrogé**
7 imparfait du subjonctif		14 plus-que-parfait du subjonctif	
interrogeasse	**interrogeassions**	**eusse interrogé**	**eussions interrogé**
interrogeasses	**interrogeassiez**	**eusses interrogé**	**eussiez interrogé**
interrogeât	**interrogeassent**	**eût interrogé**	**eussent interrogé**

Impératif
interroge
interrogeons
interrogez

Words and expressions related to this verb

une interrogation interrogation, questioning
un point d'interrogation question mark
un interrogateur, une interrogatrice interrogator
interrogatif, interrogative interrogative
interrogativement interrogatively
un interrogatoire interrogation
dérogatoire derogatory

How are you doing? Find out with the verb drills and tests with answers explained on pages 50–101.

interrompre (264) Part. pr. interrompant Part. passé interrompu

to interrupt

Regular **-re** verb endings; spelling change: 3d person sing. of Tense No. 1 adds **t**

The Seven Simple Tenses		The Seven Compound Tenses	
Singular	Plural	Singular	Plural
1 présent de l'indicatif		8 passé composé	
interromps	**interrompons**	**ai interrompu**	**avons interrompu**
interromps	**interrompez**	**as interrompu**	**avez interrompu**
interrompt	**interrompent**	**a interrompu**	**ont interrompu**
2 imparfait de l'indicatif		9 plus-que-parfait de l'indicatif	
interrompais	**interrompions**	**avais interrompu**	**avions interrompu**
interrompais	**interrompiez**	**avais interrompu**	**aviez interrompu**
interrompait	**interrompaient**	**avait interrompu**	**avaient interrompu**
3 passé simple		10 passé antérieur	
interrompis	**interrompîmes**	**eus interrompu**	**eûmes interrompu**
interrompis	**interrompîtes**	**eus interrompu**	**eûtes interrompu**
interrompit	**interrompirent**	**eut interrompu**	**eurent interrompu**
4 futur		11 futur antérieur	
interromprai	**interromprons**	**aurai interrompu**	**aurons interrompu**
interrompras	**interromprez**	**auras interrompu**	**aurez interrompu**
interrompra	**interrompront**	**aura interrompu**	**auront interrompu**
5 conditionnel		12 conditionnel passé	
interromprais	**interromprions**	**aurais interrompu**	**aurions interrompu**
interromprais	**interrompriez**	**aurais interrompu**	**auriez interrompu**
interromprait	**interrompraient**	**aurait interrompu**	**auraient interrompu**
6 présent du subjonctif		13 passé du subjonctif	
interrompe	**interrompions**	**aie interrompu**	**ayons interrompu**
interrompes	**interrompiez**	**aies interrompu**	**ayez interrompu**
interrompe	**interrompent**	**ait interrompu**	**aient interrompu**
7 imparfait du subjonctif		14 plus-que-parfait du subjonctif	
interrompisse	**interrompissions**	**eusse interrompu**	**eussions interrompu**
interrompisses	**interrompissiez**	**eusses interrompu**	**eussiez interrompu**
interrompît	**interrompissent**	**eût interrompu**	**eussent interrompu**

Impératif
interromps
interrompons
interrompez

Sentences using this verb and words related to it

—Maurice, tu m'interromps à chaque instant. Cesse de m'interrompre, s'il te plaît! C'est une mauvaise habitude et je ne l'aime pas. Est-ce que tu l'aimes quand on t'interrompt continuellement?

une interruption interruption
interrompu, interrompue interrupted

un interrupteur, une interruptrice interrupter
un interrupteur light switch

See also **corrompre** and **rompre.**

Irregular verb

to introduce, to show in

The Seven Simple Tenses		The Seven Compound Tenses	
Singular	Plural	Singular	Plural
1 présent de l'indicatif		8 passé composé	
introduis	**introduisons**	**ai introduit**	**avons introduit**
introduis	**introduisez**	**as introduit**	**avez introduit**
introduit	**introduisent**	**a introduit**	**ont introduit**
2 imparfait de l'indicatif		9 plus-que-parfait de l'indicatif	
introduisais	**introduisions**	**avais introduit**	**avions introduit**
introduisais	**introduisiez**	**avais introduit**	**aviez introduit**
introduisait	**introduisaient**	**avait introduit**	**avaient introduit**
3 passé simple		10 passé antérieur	
introduisis	**introduisîmes**	**eus introduit**	**eûmes introduit**
introduisis	**introduisîtes**	**eus introduit**	**eûtes introduit**
introduisit	**introduisirent**	**eut introduit**	**eurent introduit**
4 futur		11 futur antérieur	
introduirai	**introduirons**	**aurai introduit**	**aurons introduit**
introduiras	**introduirez**	**auras introduit**	**aurez introduit**
introduira	**introduiront**	**aura introduit**	**auront introduit**
5 conditionnel		12 conditionnel passé	
introduirais	**introduirions**	**aurais introduit**	**aurions introduit**
introduirais	**introduiriez**	**aurais introduit**	**auriez introduit**
introduirait	**introduiraient**	**aurait introduit**	**auraient introduit**
6 présent du subjonctif		13 passé du subjonctif	
introduise	**introduisions**	**aie introduit**	**ayons introduit**
introduises	**introduisiez**	**aies introduit**	**ayez introduit**
introduise	**introduisent**	**ait introduit**	**aient introduit**
7 imparfait du subjonctif		14 plus-que-parfait du subjonctif	
introduisisse	**introduisissions**	**eusse introduit**	**eussions introduit**
introduisisses	**introduisissiez**	**eusses introduit**	**eussiez introduit**
introduisît	**introduisissent**	**eût introduit**	**eussent introduit**

Impératif
introduis
introduisons
introduisez

Words related to this verb
introducteur, introductrice introducer, initiator
introductif, introductive introductory
introduction *f.* introduction; **les paroles d'introduction** introductory words

See also **conduire, déduire, produire, réduire, reproduire, séduire,** and **traduire.**

Can't remember the French verb you need? Check the back pages of this book for the English-French verb index!

inviter (266)

Part. pr. **invitant** Part. passé **invité**

to invite

Regular **-er** verb

The Seven Simple Tenses		The Seven Compound Tenses	
Singular	Plural	Singular	Plural
1 présent de l'indicatif		8 passé composé	
invite	**invitons**	**ai invité**	**avons invité**
invites	**invitez**	**as invité**	**avez invité**
invite	**invitent**	**a invité**	**ont invité**
2 imparfait de l'indicatif		9 plus-que-parfait de l'indicatif	
invitais	**invitions**	**avais invité**	**avions invité**
invitais	**invitiez**	**avais invité**	**aviez invité**
invitait	**invitaient**	**avait invité**	**avaient invité**
3 passé simple		10 passé antérieur	
invitai	**invitâmes**	**eus invité**	**eûmes invité**
invitas	**invitâtes**	**eus invité**	**eûtes invité**
invita	**invitèrent**	**eut invité**	**eurent invité**
4 futur		11 futur antérieur	
inviterai	**inviterons**	**aurai invité**	**aurons invité**
inviteras	**inviterez**	**auras invité**	**aurez invité**
invitera	**inviteront**	**aura invité**	**auront invité**
5 conditionnel		12 conditionnel passé	
inviterais	**inviterions**	**aurais invité**	**aurions invité**
inviterais	**inviteriez**	**aurais invité**	**auriez invité**
inviterait	**inviteraient**	**aurait invité**	**auraient invité**
6 présent du subjonctif		13 passé du subjonctif	
invite	**invitions**	**aie invité**	**ayons invité**
invites	**invitiez**	**aies invité**	**ayez invité**
invite	**invitent**	**ait invité**	**aient invité**
7 imparfait du subjonctif		14 plus-que-parfait du subjonctif	
invitasse	**invitassions**	**eusse invité**	**eussions invité**
invitasses	**invitassiez**	**eusses invité**	**eussiez invité**
invitât	**invitassent**	**eût invité**	**eussent invité**

Impératif
invite
invitons
invitez

Sentences using this verb and words related to it

J'ai reçu une invitation à dîner chez les Martin. C'est pour samedi soir. J'ai accepté avec plaisir et maintenant je vais en ville acheter un cadeau pour eux.

l'invitation *f.* invitation
les invités the guests
sur l'invitation de at the invitation of
sans invitation without invitation, uninvited
inviter qqn à faire qqch to invite someone to do something
Elle s'est invitée. She invited herself.
C'est moi qui invite! My treat!

Can't find the verb you're looking for? Check the back pages of this book for a list of over 2,600 additional verbs!

Regular **-er** verb endings; spelling change: **t** becomes **tt** before syllable with mute **e**

to throw, to cast

The Seven Simple Tenses		The Seven Compound Tenses	
Singular	Plural	Singular	Plural
1 présent de l'indicatif		8 passé composé	
jette	**jetons**	**ai jeté**	**avons jeté**
jettes	**jetez**	**as jeté**	**avez jeté**
jette	**jettent**	**a jeté**	**ont jeté**
2 imparfait de l'indicatif		9 plus-que-parfait de l'indicatif	
jetais	**jetions**	**avais jeté**	**avions jeté**
jetais	**jetiez**	**avais jeté**	**aviez jeté**
jetait	**jetaient**	**avait jeté**	**avaient jeté**
3 passé simple		10 passé antérieur	
jetai	**jetâmes**	**eus jeté**	**eûmes jeté**
jetas	**jetâtes**	**eus jeté**	**eûtes jeté**
jeta	**jetèrent**	**eut jeté**	**eurent jeté**
4 futur		11 futur antérieur	
jetterai	**jetterons**	**aurai jeté**	**aurons jeté**
jetteras	**jetterez**	**auras jeté**	**aurez jeté**
jettera	**jetteront**	**aura jeté**	**auront jeté**
5 conditionnel		12 conditionnel passé	
jetterais	**jetterions**	**aurais jeté**	**aurions jeté**
jetterais	**jetteriez**	**aurais jeté**	**auriez jeté**
jetterait	**jetteraient**	**aurait jeté**	**auraient jeté**
6 présent du subjonctif		13 passé du subjonctif	
jette	**jetions**	**aie jeté**	**ayons jeté**
jettes	**jetiez**	**aies jeté**	**ayez jeté**
jette	**jettent**	**ait jeté**	**aient jeté**
7 imparfait du subjonctif		14 plus-que-parfait du subjonctif	
jetasse	**jetassions**	**eusse jeté**	**eussions jeté**
jetasses	**jetassiez**	**eusses jeté**	**eussiez jeté**
jetât	**jetassent**	**eût jeté**	**eussent jeté**

Impératif
jette
jetons
jetez

Common idiomatic expressions using this verb
jeter un cri to utter a cry
jeter son argent par la fenêtre to throw one's money out the window
se jeter sur (contre) to throw oneself at (against)
un jeton de téléphone telephone slug, token
une jetée jetty
un jet d'eau fountain
jeter un coup d'oeil à to glance at; **se jeter au cou de qqn** to throw oneself at somebody
rejeter to reject, to throw back; **projeter** to plan, to project
jetable disposable
Ne jetez rien par la fenêtre. Do not throw anything out the window.

Don't miss orthographically changing verbs on pages 32–34.

joindre (268) — Part. pr. **joignant** — Part. passé **joint**

to join, to contact

Irregular verb

The Seven Simple Tenses		The Seven Compound Tenses	
Singular	Plural	Singular	Plural
1 présent de l'indicatif		8 passé composé	
joins	**joignons**	**ai joint**	**avons joint**
joins	**joignez**	**as joint**	**avez joint**
joint	**joignent**	**a joint**	**ont joint**
2 imparfait de l'indicatif		9 plus-que-parfait de l'indicatif	
joignais	**joignions**	**avais joint**	**avions joint**
joignais	**joigniez**	**avais joint**	**aviez joint**
joignait	**joignaient**	**avait joint**	**avaient joint**
3 passé simple		10 passé antérieur	
joignis	**joignîmes**	**eus joint**	**eûmes joint**
joignis	**joignîtes**	**eus joint**	**eûtes joint**
joignit	**joignirent**	**eut joint**	**eurent joint**
4 futur		11 futur antérieur	
joindrai	**joindrons**	**aurai joint**	**aurons joint**
joindras	**joindrez**	**auras joint**	**aurez joint**
joindra	**joindront**	**aura joint**	**auront joint**
5 conditionnel		12 conditionnel passé	
joindrais	**joindrions**	**aurais joint**	**aurions joint**
joindrais	**joindriez**	**aurais joint**	**auriez joint**
joindrait	**joindraient**	**aurait joint**	**auraient joint**
6 présent du subjonctif		13 passé du subjonctif	
joigne	**joignions**	**aie joint**	**ayons joint**
joignes	**joigniez**	**aies joint**	**ayez joint**
joigne	**joignent**	**ait joint**	**aient joint**
7 imparfait du subjonctif		14 plus-que-parfait du subjonctif	
joignisse	**joignissions**	**eusse joint**	**eussions joint**
joignisses	**joignissiez**	**eusses joint**	**eussiez joint**
joignît	**joignissent**	**eût joint**	**eussent joint**

Impératif
joins
joignons
joignez

Common idiomatic expressions using this verb and words related to it

joindre les deux bouts to make ends meet
les jointures des doigts knuckles
joint, jointe joined
les talons joints heels together
ci-joint herewith, attached
joindre à to join to, to add to
rejoindre to rejoin, to join together
se rejoindre to meet, to come together again
se joindre à la discussion to join in the discussion
joindre par téléphone to reach by telephone

Use the guide to French pronunciation. It's in the Appendixes.

Regular **-er** verb

to play, to act (in a play), to gamble

The Seven Simple Tenses		The Seven Compound Tenses	
Singular	Plural	Singular	Plural
1 présent de l'indicatif		8 passé composé	
joue	**jouons**	**ai joué**	**avons joué**
joues	**jouez**	**as joué**	**avez joué**
joue	**jouent**	**a joué**	**ont joué**
2 imparfait de l'indicatif		9 plus-que-parfait de l'indicatif	
jouais	**jouions**	**avais joué**	**avions joué**
jouais	**jouiez**	**avais joué**	**aviez joué**
jouait	**jouaient**	**avait joué**	**avaient joué**
3 passé simple		10 passé antérieur	
jouai	**jouâmes**	**eus joué**	**eûmes joué**
jouas	**jouâtes**	**eus joué**	**eûtes joué**
joua	**jouèrent**	**eut joué**	**eurent joué**
4 futur		11 futur antérieur	
jouerai	**jouerons**	**aurai joué**	**aurons joué**
joueras	**jouerez**	**auras joué**	**aurez joué**
jouera	**joueront**	**aura joué**	**auront joué**
5 conditionnel		12 conditionnel passé	
jouerais	**jouerions**	**aurais joué**	**aurions joué**
jouerais	**joueriez**	**aurais joué**	**auriez joué**
jouerait	**joueraient**	**aurait joué**	**auraient joué**
6 présent du subjonctif		13 passé du subjonctif	
joue	**jouions**	**aie joué**	**ayons joué**
joues	**jouiez**	**aies joué**	**ayez joué**
joue	**jouent**	**ait joué**	**aient joué**
7 imparfait du subjonctif		14 plus-que-parfait du subjonctif	
jouasse	**jouassions**	**eusse joué**	**eussions joué**
jouasses	**jouassiez**	**eusses joué**	**eussiez joué**
jouât	**jouassent**	**eût joué**	**eussent joué**

Impératif
joue
jouons
jouez

AN ESSENTIAL 55 VERB

Jouer

Jouer is an essential French verb because it is very useful for a student, especially when talking about sports and music.

Sentences using jouer

Madeleine a joué un tour au voisin. Madeleine played a trick on the neighbor.

Cela va se jouer ce soir. That will be settled tonight.

Tu dois arrêter de fumer. Ta santé est en jeu! You must stop smoking. Your health is at stake!

Sports

Paul et ses frères jouent au foot tous les jours. Paul and his brothers play soccer every day.

Claire jouait au tennis quand elle est tombée. Claire was playing tennis when she fell down.

Fred et moi, nous jouons au squash demain soir. Tomorrow evening Fred and I will play squash.

James jouera dans le championnat du polo. James will play in the polo championship.

Music

Ma tante joue du piano. My aunt plays the piano.

Jean a joué de la flûte dans un concert à New York. John played the flute in a concert in New York.

Paul joue de la guitare après l'école. Paul plays guitar after school.

Words and expressions related to this verb

jouer un tour à qqn to play a trick on someone
un jouet toy, plaything
un joueur, une joueuse player, gambler
jouer sur les mots to play with words
un jeu de mots word play, pun
jouer un rôle to play a part
se jouer de to make fun of, deride
un joujou, des joujoux toy, toys (child's language)
jouer gros jeu to play for high stakes
un jeu a game
un jeu vidéo video game
en jeu at stake
enjoué, enjouée playful
un jeu de cartes a deck of cards
un jeu d'outils a set of tools
déjouer to baffle, thwart
rejouer to replay, play again

Sports and recreation
jouer au tennis to play tennis
jouer au squash to play squash
jouer au golf to play golf
jouer au foot to play soccer
jouer aux cartes to play cards

Music
jouer d'un instrument to play an instrument
jouer de la flûte to play the flute
jouer du piano to play the piano
jouer du violon to play the violin

Regular **-ir** verb

to enjoy

The Seven Simple Tenses		The Seven Compound Tenses	
Singular	Plural	Singular	Plural
1 présent de l'indicatif		8 passé composé	
jouis	**jouissons**	**ai joui**	**avons joui**
jouis	**jouissez**	**as joui**	**avez joui**
jouit	**jouissent**	**a joui**	**ont joui**
2 imparfait de l'indicatif		9 plus-que-parfait de l'indicatif	
jouissais	**jouissions**	**avais joui**	**avions joui**
jouissais	**jouissiez**	**avais joui**	**aviez joui**
jouissait	**jouissaient**	**avait joui**	**avaient joui**
3 passé simple		10 passé antérieur	
jouis	**jouîmes**	**eus joui**	**eûmes joui**
jouis	**jouîtes**	**eus joui**	**eûtes joui**
jouit	**jouirent**	**eut joui**	**eurent joui**
4 futur		11 futur antérieur	
jouirai	**jouirons**	**aurai joui**	**aurons joui**
jouiras	**jouirez**	**auras joui**	**aurez joui**
jouira	**jouiront**	**aura joui**	**auront joui**
5 conditionnel		12 conditionnel passé	
jouirais	**jouirions**	**aurais joui**	**aurions joui**
jouirais	**jouiriez**	**aurais joui**	**auriez joui**
jouirait	**jouiraient**	**aurait joui**	**auraient joui**
6 présent du subjonctif		13 passé du subjonctif	
jouisse	**jouissions**	**aie joui**	**ayons joui**
jouisses	**jouissiez**	**aies joui**	**ayez joui**
jouisse	**jouissent**	**ait joui**	**aient joui**
7 imparfait du subjonctif		14 plus-que-parfait du subjonctif	
jouisse	**jouissions**	**eusse joui**	**eussions joui**
jouisses	**jouissiez**	**eusses joui**	**eussiez joui**
jouît	**jouissent**	**eût joui**	**eussent joui**

Impératif
jouis
jouissons
jouissez

Words and expressions related to this verb
jouir de qqch to enjoy something
la jouissance delight, enjoyment
la joie joy; **la joie de vivre** joy of living; **avec joie** gladly
la réjouissance rejoicing
se réjouir de to rejoice in, to be delighted at
réjouir to cheer up, to gladden, to rejoice
réjouir la vue to be pleasing to the eye
réjouir le coeur to gladden the heart
réjouissant, réjouissante entertaining, amusing

Don't forget to study the section on defective and impersonal verbs. It's right after this main list.

juger (271) — Part. pr. jugeant — Part. passé jugé

to judge, to deem

Regular **-er** verb endings; spelling change: retain the **ge** before **a** or **o** to keep the soft **g** sound of the verb

The Seven Simple Tenses		The Seven Compound Tenses	
Singular	Plural	Singular	Plural
1 présent de l'indicatif		8 passé composé	
juge	**jugeons**	**ai jugé**	**avons jugé**
juges	**jugez**	**as jugé**	**avez jugé**
juge	**jugent**	**a jugé**	**ont jugé**
2 imparfait de l'indicatif		9 plus-que-parfait de l'indicatif	
jugeais	**jugions**	**avais jugé**	**avions jugé**
jugeais	**jugiez**	**avais jugé**	**aviez jugé**
jugeait	**jugeaient**	**avait jugé**	**avaient jugé**
3 passé simple		10 passé antérieur	
jugeai	**jugeâmes**	**eus jugé**	**eûmes jugé**
jugeas	**jugeâtes**	**eus jugé**	**eûtes jugé**
jugea	**jugèrent**	**eut jugé**	**eurent jugé**
4 futur		11 futur antérieur	
jugerai	**jugerons**	**aurai jugé**	**aurons jugé**
jugeras	**jugerez**	**auras jugé**	**aurez jugé**
jugera	**jugeront**	**aura jugé**	**auront jugé**
5 conditionnel		12 conditionnel passé	
jugerais	**jugerions**	**aurais jugé**	**aurions jugé**
jugerais	**jugeriez**	**aurais jugé**	**auriez jugé**
jugerait	**jugeraient**	**aurait jugé**	**auraient jugé**
6 présent du subjonctif		13 passé du subjonctif	
juge	**jugions**	**aie jugé**	**ayons jugé**
juges	**jugiez**	**aies jugé**	**ayez jugé**
juge	**jugent**	**ait jugé**	**aient jugé**
7 imparfait du subjonctif		14 plus-que-parfait du subjonctif	
jugeasse	**jugeassions**	**eusse jugé**	**eussions jugé**
jugeasses	**jugeassiez**	**eusses jugé**	**eussiez jugé**
jugeât	**jugeassent**	**eût jugé**	**eussent jugé**

Impératif
juge
jugeons
jugez

Words and expressions related to this verb

juger de to judge (of); **Jugez de ma joie!** You can imagine my joy!
à en juger par . . . judging by . . .
juger par . . . to judge by . . .
mal juger qqn to misjudge someone
juger bon de faire qqch to think it wise to do something
un juge judge, magistrate; **un juge de paix** justice of the peace
un jugement judgment

Get acquainted with what preposition goes with what. See *Verbs with prepositions* in the Appendixes.

Regular **-er** verb

to swear, to vow

The Seven Simple Tenses		The Seven Compound Tenses	
Singular	Plural	Singular	Plural
1 présent de l'indicatif		8 passé composé	
jure	**jurons**	**ai juré**	**avons juré**
jures	**jurez**	**as juré**	**avez juré**
jure	**jurent**	**a juré**	**ont juré**
2 imparfait de l'indicatif		9 plus-que-parfait de l'indicatif	
jurais	**jurions**	**avais juré**	**avions juré**
jurais	**juriez**	**avais juré**	**aviez juré**
jurait	**juraient**	**avait juré**	**avaient juré**
3 passé simple		10 passé antérieur	
jurai	**jurâmes**	**eus juré**	**eûmes juré**
juras	**jurâtes**	**eus juré**	**eûtes juré**
jura	**jurèrent**	**eut juré**	**eurent juré**
4 futur		11 futur antérieur	
jurerai	**jurerons**	**aurai juré**	**aurons juré**
jureras	**jurerez**	**auras juré**	**aurez juré**
jurera	**jureront**	**aura juré**	**auront juré**
5 conditionnel		12 conditionnel passé	
jurerais	**jurerions**	**aurais juré**	**aurions juré**
jurerais	**jureriez**	**aurais juré**	**auriez juré**
jurerait	**jureraient**	**aurait juré**	**auraient juré**
6 présent du subjonctif		13 passé du subjonctif	
jure	**jurions**	**aie juré**	**ayons juré**
jures	**juriez**	**aies juré**	**ayez juré**
jure	**jurent**	**ait juré**	**aient juré**
7 imparfait du subjonctif		14 plus-que-parfait du subjonctif	
jurasse	**jurassions**	**eusse juré**	**eussions juré**
jurasses	**jurassiez**	**eusses juré**	**eussiez juré**
jurât	**jurassent**	**eût juré**	**eussent juré**

Impératif
jure
jurons
jurez

Words and expressions related to this verb

jurer sur la Bible to swear on the Bible
un juriste jurist
la jurisprudence jurisprudence
un jureur swearer
jurer contre to swear against
abjurer to abjure, renounce
un juron curse, oath
un jury jury
un jurisconsulte legal expert
Je vous le jure! I swear it!
dire des jurons to swear, to curse

It's important that you be familiar with the Subjunctive. See pages 26–31.

lâcher (273) — Part. pr. lâchant — Part. passé lâché

to loosen, to unleash, to let go

Regular **-er** verb

The Seven Simple Tenses		The Seven Compound Tenses	
Singular	Plural	Singular	Plural
1 présent de l'indicatif		8 passé composé	
lâche	**lâchons**	**ai lâché**	**avons lâché**
lâches	**lâchez**	**as lâché**	**avez lâché**
lâche	**lâchent**	**a lâché**	**ont lâché**
2 imparfait de l'indicatif		9 plus-que-parfait de l'indicatif	
lâchais	**lâchions**	**avais lâché**	**avions lâché**
lâchais	**lâchiez**	**avais lâché**	**aviez lâché**
lâchait	**lâchaient**	**avait lâché**	**avaient lâché**
3 passé simple		10 passé antérieur	
lâchai	**lâchâmes**	**eus lâché**	**eûmes lâché**
lâchas	**lâchâtes**	**eus lâché**	**eûtes lâché**
lâcha	**lâchèrent**	**eut lâché**	**eurent lâché**
4 futur		11 futur antérieur	
lâcherai	**lâcherons**	**aurai lâché**	**aurons lâché**
lâcheras	**lâcherez**	**auras lâché**	**aurez lâché**
lâchera	**lâcheront**	**aura lâché**	**auront lâché**
5 conditionnel		12 conditionnel passé	
lâcherais	**lâcherions**	**aurais lâché**	**aurions lâché**
lâcherais	**lâcheriez**	**aurais lâché**	**auriez lâché**
lâcherait	**lâcheraient**	**aurait lâché**	**auraient lâché**
6 présent du subjonctif		13 passé du subjonctif	
lâche	**lâchions**	**aie lâché**	**ayons lâché**
lâches	**lâchiez**	**aies lâché**	**ayez lâché**
lâche	**lâchent**	**ait lâché**	**aient lâché**
7 imparfait du subjonctif		14 plus-que-parfait du subjonctif	
lâchasse	**lâchassions**	**eusse lâché**	**eussions lâché**
lâchasses	**lâchassiez**	**eusses lâché**	**eussiez lâché**
lâchât	**lâchassent**	**eût lâché**	**eussent lâché**

Impératif
lâche
lâchons
lâchez

Words and expressions related to this verb

lâcher prise to let go
un lâcheur, une lâcheuse quitter
lâche cowardly; **lâchement** in a cowardly way
la lâcheté cowardice
un vêtement lâche flowing, loose garment
un relâche rest, relaxation, respite, temporary closing of a theater
relâcher to abate, to loosen, to relax, to slacken
Lâchez-moi! Let go of me!

Grammar putting you in a tense mood? Review the definitions of basic grammatical terms with examples on pages 35–49.

Regular **-er** verb

to let, to allow, to leave

The Seven Simple Tenses		The Seven Compound Tenses	
Singular	Plural	Singular	Plural
1 présent de l'indicatif		8 passé composé	
laisse	**laissons**	**ai laissé**	**avons laissé**
laisses	**laissez**	**as laissé**	**avez laissé**
laisse	**laissent**	**a laissé**	**ont laissé**
2 imparfait de l'indicatif		9 plus-que-parfait de l'indicatif	
laissais	**laissions**	**avais laissé**	**avions laissé**
laissais	**laissiez**	**avais laissé**	**aviez laissé**
laissait	**laissaient**	**avait laissé**	**avaient laissé**
3 passé simple		10 passé antérieur	
laissai	**laissâmes**	**eus laissé**	**eûmes laissé**
laissas	**laissâtes**	**eus laissé**	**eûtes laissé**
laissa	**laissèrent**	**eut laissé**	**eurent laissé**
4 futur		11 futur antérieur	
laisserai	**laisserons**	**aurai laissé**	**aurons laissé**
laisseras	**laisserez**	**auras laissé**	**aurez laissé**
laissera	**laisseront**	**aura laissé**	**auront laissé**
5 conditionnel		12 conditionnel passé	
laisserais	**laisserions**	**aurais laissé**	**aurions laissé**
laisserais	**laisseriez**	**aurais laissé**	**auriez laissé**
laisserait	**laisseraient**	**aurait laissé**	**auraient laissé**
6 présent du subjonctif		13 passé du subjonctif	
laisse	**laissions**	**aie laissé**	**ayons laissé**
laisses	**laissiez**	**aies laissé**	**ayez laissé**
laisse	**laissent**	**ait laissé**	**aient laissé**
7 imparfait du subjonctif		14 plus-que-parfait du subjonctif	
laissasse	**laissassions**	**eusse laissé**	**eussions laissé**
laissasses	**laissassiez**	**eusses laissé**	**eussiez laissé**
laissât	**laissassent**	**eût laissé**	**eussent laissé**

Impératif
laisse
laissons
laissez

Sentences using this verb and words related to it

J'ai laissé mes devoirs chez moi. I left my homework at home.
Laissez-moi tranquille! Leave me alone!
Laissez-moi passer, s'il vous plaît. Please let me get by.

laissez-faire do not interfere; **Laissez-moi faire.** Let me do as I please.
une laisse a leash
laisser entrer to let in, to allow to enter; **laisser tomber** to drop
laisser aller to let go; **se laisser aller** to let oneself go
délaisser to abandon, to forsake

lancer (275) — Part. Pr. lançant — Part. passé lancé

to hurl, to launch, to throw

Regular **-er** verb endings; spelling change: **c** changes to **ç** before **a** or **o** to keep **s** sound

The Seven Simple Tenses

Singular	Plural
1 présent de l'indicatif	
lance	**lançons**
lances	**lancez**
lance	**lancent**
2 imparfait de l'indicatif	
lançais	**lancions**
lançais	**lanciez**
lançait	**lançaient**
3 passé simple	
lançai	**lançâmes**
lanças	**lançâtes**
lança	**lancèrent**
4 futur	
lancerai	**lancerons**
lanceras	**lancerez**
lancera	**lanceront**
5 conditionnel	
lancerais	**lancerions**
lancerais	**lanceriez**
lancerait	**lanceraient**
6 présent du subjonctif	
lance	**lancions**
lances	**lanciez**
lance	**lancent**
7 imparfait du subjonctif	
lançasse	**lançassions**
lançasses	**lançassiez**
lançât	**lançassent**

The Seven Compound Tenses

Singular	Plural
8 passé composé	
ai lancé	**avons lancé**
as lancé	**avez lancé**
a lancé	**ont lancé**
9 plus-que-parfait de l'indicatif	
avais lancé	**avions lancé**
avais lancé	**aviez lancé**
avait lancé	**avaient lancé**
10 passé antérieur	
eus lancé	**eûmes lancé**
eus lancé	**eûtes lancé**
eut lancé	**eurent lancé**
11 futur antérieur	
aurai lancé	**aurons lancé**
auras lancé	**aurez lancé**
aura lancé	**auront lancé**
12 conditionnel passé	
aurais lancé	**aurions lancé**
aurais lancé	**auriez lancé**
aurait lancé	**auraient lancé**
13 passé du subjonctif	
aie lancé	**ayons lancé**
aies lancé	**ayez lancé**
ait lancé	**aient lancé**
14 plus-que-parfait du subjonctif	
eusse lancé	**eussions lancé**
eusses lancé	**eussiez lancé**
eût lancé	**eussent lancé**

Impératif
lance
lançons
lancez

Words and expressions related to this verb

se lancer contre to throw oneself at, against
un départ lancé a flying start (sports)
une lance a spear
le lancement d'un disque, d'un livre, etc. ceremony to launch a new record, book, etc.
un lancement hurling, casting
un lanceur thrower, pitcher (sports)
lancer un cri to cry out
une rampe de lancement launching pad

Can't remember the French verb you need? Check the back pages of this book for the English-French verb index!

Regular **-er** verb

to wash

The Seven Simple Tenses		The Seven Compound Tenses	
Singular	Plural	Singular	Plural
1 présent de l'indicatif		8 passé composé	
lave	**lavons**	**ai lavé**	**avons lavé**
laves	**lavez**	**as lavé**	**avez lavé**
lave	**lavent**	**a lavé**	**ont lavé**
2 imparfait de l'indicatif		9 plus-que-parfait de l'indicatif	
lavais	**lavions**	**avais lavé**	**avions lavé**
lavais	**laviez**	**avais lavé**	**aviez lavé**
lavait	**lavaient**	**avait lavé**	**avaient lavé**
3 passé simple		10 passé antérieur	
lavai	**lavâmes**	**eus lavé**	**eûmes lavé**
lavas	**lavâtes**	**eus lavé**	**eûtes lavé**
lava	**lavèrent**	**eut lavé**	**eurent lavé**
4 futur		11 futur antérieur	
laverai	**laverons**	**aurai lavé**	**aurons lavé**
laveras	**laverez**	**auras lavé**	**aurez lavé**
lavera	**laveront**	**aura lavé**	**auront lavé**
5 conditionnel		12 conditionnel passé	
laverais	**laverions**	**aurais lavé**	**aurions lavé**
laverais	**laveriez**	**aurais lavé**	**auriez lavé**
laverait	**laveraient**	**aurait lavé**	**auraient lavé**
6 présent du subjonctif		13 passé du subjonctif	
lave	**lavions**	**aie lavé**	**ayons lavé**
laves	**laviez**	**aies lavé**	**ayez lavé**
lave	**lavent**	**ait lavé**	**aient lavé**
7 imparfait du subjonctif		14 plus-que-parfait du subjonctif	
lavasse	**lavassions**	**eusse lavé**	**eussions lavé**
lavasses	**lavassiez**	**eusses lavé**	**eussiez lavé**
lavât	**lavassent**	**eût lavé**	**eussent lavé**

Impératif
lave
lavons
lavez

The subject pronouns are found on page 103.

AN ESSENTIAL 55 VERB

Laver and Se laver

Laver and **se laver** are essential verbs for you to learn because they can help you to understand the agreement of past participles.

Examples in the *présent*

Marie lave la voiture. (Marie is washing the car.) Note: **la voiture** is the direct object.

Marie se lave. (Marie is washing herself.) Note: **se** is the direct object pronoun.

Marie se lave les mains. (Marie is washing her hands.) Note: **les mains** is the direct object; **se** is an indirect object in this case.

Examples in the *passé composé*

Marie a lavé la voiture. (Marie washed the car.) Note: **la voiture** is the direct object.

Marie l'a lavée. (Marie washed it.) Note: **l'** stands for **la voiture**, so **lavée** agrees with the preceding direct object pronoun.

Marie s'est lavée. (Marie washed herself.) Note: **s'** is the direct object. What did Marie wash? She washed herself.

Marie s'est lavé les mains. (Marie washed her hands.) Note: **les mains** is the direct object; there is no feminine agreement on **lavé** because the direct object comes after; there is no preceding direct object pronoun. What did Marie wash? She washed her hands.

Sentences using se laver

—Henriette, est-ce que tu t'es bien lavée? Henrietta, did you wash yourself well?

—Oui, maman, je me suis lavée! Je me suis bien lavé les mains! Yes, Mother, I washed myself! I washed my hands well!

Lave-toi les mains, Marie. On va manger. Wash your hands, Marie. We're going to eat.

Words and expressions related to these verbs

un lavabo **washbasin, sink**

une douche **shower**

la salle de bains **bathroom**

se laver les mains de qqch **to wash one's hands of something**

lavable (en machine) **(machine) washable**

un lave-auto **car wash**

une laverie **laundry (room), launderette**

le lave-glace **windshield washer**

un lave-vaisselle **dishwasher**

une machine à laver, un lave-linge **washing machine**

laver en machine **to machine wash**

laver à la main **to hand wash**

un laveur, une laveuse **washer**

un raton laveur **raccoon**

se laver les dents (se brosser les dents) **to clean/brush one's teeth**

la lessive **laundry, laundry detergent**

le lavage **washing**

le lavement **enema**

la lavette **dish mop**

la lavure **dishwater**

For more information on **agreement of past participles**, read the entries in the section on definitions of basic grammatical terms with examples on pages 35–49.

Reflexive regular **-er** verb

to wash oneself

The Seven Simple Tenses		The Seven Compound Tenses	
Singular	Plural	Singular	Plural
1 présent de l'indicatif		8 passé composé	
me lave	**nous lavons**	**me suis lavé(e)**	**nous sommes lavé(e)s**
te laves	**vous lavez**	**t'es lavé(e)**	**vous êtes lavé(e)(s)**
se lave	**se lavent**	**s'est lavé(e)**	**se sont lavé(e)s**
2 imparfait de l'indicatif		9 plus-que-parfait de l'indicatif	
me lavais	**nous lavions**	**m'étais lavé(e)**	**nous étions lavé(e)s**
te lavais	**vous laviez**	**t'étais lavé(e)**	**vous étiez lavé(e)(s)**
se lavait	**se lavaient**	**s'était lavé(e)**	**s'étaient lavé(e)s**
3 passé simple		10 passé antérieur	
me lavai	**nous lavâmes**	**me fus lavé(e)**	**nous fûmes lavé(e)s**
te lavas	**vous lavâtes**	**te fus lavé(e)**	**vous fûtes lavé(e)(s)**
se lava	**se lavèrent**	**se fut lavé(e)**	**se furent lavé(e)s**
4 futur		11 futur antérieur	
me laverai	**nous laverons**	**me serai lavé(e)**	**nous serons lavé(e)s**
te laveras	**vous laverez**	**te seras lavé(e)**	**vous serez lavé(e)(s)**
se lavera	**se laveront**	**se sera lavé(e)**	**se seront lavé(e)s**
5 conditionnel		12 conditionnel passé	
me laverais	**nous laverions**	**me serais lavé(e)**	**nous serions lavé(e)s**
te laverais	**vous laveriez**	**te serais lavé(e)**	**vous seriez lavé(e)(s)**
se laverait	**se laveraient**	**se serait lavé(e)**	**se seraient lavé(e)s**
6 présent du subjonctif		13 passé du subjonctif	
me lave	**nous lavions**	**me sois lavé(e)**	**nous soyons lavé(e)s**
te laves	**vous laviez**	**te sois lavé(e)**	**vous soyez lavé(e)(s)**
se lave	**se lavent**	**se soit lavé(e)**	**se soient lavé(e)s**
7 imparfait du subjonctif		14 plus-que-parfait du subjonctif	
me lavasse	**nous lavassions**	**me fusse lavé(e)**	**nous fussions lavé(e)s**
te lavasses	**vous lavassiez**	**te fusses lavé(e)**	**vous fussiez lavé(e)(s)**
se lavât	**se lavassent**	**se fût lavé(e)**	**se fussent lavé(e)s**

Impératif
lave-toi; ne te lave pas
lavons-nous; ne nous lavons pas
lavez-vous; ne vous lavez pas

lever (278)

Part. pr. **levant** Part. passé **levé**

to lift, to raise

Regular **-er** verb; spelling change: **e** changes to **è** before syllable with mute **e**

The Seven Simple Tenses		The Seven Compound Tenses	
Singular	Plural	Singular	Plural
1 présent de l'indicatif		8 passé composé	
lève	**levons**	**ai levé**	**avons levé**
lèves	**levez**	**as levé**	**avez levé**
lève	**lèvent**	**a levé**	**ont levé**
2 imparfait de l'indicatif		9 plus-que-parfait de l'indicatif	
levais	**levions**	**avais levé**	**avions levé**
levais	**leviez**	**avais levé**	**aviez levé**
levait	**levaient**	**avait levé**	**avaient levé**
3 passé simple		10 passé antérieur	
levai	**levâmes**	**eus levé**	**eûmes levé**
levas	**levâtes**	**eus levé**	**eûtes levé**
leva	**levèrent**	**eut levé**	**eurent levé**
4 futur		11 futur antérieur	
lèverai	**lèverons**	**aurai levé**	**aurons levé**
lèveras	**lèverez**	**auras levé**	**aurez levé**
lèvera	**lèveront**	**aura levé**	**auront levé**
5 conditionnel		12 conditionnel passé	
lèverais	**lèverions**	**aurais levé**	**aurions levé**
lèverais	**lèveriez**	**aurais levé**	**auriez levé**
lèverait	**lèveraient**	**aurait levé**	**auraient levé**
6 présent du subjonctif		13 passé du subjonctif	
lève	**levions**	**aie levé**	**ayons levé**
lèves	**leviez**	**aies levé**	**ayez levé**
lève	**lèvent**	**ait levé**	**aient levé**
7 imparfait du subjonctif		14 plus-que-parfait du subjonctif	
levasse	**levassions**	**eusse levé**	**eussions levé**
levasses	**levassiez**	**eusses levé**	**eussiez levé**
levât	**levassent**	**eût levé**	**eussent levé**

Impératif
lève
levons
levez

Words and expressions related to this verb

voter à main levée to vote by a show of hands
le levage raising, lifting
faire lever qqn to get someone out of bed
le levant the East
le levain leaven
du pain sans levain unleavened bread
le lever du soleil sunrise
se relever to get up on one's feet
lever la main to raise one's hand
élever to raise, to rear, to bring up
enlever to remove
relever to raise again, to pick up
La séance est levée. The meeting is adjourned.
prélever to take a sample, to withdraw

See also **élever**, **enlever**, and **se lever**.

Reflexive verb; regular **-er** verb endings; spelling change: **e** changes to **è** before syllable with mute **e**

to get up

The Seven Simple Tenses		The Seven Compound Tenses	
Singular	Plural	Singular	Plural
1 présent de l'indicatif		8 passé composé	
me lève	**nous levons**	**me suis levé(e)**	**nous sommes levé(e)s**
te lèves	**vous levez**	**t'es levé(e)**	**vous êtes levé(e)(s)**
se lève	**se lèvent**	**s'est levé(e)**	**se sont levé(e)s**
2 imparfait de l'indicatif		9 plus-que-parfait de l'indicatif	
me levais	**nous levions**	**m'étais levé(e)**	**nous étions levé(e)s**
te levais	**vous leviez**	**t'étais levé(e)**	**vous étiez levé(e)(s)**
se levait	**se levaient**	**s'était levé(e)**	**s'étaient levé(e)s**
3 passé simple		10 passé antérieur	
me levai	**nous levâmes**	**me fus levé(e)**	**nous fûmes levé(e)s**
te levas	**vous levâtes**	**te fus levé(e)**	**vous fûtes levé(e)(s)**
se leva	**se levèrent**	**se fut levé(e)**	**se furent levé(e)s**
4 futur		11 futur antérieur	
me lèverai	**nous lèverons**	**me serai levé(e)**	**nous serons levé(e)s**
te lèveras	**vous lèverez**	**te seras levé(e)**	**vous serez levé(e)(s)**
se lèvera	**se lèveront**	**se sera levé(e)**	**se seront levé(e)s**
5 conditionnel		12 conditionnel passé	
me lèverais	**nous lèverions**	**me serais levé(e)**	**nous serions levé(e)s**
te lèverais	**vous lèveriez**	**te serais levé(e)**	**vous seriez levé(e)(s)**
se lèverait	**se lèveraient**	**se serait levé(e)**	**se seraient levé(e)s**
6 présent du subjonctif		13 passé du subjonctif	
me lève	**nous levions**	**me sois levé(e)**	**nous soyons levé(e)s**
te lèves	**vous leviez**	**te sois levé(e)**	**vous soyez levé(e)(s)**
se lève	**se lèvent**	**se soit levé(e)**	**se soient levé(e)s**
7 imparfait du subjonctif		14 plus-que-parfait du subjonctif	
me levasse	**nous levassions**	**me fusse levé(e)**	**nous fussions levé(e)s**
te levasses	**vous levassiez**	**te fusses levé(e)**	**vous fussiez levé(e)(s)**
se levât	**se levassent**	**se fût levé(e)**	**se fussent levé(e)s**

Impératif
lève-toi; ne te lève pas
levons-nous; ne nous levons pas
levez-vous; ne vous levez pas

AN ESSENTIAL 55 VERB

Se lever

Se lever is a very useful reflexive verb with a tricky spelling change.

Sentences using se lever

Caroline s'est levée après le petit déjeuner. Caroline got up after breakfast.

Après s'être levée, elle a quitté la maison. After getting up, she left the house.

Lève-toi! Il est temps de partir! Get up! It's time to leave!

Le soleil se lève aussi. The sun also rises.

Mon camarade de chambre est un lève-tôt. Moi, je fais souvent la grasse matinée. Je suis un lève-tard. My roommate is an early riser. As for me, I often sleep in. I'm a late riser.

Il faut que tu te lèves de bonne heure demain. You must get up early tomorrow.

Words and expressions related to this verb

le lever du soleil **sunrise**

un lève-tôt, une lève-tôt **early riser**

un lève-tard, une lève-tard **late riser**

se lever de bonne heure **to get up early**

If you can conjugate **se lever** you can also conjugate the following verbs:

s'élever **to rise, go up**

enlever **to remove**

relever **to raise**

se relever **to rise again (use être as auxiliary)**

élever **to raise, bring up**

soulever **to lift up**

Review the entry **agreement of past participle of a reflexive verb with its reflexive pronoun** in the section on definitions of basic grammatical terms with examples on pages 35–49.

Irregular verb

to read

The Seven Simple Tenses		The Seven Compound Tenses	
Singular	Plural	Singular	Plural
1 présent de l'indicatif		8 passé composé	
lis	**lisons**	**ai lu**	**avons lu**
lis	**lisez**	**as lu**	**avez lu**
lit	**lisent**	**a lu**	**ont lu**
2 imparfait de l'indicatif		9 plus-que-parfait de l'indicatif	
lisais	**lisions**	**avais lu**	**avions lu**
lisais	**lisiez**	**avais lu**	**aviez lu**
lisait	**lisaient**	**avait lu**	**avaient lu**
3 passé simple		10 passé antérieur	
lus	**lûmes**	**eus lu**	**eûmes lu**
lus	**lûtes**	**eus lu**	**eûtes lu**
lut	**lurent**	**eut lu**	**eurent lu**
4 futur		11 futur antérieur	
lirai	**lirons**	**aurai lu**	**aurons lu**
liras	**lirez**	**auras lu**	**aurez lu**
lira	**liront**	**aura lu**	**auront lu**
5 conditionnel		12 conditionnel passé	
lirais	**lirions**	**aurais lu**	**aurions lu**
lirais	**liriez**	**aurais lu**	**auriez lu**
lirait	**liraient**	**aurait lu**	**auraient lu**
6 présent du subjonctif		13 passé du subjonctif	
lise	**lisions**	**aie lu**	**ayons lu**
lises	**lisiez**	**aies lu**	**ayez lu**
lise	**lisent**	**ait lu**	**aient lu**
7 imparfait du subjonctif		14 plus-que-parfait du subjonctif	
lusse	**lussions**	**eusse lu**	**eussions lu**
lusses	**lussiez**	**eusses lu**	**eussiez lu**
lût	**lussent**	**eût lu**	**eussent lu**

Impératif
lis
lisons
lisez

The subject pronouns are found on page 103.

AN ESSENTIAL 55 VERB

Lire

Lire is used in many everyday situations and idiomatic expressions. It is a very useful verb for a beginning French student.

Sentences using lire

C'est un livre à lire. It's a book worth reading.

Frédéric, lis la prochaine phrase dans le livre. Lis-la à haute voix. Frederick, read the next sentence in the book. Read it aloud.

Guillaume, cette composition est complètement illisible. William, this essay is completely unreadable.

Lily lit un livre dans son lit. Lily is reading a book in her bed.

Anne lisait le journal quand Marie a frappé à la porte. Anne was reading the newspaper when Marie knocked on the door.

If you can conjugate **lire** you can also conjugate the following verbs:

élire **to elect**

réélire **to reelect**

relire **to reread**

Words and expressions related to this verb

lisible **legible, readable**

la lisibilité **legibility**

lisiblement **legibly**

illisible **illegible**

l'illisibilité *f.* **illegibility**

lecteur, lectrice **reader (a person who reads)**

un lecteur d'épreuves, une lectrice d'épreuves **proofreader**

la lecture **reading**

le livre **book**

livres pour la jeunesse **books for young readers**

Dans l'espoir de vous lire . . . **Hoping to receive a letter from you soon . . .**

lire à haute voix **to read aloud**

lire à voix basse **to read in a low voice**

lire tout bas **to read to oneself**

le lectorat **readership**

le lutrin **lectern**

Regular **-er** verb

to praise, to rent, to rent out

The Seven Simple Tenses		The Seven Compound Tenses	
Singular	Plural	Singular	Plural
1 présent de l'indicatif		8 passé composé	
loue	**louons**	**ai loué**	**avons loué**
loues	**louez**	**as loué**	**avez loué**
loue	**louent**	**a loué**	**ont loué**
2 imparfait de l'indicatif		9 plus-que-parfait de l'indicatif	
louais	**louions**	**avais loué**	**avions loué**
louais	**louiez**	**avais loué**	**aviez loué**
louait	**louaient**	**avait loué**	**avaient loué**
3 passé simple		10 passé antérieur	
louai	**louâmes**	**eus loué**	**eûmes loué**
louas	**louâtes**	**eus loué**	**eûtes loué**
loua	**louèrent**	**eut loué**	**eurent loué**
4 futur		11 futur antérieur	
louerai	**louerons**	**aurai loué**	**aurons loué**
loueras	**louerez**	**auras loué**	**aurez loué**
louera	**loueront**	**aura loué**	**auront loué**
5 conditionnel		12 conditionnel passé	
louerais	**louerions**	**aurais loué**	**aurions loué**
louerais	**loueriez**	**aurais loué**	**auriez loué**
louerait	**loueraient**	**aurait loué**	**auraient loué**
6 présent du subjonctif		13 passé du subjonctif	
loue	**louions**	**aie loué**	**ayons loué**
loues	**louiez**	**aies loué**	**ayez loué**
loue	**louent**	**ait loué**	**aient loué**
7 imparfait du subjonctif		14 plus-que-parfait du subjonctif	
louasse	**louassions**	**eusse loué**	**eussions loué**
louasses	**louassiez**	**eusses loué**	**eussiez loué**
louât	**louassent**	**eût loué**	**eussent loué**

Impératif
loue
louons
louez

Words and expressions related to this verb

une place louée reserved seat
maison à louer house for rent (to let)
se louer de to congratulate oneself on
allouer to allot, to allocate
Dieu soit loué! God be praised!
la location rental
le loyer rent
un loueur, une loueuse a person who rents something to someone
un loueur de voitures car rental agent
le louage renting, hiring out
la louange praise
le/la locataire renter

This verb has two very different meanings because it developed from two different Latin verbs: **locāre** (to lend) and **laudāre** (to praise).

maigrir (282) — Part. pr. maigrissant — Part. passé maigri

to reduce (one's weight), to grow thin, to lose weight

Regular **-ir** verb

The Seven Simple Tenses		The Seven Compound Tenses	
Singular	Plural	Singular	Plural
1 présent de l'indicatif		8 passé composé	
maigris	**maigrissons**	**ai maigri**	**avons maigri**
maigris	**maigrissez**	**as maigri**	**avez maigri**
maigrit	**maigrissent**	**a maigri**	**ont maigri**
2 imparfait de l'indicatif		9 plus-que-parfait de l'indicatif	
maigrissais	**maigrissions**	**avais maigri**	**avions maigri**
maigrissais	**maigrissiez**	**avais maigri**	**aviez maigri**
maigrissait	**maigrissaient**	**avait maigri**	**avaient maigri**
3 passé simple		10 passé antérieur	
maigris	**maigrîmes**	**eus maigri**	**eûmes maigri**
maigris	**maigrîtes**	**eus maigri**	**eûtes maigri**
maigrit	**maigrirent**	**eut maigri**	**eurent maigri**
4 futur		11 futur antérieur	
maigrirai	**maigrirons**	**aurai maigri**	**aurons maigri**
maigriras	**maigrirez**	**auras maigri**	**aurez maigri**
maigrira	**maigriront**	**aura maigri**	**auront maigri**
5 conditionnel		12 conditionnel passé	
maigrirais	**maigririons**	**aurais maigri**	**aurions maigri**
maigrirais	**maigririez**	**aurais maigri**	**auriez maigri**
maigrirait	**maigriraient**	**aurait maigri**	**auraient maigri**
6 présent du subjonctif		13 passé du subjonctif	
maigrisse	**maigrissions**	**aie maigri**	**ayons maigri**
maigrisses	**maigrissiez**	**aies maigri**	**ayez maigri**
maigrisse	**maigrissent**	**ait maigri**	**aient maigri**
7 imparfait du subjonctif		14 plus-que-parfait du subjonctif	
maigrisse	**maigrissions**	**eusse maigri**	**eussions maigri**
maigrisses	**maigrissiez**	**eusses maigri**	**eussiez maigri**
maigrît	**maigrissent**	**eût maigri**	**eussent maigri**

Impératif
maigris
maigrissons
maigrissez

Words and expressions related to this verb

maigre thin
la maigreur thinness
maigrement meagerly
se faire maigrir to slim down one's weight
être au régime pour maigrir to be on a diet to lose weight
s'amaigrir to lose weight
maigre comme un clou as thin as a nail
faire maigre to abstain from meat
un gamin maigrelet a skinny kid
amaigri, amaigrie gaunt
amaigrissant reducing

to eat

Regular **-er** verb endings; spelling change: retain the **ge** before **a** or **o** to keep the soft **g** sound of the verb

The Seven Simple Tenses		The Seven Compound Tenses	
Singular	Plural	Singular	Plural
1 présent de l'indicatif		8 passé composé	
mange	**mangeons**	**ai mangé**	**avons mangé**
manges	**mangez**	**as mangé**	**avez mangé**
mange	**mangent**	**a mangé**	**ont mangé**
2 imparfait de l'indicatif		9 plus-que-parfait de l'indicatif	
mangeais	**mangions**	**avais mangé**	**avions mangé**
mangeais	**mangiez**	**avais mangé**	**aviez mangé**
mangeait	**mangeaient**	**avait mangé**	**avaient mangé**
3 passé simple		10 passé antérieur	
mangeai	**mangeâmes**	**eus mangé**	**eûmes mangé**
mangeas	**mangeâtes**	**eus mangé**	**eûtes mangé**
mangea	**mangèrent**	**eut mangé**	**eurent mangé**
4 futur		11 futur antérieur	
mangerai	**mangerons**	**aurai mangé**	**aurons mangé**
mangeras	**mangerez**	**auras mangé**	**aurez mangé**
mangera	**mangeront**	**aura mangé**	**auront mangé**
5 conditionnel		12 conditionnel passé	
mangerais	**mangerions**	**aurais mangé**	**aurions mangé**
mangerais	**mangeriez**	**aurais mangé**	**auriez mangé**
mangerait	**mangeraient**	**aurait mangé**	**auraient mangé**
6 présent du subjonctif		13 passé du subjonctif	
mange	**mangions**	**aie mangé**	**ayons mangé**
manges	**mangiez**	**aies mangé**	**ayez mangé**
mange	**mangent**	**ait mangé**	**aient mangé**
7 imparfait du subjonctif		14 plus-que-parfait du subjonctif	
mangeasse	**mangeassions**	**eusse mangé**	**eussions mangé**
mangeasses	**mangeassiez**	**eusses mangé**	**eussiez mangé**
mangeât	**mangeassent**	**eût mangé**	**eussent mangé**

Impératif
mange
mangeons
mangez

AN ESSENTIAL 55 VERB

Manger

Manger is an essential verb for beginning French students because it has an important spelling change that also appears in several other verbs. You must keep the **e** after the **g** in order to retain the soft sound of **g** in the infinitive.

Sentences using manger

Y a-t-il de quoi manger? Is there something to eat?

Avez-vous quelque chose pour une démangeaison? Do you have something for an itch?

Dis-moi ce que tu manges, je te dirai ce que tu es. (Brillat-Savarin) Tell me what you eat, I'll tell you what you are.

Il faut manger pour vivre, et non pas vivre pour manger. (Molière) It is necessary to eat to live, and not to live to eat.

Proverbs

L'appétit vient en mangeant. The more you have, the more you want. (Literally: Appetite comes while eating.)

Les loups ne se mangent pas entre eux. Wolves do not eat each other.

If you can conjugate **manger** you can also conjugate the following verbs:

allonger to lengthen

démanger to itch

déménager to move

échanger to exchange

engranger to gather, store

mélanger to mix

Words and expressions related to this verb

la salle à manger dining room

une démangeaison itch

de quoi manger something to eat

le manger food

gros mangeur big eater

manger de l'argent to spend money foolishly

ne pas manger à sa faim not to have much to eat

manger à sa faim to eat until filled

manger comme quatre to eat like a horse

une mangeoire manger

mangeable edible, eatable

la mangeaille disgusting food

immangeable inedible

manger comme un oiseau to eat like a bird

The Seven Simple Tenses		The Seven Compound Tenses	
Singular	Plural	Singular	Plural
1 présent de l'indicatif		8 passé composé	
manque	**manquons**	**ai manqué**	**avons manqué**
manques	**manquez**	**as manqué**	**avez manqué**
manque	**manquent**	**a manqué**	**ont manqué**
2 imparfait de l'indicatif		9 plus-que-parfait de l'indicatif	
manquais	**manquions**	**avais manqué**	**avions manqué**
manquais	**manquiez**	**avais manqué**	**aviez manqué**
manquait	**manquaient**	**avait manqué**	**avaient manqué**
3 passé simple		10 passé antérieur	
manquai	**manquâmes**	**eus manqué**	**eûmes manqué**
manquas	**manquâtes**	**eus manqué**	**eûtes manqué**
manqua	**manquèrent**	**eut manqué**	**eurent manqué**
4 futur		11 futur antérieur	
manquerai	**manquerons**	**aurai manqué**	**aurons manqué**
manqueras	**manquerez**	**auras manqué**	**aurez manqué**
manquera	**manqueront**	**aura manqué**	**auront manqué**
5 conditionnel		12 conditionnel passé	
manquerais	**manquerions**	**aurais manqué**	**aurions manqué**
manquerais	**manqueriez**	**aurais manqué**	**auriez manqué**
manquerait	**manqueraient**	**aurait manqué**	**auraient manqué**
6 présent du subjonctif		13 passé du subjonctif	
manque	**manquions**	**aie manqué**	**ayons manqué**
manques	**manquiez**	**aies manqué**	**ayez manqué**
manque	**manquent**	**ait manqué**	**aient manqué**
7 imparfait du subjonctif		14 plus-que-parfait du subjonctif	
manquasse	**manquassions**	**eusse manqué**	**eussions manqué**
manquasses	**manquassiez**	**eusses manqué**	**eussiez manqué**
manquât	**manquassent**	**eût manqué**	**eussent manqué**

Impératif
manque
manquons
manquez

Common idiomatic expressions using this verb

manquer à to lack; **Le courage lui manque** He lacks courage.
Elle me manque. I miss her.
Est-ce que je te manque? Do you miss me?
manquer de qqch to be lacking something; **manquer de sucre** to be out of sugar
Ne manquez pas de venir. Don't fail to come.
un mariage manqué a broken engagement
un héros manqué a would-be hero
Il me manque un euro I am lacking (I need) one euro.
manquer de + inf. to fail to, to almost do something
J'ai manqué de tomber. I almost fell.
Paul a manqué de venir. Paul failed to come.
manquer à sa parole to go back on one's word

The subject pronouns are found on page 103.

marcher (285) — Part. pr. marchant — Part. passé marché

to walk, to march, to run (machine), to function

Regular **-er** verb

The Seven Simple Tenses		The Seven Compound Tenses	
Singular	Plural	Singular	Plural
1 présent de l'indicatif		8 passé composé	
marche	**marchons**	**ai marché**	**avons marché**
marches	**marchez**	**as marché**	**avez marché**
marche	**marchent**	**a marché**	**ont marché**
2 imparfait de l'indicatif		9 plus-que-parfait de l'indicatif	
marchais	**marchions**	**avais marché**	**avions marché**
marchais	**marchiez**	**avais marché**	**aviez marché**
marchait	**marchaient**	**avait marché**	**avaient marché**
3 passé simple		10 passé antérieur	
marchai	**marchâmes**	**eus marché**	**eûmes marché**
marchas	**marchâtes**	**eus marché**	**eûtes marché**
marcha	**marchèrent**	**eut marché**	**eurent marché**
4 futur		11 futur antérieur	
marcherai	**marcherons**	**aurai marché**	**aurons marché**
marcheras	**marcherez**	**auras marché**	**aurez marché**
marchera	**marcheront**	**aura marché**	**auront marché**
5 conditionnel		12 conditionnel passé	
marcherais	**marcherions**	**aurais marché**	**aurions marché**
marcherais	**marcheriez**	**aurais marché**	**auriez marché**
marcherait	**marcheraient**	**aurait marché**	**auraient marché**
6 présent du subjonctif		13 passé du subjonctif	
marche	**marchions**	**aie marché**	**ayons marché**
marches	**marchiez**	**aies marché**	**ayez marché**
marche	**marchent**	**ait marché**	**aient marché**
7 imparfait du subjonctif		14 plus-que-parfait du subjonctif	
marchasse	**marchassions**	**eusse marché**	**eussions marché**
marchasses	**marchassiez**	**eusses marché**	**eussiez marché**
marchât	**marchassent**	**eût marché**	**eussent marché**

Impératif
marche
marchons
marchez

Words and expressions related to this verb

la marche march, walking
ralentir sa marche to slow down one's pace
le marché market
le marché aux fleurs flower market
le marché aux puces flea market
à bon marché cheap
faire marcher qqn to put someone on
une démarche gait, walk
faire une démarche to take a step
marcher bien to function (go, run, work) well
marcher sur les pas de qqn to follow in someone's footsteps
faire marcher qqch to make something go (run, function)
Ça ne marche plus. It's out of order.
la course et la marche running and walking

Irregular verb

to curse

The Seven Simple Tenses		The Seven Compound Tenses	
Singular	Plural	Singular	Plural
1 présent de l'indicatif		8 passé composé	
maudis	**maudissons**	**ai maudit**	**avons maudit**
maudis	**maudissez**	**as maudit**	**avez maudit**
maudit	**maudissent**	**a maudit**	**ont maudit**
2 imparfait de l'indicatif		9 plus-que-parfait de l'indicatif	
maudissais	**maudissions**	**avais maudit**	**avions maudit**
maudissais	**maudissiez**	**avais maudit**	**aviez maudit**
maudissait	**maudissaient**	**avait maudit**	**avaient maudit**
3 passé simple		10 passé antérieur	
maudis	**maudîmes**	**eus maudit**	**eûmes maudit**
maudis	**maudîtes**	**eus maudit**	**eûtes maudit**
maudit	**maudirent**	**eut maudit**	**eurent maudit**
4 futur		11 futur antérieur	
maudirai	**maudirons**	**aurai maudit**	**aurons maudit**
maudiras	**maudirez**	**auras maudit**	**aurez maudit**
maudira	**maudiront**	**aura maudit**	**auront maudit**
5 conditionnel		12 conditionnel passé	
maudirais	**maudirions**	**aurais maudit**	**aurions maudit**
maudirais	**maudiriez**	**aurais maudit**	**auriez maudit**
maudirait	**maudiraient**	**aurait maudit**	**auraient maudit**
6 présent du subjonctif		13 passé du subjonctif	
maudisse	**maudissions**	**aie maudit**	**ayons maudit**
maudisses	**maudissiez**	**aies maudit**	**ayez maudit**
maudisse	**maudissent**	**ait maudit**	**aient maudit**
7 imparfait du subjonctif		14 plus-que-parfait du subjonctif	
maudisse	**maudissions**	**eusse maudit**	**eussions maudit**
maudisses	**maudissiez**	**eusses maudit**	**eussiez maudit**
maudît	**maudissent**	**eût maudit**	**eussent maudit**

Impératif
maudis
maudissons
maudissez

Words and expressions related to this verb

maudit, maudite cursed
Quel maudit temps! What rotten weather!
maudire un ennemi to curse an enemy
les maudits the damned
le Maudit Demon
dire to say, to tell; **dire du mal de qqn** to say something evil about someone

Careful! Although **maudire** looks like it should be conjugated like **dire**, it is conjugated like a regular **-ir** verb—and its past participle has a **t** added to it: **maudit**.

méconnaître (287) Part. pr. méconnaissant Part. passé méconnu

to misjudge, to misunderstand, not to know, not to recognize

Irregular verb

The Seven Simple Tenses		The Seven Compound Tenses	
Singular	Plural	Singular	Plural
1 présent de l'indicatif		8 passé composé	
méconnais	**méconnaissons**	**ai méconnu**	**avons méconnu**
méconnais	**méconnaissez**	**as méconnu**	**avez méconnu**
méconnaît	**méconnaissent**	**a méconnu**	**ont méconnu**
2 imparfait de l'indicatif		9 plus-que-parfait de l'indicatif	
méconnaissais	**méconnaissions**	**avais méconnu**	**avions méconnu**
méconnaissais	**méconnaissiez**	**avais méconnu**	**aviez méconnu**
méconnaissait	**méconnaissaient**	**avait méconnu**	**avaient méconnu**
3 passé simple		10 passé antérieur	
méconnus	**méconnûmes**	**eus méconnu**	**eûmes méconnu**
méconnus	**méconnûtes**	**eus méconnu**	**eûtes méconnu**
méconnut	**méconnurent**	**eut méconnu**	**eurent méconnu**
4 futur		11 futur antérieur	
méconnaîtrai	**méconnaîtrons**	**aurai méconnu**	**aurons méconnu**
méconnaîtras	**méconnaîtrez**	**auras méconnu**	**aurez méconnu**
méconnaîtra	**méconnaîtront**	**aura méconnu**	**auront méconnu**
5 conditionnel		12 conditionnel passé	
méconnaîtrais	**méconnaîtrions**	**aurais méconnu**	**aurions méconnu**
méconnaîtrais	**méconnaîtriez**	**aurais méconnu**	**auriez méconnu**
méconnaîtrait	**méconnaîtraient**	**aurait méconnu**	**auraient méconnu**
6 présent du subjonctif		13 passé du subjonctif	
méconnaisse	**méconnaissions**	**aie méconnu**	**ayons méconnu**
méconnaisses	**méconnaissiez**	**aies méconnu**	**ayez méconnu**
méconnaisse	**méconnaissent**	**ait méconnu**	**aient méconnu**
7 imparfait du subjonctif		14 plus-que-parfait du subjonctif	
méconnusse	**méconnussions**	**eusse méconnu**	**eussions méconnu**
méconnusses	**méconnussiez**	**eusses méconnu**	**eussiez méconnu**
méconnût	**méconnussent**	**eût méconnu**	**eussent méconnu**

Impératif
méconnais
méconnaissons
méconnaissez

Words related to this verb

méconnaissable unrecognizable
méconnu, méconnue misunderstood
la méconnaissance misappreciation
se méconnaître to underrate (underestimate) oneself

See also **connaître** and **reconnaître.**

Can't remember the French verb you need? Check the back pages of this book for the English-French verb index!

Irregular verb

to slander

The Seven Simple Tenses		The Seven Compound Tenses	
Singular	Plural	Singular	Plural
1 présent de l'indicatif		8 passé composé	
médis	**médisons**	**ai médit**	**avons médit**
médis	**médisez**	**as médit**	**avez médit**
médit	**médisent**	**a médit**	**ont médit**
2 imparfait de l'indicatif		9 plus-que-parfait de l'indicatif	
médisais	**médisions**	**avais médit**	**avions médit**
médisais	**médisiez**	**avais médit**	**aviez médit**
médisait	**médisaient**	**avait médit**	**avaient médit**
3 passé simple		10 passé antérieur	
médis	**médîmes**	**eus médit**	**eûmes médit**
médis	**médîtes**	**eus médit**	**eûtes médit**
médit	**médirent**	**eut médit**	**eurent médit**
4 futur		11 futur antérieur	
médirai	**médirons**	**aurai médit**	**aurons médit**
médiras	**médirez**	**auras médit**	**aurez médit**
médira	**médiront**	**aura médit**	**auront médit**
5 conditionnel		12 conditionnel passé	
médirais	**médirions**	**aurais médit**	**aurions médit**
médirais	**médiriez**	**aurais médit**	**auriez médit**
médirait	**médiraient**	**aurait médit**	**auraient médit**
6 présent du subjonctif		13 passé du subjonctif	
médise	**médisions**	**aie médit**	**ayons médit**
médises	**médisiez**	**aies médit**	**ayez médit**
médise	**médisent**	**ait médit**	**aient médit**
7 imparfait du subjonctif		14 plus-que-parfait du subjonctif	
médisse	**médissions**	**eusse médit**	**eussions médit**
médisses	**médissiez**	**eusses médit**	**eussiez médit**
médît	**médissent**	**eût médit**	**eussent médit**

Impératif
médis
médisons
médisez

Words and expressions related to this verb

la médisance slander
dire des médisances to say scandalous things
un médisant, une médisante slanderer
médire de to speak ill of, to slander

See also **contredire, dire, interdire, maudire,** and **prédire.**

Careful! Although **médire** is conjugated like **dire**, the present tense **vous** form is **médisez** and the imperative for **vous** is: **médisez**.

se méfier (289) — Part. pr. se méfiant — Part. passé méfié(e)(s)

to beware, to distrust, to mistrust

Reflexive regular **-er** verb

The Seven Simple Tenses

Singular	Plural
1 présent de l'indicatif	
me méfie	**nous méfions**
te méfies	**vous méfiez**
se méfie	**se méfient**
2 imparfait de l'indicatif	
me méfiais	**nous méfiions**
te méfiais	**vous méfiiez**
se méfiait	**se méfiaient**
3 passé simple	
me méfiai	**nous méfiâmes**
te méfias	**vous méfiâtes**
se méfia	**se méfièrent**
4 futur	
me méfierai	**nous méfierons**
te méfieras	**vous méfierez**
se méfiera	**se méfieront**
5 conditionnel	
me méfierais	**nous méfierions**
te méfierais	**vous méfieriez**
se méfierait	**se méfieraient**
6 présent du subjonctif	
me méfie	**nous méfiions**
te méfies	**vous méfiiez**
se méfie	**se méfient**
7 imparfait du subjonctif	
me méfiasse	**nous méfiassions**
te méfiasses	**vous méfiassiez**
se méfiât	**se méfiassent**

The Seven Compound Tenses

Singular	Plural
8 passé composé	
me suis méfié(e)	**nous sommes méfié(e)s**
t'es méfié(e)	**vous êtes méfié(e)(s)**
s'est méfié(e)	**se sont méfié(e)s**
9 plus-que-parfait de l'indicatif	
m'étais méfié(e)	**nous étions méfié(e)s**
t'étais méfié(e)	**vous étiez méfié(e)(s)**
s'était méfié(e)	**s'étaient méfié(e)s**
10 passé antérieur	
me fus méfié(e)	**nous fûmes méfié(e)s**
te fus méfié(e)	**vous fûtes méfié(e)(s)**
se fut méfié(e)	**se furent méfié(e)s**
11 futur antérieur	
me serai méfié(e)	**nous serons méfié(e)s**
te seras méfié(e)	**vous serez méfié(e)(s)**
se sera méfié(e)	**se seront méfié(e)s**
12 conditionnel passé	
me serais méfié(e)	**nous serions méfié(e)s**
te serais méfié(e)	**vous seriez méfié(e)(s)**
se serait méfié(e)	**se seraient méfié(e)s**
13 passé du subjonctif	
me sois méfié(e)	**nous soyons méfié(e)s**
te sois méfié(e)	**vous soyez méfié(e)(s)**
se soit méfié(e)	**se soient méfié(e)s**
14 plus-que-parfait du subjonctif	
me fusse méfié(e)	**nous fussions méfié(e)s**
te fusses méfié(e)	**vous fussiez méfié(e)(s)**
se fût méfié(e)	**se fussent méfié(e)s**

Impératif

méfie-toi; ne te méfie pas
méfions-nous; ne nous méfions pas
méfiez-vous; ne vous méfiez pas

Words and expressions related to this verb

se méfier de to distrust, to mistrust
Méfiez-vous! Watch out!
méfiant, méfiante distrustful
la méfiance distrust, mistrust
un méfait misdeed, wrongdoing
Il faut vous méfier. You must be careful.
être sans méfiance to be completely trusting
Méfiez-vous de lui (d'elle). Do not trust him (her).
avoir de la méfiance envers quelqu'un to distrust someone

It's important that you be familiar with the Subjunctive. See pages 26–31.

Regular **-er** verb; spelling change: **e** changes to **è** before syllable with mute **e**

to lead, to control

The Seven Simple Tenses		The Seven Compound Tenses	
Singular	Plural	Singular	Plural
1 présent de l'indicatif		8 passé composé	
mène	**menons**	**ai mené**	**avons mené**
mènes	**menez**	**as mené**	**avez mené**
mène	**mènent**	**a mené**	**ont mené**
2 imparfait de l'indicatif		9 plus-que-parfait de l'indicatif	
menais	**menions**	**avais mené**	**avions mené**
menais	**meniez**	**avais mené**	**aviez mené**
menait	**menaient**	**avait mené**	**avaient mené**
3 passé simple		10 passé antérieur	
menai	**menâmes**	**eus mené**	**eûmes mené**
menas	**menâtes**	**eus mené**	**eûtes mené**
mena	**menèrent**	**eut mené**	**eurent mené**
4 futur		11 futur antérieur	
mènerai	**mènerons**	**aurai mené**	**aurons mené**
mèneras	**mènerez**	**auras mené**	**aurez mené**
mènera	**mèneront**	**aura mené**	**auront mené**
5 conditionnel		12 conditionnel passé	
mènerais	**mènerions**	**aurais mené**	**aurions mené**
mènerais	**mèneriez**	**aurais mené**	**auriez mené**
mènerait	**mèneraient**	**aurait mené**	**auraient mené**
6 présent du subjonctif		13 passé du subjonctif	
mène	**menions**	**aie mené**	**ayons mené**
mènes	**meniez**	**aies mené**	**ayez mené**
mène	**mènent**	**ait mené**	**aient mené**
7 imparfait du subjonctif		14 plus-que-parfait du subjonctif	
menasse	**menassions**	**eusse mené**	**eussions mené**
menasses	**menassiez**	**eusses mené**	**eussiez mené**
menât	**menassent**	**eût mené**	**eussent mené**

Impératif
mène
menons
menez

Words and expressions related to this verb
un meneur, une meneuse leader
Cela ne mène à rien. That leads to nothing.
mener qqn par le bout du nez to lead someone around by the nose
mener une vie vagabonde to lead a vagabond life
mener tout le monde to be bossy with everyone
mener la bande to lead the group
Cela vous mènera loin. That will take you a long way.
malmener to bully

See also **amener, emmener,** and **promener.**

The subject pronouns are found on page 103.

mentir (291) — Part. pr. **mentant** — Part. passé **menti**

to lie, to tell a lie

Irregular verb

The Seven Simple Tenses		The Seven Compound Tenses	
Singular	Plural	Singular	Plural
1 présent de l'indicatif		8 passé composé	
mens	**mentons**	**ai menti**	**avons menti**
mens	**mentez**	**as menti**	**avez menti**
ment	**mentent**	**a menti**	**ont menti**
2 imparfait de l'indicatif		9 plus-que-parfait de l'indicatif	
mentais	**mentions**	**avais menti**	**avions menti**
mentais	**mentiez**	**avais menti**	**aviez menti**
mentait	**mentaient**	**avait menti**	**avaient menti**
3 passé simple		10 passé antérieur	
mentis	**mentîmes**	**eus menti**	**eûmes menti**
mentis	**mentîtes**	**eus menti**	**eûtes menti**
mentit	**mentirent**	**eut menti**	**eurent menti**
4 futur		11 futur antérieur	
mentirai	**mentirons**	**aurai menti**	**aurons menti**
mentiras	**mentirez**	**auras menti**	**aurez menti**
mentira	**mentiront**	**aura menti**	**auront menti**
5 conditionnel		12 conditionnel passé	
mentirais	**mentirions**	**aurais menti**	**aurions menti**
mentirais	**mentiriez**	**aurais menti**	**auriez menti**
mentirait	**mentiraient**	**aurait menti**	**auraient menti**
6 présent du subjonctif		13 passé du subjonctif	
mente	**mentions**	**aie menti**	**ayons menti**
mentes	**mentiez**	**aies menti**	**ayez menti**
mente	**mentent**	**ait menti**	**aient menti**
7 imparfait du subjonctif		14 plus-que-parfait du subjonctif	
mentisse	**mentissions**	**eusse menti**	**eussions menti**
mentisses	**mentissiez**	**eusses menti**	**eussiez menti**
mentît	**mentissent**	**eût menti**	**eussent menti**

Impératif
mens
mentons
mentez

Words and expressions related to this verb

un mensonge a lie
dire des mensonges to tell lies
un menteur, une menteuse a liar
Elle vit dans le mensonge. Her whole life is a lie.
Ce sont des mensonges. It's all a pack of lies.
Tu mens! You're a liar!
sans mentir quite honestly
démentir to belie, to deny, to falsify, to refute
une menterie fib

How are you doing? Find out with the verb drills and tests with answers explained on pages 50–101.

Reflexive irregular verb

to be mistaken, to mistake

The Seven Simple Tenses		The Seven Compound Tenses	
Singular	Plural	Singular	Plural
1 présent de l'indicatif		8 passé composé	
me méprends	**nous méprenons**	**me suis mépris(e)**	**nous sommes mépris(es)**
te méprends	**vous méprenez**	**t'es mépris(e)**	**vous êtes mépris(e)(es)**
se méprend	**se méprennent**	**s'est mépris(e)**	**se sont mépris(es)**
2 imparfait de l'indicatif		9 plus-que-parfait de l'indicatif	
me méprenais	**nous méprenions**	**m'étais mépris(e)**	**nous étions mépris(es)**
te méprenais	**vous méprenez**	**t'étais mépris(e)**	**vous êtiez mépris(e)(es)**
se méprenait	**se méprenaient**	**s'était mépris(e)**	**s'étaient mépris(es)**
3 passé simple		10 passé antérieur	
me mépris	**nous méprîmes**	**me fus mépris(e)**	**nous fûmes mépris(es)**
te mépris	**vous méprîtes**	**te fus mépris(e)**	**vous fûtes mépris(e)(es)**
se méprit	**se méprirent**	**se fut mépris(e)**	**se furent mépris(es)**
4 futur		11 futur antérieur	
me méprendrai	**nous méprendrons**	**me serai mépris(e)**	**nous serons mépris(es)**
te méprendras	**vous méprendrez**	**te seras mépris(e)**	**vous serez mépris(e)(es)**
se méprendra	**se méprendront**	**se sera mépris(e)**	**se seront mépris(es)**
5 conditionnel		12 conditionnel passé	
me méprendrais	**nous méprendrions**	**me serais mépris(e)**	**nous serions mépris(es)**
te méprendrais	**vous méprendriez**	**te serais mépris(e)**	**vous seriez mépris(e)(es)**
se méprendrait	**se méprendraient**	**se serait mépris(e)**	**se seraient mépris(es)**
6 présent du subjonctif		13 passé du subjonctif	
me méprenne	**nous méprenions**	**me sois mépris(e)**	**nous soyons mépris(es)**
te méprennes	**vous méprenez**	**te sois mépris(e)**	**vous soyez mépris(e)(es)**
se méprenne	**se méprennent**	**se soit mépris(e)**	**se soient mépris(es)**
7 imparfait du subjonctif		14 plus-que-parfait du subjonctif	
me méprisse	**nous méprissions**	**me fusse mépris(e)**	**nous fussions mépris(es)**
te méprisses	**vous méprissiez**	**te fusses mépris(e)**	**vous fussiez mépris(e)(es)**
se méprît	**se méprissent**	**se fût mépris(e)**	**se fussent mépris(es)**

Impératif
méprends-toi; ne te méprends pas
méprenons-nous; ne nous méprenons pas
méprenez-vous; ne vous méprenez pas

Common idiomatic expressions using this verb

se méprendre sur qqn to be mistaken about someone; to take someone for someone else

se méprendre au sujet de qqch to be mistaken about something; to take something for something else

See also **apprendre, comprendre, entreprendre, prendre, reprendre,** and **surprendre.**

Can't remember the French verb you need? Check the back pages of this book for the English-French verb index!

mériter (293) — Part. pr. méritant — Part. passé mérité

to merit, to deserve

Regular **-er** verb

The Seven Simple Tenses		The Seven Compound Tenses	
Singular	Plural	Singular	Plural
1 présent de l'indicatif		8 passé composé	
mérite	**méritons**	**ai mérité**	**avons mérité**
mérites	**méritez**	**as mérité**	**avez mérité**
mérite	**méritent**	**a mérité**	**ont mérité**
2 imparfait de l'indicatif		9 plus-que-parfait de l'indicatif	
méritais	**méritions**	**avais mérité**	**avions mérité**
méritais	**méritiez**	**avais mérité**	**aviez mérité**
méritait	**méritaient**	**avait mérité**	**avaient mérité**
3 passé simple		10 passé antérieur	
méritai	**méritâmes**	**eus mérité**	**eûmes mérité**
méritas	**méritâtes**	**eus mérité**	**eûtes mérité**
mérita	**méritèrent**	**eut mérité**	**eurent mérité**
4 futur		11 futur antérieur	
mériterai	**mériterons**	**aurai mérité**	**aurons mérité**
mériteras	**mériterez**	**auras mérité**	**aurez mérité**
méritera	**mériteront**	**aura mérité**	**auront mérité**
5 conditionnel		12 conditionnel passé	
mériterais	**mériterions**	**aurais mérité**	**aurions mérité**
mériterais	**mériteriez**	**aurais mérité**	**auriez mérité**
mériterait	**mériteraient**	**aurait mérité**	**auraient mérité**
6 présent du subjonctif		13 passé du subjonctif	
mérite	**méritions**	**aie mérité**	**ayons mérité**
mérites	**méritiez**	**aies mérité**	**ayez mérité**
mérite	**méritent**	**ait mérité**	**aient mérité**
7 imparfait du subjonctif		14 plus-que-parfait du subjonctif	
méritasse	**méritassions**	**eusse mérité**	**eussions mérité**
méritasses	**méritassiez**	**eusses mérité**	**eussiez mérité**
méritât	**méritassent**	**eût mérité**	**eussent mérité**

Impératif
mérite
méritons
méritez

Words and expressions related to this verb

un mérite merit, worthiness
méritant, méritante deserving (person)
une femme de mérite, un homme de mérite a woman, a man of merit
méritoire meritorious, commendable, deserving (things, acts, deeds)
sans mérite undeserving

Don't forget to study the section on defective and impersonal verbs. It's right after this main list.

Irregular verb

to put, to place, to put on (clothing)

The Seven Simple Tenses		The Seven Compound Tenses	
Singular	Plural	Singular	Plural
1 présent de l'indicatif		8 passé composé	
mets	**mettons**	**ai mis**	**avons mis**
mets	**mettez**	**as mis**	**avez mis**
met	**mettent**	**a mis**	**ont mis**
2 imparfait de l'indicatif		9 plus-que-parfait de l'indicatif	
mettais	**mettions**	**avais mis**	**avions mis**
mettais	**mettiez**	**avais mis**	**aviez mis**
mettait	**mettaient**	**avait mis**	**avaient mis**
3 passé simple		10 passé antérieur	
mis	**mîmes**	**eus mis**	**eûmes mis**
mis	**mîtes**	**eus mis**	**eûtes mis**
mit	**mirent**	**eut mis**	**eurent mis**
4 futur		11 futur antérieur	
mettrai	**mettrons**	**aurai mis**	**aurons mis**
mettras	**mettrez**	**auras mis**	**aurez mis**
mettra	**mettront**	**aura mis**	**auront mis**
5 conditionnel		12 conditionnel passé	
mettrais	**mettrions**	**aurais mis**	**aurions mis**
mettrais	**mettriez**	**aurais mis**	**auriez mis**
mettrait	**mettraient**	**aurait mis**	**auraient mis**
6 présent du subjonctif		13 passé du subjonctif	
mette	**mettions**	**aie mis**	**ayons mis**
mettes	**mettiez**	**aies mis**	**ayez mis**
mette	**mettent**	**ait mis**	**aient mis**
7 imparfait du subjonctif		14 plus-que-parfait du subjonctif	
misse	**missions**	**eusse mis**	**eussions mis**
misses	**missiez**	**eusses mis**	**eussiez mis**
mît	**missent**	**eût mis**	**eussent mis**

Impératif
mets
mettons
mettez

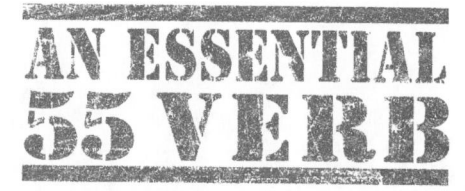

The subject pronouns are found on page 103.

AN ESSENTIAL 55 VERB

Mettre and se mettre

Mettre and **se mettre** are a very useful pair of French verbs because there are many expressions related to them. Pay special attention to the differences between these two verbs.

Sentences using mettre

Mimi a mis ses souliers blancs. Mimi put on her white shoes.

Roger était si fâché contre Julie qu'il a mis sa lettre en morceaux. Roger was so angry at Julie that he tore her letter to pieces.

Mme Petrie n'était pas contente parce que Paul avait mis douze ans pour finir ses études. Mrs. Petrie was not pleased because Paul had taken twelve years to finish his studies.

Ne remets pas à demain ce que tu peux faire après-demain. (Alphonse Allais) Don't put off until tomorrow what you can do the day after tomorrow.

M. Dupont a mis la table et a annoncé: Venez, tout le monde; mettez-vous à table! Mr. Dupont set the table and announced: Come, everybody; sit down at the table!

Proverb

Il ne faut pas se mettre à l'eau de peur de la pluie. One shouldn't jump in the water out of fear of the rain.

Words and expressions related to these verbs

mettre la table to set the table

mettre le couvert to set the table

mettre de côté to lay aside, to save

mettre en cause to question

mettre qqn à la porte to kick somebody out (the door)

mettre au courant (de) to inform (about)

mettre au point to make clear

mettre en pièces to tear to pieces, to break into pieces

mettre en scène to stage

un metteur en scène director of a film

mettre la télé to turn on the TV

mettre la radio to turn on the radio

mettre à la poste to mail, post

mettre fin à qqch to put an end to something

se mettre à + inf. to begin, to start + inf.

se mettre à table to go sit at the table

se mettre en colère to get angry

se mettre en grande toilette to dress for an occasion

se mettre en smoking to put on a dinner jacket

Can't remember the French verb you need? Check the back pages of this book for the English-French verb index!

Reflexive irregular verb

to begin, to start, to place oneself

The Seven Simple Tenses		The Seven Compound Tenses	
Singular	Plural	Singular	Plural
1 présent de l'indicatif		8 passé composé	
me mets	**nous mettons**	**me suis mis(e)**	**nous sommes mis(es)**
te mets	**vous mettez**	**t'es mis(e)**	**vous êtes mis(e)(es)**
se met	**se mettent**	**s'est mis(e)**	**se sont mis(es)**
2 imparfait de l'indicatif		9 plus-que-parfait de l'indicatif	
me mettais	**nous mettions**	**m'étais mis(e)**	**nous étions mis(es)**
te mettais	**vous mettiez**	**t'étais mis(e)**	**vous étiez mis(e)(es)**
se mettait	**se mettaient**	**s'était mis(e)**	**s'étaient mis(es)**
3 passé simple		10 passé antérieur	
me mis	**nous mîmes**	**me fus mis(e)**	**nous fûmes mis(es)**
te mis	**vous mîtes**	**te fus mis(e)**	**vous fûtes mis(e)(es)**
se mit	**se mirent**	**se fut mis(e)**	**se furent mis(es)**
4 futur		11 futur antérieur	
me mettrai	**nous mettrons**	**me serai mis(e)**	**nous serons mis(es)**
te mettras	**vous mettrez**	**te seras mis(e)**	**vous serez mis(e)(es)**
se mettra	**se mettront**	**se sera mis(e)**	**se seront mis(es)**
5 conditionnel		12 conditionnel passé	
me mettrais	**nous mettrions**	**me serais mis(e)**	**nous serions mis(es)**
te mettrais	**vous mettriez**	**te serais mis(e)**	**vous seriez mis(e)(es)**
se mettrait	**se mettraient**	**se serait mis(e)**	**se seraient mis(es)**
6 présent du subjonctif		13 passé du subjonctif	
me mette	**nous mettions**	**me sois mis(e)**	**nous soyons mis(es)**
te mettes	**vous mettiez**	**te sois mis(e)**	**vous soyez mis(e)(es)**
se mette	**se mettent**	**se soit mis(e)**	**se soient mis(es)**
7 imparfait du subjonctif		14 plus-que-parfait du subjonctif	
me misse	**nous missions**	**me fusse mis(e)**	**nous fussions mis(es)**
te misses	**vous missiez**	**te fusses mis(e)**	**vous fussiez mis(e)(es)**
se mît	**se missent**	**se fût mis(e)**	**se fussent mis(es)**

Impératif
mets-toi; ne te mets pas
mettons-nous; ne nous mettons pas
mettez-vous; ne vous mettez pas

See also **admettre, commetre, mettre, omettre, permettre, promettre, soumettre,** and **transmettre.**

mirer (296)

Part. pr. **mirant** Part. passé **miré**

to mirror

Regular **-er** verb

The Seven Simple Tenses		The Seven Compound Tenses	
Singular	Plural	Singular	Plural
1 présent de l'indicatif		8 passé composé	
mire	**mirons**	**ai miré**	**avons miré**
mires	**mirez**	**as miré**	**avez miré**
mire	**mirent**	**a miré**	**ont miré**
2 imparfait de l'indicatif		9 plus-que-parfait de l'indicatif	
mirais	**mirions**	**avais miré**	**avions miré**
mirais	**miriez**	**avais miré**	**aviez miré**
mirait	**miraient**	**avait miré**	**avaient miré**
3 passé simple		10 passé antérieur	
mirai	**mirâmes**	**eus miré**	**eûmes miré**
miras	**mirâtes**	**eus miré**	**eûtes miré**
mira	**mirèrent**	**eut miré**	**eurent miré**
4 futur		11 futur antérieur	
mirerai	**mirerons**	**aurai miré**	**aurons miré**
mireras	**mirerez**	**auras miré**	**aurez miré**
mirera	**mireront**	**aura miré**	**auront miré**
5 conditionnel		12 conditionnel passé	
mirerais	**mirerions**	**aurais miré**	**aurions miré**
mirerais	**mireriez**	**aurais miré**	**auriez miré**
mirerait	**mireraient**	**aurait miré**	**auraient miré**
6 présent du subjonctif		13 passé du subjonctif	
mire	**mirions**	**aie miré**	**ayons miré**
mires	**miriez**	**aies miré**	**ayez miré**
mire	**mirent**	**ait miré**	**aient miré**
7 imparfait du subjonctif		14 plus-que-parfait du subjonctif	
mirasse	**mirassions**	**eusse miré**	**eussions miré**
mirasses	**mirassiez**	**eusses miré**	**eussiez miré**
mirât	**mirassent**	**eût miré**	**eussent miré**

Impératif
mire
mirons
mirez

Words and expressions related to this verb

la mire aim, aiming; **point de mire** point aimed at; **prendre sa mire (viser)** to take aim
le mirage mirage; illusion
un miroir mirror
miroiter to gleam, glisten, sparkle
se mirer dans to look at oneself in (a mirror, a pool of water, a shiny surface)
admirer to admire

See also **admirer.**

Soak up some verbs used in weather expressions. There's a list in the Appendixes!

Regular **-er** verb endings; spelling change: **e** changes to **è** before syllable with mute **e**

to model, to shape

The Seven Simple Tenses		The Seven Compound Tenses	
Singular	Plural	Singular	Plural
1 présent de l'indicatif		8 passé composé	
modèle	**modelons**	**ai modelé**	**avons modelé**
modèles	**modelez**	**as modelé**	**avez modelé**
modèle	**modèlent**	**a modelé**	**ont modelé**
2 imparfait de l'indicatif		9 plus-que-parfait de l'indicatif	
modelais	**modelions**	**avais modelé**	**avions modelé**
modelais	**modeliez**	**avais modelé**	**aviez modelé**
modelait	**modelaient**	**avait modelé**	**avaient modelé**
3 passé simple		10 passé antérieur	
modelai	**modelâmes**	**eus modelé**	**eûmes modelé**
modelas	**modelâtes**	**eus modelé**	**eûtes modelé**
modela	**modelèrent**	**eut modelé**	**eurent modelé**
4 futur		11 futur antérieur	
modèlerai	**modèlerons**	**aurai modelé**	**aurons modelé**
modèleras	**modèlerez**	**auras modelé**	**aurez modelé**
modèlera	**modèleront**	**aura modelé**	**auront modelé**
5 conditionnel		12 conditionnel passé	
modèlerais	**modèlerions**	**aurais modelé**	**aurions modelé**
modèlerais	**modèleriez**	**aurais modelé**	**auriez modelé**
modèlerait	**modèleraient**	**aurait modelé**	**auraient modelé**
6 présent du subjonctif		13 passé du subjonctif	
modèle	**modelions**	**aie modelé**	**ayons modelé**
modèles	**modeliez**	**aies modelé**	**ayez modelé**
modèle	**modèlent**	**ait modelé**	**aient modelé**
7 imparfait du subjonctif		14 plus-que-parfait du subjonctif	
modelasse	**modelassions**	**eusse modelé**	**eussions modelé**
modelasses	**modelassiez**	**eusses modelé**	**eussiez modelé**
modelât	**modelassent**	**eût modelé**	**eussent modelé**

Impératif
modèle
modelons
modelez

Sentences using this verb

J'aime bien ta voiture, mais le nouveau modèle est plus économique. I like your car, but the new model is more economical.

La ville de Washington est modelée sur la ville de Paris. Washington, D.C., is modeled after the city of Paris.

Words and expressions related to this verb

le modelage modeling
le modèle model, example
un mannequin fashion model
un modèle réduit scale model
la pâte à modeler modeling clay
se modeler sur to model oneself on
un modéliste, une modéliste model maker

Don't forget to study the section on defective and impersonal verbs. It's right after this main list.

monter (298) Part. pr. **montant** Part. passé **monté**

to go up, to ascend, to take up, to bring up, to mount

Regular **-er** verb

The Seven Simple Tenses		The Seven Compound Tenses	
Singular	Plural	Singular	Plural
1 présent de l'indicatif		8 passé composé	
monte	**montons**	**suis monté(e)**	**sommes monté(e)s**
montes	**montez**	**es monté(e)**	**êtes monté(e)(s)**
monte	**montent**	**est monté(e)**	**sont monté(e)s**
2 imparfait de l'indicatif		9 plus-que-parfait de l'indicatif	
montais	**montions**	**étais monté(e)**	**étions monté(e)s**
montais	**montiez**	**étais monté(e)**	**étiez monté(e)(s)**
montait	**montaient**	**était monté(e)**	**étaient monté(e)s**
3 passé simple		10 passé antérieur	
montai	**montâmes**	**fus monté(e)**	**fûmes monté(e)s**
montas	**montâtes**	**fus monté(e)**	**fûtes monté(e)(s)**
monta	**montèrent**	**fut monté(e)**	**furent monté(e)s**
4 futur		11 futur antérieur	
monterai	**monterons**	**serai monté(e)**	**serons monté(e)s**
monteras	**monterez**	**seras monté(e)**	**serez monté(e)(s)**
montera	**monteront**	**sera monté(e)**	**seront monté(e)s**
5 conditionnel		12 conditionnel passé	
monterais	**monterions**	**serais monté(e)**	**serions monté(e)s**
monterais	**monteriez**	**serais monté(e)**	**seriez monté(e)(s)**
monterait	**monteraient**	**serait monté(e)**	**seraient monté(e)s**
6 présent du subjonctif		13 passé du subjonctif	
monte	**montions**	**sois monté(e)**	**soyons monté(e)s**
montes	**montiez**	**sois monté(e)**	**soyez monté(e)(s)**
monte	**montent**	**soit monté(e)**	**soient monté(e)s**
7 imparfait du subjonctif		14 plus-que-parfait du subjonctif	
montasse	**montassions**	**fusse monté(e)**	**fussions monté(e)s**
montasses	**montassiez**	**fusses monté(e)**	**fussiez monté(e)(s)**
montât	**montassent**	**fût monté(e)**	**fussent monté(e)s**

Impératif
monte
montons
montez

AN ESSENTIAL 55 VERB

Monter

Monter is a very important verb for you to learn because it can take either **avoir** or **être** as auxiliary in the compound tenses (tenses 8–14).

This verb is conjugated with *avoir* when it has a direct object.		
Examples:	**J'ai monté l'escalier.**	I went up the stairs.
	J'ai monté les valises.	I brought up the suitcases.
BUT:	**Elle est montée vite.**	She went up quickly.

Sentences using monter and related words

La température va remonter au cours de la semaine. The temperature will go back up during the week.

J'ai pris l'ascenseur pour monter. I took the elevator to go up.

Le prix de l'essence est monté en flèche pendant l'été. The price of gasoline shot up during the summer.

Les enfants ont monté une pièce de théâtre dans le garage. The children put on a play in the garage.

Words and expressions related to this verb

monter à bicyclette **to ride a bicycle**

monter dans un train **to get on a train**

monter une pièce de théâtre **to stage a play**

monter à cheval **to mount a horse**

monter à bord d'un navire **to get on board a ship**

monter les prix **to push prices up**

monter en flèche **to shoot up (like an arrow)**

If you can conjugate **monter** you can also conjugate the following verbs (as well as other regular **-er** verbs):

démonter **to dismantle**

remonter **to go back up**

surmonter **to overcome**

Can't find the verb you're looking for? Check the back pages of this book for a list of over 2,600 additional verbs!

The subject pronouns are found on page 103.

montrer (299) — Part. pr. montrant — Part. passé montré

to show, to display, to exhibit, to point out

Regular **-er** verb

The Seven Simple Tenses

Singular	Plural
1 présent de l'indicatif	
montre	**montrons**
montres	**montrez**
montre	**montrent**
2 imparfait de l'indicatif	
montrais	**montrions**
montrais	**montriez**
montrait	**montraient**
3 passé simple	
montrai	**montrâmes**
montras	**montrâtes**
montra	**montrèrent**
4 futur	
montrerai	**montrerons**
montreras	**montrerez**
montrera	**montreront**
5 conditionnel	
montrerais	**montrerions**
montrerais	**montreriez**
montrerait	**montreraient**
6 présent du subjonctif	
montre	**montrions**
montres	**montriez**
montre	**montrent**
7 imparfait du subjonctif	
montrasse	**montrassions**
montrasses	**montrassiez**
montrât	**montrassent**

The Seven Compound Tenses

Singular	Plural
8 passé composé	
ai montré	**avons montré**
as montré	**avez montré**
a montré	**ont montré**
9 plus-que-parfait de l'indicatif	
avais montré	**avions montré**
avais montré	**aviez montré**
avait montré	**avaient montré**
10 passé antérieur	
eus montré	**eûmes montré**
eus montré	**eûtes montré**
eut montré	**eurent montré**
11 futur antérieur	
aurai montré	**aurons montré**
auras montré	**aurez montré**
aura montré	**auront montré**
12 conditionnel passé	
aurais montré	**aurions montré**
aurais montré	**auriez montré**
aurait montré	**auraient montré**
13 passé du subjonctif	
aie montré	**ayons montré**
aies montré	**ayez montré**
ait montré	**aient montré**
14 plus-que-parfait du subjonctif	
eusse montré	**eussions montré**
eusses montré	**eussiez montré**
eût montré	**eussent montré**

Impératif
montre
montrons
montrez

Words and expressions related to this verb

une montre a watch, display
une montre-bracelet wristwatch
faire montre de sa richesse to display, to show off one's wealth
Quelle heure est-il à votre montre? What time is it on your watch?
se faire montrer la porte to be put out the door, to be shown out the door
démontrer to demonstrate
se démontrer to be proved
se montrer to show oneself, to appear
montrer du doigt to point out, to show, to indicate by pointing

Don't miss the definitions of basic grammatical terms on pages 35–49.

Reflexive regular **-er** verb

to make fun

The Seven Simple Tenses		The Seven Compound Tenses	
Singular	Plural	Singular	Plural
1 présent de l'indicatif		8 passé composé	
me moque	**nous moquons**	**me suis moqué(e)**	**nous sommes moqué(e)s**
te moques	**vous moquez**	**t'es moqué(e)**	**vous êtes moqué(e)(s)**
se moque	**se moquent**	**s'est moqué(e)**	**se sont moqué(e)s**
2 imparfait de l'indicatif		9 plus-que-parfait de l'indicatif	
me moquais	**nous moquions**	**m'étais moqué(e)**	**nous étions moqué(e)s**
te moquais	**vous moquiez**	**t'étais moqué(e)**	**vous étiez moqué(e)(s)**
se moquais	**se moquaient**	**s'était moqué(e)**	**s'étaient moqué(e)s**
3 passé simple		10 passé antérieur	
me moquai	**nous moquâmes**	**me fus moqué(e)**	**nous fûmes moqué(e)s**
te moquas	**vous moquâtes**	**te fus moqué(e)**	**vous fûtes moqué(e)(s)**
se moqua	**se moquèrent**	**se fut moqué(e)**	**se furent moqué(e)s**
4 futur		11 futur antérieur	
me moquerai	**nous moquerons**	**me serai moqué(e)**	**nous serons moqué(e)s**
te moqueras	**vous moquerez**	**te seras moqué(e)**	**vous serez moqué(e)(s)**
se moquera	**se moqueront**	**se sera moqué(e)**	**se seront moqué(e)s**
5 conditionnel		12 conditionnel passé	
me moquerais	**nous moquerions**	**me serais moqué(e)**	**nous serions moqué(e)s**
te moquerais	**vous moqueriez**	**te serais moqué(e)**	**vous seriez moqué(e)(s)**
se moquerait	**se moqueraient**	**se serait moqué(e)**	**se seraient moqué(e)s**
6 présent du subjonctif		13 passé du subjonctif	
me moque	**nous moquions**	**me sois moqué(e)**	**nous soyons moqué(e)s**
te moques	**vous moquiez**	**te sois moqué(e)**	**vous soyez moqué(e)(s)**
se moque	**se moquent**	**se soit moqué(e)**	**se soient moqué(e)s**
7 imparfait du subjonctif		14 plus-que-parfait du subjonctif	
me moquasse	**nous moquassions**	**me fusse moqué(e)**	**nous fussions moqué(e)s**
te moquasses	**vous moquassiez**	**te fusses moqué(e)**	**vous fussiez moqué(e)(s)**
se moquât	**se moquassent**	**se fût moqué(e)**	**se fussent moqué(e)s**

Impératif
moque-toi; ne te moque pas
moquons-nous; ne nous moquons pas
moquez-vous; ne vous moquez pas

Words and expressions related to this verb

se moquer de to make fun of, to laugh at
Je m'en moque! I don't give a hoot!
moquer to mock
d'un ton moqueur in a mocking way
une moquerie mockery
un moqueur, une moqueuse mocker
moqueusement mockingly

Can't remember the French verb you need? Check the back pages of this book for the English-French verb index!

mordre (301) — Part. pr. **mordant** — Part. passé **mordu**

to bite

Regular **-re** verb

The Seven Simple Tenses		The Seven Compound Tenses	
Singular	Plural	Singular	Plural
1 présent de l'indicatif		8 passé composé	
mords	**mordons**	**ai mordu**	**avons mordu**
mords	**mordez**	**as mordu**	**avez mordu**
mord	**mordent**	**a mordu**	**ont mordu**
2 imparfait de l'indicatif		9 plus-que-parfait de l'indicatif	
mordais	**mordions**	**avais mordu**	**avions mordu**
mordais	**mordiez**	**avais mordu**	**aviez mordu**
mordait	**mordaient**	**avait mordu**	**avaient mordu**
3 passé simple		10 passé antérieur	
mordis	**mordîmes**	**eus mordu**	**eûmes mordu**
mordis	**mordîtes**	**eus mordu**	**eûtes mordu**
mordit	**mordirent**	**eut mordu**	**eurent mordu**
4 futur		11 futur antérieur	
mordrai	**mordrons**	**aurai mordu**	**aurons mordu**
mordras	**mordrez**	**auras mordu**	**aurez mordu**
mordra	**mordront**	**aura mordu**	**auront mordu**
5 conditionnel		12 conditionnel passé	
mordrais	**mordrions**	**aurais mordu**	**aurions mordu**
mordrais	**mordriez**	**aurais mordu**	**auriez mordu**
mordrait	**mordraient**	**aurait mordu**	**auraient mordu**
6 présent du subjonctif		13 passé du subjonctif	
morde	**mordions**	**aie mordu**	**ayons mordu**
mordes	**mordiez**	**aies mordu**	**ayez mordu**
morde	**mordent**	**ait mordu**	**aient mordu**
7 imparfait du subjonctif		14 plus-que-parfait du subjonctif	
mordisse	**mordissions**	**eusse mordu**	**eussions mordu**
mordisses	**mordissiez**	**eusses mordu**	**eussiez mordu**
mordît	**mordissent**	**eût mordu**	**eussent mordu**

Impératif
mords
mordons
mordez

Words and expressions related to this verb

Chien qui aboie ne mord pas. A barking dog does not bite. (His bark is worse than his bite.)
Tous les chiens qui aboient ne mordent pas. All dogs that bark do not bite.
mordre la poussière to bite the dust
se mordre les lèvres to bite one's lips
mordeur, mordeuse biter (one who bites)
mordiller to bite playfully, to nibble
mordant, mordante biting, trenchant
une morsure bite
mordre dans une pomme to bite into an apple
un mordu de l'ordinateur a computer fanatic, buff
C'est un mordu du jazz. He's jazz crazy.

Irregular verb

to grind, to mill

The Seven Simple Tenses		The Seven Compound Tenses	
Singular	Plural	Singular	Plural
1 présent de l'indicatif		8 passé composé	
mouds	**moulons**	**ai moulu**	**avons moulu**
mouds	**moulez**	**as moulu**	**avez moulu**
moud	**moulent**	**a moulu**	**ont moulu**
2 imparfait de l'indicatif		9 plus-que-parfait de l'indicatif	
moulais	**moulions**	**avais moulu**	**avions moulu**
moulais	**mouliez**	**avais moulu**	**aviez moulu**
moulait	**moulaient**	**avait moulu**	**avaient moulu**
3 passé simple		10 passé antérieur	
moulus	**moulûmes**	**eus moulu**	**eûmes moulu**
moulus	**moulûtes**	**eus moulu**	**eûtes moulu**
moulut	**moulurent**	**eut moulu**	**eurent moulu**
4 futur		11 futur antérieur	
moudrai	**moudrons**	**aurai moulu**	**aurons moulu**
moudras	**moudrez**	**auras moulu**	**aurez moulu**
moudra	**moudront**	**aura moulu**	**auront moulu**
5 conditionnel		12 conditionnel passé	
moudrais	**moudrions**	**aurais moulu**	**aurions moulu**
moudrais	**moudriez**	**aurais moulu**	**auriez moulu**
moudrait	**moudraient**	**aurait moulu**	**auraient moulu**
6 présent du subjonctif		13 passé du subjonctif	
moule	**moulions**	**aie moulu**	**ayons moulu**
moules	**mouliez**	**aies moulu**	**ayez moulu**
moule	**moulent**	**ait moulu**	**aient moulu**
7 imparfait du subjonctif		14 plus-que-parfait du subjonctif	
moulusse	**moulussions**	**eusse moulu**	**eussions moulu**
moulusses	**moulussiez**	**eusses moulu**	**eussiez moulu**
moulût	**moulussent**	**eût moulu**	**eussent moulu**

Impératif
mouds
moulons
moulez

Words and expressions related to this verb

moudre du café to grind coffee; **moudre du poivre** to grind pepper

un moulin à café coffee mill, coffee grinder

un petit moulin à légumes vegetable blender

un moulin mill; **un moulin à eau** watermill; **un moulin à vent** windmill; **un moulin rouge** red mill

un moulin à paroles person who talks constantly without ever stopping; excessively talkative; chatterbox

Don't forget to check the list of 2,600 additional verbs keyed to the 501 model verbs. It's in the Appendixes!

mourir (303) — Part. pr. mourant — Part. passé mort(e)(s)

to die

Irregular verb

The Seven Simple Tenses		The Seven Compound Tenses	
Singular	Plural	Singular	Plural
1 présent de l'indicatif		8 passé composé	
meurs	**mourons**	**suis mort(e)**	**sommes mort(e)s**
meurs	**mourez**	**es mort(e)**	**êtes mort(e)(s)**
meurt	**meurent**	**est mort(e)**	**sont mort(e)s**
2 imparfait de l'indicatif		9 plus-que-parfait de l'indicatif	
mourais	**mourions**	**étais mort(e)**	**étions mort(e)s**
mourais	**mouriez**	**étais mort(e)**	**étiez mort(e)(s)**
mourait	**mouraient**	**était mort(e)**	**étaient mort(e)s**
3 passé simple		10 passé antérieur	
mourus	**mourûmes**	**fus mort(e)**	**fûmes mort(e)s**
mourus	**mourûtes**	**fus mort(e)**	**fûtes mort(e)(s)**
mourut	**moururent**	**fut mort(e)**	**furent mort(e)s**
4 futur		11 futur antérieur	
mourrai	**mourrons**	**serai mort(e)**	**serons mort(e)s**
mourras	**mourrez**	**seras mort(e)**	**serez mort(e)(s)**
mourra	**mourront**	**sera mort(e)**	**seront mort(e)s**
5 conditionnel		12 conditionnel passé	
mourrais	**mourrions**	**serais mort(e)**	**serions mort(e)s**
mourrais	**mourriez**	**serais mort(e)**	**seriez mort(e)(s)**
mourrait	**mourraient**	**serait mort(e)**	**seraient mort(e)s**
6 présent du subjonctif		13 passé du subjonctif	
meure	**mourions**	**sois mort(e)**	**soyons mort(e)s**
meures	**mouriez**	**sois mort(e)**	**soyez mort(e)(s)**
meure	**meurent**	**soit mort(e)**	**soient mort(e)s**
7 imparfait du subjonctif		14 plus-que-parfait du subjonctif	
mourusse	**mourussions**	**fusse mort(e)**	**fussions mort(e)s**
mourusses	**mourussiez**	**fusses mort(e)**	**fussiez mort(e)(s)**
mourût	**mourussent**	**fût mort(e)**	**fussent mort(e)s**

Impératif
meurs
mourons
mourez

Words and expressions related to this verb
mourir de faim to starve to death
la mort death
Elle est mourante. She is dying; **Elle se meurt.** She is dying.
mourir d'ennui to be bored to tears
mourir de chagrin to die of a broken heart
mourir de soif to die of thirst
mourir de rire to die laughing
mourir d'envie de faire qqch to be very eager to do something
C'est triste à mourir. It's horribly sad.

Can't recognize an irregular verb form? Check out the index of common irregular French verb forms in the Appendixes.

Irregular verb

to move

The Seven Simple Tenses

Singular	Plural
1 présent de l'indicatif	
meus	**mouvons**
meus	**mouvez**
meut	**meuvent**
2 imparfait de l'indicatif	
mouvais	**mouvions**
mouvais	**mouviez**
mouvait	**mouvaient**
3 passé simple	
mus	**mûmes**
mus	**mûtes**
mut	**murent**
4 futur	
mouvrai	**mouvrons**
mouvras	**mouvrez**
mouvra	**mouvront**
5 conditionnel	
mouvrais	**mouvrions**
mouvrais	**mouvriez**
mouvrait	**mouvraient**
6 présent du subjonctif	
meuve	**mouvions**
meuves	**mouviez**
meuve	**meuvent**
7 imparfait du subjonctif	
musse	**mussions**
musses	**mussiez**
mût	**mussent**

Impératif
meus
mouvons
mouvez

The Seven Compound Tenses

Singular	Plural
8 passé composé	
ai mû	**avons mû**
as mû	**avez mû**
a mû	**ont mû**
9 plus-que-parfait de l'indicatif	
avais mû	**avions mû**
avais mû	**aviez mû**
avait mû	**avaient mû**
10 passé antérieur	
eus mû	**eûmes mû**
eus mû	**eûtes mû**
eut mû	**eurent mû**
11 futur antérieur	
aurai mû	**aurons mû**
auras mû	**aurez mû**
aura mû	**auront mû**
12 conditionnel passé	
aurais mû	**aurions mû**
aurais mû	**auriez mû**
aurait mû	**auraient mû**
13 passé du subjonctif	
aie mû	**ayons mû**
aies mû	**ayez mû**
ait mû	**aient mû**
14 plus-que-parfait du subjonctif	
eusse mû	**eussions mû**
eusses mû	**eussiez mû**
eût mû	**eussent mû**

M

Words and expressions related to this verb
émouvoir to move, to affect (emotionally)
s'émouvoir to be moved, to be touched, to be affected (emotionally)
faire mouvoir to move, to set in motion
promouvoir to promote

Do not confuse this verb with **déménager**, which means to move from one dwelling to another or from one city to another.

nager (305) — Part. pr. nageant — Part. passé nagé

to swim

Regular **-er** verb endings; spelling change: retain the **ge** before **a** or **o** to keep the soft **g** sound of the verb

The Seven Simple Tenses

Singular	Plural
1 présent de l'indicatif	
nage	**nageons**
nages	**nagez**
nage	**nagent**
2 imparfait de l'indicatif	
nageais	**nagions**
nageais	**nagiez**
nageait	**nageaient**
3 passé simple	
nageai	**nageâmes**
nageas	**nageâtes**
nagea	**nagèrent**
4 futur	
nagerai	**nagerons**
nageras	**nagerez**
nagera	**nageront**
5 conditionnel	
nagerais	**nagerions**
nagerais	**nageriez**
nagerait	**nageraient**
6 présent du subjonctif	
nage	**nagions**
nages	**nagiez**
nage	**nagent**
7 imparfait du subjonctif	
nageasse	**nageassions**
nageasses	**nageassiez**
nageât	**nageassent**

The Seven Compound Tenses

Singular	Plural
8 passé composé	
ai nagé	**avons nagé**
as nagé	**avez nagé**
a nagé	**ont nagé**
9 plus-que-parfait de l'indicatif	
avais nagé	**avions nagé**
avais nagé	**aviez nagé**
avait nagé	**avaient nagé**
10 passé antérieur	
eus nagé	**eûmes nagé**
eus nagé	**eûtes nagé**
eut nagé	**eurent nagé**
11 futur antérieur	
aurai nagé	**aurons nagé**
auras nagé	**aurez nagé**
aura nagé	**auront nagé**
12 conditionnel passé	
aurais nagé	**aurions nagé**
aurais nagé	**auriez nagé**
aurait nagé	**auraient nagé**
13 passé du subjonctif	
aie nagé	**ayons nagé**
aies nagé	**ayez nagé**
ait nagé	**aient nagé**
14 plus-que-parfait du subjonctif	
eusse nagé	**eussions nagé**
eusses nagé	**eussiez nagé**
eût nagé	**eussent nagé**

Impératif
nage
nageons
nagez

Words and expressions related to this verb

un nageur, une nageuse swimmer
la piscine swimming pool
savoir nager to know how to swim
la natation swimming
nager entre deux eaux to sit on the fence
la nage swimming; **la nage libre** free style swimming
se sauver à la nage to swim to safety
nager sous l'eau to swim underwater
Il nage dans ses vêtements. His clothes are too big on him.
un maillot de bain swimsuit
nager comme un poisson to swim like a fish
nager dans l'opulence to be rolling in money
aller nager to go swimming
faire de la natation to swim

Don't miss orthographically changing verbs on pages 32–34.

Irregular verb

to be born

The Seven Simple Tenses		The Seven Compound Tenses	
Singular	Plural	Singular	Plural
1 présent de l'indicatif		8 passé composé	
nais	**naissons**	**suis né(e)**	**sommes né(e)s**
nais	**naissez**	**es né(e)**	**êtes né(e)(s)**
naît	**naissent**	**est né(e)**	**sont né(e)s**
2 imparfait de l'indicatif		9 plus-que-parfait de l'indicatif	
naissais	**naissions**	**étais né(e)**	**étions né(e)s**
naissais	**naissiez**	**étais né(e)**	**étiez né(e)(s)**
naissait	**naissaient**	**était né(e)**	**étaient né(e)s**
3 passé simple		10 passé antérieur	
naquis	**naquîmes**	**fus né(e)**	**fûmes né(e)s**
naquis	**naquîtes**	**fus né(e)**	**fûtes né(e)(s)**
naquit	**naquirent**	**fut né(e)**	**furent né(e)s**
4 futur		11 futur antérieur	
naîtrai	**naîtrons**	**serai né(e)**	**serons né(e)s**
naîtras	**naîtrez**	**seras né(e)**	**serez né(e)(s)**
naîtra	**naîtront**	**sera né(e)**	**seront né(e)s**
5 conditionnel		12 conditionnel passé	
naîtrais	**naîtrions**	**serais né(e)**	**serions né(e)s**
naîtrais	**naîtriez**	**serais né(e)**	**seriez né(e)(s)**
naîtrait	**naîtraient**	**serait né(e)**	**seraient né(e)s**
6 présent du subjonctif		13 passé du subjonctif	
naisse	**naissions**	**sois né(e)**	**soyons né(e)s**
naisses	**naissiez**	**sois né(e)**	**soyez né(e)(s)**
naisse	**naissent**	**soit né(e)**	**soient né(e)s**
7 imparfait du subjonctif		14 plus-que-parfait du subjonctif	
naquisse	**naquissions**	**fusse né(e)**	**fussions né(e)s**
naquisses	**naquissiez**	**fusses né(e)**	**fussiez né(e)(s)**
naquît	**naquissent**	**fût né(e)**	**fussent né(e)s**

Impératif
nais
naissons
naissez

Words and expressions related to this verb
la naissance birth
un anniversaire de naissance a birthday anniversary
donner naissance à to give birth to; **la naissance du monde** beginning of the world
Anne est Française de naissance. Anne was born French.
renaître to be born again
faire naître to cause, to give rise to
Je ne suis pas né(e) d'hier! I wasn't born yesterday!
la Nativité Nativity

Don't forget to study the section on defective and impersonal verbs. It's right after this main list.

naviguer (307) — Part. pr. **naviguant** — Part. passé **navigué**

to navigate, to sail; to browse, to surf (Internet)

Regular **-er** verb

The Seven Simple Tenses

Singular	Plural
1 présent de l'indicatif	
navigue	**naviguons**
navigues	**naviguez**
navigue	**naviguent**
2 imparfait de l'indicatif	
naviguais	**naviguions**
naviguais	**naviguiez**
naviguait	**naviguaient**
3 passé simple	
naviguai	**naviguâmes**
naviguas	**naviguâtes**
navigua	**naviguèrent**
4 futur	
naviguerai	**naviguerons**
navigueras	**naviguerez**
naviguera	**navigueront**
5 conditionnel	
naviguerais	**naviguerions**
naviguerais	**navigueriez**
naviguerait	**navigueraient**
6 présent du subjonctif	
navigue	**naviguions**
navigues	**naviguiez**
navigue	**naviguent**
7 imparfait du subjonctif	
naviguasse	**naviguassions**
naviguasses	**naviguassiez**
naviguât	**naviguassent**

The Seven Compound Tenses

Singular	Plural
8 passé composé	
ai navigué	**avons navigué**
as navigué	**avez navigué**
a navigué	**ont navigué**
9 plus-que-parfait de l'indicatif	
avais navigué	**avions navigué**
avais navigué	**aviez navigué**
avait navigué	**avaient navigué**
10 passé antérieur	
eus navigué	**eûmes navigué**
eus navigué	**eûtes navigué**
eut navigué	**eurent navigué**
11 futur antérieur	
aurai navigué	**aurons navigué**
auras navigué	**aurez navigué**
aura navigué	**auront navigué**
12 conditionnel passé	
aurais navigué	**aurions navigué**
aurais navigué	**auriez navigué**
aurait navigué	**auraient navigué**
13 passé du subjonctif	
aie navigué	**ayons navigué**
aies navigué	**ayez navigué**
ait navigué	**aient navigué**
14 plus-que-parfait du subjonctif	
eusse navigué	**eussions navigué**
eusses navigué	**eussiez navigué**
eût navigué	**eussent navigué**

Impératif
navigue
naviguons
naviguez

Sentences using this verb and words related to it

Je naviguais sur le Web quand mon ordinateur est tombé en panne. I was surfing the Web when my computer crashed.

Jacques Cartier est le navigateur qui a découvert le Saint-Laurent. Jacques Cartier is the navigator who discovered the Saint Lawrence River.

Words and expressions related to this verb

un navigateur, une navigatrice navigator, sailor
un navigateur Web Web browser
la navigation navigation, sailing
navigable *adj.* navigable
naviguer sur Internet, naviguer sur le Web to surf the Internet (You can also use **surfer**.)
un navire ship
naviguer à vue to fly visually (VFR)

Can't find the verb you're looking for? Check the back pages of this book for a list of over 2,600 additional verbs!

Regular **-er** verb endings; spelling change: **-oyer** verbs must change **y** to **i** in front of a mute **e**

to clean

The Seven Simple Tenses		The Seven Compound Tenses	
Singular	Plural	Singular	Plural
1 présent de l'indicatif		8 passé composé	
nettoie	**nettoyons**	**ai nettoyé**	**avons nettoyé**
nettoies	**nettoyez**	**as nettoyé**	**avez nettoyé**
nettoie	**nettoient**	**a nettoyé**	**ont nettoyé**
2 imparfait de l'indicatif		9 plus-que-parfait de l'indicatif	
nettoyais	**nettoyions**	**avais nettoyé**	**avions nettoyé**
nettoyais	**nettoyiez**	**avais nettoyé**	**aviez nettoyé**
nettoyait	**nettoyaient**	**avait nettoyé**	**avaient nettoyé**
3 passé simple		10 passé antérieur	
nettoyai	**nettoyâmes**	**eus nettoyé**	**eûmes nettoyé**
nettoyas	**nettoyâtes**	**eus nettoyé**	**eûtes nettoyé**
nettoya	**nettoyèrent**	**eut nettoyé**	**eurent nettoyé**
4 futur		11 futur antérieur	
nettoierai	**nettoierons**	**aurai nettoyé**	**aurons nettoyé**
nettoieras	**nettoierez**	**auras nettoyé**	**aurez nettoyé**
nettoiera	**nettoieront**	**aura nettoyé**	**auront nettoyé**
5 conditionnel		12 conditionnel passé	
nettoierais	**nettoierions**	**aurais nettoyé**	**aurions nettoyé**
nettoierais	**nettoieriez**	**aurais nettoyé**	**auriez nettoyé**
nettoierait	**nettoieraient**	**aurait nettoyé**	**auraient nettoyé**
6 présent du subjonctif		13 passé du subjonctif	
nettoie	**nettoyions**	**aie nettoyé**	**ayons nettoyé**
nettoies	**nettoyiez**	**aies nettoyé**	**ayez nettoyé**
nettoie	**nettoient**	**ait nettoyé**	**aient nettoyé**
7 imparfait du subjonctif		14 plus-que-parfait du subjonctif	
nettoyasse	**nettoyassions**	**eusse nettoyé**	**eussions nettoyé**
nettoyasses	**nettoyassiez**	**eusses nettoyé**	**eussiez nettoyé**
nettoyât	**nettoyassent**	**eût nettoyé**	**eussent nettoyé**

Impératif
nettoie
nettoyons
nettoyez

Words and expressions related to this verb

le nettoyage cleaning; **le nettoyage à sec** dry cleaning
nettoyer à sec to dry clean
une nettoyeuse cleaning machine
un nettoyant cleanser
un nettoyeur de fenêtres window cleaner
Elle refuse nettement. She flatly refuses.
se faire nettoyer au jeu to be cleaned out at gambling

The subject pronouns are found on page 103.

nier (309)

Part. pr. **niant** Part. passé **nié**

to deny

Regular **-er** verb

The Seven Simple Tenses		The Seven Compound Tenses	
Singular	Plural	Singular	Plural
1 présent de l'indicatif		8 passé composé	
nie	**nions**	**ai nié**	**avons nié**
nies	**niez**	**as nié**	**avez nié**
nie	**nient**	**a nié**	**ont nié**
2 imparfait de l'indicatif		9 plus-que-parfait de l'indicatif	
niais	**niions**	**avais nié**	**avions nié**
niais	**niiez**	**avais nié**	**aviez nié**
niait	**niaient**	**avait nié**	**avaient nié**
3 passé simple		10 passé antérieur	
niai	**niâmes**	**eus nié**	**eûmes nié**
nias	**niâtes**	**eus nié**	**eûtes nié**
nia	**nièrent**	**eut nié**	**eurent nié**
4 futur		11 futur antérieur	
nierai	**nierons**	**aurai nié**	**aurons nié**
nieras	**nierez**	**auras nié**	**aurez nié**
niera	**nieront**	**aura nié**	**auront nié**
5 conditionnel		12 conditionnel passé	
nierais	**nierions**	**aurais nié**	**aurions nié**
nierais	**nieriez**	**aurais nié**	**auriez nié**
nierait	**nieraient**	**aurait nié**	**auraient nié**
6 présent du subjonctif		13 passé du subjonctif	
nie	**niions**	**aie nié**	**ayons nié**
nies	**niiez**	**aies nié**	**ayez nié**
nie	**nient**	**ait nié**	**aient nié**
7 imparfait du subjonctif		14 plus-que-parfait du subjonctif	
niasse	**niassions**	**eusse nié**	**eussions nié**
niasses	**niassiez**	**eusses nié**	**eussiez nié**
niât	**niassent**	**eût nié**	**eussent nié**

Impératif
nie
nions
niez

Words and expressions related to this verb

nier un fait to deny a fact
dénier qqch à qqn to deny someone something, to refuse someone something
un déni denial; **un déni de justice** denial of justice
renier to deny openly, to reject
renier un ami to reject a friend
renier sa promesse to go back on, to break one's promise
un renégat, une renégate renegade
un reniement denial
indéniable undeniable

Get acquainted with what preposition goes with what verb. See *Verbs with prepositions* in the Appendixes.

Regular **-er** verb

to name, to appoint

The Seven Simple Tenses		The Seven Compound Tenses	
Singular	Plural	Singular	Plural
1 présent de l'indicatif		8 passé composé	
nomme	**nommons**	**ai nommé**	**avons nommé**
nommes	**nommez**	**as nommé**	**avez nommé**
nomme	**nomment**	**a nommé**	**ont nommé**
2 imparfait de l'indicatif		9 plus-que-parfait de l'indicatif	
nommais	**nommions**	**avais nommé**	**avions nommé**
nommais	**nommiez**	**avais nommé**	**aviez nommé**
nommait	**nommaient**	**avait nommé**	**avaient nommé**
3 passé simple		10 passé antérieur	
nommai	**nommâmes**	**eus nommé**	**eûmes nommé**
nommas	**nommâtes**	**eus nommé**	**eûtes nommé**
nomma	**nommèrent**	**eut nommé**	**eurent nommé**
4 futur		11 futur antérieur	
nommerai	**nommerons**	**aurai nommé**	**aurons nommé**
nommeras	**nommerez**	**auras nommé**	**aurez nommé**
nommera	**nommeront**	**aura nommé**	**auront nommé**
5 conditionnel		12 conditionnel passé	
nommerais	**nommerions**	**aurais nommé**	**aurions nommé**
nommerais	**nommeriez**	**aurais nommé**	**auriez nommé**
nommerait	**nommeraient**	**aurait nommé**	**auraient nommé**
6 présent du subjonctif		13 passé du subjonctif	
nomme	**nommions**	**aie nommé**	**ayons nommé**
nommes	**nommiez**	**aies nommé**	**ayez nommé**
nomme	**nomment**	**ait nommé**	**aient nommé**
7 imparfait du subjonctif		14 plus-que-parfait du subjonctif	
nommasse	**nommassions**	**eusse nommé**	**eussions nommé**
nommasses	**nommassiez**	**eusses nommé**	**eussiez nommé**
nommât	**nommassent**	**eût nommé**	**eussent nommé**

Impératif
nomme
nommons
nommez

Common idiomatic expressions using this verb and words related to it

nommément namely, by name
un pronom a pronoun
un pseudonyme pseudonym
un nom de théâtre stage name
le petit nom a person's first name
appeler les choses par leur nom to call a spade a spade
anonyme anonymous
un nom de plume pen name (a name used by an author other than the real name)
un nom de guerre false (assumed) name
nominalement nominally
au nom du Père, du Fils, et du Saint-Esprit in the name of the Father, the Son, and the Holy Spirit
le renom renown

The subject pronouns are found on page 103.

nourrir (311) — Part. pr. nourrissant — Part. passé nourri

to feed, to nourish

Regular -ir verb

The Seven Simple Tenses		The Seven Compound Tenses	
Singular	Plural	Singular	Plural
1 présent de l'indicatif		8 passé composé	
nourris	**nourrissons**	**ai nourri**	**avons nourri**
nourris	**nourrissez**	**as nourri**	**avez nourri**
nourrit	**nourrissent**	**a nourri**	**ont nourri**
2 imparfait de l'indicatif		9 plus-que-parfait de l'indicatif	
nourrissais	**nourrissions**	**avais nourri**	**avions nourri**
nourrissais	**nourrissiez**	**avais nourri**	**aviez nourri**
nourrissait	**nourrissaient**	**avait nourri**	**avaient nourri**
3 passé simple		10 passé antérieur	
nourris	**nourrîmes**	**eus nourri**	**eûmes nourri**
nourris	**nourrîtes**	**eus nourri**	**eûtes nourri**
nourrit	**nourrirent**	**eut nourri**	**eurent nourri**
4 futur		11 futur antérieur	
nourrirai	**nourrirons**	**aurai nourri**	**aurons nourri**
nourriras	**nourrirez**	**auras nourri**	**aurez nourri**
nourrira	**nourriront**	**aura nourri**	**auront nourri**
5 conditionnel		12 conditionnel passé	
nourrirais	**nourririons**	**aurais nourri**	**aurions nourri**
nourrirais	**nourririez**	**aurais nourri**	**auriez nourri**
nourrirait	**nourriraient**	**aurait nourri**	**auraient nourri**
6 présent du subjonctif		13 passé du subjonctif	
nourrisse	**nourrissions**	**aie nourri**	**ayons nourri**
nourrisses	**nourrissiez**	**aies nourri**	**ayez nourri**
nourrisse	**nourrissent**	**ait nourri**	**aient nourri**
7 imparfait du subjonctif		14 plus-que-parfait du subjonctif	
nourrisse	**nourrissions**	**eusse nourri**	**eussions nourri**
nourrisses	**nourrissiez**	**eusses nourri**	**eussiez nourri**
nourrît	**nourrissent**	**eût nourri**	**eussent nourri**

Impératif
nourris
nourrissons
nourrissez

Words and expressions related to this verb

la nourriture nourishment, food
une nourrice wet nurse
bien nourri well fed
mal nourri poorly fed
nourrissant, nourrissante nourishing
un nourrisson infant
nourricier, nourricière nutritious
une mère nourricière foster mother
un père nourricier foster father
se nourrir to feed oneself

Grammar putting you in a tense mood? Review the definitions of basic grammatical terms with examples on pages 35–49.

Reflexive regular **-er** verb endings; spelling change: **-oyer** verbs must change **y** to **i** in front of a mute **e**

to drown

The Seven Simple Tenses		The Seven Compound Tenses	
Singular	Plural	Singular	Plural
1 présent de l'indicatif		8 passé composé	
me noie	**nous noyons**	**me suis noyé(e)**	**nous sommes noyé(e)s**
te noies	**vous noyez**	**t'es noyé(e)**	**vous êtes noyé(e)(s)**
se noie	**se noient**	**s'est noyé(e)**	**se sont noyé(e)s**
2 imparfait de l'indicatif		9 plus-que-parfait de l'indicatif	
me noyais	**nous noyions**	**m'étais noyé(e)**	**nous étions noyé(e)s**
te noyais	**vous noyiez**	**t'étais noyé(e)**	**vous étiez noyé(e)(s)**
se noyait	**se noyaient**	**s'était noyé(e)**	**s'étaient noyé(e)s**
3 passé simple		10 passé antérieur	
me noyai	**nous noyâmes**	**me fus noyé(e)**	**nous fûmes noyé(e)s**
te noyas	**vous noyâtes**	**te fus noyé(e)**	**vous fûtes noyé(e)(s)**
se noya	**se noyèrent**	**se fut noyé(e)**	**se furent noyé(e)s**
4 futur		11 futur antérieur	
me noierai	**nous noierons**	**me serai noyé(e)**	**nous serons noyé(e)s**
te noieras	**vous noierez**	**te seras noyé(e)**	**vous serez noyé(e)(s)**
se noiera	**se noieront**	**se sera noyé(e)**	**se seront noyé(e)s**
5 conditionnel		12 conditionnel passé	
me noierais	**nous noierions**	**me serais noyé(e)**	**nous serions noyé(e)s**
te noierais	**vous noieriez**	**te serais noyé(e)**	**vous seriez noyé(e)(s)**
se noierait	**se noieraient**	**se serait noyé(e)**	**se seraient noyé(e)s**
6 présent du subjonctif		13 passé du subjonctif	
me noie	**nous noyions**	**me sois noyé(e)**	**nous soyons noyé(e)s**
te noies	**vous noyiez**	**te sois noyé(e)**	**vous soyez noyé(e)(s)**
se noie	**se noient**	**se soit noyé(e)**	**se soient noyé(e)s**
7 imparfait du subjonctif		14 plus-que-parfait du subjonctif	
me noyasse	**nous noyassions**	**me fusse noyé(e)**	**nous fussions noyé(e)s**
te noyasses	**vous noyassiez**	**te fusses noyé(e)**	**vous fussiez noyé(e)(s)**
se noyât	**se noyassent**	**se fût noyé(e)**	**se fussent noyé(e)s**

Impératif
noie-toi; ne te noie pas
noyons-nous; ne nous noyons pas
noyez-vous; ne vous noyez pas

Words and expressions related to this verb

Suzanne se noyait quand le maître-nageur est arrivé lui sauver la vie.
Suzanne was drowning when the lifeguard arrived to save her life.

une noyade drowning
noyer to drown (an animal or person), to water down (liquid)
se noyer dans to get bogged down in
le noyé, la noyée drowned person

Can't remember the French verb you need? Check the back pages of this book for the English-French verb index!

nuire (313) — Part. pr. **nuisant** — Part. passé **nui**

to harm, to hinder

Irregular verb

The Seven Simple Tenses		The Seven Compound Tenses	
Singular	Plural	Singular	Plural
1 présent de l'indicatif		8 passé composé	
nuis	**nuisons**	**ai nui**	**avons nui**
nuis	**nuisez**	**as nui**	**avez nui**
nuit	**nuisent**	**a nui**	**ont nui**
2 imparfait de l'indicatif		9 plus-que-parfait de l'indicatif	
nuisais	**nuisions**	**avais nui**	**avions nui**
nuisais	**nuisiez**	**avais nui**	**aviez nui**
nuisait	**nuisaient**	**avait nui**	**avaient nui**
3 passé simple		10 passé antérieur	
nuisis	**nuisîmes**	**eus nui**	**eûmes nui**
nuisis	**nuisîtes**	**eus nui**	**eûtes nui**
nuisit	**nuisirent**	**eut nui**	**eurent nui**
4 futur		11 futur antérieur	
nuirai	**nuirons**	**aurai nui**	**aurons nui**
nuiras	**nuirez**	**auras nui**	**aurez nui**
nuira	**nuiront**	**aura nui**	**auront nui**
5 conditionnel		12 conditionnel passé	
nuirais	**nuirions**	**aurais nui**	**aurions nui**
nuirais	**nuiriez**	**aurais nui**	**auriez nui**
nuirait	**nuiraient**	**aurait nui**	**auraient nui**
6 présent du subjonctif		13 passé du subjonctif	
nuise	**nuisions**	**aie nui**	**ayons nui**
nuises	**nuisiez**	**aies nui**	**ayez nui**
nuise	**nuisent**	**ait nui**	**aient nui**
7 imparfait du subjonctif		14 plus-que-parfait du subjonctif	
nuisisse	**nuisissions**	**eusse nui**	**eussions nui**
nuisisses	**nuisissiez**	**eusses nui**	**eussiez nui**
nuisît	**nuisissent**	**eût nui**	**eussent nui**

Impératif
nuis
nuisons
nuisez

Words and expressions related to this verb

la nuisance nuisance
les nuisances sonores noise pollution
nuisible harmful
nuire à to do harm to, to be injurious to, to be harmful to

Cela peut nuire à la réputation de votre famille. That may harm the reputation of your family.

How are you doing? Find out with the verb drills and tests with answers explained on pages 50–101.

The Seven Simple Tenses		The Seven Compound Tenses	
Singular	Plural	Singular	Plural
1 présent de l'indicatif		8 passé composé	
obéis	**obéissons**	**ai obéi**	**avons obéi**
obéis	**obéissez**	**as obéi**	**avez obéi**
obéit	**obéissent**	**a obéi**	**ont obéi**
2 imparfait de l'indicatif		9 plus-que-parfait de l'indicatif	
obéissais	**obéissions**	**avais obéi**	**avions obéi**
obéissais	**obéissiez**	**avais obéi**	**aviez obéi**
obéissait	**obéissaient**	**avait obéi**	**avaient obéi**
3 passé simple		10 passé antérieur	
obéis	**obéîmes**	**eus obéi**	**eûmes obéi**
obéis	**obéîtes**	**eus obéi**	**eûtes obéi**
obéit	**obéirent**	**eut obéi**	**eurent obéi**
4 futur		11 futur antérieur	
obéirai	**obéirons**	**aurai obéi**	**aurons obéi**
obéiras	**obéirez**	**auras obéi**	**aurez obéi**
obéira	**obéiront**	**aura obéi**	**auront obéi**
5 conditionnel		12 conditionnel passé	
obéirais	**obéirions**	**aurais obéi**	**aurions obéi**
obéirais	**obéiriez**	**aurais obéi**	**auriez obéi**
obéirait	**obéiraient**	**aurait obéi**	**auraient obéi**
6 présent du subjonctif		13 passé du subjonctif	
obéisse	**obéissions**	**aie obéi**	**ayons obéi**
obéisses	**obéissiez**	**aies obéi**	**ayez obéi**
obéisse	**obéissent**	**ait obéi**	**aient obéi**
7 imparfait du subjonctif		14 plus-que-parfait du subjonctif	
obéisse	**obéissions**	**eusse obéi**	**eussions obéi**
obéisses	**obéissiez**	**eusses obéi**	**eussiez obéi**
obéît	**obéissent**	**eût obéi**	**eussent obéi**

Impératif
obéis
obéissons
obéissez

Words and expressions related to this verb
obéir à qqn to obey someone
désobéir à qqn to disobey someone
l'obéissance *f.* obedience
obéissant, obéissante obedient
désobéissant, désobéissante disobedient
obéir à ses instincts to obey one's instincts

Get acquainted with what preposition goes with what verb. See *Verbs with prepositions* in the Appendixes.

obliger (315) — Part. pr. obligeant — Part. passé obligé

to oblige

Regular **-er** verb endings; spelling change: retain the **ge** before **a** or **o** to keep the soft **g** sound of the verb

The Seven Simple Tenses

Singular	Plural
1 présent de l'indicatif	
oblige	**obligeons**
obliges	**obligez**
oblige	**obligent**
2 imparfait de l'indicatif	
obligeais	**obligions**
obligeais	**obligiez**
obligeait	**obligeaient**
3 passé simple	
obligeai	**obligeâmes**
obligeas	**obligeâtes**
obligea	**obligèrent**
4 futur	
obligerai	**obligerons**
obligeras	**obligerez**
obligera	**obligeront**
5 conditionnel	
obligerais	**obligerions**
obligerais	**obligeriez**
obligerait	**obligeraient**
6 présent du subjonctif	
oblige	**obligions**
obliges	**obligiez**
oblige	**obligent**
7 imparfait du subjonctif	
obligeasse	**obligeassions**
obligeasses	**obligeassiez**
obligeât	**obligeassent**

The Seven Compound Tenses

Singular	Plural
8 passé composé	
ai obligé	**avons obligé**
as obligé	**avez obligé**
a obligé	**ont obligé**
9 plus-que-parfait de l'indicatif	
avais obligé	**avions obligé**
avais obligé	**aviez obligé**
avait obligé	**avaient obligé**
10 passé antérieur	
eus obligé	**eûmes obligé**
eus obligé	**eûtes obligé**
eut obligé	**eurent obligé**
11 futur antérieur	
aurai obligé	**aurons obligé**
auras obligé	**aurez obligé**
aura obligé	**auront obligé**
12 conditionnel passé	
aurais obligé	**aurions obligé**
aurais obligé	**auriez obligé**
aurait obligé	**auraient obligé**
13 passé du subjonctif	
aie obligé	**ayons obligé**
aies obligé	**ayez obligé**
ait obligé	**aient obligé**
14 plus-que-parfait du subjonctif	
eusse obligé	**eussions obligé**
eusses obligé	**eussiez obligé**
eût obligé	**eussent obligé**

Impératif
oblige
obligeons
obligez

Words and expressions related to this verb

obligatoire obligatory
l'obligation *f.* obligation
avoir beaucoup d'obligation à qqn to be much obliged to someone
obligeant, obligeante obliging
se montrer obligeant envers qqn to show kindness to someone
obligé, obligée obliged
Noblesse oblige. Nobility obliges. (*i.e.*, the moral obligation of a highborn person is to show honorable conduct)

If you want to see a sample English verb fully conjugated in all the tenses, check out pages 8 and 9.

Irregular verb

to obtain, to get

The Seven Simple Tenses		The Seven Compound Tenses	
Singular	Plural	Singular	Plural
1 présent de l'indicatif		8 passé composé	
obtiens	**obtenons**	**ai obtenu**	**avons obtenu**
obtiens	**obtenez**	**as obtenu**	**avez obtenu**
obtient	**obtiennent**	**a obtenu**	**ont obtenu**
2 imparfait de l'indicatif		9 plus-que-parfait de l'indicatif	
obtenais	**obtenions**	**avais obtenu**	**avions obtenu**
obtenais	**obteniez**	**avais obtenu**	**aviez obtenu**
obtenait	**obtenaient**	**avait obtenu**	**avaient obtenu**
3 passé simple		10 passé antérieur	
obtins	**obtînmes**	**eus obtenu**	**eûmes obtenu**
obtins	**obtîntes**	**eus obtenu**	**eûtes obtenu**
obtint	**obtinrent**	**eut obtenu**	**eurent obtenu**
4 futur		11 futur antérieur	
obtiendrai	**obtiendrons**	**aurai obtenu**	**aurons obtenu**
obtiendras	**obtiendrez**	**auras obtenu**	**aurez obtenu**
obtiendra	**obtiendront**	**aura obtenu**	**auront obtenu**
5 conditionnel		12 conditionnel passé	
obtiendrais	**obtiendrions**	**aurais obtenu**	**aurions obtenu**
obtiendrais	**obtiendriez**	**aurais obtenu**	**auriez obtenu**
obtiendrait	**obtiendraient**	**aurait obtenu**	**auraient obtenu**
6 présent du subjonctif		13 passé du subjonctif	
obtienne	**obtenions**	**aie obtenu**	**ayons obtenu**
obtiennes	**obteniez**	**aies obtenu**	**ayez obtenu**
obtienne	**obtiennent**	**ait obtenu**	**aient obtenu**
7 imparfait du subjonctif		14 plus-que-parfait du subjonctif	
obtinsse	**obtinssions**	**eusse obtenu**	**eussions obtenu**
obtinsses	**obtinssiez**	**eusses obtenu**	**eussiez obtenu**
obtînt	**obtinssent**	**eût obtenu**	**eussent obtenu**

Impératif
obtiens
obtenons
obtenez

Words and expressions related to this verb
l'obtention *f.* obtainment
obtenir de qqn qqch de force to get something out of someone by force
s'obtenir de to be obtained from

See also **contenir, retenir,** and **tenir.**

It's important that you be familiar with the Subjunctive. See pages 26–31.

to occupy

Regular **-er** verb

The Seven Simple Tenses		The Seven Compound Tenses	
Singular	Plural	Singular	Plural
1 présent de l'indicatif		8 passé composé	
occupe	**occupons**	**ai occupé**	**avons occupé**
occupes	**occupez**	**as occupé**	**avez occupé**
occupe	**occupent**	**a occupé**	**ont occupé**
2 imparfait de l'indicatif		9 plus-que-parfait de l'indicatif	
occupais	**occupions**	**avais occupé**	**avions occupé**
occupais	**occupiez**	**avais occupé**	**aviez occupé**
occupait	**occupaient**	**avait occupé**	**avaient occupé**
3 passé simple		10 passé antérieur	
occupai	**occupâmes**	**eus occupé**	**eûmes occupé**
occupas	**occupâtes**	**eus occupé**	**eûtes occupé**
occupa	**occupèrent**	**eut occupé**	**eurent occupé**
4 futur		11 futur antérieur	
occuperai	**occuperons**	**aurai occupé**	**aurons occupé**
occuperas	**occuperez**	**auras occupé**	**aurez occupé**
occupera	**occuperont**	**aura occupé**	**auront occupé**
5 conditionnel		12 conditionnel passé	
occuperais	**occuperions**	**aurais occupé**	**aurions occupé**
occuperais	**occuperiez**	**aurais occupé**	**auriez occupé**
occuperait	**occuperaient**	**aurait occupé**	**auraient occupé**
6 présent du subjonctif		13 passé du subjonctif	
occupe	**occupions**	**aie occupé**	**ayons occupé**
occupes	**occupiez**	**aies occupé**	**ayez occupé**
occupe	**occupent**	**ait occupé**	**aient occupé**
7 imparfait du subjonctif		14 plus-que-parfait du subjonctif	
occupasse	**occupassions**	**eusse occupé**	**eussions occupé**
occupasses	**occupassiez**	**eusses occupé**	**eussiez occupé**
occupât	**occupassent**	**eût occupé**	**eussent occupé**

Impératif
occupe
occupons
occupez

Words and expressions related to this verb
l'occupation *f.* occupation
être occupé(e) to be busy
occuper qqn to keep someone busy
occuper trop de place to take up too much room
occupant, occupante occupying; **du travail occupant** engrossing work
occuper l'attention de qqn to hold someone's attention
préoccuper to preoccupy; **une préoccupation** preoccupation
La ligne est occupée. The line is busy.

See also **s'occuper.**

Reflexive regular **-er** verb

to be busy, to keep oneself busy

The Seven Simple Tenses		The Seven Compound Tenses	
Singular	Plural	Singular	Plural
1 présent de l'indicatif		8 passé composé	
m'occupe	**nous occupons**	**me suis occupé(e)**	**nous sommes occupé(e)s**
t'occupes	**vous occupez**	**t'es occupé(e)**	**vous êtes occupé(e)(s)**
s'occupe	**s'occupent**	**s'est occupé(e)**	**se sont occupé(e)s**
2 imparfait de l'indicatif		9 plus-que-parfait de l'indicatif	
m'occupais	**nous occupions**	**m'étais occupé(e)**	**nous étions occupé(e)s**
t'occupais	**vous occupiez**	**t'étais occupé(e)**	**vous étiez occupé(e)(s)**
s'occupait	**s'occupaient**	**s'était occupé(e)**	**s'étaient occupé(e)s**
3 passé simple		10 passé antérieur	
m'occupai	**nous occupâmes**	**me fus occupé(e)**	**nous fûmes occupé(e)s**
t'occupas	**vous occupâtes**	**te fus occupé(e)**	**vous fûtes occupé(e)(s)**
s'occupa	**s'occupèrent**	**se fut occupé(e)**	**se furent occupé(e)s**
4 futur		11 futur antérieur	
m'occuperai	**nous occuperons**	**me serai occupé(e)**	**nous serons occupé(e)s**
t'occuperas	**vous occuperez**	**te seras occupé(e)**	**vous serez occupé(e)(s)**
s'occupera	**s'occuperont**	**se sera occupé(e)**	**se seront occupé(e)s**
5 conditionnel		12 conditionnel passé	
m'occuperais	**nous occuperions**	**me serais occupé(e)**	**nous serions occupé(e)s**
t'occuperais	**vous occuperiez**	**te serais occupé(e)**	**vous seriez occupé(e)(s)**
s'occuperait	**s'occuperaient**	**se serait occupé(e)**	**se seraient occupé(e)s**
6 présent du subjonctif		13 passé du subjonctif	
m'occupe	**nous occupions**	**me sois occupé(e)**	**nous soyons occupé(e)s**
t'occupes	**vous occupiez**	**te sois occupé(e)**	**vous soyez occupé(e)(s)**
s'occupe	**s'occupent**	**se soit occupé(e)**	**se soient occupé(e)s**
7 imparfait du subjonctif		14 plus-que-parfait du subjonctif	
m'occupasse	**nous occupassions**	**me fusse occupé(e)**	**nous fussions occupé(e)s**
t'occupasses	**vous occupassiez**	**te fusses occupé(e)**	**vous fussiez occupé(e)(s)**
s'occupât	**s'occupassent**	**se fût occupé(e)**	**se fussent occupé(e)s**

Impératif
occupe-toi; ne t'occupe pas
occupons-nous; ne nous occupons pas
occupez-vous; ne vous occupez pas

Words and expressions related to this verb

s'occuper de ses affaires to mind one's own business

Je m'occupe de mes affaires. I mind my own business.

s'occuper des enfants to look after children

s'occuper de to look after, to tend to

s'occuper à to be engaged in

Occupez-vous de vos affaires! Mind your own business!

Ne vous occupez pas de mes affaires! Don't mind my business!

Est-ce qu'on s'occupe de vous? Is someone helping you?

See also the verb **occuper.**

Don't forget to study the section on defective and impersonal verbs. It's right after this main list.

to offer

Irregular verb

The Seven Simple Tenses		The Seven Compound Tenses	
Singular	Plural	Singular	Plural
1 présent de l'indicatif		8 passé composé	
offre	**offrons**	**ai offert**	**avons offert**
offres	**offrez**	**as offert**	**avez offert**
offre	**offrent**	**a offert**	**ont offert**
2 imparfait de l'indicatif		9 plus-que-parfait de l'indicatif	
offrais	**offrions**	**avais offert**	**avions offert**
offrais	**offriez**	**avais offert**	**aviez offert**
offrait	**offraient**	**avait offert**	**avaient offert**
3 passé simple		10 passé antérieur	
offris	**offrîmes**	**eus offert**	**eûmes offert**
offris	**offrîtes**	**eus offert**	**eûtes offert**
offrit	**offrirent**	**eut offert**	**eurent offert**
4 futur		11 futur antérieur	
offrirai	**offrirons**	**aurai offert**	**aurons offert**
offriras	**offrirez**	**auras offert**	**aurez offert**
offrira	**offriront**	**aura offert**	**auront offert**
5 conditionnel		12 conditionnel passé	
offrirais	**offririons**	**aurais offert**	**aurions offert**
offrirais	**offririez**	**aurais offert**	**auriez offert**
offrirait	**offriraient**	**aurait offert**	**auraient offert**
6 présent du subjonctif		13 passé du subjonctif	
offre	**offrions**	**aie offert**	**ayons offert**
offres	**offriez**	**aies offert**	**ayez offert**
offre	**offrent**	**ait offert**	**aient offert**
7 imparfait du subjonctif		14 plus-que-parfait du subjonctif	
offrisse	**offrissions**	**eusse offert**	**eussions offert**
offrisses	**offrissiez**	**eusses offert**	**eussiez offert**
offrît	**offrissent**	**eût offert**	**eussent offert**

Impératif
offre
offrons
offrez

Words and expressions related to this verb

offrir qqch à qqn to offer (to present) something to someone
une offre an offer, a proposal
une offrande gift, offering
l'offre et la demande supply and demand
une offre d'emploi a job offer
les offres d'emploi employment opportunities
C'est pour offrir? Is it to give as a gift?

Get acquainted with what preposition goes with what verb. See *Verbs with prepositions* in the Appendixes.

Irregular verb

to omit

The Seven Simple Tenses		The Seven Compound Tenses	
Singular	Plural	Singular	Plural
1 présent de l'indicatif		8 passé composé	
omets	**omettons**	**ai omis**	**avons omis**
omets	**omettez**	**as omis**	**avez omis**
omet	**omettent**	**a omis**	**ont omis**
2 imparfait de l'indicatif		9 plus-que-parfait de l'indicatif	
omettais	**omettions**	**avais omis**	**avions omis**
omettais	**omettiez**	**avais omis**	**aviez omis**
omettait	**omettaient**	**avait omis**	**avaient omis**
3 passé simple		10 passé antérieur	
omis	**omîmes**	**eus omis**	**eûmes omis**
omis	**omîtes**	**eus omis**	**eûtes omis**
omit	**omirent**	**eut omis**	**eurent omis**
4 futur		11 futur antérieur	
omettrai	**omettrons**	**aurai omis**	**aurons omis**
omettras	**omettrez**	**auras omis**	**aurez omis**
omettra	**omettront**	**aura omis**	**auront omis**
5 conditionnel		12 conditionnel passé	
omettrais	**omettrions**	**aurais omis**	**aurions omis**
omettrais	**omettriez**	**aurais omis**	**auriez omis**
omettrait	**omettraient**	**aurait omis**	**auraient omis**
6 présent du subjonctif		13 passé du subjonctif	
omette	**omettions**	**aie omis**	**ayons omis**
omettes	**omettiez**	**aies omis**	**ayez omis**
omette	**omettent**	**ait omis**	**aient omis**
7 imparfait du subjonctif		14 plus-que-parfait du subjonctif	
omisse	**omissions**	**eusse omis**	**eussions omis**
omisses	**omissiez**	**eusses omis**	**eussiez omis**
omît	**omissent**	**eût omis**	**eussent omis**

Impératif
omets
omettons
omettez

Words and expressions related to this verb
omettre de faire qqch to neglect to do something
une omission an omission
omis, omise omitted
commettre to commit

See also **admettre, commettre, mettre, permettre, promettre, remettre, soumettre,** and **transmettre.**

Don't forget to check the list of 2,600 additional verbs keyed to the 501 model verbs. It's in the Appendixes!

oser (321)

Part. pr. **osant** Part. passé **osé**

to dare

Regular **-er** verb

The Seven Simple Tenses

Singular	Plural
1 présent de l'indicatif	
ose	**osons**
oses	**osez**
ose	**osent**
2 imparfait de l'indicatif	
osais	**osions**
osais	**osiez**
osait	**osaient**
3 passé simple	
osai	**osâmes**
osas	**osâtes**
osa	**osèrent**
4 futur	
oserai	**oserons**
oseras	**oserez**
osera	**oseront**
5 conditionnel	
oserais	**oserions**
oserais	**oseriez**
oserait	**oseraient**
6 présent du subjonctif	
ose	**osions**
oses	**osiez**
ose	**osent**
7 imparfait du subjonctif	
osasse	**osassions**
osasses	**osassiez**
osât	**osassent**

The Seven Compound Tenses

Singular	Plural
8 passé composé	
ai osé	**avons osé**
as osé	**avez osé**
a osé	**ont osé**
9 plus-que-parfait de l'indicatif	
avais osé	**avions osé**
avais osé	**aviez osé**
avait osé	**avaient osé**
10 passé antérieur	
eus osé	**eûmes osé**
eus osé	**eûtes osé**
eut osé	**eurent osé**
11 futur antérieur	
aurai osé	**aurons osé**
auras osé	**aurez osé**
aura osé	**auront osé**
12 conditionnel passé	
aurais osé	**aurions osé**
aurais osé	**auriez osé**
aurait osé	**auraient osé**
13 passé du subjonctif	
aie osé	**ayons osé**
aies osé	**ayez osé**
ait osé	**aient osé**
14 plus-que-parfait du subjonctif	
eusse osé	**eussions osé**
eusses osé	**eussiez osé**
eût osé	**eussent osé**

Impératif
ose
osons
osez

Words and expressions related to this verb

Si j'ose dire . . . If I may be so bold as to say . . .
Je n'ose le dire. I dare not say so.
oser faire qqch to dare to do something; to have the courage, audacity to do something
Je n'ose rien dire. I don't dare say anything.
osé, osée bold, daring

Can't remember the French verb you need? Check the back pages of this book for the English-French verb index!

Regular **-er** verb

to forget

The Seven Simple Tenses		The Seven Compound Tenses	
Singular	Plural	Singular	Plural
1 présent de l'indicatif		8 passé composé	
oublie	**oublions**	**ai oublié**	**avons oublié**
oublies	**oubliez**	**as oublié**	**avez oublié**
oublie	**oublient**	**a oublié**	**ont oublié**
2 imparfait de l'indicatif		9 plus-que-parfait de l'indicatif	
oubliais	**oubliions**	**avais oublié**	**avions oublié**
oubliais	**oubliiez**	**avais oublié**	**aviez oublié**
oubliait	**oubliaient**	**avait oublié**	**avaient oublié**
3 passé simple		10 passé antérieur	
oubliai	**oubliâmes**	**eus oublié**	**eûmes oublié**
oublias	**oubliâtes**	**eus oublié**	**eûtes oublié**
oublia	**oublièrent**	**eut oublié**	**eurent oublié**
4 futur		11 futur antérieur	
oublierai	**oublierons**	**aurai oublié**	**aurons oublié**
oublieras	**oublierez**	**auras oublié**	**aurez oublié**
oubliera	**oublieront**	**aura oublié**	**auront oublié**
5 conditionnel		12 conditionnel passé	
oublierais	**oublierions**	**aurais oublié**	**aurions oublié**
oublierais	**oublieriez**	**aurais oublié**	**auriez oublié**
oublierait	**oublieraient**	**aurait oublié**	**auraient oublié**
6 présent du subjonctif		13 passé du subjonctif	
oublie	**oubliions**	**aie oublié**	**ayons oublié**
oublies	**oubliiez**	**aies oublié**	**ayez oublié**
oublie	**oublient**	**ait oublié**	**aient oublié**
7 imparfait du subjonctif		14 plus-que-parfait du subjonctif	
oubliasse	**oubliassions**	**eusse oublié**	**eussions oublié**
oubliasses	**oubliassiez**	**eusses oublié**	**eussiez oublié**
oubliât	**oubliassent**	**eût oublié**	**eussent oublié**

Impératif
oublie
oublions
oubliez

Words and expressions related to this verb

un oubli oversight; oblivion
tomber dans l'oubli to be forgotten (over time)
oubliable forgettable
inoubliable unforgettable
s'oublier to forget oneself, to be unmindful of oneself
oublier de faire qqch to forget to do something
oublieux, oublieuse oblivious; **oublieux de** unmindful of; forgetful
Nous n'oublierons jamais. We will never forget.

How are you doing? Find out with the verb drills and tests with answers explained on pages 50–101.

to open

Irregular verb

The Seven Simple Tenses		The Seven Compound Tenses	
Singular	Plural	Singular	Plural
1 présent de l'indicatif		8 passé composé	
ouvre	**ouvrons**	**ai ouvert**	**avons ouvert**
ouvres	**ouvrez**	**as ouvert**	**avez ouvert**
ouvre	**ouvrent**	**a ouvert**	**ont ouvert**
2 imparfait de l'indicatif		9 plus-que-parfait de l'indicatif	
ouvrais	**ouvrions**	**avais ouvert**	**avions ouvert**
ouvrais	**ouvriez**	**avais ouvert**	**aviez ouvert**
ouvrait	**ouvraient**	**avait ouvert**	**avaient ouvert**
3 passé simple		10 passé antérieur	
ouvris	**ouvrîmes**	**eus ouvert**	**eûmes ouvert**
ouvris	**ouvrîtes**	**eus ouvert**	**eûtes ouvert**
ouvrit	**ouvrirent**	**eut ouvert**	**eurent ouvert**
4 futur		11 futur antérieur	
ouvrirai	**ouvrirons**	**aurai ouvert**	**aurons ouvert**
ouvriras	**ouvrirez**	**auras ouvert**	**aurez ouvert**
ouvrira	**ouvriront**	**aura ouvert**	**auront ouvert**
5 conditionnel		12 conditionnel passé	
ouvrirais	**ouvririons**	**aurais ouvert**	**aurions ouvert**
ouvrirais	**ouvririez**	**aurais ouvert**	**auriez ouvert**
ouvrirait	**ouvriraient**	**aurait ouvert**	**auraient ouvert**
6 présent du subjonctif		13 passé du subjonctif	
ouvre	**ouvrions**	**aie ouvert**	**ayons ouvert**
ouvres	**ouvriez**	**aies ouvert**	**ayez ouvert**
ouvre	**ouvrent**	**ait ouvert**	**aient ouvert**
7 imparfait du subjonctif		14 plus-que-parfait du subjonctif	
ouvrisse	**ouvrissions**	**eusse ouvert**	**eussions ouvert**
ouvrisses	**ouvrissiez**	**eusses ouvert**	**eussiez ouvert**
ouvrît	**ouvrissent**	**eût ouvert**	**eussent ouvert**

Impératif
ouvre
ouvrons
ouvrez

Words and expressions related to this verb

ouvert, ouverte open
l'ouverture *f.* opening
ouvrir le gaz to turn on the gas
ouvrir de force to force open
un ouvre-boîte (des ouvre-boîtes) can opener
entrouvert, entrouverte ajar
un ouvre-bouteille (des ouvre-bouteilles) bottle opener
rouvrir to reopen, to open again
entrouvrir to open just a bit
s'ouvrir à to confide in
les heures ouvrables business hours
ouvrir une session to log in, log on (computer)

Irregular verb

to appear, to seem

The Seven Simple Tenses		The Seven Compound Tenses	
Singular	Plural	Singular	Plural
1 présent de l'indicatif		8 passé composé	
parais	**paraissons**	**ai paru**	**avons paru**
parais	**paraissez**	**as paru**	**avez paru**
paraît	**paraissent**	**a paru**	**ont paru**
2 imparfait de l'indicatif		9 plus-que-parfait de l'indicatif	
paraissais	**paraissions**	**avais paru**	**avions paru**
paraissais	**paraissiez**	**avais paru**	**aviez paru**
paraissait	**paraissaient**	**avait paru**	**avaient paru**
3 passé simple		10 passé antérieur	
parus	**parûmes**	**eus paru**	**eûmes paru**
parus	**parûtes**	**eus paru**	**eûtes paru**
parut	**parurent**	**eut paru**	**eurent paru**
4 futur		11 futur antérieur	
paraîtrai	**paraîtrons**	**aurai paru**	**aurons paru**
paraîtras	**paraîtrez**	**auras paru**	**aurez paru**
paraîtra	**paraîtront**	**aura paru**	**auront paru**
5 conditionnel		12 conditionnel passé	
paraîtrais	**paraîtrions**	**aurais paru**	**aurions paru**
paraîtrais	**paraîtriez**	**aurais paru**	**auriez paru**
paraîtrait	**paraîtraient**	**aurait paru**	**auraient paru**
6 présent du subjonctif		13 passé du subjonctif	
paraisse	**paraissions**	**aie paru**	**ayons paru**
paraisses	**paraissiez**	**aies paru**	**ayez paru**
paraisse	**paraissent**	**ait paru**	**aient paru**
7 imparfait du subjonctif		14 plus-que-parfait du subjonctif	
parusse	**parussions**	**eusse paru**	**eussions paru**
parusses	**parussiez**	**eusses paru**	**eussiez paru**
parût	**parussent**	**eût paru**	**eussent paru**

Impératif
parais
paraissons
paraissez

Words and expressions related to this verb
l'apparition *f.* apparition, appearance
Cela me paraît incroyable. That seems unbelievable to me.
Le jour paraît. Day is breaking.
apparaître to appear, to come into view
disparaître to disappear
réapparaître to reappear
Ce livre vient de paraître. This book has just been published.
la parution (act of) publication

See also **apparaître, disparaître,** and **reparaître.**

Review the Subjunctive clearly and simply on pages 26–31.

The subject pronouns are found on page 103.

pardonner (325) — Part. pr. pardonnant — Part. passé pardonné

to pardon, to forgive

Regular **-er** verb

The Seven Simple Tenses

Singular	Plural
1 présent de l'indicatif	
pardonne	**pardonnons**
pardonnes	**pardonnez**
pardonne	**pardonnent**
2 imparfait de l'indicatif	
pardonnais	**pardonnions**
pardonnais	**pardonniez**
pardonnait	**pardonnaient**
3 passé simple	
pardonnai	**pardonnâmes**
pardonnas	**pardonnâtes**
pardonna	**pardonnèrent**
4 futur	
pardonnerai	**pardonnerons**
pardonneras	**pardonnerez**
pardonnera	**pardonneront**
5 conditionnel	
pardonnerais	**pardonnerions**
pardonnerais	**pardonneriez**
pardonnerait	**pardonneraient**
6 présent du subjonctif	
pardonne	**pardonnions**
pardonnes	**pardonniez**
pardonne	**pardonnent**
7 imparfait du subjonctif	
pardonnasse	**pardonnassions**
pardonnasses	**pardonnassiez**
pardonnât	**pardonnassent**

The Seven Compound Tenses

Singular	Plural
8 passé composé	
ai pardonné	**avons pardonné**
as pardonné	**avez pardonné**
a pardonné	**ont pardonné**
9 plus-que-parfaît de l'indicatif	
avais pardonné	**avions pardonné**
avais pardonné	**aviez pardonné**
avait pardonné	**avaient pardonné**
10 passé antérieur	
eus pardonné	**eûmes pardonné**
eus pardonné	**eûtes pardonné**
eut pardonné	**eurent pardonné**
11 futur antérieur	
aurai pardonné	**aurons pardonné**
auras pardonné	**aurez pardonné**
aura pardonné	**auront pardonné**
12 conditionnel passé	
aurais pardonné	**aurions pardonné**
aurais pardonné	**auriez pardonné**
aurait pardonné	**auraient pardonné**
13 passé du subjonctif	
aie pardonné	**ayons pardonné**
aies pardonné	**ayez pardonné**
ait pardonné	**aient pardonné**
14 plus-que-parfait du subjonctif	
eusse pardonné	**eussions pardonné**
eusses pardonné	**eussiez pardonné**
eût pardonné	**eussent pardonné**

Impératif
pardonne
pardonnons
pardonnez

Sentences using this verb and words related to it

pardonner à qqn de qqch to forgive someone for something

J'ai pardonné à mon ami d'être arrivé en retard. I forgave my friend for having arrived late.

un pardon forgiveness, pardon

un don gift

pardonnable forgivable, pardonable

Pardonnez-moi. Pardon me.

Marie-Thérèse, ce que vous venez de faire est impardonnable. Marie-Thérèse, what you just did is unforgivable.

See also **donner.**

Can't find the verb you're looking for? Check the back pages of this book for a list of over 2,600 additional verbs!

The Seven Simple Tenses		The Seven Compound Tenses	
Singular	Plural	Singular	Plural
1 présent de l'indicatif		8 passé composé	
parle	**parlons**	**ai parlé**	**avons parlé**
parles	**parlez**	**as parlé**	**avez parlé**
parle	**parlent**	**a parlé**	**ont parlé**
2 imparfait de l'indicatif		9 plus-que-parfait de l'indicatif	
parlais	**parlions**	**avais parlé**	**avions parlé**
parlais	**parliez**	**avais parlé**	**aviez parlé**
parlait	**parlaient**	**avait parlé**	**avaient parlé**
3 passé simple		10 passé antérieur	
parlai	**parlâmes**	**eus parlé**	**eûmes parlé**
parlas	**parlâtes**	**eus parlé**	**eûtes parlé**
parla	**parlèrent**	**eut parlé**	**eurent parlé**
4 futur		11 futur antérieur	
parlerai	**parlerons**	**aurai parlé**	**aurons parlé**
parleras	**parlerez**	**auras parlé**	**aurez parlé**
parlera	**parleront**	**aura parlé**	**auront parlé**
5 conditionnel		12 conditionnel passé	
parlerais	**parlerions**	**aurais parlé**	**aurions parlé**
parlerais	**parleriez**	**aurais parlé**	**auriez parlé**
parlerait	**parleraient**	**aurait parlé**	**auraient parlé**
6 présent du subjonctif		13 passé du subjonctif	
parle	**parlions**	**aie parlé**	**ayons parlé**
parles	**parliez**	**aies parlé**	**ayez parlé**
parle	**parlent**	**ait parlé**	**aient parlé**
7 imparfait du subjonctif		14 plus-que-parfait du subjonctif	
parlasse	**parlassions**	**eusse parlé**	**eussions parlé**
parlasses	**parlassiez**	**eusses parlé**	**eussiez parlé**
parlât	**parlassent**	**eût parlé**	**eussent parlé**

Impératif
parle
parlons
parlez

AN ESSENTIAL 55 VERB

Parler

Parler is an essential verb because it is used in many everyday situations and idiomatic expressions. It is an essential verb for a beginning student.

Sentences using parler

Ce n'est qu'une façon de parler. It's just a way of speaking.

Avez-vous jamais entendu parler de cela? Have you ever heard of that?

Je ne peux pas vous entendre. Parlez plus fort, s'il vous plaît. I can't hear you. Please speak more loudly.

Écoutez, le professeur va nous adresser la parole. Listen, the professor is going to speak to us.

Ici on parle français. French is spoken here.

Grand parleur, petit faiseur. All talk no action.

Proverbs and expressions

Il est bon de parler et meilleur de se taire. **(La Fontaine) Speech is silver; silence is golden.**

Toute parole n'est pas bonne à dire. **Not everything is worth saying.**

J'en parlerai à mon cheval. **I don't care what you're talking about. (Literally: I'll talk to my horse about it.)**

Words and expressions related to this verb

parler à haute voix **to speak in a loud voice**

parler haut **to speak loudly**

parler bas **to speak softly**

la parole **spoken word**

parler à **to talk to**

parler de **to talk about (of)**

le don de la parole **the gift of gab**

les pourparlers **negotiations**

francophone **French-speaking**

anglophone **English-speaking**

hispanophone **Spanish-speaking**

parler affaires **to talk business, to talk shop**

sans parler de . . . **not to mention . . .**

parler pour qqn **to speak for someone**

parler contre qqn **to speak against someone**

un parloir **parlor (room where people talk)**

le franc-parler **outspokenness**

à proprement parler **strictly speaking**

adresser la parole à **to speak to, to direct one's words at**

entendre parler de **to hear about**

reparler **to speak again**

le parleur, la parleuse **talker**

Irregular verb

to leave, to depart

The Seven Simple Tenses		The Seven Compound Tenses	
Singular	Plural	Singular	Plural
1 présent de l'indicatif		8 passé composé	
pars	**partons**	**suis parti(e)**	**sommes parti(e)s**
pars	**partez**	**es parti(e)**	**êtes parti(e)(s)**
part	**partent**	**est parti(e)**	**sont parti(e)s**
2 imparfait de l'indicatif		9 plus-que-parfaît de l'indicatif	
partais	**partions**	**étais parti(e)**	**étions parti(e)s**
partais	**partiez**	**étais parti(e)**	**étiez parti(e)(s)**
partait	**partaient**	**était parti(e)**	**étaient parti(e)s**
3 passé simple		10 passé antérieur	
partis	**partîmes**	**fus parti(e)**	**fûmes parti(e)s**
partis	**partîtes**	**fus parti(e)**	**fûtes parti(e)(s)**
partit	**partirent**	**fut parti(e)**	**furent parti(e)s**
4 futur		11 futur antérieur	
partirai	**partirons**	**serai parti(e)**	**serons parti(e)s**
partiras	**partirez**	**seras parti(e)**	**serez parti(e)(s)**
partira	**partiront**	**sera parti(e)**	**seront parti(e)s**
5 conditionnel		12 conditionnel passé	
partirais	**partirions**	**serais parti(e)**	**serions parti(e)s**
partirais	**partiriez**	**serais parti(e)**	**seriez parti(e)(s)**
partirait	**partiraient**	**serait parti(e)**	**seraient parti(e)s**
6 présent du subjonctif		13 passé du subjonctif	
parte	**partions**	**sois parti(e)**	**soyons parti(e)s**
partes	**partiez**	**sois parti(e)**	**soyez parti(e)(s)**
parte	**partent**	**soit parti(e)**	**soient parti(e)s**
7 imparfait du subjonctif		14 plus-que-parfait du subjonctif	
partisse	**partissions**	**fusse parti(e)**	**fussions parti(e)s**
partisses	**partissiez**	**fusses parti(e)**	**fussiez parti(e)(s)**
partît	**partissent**	**fût parti(e)**	**fussent parti(e)s**

Impératif
pars
partons
partez

AN ESSENTIAL 55 VERB

Partir

Partir is an important verb for a beginning student because there are many words and idiomatic expressions that are based on it.

Sentences using partir

À quelle heure part le train pour Paris? At what time does the train for Paris leave?

Le train en partance pour Paris est sur la voie deux. The train leaving for Paris is on track two.

Dépêche-toi, Nathalie, nous partons tout de suite. Hurry up, Nathalie, we're leaving right away.

À partir de cet instant, tu vas faire tes devoirs avant de regarder la télévision. From this moment on, you are going to do your homework before watching television.

Je voudrais savoir à quelle heure l'avion part pour Montréal. I would like to know at what time the plane leaves for Montreal.

Proverbs

Le chat parti, les souris dansent. **When the cat is away, the mice will play.**

Rien ne sert de courir; il faut partir à point. **(La Fontaine, *le Lièvre et la Tortue*) There's no point in running; you have to leave at the right moment.**

Words and expressions related to this verb

en partance **due to depart**

à partir de **beginning with**

à partir de maintenant **from now on**

à partir d'aujourd'hui **from today on**

partir en voyage **to go on a trip**

partir en vacances **to leave for a vacation**

un département **department**

départir **to assign (regular -ir verb)**

se départir de **to depart from (Use être as auxiliary)**

repartir **to leave again, to set out again (Use être as auxiliary); to reply (Use avoir as auxiliary)**

Careful! répartir (to divide up, share) is a regular -ir verb.

un faux départ **false start**

Regular **-er** verb

to pass, to spend (time)

The Seven Simple Tenses		The Seven Compound Tenses	
Singular	Plural	Singular	Plural
1 présent de l'indicatif		8 passé composé	
passe	**passons**	**ai passé**	**avons passé**
passes	**passez**	**as passé**	**avez passé**
passe	**passent**	**a passé**	**ont passé**
2 imparfait de l'indicatif		9 plus-que-parfait de l'indicatif	
passais	**passions**	**avais passé**	**avions passé**
passais	**passiez**	**avais passé**	**aviez passé**
passait	**passaient**	**avait passé**	**avaient passé**
3 passé simple		10 passé antérieur	
passai	**passâmes**	**eus passé**	**eûmes passé**
passas	**passâtes**	**eus passé**	**eûtes passé**
passa	**passèrent**	**eut passé**	**eurent passé**
4 futur		11 futur antérieur	
passerai	**passerons**	**aurai passé**	**aurons passé**
passeras	**passerez**	**auras passé**	**aurez passé**
passera	**passeront**	**aura passé**	**auront passé**
5 conditionnel		12 conditionnel passé	
passerais	**passerions**	**aurais passé**	**aurions passé**
passerais	**passeriez**	**aurais passé**	**auriez passé**
passerait	**passeraient**	**aurait passé**	**auraient passé**
6 présent du subjonctif		13 passé du subjonctif	
passe	**passions**	**aie passé**	**ayons passé**
passes	**passiez**	**aies passé**	**ayez passé**
passe	**passent**	**ait passé**	**aient passé**
7 imparfait du subjonctif		14 plus-que-parfait du subjonctif	
passasse	**passassions**	**eusse passé**	**eussions passé**
passasses	**passassiez**	**eusses passé**	**eussiez passé**
passât	**passassent**	**eût passé**	**eussent passé**

Impératif
passe
passons
passez

This verb is conjugated with **être** to indicate a state.

Example: **Ses soupçons sont passés en certitudes.**

This verb is conjugated with **être** when it means *to pass by, go by.*

Example: **Elle est passée chez moi.** She came by my house.

BUT This verb is conjugated with **avoir** when it has a direct object.

Examples: **Elle m'a passé le sel.** She passed me the salt.

Elle a passé un examen. She took an exam.

Passez une bonne journée! Au revoir! Have a nice day! Good bye!

repasser to pass again; to iron

dépasser to protrude, to exceed, to surpass, to pass (a vehicle)

passable acceptable

passer un examen to take an exam

passer chez qqn to drop in on someone

passer un coup de fil à qqn to give someone a ring (a telephone call)

See also **repasser** and **se passer.** Review page 6.

The subject pronouns are found on page 103.

patiner (329) — Part. pr. patinant — Part. passé patiné

to skate

Regular **-er** verb

The Seven Simple Tenses		The Seven Compound Tenses	
Singular	Plural	Singular	Plural
1 présent de l'indicatif		8 passé composé	
patine	**patinons**	**ai patiné**	**avons patiné**
patines	**patinez**	**as patiné**	**avez patiné**
patine	**patinent**	**a patiné**	**ont patiné**
2 imparfait de l'indicatif		9 plus-que-parfait de l'indicatif	
patinais	**patinions**	**avais patiné**	**avions patiné**
patinais	**patiniez**	**avais patiné**	**aviez patiné**
patinait	**patinaient**	**avait patiné**	**avaient patiné**
3 passé simple		10 passé antérieur	
patinai	**patinâmes**	**eus patiné**	**eûmes patiné**
patinas	**patinâtes**	**eus patiné**	**eûtes patiné**
patina	**patinèrent**	**eut patiné**	**eurent patiné**
4 futur		11 futur antérieur	
patinerai	**patinerons**	**aurai patiné**	**aurons patiné**
patineras	**patinerez**	**auras patiné**	**aurez patiné**
patinera	**patineront**	**aura patiné**	**auront patiné**
5 conditionnel		12 conditionnel passé	
patinerais	**patinerions**	**aurais patiné**	**aurions patiné**
patinerais	**patineriez**	**aurais patiné**	**auriez patiné**
patinerait	**patineraient**	**aurait patiné**	**auraient patiné**
6 présent du subjonctif		13 passé du subjonctif	
patine	**patinions**	**aie patiné**	**ayons patiné**
patines	**patiniez**	**aies patiné**	**ayez patiné**
patine	**patinent**	**ait patiné**	**aient patiné**
7 imparfait du subjonctif		14 plus-que-parfait du subjonctif	
patinasse	**patinassions**	**eusse patiné**	**eussions patiné**
patinasses	**patinassiez**	**eusses patiné**	**eussiez patiné**
patinât	**patinassent**	**eût patiné**	**eussent patiné**

Impératif
patine
patinons
patinez

Words and expressions related to this verb

patiner sur glace to skate on ice
une patinette scooter
un patineur, une patineuse skater
le patinage skating
le patinage artistique figure skating
les patins à roues alignées inline skates
une patinoire skating rink
patiner sur roulettes, patiner à roulettes to roller-skate
le patinage à roulettes roller-skating
le patinage de vitesse speed skating

Soak up some verbs used in weather expressions. There's a list in the Appendixes!

Regular **-er** verb endings; spelling change: **-ayer** verbs may change **y** to **i** before a mute **e** or may keep **y**

to pay (for)

The Seven Simple Tenses		The Seven Compound Tenses	
Singular	Plural	Singular	Plural
1 présent de l'indicatif		8 passé composé	
paye	**payons**	**ai payé**	**avons payé**
payes	**payez**	**as payé**	**avez payé**
paye	**payent**	**a payé**	**ont payé**
2 imparfait de l'indicatif		9 plus-que-parfait de l'indicatif	
payais	**payions**	**avais payé**	**avions payé**
payais	**payiez**	**avais payé**	**aviez payé**
payait	**payaient**	**avait payé**	**avaient payé**
3 passé simple		10 passé antérieur	
payai	**payâmes**	**eus payé**	**eûmes payé**
payas	**payâtes**	**eus payé**	**eûtes payé**
paya	**payèrent**	**eut payé**	**eurent payé**
4 futur		11 futur antérieur	
payerai	**payerons**	**aurai payé**	**aurons payé**
payeras	**payerez**	**auras payé**	**aurez payé**
payera	**payeront**	**aura payé**	**auront payé**
5 conditionnel		12 conditionnel passé	
payerais	**payerions**	**aurais payé**	**aurions payé**
payerais	**payeriez**	**aurais payé**	**auriez payé**
payerait	**payeraient**	**aurait payé**	**auraient payé**
6 présent du subjonctif		13 passé du subjonctif	
paye	**payions**	**aie payé**	**ayons payé**
payes	**payiez**	**aies payé**	**ayez payé**
paye	**payent**	**ait payé**	**aient payé**
7 imparfait du subjonctif		14 plus-que-parfait du subjonctif	
payasse	**payassions**	**eusse payé**	**eussions payé**
payasses	**payassiez**	**eusses payé**	**eussiez payé**
payât	**payassent**	**eût payé**	**eussent payé**

Impératif
paye
payons
payez

AN ESSENTIAL 55 VERB

Payer

Payer is an important verb for you to know because of its spelling change before a mute **e**. **Payer** is also useful for shopping when you travel!

Sentences using payer and related words

Payez à la caisse, s'il vous plaît. Please pay at the cashier.

Nous payons toutes nos factures à la fin du mois. We pay all our bills at the end of the month.

Roland paye par carte bancaire, mais Olivier paye comptant. Roland pays by credit card, but Olivier pays cash.

If you can conjugate **payer** you can also conjugate the following verbs:

débrayer **to disengage the clutch**

défrayer **to pay expenses**

repayer **to pay again**

sous-payer **to underpay**

surpayer **to overpay**

Words and expressions related to this verb

un paiement (or paiement) **payment**

avoir de quoi payer **to have the means to pay**

payable **payable**

se faire payer à dîner par qqn **to get your dinner paid for by someone**

payer cher **to pay a lot**

payer peu **to pay little**

payer comptant, payer en espèces **to pay in cash**

payer l'addition **to pay the check**

payer à la caisse **to pay at the counter (cashier's desk)**

Proverb

Les gens payent bien quand ils payent comptant. **People pay well when they pay cash.**

Can't find the verb you're looking for? Check the back pages of this book for a list of over 2,600 additional verbs!

Regular **-er** verb endings; spelling change: **é** changes to **è** before syllable with mute **e**

to sin, to commit a sin

The Seven Simple Tenses		The Seven Compound Tenses	
Singular	Plural	Singular	Plural
1 présent de l'indicatif		8 passé composé	
pèche	**péchons**	**ai péché**	**avons péché**
pèches	**péchez**	**as péché**	**avez péché**
pèche	**pèchent**	**a péché**	**ont péché**
2 imparfait de l'indicatif		9 plus-que-parfait de l'indicatif	
péchais	**péchions**	**avais péché**	**avions péché**
péchais	**péchiez**	**avais péché**	**aviez péché**
péchait	**péchaient**	**avait péché**	**avaient péché**
3 passé simple		10 passé antérieur	
péchai	**péchâmes**	**eus péché**	**eûmes péché**
péchas	**péchâtes**	**eus péché**	**eûtes péché**
pécha	**péchèrent**	**eut péché**	**eurent péché**
4 futur		11 futur antérieur	
pécherai	**pécherons**	**aurai péché**	**aurons péché**
pécheras	**pécherez**	**auras péché**	**aurez péché**
péchera	**pécheront**	**aura péché**	**auront péché**
5 conditionnel		12 conditionnel passé	
pécherais	**pécherions**	**aurais péché**	**aurions péché**
pécherais	**pécheriez**	**aurais péché**	**auriez péché**
pécherait	**pécheraient**	**aurait péché**	**auraient péché**
6 présent du subjonctif		13 passé du subjonctif	
pèche	**péchions**	**aie péché**	**ayons péché**
pèches	**péchiez**	**aies péché**	**ayez péché**
pèche	**pèchent**	**ait péché**	**aient péché**
7 imparfait du subjonctif		14 plus-que-parfait du subjonctif	
péchasse	**péchassions**	**eusse péché**	**eussions péché**
péchasses	**péchassiez**	**eusses péché**	**eussiez péché**
péchât	**péchassent**	**eût péché**	**eussent péché**

Impératif
pèche
péchons
péchez

Words and expressions related to this verb

le péché sin
un pécheur, une pécheresse sinner
à tout péché miséricorde forgiveness for every sin
commettre, faire un péché to commit sin
vivre dans le péché to lead a sinful life
les sept péchés capitaux the seven deadly sins

Do not confuse this verb with **pêcher,** *to fish.*

Don't forget to study the section on defective and impersonal verbs. It's right after this main list.

pêcher (332) — Part. pr. pêchant — Part. passé pêché

to fish

Regular **-er** verb

The Seven Simple Tenses		The Seven Compound Tenses	
Singular	Plural	Singular	Plural
1 présent de l'indicatif		8 passé composé	
pêche	**pêchons**	**ai pêché**	**avons pêché**
pêches	**pêchez**	**as pêché**	**avez pêché**
pêche	**pêchent**	**a pêché**	**ont pêché**
2 imparfait de l'indicatif		9 plus-que-parfait de l'indicatif	
pêchais	**pêchions**	**avais pêché**	**avions pêché**
pêchais	**pêchiez**	**avais pêché**	**aviez pêché**
pêchait	**pêchaient**	**avait pêché**	**avaient pêché**
3 passé simple		10 passé antérieur	
pêchai	**pêchâmes**	**eus pêché**	**eûmes pêché**
pêchas	**pêchâtes**	**eus pêché**	**eûtes pêché**
pâcha	**pêchèrent**	**eut pêché**	**eurent pêché**
4 futur		11 futur antérieur	
pêcherai	**pêcherons**	**aurai pêché**	**aurons pêché**
pêcheras	**pêcherez**	**auras pêché**	**aurez pêché**
pêchera	**pêcheront**	**aura pêché**	**auront pêché**
5 conditionnel		12 conditionnel passé	
pêcherais	**pêcherions**	**aurais pêché**	**aurions pêché**
pêcherais	**pêcheriez**	**aurais pêché**	**auriez pêché**
pêcherait	**pêcheraient**	**aurait pêché**	**auraient pêché**
6 présent du subjonctif		13 passé du subjonctif	
pêche	**pêchions**	**aie pêché**	**ayons pêché**
pêches	**pêchiez**	**aies pêché**	**ayez pêché**
pêche	**pêchent**	**ait pêché**	**aient pêché**
7 imparfait du subjonctif		14 plus-que-parfait du subjonctif	
pêchasse	**pêchassions**	**eusse pêché**	**eussions pêché**
pêchasses	**pêchassiez**	**eusses pêché**	**eussiez pêché**
pêchât	**pêchassent**	**eût pêché**	**eussent pêché**

Impératif
pêche
pêchons
pêchez

Common idiomatic expressions using this verb

Samedi nous irons à la pêche. Je connais un lac à la campagne où il y a beaucoup de poissons.

aller à la pêche to go fishing
un pêcheur fisherman; **une pêcheuse** fisherwoman
un bateau pêcheur fishing boat
le repêchage recovery, (act of) fishing out
la pêche au filet net fishing
un pêcheur de perles pearl diver
repêcher to fish out

Do not confuse this verb with **pécher**, *to sin*. And do not confuse **une pêche** (*peach*), which is a

Reflexive regular **-er** verb

to comb one's hair

The Seven Simple Tenses		The Seven Compound Tenses	
Singular	Plural	Singular	Plural
1 présent de l'indicatif		8 passé composé	
me peigne	**nous peignons**	**me suis peigné(e)**	**nous sommes peigné(e)s**
te peignes	**vous peignez**	**t'es peigné(e)**	**vous êtes peigné(e)(s)**
se peigne	**se peignent**	**s'est peigné(e)**	**se sont peigné(e)s**
2 imparfait de l'indicatif		9 plus-que-parfait de l'indicatif	
me peignais	**nous peignions**	**m'étais peigné(e)**	**nous étions peigné(e)s**
te peignais	**vous peigniez**	**t'étais peigné(e)**	**vous étiez peigné(e)(s)**
se peignait	**se peignaient**	**s'était peigné(e)**	**s'étaient peigné(e)s**
3 passé simple		10 passé antérieur	
me peignai	**nous peignâmes**	**me fus peigné(e)**	**nous fûmes peigné(e)s**
te peignas	**vous peignâtes**	**te fus peigné(e)**	**vous fûtes peigné(e)(s)**
se peigna	**se peignèrent**	**se fut peigné(e)**	**se furent peigné(e)s**
4 futur		11 futur antérieur	
me peignerai	**nous peignerons**	**me serai peigné(e)**	**nous serons peigné(e)s**
te peigneras	**vous peignerez**	**te seras peigné(e)**	**vous serez peigné(e)(s)**
se peignera	**se peigneront**	**se sera peigné(e)**	**se seront peigné(e)s**
5 conditionnel		12 conditionnel passé	
me peignerais	**nous peignerions**	**me serais peigné(e)**	**nous serions peigné(e)s**
te peignerais	**vous peigneriez**	**te serais peigné(e)**	**vous seriez peigné(e)(s)**
se peignerait	**se peigneraient**	**se serait peigné(e)**	**se seraient peigné(e)s**
6 présent du subjonctif		13 passé du subjonctif	
me peigne	**nous peignions**	**me sois peigné(e)**	**nous soyons peigné(e)s**
te peignes	**vous peigniez**	**te sois peigné(e)**	**vous soyez peigné(e)(s)**
se peigne	**se peignent**	**se soit peigné(e)**	**se soient peigné(e)s**
7 imparfait du subjonctif		14 plus-que-parfait du subjonctif	
me peignasse	**nous peignassions**	**me fusse peigné(e)**	**nous fussions peigné(e)s**
te peignasses	**vous peignassiez**	**te fusses peigné(e)**	**vous fussiez peigné(e)(s)**
se peignât	**se peignassent**	**se fût peigné(e)**	**se fussent peigné(e)s**

Impératif
peigne-toi; ne te peigne pas
peignons-nous; ne nous peignons pas
peignez-vous; ne vous peignez pas

Sentences using this verb and words related to it

Mon frère a peigné notre petit chien. Ma mère a lavé les cheveux de ma petite soeur et elle l'a peignée. Après cela, elle s'est lavé les cheveux et elle s'est peignée.

peigner qqn to comb someone
un peigne a comb
un peignoir dressing gown
mal peigné(e)(s) untidy hair, dishevelled
bien peigné(e)(s) well combed
un peignoir de bain bathrobe

Review the entry agreement of past participle of a reflexive verb with its reflexive pronoun in the section on definitions of basic grammatical terms with examples on pages 35–49.

to paint, to portray

Irregular verb

The Seven Simple Tenses		The Seven Compound Tenses	
Singular	Plural	Singular	Plural
1 présent de l'indicatif		8 passé composé	
peins	**peignons**	**ai peint**	**avons peint**
peins	**peignez**	**as peint**	**avez peint**
peint	**peignent**	**a peint**	**ont peint**
2 imparfait de l'indicatif		9 plus-que-parfait de l'indicatif	
peignais	**peignions**	**avais peint**	**avions peint**
peignais	**peigniez**	**avais peint**	**aviez peint**
peignait	**peignaient**	**avait peint**	**avaient peint**
3 passé simple		10 passé antérieur	
peignis	**peignîmes**	**eus peint**	**eûmes peint**
peignis	**peignîtes**	**eus peint**	**eûtes peint**
peignit	**peignirent**	**eut peint**	**eurent peint**
4 futur		11 futur antérieur	
peindrai	**peindrons**	**aurai peint**	**aurons peint**
peindras	**peindrez**	**auras peint**	**aurez peint**
peindra	**peindront**	**aura peint**	**auront peint**
5 conditionnel		12 conditionnel passé	
peindrais	**peindrions**	**aurais peint**	**aurions peint**
peindrais	**peindriez**	**aurais peint**	**auriez peint**
peindrait	**peindraient**	**aurait peint**	**auraient peint**
6 présent du subjonctif		13 passé du subjonctif	
peigne	**peignions**	**aie peint**	**ayons peint**
peignes	**peigniez**	**aies peint**	**ayez peint**
peigne	**peignent**	**ait peint**	**aient peint**
7 imparfait du subjonctif		14 plus-que-parfait du subjonctif	
peignisse	**peignissions**	**eusse peint**	**eussions peint**
peignisses	**peignissiez**	**eusses peint**	**eussiez peint**
peignît	**peignissent**	**eût peint**	**eussent peint**

Impératif
peins
peignons
peignez

Sentences using this verb and words related to it
—Qui a peint ce tableau? Mon fils. Il est artiste peintre.
—Est-ce que Renoir a jamais peint une reine noire?

une peinture painting, picture
un tableau painting, picture
une peinture à l'huile oil painting
peintre en bâtiments house painter
dépeindre to depict, to describe
PEINTURE FRAÎCHE WET PAINT
un peintre painter
un artiste peintre artist
une femme peintre woman artist
une palette de peintre artist's palette
se faire peindre to have one's portrait painted

See also **dépeindre.**

Regular **-re** verb

to hang, to suspend

The Seven Simple Tenses		The Seven Compound Tenses	
Singular	Plural	Singular	Plural
1 présent de l'indicatif		8 passé composé	
pends	**pendons**	**ai pendu**	**avons pendu**
pends	**pendez**	**as pendu**	**avez pendu**
pend	**pendent**	**a pendu**	**ont pendu**
2 imparfait de l'indicatif		9 plus-que-parfait de l'indicatif	
pendais	**pendions**	**avais pendu**	**avions pendu**
pendais	**pendiez**	**avais pendu**	**aviez pendu**
pendait	**pendaient**	**avait pendu**	**avaient pendu**
3 passé simple		10 passé antérieur	
pendis	**pendîmes**	**eus pendu**	**eûmes pendu**
pendis	**pendîtes**	**eus pendu**	**eûtes pendu**
pendit	**pendirent**	**eut pendu**	**eurent pendu**
4 futur		11 futur antérieur	
pendrai	**pendrons**	**aurai pendu**	**aurons pendu**
pendras	**pendrez**	**auras pendu**	**aurez pendu**
pendra	**pendront**	**aura pendu**	**auront pendu**
5 conditionnel		12 conditionnel passé	
pendrais	**pendrions**	**aurais pendu**	**aurions pendu**
pendrais	**pendriez**	**aurais pendu**	**auriez pendu**
pendrait	**pendraient**	**aurait pendu**	**auraient pendu**
6 présent du subjonctif		13 passé du subjonctif	
pende	**pendions**	**aie pendu**	**ayons pendu**
pendes	**pendiez**	**aies pendu**	**ayez pendu**
pende	**pendent**	**ait pendu**	**aient pendu**
7 imparfait du subjonctif		14 plus-que-parfait du subjonctif	
pendisse	**pendissions**	**eusse pendu**	**eussions pendu**
pendisses	**pendissiez**	**eusses pendu**	**eussiez pendu**
pendît	**pendissent**	**eût pendu**	**eussent pendu**

Impératif
pends
pendons
pendez

Words and expressions related to this verb

pendre des rideaux to hang curtains
pendre qqch to hang something
pendre qqn to hang someone
se pendre to hang oneself
dépendre de to depend on
pendant during; **pendant que** while
un pendant pendant, main piece of a necklace, hanging ornament
suspendre un lustre to hang a chandelier (ceiling lighting fixture)
pendu, pendue *adj.* hung (thing); hanged (person)
un pendule pendulum
une pendule clock
un pendant d'oreille pendant earring, drop earring

See also **dépendre.**

For an explanation of meanings and uses of French and English verb tenses and moods, see pages 10–21.

penser (336) — Part. pr. pensant — Part. passé pensé

to think

Regular **-er** verb

The Seven Simple Tenses		The Seven Compound Tenses	
Singular	Plural	Singular	Plural
1 présent de l'indicatif		8 passé composé	
pense	**pensons**	**ai pensé**	**avons pensé**
penses	**pensez**	**as pensé**	**avez pensé**
pense	**pensent**	**a pensé**	**ont pensé**
2 imparfait de l'indicatif		9 plus-que-parfait de l'indicatif	
pensais	**pensions**	**avais pensé**	**avions pensé**
pensais	**pensiez**	**avais pensé**	**aviez pensé**
pensait	**pensaient**	**avait pensé**	**avaient pensé**
3 passé simple		10 passé antérieur	
pensai	**pensâmes**	**eus pensé**	**eûmes pensé**
pensas	**pensâtes**	**eus pensé**	**eûtes pensé**
pensa	**pensèrent**	**eut pensé**	**eurent pensé**
4 futur		11 futur antérieur	
penserai	**penserons**	**aurai pensé**	**aurons pensé**
penseras	**penserez**	**auras pensé**	**aurez pensé**
pensera	**penseront**	**aura pensé**	**auront pensé**
5 conditionnel		12 conditionnel passé	
penserais	**penserions**	**aurais pensé**	**aurions pensé**
penserais	**penseriez**	**aurais pensé**	**auriez pensé**
penserait	**penseraient**	**aurait pensé**	**auraient pensé**
6 présent du subjonctif		13 passé du subjonctif	
pense	**pensions**	**aie pensé**	**ayons pensé**
penses	**pensiez**	**aies pensé**	**ayez pensé**
pense	**pensent**	**ait pensé**	**aient pensé**
7 imparfait du subjonctif		14 plus-que-parfait du subjonctif	
pensasse	**pensassions**	**eusse pensé**	**eussions pensé**
pensasses	**pensassiez**	**eusses pensé**	**eussiez pensé**
pensât	**pensassent**	**eût pensé**	**eussent pensé**

Impératif
pense
pensons
pensez

Common idiomatic expressions using this verb

—Robert, tu as l'air pensif; à quoi penses-tu?
—Je pense à mon examen de français.
—Moi, je pense aux vacances de Noël.
—Que penses-tu de cette classe de français?
—Je trouve que cette classe est excellente.
—Penses-tu continuer à étudier le français l'année prochaine?
—Certainement.

penser à to think of, to think about; **penser de** to think about (*i.e.*, to have an opinion about); **un pense-bête** reminder (*e.g.*, string around one's finger); **repenser** to rethink

Note: If you want to say that you're making up your mind (reflecting on something) use **réfléchir.**

Regular **-re** verb

to lose

The Seven Simple Tenses		The Seven Compound Tenses	
Singular	Plural	Singular	Plural
1 présent de l'indicatif		8 passé composé	
perds	**perdons**	**ai perdu**	**avons perdu**
perds	**perdez**	**as perdu**	**avez perdu**
perd	**perdent**	**a perdu**	**ont perdu**
2 imparfait de l'indicatif		9 plus-que-parfait de l'indicatif	
perdais	**perdions**	**avais perdu**	**avions perdu**
perdais	**perdiez**	**avais perdu**	**aviez perdu**
perdait	**perdaient**	**avait perdu**	**avaient perdu**
3 passé simple		10 passé antérieur	
perdis	**perdîmes**	**eus perdu**	**eûmes perdu**
perdis	**perdîtes**	**eus perdu**	**eûtes perdu**
perdit	**perdirent**	**eut perdu**	**eurent perdu**
4 futur		11 futur antérieur	
perdrai	**perdrons**	**aurai perdu**	**aurons perdu**
perdras	**perdrez**	**auras perdu**	**aurez perdu**
perdra	**perdront**	**aura perdu**	**auront perdu**
5 conditionnel		12 conditionnel passé	
perdrais	**perdrions**	**aurais perdu**	**aurions perdu**
perdrais	**perdriez**	**aurais perdu**	**auriez perdu**
perdrait	**perdraient**	**aurait perdu**	**auraient perdu**
6 présent du subjonctif		13 passé du subjonctif	
perde	**perdions**	**aie perdu**	**ayons perdu**
perdes	**perdiez**	**aies perdu**	**ayez perdu**
perde	**perdent**	**ait perdu**	**aient perdu**
7 imparfait du subjonctif		14 plus-que-parfait du subjonctif	
perdisse	**perdissions**	**eusse perdu**	**eussions perdu**
perdisses	**perdissiez**	**eusses perdu**	**eussiez perdu**
perdît	**perdissent**	**eût perdu**	**eussent perdu**

Impératif
perds
perdons
perdez

AN ESSENTIAL 55 VERB

Perdre

Perdre is an important verb for a beginning French student because it is a regular **-re** verb and because it is used in numerous everyday situations and idiomatic expressions.

Sentences using perdre

Vous n'avez rien à perdre. You have nothing to lose.

Je me suis perdu(e). I'm lost.

À cause du verglas, le chauffeur a perdu la maîtrise de sa voiture. Because of the black ice, the driver lost control of his car.

Quand on n'a rien à perdre, on peut bien tout risquer. (Jean-Louis Laya) When one has nothing to lose, one can risk everything.

Words and expressions related to this verb

se perdre **to lose oneself, to lose one's way, to be ruined**

perdre son temps **to waste one's time**

perdre son chemin **to lose one's way**

perdre pied **to lose one's footing**

perdre les pédales **to lose one's head**

perdre le nord, perdre la boule **to go crazy**

perdre connaissance **to faint**

perdre l'esprit **to go out of one's mind**

une perte **loss**

perdre de vue **to lose sight of**

perdre la raison **to take leave of one's senses**

éperdu, éperdue **distraught, overcome**

éperdument **passionately**

reperdre **to lose again**

Can't remember the French verb you need? Check the back pages of this book for the English-French verb index!

Regular **-ir** verb

to perish, to die

The Seven Simple Tenses		The Seven Compound Tenses	
Singular	Plural	Singular	Plural
1 présent de l'indicatif		8 passé composé	
péris	**périssons**	**ai péri**	**avons péri**
péris	**périssez**	**as péri**	**avez péri**
périt	**périssent**	**a péri**	**ont péri**
2 imparfait de l'indicatif		9 plus-que-parfait de l'indicatif	
périssais	**périssions**	**avais péri**	**avions péri**
périssais	**périssiez**	**avais péri**	**aviez péri**
périssait	**périssaient**	**avait péri**	**avaient péri**
3 passé simple		10 passé antérieur	
péris	**périmes**	**eus péri**	**eûmes péri**
péris	**pérites**	**eus péri**	**eûtes péri**
périt	**périrent**	**eut péri**	**eurent péri**
4 futur		11 futur antérieur	
périrai	**périrons**	**aurai péri**	**aurons péri**
périras	**périrez**	**auras péri**	**aurez péri**
périra	**périront**	**aura péri**	**auront péri**
5 conditionnel		12 conditionnel passé	
périrais	**péririons**	**aurais péri**	**aurions péri**
périrais	**péririez**	**aurais péri**	**auriez péri**
périrait	**périraient**	**aurait péri**	**auraient péri**
6 présent du subjonctif		13 passé du subjonctif	
périsse	**périssions**	**aie péri**	**ayons péri**
périsses	**périssiez**	**aies péri**	**ayez péri**
périsse	**périssent**	**ait péri**	**aient péri**
7 imparfait du subjonctif		14 plus-que-parfait du subjonctif	
périsse	**périssions**	**eusse péri**	**eussions péri**
périsses	**périssiez**	**eusses péri**	**eussiez péri**
périt	**périssent**	**eût péri**	**eussent péri**

Impératif
péris
périssons
périssez

Common idiomatic expressions using this verb

faire périr to kill
s'ennuyer à périr to be bored to death
périssable perishable
périr d'ennui to be bored to death
péri en mer lost at sea
périr de froid to freeze to death
les denrées périssables perishable foods
impérissable imperishable, eternal

Can't find the verb you're looking for? Check the back pages of this book for a list of over 2,600 additional verbs!

permettre (339) — Part. pr. **permettant** — Part. passé **permis**

to permit, to allow, to let

Irregular verb

The Seven Simple Tenses		The Seven Compound Tenses	
Singular	Plural	Singular	Plural
1 présent de l'indicatif		8 passé composé	
permets	**permettons**	**ai permis**	**avons permis**
permets	**permettez**	**as permis**	**avez permis**
permet	**permettent**	**a permis**	**ont permis**
2 imparfait de l'indicatif		9 plus-que-parfait de l'indicatif	
permettais	**permettions**	**avais permis**	**avions permis**
permettais	**permettiez**	**avais permis**	**aviez permis**
permettait	**permettaient**	**avait permis**	**avaient permis**
3 passé simple		10 passé antérieur	
permis	**permîmes**	**eus permis**	**eûmes permis**
permis	**permîtes**	**eus permis**	**eûtes permis**
permit	**permirent**	**eut permis**	**eurent permis**
4 futur		11 futur antérieur	
permettrai	**permettrons**	**aurai permis**	**aurons permis**
permettras	**permettrez**	**auras permis**	**aurez permis**
permettra	**permettront**	**aura permis**	**auront permis**
5 conditionnel		12 conditionnel passé	
permettrais	**permettrions**	**aurais permis**	**aurions permis**
permettrais	**permettriez**	**aurais permis**	**auriez permis**
permettrait	**permettraient**	**aurait permis**	**auraient permis**
6 présent du subjonctif		13 passé du subjonctif	
permette	**permettions**	**aie permis**	**ayons permis**
permettes	**permettiez**	**aies permis**	**ayez permis**
permette	**permettent**	**ait permis**	**aient permis**
7 imparfait du subjonctif		14 plus-que-parfait du subjonctif	
permisse	**permissions**	**eusse permis**	**eussions permis**
permisses	**permissiez**	**eusses permis**	**eussiez permis**
permît	**permissent**	**eût permis**	**eussent permis**

Impératif
permets
permettons
permettez

Common idiomatic expressions using this verb and words related to it

La maîtresse de français a permis à l'élève de quitter la salle de classe quelques minutes avant la fin de la leçon.

permettre à qqn de faire qqch to permit (to allow) someone to do something
Vous permettez? May I? Do you mind?
s'il est permis if it is allowed, permitted
un permis permit
un permis de conduire driving license
la permission permission
se permettre de faire qqch to take the liberty to do something; to venture to do something
un permis de construction building permit

See also **commettre, mettre, omettre, promettre, remettre, soumettre,** and **transmettre.**

Regular **-er** verb

to persuade, to convince, to induce

The Seven Simple Tenses		The Seven Compound Tenses	
Singular	Plural	Singular	Plural
1 présent de l'indicatif		8 passé composé	
persuade	**persuadons**	**ai persuadé**	**avons persuadé**
persuades	**persuadez**	**as persuadé**	**avez persuadé**
persuade	**persuadent**	**a persuadé**	**ont persuadé**
2 imparfait de l'indicatif		9 plus-que-parfait de l'indicatif	
persuadais	**persuadions**	**avais persuadé**	**avions persuadé**
persuadais	**persuadiez**	**avais persuadé**	**aviez persuadé**
persuadait	**persuadaient**	**avait persuadé**	**avaient persuadé**
3 passé simple		10 passé antérieur	
persuadai	**persuadâmes**	**eus persuadé**	**eûmes persuadé**
persuadas	**persuadâtes**	**eus persuadé**	**eûtes persuadé**
persuada	**persuadèrent**	**eut persuadé**	**eurent persuadé**
4 futur		11 futur antérieur	
persuaderai	**persuaderons**	**aurai persuadé**	**aurons persuadé**
persuaderas	**persuaderez**	**auras persuadé**	**aurez persuadé**
persuadera	**persuaderont**	**aura persuadé**	**auront persuadé**
5 conditionnel		12 conditionnel passé	
persuaderais	**persuaderions**	**aurais persuadé**	**aurions persuadé**
persuaderais	**persuaderiez**	**aurais persuadé**	**auriez persuadé**
persuaderait	**persuaderaient**	**aurait persuadé**	**auraient persuadé**
6 présent du subjonctif		13 passé du subjonctif	
persuade	**persuadions**	**aie persuadé**	**ayons persuadé**
persuades	**persuadiez**	**aies persuadé**	**ayez persuadé**
persuade	**persuadent**	**ait persuadé**	**aient persuadé**
7 imparfait du subjonctif		14 plus-que-parfait du subjonctif	
persuadasse	**persuadassions**	**eusse persuadé**	**eussions persuadé**
persuadasses	**persuadassiez**	**eusses persuadé**	**eussiez persuadé**
persuadât	**persuadassent**	**eût persuadé**	**eussent persuadé**

Impératif
persuade
persuadons
persuadez

Words and expressions related to this verb

persuader à qqn de faire qqch to induce someone to do something

persuader qqn de qqch to persuade someone of something

dissuader de to dissuade from

la persuasion persuasion

persuasif, persuasive persuasive

persuasivement persuasively

se persuader de qqch to persuade (convince) oneself of something

Can't remember the French verb you need? Check the back pages of this book for the English-French verb index!

peser (341) — Part. pr. pesant — Part. passé pesé

to weigh

Regular **-er** verb endings; spelling change: **e** changes to **è** before syllable with mute **e**

The Seven Simple Tenses		The Seven Compound Tenses	
Singular	Plural	Singular	Plural
1 présent de l'indicatif		8 passé composé	
pèse	**pesons**	**ai pesé**	**avons pesé**
pèses	**pesez**	**as pesé**	**avez pesé**
pèse	**pèsent**	**a pesé**	**ont pesé**
2 imparfait de l'indicatif		9 plus-que-parfait de l'indicatif	
pesais	**pesions**	**avais pesé**	**avions pesé**
pesais	**pesiez**	**avais pesé**	**aviez pesé**
pesait	**pesaient**	**avait pesé**	**avaient pesé**
3 passé simple		10 passé antérieur	
pesai	**pesâmes**	**eus pesé**	**eûmes pesé**
pesas	**pesâtes**	**eus pesé**	**eûtes pesé**
pesa	**pesèrent**	**eut pesé**	**eurent pesé**
4 futur		11 futur antérieur	
pèserai	**pèserons**	**aurai pesé**	**aurons pesé**
pèseras	**pèserez**	**auras pesé**	**aurez pesé**
pèsera	**pèseront**	**aura pesé**	**auront pesé**
5 conditionnel		12 conditionnel passé	
pèserais	**pèserions**	**aurais pesé**	**aurions pesé**
pèserais	**pèseriez**	**aurais pesé**	**auriez pesé**
pèserait	**pèseraient**	**aurait pesé**	**auraient pesé**
6 présent du subjonctif		13 passé du subjonctif	
pèse	**pesions**	**aie pesé**	**ayons pesé**
pèses	**pesiez**	**aies pesé**	**ayez pesé**
pèse	**pèsent**	**ait pesé**	**aient pesé**
7 imparfait du subjonctif		14 plus-que-parfait du subjonctif	
pesasse	**pesassions**	**eusse pesé**	**eussions pesé**
pesasses	**pesassiez**	**eusses pesé**	**eussiez pesé**
pesât	**pesassent**	**eût pesé**	**eussent pesé**

Impératif
pèse
pesons
pesez

Words and expressions related to this verb

peser qqch to weigh something; to ponder; to think out, to consider
peser sur to weigh upon
se peser to weigh oneself
pesamment heavily
un pèse-lettre weight scale for letters **(des pèse-lettres)**
le poids weight (measured)
la pesanteur weight, gravity
pesant, pesante heavy, weighty
poids et mesures weights and measures
perdre du poids to lose weight
un pèse-personne a bathroom scale

Grammar putting you in a tense mood? Review the definitions of basic grammatical terms on pages 35–49.

Regular **-er** verb endings; spelling change:
c changes to **ç** before **a** or **o** to keep **s** sound

to place, to put

The Seven Simple Tenses		The Seven Compound Tenses	
Singular	Plural	Singular	Plural
1 présent de l'indicatif		8 passé composé	
place	**plaçons**	**ai placé**	**avons placé**
places	**placez**	**as placé**	**avez placé**
place	**placent**	**a placé**	**ont placé**
2 imparfait de l'indicatif		9 plus-que-parfait de l'indicatif	
plaçais	**placions**	**avais placé**	**avions placé**
plaçais	**placiez**	**avais placé**	**aviez placé**
plaçait	**plaçaient**	**avait placé**	**avaient placé**
3 passé simple		10 passé antérieur	
plaçai	**plaçâmes**	**eus placé**	**eûmes placé**
plaças	**plaçâtes**	**eus placé**	**eûtes placé**
plaça	**placèrent**	**eut placé**	**eurent placé**
4 futur		11 futur antérieur	
placerai	**placerons**	**aurai placé**	**aurons placé**
placeras	**placerez**	**auras placé**	**aurez placé**
placera	**placeront**	**aura placé**	**auront placé**
5 conditionnel		12 conditionnel passé	
placerais	**placerions**	**aurais placé**	**aurions placé**
placerais	**placeriez**	**aurais placé**	**auriez placé**
placerait	**placeraient**	**aurait placé**	**auraient placé**
6 présent du subjonctif		13 passé du subjonctif	
place	**placions**	**aie placé**	**ayons placé**
places	**placiez**	**aies placé**	**ayez placé**
place	**placent**	**ait placé**	**aient placé**
7 imparfait du subjonctif		14 plus-que-parfait du subjonctif	
plaçasse	**plaçassions**	**eusse placé**	**eussions placé**
plaçasses	**plaçassiez**	**eusses placé**	**eussiez placé**
plaçât	**plaçassent**	**eût placé**	**eussent placé**

Impératif
place
plaçons
placez

Sentences using this verb and words related to it

Nous pouvons déjeuner maintenant. Ma place est ici près de la fenêtre, ta place est là-bas près de la porte. Marie, place-toi à côté de Pierre. Combien de places y a-t-il? Y a-t-il assez de places pour tout le monde?

une place a seat, a place
chaque chose à sa place everything in its place
un placement placing
un bureau de placement employment agency
se placer to place oneself, to take a seat, to find employment
replacer to replace, put back

See also **remplacer.**

plaindre (343) — Part. pr. plaignant — Part. passé plaint

to pity

Irregular verb

The Seven Simple Tenses		The Seven Compound Tenses	
Singular	Plural	Singular	Plural
1 présent de l'indicatif		8 passé composé	
plains	**plaignons**	**ai plaint**	**avons plaint**
plains	**plaignez**	**as plaint**	**avez plaint**
plaint	**plaignent**	**a plaint**	**ont plaint**
2 imparfait de l'indicatif		9 plus-que-parfait de l'indicatif	
plaignais	**plaignions**	**avais plaint**	**avions plaint**
plaignais	**plaigniez**	**avais plaint**	**aviez plaint**
plaignait	**plaignaient**	**avait plaint**	**avaient plaint**
3 passé simple		10 passé antérieur	
plaignis	**plaignîmes**	**eus plaint**	**eûmes plaint**
plaignis	**plaignîtes**	**eus plaint**	**eûtes plaint**
plaignit	**plaignirent**	**eut plaint**	**eurent plaint**
4 futur		11 futur antérieur	
plaindrai	**plaindrons**	**aurai plaint**	**aurons plaint**
plaindras	**plaindrez**	**auras plaint**	**aurez plaint**
plaindra	**plaindront**	**aura plaint**	**auront plaint**
5 conditionnel		12 conditionnel passé	
plaindrais	**plaindrions**	**aurais plaint**	**aurions plaint**
plaindrais	**plaindriez**	**aurais plaint**	**auriez plaint**
plaindrait	**plaindraient**	**aurait plaint**	**auraient plaint**
6 présent du subjonctif		13 passé du subjonctif	
plaigne	**plaignions**	**aie plaint**	**ayons plaint**
plaignes	**plaigniez**	**aies plaint**	**ayez plaint**
plaigne	**plaignent**	**ait plaint**	**aient plaint**
7 imparfait du subjonctif		14 plus-que-parfait du subjonctif	
plaignisse	**plaignissions**	**eusse plaint**	**eussions plaint**
plaignisses	**plaignissiez**	**eusses plaint**	**eussiez plaint**
plaignît	**plaignissent**	**eût plaint**	**eussent plaint**

Impératif
plains
plaignons
plaignez

Sentences using this verb and words related to it

Pauvre Madame Bayou! Elle a des ennuis et je la plains.

une plainte groan, moan, protest, complaint
porter plainte contre to bring charges against
déposer/faire une plainte to file a complaint
plaintif, plaintive plaintive
plaintivement plaintively, mournfully
Je te plains. I feel for you; I feel sorry for you; I pity you.
être à plaindre to be pitied
Elle est à plaindre. She is to be pitied.
For additional related words, see **se plaindre.**

Soak up some verbs used in weather expressions. There's a list in the Appendixes.

Reflexive irregular verb

to complain, to lament, to moan

The Seven Simple Tenses		The Seven Compound Tenses	
Singular	Plural	Singular	Plural
1 présent de l'indicatif		8 passé composé	
me plains	**nous plaignons**	**me suis plaint(e)**	**nous sommes plaint(e)s**
te plains	**vous plaignez**	**t'es plaint(e)**	**vous êtes plaint(e)(s)**
se plaint	**se plaignent**	**s'est plaint(e)**	**se sont plaint(e)s**
2 imparfait de l'indicatif		9 plus-que-parfait de l'indicatif	
me plaignais	**nous plaignions**	**m'étais plaint(e)**	**nous étions plaint(e)s**
te plaignais	**vous plaigniez**	**t'étais plaint(e)**	**vous étiez plaint(e)(s)**
se plaignait	**se plaignaient**	**s'était plaint(e)**	**s'étaient plaint(e)s**
3 passé simple		10 passé antérieur	
me plaignis	**nous plaignîmes**	**me fus plaint(e)**	**nous fûmes plaint(e)s**
te plaignis	**vous plaignîtes**	**te fus plaint(e)**	**vous fûtes plaint(e)(s)**
se plaignit	**se plaignirent**	**se fut plaint(e)**	**se furent plaint(e)s**
4 futur		11 futur antérieur	
me plaindrai	**nous plaindrons**	**me serai plaint(e)**	**nous serons plaint(e)s**
te plaindras	**vous plaindrez**	**te seras plaint(e)**	**vous serez plaint(e)(s)**
se plaindra	**se plaindront**	**se sera plaint(e)**	**se seront plaint(e)s**
5 conditionnel		12 conditionnel passé	
me plaindrais	**nous plaindrions**	**me serais plaint(e)**	**nous serions plaint(e)s**
te plaindrais	**vous plaindriez**	**te serais plaint(e)**	**vous seriez plaint(e)(s)**
se plaindrait	**se plaindraient**	**se serait plaint(e)**	**se seraient plaint(e)s**
6 présent du subjonctif		13 passé du subjonctif	
me plaigne	**nous plaignions**	**me sois plaint(e)**	**nous soyons plaint(e)s**
te plaignes	**vous plaigniez**	**te sois plaint(e)**	**vous soyez plaint(e)(s)**
se plaigne	**se plaignent**	**se soit plaint(e)**	**se soient plaint(e)s**
7 imparfait du subjonctif		14 plus-que-parfait du subjonctif	
me plaignisse	**nous plaignissions**	**me fusse plaint(e)**	**nous fussions plaint(e)s**
te plaignisses	**vous plaignissiez**	**te fusses plaint(e)**	**vous fussiez plaint(e)(s)**
se plaignît	**se plaignissent**	**se fût plaint(e)**	**se fussent plaint(e)s**

Impératif
plains-toi; ne te plains pas
plaignons-nous; ne nous plaignons pas
plaignez-vous; ne vous plaignez pas

Common idiomatic expressions using this verb

Quelle jeune fille! Elle se plaint toujours de tout! Hier elle s'est plainte de son professeur de français, aujourd'hui elle se plaint de ses devoirs, et je suis certain que demain elle se plaindra du temps.

se plaindre du temps to complain about the weather
se plaindre de qqn ou de qqch to complain of, to find fault with, someone or something
avoir bonne raison de se plaindre to have a good reason to complain

For other words related to this verb, see **plaindre.**

It's important that you be familiar with the Subjunctive. See pages 26–31.

to please

Irregular verb

The Seven Simple Tenses		The Seven Compound Tenses	
Singular	Plural	Singular	Plural
1 présent de l'indicatif		8 passé composé	
plais	**plaisons**	**ai plu**	**avons plu**
plais	**plaisez**	**as plu**	**avez plu**
plaît	**plaisent**	**a plu**	**ont plu**
2 imparfait de l'indicatif		9 plus-que-parfait de l'indicatif	
plaisais	**plaisions**	**avais plu**	**avions plu**
plaisais	**plaisiez**	**avais plu**	**aviez plu**
plaisait	**plaisaient**	**avait plu**	**avaient plu**
3 passé simple		10 passé antérieur	
plus	**plûmes**	**eus plu**	**eûmes plu**
plus	**plûtes**	**eus plu**	**eûtes plu**
plut	**plurent**	**eut plu**	**eurent plu**
4 futur		11 futur antérieur	
plairai	**plairons**	**aurai plu**	**aurons plu**
plairas	**plairez**	**auras plu**	**aurez plu**
plaira	**plairont**	**aura plu**	**auront plu**
5 conditionnel		12 conditionnel passé	
plairais	**plairions**	**aurais plu**	**aurions plu**
plairais	**plairiez**	**aurais plu**	**auriez plu**
plairait	**plairaient**	**aurait plu**	**auraient plu**
6 présent du subjonctif		13 passé du subjonctif	
plaise	**plaisions**	**aie plu**	**ayons plu**
plaises	**plaisiez**	**aies plu**	**ayez plu**
plaise	**plaisent**	**ait plu**	**aient plu**
7 imparfait du subjonctif		14 plus-que-parfait du subjonctif	
plusse	**plussions**	**eusse plu**	**eussions plu**
plusses	**plussiez**	**eusses plu**	**eussiez plu**
plût	**plussent**	**eût plu**	**eussent plu**

Impératif
plais
plaisons
plaisez

Common idiomatic expressions using this verb

plaire à qqn to please, to be pleasing to someone; **Son mariage a plu à sa famille.** Her (his) marriage pleased her (his) family. **Est-ce que ce cadeau lui plaira?** Will this present please her (him)? Will this gift be pleasing to her (to him)?

se plaire à to take pleasure in; **Robert se plaît à ennuyer son petit frère.** Robert takes pleasure in bothering his little brother.

le plaisir delight, pleasure; **complaire à** to please; **déplaire à** to displease

s'il vous plaît; s'il te plaît please (if it is pleasing to you); **avec plaisir** with pleasure

Il a beaucoup plu hier et cela m'a beaucoup plu. It rained a lot yesterday and that pleased me a great deal. (See **pleuvoir**)

See also **déplaire.**

Can't recognize an irregular verb form? Check out the index of common irregular French verb forms in the Appendixes.

Regular **-er** verb

to joke

The Seven Simple Tenses		The Seven Compound Tenses	
Singular	Plural	Singular	Plural
1 présent de l'indicatif		8 passé composé	
plaisante	**plaisantons**	**ai plaisanté**	**avons plaisanté**
plaisantes	**plaisantez**	**as plaisanté**	**avez plaisanté**
plaisante	**plaisantent**	**a plaisanté**	**ont plaisanté**
2 imparfait de l'indicatif		9 plus-que-parfait de l'indicatif	
plaisantais	**plaisantions**	**avais plaisanté**	**avions plaisanté**
plaisantais	**plaisantiez**	**avais plaisanté**	**aviez plaisanté**
plaisantait	**plaisantaient**	**avait plaisanté**	**avaient plaisanté**
3 passé simple		10 passé antérieur	
plaisantai	**plaisantâmes**	**eus plaisanté**	**eûmes plaisanté**
plaisantas	**plaisantâtes**	**eus plaisanté**	**eûtes plaisanté**
plaisanta	**plaisantèrent**	**eut plaisanté**	**eurent plaisanté**
4 futur		11 futur antérieur	
plaisanterai	**plaisanterons**	**aurai plaisanté**	**aurons plaisanté**
plaisanteras	**plaisanterez**	**auras plaisanté**	**aurez plaisanté**
plaisantera	**plaisanteront**	**aura plaisanté**	**auront plaisanté**
5 conditionnel		12 conditionnel passé	
plaisanterais	**plaisanterions**	**aurais plaisanté**	**aurions plaisanté**
plaisanterais	**plaisanteriez**	**aurais plaisanté**	**auriez plaisanté**
plaisanterait	**plaisanteraient**	**aurait plaisanté**	**auraient plaisanté**
6 présent du subjonctif		13 passé du subjonctif	
plaisante	**plaisantions**	**aie plaisanté**	**ayons plaisanté**
plaisantes	**plaisantiez**	**aies plaisanté**	**ayez plaisanté**
plaisante	**plaisantent**	**ait plaisanté**	**aient plaisanté**
7 imparfait du subjonctif		14 plus-que-parfait du subjonctif	
plaisantasse	**plaisantassions**	**eusse plaisanté**	**eussions plaisanté**
plaisantasses	**plaisantassiez**	**eusses plaisanté**	**eussiez plaisanté**
plaisantât	**plaisantassent**	**eût plaisanté**	**eussent plaisanté**

Impératif
plaisante
plaisantons
plaisantez

Words and expressions related to this verb

pour plaisanter for fun
une plaisanterie joke, joking
dire des plaisanteries to crack jokes
en plaisantant in fun
dire une chose par plaisanterie to say something in a joking way
prendre bien une plaisanterie to know how to take a joke

Can't find the verb you're looking for? Check the back pages of this book for a list of over 2,600 additional verbs!

pleurer (347) — Part. pr. pleurant — Part. passé pleuré

to cry, to weep, to mourn

Regular **-er** verb

The Seven Simple Tenses		The Seven Compound Tenses	
Singular	Plural	Singular	Plural
1 présent de l'indicatif		8 passé composé	
pleure	**pleurons**	**ai pleuré**	**avons pleuré**
pleures	**pleurez**	**as pleuré**	**avez pleuré**
pleure	**pleurent**	**a pleuré**	**ont pleuré**
2 imparfait de l'indicatif		9 plus-que-parfait de l'indicatif	
pleurais	**pleurions**	**avais pleuré**	**avions pleuré**
pleurais	**pleuriez**	**avais pleuré**	**aviez pleuré**
pleurait	**pleuraient**	**avait pleuré**	**avaient pleuré**
3 passé simple		10 passé antérieur	
pleurai	**pleurâmes**	**eus pleuré**	**eûmes pleuré**
pleuras	**pleurâtes**	**eus pleuré**	**eûtes pleuré**
pleura	**pleurèrent**	**eut pleuré**	**eurent pleuré**
4 futur		11 futur antérieur	
pleurerai	**pleurerons**	**aurai pleuré**	**aurons pleuré**
pleureras	**pleurerez**	**auras pleuré**	**aurez pleuré**
pleurera	**pleureront**	**aura pleuré**	**auront pleuré**
5 conditionnel		12 conditionnel passé	
pleurerais	**pleurerions**	**aurais pleuré**	**aurions pleuré**
pleurerais	**pleureriez**	**aurais pleuré**	**auriez pleuré**
pleurerait	**pleureraient**	**aurait pleuré**	**auraient pleuré**
6 présent du subjonctif		13 passé du subjonctif	
pleure	**pleurions**	**aie pleuré**	**ayons pleuré**
pleures	**pleuriez**	**aies pleuré**	**ayez pleuré**
pleure	**pleurent**	**ait pleuré**	**aient pleuré**
7 imparfait du subjonctif		14 plus-que-parfait du subjonctif	
pleurasse	**pleurassions**	**eusse pleuré**	**eussions pleuré**
pleurasses	**pleurassiez**	**eusses pleuré**	**eussiez pleuré**
pleurât	**pleurassent**	**eût pleuré**	**eussent pleuré**

Impératif
pleure
pleurons
pleurez

Common idiomatic expressions using this verb and words related to it

pleurer toutes les larmes de son corps to cry one's eyes out
une larme a tear
un pleur a tear
pleurard, pleurarde whimpering person
une pièce pleurnicharde soap opera
larmoyant, larmoyante tearful, lachrymose
pleurnicher to snivel, to whine
un pleurnicheur, une pleurnicheuse crybaby

How are you doing? Find out with the verb drills and tests with answers explained on pages 50–101.

Regular **-er** verb

to fold, to bend

The Seven Simple Tenses		The Seven Compound Tenses	
Singular	Plural	Singular	Plural
1 présent de l'indicatif		8 passé composé	
plie	**plions**	**ai plié**	**avons plié**
plies	**pliez**	**as plié**	**avez plié**
plie	**plient**	**a plié**	**ont plié**
2 imparfait de l'indicatif		9 plus-que-parfait de l'indicatif	
pliais	**pliions**	**avais plié**	**avions plié**
pliais	**pliiez**	**avais plié**	**aviez plié**
pliait	**pliaient**	**avait plié**	**avaient plié**
3 passé simple		10 passé antérieur	
pliai	**pliâmes**	**eus plié**	**eûmes plié**
plias	**pliâtes**	**eus plié**	**eûtes plié**
plia	**plièrent**	**eut plié**	**eurent plié**
4 futur		11 futur antérieur	
plierai	**plierons**	**aurai plié**	**aurons plié**
plieras	**plierez**	**auras plié**	**aurez plié**
pliera	**plieront**	**aura plié**	**auront plié**
5 conditionnel		12 conditionnel passé	
plierais	**plierions**	**aurais plié**	**aurions plié**
plierais	**plieriez**	**aurais plié**	**auriez plié**
plierait	**plieraient**	**aurait plié**	**auraient plié**
6 présent du subjonctif		13 passé du subjonctif	
plie	**pliions**	**aie plié**	**ayons plié**
plies	**pliiez**	**aies plié**	**ayez plié**
plie	**plient**	**ait plié**	**aient plié**
7 imparfait du subjonctif		14 plus-que-parfait du subjonctif	
pliasse	**pliassions**	**eusse plié**	**eussions plié**
pliasses	**pliassiez**	**eusses plié**	**eussiez plié**
pliât	**pliassent**	**eût plié**	**eussent plié**

Impératif
plie
plions
pliez

Sentences using this verb and words related to it

En pliant un morceau de papier ainsi, tu peux faire un petit avion en papier. By folding a piece of paper in this way, you can make a little paper airplane.

Je plie et ne romps pas. (La Fontaine, le roseau dans "Le Chêne et le Roseau") I bend and do not break. (La Fontaine, the reed in "The Oak and the Reed")

Words and expressions related to this verb

plier en deux to double over
un pli fold, wrinkle, crease
sous pli séparé under separate cover
se plier à to submit to
plier devant qqn to submit to someone
un dépliant brochure
plier bagage to pack up, to pack one's bags
un plié plié (ballet)
replier to fold up
se replier to fold back

The subject pronouns are found on page 103.

to wear, to carry

Regular **-er** verb

The Seven Simple Tenses		The Seven Compound Tenses	
Singular	Plural	Singular	Plural
1 présent de l'indicatif		8 passé composé	
porte	**portons**	**ai porté**	**avons porté**
portes	**portez**	**as porté**	**avez porté**
porte	**portent**	**a porté**	**ont porté**
2 imparfait de l'indicatif		9 plus-que-parfait de l'indicatif	
portais	**portions**	**avais porté**	**avions porté**
portais	**portiez**	**avais porté**	**aviez porté**
portait	**portaient**	**avait porté**	**avaient porté**
3 passé simple		10 passé antérieur	
portai	**portâmes**	**eus porté**	**eûmes porté**
portas	**portâtes**	**eus porté**	**eûtes porté**
porta	**portèrent**	**eut porté**	**eurent porté**
4 futur		11 futur antérieur	
porterai	**porterons**	**aurai porté**	**aurons porté**
porteras	**porterez**	**auras porté**	**aurez porté**
portera	**porteront**	**aura porté**	**auront porté**
5 conditionnel		12 conditionnel passé	
porterais	**porterions**	**aurais porté**	**aurions porté**
porterais	**porteriez**	**aurais porté**	**auriez porté**
porterait	**porteraient**	**aurait porté**	**auraient porté**
6 présent du subjonctif		13 passé du subjonctif	
porte	**portions**	**aie porté**	**ayons porté**
portes	**portiez**	**aies porté**	**ayez porté**
porte	**portent**	**ait porté**	**aient porté**
7 imparfait du subjonctif		14 plus-que-parfait du subjonctif	
portasse	**portassions**	**eusse porté**	**eussions porté**
portasses	**portassiez**	**eusses porté**	**eussiez porté**
portât	**portassent**	**eût porté**	**eussent porté**

Impératif
porte
portons
portez

Common idiomatic expressions using this verb and words related to it

porter la main sur qqn to raise one's hand against someone
porter son âge to look one's age
se porter to feel (health); **Comment vous portez-vous aujourd'hui?** How do you feel today?
apporter to bring; **rapporter** to bring back
exporter to export
importer to import; to matter, to be of importance
un porte-monnaie change purse (**des porte-monnaie**)
comporter to comprise
déporter to deport
se comporter to behave
emporter to carry away; *Autant en emporte le vent* (*Gone with the Wind*)
Elle porte de jolies robes. She wears pretty dresses.
un portable cell phone, laptop computer

See also **apporter** and **supporter.**

Regular **-er** verb

to lay, to place, to put, to set, to pose

The Seven Simple Tenses		The Seven Compound Tenses	
Singular	Plural	Singular	Plural
1 présent de l'indicatif		8 passé composé	
pose	**posons**	**ai posé**	**avons posé**
poses	**posez**	**as posé**	**avez posé**
pose	**posent**	**a posé**	**ont posé**
2 imparfait de l'indicatif		9 plus-que-parfait de l'indicatif	
posais	**posions**	**avais posé**	**avions posé**
posais	**posiez**	**avais posé**	**aviez posé**
posait	**posaient**	**avait posé**	**avaient posé**
3 passé simple		10 passé antérieur	
posai	**posâmes**	**eus posé**	**eûmes posé**
posas	**posâtes**	**eus posé**	**eûtes posé**
posa	**posèrent**	**eut posé**	**eurent posé**
4 futur		11 futur antérieur	
poserai	**poserons**	**aurai posé**	**aurons posé**
poseras	**poserez**	**auras posé**	**aurez posé**
posera	**poseront**	**aura posé**	**auront posé**
5 conditionnel		12 conditionnel passé	
poserais	**poserions**	**aurais posé**	**aurions posé**
poserais	**poseriez**	**aurais posé**	**auriez posé**
poserait	**poseraient**	**aurait posé**	**auraient posé**
6 présent du subjonctif		13 passé du subjonctif	
pose	**posions**	**aie posé**	**ayons posé**
poses	**posiez**	**aies posé**	**ayez posé**
pose	**posent**	**ait posé**	**aient posé**
7 imparfait du subjonctif		14 plus-que-parfait du subjonctif	
posasse	**posassions**	**eusse posé**	**eussions posé**
posasses	**posassiez**	**eusses posé**	**eussiez posé**
posât	**posassent**	**eût posé**	**eussent posé**

Impératif
pose
posons
posez

Words and expressions related to this verb

poser une question to ask a question
poser pour son portrait to sit for a portrait painting
faire poser qqn to keep someone waiting
déposer to deposit, to set (put) down
composer to compose
supposer to suppose
opposer to oppose; **s'opposer à** to be opposed to
reposer to set down again; **se reposer** to rest
exposer to exhibit, to expose

Can't find the verb you're looking for? Check the back pages of this book for a list of over 2,600 additional verbs!

posséder (351) — Part. pr. possédant — Part. passé possédé

to possess, to own, to master

Regular **-er** verb endings; spelling change: **é** changes to **è** before syllable with mute **e**

The Seven Simple Tenses

Singular	Plural
1 présent de l'indicatif	
possède	**possédons**
possèdes	**possédez**
possède	**possèdent**
2 imparfait de l'indicatif	
possédais	**possédions**
possédais	**possédiez**
possédait	**possédaient**
3 passé simple	
possédai	**possédâmes**
possédas	**possédâtes**
posséda	**possédèrent**
4 futur	
posséderai	**posséderons**
posséderas	**posséderez**
possédera	**posséderont**
5 conditionnel	
posséderais	**posséderions**
posséderais	**posséderiez**
posséderait	**posséderaient**
6 présent du subjonctif	
possède	**possédions**
possèdes	**possédiez**
possède	**possèdent**
7 imparfait du subjonctif	
possédasse	**possédassions**
possédasses	**possédassiez**
possédât	**possédassent**

The Seven Compound Tenses

Singular	Plural
8 passé composé	
ai possédé	**avons possédé**
as possédé	**avez possédé**
a possédé	**ont possédé**
9 plus-que-parfait de l'indicatif	
avais possédé	**avions possédé**
avais possédé	**aviez possédé**
avait possédé	**avaient possédé**
10 passé antérieur	
eus possédé	**eûmes possédé**
eus possédé	**eûtes possédé**
eut possédé	**eurent possédé**
11 futur antérieur	
aurai possédé	**aurons possédé**
auras possédé	**aurez possédé**
aura possédé	**auront possédé**
12 conditionnel passé	
aurais possédé	**aurions possédé**
aurais possédé	**auriez possédé**
aurait possédé	**auraient possédé**
13 passé du subjonctif	
aie possédé	**ayons possédé**
aies possédé	**ayez possédé**
ait possédé	**aient possédé**
14 plus-que-parfait du subjonctif	
eusse possédé	**eussions possédé**
eusses possédé	**eussiez possédé**
eût possédé	**eussent possédé**

Impératif
possède
possédons
possédez

Words and expressions related to this verb

se faire posséder to be taken in
la possession possession, ownership
possessif, possessive possessive
se posséder to have control of oneself
un possesseur possessor, owner; **Madame Goulu est possesseur d'un grand château.**
déposséder de to dispossess of (from)
une dépossession dispossession

Don't forget to study the section on defective and impersonal verbs. It's right after this main list.

Irregular verb

to pursue, to prosecute

The Seven Simple Tenses		The Seven Compound Tenses	
Singular	Plural	Singular	Plural
1 présent de l'indicatif		8 passé composé	
poursuis	**poursuivons**	**ai poursuivi**	**avons poursuivi**
poursuis	**poursuivez**	**as poursuivi**	**avez poursuivi**
poursuit	**poursuivent**	**a poursuivi**	**ont poursuivi**
2 imparfait de l'indicatif		9 plus-que-parfait de l'indicatif	
poursuivais	**poursuivions**	**avais poursuivi**	**avions poursuivi**
poursuivais	**poursuiviez**	**avais poursuivi**	**aviez poursuivi**
poursuivait	**poursuivaient**	**avait poursuivi**	**avaient poursuivi**
3 passé simple		10 passé antérieur	
poursuivis	**poursuivîmes**	**eus poursuivi**	**eûmes poursuivi**
poursuivis	**poursuivîtes**	**eus poursuivi**	**eûtes poursuivi**
poursuivit	**poursuivirent**	**eut poursuivi**	**eurent poursuivi**
4 futur		11 futur antérieur	
poursuivrai	**poursuivrons**	**aurai poursuivi**	**aurons poursuivi**
poursuivras	**poursuivrez**	**auras poursuivi**	**aurez poursuivi**
poursuivra	**poursuivront**	**aura poursuivi**	**auront poursuivi**
5 conditionnel		12 conditionnel passé	
poursuivrais	**poursuivrions**	**aurais poursuivi**	**aurions poursuivi**
poursuivrais	**poursuivriez**	**aurais poursuivi**	**auriez poursuivi**
poursuivrait	**poursuivraient**	**aurait poursuivi**	**auraient poursuivi**
6 présent du subjonctif		13 passé du subjonctif	
poursuive	**poursuivions**	**aie poursuivi**	**ayons poursuivi**
poursuives	**poursuiviez**	**aies poursuivi**	**ayez poursuivi**
poursuive	**poursuivent**	**ait poursuivi**	**aient poursuivi**
7 imparfait du subjonctif		14 plus-que-parfait du subjonctif	
poursuivisse	**poursuivissions**	**eusse poursuivi**	**eussions poursuivi**
poursuivisses	**poursuivissiez**	**eusses poursuivi**	**eussiez poursuivi**
poursuivît	**poursuivissent**	**eût poursuivi**	**eussent poursuivi**

Impératif
poursuis
poursuivons
poursuivez

Words and expressions related to this verb

se poursuivre to pursue each other
poursuivre qqn en justice to sue someone, to prosecute
poursuivre ses études to carry on one's studies
une poursuite pursuit
à la poursuite de in pursuit of
poursuivre son chemin to continue on one's way

See also **suivre.**

Can't remember the French verb you need? Check the back pages of this book for the English-French verb index!

pousser (353) — Part. pr. poussant — Part. passé poussé

to push, to grow

Regular **-er** verb

The Seven Simple Tenses		The Seven Compound Tenses	
Singular	Plural	Singular	Plural
1 présent de l'indicatif		8 passé composé	
pousse	**poussons**	**ai poussé**	**avons poussé**
pousses	**poussez**	**as poussé**	**avez poussé**
pousse	**poussent**	**a poussé**	**ont poussé**
2 imparfait de l'indicatif		9 plus-que-parfait de l'indicatif	
poussais	**poussions**	**avais poussé**	**avions poussé**
poussais	**poussiez**	**avais poussé**	**aviez poussé**
poussait	**poussaient**	**avait poussé**	**avaient poussé**
3 passé simple		10 passé antérieur	
poussai	**poussâmes**	**eus poussé**	**eûmes poussé**
poussas	**poussâtes**	**eus poussé**	**eûtes poussé**
poussa	**poussèrent**	**eut poussé**	**eurent poussé**
4 futur		11 futur antérieur	
pousserai	**pousserons**	**aurai poussé**	**aurons poussé**
pousseras	**pousserez**	**auras poussé**	**aurez poussé**
poussera	**pousseront**	**aura poussé**	**auront poussé**
5 conditionnel		12 conditionnel passé	
pousserais	**pousserions**	**aurais poussé**	**aurions poussé**
pousserais	**pousseriez**	**aurais poussé**	**auriez poussé**
pousserait	**pousseraient**	**aurait poussé**	**auraient poussé**
6 présent du subjonctif		13 passé du subjonctif	
pousse	**poussions**	**aie poussé**	**ayons poussé**
pousses	**poussiez**	**aies poussé**	**ayez poussé**
pousse	**poussent**	**ait poussé**	**aient poussé**
7 imparfait du subjonctif		14 plus-que-parfait du subjonctif	
poussasse	**poussassions**	**eusse poussé**	**eussions poussé**
poussasses	**poussassiez**	**eusses poussé**	**eussiez poussé**
poussât	**poussassent**	**eût poussé**	**eussent poussé**

Impératif
pousse
poussons
poussez

Common idiomatic expressions using this verb

une poussée a push, a thrust

pousser qqn à faire qqch to egg someone on to do something

Robert pousse une barbe. Robert is growing a beard.

pousser un cri to utter a cry; **pousser un soupir** to heave a sigh

repousser to repulse, to drive back; to grow in again, to grow back in

se pousser to push oneself; to push each other

un pousse-pousse rickshaw

pousser qqn à bout to corner someone

une poussette a stroller

Don't forget to study the section on defective and impersonal verbs. It's right after this main list.

Irregular verb

to be able, can

The Seven Simple Tenses		The Seven Compound Tenses	
Singular	Plural	Singular	Plural
1 présent de l'indicatif		8 passé composé	
peux *or* puis	**pouvons**	**ai pu**	**avons pu**
peux	**pouvez**	**as pu**	**avez pu**
peut	**peuvent**	**a pu**	**ont pu**
2 imparfait de l'indicatif		9 plus-que-parfait de l'indicatif	
pouvais	**pouvions**	**avais pu**	**avions pu**
pouvais	**pouviez**	**avais pu**	**aviez pu**
pouvait	**pouvaient**	**avait pu**	**avaient pu**
3 passé simple		10 passé antérieur	
pus	**pûmes**	**eus pu**	**eûmes pu**
pus	**pûtes**	**eus pu**	**eûtes pu**
put	**purent**	**eut pu**	**eurent pu**
4 futur		11 futur antérieur	
pourrai	**pourrons**	**aurai pu**	**aurons pu**
pourras	**pourrez**	**auras pu**	**aurez pu**
pourra	**pourront**	**aura pu**	**auront pu**
5 conditionnel		12 conditionnel passé	
pourrais	**pourrions**	**aurais pu**	**aurions pu**
pourrais	**pourriez**	**aurais pu**	**auriez pu**
pourrait	**pourraient**	**aurait pu**	**auraient pu**
6 présent du subjonctif		13 passé du subjonctif	
puisse	**puissions**	**aie pu**	**ayons pu**
puisses	**puissiez**	**aies pu**	**ayez pu**
puisse	**puissent**	**ait pu**	**aient pu**
7 imparfait du subjonctif		14 plus-que-parfait du subjonctif	
pusse	**pussions**	**eusse pu**	**eussions pu**
pusses	**pussiez**	**eusses pu**	**eussiez pu**
pût	**pussent**	**eût pu**	**eussent pu**

Impératif
[not in use]

AN ESSENTIAL 55 VERB

Pouvoir

Pouvoir is a very important verb for a beginning French student because it is useful in many everyday situations and idiomatic expressions.

Sentences using pouvoir

Que me voulez-vous? What do you want from me?

Je n'y peux rien. I can't help it; I can't do anything about it.

Puis-je entrer?/Est-ce que je peux entrer? May I come in?

Cela se peut. That may be./That's possible.

Sauve qui peut! Run for your life!

Vouloir, c'est pouvoir. Where there's a will, there's a way.

Pouvez-vous me dire où se trouvent les toilettes? Can you tell me where the restrooms are located?

Je ne peux pas vous entendre. Parlez plus fort, s'il vous plaît. I cannot hear you. Please speak more loudly.

Où est-ce que je peux envoyer un courriel? Where can I send an e-mail?

Words and expressions related to this verb

le pouvoir **power**

la puissance **power**

si l'on peut dire **if one may say so**

se pouvoir **to be possible**

la course au pouvoir **the race for power**

le sauve-qui-peut **panic**

avoir du pouvoir sur soi-même **to have self-control**

n'y pouvoir rien **not to be able to do anything about it**

Do you need more drills? Have fun with the *501 French Verbs* CD-ROM!

Irregular verb

to predict, to foretell

The Seven Simple Tenses		The Seven Compound Tenses	
Singular	Plural	Singular	Plural
1 présent de l'indicatif		8 passé composé	
prédis	**prédisons**	**ai prédit**	**avons prédit**
prédis	**prédisez**	**as prédit**	**avez prédit**
prédit	**prédisent**	**a prédit**	**ont prédit**
2 imparfait de l'indicatif		9 plus-que-parfait de l'indicatif	
prédisais	**prédisions**	**avais prédit**	**avions prédit**
prédisais	**prédisiez**	**avais prédit**	**aviez prédit**
prédisait	**prédisaient**	**avait prédit**	**avaient prédit**
3 passé simple		10 passé antérieur	
prédis	**prédîmes**	**eus prédit**	**eûmes prédit**
prédis	**prédîtes**	**eus prédit**	**eûtes prédit**
prédit	**prédirent**	**eut prédit**	**eurent prédit**
4 futur		11 futur antérieur	
prédirai	**prédirons**	**aurai prédit**	**aurons prédit**
prédiras	**prédirez**	**auras prédit**	**aurez prédit**
prédira	**prédiront**	**aura prédit**	**auront prédit**
5 conditionnel		12 conditionnel passé	
prédirais	**prédirions**	**aurais prédit**	**aurions prédit**
prédirais	**prédiriez**	**aurais prédit**	**auriez prédit**
prédirait	**prédiraient**	**aurait prédit**	**auraient prédit**
6 présent du subjonctif		13 passé du subjonctif	
prédise	**prédisions**	**aie prédit**	**ayons prédit**
prédises	**prédisiez**	**aies prédit**	**ayez prédit**
prédise	**prédisent**	**ait prédit**	**aient prédit**
7 imparfait du subjonctif		14 plus-que-parfait du subjonctif	
prédisse	**prédissions**	**eusse prédit**	**eussions prédit**
prédisses	**prédissiez**	**eusses prédit**	**eussiez prédit**
prédît	**prédissent**	**eût prédit**	**eussent prédit**

Impératif
prédis
prédisons
prédisez

Words related to this verb
une prédiction prediction
prédire l'avenir to predict the future

See also **contredire, dire, interdire, maudire,** and **médire.**

Compare (**vous**) **prédisez** with (**vous**) **dites** of **dire** on page 290.

Can't find the verb you're looking for? Check the back pages of this book for a list of over 2,600 additional verbs!

préférer (356) — Part. pr. préférant — Part. passé préféré

to prefer

Regular **-er** verb endings; spelling change: **é** changes to **è** before syllable with mute **e**

The Seven Simple Tenses

Singular	Plural
1 présent de l'indicatif	
préfère	**préférons**
préfères	**préférez**
préfère	**préfèrent**
2 imparfait de l'indicatif	
préférais	**préférions**
préférais	**préfériez**
préférait	**préféraient**
3 passé simple	
préférai	**préférâmes**
préféras	**préférâtes**
préféra	**préférèrent**
4 futur	
préférerai	**préférerons**
préféreras	**préférerez**
préférera	**préféreront**
5 conditionnel	
préférerais	**préférerions**
préférerais	**préféreriez**
préférerait	**préféreraient**
6 présent du subjonctif	
préfère	**préférions**
préfères	**préfériez**
préfère	**préfèrent**
7 imparfait du subjonctif	
préférasse	**préférassions**
préférasses	**préférassiez**
préférât	**préférassent**

The Seven Compound Tenses

Singular	Plural
8 passé composé	
ai préféré	**avons préféré**
as préféré	**avez préféré**
a préféré	**ont préféré**
9 plus-que-parfait de l'indicatif	
avais préféré	**avions préféré**
avais préféré	**aviez préféré**
avait préféré	**avaient préféré**
10 passé antérieur	
eus préféré	**eûmes préféré**
eus préféré	**eûtes préféré**
eut préféré	**eurent préféré**
11 futur antérieur	
aurai préféré	**aurons préféré**
auras préféré	**aurez préféré**
aura préféré	**auront préféré**
12 conditionnel passé	
aurais préféré	**aurions préféré**
aurais préféré	**auriez préféré**
aurait préféré	**auraient préféré**
13 passé du subjonctif	
aie préféré	**ayons préféré**
aies préféré	**ayez préféré**
ait préféré	**aient préféré**
14 plus-que-parfait du subjonctif	
eusse préféré	**eussions préféré**
eusses préféré	**eussiez préféré**
eût préféré	**eussent préféré**

Impératif
préfère
préférons
préférez

Sentences using this verb and words related to it

—Qu'est-ce que vous préférez faire ce soir?
—Je préfère aller voir un bon film. Et vous?
—Je préfère rester à la maison. Ne préféreriez-vous pas rester ici avec moi?

Mon père préfère monter l'escalier. Il n'aime pas les ascenseurs! My father prefers to walk up the stairs. He doesn't like elevators!

une préférence a preference
préférentiel, préférentielle preferential
préférable preferable
préférablement preferably
de préférence à in preference to
Je n'ai pas de préférence. I have no preference.
par ordre de préférence in order of preference

Don't miss orthographically changing verbs on pages 32–34.

Irregular verb

to take

The Seven Simple Tenses		The Seven Compound Tenses	
Singular	Plural	Singular	Plural
1 présent de l'indicatif		8 passé composé	
prends	**prenons**	**ai pris**	**avons pris**
prends	**prenez**	**as pris**	**avez pris**
prend	**prennent**	**a pris**	**ont pris**
2 imparfait de l'indicatif		9 plus-que-parfait de l'indicatif	
prenais	**prenions**	**avais pris**	**avions pris**
prenais	**preniez**	**avais pris**	**aviez pris**
prenait	**prenaient**	**avait pris**	**avaient pris**
3 passé simple		10 passé antérieur	
pris	**prîmes**	**eus pris**	**eûmes pris**
pris	**prîtes**	**eus pris**	**eûtes pris**
prit	**prirent**	**eut pris**	**eurent pris**
4 futur		11 futur antérieur	
prendrai	**prendrons**	**aurai pris**	**aurons pris**
prendras	**prendrez**	**auras pris**	**aurez pris**
prendra	**prendront**	**aura pris**	**auront pris**
5 conditionnel		12 conditionnel passé	
prendrais	**prendrions**	**aurais pris**	**aurions pris**
prendrais	**prendriez**	**aurais pris**	**auriez pris**
prendrait	**prendraient**	**aurait pris**	**auraient pris**
6 présent du subjonctif		13 passé du subjonctif	
prenne	**prenions**	**aie pris**	**ayons pris**
prennes	**preniez**	**aies pris**	**ayez pris**
prenne	**prennent**	**ait pris**	**aient pris**
7 imparfait du subjonctif		14 plus-que-parfait du subjonctif	
prisse	**prissions**	**eusse pris**	**eussions pris**
prisses	**prissiez**	**eusses pris**	**eussiez pris**
prît	**prissent**	**eût pris**	**eussent pris**

Impératif
prends
prenons
prenez

The subject pronouns are found on page 103.

AN ESSENTIAL 55 VERB

Prendre

Prendre is a very useful French verb because, although it is irregular, many verbs are conjugated like it. It is used in numerous everyday situations and idiomatic expressions.

Sentences using prendre

Qu'est-ce qui vous prend? What's got into you?

J'ai pris assez de soleil. Je vais nager maintenant. I've had enough sun. I'm going to swim now.

Prenez garde de ne pas tomber. Take care not to fall.

Prenez garde de tomber. Avoid falling.

C'est à prendre ou à laisser. Take it or leave it.

Je ne sais comment m'y prendre. I don't know how to go about it.

—Qui a pris les fleurs qui étaient sur la table?
—C'est moi qui les ai prises.

—Who took the flowers that were on the table?
—I took them. (It is I who took them.)

Tel est pris qui croyait prendre. (La Fontaine, "Le Rat et l'Huître") He who believed he would take is taken. (That is, one can be hurt by one's own ignorance. La Fontaine, "The Rat and the Oyster")

Words and expressions related to this verb

à tout prendre **on the whole, all in all**

un preneur, une preneuse **taker, purchaser**

s'y prendre **to go about it, to handle it, to set about it**

prendre à témoin **to call to witness**

la prise **seize, capture; La Prise de la Bastille The Storming of the Bastille (July 14, 1789)**

prendre un bain **to take a bath**

prendre des photos **to take pictures**

prendre un bain de soleil **to sunbathe**

prendre garde de + inf. **to avoid + pres. part., to take care not + inf.**

prendre le parti de + inf. **to decide + inf.**

prendre un billet **to buy a ticket**

If you can conjugate **prendre** you can also conjugate the following verbs:

apprendre **to learn**

comprendre **to understand**

se déprendre de qqn/qqch **to give up someone/something (Use être as auxiliary)**

désapprendre **to unlearn, forget**

entreprendre **to undertake**

s'éprendre de qqn **to fall for someone (Use être as auxiliary)**

se méprendre **to be mistaken (Use être as auxiliary)**

réapprendre **to relearn, learn again**

Regular **-er** verb

to prepare

The Seven Simple Tenses		The Seven Compound Tenses	
Singular	Plural	Singular	Plural
1 présent de l'indicatif		8 passé composé	
prépare	**préparons**	**ai préparé**	**avons préparé**
prépares	**préparez**	**as préparé**	**avez préparé**
prépare	**préparent**	**a préparé**	**ont préparé**
2 imparfait de l'indicatif		9 plus-que-parfait de l'indicatif	
préparais	**préparions**	**avais préparé**	**avions préparé**
préparais	**prépariez**	**avais préparé**	**aviez préparé**
préparait	**préparaient**	**avait préparé**	**avaient préparé**
3 passé simple		10 passé antérieur	
préparai	**préparâmes**	**eus préparé**	**eûmes préparé**
préparas	**préparâtes**	**eus préparé**	**eûtes préparé**
prépara	**préparèrent**	**eut préparé**	**eurent préparé**
4 futur		11 futur antérieur	
préparerai	**préparerons**	**aurai préparé**	**aurons préparé**
prépareras	**préparerez**	**auras préparé**	**aurez préparé**
préparera	**prépareront**	**aura préparé**	**auront préparé**
5 conditionnel		12 conditionnel passé	
préparerais	**préparerions**	**aurais préparé**	**aurions préparé**
préparerais	**prépareriez**	**aurais préparé**	**auriez préparé**
préparerait	**prépareraient**	**aurait préparé**	**auraient préparé**
6 présent du subjonctif		13 passé du subjonctif	
prépare	**préparions**	**aie préparé**	**ayons préparé**
prépares	**prépariez**	**aies préparé**	**ayez préparé**
prépare	**préparent**	**ait préparé**	**aient préparé**
7 imparfait du subjonctif		14 plus-que-parfait du subjonctif	
préparasse	**préparassions**	**eusse préparé**	**eussions préparé**
préparasses	**préparassiez**	**eusses préparé**	**eussiez préparé**
préparât	**préparassent**	**eût préparé**	**eussent préparé**

Impératif
prépare
préparons
préparez

Sentences using this verb and words related to it

Si Albert avait préparé sa leçon, il aurait reçu une bonne note. Il prépare toujours ses leçons, mais, cette fois, il ne les a pas préparées.

la préparation preparation
les préparatifs *m.* preparations
préparatoire preparatory
se préparer to prepare oneself
préparer un examen to study for an exam

Get acquainted with what preposition goes with what verb. See *Verbs with prepositions* in the Appendixes.

The subject pronouns are found on page 103.

présenter (359) — Part. pr. présentant — Part. passé présenté

to present, to introduce

Regular **-er** verb

The Seven Simple Tenses		The Seven Compound Tenses	
Singular	Plural	Singular	Plural
1 présent de l'indicatif		8 passé composé	
présente	**présentons**	**ai présenté**	**avons présenté**
présentes	**présentez**	**as présenté**	**avez présenté**
présente	**présentent**	**a présenté**	**ont présenté**
2 imparfait de l'indicatif		9 plus-que-parfait de l'indicatif	
présentais	**présentions**	**avais présenté**	**avions présenté**
présentais	**présentiez**	**avais présenté**	**aviez présenté**
présentait	**présentaient**	**avait présenté**	**avaient présenté**
3 passé simple		10 passé antérieur	
présentai	**présentâmes**	**eus présenté**	**eûmes présenté**
présentas	**présentâtes**	**eus présenté**	**eûtes présenté**
présenta	**présentèrent**	**eut présenté**	**eurent présenté**
4 futur		11 futur antérieur	
présenterai	**présenterons**	**aurai présenté**	**aurons présenté**
présenteras	**présenterez**	**auras présenté**	**aurez présenté**
présentera	**présenteront**	**aura présenté**	**auront présenté**
5 conditionnel		12 conditionnel passé	
présenterais	**présenterions**	**aurais présenté**	**aurions présenté**
présenterais	**présenteriez**	**aurais présenté**	**auriez présenté**
présenterait	**présenteraient**	**aurait présenté**	**auraient présenté**
6 présent du subjonctif		13 passé du subjonctif	
présente	**présentions**	**aie présenté**	**ayons présenté**
présentes	**présentiez**	**aies présenté**	**ayez présenté**
présente	**présentent**	**ait présenté**	**aient présenté**
7 imparfait du subjonctif		14 plus-que-parfait du subjonctif	
présentasse	**présentassions**	**eusse présenté**	**eussions présenté**
présentasses	**présentassiez**	**eusses présenté**	**eussiez présenté**
présentât	**présentassent**	**eût présenté**	**eussent présenté**

Impératif
présente
présentons
présentez

Common idiomatic expressions using this verb

présenter qqn à qqn to introduce someone to someone
Je vous présente à mon professeur de français. May I introduce you to my French teacher?
un présentateur, une présentatrice newscaster, announcer
se présenter to introduce oneself
Permettez-moi de me présenter. Allow me to introduce myself.
présenter bien to make a good impression
présenter mal to make a bad impression
un présentoir display

Do you need more drills? Have fun with the *501 French Verbs* CD-ROM!

Regular **-er** verb

to press, to squeeze

The Seven Simple Tenses		The Seven Compound Tenses	
Singular	Plural	Singular	Plural
1 présent de l'indicatif		8 passé composé	
presse	**pressons**	**ai pressé**	**avons pressé**
presses	**pressez**	**as pressé**	**avez pressé**
presse	**pressent**	**a pressé**	**ont pressé**
2 imparfait de l'indicatif		9 plus-que-parfait de l'indicatif	
pressais	**pressions**	**avais pressé**	**avions pressé**
pressais	**pressiez**	**avais pressé**	**aviez pressé**
pressait	**pressaient**	**avait pressé**	**avaient pressé**
3 passé simple		10 passé antérieur	
pressai	**pressâmes**	**eus pressé**	**eûmes pressé**
pressas	**pressâtes**	**eus pressé**	**eûtes pressé**
pressa	**pressèrent**	**eut pressé**	**eurent pressé**
4 futur		11 futur antérieur	
presserai	**presserons**	**aurai pressé**	**aurons pressé**
presseras	**presserez**	**auras pressé**	**aurez pressé**
pressera	**presseront**	**aura pressé**	**auront pressé**
5 conditionnel		12 conditionnel passé	
presserais	**presserions**	**aurais pressé**	**aurions pressé**
presserais	**presseriez**	**aurais pressé**	**auriez pressé**
presserait	**presseraient**	**aurait pressé**	**auraient pressé**
6 présent du subjonctif		13 passé du subjonctif	
presse	**pressions**	**aie pressé**	**ayons pressé**
presses	**pressiez**	**aies pressé**	**ayez pressé**
presse	**pressent**	**ait pressé**	**aient pressé**
7 imparfait du subjonctif		14 plus-que-parfait du subjonctif	
pressasse	**pressassions**	**eusse pressé**	**eussions pressé**
pressasses	**pressassiez**	**eusses pressé**	**eussiez pressé**
pressât	**pressassent**	**eût pressé**	**eussent pressé**

Impératif
presse
pressons
pressez

Words and expressions related to this verb

presser qqn to hurry someone
la pression pressure
un presse-bouton push button (**presse-bouton** *adj. pl.*)
un presse-papiers paperweight (**des presse-papiers**)
un pressoir press
un presseur, une presseuse press worker
presser qqn de se décider to urge someone to make a decision
être sous pression to be under pressure
un presse-citron lemon squeezer (**des presse-citrons**)
faire le coup du presse-citron à qqn to put the squeeze on someone
le pressing steam pressing (dry cleaner's)

Get acquainted with what preposition goes with what verb. See *Verbs with prepositions* in the Appendixes.

se presser (361) — Part. pr. se pressant — Part. passé pressé(e)(s)

to be in a hurry, to make haste, to rush, to crowd

Reflexive regular **-er** verb

The Seven Simple Tenses

Singular	Plural
1 présent de l'indicatif	
me presse	**nous pressons**
te presses	**vous pressez**
se presse	**se pressent**
2 imparfait de l'indicatif	
me pressais	**nous pressions**
te pressais	**vous pressiez**
se pressait	**se pressaient**
3 passé simple	
me pressai	**nous pressâmes**
te pressas	**vous pressâtes**
se pressa	**se pressèrent**
4 futur	
me presserai	**nous presserons**
te presseras	**vous presserez**
se pressera	**se presseront**
5 conditionnel	
me presserais	**nous presserions**
te presserais	**vous presseriez**
se presserait	**se presseraient**
6 présent du subjonctif	
me presse	**nous pressions**
te presses	**vous pressiez**
se presse	**se pressent**
7 imparfait du subjonctif	
me pressasse	**nous pressassions**
te pressasses	**vous pressassiez**
se pressât	**se pressassent**

The Seven Compound Tenses

Singular	Plural
8 passé composé	
me suis pressé(e)	**nous sommes pressé(e)s**
t'es pressé(e)	**vous êtes pressé(e)(s)**
s'est pressé(e)	**se sont pressé(e)s**
9 plus-que-parfait de l'indicatif	
m'étais pressé(e)	**nous étions pressé(e)s**
t'étais pressé(e)	**vous étiez pressé(e)(s)**
s'était pressé(e)	**s'étaient pressé(e)s**
10 passé antérieur	
me fus pressé(e)	**nous fûmes pressé(e)s**
te fus pressé(e)	**vous fûtes pressé(e)(s)**
se fut pressé(e)	**se furent pressé(e)s**
11 futur antérieur	
me serai pressé(e)	**nous serons pressé(e)s**
te seras pressé(e)	**vous serez pressé(e)(s)**
se sera pressé(e)	**se seront pressé(e)s**
12 conditionnel passé	
me serais pressé(e)	**nous serions pressé(e)s**
te serais pressé(e)	**vous seriez pressé(e)(s)**
se serait pressé(e)	**se seraient pressé(e)s**
13 passé du subjonctif	
me sois pressé(e)	**nous soyons pressé(e)s**
te sois pressé(e)	**vous soyez pressé(e)(s)**
se soit pressé(e)	**se soient pressé(e)s**
14 plus-que-parfait du subjonctif	
me fusse pressé(e)	**nous fussions pressé(e)s**
te fusses pressé(e)	**vous fussiez pressé(e)(s)**
se fût pressé(e)	**se fussent pressé(e)s**

Impératif

presse-toi; ne te presse pas
pressons-nous; ne nous pressons pas
pressez-vous; ne vous pressez pas

Words and expressions related to this verb

se presser contre qqn to press oneself against someone
se presser de faire qqch to hurry to do something
se presser en foule to press against each other in a crowd
presser to press, to squeeze
presser le pas to walk more quickly
presser qqn to urge someone, to hurry someone
une pression pressure
faire pression sur qqn to exert pressure on someone

Get acquainted with what preposition goes with what verb. See *Verbs with prepositions* in the Appendixes.

Regular **-re** verb

to pretend, to claim, to lay claim, to maintain

The Seven Simple Tenses		The Seven Compound Tenses	
Singular	Plural	Singular	Plural
1 présent de l'indicatif		8 passé composé	
prétends	**prétendons**	**ai prétendu**	**avons prétendu**
prétends	**prétendez**	**as prétendu**	**avez prétendu**
prétend	**prétendent**	**a prétendu**	**ont prétendu**
2 imparfait de l'indicatif		9 plus-que-parfait de l'indicatif	
prétendais	**prétendions**	**avais prétendu**	**avions prétendu**
prétendais	**prétendiez**	**avais prétendu**	**aviez prétendu**
prétendait	**prétendaient**	**avait prétendu**	**avaient prétendu**
3 passé simple		10 passé antérieur	
prétendis	**prétendîmes**	**eus prétendu**	**eûmes prétendu**
prétendis	**prétendîtes**	**eus prétendu**	**eûtes prétendu**
prétendit	**prétendirent**	**eut prétendu**	**eurent prétendu**
4 futur		11 futur antérieur	
prétendrai	**prétendrons**	**aurai prétendu**	**aurons prétendu**
prétendras	**prétendrez**	**auras prétendu**	**aurez prétendu**
prétendra	**prétendront**	**aura prétendu**	**auront prétendu**
5 conditionnel		12 conditionnel passé	
prétendrais	**prétendrions**	**aurais prétendu**	**aurions prétendu**
prétendrais	**prétendriez**	**aurais prétendu**	**auriez prétendu**
prétendrait	**prétendraient**	**aurait prétendu**	**auraient prétendu**
6 présent du subjonctif		13 passé du subjonctif	
prétende	**prétendions**	**aie prétendu**	**ayons prétendu**
prétendes	**prétendiez**	**aies prétendu**	**ayez prétendu**
prétende	**prétendent**	**ait prétendu**	**aient prétendu**
7 imparfait du subjonctif		14 plus-que-parfait du subjonctif	
prétendisse	**prétendissions**	**eusse prétendu**	**eussions prétendu**
prétendisses	**prétendissiez**	**eusses prétendu**	**eussiez prétendu**
prétendît	**prétendissent**	**eût prétendu**	**eussent prétendu**

Impératif
prétends
prétendons
prétendez

Words and expressions related to this verb

prétendre savoir qqch to claim to know something
prétentieux, prétentieuse pretentious
un prétendu spécialiste self-styled specialist
prétendre à to lay claim to
la prétention pretention
sans prétentions unpretentious, unpretentiously
prétentieusement pretentiously

How are you doing? Find out with the verb drills and tests with answers explained on pages 50–101.

prêter (363) — Part. pr. prêtant — Part. passé prêté

to lend

Regular **-er** verb

The Seven Simple Tenses		The Seven Compound Tenses	
Singular	Plural	Singular	Plural
1 présent de l'indicatif		8 passé composé	
prête	**prêtons**	**ai prêté**	**avons prêté**
prêtes	**prêtez**	**as prêté**	**avez prêté**
prête	**prêtent**	**a prêté**	**ont prêté**
2 imparfait de l'indicatif		9 plus-que-parfait de l'indicatif	
prêtais	**prêtions**	**avais prêté**	**avions prêté**
prêtais	**prêtiez**	**avais prêté**	**aviez prêté**
prêtait	**prêtaient**	**avait prêté**	**avaient prêté**
3 passé simple		10 passé antérieur	
prêtai	**prêtâmes**	**eus prêté**	**eûmes prêté**
prêtas	**prêtâtes**	**eus prêté**	**eûtes prêté**
prêta	**prêtèrent**	**eut prêté**	**eurent prêté**
4 futur		11 futur antérieur	
prêterai	**prêterons**	**aurai prêté**	**aurons prêté**
prêteras	**prêterez**	**auras prêté**	**aurez prêté**
prêtera	**prêteront**	**aura prêté**	**auront prêté**
5 conditionnel		12 conditionnel passé	
prêterais	**prêterions**	**aurais prêté**	**aurions prêté**
prêterais	**prêteriez**	**aurais prêté**	**auriez prêté**
prêterait	**prêteraient**	**aurait prêté**	**auraient prêté**
6 présent du subjonctif		13 passé du subjonctif	
prête	**prêtions**	**aie prêté**	**ayons prêté**
prêtes	**prêtiez**	**aies prêté**	**ayez prêté**
prête	**prêtent**	**ait prêté**	**aient prêté**
7 imparfait du subjonctif		14 plus-que-parfait du subjonctif	
prêtasse	**prêtassions**	**eusse prêté**	**eussions prêté**
prêtasses	**prêtassiez**	**eusses prêté**	**eussiez prêté**
prêtât	**prêtassent**	**eût prêté**	**eussent prêté**

Impératif
prête
prêtons
prêtez

Common idiomatic expressions using this verb

prêter à intérêt to lend at interest
prêter attention à qqn ou à qqch to pay attention to someone or something
un prêteur sur gages pawnbroker
prêter la main à qqn to give a helping hand to someone
prêter secours à qqn to go to someone's rescue (help)
apprêter to prepare, to get (something) ready
s'apprêter to get oneself ready
prêter l'oreille to listen, to lend an ear

NOTE: Don't confuse **prêter** with **emprunter** (to borrow).

Irregular verb

to warn, to forestall, to ward off

The Seven Simple Tenses		The Seven Compound Tenses	
Singular	Plural	Singular	Plural
1 présent de l'indicatif		8 passé composé	
préviens	**prévenons**	**ai prévenu**	**avons prévenu**
préviens	**prévenez**	**as prévenu**	**avez prévenu**
prévient	**préviennent**	**a prévenu**	**ont prévenu**
2 imparfait de l'indicatif		9 plus-que-parfait de l'indicatif	
prévenais	**prévenions**	**avais prévenu**	**avions prévenu**
prévenais	**préveniez**	**avais prévenu**	**aviez prévenu**
prévenait	**prévenaient**	**avait prévenu**	**avaient prévenu**
3 passé simple		10 passé antérieur	
prévins	**prévînmes**	**eus prévenu**	**eûmes prévenu**
prévins	**prévîntes**	**eus prévenu**	**eûtes prévenu**
prévint	**prévinrent**	**eut prévenu**	**eurent prévenu**
4 futur		11 futur antérieur	
préviendrai	**préviendrons**	**aurai prévenu**	**aurons prévenu**
préviendras	**préviendrez**	**auras prévenu**	**aurez prévenu**
préviendra	**préviendront**	**aura prévenu**	**auront prévenu**
5 conditionnel		12 conditionnel passé	
préviendrais	**préviendrions**	**aurais prévenu**	**aurions prévenu**
préviendrais	**préviendriez**	**aurais prévenu**	**auriez prévenu**
préviendrait	**préviendraient**	**aurait prévenu**	**auraient prévenu**
6 présent du subjonctif		13 passé du subjonctif	
prévienne	**prévenions**	**aie prévenu**	**ayons prévenu**
préviennes	**préveniez**	**aies prévenu**	**ayez prévenu**
prévienne	**préviennent**	**ait prévenu**	**aient prévenu**
7 imparfait du subjonctif		14 plus-que-parfait du subjonctif	
prévinsse	**prévinssions**	**eusse prévenu**	**eussions prévenu**
prévinsses	**prévinssiez**	**eusses prévenu**	**eussiez prévenu**
prévînt	**prévinssent**	**eût prévenu**	**eussent prévenu**

Impératif
préviens
prévenons
prévenez

Words and expressions related to this verb

Mieux vaut prévenir que guérir. Prevention is better than cure.
la prévenance considerateness, kindness
la prévention prevention
prévenant, prévenante considerate, kind, thoughtful
entourer qqn de prévenances to shower someone with kindness, attention

See also **convenir, devenir, revenir, se souvenir,** and **venir.**

Can't find the verb you're looking for? Check the back pages of this book for a list of over 2,600 additional verbs!

to foresee

Irregular verb

The Seven Simple Tenses		The Seven Compound Tenses	
Singular	Plural	Singular	Plural
1 présent de l'indicatif		8 passé composé	
prévois	**prévoyons**	**ai prévu**	**avons prévu**
prévois	**prévoyez**	**as prévu**	**avez prévu**
prévoit	**prévoient**	**a prévu**	**ont prévu**
2 imparfait de l'indicatif		9 plus-que-parfait de l'indicatif	
prévoyais	**prévoyions**	**avais prévu**	**avions prévu**
prévoyais	**prévoyiez**	**avais prévu**	**aviez prévu**
prévoyait	**prévoyaient**	**avait prévu**	**avaient prévu**
3 passé simple		10 passé antérieur	
prévis	**prévîmes**	**eus prévu**	**eûmes prévu**
prévis	**prévîtes**	**eus prévu**	**eûtes prévu**
prévit	**prévirent**	**eut prévu**	**eurent prévu**
4 futur		11 futur antérieur	
prévoirai	**prévoirons**	**aurai prévu**	**aurons prévu**
prévoiras	**prévoirez**	**auras prévu**	**aurez prévu**
prévoira	**prévoiront**	**aura prévu**	**auront prévu**
5 conditionnel		12 conditionnel passé	
prévoirais	**prévoirions**	**aurais prévu**	**aurions prévu**
prévoirais	**prévoiriez**	**aurais prévu**	**auriez prévu**
prévoirait	**prévoiraient**	**aurait prévu**	**auraient prévu**
6 présent du subjonctif		13 passé du subjonctif	
prévoie	**prévoyions**	**aie prévu**	**ayons prévu**
prévoies	**prévoyiez**	**aies prévu**	**ayez prévu**
prévoie	**prévoient**	**ait prévu**	**aient prévu**
7 imparfait du subjonctif		14 plus-que-parfait du subjonctif	
prévisse	**prévissions**	**eusse prévu**	**eussions prévu**
prévisses	**prévissiez**	**eusses prévu**	**eussiez prévu**
prévît	**prévissent**	**eût prévu**	**eussent prévu**

Impératif
prévois
prévoyons
prévoyez

Words and expressions related to this verb

la prévision forecast
en prévision de in anticipation of
prévisible foreseeable; **visible** visible
la prévoyance foresight
une avant-première preview
prévoir le temps to forecast the weather
les prévisions météorologiques weather forecasts
voir to see
prévoyant, prévoyante provident

See also **voir.**

Soak up some verbs used in weather expressions. There's a list in the Appendixes!

Regular **-er** verb

to pray, to supplicate, to entreat, to beg, to request

The Seven Simple Tenses		The Seven Compound Tenses	
Singular	Plural	Singular	Plural
1 présent de l'indicatif		8 passé composé	
prie	**prions**	**ai prié**	**avons prié**
pries	**priez**	**as prié**	**avez prié**
prie	**prient**	**a prié**	**ont prié**
2 imparfait de l'indicatif		9 plus-que-parfait de l'indicatif	
priais	**priions**	**avais prié**	**avions prié**
priais	**priiez**	**avais prié**	**aviez prié**
priait	**priaient**	**avait prié**	**avaient prié**
3 passé simple		10 passé antérieur	
priai	**priâmes**	**eus prié**	**eûmes prié**
prias	**priâtes**	**eus prié**	**eûtes prié**
pria	**prièrent**	**eut prié**	**eurent prié**
4 futur		11 futur antérieur	
prierai	**prierons**	**aurai prié**	**aurons prié**
prieras	**prierez**	**auras prié**	**aurez prié**
priera	**prieront**	**aura prié**	**auront prié**
5 conditionnel		12 conditionnel passé	
prierais	**prierions**	**aurais prié**	**aurions prié**
prierais	**prieriez**	**aurais prié**	**auriez prié**
prierait	**prieraient**	**aurait prié**	**auraient prié**
6 présent du subjonctif		13 passé du subjonctif	
prie	**priions**	**aie prié**	**ayons prié**
pries	**priiez**	**aies prié**	**ayez prié**
prie	**prient**	**ait prié**	**aient prié**
7 imparfait du subjonctif		14 plus-que-parfait du subjonctif	
priasse	**priassions**	**eusse prié**	**eussions prié**
priasses	**priassiez**	**eusses prié**	**eussiez prié**
priât	**priassent**	**eût prié**	**eussent prié**

Impératif
prie
prions
priez

Words and expressions related to this verb

prier qqn de faire qqch to beg (entreat, request) someone to do something

Je vous en prie! You're welcome! I beg of you!

On vous prie de + inf. You are requested + inf.

prier qqn à faire qqch to invite someone to do something

une prière prayer; **Prière d'entrer sans frapper.** Please enter without knocking.

Prière de ne pas fumer. You are requested not to smoke.

Puis-je entrer? May I come in?—**Je vous en prie!** Please do! (I beg you to do so)

vouloir se faire prier to desire to be urged; **Madame Duchemin veut toujours se faire prier.** Mrs. Duchemin always wants to be urged.

sans se faire prier willingly

The subject pronouns are found on page 103.

to produce

Irregular verb

The Seven Simple Tenses		The Seven Compound Tenses	
Singular	Plural	Singular	Plural
1 présent de l'indicatif		8 passé composé	
produis	**produisons**	**ai produit**	**avons produit**
produis	**produisez**	**as produit**	**avez produit**
produit	**produisent**	**a produit**	**ont produit**
2 imparfait de l'indicatif		9 plus-que-parfait de l'indicatif	
produisais	**produisions**	**avais produit**	**avions produit**
produisais	**produisiez**	**avais produit**	**aviez produit**
produisait	**produisaient**	**avait produit**	**avaient produit**
3 passé simple		10 passé antérieur	
produisis	**produisîmes**	**eus produit**	**eûmes produit**
produisis	**produisîtes**	**eus produit**	**eûtes produit**
produisit	**produisirent**	**eut produit**	**eurent produit**
4 futur		11 futur antérieur	
produirai	**produirons**	**aurai produit**	**aurons produit**
produiras	**produirez**	**auras produit**	**aurez produit**
produira	**produiront**	**aura produit**	**auront produit**
5 conditionnel		12 conditionnel passé	
produirais	**produirions**	**aurais produit**	**aurions produit**
produirais	**produiriez**	**aurais produit**	**auriez produit**
produirait	**produiraient**	**aurait produit**	**auraient produit**
6 présent du subjonctif		13 passé du subjonctif	
produise	**produisions**	**aie produit**	**ayons produit**
produises	**produisiez**	**aies produit**	**ayez produit**
produise	**produisent**	**ait produit**	**aient produit**
7 imparfait du subjonctif		14 plus-que-parfait du subjonctif	
produisisse	**produisissions**	**eusse produit**	**eussions produit**
produisisses	**produisissiez**	**eusses produit**	**eussiez produit**
produisît	**produisissent**	**eût produit**	**eussent produit**

Impératif
produis
produisons
produisez

Words related to this verb

un produit product
la production production
productible producible
productif, productive productive
le produit national brut the gross national product
la productivité productivity
se produire to happen, to occur, to be brought about
les produits alimentaires food products
se produire en public to appear in public

See also **conduire, déduire, introduire, réduire, reproduire, séduire,** and **traduire.**

Get acquainted with what preposition goes with what verb. See *Verbs with prepositions* in the Appendixes.

Regular **-er** verb

to program, to plan

The Seven Simple Tenses		The Seven Compound Tenses	
Singular	Plural	Singular	Plural
1 présent de l'indicatif		8 passé composé	
programme	**programmons**	**ai programmé**	**avons programmé**
programmes	**programmez**	**as programmé**	**avez programmé**
programme	**programment**	**a programmé**	**ont programmé**
2 imparfait de l'indicatif		9 plus-que-parfait de l'indicatif	
programmais	**programmions**	**avais programmé**	**avions programmé**
programmais	**programmiez**	**avais programmé**	**aviez programmé**
programmait	**programmaient**	**avait programmé**	**avaient programmé**
3 passé simple		10 passé antérieur	
programmai	**programmâmes**	**eus programmé**	**eûmes programmé**
programmas	**programmâtes**	**eus programmé**	**eûtes programmé**
programma	**programmèrent**	**eut programmé**	**eurent programmé**
4 futur		11 futur antérieur	
programmerai	**programmerons**	**aurai programmé**	**aurons programmé**
programmeras	**programmerez**	**auras programmé**	**aurez programmé**
programmera	**programmeront**	**aura programmé**	**auront programmé**
5 conditionnel		12 conditionnel passé	
programmerais	**programmerions**	**aurais programmé**	**aurions programmé**
programmerais	**programmeriez**	**aurais programmé**	**auriez programmé**
programmerait	**programmeraient**	**aurait programmé**	**auraient programmé**
6 présent du subjonctif		13 passé du subjonctif	
programme	**programmions**	**aie programmé**	**ayons programmé**
programmes	**programmiez**	**aies programmé**	**ayez programmé**
programme	**programment**	**ait programmé**	**aient programmé**
7 imparfait du subjonctif		14 plus-que-parfait du subjonctif	
programmasse	**programmassions**	**eusse programmé**	**eussions programmé**
programmasses	**programmassiez**	**eusses programmé**	**eussiez programmé**
programmât	**programmassent**	**eût programmé**	**eussent programmé**

Impératif
programme
programmons
programmez

Sentences using this verb and words related to it

Marie est programmeuse. Elle a créé et programmé un site Web pour son entreprise.
Marie is a programmer. She created and programmed a web site for her company.

Qu'est-ce que tu as au programme demain? What's on your schedule for tomorrow?

Words and expressions related to this verb

un programmateur, une programmatrice programmer (radio and television)
un programmeur, une programmeuse programmer (computer)
un programme program, schedule, curriculum
la programmation programming
déprogrammer to remove from a program, schedule
programmable *adj.* programmable
programmé, programmée computerized
une émission radio, television broadcast
un logiciel software

Do you need more drills? Have fun with the *501 French Verbs* CD-ROM.

The subject pronouns are found on page 103.

se promener (369) Part. pr. se promenant Part. passé promené(e)(s)

to take a walk

Regular **-er** verb endings; spelling change: **e** changes to **è** before syllable with mute **e**

The Seven Simple Tenses		The Seven Compound Tenses	
Singular	Plural	Singular	Plural
1 présent de l'indicatif		8 passé composé	
me promène	**nous promenons**	**me suis promené(e)**	**nous sommes promené(e)s**
te promènes	**vous promenez**	**t'es promené(e)**	**vous êtes promené(e)(s)**
se promène	**se promènent**	**s'est promené(e)**	**se sont promené(e)s**
2 imparfait de l'indicatif		9 plus-que-parfait de l'indicatif	
me promenais	**nous promenions**	**m'étais promené(e)**	**nous étions promené(e)s**
te promenais	**vous promeniez**	**t'étais promené(e)**	**vous étiez promené(e)(s)**
se promenait	**se promenaient**	**s'était promené(e)**	**s'étaient promené(e)s**
3 passé simple		10 passé antérieur	
me promenai	**nous promenâmes**	**me fus promené(e)**	**nous fûmes promené(e)s**
te promenas	**vous promenâtes**	**te fus promené(e)**	**vous fûtes promené(e)(s)**
se promena	**se promenèrent**	**se fut promené(e)**	**se furent promené(e)s**
4 futur		11 futur antérieur	
me promènerai	**nous promènerons**	**me serai promené(e)**	**nous serons promené(e)s**
te promèneras	**vous promènerez**	**te seras promené(e)**	**vous serez promené(e)(s)**
se promènera	**se promèneront**	**se sera promené(e)**	**se seront promené(e)s**
5 conditionnel		12 conditionnel passé	
me promènerais	**nous promènerions**	**me serais promené(e)**	**nous serions promené(e)s**
te promènerais	**vous promèneriez**	**te serais promené(e)**	**vous seriez promené(e)(s)**
se promènerait	**se promèneraient**	**se serait promené(e)**	**se seraient promené(e)s**
6 présent du subjonctif		13 passé du subjonctif	
me promène	**nous promenions**	**me sois promené(e)**	**nous soyons promené(e)s**
te promènes	**vous promeniez**	**te sois promené(e)**	**vous soyez promené(e)(s)**
se promène	**se promènent**	**se soit promené(e)**	**se soient promené(e)s**
7 imparfait du subjonctif		14 plus-que-parfait du subjonctif	
me promenasse	**nous promenassions**	**me fusse promené(e)**	**nous fussions promené(e)s**
te promenasses	**vous promenassiez**	**te fusses promené(e)**	**vous fussiez promené(e)(s)**
se promenât	**se promenassent**	**se fût promené(e)**	**se fussent promené(e)s**

Impératif
promène-toi; ne te promène pas
promenons-nous; ne nous promenons pas
promenez-vous; ne vous promenez pas

Common idiomatic expressions using this verb

Je me promène tous les matins. I take a walk every morning.

Cette promenade est merveilleuse. This walk is marvelous.

Janine et Robert se sont promenés dans le parc. Janine and Robert took a walk in the park.

faire une promenade to take a walk

faire une promenade en voiture to go for a drive

promener son chien to take one's dog out for a walk

promener ses regards sur to cast one's eyes on, to look over

un promenoir indoor mall for walking, strolling

See also **amener, emmener,** and **mener.**

Irregular verb

to promise

The Seven Simple Tenses		The Seven Compound Tenses	
Singular	Plural	Singular	Plural
1 présent de l'indicatif		8 passé composé	
promets	**promettons**	**ai promis**	**avons promis**
promets	**promettez**	**as promis**	**avez promis**
promet	**promettent**	**a promis**	**ont promis**
2 imparfait de l'indicatif		9 plus-que-parfait de l'indicatif	
promettais	**promettions**	**avais promis**	**avions promis**
promettais	**promettiez**	**avais promis**	**aviez promis**
promettait	**promettaient**	**avait promis**	**avaient promis**
3 passé simple		10 passé antérieur	
promis	**promîmes**	**eus promis**	**eûmes promis**
promis	**promîtes**	**eus promis**	**eûtes promis**
promit	**promirent**	**eut promis**	**eurent promis**
4 futur		11 futur antérieur	
promettrai	**promettrons**	**aurai promis**	**aurons promis**
promettras	**promettrez**	**auras promis**	**aurez promis**
promettra	**promettront**	**aura promis**	**auront promis**
5 conditionnel		12 conditionnel passé	
promettrais	**promettrions**	**aurais promis**	**aurions promis**
promettrais	**promettriez**	**aurais promis**	**auriez promis**
promettrait	**promettraient**	**aurait promis**	**auraient promis**
6 présent du subjonctif		13 passé du subjonctif	
promette	**promettions**	**aie promis**	**ayons promis**
promettes	**promettiez**	**aies promis**	**ayez promis**
promette	**promettent**	**ait promis**	**aient promis**
7 imparfait du subjonctif		14 plus-que-parfait du subjonctif	
promisse	**promissions**	**eusse promis**	**eussions promis**
promisses	**promissiez**	**eusses promis**	**eussiez promis**
promît	**promissent**	**eût promis**	**eussent promis**

Impératif
promets
promettons
promettez

Common idiomatic expressions using this verb
promettre de faire qqch to promise to do something
une promesse promise
tenir sa promesse to keep one's promise
promettre à qqn de faire qqch to promise someone to do something
Ça promet! It looks promising!
se promettre to promise oneself
compromettre to compromise

See also **commettre, mettre, se mettre, omettre, permettre, remettre, soumettre,** and **transmettre.**

The subject pronouns are found on page 103.

prononcer (371) — Part. pr. prononçant — Part. passé prononcé

to pronounce, to declare

Regular **-er** verb endings; spelling change: **c** changes to **ç** before **a** or **o** to keep **s** sound

The Seven Simple Tenses

Singular	Plural
1 présent de l'indicatif	
prononce	**prononçons**
prononces	**prononcez**
prononce	**prononcent**
2 imparfait de l'indicatif	
prononçais	**prononcions**
prononçais	**prononciez**
prononçait	**prononçaient**
3 passé simple	
prononçai	**prononçâmes**
prononças	**prononçâtes**
prononça	**prononcèrent**
4 futur	
prononcerai	**prononcerons**
prononceras	**prononcerez**
prononcera	**prononceront**
5 conditionnel	
prononcerais	**prononcerions**
prononcerais	**prononceriez**
prononcerait	**prononceraient**
6 présent du subjonctif	
prononce	**prononcions**
prononces	**prononciez**
prononce	**prononcent**
7 imparfait du subjonctif	
prononçasse	**prononçassions**
prononçasses	**prononçassiez**
prononçât	**prononçassent**

The Seven Compound Tenses

Singular	Plural
8 passé composé	
ai prononcé	**avons prononcé**
as prononcé	**avez prononcé**
a prononcé	**ont prononcé**
9 plus-que-parfait de l'indicatif	
avais prononcé	**avions prononcé**
avais prononcé	**aviez prononcé**
avait prononcé	**avaient prononcé**
10 passé antérieur	
eus prononcé	**eûmes prononcé**
eus prononcé	**eûtes prononcé**
eut prononcé	**eurent prononcé**
11 futur antérieur	
aurai prononcé	**aurons prononcé**
auras prononcé	**aurez prononcé**
aura prononcé	**auront prononcé**
12 conditionnel passé	
aurais prononcé	**aurions prononcé**
aurais prononcé	**auriez prononcé**
aurait prononcé	**auraient prononcé**
13 passé du subjonctif	
aie prononcé	**ayons prononcé**
aies prononcé	**ayez prononcé**
ait prononcé	**aient prononcé**
14 plus-que-parfait du subjonctif	
eusse prononcé	**eussions prononcé**
eusses prononcé	**eussiez prononcé**
eût prononcé	**eussent prononcé**

Impératif
prononce
prononçons
prononcez

Words and expressions related to this verb

prononcer un discours to deliver a speech
la prononciation pronunciation
prononçable pronounceable
se prononcer pour to decide in favor of
énoncer to enunciate
annoncer to announce
dénoncer to denounce
se prononcer to declare, to be pronounced (as a word)
se prononcer contre to decide against

See also **annoncer.**

Don't miss orthographically changing verbs on pages 32–34.

Use the guide to French pronunciation. It's in the Appendixes!

Regular **-er** verb

to prove

The Seven Simple Tenses		The Seven Compound Tenses	
Singular	Plural	Singular	Plural
1 présent de l'indicatif		8 passé composé	
prouve	**prouvons**	**ai prouvé**	**avons prouvé**
prouves	**prouvez**	**as prouvé**	**avez prouvé**
prouve	**prouvent**	**a prouvé**	**ont prouvé**
2 imparfait de l'indicatif		9 plus-que-parfait de l'indicatif	
prouvais	**prouvions**	**avais prouvé**	**avions prouvé**
prouvais	**prouviez**	**avais prouvé**	**aviez prouvé**
prouvait	**prouvaient**	**avait prouvé**	**avaient prouvé**
3 passé simple		10 passé antérieur	
prouvai	**prouvâmes**	**eus prouvé**	**eûmes prouvé**
prouvas	**prouvâtes**	**eus prouvé**	**eûtes prouvé**
prouva	**prouvèrent**	**eut prouvé**	**eurent prouvé**
4 futur		11 futur antérieur	
prouverai	**prouverons**	**aurai prouvé**	**aurons prouvé**
prouveras	**prouverez**	**auras prouvé**	**aurez prouvé**
prouvera	**prouveront**	**aura prouvé**	**auront prouvé**
5 conditionnel		12 conditionnel passé	
prouverais	**prouverions**	**aurais prouvé**	**aurions prouvé**
prouverais	**prouveriez**	**aurais prouvé**	**auriez prouvé**
prouverait	**prouveraient**	**aurait prouvé**	**auraient prouvé**
6 présent du subjonctif		13 passé du subjonctif	
prouve	**prouvions**	**aie prouvé**	**ayons prouvé**
prouves	**prouviez**	**aies prouvé**	**ayez prouvé**
prouve	**prouvent**	**ait prouvé**	**aient prouvé**
7 imparfait du subjonctif		14 plus-que-parfait du subjonctif	
prouvasse	**prouvassions**	**eusse prouvé**	**eussions prouvé**
prouvasses	**prouvassiez**	**eusses prouvé**	**eussiez prouvé**
prouvât	**prouvassent**	**eût prouvé**	**eussent prouvé**

Impératif
prouve
prouvons
prouvez

Words and expressions related to this verb
une preuve proof
comme preuve by way of proof
prouvable provable
une épreuve test, proof
faire la preuve de qqch to prove something
éprouver to test, to try, to experience
éprouver de la sympathie pour to feel sympathy for
mettre à l'épreuve to put to the test
avoir la preuve de to have proof of
désapprouver to disapprove of

See also **approuver** and **éprouver.**

It's important that you be familiar with the Subjunctive. See pages 26–31.

to punish

Regular **-ir** verb

The Seven Simple Tenses		The Seven Compound Tenses	
Singular	Plural	Singular	Plural
1 présent de l'indicatif		8 passé composé	
punis	**punissons**	**ai puni**	**avons puni**
punis	**punissez**	**as puni**	**avez puni**
punit	**punissent**	**a puni**	**ont puni**
2 imparfait de l'indicatif		9 plus-que-parfait de l'indicatif	
punissais	**punissions**	**avais puni**	**avions puni**
punissais	**punissiez**	**avais puni**	**aviez puni**
punissait	**punissaient**	**avait puni**	**avaient puni**
3 passé simple		10 passé antérieur	
punis	**punîmes**	**eus puni**	**eûmes puni**
punis	**punîtes**	**eus puni**	**eûtes puni**
punit	**punirent**	**eut puni**	**eurent puni**
4 futur		11 futur antérieur	
punirai	**punirons**	**aurai puni**	**aurons puni**
puniras	**punirez**	**auras puni**	**aurez puni**
punira	**puniront**	**aura puni**	**auront puni**
5 conditionnel		12 conditionnel passé	
punirais	**punirions**	**aurais puni**	**aurions puni**
punirais	**puniriez**	**aurais puni**	**auriez puni**
punirait	**puniraient**	**aurait puni**	**auraient puni**
6 présent du subjonctif		13 passé du subjonctif	
punisse	**punissions**	**aie puni**	**ayons puni**
punisses	**punissiez**	**aies puni**	**ayez puni**
punisse	**punissent**	**ait puni**	**aient puni**
7 imparfait du subjonctif		14 plus-que-parfait du subjonctif	
punisse	**punissions**	**eusse puni**	**eussions puni**
punisses	**punissiez**	**eusses puni**	**eussiez puni**
punît	**punissent**	**eût puni**	**eussent puni**

Impératif
punis
punissons
punissez

Words and expressions related to this verb

punisseur, punisseuse punisher
punissable punishable
la punition punishment
punitif, punitive punitive
échapper à la punition to escape punishment
la peine capitale capital punishment
en punition as a punishment

Grammar putting you in a tense mood? Review the definitions of basic grammatical terms with examples on pages 35–49.

Regular **-er** verb

to leave

The Seven Simple Tenses		The Seven Compound Tenses	
Singular	Plural	Singular	Plural
1 présent de l'indicatif		8 passé composé	
quitte	**quittons**	**ai quitté**	**avons quitté**
quittes	**quittez**	**as quitté**	**avez quitté**
quitte	**quittent**	**a quitté**	**ont quitté**
2 imparfait de l'indicatif		9 plus-que-parfait de l'indicatif	
quittais	**quittions**	**avais quitté**	**avions quitté**
quittais	**quittiez**	**avais quitté**	**aviez quitté**
quittait	**quittaient**	**avait quitté**	**avaient quitté**
3 passé simple		10 passé antérieur	
quittai	**quittâmes**	**eus quitté**	**eûmes quitté**
quittas	**quittâtes**	**eus quitté**	**eûtes quitté**
quitta	**quittèrent**	**eut quitté**	**eurent quitté**
4 futur		11 futur antérieur	
quitterai	**quitterons**	**aurai quitté**	**aurons quitté**
quitteras	**quitterez**	**auras quitté**	**aurez quitté**
quittera	**quitteront**	**aura quitté**	**auront quitté**
5 conditionnel		12 conditionnel passé	
quitterais	**quitterions**	**aurais quitté**	**aurions quitté**
quitterais	**quitteriez**	**aurais quitté**	**auriez quitté**
quitterait	**quitteraient**	**aurait quitté**	**auraient quitté**
6 présent du subjonctif		13 passé du subjonctif	
quitte	**quittions**	**aie quitté**	**ayons quitté**
quittes	**quittiez**	**aies quitté**	**ayez quitté**
quitte	**quittent**	**ait quitté**	**aient quitté**
7 imparfait du subjonctif		14 plus-que-parfait du subjonctif	
quittasse	**quittassions**	**eusse quitté**	**eussions quitté**
quittasses	**quittassiez**	**eusses quitté**	**eussiez quitté**
quittât	**quittassent**	**eût quitté**	**eussent quitté**

Impératif
quitte
quittons
quittez

Q

Words and expressions related to this verb

une quittance acquittance, discharge
quitter son chapeau to take off one's hat
se quitter to separate, to leave each other
Ne quittez pas, s'il vous plaît! Hold the line, please! (on the phone)
être quitte to be free of an obligation
quitte ou double double or nothing
Elle a quitté son mari. She left her husband.
Avant quelle heure dois-je quitter la chambre? Before what time must I leave the room?
acquitter to acquit
s'acquitter de to fulfill
un acquittement acquittal, payment
Je vous ai payé la dette; maintenant nous sommes quittes! I paid you the debt; now we're even!
Il a quitté sa femme. He left his wife.

The subject pronouns are found on page 103.

raconter (375) — Part. pr. **racontant** — Part. passé **raconté**

to relate, to tell about, to tell (a story)

Regular **-er** verb

The Seven Simple Tenses		The Seven Compound Tenses	
Singular	Plural	Singular	Plural
1 présent de l'indicatif		8 passé composé	
raconte	**racontons**	**ai raconté**	**avons raconté**
racontes	**racontez**	**as raconté**	**avez raconté**
raconte	**racontent**	**a raconté**	**ont raconté**
2 imparfait de l'indicatif		9 plus-que-parfait de l'indicatif	
racontais	**racontions**	**avais raconté**	**avions raconté**
racontais	**racontiez**	**avais raconté**	**aviez raconté**
racontait	**racontaient**	**avait raconté**	**avaient raconté**
3 passé simple		10 passé antérieur	
racontai	**racontâmes**	**eus raconté**	**eûmes raconté**
racontas	**racontâtes**	**eus raconté**	**eûtes raconté**
raconta	**racontèrent**	**eut raconté**	**eurent raconté**
4 futur		11 futur antérieur	
raconterai	**raconterons**	**aurai raconté**	**aurons raconté**
raconteras	**raconterez**	**auras raconté**	**aurez raconté**
racontera	**raconteront**	**aura raconté**	**auront raconté**
5 conditionnel		12 conditionnel passé	
raconterais	**raconterions**	**aurais raconté**	**aurions raconté**
raconterais	**raconteriez**	**aurais raconté**	**auriez raconté**
raconterait	**raconteraient**	**aurait raconté**	**auraient raconté**
6 présent du subjonctif		13 passé du subjonctif	
raconte	**racontions**	**aie raconté**	**ayons raconté**
racontes	**racontiez**	**aies raconté**	**ayez raconté**
raconte	**racontent**	**ait raconté**	**aient raconté**
7 imparfait du subjonctif		14 plus-que-parfait du subjonctif	
racontasse	**racontassions**	**eusse raconté**	**eussions raconté**
racontasses	**racontassiez**	**eusses raconté**	**eussiez raconté**
racontât	**racontassent**	**eût raconté**	**eussent raconté**

Impératif
raconte
racontons
racontez

Sentences using this verb and words related to it

Mon professeur de français aime nous raconter des anecdotes en français dans la classe de français. C'est un bon raconteur.

un raconteur, une raconteuse storyteller
Qu'est-ce que vous racontez? What are you talking about?

See also **conter.**

Can't find the verb you're looking for? Check the back pages of this book for a list of over 2,600 additional verbs!

Regular **-er** verb endings; spelling change: retain the **ge** before **a** or **o** to keep the soft **g** sound of the verb

to set (put) in order, to tidy up

The Seven Simple Tenses		The Seven Compound Tenses	
Singular	Plural	Singular	Plural
1 présent de l'indicatif		8 passé composé	
range	**rangeons**	**ai rangé**	**avons rangé**
ranges	**rangez**	**as rangé**	**avez rangé**
range	**rangent**	**a rangé**	**ont rangé**
2 imparfait de l'indicatif		9 plus-que-parfait de l'indicatif	
rangeais	**rangions**	**avais rangé**	**avions rangé**
rangeais	**rangiez**	**avais rangé**	**aviez rangé**
rangeait	**rangeaient**	**avait rangé**	**avaient rangé**
3 passé simple		10 passé antérieur	
rangeai	**rangeâmes**	**eus rangé**	**eûmes rangé**
rangeas	**rangeâtes**	**eus rangé**	**eûtes rangé**
rangea	**rangèrent**	**eut rangé**	**eurent rangé**
4 futur		11 futur antérieur	
rangerai	**rangerons**	**aurai rangé**	**aurons rangé**
rangeras	**rangerez**	**auras rangé**	**aurez rangé**
rangera	**rangeront**	**aura rangé**	**auront rangé**
5 conditionnel		12 conditionnel passé	
rangerais	**rangerions**	**aurais rangé**	**aurions rangé**
rangerais	**rangeriez**	**aurais rangé**	**auriez rangé**
rangerait	**rangeraient**	**aurait rangé**	**auraient rangé**
6 présent du subjonctif		13 passé du subjonctif	
range	**rangions**	**aie rangé**	**ayons rangé**
ranges	**rangiez**	**aies rangé**	**ayez rangé**
range	**rangent**	**ait rangé**	**aient rangé**
7 imparfait du subjonctif		14 plus-que-parfait du subjonctif	
rangeasse	**rangeassions**	**eusse rangé**	**eussions rangé**
rangeasses	**rangeassiez**	**eusses rangé**	**eussiez rangé**
rangeât	**rangeassent**	**eût rangé**	**eussent rangé**

Impératif
range
rangeons
rangez

R

Words and expressions related to this verb

un rang row; rank
sortir du rang to rise from the ranks
une rangée d'arbres a line of trees
déranger to disturb
se déranger to inconvenience oneself
de premier rang first-rate
se mettre sur les rangs to join the ranks
se ranger to stand back (out of the way)
arranger to arrange; **s'arranger avec** to come to terms with, to come to an agreement with; to manage

rappeler (377)

Part. pr. **rappelant** Part. passé **rappelé**

to call again, to call back, to recall, to remind

Regular **-er** verb endings; spelling change: **l** becomes **ll** before syllable with a mute **e**

The Seven Simple Tenses		The Seven Compound Tenses	
Singular	Plural	Singular	Plural
1 présent de l'indicatif		8 passé composé	
rappelle	**rappelons**	**ai rappelé**	**avons rappelé**
rappelles	**rappelez**	**as rappelé**	**avez rappelé**
rappelle	**rappellent**	**a rappelé**	**ont rappelé**
2 imparfait de l'indicatif		9 plus-que-parfait de l'indicatif	
rappelais	**rappelions**	**avais rappelé**	**avions rappelé**
rappelais	**rappeliez**	**avais rappelé**	**aviez rappelé**
rappelait	**rappelaient**	**avait rappelé**	**avaient rappelé**
3 passé simple		10 passé antérieur	
rappelai	**rappelâmes**	**eus rappelé**	**eûmes rappelé**
rappelas	**rappelâtes**	**eus rappelé**	**eûtes rappelé**
rappela	**rappelèrent**	**eut rappelé**	**eurent rappelé**
4 futur		11 futur antérieur	
rappellerai	**rappellerons**	**aurai rappelé**	**aurons rappelé**
rappelleras	**rappellerez**	**auras rappelé**	**aurez rappelé**
rappellera	**rappelleront**	**aura rappelé**	**auront rappelé**
5 conditionnel		12 conditionnel passé	
rappellerais	**rappellerions**	**aurais rappelé**	**aurions rappelé**
rappellerais	**rappelleriez**	**aurais rappelé**	**auriez rappelé**
rappellerait	**rappelleraient**	**aurait rappelé**	**auraient rappelé**
6 présent du subjonctif		13 passé du subjonctif	
rappelle	**rappelions**	**aie rappelé**	**ayons rappelé**
rappelles	**rappeliez**	**aies rappelé**	**ayez rappelé**
rappelle	**rappellent**	**ait rappelé**	**aient rappelé**
7 imparfait du subjonctif		14 plus-que-parfait du subjonctif	
rappelasse	**rappelassions**	**eusse rappelé**	**eussions rappelé**
rappelasses	**rappelassiez**	**eusses rappelé**	**eussiez rappelé**
rappelât	**rappelassent**	**eût rappelé**	**eussent rappelé**

Impératif
rappelle
rappelons
rappelez

Sentences using this verb and words related to it
—Je ne peux pas vous parler maintenant. Rappelez-moi demain.
—D'accord. Je vous rappellerai demain.

un rappel recall, call back, recalling
rappeler à la vie to restore to life
Rappelez-moi votre nom. Remind me of your name.
rappeler qqn à l'ordre to call someone to order

See also **appeler, s'appeler,** and **se rappeler.**

Don't miss orthographically changing verbs on pages 32–34.

Part. pr. **se rappelant** Part. passé **rappelé(e)(s)** **se rappeler (378)**

Regular **-er** verb endings; spelling change: **l** becomes **ll** before syllable with a mute **e**

to remember, to recall, to recollect

The Seven Simple Tenses		The Seven Compound Tenses	
Singular	Plural	Singular	Plural
1 présent de l'indicatif		8 passé composé	
me rappelle	**nous rappelons**	**me suis rappelé(e)**	**nous sommes rappelé(e)s**
te rappelles	**vous rappelez**	**t'es rappelé(e)**	**vous êtes rappelé(e)(s)**
se rappelle	**se rappellent**	**s'est rappelé(e)**	**se sont rappelé(e)s**
2 imparfait de l'indicatif		9 plus-que-parfait de l'indicatif	
me rappelais	**nous rappelions**	**m'étais rappelé(e)**	**nous étions rappelé(e)s**
te rappelais	**vous rappeliez**	**t'étais rappelé(e)**	**vous étiez rappelé(e)(s)**
se rappelait	**se rappelaient**	**s'était rappelé(e)**	**s'étaient rappelé(e)s**
3 passé simple		10 passé antérieur	
me rappelai	**nous rappelâmes**	**me fus rappelé(e)**	**nous fûmes rappelé(e)s**
te rappelas	**vous rappelâtes**	**te fus rappelé(e)**	**vous fûtes rappelé(e)(s)**
se rappela	**se rappelèrent**	**se fut rappelé(e)**	**se furent rappelé(e)s**
4 futur		11 futur antérieur	
me rappellerai	**nous rappellerons**	**me serai rappelé(e)**	**nous serons rappelé(e)s**
te rappelleras	**vous rappellerez**	**te seras rappelé(e)**	**vous serez rappelé(e)(s)**
se rappellera	**se rappelleront**	**se sera rappelé(e)**	**se seront rappelé(e)s**
5 conditionnel		12 conditionnel passé	
me rappellerais	**nous rappellerions**	**me serais rappelé(e)**	**nous serions rappelé(e)s**
te rappellerais	**vous rappelleriez**	**te serais rappelé(e)**	**vous seriez rappelé(e)(s)**
se rappellerait	**se rappelleraient**	**se serait rappelé(e)**	**se seraient rappelé(e)s**
6 présent du subjonctif		13 passé du subjonctif	
me rappelle	**nous rappelions**	**me sois rappelé(e)**	**nous soyons rappelé(e)s**
te rappelles	**vous rappeliez**	**te sois rappelé(e)**	**vous soyez rappelé(e)(s)**
se rappelle	**se rappellent**	**se soit rappelé(e)**	**se soient rappelé(e)s**
7 imparfait du subjonctif		14 plus-que-parfait du subjonctif	
me rappelasse	**nous rappelassions**	**me fusse rappelé(e)**	**nous fussions rappelé(e)**
te rappelasses	**vous rappelassiez**	**te fusses rappelé(e)**	**vous fussiez rappelé(e)(s)**
se rappelât	**se rappelassent**	**se fût rappelé(e)**	**se fussent rappelé(e)s**

Impératif
rappelle-toi; ne te rappelle pas
rappelons-nous; ne nous rappelons pas
rappelez-vous; ne vous rappelez pas

Sentences using this verb and words related to it
Je me rappelle bien le premier jour où j'ai vu la belle Hélène. C'était un jour inoubliable.

See also **appeler, s'appeler,** and **rappeler.**

How are you doing? Find out with the verb drills and tests with answers explained on pages 50–101.

recevoir (379) — Part. pr. recevant — Part. passé reçu

to receive, to get

Irregular verb with spelling change: **c** changes to **ç** before **a** or **u** to keep **s** sound

The Seven Simple Tenses		The Seven Compound Tenses	
Singular	Plural	Singular	Plural
1 présent de l'indicatif		8 passé composé	
reçois	**recevons**	**ai reçu**	**avons reçu**
reçois	**recevez**	**as reçu**	**avez reçu**
reçoit	**reçoivent**	**a reçu**	**ont reçu**
2 imparfait de l'indicatif		9 plus-que-parfait de l'indicatif	
recevais	**recevions**	**avais reçu**	**avions reçu**
recevais	**receviez**	**avais reçu**	**aviez reçu**
recevait	**recevaient**	**avait reçu**	**avaient reçu**
3 passé simple		10 passé antérieur	
reçus	**reçûmes**	**eus reçu**	**eûmes reçu**
reçus	**reçûtes**	**eus reçu**	**eûtes reçu**
reçut	**reçurent**	**eut reçu**	**eurent reçu**
4 futur		11 futur antérieur	
recevrai	**recevrons**	**aurai reçu**	**aurons reçu**
recevras	**recevrez**	**auras reçu**	**aurez reçu**
recevra	**recevront**	**aura reçu**	**auront reçu**
5 conditionnel		12 conditionnel passé	
recevrais	**recevrions**	**aurais reçu**	**aurions reçu**
recevrais	**recevriez**	**aurais reçu**	**auriez reçu**
recevrait	**recevraient**	**aurait reçu**	**auraient reçu**
6 présent du subjonctif		13 passé du subjonctif	
reçoive	**recevions**	**aie reçu**	**ayons reçu**
reçoives	**receviez**	**aies reçu**	**ayez reçu**
reçoive	**reçoivent**	**ait reçu**	**aient reçu**
7 imparfait du subjonctif		14 plus-que-parfait du subjonctif	
reçusse	**reçussions**	**eusse reçu**	**eussions reçu**
reçusses	**reçussiez**	**eusses reçu**	**eussiez reçu**
reçût	**reçussent**	**eût reçu**	**eussent reçu**

Impératif
reçois
recevons
recevez

Words and expressions related to this verb

réceptif, réceptive receptive
une réception reception, welcome
un, une réceptionniste receptionist
un reçu a receipt
au reçu de on receipt of
recevable receivable
un receveur, une receveuse receiver
être reçu à un examen to pass an exam
Est-ce que tu as reçu mon courriel? Did you receive my e-mail?

Proverb:
Il y a plus de bonheur à donner qu'à recevoir. It is better to give than to receive.

Don't miss the definitions of basic grammatical terms on pages 35–49.

Irregular verb

to recognize, to acknowledge

The Seven Simple Tenses		The Seven Compound Tenses	
Singular	Plural	Singular	Plural
1 présent de l'indicatif		8 passé composé	
reconnais	**reconnaissons**	**ai reconnu**	**avons reconnu**
reconnais	**reconnaissez**	**as reconnu**	**avez reconnu**
reconnaît	**reconnaissent**	**a reconnu**	**ont reconnu**
2 imparfait de l'indicatif		9 plus-que-parfait de l'indicatif	
reconnaissais	**reconnaissions**	**avais reconnu**	**avions reconnu**
reconnaissais	**reconnaissiez**	**avais reconnu**	**aviez reconnu**
reconnaissait	**reconnaissaient**	**avait reconnu**	**avaient reconnu**
3 passé simple		10 passé antérieur	
reconnus	**reconnûmes**	**eus reconnu**	**eûmes reconnu**
reconnus	**reconnûtes**	**eus reconnu**	**eûtes reconnu**
reconnut	**reconnurent**	**eut reconnu**	**eurent reconnu**
4 futur		11 futur antérieur	
reconnaîtrai	**reconnaîtrons**	**aurai reconnu**	**aurons reconnu**
reconnaîtras	**reconnaîtrez**	**auras reconnu**	**aurez reconnu**
reconnaîtra	**reconnaîtront**	**aura reconnu**	**auront reconnu**
5 conditionnel		12 conditionnel passé	
reconnaîtrais	**reconnaîtrions**	**aurais reconnu**	**aurions reconnu**
reconnaîtrais	**reconnaîtriez**	**aurais reconnu**	**auriez reconnu**
reconnaîtrait	**reconnaîtraient**	**aurait reconnu**	**auraient reconnu**
6 présent du subjonctif		13 passé du subjonctif	
reconnaisse	**reconnaissions**	**aie reconnu**	**ayons reconnu**
reconnaisses	**reconnaissiez**	**aies reconnu**	**ayez reconnu**
reconnaisse	**reconnaissent**	**ait reconnu**	**aient reconnu**
7 imparfait du subjonctif		14 plus-que-parfait du subjonctif	
reconnusse	**reconnussions**	**eusse reconnu**	**eussions reconnu**
reconnusses	**reconnussiez**	**eusses reconnu**	**eussiez reconnu**
reconnût	**reconnussent**	**eût reconnu**	**eussent reconnu**

Impératif
reconnais
reconnaissons
reconnaissez

Words and expressions related to this verb

la reconnaissance gratitude, gratefulness, recognition

être reconnaissant à qqn de to be grateful (thankful, obliged) to someone for

la reconnaissance vocale speech/voice recognition (computer)

se reconnaître to recognize oneself, to recognize each other

reconnaissable recognizable

See also **connaître** and **méconnaître.**

Don't forget to study the section on defective and impersonal verbs. It's right after this main list.

to collect, to gather, to harvest

Irregular verb

The Seven Simple Tenses		The Seven Compound Tenses	
Singular	Plural	Singular	Plural
1 présent de l'indicatif		8 passé composé	
recueille	**recueillons**	**ai recueilli**	**avons recueilli**
recueilles	**recueillez**	**as recueilli**	**avez recueilli**
recueille	**recueillent**	**a recueilli**	**ont recueilli**
2 imparfait de l'indicatif		9 plus-que-parfait de l'indicatif	
recueillais	**recueillions**	**avais recueilli**	**avions recueilli**
recueillais	**recueilliez**	**avais recueilli**	**aviez recueilli**
recueillait	**recueillaient**	**avait recueilli**	**avaient recueilli**
3 passé simple		10 passé antérieur	
recueillis	**recueillîmes**	**eus recueilli**	**eûmes recueilli**
recueillis	**recueillîtes**	**eus recueilli**	**eûtes recueilli**
recueillit	**recueillirent**	**eut recueilli**	**eurent recueilli**
4 futur		11 futur antérieur	
recueillerai	**recueillerons**	**aurai recueilli**	**aurons recueilli**
recueilleras	**recueillerez**	**auras recueilli**	**aurez recueilli**
recueillera	**recueilleront**	**aura recueilli**	**auront recueilli**
5 conditionnel		12 conditionnel passé	
recueillerais	**recueillerions**	**aurais recueilli**	**aurions recueilli**
recueillerais	**recueilleriez**	**aurais recueilli**	**auriez recueilli**
recueillerait	**recueilleraient**	**aurait recueilli**	**auraient recueilli**
6 présent du subjonctif		13 passé du subjonctif	
recueille	**recueillions**	**aie recueilli**	**ayons recueilli**
recueilles	**recueilliez**	**aies recueilli**	**ayez recueilli**
recueille	**recueillent**	**ait recueilli**	**aient recueilli**
7 imparfait du subjonctif		14 plus-que-parfait du subjonctif	
recueillisse	**recueillissions**	**eusse recueilli**	**eussions recueilli**
recueillisses	**recueillissiez**	**eusses recueilli**	**eussiez recueilli**
recueillît	**recueillissent**	**eût recueilli**	**eussent recueilli**

Impératif
recueille
recueillons
recueillez

Words and expressions related to this verb

recueillir le fruit de son travail to reap the fruit of one's labor

un recueil collection; **un recueil de contes** collection of stories

le recueillement meditation, contemplation

se recueillir to meditate, to collect one's thoughts

Avez-vous jamais lu le poème *Recueillement* de Charles Baudelaire? Have you ever read the poem *Recueillement* by Charles Baudelaire?

See also **accueillir** and **cueillir.**

Do you need more drills? Have fun with the *501 French Verbs* CD-ROM!

Irregular verb

to reduce, to decrease, to diminish

The Seven Simple Tenses		The Seven Compound Tenses	
Singular	Plural	Singular	Plural
1 présent de l'indicatif		8 passé composé	
réduis	**réduisons**	**ai réduit**	**avons réduit**
réduis	**réduisez**	**as réduit**	**avez réduit**
réduit	**réduisent**	**a réduit**	**ont réduit**
2 imparfait de l'indicatif		9 plus-que-parfait de l'indicatif	
réduisais	**réduisions**	**avais réduit**	**avions réduit**
réduisais	**réduisiez**	**avais réduit**	**aviez réduit**
réduisait	**réduisaient**	**avait réduit**	**avaient réduit**
3 passé simple		10 passé antérieur	
réduisis	**réduisîmes**	**eus réduit**	**eûmes réduit**
réduisis	**réduisîtes**	**eus réduit**	**eûtes réduit**
réduisit	**réduisirent**	**eut réduit**	**eurent réduit**
4 futur		11 futur antérieur	
réduirai	**réduirons**	**aurai réduit**	**aurons réduit**
réduiras	**réduirez**	**auras réduit**	**aurez réduit**
réduira	**réduiront**	**aura réduit**	**auront réduit**
5 conditionnel		12 conditionnel passé	
réduirais	**réduirions**	**aurais réduit**	**aurions réduit**
réduirais	**réduiriez**	**aurais réduit**	**auriez réduit**
réduirait	**réduiraient**	**aurait réduit**	**auraient réduit**
6 présent du subjonctif		13 passé du subjonctif	
réduise	**réduisions**	**aie réduit**	**ayons réduit**
réduises	**réduisiez**	**aies réduit**	**ayez réduit**
réduise	**réduisent**	**ait réduit**	**aient réduit**
7 imparfait du subjonctif		14 plus-que-parfait du subjonctif	
réduisisse	**réduisissions**	**eusse réduit**	**eussions réduit**
réduisisses	**réduisissiez**	**eusses réduit**	**eussiez réduit**
réduisît	**réduisissent**	**eût réduit**	**eussent réduit**

Impératif
réduis
réduisons
réduisez

Words and expressions related to this verb

une réduction reduction, decrease
réductible reducible
une tête réduite shrunken head
la réductibilité reductibility
se réduire à to be reduced to
à prix réduit at a reduced price

See also **conduire, déduire, introduire, produire, reproduire, séduire,** and **traduire.**

Consult the back pages for over 2,600 verbs conjugated like model verbs among the 501 in this book.

How are you doing? Find out with the verb drills and tests with answers explained on pages 50–101.

to think, to meditate, to reflect, to ponder

Regular **-ir** verb

The Seven Simple Tenses		The Seven Compound Tenses	
Singular	Plural	Singular	Plural
1 présent de l'indicatif		8 passé composé	
réfléchis	**réfléchissons**	**ai réfléchi**	**avons réfléchi**
réfléchis	**réfléchissez**	**as réfléchi**	**avez réfléchi**
réfléchit	**réfléchissent**	**a réfléchi**	**ont réfléchi**
2 imparfait de l'indicatif		9 plus-que-parfait de l'indicatif	
réfléchissais	**réfléchissions**	**avais réfléchi**	**avions réfléchi**
réfléchissais	**réfléchissiez**	**avais réfléchi**	**aviez réfléchi**
réfléchissait	**réfléchissaient**	**avait réfléchi**	**avaient réfléchi**
3 passé simple		10 passé antérieur	
réfléchis	**réfléchîmes**	**eus réfléchi**	**eûmes réfléchi**
réfléchis	**réfléchîtes**	**eus réfléchi**	**eûtes réfléchi**
réfléchit	**réfléchirent**	**eut réfléchi**	**eurent réfléchi**
4 futur		11 futur antérieur	
réfléchirai	**réfléchirons**	**aurai réfléchi**	**aurons réfléchi**
réfléchiras	**réfléchirez**	**auras réfléchi**	**aurez réfléchi**
réfléchira	**réfléchiront**	**aura réfléchi**	**auront réfléchi**
5 conditionnel		12 conditionnel passé	
réfléchirais	**réfléchirions**	**aurais réfléchi**	**aurions réfléchi**
réfléchirais	**réfléchiriez**	**aurais réfléchi**	**auriez réfléchi**
réfléchirait	**réfléchiraient**	**aurait réfléchi**	**auraient réfléchi**
6 présent du subjonctif		13 passé du subjonctif	
réfléchisse	**réfléchissions**	**aie réfléchi**	**ayons réfléchi**
réfléchisses	**réfléchissiez**	**aies réfléchi**	**ayez réfléchi**
réfléchisse	**réfléchissent**	**ait réfléchi**	**aient réfléchi**
7 imparfait du subjonctif		14 plus-que-parfait du subjonctif	
réfléchisse	**réfléchissions**	**eusse réfléchi**	**eussions réfléchi**
réfléchisses	**réfléchissiez**	**eusses réfléchi**	**eussiez réfléchi**
réfléchît	**réfléchissent**	**eût réfléchi**	**eussent réfléchi**

Impératif
réfléchis
réfléchissons
réfléchissez

Sentences using this verb and expressions related to it

Mathide: **Yvette, vas-tu au bal samedi soir?**
Yvette: **Je ne sais pas si j'y vais. Je demande à réfléchir.**
Mathilde: **Bon, alors, réfléchis avant de me donner ta réponse.**

réfléchir à qqch to think over (ponder) something
Il faut que j'y réfléchisse. I must think it over.
réfléchir avant de parler to think before speaking
La mer réfléchit le ciel. The sea reflects the sky.
un reflet reflection
tout bien réfléchi after careful thought

Review the Subjunctive clearly and simply on pages 26–31.

Regular **-er** verb

to refuse, to withhold

The Seven Simple Tenses		The Seven Compound Tenses	
Singular	Plural	Singular	Plural
1 présent de l'indicatif		8 passé composé	
refuse	**refusons**	**ai refusé**	**avons refusé**
refuses	**refusez**	**as refusé**	**avez refusé**
refuse	**refusent**	**a refusé**	**ont refusé**
2 imparfait de l'indicatif		9 plus-que-parfait de l'indicatif	
refusais	**refusions**	**avais refusé**	**avions refusé**
refusais	**refusiez**	**avais refusé**	**aviez refusé**
refusait	**refusaient**	**avait refusé**	**avaient refusé**
3 passé simple		10 passé antérieur	
refusai	**refusâmes**	**eus refusé**	**eûmes refusé**
refusas	**refusâtes**	**eus refusé**	**eûtes refusé**
refusa	**refusèrent**	**eut refusé**	**eurent refusé**
4 futur		11 futur antérieur	
refuserai	**refuserons**	**aurai refusé**	**aurons refusé**
refuseras	**refuserez**	**auras refusé**	**aurez refusé**
refusera	**refuseront**	**aura refusé**	**auront refusé**
5 conditionnel		12 conditionnel passé	
refuserais	**refuserions**	**aurais refusé**	**aurions refusé**
refuserais	**refuseriez**	**aurais refusé**	**auriez refusé**
refuserait	**refuseraient**	**aurait refusé**	**auraient refusé**
6 présent du subjonctif		13 passé du subjonctif	
refuse	**refusions**	**aie refusé**	**ayons refusé**
refuses	**refusiez**	**aies refusé**	**ayez refusé**
refuse	**refusent**	**ait refusé**	**aient refusé**
7 imparfait du subjonctif		14 plus-que-parfait du subjonctif	
refusasse	**refusassions**	**eusse refusé**	**eussions refusé**
refusasses	**refusassiez**	**eusses refusé**	**eussiez refusé**
refusât	**refusassent**	**eût refusé**	**eussent refusé**

Impératif
refuse
refusons
refusez

R

Sentences using this verb and words related to it

Je refuse absolument de vous écouter. Sortez, s'il vous plaît! Si vous refusez, vous le regretterez.

refuser de faire qqch to refuse to do something
se refuser qqch to deny oneself something
refusable refusable
un refus refusal
refuser l'entrée à qqn to turn someone away
refuser la vie routinière to refuse a routine life
Elle a été refusée. She was refused.

Use the guide to French pronunciation. It's in the Appendixes.

regarder (385) — Part. pr. regardant — Part. passé regardé

to look (at), to watch

Regular **-er** verb

The Seven Simple Tenses		The Seven Compound Tenses	
Singular	Plural	Singular	Plural
1 présent de l'indicatif		8 passé composé	
regarde	**regardons**	**ai regardé**	**avons regardé**
regardes	**regardez**	**as regardé**	**avez regardé**
regarde	**regardent**	**a regardé**	**ont regardé**
2 imparfait de l'indicatif		9 plus-que-parfait de l'indicatif	
regardais	**regardions**	**avais regardé**	**avions regardé**
regardais	**regardiez**	**avais regardé**	**aviez regardé**
regardait	**regardaient**	**avait regardé**	**avaient regardé**
3 passé simple		10 passé antérieur	
regardai	**regardâmes**	**eus regardé**	**eûmes regardé**
regardas	**regardâtes**	**eus regardé**	**eûtes regardé**
regarda	**regardèrent**	**eut regardé**	**eurent regardé**
4 futur		11 futur antérieur	
regarderai	**regarderons**	**aurai regardé**	**aurons regardé**
regarderas	**regarderez**	**auras regardé**	**aurez regardé**
regardera	**regarderont**	**aura regardé**	**auront regardé**
5 conditionnel		12 conditionnel passé	
regarderais	**regarderions**	**aurais regardé**	**aurions regardé**
regarderais	**regarderiez**	**aurais regardé**	**auriez regardé**
regarderait	**regarderaient**	**aurait regardé**	**auraient regardé**
6 présent du subjonctif		13 passé du subjonctif	
regarde	**regardions**	**aie regardé**	**ayons regardé**
regardes	**regardiez**	**aies regardé**	**ayez regardé**
regarde	**regardent**	**ait regardé**	**aient regardé**
7 imparfait du subjonctif		14 plus-que-parfait du subjonctif	
regardasse	**regardassions**	**eusse regardé**	**eussions regardé**
regardasses	**regardassiez**	**eusses regardé**	**eussiez regardé**
regardât	**regardassent**	**eût regardé**	**eussent regardé**

Impératif
regarde
regardons
regardez

Sentences using this verb and words related to it
—Qu'est-ce que tu regardes, Bernard?
—Je regarde le ciel. Il est beau et clair.
—Pourquoi ne me regardes-tu pas?
Cela ne vous regarde pas. That's none of your business.

regarder qqch to look at (to watch) something; **regarder la télé** to watch TV
un regard glance, look; **au regard de** compared to, with regard to

See *Verbs with prepositions* in the Appendixes.

Regular **-er** verb

to regret, to miss

The Seven Simple Tenses		The Seven Compound Tenses	
Singular	Plural	Singular	Plural
1 présent de l'indicatif		8 passé composé	
regrette	**regrettons**	**ai regretté**	**avons regretté**
regrettes	**regrettez**	**as regretté**	**avez regretté**
regrette	**regrettent**	**a regretté**	**ont regretté**
2 imparfait de l'indicatif		9 plus-que-parfait de l'indicatif	
regrettais	**regrettions**	**avais regretté**	**avions regretté**
regrettais	**regrettiez**	**avais regretté**	**aviez regretté**
regrettait	**regrettaient**	**avait regretté**	**avaient regretté**
3 passé simple		10 passé antérieur	
regrettai	**regrettâmes**	**eus regretté**	**eûmes regretté**
regrettas	**regrettâtes**	**eus regretté**	**eûtes regretté**
regretta	**regrettèrent**	**eut regretté**	**eurent regretté**
4 futur		11 futur antérieur	
regretterai	**regretterons**	**aurai regretté**	**aurons regretté**
regretteras	**regretterez**	**auras regretté**	**aurez regretté**
regrettera	**regretteront**	**aura regretté**	**auront regretté**
5 conditionnel		12 conditionnel passé	
regretterais	**regretterions**	**aurais regretté**	**aurions regretté**
regretterais	**regretteriez**	**aurais regretté**	**auriez regretté**
regretterait	**regretteraient**	**aurait regretté**	**auraient regretté**
6 présent du subjonctif		13 passé du subjonctif	
regrette	**regrettions**	**aie regretté**	**ayons regretté**
regrettes	**regrettiez**	**aies regretté**	**ayez regretté**
regrette	**regrettent**	**ait regretté**	**aient regretté**
7 imparfait du subjonctif		14 plus-que-parfait du subjonctif	
regrettasse	**regrettassions**	**eusse regretté**	**eussions regretté**
regrettasses	**regrettassiez**	**eusses regretté**	**eussiez regretté**
regrettât	**regrettassent**	**eût regretté**	**eussent regretté**

Impératif
regrette
regrettons
regrettez

Common idiomatic expressions using this verb and words related to it
regretter d'avoir fait qqch to regret (to be sorry for) having done something
regrettable regrettable; **Il est regrettable que + subjunctive** It is regrettable (It is a pity) that . . .
Je ne regrette rien. I regret nothing.
Je le regrette. I'm sorry. (I regret it.)
un regret regret; **avoir regret de qqch** to regret something, to feel sorry about something

It's important that you be familiar with the Subjunctive. See pages 26–31.

to read again, to reread

Irregular verb

The Seven Simple Tenses		The Seven Compound Tenses	
Singular	Plural	Singular	Plural
1 présent de l'indicatif		8 passé composé	
relis	**relisons**	**ai relu**	**avons relu**
relis	**relisez**	**as relu**	**avez relu**
relit	**relisent**	**a relu**	**ont relu**
2 imparfait de l'indicatif		9 plus-que-parfait de l'indicatif	
relisais	**relisions**	**avais relu**	**avions relu**
relisais	**relisiez**	**avais relu**	**aviez relu**
relisait	**relisaient**	**avait relu**	**avaient relu**
3 passé simple		10 passé antérieur	
relus	**relûmes**	**eus relu**	**eûmes relu**
relus	**relûtes**	**eus relu**	**eûtes relu**
relut	**relurent**	**eut relu**	**eurent relu**
4 futur		11 futur antérieur	
relirai	**relirons**	**aurai relu**	**aurons relu**
reliras	**relirez**	**auras relu**	**aurez relu**
relira	**reliront**	**aura relu**	**auront relu**
5 conditionnel		12 conditionnel passé	
relirais	**relirions**	**aurais relu**	**aurions relu**
relirais	**reliriez**	**aurais relu**	**auriez relu**
relirait	**reliraient**	**aurait relu**	**auraient relu**
6 présent du subjonctif		13 passé du subjonctif	
relise	**relisions**	**aie relu**	**ayons relu**
relises	**relisiez**	**aies relu**	**ayez relu**
relise	**relisent**	**ait relu**	**aient relu**
7 imparfait du subjonctif		14 plus-que-parfait du subjonctif	
relusse	**relussions**	**eusse relu**	**eussions relu**
relusses	**relussiez**	**eusses relu**	**eussiez relu**
relût	**relussent**	**eût relu**	**eussent relu**

Impératif
relis
relisons
relisez

Words and expressions related to this verb

lire to read
la lecture reading; reading selection
la relecture rereading

relire une composition en vue de la corriger to reread a composition for the purpose of correcting it

For other words related to this verb see **lire.**

Grammar putting you in a tense mood? Review the definitions of basic grammatical terms with examples on pages 35–49.

Regular **-er** verb

to remark, to notice, to observe, to distinguish

The Seven Simple Tenses		The Seven Compound Tenses	
Singular	Plural	Singular	Plural
1 présent de l'indicatif		8 passé composé	
remarque	**remarquons**	**ai remarqué**	**avons remarqué**
remarques	**remarquez**	**as remarqué**	**avez remarqué**
remarque	**remarquent**	**a remarqué**	**ont remarqué**
2 imparfait de l'indicatif		9 plus-que-parfait de l'indicatif	
remarquais	**remarquions**	**avais remarqué**	**avions remarqué**
remarquais	**remarquiez**	**avais remarqué**	**aviez remarqué**
remarquait	**remarquaient**	**avait remarqué**	**avaient remarqué**
3 passé simple		10 passé antérieur	
remarquai	**remarquâmes**	**eus remarqué**	**eûmes remarqué**
remarquas	**remarquâtes**	**eus remarqué**	**eûtes remarqué**
remarqua	**remarquèrent**	**eut remarqué**	**eurent remarqué**
4 futur		11 futur antérieur	
remarquerai	**remarquerons**	**aurai remarqué**	**aurons remarqué**
remarqueras	**remarquerez**	**auras remarqué**	**aurez remarqué**
remarquera	**remarqueront**	**aura remarqué**	**auront remarqué**
5 conditionnel		12 conditionnel passé	
remarquerais	**remarquerions**	**aurais remarqué**	**aurions remarqué**
remarquerais	**remarqueriez**	**aurais remarqué**	**auriez remarqué**
remarquerait	**remarqueraient**	**aurait remarqué**	**auraient remarqué**
6 présent du subjonctif		13 passé du subjonctif	
remarque	**remarquions**	**aie remarqué**	**ayons remarqué**
remarques	**remarquiez**	**aies remarqué**	**ayez remarqué**
remarque	**remarquent**	**ait remarqué**	**aient remarqué**
7 imparfait du subjonctif		14 plus-que-parfait du subjonctif	
remarquasse	**remarquassions**	**eusse remarqué**	**eussions remarqué**
remarquasses	**remarquassiez**	**eusses remarqué**	**eussiez remarqué**
remarquât	**remarquassent**	**eût remarqué**	**eussent remarqué**

Impératif
remarque
remarquons
remarquez

Words and expressions related to this verb

une remarque remark, observation, comment
marquer to mark
faire remarquer qqch à qqn to bring something to someone's attention, to point out something to someone
se faire remarquer to make oneself noticed, draw attention
remarquable remarkable

Can't find the verb you're looking for? Check the back pages of this book for a list of over 2,600 additional verbs!

to thank

Regular **-er** verb

The Seven Simple Tenses		The Seven Compound Tenses	
Singular	Plural	Singular	Plural
1 présent de l'indicatif		8 passé composé	
remercie	**remercions**	**ai remercié**	**avons remercié**
remercies	**remerciez**	**as remercié**	**avez remercié**
remercie	**remercient**	**a remercié**	**ont remercié**
2 imparfait de l'indicatif		9 plus-que-parfait de l'indicatif	
remerciais	**remerciions**	**avais remercié**	**avions remercié**
remerciais	**remerciiez**	**avais remercié**	**aviez remercié**
remerciait	**remerciaient**	**avait remercié**	**avaient remercié**
3 passé simple		10 passé antérieur	
remerciai	**remerciâmes**	**eus remercié**	**eûmes remercié**
remercias	**remerciâtes**	**eus remercié**	**eûtes remercié**
remercia	**remercièrent**	**eut remercié**	**eurent remercié**
4 futur		11 futur antérieur	
remercierai	**remercierons**	**aurai remercié**	**aurons remercié**
remercieras	**remercierez**	**auras remercié**	**aurez remercié**
remerciera	**remercieront**	**aura remercié**	**auront remercié**
5 conditionnel		12 conditionnel passé	
remercierais	**remercierions**	**aurais remercié**	**aurions remercié**
remercierais	**remercieriez**	**aurais remercié**	**auriez remercié**
remercierait	**remercieraient**	**aurait remercié**	**auraient remercié**
6 présent du subjonctif		13 passé du subjonctif	
remercie	**remerciions**	**aie remercié**	**ayons remercié**
remercies	**remerciiez**	**aies remercié**	**ayez remercié**
remercie	**remercient**	**ait remercié**	**aient remercié**
7 imparfait du subjonctif		14 plus-que-parfait du subjonctif	
remerciasse	**remerciassions**	**eusse remercié**	**eussions remercié**
remerciasses	**remerciassiez**	**eusses remercié**	**eussiez remercié**
remerciât	**remerciassent**	**eût remercié**	**eussent remercié**

Impératif
remercie
remercions
remerciez

Common idiomatic expressions using this verb and words related to it

remercier qqn de qqch to thank someone for something; **Je vous remercie de votre aimable invitation.** I thank you for your kind invitation.

un remerciement acknowledgment, thanks

Merci! Thank you!

Merci bien! Thank you very much!

sans merci without mercy, mercilessly

être à la merci de to be at the mercy of; **la merci** mercy, good will

Can't remember the French verb you need? Check the back pages of this book for the English-French verb index!

Irregular verb

to put (on) again, to replace, to put back, to give back, to postpone

The Seven Simple Tenses		The Seven Compound Tenses	
Singular	Plural	Singular	Plural
1 présent de l'indicatif		8 passé composé	
remets	**remettons**	**ai remis**	**avons remis**
remets	**remettez**	**as remis**	**avez remis**
remet	**remettent**	**a remis**	**ont remis**
2 imparfait de l'indicatif		9 plus-que-parfait de l'indicatif	
remettais	**remettions**	**avais remis**	**avions remis**
remettais	**remettiez**	**avais remis**	**aviez remis**
remettait	**remettaient**	**avait remis**	**avaient remis**
3 passé simple		10 passé antérieur	
remis	**remîmes**	**eus remis**	**eûmes remis**
remis	**remîtes**	**eus remis**	**eûtes remis**
remit	**remirent**	**eut remis**	**eurent remis**
4 futur		11 futur antérieur	
remettrai	**remettrons**	**aurai remis**	**aurons remis**
remettras	**remettrez**	**auras remis**	**aurez remis**
remettra	**remettront**	**aura remis**	**auront remis**
5 conditionnel		12 conditionnel passé	
remettrais	**remettrions**	**aurais remis**	**aurions remis**
remettrais	**remettriez**	**aurais remis**	**auriez remis**
remettrait	**remettraient**	**aurait remis**	**auraient remis**
6 présent du subjonctif		13 passé du subjonctif	
remette	**remettions**	**aie remis**	**ayons remis**
remettes	**remettiez**	**aies remis**	**ayez remis**
remette	**remettent**	**ait remis**	**aient remis**
7 imparfait du subjonctif		14 plus-que-parfait du subjonctif	
remisse	**remissions**	**eusse remis**	**eussions remis**
remisses	**remissiez**	**eusses remis**	**eussiez remis**
remît	**remissent**	**eût remis**	**eussent remis**

Impératif
remets
remettons
remettez

Sentences using this verb and words and expressions related to it
—Où avez-vous remis les fleurs que je vous ai données?
—Je les ai remises là-bas. Ne les voyez-vous pas?

se remettre de to recover from
se remettre à faire qqch to start to do something again
s'en remettre à to depend on, to rely on
Remettez-vous! Pull yourself together!
une remise remittance, postponement, discount

See also **commettre, mettre, se mettre, omettre, permettre, promettre, soumettre,** and **transmettre.**

remplacer (391) — Part. pr. remplaçant — Part. passé remplacé

to replace

Regular **-er** verb endings; spelling change: **c** changes to **ç** before **a** or **o** to keep **s** sound

The Seven Simple Tenses		The Seven Compound Tenses	
Singular	Plural	Singular	Plural
1 présent de l'indicatif		8 passé composé	
remplace	**remplaçons**	**ai remplacé**	**avons remplacé**
remplaces	**remplacez**	**as remplacé**	**avez remplacé**
remplace	**remplacent**	**a remplacé**	**ont remplacé**
2 imparfait de l'indicatif		9 plus-que-parfait de l'indicatif	
remplaçais	**remplacions**	**avais remplacé**	**avions remplacé**
remplaçais	**remplaciez**	**avais remplacé**	**aviez remplacé**
remplaçait	**remplaçaient**	**avait remplacé**	**avaient remplacé**
3 passé simple		10 passé antérieur	
remplaçai	**remplaçâmes**	**eus remplacé**	**eûmes remplacé**
remplaças	**remplaçâtes**	**eus remplacé**	**eûtes remplacé**
remplaça	**remplacèrent**	**eut remplacé**	**eurent remplacé**
4 futur		11 futur antérieur	
remplacerai	**remplacerons**	**aurai remplacé**	**aurons remplacé**
remplaceras	**remplacerez**	**auras remplacé**	**aurez remplacé**
remplacera	**remplaceront**	**aura remplacé**	**auront remplacé**
5 conditionnel		12 conditionnel passé	
remplacerais	**remplacerions**	**aurais remplacé**	**aurions remplacé**
remplacerais	**remplaceriez**	**aurais remplacé**	**auriez remplacé**
remplacerait	**remplaceraient**	**aurait remplacé**	**auraient remplacé**
6 présent du subjonctif		13 passé du subjonctif	
remplace	**remplacions**	**aie remplacé**	**ayons remplacé**
remplaces	**remplaciez**	**aies remplacé**	**ayez remplacé**
remplace	**remplacent**	**ait remplacé**	**aient remplacé**
7 imparfait du subjonctif		14 plus-que-parfait du subjonctif	
remplaçasse	**remplaçassions**	**eusse remplacé**	**eussions remplacé**
remplaçasses	**remplaçassiez**	**eusses remplacé**	**eussiez remplacé**
remplaçât	**remplaçassent**	**eût remplacé**	**eussent remplacé**

Impératif
remplace
remplaçons
remplacez

Words and expressions related to this verb

remplacer par to replace with
un remplacement replacement (thing)
un remplaçant, une remplaçante replacement (person), substitute
remplaçable replaceable; **irremplaçable** irreplaceable
en remplacement de in place of

See also **placer.**

Use the guide to French pronunciation. It's in the Appendixes!

Regular **-ir** verb

to fill, to fulfill, to fill in, to fill out

The Seven Simple Tenses		The Seven Compound Tenses	
Singular	Plural	Singular	Plural
1 présent de l'indicatif		8 passé composé	
remplis	**remplissons**	**ai rempli**	**avons rempli**
remplis	**remplissez**	**as rempli**	**avez rempli**
remplit	**remplissent**	**a rempli**	**ont rempli**
2 imparfait de l'indicatif		9 plus-que-parfait de l'indicatif	
remplissais	**remplissions**	**avais rempli**	**avions rempli**
remplissais	**remplissiez**	**avais rempli**	**aviez rempli**
remplissait	**remplissaient**	**avait rempli**	**avaient rempli**
3 passé simple		10 passé antérieur	
remplis	**remplîmes**	**eus rempli**	**eûmes rempli**
remplis	**remplîtes**	**eus rempli**	**eûtes rempli**
remplit	**remplirent**	**eut rempli**	**eurent rempli**
4 futur		11 futur antérieur	
remplirai	**remplirons**	**aurai rempli**	**aurons rempli**
rempliras	**remplirez**	**auras rempli**	**aurez rempli**
remplira	**rempliront**	**aura rempli**	**auront rempli**
5 conditionnel		12 conditionnel passé	
remplirais	**remplirions**	**aurais rempli**	**aurions rempli**
remplirais	**rempliriez**	**aurais rempli**	**auriez rempli**
remplirait	**rempliraient**	**aurait rempli**	**auraient rempli**
6 présent du subjonctif		13 passé du subjonctif	
remplisse	**remplissions**	**aie rempli**	**ayons rempli**
remplisses	**remplissiez**	**aies rempli**	**ayez rempli**
remplisse	**remplissent**	**ait rempli**	**aient rempli**
7 imparfait du subjonctif		14 plus-que-parfait du subjonctif	
remplisse	**remplissions**	**eusse rempli**	**eussions rempli**
remplisses	**remplissiez**	**eusses rempli**	**eussiez rempli**
remplît	**remplissent**	**eût rempli**	**eussent rempli**

Impératif
remplis
remplissons
remplissez

Words and expressions related to this verb

remplir de to fill with
remplir qqch de qqch to fill something with something
se remplir to fill up
un remplissage filling up
emplir to fill
remplir des conditions to fulfill requirements, conditions
remplir une tâche to carry out (perform) a task
remplir quelqu'un d'admiration to fill someone with admiration

Grammar putting you in a tense mood? Review the definitions of basic grammatical terms with examples on pages 35–49.

rencontrer (393) — Part. pr. rencontrant — Part. passé rencontré

to meet, to encounter

Regular **-er** verb

The Seven Simple Tenses		The Seven Compound Tenses	
Singular	Plural	Singular	Plural
1 présent de l'indicatif		8 passé composé	
rencontre	**rencontrons**	**ai rencontré**	**avons rencontré**
rencontres	**rencontrez**	**as rencontré**	**avez rencontré**
rencontre	**rencontrent**	**a rencontré**	**ont rencontré**
2 imparfait de l'indicatif		9 plus-que-parfait de l'indicatif	
rencontrais	**rencontrions**	**avais rencontré**	**avions rencontré**
rencontrais	**rencontriez**	**avais rencontré**	**aviez rencontré**
rencontrait	**rencontraient**	**avait rencontré**	**avaient rencontré**
3 passé simple		10 passé antérieur	
rencontrai	**rencontrâmes**	**eus rencontré**	**eûmes rencontré**
rencontras	**rencontrâtes**	**eus rencontré**	**eûtes rencontré**
rencontra	**rencontrèrent**	**eut rencontré**	**eurent rencontré**
4 futur		11 futur antérieur	
rencontrerai	**rencontrerons**	**aurai rencontré**	**aurons rencontré**
rencontreras	**rencontrerez**	**auras rencontré**	**aurez rencontré**
rencontrera	**rencontreront**	**aura rencontré**	**auront rencontré**
5 conditionnel		12 conditionnel passé	
rencontrerais	**rencontrerions**	**aurais rencontré**	**aurions rencontré**
rencontrerais	**rencontreriez**	**aurais rencontré**	**auriez rencontré**
rencontrerait	**rencontreraient**	**aurait rencontré**	**auraient rencontré**
6 présent du subjonctif		13 passé du subjonctif	
rencontre	**rencontrions**	**aie rencontré**	**ayons rencontré**
rencontres	**rencontriez**	**aies rencontré**	**ayez rencontré**
rencontre	**rencontrent**	**ait rencontré**	**aient rencontré**
7 imparfait du subjonctif		14 plus-que-parfait du subjonctif	
rencontrasse	**rencontrassions**	**eusse rencontré**	**eussions rencontré**
rencontrasses	**rencontrassiez**	**eusses rencontré**	**eussiez rencontré**
rencontrât	**rencontrassent**	**eût rencontré**	**eussent rencontré**

Impératif
rencontre
rencontrons
rencontrez

Words and expressions related to this verb

se rencontrer to meet each other
une rencontre encounter, meeting
aller à la rencontre de qqn to go to meet someone
rencontrer par hasard to meet someone by chance (bump into)
une rencontre au sommet summit meeting
faire une rencontre inattendue to have an unexpected encounter
de mauvaises rencontres the wrong sort of people

Do you need more drills? Have fun with the *501 French Verbs* CD-ROM!

Regular **-re** verb

to give back, to return (something), to render; to vomit

The Seven Simple Tenses		The Seven Compound Tenses	
Singular	Plural	Singular	Plural
1 présent de l'indicatif		8 passé composé	
rends	**rendons**	**ai rendu**	**avons rendu**
rends	**rendez**	**as rendu**	**avez rendu**
rend	**rendent**	**a rendu**	**ont rendu**
2 imparfait de l'indicatif		9 plus-que-parfait de l'indicatif	
rendais	**rendions**	**avais rendu**	**avions rendu**
rendais	**rendiez**	**avais rendu**	**aviez rendu**
rendait	**rendaient**	**avait rendu**	**avaient rendu**
3 passé simple		10 passé antérieur	
rendis	**rendîmes**	**eus rendu**	**eûmes rendu**
rendis	**rendîtes**	**eus rendu**	**eûtes rendu**
rendit	**rendirent**	**eut rendu**	**eurent rendu**
4 futur		11 futur antérieur	
rendrai	**rendrons**	**aurai rendu**	**aurons rendu**
rendras	**rendrez**	**auras rendu**	**aurez rendu**
rendra	**rendront**	**aura rendu**	**auront rendu**
5 conditionnel		12 conditionnel passé	
rendrais	**rendrions**	**aurais rendu**	**aurions rendu**
rendrais	**rendriez**	**aurais rendu**	**auriez rendu**
rendrait	**rendraient**	**aurait rendu**	**auraient rendu**
6 présent du subjonctif		13 passé du subjonctif	
rende	**rendions**	**aie rendu**	**ayons rendu**
rendes	**rendiez**	**aies rendu**	**ayez rendu**
rende	**rendent**	**ait rendu**	**aient rendu**
7 imparfait du subjonctif		14 plus-que-parfait du subjonctif	
rendisse	**rendissions**	**eusse rendu**	**eussions rendu**
rendisses	**rendissiez**	**eusses rendu**	**eussiez rendu**
rendît	**rendissent**	**eût rendu**	**eussent rendu**

Impératif
rends
rendons
rendez

AN ESSENTIAL 55 VERB

Rendre

Rendre is a very useful verb for beginning students because it is used in numerous everyday situations and idiomatic expressions. It is a regular **-re** verb.

Sentences using rendre

J'ai rendu le livre à la bibliothèque. I returned the book to the library.

Elle a rendu tout ce qu'elle a mangé. She vomited everything she ate.

Prière de rendre la clé de la chambre avant de partir. Please return the room key before leaving. (When going out for the day or checking out of a hotel.)

Tous les citoyens se sont rendus aux urnes afin d'élire un nouveau président. All the citizens voted in order to elect a new president.

Rendez à César ce qui est à César, et à Dieu ce qui est à Dieu. (Luc 20, 25) Render unto Caesar that which is Caesar's, and unto God that which is God's. (Luke 20, 25)

Pendant les vacances nous rendrons visite à notre grand-père. During vacation we will pay a visit to our grandfather.

Words and expressions related to this verb

un rendez-vous **appointment, date**

fixer un rendez-vous **to make an appointment, a date**

un compte rendu **report, account**

se rendre à **to go to, to surrender to**

rendre un service à qqn **to do someone a favor**

rendre service à qqn **to be of service to someone**

rendre qqn + adj. **to make someone + adj.**

rendre grâce à qqn **to give thanks to someone**

rendre compte de qqch **to give an account of something**

se rendre compte de **to realize**

rendre justice **to uphold justice**

rendre qqch **to return something**

se rendre aux urnes **to vote**

rendre hommage à qqn/qqch **to pay someone/something homage**

rendre visite à **to pay a visit to**

Can't remember the French verb you need? Check the back pages of this book for the English-French verb index!

Regular **-er** verb

to return

The Seven Simple Tenses		The Seven Compound Tenses	
Singular	Plural	Singular	Plural
1 présent de l'indicatif		8 passé composé	
rentre	**rentrons**	**suis rentré(e)**	**sommes rentré(e)s**
rentres	**rentrez**	**es rentré(e)**	**êtes rentré(e)(s)**
rentre	**rentrent**	**est rentré(e)**	**sont rentré(e)s**
2 imparfait de l'indicatif		9 plus-que-parfait de l'indicatif	
rentrais	**rentrions**	**étais rentré(e)**	**étions rentré(e)s**
rentrais	**rentriez**	**étais rentré(e)**	**étiez rentré(e)(s)**
rentrait	**rentraient**	**était rentré(e)**	**étaient rentré(e)s**
3 passé simple		10 passé antérieur	
rentrai	**rentrâmes**	**fus rentré(e)**	**fûmes rentré(e)s**
rentras	**rentrâtes**	**fus rentré(e)**	**fûtes rentré(e)(s)**
rentra	**rentrèrent**	**fut rentré(e)**	**furent rentré(e)s**
4 futur		11 futur antérieur	
rentrerai	**rentrerons**	**serai rentré(e)**	**serons rentré(e)s**
rentreras	**rentrerez**	**seras rentré(e)**	**serez rentré(e)(s)**
rentrera	**rentreront**	**sera rentré(e)**	**seront rentré(e)s**
5 conditionnel		12 conditionnel passé	
rentrerais	**rentrerions**	**serais rentré(e)**	**serions rentré(e)s**
rentrerais	**rentreriez**	**serais rentré(e)**	**seriez rentré(e)(s)**
rentrerait	**rentreraient**	**serait rentré(e)**	**seraient rentré(e)s**
6 présent du subjonctif		13 passé du subjonctif	
rentre	**rentrions**	**sois rentré(e)**	**soyons rentré(e)s**
rentres	**rentriez**	**sois rentré(e)**	**soyez rentré(e)(s)**
rentre	**rentrent**	**soit rentré(e)**	**soient rentré(e)s**
7 imparfait du subjonctif		14 plus-que-parfait du subjonctif	
rentrasse	**rentrassions**	**fusse rentré(e)**	**fussions rentré(e)s**
rentrasses	**rentrassiez**	**fusses rentré(e)**	**fussiez rentré(e)(s)**
rentrât	**rentrassent**	**fût rentré(e)**	**fussent rentré(e)s**

Impératif
rentre
rentrons
rentrez

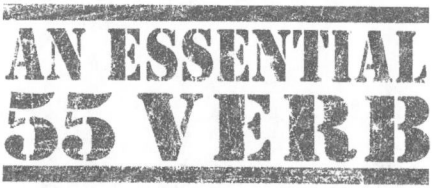

The subject pronouns are found on page 103.

AN ESSENTIAL 55 VERB

Rentrer

Rentrer is an important verb because it is used in many everyday situations and because it is a non-reflexive verb that takes **être** as an auxiliary (see page 6).

This verb is conjugated with **avoir** when it has a direct object.

Example: **Elle a rentré le chat dans la maison.** She brought (took) the cat into the house.
BUT: **Elle est rentrée tôt.** She returned home early.

Sentences using rentrer

—À quelle heure es-tu rentré à la maison, Alexandre?
—Je suis rentré à dix heures du soir, maman.

—What time did you get home, Alexander?
—I got home at ten in the evening, Mom.

Aide-moi, s'il te plaît, je ne parviens pas à faire rentrer ce téléviseur dans le coffre de ma voiture. Please help me, I cannot manage to make this television set fit in the trunk of my car.

J'ai hâte de voir tous mes amis à la rentrée des classes. I can't wait to see all my friends when we go back to school.

Words and expressions related to this verb

rentrer chez soi **to go back home**

rentrer les enfants **to take the children home**

rentrer ses larmes **to hold back one's tears**

la rentrée **return, homecoming**

la rentrée des classes, la rentrée scolaire **back to school**

rentrer ses griffes **to calm down (Literally, to pull in one's claws)**

rentrer dans **to crash into**

Can't find the verb you're looking for? Check the back pages of this book for a list of over 2,600 additional verbs!

Regular **-re** verb

to spread, to scatter, to spill

The Seven Simple Tenses		The Seven Compound Tenses	
Singular	Plural	Singular	Plural
1 présent de l'indicatif		8 passé composé	
répands	**répandons**	**ai répandu**	**avons répandu**
répands	**répandez**	**as répandu**	**avez répandu**
répand	**répandent**	**a répandu**	**ont répandu**
2 imparfait de l'indicatif		9 plus-que-parfait de l'indicatif	
répandais	**répandions**	**avais répandu**	**avions répandu**
répandais	**répandiez**	**avais répandu**	**aviez répandu**
répandait	**répandaient**	**avait répandu**	**avaient répandu**
3 passé simple		10 passé antérieur	
répandis	**répandîmes**	**eus répandu**	**eûmes répandu**
répandis	**répandîtes**	**eus répandu**	**eûtes répandu**
répandit	**répandirent**	**eut répandu**	**eurent répandu**
4 futur		11 futur antérieur	
répandrai	**répandrons**	**aurai répandu**	**aurons répandu**
répandras	**répandrez**	**auras répandu**	**aurez répandu**
répandra	**répandront**	**aura répandu**	**auront répandu**
5 conditionnel		12 conditionnel passé	
répandrais	**répandrions**	**aurais répandu**	**aurions répandu**
répandrais	**répandriez**	**aurais répandu**	**auriez répandu**
répandrait	**répandraient**	**aurait répandu**	**auraient répandu**
6 présent du subjonctif		13 passé du subjonctif	
répande	**répandions**	**aie répandu**	**ayons répandu**
répandes	**répandiez**	**aies répandu**	**ayez répandu**
répande	**répandent**	**ait répandu**	**aient répandu**
7 imparfait du subjonctif		14 plus-que-parfait du subjonctif	
répandisse	**répandissions**	**eusse répandu**	**eussions répandu**
répandisses	**répandissiez**	**eusses répandu**	**eussiez répandu**
répandît	**répandissent**	**eût répandu**	**eussent répandu**

Impératif
répands
répandons
répandez

Words and expressions related to this verb

répandre l'effroi to spread fear
une personne répandue widely known person
une opinion répandue widely accepted opinion
répandre du sang to shed blood
répandre une nouvelle to spread news
se répandre en injures to pour out insults
répandre la joie to spread joy

Don't forget to study the section on defective and impersonal verbs. It's right after this main list.

to reappear, to appear again

Irregular verb

The Seven Simple Tenses		The Seven Compound Tenses	
Singular	Plural	Singular	Plural
1 présent de l'indicatif		8 passé composé	
reparais	**reparaissons**	**ai reparu**	**avons reparu**
reparais	**reparaissez**	**as reparu**	**avez reparu**
reparaît	**reparaissent**	**a reparu**	**ont reparu**
2 imparfait de l'indicatif		9 plus-que-parfait de l'indicatif	
reparaissais	**reparaissions**	**avais reparu**	**avions reparu**
reparaissais	**reparaissiez**	**avais reparu**	**aviez reparu**
reparaissait	**reparaissaient**	**avait reparu**	**avaient reparu**
3 passé simple		10 passé antérieur	
reparus	**reparûmes**	**eus reparu**	**eûmes reparu**
reparus	**reparûtes**	**eus reparu**	**eûtes reparu**
reparut	**reparurent**	**eut reparu**	**eurent reparu**
4 futur		11 futur antérieur	
reparaîtrai	**reparaîtrons**	**aurai reparu**	**aurons reparu**
reparaîtras	**reparaîtrez**	**auras reparu**	**aurez reparu**
reparaîtra	**reparaîtront**	**aura reparu**	**auront reparu**
5 conditionnel		12 conditionnel passé	
reparaîtrais	**reparaîtrions**	**aurais reparu**	**aurions reparu**
reparaîtrais	**reparaîtriez**	**aurais reparu**	**auriez reparu**
reparaîtrait	**reparaîtraient**	**aurait reparu**	**auraient reparu**
6 présent du subjonctif		13 passé du subjonctif	
reparaisse	**reparaissions**	**aie reparu**	**ayons reparu**
reparaisses	**reparaissiez**	**aies reparu**	**ayez reparu**
reparaisse	**reparaissent**	**ait reparu**	**aient reparu**
7 imparfait du subjonctif		14 plus-que-parfait du subjonctif	
reparusse	**reparussions**	**eusse reparu**	**eussions reparu**
reparusses	**reparussiez**	**eusses reparu**	**eussiez reparu**
reparût	**reparussent**	**eût reparu**	**eussent reparu**

Impératif
reparais
reparaissons
reparaissez

Words related to this verb

paraître to appear, to seem
réapparaître to appear again, to reappear
la réapparition reappearance
disparaître to disappear
apparaître to appear, to come into view

See also **apparaître, disparaître,** and **paraître.**

Do you need more drills? Have fun with the *501 French Verbs* CD-ROM!

Regular **-er** verb

to repair

The Seven Simple Tenses		The Seven Compound Tenses	
Singular	Plural	Singular	Plural
1 présent de l'indicatif		8 passé composé	
répare	**réparons**	**ai réparé**	**avons réparé**
répares	**réparez**	**as réparé**	**avez réparé**
répare	**réparent**	**a réparé**	**ont réparé**
2 imparfait de l'indicatif		9 plus-que-parfait de l'indicatif	
réparais	**réparions**	**avais réparé**	**avions réparé**
réparais	**répariez**	**avais réparé**	**aviez réparé**
réparait	**réparaient**	**avait réparé**	**avaient réparé**
3 passé simple		10 passé antérieur	
réparai	**réparâmes**	**eus réparé**	**eûmes réparé**
réparas	**réparâtes**	**eus réparé**	**eûtes réparé**
répara	**réparèrent**	**eut réparé**	**eurent réparé**
4 futur		11 futur antérieur	
réparerai	**réparerons**	**aurai réparé**	**aurons réparé**
répareras	**réparerez**	**auras réparé**	**aurez réparé**
réparera	**répareront**	**aura réparé**	**auront réparé**
5 conditionnel		12 conditionnel passé	
réparerais	**réparerions**	**aurais réparé**	**aurions réparé**
réparerais	**répareriez**	**aurais réparé**	**auriez réparé**
réparerait	**répareraient**	**aurait réparé**	**auraient réparé**
6 présent du subjonctif		13 passé du subjonctif	
répare	**réparions**	**aie réparé**	**ayons réparé**
répares	**répariez**	**aies réparé**	**ayez réparé**
répare	**réparent**	**ait réparé**	**aient réparé**
7 imparfait du subjonctif		14 plus-que-parfait du subjonctif	
réparasse	**réparassions**	**eusse réparé**	**eussions réparé**
réparasses	**réparassiez**	**eusses réparé**	**eussiez réparé**
réparât	**réparassent**	**eût réparé**	**eussent réparé**

Impératif
répare
réparons
réparez

Words and expressions related to this verb

faire réparer ses chaussures to have one's shoes repaired
un réparateur, une réparatrice repairer
réparable reparable
irréparable irreparable
réparer une maison to restore a house
la réparation repair, repairing; **en réparation** in repair, under repair
réparer une offense to correct an offense
irréparablement irreparably

How are you doing? Find out with the verb drills and tests with answers explained on pages 50–101.

repasser (399) Part. pr. repassant Part. passé repassé

to iron, to pass again, to pass by again

Regular **-er** verb

The Seven Simple Tenses		The Seven Compound Tenses	
Singular	Plural	Singular	Plural
1 présent de l'indicatif		8 passé composé	
repasse	**repassons**	**ai repassé**	**avons repassé**
repasses	**repassez**	**as repassé**	**avez repassé**
repasse	**repassent**	**a repassé**	**ont repassé**
2 imparfait de l'indicatif		9 plus-que-parfait de l'indicatif	
repassais	**repassions**	**avais repassé**	**avions repassé**
repassais	**repassiez**	**avais repassé**	**aviez repassé**
repassait	**repassaient**	**avait repassé**	**avaient repassé**
3 passé simple		10 passé antérieur	
repassai	**repassâmes**	**eus repassé**	**eûmes repassé**
repassas	**repassâtes**	**eus repassé**	**eûtes repassé**
repassa	**repassèrent**	**eut repassé**	**eurent repassé**
4 futur		11 futur antérieur	
repasserai	**repasserons**	**aurai repassé**	**aurons repassé**
repasseras	**repasserez**	**auras repassé**	**aurez repassé**
repassera	**repasseront**	**aura repassé**	**auront repassé**
5 conditionnel		12 conditionnel passé	
repasserais	**repasserions**	**aurais repassé**	**aurions repassé**
repasserais	**repasseriez**	**aurais repassé**	**auriez repassé**
repasserait	**repasseraient**	**aurait repassé**	**auraient repassé**
6 présent du subjonctif		13 passé du subjonctif	
repasse	**repassions**	**aie repassé**	**ayons repassé**
repasses	**repassiez**	**aies repassé**	**ayez repassé**
repasse	**repassent**	**ait repassé**	**aient repassé**
7 imparfait du subjonctif		14 plus-que-parfait du subjonctif	
repassasse	**repassassions**	**eusse repassé**	**eussions repassé**
repassasses	**repassassiez**	**eusses repassé**	**eussiez repassé**
repassât	**repassassent**	**eût repassé**	**eussent repassé**

Impératif
repasse
repassons
repassez

Common idiomatic expressions using this verb and words related to it

une planche à repasser ironing board
un fer à repasser flat iron (for ironing clothes)
passer un examen to take (sit for) an exam
repasser un examen to take an exam over again
repasser un couteau, des ciseaux to sharpen a knife, scissors
repasser une leçon to review a lesson
repasser une chemise to iron a shirt
repasser un autre jour to stop in again another day
du linge à repasser laundry to iron

See also **passer.**

Can't remember the French verb you need? Check the back pages of this book for the English-French verb index!

Regular **-er** verb with spelling change: **é** changes to **è** before syllable with mute **e**

to repeat, to rehearse

The Seven Simple Tenses		The Seven Compound Tenses	
Singular	Plural	Singular	Plural
1 présent de l'indicatif		8 passé composé	
répète	**répétons**	**ai répété**	**avons répété**
répètes	**répétez**	**as répété**	**avez répété**
répète	**répètent**	**a répété**	**ont répété**
2 imparfait de l'indicatif		9 plus-que-parfait de l'indicatif	
répétais	**répétions**	**avais répété**	**avions répété**
répétais	**répétiez**	**avais répété**	**aviez répété**
répétait	**répétaient**	**avait répété**	**avaient répété**
3 passé simple		10 passé antérieur	
répétai	**répétâmes**	**eus répété**	**eûmes répété**
répétas	**répétâtes**	**eus répété**	**eûtes répété**
répéta	**répétèrent**	**eut répété**	**eurent répété**
4 futur		11 futur antérieur	
répéterai	**répéterons**	**aurai répété**	**aurons répété**
répéteras	**répéterez**	**auras répété**	**aurez répété**
répétera	**répéteront**	**aura répété**	**auront répété**
5 conditionnel		12 conditionnel passé	
répéterais	**répéterions**	**aurais répété**	**aurions répété**
répéterais	**répéteriez**	**aurais répété**	**auriez répété**
répéterait	**répéteraient**	**aurait répété**	**auraient répété**
6 présent du subjonctif		13 passé du subjonctif	
répète	**répétions**	**aie répété**	**ayons répété**
répètes	**répétiez**	**aies répété**	**ayez répété**
répète	**répètent**	**ait répété**	**aient répété**
7 imparfait du subjonctif		14 plus-que-parfait du subjonctif	
répétasse	**répétassions**	**eusse répété**	**eussions répété**
répétasses	**répétassiez**	**eusses répété**	**eussiez répété**
répétât	**répétassent**	**eût répété**	**eussent répété**

Impératif
répète
répétons
répétez

Words and expressions related to this verb

répéter une pièce de théâtre to rehearse a play

une répétition repetition

La pièce est en répétition. The play is in rehearsal.

se répéter to repeat oneself; to recur

Soak up some verbs used in weather expressions. There's a list in the Appendixes!

répondre (401) — Part. pr. répondant — Part. passé répondu

to respond, to reply, to answer

Regular **-re** verb

The Seven Simple Tenses		The Seven Compound Tenses	
Singular	Plural	Singular	Plural
1 présent de l'indicatif		8 passé composé	
réponds	**répondons**	**ai répondu**	**avons répondu**
réponds	**répondez**	**as répondu**	**avez répondu**
répond	**répondent**	**a répondu**	**ont répondu**
2 imparfait de l'indicatif		9 plus-que-parfait de l'indicatif	
répondais	**répondions**	**avais répondu**	**avions répondu**
répondais	**répondiez**	**avais répondu**	**aviez répondu**
répondait	**répondaient**	**avait répondu**	**avaient répondu**
3 passé simple		10 passé antérieur	
répondis	**répondîmes**	**eus répondu**	**eûmes répondu**
répondis	**répondîtes**	**eus répondu**	**eûtes répondu**
répondit	**répondirent**	**eut répondu**	**eurent répondu**
4 futur		11 futur antérieur	
répondrai	**répondrons**	**aurai répondu**	**aurons répondu**
répondras	**répondrez**	**auras répondu**	**aurez répondu**
répondra	**répondront**	**aura répondu**	**auront répondu**
5 conditionnel		12 conditionnel passé	
répondrais	**répondrions**	**aurais répondu**	**aurions répondu**
répondrais	**répondriez**	**aurais répondu**	**auriez répondu**
répondrait	**répondraient**	**aurait répondu**	**auraient répondu**
6 présent du subjonctif		13 passé du subjonctif	
réponde	**répondions**	**aie répondu**	**ayons répondu**
répondes	**répondiez**	**aies répondu**	**ayez répondu**
réponde	**répondent**	**ait répondu**	**aient répondu**
7 imparfait du subjonctif		14 plus-que-parfait du subjonctif	
répondisse	**répondissions**	**eusse répondu**	**eussions répondu**
répondisses	**répondissiez**	**eusses répondu**	**eussiez répondu**
répondît	**répondissent**	**eût répondu**	**eussent répondu**

Impératif
réponds
répondons
répondez

Words and expressions related to this verb

répondre à qqn to answer someone; to reply to someone

répondre de qqn to be responsible for, to vouch for someone

répondre de qqch to vouch for something, to guarantee something

une réponse answer, reply; **en réponse à votre lettre . . .** in reply to your letter . . .

pour répondre à la question de . . . in answer to the question of . . .

un répondeur téléphonique telephone answering machine

Elle m'a répondu en claquant la porte. She answered me by slamming the door.

un coupon-réponse reply coupon

Get acquainted with what preposition goes with what verb. See *Verbs with prepositions* in the Appendixes.

Reflexive regular **-er** verb

to rest

The Seven Simple Tenses		The Seven Compound Tenses	
Singular	Plural	Singular	Plural
1 présent de l'indicatif		8 passé composé	
me repose	**nous reposons**	**me suis reposé(e)**	**nous sommes reposé(e)s**
te reposes	**vous reposez**	**t'es reposé(e)**	**vous êtes reposé(e)(s)**
se repose	**se reposent**	**s'est reposé(e)**	**se sont reposé(e)s**
2 imparfait de l'indicatif		9 plus-que-parfait de l'indicatif	
me reposais	**nous reposions**	**m'étais reposé(e)**	**nous étions reposé(e)s**
te reposais	**vous reposiez**	**t'étais reposé(e)**	**vous étiez reposé(e)(s)**
se reposait	**se reposaient**	**s'était reposé(e)**	**s'étaient reposé(e)s**
3 passé simple		10 passé antérieur	
me reposai	**nous reposâmes**	**me fus reposé(e)**	**nous fûmes reposé(e)s**
te reposas	**vous reposâtes**	**te fus reposé(e)**	**vous fûtes reposé(e)(s)**
se reposa	**se reposèrent**	**se fut reposé(e)**	**se furent reposé(e)s**
4 futur		11 futur antérieur	
me reposerai	**nous reposerons**	**me serai reposé(e)**	**nous serons reposé(e)s**
te reposeras	**vous reposerez**	**te seras reposé(e)**	**vous serez reposé(e)(s)**
se reposera	**se reposeront**	**se sera reposé(e)**	**se seront reposé(e)s**
5 conditionnel		12 conditionnel passé	
me reposerais	**nous reposerions**	**me serais reposé(e)**	**nous serions reposé(e)s**
te reposerais	**vous reposeriez**	**te serais reposé(e)**	**vous seriez reposé(e)(s)**
se reposerait	**se reposeraient**	**se serait reposé(e)**	**se seraient reposé(e)s**
6 présent du subjonctif		13 passé du subjonctif	
me repose	**nous reposions**	**me sois reposé(e)**	**nous soyons reposé(e)s**
te reposes	**vous reposiez**	**te sois reposé(e)**	**vous soyez reposé(e)(s)**
se repose	**se reposent**	**se soit reposé(e)**	**se soient reposé(e)s**
7 imparfait du subjonctif		14 plus-que-parfait du subjonctif	
me reposasse	**nous reposassions**	**me fusse reposé(e)**	**nous fussions reposé(e)s**
te reposasses	**vous reposassiez**	**te fusses reposé(e)**	**vous fussiez reposé(e)(s)**
se reposât	**se reposassent**	**se fût reposé(e)**	**se fussent reposé(e)s**

Impératif
repose-toi; ne te repose pas
reposons-nous; ne nous reposons pas
reposez-vous; ne vous reposez pas

Words and expressions related to this verb

reposer to put down again; **reposer la tête sur** to rest one's head on; **reposer sur** to be based on

le repos rest, repose; **Au repos!** At ease!

se reposer sur qqn, qqch to put one's trust in someone, something

un repose-pied footrest; **un repose-bras** armrest

Je suis fatigué; je vais me reposer. I'm tired; I'm going to rest.

Do you need more drills? Have fun with the *501 French Verbs* CD-ROM!

reprendre (403) — Part. pr. reprenant — Part. passé repris

to take again, to take back, to recover, to resume

Irregular verb

The Seven Simple Tenses		The Seven Compound Tenses	
Singular	Plural	Singular	Plural
1 présent de l'indicatif		8 passé composé	
reprends	**reprenons**	**ai repris**	**avons repris**
reprends	**reprenez**	**as repris**	**avez repris**
reprend	**reprennent**	**a repris**	**ont repris**
2 imparfait de l'indicatif		9 plus-que-parfait de l'indicatif	
reprenais	**reprenions**	**avais repris**	**avions repris**
reprenais	**repreniez**	**avais repris**	**aviez repris**
reprenait	**reprenaient**	**avait repris**	**avaient repris**
3 passé simple		10 passé antérieur	
repris	**reprîmes**	**eus repris**	**eûmes repris**
repris	**reprîtes**	**eus repris**	**eûtes repris**
reprit	**reprirent**	**eut repris**	**eurent repris**
4 futur		11 futur antérieur	
reprendrai	**reprendrons**	**aurai repris**	**aurons repris**
reprendras	**reprendrez**	**auras repris**	**aurez repris**
reprendra	**reprendront**	**aura repris**	**auront repris**
5 conditionnel		12 conditionnel passé	
reprendrais	**reprendrions**	**aurais repris**	**aurions repris**
reprendrais	**reprendriez**	**aurais repris**	**auriez repris**
reprendrait	**reprendraient**	**aurait repris**	**auraient repris**
6 présent du subjonctif		13 passé du subjonctif	
reprenne	**reprenions**	**aie repris**	**ayons repris**
reprennes	**repreniez**	**aies repris**	**ayez repris**
reprenne	**reprennent**	**ait repris**	**aient repris**
7 imparfait du subjonctif		14 plus-que-parfait du subjonctif	
reprisse	**reprissions**	**eusse repris**	**eussions repris**
reprisses	**reprissiez**	**eusses repris**	**eussiez repris**
reprît	**reprissent**	**eût repris**	**eussent repris**

Impératif
reprends
reprenons
reprenez

Words and expressions related to this verb

reprendre froid to catch cold again
reprendre ses esprits to recover one's senses
reprendre le dessus to regain the upper hand
reprendre ses forces to recover one's strength
se reprendre to take hold of oneself, to recover oneself
une reprise resumption, renewal, repetition (*music*)
à maintes reprises over and over again
reprendre la parole to go on speaking, to resume speaking

See also **apprendre, comprendre, entreprendre, se méprendre, prendre,** and **surprendre.**

Don't forget to study the section on defective and impersonal verbs. It's right after this main list.

Regular **-er** verb

to reprimand, to rebuke

The Seven Simple Tenses		The Seven Compound Tenses	
Singular	Plural	Singular	Plural
1 présent de l'indicatif		8 passé composé	
réprimande	**réprimandons**	**ai réprimandé**	**avons réprimandé**
réprimandes	**réprimandez**	**as réprimandé**	**avez réprimandé**
réprimande	**réprimandent**	**a réprimandé**	**ont réprimandé**
2 imparfait de l'indicatif		9 plus-que-parfait de l'indicatif	
réprimandais	**réprimandions**	**avais réprimandé**	**avions réprimandé**
réprimandais	**réprimandiez**	**avais réprimandé**	**aviez réprimandé**
réprimandait	**réprimandaient**	**avait réprimandé**	**avaient réprimandé**
3 passé simple		10 passé antérieur	
réprimandai	**réprimandâmes**	**eus réprimandé**	**eûmes réprimandé**
réprimandas	**réprimandâtes**	**eus réprimandé**	**eûtes réprimandé**
réprimanda	**réprimandèrent**	**eut réprimandé**	**eurent réprimandé**
4 futur		11 futur antérieur	
réprimanderai	**réprimanderons**	**aurai réprimandé**	**aurons réprimandé**
réprimanderas	**réprimanderez**	**auras réprimandé**	**aurez réprimandé**
réprimandera	**réprimanderont**	**aura réprimandé**	**auront réprimandé**
5 conditionnel		12 conditionnel passé	
réprimanderais	**réprimanderions**	**aurais réprimandé**	**aurions réprimandé**
réprimanderais	**réprimanderiez**	**aurais réprimandé**	**auriez réprimandé**
réprimanderait	**réprimanderaient**	**aurait réprimandé**	**auraient réprimandé**
6 présent du subjonctif		13 passé du subjonctif	
réprimande	**réprimandions**	**aie réprimandé**	**ayons réprimandé**
réprimandes	**réprimandiez**	**aies réprimandé**	**ayez réprimandé**
réprimande	**réprimandent**	**ait réprimandé**	**aient réprimandé**
7 imparfait du subjonctif		14 plus-que-parfait du subjonctif	
réprimandasse	**réprimandassions**	**eusse réprimandé**	**eussions réprimandé**
réprimandasses	**réprimandassiez**	**eusses réprimandé**	**eussiez réprimandé**
réprimandât	**réprimandassent**	**eût réprimandé**	**eussent réprimandé**

Impératif
réprimande
réprimandons
réprimandez

Words and expressions related to this verb

une réprimande reprimand, rebuke
faire des réprimandes to make rebukes
réprimandable blameworthy
prononcer une réprimande to issue a reprimand

If you want to see a sample English verb fully conjugated in all the tenses, check out pages 8 and 9.

to reproduce

Irregular verb

The Seven Simple Tenses		The Seven Compound Tenses	
Singular	Plural	Singular	Plural
1 présent de l'indicatif		8 passé composé	
reproduis	**reproduisons**	**ai reproduit**	**avons reproduit**
reproduis	**reproduisez**	**as reproduit**	**avez reproduit**
reproduit	**reproduisent**	**a reproduit**	**ont reproduit**
2 imparfait de l'indicatif		9 plus-que-parfait de l'indicatif	
reproduisais	**reproduisions**	**avais reproduit**	**avions reproduit**
reproduisais	**reproduisiez**	**avais reproduit**	**aviez reproduit**
reproduisait	**reproduisaient**	**avait reproduit**	**avaient reproduit**
3 passé simple		10 passé antérieur	
reproduisis	**reproduisîmes**	**eus reproduit**	**eûmes reproduit**
reproduisis	**reproduisîtes**	**eus reproduit**	**eûtes reproduit**
reproduisit	**reproduisirent**	**eut reproduit**	**eurent reproduit**
4 futur		11 futur antérieur	
reproduirai	**reproduirons**	**aurai reproduit**	**aurons reproduit**
reproduiras	**reproduirez**	**auras reproduit**	**aurez reproduit**
reproduira	**reproduiront**	**aura reproduit**	**auront reproduit**
5 conditionnel		12 conditionnel passé	
reproduirais	**reproduirions**	**aurais reproduit**	**aurions reproduit**
reproduirais	**reproduiriez**	**aurais reproduit**	**auriez reproduit**
reproduirait	**reproduiraient**	**aurait reproduit**	**auraient reproduit**
6 présent du subjonctif		13 passé du subjonctif	
reproduise	**reproduisions**	**aie reproduit**	**ayons reproduit**
reproduises	**reproduisiez**	**aies reproduit**	**ayez reproduit**
reproduise	**reproduisent**	**ait reproduit**	**aient reproduit**
7 imparfait du subjonctif		14 plus-que-parfait du subjonctif	
reproduisisse	**reproduisissions**	**eusse reproduit**	**eussions reproduit**
reproduisisses	**reproduisissiez**	**eusses reproduit**	**eussiez reproduit**
reproduisît	**reproduisissent**	**eût reproduit**	**eussent reproduit**

Impératif
reproduis
reproduisons
reproduisez

Words and expressions related to this verb

se reproduire to reproduce itself, to multiply, to recur, to happen again
une reproduction reproduction; **les droits de reproduction** copyright
reproductif, reproductive reproductive
reproductible reproductible
le clonage cloning
cloner to clone

See also **conduire, déduire, introduire, produire, réduire, séduire,** and **traduire.**

Grammar putting you in a tense mood? Review the definitions of basic grammatical terms with examples on pages 35–49.

Irregular verb

to resolve, to solve

The Seven Simple Tenses		The Seven Compound Tenses	
Singular	Plural	Singular	Plural
1 présent de l'indicatif		8 passé composé	
résous	**résolvons**	**ai résolu**	**avons résolu**
résous	**résolvez**	**as résolu**	**avez résolu**
résout	**résolvent**	**a résolu**	**ont résolu**
2 imparfait de l'indicatif		9 plus-que-parfait de l'indicatif	
résolvais	**résolvions**	**avais résolu**	**avions résolu**
résolvais	**résolviez**	**avais résolu**	**aviez résolu**
résolvait	**résolvaient**	**avait résolu**	**avaient résolu**
3 passé simple		10 passé antérieur	
résolus	**résolûmes**	**eus résolu**	**eûmes résolu**
résolus	**résolûtes**	**eus résolu**	**eûtes résolu**
résolut	**résolurent**	**eut résolu**	**eurent résolu**
4 futur		11 futur antérieur	
résoudrai	**résoudrons**	**aurai résolu**	**aurons résolu**
résoudras	**résoudrez**	**auras résolu**	**aurez résolu**
résoudra	**résoudront**	**aura résolu**	**auront résolu**
5 conditionnel		12 conditionnel passé	
résoudrais	**résoudrions**	**aurais résolu**	**aurions résolu**
résoudrais	**résoudriez**	**aurais résolu**	**auriez résolu**
résoudrait	**résoudraient**	**aurait résolu**	**auraient résolu**
6 présent du subjonctif		13 passé du subjonctif	
résolve	**résolvions**	**aie résolu**	**ayons résolu**
résolves	**résolviez**	**aies résolu**	**ayez résolu**
résolve	**résolvent**	**ait résolu**	**aient résolu**
7 imparfait du subjonctif		14 plus-que-parfait du subjonctif	
résolusse	**résolussions**	**eusse résolu**	**eussions résolu**
résolusses	**résolussiez**	**eusses résolu**	**eussiez résolu**
résolût	**résolussent**	**eût résolu**	**eussent résolu**

Impératif
résous
résolvons
résolvez

Words and expressions related to this verb

se résoudre à to make up one's mind to

résoudre qqn à faire qqch to induce someone to do something

résoudre un problème mathématique to solve a math problem

une résolution resolution

être résolu(e) à faire qqch to be resolved to doing something

Le feu a résous le bois en cendres. The fire has changed the wood into ashes. (The past part. **résous** is used for things that have undergone a physical change.)

See also **absoudre.**

Soak up some verbs used in weather expressions. There's a list in the Appendixes!

ressembler (407) Part. pr. **ressemblant** Part. passé **ressemblé**

to resemble, to be like, to look like

Regular **-er** verb

The Seven Simple Tenses		The Seven Compound Tenses	
Singular	Plural	Singular	Plural
1 présent de l'indicatif		8 passé composé	
ressemble	**ressemblons**	**ai ressemblé**	**avons ressemblé**
ressembles	**ressemblez**	**as ressemblé**	**avez ressemblé**
ressemble	**ressemblent**	**a ressemblé**	**ont ressemblé**
2 imparfait de l'indicatif		9 plus-que-parfait de l'indicatif	
ressemblais	**ressemblions**	**avais ressemblé**	**avions ressemblé**
ressemblais	**ressembliez**	**avais ressemblé**	**aviez ressemblé**
ressemblait	**ressemblaient**	**avait ressemblé**	**avaient ressemblé**
3 passé simple		10 passé antérieur	
ressemblai	**ressemblâmes**	**eus ressemblé**	**eûmes ressemblé**
ressemblas	**ressemblâtes**	**eus ressemblé**	**eûtes ressemblé**
ressembla	**ressemblèrent**	**eut ressemblé**	**eurent ressemblé**
4 futur		11 futur antérieur	
ressemblerai	**ressemblerons**	**aurai ressemblé**	**aurons ressemblé**
ressembleras	**ressemblerez**	**auras ressemblé**	**aurez ressemblé**
ressemblera	**ressembleront**	**aura ressemblé**	**auront ressemblé**
5 conditionnel		12 conditionnel passé	
ressemblerais	**ressemblerions**	**aurais ressemblé**	**aurions ressemblé**
ressemblerais	**ressembleriez**	**aurais ressemblé**	**auriez ressemblé**
ressemblerait	**ressembleraient**	**aurait ressemblé**	**auraient ressemblé**
6 présent du subjonctif		13 passé du subjonctif	
ressemble	**ressemblions**	**aie ressemblé**	**ayons ressemblé**
ressembles	**ressembliez**	**aies ressemblé**	**ayez ressemblé**
ressemble	**ressemblent**	**ait ressemblé**	**aient ressemblé**
7 imparfait du subjonctif		14 plus-que-parfait du subjonctif	
ressemblasse	**ressemblassions**	**eusse ressemblé**	**eussions ressemblé**
ressemblasses	**ressemblassiez**	**eusses ressemblé**	**eussiez ressemblé**
ressemblât	**ressemblassent**	**eût ressemblé**	**eussent ressemblé**

Impératif
ressemble
ressemblons
ressemblez

Words and expressions related to this verb

ressembler à qqn to resemble someone

Paulette ressemble beaucoup à sa mère. Paulette looks very much like her mother.

se ressembler to resemble each other, to look alike

Qui se ressemble s'assemble. Birds of a feather flock together.

sembler to seem, to appear

une ressemblance resemblance

Cela ne te ressemble pas! That's not like you!

Ils se ressemblent comme deux gouttes d'eau. They are as alike as two peas in a pod (like two drops of water).

Regular **-er** verb

to remain, to stay; to be left (over)

The Seven Simple Tenses		The Seven Compound Tenses	
Singular	Plural	Singular	Plural
1 présent de l'indicatif		8 passé composé	
reste	**restons**	**suis resté(e)**	**sommes resté(e)s**
restes	**restez**	**es resté(e)**	**êtes resté(e)(s)**
reste	**restent**	**est resté(e)**	**sont resté(e)s**
2 imparfait de l'indicatif		9 plus-que-parfait de l'indicatif	
restais	**restions**	**étais resté(e)**	**étions resté(e)s**
restais	**restiez**	**étais resté(e)**	**étiez resté(e)(s)**
restait	**restaient**	**était resté(e)**	**étaient resté(e)s**
3 passé simple		10 passé antérieur	
restai	**restâmes**	**fus resté(e)**	**fûmes resté(e)s**
restas	**restâtes**	**fus resté(e)**	**fûtes resté(e)(s)**
resta	**restèrent**	**fut resté(e)**	**furent resté(e)s**
4 futur		11 futur antérieur	
resterai	**resterons**	**serai resté(e)**	**serons resté(e)s**
resteras	**resterez**	**seras resté(e)**	**serez resté(e)(s)**
restera	**resteront**	**sera resté(e)**	**seront resté(e)s**
5 conditionnel		12 conditionnel passé	
resterais	**resterions**	**serais resté(e)**	**serions resté(e)s**
resterais	**resteriez**	**serais resté(e)**	**seriez resté(e)(s)**
resterait	**resteraient**	**serait resté(e)**	**seraient resté(e)s**
6 présent du subjonctif		13 passé du subjonctif	
reste	**restions**	**sois resté(e)**	**soyons resté(e)s**
restes	**restiez**	**sois resté(e)**	**soyez resté(e)(s)**
reste	**restent**	**soit resté(e)**	**soient resté(e)s**
7 imparfait du subjonctif		14 plus-que-parfait du subjonctif	
restasse	**restassions**	**fusse resté(e)**	**fussions resté(e)s**
restasses	**restassiez**	**fusses resté(e)**	**fussiez resté(e)(s)**
restât	**restassent**	**fût resté(e)**	**fussent resté(e)s**

Impératif
reste
restons
restez

Sentences using this verb and words related to it

Combien d'argent vous reste-t-il? How much money do you have left (over)?
Il me reste deux cents euros. I have two hundred euros left.
Restez là; je reviens tout de suite. Stay there; I'll be right back.
Simone est restée au lit toute la journée. Simone stayed in bed all day.
les restes leftovers; **le reste du temps** the rest of the time
le restant remainder
rester au lit to stay in bed

Can't find the verb you're looking for? Check the back pages of this book for a list of over 2,600 additional verbs!

to retain, to keep, to detain, to hold back

Irregular verb

The Seven Simple Tenses		The Seven Compound Tenses	
Singular	Plural	Singular	Plural
1 présent de l'indicatif		8 passé composé	
retiens	**retenons**	**ai retenu**	**avons retenu**
retiens	**retenez**	**as retenu**	**avez retenu**
retient	**retiennent**	**a retenu**	**ont retenu**
2 imparfait de l'indicatif		9 plus-que-parfait de l'indicatif	
retenais	**retenions**	**avais retenu**	**avions retenu**
retenais	**reteniez**	**avais retenu**	**aviez retenu**
retenait	**retenaient**	**avait retenu**	**avaient retenu**
3 passé simple		10 passé antérieur	
retins	**retînmes**	**eus retenu**	**eûmes retenu**
retins	**retîntes**	**eus retenu**	**eûtes retenu**
retint	**retinrent**	**eut retenu**	**eurent retenu**
4 futur		11 futur antérieur	
retiendrai	**retiendrons**	**aurai retenu**	**aurons retenu**
retiendras	**retiendrez**	**auras retenu**	**aurez retenu**
retiendra	**retiendront**	**aura retenu**	**auront retenu**
5 conditionnel		12 conditionnel passé	
retiendrais	**retiendrions**	**aurais retenu**	**aurions retenu**
retiendrais	**retiendriez**	**aurais retenu**	**auriez retenu**
retiendrait	**retiendraient**	**aurait retenu**	**auraient retenu**
6 présent du subjonctif		13 passé du subjonctif	
retienne	**retenions**	**aie retenu**	**ayons retenu**
retiennes	**reteniez**	**aies retenu**	**ayez retenu**
retienne	**retiennent**	**ait retenu**	**aient retenu**
7 imparfait du subjonctif		14 plus-que-parfait du subjonctif	
retinsse	**retinssions**	**eusse retenu**	**eussions retenu**
retinsses	**retinssiez**	**eusses retenu**	**eussiez retenu**
retînt	**retinssent**	**eût retenu**	**eussent retenu**

Impératif
retiens
retenons
retenez

Words and expressions related to this verb

retenir au lit to confine to bed
retenir qqn to detain someone
se retenir to restrain oneself
retenir une chambre to reserve a room
retenir une place to reserve a place, a seat
une rétention retention
une retenue deduction, detention (in school)

See also **contenir, obtenir,** and **tenir.**

Do you need more drills? Have fun with the *501 French Verbs* CD-ROM!

Regular **-er** verb

to draw (out) again, to pull again

The Seven Simple Tenses		The Seven Compound Tenses	
Singular	Plural	Singular	Plural
1 présent de l'indicatif		8 passé composé	
retire	**retirons**	**ai retiré**	**avons retiré**
retires	**retirez**	**as retiré**	**avez retiré**
retire	**retirent**	**a retiré**	**ont retiré**
2 imparfait de l'indicatif		9 plus-que-parfait de l'indicatif	
retirais	**retirions**	**avais retiré**	**avions retiré**
retirais	**retiriez**	**avais retiré**	**aviez retiré**
retirait	**retiraient**	**avait retiré**	**avaient retiré**
3 passé simple		10 passé antérieur	
retirai	**retirâmes**	**eus retiré**	**eûmes retiré**
retiras	**retirâtes**	**eus retiré**	**eûtes retiré**
retira	**retirèrent**	**eut retiré**	**eurent retiré**
4 futur		11 futur antérieur	
retirerai	**retirerons**	**aurai retiré**	**aurons retiré**
retireras	**retirerez**	**auras retiré**	**aurez retiré**
retirera	**retireront**	**aura retiré**	**auront retiré**
5 conditionnel		12 conditionnel passé	
retirerais	**retirerions**	**aurais retiré**	**aurions retiré**
retirerais	**retireriez**	**aurais retiré**	**auriez retiré**
retirerait	**retireraient**	**aurait retiré**	**auraient retiré**
6 présent du subjonctif		13 passé du subjonctif	
retire	**retirions**	**aie retiré**	**ayons retiré**
retires	**retiriez**	**aies retiré**	**ayez retiré**
retire	**retirent**	**ait retiré**	**aient retiré**
7 imparfait du subjonctif		14 plus-que-parfait du subjonctif	
retirasse	**retirassions**	**eusse retiré**	**eussions retiré**
retirasses	**retirassiez**	**eusses retiré**	**eussiez retiré**
retirât	**retirassent**	**eût retiré**	**eussent retiré**

Impératif
retire
retirons
retirez

Words and expressions related to this verb

retirer qqch à qqn to take something back from someone
retirer qqn de to take someone out of, to withdraw someone from
retirer une promesse to take back a promise
retirer ses chaussures to take off one's shoes
retirer qqch de to take something out of
retirer ses paroles to withdraw, to take back one's words
la carte de retrait debit card

See also **attirer, se retirer,** and **tirer.**

How are you doing? Find out with the verb drills and tests with answers explained on pages 50–101.

se retirer (411) — Part. pr. se retirant — Part. passé retiré(e)(s)

to retire, to withdraw

Reflexive regular **-er** verb

The Seven Simple Tenses

Singular	Plural
1 présent de l'indicatif	
me retire	**nous retirons**
te retires	**vous retirez**
se retire	**se retirent**
2 imparfait de l'indicatif	
me retirais	**nous retirions**
te retirais	**vous retiriez**
se retirait	**se retiraient**
3 passé simple	
me retirai	**nous retirâmes**
te retiras	**vous retirâtes**
se retira	**se retirèrent**
4 futur	
me retirerai	**nous retirerons**
te retireras	**vous retirerez**
se retirera	**se retireront**
5 conditionnel	
me retirerais	**nous retirerions**
te retirerais	**vous retireriez**
se retirerait	**se retireraient**
6 présent du subjonctif	
me retire	**nous retirions**
te retires	**vous retiriez**
se retire	**se retirent**
7 imparfait du subjonctif	
me retirasse	**nous retirassions**
te retirasses	**vous retirassiez**
se retirât	**se retirassent**

The Seven Compound Tenses

Singular	Plural
8 passé composé	
me suis retiré(e)	**nous sommes retiré(e)s**
t'es retiré(e)	**vous êtes retiré(e)(s)**
s'est retiré(e)	**se sont retiré(e)s**
9 plus-que-parfait de l'indicatif	
m'étais retiré(e)	**nous étions retiré(e)s**
t'étais retiré(e)	**vous étiez retiré(e)(s)**
s'était retiré(e)	**s'étaient retiré(e)s**
10 passé antérieur	
me fus retiré(e)	**nous fûmes retiré(e)s**
te fus retiré(e)	**vous fûtes retiré(e)(s)**
se fut retiré(e)	**se furent retiré(e)s**
11 futur antérieur	
me serai retiré(e)	**nous serons retiré(e)s**
te seras retiré(e)	**vous serez retiré(e)(s)**
se sera retiré(e)	**se seront retiré(e)s**
12 conditionnel passé	
me serais retiré(e)	**nous serions retiré(e)s**
te serais retiré(e)	**vous seriez retiré(e)(s)**
se serait retiré(e)	**se seraient retiré(e)s**
13 passé du subjonctif	
me sois retiré(e)	**nous soyons retiré(e)s**
te sois retiré(e)	**vous soyez retiré(e)(s)**
se soit retiré(e)	**se soient retiré(e)s**
14 plus-que-parfait du subjonctif	
me fusse retiré(e)	**nous fussions retiré(e)s**
te fusses retiré(e)	**vous fussiez retiré(e)(s)**
se fût retiré(e)	**se fussent retiré(e)s**

Impératif

retire-toi; ne te retire pas
retirons-nous; ne nous retirons pas
retirez-vous; ne vous retirez pas

Words and expressions related to this verb

se retirer des affaires to retire from business
retraité, retraitée retired, pensioned off
un officier en retraite retired officer
une retraite retreat, retirement; **vivre à la retraite** to live in retirement
un retrait withdrawal; **en retrait** set back; out of line; **un mur en retrait** recess of a wall

See also **attirer, retirer,** and **tirer.**

It's important that you be familiar with the Subjunctive. See pages 26–31.

Regular **-er** verb

to return, to go back, to turn again

The Seven Simple Tenses		The Seven Compound Tenses	
Singular	Plural	Singular	Plural
1 présent de l'indicatif		8 passé composé	
retourne	**retournons**	**suis retourné(e)**	**sommes retourné(e)s**
retournes	**retournez**	**es retourné(e)**	**êtes retourné(e)(s)**
retourne	**retournent**	**est retourné(e)**	**sont retourné(e)s**
2 imparfait de l'indicatif		9 plus-que-parfait de l'indicatif	
retournais	**retournions**	**étais retourné(e)**	**étions retourné(e)s**
retournais	**retourniez**	**étais retourné(e)**	**étiez retourné(e)(s)**
retournait	**retournaient**	**était retourné(e)**	**étaient retourné(e)s**
3 passé simple		10 passé antérieur	
retournai	**retournâmes**	**fus retourné(e)**	**fûmes retourné(e)s**
retournas	**retournâtes**	**fus retourné(e)**	**fûtes retourné(e)(s)**
retourna	**retournèrent**	**fut retourné(e)**	**furent retourné(e)s**
4 futur		11 futur antérieur	
retournerai	**retournerons**	**serai retourné(e)**	**serons retourné(e)s**
retourneras	**retournerez**	**seras retourné(e)**	**serez retourné(e)(s)**
retournera	**retourneront**	**sera retourné(e)**	**seront retourné(e)s**
5 conditionnel		12 conditionnel passé	
retournerais	**retournerions**	**serais retourné(e)**	**serions retourné(e)s**
retournerais	**retourneriez**	**serais retourné(e)**	**seriez retourné(e)(s)**
retournerait	**retourneraient**	**serait retourné(e)**	**seraient retourné(e)s**
6 présent du subjonctif		13 passé du subjonctif	
retourne	**retournions**	**sois retourné(e)**	**soyons retourné(e)s**
retournes	**retourniez**	**sois retourné(e)**	**soyez retourné(e)(s)**
retourne	**retournent**	**soit retourné(e)**	**soient retourné(e)s**
7 imparfait du subjonctif		14 plus-que-parfait du subjonctif	
retournasse	**retournassions**	**fusse retourné(e)**	**fussions retourné(e)s**
retournasses	**retournassiez**	**fusses retourné(e)**	**fussiez retourné(e)(s)**
retournât	**retournassent**	**fût retourné(e)**	**fussent retourné(e)s**

Impératif
retourne
retournons
retournez

Words and expressions related to this verb

retourner une chaussette to turn a sock inside out
retourner un matelas to turn over a mattress
retourner qqn to change someone's mind
se retourner to turn around; **se retourner sur le dos** to turn over on one's back
un retour return; **un billet de retour** return ticket
un billet d'aller et retour a round trip ticket
être de retour to be back; **Madame Dupin sera de retour demain.** Mrs. Dupin will be back tomorrow.

See also **détourner** and **tourner.**

Can't remember the French verb you need? Check the back pages of this book for the English-French verb index.

to succeed, to result

Regular **-ir** verb

The Seven Simple Tenses		The Seven Compound Tenses	
Singular	Plural	Singular	Plural
1 présent de l'indicatif		8 passé composé	
réussis	**réussissons**	**ai réussi**	**avons réussi**
réussis	**réussissez**	**as réussi**	**avez réussi**
réussit	**réussissent**	**a réussi**	**ont réussi**
2 imparfait de l'indicatif		9 plus-que-parfait de l'indicatif	
réussissais	**réussissions**	**avais réussi**	**avions réussi**
réussissais	**réussissiez**	**avais réussi**	**aviez réussi**
réussissait	**réussissaient**	**avait réussi**	**avaient réussi**
3 passé simple		10 passé antérieur	
réussis	**réussîmes**	**eus réussi**	**eûmes réussi**
réussis	**réussîtes**	**eus réussi**	**eûtes réussi**
réussit	**réussirent**	**eut réussi**	**eurent réussi**
4 futur		11 futur antérieur	
réussirai	**réussirons**	**aurai réussi**	**aurons réussi**
réussiras	**réussirez**	**auras réussi**	**aurez réussi**
réussira	**réussiront**	**aura réussi**	**auront réussi**
5 conditionnel		12 conditionnel passé	
réussirais	**réussirions**	**aurais réussi**	**aurions réussi**
réussirais	**réussiriez**	**aurais réussi**	**auriez réussi**
réussirait	**réussiraient**	**aurait réussi**	**auraient réussi**
6 présent du subjonctif		13 passé du subjonctif	
réussisse	**réussissions**	**aie réussi**	**ayons réussi**
réussisses	**réussissiez**	**aies réussi**	**ayez réussi**
réussisse	**réussissent**	**ait réussi**	**aient réussi**
7 imparfait du subjonctif		14 plus-que-parfait du subjonctif	
réussisse	**réussissions**	**eusse réussi**	**eussions réussi**
réussisses	**réussissiez**	**eusses réussi**	**eussiez réussi**
réussît	**réussissent**	**eût réussi**	**eussent réussi**

Impératif
réussis
réussissons
réussissez

Words and expressions related to this verb

réussir à qqch to succeed in something
réussir à un examen to pass an exam
une réussite success; **une réussite sociale** social success
réussir to result; **Le projet a mal réussi.** The plan turned out badly; **Le projet a bien réussi.** The plan turned out well.
une soirée réussie a successful evening
réussir dans la vie to succeed in life
Les fritures ne me réussissent pas. Fried food doesn't agree with me.

Get acquainted with what preposition goes with what verb. See *Verbs with prepositions* in the Appendixes.

Reflexive regular **-er** verb

to wake up

The Seven Simple Tenses		The Seven Compound Tenses	
Singular	Plural	Singular	Plural
1 présent de l'indicatif		8 passé composé	
me réveille	**nous réveillons**	**me suis réveillé(e)**	**nous sommes réveillé(e)s**
te réveilles	**vous réveillez**	**t'es réveillé(e)**	**vous êtes réveillé(e)(s)**
se réveille	**se réveillent**	**s'est réveillé(e)**	**se sont réveillé(e)s**
2 imparfait de l'indicatif		9 plus-que-parfait de l'indicatif	
me réveillais	**nous réveillions**	**m'étais réveillé(e)**	**nous étions réveillé(e)s**
te réveillais	**vous réveilliez**	**t'étais réveillé(e)**	**vous étiez réveillé(e)(s)**
se réveillait	**se réveillaient**	**s'était réveillé(e)**	**s'étaient réveillé(e)s**
3 passé simple		10 passé antérieur	
me réveillai	**nous réveillâmes**	**me fus réveillé(e)**	**nous fûmes réveillé(e)s**
te réveillas	**vous réveillâtes**	**te fus réveillé(e)**	**vous fûtes réveillé(e)(s)**
se réveilla	**se réveillèrent**	**se fut réveillé(e)**	**se furent réveillé(e)s**
4 futur		11 futur antérieur	
me réveillerai	**nous réveillerons**	**me serai réveillé(e)**	**nous serons réveillé(e)s**
te réveilleras	**vous réveillerez**	**te seras réveillé(e)**	**vous serez réveillé(e)(s)**
se réveillera	**se réveilleront**	**se sera réveillé(e)**	**se seront réveillé(e)s**
5 conditionnel		12 conditionnel passé	
me réveillerais	**nous réveillerions**	**me serais réveillé(e)**	**nous serions réveillé(e)s**
te réveillerais	**vous réveilleriez**	**te serais réveillé(e)**	**vous seriez réveillé(e)(s)**
se réveillerait	**se réveilleraient**	**se serait réveillé(e)**	**se seraient réveillé(e)s**
6 présent du subjonctif		13 passé du subjonctif	
me réveille	**nous réveillions**	**me sois réveillé(e)**	**nous soyons réveillé(e)s**
te réveilles	**vous réveilliez**	**te sois réveillé(e)**	**vous soyez réveillé(e)(s)**
se réveille	**se réveillent**	**se soit réveillé(e)**	**se soient réveillé(e)s**
7 imparfait du subjonctif		14 plus-que-parfait du subjonctif	
me réveillasse	**nous réveillassions**	**me fusse réveillé(e)**	**nous fussions réveillé(e)s**
te réveillasses	**vous réveillassiez**	**te fusses réveillé(e)**	**vous fussiez réveillé(e)(s)**
se réveillât	**se réveillassent**	**se fût réveillé(e)**	**se fussent réveillé(e)s**

Impératif
réveille-toi; ne te réveille pas
réveillons-nous; ne nous réveillons pas
réveillez-vous; ne vous réveillez pas

Words and expressions related to this verb

le réveillon Christmas or New Year's Eve party

faire réveillon to see the New Year in, to see Christmas in on Christmas Eve

un réveille-matin alarm clock

éveiller (réveiller) qqn to wake up, awaken someone; **éveiller** implies to awaken or wake up gently; **réveiller** suggests with some effort

veiller to stay awake; **veiller à** to look after

veiller sur to watch over; **surveiller** to keep an eye on

la veille de Noël Christmas Eve

La tempête a réveillé le chien. The storm woke up the dog.

Marie s'est réveillée à six heures. Mary woke up at six o'clock.

to come back

Irregular verb

The Seven Simple Tenses		The Seven Compound Tenses	
Singular	Plural	Singular	Plural
1 présent de l'indicatif		8 passé composé	
reviens	**revenons**	**suis revenu(e)**	**sommes revenu(e)s**
reviens	**revenez**	**es revenu(e)**	**êtes revenu(e)(s)**
revient	**reviennent**	**est revenu(e)**	**sont revenu(e)s**
2 imparfait de l'indicatif		9 plus-que-parfait de l'indicatif	
revenais	**revenions**	**étais revenu(e)**	**étions revenu(e)s**
revenais	**reveniez**	**étais revenu(e)**	**étiez revenu(e)(s)**
revenait	**revenaient**	**était revenu(e)**	**étaient revenu(e)s**
3 passé simple		10 passé antérieur	
revins	**revînmes**	**fus revenu(e)**	**fûmes revenu(e)s**
revins	**revîntes**	**fus revenu(e)**	**fûtes revenu(e)(s)**
revint	**revinrent**	**fut revenu(e)**	**furent revenu(e)s**
4 futur		11 futur antérieur	
reviendrai	**reviendrons**	**serai revenu(e)**	**serons revenu(e)s**
reviendras	**reviendrez**	**seras revenu(e)**	**serez revenu(e)(s)**
reviendra	**reviendront**	**sera revenu(e)**	**seront revenu(e)s**
5 conditionnel		12 conditionnel passé	
reviendrais	**reviendrions**	**serais revenu(e)**	**serions revenu(e)s**
reviendrais	**reviendriez**	**serais revenu(e)**	**seriez revenu(e)(s)**
reviendrait	**reviendraient**	**serait revenu(e)**	**seraient revenu(e)s**
6 présent du subjonctif		13 passé du subjonctif	
revienne	**revenions**	**sois revenu(e)**	**soyons revenu(e)s**
reviennes	**reveniez**	**sois revenu(e)**	**soyez revenu(e)(s)**
revienne	**reviennent**	**soit revenu(e)**	**soient revenu(e)s**
7 imparfait du subjonctif		14 plus-que-parfait du subjonctif	
revinsse	**revinssions**	**fusse revenu(e)**	**fussions revenu(e)s**
revinsses	**revinssiez**	**fusses revenu(e)**	**fussiez revenu(e)(s)**
revînt	**revinssent**	**fût revenu(e)**	**fussent revenu(e)s**

Impératif
reviens
revenons
revenez

Words and expressions related to this verb

le revenu revenue, income
à revenu fixe fixed interest
revenir d'une erreur to realize one's mistake
revenir au même to amount to the same thing
revenir sur ses pas to retrace one's steps
revenir sur le sujet to get back to the subject
revenir sur sa parole to go back on one's word
Tout revient à ceci . . . It all boils down to this . . .
Il/Elle s'appelle "reviens." Make sure you return it (*m.* or *f.* object that is being lent to someone). (Literally: Its name is "come back.")

See also **convenir, devenir, prévenir, se souvenir,** and **venir.**

Regular **-er** verb

to dream

The Seven Simple Tenses		The Seven Compound Tenses	
Singular	Plural	Singular	Plural
1 présent de l'indicatif		8 passé composé	
rêve	**rêvons**	**ai rêvé**	**avons rêvé**
rêves	**rêvez**	**as rêvé**	**avez rêvé**
rêve	**rêvent**	**a rêvé**	**ont rêvé**
2 imparfait de l'indicatif		9 plus-que-parfait de l'indicatif	
rêvais	**rêvions**	**avais rêvé**	**avions rêvé**
rêvais	**rêviez**	**avais rêvé**	**aviez rêvé**
rêvait	**rêvaient**	**avait rêvé**	**avaient rêvé**
3 passé simple		10 passé antérieur	
rêvai	**rêvâmes**	**eus rêvé**	**eûmes rêvé**
rêvas	**rêvâtes**	**eus rêvé**	**eûtes rêvé**
rêva	**rêvèrent**	**eut rêvé**	**eurent rêvé**
4 futur		11 futur antérieur	
rêverai	**rêverons**	**aurai rêvé**	**aurons rêvé**
rêveras	**rêverez**	**auras rêvé**	**aurez rêvé**
rêvera	**rêveront**	**aura rêvé**	**auront rêvé**
5 conditionnel		12 conditionnel passé	
rêverais	**rêverions**	**aurais rêvé**	**aurions rêvé**
rêverais	**rêveriez**	**aurais rêvé**	**auriez rêvé**
rêverait	**rêveraient**	**aurait rêvé**	**auraient rêvé**
6 présent du subjonctif		13 passé du subjonctif	
rêve	**rêvions**	**aie rêvé**	**ayons rêvé**
rêves	**rêviez**	**aies rêvé**	**ayez rêvé**
rêve	**rêvent**	**ait rêvé**	**aient rêvé**
7 imparfait du subjonctif		14 plus-que-parfait du subjonctif	
rêvasse	**rêvassions**	**eusse rêvé**	**eussions rêvé**
rêvasses	**rêvassiez**	**eusses rêvé**	**eussiez rêvé**
rêvât	**rêvassent**	**eût rêvé**	**eussent rêvé**

Impératif
rêve
rêvons
rêvez

R

Common idiomatic expressions using this verb and words related to it

rêver de to dream of, to dream about, to yearn for

J'ai rêvé de toi toute la nuit. I dreamt of you all night long.

rêver tout éveillé(e) to daydream

rêver à to imagine, to think vaguely about something, to daydream

Janine, tu ne fais pas attention! A quoi rêves-tu? Janine, you are not paying attention! What are you dreaming about?

un rêveur, une rêveuse dreamer

une rêverie reverie, meditation

un rêve dream

Use the guide to French pronunciation. It's in the Appendixes.

to see again, to see once more

Irregular verb

The Seven Simple Tenses		The Seven Compound Tenses	
Singular	Plural	Singular	Plural
1 présent de l'indicatif		8 passé composé	
revois	**revoyons**	**ai revu**	**avons revu**
revois	**revoyez**	**as revu**	**avez revu**
revoit	**revoient**	**a revu**	**ont revu**
2 imparfait de l'indicatif		9 plus-que-parfait de l'indicatif	
revoyais	**revoyions**	**avais revu**	**avions revu**
revoyais	**revoyiez**	**avais revu**	**aviez revu**
revoyait	**revoyaient**	**avait revu**	**avaient revu**
3 passé simple		10 passé antérieur	
revis	**revîmes**	**eus revu**	**eûmes revu**
revis	**revîtes**	**eus revu**	**eûtes revu**
revit	**revirent**	**eut revu**	**eurent revu**
4 futur		11 futur antérieur	
reverrai	**reverrons**	**aurai revu**	**aurons revu**
reverras	**reverrez**	**auras revu**	**aurez revu**
reverra	**reverront**	**aura revu**	**auront revu**
5 conditionnel		12 conditionnel passé	
reverrais	**reverrions**	**aurais revu**	**aurions revu**
reverrais	**reverriez**	**aurais revu**	**auriez revu**
reverrait	**reverraient**	**aurait revu**	**auraient revu**
6 présent du subjonctif		13 passé du subjonctif	
revoie	**revoyions**	**aie revu**	**ayons revu**
revoies	**revoyiez**	**aies revu**	**ayez revu**
revoie	**revoient**	**ait revu**	**aient revu**
7 imparfait du subjonctif		14 plus-que-parfait du subjonctif	
revisse	**revissions**	**eusse revu**	**eussions revu**
revisses	**revissiez**	**eusses revu**	**eussiez revu**
revît	**revissent**	**eût revu**	**eussent revu**

Impératif
revois
revoyons
revoyez

Words and expressions related to this verb

au revoir good-bye, see you again, until we meet again
se revoir to see each other again
une revue review, magazine
un, une revuiste a writer of reviews
une révision revision; **à revoir** to be revised
passer en revue to review, look through

See also **prévoir** and **voir.**

Irregular verb

to laugh

The Seven Simple Tenses		The Seven Compound Tenses	
Singular	Plural	Singular	Plural
1 présent de l'indicatif		8 passé composé	
ris	**rions**	**ai ri**	**avons ri**
ris	**riez**	**as ri**	**avez ri**
rit	**rient**	**a ri**	**ont ri**
2 imparfait de l'indicatif		9 plus-que-parfait de l'indicatif	
riais	**riions**	**avais ri**	**avions ri**
riais	**riiez**	**avais ri**	**aviez ri**
riait	**riaient**	**avait ri**	**avaient ri**
3 passé simple		10 passé antérieur	
ris	**rîmes**	**eus ri**	**eûmes ri**
ris	**rîtes**	**eus ri**	**eûtes ri**
rit	**rirent**	**eut ri**	**eurent ri**
4 futur		11 futur antérieur	
rirai	**rirons**	**aurai ri**	**aurons ri**
riras	**rirez**	**auras ri**	**aurez ri**
rira	**riront**	**aura ri**	**auront ri**
5 conditionnel		12 conditionnel passé	
rirais	**ririons**	**aurais ri**	**aurions ri**
rirais	**ririez**	**aurais ri**	**auriez ri**
rirait	**riraient**	**aurait ri**	**auraient ri**
6 présent du subjonctif		13 passé du subjonctif	
rie	**riions**	**aie ri**	**ayons ri**
ries	**riiez**	**aies ri**	**ayez ri**
rie	**rient**	**ait ri**	**aient ri**
7 imparfait du subjonctif		14 plus-que-parfait du subjonctif	
risse	**rissions**	**eusse ri**	**eussions ri**
risses	**rissiez**	**eusses ri**	**eussiez ri**
rît	**rissent**	**eût ri**	**eussent ri**

Impératif
ris
rions
riez

Words and expressions related to this verb

éclater de rire to burst out laughing; **rire de** to laugh at
dire qqch pour rire to say something just for a laugh
rire au nez de qqn to laugh in someone's face
rire de bon coeur to laugh heartily
le rire laughter; **un sourire** smile; **risible** laughable
le fou rire fit of laughter, giggles
rire aux éclats to roar with laughter
le rire franc a hearty laugh, an open laugh
se rire de to make fun of
la risette a little smile (as a child's smile)
Rira bien qui rira le dernier. Whoever laughs last laughs best.

See also **sourire.**

Grammar putting you in a tense mood? Review the definitions of basic grammatical terms with examples on pages 35–49.

rompre (419) — Part. pr. **rompant** — Part. passé **rompu**

to break, to burst, to shatter, to break off

Regular **-re** verb endings; spelling change: 3rd person sing. of Tense No. 1 adds **t**

The Seven Simple Tenses		The Seven Compound Tenses	
Singular	Plural	Singular	Plural
1 présent de l'indicatif		8 passé composé	
romps	**rompons**	**ai rompu**	**avons rompu**
romps	**rompez**	**as rompu**	**avez rompu**
rompt	**rompent**	**a rompu**	**ont rompu**
2 imparfait de l'indicatif		9 plus-que-parfait de l'indicatif	
rompais	**rompions**	**avais rompu**	**avions rompu**
rompais	**rompiez**	**avais rompu**	**aviez rompu**
rompait	**rompaient**	**avait rompu**	**avaient rompu**
3 passé simple		10 passé antérieur	
rompis	**rompîmes**	**eus rompu**	**eûmes rompu**
rompis	**rompîtes**	**eus rompu**	**eûtes rompu**
rompit	**rompirent**	**eut rompu**	**eurent rompu**
4 futur		11 futur antérieur	
romprai	**romprons**	**aurai rompu**	**aurons rompu**
rompras	**romprez**	**auras rompu**	**aurez rompu**
rompra	**rompront**	**aura rompu**	**auront rompu**
5 conditionnel		12 conditionnel passé	
romprais	**romprions**	**aurais rompu**	**aurions rompu**
romprais	**rompriez**	**aurais rompu**	**auriez rompu**
romprait	**rompraient**	**aurait rompu**	**auraient rompu**
6 présent du subjonctif		13 passé du subjonctif	
rompe	**rompions**	**aie rompu**	**ayons rompu**
rompes	**rompiez**	**aies rompu**	**ayez rompu**
rompe	**rompent**	**ait rompu**	**aient rompu**
7 imparfait du subjonctif		14 plus-que-parfait du subjonctif	
rompisse	**rompissions**	**eusse rompu**	**eussions rompu**
rompisses	**rompissiez**	**eusses rompu**	**eussiez rompu**
rompît	**rompissent**	**eût rompu**	**eussent rompu**

Impératif
romps
rompons
rompez

Common idiomatic expressions using this verb and words related to it

rompu de fatigue worn out
rompu aux affaires experienced in business
se rompre à to get used to
se rompre la tête to rack one's brains
une rupture de contrat breach of contract
corrompre to corrupt
interrompre to interrupt
une rupture rupture, bursting
un rupteur circuit breaker
rompre avec qqn to have a falling out with someone

See also **corrompre** and **interrompre.**

How are you doing? Find out with the verb drills and tests with answers explained on pages 50–101.

Regular **-ir** verb

to blush, to redden

The Seven Simple Tenses		The Seven Compound Tenses	
Singular	Plural	Singular	Plural
1 présent de l'indicatif		8 passé composé	
rougis	**rougissons**	**ai rougi**	**avons rougi**
rougis	**rougissez**	**as rougi**	**avez rougi**
rougit	**rougissent**	**a rougi**	**ont rougi**
2 imparfait de l'indicatif		9 plus-que-parfait de l'indicatif	
rougissais	**rougissions**	**avais rougi**	**avions rougi**
rougissais	**rougissiez**	**avais rougi**	**aviez rougi**
rougissait	**rougissaient**	**avait rougi**	**avaient rougi**
3 passé simple		10 passé antérieur	
rougis	**rougîmes**	**eus rougi**	**eûmes rougi**
rougis	**rougîtes**	**eus rougi**	**eûtes rougi**
rougit	**rougirent**	**eut rougi**	**eurent rougi**
4 futur		11 futur antérieur	
rougirai	**rougirons**	**aurai rougi**	**aurons rougi**
rougiras	**rougirez**	**auras rougi**	**aurez rougi**
rougira	**rougiront**	**aura rougi**	**auront rougi**
5 conditionnel		12 conditionnel passé	
rougirais	**rougirions**	**aurais rougi**	**aurions rougi**
rougirais	**rougiriez**	**aurais rougi**	**auriez rougi**
rougirait	**rougiraient**	**aurait rougi**	**auraient rougi**
6 présent du subjonctif		13 passé du subjonctif	
rougisse	**rougissions**	**aie rougi**	**ayons rougi**
rougisses	**rougissiez**	**aies rougi**	**ayez rougi**
rougisse	**rougissent**	**ait rougi**	**aient rougi**
7 imparfait du subjonctif		14 plus-que-parfait du subjonctif	
rougisse	**rougissions**	**eusse rougi**	**eussions rougi**
rougisses	**rougissiez**	**eusses rougi**	**eussiez rougi**
rougît	**rougissent**	**eût rougi**	**eussent rougi**

Impératif
rougis
rougissons
rougissez

Words and expressions related to this verb

faire rougir qqn to make someone blush
le rouge red; **rougeâtre** reddish
un rouge-gorge robin redbreast; **(des rouges-gorges)**
rougir de qqn to feel shame for someone
la rougeole measles
rougeaud, rougeaude ruddy complexion
le rouge à lèvres lipstick; **le rouge à joues** rouge (for cheeks)
voir rouge to see red
une jeune mariée rougissante a blushing bride

Can't find the verb you're looking for? Check the back pages of this book for a list of over 2,600 additional verbs!

rouler (421) — Part. pr. roulant — Part. passé roulé

to roll, to roll along, to drive (a car), to ride along

Regular **-er** verb

The Seven Simple Tenses		The Seven Compound Tenses	
Singular	Plural	Singular	Plural
1 présent de l'indicatif		8 passé composé	
roule	**roulons**	**ai roulé**	**avons roulé**
roules	**roulez**	**as roulé**	**avez roulé**
roule	**roulent**	**a roulé**	**ont roulé**
2 imparfait de l'indicatif		9 plus-que-parfait de l'indicatif	
roulais	**roulions**	**avais roulé**	**avions roulé**
roulais	**rouliez**	**avais roulé**	**aviez roulé**
roulait	**roulaient**	**avait roulé**	**avaient roulé**
3 passé simple		10 passé antérieur	
roulai	**roulâmes**	**eus roulé**	**eûmes roulé**
roulas	**roulâtes**	**eus roulé**	**eûtes roulé**
roula	**roulèrent**	**eut roulé**	**eurent roulé**
4 futur		11 futur antérieur	
roulerai	**roulerons**	**aurai roulé**	**aurons roulé**
rouleras	**roulerez**	**auras roulé**	**aurez roulé**
roulera	**rouleront**	**aura roulé**	**auront roulé**
5 conditionnel		12 conditionnel passé	
roulerais	**roulerions**	**aurais roulé**	**aurions roulé**
roulerais	**rouleriez**	**aurais roulé**	**auriez roulé**
roulerait	**rouleraient**	**aurait roulé**	**auraient roulé**
6 présent du subjonctif		13 passé du subjonctif	
roule	**roulions**	**aie roulé**	**ayons roulé**
roules	**rouliez**	**aies roulé**	**ayez roulé**
roule	**roulent**	**ait roulé**	**aient roulé**
7 imparfait du subjonctif		14 plus-que-parfait du subjonctif	
roulasse	**roulassions**	**eusse roulé**	**eussions roulé**
roulasses	**roulassiez**	**eusses roulé**	**eussiez roulé**
roulât	**roulassent**	**eût roulé**	**eussent roulé**

Impératif
roule
roulons
roulez

Words and expressions related to this verb

rouler les *r* to roll one's r's
rouler sur l'or to be rolling in dough (money)
se rouler to roll over
dérouler to unroll
un rouleau roll; **un rouleau de papier peint** roll of wallpaper
un rouleau de pièces de monnaie a roll of coins
un rouleau de pellicule roll of film
un rouleau à pâtisserie rolling pin
se dérouler to take place, to develop, to unfold

Review the Subjunctive clearly and simply on pages 26–31.

Regular **-ir** verb

to seize, to grasp, to comprehend

The Seven Simple Tenses		The Seven Compound Tenses	
Singular	Plural	Singular	Plural
1 présent de l'indicatif		8 passé composé	
saisis	**saisissons**	**ai saisi**	**avons saisi**
saisis	**saisissez**	**as saisi**	**avez saisi**
saisit	**saisissent**	**a saisi**	**ont saisi**
2 imparfait de l'indicatif		9 plus-que-parfait de l'indicatif	
saisissais	**saisissions**	**avais saisi**	**avions saisi**
saisissais	**saisissiez**	**avais saisi**	**aviez saisi**
saisissait	**saisissaient**	**avait saisi**	**avaient saisi**
3 passé simple		10 passé antérieur	
saisis	**saisîmes**	**eus saisi**	**eûmes saisi**
saisis	**saisîtes**	**eus saisi**	**eûtes saisi**
saisit	**saisirent**	**eut saisi**	**eurent saisi**
4 futur		11 futur antérieur	
saisirai	**saisirons**	**aurai saisi**	**aurons saisi**
saisiras	**saisirez**	**auras saisi**	**aurez saisi**
saisira	**saisiront**	**aura saisi**	**auront saisi**
5 conditionnel		12 conditionnel passé	
saisirais	**saisirions**	**aurais saisi**	**aurions saisi**
saisirais	**saisiriez**	**aurais saisi**	**auriez saisi**
saisirait	**saisiraient**	**aurait saisi**	**auraient saisi**
6 présent du subjonctif		13 passé du subjonctif	
saisisse	**saisissions**	**aie saisi**	**ayons saisi**
saisisses	**saisissiez**	**aies saisi**	**ayez saisi**
saisisse	**saisissent**	**ait saisi**	**aient saisi**
7 imparfait du subjonctif		14 plus-que-parfait du subjonctif	
saisisse	**saisissions**	**eusse saisi**	**eussions saisi**
saisisses	**saisissiez**	**eusses saisi**	**eussiez saisi**
saisît	**saisissent**	**eût saisi**	**eussent saisi**

Impératif
saisis
saisissons
saisissez

Words and expressions related to this verb

un saisissement shock
saisissable seizable
saisissant, saisissante thrilling, piercing
une saisie seizure
saisir des données to input data (comp.)
la saisie de données data input (comp.)
saisir l'occasion to seize the opportunity
saisi de joie overcome with joy
saisir la signification de qqch to grasp the meaning of something
insaisissable elusive
se saisir de to take possession of

Seize the opportunity! Read pages 26–31 and grasp the basics of the Subjunctive.

salir (423) — Part. pr. salissant — Part. passé sali

to soil, to dirty

Regular -ir verb

The Seven Simple Tenses		The Seven Compound Tenses	
Singular	Plural	Singular	Plural
1 présent de l'indicatif		8 passé composé	
salis	**salissons**	**ai sali**	**avons sali**
salis	**salissez**	**as sali**	**avez sali**
salit	**salissent**	**a sali**	**ont sali**
2 imparfait de l'indicatif		9 plus-que-parfait de l'indicatif	
salissais	**salissions**	**avais sali**	**avions sali**
salissais	**salissiez**	**avais sali**	**aviez sali**
salissait	**salissaient**	**avait sali**	**avaient sali**
3 passé simple		10 passé antérieur	
salis	**salîmes**	**eus sali**	**eûmes sali**
salis	**salîtes**	**eus sali**	**eûtes sali**
salit	**salirent**	**eut sali**	**eurent sali**
4 futur		11 futur antérieur	
salirai	**salirons**	**aurai sali**	**aurons sali**
saliras	**salirez**	**auras sali**	**aurez sali**
salira	**saliront**	**aura sali**	**auront sali**
5 conditionnel		12 conditionnel passé	
salirais	**salirions**	**aurais sali**	**aurions sali**
salirais	**saliriez**	**aurais sali**	**auriez sali**
salirait	**saliraient**	**aurait sali**	**auraient sali**
6 présent du subjonctif		13 passé du subjonctif	
salisse	**salissions**	**aie sali**	**ayons sali**
salisses	**salissiez**	**aies sali**	**ayez sali**
salisse	**salissent**	**ait sali**	**aient sali**
7 imparfait du subjonctif		14 plus-que-parfait du subjonctif	
salisse	**salissions**	**eusse sali**	**eussions sali**
salisses	**salissiez**	**eusses sali**	**eussiez sali**
salît	**salissent**	**eût sali**	**eussent sali**

Impératif
salis
salissons
salissez

Words and expressions related to this verb

sale dirty, soiled
salement disgustingly
la saleté filth
dire des saletés to use filthy language
se salir to get dirty
une réputation salie a tarnished reputation
les mains sales soiled hands
Avez-vous jamais lu ou vu la pièce de théâtre *Les Mains sales* de Jean-Paul Sartre?

How are you doing? Find out with the verb drills and tests with answers explained on pages 50–101.

Irregular verb

to satisfy

The Seven Simple Tenses		The Seven Compound Tenses	
Singular	Plural	Singular	Plural
1 présent de l'indicatif		8 passé composé	
satisfais	**satisfaisons**	**ai satisfait**	**avons satisfait**
satisfais	**satisfaites**	**as satisfait**	**avez satisfait**
satisfait	**satisfont**	**a satisfait**	**ont satisfait**
2 imparfait de l'indicatif		9 plus-que-parfait de l'indicatif	
satisfaisais	**satisfaisions**	**avais satisfait**	**avions satisfait**
satisfaisais	**satisfaisiez**	**avais satisfait**	**aviez satisfait**
satisfaisait	**satisfaisaient**	**avait satisfait**	**avaient satisfait**
3 passé simple		10 passé antérieur	
satisfis	**satisfîmes**	**eus satisfait**	**eûmes satisfait**
satisfis	**satisfîtes**	**eus satisfait**	**eûtes satisfait**
satisfit	**satisfirent**	**eut satisfait**	**eurent satisfait**
4 futur		11 futur antérieur	
satisferai	**satisferons**	**aurai satisfait**	**aurons satisfait**
satisferas	**satisferez**	**auras satisfait**	**aurez satisfait**
satisfera	**satisferont**	**aura satisfait**	**auront satisfait**
5 conditionnel		12 conditionnel passé	
satisferais	**satisferions**	**aurais satisfait**	**aurions satisfait**
satisferais	**satisferiez**	**aurais satisfait**	**auriez satisfait**
satisferait	**satisferaient**	**aurait satisfait**	**auraient satisfait**
6 présent du subjonctif		13 passé du subjonctif	
satisfasse	**satisfassions**	**aie satisfait**	**ayons satisfait**
satisfasses	**satisfassiez**	**aies satisfait**	**ayez satisfait**
satisfasse	**satisfassent**	**ait satisfait**	**aient satisfait**
7 imparfait du subjonctif		14 plus-que-parfait du subjonctif	
satisfisse	**satisfissions**	**eusse satisfait**	**eussions satisfait**
satisfisses	**satisfissiez**	**eusses satisfait**	**eussiez satisfait**
satisfît	**satisfissent**	**eût satisfait**	**eussent satisfait**

Impératif
satisfais
satisfaisons
satisfaites

Words and expressions related to this verb

satisfaire sa faim to satisfy one's hunger; **satisfaire sa soif** to satisfy one's thirst
satisfaisant, satisfaisante satisfying
la satisfaction satisfaction
demander satisfaction à to demand satisfaction from
être satisfait (satisfaite) de to be satisfied with

See also **défaire** and **faire.**

Do you need more drills? Have fun with the *501 French Verbs* CD-ROM!

sauter (425) — Part. pr. **sautant** — Part. passé **sauté**

to jump, to leap

Regular **-er** verb

The Seven Simple Tenses		The Seven Compound Tenses	
Singular	Plural	Singular	Plural
1 présent de l'indicatif		8 passé composé	
saute	**sautons**	**ai sauté**	**avons sauté**
sautes	**sautez**	**as sauté**	**avez sauté**
saute	**sautent**	**a sauté**	**ont sauté**
2 imparfait de l'indicatif		9 plus-que-parfait de l'indicatif	
sautais	**sautions**	**avais sauté**	**avions sauté**
sautais	**sautiez**	**avais sauté**	**aviez sauté**
sautait	**sautaient**	**avait sauté**	**avaient sauté**
3 passé simple		10 passé antérieur	
sautai	**sautâmes**	**eus sauté**	**eûmes sauté**
sautas	**sautâtes**	**eus sauté**	**eûtes sauté**
sauta	**sautèrent**	**eut sauté**	**eurent sauté**
4 futur		11 futur antérieur	
sauterai	**sauterons**	**aurai sauté**	**aurons sauté**
sauteras	**sauterez**	**auras sauté**	**aurez sauté**
sautera	**sauteront**	**aura sauté**	**auront sauté**
5 conditionnel		12 conditionnel passé	
sauterais	**sauterions**	**aurais sauté**	**aurions sauté**
sauterais	**sauteriez**	**aurais sauté**	**auriez sauté**
sauterait	**sauteraient**	**aurait sauté**	**auraient sauté**
6 présent du subjonctif		13 passé du subjonctif	
saute	**sautions**	**aie sauté**	**ayons sauté**
sautes	**sautiez**	**aies sauté**	**ayez sauté**
saute	**sautent**	**ait sauté**	**aient sauté**
7 imparfait du subjonctif		14 plus-que-parfait du subjonctif	
sautasse	**sautassions**	**eusse sauté**	**eussions sauté**
sautasses	**sautassiez**	**eusses sauté**	**eussiez sauté**
sautât	**sautassent**	**eût sauté**	**eussent sauté**

Impératif
saute
sautons
sautez

Words and expressions related to this verb

un saut leap, jump
une sauterelle grasshopper
sautiller to skip, to hop
sauter à la corde to jump (skip) rope
sauter au bas du lit to jump out of bed
faire sauter une crêpe to toss a pancake
sauter aux yeux to be evident, self-evident
Cela saute aux yeux. That's obvious.
sursauter to jump, start

Don't forget to study the section on defective and impersonal verbs. It's right after this main list.

Regular **-er** verb

to rescue, to save

The Seven Simple Tenses		The Seven Compound Tenses	
Singular	Plural	Singular	Plural
1 présent de l'indicatif		8 passé composé	
sauve	**sauvons**	**ai sauvé**	**avons sauvé**
sauves	**sauvez**	**as sauvé**	**avez sauvé**
sauve	**sauvent**	**a sauvé**	**ont sauvé**
2 imparfait de l'indicatif		9 plus-que-parfait de l'indicatif	
sauvais	**sauvions**	**avais sauvé**	**avions sauvé**
sauvais	**sauviez**	**avais sauvé**	**aviez sauvé**
sauvait	**sauvaient**	**avait sauvé**	**avaient sauvé**
3 passé simple		10 passé antérieur	
sauvai	**sauvâmes**	**eus sauvé**	**eûmes sauvé**
sauvas	**sauvâtes**	**eus sauvé**	**eûtes sauvé**
sauva	**sauvèrent**	**eut sauvé**	**eurent sauvé**
4 futur		11 futur antérieur	
sauverai	**sauverons**	**aurai sauvé**	**aurons sauvé**
sauveras	**sauverez**	**auras sauvé**	**aurez sauvé**
sauvera	**sauveront**	**aura sauvé**	**auront sauvé**
5 conditionnel		12 conditionnel passé	
sauverais	**sauverions**	**aurais sauvé**	**aurions sauvé**
sauverais	**sauveriez**	**aurais sauvé**	**auriez sauvé**
sauverait	**sauveraient**	**aurait sauvé**	**auraient sauvé**
6 présent du subjonctif		13 passé du subjonctif	
sauve	**sauvions**	**aie sauvé**	**ayons sauvé**
sauves	**sauviez**	**aies sauvé**	**ayez sauvé**
sauve	**sauvent**	**ait sauvé**	**aient sauvé**
7 imparfait du subjonctif		14 plus-que-parfait du subjonctif	
sauvasse	**sauvassions**	**eusse sauvé**	**eussions sauvé**
sauvasses	**sauvassiez**	**eusses sauvé**	**eussiez sauvé**
sauvât	**sauvassent**	**eût sauvé**	**eussent sauvé**

Impératif
sauve
sauvons
sauvez

Words and expressions related to this verb

sauvegarder to safeguard
le sauvetage life-saving, rescue
Sauve qui peut! Run for your life!
le sauve-qui-peut panic
sauver les apparences to preserve appearances
se sauver to run away, to escape, to rush off
sauver la vie à qqn to save someone's life
une échelle de sauvetage fire escape
un gilet de sauvetage a life jacket

See also **se sauver.**

Grammar putting you in a tense mood? Review the definitions of basic grammatical terms with examples on pages 35–49.

se sauver (427) — Part. pr. se sauvant — Part. passé sauvé(e)(s)

to run away, to rush off, to escape

Reflexive regular **-er** verb

The Seven Simple Tenses		The Seven Compound Tenses	
Singular	Plural	Singular	Plural
1 présent de l'indicatif		8 passé composé	
me sauve	**nous sauvons**	**me suis sauvé(e)**	**nous sommes sauvé(e)s**
te sauves	**vous sauvez**	**t'es sauvé(e)**	**vous êtes sauvé(e)(s)**
se sauve	**se sauvent**	**s'est sauvé(e)**	**se sont sauvé(e)s**
2 imparfait de l'indicatif		9 plus-que-parfait de l'indicatif	
me sauvais	**nous sauvions**	**m'étais sauvé(e)**	**nous étions sauvé(e)s**
te sauvais	**vous sauviez**	**t'étais sauvé(e)**	**vous étiez sauvé(e)(s)**
se sauvait	**se sauvaient**	**s'était sauvé(e)**	**s'étaient sauvé(e)s**
3 passé simple		10 passé antérieur	
me sauvai	**nous sauvâmes**	**me fus sauvé(e)**	**nous fûmes sauvé(e)s**
te sauvas	**vous sauvâtes**	**te fus sauvé(e)**	**vous fûtes sauvé(e)(s)**
se sauva	**se sauvèrent**	**se fut sauvé(e)**	**se furent sauvé(e)s**
4 futur		11 futur antérieur	
me sauverai	**nous sauverons**	**me serai sauvé(e)**	**nous serons sauvé(e)s**
te sauveras	**vous sauverez**	**te seras sauvé(e)**	**vous serez sauvé(e)(s)**
se sauvera	**se sauveront**	**se sera sauvé(e)**	**se seront sauvé(e)s**
5 conditionnel		12 conditionnel passé	
me sauverais	**nous sauverions**	**me serais sauvé(e)**	**nous serions sauvé(e)s**
te sauverais	**vous sauveriez**	**te serais sauvé(e)**	**vous seriez sauvé(e)(s)**
se sauverait	**se sauveraient**	**se serait sauvé(e)**	**se seraient sauvé(e)s**
6 présent du subjonctif		13 passé du subjonctif	
me sauve	**nous sauvions**	**me sois sauvé(e)**	**nous soyons sauvé(e)s**
te sauves	**vous sauviez**	**te sois sauvé(e)**	**vous soyez sauvé(e)(s)**
se sauve	**se sauvent**	**se soit sauvé(e)**	**se soient sauvé(e)s**
7 imparfait du subjonctif		14 plus-que-parfait du subjonctif	
me sauvasse	**nous sauvassions**	**me fusse sauvé(e)**	**nous fussions sauvé(e)s**
te sauvasses	**vous sauvassiez**	**te fusses sauvé(e)**	**vous fussiez sauvé(e)(s)**
se sauvât	**se sauvassent**	**se fût sauvé(e)**	**se fussent sauvé(e)s**

Impératif
sauve-toi; ne te sauve pas
sauvons-nous; ne nous sauvons pas
sauvez-vous; ne vous sauvez pas

Words and expressions related to this verb

se sauver de prison to get out of prison
sauvegarder to safeguard
le sauvetage life-saving, rescue
Sauve qui peut! Run for your life!
Je me sauve! I'm out of here!
sauver to rescue, to save
sauver la vie à qqn to save someone's life
vendre à la sauvette to peddle in the streets
une vente à la sauvette street peddling

See also **sauver.**

Get acquainted with what preposition goes with what verb. See *Verbs with prepositions* in the Appendixes.

The Seven Simple Tenses		The Seven Compound Tenses	
Singular	Plural	Singular	Plural
1 présent de l'indicatif		8 passé composé	
sais	**savons**	**ai su**	**avons su**
sais	**savez**	**as su**	**avez su**
sait	**savent**	**a su**	**ont su**
2 imparfait de l'indicatif		9 plus-que-parfait de l'indicatif	
savais	**savions**	**avais su**	**avions su**
savais	**saviez**	**avais su**	**aviez su**
savait	**savaient**	**avait su**	**avaient su**
3 passé simple		10 passé antérieur	
sus	**sûmes**	**eus su**	**eûmes su**
sus	**sûtes**	**eus su**	**eûtes su**
sut	**surent**	**eut su**	**eurent su**
4 futur		11 futur antérieur	
saurai	**saurons**	**aurai su**	**aurons su**
sauras	**saurez**	**auras su**	**aurez su**
saura	**sauront**	**aura su**	**auront su**
5 conditionnel		12 conditionnel passé	
saurais	**saurions**	**aurais su**	**aurions su**
saurais	**sauriez**	**aurais su**	**auriez su**
saurait	**sauraient**	**aurait su**	**auraient su**
6 présent du subjonctif		13 passé du subjonctif	
sache	**sachions**	**aie su**	**ayons su**
saches	**sachiez**	**aies su**	**ayez su**
sache	**sachent**	**ait su**	**aient su**
7 imparfait du subjonctif		14 plus-que-parfait du subjonctif	
susse	**sussions**	**eusse su**	**eussions su**
susses	**sussiez**	**eusses su**	**eussiez su**
sût	**sussent**	**eût su**	**eussent su**

Impératif
sache
sachons
sachez

AN ESSENTIAL 55 VERB

Savoir

Savoir is an important verb to know, especially if you are a beginning student. It is used in many idiomatic expressions and everyday situations.

Sentences using savoir

Savez-vous jouer du piano? Do you know how to play the piano?

C'est à savoir. That remains to be seen.

Pas que je sache. Not to my knowledge.

Je voudrais savoir à quelle heure l'avion va partir pour Toronto. I would like to know at what time the plane is going to leave for Toronto.

—Sais-tu que nous déménageons en Europe?
—Oui, je l'ai su hier.

—Do you know that we're moving to Europe?
—Yes, I found out yesterday.

Généralement, les gens qui savent peu parlent beaucoup, et les gens qui savent beaucoup parlent peu. (Rousseau) In general, people who know little talk a lot, and people who know a lot talk little.

Careful! If you're talking about knowing a person, use connaître:

Je le connais. I know him.

Words and expressions related to this verb

le savoir **knowledge**

le savoir-faire **know-how, tact, ability**

savoir faire qqch **to know how to do something**

avoir le savoir-vivre **to be well-mannered, well-bred**

faire savoir **to inform**

sans le savoir **without knowing it**

savoir bon gré à qqn **to be thankful, grateful to someone**

Proverb

Savoir, c'est pouvoir. **Knowledge is power.**

Tongue Twister

Le chasseur, sachant chasser sans son chien, chassera. **The hunter, knowing how to hunt without his dog, will hunt.**

Can't remember the French verb you need? Check the back pages of this book for the English-French verb index!

to dry

Regular **-er** verb endings; spelling change:
é changes to **è** before syllable with mute **e**

The Seven Simple Tenses		The Seven Compound Tenses	
Singular	Plural	Singular	Plural
1 présent de l'indicatif		8 passé composé	
sèche	**séchons**	**ai séché**	**avons séché**
sèches	**séchez**	**as séché**	**avez séché**
sèche	**sèchent**	**a séché**	**ont séché**
2 imparfait de l'indicatif		9 plus-que-parfait de l'indicatif	
séchais	**séchions**	**avais séché**	**avions séché**
séchais	**séchiez**	**avais séché**	**aviez séché**
séchait	**séchaient**	**avait séché**	**avaient séché**
3 passé simple		10 passé antérieur	
séchai	**séchâmes**	**eus séché**	**eûmes séché**
séchas	**séchâtes**	**eus séché**	**eûtes séché**
sécha	**séchèrent**	**eut séché**	**eurent séché**
4 futur		11 futur antérieur	
sécherai	**sécherons**	**aurai séché**	**aurons séché**
sécheras	**sécherez**	**auras séché**	**aurez séché**
séchera	**sécheront**	**aura séché**	**auront séché**
5 conditionnel		12 conditionnel passé	
sécherais	**sécherions**	**aurais séché**	**aurions séché**
sécherais	**sécheriez**	**aurais séché**	**auriez séché**
sécherait	**sécheraient**	**aurait séché**	**auraient séché**
6 présent du subjonctif		13 passé du subjonctif	
sèche	**séchions**	**aie séché**	**ayons séché**
sèches	**séchiez**	**aies séché**	**ayez séché**
sèche	**sèchent**	**ait séché**	**aient séché**
7 imparfait du subjonctif		14 plus-que-parfait du subjonctif	
séchasse	**séchassions**	**eusse séché**	**eussions séché**
séchasses	**séchassiez**	**eusses séché**	**eussiez séché**
séchât	**séchassent**	**eût séché**	**eussent séché**

Impératif
sèche
séchons
séchez

S

Sentences using this verb and words related to it

Les fermiers ont perdu la moitié de leur récolte à cause de la sécheresse. The farmers lost half of their harvest because of the drought.

Sèche tes pleurs, sèche tes pleurs, je t'en prie sèche tes pleurs. Dry your tears, dry your tears, please (I beg of you) dry your tears. ("Sèche tes pleurs," song by Daniel Bélanger)

Words and expressions related to this verb

sec, sèche dry
sèchement dryly, tersely
sécher un cours to skip a class
la sécheresse dryness, drought
mettre à sec to drain, dry up
le séchage drying
un sèche-cheveux, un séchoir à cheveux hair dryer
une sécheuse clothes dryer

secouer (430) — Part. pr. secouant — Part. passé secoué

to shake, to shake down (off)

Regular **-er** verb

The Seven Simple Tenses		The Seven Compound Tenses	
Singular	Plural	Singular	Plural
1 présent de l'indicatif		8 passé composé	
secoue	**secouons**	**ai secoué**	**avons secoué**
secoues	**secouez**	**as secoué**	**avez secoué**
secoue	**secouent**	**a secoué**	**ont secoué**
2 imparfait de l'indicatif		9 plus-que-parfait de l'indicatif	
secouais	**secouions**	**avais secoué**	**avions secoué**
secouais	**secouiez**	**avais secoué**	**aviez secoué**
secouait	**secouaient**	**avait secoué**	**avaient secoué**
3 passé simple		10 passé antérieur	
secouai	**secouâmes**	**eus secoué**	**eûmes secoué**
secouas	**secouâtes**	**eus secoué**	**eûtes secoué**
secoua	**secouèrent**	**eut secoué**	**eurent secoué**
4 futur		11 futur antérieur	
secouerai	**secouerons**	**aurai secoué**	**aurons secoué**
secoueras	**secouerez**	**auras secoué**	**aurez secoué**
secouera	**secoueront**	**aura secoué**	**auront secoué**
5 conditionnel		12 conditionnel passé	
secouerais	**secouerions**	**aurais secoué**	**aurions secoué**
secouerais	**secoueriez**	**aurais secoué**	**auriez secoué**
secouerait	**secoueraient**	**aurait secoué**	**auraient secoué**
6 présent du subjonctif		13 passé du subjonctif	
secoue	**secouions**	**aie secoué**	**ayons secoué**
secoues	**secouiez**	**aies secoué**	**ayez secoué**
secoue	**secouent**	**ait secoué**	**aient secoué**
7 imparfait du subjonctif		14 plus-que-parfait du subjonctif	
secouasse	**secouassions**	**eusse secoué**	**eussions secoué**
secouasses	**secouassiez**	**eusses secoué**	**eussiez secoué**
secouât	**secouassent**	**eût secoué**	**eussent secoué**

Impératif
secoue
secouons
secouez

Words and expressions related to this verb

secouer la tête to shake one's head
le secouement shaking
secouer la poussière to shake off the dust
une secousse jolt; **sans secousse** smoothly

Do you need more drills? Have fun with the *501 French Verbs* CD-ROM!

Irregular verb

to help, to relieve, to succor

The Seven Simple Tenses		The Seven Compound Tenses	
Singular	Plural	Singular	Plural
1 présent de l'indicatif		8 passé composé	
secours	**secourons**	**ai secouru**	**avons secouru**
secours	**secourez**	**as secouru**	**avez secouru**
secourt	**secourent**	**a secouru**	**ont secouru**
2 imparfait de l'indicatif		9 plus-que-parfait de l'indicatif	
secourais	**secourions**	**avais secouru**	**avions secouru**
secourais	**secouriez**	**avais secouru**	**aviez secouru**
secourait	**secouraient**	**avait secouru**	**avaient secouru**
3 passé simple		10 passé antérieur	
secourus	**secourûmes**	**eus secouru**	**eûmes secouru**
secourus	**secourûtes**	**eus secouru**	**eûtes secouru**
secourut	**secoururent**	**eut secouru**	**eurent secouru**
4 futur		11 futur antérieur	
secourrai	**secourrons**	**aurai secouru**	**aurons secouru**
secourras	**secourrez**	**auras secouru**	**aurez secouru**
secourra	**secourront**	**aura secouru**	**auront secouru**
5 conditionnel		12 conditionnel passé	
secourrais	**secourrions**	**aurais secouru**	**aurions secouru**
secourrais	**secourriez**	**aurais secouru**	**auriez secouru**
secourrait	**secourraient**	**aurait secouru**	**auraient secouru**
6 présent du subjonctif		13 passé du subjonctif	
secoure	**secourions**	**aie secouru**	**ayons secouru**
secoures	**secouriez**	**aies secouru**	**ayez secouru**
secoure	**secourent**	**ait secouru**	**aient secouru**
7 imparfait du subjonctif		14 plus-que-parfait du subjonctif	
secourusse	**secourussions**	**eusse secouru**	**eussions secouru**
secourusses	**secourussiez**	**eusses secouru**	**eussiez secouru**
secourût	**secourussent**	**eût secouru**	**eussent secouru**

Impératif
secours
secourons
secourez

Common idiomatic expressions using this verb and words related to it

le secours help, assistance
Au secours! Help!
crier au secours to shout for help
une roue de secours spare wheel
une sortie de secours emergency exit
secourir qqn contre un ennemi to help someone from an enemy
aller au secours de qqn to go to someone's aid
prêter secours à qqn to go to someone's rescue, assistance
une équipe de secours rescue squad
courir to run

Don't forget to study the section on defective and impersonal verbs. It's right after this main list.

séduire (432) — Part. pr. séduisant — Part. passé séduit

to seduce

Irregular verb

The Seven Simple Tenses		The Seven Compound Tenses	
Singular	Plural	Singular	Plural
1 présent de l'indicatif		8 passé composé	
séduis	**séduisons**	**ai séduit**	**avons séduit**
séduis	**séduisez**	**as séduit**	**avez séduit**
séduit	**séduisent**	**a séduit**	**ont séduit**
2 imparfait de l'indicatif		9 plus-que-parfait de l'indicatif	
séduisais	**séduisions**	**avais séduit**	**avions séduit**
séduisais	**séduisiez**	**avais séduit**	**aviez séduit**
séduisait	**séduisaient**	**avait séduit**	**avaient séduit**
3 passé simple		10 passé antérieur	
séduisis	**séduisîmes**	**eus séduit**	**eûmes séduit**
séduisis	**séduisîtes**	**eus séduit**	**eûtes séduit**
séduisit	**séduisirent**	**eut séduit**	**eurent séduit**
4 futur		11 futur antérieur	
séduirai	**séduirons**	**aurai séduit**	**aurons séduit**
séduiras	**séduirez**	**auras séduit**	**aurez séduit**
séduira	**séduiront**	**aura séduit**	**auront séduit**
5 conditionnel		12 conditionnel passé	
séduirais	**séduirions**	**aurais séduit**	**aurions séduit**
séduirais	**séduiriez**	**aurais séduit**	**auriez séduit**
séduirait	**séduiraient**	**aurait séduit**	**auraient séduit**
6 présent du subjonctif		13 passé du subjonctif	
séduise	**séduisions**	**aie séduit**	**ayons séduit**
séduises	**séduisiez**	**aies séduit**	**ayez séduit**
séduise	**séduisent**	**ait séduit**	**aient séduit**
7 imparfait du subjonctif		14 plus-que-parfait du subjonctif	
séduisisse	**séduisissions**	**eusse séduit**	**eussions séduit**
séduisisses	**séduisissiez**	**eusses séduit**	**eussiez séduit**
séduisît	**séduisissent**	**eût séduit**	**eussent séduit**

Impératif
séduis
séduisons
séduisez

Words related to this verb
séduisant, séduisante fascinating, seductive, attractive
un séducteur, une séductrice tempter (temptress), seducer (seductress)
une séduction seduction, enticement

See also **conduire, déduire, introduire, produire, réduire, reproduire,** and **traduire.**

Soak up some verbs used in weather expressions. There's a list in the Appendixes!

Regular **-er** verb

to sojourn, to live somewhere temporarily

The Seven Simple Tenses		The Seven Compound Tenses	
Singular	Plural	Singular	Plural
1 présent de l'indicatif		8 passé composé	
séjourne	**séjournons**	**ai séjourné**	**avons séjourné**
séjournes	**séjournez**	**as séjourné**	**avez séjourné**
séjourne	**séjournent**	**a séjourné**	**ont séjourné**
2 imparfait de l'indicatif		9 plus-que-parfait de l'indicatif	
séjournais	**séjournions**	**avais séjourné**	**avions séjourné**
séjournais	**séjourniez**	**avais séjourné**	**aviez séjourné**
séjournait	**séjournaient**	**avait séjourné**	**avaient séjourné**
3 passé simple		10 passé antérieur	
séjournai	**séjournâmes**	**eus séjourné**	**eûmes séjourné**
séjournas	**séjournâtes**	**eus séjourné**	**eûtes séjourné**
séjourna	**séjournèrent**	**eut séjourné**	**eurent séjourné**
4 futur		11 futur antérieur	
séjournerai	**séjournerons**	**aurai séjourné**	**aurons séjourné**
séjourneras	**séjournerez**	**auras séjourné**	**aurez séjourné**
séjournera	**séjourneront**	**aura séjourné**	**auront séjourné**
5 conditionnel		12 conditionnel passé	
séjournerais	**séjournerions**	**aurais séjourné**	**aurions séjourné**
séjournerais	**séjourneriez**	**aurais séjourné**	**auriez séjourné**
séjournerait	**séjourneraient**	**aurait séjourné**	**auraient séjourné**
6 présent du subjonctif		13 passé du subjonctif	
séjourne	**séjournions**	**aie séjourné**	**ayons séjourné**
séjournes	**séjourniez**	**aies séjourné**	**ayez séjourné**
séjourne	**séjournent**	**ait séjourné**	**aient séjourné**
7 imparfait du subjonctif		14 plus-que-parfait du subjonctif	
séjournasse	**séjournassions**	**eusse séjourné**	**eussions séjourné**
séjournasses	**séjournassiez**	**eusses séjourné**	**eussiez séjourné**
séjournât	**séjournassent**	**eût séjourné**	**eussent séjourné**

Impératif
séjourne
séjournons
séjournez

Words and expressions related to this verb

séjourner à un hôtel to stay (stop) at a hotel
un séjour sojourn, stay
faire un séjour à la campagne to stay in the country
séjourner chez des amis to stay with friends
le jour day
une salle de séjour living room
un bref séjour a brief stay
Mon séjour dans votre hôtel a été très agréable. My stay in your hotel has been very pleasuant.

Can't find the verb you're looking for? Check the back pages of this book for a list of over 2,600 additional verbs!

to feel, to smell, to perceive

Irregular verb

The Seven Simple Tenses		The Seven Compound Tenses	
Singular	Plural	Singular	Plural
1 présent de l'indicatif		8 passé composé	
sens	**sentons**	**ai senti**	**avons senti**
sens	**sentez**	**as senti**	**avez senti**
sent	**sentent**	**a senti**	**ont senti**
2 imparfait de l'indicatif		9 plus-que-parfait de l'indicatif	
sentais	**sentions**	**avais senti**	**avions senti**
sentais	**sentiez**	**avais senti**	**aviez senti**
sentait	**sentaient**	**avait senti**	**avaient senti**
3 passé simple		10 passé antérieur	
sentis	**sentîmes**	**eus senti**	**eûmes senti**
sentis	**sentîtes**	**eus senti**	**eûtes senti**
sentit	**sentirent**	**eut senti**	**eurent senti**
4 futur		11 futur antérieur	
sentirai	**sentirons**	**aurai senti**	**aurons senti**
sentiras	**sentirez**	**auras senti**	**aurez senti**
sentira	**sentiront**	**aura senti**	**auront senti**
5 conditionnel		12 conditionnel passé	
sentirais	**sentirions**	**aurais senti**	**aurions senti**
sentirais	**sentiriez**	**aurais senti**	**auriez senti**
sentirait	**sentiraient**	**aurait senti**	**auraient senti**
6 présent du subjonctif		13 passé du subjonctif	
sente	**sentions**	**aie senti**	**ayons senti**
sentes	**sentiez**	**aies senti**	**ayez senti**
sente	**sentent**	**ait senti**	**aient senti**
7 imparfait du subjonctif		14 plus-que-parfait du subjonctif	
sentisse	**sentissions**	**eusse senti**	**eussions senti**
sentisses	**sentissiez**	**eusses senti**	**eussiez senti**
sentît	**sentissent**	**eût senti**	**eussent senti**

Impératif
sens
sentons
sentez

AN ESSENTIAL 55 VERB

Sentir

Sentir is a very improtant verb for a beginning student because, although it is irregular, several useful verbs are conjugated like it. There are also many idiomatic expressions related to **sentir**.

Sentences using sentir

Qu'est-ce que tu fais pour le dîner? Ça sent bon! What are you making for dinner? That smells good!

Je me sens mal. I feel ill.

Je ne me sens pas bien. I don't feel well.

Ouvre la fenêtre, Claire. Ça sent le renfermé ici! Open the window, Claire. It smells stuffy here!

If you can conjugate **sentir** you can also conjugate the following verbs:

consentir **to allow; consentir à** **to agree to**

pressentir **to sense**

Words and expressions related to this verb

un sentiment **feeling, sense, impression**

un sentiment d'appartenance **feeling of membership, belonging**

sentimental, sentimentale **sentimental**

la sentimentalité **sentimentality**

le sentimentalisme **sentimentalism**

sentir le chagrin **to feel sorrow**

se sentir + adj. **to feel + adj.**

ressentir **to feel**

le ressentiment **resentment**

sentir bon **to smell good**

sentir mauvais **to smell bad**

faire sentir qqch à qqn **to make someone feel something**

se faire sentir **to make itself felt**

ne se sentir pas bien **not to feel well**

S

Don't forget to study the section on defective and impersonal verbs. It's right after this main list.

The subject pronouns are found on page 103.

to separate

Regular **-er** verb

The Seven Simple Tenses		The Seven Compound Tenses	
Singular	Plural	Singular	Plural
1 présent de l'indicatif		8 passé composé	
sépare	**séparons**	**ai séparé**	**avons séparé**
sépares	**séparez**	**as séparé**	**avez séparé**
sépare	**séparent**	**a séparé**	**ont séparé**
2 imparfait de l'indicatif		9 plus-que-parfait de l'indicatif	
séparais	**séparions**	**avais séparé**	**avions séparé**
séparais	**sépariez**	**avais séparé**	**aviez séparé**
séparait	**séparaient**	**avait séparé**	**avaient séparé**
3 passé simple		10 passé antérieur	
séparai	**séparâmes**	**eus séparé**	**eûmes séparé**
séparas	**séparâtes**	**eus séparé**	**eûtes séparé**
sépara	**séparèrent**	**eut séparé**	**eurent séparé**
4 futur		11 futur antérieur	
séparerai	**séparerons**	**aurai séparé**	**aurons séparé**
sépareras	**séparerez**	**auras séparé**	**aurez séparé**
séparera	**sépareront**	**aura séparé**	**auront séparé**
5 conditionnel		12 conditionnel passé	
séparerais	**séparerions**	**aurais séparé**	**aurions séparé**
séparerais	**sépareriez**	**aurais séparé**	**auriez séparé**
séparerait	**sépareraient**	**aurait séparé**	**auraient séparé**
6 présent du subjonctif		13 passé du subjonctif	
sépare	**séparions**	**aie séparé**	**ayons séparé**
séparés	**sépariez**	**aies séparé**	**ayez séparé**
sépare	**séparent**	**ait séparé**	**aient séparé**
7 imparfait du subjonctif		14 plus-que-parfait du subjonctif	
séparasse	**séparassions**	**eusse séparé**	**eussions séparé**
séparasses	**séparassiez**	**eusses séparé**	**eussiez séparé**
séparât	**séparassent**	**eût séparé**	**eussent séparé**

Impératif
sépare
séparons
séparez

Words and expressions related to this verb

séparer de to sever from, to separate from

Les Pyrénées séparent la France et l'Espagne. France is separated from Spain by the Pyrenees.

se séparer de to be separated from, to separate oneself from

Madame Dubois se sépare de son mari. Mrs. Dubois is separating from her husband.

une séparation separation, parting

Get acquainted with what preposition goes with what verb. See *Verbs with prepositions* in the Appendixes.

Regular **-er** verb

to grasp, to press, to squeeze, to shake (hands)

The Seven Simple Tenses		The Seven Compound Tenses	
Singular	Plural	Singular	Plural
1 présent de l'indicatif		8 passé composé	
serre	**serrons**	**ai serré**	**avons serré**
serres	**serrez**	**as serré**	**avez serré**
serre	**serrent**	**a serré**	**ont serré**
2 imparfait de l'indicatif		9 plus-que-parfait de l'indicatif	
serrais	**serrions**	**avais serré**	**avions serré**
serrais	**serriez**	**avais serré**	**aviez serré**
serrait	**serraient**	**avait serré**	**avaient serré**
3 passé simple		10 passé antérieur	
serrai	**serrâmes**	**eus serré**	**eûmes serré**
serras	**serrâtes**	**eus serré**	**eûtes serré**
serra	**serrèrent**	**eut serré**	**eurent serré**
4 futur		11 futur antérieur	
serrerai	**serrerons**	**aurai serré**	**aurons serré**
serreras	**serrerez**	**auras serré**	**aurez serré**
serrera	**serreront**	**aura serré**	**auront serré**
5 conditionnel		12 conditionnel passé	
serrerais	**serrerions**	**aurais serré**	**aurions serré**
serrerais	**serreriez**	**aurais serré**	**auriez serré**
serrerait	**serreraient**	**aurait serré**	**auraient serré**
6 présent du subjonctif		13 passé du subjonctif	
serre	**serrions**	**aie serré**	**ayons serré**
serres	**serriez**	**aies serré**	**ayez serré**
serre	**serrent**	**ait serré**	**aient serré**
7 imparfait du subjonctif		14 plus-que-parfait du subjonctif	
serrasse	**serrassions**	**eusse serré**	**eussions serré**
serrasses	**serrassiez**	**eusses serré**	**eussiez serré**
serrât	**serrassent**	**eût serré**	**eussent serré**

Impératif
serre
serrons
serrez

Words and expressions related to this verb

serrer la main à qqn to shake hands with someone
serrer un noeud to tighten a knot
un serre-livres book end (**des serre-livres**)
serrer les rangs to close up ranks
serrer le coeur to wring one's heart
serrés comme des harengs packed like sardines
une serrure lock; **le trou de la serrure** keyhole
Serrez à droite./Serrez à gauche. Keep (Squeeze) right/left.

Grammar putting you in a tense mood? Review the definitions of basic grammatical terms with examples on pages 35–49.

to serve, to be useful

Irregular verb

The Seven Simple Tenses		The Seven Compound Tenses	
Singular	Plural	Singular	Plural
1 présent de l'indicatif		8 passé composé	
sers	**servons**	**ai servi**	**avons servi**
sers	**servez**	**as servi**	**avez servi**
sert	**servent**	**a servi**	**ont servi**
2 imparfait de l'indicatif		9 plus-que-parfait de l'indicatif	
servais	**servions**	**avais servi**	**avions servi**
servais	**serviez**	**avais servi**	**aviez servi**
servait	**servaient**	**avait servi**	**avaient servi**
3 passé simple		10 passé antérieur	
servis	**servîmes**	**eus servi**	**eûmes servi**
servis	**servîtes**	**eus servi**	**eûtes servi**
servit	**servirent**	**eut servi**	**eurent servi**
4 futur		11 futur antérieur	
servirai	**servirons**	**aurai servi**	**aurons servi**
serviras	**servirez**	**auras servi**	**aurez servi**
servira	**serviront**	**aura servi**	**auront servi**
5 conditionnel		12 conditionnel passé	
servirais	**servirions**	**aurais servi**	**aurions servi**
servirais	**serviriez**	**aurais servi**	**auriez servi**
servirait	**serviraient**	**aurait servi**	**auraient servi**
6 présent du subjonctif		13 passé du subjonctif	
serve	**servions**	**aie servi**	**ayons servi**
serves	**serviez**	**aies servi**	**ayez servi**
serve	**servent**	**ait servi**	**aient servi**
7 imparfait du subjonctif		14 plus-que-parfait du subjonctif	
servisse	**servissions**	**eusse servi**	**eussions servi**
servisses	**servissiez**	**eusses servi**	**eussiez servi**
servît	**servissent**	**eût servi**	**eussent servi**

Impératif
sers
servons
servez

Words and expressions related to this verb

le serveur waiter
la serveuse waitress
le service service
une serviette napkin
un serviteur servant
la servitude servitude
desservir to clear off the table
un serveur server (computer)

See also **se servir.**

se servir to serve oneself, to help oneself
se servir de qqch to use something, to avail oneself of something, to make use of something
servir à qqch to be of some use
servir à rien to be of no use; **Cela ne sert à rien.** That serves no purpose.

Refelxive irregular verb

to serve oneself, to help oneself (to food and drink)

The Seven Simple Tenses		The Seven Compound Tenses	
Singular	Plural	Singular	Plural
1 présent de l'indicatif		8 passé composé	
me sers	**nous servons**	**me suis servi(e)**	**nous sommes servi(e)s**
te sers	**vous servez**	**t'es servi(e)**	**vous êtes servi(e)(s)**
se sert	**se servent**	**s'est servi(e)**	**se sont servi(e)s**
2 imparfait de l'indicatif		9 plus-que-parfait de l'indicatif	
me servais	**nous servions**	**m'étais servi(e)**	**nous étions servi(e)s**
te servais	**vous serviez**	**t'étais servi(e)**	**vous étiez servi(e)(s)**
se servait	**se servaient**	**s'était servi(e)**	**s'étaient servi(e)s**
3 passé simple		10 passé antérieur	
me servis	**nous servîmes**	**me fus servi(e)**	**nous fûmes servi(e)s**
te servis	**vous servîtes**	**te fus servi(e)**	**vous fûtes servi(e)(s)**
se servit	**se servirent**	**se fut servi(e)**	**se furent servi(e)s**
4 futur		11 futur antérieur	
me servirai	**nous servirons**	**me serai servi(e)**	**nous serons servi(e)s**
te serviras	**vous servirez**	**te seras servi(e)**	**vous serez servi(e)(s)**
se servira	**se serviront**	**se sera servi(e)**	**se seront servi(e)s**
5 conditionnel		12 conditionnel passé	
me servirais	**nous servirions**	**me serais servi(e)**	**nous serions servi(e)s**
te servirais	**vous serviriez**	**te serais servi(e)**	**vous seriez servi(e)(s)**
se servirait	**se serviraient**	**se serait servi(e)**	**se seraient servi(e)s**
6 présent du subjonctif		13 passé du subjonctif	
me serve	**nous servions**	**me sois servi(e)**	**nous soyons servi(e)s**
te serves	**vous serviez**	**te sois servi(e)**	**vous soyez servi(e)(s)**
se serve	**se servent**	**se soit servi(e)**	**se soient servi(e)s**
7 imparfait du subjonctif		14 plus-que-parfait du subjonctif	
me servisse	**nous servissions**	**me fusse servi(e)**	**nous fussions servi(e)s**
te servisses	**vous servissiez**	**te fusses servi(e)**	**vous fussiez servi(e)(s)**
se servît	**se servissent**	**se fût servi(e)**	**se fussent servi(e)s**

Impératif
sers-toi; ne te sers pas
servons-nous; ne nous servons pas
servez-vous; ne vous servez pas

Words and expressions related to this verb

un serviteur servant
la servitude servitude
le serveur waiter
la serveuse waitress
le service service
une serviette napkin

See also **servir.**

se servir de qqch to use something, to make use of something
Servez-vous, je vous en prie! Help yourself, please!
Est-ce qu'on se sert seul dans ce restaurant?—Oui, c'est un restaurant self-service.

Can't find the verb you're looking for? Check the back pages of this book for a list of over 2,600 additional verbs!

to whistle, to hiss, to boo

Regular **-er** verb

The Seven Simple Tenses		The Seven Compound Tenses	
Singular	Plural	Singular	Plural
1 présent de l'indicatif		8 passé composé	
siffle	**sifflons**	**ai sifflé**	**avons sifflé**
siffles	**sifflez**	**as sifflé**	**avez sifflé**
siffle	**sifflent**	**a sifflé**	**ont sifflé**
2 imparfait de l'indicatif		9 plus-que-parfait de l'indicatif	
sifflais	**sifflions**	**avais sifflé**	**avions sifflé**
sifflais	**siffliez**	**avais sifflé**	**aviez sifflé**
sifflait	**sifflaient**	**avait sifflé**	**avaient sifflé**
3 passé simple		10 passé antérieur	
sifflai	**sifflâmes**	**eus sifflé**	**eûmes sifflé**
sifflas	**sifflâtes**	**eus sifflé**	**eûtes sifflé**
siffla	**sifflèrent**	**eut sifflé**	**eurent sifflé**
4 futur		11 futur antérieur	
sifflerai	**sifflerons**	**aurai sifflé**	**aurons sifflé**
siffleras	**sifflerez**	**auras sifflé**	**aurez sifflé**
sifflera	**siffleront**	**aura sifflé**	**auront sifflé**
5 conditionnel		12 conditionnel passé	
sifflerais	**sifflerions**	**aurais sifflé**	**aurions sifflé**
sifflerais	**siffleriez**	**aurais sifflé**	**auriez sifflé**
sifflerait	**siffleraient**	**aurait sifflé**	**auraient sifflé**
6 présent du subjonctif		13 passé du subjonctif	
siffle	**sifflions**	**aie sifflé**	**ayons sifflé**
siffles	**siffliez**	**aies sifflé**	**ayez sifflé**
siffle	**sifflent**	**ait sifflé**	**aient sifflé**
7 imparfait du subjonctif		14 plus-que-parfait du subjonctif	
sifflasse	**sifflassions**	**eusse sifflé**	**eussions sifflé**
sifflasses	**sifflassiez**	**eusses sifflé**	**eussiez sifflé**
sifflât	**sifflassent**	**eût sifflé**	**eussent sifflé**

Impératif
siffle
sifflons
sifflez

Words and expressions related to this verb

un sifflet whistle
un sifflet d'alarme alarm whistle
un siffleur, une siffleuse whistler, booer, hisser
le sifflet d'un agent de police policeman's whistle
le sifflement whistling, hissing

Do you need more drills? Have fun with the *501 French Verbs* CD-ROM!

Regular **-er** verb

to point out, to signal

The Seven Simple Tenses		The Seven Compound Tenses	
Singular	Plural	Singular	Plural
1 présent de l'indicatif		8 passé composé	
signale	**signalons**	**ai signalé**	**avons signalé**
signales	**signalez**	**as signalé**	**avez signalé**
signale	**signalent**	**a signalé**	**ont signalé**
2 imparfait de l'indicatif		9 plus-que-parfait de l'indicatif	
signalais	**signalions**	**avais signalé**	**avions signalé**
signalais	**signaliez**	**avais signalé**	**aviez signalé**
signalait	**signalaient**	**avait signalé**	**avaient signalé**
3 passé simple		10 passé antérieur	
signalai	**signalâmes**	**eus signalé**	**eûmes signalé**
signalas	**signalâtes**	**eus signalé**	**eûtes signalé**
signala	**signalèrent**	**eut signalé**	**eurent signalé**
4 futur		11 futur antérieur	
signalerai	**signalerons**	**aurai signalé**	**aurons signalé**
signaleras	**signalerez**	**auras signalé**	**aurez signalé**
signalera	**signaleront**	**aura signalé**	**auront signalé**
5 conditionnel		12 conditionnel passé	
signalerais	**signalerions**	**aurais signalé**	**aurions signalé**
signaierais	**signaleriez**	**aurais signalé**	**auriez signalé**
signalerait	**signaleraient**	**aurait signalé**	**auraient signalé**
6 présent du subjonctif		13 passé du subjonctif	
signale	**signalions**	**aie signalé**	**ayons signalé**
signales	**signaliez**	**aies signalé**	**ayez signalé**
signale	**signalent**	**ait signalé**	**aient signalé**
7 imparfait du subjonctif		14 plus-que-parfait du subjonctif	
signalasse	**signalassions**	**eusse signalé**	**eussions signalé**
signalasses	**signalassiez**	**eusses signalé**	**eussiez signalé**
signalât	**signalassent**	**eût signalé**	**eussent signalé**

Impératif
signale
signalons
signalez

Words and expressions related to this verb

se signaler to distinguish oneself
un signal signal
le signal d'alarme alarm signal
les signaux de route road signs
signaliser to mark with signs
le signal de détresse distress signal
tirer le signal d'alarme to pull the alarm
les moyens de signalisation means of signaling

Don't forget to study the section on defective and impersonal verbs. It's right after this main list.

signer (441)

Part. pr. **signant** Part. passé **signé**

to sign

Regular **-er** verb

The Seven Simple Tenses		The Seven Compound Tenses	
Singular	Plural	Singular	Plural
1 présent de l'indicatif		8 passé composé	
signe	**signons**	**ai signé**	**avons signé**
signes	**signez**	**as signé**	**avez signé**
signe	**signent**	**a signé**	**ont signé**
2 imparfait de l'indicatif		9 plus-que-parfait de l'indicatif	
signais	**signions**	**avais signé**	**avions signé**
signais	**signiez**	**avais signé**	**aviez signé**
signait	**signaient**	**avait signé**	**avaient signé**
3 passé simple		10 passé antérieur	
signai	**signâmes**	**eus signé**	**eûmes signé**
signas	**signâtes**	**eus signé**	**eûtes signé**
signa	**signèrent**	**eut signé**	**eurent signé**
4 futur		11 futur antérieur	
signerai	**signerons**	**aurai signé**	**aurons signé**
signeras	**signerez**	**auras signé**	**aurez signé**
signera	**signeront**	**aura signé**	**auront signé**
5 conditionnel		12 conditionnel passé	
signerais	**signerions**	**aurais signé**	**aurions signé**
signerais	**signeriez**	**aurais signé**	**auriez signé**
signerait	**signeraient**	**aurait signé**	**auraient signé**
6 présent du subjonctif		13 passé du subjonctif	
signe	**signions**	**aie signé**	**ayons signé**
signes	**signiez**	**aies signé**	**ayez signé**
signe	**signent**	**ait signé**	**aient signé**
7 imparfait du subjonctif		14 plus-que-parfait du subjonctif	
signasse	**signassions**	**eusse signé**	**eussions signé**
signasses	**signassiez**	**eusses signé**	**eussiez signé**
signât	**signassent**	**eût signé**	**eussent signé**

Impératif
signe
signons
signez

Words and expressions related to this verb

se signer to cross oneself (to make the sign of the Cross)
un signe gesture, sign; **un signe de tête** nod
faire le signe de la Croix to make the sign of the Cross
la signature signature, signing
assigner to assign
consigner to deposit (money); to consign (merchandise)
la consignation consignment, deposit
le, la consignataire consignee
le, la signataire signer
les signes de vie signs of life
Veuillez signer le document ici. Please sign the document here.

If you don't know the French verb for an English verb you have in mind, try the index in the Appendixes.

Regular **-er** verb endings; spelling change: retain the **ge** before **a** or **o** to keep the soft **g** sound of the verb

to dream, to think

The Seven Simple Tenses		The Seven Compound Tenses	
Singular	Plural	Singular	Plural
1 présent de l'indicatif		8 passé composé	
songe	**songeons**	**ai songé**	**avons songé**
songes	**songez**	**as songé**	**avez songé**
songe	**songent**	**a songé**	**ont songé**
2 imparfait de l'indicatif		9 plus-que-parfait de l'indicatif	
songeais	**songions**	**avais songé**	**avions songé**
songeais	**songiez**	**avais songé**	**aviez songé**
songeait	**songeaient**	**avait songé**	**avaient songé**
3 passé simple		10 passé antérieur	
songeai	**songeâmes**	**eus songé**	**eûmes songé**
songeas	**songeâtes**	**eus songé**	**eûtes songé**
songea	**songèrent**	**eut songé**	**eurent songé**
4 futur		11 futur antérieur	
songerai	**songerons**	**aurai songe**	**aurons songé**
songeras	**songerez**	**auras songé**	**aurez songé**
songera	**songeront**	**aura songé**	**auront songé**
5 conditionnel		12 conditionnel passé	
songerais	**songerions**	**aurais songé**	**aurions songé**
songerais	**songeriez**	**aurais songé**	**auriez songé**
songerait	**songeraient**	**aurait songé**	**auraient songé**
6 présent du subjonctif		13 passé du subjonctif	
songe	**songions**	**aie songé**	**ayons songé**
songes	**songiez**	**aies songé**	**ayez songé**
songe	**songent**	**ait songé**	**aient songé**
7 imparfait du subjonctif		14 plus-que-parfait du subjonctif	
songeasse	**songeassions**	**eusse songé**	**eussions songé**
songeasses	**songeassiez**	**eusses songé**	**eussiez songé**
songeât	**songeassent**	**eût songé**	**eussent songé**

Impératif
songe
songeons
songez

Words and expressions related to this verb

un songe dream
un songeur, une songeuse dreamer
songer à l'avenir to think of the future
faire un songe to have a dream
songer à to think of something, to give thought to something
Songez-y bien! Think it over carefully!
songer à faire qqch to contemplate doing something

Get acquainted with what preposition goes with what. See *Verbs with prepositions* in the Appendixes.

sonner (443) — Part. pr. sonnant — Part. passé sonné

to ring

Regular **-er** verb

The Seven Simple Tenses		The Seven Compound Tenses	
Singular	Plural	Singular	Plural
1 présent de l'indicatif		8 passé composé	
sonne	**sonnons**	**ai sonné**	**avons sonné**
sonnes	**sonnez**	**as sonné**	**avez sonné**
sonne	**sonnent**	**a sonné**	**ont sonné**
2 imparfait de l'indicatif		9 plus-que-parfait de l'indicatif	
sonnais	**sonnions**	**avais sonné**	**avions sonné**
sonnais	**sonniez**	**avais sonné**	**aviez sonné**
sonnait	**sonnaient**	**avait sonné**	**avaient sonné**
3 passé simple		10 passé antérieur	
sonnai	**sonnâmes**	**eus sonné**	**eûmes sonné**
sonnas	**sonnâtes**	**eus sonné**	**eûtes sonné**
sonna	**sonnèrent**	**eut sonné**	**eurent sonné**
4 futur		11 futur antérieur	
sonnerai	**sonnerons**	**aurai sonné**	**aurons sonné**
sonneras	**sonnerez**	**auras sonné**	**aurez sonné**
sonnera	**sonneront**	**aura sonné**	**auront sonné**
5 conditionnel		12 conditionnel passé	
sonnerais	**sonnerions**	**aurais sonné**	**aurions sonné**
sonnerais	**sonneriez**	**aurais sonné**	**auriez sonné**
sonnerait	**sonneraient**	**aurait sonné**	**auraient sonné**
6 présent du subjonctif		13 passé du subjonctif	
sonne	**sonnions**	**aie sonné**	**ayons sonné**
sonnes	**sonniez**	**aies sonné**	**ayez sonné**
sonne	**sonnent**	**ait sonné**	**aient sonné**
7 imparfait du subjonctif		14 plus-que-parfait du subjonctif	
sonnasse	**sonnassions**	**eusse sonné**	**eussions sonné**
sonnasses	**sonnassiez**	**eusses sonné**	**eussiez sonné**
sonnât	**sonnassent**	**eût sonné**	**eussent sonné**

Impératif
sonne
sonnons
sonnez

Words and expressions related to this verb

une sonnerie ringing, chiming
une sonnette house bell, doorbell
une sonnette électrique electric bell
le son sound, ringing
une sonnette de nuit night bell
sonner creux to sound hollow
une sonnette d'alarme alarm bell
faire sonner un mot to emphasize a word
une clochette hand bell
la sonnerie du téléphone the ringing of the telephone

Use the guide to French pronunciation. It's in the Appendixes.

Irregular verb

to go out, to leave

The Seven Simple Tenses		The Seven Compound Tenses	
Singular	Plural	Singular	Plural
1 présent de l'indicatif		8 passé composé	
sors	**sortons**	**suis sorti(e)**	**sommes sorti(e)s**
sors	**sortez**	**es sorti(e)**	**êtes sorti(e)(s)**
sort	**sortent**	**est sorti(e)**	**sont sorti(e)s**
2 imparfait de l'indicatif		9 plus-que-parfait de l'indicatif	
sortais	**sortions**	**étais sorti(e)**	**étions sorti(e)s**
sortais	**sortiez**	**étais sorti(e)**	**étiez sorti(e)(s)**
sortait	**sortaient**	**était sorti(e)**	**étaient sorti(e)s**
3 passé simple		10 passé antérieur	
sortis	**sortîmes**	**fus sorti(e)**	**fûmes sorti(e)s**
sortis	**sortîtes**	**fus sorti(e)**	**fûtes sorti(e)(s)**
sortit	**sortirent**	**fut sorti(e)**	**furent sorti(e)s**
4 futur		11 futur antérieur	
sortirai	**sortirons**	**serai sorti(e)**	**serons sorti(e)s**
sortiras	**sortirez**	**seras sorti(e)**	**serez sorti(e)(s)**
sortira	**sortiront**	**sera sorti(e)**	**seront sorti(e)s**
5 conditionnel		12 conditionnel passé	
sortirais	**sortirions**	**serais sorti(e)**	**serions sorti(e)s**
sortirais	**sortiriez**	**serais sorti(e)**	**seriez sorti(e)(s)**
sortirait	**sortiraient**	**serait sorti(e)**	**seraient sorti(e)s**
6 présent du subjonctif		13 passé du subjonctif	
sorte	**sortions**	**sois sorti(e)**	**soyons sorti(e)s**
sortes	**sortiez**	**sois sorti(e)**	**soyez sorti(e)(s)**
sorte	**sortent**	**soit sorti(e)**	**soient sorti(e)s**
7 imparfait du subjonctif		14 plus-que-parfait du subjonctif	
sortisse	**sortissions**	**fusse sorti(e)**	**fussions sorti(e)s**
sortisses	**sortissiez**	**fusses sorti(e)**	**fussiez sorti(e)(s)**
sortît	**sortissent**	**fût sorti(e)**	**fussent sorti(e)s**

Impératif
sors
sortons
sortez

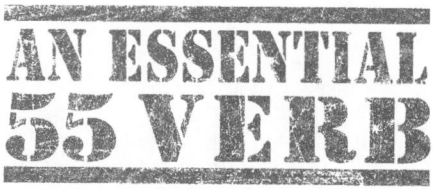

AN ESSENTIAL 55 VERB

Sortir

Sortir is useful in many everyday situations and idiomatic expressions. Although **sortir** is an irregular verb, many verbs are conjugated like it.

This verb is conjugated with **avoir** when it has a direct object. Review page 6.

Example: **Elle a sorti son mouchoir.** She took out her handkerchief.
BUT: **Elle est sortie hier soir.** She went out last night.

Sentences using sortir

Le cambrioleur est entré par la fenêtre, mais il est sorti par la porte. The burglar came in through the window, but he left through the door.

René et Nathalie sortent ensemble depuis longtemps. René and Nathalie have been going out for a long time.

Le magicien a sorti un lapin de son chapeau haut-de-forme. The magician took a rabbit out of his top hat.

Words and expressions related to this verb

une sortie **exit**

une sortie de secours **emergency exit**

sortir du lit **to get out of bed**

se sortir d'une situation **to get oneself out of a situation**

sortir d'une bonne famille **to come from a good family**

If you can conjugate **sortir** you can also conjugate the following verbs:

démentir **to contradict**

partir **to leave**

ressortir **to go out again (Note: Ressortir à means "to pertain to." In this usage ressortir is conjugated like a regular -ir verb.)**

Careful! Assortir (to match) looks like it should be conjugated like sortir, but it is a regular -ir verb.

Proverb

La faim fait sortir le loup du bois. **Hunger makes the wolf leave the woods.**

Can't remember the French verb you need? Check the back pages of this book for the English-French verb index!

Regular **-er** verb

to blow, to pant, to prompt (an actor/actress with a cue)

The Seven Simple Tenses		The Seven Compound Tenses	
Singular	Plural	Singular	Plural
1 présent de l'indicatif		8 passé composé	
souffle	**soufflons**	**ai soufflé**	**avons soufflé**
souffles	**soufflez**	**as soufflé**	**avez soufflé**
souffle	**soufflent**	**a soufflé**	**ont soufflé**
2 imparfait de l'indicatif		9 plus-que-parfait de l'indicatif	
soufflais	**soufflions**	**avais soufflé**	**avions soufflé**
soufflais	**souffliez**	**avais soufflé**	**aviez soufflé**
soufflait	**soufflaient**	**avait soufflé**	**avaient soufflé**
3 passé simple		10 passé antérieur	
soufflai	**soufflâmes**	**eus soufflé**	**eûmes soufflé**
soufflas	**soufflâtes**	**eus soufflé**	**eûtes soufflé**
souffla	**soufflèrent**	**eut soufflé**	**eurent soufflé**
4 futur		11 futur antérieur	
soufflerai	**soufflerons**	**aurai soufflé**	**aurons soufflé**
souffleras	**soufflerez**	**auras soufflé**	**aurez soufflé**
soufflera	**souffleront**	**aura soufflé**	**auront soufflé**
5 conditionnel		12 conditionnel passé	
soufflerais	**soufflerions**	**aurais soufflé**	**aurions soufflé**
soufflerais	**souffleriez**	**aurais soufflé**	**auriez soufflé**
soufflerait	**souffleraient**	**aurait soufflé**	**auraient soufflé**
6 présent du subjonctif		13 passé du subjonctif	
souffle	**soufflions**	**aie soufflé**	**ayons soufflé**
souffles	**souffliez**	**aies soufflé**	**ayez soufflé**
souffle	**soufflent**	**ait soufflé**	**aient soufflé**
7 imparfait du subjonctif		14 plus-que-parfait du subjonctif	
soufflasse	**soufflassions**	**eusse soufflé**	**eussions soufflé**
soufflasses	**soufflassiez**	**eusses soufflé**	**eussiez soufflé**
soufflât	**soufflassent**	**eût soufflé**	**eussent soufflé**

Impératif
souffle
soufflons
soufflez

Words and expressions related to this verb

le souffle breath, breathing
à bout de souffle out of breath
retenir son souffle to hold one's breath
couper le souffle à qqn to take someone's breath away
un soufflé au fromage cheese soufflé
souffler le verre to blow glass
le souffle cardiaque heart murmur
une souffleuse snowblower

Do you need more drills? Have fun with the *501 French Verbs* CD-ROM!

to suffer, to endure

Irregular verb

The Seven Simple Tenses		The Seven Compound Tenses	
Singular	Plural	Singular	Plural
1 présent de l'indicatif		8 passé composé	
souffre	**souffrons**	**ai souffert**	**avons souffert**
souffres	**souffrez**	**as souffert**	**avez souffert**
souffre	**souffrent**	**a souffert**	**ont souffert**
2 imparfait de l'indicatif		9 plus-que-parfait de l'indicatif	
souffrais	**souffrions**	**avais souffert**	**avions souffert**
souffrais	**souffriez**	**avais souffert**	**aviez souffert**
souffrait	**souffraient**	**avait souffert**	**avaient souffert**
3 passé simple		10 passé antérieur	
souffris	**souffrîmes**	**eus souffert**	**eûmes souffert**
souffris	**souffrîtes**	**eus souffert**	**eûtes souffert**
souffrit	**souffrirent**	**eut souffert**	**eurent souffert**
4 futur		11 futur antérieur	
souffrirai	**souffrirons**	**aurai souffert**	**aurons souffert**
souffriras	**souffrirez**	**auras souffert**	**aurez souffert**
souffrira	**souffriront**	**aura souffert**	**auront souffert**
5 conditionnel		12 conditionnel passé	
souffrirais	**souffririons**	**aurais souffert**	**aurions souffert**
souffrirais	**souffririez**	**aurais souffert**	**auriez souffert**
souffrirait	**souffriraient**	**aurait souffert**	**auraient souffert**
6 présent du subjonctif		13 passé du subjonctif	
souffre	**souffrions**	**aie souffert**	**ayons souffert**
souffres	**souffriez**	**aies souffert**	**ayez souffert**
souffre	**souffrent**	**ait souffert**	**aient souffert**
7 imparfait du subjonctif		14 plus-que-parfait du subjonctif	
souffrisse	**souffrissions**	**eusse souffert**	**eussions souffert**
souffrisses	**souffrissiez**	**eusses souffert**	**eussiez souffert**
souffrît	**souffrissent**	**eût souffert**	**eussent souffert**

Impératif
souffre
souffrons
souffrez

Words and expressions related to this verb

la souffrance suffering
souffrant, souffrante ailing, sick
souffreteux, souffreteuse sickly, feeble
souffrir le froid to withstand the cold
Cela me fait souffrir. That hurts me.

Can't find the verb you're looking for? Check the back pages of this book for a list of over 2,600 additional verbs!

Regular **-er** verb

to wish

The Seven Simple Tenses		The Seven Compound Tenses	
Singular	Plural	Singular	Plural
1 présent de l'indicatif		8 passé composé	
souhaite	**souhaitons**	**ai souhaité**	**avons souhaité**
souhaites	**souhaitez**	**as souhaité**	**avez souhaité**
souhaite	**souhaitent**	**a souhaité**	**ont souhaité**
2 imparfait de l'indicatif		9 plus-que-parfait de l'indicatif	
souhaitais	**souhaitions**	**avais souhaité**	**avions souhaité**
souhaitais	**souhaitiez**	**avais souhaité**	**aviez souhaité**
souhaitait	**souhaitaient**	**avait souhaité**	**avaient souhaité**
3 passé simple		10 passé antérieur	
souhaitai	**souhaitâmes**	**eus souhaité**	**eûmes souhaité**
souhaitas	**souhaitâtes**	**eus souhaité**	**eûtes souhaité**
souhaita	**souhaitèrent**	**eut souhaité**	**eurent souhaité**
4 futur		11 futur antérieur	
souhaiterai	**souhaiterons**	**aurai souhaité**	**aurons souhaité**
souhaiteras	**souhaiterez**	**auras souhaité**	**aurez souhaité**
souhaitera	**souhaiteront**	**aura souhaité**	**auront souhaité**
5 conditionnel		12 conditionnel passé	
souhaiterais	**souhaiterions**	**aurais souhaité**	**aurions souhaité**
souhaiterais	**souhaiteriez**	**aurais souhaité**	**auriez souhaité**
souhaiterait	**souhaiteraient**	**aurait souhaité**	**auraient souhaité**
6 présent du subjonctif		13 passé du subjonctif	
souhaite	**souhaitions**	**aie souhaité**	**ayons souhaité**
souhaites	**souhaitiez**	**aies souhaité**	**ayez souhaité**
souhaite	**souhaitent**	**ait souhaité**	**aient souhaité**
7 imparfait du subjonctif		14 plus-que-parfait du subjonctif	
souhaitasse	**souhaitassions**	**eusse souhaité**	**eussions souhaité**
souhaitasses	**souhaitassiez**	**eusses souhaité**	**eussiez souhaité**
souhaitât	**souhaitassent**	**eût souhaité**	**eussent souhaité**

Impératif
souhaite
souhaitons
souhaitez

Words and expressions related to this verb

un souhait a wish
à souhait to one's liking
souhaits de bonne année New Year's greetings
souhaiter bon voyage à qqn to wish someone a good trip
souhaiter la bienvenue à qqn to welcome someone
souhaiter le bonjour à qqn to greet someone
souhaitable desirable

Don't miss the definitions of basic grammatical terms with examples in English and French on pages 35–49.

souiller (448) — Part. pr. souillant — Part. passé souillé

to dirty, to muddy, to soil

Regular **-er** verb

The Seven Simple Tenses		The Seven Compound Tenses	
Singular	Plural	Singular	Plural
1 présent de l'indicatif		8 passé composé	
souille	**souillons**	**ai souillé**	**avons souillé**
souilles	**souillez**	**as souillé**	**avez souillé**
souille	**souillent**	**a souillé**	**ont souillé**
2 imparfait de l'indicatif		9 plus-que-parfait de l'indicatif	
souillais	**souillions**	**avais souillé**	**avions souillé**
souillais	**souilliez**	**avais souillé**	**aviez souillé**
souillait	**souillaient**	**avait souillé**	**avaient souillé**
3 passé simple		10 passé antérieur	
souillai	**souillâmes**	**eus souillé**	**eûmes souillé**
souillas	**souillâtes**	**eus souillé**	**eûtes souillé**
souilla	**souillèrent**	**eut souillé**	**eurent souillé**
4 futur		11 futur antérieur	
souillerai	**souillerons**	**aurai souillé**	**aurons souillé**
souilleras	**souillerez**	**auras souillé**	**aurez souillé**
souillera	**souilleront**	**aura souillé**	**auront souillé**
5 conditionnel		12 conditionnel passé	
souillerais	**souillerions**	**aurais souillé**	**aurions souillé**
souillerais	**souilleriez**	**aurais souillé**	**auriez souillé**
souillerait	**souilleraient**	**aurait souillé**	**auraient souillé**
6 présent du subjonctif		13 passé du subjonctif	
souille	**souillions**	**aie souillé**	**ayons souillé**
souilles	**souilliez**	**aies souillé**	**ayez souillé**
souille	**souillent**	**ait souillé**	**aient souillé**
7 imparfait du subjonctif		14 plus-que-parfait du subjonctif	
souillasse	**souillassions**	**eusse souillé**	**eussions souillé**
souillasses	**souillassiez**	**eusses souillé**	**eussiez souillé**
souillât	**souillassent**	**eût souillé**	**eussent souillé**

Impératif
souille
souillons
souillez

Sentences using this verb and words related to it

Monsieur Beauregard dîne seul dans un restaurant. Le garçon lui apporte du poisson et après quelques minutes il demande au monsieur.

—Eh bien, monsieur. Comment trouvez-vous le poisson? Il est bon, n'est-ce pas?
—Non, je le trouve dégoûtant. Ce poisson salé est souillé. Emportez-le!

dégoûtant, dégoûtante disgusting
salé, salée salty
Comment trouvez-vous le poisson? How do you like the fish?
souillé, souillée dirty, soiled
Emportez-le! Take it away!
un, une souillon filthy slob
une souillure spot, stain

Irregular verb

to submit

The Seven Simple Tenses		The Seven Compound Tenses	
Singular	Plural	Singular	Plural
1 présent de l'indicatif		8 passé composé	
soumets	**soumettons**	**ai soumis**	**avons soumis**
soumets	**soumettez**	**as soumis**	**avez soumis**
soumet	**soumettent**	**a soumis**	**ont soumis**
2 imparfait de l'indicatif		9 plus-que-parfait de l'indicatif	
soumettais	**soumettions**	**avais soumis**	**avions soumis**
soumettais	**soumettiez**	**avais soumis**	**aviez soumis**
soumettait	**soumettaient**	**avait soumis**	**avaient soumis**
3 passé simple		10 passé antérieur	
soumis	**soumîmes**	**eus soumis**	**eûmes soumis**
soumis	**soumîtes**	**eus soumis**	**eûtes soumis**
soumit	**soumirent**	**eut soumis**	**eurent soumis**
4 futur		11 futur antérieur	
soumettrai	**soumettrons**	**aurai soumis**	**aurons soumis**
soumettras	**soumettrez**	**auras soumis**	**aurez soumis**
soumettra	**soumettront**	**aura soumis**	**auront soumis**
5 conditionnel		12 conditionnel passé	
soumettrais	**soumettrions**	**aurais soumis**	**aurions soumis**
soumettrais	**soumettriez**	**aurais soumis**	**auriez soumis**
soumettrait	**soumettraient**	**aurait soumis**	**auraient soumis**
6 présent du subjonctif		13 passé du subjonctif	
soumette	**soumettions**	**aie soumis**	**ayons soumis**
soumettes	**soumettiez**	**aies soumis**	**ayez soumis**
soumette	**soumettent**	**ait soumis**	**aient soumis**
7 imparfait du subjonctif		14 plus-que-parfait du subjonctif	
soumisse	**soumissions**	**eusse soumis**	**eussions soumis**
soumisses	**soumissiez**	**eusses soumis**	**eussiez soumis**
soumît	**soumissent**	**eût soumis**	**eussent soumis**

Impératif
soumets
soumettons
soumettez

Words and expressions related to this verb
se soumettre à to give in to, to comply with
se soumettre à une décision to comply with a decision
la soumission submission

See also **commettre, mettre, se mettre, permettre, promettre, remettre,** and **transmettre.**

It's important that you be familiar with the Subjunctive. See pages 26–31.

The subject pronouns are found on page 103.

to smile

Irregular verb

The Seven Simple Tenses		The Seven Compound Tenses	
Singular	Plural	Singular	Plural
1 présent de l'indicatif		8 passé composé	
souris	**sourions**	**ai souri**	**avons souri**
souris	**souriez**	**as souri**	**avez souri**
sourit	**sourient**	**a souri**	**ont souri**
2 imparfait de l'indicatif		9 plus-que-parfait de l'indicatif	
souriais	**souriions**	**avais souri**	**avions souri**
souriais	**souriiez**	**avais souri**	**aviez souri**
souriait	**souriaient**	**avait souri**	**avaient souri**
3 passé simple		10 passé antérieur	
souris	**sourîmes**	**eus souri**	**eûmes souri**
souris	**sourîtes**	**eus souri**	**eûtes souri**
sourit	**sourirent**	**eut souri**	**eurent souri**
4 futur		11 futur antérieur	
sourirai	**sourirons**	**aurai souri**	**aurons souri**
souriras	**sourirez**	**auras souri**	**aurez souri**
sourira	**souriront**	**aura souri**	**auront souri**
5 conditionnel		12 conditionnel passé	
sourirais	**souririons**	**aurais souri**	**aurions souri**
sourirais	**souririez**	**aurais souri**	**auriez souri**
sourirait	**souriraient**	**aurait souri**	**auraient souri**
6 présent du subjonctif		13 passé du subjonctif	
sourie	**souriions**	**aie souri**	**ayons souri**
souries	**souriiez**	**aies souri**	**ayez souri**
sourie	**sourient**	**ait souri**	**aient souri**
7 imparfait du subjonctif		14 plus-que-parfait du subjonctif	
sourisse	**sourissions**	**eusse souri**	**eussions souri**
sourisses	**sourissiez**	**eusses souri**	**eussiez souri**
sourît	**sourissent**	**eût souri**	**eussent souri**

Impératif
souris
sourions
souriez

Words and expressions related to this verb

un sourire a smile
Gardez le sourire! Keep smiling!
un large sourire a broad smile
le rire laughter
sourire à to favor, to be favorable to, to smile on; **Claudine est heureuse; la vie lui sourit.**
faire un sourire à qqn to give someone a smile
Souris à la vie, et la vie te sourira. Smile at life and life will smile at you.

See also **rire.**

Don't forget to study the section on defective and impersonal verbs. It's right after this main list.

Irregular verb

to remember, to recall

The Seven Simple Tenses		The Seven Compound Tenses	
Singular	Plural	Singular	Plural
1 présent de l'indicatif		8 passé composé	
me souviens	**nous souvenons**	**me suis souvenu(e)**	**nous sommes souvenu(e)s**
te souviens	**vous souvenez**	**t'es souvenu(e)**	**vous êtes souvenu(e)(s)**
se souvient	**se souviennent**	**s'est souvenu(e)**	**se sont souvenu(e)s**
2 imparfait de l'indicatif		9 plus-que-parfait de l'indicatif	
me souvenais	**nous souvenions**	**m'étais souvenu(e)**	**nous étions souvenu(e)s**
te souvenais	**vous souveniez**	**t'étais souvenu(e)**	**vous étiez souvenu(e)(s)**
se souvenait	**se souvenaient**	**s'était souvenu(e)**	**s'étaient souvenu(e)s**
3 passé simple		10 passé antérieur	
me souvins	**nous souvînmes**	**me fus souvenu(e)**	**nous fûmes souvenu(e)s**
te souvins	**vous souvîntes**	**te fus souvenu(e)**	**vous fûtes souvenu(e)(s)**
se souvint	**se souvinrent**	**se fut souvenu(e)**	**se furent souvenu(e)s**
4 futur		11 futur antérieur	
me souviendrai	**nous souviendrons**	**me serai souvenu(e)**	**nous serons souvenu(e)s**
te souviendras	**vous souviendrez**	**te seras souvenu(e)**	**vous serez souvenu(e)(s)**
se souviendra	**se souviendront**	**se sera souvenu(e)**	**se seront souvenu(e)s**
5 conditionnel		12 conditionnel passé	
me souviendrais	**nous souviendrions**	**me serais souvenu(e)**	**nous serions souvenu(e)s**
te souviendrais	**vous souviendriez**	**te serais souvenu(e)**	**vous seriez souvenu(e)(s)**
se souviendrait	**se souviendraient**	**se serait souvenu(e)**	**se seraient souvenu(e)s**
6 présent du subjonctif		13 passé du subjonctif	
me souvienne	**nous souvenions**	**me sois souvenu(e)**	**nous soyons souvenu(e)s**
te souviennes	**vous souveniez**	**te sois souvenu(e)**	**vous soyez souvenu(e)(s)**
se souvienne	**se souviennent**	**se soit souvenu(e)**	**se soient souvenu(e)s**
7 imparfait du subjonctif		14 plus-que-parfait du subjonctif	
me souvinsse	**nous souvinssions**	**me fusse souvenu(e)**	**nous fussions souvenu(e)s**
te souvinsses	**vous souvinssiez**	**te fusses souvenu(e)**	**vous fussiez souvenu(e)(s)**
se souvînt	**se souvinssent**	**se fût souvenu(e)**	**se fussent souvenu(e)s**

Impératif
souviens-toi; ne te souviens pas
souvenons-nous; ne nous souvenons pas
souvenez-vous; ne vous souvenez pas

Words and expressions related to this verb

un souvenir souvenir, remembrance
Je m'en souviendrai! I'll remember that! I won't forget that!
se souvenir de qqn ou de qqch to remember someone or something
conserver le souvenir de qqch to retain the memory of something
raconter des souvenirs d'enfance to recount memories of one's childhood
les souvenirs memoirs
en souvenir de in remembrance of
Je me souviens. I remember. (Motto of the Province of Québec)

See also **convenir, devenir, prévenir, revenir,** and **venir.**

The subject pronouns are found on page 103.

to suck

Regular **-er** verb endings; spelling change: **c** changes to **ç** before **a** or **o** to keep **s** sound

The Seven Simple Tenses		The Seven Compound Tenses	
Singular	Plural	Singular	Plural
1 présent de l'indicatif		8 passé composé	
suce	**suçons**	**ai sucé**	**avons sucé**
suces	**sucez**	**as sucé**	**avez sucé**
suce	**sucent**	**a sucé**	**ont sucé**
2 imparfait de l'indicatif		9 plus-que-parfait de l'indicatif	
suçais	**sucions**	**avais sucé**	**avions sucé**
suçais	**suciez**	**avais sucé**	**aviez sucé**
suçait	**suçaient**	**avait sucé**	**avaient sucé**
3 passé simple		10 passé antérieur	
suçai	**suçâmes**	**eus sucé**	**eûmes sucé**
suças	**suçâtes**	**eus sucé**	**eûtes sucé**
suça	**sucèrent**	**eut sucé**	**eurent sucé**
4 futur		11 futur antérieur	
sucerai	**sucerons**	**aurai sucé**	**aurons sucé**
suceras	**sucerez**	**auras sucé**	**aurez sucé**
sucera	**suceront**	**aura sucé**	**auront sucé**
5 conditionnel		12 conditionnel passé	
sucerais	**sucerions**	**aurais sucé**	**aurions sucé**
sucerais	**suceriez**	**aurais sucé**	**auriez sucé**
sucerait	**suceraient**	**aurait sucé**	**auraient sucé**
6 présent du subjonctif		13 passé du subjonctif	
suce	**sucions**	**aie sucé**	**ayons sucé**
suces	**suciez**	**aies sucé**	**ayez sucé**
suce	**sucent**	**ait sucé**	**aient sucé**
7 imparfait du subjonctif		14 plus-que-parfait du subjonctif	
suçasse	**suçassions**	**eusse sucé**	**eussions sucé**
suçasses	**suçassiez**	**eusses sucé**	**eussiez sucé**
suçât	**suçassent**	**eût sucé**	**eussent sucé**

Impératif
suce
suçons
sucez

Words and expressions related to this verb

une sucette lollipop; **une sucette de bébé** teething ring

sucer le jus d'une orange to suck the juice of an orange

un suceur, une suceuse sucker; **suceur de sang** bloodsucker

suçoter to suck away on a candy; **toujours à sucer des bonbons** always sucking candies

un suçon hickey

Don't miss the definitions of basic grammatical terms with examples in English and French on pages 35–49.

Irregular verb

to follow

The Seven Simple Tenses		The Seven Compound Tenses	
Singular	Plural	Singular	Plural
1 présent de l'indicatif		8 passé composé	
suis	**suivons**	**ai suivi**	**avons suivi**
suis	**suivez**	**as suivi**	**avez suivi**
suit	**suivent**	**a suivi**	**ont suivi**
2 imparfait de l'indicatif		9 plus-que-parfait de l'indicatif	
suivais	**suivions**	**avais suivi**	**avions suivi**
suivais	**suiviez**	**avais suivi**	**aviez suivi**
suivait	**suivaient**	**avait suivi**	**avaient suivi**
3 passé simple		10 passe antérieur	
suivis	**suivîmes**	**eus suivi**	**eûmes suivi**
suivis	**suivîtes**	**eus suivi**	**eûtes suivi**
suivit	**suivirent**	**eut suivi**	**eurent suivi**
4 futur		11 futur antérieur	
suivrai	**suivrons**	**aurai suivi**	**aurons suivi**
suivras	**suivrez**	**auras suivi**	**aurez suivi**
suivra	**suivront**	**aura suivi**	**auront suivi**
5 conditionnel		12 conditionnel passé	
suivrais	**suivrions**	**aurais suivi**	**aurions suivi**
suivrais	**suivriez**	**aurais suivi**	**auriez suivi**
suivrait	**suivraient**	**aurait suivi**	**auraient suivi**
6 présent du subjonctif		13 passé du subjonctif	
suive	**suivions**	**aie suivi**	**ayons suivi**
suives	**suiviez**	**aies suivi**	**ayez suivi**
suive	**suivent**	**ait suivi**	**aient suivi**
7 imparfait du subjonctif		14 plus-que-parfait du subjonctif	
suivisse	**suivissions**	**eusse suivi**	**eussions suivi**
suivisses	**suivissiez**	**eusses suivi**	**eussiez suivi**
suivît	**suivissent**	**eût suivi**	**eussent suivi**

Impératif
suis
suivons
suivez

Words and expressions related to this verb

suivant according to
suivant que . . . according as . . .
la suite continuation
à la suite de coming after
de suite in succession, right away
à suivre to be continued
Je vais suivre un cours de français cet été. I'm going to take a course in French this summer.
Pourquoi me suivez-vous? Why are you following me?
le jour suivant on the following day
les questions suivantes the following questions
tout de suite immediately
suivre un cours to take a course
suivre un régime to be on a diet

See also **poursuivre.**

supplier (454) — Part. pr. suppliant — Part. passé supplié

to beg, to beseech, to implore, to supplicate

Regular **-er** verb

The Seven Simple Tenses		The Seven Compound Tenses	
Singular	Plural	Singular	Plural
1 présent de l'indicatif		8 passé composé	
supplie	**supplions**	**ai supplié**	**avons supplié**
supplies	**suppliez**	**as supplié**	**avez supplié**
supplie	**supplient**	**a supplié**	**ont supplié**
2 imparfait de l'indicatif		9 plus-que-parfait de l'indicatif	
suppliais	**suppliions**	**avais supplié**	**avions supplié**
suppliais	**suppliiez**	**avais supplié**	**aviez supplié**
suppliait	**suppliaient**	**avait supplié**	**avaient supplié**
3 passé simple		10 passé antérieur	
suppliai	**suppliâmes**	**eus supplié**	**eûmes supplié**
supplias	**suppliâtes**	**eus supplié**	**eûtes supplié**
supplia	**supplièrent**	**eut supplié**	**eurent supplié**
4 futur		11 futur antérieur	
supplierai	**supplierons**	**aurai supplié**	**aurons supplié**
supplieras	**supplierez**	**auras supplié**	**aurez supplié**
suppliera	**supplieront**	**aura supplié**	**auront supplié**
5 conditionnel		12 conditionnel passé	
supplierais	**supplierions**	**aurais supplié**	**aurions supplié**
supplierais	**supplieriez**	**aurais supplié**	**auriez supplié**
supplierait	**supplieraient**	**aurait supplié**	**auraient supplié**
6 présent du subjonctif		13 passé du subjonctif	
supplie	**suppliions**	**aie supplié**	**ayons supplié**
supplies	**suppliiez**	**aies supplié**	**ayez supplié**
supplie	**supplient**	**ait supplié**	**aient supplié**
7 imparfait du subjonctif		14 plus-que-parfait du subjonctif	
suppliasse	**suppliassions**	**eusse supplié**	**eussions supplié**
suppliasses	**suppliassiez**	**eusses supplié**	**eussiez supplié**
suppliât	**suppliassent**	**eût supplié**	**eussent supplié**

Impératif
supplie
supplions
suppliez

Words and expressions related to this verb

une supplique request, petition
suppliant, suppliante imploring, supplicating
supplicier to torture
un supplice torture
une supplication supplication, plea
supplier qqn à genoux to beg someone on hands and knees

Try the verb drills and verb tests with answers explained on pages 50–101.

Regular **-er** verb

to hold up, to prop up, to support, to endure, to tolerate

The Seven Simple Tenses		The Seven Compound Tenses	
Singular	Plural	Singular	Plural
1 présent de l'indicatif		8 passé composé	
supporte	**supportons**	**ai supporté**	**avons supporté**
supportes	**supportez**	**as supporté**	**avez supporté**
supporte	**supportent**	**a supporté**	**ont supporté**
2 imparfait de l'indicatif		9 plus-que-parfait de l'indicatif	
supportais	**supportions**	**avais supporté**	**avions supporté**
supportais	**supportiez**	**avais supporté**	**aviez supporté**
supportait	**supportaient**	**avait supporté**	**avaient supporté**
3 passé simple		10 passé antérieur	
supportai	**supportâmes**	**eus supporté**	**eûmes supporté**
supportas	**supportâtes**	**eus supporté**	**eûtes supporté**
supporta	**supportèrent**	**eut supporté**	**eurent supporté**
4 futur		11 futur antérieur	
supporterai	**supporterons**	**aurai supporté**	**aurons supporté**
supporteras	**supporterez**	**auras supporté**	**aurez supporté**
supportera	**supporteront**	**aura supporté**	**auront supporté**
5 conditionnel		12 conditionnel passé	
supporterais	**supporterions**	**aurais supporté**	**aurions supporté**
supporterais	**supporteriez**	**aurais supporté**	**auriez supporté**
supporterait	**supporteraient**	**aurait supporté**	**auraient supporté**
6 présent du subjonctif		13 passé du subjonctif	
supporte	**supportions**	**aie supporté**	**ayons supporté**
supportes	**supportiez**	**aies supporté**	**ayez supporté**
supporte	**supportent**	**ait supporté**	**aient supporté**
7 imparfait du subjonctif		14 plus-que-parfait du subjonctif	
supportasse	**supportassions**	**eusse supporté**	**eussions supporté**
supportasses	**supportassiez**	**eusses supporté**	**eussiez supporté**
supportât	**supportassent**	**eût supporté**	**eussent supporté**

Impératif
supporte
supportons
supportez

Words and expressions related to this verb

supportable endurable, bearable, supportable
porter to carry
insupportable unbearable, insufferable
un support support, prop
un support-chaussette elastic band support (for socks) **(des supports-chaussettes)**

See also **apporter** and **porter.**

Grammar putting you in a tense mood? Review the definitions of basic grammatical terms with examples on pages 35–49.

to surprise

Irregular verb

The Seven Simple Tenses		The Seven Compound Tenses	
Singular	Plural	Singular	Plural
1 présent de l'indicatif		8 passé composé	
surprends	**surprenons**	**ai surpris**	**avons surpris**
surprends	**surprenez**	**as surpris**	**avez surpris**
surprend	**surprennent**	**a surpris**	**ont surpris**
2 imparfait de l'indicatif		9 plus-que-parfait de l'indicatif	
surprenais	**surprenions**	**avais surpris**	**avions surpris**
surprenais	**surpreniez**	**avais surpris**	**aviez surpris**
surprenait	**surprenaient**	**avait surpris**	**avaient surpris**
3 passé simple		10 passé antérieur	
surpris	**surprîmes**	**eus surpris**	**eûmes surpris**
surpris	**surprîtes**	**eus surpris**	**eûtes surpris**
surprit	**surprirent**	**eut surpris**	**eurent surpris**
4 futur		11 futur antérieur	
surprendrai	**surprendrons**	**aurai surpris**	**aurons surpris**
surprendras	**surprendrez**	**auras surpris**	**aurez surpris**
surprendra	**surprendront**	**aura surpris**	**auront surpris**
5 conditionnel		12 conditionnel passé	
surprendrais	**surprendrions**	**aurais surpris**	**aurions aurpris**
surprendrais	**surprendriez**	**aurais surpris**	**auriez surpris**
surprendrait	**surprendraient**	**aurait surpris**	**auraient surpris**
6 présent du subjonctif		13 passé du subjonctif	
surprenne	**surprenions**	**aie surpris**	**ayons surpris**
surprennes	**surpreniez**	**aies surpirs**	**ayez surpris**
surprenne	**surprennent**	**ait surpris**	**aient surpris**
7 imparfait du subjonctif		14 plus-que-parfait du subjonctif	
surprisse	**surprissions**	**eusse surpris**	**eussions surpris**
surprisses	**surprissiez**	**eusses surpris**	**eussiez surpris**
surprît	**surprissent**	**eût surpris**	**eussent surpris**

Impératif
surprends
surprenons
surprenez

Words and expressions related to this verb

surprendre qqn chez soi to surprise someone at home
une surprise surprise
surprenant, surprenante surprising
une boîte à surprise jack-in-the-box
surpris par qqn surprised by someone
surpris par qqch surprised by something
par surprise by surprise
à ma grande surprise to my great surprise
une surprise partie (une surprise-party) surprise party; **des surprises-parties**

See also **apprendre, comprendre, entreprendre, se méprendre, prendre,** and **reprendre.**

Do you need more drills? Have fun with the *501 French Verbs* CD-ROM!

Irregular verb

to survive

The Seven Simple Tenses		The Seven Compound Tenses	
Singular	Plural	Singular	Plural
1 présent de l'indicatif		8 passé composé	
survis	**survivons**	**ai survécu**	**avons survécu**
survis	**survivez**	**as survécu**	**avez survécu**
survit	**survivent**	**a survécu**	**ont survécu**
2 imparfait de l'indicatif		9 plus-que-parfait de l'indicatif	
survivais	**survivions**	**avais survécu**	**avions survécu**
survivais	**survivez**	**avais survécu**	**aviez survécu**
survivait	**survivaient**	**avait survécu**	**avaient survécu**
3 passé simple		10 passé antérieur	
survécus	**survécûmes**	**eus survécu**	**eûmes survécu**
survécus	**survécûtes**	**eus survécu**	**eûtes survécu**
survécut	**survécurent**	**eut survécu**	**eurent survécu**
4 futur		11 futur antérieur	
survivrai	**survivrons**	**aurai survécu**	**aurons survécu**
survivras	**survivrez**	**auras survécu**	**aurez survécu**
survivra	**survivront**	**aura survécu**	**auront survécu**
5 conditionnel		12 conditionnel passé	
survivrais	**survivrions**	**aurais survécu**	**aurions survécu**
survivrais	**survivriez**	**aurais survécu**	**auriez survécu**
survivrait	**survivraient**	**aurait survécu**	**auraient survécu**
6 présent du subjonctif		13 passé du subjonctif	
survive	**survivions**	**aie survécu**	**ayons survécu**
survives	**survivez**	**aies survécu**	**ayez survécu**
survive	**survivent**	**ait survécu**	**aient survécu**
7 imparfait du subjonctif		14 plus-que-parfait du subjonctif	
survécusse	**survécussions**	**eusse survécu**	**eussions survécu**
survécusses	**survécussiez**	**eusses survécu**	**eussiez survécu**
survécût	**survécussent**	**eût survécu**	**eussent survécu**

Impératif
survis
survivons
survivez

Words and expressions related to this verb

survivre à qqn to survive someone
survivant, survivante surviving; survivor
la survivance survival
se survivre to live on
survivre à l'humiliation to survive humiliation
la survie survival

See also **vivre.**

For an explanation of meanings and uses of French and English verb tenses and moods, see pages 10–21.

survoler (458) — Part. pr. survolant — Part. passé survolé

to fly over

Regular **-er** verb

The Seven Simple Tenses		The Seven Compound Tenses	
Singular	Plural	Singular	Plural
1 présent de l'indicatif		8 passé composé	
survole	**survolons**	**ai survolé**	**avons survolé**
survoles	**survolez**	**as survolé**	**avez survolé**
survole	**survolent**	**a survolé**	**ont survolé**
2 imparfait de l'indicatif		9 plus-que-parfait de l'indicatif	
survolais	**survolions**	**avais survolé**	**avions survolé**
survolais	**survoliez**	**avais survolé**	**aviez survolé**
survolait	**survolaient**	**avait survolé**	**avaient survolé**
3 passé simple		10 passé antérieur	
survolai	**survolâmes**	**eus survolé**	**eûmes survolé**
survolas	**survolâtes**	**eus survolé**	**eûtes survolé**
survola	**survolèrent**	**eut survolé**	**eurent survolé**
4 futur		11 futur antérieur	
survolerai	**survolerons**	**aurai survolé**	**aurons survolé**
survoleras	**survolerez**	**auras survolé**	**aurez survolé**
survolera	**survoleront**	**aura survolé**	**auront survolé**
5 conditionnel		12 conditionnel passé	
survolerais	**survolerions**	**aurais survolé**	**aurions survolé**
survolerais	**survoleriez**	**aurais survolé**	**auriez survolé**
survolerait	**survoleraient**	**aurait survolé**	**auraient survolé**
6 présent du subjonctif		13 passé du subjonctif	
survole	**survolions**	**aie survolé**	**ayons survolé**
survoles	**survoliez**	**aies survolé**	**ayez survolé**
survole	**survolent**	**ait survolé**	**aient survolé**
7 imparfait du subjonctif		14 plus-que-parfait du subjonctif	
survolasse	**survolassions**	**eusse survolé**	**eussions survolé**
survolasses	**survolassiez**	**eusses survolé**	**eussiez survolé**
survolât	**survolassent**	**eût survolé**	**eussent survolé**

Impératif
survole
survolons
survolez

Words and expressions related to this verb
le survol flying over
voler to fly, to steal
le vol flight, theft
faire un survol à basse altitude to make a low flight

See also **voler.**

If you want to see a sample English verb fully conjugated in all the tenses, check out pages 8 and 9.

Reflexive irregular verb

to be silent, to be quiet, not to speak

The Seven Simple Tenses		The Seven Compound Tenses	
Singular	Plural	Singular	Plural
1 présent de l'indicatif		8 passé composé	
me tais	**nous taisons**	**me suis tu(e)**	**nous sommes tu(e)s**
te tais	**vous taisez**	**t'es tu(e)**	**vous êtes tu(e)(s)**
se tait	**se taisent**	**s'est tu(e)**	**se sont tu(e)s**
2 imparfait de l'indicatif		9 plus-que-parfait de l'indicatif	
me taisais	**nous taisions**	**m'étais tu(e)**	**nous étions tu(e)s**
te taisais	**vous taisiez**	**t'étais tu(e)**	**vous étiez tu(e)(s)**
se taisait	**se taisaient**	**s'était tu(e)**	**s'étaient tu(e)s**
3 passé simple		10 passé antérieur	
me tus	**nous tûmes**	**me fus tu(e)**	**nous fûmes tu(e)s**
te tus	**vous tûtes**	**te fus tu(e)**	**vous fûtes tu(e)(s)**
se tut	**se turent**	**se fut tu(e)**	**se furent tu(e)s**
4 futur		11 futur antérieur	
me tairai	**nous tairons**	**me serai tu(e)**	**nous serons tu(e)s**
te tairas	**vous tairez**	**te seras tu(e)**	**vous serez tu(e)(s)**
se taira	**se tairont**	**se sera tu(e)**	**se seront tu(e)s**
5 conditionnel		12 conditionnel passé	
me tairais	**nous tairions**	**me serais tu(e)**	**nous serions tu(e)s**
te tairais	**vous tairiez**	**te serais tu(e)**	**vous seriez tu(e)(s)**
se tairait	**se tairaient**	**se serait tu(e)**	**se seraient tu(e)s**
6 présent du subjonctif		13 passé du subjonctif	
me taise	**nous taisions**	**me sois tu(e)**	**nous soyons tu(e)s**
te taises	**vous taisiez**	**te sois tu(e)**	**vous soyez tu(e)(s)**
se taise	**se taisent**	**se soit tu(e)**	**se soient tu(e)s**
7 imparfait du subjonctif		14 plus-que-parfait du subjonctif	
me tusse	**nous tussions**	**me fusse tu(e)**	**nous fussions tu(e)s**
te tusses	**vous tussiez**	**te fusses tu(e)**	**vous fussiez tu(e)(s)**
se tût	**se tussent**	**se fût tu(e)**	**se fussent tu(e)s**

Impératif
tais-toi; ne te tais pas
taisons-nous; ne nous taisons pas
taisez-vous; ne vous taisez pas

Sentences using this verb

—Marie, veux-tu te taire! Tu es trop bavarde. Et toi, Hélène, tais-toi aussi.

Les deux élèves ne se taisent pas. La maîtresse de chimie continue:

—Taisez-vous, je vous dis, toutes les deux; autrement, vous resterez dans cette salle après la classe.

Les deux jeunes filles se sont tues.

Il est bon de parler et meilleur de se taire. Speech is silver, silence is golden.

See also **bavarder** and **cesser.**

For an explanation of meanings and uses of French and English verb tenses and moods, see pages 10–21.

The subject pronouns are found on page 103.

to dye

Irregular verb

The Seven Simple Tenses		The Seven Compound Tenses	
Singular	Plural	Singular	Plural
1 présent de l'indicatif		8 passé composé	
teins	**teignons**	**ai teint**	**avons teint**
teins	**teignez**	**as teint**	**avez teint**
teint	**teignent**	**a teint**	**ont teint**
2 imparfait de l'indicatif		9 plus-que-parfait de l'indicatif	
teignais	**teignions**	**avais teint**	**avions teint**
teignais	**teigniez**	**avais teint**	**aviez teint**
teignait	**teignaient**	**avait teint**	**avaient teint**
3 passé simple		10 passé antérieur	
teignis	**teignîmes**	**eus teint**	**eûmes teint**
teignis	**teignîtes**	**eus teint**	**eûtes teint**
teignit	**teignirent**	**eut teint**	**eurent teint**
4 futur		11 futur antérieur	
teindrai	**teindrons**	**aurai teint**	**aurons teint**
teindras	**teindrez**	**auras teint**	**aurez teint**
teindra	**teindront**	**aura teint**	**auront teint**
5 conditionnel		12 conditionnel passé	
teindrais	**teindrions**	**aurais teint**	**aurions teint**
teindrais	**teindriez**	**aurais teint**	**auriez teint**
teindrait	**teindraient**	**aurait teint**	**auraient teint**
6 présent du subjonctif		13 passé du subjonctif	
teigne	**teignions**	**aie teint**	**ayons teint**
teignes	**teigniez**	**aies teint**	**ayez teint**
teigne	**teignent**	**ait teint**	**aient teint**
7 imparfait du subjonctif		14 plus-que-parfait du subjonctif	
teignisse	**teignissions**	**eusse teint**	**eussions teint**
teignisses	**teignissiez**	**eusses teint**	**eussiez teint**
teignît	**teignissent**	**eût teint**	**eussent teint**

Impératif
teins
teignons
teignez

Words and expressions related to this verb

déteindre to fade, to lose color, to remove the color
faire teindre qqch to have something dyed
la teinture dyeing
un teinturier, une teinturière dyer
des cheveux teints dyed hair
teindre en noir to dye black
le teint color, dye; complexion
teinter to tint
la teinturerie cleaning and dyeing
des lunettes à verres teintés tinted eyeglasses
se teindre les cheveux to dye one's hair

Use the guide to French pronunciation. It's in the Appendixes.

Regular **-er** verb

to telephone

The Seven Simple Tenses		The Seven Compound Tenses	
Singular	Plural	Singular	Plural
1 présent de l'indicatif		8 passé composé	
téléphone	**téléphonons**	**ai téléphoné**	**avons téléphoné**
téléphones	**téléphonez**	**as téléphoné**	**avez téléphoné**
téléphone	**téléphonent**	**a téléphoné**	**ont téléphoné**
2 imparfait de l'indicatif		9 plus-que-parfait de l'indicatif	
téléphonais	**téléphonions**	**avais téléphoné**	**avions téléphoné**
téléphonais	**téléphoniez**	**avais téléphoné**	**aviez téléphoné**
téléphonait	**téléphonaient**	**avait téléphoné**	**avaient téléphoné**
3 passé simple		10 passé antérieur	
téléphonai	**téléphonâmes**	**eus téléphoné**	**eûmes téléphoné**
téléphonas	**téléphonâtes**	**eus téléphoné**	**eûtes téléphoné**
téléphona	**téléphonèrent**	**eut téléphoné**	**eurent téléphoné**
4 futur		11 futur antérieur	
téléphonerai	**téléphonerons**	**aurai téléphoné**	**aurons téléphoné**
téléphoneras	**téléphonerez**	**auras téléphoné**	**aurez téléphoné**
téléphonera	**téléphoneront**	**aura téléphoné**	**auront téléphoné**
5 conditionnel		12 conditionnel passé	
téléphonerais	**téléphonerions**	**aurais téléphoné**	**aurions téléphoné**
téléphonerais	**téléphoneriez**	**aurais téléphoné**	**auriez téléphoné**
téléphonerait	**téléphoneraient**	**aurait téléphoné**	**auraient téléphoné**
6 présent du subjonctif		13 passé du subjonctif	
téléphone	**téléphonions**	**aie téléphoné**	**ayons téléphoné**
téléphones	**téléphoniez**	**aies téléphoné**	**ayez téléphoné**
téléphone	**téléphonent**	**ait téléphoné**	**aient téléphoné**
7 imparfait du subjonctif		14 plus-que-parfait du subjonctif	
téléphonasse	**téléphonassions**	**eusse téléphoné**	**eussions téléphoné**
téléphonasses	**téléphonassiez**	**eusses téléphoné**	**eussiez téléphoné**
téléphonât	**téléphonassent**	**eût téléphoné**	**eussent téléphoné**

Impératif
téléphone
téléphonons
téléphonez

Words and expressions related to this verb

le téléphone telephone
téléphonique telephonic
téléphoniquement telephonically (by telephone)
un, une téléphoniste telephone operator
téléphoner à qqn to telephone someone
Marie? Je lui ai téléphoné hier Mary? I telephoned her yesterday.
le téléphone rouge hot line
un téléphone cellulaire, un téléphone portable cell phone
faire un appel téléphonique to make a telephone call

Check out the principal parts of some important French verbs on page 7.

tendre (462) — Part. pr. tendant — Part. passé tendu

to strain, to stretch, to tighten, to tend

Regular **-re** verb

The Seven Simple Tenses		The Seven Compound Tenses	
Singular	Plural	Singular	Plural
1 présent de l'indicatif		8 passé composé	
tends	**tendons**	**ai tendu**	**avons tendu**
tends	**tendez**	**as tendu**	**avez tendu**
tend	**tendent**	**a tendu**	**ont tendu**
2 imparfait de l'indicatif		9 plus-que-parfait de l'indicatif	
tendais	**tendions**	**avais tendu**	**avions tendu**
tendais	**tendiez**	**avais tendu**	**aviez tendu**
tendait	**tendaient**	**avait tendu**	**avaient tendu**
3 passé simple		10 passé antérieur	
tendis	**tendîmes**	**eus tendu**	**eûmes tendu**
tendis	**tendîtes**	**eus tendu**	**eûtes tendu**
tendit	**tendirent**	**eut tendu**	**eurent tendu**
4 futur		11 futur antérieur	
tendrai	**tendrons**	**aurai tendu**	**aurons tendu**
tendras	**tendrez**	**auras tendu**	**aurez tendu**
tendra	**tendront**	**aura tendu**	**auront tendu**
5 conditionnel		12 conditionnel passé	
tendrais	**tendrions**	**aurais tendu**	**aurions tendu**
tendrais	**tendriez**	**aurais tendu**	**auriez tendu**
tendrait	**tendraient**	**aurait tendu**	**auraient tendu**
6 présent du subjonctif		13 passé du subjonctif	
tende	**tendions**	**aie tendu**	**ayons tendu**
tendes	**tendiez**	**aies tendu**	**ayez tendu**
tende	**tendent**	**ait tendu**	**aient tendu**
7 imparfait du subjonctif		14 plus-que-parfait du subjonctif	
tendisse	**tendissions**	**eusse tendu**	**eussions tendu**
tendisses	**tendissiez**	**eusses tendu**	**eussiez tendu**
tendît	**tendissent**	**eût tendu**	**eussent tendu**

Impératif
tends
tendons
tendez

Words and expressions related to this verb

tendre la main à qqn to hold out one's hand to someone
attendre to wait (for)
détendre to slacken
se détendre to bend, to relax
étendre to extend, to spread
une détente relaxing, slackening, release of tension
s'attendre à to expect
entendre to hear, to understand
s'entendre avec qqn to get along with someone, to understand each other, to agree
s'étendre to stretch out, to lie down
tendre l'autre joue to turn the other cheek
tendre l'oreille to prick up one's ears
tendre un piège to set a trap

See the summary of sequence of tenses with *si* (if) clauses on page 26.

Irregular verb

to hold, to grasp

The Seven Simple Tenses		The Seven Compound Tenses	
Singular	Plural	Singular	Plural
1 présent de l'indicatif		8 passé composé	
tiens	**tenons**	**ai tenu**	**avons tenu**
tiens	**tenez**	**as tenu**	**avez tenu**
tient	**tiennent**	**a tenu**	**ont tenu**
2 imparfait de l'indicatif		9 plus-que-parfait de l'indicatif	
tenais	**tenions**	**avais tenu**	**avions tenu**
tenais	**teniez**	**avais tenu**	**aviez tenu**
tenait	**tenaient**	**avait tenu**	**avaient tenu**
3 passé simple		10 passé antérieur	
tins	**tînmes**	**eus tenu**	**eûmes tenu**
tins	**tîntes**	**eus tenu**	**eûtes tenu**
tint	**tinrent**	**eut tenu**	**eurent tenu**
4 futur		11 futur antérieur	
tiendrai	**tiendrons**	**aurai tenu**	**aurons tenu**
tiendras	**tiendrez**	**auras tenu**	**aurez tenu**
tiendra	**tiendront**	**aura tenu**	**auront tenu**
5 conditionnel		12 conditionnel passé	
tiendrais	**tiendrions**	**aurais tenu**	**aurions tenu**
tiendrais	**tiendriez**	**aurais tenu**	**auriez tenu**
tiendrait	**tiendraient**	**aurait tenu**	**auraient tenu**
6 présent du subjonctif		13 passé du subjonctif	
tienne	**tenions**	**aie tenu**	**ayons tenu**
tiennes	**teniez**	**aies tenu**	**ayez tenu**
tienne	**tiennent**	**ait tenu**	**aient tenu**
7 imparfait du subjonctif		14 plus-que-parfait du subjonctif	
tinsse	**tinssions**	**eusse tenu**	**eussions tenu**
tinsses	**tinssiez**	**eusses tenu**	**eussiez tenu**
tînt	**tinssent**	**eût tenu**	**eussent tenu**

Impératif
tiens
tenons
tenez

AN ESSENTIAL 55 VERB

Tenir

Tenir is an essential verb for beginning students because it is used in many idiomatic expressions and because there are several useful verbs that are conjugated like it.

Sentences using tenir

Robert tient de son père. Robert takes after his father.

Cette maîtresse tient bien sa classe. This teacher controls her class well.

Tiens! Voilà Bob! Look! There's Bob!

Ma nouvelle voiture a une excellente tenue de route. My new car holds the road very well.

Tenez votre droite. Keep to your right.

Proverb

Il vaut mieux "je tiens" que "je tiendrai." **It's better to say "I hold" than "I will hold." (Similar to: A bird in the hand is worth two in the bush.)**

If you can conjugate **tenir** you can also conjugate these verbs:

entretenir **to maintain**

s'entretenir avec **to talk with (Use être as auxiliary)**

maintenir **to keep, to maintain**

soutenir **to support**

Words and expressions related to this verb

tenir de qqn **to take after (to favor) someone**

tenir de bonne source **to have on good authority**

tenir à qqch **to cherish something**

tenir qqn au courant **to keep someone informed**

tenir sa promsesse **to keep one's promise**

tenir le pari **to take on the bet**

tenir les bras levés **to keep one's arms up**

tenir les yeux fermés **to keep one's eyes closed**

tenir un chien en laisse **to keep a dog on a leash**

la tenue **behavior, attitude, uniform**

bien tenu, bien tenue **well-kept**

Tiens, tiens! **Well, well! Fancy that!**

Regular **-er** verb

to tempt, to attempt, to try

The Seven Simple Tenses		The Seven Compound Tenses	
Singular	Plural	Singular	Plural
1 présent de l'indicatif		8 passé composé	
tente	**tentons**	**ai tenté**	**avons tenté**
tentes	**tentez**	**as tenté**	**avez tenté**
tente	**tentent**	**a tenté**	**ont tenté**
2 imparfait de l'indicatif		9 plus-que-parfait de l'indicatif	
tentais	**tentions**	**avais tenté**	**avions tenté**
tentais	**tentiez**	**avais tenté**	**aviez tenté**
tentait	**tentaient**	**avait tenté**	**avaient tenté**
3 passé simple		10 passé antérieur	
tentai	**tentâmes**	**eus tenté**	**eûmes tenté**
tentas	**tentâtes**	**eus tenté**	**eûtes tenté**
tenta	**tentèrent**	**eut tenté**	**eurent tenté**
4 futur		11 futur antérieur	
tenterai	**tenterons**	**aurai tenté**	**aurons tenté**
tenteras	**tenterez**	**auras tenté**	**aurez tenté**
tentera	**tenteront**	**aura tenté**	**auront tenté**
5 conditionnel		12 conditionnel passé	
tenterais	**tenterions**	**aurais tenté**	**aurions tenté**
tenterais	**tenteriez**	**aurais tenté**	**auriez tenté**
tenterait	**tenteraient**	**aurait tenté**	**auraient tenté**
6 présent du subjonctif		13 passé du subjonctif	
tente	**tentions**	**aie tenté**	**ayons tenté**
tentes	**tentiez**	**aies tenté**	**ayez tenté**
tente	**tentent**	**ait tenté**	**aient tenté**
7 imparfait du subjonctif		14 plus-que-parfait du subjonctif	
tentasse	**tentassions**	**eusse tenté**	**eussions tenté**
tentasses	**tentassiez**	**eusses tenté**	**eussiez tenté**
tentât	**tentassent**	**eût tenté**	**eussent tenté**

Impératif
tente
tentons
tentez

Words and expressions related to this verb

se laisser tenter to allow oneself to be tempted
une tentative attempt
tenter sa chance to try one's luck
un tentateur, une tentatrice tempter, temptress
tenter de faire qqch to try, to attempt to do something
tentant, tentante tempting, inviting

Tongue twister:
Tas de riz, tas de rats. Tas de riz tentant, tas de rats tentés. Pile of rice, pile of rats. Tempting pile of rice, pile of tempted rats.

Use the guide to French pronunciation. It's in the Appendixes.

terminer (465) — Part. pr. terminant — Part. passé terminé

to terminate, to finish, to end

Regular **-er** verb

The Seven Simple Tenses		The Seven Compound Tenses	
Singular	Plural	Singular	Plural
1 présent de l'indicatif		8 passé composé	
termine	**terminons**	**ai terminé**	**avons terminé**
termines	**terminez**	**as terminé**	**avez terminé**
termine	**terminent**	**a terminé**	**ont terminé**
2 imparfait de l'indicatif		9 plus-que-parfait de l'indicatif	
terminais	**terminions**	**avais terminé**	**avions terminé**
terminais	**terminiez**	**avais terminé**	**aviez terminé**
terminait	**terminaient**	**avait terminé**	**avaient terminé**
3 passé simple		10 passé antérieur	
terminai	**terminâmes**	**eus terminé**	**eûmes terminé**
terminas	**terminâtes**	**eus terminé**	**eûtes terminé**
termina	**terminèrent**	**eut terminé**	**eurent terminé**
4 futur		11 futur antérieur	
terminerai	**terminerons**	**aurai terminé**	**aurons terminé**
termineras	**terminerez**	**auras terminé**	**aurez terminé**
terminera	**termineront**	**aura terminé**	**auront terminé**
5 conditionnel		12 conditionnel passé	
terminerais	**terminerions**	**aurais terminé**	**aurions terminé**
terminerais	**termineriez**	**aurais terminé**	**auriez terminé**
terminerait	**termineraient**	**aurait terminé**	**auraient terminé**
6 présent du subjonctif		13 passé du subjonctif	
termine	**terminions**	**aie terminé**	**ayons terminé**
termines	**terminiez**	**aies terminé**	**ayez terminé**
termine	**terminent**	**ait terminé**	**aient terminé**
7 imparfait du subjonctif		14 plus-que-parfait du subjonctif	
terminasse	**terminassions**	**eusse terminé**	**eussions terminé**
terminasses	**terminassiez**	**eusses terminé**	**eussiez terminé**
terminât	**terminassent**	**eût terminé**	**eussent terminé**

Impératif
termine
terminons
terminez

Words and expressions related to this verb

terminal, terminale terminal
la terminaison ending, termination
terminable terminable
interminable interminable, endless
exterminer to exterminate
terminer la journée chez un ami to end the day at a friend's house
terminer une session to log off (computer)
J'attends qu'elle termine le travail. I'm waiting for her to finish the work.
Les vacances de Noël se terminent demain. Christmas vacation ends tomorrow.
se terminer to end (itself)
se terminer en to end in; **un verbe qui se termine en *er* . . .** a verb that ends in *er* . . .
terminer un repas to finish a meal

Check out the principal parts of some important French verbs on page 7.

Regular **-er** verb

to draw out, to shoot, to pull

The Seven Simple Tenses		The Seven Compound Tenses	
Singular	Plural	Singular	Plural
1 présent de l'indicatif		8 passé composé	
tire	**tirons**	**ai tiré**	**avons tiré**
tires	**tirez**	**as tiré**	**avez tiré**
tire	**tirent**	**a tiré**	**ont tiré**
2 imparfait de l'indicatif		9 plus-que-parfait de l'indicatif	
tirais	**tirions**	**avais tiré**	**avions tiré**
tirais	**tiriez**	**avais tiré**	**aviez tiré**
tirait	**tiraient**	**avait tiré**	**avaient tiré**
3 passé simple		10 passé antérieur	
tirai	**tirâmes**	**eus tiré**	**eûmes tiré**
tiras	**tirâtes**	**eus tiré**	**eûtes tiré**
tira	**tirèrent**	**eut tiré**	**eurent tiré**
4 futur		11 futur antérieur	
tirerai	**tirerons**	**aurai tiré**	**aurons tiré**
tireras	**tirerez**	**auras tiré**	**aurez tiré**
tirera	**tireront**	**aura tiré**	**auront tiré**
5 conditionnel		12 conditionnel passé	
tirerais	**tirerions**	**aurais tiré**	**aurions tiré**
tirerais	**tireriez**	**aurais tiré**	**auriez tiré**
tirerait	**tireraient**	**aurait tiré**	**auraient tiré**
6 présent du subjonctif		13 passé du subjonctif	
tire	**tirions**	**aie tiré**	**ayons tiré**
tires	**tiriez**	**aies tiré**	**ayez tiré**
tire	**tirent**	**ait tiré**	**aient tiré**
7 imparfait du subjonctif		14 plus-que-parfait du subjonctif	
tirasse	**tirassions**	**eusse tiré**	**eussions tiré**
tirasses	**tirassiez**	**eusses tiré**	**eussiez tiré**
tirât	**tirassent**	**eût tiré**	**eussent tiré**

Impératif
tire
tirons
tirez

Words and expressions related to this verb

tirer une affaire au clair to clear up a matter
tirer parti de to take advantage of, to make the best of
un tireur, une tireuse marksman, markswoman
un tire-bouchon corkscrew (**des tire-bouchons**)
Tirez la langue. Stick out your tongue.
s'en tirer to pull through
s'en tirer bien to get off well, to come through well
tirer sur to fire (shoot) at
un tiroir drawer (of a desk, etc.)
se tirer d'affaire to get out of a jam
un tire-clou nail puller (**des tire-clous**)

See also **attirer, retirer,** and **se retirer.**

The subject pronouns are found on page 103.

tomber (467) — Part. pr. tombant — Part. passé tombé(e)(s)

to fall

Regular **-er** verb

The Seven Simple Tenses

Singular	Plural
1 présent de l'indicatif	
tombe	**tombons**
tombes	**tombez**
tombe	**tombent**
2 imparfait de l'indicatif	
tombais	**tombions**
tombais	**tombiez**
tombait	**tombaient**
3 passé simple	
tombai	**tombâmes**
tombas	**tombâtes**
tomba	**tombèrent**
4 futur	
tomberai	**tomberons**
tomberas	**tomberez**
tombera	**tomberont**
5 conditionnel	
tomberais	**tomberions**
tomberais	**tomberiez**
tomberait	**tomberaient**
6 présent du subjonctif	
tombe	**tombions**
tombes	**tombiez**
tombe	**tombent**
7 imparfait du subjonctif	
tombasse	**tombassions**
tombasses	**tombassiez**
tombât	**tombassent**

The Seven Compound Tenses

Singular	Plural
8 passé composé	
suis tombé(e)	**sommes tombé(e)s**
es tombé(e)	**êtes tombé(e)(s)**
est tombé(e)	**sont tombé(e)s**
9 plus-que-parfait de l'indicatif	
étais tombé(e)	**étions tombé(e)s**
étais tombé(e)	**étiez tombé(e)(s)**
était tombé(e)	**étaient tombé(e)s**
10 passé antérieur	
fus tombé(e)	**fûmes tombé(e)s**
fus tombé(e)	**fûtes tombé(e)(s)**
fut tombé(e)	**furent tombé(e)s**
11 futur antérieur	
serai tombé(e)	**serons tombé(e)s**
seras tombé(e)	**serez tombé(e)(s)**
sera tombé(e)	**seront tombé(e)s**
12 conditionnel passé	
serais tombé(e)	**serions tombé(e)s**
serais tombé(e)	**seriez tombé(e)(s)**
serait tombé(e)	**seraient tombé(e)s**
13 passé du subjonctif	
sois tombé(e)	**soyons tombé(e)s**
sois tombé(e)	**soyez tombé(e)(s)**
soit tombé(e)	**soient tombé(e)s**
14 plus-que-parfait du subjonctif	
fusse tombé(e)	**fussions tombé(e)s**
fusses tombé(e)	**fussiez tombé(e)(s)**
fût tombé(e)	**fussent tombé(e)s**

Impératif
tombe
tombons
tombez

AN ESSENTIAL 55 VERB

Tomber

Tomber is a very useful verb for a beginning French student. Note that it is one of the nonreflexive verbs that take **être** as an auxiliary in the compound tenses (see page 6).

Sentences using tomber

Oups! J'ai laissé tomber mes clés. Oops! I dropped my keys.

David est tombé de l'échelle et il s'est cassé le bras. David fell from the ladder and broke his arm.

Cela tombe bien. That's fortunate.

Nous nous sommes pressés pour arriver avant la tombée du jour. We hurried to arrive before nightfall.

Il tombe des clous. It's raining cats and dogs. (Literally: Nails are falling.)

Words and expressions related to this verb

tomber amoureux (amoureuse) de qqn **to fall in love with someone**

tomber sur **to run into, to come across**

laisser tomber **to drop**

tomber malade **to fall sick**

faire tomber **to knock down**

tomber en panne **to break down, to crash (computer)**

tomber dans les pommes **to pass out, to faint**

tomber à la renverse **to fall backward**

tomber à pic **to fall/come at the right time**

retomber **to fall again**

la tombée du jour **nightfall**

Can't find the verb you're looking for? Check the back pages of this book for a list of over 2,600 additional verbs!

tordre (468) — Part. pr. **tordant** — Part. passé **tordu**

to twist

Regular **-re** verb

The Seven Simple Tenses		The Seven Compound Tenses	
Singular	Plural	Singular	Plural
1 présent de l'indicatif		8 passé composé	
tords	**tordons**	**ai tordu**	**avons tordu**
tords	**tordez**	**as tordu**	**avez tordu**
tord	**tordent**	**a tordu**	**ont tordu**
2 imparfait de l'indicatif		9 plus-que-parfait de l'indicatif	
tordais	**tordions**	**avais tordu**	**avions tordu**
tordais	**tordiez**	**avais tordu**	**aviez tordu**
tordait	**tordaient**	**avait tordu**	**avaient tordu**
3 passé simple		10 passé antérieur	
tordis	**tordîmes**	**eus tordu**	**eûmes tordu**
tordis	**tordîtes**	**eus tordu**	**eûtes tordu**
tordit	**tordirent**	**eut tordu**	**eurent tordu**
4 futur		11 futur antérieur	
tordrai	**tordrons**	**aurai tordu**	**aurons tordu**
tordras	**tordrez**	**auras tordu**	**aurez tordu**
tordra	**tordront**	**aura tordu**	**auront tordu**
5 conditionnel		12 conditionnel passé	
tordrais	**tordrions**	**aurais tordu**	**aurions tordu**
tordrais	**tordriez**	**aurais tordu**	**auriez tordu**
tordrait	**tordraient**	**aurait tordu**	**auraient tordu**
6 présent du subjonctif		13 passé du subjonctif	
torde	**tordions**	**aie tordu**	**ayons tordu**
tordes	**tordiez**	**aies tordu**	**ayez tordu**
torde	**tordent**	**ait tordu**	**aient tordu**
7 imparfait du subjonctif		14 plus-que-parfait du subjonctif	
tordisse	**tordissions**	**eusse tordu**	**eussions tordu**
tordisses	**tordissiez**	**eusses tordu**	**eussiez tordu**
tordît	**tordissent**	**eût tordu**	**eussent tordu**

Impératif
tords
tordons
tordez

Words and expressions related to this verb

tordre le cou à qqn to twist someone's neck
tordu, tordue twisted
tortueux twisting
être tordu (tordue) to be crazy
une rue tortueuse winding street
se tordre les mains to wring one's hands
se tordre de rire to split one's sides laughing
avoir la gueule tordue to have an ugly puss (face)
avoir l'esprit tordu to have a twisted mind

How are you doing? Find out with the verb drills and tests with answers explained on pages 50–101.

Regular **-er** verb

to touch, to affect

The Seven Simple Tenses		The Seven Compound Tenses	
Singular	Plural	Singular	Plural
1 présent de l'indicatif		8 passé composé	
touche	**touchons**	**ai touché**	**avons touché**
touches	**touchez**	**as touché**	**avez touché**
touche	**touchent**	**a touché**	**ont touché**
2 imparfait de l'indicatif		9 plus-que-parfait de l'indicatif	
touchais	**touchions**	**avais touché**	**avions touché**
touchais	**touchiez**	**avais touché**	**aviez touché**
touchait	**touchaient**	**avait touché**	**avaient touché**
3 passé simple		10 passé antérieur	
touchai	**touchâmes**	**eus touché**	**eûmes touché**
touchas	**touchâtes**	**eus touché**	**eûtes touché**
toucha	**touchèrent**	**eut touché**	**eurent touché**
4 futur		11 futur antérieur	
toucherai	**toucherons**	**aurai touché**	**aurons touché**
toucheras	**toucherez**	**auras touché**	**aurez touché**
touchera	**toucheront**	**aura touché**	**auront touché**
5 conditionnel		12 conditionnel passé	
toucherais	**toucherions**	**aurais touché**	**aurions touché**
toucherais	**toucheriez**	**aurais touché**	**auriez touché**
toucherait	**toucheraient**	**aurait touché**	**auraient touché**
6 présent du subjonctif		13 passé du subjonctif	
touche	**touchions**	**aie touché**	**ayons touché**
touches	**touchiez**	**aies touché**	**ayez touché**
touche	**touchent**	**ait touché**	**aient touché**
7 imparfait du subjonctif		14 plus-que-parfait du subjonctif	
touchasse	**touchassions**	**eusse touché**	**eussions touché**
touchasses	**touchassiez**	**eusses touché**	**eussiez touché**
touchât	**touchassent**	**eût touché**	**eussent touché**

Impératif
touche
touchons
touchez

Words and expressions related to this verb

une personne qui touche à tout a meddlesome person
Touchez là! Put it there! Shake!
toucher à qqch to touch something
N'y touchez pas! Don't touch!
retoucher to touch up
le toucher touch, feeling, sense of touch
toucher de l'argent to get some money
toucher un chèque to cash a check
Cela me touche profondément. That touches me deeply.
un, une touche-à-tout meddler

tourner (470) — Part. pr. tournant — Part. passé tourné

to turn

Regular **-er** verb

The Seven Simple Tenses		The Seven Compound Tenses	
Singular	Plural	Singular	Plural
1 présent de l'indicatif		8 passé composé	
tourne	**tournons**	**ai tourné**	**avons tourné**
tournes	**tournez**	**as tourné**	**avez tourné**
tourne	**tournent**	**a tourné**	**ont tourné**
2 imparfait de l'indicatif		9 plus-que-parfait de l'indicatif	
tournais	**tournions**	**avais tourné**	**avions tourné**
tournais	**tourniez**	**avais tourné**	**aviez tourné**
tournait	**tournaient**	**avait tourné**	**avaient tourné**
3 passé simple		10 passé antérieur	
tournai	**tournâmes**	**eus tourné**	**eûmes tourné**
tournas	**tournâtes**	**eus tourné**	**eûtes tourné**
tourna	**tournèrent**	**eut tourné**	**eurent tourné**
4 futur		11 futur antérieur	
tournerai	**tournerons**	**aurai tourné**	**aurons tourné**
tourneras	**tournerez**	**auras tourné**	**aurez tourné**
tournera	**tourneront**	**aura tourné**	**auront tourné**
5 conditionnel		12 conditionnel passé	
tournerais	**tournerions**	**aurais tourné**	**aurions tourné**
tournerais	**tourneriez**	**aurais tourné**	**auriez tourné**
tournerait	**tourneraient**	**aurait tourné**	**auraient tourné**
6 présent du subjonctif		13 passé du subjonctif	
tourne	**tournions**	**aie tourné**	**ayons tourné**
tournes	**tourniez**	**aies tourné**	**ayez tourné**
tourne	**tournent**	**ait tourné**	**aient tourné**
7 imparfait du subjonctif		14 plus-que-parfait du subjonctif	
tournasse	**tournassions**	**eusse tourné**	**eussions tourné**
tournasses	**tournassiez**	**eusses tourné**	**eussiez tourné**
tournât	**tournassent**	**eût tourné**	**eussent tourné**

Impératif
tourne
tournons
tournez

Words and expressions related to this verb

se tourner to turn around
tourner qqn en ridicule to ridicule someone
un tourne-disque record player (**des tourne-disques**)
un tournevis screwdriver
retourner to return
tourner l'estomac à qqn to turn someone's stomach
faire une tournée to go on a tour
tourner autour du pot to beat around the bush

See also **détourner** and **retourner.**

If you don't know the French verb for an English verb you have in mind, try the index in the Appendixes.

The Seven Simple Tenses		The Seven Compound Tenses	
Singular	Plural	Singular	Plural
1 présent de l'indicatif		8 passé composé	
tousse	**toussons**	**ai toussé**	**avons toussé**
tousses	**toussez**	**as toussé**	**avez toussé**
tousse	**toussent**	**a toussé**	**ont toussé**
2 imparfait de l'indicatif		9 plus-que-parfait de l'indicatif	
toussais	**toussions**	**avais toussé**	**avions toussé**
toussais	**toussiez**	**avais toussé**	**aviez toussé**
toussait	**toussaient**	**avait toussé**	**avaient toussé**
3 passé simple		10 passé antérieur	
toussai	**toussâmes**	**eus toussé**	**eûmes toussé**
toussas	**toussâtes**	**eus toussé**	**eûtes toussé**
toussa	**toussèrent**	**eut toussé**	**eurent toussé**
4 futur		11 futur antérieur	
tousserai	**tousserons**	**aurai toussé**	**aurons toussé**
tousseras	**tousserez**	**auras toussé**	**aurez toussé**
toussera	**tousseront**	**aura toussé**	**auront toussé**
5 conditionnel		12 conditionnel passé	
tousserais	**tousserions**	**aurais toussé**	**aurions toussé**
tousserais	**tousseriez**	**aurais toussé**	**auriez toussé**
tousserait	**tousseraient**	**aurait toussé**	**auraient toussé**
6 présent du subjonctif		13 passé du subjonctif	
tousse	**toussions**	**aie toussé**	**ayons toussé**
tousses	**toussiez**	**aies toussé**	**ayez toussé**
tousse	**toussent**	**ait toussé**	**aient toussé**
7 imparfait du subjonctif		14 plus-que-parfait du subjonctif	
toussasse	**toussassions**	**eusse toussé**	**eussions toussé**
toussasses	**toussassiez**	**eusses toussé**	**eussiez toussé**
toussât	**toussassent**	**eût toussé**	**eussent toussé**

Impératif
tousse
toussons
toussez

Words and expressions related to this verb

une toux cough; **une toux grasse** crackling cough, heavy cough; **une toux sèche** dry cough
une toux nerveuse nervous cough
toussoter to have a minor, slight cough
un tousseur, une tousseuse cougher
un toussotement slight cough
Je voudrais acheter des pastilles contre la toux. I would also like to buy some cough drops.

How are you doing? Find out with the verb drills and tests with answers explained on pages 50–101.

to translate

Irregular verb

The Seven Simple Tenses		The Seven Compound Tenses	
Singular	Plural	Singular	Plural
1 présent de l'indicatif		8 passé composé	
traduis	**traduisons**	**ai traduit**	**avons traduit**
traduis	**traduisez**	**as traduit**	**avez traduit**
traduit	**traduisent**	**a traduit**	**ont traduit**
2 imparfait de l'indicatif		9 plus-que-parfait de l'indicatif	
traduisais	**traduisions**	**avais traduit**	**avions traduit**
traduisais	**traduisiez**	**avais traduit**	**aviez traduit**
traduisait	**traduisaient**	**avait traduit**	**avaient traduit**
3 passé simple		10 passé antérieur	
traduisis	**traduisîmes**	**eus traduit**	**eûmes traduit**
traduisis	**traduisîtes**	**eus traduit**	**eûtes traduit**
traduisit	**traduisirent**	**eut traduit**	**eurent traduit**
4 futur		11 futur antérieur	
traduirai	**traduirons**	**aurai traduit**	**aurons traduit**
traduiras	**traduirez**	**auras traduit**	**aurez traduit**
traduira	**traduiront**	**aura traduit**	**auront traduit**
5 conditionnel		12 conditionnel passé	
traduirais	**traduirions**	**aurais traduit**	**aurions traduit**
traduirais	**traduiriez**	**aurais traduit**	**auriez traduit**
traduirait	**traduiraient**	**aurait traduit**	**auraient traduit**
6 présent du subjonctif		13 passé du subjonctif	
traduise	**traduisions**	**aie traduit**	**ayons traduit**
traduises	**tradusiez**	**aies traduit**	**ayez traduit**
traduise	**traduisent**	**ait traduit**	**aient traduit**
7 imparfait du subjonctif		14 plus-que-parfait du subjonctif	
traduisisse	**traduisissions**	**eusse traduit**	**eussions traduit**
traduisisses	**traduisissiez**	**eusses traduit**	**eussiez traduit**
traduisît	**traduisissent**	**eût traduit**	**eussent traduit**

Impératif
traduis
traduisons
traduisez

Words and expressions related to this verb

un traducteur, une traductrice translator
une traduction a translation
traduisible translatable
une traduction littérale a literal translation
une traduction libre a free translation
traduire du français en anglais to translate from French to English
se traduire to be translated; **Cette phrase se traduit facilement.** This sentence is easily translated.
une traduction fidèle a faithful translation
traduire de l'anglais en français to translate from English to French

See also **conduire, déduire, introduire, produire, réduire, reproduire,** and **séduire.**

The Seven Simple Tenses		The Seven Compound Tenses	
Singular	Plural	Singular	Plural
1 présent de l'indicatif		8 passé composé	
trahis	**trahissons**	**ai trahi**	**avons trahi**
trahis	**trahissez**	**as trahi**	**avez trahi**
trahit	**trahissent**	**a trahi**	**ont trahi**
2 imparfait de l'indicatif		9 plus-que-parfait de l'indicatif	
trahissais	**trahissions**	**avais trahi**	**avions trahi**
trahissais	**trahissiez**	**avais trahi**	**aviez trahi**
trahissait	**trahissaient**	**avait trahi**	**avaient trahi**
3 passé simple		10 passé antérieur	
trahis	**trahîmes**	**eus trahi**	**eûmes trahi**
trahis	**trahîtes**	**eus trahi**	**eûtes trahi**
trahit	**trahirent**	**eut trahi**	**eurent trahi**
4 futur		11 futur antérieur	
trahirai	**trahirons**	**aurai trahi**	**aurons trahi**
trahiras	**trahirez**	**auras trahi**	**aurez trahi**
trahira	**trahiront**	**aura trahi**	**auront trahi**
5 conditionnel		12 conditionnel passé	
trahirais	**trahirions**	**aurais trahi**	**aurions trahi**
trahirais	**trahiriez**	**aurais trahi**	**auriez trahi**
trahirait	**trahiraient**	**aurait trahi**	**auraient trahi**
6 présent du subjonctif		13 passé du subjonctif	
trahisse	**trahissions**	**aie trahi**	**ayons trahi**
trahisses	**trahissiez**	**aies trahi**	**ayez trahi**
trahisse	**trahissent**	**ait trahi**	**aient trahi**
7 imparfait du subjonctif		14 plus-que-parfait du subjonctif	
trahisse	**trahissions**	**eusse trahi**	**eussions trahi**
trahisses	**trahissiez**	**eusses trahi**	**eussiez trahi**
trahît	**trahissent**	**eût trahi**	**eussent trahi**

Impératif
trahis
trahissons
trahissez

Words and expressions related to this verb

se trahir to give oneself away, to betray each other, to deceive each other
traîtreusement treacherously
la trahison betrayal, treason
la haute trahison high treason
un traître traitor, betrayer
une traîtresse traitress, betrayer

Don't miss the definitions of basic grammatical terms with examples in English and French on pages 35–49.

to milk, to draw (milk)

Irregular verb

The Seven Simple Tenses		The Seven Compound Tenses	
Singular	Plural	Singular	Plural
1 présent de l'indicatif		8 passé composé	
trais	**trayons**	**ai trait**	**avons trait**
trais	**trayez**	**as trait**	**avez trait**
trait	**traient**	**a trait**	**ont trait**
2 imparfait de l'indicatif		9 plus-que-parfait de l'indicatif	
trayais	**trayions**	**avais trait**	**avions trait**
trayais	**trayiez**	**avais trait**	**aviez trait**
trayait	**trayaient**	**avait trait**	**avaient trait**
3 passé simple		10 passé antérieur	
—		**eus trait**	**eûmes trait**
—		**eus trait**	**eûtes trait**
		eut trait	**eurent trait**
4 futur		11 futur antérieur	
trairai	**trairons**	**aurai trait**	**aurons trait**
trairas	**trairez**	**auras trait**	**aurez trait**
traira	**trairont**	**aura trait**	**auront trait**
5 conditionnel		12 conditionnel passé	
trairais	**trairions**	**aurais trait**	**aurions trait**
trairais	**trairiez**	**aurais trait**	**auriez trait**
trairait	**trairaient**	**aurait trait**	**auraient trait**
6 présent du subjonctif		13 passé du subjonctif	
traie	**trayions**	**aie trait**	**ayons trait**
traies	**trayiez**	**aies trait**	**ayez trait**
traie	**traient**	**ait trait**	**aient trait**
7 imparfait du subjonctif		14 plus-que-parfait du subjonctif	
—		**eusse trait**	**eussions trait**
—		**eusses trait**	**eussiez trait**
		eût trait	**eussent trait**

Impératif
trais
trayons
trayez

Sentences using this verb and words related to it

M. Verjean se lève tôt pour traire les vaches. Mr. Verjean gets up early to milk the cows.
Le trayeur trait les vaches deux fois par jour. The milker milks the cows twice a day.

Words and expressions related to this verb

traire les vaches, traire les chèvres to milk the cows, milk the goats
une trayeuse, une machine à traire milking machine
un trayeur milker, milkman
une trayeuse milker, milkwoman
le laitier milkman (delivery)
la laitière milkwoman (delivery)
la traite milking
la laiterie dairy
un tabouret à traire milking stool

Regular -er verb

to treat, to negotiate

The Seven Simple Tenses		The Seven Compound Tenses	
Singular	Plural	Singular	Plural
1 présent de l'indicatif		8 passé composé	
traite	**traitons**	**ai traité**	**avons traité**
traites	**traitez**	**as traité**	**avez traité**
traite	**traitent**	**a traité**	**ont traité**
2 imparfait de l'indicatif		9 plus-que-parfait de l'indicatif	
traitais	**traitions**	**avais traité**	**avions traité**
traitais	**traitiez**	**avais traité**	**aviez traité**
traitait	**traitaient**	**avait traité**	**avaient traité**
3 passé simple		10 passé antérieur	
traitai	**traitâmes**	**eus traité**	**eûmes traité**
traitas	**traitâtes**	**eus traité**	**eûtes traité**
traita	**traitèrent**	**eut traité**	**eurent traité**
4 futur		11 futur antérieur	
traiterai	**traiterons**	**aurai traité**	**aurons traité**
traiteras	**traiterez**	**auras traité**	**aurez traité**
traitera	**traiteront**	**aura traité**	**auront traité**
5 conditionnel		12 conditionnel passé	
traiterais	**traiterions**	**aurais traité**	**aurions traité**
traiterais	**traiteriez**	**aurais traité**	**auriez traité**
traiterait	**traiteraient**	**aurait traité**	**auraient traité**
6 présent du subjonctif		13 passé du subjonctif	
traite	**traitions**	**aie traité**	**ayons traité**
traites	**traitiez**	**aies traité**	**ayez traité**
traite	**traitent**	**ait traité**	**aient traité**
7 imparfait du subjonctif		14 plus-que-parfait du subjonctif	
traitasse	**traitassions**	**eusse traité**	**eussions traité**
traitasses	**traitassiez**	**eusses traité**	**eussiez traité**
traitât	**traitassent**	**eût traité**	**eussent traité**

Impératif
traite
traitons
traitez

Words and expressions related to this verb

traiter qqn mal to treat someone badly; **traiter qqn bien** to treat someone well

maltraiter to maltreat, to mistreat; **traiter de** to deal with

traiter qqn de qqch to call someone something; **traiter qqn de menteur** to call someone a liar

un traitement treatment; salary

un traité treatise; treaty

boire d'une seule traite to drink in one gulp

le traitement de texte word processing

Do you need more drills? Have fun with the *501 French Verbs* CD-ROM!

to transmit, to transfer

Irregular verb

The Seven Simple Tenses		The Seven Compound Tenses	
Singular	Plural	Singular	Plural
1 présent de l'indicatif		8 passé composé	
transmets	**transmettons**	**ai transmis**	**avons transmis**
transmets	**transmettez**	**as transmis**	**avez transmis**
transmet	**transmettent**	**a transmis**	**ont transmis**
2 imparfait de l'indicatif		9 plus-que-parfait de l'indicatif	
transmettais	**transmettions**	**avais transmis**	**avions transmis**
transmettais	**transmettiez**	**avais transmis**	**aviez transmis**
transmettait	**transmettaient**	**avait transmis**	**avaient transmis**
3 passé simple		10 passé antérieur	
transmis	**transmîmes**	**eus transmis**	**eûmes transmis**
transmis	**transmîtes**	**eus transmis**	**eûtes transmis**
transmit	**transmirent**	**eut transmis**	**eurent transmis**
4 futur		11 futur antérieur	
transmettrai	**transmettrons**	**aurai transmis**	**aurons transmis**
transmettras	**transmettrez**	**auras transmis**	**aurez transmis**
transmettra	**transmettront**	**aura transmis**	**auront transmis**
5 conditionnel		12 conditionnel passé	
transmettrais	**transmettrions**	**aurais transmis**	**aurions transmis**
transmettrais	**transmettriez**	**aurais transmis**	**auriez transmis**
transmettrait	**transmettraient**	**aurait transmis**	**auraient transmis**
6 présent du subjonctif		13 passé du subjonctif	
transmette	**transmettions**	**aie transmis**	**ayons transmis**
transmettes	**transmettiez**	**aies transmis**	**ayez transmis**
transmette	**transmettent**	**ait transmis**	**aient transmis**
7 imparfait du subjonctif		14 plus-que-parfait du subjonctif	
transmisse	**transmissions**	**eusse transmis**	**eussions transmis**
transmisses	**transmissiez**	**eusses transmis**	**eussiez transmis**
transmît	**transmissent**	**eût transmis**	**eussent transmis**

Impératif
transmets
transmettons
transmettez

Words and expressions related to this verb

transmettre une maladie to transmit an illness
transmettre un message to relay, to transmit a message
transmettre son autorité to transfer one's authority
transmettre une lettre to forward a letter
une transmission transmission
transmissible transmissible, transferable
une maladie transmissible contagious disease
Le SIDA est une maladie transmissible. AIDS is a transmittable disease.

See also **commettre, mettre, se mettre, omettre, permettre, promettre, remettre,** and **soumettre.**

Regular **-er** verb

to work

The Seven Simple Tenses		The Seven Compound Tenses	
Singular	Plural	Singular	Plural
1 présent de l'indicatif		8 passé composé	
travaille	**travaillons**	**ai travaillé**	**avons travaillé**
travailles	**travaillez**	**as travaillé**	**avez travaillé**
travaille	**travaillent**	**a travaillé**	**ont travaillé**
2 imparfait de l'indicatif		9 plus-que-parfait de l'indicatif	
travaillais	**travaillions**	**avais travaillé**	**avions travaillé**
travaillais	**travailliez**	**avais travaillé**	**aviez travaillé**
travaillait	**travaillaient**	**avait travaillé**	**avaient travaillé**
3 passé simple		10 passé antérieur	
travaillai	**travaillâmes**	**eus travaillé**	**eûmes travaillé**
travaillas	**travaillâtes**	**eus travaillé**	**eûtes travaillé**
travailla	**travaillèrent**	**eut travaillé**	**eurent travaillé**
4 futur		11 futur antérieur	
travaillerai	**travaillerons**	**aurai travaillé**	**aurons travaillé**
travailleras	**travaillerez**	**auras travaillé**	**aurez travaillé**
travaillera	**travailleront**	**aura travaillé**	**auront travaillé**
5 conditionnel		12 conditionnel passé	
travaillerais	**travaillerions**	**aurais travaillé**	**aurions travaillé**
travaillerais	**travailleriez**	**aurais travaillé**	**auriez travaillé**
travaillerait	**travailleraient**	**aurait travaillé**	**auraient travaillé**
6 présent du subjonctif		13 passé du subjonctif	
travaille	**travaillions**	**aie travaillé**	**ayons travaillé**
travailles	**travailliez**	**aies travaillé**	**ayez travaillé**
travaille	**travaillent**	**ait travaillé**	**aient travaillé**
7 imparfait du subjonctif		14 plus-que-parfait du subjonctif	
travaillasse	**travaillassions**	**eusse travaillé**	**eussions travaillé**
travaillasses	**travaillassiez**	**eusses travaillé**	**eussiez travaillé**
travaillât	**travaillassent**	**eût travaillé**	**eussent travaillé**

Impératif
travaille
travaillons
travaillez

Words and expressions related to this verb

travailleur, travailleuse industrious, worker

être sans travail to be out of work

faire travailler son argent to put one's money to work (to earn interest)

Madame Reed fait travailler ses élèves dans la classe de français. Mrs. Reed makes her students work in French class.

le travail work, labor, travail (**les travaux**)

les travaux publics public works

les vêtements de travail work clothes

Proverb:

Choisissez un travail que vous aimez et vous n'aurez pas à travailler un seul jour de votre vie. Choose a job you love and you will never have to work a day in your life. (Confucius)

Consult the entry *causative* **faire** (page 37) in the section on definitions of basic grammatical terms.

traverser (478) — Part. pr. traversant — Part. passé traversé

to traverse, to cross

Regular **-er** verb

The Seven Simple Tenses		The Seven Compound Tenses	
Singular	Plural	Singular	Plural
1 présent de l'indicatif		8 passé composé	
traverse	**traversons**	**ai traversé**	**avons traversé**
traverses	**traversez**	**as traversé**	**avez traversé**
traverse	**traversent**	**a traversé**	**ont traversé**
2 imparfait de l'indicatif		9 plus-que-parfait de l'indicatif	
traversais	**traversions**	**avais traversé**	**avions traversé**
traversais	**traversiez**	**avais traversé**	**aviez traversé**
traversait	**traversaient**	**avait traversé**	**avaient traversé**
3 passé simple		10 passé antérieur	
traversai	**traversâmes**	**eus traversé**	**eûmes traversé**
traversas	**traversâtes**	**eus traversé**	**eûtes traversé**
traversa	**traversèrent**	**eut traversé**	**eurent traversé**
4 futur		11 futur antérieur	
traverserai	**traverserons**	**aurai traversé**	**aurons traversé**
traverseras	**traverserez**	**auras traversé**	**aurez traversé**
traversera	**traverseront**	**aura traversé**	**auront traversé**
5 conditionnel		12 conditionnel passé	
traverserais	**traverserions**	**aurais traversé**	**aurions traversé**
traverserais	**traverseriez**	**aurais traversé**	**auriez traversé**
traverserait	**traverseraient**	**aurait traversé**	**auraient traversé**
6 présent du subjonctif		13 passé du subjonctif	
traverse	**traversions**	**aie traversé**	**ayons traversé**
traverses	**traversiez**	**aies traversé**	**ayez traversé**
traverse	**traversent**	**ait traversé**	**aient traversé**
7 imparfait du subjonctif		14 plus-que-parfait du subjonctif	
traversasse	**traversassions**	**eusse traversé**	**eussions traversé**
traversasses	**traversassiez**	**eusses traversé**	**eussiez traversé**
traversât	**traversassent**	**eût traversé**	**eussent traversé**

Impératif
traverse
traversons
traversez

Words and expressions related to this verb

la traversée the crossing
à travers through
de travers askew, awry, crooked
une traversée de voie railroad crossing
marcher de travers to stagger

Check out the principal parts of some important French verbs on page 7.

Regular **-er** verb

to cheat, to trick

The Seven Simple Tenses		The Seven Compound Tenses	
Singular	Plural	Singular	Plural
1 présent de l'indicatif		8 passé composé	
triche	**trichons**	**ai triché**	**avons triché**
triches	**trichez**	**as triché**	**avez triché**
triche	**trichent**	**a triché**	**ont triché**
2 imparfait de l'indicatif		9 plus-que-parfait de l'indicatif	
trichais	**trichions**	**avais triché**	**avions triché**
trichais	**trichiez**	**avais triché**	**aviez triché**
trichait	**trichaient**	**avait triché**	**avaient triché**
3 passé simple		10 passé antérieur	
trichai	**trichâmes**	**eus triché**	**eûmes triché**
trichas	**trichâtes**	**eus triché**	**eûtes triché**
tricha	**trichèrent**	**eut triché**	**eurent triché**
4 futur		11 futur antérieur	
tricherai	**tricherons**	**aurai triché**	**aurons triché**
tricheras	**tricherez**	**auras triché**	**aurez triché**
trichera	**tricheront**	**aura triché**	**auront triché**
5 conditionnel		12 conditionnel passé	
tricherais	**tricherions**	**aurais triché**	**aurions triché**
tricherais	**tricheriez**	**aurais triché**	**auriez triché**
tricherait	**tricheraient**	**aurait triché**	**auraient triché**
6 présent du subjonctif		13 passé du subjonctif	
triche	**trichions**	**aie triché**	**ayons triché**
triches	**trichiez**	**aies triché**	**ayez triché**
triche	**trichent**	**ait triché**	**aient triché**
7 imparfait du subjonctif		14 plus-que-parfait du subjonctif	
trichasse	**trichassions**	**eusse triché**	**eussions triché**
trichasses	**trichassiez**	**eusses triché**	**eussiez triché**
trichât	**trichassent**	**eût triché**	**eussent triché**

Impératif
triche
trichons
trichez

Words and expressions related to this verb

une tricherie cheating
gagner par tricherie to win by cheating
une triche cheating
un tricheur, une tricheuse cheater
tricher aux cartes to cheat at cards

If you want to see a sample English verb fully conjugated in all the tenses, check out pages 8 and 9.

se tromper (480) — Part. pr. se trompant — Part. passé trompé(e)(s)

to be mistaken, to be wrong (about something)

Reflexive regular **-er** verb

The Seven Simple Tenses

Singular	Plural
1 présent de l'indicatif	
me trompe	**nous trompons**
te trompes	**vous trompez**
se trompe	**se trompent**
2 imparfait de l'indicatif	
me trompais	**nous trompions**
te trompais	**vous trompiez**
se trompait	**se trompaient**
3 passé simple	
me trompai	**nous trompâmes**
te trompas	**vous trompâtes**
se trompa	**se trompèrent**
4 futur	
me tromperai	**nous tromperons**
te tromperas	**vous tromperez**
se trompera	**se tromperont**
5 conditionnel	
me tromperais	**nous tromperions**
te tromperais	**vous tromperiez**
se tromperait	**se tromperaient**
6 présent du subjonctif	
me trompe	**nous trompions**
te trompes	**vous trompiez**
se trompe	**se trompent**
7 imparfait du subjonctif	
me trompasse	**nous trompassions**
te trompasses	**vous trompassiez**
se trompât	**se trompassent**

The Seven Compound Tenses

Singular	Plural
8 passé composé	
me suis trompé(e)	**nous sommes trompé(e)s**
t'es trompé(e)	**vous êtes trompé(e)(s)**
s'est trompé(e)	**se sont trompé(e)s**
9 plus-que-parfait de l'indicatif	
m'étais trompé(e)	**nous étions trompé(e)s**
t'étais trompé(e)	**vous étiez trompé(e)(s)**
s'était trompé(e)	**s'étaient trompé(e)s**
10 passé antérieur	
me fus trompé(e)	**nous fûmes trompé(e)s**
te fus trompé(e)	**vous fûtes trompé(e)(s)**
se fut trompé(e)	**se furent trompé(e)s**
11 futur antérieur	
me serai trompé(e)	**nous serons trompé(e)s**
te seras trompé(e)	**vous serez trompé(e)(s)**
se sera trompé(e)	**se seront trompé(e)s**
12 conditionnel passé	
me serais trompé(e)	**nous serions trompé(e)s**
te serais trompé(e)	**vous seriez trompé(e)(s)**
se serait trompé(e)	**se seraient trompé(e)s**
13 passé du subjonctif	
me sois trompé(e)	**nous soyons trompé(e)s**
te sois trompé(e)	**vous soyez trompé(e)(s)**
se soit trompé(e)	**se soient trompé(e)s**
14 plus-que-parfait du subjonctif	
me fusse trompé(e)	**nous fussions trompé(e)s**
te fusses trompé(e)	**vous fussiez trompé(e)(s)**
se fût trompé(e)	**se fussent trompé(e)s**

Impératif

trompe-toi; ne te trompe pas
trompons-nous; ne nous trompons pas
trompez-vous; ne vous trompez pas

Words and expressions related to this verb

tromper to cheat, to deceive
détromper to free from deception, to set a matter straight
se laisser tromper to be taken in (fooled, deceived)
un trompeur, une trompeuse deceiver
se détromper to see the truth about a matter
se tromper de chemin to take the wrong route
une tromperie deceit, deception

For an explanation of meanings and uses of French and English verb tenses and moods, see pages 10–21.

Regular **-er** verb

to find

The Seven Simple Tenses		The Seven Compound Tenses	
Singular	Plural	Singular	Plural
1 présent de l'indicatif		8 passé composé	
trouve	**trouvons**	**ai trouvé**	**avons trouvé**
trouves	**trouvez**	**as trouvé**	**avez trouvé**
trouve	**trouvent**	**a trouvé**	**ont trouvé**
2 imparfait de l'indicatif		9 plus-que-parfait de l'indicatif	
trouvais	**trouvions**	**avais trouvé**	**avions trouvé**
trouvais	**trouviez**	**avais trouvé**	**aviez trouvé**
trouvait	**trouvaient**	**avait trouvé**	**avaient trouvé**
3 passé simple		10 passé antérieur	
trouvai	**trouvâmes**	**eus trouvé**	**eûmes trouvé**
trouvas	**trouvâtes**	**eus trouvé**	**eûtes trouvé**
trouva	**trouvèrent**	**eut trouvé**	**eurent trouvé**
4 futur		11 futur antérieur	
trouverai	**trouverons**	**aurai trouvé**	**aurons trouvé**
trouveras	**trouverez**	**auras trouvé**	**aurez trouvé**
trouvera	**trouveront**	**aura trouvé**	**auront trouvé**
5 conditionnel		12 conditionnel passé	
trouverais	**trouverions**	**aurais trouvé**	**aurions trouvé**
trouverais	**trouveriez**	**aurais trouvé**	**auriez trouvé**
trouverait	**trouveraient**	**aurait trouvé**	**auraient trouvé**
6 présent du subjonctif		13 passé du subjonctif	
trouve	**trouvions**	**aie trouvé**	**ayons trouvé**
trouves	**trouviez**	**aies trouvé**	**ayez trouvé**
trouve	**trouvent**	**ait trouvé**	**aient trouvé**
7 imparfait du subjonctif		14 plus-que-parfait du subjonctif	
trouvasse	**trouvassions**	**eusse trouvé**	**eussions trouvé**
trouvasses	**trouvassiez**	**eusses trouvé**	**eussiez trouvé**
trouvât	**trouvassent**	**eût trouvé**	**eussent trouvé**

Impératif
trouve
trouvons
trouvez

Words and expressions related to this verb

J'ai une nouvelle voiture; comment la trouvez-vous? I have a new car; how do you like it?

trouver un emploi to find a job

trouver bon de faire qqch to think fit to do something

retrouver to find again, to recover, to retrieve

trouver porte close, trouver visage de bois not to find anyone answering the door after knocking

une trouvaille a discovery, a find

les retrouvailles *f.* reunion, rediscovery

le bueau d'objets trouvés lost and found

See also **se trouver.**

Review the Subjunctive clearly and simply on pages 26–31.

The subject pronouns are found on page 103.

se trouver (482) — Part. pr. se trouvant — Part. passé trouvé(e)(s)

to be located, to be situated

Reflexive regular **-er** verb

The Seven Simple Tenses		The Seven Compound Tenses	
Singular	Plural	Singular	Plural
1 présent de l'indicatif		8 passé composé	
me trouve	**nous trouvons**	**me suis trouvé(e)**	**nous sommes trouvé(e)s**
te trouves	**vous trouvez**	**t'es trouvé(e)**	**vous êtes trouvé(e)(s)**
se trouve	**se trouvent**	**s'est trouvé(e)**	**se sont trouvé(e)s**
2 imparfait de l'indicatif		9 plus-que-parfait de l'indicatif	
me trouvais	**nous trouvions**	**m'étais trouvé(e)**	**nous étions trouvé(e)s**
te trouvais	**vous trouviez**	**t'étais trouvé(e)**	**vous étiez trouvé(e)(s)**
se trouvait	**se trouvaient**	**s'était trouvé(e)**	**s'étaient trouvé(e)s**
3 passé simple		10 passé antérieur	
me trouvai	**nous trouvâmes**	**me fus trouvé(e)**	**nous fûmes trouvé(e)s**
te trouvas	**vous trouvâtes**	**te fus trouvé(e)**	**vous fûtes trouvé(e)(s)**
se trouva	**se trouvèrent**	**se fut trouvé(e)**	**se furent trouvé(e)s**
4 futur		11 futur antérieur	
me trouverai	**nous trouverons**	**me serai trouvé(e)**	**nous serons trouvé(e)s**
te trouveras	**vous trouverez**	**te seras trouvé(e)**	**vous serez trouvé(e)(s)**
se trouvera	**se trouveront**	**se sera trouvé(e)**	**se seront trouvé(e)s**
5 conditionnel		12 conditionnel passé	
me trouverais	**nous trouverions**	**me serais trouvé(e)**	**nous serions trouvé(e)s**
te trouverais	**vous trouveriez**	**te serais trouvé(e)**	**vous seriez trouvé(e)(s)**
se trouverait	**se trouveraient**	**se serait trouvé(e)**	**se seraient trouvé(e)s**
6 présent du subjonctif		13 passé du subjonctif	
me trouve	**nous trouvions**	**me sois trouvé(e)**	**nous soyons trouvé(e)s**
te trouves	**vous trouviez**	**te sois trouvé(e)**	**vous soyez trouvé(e)(s)**
se trouve	**se trouvent**	**se soit trouvé(e)**	**se soient trouvé(e)s**
7 imparfait du subjonctif		14 plus-que-parfait du subjonctif	
me trouvasse	**nous trouvassions**	**me fusse trouvé(e)**	**nous fussions trouvé(e)s**
te trouvasses	**vous trouvassiez**	**te fusses trouvé(e)**	**vous fussiez trouvé(e)(s)**
se trouvât	**se trouvassent**	**se fût trouvé(e)**	**se fussent trouvé(e)s**

Impératif

trouve-toi; ne te trouve pas
trouvons-nous; ne nous trouvons pas
trouvez-vous; ne vous trouvez pas

Words and expressions related to this verb

Où se trouve le bureau de poste? Where is the post office located?

Pouvez-vous me dire où se trouvent les toilettes? Can you tell me where the rest rooms are located?

Trouve-toi dans ce café à huit heures ce soir. Be in this café at 8 o'clock tonight.

Vous avez été malade; allez-vous mieux maintenant?—Oui, je me trouve mieux, merci! You have been sick; are you feeling better now?—Yes, I'm feeling better, thank you!

See also **trouver.**

Use the guide to French pronunciation. It's in the Appendixes.

Regular **-er** verb

to kill

The Seven Simple Tenses		The Seven Compound Tenses	
Singular	Plural	Singular	Plural
1 présent de l'indicatif		8 passé composé	
tue	**tuons**	**ai tué**	**avons tué**
tues	**tuez**	**as tué**	**avez tué**
tue	**tuent**	**a tué**	**ont tué**
2 imparfait de l'indicatif		9 plus-que-parfait de l'indicatif	
tuais	**tuions**	**avais tué**	**avions tué**
tuais	**tuiez**	**avais tué**	**aviez tué**
tuait	**tuaient**	**avait tué**	**avaient tué**
3 passé simple		10 passé antérieur	
tuai	**tuâmes**	**eus tué**	**eûmes tué**
tuas	**tuâtes**	**eus tué**	**eûtes tué**
tua	**tuèrent**	**eut tué**	**eurent tué**
4 futur		11 futur antérieur	
tuerai	**tuerons**	**aurai tué**	**aurons tué**
tueras	**tuerez**	**auras tué**	**aurez tué**
tuera	**tueront**	**aura tué**	**auront tué**
5 conditionnel		12 conditionnel passé	
tuerais	**tuerions**	**aurais tué**	**aurions tué**
tuerais	**tueriez**	**aurais tué**	**auriez tué**
tuerait	**tueraient**	**aurait tué**	**auraient tué**
6 présent du subjonctif		13 passé du subjonctif	
tue	**tuions**	**aie tué**	**ayons tué**
tues	**tuiez**	**aies tué**	**ayez tué**
tue	**tuent**	**ait tué**	**aient tué**
7 imparfait du subjonctif		14 plus-que-parfait du subjonctif	
tuasse	**tuassions**	**eusse tué**	**eussions tué**
tuasses	**tuassiez**	**eusses tué**	**eussiez tué**
tuât	**tuassent**	**eût tué**	**eussent tué**

Impératif
tue
tuons
tuez

Words and expressions related to this verb

tuer le temps to kill time
Ce travail me tue! This work is killing me!
se tuer to kill oneself; to get killed
un tueur, une tueuse killer
une tuerie slaughter
La drogue tue. Drugs kill.
un tue-mouche fly swatter (**des tue-mouches**)
crier à tue-tête to shout at the top of one's voice.
chanter à tue-tête to sing at the top of one's voice

French Proverb:

Il ne faut pas vendre la peau de l'ours avant de l'avoir tué. Don't count your chickens before they're hatched. (Lit.: Don't sell the bear's pelt before you've killed it.)

The subject pronouns are found on page 103.

to use **tu** when speaking, to be on familiar terms with someone

Regular **-er** verb endings; spelling change: **-oyer** verbs must change **y** to **i** in front of a mute **e**

The Seven Simple Tenses

Singular	Plural
1 présent de l'indicatif	
tutoie	**tutoyons**
tutoies	**tutoyez**
tutoie	**tutoient**
2 imparfait de l'indicatif	
tutoyais	**tutoyions**
tutoyais	**tutoyiez**
tutoyait	**tutoyaient**
3 passé simple	
tutoyai	**tutoyâmes**
tutoyas	**tutoyâtes**
tutoya	**tutoyèrent**
4 futur	
tutoierai	**tutoierons**
tutoieras	**tutoierez**
tutoiera	**tutoieront**
5 conditionnel	
tutoierais	**tutoierions**
tutoierais	**tutoieriez**
tutoierait	**tutoieraient**
6 présent du subjonctif	
tutoie	**tutoyions**
tutoies	**tutoyiez**
tutoie	**tutoient**
7 imparfait du subjonctif	
tutoyasse	**tutoyassions**
tutoyasses	**tutoyassiez**
tutoyât	**tutoyassent**

The Seven Compound Tenses

Singular	Plural
8 passé composé	
ai tutoyé	**avons tutoyé**
as tutoyé	**avez tutoyé**
a tutoyé	**ont tutoyé**
9 plus-que-parfait de l'indicatif	
avais tutoyé	**avions tutoyé**
avais tutoyé	**aviez tutoyé**
avait tutoyé	**avaient tutoyé**
10 passé antérieur	
eus tutoyé	**eûmes tutoyé**
eus tutoyé	**eûtes tutoyé**
eut tutoyé	**eurent tutoyé**
11 futur antérieur	
aurai tutoyé	**aurons tutoyé**
auras tutoyé	**aurez tutoyé**
aura tutoyé	**auront tutoyé**
12 conditionnel passé	
aurais tutoyé	**aurions tutoyé**
aurais tutoyé	**auriez tutoyé**
aurait tutoyé	**auraient tutoyé**
13 passé du subjonctif	
aie tutoyé	**ayons tutoyé**
aies tutoyé	**ayez tutoyé**
ait tutoyé	**aient tutoyé**
14 plus-que-parfait du subjonctif	
eusse tutoyé	**eussions tutoyé**
eusses tutoyé	**eussiez tutoyé**
eût tutoyé	**eussent tutoyé**

Impératif
tutoie
tutoyons
tutoyez

Sentences using this verb and words related to it

Est-ce que cela vous dérangerait si on se tutoyait? (Cela vous dérange si on se tutoie?)
Would it bother you if we used **tu** with each other?

Words and expressions related to this verb

le tutoiement use of **tu** when speaking with someone

se tutoyer to use **tu** with each other
See **vouvoyer**.

In French, **tu** is used when you are speaking to a member of your family, a close friend, a classmate, or someone younger than you. **Tu** is also used when speaking to an animal. **Vous** is the polite form of *you* and is used at all other times. **Vous** is also the plural of **tu**; when you are speaking to two or more strangers, two or more members of your family at the same time, or two or more close friends at the same time, use **vous**. If you're not sure, use **vous** until someone tells you otherwise!

Regular **-ir** verb

to unite, to join

The Seven Simple Tenses		The Seven Compound Tenses	
Singular	Plural	Singular	Plural
1 présent de l'indicatif		8 passé composé	
unis	**unissons**	**ai uni**	**avons uni**
unis	**unissez**	**as uni**	**avez uni**
unit	**unissent**	**a uni**	**ont uni**
2 imparfait de l'indicatif		9 plus-que-parfait de l'indicatif	
unissais	**unissions**	**avais uni**	**avions uni**
unissais	**unissiez**	**avais uni**	**aviez uni**
unissait	**unissaient**	**avait uni**	**avaient uni**
3 passé simple		10 passé antérieur	
unis	**unîmes**	**eus uni**	**eûmes uni**
unis	**unîtes**	**eus uni**	**eûtes uni**
unit	**unirent**	**eut uni**	**eurent uni**
4 futur		11 futur antérieur	
unirai	**unirons**	**aurai uni**	**aurons uni**
uniras	**unirez**	**auras uni**	**aurez uni**
unira	**uniront**	**aura uni**	**auront uni**
5 conditionnel		12 conditionnel passé	
unirais	**unirions**	**aurais uni**	**aurions uni**
unirais	**uniriez**	**aurais uni**	**auriez uni**
unirait	**uniraient**	**aurait uni**	**auraient uni**
6 présent du subjonctif		13 passé du subjonctif	
unisse	**unissions**	**aie uni**	**ayons uni**
unisses	**unissiez**	**aies uni**	**ayez uni**
unisse	**unissent**	**ait uni**	**aient uni**
7 imparfait du subjonctif		14 plus-que-parfait du subjonctif	
unisse	**unissions**	**eusse uni**	**eussions uni**
unisses	**unissiez**	**eusses uni**	**eussiez uni**
unît	**unissent**	**eût uni**	**eussent uni**

Impératif
unis
unissons
unissez

U

Words and expressions related to this verb

s'unir to join together, to marry
réunir to reunite; **se réunir** to meet together
les Etats-Unis the United States
les Nations-Unies (l'ONU) the United Nations
une union union, alliance
un trait d'union hyphen
unisexe unisex
unir ses forces to combine one's forces
chanter à l'unisson to sing in unison

Don't forget to study the section on defective and impersonal verbs. It's right after this main list.

utiliser (486) — Part. pr. utilisant — Part. passé utilisé

to utilize, to use, to make use of, to put to use

Regular **-er** verb

The Seven Simple Tenses		The Seven Compound Tenses	
Singular	Plural	Singular	Plural
1 présent de l'indicatif		8 passé composé	
utilise	**utilisons**	**ai utilisé**	**avons utilisé**
utilises	**utilisez**	**as utilisé**	**avez utilisé**
utilise	**utilisent**	**a utilisé**	**ont utilisé**
2 imparfait de l'indicatif		9 plus-que-parfait de l'indicatif	
utilisais	**utilisions**	**avais utilisé**	**avions utilisé**
utilisais	**utilisiez**	**avais utilisé**	**aviez utilisé**
utilisait	**utilisaient**	**avait utilisé**	**avaient utilisé**
3 passé simple		10 passé antérieur	
utilisai	**utilisâmes**	**eus utilisé**	**eûmes utilisé**
utilisas	**utilisâtes**	**eus utilisé**	**eûtes utilisé**
utilisa	**utilisèrent**	**eut utilisé**	**eurent utilisé**
4 futur		11 futur antérieur	
utiliserai	**utiliserons**	**aurai utilisé**	**aurons utilisé**
utiliseras	**utiliserez**	**auras utilisé**	**aurez utilisé**
utilisera	**utiliseront**	**aura utilisé**	**auront utilisé**
5 conditionnel		12 conditionnel passé	
utiliserais	**utiliserions**	**aurais utilisé**	**aurions utilisé**
utiliserais	**utiliseriez**	**aurais utilisé**	**auriez utilisé**
utiliserait	**utiliseraient**	**aurait utilisé**	**auraient utilisé**
6 présent du subjonctif		13 passé du subjonctif	
utilise	**utilisions**	**aie utilisé**	**ayons utilisé**
utilises	**utilisiez**	**aies utilisé**	**ayez utilisé**
utilise	**utilisent**	**ait utilisé**	**aient utilisé**
7 imparfait du subjonctif		14 plus-que-parfait du subjonctif	
utilisasse	**utilisassions**	**eusse utilisé**	**eussions utilisé**
utilisasses	**utilisassiez**	**eusses utilisé**	**eussiez utilisé**
utilisât	**utilisassent**	**eût utilisé**	**eussent utilisé**

Impératif
utilise
utilisons
utilisez

Words and expressions related to this verb

utile useful
inutile useless
une utilité utility, usefulness
un utilisateur, une utilisatrice user
utilitaire utilitarian
une utilisation utilization
Il est utile de + inf. It is useful + inf.
utilement usefully

Get acquainted with what preposition (if any) goes with what verb. See *Verbs with prepositions* in the Appendixes.

Irregular verb

to vanquish, to conquer

The Seven Simple Tenses		The Seven Compound Tenses	
Singular	Plural	Singular	Plural
1 présent de l'indicatif		8 passé composé	
vaincs	**vainquons**	**ai vaincu**	**avons vaincu**
vaincs	**vainquez**	**as vaincu**	**avez vaincu**
vainc	**vainquent**	**a vaincu**	**ont vaincu**
2 imparfait de l'indicatif		9 plus-que-parfait de l'indicatif	
vainquais	**vainquions**	**avais vaincu**	**avions vaincu**
vainquais	**vainquiez**	**avais vaincu**	**aviez vaincu**
vainquait	**vainquaient**	**avait vaincu**	**avaient vaincu**
3 passé simple		10 passé antérieur	
vainquis	**vainquîmes**	**eus vaincu**	**eûmes vaincu**
vainquis	**vainquîtes**	**eus vaincu**	**eûtes vaincu**
vainquit	**vainquirent**	**eut vaincu**	**eurent vaincu**
4 futur		11 futur antérieur	
vaincrai	**vaincrons**	**aurai vaincu**	**aurons vaincu**
vaincras	**vaincrez**	**auras vaincu**	**aurez vaincu**
vaincra	**vaincront**	**aura vaincu**	**auront vaincu**
5 conditionnel		12 conditionnel passé	
vaincrais	**vaincrions**	**aurais vaincu**	**aurions vaincu**
vaincrais	**vaincriez**	**aurais vaincu**	**auriez vaincu**
vaincrait	**vaincraient**	**aurait vaincu**	**auraient vaincu**
6 présent du subjonctif		13 passé du subjonctif	
vainque	**vainquions**	**aie vaincu**	**ayons vaincu**
vainques	**vainquiez**	**aies vaincu**	**ayez vaincu**
vainque	**vainquent**	**ait vaincu**	**aient vaincu**
7 imparfait du subjonctif		14 plus-que-parfait du subjonctif	
vainquisse	**vainquissions**	**eusse vaincu**	**eussions vaincu**
vainquisses	**vainquissiez**	**eusses vaincu**	**eussiez vaincu**
vainquît	**vainquissent**	**eût vaincu**	**eussent vaincu**

Impératif
vaincs
vainquons
vainquez

Words and expressions related to this verb

convaincre qqn de qqch to convince, to persuade someone of something

vainqueur victor, victorious; conqueror, conquering

convaincant, convaincante convincing

vaincu defeated

See also **convaincre.**

How are you doing? Find out with the verb drills and tests with answers explained on pages 50–101.

to be worth, to be as good as, to deserve, to merit, to be equal to

Irregular verb

The Seven Simple Tenses		The Seven Compound Tenses	
Singular	Plural	Singular	Plural
1 présent de l'indicatif		8 passé composé	
vaux	**valons**	**ai valu**	**avons valu**
vaux	**valez**	**as valu**	**avez valu**
vaut	**valent**	**a valu**	**ont valu**
2 imparfait de l'indicatif		9 plus-que-parfait de l'indicatif	
valais	**valions**	**avais valu**	**avions valu**
valais	**valiez**	**avais valu**	**aviez valu**
valait	**valaient**	**avait valu**	**avaient valu**
3 passé simple		10 passé antérieur	
valus	**valûmes**	**eus valu**	**eûmes valu**
valus	**valûtes**	**eus valu**	**eûtes valu**
valut	**valurent**	**eut valu**	**eurent valu**
4 futur		11 futur antérieur	
vaudrai	**vaudrons**	**aurai valu**	**aurons valu**
vaudras	**vaudrez**	**auras valu**	**aurez valu**
vaudra	**vaudront**	**aura valu**	**auront valu**
5 conditionnel		12 conditionnel passé	
vaudrais	**vaudrions**	**aurais valu**	**aurions valu**
vaudrais	**vaudriez**	**aurais valu**	**auriez valu**
vaudrait	**vaudraient**	**aurait valu**	**auraient valu**
6 présent du subjonctif		13 passé du subjonctif	
vaille	**valions**	**aie valu**	**ayons valu**
vailles	**valiez**	**aies valu**	**ayez valu**
vaille	**vaillent**	**ait valu**	**aient valu**
7 imparfait du subjonctif		14 plus-que-parfait du subjonctif	
valusse	**valussions**	**eusse valu**	**eussions valu**
valusses	**valussiez**	**eusses valu**	**eussiez valu**
valût	**valussent**	**eût valu**	**eussent valu**

Impératif
vaux
valons
valez

Words and expressions related to this verb

la valeur value, worth
valeureusement valorously
valeureux, valeureuse valorous
la validation validation
valide valid
Mieux vaut tard que jamais. Better late than never.
Cela vaut la peine. It's worth the trouble.
faire valoir to make the most of, to invest one's money
valoir cher to be worth a lot
valoir de l'argent to be worth money

Can't recognize an irregular verb form? Check out the index of common irregular French verb forms in the Appendixes.

The Seven Simple Tenses		The Seven Compound Tenses	
Singular	Plural	Singular	Plural
1 présent de l'indicatif		8 passé composé	
vends	**vendons**	**ai vendu**	**avons vendu**
vends	**vendez**	**as vendu**	**avez vendu**
vend	**vendent**	**a vendu**	**ont vendu**
2 imparfait de l'indicatif		9 plus-que-parfait de l'indicatif	
vendais	**vendions**	**avais vendu**	**avions vendu**
vendais	**vendiez**	**avais vendu**	**aviez vendu**
vendait	**vendaient**	**avait vendu**	**avaient vendu**
3 passé simple		10 passé antérieur	
vendis	**vendîmes**	**eus vendu**	**eûmes vendu**
vendis	**vendîtes**	**eus vendu**	**eûtes vendu**
vendit	**vendirent**	**eut vendu**	**eurent vendu**
4 futur		11 futur antérieur	
vendrai	**vendrons**	**aurai vendu**	**aurons vendu**
vendras	**vendrez**	**auras vendu**	**aurez vendu**
vendra	**vendront**	**aura vendu**	**auront vendu**
5 conditionnel		12 conditionnel passé	
vendrais	**vendrions**	**aurais vendu**	**aurions vendu**
vendrais	**vendriez**	**aurais vendu**	**auriez vendu**
vendrait	**vendraient**	**aurait vendu**	**auraient vendu**
6 présent du subjonctif		13 passé du subjonctif	
vende	**vendions**	**aie vendu**	**ayons vendu**
vendes	**vendiez**	**aies vendu**	**ayez vendu**
vende	**vendent**	**ait vendu**	**aient vendu**
7 imparfait du subjonctif		14 plus-que-parfait du subjonctif	
vendisse	**vendissions**	**eusse vendu**	**eussions vendu**
vendisses	**vendissiez**	**eusses vendu**	**eussiez vendu**
vendît	**vendissent**	**eût vendu**	**eussent vendu**

Impératif
vends
vendons
vendez

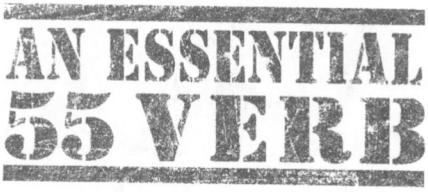

AN ESSENTIAL 55 VERB

Vendre

Vendre is an important verb because of its usefulness in many idiomatic expressions and everyday situations. **Vendre** is a regular **-re** verb, so many verbs are conjugated like it.

Sentences using vendre

Ce comédien a commencé sa carrière comme vendeur de chaussures. This actor began his career as a shoe salesman.

On vend des livres ici. Books are sold here.

Proverb

Il ne faut pas vendre la peau de l'ours avant de l'avoir tué. Don't count your chickens before they're hatched. (Literally: Don't sell the bear's pelt before you've killed it.)

Words and expressions related to this verb

un vendeur, une vendeuse **salesperson**

une vente **sale**

en vente **on sale**

maison à vendre **house for sale**

une salle de ventes **salesroom**

vendre à bon marché **to sell at a reasonably low price (a good buy)**

une vente aux enchères **auction**

vendre au rabais **to sell at a discount**

vendre à la sauvette **to peddle on the streets**

une vente à la sauvette **street peddling**

la mévente **a drop in sales, a sale at a loss**

À Vendre
Ordinateur portable, 512 Mo, 80 Gig, graveur CD, 700€.

For Sale
Laptop computer, 512 Meg, 80 Gig, CD burner, 700€.

If you can conjugate **vendre** you can also conjugate the following verbs (as well as other regular **-re** verbs):

fendre **to split**

revendre **to resell**

suspendre **to hang**

Regular **-er** verb endings; spelling change: retain the **ge** before **a** or **o** to keep the soft **g** sound of the verb

to avenge

The Seven Simple Tenses		The Seven Compound Tenses	
Singular	Plural	Singular	Plural
1 présent de l'indicatif		8 passé composé	
venge	**vengeons**	**ai vengé**	**avons vengé**
venges	**vengez**	**as vengé**	**avez vengé**
venge	**vengent**	**a vengé**	**ont vengé**
2 imparfait de l'indicatif		9 plus-que-parfait de l'indicatif	
vengeais	**vengions**	**avais vengé**	**avions vengé**
vengeais	**vengiez**	**avais vengé**	**aviez vengé**
vengeait	**vengeaient**	**avait vengé**	**avaient vengé**
3 passé simple		10 passé antérieur	
vengeai	**vengeâmes**	**eus vengé**	**eûmes vengé**
vengeas	**vengeâtes**	**eus vengé**	**eûtes vengé**
vengea	**vengèrent**	**eut vengé**	**eurent vengé**
4 futur		11 futur antérieur	
vengerai	**vengerons**	**aurai vengé**	**aurons vengé**
vengeras	**vengerez**	**auras vengé**	**aurez vengé**
vengera	**vengeront**	**aura vengé**	**auront vengé**
5 conditionnel		12 conditionnel passé	
vengerais	**vengerions**	**aurais vengé**	**aurions vengé**
vengerais	**vengeriez**	**aurais vengé**	**auriez vengé**
vengerait	**vengeraient**	**aurait vengé**	**auraient vengé**
6 présent du subjonctif		13 passé du subjonctif	
venge	**vengions**	**aie vengé**	**ayons vengé**
venges	**vengiez**	**aies vengé**	**ayez vengé**
venge	**vengent**	**ait vengé**	**aient vengé**
7 imparfait du subjonctif		14 plus-que-parfait du subjonctif	
vengeasse	**vengeassions**	**eusse vengé**	**eussions vengé**
vengeasses	**vengeassiez**	**eusses vengé**	**eussiez vengé**
vengeât	**vengeassent**	**eût vengé**	**eussent vengé**

Impératif
venge
vengeons
vengez

Words and expressions related to this verb

se venger to avenge oneself
venger son honneur to avenge one's honor
par vengeance out of revenge
un vengeur, une vengeresse avenger
se venger de to avenge oneself for
la vengeance vengeance, revenge
la vengeance divine divine vengeance

Don't miss orthographically changing verbs on pages 32–34.

venir (491) Part. pr. **venant** Part. passé **venu(e)(s)**

to come

Irregular verb

The Seven Simple Tenses		The Seven Compound Tenses	
Singular	Plural	Singular	Plural
1 présent de l'indicatif		8 passé composé	
viens	**venons**	**suis venu(e)**	**sommes venu(e)s**
viens	**venez**	**es venu(e)**	**êtes venu(e)(s)**
vient	**viennent**	**est venu(e)**	**sont venu(e)s**
2 imparfait de l'indicatif		9 plus-que-parfait de l'indicatif	
venais	**venions**	**étais venu(e)**	**étions venu(e)s**
venais	**veniez**	**étais venu(e)**	**étiez venu(e)(s)**
venait	**venaient**	**était venu(e)**	**étaient venu(e)s**
3 passé simple		10 passé antérieur	
vins	**vînmes**	**fus venu(e)**	**fûmes venu(e)s**
vins	**vîntes**	**fus venu(e)**	**fûtes venu(e)(s)**
vint	**vinrent**	**fut venu(e)**	**furent venu(e)s**
4 futur		11 futur antérieur	
viendrai	**viendrons**	**serai venu(e)**	**serons venu(e)s**
viendras	**viendrez**	**seras venu(e)**	**serez venu(e)(s)**
viendra	**viendront**	**sera venu(e)**	**seront venu(e)s**
5 conditionnel		12 conditionnel passé	
viendrais	**viendrions**	**serais venu(e)**	**serions venu(e)s**
viendrais	**viendriez**	**serais venu(e)**	**seriez venu(e)(s)**
viendrait	**viendraient**	**serait venu(e)**	**seraient venu(e)s**
6 présent du subjonctif		13 passé du subjonctif	
vienne	**venions**	**sois venu(e)**	**soyons venu(e)s**
viennes	**veniez**	**sois venu(e)**	**soyez venu(e)(s)**
vienne	**viennent**	**soit venu(e)**	**soient venu(e)s**
7 imparfait du subjonctif		14 plus-que-parfait du subjonctif	
vinsse	**vinssions**	**fusse venu(e)**	**fussions venu(e)s**
vinsses	**vinssiez**	**fusses venu(e)**	**fussiez venu(e)(s)**
vînt	**vinssent**	**fût venu(e)**	**fussent venu(e)s**

Impératif
viens
venons
venez

AN ESSENTIAL 55 VERB

Venir

Venir is an important verb for a beginning student because it is used in numerous situations and idiomatic expressions. There are also many useful verbs that are conjugated like **venir**. Note that the auxiliary of **venir** is **être** (see page 6).

Sentences using venir

Je viens de manger. I have just eaten.

D'où vient cela? Where does that come from?

Venons-en au fait. Let's get to the point.

Si nous venons à nous voir en ville, nous pouvons prendre un café ensemble. If we happen to see each other downtown, we can have coffee together.

Tina venait de sortir avec Alexandre quand le téléphone a sonné. Tina had just gone out with Alexander when the telephone rang.

Tu viens avec moi? Are you coming with me?

Words and expressions related to this verb

venir de faire qqch **to have just done something**

venir à + inf. **to happen to; Si je viens à devenir riche . . . If I happen to become rich . . .**

venir à bout de + inf. **to manage, to succeed + inf.**

s'en venir **to come**

faire venir **to send for**

venir chercher **to call for, to come to get**

le va et vient **coming and going (of people, cars, etc.)**

Proverbs

Tout vient à temps (à point) à qui sait attendre. **Everything comes to him who waits.**

L'appétit vient en mangeant. **The more you have, the more you want. (Literally: Appetite comes while eating.)**

Note: If you want to tell someone that you're on the way, say "J'arrive!" (I'm on the way! I'm coming!)

V

If you can conjugate **venir** you can also conjugate the following verbs:

intervenir **to intervene**

parvenir à **to reach, succeed**

survenir **to occur, arise**

The subject pronouns are found on page 103.

verser (492) — Part. pr. versant — Part. passé versé

to pour

Regular **-er** verb

The Seven Simple Tenses		The Seven Compound Tenses	
Singular	Plural	Singular	Plural
1 présent de l'indicatif		8 passé composé	
verse	**versons**	**ai versé**	**avons versé**
verses	**versez**	**as versé**	**avez versé**
verse	**versent**	**a versé**	**ont versé**
2 imparfait de l'indicatif		9 plus-que-parfait de l'indicatif	
versais	**versions**	**avais versé**	**avions versé**
versais	**versiez**	**avais versé**	**aviez versé**
versait	**versaient**	**avait versé**	**avaient versé**
3 passé simple		10 passé antérieur	
versai	**versâmes**	**eus versé**	**eûmes versé**
versas	**versâtes**	**eus versé**	**eûtes versé**
versa	**versèrent**	**eut versé**	**eurent versé**
4 futur		11 futur antérieur	
verserai	**verserons**	**aurai versé**	**aurons versé**
verseras	**verserez**	**auras versé**	**aurez versé**
versera	**verseront**	**aura versé**	**auront versé**
5 conditionnel		12 conditionnel passé	
verserais	**verserions**	**aurais versé**	**aurions versé**
verserais	**verseriez**	**aurais versé**	**auriez versé**
verserait	**verseraient**	**aurait versé**	**auraient versé**
6 présent du subjonctif		13 passé du subjonctif	
verse	**versions**	**aie versé**	**ayons versé**
verses	**versiez**	**aies versé**	**ayez versé**
verse	**versent**	**ait versé**	**aient versé**
7 imparfait du subjonctif		14 plus-que-parfait du subjonctif	
versasse	**versassions**	**eusse versé**	**eussions versé**
versasses	**versassiez**	**eusses versé**	**eussiez versé**
versât	**versassent**	**eût versé**	**eussent versé**

Impératif
verse
versons
versez

Common idiomatic expressions using this verb and words related to it

verser des larmes to shed tears
verser de l'argent to deposit money
verser des fonds to invest capital
un versement deposit, payment
verser du sang to shed blood
verser à boire à qqn to pour someone a drink
pleuvoir à verse to rain hard

Soak up some verbs used in weather expressions. There's a list in the Appendixes!

Irregular verb

to clothe, to dress

The Seven Simple Tenses		The Seven Compound Tenses	
Singular	Plural	Singular	Plural
1 présent de l'indicatif		8 passé composé	
vêts	**vêtons**	**ai vêtu**	**avons vêtu**
vêts	**vêtez**	**as vêtu**	**avez vêtu**
vêt	**vêtent**	**a vêtu**	**ont vêtu**
2 imparfait de l'indicatif		9 plus-que-parfait de l'indicatif	
vêtais	**vêtions**	**avais vêtu**	**avions vêtu**
vêtais	**vêtiez**	**avais vêtu**	**aviez vêtu**
vêtait	**vêtaient**	**avait vêtu**	**avaient vêtu**
3 passé simple		10 passé antérieur	
vêtis	**vêtîmes**	**eus vêtu**	**eûmes vêtu**
vêtis	**vêtîtes**	**eus vêtu**	**eûtes vêtu**
vêtit	**vêtirent**	**eut vêtu**	**eurent vêtu**
4 futur		11 futur antérieur	
vêtirai	**vêtirons**	**aurai vêtu**	**aurons vêtu**
vêtiras	**vêtirez**	**auras vêtu**	**aurez vêtu**
vêtira	**vêtiront**	**aura vêtu**	**auront vêtu**
5 conditionnel		12 conditionnel passé	
vêtirais	**vêtirions**	**aurais vêtu**	**aurions vêtu**
vêtirais	**vêtiriez**	**aurais vêtu**	**auriez vêtu**
vêtirait	**vêtiraient**	**aurait vêtu**	**auraient vêtu**
6 présent du subjonctif		13 passé du subjonctif	
vête	**vêtions**	**aie vêtu**	**ayons vêtu**
vêtes	**vêtiez**	**aies vêtu**	**ayez vêtu**
vête	**vêtent**	**ait vêtu**	**aient vêtu**
7 imparfait du subjonctif		14 plus-que-parfait du subjonctif	
vêtisse	**vêtissions**	**eusse vêtu**	**eussions vêtu**
vêtisses	**vêtissiez**	**eusses vêtu**	**eussiez vêtu**
vêtît	**vêtissent**	**eût vêtu**	**eussent vêtu**

Impératif
vêts
vêtons
vêtez

Words and expressions related to this verb

un vêtement garment, wearing apparel;
des vêtements clothes
les vêtements de dessus outerwear
les sous-vêtements underwear
vêtir un enfant to dress a child
dévêtir to undress
mettre sur soi un vêtement to put on clothing
les vêtements de deuil mourning clothes
le vestiaire coatroom
les vêtements de travail work clothes
se vêtir to dress oneself
se dévêtir to undress oneself
être bien vêtu (vêtue) to be well dressed;
mal vêtu badly dressed;
à demi-vêtu half dressed

See also **s'habiller.**

The subject pronouns are found on page 103.

vieillir (494) — Part. pr. vieillissant — Part. passé vieilli

to grow old, to become old, to age

Regular **-ir** verb

The Seven Simple Tenses		The Seven Compound Tenses	
Singular	Plural	Singular	Plural
1 présent de l'indicatif		8 passé composé	
vieillis	**vieillissons**	**ai vieilli**	**avons vieilli**
vieillis	**vieillissez**	**as vieilli**	**avez vieilli**
vieillit	**vieillissent**	**a vieilli**	**ont vieilli**
2 imparfait de l'indicatif		9 plus-que-parfait de l'indicatif	
vieillissais	**vieillissions**	**avais vieilli**	**avions vieilli**
vieillissais	**vieillissiez**	**avais vieilli**	**aviez vieilli**
vieillissait	**vieillissaient**	**avait vieilli**	**avaient vieilli**
3 passé simple		10 passé antérieur	
vieillis	**vieillîmes**	**eus vieilli**	**eûmes vieilli**
vieillis	**vieillîtes**	**eus vieilli**	**eûtes vieilli**
vieillit	**vieillirent**	**eut vieilli**	**eurent vieilli**
4 futur		11 futur antérieur	
vieillirai	**vieillirons**	**aurai vieilli**	**aurons vieilli**
vieilliras	**vieillirez**	**auras vieilli**	**aurez vieilli**
vieillira	**vieilliront**	**aura vieilli**	**auront vieilli**
5 conditionnel		12 conditionnel passé	
vieillirais	**vieillirions**	**aurais vieilli**	**aurions vieilli**
vieillirais	**vieilliriez**	**aurais vieilli**	**auriez vieilli**
vieillirait	**vieilliraient**	**aurait vieilli**	**auraient vieilli**
6 présent du subjonctif		13 passé du subjonctif	
vieillisse	**vieillissions**	**aie vieilli**	**ayons vieilli**
vieillisses	**vieillissiez**	**aies vieilli**	**ayez vieilli**
vieillisse	**vieillissent**	**ait vieilli**	**aient vieilli**
7 imparfait du subjonctif		14 plus-que-parfait du subjonctif	
vieillisse	**vieillissions**	**eusse vieilli**	**eussions vieilli**
vieillisses	**vieillissiez**	**eusses vieilli**	**eussiez vieilli**
vieillît	**vieillissent**	**eût vieilli**	**eussent vieilli**

Impératif
vieillis
vieillissons
vieillissez

Words related to this verb

vieux, vieil, vieille old
- **un vieux chapeau** an old hat
- **un vieil arbre** an old tree
- **un vieil homme** an old man
- **deux vieux hommes** two old men
- **une vieille dame** an old lady

la vieillesse old age
un vieillard old man
une vieille old woman
vieillissant, vieillissante *adj.* aging
le vieillissement aging, growing old

Can't find the verb you're looking for? Check the back pages of this book for a list of over 2,600 additional verbs!

Regular **-er** verb

to visit

The Seven Simple Tenses		The Seven Compound Tenses	
Singular	Plural	Singular	Plural
1 présent de l'indicatif		8 passé composé	
visite	**visitons**	**ai visité**	**avons visité**
visites	**visitez**	**as visité**	**avez visité**
visite	**visitent**	**a visité**	**ont visité**
2 imparfait de l'indicatif		9 plus-que-parfait de l'indicatif	
visitais	**visitions**	**avais visité**	**avions visité**
visitais	**visitiez**	**avais visité**	**aviez visité**
visitait	**visitaient**	**avait visité**	**avaient visité**
3 passé simple		10 passé antérieur	
visitai	**visitâmes**	**eus visité**	**eûmes visité**
visitas	**visitâtes**	**eus visité**	**eûtes visité**
visita	**visitèrent**	**eut visité**	**eurent visité**
4 futur		11 futur antérieur	
visiterai	**visiterons**	**aurai visité**	**aurons visité**
visiteras	**visiterez**	**auras visité**	**aurez visité**
visitera	**visiteront**	**aura visité**	**auront visité**
5 conditionnel		12 conditionnel passé	
visiterais	**visiterions**	**aurais visité**	**aurions visité**
visiterais	**visiteriez**	**aurais visité**	**auriez visité**
visiterait	**visiteraient**	**aurait visité**	**auraient visité**
6 présent du subjonctif		13 passé du subjonctif	
visite	**visitions**	**aie visité**	**ayons visité**
visites	**visitiez**	**aies visité**	**ayez visité**
visite	**visitent**	**ait visité**	**aient visité**
7 imparfait du subjonctif		14 plus-que-parfait du subjonctif	
visitasse	**visitassions**	**eusse visité**	**eussions visité**
visitasses	**visitassiez**	**eusses visité**	**eussiez visité**
visitât	**visitassent**	**eût visité**	**eussent visité**

Impératif
visite
visitons
visitez

Words and expressions related to this verb

rendre visite à qqn to visit someone, to pay a call
un visiteur, une visiteuse visitor, caller
une visite guidée a guided tour
rendre une visite à qqn to return a visit
les heures de visite visiting hours
une visitation visitation

Can't remember the French verb you need? Check the back pages of this book for the English-French verb index!

to live

Irregular verb

The Seven Simple Tenses		The Seven Compound Tenses	
Singular	Plural	Singular	Plural
1 présent de l'indicatif		8 passé composé	
vis	**vivons**	**ai vécu**	**avons vécu**
vis	**vivez**	**as vécu**	**avez vécu**
vit	**vivent**	**a vécu**	**ont vécu**
2 imparfait de l'indicatif		9 plus-que-parfait de l'indicatif	
vivais	**vivions**	**avais vécu**	**avions vécu**
vivais	**viviez**	**avais vécu**	**aviez vécu**
vivait	**vivaient**	**avait vécu**	**avaient vécu**
3 passé simple		10 passé antérieur	
vécus	**vécûmes**	**eus vécu**	**eûmes vécu**
vécus	**vécûtes**	**eus vécu**	**eûtes vécu**
vécut	**vécurent**	**eut vécu**	**eurent vécu**
4 futur		11 futur antérieur	
vivrai	**vivrons**	**aurai vécu**	**aurons vécu**
vivras	**vivrez**	**auras vécu**	**aurez vécu**
vivra	**vivront**	**aura vécu**	**auront vécu**
5 conditionnel		12 conditionnel passé	
vivrais	**vivrions**	**aurais vécu**	**aurions vécu**
vivrais	**vivriez**	**aurais vécu**	**auriez vécu**
vivrait	**vivraient**	**aurait vécu**	**auraient vécu**
6 présent du subjonctif		13 passé du subjonctif	
vive	**vivions**	**aie vécu**	**ayons vécu**
vives	**viviez**	**aies vécu**	**ayez vécu**
vive	**vivent**	**ait vécu**	**aient vécu**
7 imparfait du subjonctif		14 plus-que-parfait du subjonctif	
vécusse	**vécussions**	**eusse vécu**	**eussions vécu**
vécusses	**vécussiez**	**eusses vécu**	**eussiez vécu**
vécût	**vécussent**	**eût vécu**	**eussent vécu**

Impératif
vis
vivons
vivez

Words and expressions related to this verb

revivre to relive, to revive
survivre à to survive
Vive la France! Long live France!
avoir de quoi vivre to have enough to live on
vivre de to subsist on
savoir-vivre to be well-mannered
Qui vivra verra. Time will tell.
Vivent les Etats-Unis! Long live the United States!
le vivre et le couvert room and board
vivre largement to live well
Nous vivons des temps troublés. We are living in troubled times.

See also **survivre.**

Can't recognize an irregular verb form? Check out the index of common irregular French verb forms in the Appendixes.

Irregular verb

to see

The Seven Simple Tenses		The Seven Compound Tenses	
Singular	Plural	Singular	Plural
1 présent de l'indicatif		8 passé composé	
vois	**voyons**	**ai vu**	**avons vu**
vois	**voyez**	**as vu**	**avez vu**
voit	**voient**	**a vu**	**ont uv**
2 imparfait de l'indicatif		9 plus-que-parfait de l'indicatif	
voyais	**voyions**	**avais vu**	**avions vu**
voyais	**voyiez**	**avais vu**	**aviez vu**
voyait	**voyaient**	**avait vu**	**avaient vu**
3 passé simple		10 passé antérieur	
vis	**vîmes**	**eus vu**	**eûmes vu**
vis	**vîtes**	**eus vu**	**eûtes vu**
vit	**virent**	**eut vu**	**eurent vu**
4 futur		11 futur antérieur	
verrai	**verrons**	**aurai vu**	**aurons vu**
verras	**verrez**	**auras vu**	**aurez vu**
verra	**verront**	**aura vu**	**auront vu**
5 conditionnel		12 conditionnel passé	
verrais	**verrions**	**aurais vu**	**aurions vu**
verrais	**verriez**	**aurais vu**	**auriez vu**
verrait	**verraient**	**aurait vu**	**auraient vu**
6 présent du subjonctif		13 passé du subjonctif	
voie	**voyions**	**aie vu**	**ayons vu**
voies	**voyiez**	**aies vu**	**ayez vu**
voie	**voient**	**ait vu**	**aient vu**
7 imparfait du subjonctif		14 plus-que-parfait du subjonctif	
visse	**vissions**	**eusse vu**	**eussions vu**
visses	**vissiez**	**eusses vu**	**eussiez vu**
vît	**vissent**	**eût vu**	**eussent vu**

Impératif
vois
voyons
voyez

AN ESSENTIAL 55 VERB

Voir

Voir is an important verb for a beginning French student to learn because it is used in many everyday situations and idiomatic expressions.

Sentences using voir

Cela se voit. That's obvious.

Voyez vous-même! See for yourself!

C'est à voir. It remains to be seen.

Voir c'est croire. Seeing is believing

Il m'a frappé si fort que j'ai vu trente-six chandelles. He hit me so hard I saw stars.

Édith a tendance à voir la vie en rose. Edith tends to see life through rose-colored glasses.

Voyons! See here now!

Qu'est-ce que tu caches dans ton sac-à-dos? Fais voir. What are you hiding in your backpack? Show me.

Words and expressions related to this verb

à vue d'oeil **visibly**

voir de loin **to be farsighted**

faire voir **to show**

voir la vie en rose **to see the bright side of life, to see life through rose-colored glasses**

voir tout en rose **to see the bright side of things, to be optimistic**

If you can conjugate **voir** you can also conjugate the following verbs:

entrevoir **to glimpse, to catch a glimpse**

prévoir **to foresee (Note: The future and conditional stem is prévoir-)**

revoir **to see again**

Can't find the verb you're looking for? Check the back pages of this book for a list of over 2,600 additional verbs!

Regular **-er** verb

to fly, to steal

The Seven Simple Tenses		The Seven Compound Tenses	
Singular	Plural	Singular	Plural
1 présent de l'indicatif		8 passé composé	
vole	**volons**	**ai volé**	**avons volé**
voles	**volez**	**as volé**	**avez volé**
vole	**volent**	**a volé**	**ont volé**
2 imparfait de l'indicatif		9 plus-que-parfait de l'indicatif	
volais	**volions**	**avais volé**	**avions volé**
volais	**voliez**	**avais volé**	**aviez volé**
volait	**volaient**	**avait volé**	**avaient volé**
3 passé simple		10 passé antérieur	
volai	**volâmes**	**eus volé**	**eûmes volé**
volas	**volâtes**	**eus volé**	**eûtes volé**
vola	**volèrent**	**eut volé**	**eurent volé**
4 futur		11 futur antérieur	
volerai	**volerons**	**aurai volé**	**aurons volé**
voleras	**volerez**	**auras volé**	**aurez volé**
volera	**voleront**	**aura volé**	**auront volé**
5 conditionnel		12 conditionnel passé	
volerais	**volerions**	**aurais volé**	**aurions volé**
volerais	**voleriez**	**aurais volé**	**auriez volé**
volerait	**voleraient**	**aurait volé**	**auraient volé**
6 présent du subjonctif		13 passé du subjonctif	
vole	**volions**	**aie volé**	**ayons volé**
voles	**voliez**	**aies volé**	**ayez volé**
vole	**volent**	**ait volé**	**aient volé**
7 imparfait du subjonctif		14 plus-que-parfait du subjonctif	
volasse	**volassions**	**eusse volé**	**eussions volé**
volasses	**volassiez**	**eusses volé**	**eussiez volé**
volât	**volassent**	**eût volé**	**eussent volé**

Impératif
vole
volons
volez

V

Words and expressions related to this verb

un vol flight, theft
le voleur thief
Au voleur! Stop thief!
à vol d'oiseau as the crow flies
vol de nuit night flying (airplane), night flight
New York à vol d'oiseau bird's eye view of New York
survoler to fly over
le volant steering wheel
se mettre au volant to take the (steering) wheel
voler un baiser à qqn to steal a kiss from someone
voler dans les bras de qqn to fly into someone's arms

See also **s'envoler** and **survoler.**

to want

Irregular verb

The Seven Simple Tenses		The Seven Compound Tenses	
Singular	Plural	Singular	Plural
1 présent de l'indicatif		8 passé composé	
veux	**voulons**	**ai voulu**	**avons voulu**
veux	**voulez**	**as voulu**	**avez voulu**
veut	**veulent**	**a voulu**	**ont voulu**
2 imparfait de l'indicatif		9 plus-que-parfait de l'indicatif	
voulais	**voulions**	**avais voulu**	**avions voulu**
voulais	**vouliez**	**avais voulu**	**aviez voulu**
voulait	**voulaient**	**avait voulu**	**avaient voulu**
3 passé simple		10 passé antérieur	
voulus	**voulûmes**	**eus voulu**	**eûmes voulu**
voulus	**voulûtes**	**eus voulu**	**eûtes voulu**
voulut	**voulurent**	**eut voulu**	**eurent voulu**
4 futur		11 futur antérieur	
voudrai	**voudrons**	**aurai voulu**	**aurons voulu**
voudras	**voudrez**	**auras voulu**	**aurez voulu**
voudra	**voudront**	**aura voulu**	**auront voulu**
5 conditionnel		12 conditionnel passé	
voudrais	**voudrions**	**aurais voulu**	**aurions voulu**
voudrais	**voudriez**	**aurais voulu**	**auriez voulu**
voudrait	**voudraient**	**aurait voulu**	**auraient voulu**
6 présent du subjonctif		13 passé du subjonctif	
veuille	**voulions**	**aie voulu**	**ayons voulu**
veuilles	**vouliez**	**aies voulu**	**ayez voulu**
veuille	**veuillent**	**ait voulu**	**aient voulu**
7 imparfait du subjonctif		14 plus-que-parfait du subjonctif	
voulusse	**voulussions**	**eusse voulu**	**eussions voulu**
voulusses	**voulussiez**	**eusses voulu**	**eussiez voulu**
voulût	**voulussent**	**eût voulu**	**eussent voulu**

Impératif
veuille
veuillons
veuillez

AN ESSENTIAL 55 VERB

Vouloir

Vouloir is an important verb for beginning students because it is used in many everyday situations and idiomatic expressions.

Sentences using vouloir

Que voulez-vous dire par là? What do you mean by that remark?

Vouloir c'est pouvoir. Where there's a will there's a way.

Pourriez-vous m'aider? Je voudrais installer ce logiciel. Could you please help me? I would like to install this software.

—Est-ce que tu veux m'accompagner?
—Oui, je veux bien!

—Do you want to accompany me?
—Yes, I'd really like to!

Que voulez-vous? What do you expect?

Qu'est-ce que cela veut dire? What does that mean?

Veuillez éteindre vos téléphones cellulaires. Please turn off your cell phones.

Veuillez agréer, Monsieur (Madame), mes sincères salutations. Please be good enough, Sir (Madam) to accept my sincere greetings. (This is one of many possible closing statements in correspondence. Of course, in English we simply say: Sincerely.)

Words and expressions related to this verb

vouloir dire **to mean**

Que veut dire . . .? **What does . . . mean?**

un voeu **wish**

meilleurs voeux **best wishes**

vouloir bien faire qqch **to be willing to do something**

sans le vouloir **without meaning to, unintentionally**

en temps voulu **in due time**

en vouloir à qqn **to bear a grudge against someone**

vouloir du bien à qqn **to wish someone well**

V

Can't remember the French verb you need? Check the back pages of this book for the English-French verb index!

The subject pronouns are found on page 103.

to use **vous** when speaking, to be on formal or polite terms with someone

Regular **-er** verb endings; spelling change: **-oyer** verbs must change **y** to **i** before a mute **e**

The Seven Simple Tenses

Singular	Plural
1 présent de l'indicatif	
vouvoie	**vouvoyons**
vouvoies	**vouvoyez**
vouvoie	**vouvoient**
2 imparfait de l'indicatif	
vouvoyais	**vouvoyions**
vouvoyais	**vouvoyiez**
vouvoyait	**vouvoyaient**
3 passé simple	
vouvoyai	**vouvoyâmes**
vouvoyas	**vouvoyâtes**
vouvoya	**vouvoyèrent**
4 futur	
vouvoierai	**vouvoierons**
vouvoieras	**vouvoierez**
vouvoiera	**vouvoieront**
5 conditionnel	
vouvoierais	**vouvoierions**
vouvoierais	**vouvoieriez**
vouvoierait	**vouvoieraient**
6 présent du subjonctif	
vouvoie	**vouvoyions**
vouvoies	**vouvoyiez**
vouvoie	**vouvoient**
7 imparfait du subjonctif	
vouvoyasse	**vouvoyassions**
vouvoyasses	**vouvoyassiez**
vouvoyât	**vouvoyassent**

The Seven Compound Tenses

Singular	Plural
8 passé composé	
ai vouvoyé	**avons vouvoyé**
as vouvoyé	**avez vouvoyé**
a vouvoyé	**ont vouvoyé**
9 plus-que-parfait de l'indicatif	
avais vouvoyé	**avions vouvoyé**
avais vouvoyé	**aviez vouvoyé**
avait vouvoyé	**avaient vouvoyé**
10 passé antérieur	
eus vouvoyé	**eûmes vouvoyé**
eus vouvoyé	**eûtes vouvoyé**
eut vouvoyé	**eurent vouvoyé**
11 futur antérieur	
aurai vouvoyé	**aurons vouvoyé**
auras vouvoyé	**aurez vouvoyé**
aura vouvoyé	**auront vouvoyé**
12 conditionnel passé	
aurais vouvoyé	**aurions vouvoyé**
aurais vouvoyé	**auriez vouvoyé**
aurait vouvoyé	**auraient vouvoyé**
13 passé du subjonctif	
aie vouvoyé	**ayons vouvoyé**
aies vouvoyé	**ayez vouvoyé**
ait vouvoyé	**aient vouvoyé**
14 plus-que-parfait du subjonctif	
eusse vouvoyé	**eussions vouvoyé**
eusses vouvoyé	**eussiez vouvoyé**
eût vouvoyé	**eussent vouvoyé**

Impératif
vouvoie
vouvoyons
vouvoyez

Sentences using this verb and words related to it

Quand je l'ai connu on se vouvoyait, mais maintenant je le tutoie. When I met him we used **vous**, but now I use **tu** with him.

Words and expressions related to this verb

le vouvoiement use of **vous** when speaking with someone

se vouvoyer to use **vous** with each other

See **tutoyer**.

In French, **tu** is used when you are speaking to a member of your family, a close friend, a classmate, or someone younger than you. **Tu** is also used when speaking to an animal. **Vous** is the polite form of *you* and is used at all other times. **Vous** is also the plural of **tu**; when you are speaking to two or more strangers, two or more members of your family at the same time, or two or more close friends at the same time, use **vous**. If you're not sure, use **vous** until someone tells you otherwise!

to travel

Regular **-er** verb endings; spelling change: retain the **ge** before **a** or **o** to keep the soft **g** sound of the verb

The Seven Simple Tenses		The Seven Compound Tenses	
Singular	Plural	Singular	Plural
1 présent de l'indicatif		8 passé composé	
voyage	**voyageons**	**ai voyagé**	**avons voyagé**
voyages	**voyagez**	**as voyagé**	**avez voyagé**
voyage	**voyagent**	**a voyagé**	**ont voyagé**
2 imparfait de l'indicatif		9 plus-que-parfait de l'indicatif	
voyageais	**voyagions**	**avais voyagé**	**avions voyagé**
voyageais	**voyagiez**	**avais voyagé**	**aviez voyagé**
voyageait	**voyageaient**	**avait voyagé**	**avaient voyagé**
3 passé simple		10 passé antérieur	
voyageai	**voyageâmes**	**eus voyagé**	**eûmes voyagé**
voyageas	**voyageâtes**	**eus voyagé**	**eûtes voyagé**
voyagea	**voyagèrent**	**eut voyagé**	**eurent voyagé**
4 futur		11 futur antérieur	
voyagerai	**voyagerons**	**aurai voyagé**	**aurons voyagé**
voyageras	**voyagerez**	**auras voyagé**	**aurez voyagé**
voyagera	**voyageront**	**aura voyagé**	**auront voyagé**
5 conditionnel		12 conditionnel passé	
voyagerais	**voyagerions**	**aurais voyagé**	**aurions voyagé**
voyagerais	**voyageriez**	**aurais voyagé**	**auriez voyagé**
voyagerait	**voyageraient**	**aurait voyagé**	**auraient voyagé**
6 présent du subjonctif		13 passé du subjonctif	
voyage	**voyagions**	**aie voyagé**	**ayons voyagé**
voyages	**voyagiez**	**aies voyagé**	**ayez voyagé**
voyage	**voyagent**	**ait voyagé**	**aient voyagé**
7 imparfait du subjonctif		14 plus-que-parfait du subjonctif	
voyageasse	**voyageassions**	**eusse voyagé**	**eussions voyagé**
voyageasses	**voyageassiez**	**eusses voyagé**	**eussiez voyagé**
voyageât	**voyageassent**	**eût voyagé**	**eussent voyagé**

Impératif
voyage
voyageons
voyagez

V

Words and expressions related to this verb

un voyage a trip
faire un voyage to take a trip
un voyageur, une voyageuse traveler
une agence de voyages tourist agency
Bon voyage! Have a good trip!
Bon voyage et bon retour! Have a good trip and a safe return!
Les Voyages de Gulliver *Gulliver's Travels*
les frais de voyage travel expenses
un voyage d'affaires business trip
un voyage d'agrément pleasure trip
Quand je fais un voyage, j'envoie des cartes postales à mes amis. When I take a trip, I send postcards to my friends.

Don't miss orthographically changing verbs on pages 32–34.

Appendixes

Defective and impersonal verbs 665

Guide to French pronunciation 686

Verbs used in weather expressions 688

Verbs with prepositions 690

Index of common irregular French verb forms 701

English-French verb index 705

Index of 2,600 additional verbs keyed to listing of 501 French verbs 733

Defective and impersonal verbs

Part. pr. **advenant** Part. passé **advenu** **advenir**

Irregular verb

to happen, to occur, to come to pass

The Seven Simple Tenses		The Seven Compound Tenses	
Singular	Plural	Singular	Plural
1 présent de l'indicatif **il advient**		8 passé composé **il est advenu**	
2 imparfait de l'indicatif **il advenait**		9 plus-que-parfait de l'indicatif **il était advenu**	
3 passé simple **il advint**		10 passé antérieur **il fut advenu**	
4 futur **il adviendra**		11 futur antérieur **il sera advenu**	
5 conditionnel **il adviendrait**		12 conditionnel passé **il serait advenu**	
6 présent du subjonctif **qu'il advienne**		13 passé du subjonctif **qu'il soit advenu**	
7 imparfait du subjonctif **qu'il advînt**		14 plus-que-parfait du subjonctif **qu'il fût advenu**	

Impératif
Qu'il advienne!
Let it come to pass!

Words and expressions related to this verb
Il advint que . . . It came to pass that . . .
Advienne que pourra . . . Come what may . . .
Voilà ce qu'il advint. That's what happened.
quoiqu'il advienne whatever may happen

This is an impersonal verb used in the third person singular only.

s'agir Part. pr. **s'agissant** Part. passé **agi**

to be the matter, to be a question of

Reflexive regular **-ir** verb

The Seven Simple Tenses	The Seven Compound Tenses
Singular Plural	Singular Plural
1 présent de l'indicatif **il s'agit**	8 passé composé **il s'est agi**
2 imparfait de l'indicatif **il s'agissait**	9 plus-que-parfait de l'indicatif **il s'était agi**
3 passé simple **il s'agit**	10 passé antérieur **il se fut agi**
4 futur **il s'agira**	11 futur antérieur **il se sera agi**
5 conditionnel **il s'agirait**	12 conditionnel passé **il se serait agi**
6 présent du subjonctif **qu'il s'agisse**	13 passé du subjonctif **qu'il se soit agi**
7 imparfait du subjonctif **qu'il s'agît**	14 plus-que-parfait du subjonctif **qu'il se fût agi**

Impératif
[not in use]

Common idiomatic expressions using this verb

s'agir de to have to do with, to be a matter of
De quoi s'agit-il? What's the matter? What's up?
Voici ce dont il s'agit. This is what it's about.
Il s'agit de mon vélo. It's about my bike.

Note that this verb is impersonal and is used primarily in the tenses given above.

The Seven Simple Tenses		The Seven Compound Tenses	
Singular	Plural	Singular	Plural
1 présent de l'indicatif		8 passé composé	
il choit	**ils choient**	**ai chu**	**avons chu**
		as chu	**avez chu**
		a chu	**ont chu**
		9 plus-que-parfait de l'indicatif	
		avais chu	**avions chu**
		avais chu	**aviez chu**
		avait chu	**avaient chu**
3 passé simple		10 passé antérieur	
il chut	**ils churent**	**eus chu**	**eûmes chu**
		eus chu	**eûtes chu**
		eut chu	**eurent chu**
		11 futur antérieur	
		aurai chu	**aurons chu**
		auras chu	**aurez chu**
		aura chu	**auront chu**
		12 conditionnel passé	
		aurais chu	**aurions chu**
		aurais chu	**auriez chu**
		aurait chu	**auraient chu**

This is a defective verb. It is generally used in the above tenses.

to close

The Seven Simple Tenses		The Seven Compound Tenses	
Singular	Plural	Singular	Plural
1 présent de l'indicatif		8 passé composé	
clos	—	**ai clos**	**avons clos**
clos	—	**as clos**	**avez clos**
clôt	**closent**	**a clos**	**ont clos**
		9 plus-que-parfait de l'indicatif	
		avais clos	**avions clos**
		avais clos	**aviez clos**
		avait clos	**avaient clos**
		10 passé antérieur	
		eus clos	**eûmes clos**
		eus clos	**eûtes clos**
		eut clos	**eurent clos**
4 futur		11 futur antérieur	
clorai	**clorons**	**aurai clos**	**aurons clos**
cloras	**clorez**	**auras clos**	**aurez clos**
clora	**cloront**	**aura clos**	**auront clos**
5 conditionnel		12 conditionnel passé	
clorais	**clorions**	**aurais clos**	**aurions clos**
clorais	**cloriez**	**aurais clos**	**auriez clos**
clorait	**cloraient**	**aurait clos**	**auraient clos**
6 présent du subjonctif		13 passé du subjonctif	
close	**closions**	**aie clos**	**ayons clos**
closes	**closiez**	**aies clos**	**ayez clos**
close	**closent**	**ait clos**	**aient clos**
		14 plus-que-parfait du subjonctif	
		eusse clos	**eussions clos**
		eusses clos	**eussiez clos**
		eût clos	**eussent clos**

Impératif
clos

This is a defective verb. It is generally used in the above tenses.

The Seven Simple Tenses		The Seven Compound Tenses	
Singular	Plural	Singular	Plural
1 présent de l'indicatif		8 passé composé	
il coûte	**ils coûtent**	**il a coûté**	**ils ont coûté**
2 imparfait de l'indicatif		9 plus-que-parfait de l'indicatif	
il coûtait	**ils coûtaient**	**il avait coûté**	**ils avaient coûté**
3 passé simple		10 passé antérieur	
il coûta	**ils coûtèrent**	**il eut coûté**	**ils eurent coûté**
4 futur		11 futur antérieur	
il coûtera	**ils coûteront**	**il aura coûté**	**ils auront coûté**
5 conditionnel		12 conditionnel passé	
il coûterait	**ils coûteraient**	**il aurait coûté**	**ils auraient coûté**
6 présent du subjonctif		13 passé du subjonctif	
qu'il coûte	**qu'ils coûtent**	**qu'il ait coûté**	**qu'ils aient coûté**
7 imparfait du subjonctif		14 plus-que-parfait du subjonctif	
qu'il coûtât	**qu'ils coûtassent**	**qu'il eût coûté**	**qu'ils eussent coûté**

Impératif
[not in use]

Sentences using this verb and words related to it

—Combien coûte cette table?
—Elle coûte dix mille euros.
—Et combien coûte ce lit?
—Il coûte dix mille euros aussi.
—Ils coûtent joliment cher!

coûteusement expensively, dearly
coûte que coûte at any cost
coûteux, coûteuse costly, expensive
Cela coûte joliment cher. That costs a pretty penny.
coûter cher, coûter peu to be expensive, inexpensive
coûter à qqn to cost someone;
Cela lui en a coûté la vie. That cost him his life.
coûter les yeux de la tête to be very expensive
le coût de la vie the cost of living

This verb is generally regarded as impersonal and is used primarily in the third person singular and plural.

échoir — Part. pr. **échéant** — Part. passé **échu**

to fall due

The Seven Simple Tenses		The Seven Compound Tenses	
Singular	Plural	Singular	Plural
1 présent de l'indicatif		8 passé composé	
échoit	**échoient**	**est échu**	**sont échus**
2 imparfait de l'indicatif		9 plus-que-parfait de l'indicatif	
échoyait	**échoyaient**	**était échu**	**étaient échus**
3 passé simple		10 passé antérieur	
échut	**échurent**	**fut échu**	**furent échus**
4 futur		11 futur antérieur	
échoira	**échoiront**	**sera échu**	**seront échus**
5 conditionnel		12 conditionnel passé	
échoirait	**échoiraient**	**serait échu**	**seraient échus**
6 présent du subjonctif		13 passé du subjonctif	
échoie	**échoient**	**soit échu**	**soient échus**
7 imparfait du subjonctif		14 plus-que-parfait du subjonctif	
échût	**échussent**	**fût échu**	**fussent échus**

Expression related to this verb
échoir à to fall to

This verb is used only in the third person singular and plural.

to be necessary, must, to be lacking to (à), to need

The Seven Simple Tenses		The Seven Compound Tenses	
Singular	Plural	Singular	Plural
1 présent de l'indicatif **il faut**		8 passé composé **il a fallu**	
2 imparfait de l'indicatif **il fallait**		9 plus-que-parfait de l'indicatif **il avait fallu**	
3 passé simple **il fallut**		10 passé antérieur **il eut fallu**	
4 futur **il faudra**		11 futur antérieur **il aura fallu**	
5 conditionnel **il faudrait**		12 conditionnel passé **il aurait fallu**	
6 présent du subjonctif **qu'il faille**		13 passé du subjonctif **qu'il ait fallu**	
7 imparfait du subjonctif **qu'il fallût**		14 plus-que-parfait du subjonctif **qu'il eût fallu**	

Impératif
[not in use]

Common idiomatic expressions using this verb

comme il faut as is proper
agir comme il faut to behave properly
Il me faut de l'argent. I need some money.
Il faut manger pour vivre. It is necessary to eat in order to live.
Il ne faut pas parler sans politesse. One must not talk impolitely.
Il faut . . . It is necessary; one must
Il ne faut pas . . . One must not . . .
Peu s'en faut . . . It takes only a little . . .
s'en falloir to be lacking
Il s'en faut de beaucoup . . . It takes a lot . . .

This is an impersonal verb and it is used in the tenses given above with the subject *il*.

frire Part. pr. [not in use] Part. passé **frit**

to fry

The Seven Simple Tenses		The Seven Compound Tenses	
Singular	Plural	Singular	Plural
1 présent de l'indicatif		8 passé composé	
fris		**ai frit**	**avons frit**
fris		**as frit**	**avez frit**
frit		**a frit**	**ont frit**
		9 plus-que-parfait de l'indicatif	
		avais frit	**avions frit**
		avais frit	**aviez frit**
		avait frit	**avaient frit**
		10 passé antérieur	
		eus frit	**eûmes frit**
		eus frit	**eûtes frit**
		eut frit	**eurent frit**
4 futur		11 futur antérieur	
frirai	**frirons**	**aurai frit**	**aurons frit**
friras	**frirez**	**auras frit**	**aurez frit**
frira	**friront**	**aura frit**	**auront frit**
5 conditionnel		12 conditionnel passé	
frirais	**fririons**	**aurais frit**	**aurions frit**
frirais	**fririez**	**aurais frit**	**auriez frit**
frirait	**friraient**	**aurait frit**	**auraient frit**
		13 passé du subjonctif	
		aie frit	**ayons frit**
		aies frit	**ayez frit**
		ait frit	**aient frit**
		14 plus-que-parfait du subjonctif	
		eusse frit	**eussions frit**
		eusses frit	**eussiez frit**
		eût frit	**eussent frit**

Impératif
fris
faisons frire
faites frire

Words and expressions related to this verb

faire frire to fry (see note below)
pommes frites French fries
une friteuse frying basket
la friture frying
des pommes de terre frites fried potatoes (French style)
un bifteck-frites, un steak-frites steak with French fries

This verb is generally used only in the persons and tenses given above. To supply the forms that are lacking, use the appropriate form of **faire** plus the infinitive **frire**, *e.g.*, the plural of the present indicative is: **nous faisons frire, vous faites frire, ils font frire**.

Part. pr. **gisant** Part. passé [not in use] **gésir**

to lie down, to be lying down

The Seven Simple Tenses		The Seven Compound Tenses	
Singular	Plural	Singular	Plural
1 présent de l'indicatif			
gis	**gisons**		
gis	**gisez**		
gît	**gisent**		
2 imparfait de l'indicatif			
gisais	**gisions**		
gisais	**gisiez**		
gisait	**gisaient**		

Words and expressions related to this verb

un gisement layer, deposit
un gisement de charbon coal field
Ci-gît . . . Here lies . . .
Ci-gisent . . . Here lie . . .
gisant, gisante lying, fallen, felled
un gîte lodging, refuge, shelter
gîter to lodge

This is a defective verb. It is generally used only in the above tenses. **Gésir** is used primarily in reference to the dead, to sick persons lying down, and to inanimate objects that have been felled.

grêler Part. pr. **grêlant** Part. passé **grêlé**

to hail (weather)

The Seven Simple Tenses	The Seven Compound Tenses
Singular Plural	Singular Plural
1 présent de l'indicatif **il grêle**	8 passé composé **il a grêlé**
2 imparfait de l'indicatif **il grêlait**	9 plus-que-parfait de l'indicatif **il avait grêlé**
3 passé simple **il grêla**	10 passé antérieur **il eut grêlé**
4 futur **il grêlera**	11 futur antérieur **il aura grêlé**
5 conditionnel **il grêlerait**	12 conditionnel passé **il aurait grêlé**
6 présent du subjonctif **qu'il grêle**	13 passé du subjonctif **qu'il ait grêlé**
7 imparfait du subjonctif **qu'il grêlât**	14 plus-que-parfait du subjonctif **qu'il eût grêlé**

Impératif
Qu'il grêle! Let it hail!

Words and expressions related to this verb
la grêle hail (weather)
une averse de grêle hail storm
un grêlon hailstone

grêle *adj.* thin, slender, slim; **un bras grêle** thin arm; **une voix grêle** shrill voice to shine, to gleam, to glisten

The Seven Simple Tenses		The Seven Compound Tenses	
Singular	Plural	Singular	Plural
1 présent de l'indicatif **il luit**		8 passé composé **il a lui**	
2 imparfait de l'indicatif **il luisait**		9 plus-que-parfait de l'indicatif **il avait lui**	
3 passé simple **il luisit**		10 passé antérieur **il eut lui**	
4 futur **il luira**		11 futur antérieur **il aura lui**	
5 conditionnel **il luirait**		12 conditionnel passé **il aurait lui**	
6 présent du subjonctif **qu'il luise**		13 passé du subjonctif **qu'il ait lui**	
7 imparfait du subjonctif **qu'il luisît**		14 plus-que-parfait du subjonctif **qu'il eût lui**	

Impératif
Qu'il luise! Let it shine!

Words and expressions related to this verb

la lueur glimmer, gleam, glow
luisant, luisante shining
à la lueur d'une bougie by candlelight
l'espoir luit encore there is still a glimmer of hope
le lac luisait au soleil du matin the lake glistened in the morning sunlight
Le soleil luit. The sun is shining.
J'ai le nez qui luit. My nose is shiny.
une lueur d'espoir a glimmer of hope

messeoir (à) Part. pr. **messéant** Part. passé [not in use]

to be unbecoming to

The Seven Simple Tenses		The Seven Compound Tenses	
Singular	Plural	Singular	Plural
1 présent de l'indicatif			
messied	**messiéent**		
2 imparfait de l'indicatif			
messeyait	**messeyaient**		
4 futur			
messiéra	**messiéront**		
5 conditionnel			
messiérait	**messiéraient**		
6 présent du subjonctif			
messiée	**messiéent**		

This verb is defective and it is only used in the third person singular and plural.

The Seven Simple Tenses	The Seven Compound Tenses
Singular Plural	Singular Plural
1 présent de l'indicatif **il neige**	8 passé composé **il a neigé**
2 imparfait de l'indicatif **il neigeait**	9 plus-que-parfait de l'indicatif **il avait neigé**
3 passé simple **il neigea**	10 passé antérieur **il eut neigé**
4 futur **il neigera**	11 futur antérieur **il aura neigé**
5 conditionnel **il neigerait**	12 conditionnel passé **il aurait neigé**
6 présent du subjonctif **qu'il neige**	13 passé du subjonctif **qu'il ait neigé**
7 imparfait du subjonctif **qu'il neigeât**	14 plus-que-parfait du subjonctif **qu'il eût neigé**

Impératif
Qu'il neige! Let it snow!

Words and expressions related to this verb

la neige snow
un bonhomme de neige a snowman
neige fondue slush
neigeux, neigeuse snowy
Blanche-Neige Snow White
une boule de neige snowball
lancer des boules de neige to throw snowballs
une chute de neige snowfall
déneiger to clear the snow
la neige artificielle artificial snow
la neige poudreuse dusting of snow
la bataille de boules de neige snowball fight
être submergé de travail to be snowed under with work
les conditions d'enneigement snow conditions
le bulletin d'enneigement snow report
un chasse-neige snowplow

paître Part. pr. **paissant** Part. passé [not in use]

to graze, to feed

The Seven Simple Tenses		The Seven Compound Tenses	
Singular	Plural	Singular	Plural
1 présent de l'indicatif			
pais	**paissons**		
pais	**paissez**		
paît	**paissent**		
2 imparfait de l'indicatif			
paissais	**paissions**		
paissais	**paissiez**		
paissait	**paissaient**		
4 futur			
paîtrai	**paîtrons**		
paîtras	**paîtrez**		
paîtra	**paîtront**		
5 conditionnel			
paîtrais	**paîtrions**		
paîtrais	**paîtriez**		
paîtrait	**paîtraient**		
6 présent du subjonctif			
paisse	**paissions**		
paisses	**paissiez**		
paisse	**paissent**		

Impératif
pais
paissons
paissez

This verb is used only in the above tenses.

Part. pr. **se passant** Part passé **passé** **se passer**

to happen, to take place

The Seven Simple Tenses	The Seven Compound Tenses
Singular Plural	Singular Plural
1 présent de l'indicatif **il se passe**	8 passé composé **il s'est passé**
2 imparfait de l'indicatif **il se passait**	9 plus-que-parfait de l'indicatif **il s'était passé**
3 passé simple **il se passa**	10 passé antérieur **il se fut passé**
4 futur **il se passera**	11 futur antérieur **il se sera passé**
5 conditionnel **il se passerait**	12 conditionnel passé **il se serait passé**
6 présent du subjonctif **qu'il se passe**	13 passé du subjonctif **qu'il se soit passé**
7 imparfait du subjonctif **qu'il se passât**	14 plus-que-parfait du subjonctif **qu'il se fût passé**

Impératif
Qu'il se passe! Let it happen!

Words and expressions related to this verb
Que se passe-t-il? What's going on? What's happening?
Qu'est-ce qui se passe? What's going on? What's happening?
Qu'est-ce qui s'est passé? What happened?
se passer de qqch to do without something
Je peux me passer de fumer. I can do without smoking.

See also **passer** and **repasser.**

This verb is impersonal and is generally used in the third person singular only.

pleuvoir Part. pr. **pleuvant** Part. passé **plu**

to rain

The Seven Simple Tenses	The Seven Compound Tenses
Singular Plural	Singular Plural
1 présent de l'indicatif **il pleut**	8 passé composé **il a plu**
2 imparfait de l'indicatif **il pleuvait**	9 plus-que-parfait de l'indicatif **il avait plu**
3 passé simple **il plut**	10 passé antérieur **il eut plu**
4 futur **il pleuvra**	11 futur antérieur **il aura plu**
5 conditionnel **il pleuvrait**	12 conditionnel passé **il aurait plu**
6 présent du subjonctif **qu'il pleuve**	13 passé du subjonctif **qu'il ait plu**
7 imparfait du subjonctif **qu'il plût**	14 plus-que-parfait du subjonctif **qu'il eût plu**

Impératif
Qu'il pleuve! Let it rain!

Sentences using this verb and words related to it

Hier il a plu, il pleut maintenant, et je suis certain qu'il pleuvra demain.

la pluie the rain
pluvieux, pluvieuse rainy
pleuvoter to drizzle
bruiner to drizzle; **un parapluie** umbrella
Il pleut à seaux. It's raining buckets.
Il pleut à verse. It's raining hard.
Il a beaucoup plu hier et cela m'a beaucoup plu. It rained a lot yesterday and that pleased me a great deal. (See **plaire**)

Do not confuse the past part. of this verb with the past part. of **plaire**, which is identical.

The Seven Simple Tenses

Singular	Plural
1 présent de l'indicatif	
pue	**puons**
pues	**puez**
pue	**puent**
2 imparfait de l'indicatif	
puais	**puions**
puais	**puiez**
puait	**puaient**
4 futur	
puerai	**puerons**
pueras	**puerez**
puera	**pueront**
5 conditionnel	
puerais	**puerions**
puerais	**pueriez**
puerait	**pueraient**

Words and expressions related to this verb
puant, puante stinking; conceited
la puanteur stink, foul smell
Robert est un type puant. Robert is a stinker.
Cet ivrogne pue l'alcool; je me bouche le nez. This drunkard stinks of alcohol; I'm plugging my nose.
Joseph, ta chambre pue la porcherie. Joseph, your room smells like a pigsty.

This verb is used mainly in the above tenses.

If you have the need to use this verb in all the 14 tenses and the imperative, the forms are the same as for the verb **tuer** among the 501 verbs. Just replace the letter **t** with the letter **p**.

sembler Part. pr. [not in use] Part. passé **semblé**

to seem

The Seven Simple Tenses		The Seven Compound Tenses	
Singular	Plural	Singular	Plural
1 présent de l'indicatif **il semble**		8 passé composé **il a semblé**	
2 imparfait de l'indicatif **il semblait**		9 plus-que-parfait de l'indicatif **il avait semblé**	
3 passé simple **il sembla**		10 passé antérieur **il eut semblé**	
4 futur **il semblera**		11 futur antérieur **il aura semblé**	
5 conditionnel **il semblerait**		12 conditionnel passé **il aurait semblé**	
6 présent du subjonctif **qu'il semble**		13 passé du subjonctif **qu'il ait semblé**	
7 imparfait du subjonctif **qu'il semblât**		14 plus-que-parfait du subjonctif **qu'il eût semblé**	

Impératif
[not in use]

Words and expressions related to this verb

Il me semble difficile. It seems difficult to me.
Il me semble que . . . It seems to me that . . .
Il semble bon It seems good.
Il semble inutile. It seems useless.
à ce qu'il me semble . . . to my mind . . .
C'est ce qui me semble. That's what it looks like to me.

This verb has regular forms in all the tenses (like **ressembler** among the 501 verbs in this book) but much of the time it is used impersonally in the forms given above with **il** (*it*) as the subject.

to be becoming, to suit

The Seven Simple Tenses

Singular	Plural
1 présent de l'indicatif	
il sied	**ils siéent**
2 imparfait de l'indicatif	
il seyait	**ils seyaient**
4 futur	
il siéra	**ils siéront**
5 conditionnel	
il siérait	**ils siéraient**
6 présent du subjonctif	
qu'il siée	**qu'ils siéent**

This verb is defective and it is generally used only in the above persons and tenses.
Cela vous sied. That suits you well.
Ce chapeau te sied si bien! That hat looks so good on you!
Connaissez-vous la pièce *Le Deuil sied à Electre* d'Eugene O'Neill? Do you know the play *Mourning Becomes Electra* by Eugene O'Neill?
seoir à to be becoming to

See also **s'asseoir.**

The form **séant** is used as an adj.: **Il n'est pas séant de faire cela.** It's unbecoming to do that.

to suffice, to be sufficient, to be enough

The Seven Simple Tenses		The Seven Compound Tenses	
Singular	Plural	Singular	Plural
1 présent de l'indicatif **il suffit**		8 passé composé **il a suffi**	
2 imparfait de l'indicatif **il suffisait**		9 plus-que-parfait de l'indicatif **il avait suffi**	
3 passé simple **il suffit**		10 passé antérieur **il eut suffi**	
4 futur **il suffira**		11 futur antérieur **il aura suffi**	
5 conditionnel **il suffirait**		12 conditionnel passé **il aurait suffi**	
6 présent du subjonctif **qu'il suffise**		13 passé du subjonctif **qu'il ait suffi**	
7 imparfait du subjonctif **qu'il suffît**		14 plus-que-parfait du subjonctif **qu'il eût suffi**	

Impératif
Qu'il suffise!

Words and expressions related to this verb

la suffisance sufficiency
suffisamment sufficiently
Cela suffit! That's quite enough!
Suffit! Enough! Stop it!
Ma famille suffit à mon bonheur. My family is enough for my happiness.
Ça ne te suffit pas? That's not enough for you?
Y a-t-il suffisamment à manger? Is there enough to eat?

This verb is generally impersonal and is used in the third person singular as given in the above tenses.

to thunder

The Seven Simple Tenses		The Seven Compound Tenses	
Singular	Plural	Singular	Plural
1 présent de l'indicatif **il tonne**		8 passé composé **il a tonné**	
2 imparfait de l'indicatif **il tonnait**		9 plus-que-parfait de l'indicatif **il avait tonné**	
3 passé simple **il tonna**		10 passé antérieur **il eut tonné**	
4 futur **il tonnera**		11 futur antérieur **il aura tonné**	
5 conditionnel **il tonnerait**		12 conditionnel passé **il aurait tonné**	
6 présent du subjonctif **qu'il tonne**		13 passé du subjonctif **qu'il ait tonné**	
7 imparfait du subjonctif **qu'il tonnât**		14 plus-que-parfait du subjonctif **qu'il eût tonné**	

Impératif
Qu'il tonne! Let it thunder!

Common idiomatic expressions using this verb and words related to it

le tonnerre thunder
Tonnerre! By thunder!
C'est du tonnerre! That's terrific!
un coup de tonnerre a clap of thunder
un tonnerre d'acclamations thundering applause

This verb is impersonal and is used in the third person singular.

Guide to French pronunciation

The purpose of the guide on the next page is to help you pronounce French words as correctly as possible. However, the best way to improve your pronunciation is to imitate spoken French that you hear from speakers who pronounce French accurately. To accomplish this, you may want to consult the Barron's book *Pronounce It Perfectly in French*, which comes with three CDs that give you practice, during pauses, in imitating French spoken by French speakers.

In French there are several spellings for the same sound; for example, the following spellings are all pronounced **ay**, as in the English word *say*.

et (j')**ai** (parl)**é** (av)**ez** (all)**er** (l)**es**

Consonant sounds are approximately the same in French and English. When speaking French, you must raise your voice slightly on the last sound when there is more than one in a group; for example, in pronouncing **s'il vous plaît** (please), raise your voice slightly on *plaît*.

There are only four nasal vowel sounds in French. They are expressed in the following catchy phrase, which means "a good white wine."

un bon vin blanc

How do you nasalize a vowel in French? Instead of letting breath (air) out your mouth, you must push it up your nose so that it does not come out your mouth.

Now, become familiar with the guide to French pronunciation. Practice pronouncing each sound first and then try it out by reading aloud some of the words and expressions on the pages that follow.

Approximate pronunciation

IPA Phonetic Symbol	English Word	French Word
[a]	something like the vowel sound in T**o**m	l**a**
[ɑ]	**ah**!	p**a**s
[e]	s**ay**	a**i**
[ə]	th**e**	l**e**
[i]	s**ee**	**ici**
[ɛ]	**e**gg	m**è**re
[y]	(not an English sound, but close to the sound of f**ew** without pronouncing the **y** sound that comes before the **u** sound or the **w** that comes after it)	l**u**
[ɥ]	(not an English sound, but close to "**you + ee**" without the *y* sound)	h**ui**t
[ɲ]	ca**ny**on	monta**gne**
[o]	als**o**	h**ô**tel
[ɔ]	d**o**ne	d**o**nne
[u]	t**oo**	**ou**
[ʃ]	**sh**ip	**ch**ose
[s]	ki**ss**	ce**sse**
[ø]	(not an English sound, but close to p**u**dding)	p**eux**
[œ]	(not an English sound, but close to p**ur**r)	h**eure**
[j]	**y**es	jo**y**eux
[z]	**z**ero	**z**éro
[ʒ]	mea**s**ure	**j**e

Nasal Vowels

[œ̃]	(not an English sound, but close to s**un**g)	**un**
[ɔ̃]	(not an English sound, but close to s**on**g)	b**on**
[ɛ̃]	(not an English sound, but close to s**an**g)	v**in**
[ɑ̃]	(not an English sound, but close to thr**on**g)	bl**anc**

Verbs used in weather expressions

Quel temps fait-il? / What's the weather like?

(a) With **Il fait . . .**
Il fait beau / The weather is fine; The weather is beautiful.
Il fait beau temps / The weather is beautiful.
Il fait bon / It's nice; It's good.
Il fait brumeux / It's misty.
Il fait chaud / It's warm.
Il fait clair / It is clear.
Il fait de l'orage / It's storming; there is a thunderstorm.
Il fait des éclairs / There's lightning.
Il fait doux / It's mild.
Il fait du soleil / It's sunny.
Il fait du tonnerre / It's thundering. (You can also say: **Il tonne.**)
Il fait du vent / It's windy.
Il fait frais / It is cool.
Il fait froid / It's cold.
Il fait glissant / It is slippery.
Il fait humide / It's humid.
Il fait jour / It is daylight.
Il fait lourd / The weather is sultry.
Il fait mauvais / The weather is bad.
Il fait nuit / It is dark.
Il fait sec / It's dry.
Il fait une chaleur épouvantable / It's awfully (frightfully) hot.

(b) With **Il fait un temps . . .**
Il fait un temps affreux / The weather is frightful.
Il fait un temps calme / The weather is calm.
Il fait un temps couvert / The weather is cloudy.
Il fait un temps de saison / The weather is seasonal.
Il fait un temps épouvantable / The weather is frightful.
Il fait un temps lourd / It's muggy.
Il fait un temps magnifique / The weather is magnificent.
Il fait un temps pourri / The weather is rotten.
Il fait un temps serein / The weather is serene.
Il fait un temps superbe / The weather is superb.

(c) With **Le temps + verb . . .**
Le temps menace / The weather is threatening.
Le temps s'éclaircit / The weather is clearing up.
Le temps se couvre / The sky is overcast.
Le temps se gâte / The weather is getting bad.
Le temps se met au beau / The weather is getting beautiful.
Le temps se met au froid / It's getting cold.
Le temps se radoucit / The weather is getting nice again.

Le temps se rafraîchit / The weather is getting cold.
Le temps se remet / The weather is clearing up.

(d) With **Le ciel est . . .**
Le ciel est bleu / The sky is blue.
Le ciel est calme / The sky is calm.
Le ciel est couvert / The sky is cloudy.
Le ciel est gris / The sky is gray.
Le ciel est serein / The sky is serene.

(e) With other verbs
Il gèle / It's freezing.
Il grêle / It's hailing.
Il neige / It's snowing.
Il pleut / It's raining.
Il pleut à verse / It's raining hard.
Il tombe de la grêle / It's hailing.
Il va grêler / It's going to hail.
Il tonne / It's thundering.
Je sors par tous les temps / I go out in all kinds of weather.
Quelle est la prévision scientifique du temps? Quelle est la météo? / What is the weather forecast?

Verbs with prepositions

French verbs are used with certain prepositions or no preposition at all. At times, the preposition used with a particular verb changes the meaning entirely, *e.g.*, **se passer** means *to happen* and **se passer de** means *to do without*.

When you look up a verb among the 501 to find its verb forms (or in the section of over 2,600 verbs), also consult the following categories so that you will learn what preposition that verb requires, if any.

Consult all the categories that are given below; *e.g.*, verbs that take **à** + noun, verbs that take **à** + inf., verbs that take **de** + noun, verbs that take **de** + inf., verbs that take **à** + noun + **de** + inf., verbs that take prepositions other than **à** or **de**, verbs that require no preposition, and verbs that do not require any preposition in French whereas in English a preposition is used.

The following are used frequently in French readings and in conversation.

A. *The following verbs take* à + *noun*

assister à qqch (à une assemblée, à une réunion, à un spectacle, *etc.*) to attend a gathering, a meeting, a theatrical presentation, *etc.*, or to be present at: **Allez-vous assister à la conférence du professeur Godard?** Are you going to attend (to be present at) Prof. Godard's lecture? **Oui, je vais y assister.** Yes, I am going to attend it.

convenir à qqn ou à qqch to please (to be pleasing to), to suit (to be suitable to): **Cette robe ne convient pas à la circonstance.** This dress does not suit the occasion. **Cela ne convient pas à mon père.** That is not suitable to my father.

demander à qqn to ask someone: **Demandez à la dame où s'arrête l'autobus.** Ask the lady where the bus stops.

déplaire à qqn to displease someone, to be displeasing to someone: **Cet homme-là déplaît à ma soeur.** That man is displeasing to my sister. **Cet homme-là lui déplaît.** That man is displeasing to her.

désobéir à qqn to disobey someone: **Ce chien ne désobéit jamais à son maître.** This dog never disobeys his master. **Il ne lui désobéit jamais.** He never disobeys him.

être à qqn to belong to someone: **Ce livre est à Victor.** This book belongs to Victor. [Note this special possessive meaning when you use **être** + **à**.]

faire attention à qqn ou à qqch to pay attention to someone or to something: **Faites attention au professeur.** Pay attention to the professor. **Faites attention aux marches.** Pay attention to the steps.

se fier à qqn to trust someone: **Je me fie à mes parents.** I trust my parents. **Je me fie à eux.** I trust them.

goûter à qqch to taste a little, to sample a little something: **Goûtez à ce gâteau; il est délicieux et vous m'en direz des nouvelles.** Taste a little of this cake; it is delicious and you will rave about it. **Goûtez-y!** Taste it!

s'habituer à qqn ou à qqch to get used to someone or something: **Je m'habitue à mon nouveau professeur.** I am getting used to my new teacher. **Je m'habitue à lui.** I am getting used to him. **Je m'habitue à ce travail.** I am getting used to this work. **Je m'y habitue.** I am getting used to it.

s'intéresser à qqn ou à qqch to be interested in someone or something: **Je m'intéresse aux sports.** I am interested in sports.

jouer à to play (a game or sport): **Il aime bien jouer à la balle.** He likes to play ball. **Elle aime bien jouer au tennis.** She likes to play tennis.

manquer à qqn to miss someone (because of an absence): **Vous me manquez.** I miss you. **Ses enfants lui manquent.** He (or She) misses his (or her) children.

se mêler à qqch to mingle with, to mix with, to join in: **Il se mêle à tous les groupes à l'école.** He mixes with all the groups at school.

nuire à qqn ou à qqch to harm someone or something: **Ce que vous faites peut nuire à la réputation de votre famille.** What you are doing may harm the reputation of your family.

obéir à qqn to obey someone: **Une personne honorable obéit à ses parents.** An honorable person obeys his (her) parents.

s'opposer à qqn ou à qqch to oppose someone or something: **Je m'oppose aux idées du président.** I am opposed to the president's ideas.

penser à qqn ou à qqch to think of (about) someone or something: **Je pense à mes amis.** I am thinking of my friends. **Je pense à eux.** I am thinking of them. **Je pense à mon travail.** I am thinking about my work. **J'y pense.** I am thinking about it. BUT: **Que pensez-vous de cela?** What do you think of that?

plaire à qqn to please, to be pleasing to someone: **Mon mariage plaît à ma famille.** My marriage pleases my family. **Mon mariage leur plaît.** My marriage pleases them (is pleasing to them).

réfléchir à qqch to think over something: **Il faut que j'y réfléchisse.** I must think it over.

répondre à qqn ou à qqch to answer someone or something: **J'ai répondu au professeur.** I answered the teacher. **Je lui ai répondu.** I answered him. **J'ai répondu à la lettre.** I answered the letter. **J'y ai répondu.** I answered it.

résister à qqn ou à qqch to resist someone or something: **Le criminel a résisté à l'agent de police.** The criminal resisted the police officer.

ressembler à qqn to resemble someone: **Il ressemble beaucoup à sa mère.** He resembles his mother a lot.

réussir à qqch to succeed in something. **réussir à un examen** to pass an examination: **Il a réussi à l'examen.** He passed the exam.

serrer la main à qqn to shake hands with someone: **Bobby, va serrer la main à la dame.** Bobby, go shake hands with the lady.

songer à qqn ou à qqch to dream (to think) of someone or something: **Je songe aux grandes vacances.** I'm dreaming of the summer vacation.

survivre à qqn ou à qqch to survive someone or something: **Il a survécu à l'ouragan.** He survived the hurricane.

téléphoner à qqn to telephone someone: **Marie a téléphoné à Paul.** Marie telephoned Paul. **Elle lui a téléphoné.** She telephoned him.

B. *The following verbs take* à + *inf.*

aider à to help: **Roger aide son petit frère à faire sa leçon de mathématiques.** Roger is helping his little brother do the math lesson.

aimer à to like: **J'aime à lire.** I like to read. [Note that **aimer à + inf.** is used primarily in literary style; ordinarily, use **aimer + inf.**]

s'amuser à to amuse oneself, to enjoy, to have fun: **Il y a des élèves qui s'amusent à mettre le professeur en colère.** There are pupils who have fun making the teacher angry.

apprendre à to learn: **J'apprends à lire.** I am learning to read.

s'apprêter à to get ready: **Je m'apprête à aller au bal.** I am getting ready to go to the dance.

arriver à to succeed in: **Jacques arrive à comprendre le subjonctif.** Jack is succeeding in learning the subjunctive.

s'attendre à to expect: **Je m'attendais à trouver une salle de classe vide.** I was expecting to find an empty classroom.

autoriser à to authorize, to allow: **Je vous autorise à quitter cette salle de classe tout de suite.** I authorize you to leave this classroom immediately.

avoir à to have, to be obliged (to do something): **J'ai à faire mes devoirs ce soir.** I have to do my homework tonight.

commencer à to begin: **Il commence à pleuvoir.** It is beginning to rain. [Note that **commencer de + inf.** is also correct.]

consentir à to consent: **Je consens à venir chez vous après le dîner.** I consent (agree) to come to your house after dinner.

continuer à to continue: **Je continue à étudier le français.** I am continuing to study French. [Note that **continuer de + inf.** is also correct.]

décider qqn à to persuade someone: **J'ai décidé mon père à me prêter quelques euros.** I persuaded my father to lend me a few euros.

se décider à to make up one's mind: **Il s'est décidé à l'épouser.** He made up his mind to marry her.

demander à to ask, to request: **Elle demande à parler.** She asks to speak. [Note that here the subjects are the same—she is the one who is asking to speak. If the subjects are different, use **demander de**: **Je vous demande de parler.** I am asking you to talk.]

encourager à to encourage: **Je l'ai encouragé à suivre un cours de français.** I encouraged him to take a course in French.

s'engager à to get oneself around (to doing something): **Je ne peux pas m'engager à accepter ses idées frivoles.** I can't get myself around to accepting his (her) frivolous ideas.

enseigner à to teach: **Je vous enseigne à lire en français.** I am teaching you to read in French.

s'habituer à to get used (to): **Je m'habitue à parler français couramment.** I am getting used to speaking French fluently.

hésiter à to hesitate: **J'hésite à répondre à sa lettre.** I hesitate to reply to her (his) letter.

inviter à to invite: **Monsieur et Madame Boivin ont invité les Béry à dîner chez eux.** Mr. and Mrs. Boivin invited the Bérys to have dinner at their house.

se mettre à to begin: **L'enfant se met à rire.** The child is beginning to laugh.

parvenir à to succeed: **Elle est parvenue à devenir docteur.** She succeeded in becoming a doctor.

persister à to persist: **Je persiste à croire que cet homme est innocent.** I persist in believing that this man is innocent.

se plaire à to take pleasure in: **Il se plaît à taquiner ses amis.** He takes pleasure in teasing his friends.

recommencer à to begin again: **Il recommence à pleuvoir.** It is beginning to rain again.

résister à to resist: **Je résiste à croire qu'il est malhonnête.** I resist believing that he is dishonest.

réussir à to succeed in: **Henri a réussi à me convaincre.** Henry succeeded in convincing me.

songer à to dream, to think: **Elle songe à trouver un millionnaire.** She is dreaming of finding a millionaire.

tarder à to delay: **Mes amis tardent à venir.** My friends are late in coming.

tenir à to insist, to be anxious: **Je tiens absolument à voir mon enfant cet instant.** I am very anxious to see my child this instant.

venir à to happen (to): **Si je viens à voir mes amis en ville, je vous le dirai.** If I happen to see my friends downtown, I will tell you (so).

C. *The following verbs take* de + *noun*

s'agir de to be a question of, to be a matter of: **Il s'agit de l'amour.** It is a matter of love.

s'approcher de to approach: **La dame s'approche de la porte et elle l'ouvre.** The lady approaches the door and opens it.

changer de to change: **Je dois changer de train à Paris.** I have to change trains in Paris.

dépendre de to depend on: **Je veux sortir avec toi mais cela dépend des circonstances.** I want to go out with you but that depends on the circumstances.

douter de to doubt: **Je doute de la véracité de ce que vous dites.** I doubt the veracity of what you are saying.

se douter de to suspect: **Je me doute de ses actions.** I suspect his (her) actions.

féliciter de to congratulate on: **Je vous félicite de vos progrès.** I congratulate you on your progress.

jouer de to play (a musical instrument): **Je sais jouer du piano.** I know how to play the piano.

jouir de to enjoy: **Mon père jouit d'une bonne santé.** My father enjoys good health.

manquer de to lack: **Cette personne manque de politesse.** This person lacks courtesy. **Mon frère manque de bon sens.** My brother lacks common sense.

se méfier de to distrust, to mistrust, to beware of: **Je me méfie des personnes que je ne connais pas.** I distrust persons whom I do not know.

se moquer de to make fun of: **Les enfants aiment se moquer d'un singe.** Children like to make fun of a monkey.

s'occuper de to be busy with: **Madame Boulanger s'occupe de son mari infirme.** Mrs. Boulanger is busy with her disabled husband. **Je m'occupe de mes affaires.** I mind my own business. **Occupez-vous de vos affaires!** Mind your own business!

partir de to leave: **Il est parti de la maison à 8 h.** He left the house at 8 o'clock.

se passer de to do without: **Je me passe de sel.** I do without salt.

se plaindre de to complain about: **Il se plaint toujours de son travail.** He always complains about his work.

remercier de to thank: **Je vous remercie de votre bonté.** I thank you for your kindness. [Use **remercier de + an abstract noun** or **+ inf.**; Use **remercier pour + a concrete object**; *e.g.*, **Je vous remercie pour le cadeau.** I thank you for the present.]

se rendre compte de to realize: **Je me rends compte de la condition de cette personne.** I realize the condition of this person.

rire de to laugh at; **Tout le monde rit de cette personne.** Everybody laughs at this person.

se servir de to employ, to use, to make use of: **Je me sers d'un stylo quand j'écris une lettre.** I use a pen when I write a letter.

se soucier de to care about, to be concerned about: **Marc se soucie de ses amis.** Marc cares about his friends.

se souvenir de to remember: **Oui, je me souviens de Gervaise.** Yes, I remember Gervaise. **Je me souviens de lui.** I remember him. **Je me souviens d'elle.** I remember her. **Je me souviens de l'été passé.** I remember last summer. **Je m'en souviens.** I remember it.

tenir de to take after (to resemble): **Julie tient de sa mère.** Julie takes after her mother.

D. *The following verbs take* de + *inf.*

s'agir de to be a question of, to be a matter of: **Il s'agit de faire les devoirs tous les jours.** It is a matter of doing the homework every day.

avoir peur de to be afraid of: **Le petit garçon a peur de traverser la rue seul.** The little boy is afraid of crossing the street alone.

cesser de to stop, to cease: **Il a cessé de pleuvoir.** It has stopped raining.

commencer de to begin: **Il a commencé de pleuvoir.** It has started to rain. [Note that **commencer à + inf.** is also correct.]

continuer de to continue: **Il continue de pleuvoir.** It's still raining OR It's continuing to rain. [Note that **continuer à + inf.** is also correct.]

convenir de faire qqch to agree to do something: **Nous avons convenu de venir chez vous.** We agreed to coming to your place.

craindre de to be afraid of, to fear: **La petite fille craint de traverser la rue seule.** The little girl is afraid of crossing the street alone.

décider de to decide: **J'ai décidé de partir tout de suite.** I decided to leave immediately. **Il a décidé d'acheter la maison.** He decided to buy the house.

demander de to ask, to request: **Je vous demande de parler.** I am asking you to speak. [Note that here the subjects are different: I am asking you to speak; whereas, when the subjects are the same, use **damander à**: **Elle demande à parler.** She is asking to speak. **Je demande à parler.** I am asking to speak.]

se dépêcher de to hurry: **Je me suis dépêché de venir chez vous pour vous dire quelque chose.** I hurried to come to your place in order to tell you something.

empêcher de to keep from, to prevent: **Je vous empêche de sortir.** I prevent you from going out.

s'empresser de to hurry: **Je m'empresse de venir chez toi.** I am hurrying to come to your place.

essayer de to try: **J'essaye d'ouvrir la porte mais je ne peux pas.** I'm trying to open the door but I can't.

féliciter de to congratulate: **On m'a félicité d'avoir gagné le prix.** I was congratulated on having won the prize.

finir de to finish: **J'ai fini de travailler sur cette composition.** I have finished working on this composition.

gronder de to scold: **La maîtresse a grondé l'élève d'avoir fait beaucoup de fautes dans le devoir.** The teacher scolded the pupil for having made many errors in the homework.

se hâter de to hurry: **Je me hâte de venir chez toi.** I am hurrying to come to your house.

manquer de to neglect to, to fail to, to forget to: **Guy a manqué de compléter sa leçon de français.** Guy neglected to complete his French lesson.

offrir de to offer: **J'ai offert d'écrire une lettre pour elle.** I offered to write a letter for her.

oublier de to forget: **J'ai oublié de vous donner la monnaie.** I forgot to give you the change.

persuader de to persuade: **J'ai persuadé mon père de me prêter quelques euros.** I persuaded my father to lend me a few euros.

prendre garde de to take care not to: **Prenez garde de tomber.** Be careful not to fall.

prendre le parti de faire qqch to decide to do something: **Théodore n'a pas hésité à prendre le parti de voter pour elle.** Theodore did not hesitate to decide to vote for her.

prier de to beg: **Je vous prie d'arrêter.** I beg you to stop.

promettre de to promise: **J'ai promis de venir chez toi à 8 h.** I promised to come to your place at 8 o'clock.

refuser de to refuse: **Je refuse de le croire.** I refuse to believe it.

regretter de to regret, to be sorry: **Je regrette d'être obligé de vous dire cela.** I am sorry to be obliged to tell you that.

remercier de to thank: **Je vous remercie d'être venu si vite.** I thank you for coming (having come) so quickly. [Use **remercier de + inf.** or **+ abstract noun**. Use **remercier pour + concrete object.**]

se souvenir de to remember: **Tu vois? Je me suis souvenu de venir chez toi.** You see? I remembered to come to your house.

tâcher de to try: **Tâche de finir tes devoirs avant de sortir.** Try to finish your homework before going out.

venir de to have just (done something): **Je viens de manger.** I have just eaten *or* I just ate.

E. *The following verbs commonly take* à + *noun* + de + *inf.*

The model to follow is: **J'ai conseillé à Robert de suivre un cours de français.** I advised Robert to take a course in French.

conseiller à to advise: **J'ai conseillé à Jeanne de se marier.** I advised Joan to get married.

défendre à to forbid: **Mon père défend à mon frère de fumer.** My father forbids my brother to smoke.

demander à to ask, to request: **J'ai demandé à Marie de venir.** I asked Mary to come.

dire à to say, to tell: **J'ai dit à Charles de venir.** I told Charles to come.

interdire à to forbid: **Mon père interdit à mon frère de fumer.** My father forbids my brother to smoke.

ordonner à to order: **J'ai ordonné au chauffeur de ralentir.** I ordered the driver to slow down.

permettre à to permit: **J'ai permis à l'étudiant de partir quelques minutes avant la fin de la classe.** I permitted the student to leave a few minutes before the end of class.

promettre à to promise: **J'ai promis à mon ami d'arriver à l'heure.** I promised my friend to arrive on time.

téléphoner à to telephone: **J'ai téléphoné à Marcel de venir me voir.** I phoned Marcel to come to see me.

F. *The following verbs take prepositions other than* à *or* de

commencer par + inf. to begin by + present participle: **La présidente a commencé par discuter les problèmes de la société.** The president began by discussing the problems in society.

continuer par + inf. to continue by + pres. part.: **La maîtresse a continué la conférence par lire un poème.** The teacher continued the lecture by reading a poem.

entrer dans + noun to enter, to go in: **Elle est entrée dans le restaurant.** She went in the restaurant.

être en colère contre qqn to be angry with someone: **Monsieur Laroche est toujours en colère contre ses voisins.** Mr. Laroche is always angry with his neighbors.

finir par + inf. to end up by + pres. part.: **Clément a fini par épouser une femme plus âgée que lui.** Clement ended up marrying a woman older than he.

s'incliner devant qqn to bow to someone: **La princesse s'incline devant la reine.** The princess is bowing to the queen.

insister pour + inf. to insist on, upon: **J'insiste pour obtenir tous mes droits.** I insist on obtaining all my rights.

se marier avec qqn to marry someone: **Elle va se marier avec lui.** She is going to marry him.

se mettre en colère to become angry, upset: **Monsieur Leduc se met en colère facilement.** Mr. Leduc gets angry easily.

se mettre en route to start out, to set out: **Ils se sont mis en route dès l'aube.** They started out at dawn.

remercier pour + a concrete noun to thank for: **Je vous remercie pour le joli cadeau.** I thank you for the pretty present. [Remember to use **remercier pour + a concrete object;** use **remercier de + an abstract noun** or **+ inf.** **Je vous remercie de votre bonté.** I thank you for your kindness. **Je vous remercie d'être venue si vite.** I thank you for coming so quickly.]

G. *The following verbs require no preposition before the infinitive*

adorer + inf. to adore, to love: **Madame Morin adore mettre tous ses bijoux avant de sortir.** Mrs. Morin loves to put on all her jewelry before going out.

aimer + inf. to like: **J'aime lire.** I like to read. [You may also say: **J'aime à lire**, but **aimer + à + inf.** is used primarily in literary style.]

aimer mieux + inf. to prefer: **J'aime mieux rester ici.** I prefer to stay here.

aller + inf. to go: **Je vais faire mes devoirs maintenant.** I am going to do my homework now.

apercevoir + inf. to perceive: **J'aperçois avancer l'ouragan.** I notice the hurricane advancing. [This is a verb of perception. You may also say: **J'aperçois l'ouragan qui s'avance.**]

compter + inf. to intend: **Je compte aller en France l'été prochain.** I intend to go to France next summer.

croire + inf. to believe: **Il croit être innocent.** He believes he is innocent.

désirer + inf. to desire, to wish: **Je désire prendre une tasse de café.** I desire to have a cup of coffee.

devoir + inf. to have to, ought to: **Je dois faire mes devoirs avant de sortir.** I have to do my homework before going out.

écouter + inf. to listen to: **J'écoute chanter les enfants.** I am listening to the children singing. [This is a verb of perception. You may also say: **J'écoute les enfants qui chantent.**]

entendre + inf. to hear: **J'entends chanter les enfants.** I hear the children singing. [This is a verb of perception. You may also say: **J'entends les enfants qui chantent.**]

espérer + inf. to hope: **J'espère aller en France.** I hope to go to France.

faire + inf. to cause, to make, to have something done by someone: **Le professeur fait travailler les élèves dans la salle de classe.** The teacher has the pupils work in the classroom. (See **causative faire**, page 676.)

falloir + inf. to be necessary: **Il faut être honnête.** One must be honest.

laisser + inf. to let, to allow: **Je vous laisse partir.** I am letting you go.

oser + inf. to dare: **Ce garçon ose dire n'importe quoi.** This boy dares to say anything.

paraître + inf. to appear, to seem: **Elle paraît être capable.** She appears to be capable.

penser + inf. to think, to plan, to intend: **Je pense aller à Paris.** I intend to go to Paris.

pouvoir + inf. to be able, can: **Je peux marcher mieux maintenant après l'accident.** I can walk better now after the accident.

préférer + inf. to prefer: **Je préfère manger maintenant.** I prefer to eat now.

regarder + inf. to look at: **Je regarde voler les oiseaux.** I am looking at the birds flying. [This is a verb of perception. You may also say: **Je regarde les oiseaux qui volent.**]

savoir + inf. to know, to know how: **Je sais nager.** I know how to swim.

sentir + inf. to feel: **Je sens s'approcher l'ouragan.** I feel the hurricane approaching. [This is a verb of perception. You can also say: **Je sens l'ouragan qui s'approche.**]

sentir + inf. to smell: **Je sens venir une odeur agréable du jardin.** I smell a pleasant fragrance coming from the garden. [This is another verb of perception. You may also say: **Je sens une odeur agréable qui vient du jardin.**]

valoir mieux + inf. to be better: **Il vaut mieux être honnête.** It is better to be honest.

venir + inf. to come: **Gérard vient voir ma nouvelle voiture.** Gerard is coming to see my new car.

voir + inf. to see: **Je vois courir les enfants.** I see the children running. [This is another verb of perception. You may also say: **Je vois les enfants qui courent.**]

vouloir + inf. to want: **Je veux venir chez vous.** I want to come to your house.

H. ***The following verbs do not require a preposition, whereas in English a preposition is used***

approuver to approve of: **J'approuve votre décision.** I approve of your decision.

attendre to wait for: **J'attends l'autobus depuis vingt minutes.** I have been waiting for the bus for twenty minutes.

chercher to look for: **Je cherche mon livre.** I'm looking for my book.

demander to ask for: **Je demande une réponse.** I am asking for a reply

écouter to listen to: **J'écoute la musique.** I am listening to the music. **J'écoute le professeur.** I am listening to the teacher.

envoyer chercher to send for: **J'ai envoyé chercher le docteur.** I sent for the doctor.

essayer to try on: **Elle a essayé une jolie robe.** She tried on a pretty dress.

habiter to live in: **J'habite cette maison.** I live in this house.

ignorer to be unaware of: **J'ignore ce fait.** I am unaware of this fact.

mettre to put on: **Elle a mis la robe rouge.** She put on the red dress.

payer to pay for: **J'ai payé le dîner.** I paid for the dinner.

pleurer to cry about, to cry over: **Elle pleure la perte de son petit chien.** She is crying over the loss of her little dog.

prier to pray to: **Elle prie le ciel.** She is praying to the heavens. **Elle prie la Vierge.** She is praying to the Holy Mother.

puer to stink of: **Cet ivrogne pue l'alcool.** This drunkard stinks of alcohol.

regarder to look at: **Je regarde le ciel.** I am looking at the sky.

sentir to smell of: **Robert, ta chambre sent la porcherie.** Robert, your room smells like a pigsty (pigpen).

soigner to take care of: **Cette personne soigne les pauvres.** This person takes care of (cares for) poor people.

Index of common irregular French verb forms identified by infinitive

The purpose of this index is to help you identify those verb forms that cannot be readily identified because they are irregular in some way. For example, if you come across the verb form ***fut*** (which is very common) in your French readings, this index will tell you that *fut* is a form of **être**. Then you look up **être** in this book and you will find that verb form on the page where all the forms of **être** are given.

Verb forms whose first few letters are the same as the infinitive have not been included because they can easily be identified by referring to the alphabetical listing of the 501 verbs in this book.

After you find the verb of an irregular verb form, if it is not among the 501 verbs, consult the list of over 2,600 French verbs conjugated like model verbs.

A

a **avoir**
ai **avoir**
aie **avoir**
aient **avoir**
aies **avoir**
aille **aller**
ait **avoir**
as **avoir**
asseyais, *etc.* **asseoir**
assieds **asseoir**
assiérai, *etc.* **asseoir**
assis **asseoir**
assoie **asseoir**
assoirai, *etc.* **asseoir**
assoyais, *etc.* **asseoir**
aurai, *etc.* **avoir**
avaient **avoir**
avais **avoir**
avait **avoir**
avez **avoir**
aviez **avoir**
avions **avoir**
avons **avoir**
ayant **avoir**
ayons, *etc.* **avoir**

B

bats **battre**
bois **boire**
boivent **boire**
bu **boire**
bûmes **boire**
burent **boire**
bus, bût **boire**
busse, *etc.* **boire**
but **boire**
bûtes **boire**
buvant **boire**
buvez **boire**
buvons **boire**

C

connu **connaître**
craignis, *etc.* **craindre**
crois **croire**
croîs **croître**
croissais, *etc.* **croître**
croit **croire**
croît **croître**
croyais, *etc.* **croire**
cru **croire**
crû, crue **croître**
crûmes **croire, croître**
crurent **croire**
crûrent **croître**
crus **croire**
crûs **croître**
crûsse, *etc.* **croître**
crût **croire, croître**

D

devais, *etc.* **devoir**
dîmes **dire**
dis, disais, *etc.* **dire**
disse, *etc.* **dire**
dit, dît **dire**
dois, *etc.* **devoir**
doive, *etc.* **devoir**
dors, *etc.* **dormir**
dû, due **devoir**
dûmes **devoir**
dus, dussent **devoir**
dut, dût, dûtes **devoir**

E

es **être**
est **être**
étais, *etc.* **être**
été **être**
êtes **être**
étiez **être**
eu **avoir**
eûmes **avoir**
eurent **avoir**
eus **avoir**
eusse, *etc.* **avoir**
eut, eût **avoir**
eûtes **avoir**

F

faille **faillir, falloir** (Def. and Imp.)
fais, *etc.* **faire**
fallut, *etc.* **falloir** (Def. and Imp.)
fasse, *etc.* **faire**
faudra **faillir, falloir** (Def. and Imp.)
faudrait **faillir, falloir** (Def. and Imp.)
faut **faillir, falloir** (Def. and Imp.)
faux **faillir**
ferai, *etc.* **faire**
fîmes **faire**
firent **faire**
fis, *etc.* **faire**
font **faire**
fûmes **être**
furent **être**
fus, *etc.* **être**
fut, fût **être**
fuyais, *etc.* **fuir**

G

gis, gisons, *etc.* **gésir** (Def. and Imp.)
gît **gésir** (Def. and Imp.)

I

ira, irai, iras, *etc.* **aller**

L

lis, *etc.* **lire**
lu **lire**
lus, *etc.* **lire**

M

mens **mentir**
mets **mettre**
meure, *etc.* **mourir**
meus, *etc.* **mouvoir**
mîmes **mettre**
mirent **mettre, mirer**
mis **mettre**
misses, *etc.* **mettre**
mit **mettre**
mort **mourir**
moulons, *etc.* **moudre**
moulu **moudre**
mû, mue **mouvoir**
mussent **mouvoir**
mut **mouvoir**

N

nais, *etc.* **naître**
naquîmes, *etc.* **naître**
né **naître**
nuis, nuit, *etc.* **nuire**

O

offert **offrir**
omis **omettre**
ont **avoir**

P

paie (paye) **payer**
pars **partir**
paru, *etc.* **paraître**
peignis, *etc.* **peindre**
peins, *etc.* **peindre**
pendant **pendre**
peut, *etc.* **pouvoir**
peuvent **pouvoir**
plaigne, *etc.* **plaindre**
plu **plaire, pleuvoir** (Def. and Imp.)
plurent **plaire**
plut, plût, *etc.* **plaire, pleuvoir** (Def. and Imp.)
plûtes **plaire**
pourrai, *etc.* **pouvoir**
prenne, *etc.* **prendre**
prîmes **prendre**
prirent **prendre**
pris **prendre**
prisse, *etc.* **prendre**
pu **pouvoir**
puis **pouvoir**
puisse, *etc.* **pouvoir**
pûmes, *etc.* **pouvoir**
purent **pouvoir**
pus **pouvoir**
pusse **pouvoir**
put, pût **pouvoir**

R

reçois, *etc.* **recevoir**
reçûmes, *etc.* **recevoir**
relu **relire**
résolu, *etc.* **résoudre**
reviens, *etc.* **revenir**
revins, *etc.* **revenir**
ri, rie, riant, *etc.* **rire**
riiez **rire**
ris, *etc.* **rire**

S

sache, *etc.* **savoir**
sais, *etc.* **savoir**
saurai, *etc.* **savoir**
séant **seoir** (Def. and Imp.)
sens, *etc.* **sentir**
serai, *etc.* **être**
sers, *etc.* **servir**
seyant **seoir** (Def. and Imp.)
sied **seoir** (Def. and Imp.)
siéent **seoir** (Def. and Imp.)
siéra, *etc.* **seoir** (Def. and Imp.)
sois, *etc.* **être**
sommes **être**
sont **être**
sors, *etc.* **sortir**
soyez **être**
soyons **être**
su **savoir**
suis **être, suivre**
suit **suivre**
sûmes **savoir**
surent **savoir**
survécu **survivre**
sus, susse, *etc.* **savoir**
sut, sût **savoir**

T

tais, *etc.* **se taire**
teigne, *etc.* **teindre**
tiendrai, *etc.* **tenir**
tienne, *etc.* **tenir**
tînmes **tenir**
tins, *etc.* **tenir**
trayant **traire**
tu **se taire**
tûmes **se taire**
turent **se taire**
tus **se taire**
tusse, *etc.* **se taire**
tut, tût **se taire**

V

va **aller**
vaille **valoir**
vainque, *etc.* **vaincre**
vais **aller**
vas **aller**
vaudrai, *etc.* **valoir**
vaux, *etc.* **valoir**
vécu, *etc.* **vivre**
vécûmes, *etc.* **vivre**
verrai, *etc.* **voir**
veuille, *etc.* **vouloir**
veulent **vouloir**
veut, *etc.* **vouloir**
viendrai, *etc.* **venir**
vienne, *etc.* **venir**
viens, *etc.* **venir**
vîmes **voir**
vînmes **venir**
vinrent **venir**
vins, *etc.* **venir**
virent **voir**
vis **vivre, voir**
visse, *etc.* **voir**
vit **vivre, voir**
vît **voir**
vîtes **voir**
voie, *etc.* **voir**
vont **aller**
voudrai, *etc.* **vouloir**
voulu, *etc.* **vouloir**
voyais, *etc.* **voir**
vu **voir**

English-French verb index

The purpose of this index is to give you instantly the French verb for the English verb you have in mind to use. We have listed the most common definition to save you time if you do not have at your fingertips a standard English-French dictionary.

If the French verb you want is reflexive (*e.g.*, **s'appeler** or **se lever**), you will find it listed alphabetically under the first letter of the verb and not under the reflexive pronoun *s'* or *se*.

When you find the French verb you need, look up the form of the model verb that has a similar conjugation (*e.g.,* bark is **aboyer**, which is conjugated like verb 187, which is **envoyer**). If there is no verb number listed (*e.g.,* **amuser**) that means that the French verb is one of the 501 model verbs.

Note: The mark * in front of the letter *h* in a French verb denotes that it is aspirate; make no liaison and use *je* instead of *j'*; *me* instead of *m'*.

A

abandon **abandonner** (171)
abandon, quit **délaisser** (274)
abdicate **abdiquer** (219)
abhor **exécrer** (203)
abhor **abhorrer** (27)
abjure **abjurer** (148)
able, to be **pouvoir**
abolish **abolir**
abominate **abominer** (465)
abort **avorter** (27)
abound **affluer** (114)
abound **foisonner** (171)
abound **surabonder** (27)
abound in **abonder en** (26)
abound in **regorger de** (283)
abrade **abraser** (27)
abridge **abréger** (52)
absent oneself from **s'absenter de** (26)
absolve **absoudre**
absorb **absorber** (385)
absorb **résorber** (240)
abstain **s'abstenir**
abstract **abstraire** (474) (no passé simple or imp. subj.)
abuse **injurier** (389)
abuse **abuser de qqch** (32)
abuse **maltraiter** (475)
accelerate **accélérer** (356)
accentuate, stress **accentuer** (483)
accept **agréer** (128)
accept **accepter**
accessorize **accessoiriser** (486)
acclaim **acclamer**
acclimate **acclimater** (27)
accommodate **accommoder** (147)
accompany **accompagner**
accomplish **accomplir** (392)
accord **accorder**
accost **accoster** (160)
accost **aborder** (26)
accredit **accréditer** (251)
acculturate **acculturer** (27)
accumulate **accumuler** (81)
accuse **accuser**
accuse oneself **s'accuser** (16, 33)
accustom **habituer** (483)
accustom oneself **s'habituer** (33, 483)
achieve **achever**
acquire **aquérir**
acquit **acquitter (de)** (374)
act **agir**
activate **actionner** (171)
activist/militant, to be an **militer** (251)
adapt to **adapter à** (8)
add **ajouter**
add a sound track **sonoriser** (486)
add more **rajouter** (28)
add up **additionner** (171)
address **adresser**
address someone **s'adresser à qqn** (33, 79)
adhere to **adhérer à** (87)
adjust **ajuster** (28)
administer **administrer** (26)
admire **admirer**
admit **avouer** (269)
admit **admettre**
admonish **admonester** (27)
adopt **adopter** (8)
adore **adorer**
adorn **parer** (435)
adulate **aduler** (81)
advance **avancer**
advance (oneself) **s'avancer** (33, 61)
advise **conseiller**
advise against **déconseiller** (109)
advocate **préconiser** (486)

advocate **prôner** (27)
aerate **aérer** (87)
affiliate to **s'affilier à** (33, 41)
affirm **affirmer** (227)
afflict with **affliger de** (119)
age **vieillir**
agglutinate **agglutiner** (329)
aggravate **exacerber** (27)
aggravate **aggraver** (276)
agree **consentir**
agree **acquiescer** (342)
agree with **concorder avec** (11)
aid **aider**
aim at **viser à** (486)
aim, point **braquer** (284)
air **aérer** (87)
air condition **climatiser** (486)
alarm **alarmer** (310)
alarm **effarer** (22)
alienate **aliéner** (87)
align **aligner** (26)
allocate **allouer** (281)
allow **laisser**
allow **permettre**
ally **allier** (41)
almost (do something) **faillir**
alter **altérer** (87)
alternate **alterner** (27)
amass **amasser** (92)
amass **amonceler** (38)
amaze **épater** (241)
ambush **s'embusquer** (33, 284)
amend **amender** (27)
Americanize **américaniser** (32)
amplify with/by **amplifier de** (322)
amputate **amputer** (251)
amuse **amuser**
amuse **divertir** (210)
amuse **récréer** (128)
amuse oneself **s'amuser**
analyze **analyser** (32)
anchor **ancrer** (27)
anger **courroucer** (342)
anger someone **fâcher qqn** (82) (See 216; aux. **avoir**)
anglicize **angliciser** (23)
angry, to become **se fâcher**
anguish, to cause **angoisser** (27)
animate **animer** (27)
annex **annexer** (27)
annihilate **anéantir** (229)
annihilate **annihiler** (27)
announce **annoncer**
annoy **agacer**
annoy **enquiquiner** (329)
annoy **contrarier** (41)
annoy **embêter** (47)
annoy **vexer** (27)
annoyed, to become **s'énerver** (33, 276)
annul **annuler** (81)
anoint **oindre** (268)
answer **répondre**
antedate **antidater** (28)
anticipate **anticiper** (329)
ape **singer** (283)
apologize **s'excuser**
appall **consterner** (27)
appear **apparaître**
appear **paraître**
appear before court **comparaître** (324)
applaud for **applaudir de** (229)
apply **appliquer** (219)
apply for (a position) **postuler** (81)
apply makeup to one's own face **se farder** (83, 240)
apply makeup to someone's face **farder** (240)
appoint **mandater** (241)
appoint to **préposer à** (350)
appreciate **apprécier**
apprehend (legal term) **appréhender** (27)
approach **approcher**
approach **s'approcher** (33, 43)
appropriate **s'approprier** (83, 212)
approve **homologuer** (307)
approve (of) **approuver**
arabize **arabiser** (486)
arbitrate **arbitrer** (27)
arch **cambrer** (27)
arch **arquer** (284)
arch **cintrer** (27)
archive **archiver** (27)
argue **bagarrer** (435)
arise **survenir** (491)
arise **procéder de** (87)
arm **armer** (238)
arrange **disposer** (350)
arrange **arranger**
arrange **agencer** (342)
arrange **ordonner** (171)
arrest **arrêter**
arrive **arriver**
arrive ahead of **devancer** (61)
articulate **articuler** (81)
ascend **monter**
ask (for) **demander**
ask again **redemander** (147)
ask for **réclamer** (71)
asphyxiate **asphyxier** (41)
aspire to **ambitionner de** (171)
assail **assaillir**
assassinate **assassiner** (159)
assemble **assembler** (407)
assemble **rassembler** (407)
assign **assigner** (441)
assimilate **assimiler** (27)
assist **seconder** (240)
associate (something with) **associer (qqch à)** (41)
associate (with) **adjoindre à** (268)
assume **assumer** (27)
assure **assurer**
astonish **étonner**
astound **ahurir** (229)
atomize **atomiser** (486)
atone **se racheter** (17, 122)
attach again **rattacher** (82)
attack **agresser** (23)
attack **attaquer** (219)
attack **assaillir**
attain **atteindre**
attain **accéder à** (87)
attend **assister (à)**
attract **attirer**
attribute to **attribuer à** (114)
authorize **autoriser** (16)

authorize **habiliter** (251)
automate **automatiser** (486)
avenge **venger**
avoid **esquiver** (276)
avoid **éviter**
awaken **éveiller** (109)
award **adjuger** (283)
award **décerner** (470)

B

back, to give **rendre**
backdate **antidater** (28)
badger, pester someone **tanner qqn** (171)
balance **équilibrer** (158)
balance **pondérer** (203)
balance **balancer**
ban **proscrire** (177)
bandage **panser** (134)
bandage **bander** (27)
bang **claquer** (284)
banish from **bannir de** (229)
banter **marivauder** (27)
banter, to exchange **badiner** (167)
baptize **baptiser** (32)
bar **barrer** (21)
bark **aboyer** (187)
base upon **baser sur** (32)
bathe **baigner** (10)
battle **batailler** (477)
bawl, cry **brailler** (477)
be **être**
be green **verdoyer** (187)
bead **perler** (326)
beat **battre**
beat up **rouer (de coups)** (269)
beat with a stick **bâtonner** (171)
beautify **embellir** (229)
become **devenir**
become again **redevenir** (164)
becoming, to be **seoir** (Def. and Imp.)
bed, to go back to **se recoucher** (122)
bed, to go to **se coucher**
bed, to put to **coucher**
beg **mendier** (212)
beg **prier**
beg **supplier**
begin **débuter** (173)
begin **commencer**
begin **se mettre**
begin **entamer** (71)
begin again **recommencer** (99)
behave **se comporter** (80, 349)
belch **éructer** (28)
believe **croire**
belong **appartenir**
bend **courber** (481)
bend **recourber** (240)
bend **plier**
bend **fléchir** (383)
bend **ployer** (187)
bequeath **léguer** (87, 307)
beseech **conjurer** (54)
besiege **assiéger**
bet **miser** (486)
bet **gager** (305)
bet on **parier sur** (129)
betray **trahir**
beware **se méfier**
bewitch **ensorceler** (38)
bid, to increase **renchérir** (94)
bifurcate **bifurquer** (284)
bill **facturer** (54)
billet **cantonner** (171)
bite **mordre**
bivouac **bivouaquer** (219)
black, to stain **mâchurer** (54)
blacken **noircir** (229)
blame **blâmer**
blame **reprocher qqch à qqn** (43)
blaspheme **blasphémer** (356)
blaze **flamboyer** (187)
bleach **javelliser** (486)
bleach hair **blondir** (210)
bleed **saigner** (441)
blend **malaxer** (27)
bless **bénir**
blind **aveugler** (27)
blindfold **bander** (27)
blink **cligner** (10)
blink **clignoter** (27)
bloat **boursoufler** (445)
block **enrayer** (330)
block up **bloquer** (219)
block up **boucher** (469)
blog **bloguer** (307)
blond, to become **blondir** (210)
bloody **ensanglanter** (90)
bloom **s'épanouir** (214)
blow **souffler**
blow away (slang) **flinguer** (307)
blow one's nose **se moucher** (122)
blow up **péter** (87)
bluff **bluffer** (26)
blur **estomper** (247)
blur **brouiller** (233)
blush **rougir**
boast **se targuer de** (122, 307)
boil **bouillir**
bold, to make **enhardir** (210)
bombard **bombarder** (385)
bone (remove bones) **désosser** (79)
boo ***huer** (483)
boot (computer) **démarrer** (27)
boot (computer) **amorcer** (342)
border **border** (248)
bore **barber** (27)
bore **ennuyer**
bored, to be **s'ennuyer** (55, 192)
bored, to be **s'ennuyer**
born, to be **naître**
borrow **emprunter**
borrow again **remprunter** (188)
botch **torchonner** (171)
botch up **bâcler** (445)
bother **contrarier** (41)
bother **embêter** (47)
bother **gêner**

bother **emmerder** (240)
bother **incommoder** (96)
bother **tracasser** (84)
bow down before **s'incliner devant** (33, 329)
box **boxer** (26)
boycott **boycotter** (373)
brag **se vanter** (90, 122)
braid **tresser** (73)
braid **natter** (246)
brake **freiner** (329)
brandish **brandir** (210)
bread **paner** (27)
break **casser**
break **rompre**
break **briser** (32)
break (body part) **se casser**
break (wave) **déferler** (326)
break in (mechanical) **roder** (96)
break one's pledge **se parjurer** (122, 272)
break through **poindre** (268)
breakfast, to have **déjeuner**
breast-feed **allaiter** (27)
breathe **respirer** (466)
brew **brasser** (79)
bridle **brider** (329)
brighten with sunlight **ensoleiller** (109)
bring **amener**
bring **apporter**
bring back **ramener** (31)
bring back **rapporter** (40)
bring back **remmener** (290)
bring closer to **rapprocher de** (43)
bring up to date **actualiser** (16)
bristle **se *hérisser** (122, 486)
broadcast **retransmettre** (294)
broadcast **diffuser** (32)
broadcast **radiodiffuser** (32)
bronze **bronzer** (134)
brown **brunir** (229)
brown **rissoler** (498)
browse books **bouquiner** (329)
bruise **contusionner** (171)
bruise **meurtrir** (249)
brush **brosser**
brush **effleurer** (466)
brush against **frôler** (498)
brush oneself **se brosser**
brutalize, bully **brutaliser** (486)
bubble **bouillonner** (171)
bubble **pétiller** (477)
buckle **boucler** (469)
bud **bourgeonner** (171)
build **bâtir**
build **construire**
build **édifier** (41)
build (with masonry) **maçonner** (171)
bully **brimer** (27)
bump into someone **croiser** (86)
bump off **zigouiller** (233)
burglarize **cambrioler** (26)
burn **flamber** (240)
burn **brûler**
burn up **consumer** (32)
burn up **carboniser** (486)
burp **éructer** (28)
burp **roter** (96)
burst forth **fuser** (32)
burst into **éclater en** (176)
burst with **crever de** (278)
bury **enfouir** (270)
bury **ensevelir** (229)
bury **inhumer** (238)
bury **enterrer**
busy, to be **s'occuper**
butter **beurrer** (26)
button **boutonner** (171)
buy **acheter**
buy back **racheter** (17)
buzz **bourdonner** (171)
by, to get **se débrouiller**
bypass **contourner** (470)

C

cackle **caqueter** (267)
cajole **enjôler** (498)
cajole **cajoler** (27)
calcify **calcifier** (41)
calculate **calculer** (81)
calibrate **calibrer** (27)
call **appeler**
call again **rappeler**
call onself **s'appeler**
calm **calmer** (27)
calm down **se calmer** (27)
calm down, pacify **apaiser** (27)
camouflage **camoufler** (445)
camp **camper** (235)
can **pouvoir**
cancel **annuler** (81)
cancel an order **décommander** (98)
canonize **canoniser** (486)
capitalize **capitaliser** (486)
capitulate **capituler** (81)
capsize **chavirer** (27)
captivate **captiver** (167)
capture **capturer** (27)
capture **accaparer** (27)
carbonate **gazéifier** (212)
care about **se soucier de** (41 (aux. être))
caress **caresser** (353)
caricature **caricaturer** (21)
carry **porter**
carry away **emporter** (349)
carry away **entraîner** (27)
carry forward **reporter** (349)
carry out **réaliser** (486)
cart (something) around **trimbaler** (326)
cash **encaisser** (274)
castrate **castrer** (27)
catalog **cataloguer** (307)
catch (a ball) **réceptionner** (443)
catch a cold **s'enrhumer** (33, 238)
catch a glimpse **entrevoir** (497)
catch on **piger** (218)
catch up **rattraper** (59)
catechize **catéchiser** (486)
cause **occasionner** (171)
cause **causer**
cease **cesser**
celebrate **célébrer** (356)
celebrate **fêter** (363)
celebrate at a carnival (Qué.) **carnavaler** (27)

celebrate on Christmas Eve or New Year's Eve **réveillonner** (171)
cement **cimenter** (464)
censor **caviarder** (27)
censure **censurer** (54)
centralize **centraliser** (486)
certify **certifier** (212)
chain **chaîner** (167)
chains, to put in **enchaîner** (167)
challenge **défier** (212)
change **changer**
change channels **zapper** (235)
change one's mind **se raviser** (122, 486)
channel **canaliser** (26)
chant **psalmodier** (212)
chap **gercer** (342)
chaperon **chaperonner** (171)
char **calciner** (329)
characterize **caractériser** (486)
charge someone to do **enjoindre à qqn de faire** (268)
charm **charmer** (238)
charter (boat, plane) **affréter** (87)
charter (boat, plane) **noliser** (486)
chat **bavarder**
chat **causer**
chat (Internet) **clavarder** (69)
chatter **jacasser** (84)
chatter **jaser** (84)
cheat **escroquer** (219)
cheat **tricher**
cheat **arnaquer** (284)
check off **cocher** (121)
checkmate **mater** (241)
cherish **chérir**
chew **mâcher** (82)
chew **mâchonner** (171)
chew **mastiquer** (219)
chirp **gazouiller** (233)
chisel **ciseler** (297)
chloroform **chloroformer** (227)
chop up ***hacher** (285)
circulate **circuler** (81)
circumscribe **circonscrire** (177)
circumvent **circonvenir** (491)
civilize **civiliser** (486)
claim **revendiquer** (256)
claim falsely **s'arroger** (33, 305)
clarify **clarifier** (212)
classify **classer** (84)
classify **classifier** (212)
clean **nettoyer**
clean **décrasser** (79)
clean **ravaler** (326)
clean (ears, nails, teeth) by scraping) **curer** (32)
clean mud off **décrotter** (163)
clear **frayer** (330)
clear (land) **défricher** (285)
clear (out) **dégager**
clear away (the table) **desservir (la table)** (437)
clear off **débarrasser** (183)
clear off (snow, dirt) **déblayer** (330)
clear up **éclaircir** (229)
clear, cross **franchir** (383)
click **cliquer** (219)
click (one's tongue) **clapper (de la langue)** (235)
climb **gravir** (95)
climb **grimper**
clone **cloner** (461)
close **fermer**
close to, to be **voisiner** (159)
close to, to be **avoisiner** (159)
clothe **vêtir**
club **matraquer** (219)
cluck **glousser** (353)
clutch, disengage the **débrayer** (330)
clutch, to engage the **embrayer** (330)
coat, to top with a **napper de** (59)
coax **amadouer** (269)
code **coder** (26)
codify **codifier** (41)
coexist **coexister** (259)
cogitate **cogiter** (215)
collaborate **collaborer** (22)
collapse **s'écrouler** (33, 421)
collapse **crouler** (421)
collapse **s'affaisser** (33, 274)
collate **collationner** (171)
collect **collectionner** (171)
collect **recueillir**
colonize, settle **coloniser** (486)
color **colorer** (22)
color (in) **colorier** (212)
comb (hair) **se peigner**
combat **combattre**
combine **combiner** (329)
come **venir**
come to an agreement **s'arranger** (33, 46)
come back **rappliquer** (219)
come back **revenir**
comfort **réconforter**
command **commander**
command, summon **mander** (147)
commemorate **commémorer** (22)
commence **commencer**
commercialize **commercialiser** (486)
commit **commettre**
commit oneself to do **s'engager** (305, 318)
communicate **communiquer** (219)
communion, to receive **communier** (389)
commute (legal term) **commuer** (114)
commute (mathematics) **commuter** (173)
compare **comparer**
compare someone/something to **assimiler qqn/qqch à** (27)

compensate **compenser** (336)
compensate **dédommager** (305)
compete **concurrencer** (342)
compete with **concourir avec** (125)
compile **compiler** (251)
complain **rouspéter** (87)
complain **se plaindre**
complete **compléter** (87)
complicate **compliquer** (219)
complicate **embrouiller** (233)
compliment **complimenter** (60)
comply with **obtempérer à** (203)
compose **composer** (350)
comprise **comporter** (349)
compromise **compromettre** (294)
compromise **transiger** (218)
computerize **informatiser** (486)
conceal **celer** (297)
conceal **dissimuler** (81)
concede **concéder** (87)
conceive **concevoir**
concentrate (oneself) on **se concentrer sur** (80, 299)
concentrate on **concentrer sur** (299)
conclude **conclure**
concoct **concocter** (349)
condemn **condamner** (98)
condescend to **condescendre à** (394)
condition **conditionner** (171)
conduct **conduire**
confer **conférer** (356)
confess **confesser** (73)
configure **configurer** (27)
confine **confiner** (329)
confirm **confirmer** (227)
confiscate **confisquer** (219)
conform to **se conformer à** (122, 227)
confound **confondre** (231)
confront **affronter** (113)
confront **confronter** (113)
confuse **tournebouler** (421)
confuse **troubler** (407)
congratulate **féliciter** (251)
conjecture **conjecturer** (54)
conjugate **conjuguer** (307)
connect **connecter** (349)
connect **brancher**
connect (Internet) **se connecter à** (122, 349)
connect to **raccorder à** (11)
conquer **conquérir**
conquer **vaincre**
consecrate **consacrer** (54)
consecrate **sacrer** (22)
consent **consentir**
consider **considérer** (87)
consist of **consister en** (215)
console **consoler** (27)
consolidate **consolider** (329)
conspire **conspirer** (21)
constitute **constituer** (483)
constrain **contraindre**
construct **bâtir**
construct **construire**
consult **compulser** (32)
consult **consulter** (375)
consume **consommer** (310)
contact **contacter** (28)
contain **contenir**
contaminate **contaminer** (329)
contemplate **contempler** (407)
content **contenter** (464)
continue **continuer**
contradict **contredire**
contrast with **contraster avec** (160)
contribute **contribuer** (114)
contribute **cotiser** (32)
control **contrôler** (498)
control by radio **téléguider** (27)
convene **convoquer** (219)
converge **converger** (283)
converge **confluer** (114)
converse **converser** (492)
converse **dialoguer** (307)
convert **convertir** (229)
convince **convaincre**
convulse **convulser** (336)
coo **roucouler** (421)
cook **cuisiner** (159)
cook **cuire**
cool **refroidir** (229)
cooler, to get **fraîchir** (383)
cooperate **coopérer** (356)
coordinate **coordonner** (171)
cope **se débrouiller** (122, 233)
copy **copier** (212)
corner somebody **acculer** (81)
correct **amender** (27)
correct **corriger**
correspond **correspondre** (401)
correspond (with) **cadrer** (27)
corroborate **corroborer** (27)
corrupt **corrompre**
corset **corseter** (297)
cost **coûter** (Def. and Imp.)
cough **tousser**
cough, to have a slight **toussoter** (96)
cough, to have a slight **toussailler** (477)
counsel **conseiller**
count **dénombrer** (407)
count **nombrer** (22)
count **compter**
count again **recompter** (103)
count on **tabler sur** (407)
counterfeit **contrefaire** (223)
couple **accoupler** (27)
couple **coupler** (421)
couple **jumeler** (38)
cover **couvrir**
cover again **recouvrir** (126)

cover in sand **ensabler** (407)
covet **convoiter** (447)
crack **craquer** (219)
crack **fendiller** (477)
crack **crevasser** (84)
crackle **pétiller** (477)
crackle (object) **craqueler** (38)
crackle (sound) **crépiter** (215)
cram (for a test) **potasser** (84)
cram for an exam **bachoter** (96)
cram, shove in **fourrer** (22)
crawl **ramper** (247)
crazy about, to be **raffoler de** (498)
creak, grind **grincer** (99)
crease **froisser** (353)
crease **plisser** (73)
create **créer**
create an uproar **chahuter** (8)
credit with **créditer de** (251)
crisscross **quadriller** (477)
criticize **critiquer** (219)
crochet **crocheter** (17)
cross **traverser**
cross **croiser** (86)
cross off (a list) **radier** (212)
cross out **raturer** (54)
cross out **rayer** (330)
crossbreed **métisser** (274)
crouch **se tapir** (66) (aux. **être**)
crown **couronner** (171)
crucify **crucifier** (212)
crumple **chiffonner** (171)
crumple **froisser** (353)
crunch **croquer** (219)
crush **concasser** (84)
crush **écrabouiller** (233)
crush **écraser** (183)
crush **broyer** (187)
cry **chialer** (421)
cry **pleurer**
cry out **s'écrier** (33, 41)
cry out **s'exclamer** (9)
cry out **crier**
crystallize **cristalliser** (486)
cuddle **se blottir** (214, 229)
cuddle **câliner** (329)
culminate **culminer** (329)
cultivate **cultiver** (329)
curl **friser** (486)
curl up **se recroqueviller** (414)
curse **pester** (27)
curse **maudire**
curve **arquer** (284)
curve **cintrer** (27)
cushion **amortir** (229)
cut **couper**
cut **tailler** (477)
cut again **recouper** (124)
cut down trees (Qué.) **bûcher** (285)
cut into sections **tronçonner** (483)
cut the head off of something **étêter** (47)
cut the throat of **égorger** (283)
cut up **découper** (124)

D

damage **endommager** (305)
damage **accidenter** (27)
damage **abîmer** (27)
damn **damner** (239)
dance **dancer**
dare **oser**
darken **assombrir** (229)
darken **obscurcir** (229)
darken **foncer** (371)
date from **dater de** (241)
daub (with) **barbouiller (de)** (233)
dawdle **lambiner** (329)
dawdle **s'attarder** (33)
daydream **rêvasser** (84)
dazzle **éblouir** (229)
deafen **assourdir** (229)
debit **débiter** (251)
debug (computer) **déboguer** (307)
decalcify **décalcifier** (41)
decamp **décamper** (27)
decant **soutirer** (466)
decapitate **décapiter** (251)
deceive **leurrer** (22)
deceive **tromper** (247) (See 480)
deceive **décevoir**
decide **décider**
decimate **décimer** (27)
decipher **déchiffrer** (27)
declaim **déclamer** (71)
declare **déclarer** (69)
decline **décliner** (465)
decolorize **décolorer** (22)
decompose **décomposer** (350)
decongest **décongestionner** (171)
deconstruct **déconstruire** (133)
decorate with **décorer de** (22)
decorate with **orner de** (470)
decrease **décroître**
decrease **diminuer**
decree **décréter** (87)
decry **décrier** (129)
dedicate (a book) **dédicacer à** (342)
dedicate to **dédier à** (212)
deduce **déduire**
deduct **déduire**
deepen **approfondir** (229)
defame **diffamer** (71)
defend **défendre**
defer to **déférer à** (356)
define **définir** (229)
deflate **dégonfler** (498)
deforest **déboiser** (486)
deform **déformer** (227)
defraud **frauder** (27)
defrost **dégivrer** (27)
defuse **désamorcer** (342)
defy **braver** (276)
degrade **dégrader** (27)
degrade **avilir** (423)

dehydrate **déshydrater** (241)
deign **daigner** (10)
delay **attarder** (240)
delay **retarder** (240)
delay **tarder** (240)
delay **temporiser** (486)
delegate **déléguer** (87, 307)
deliberate **délibérer** (356)
delight **ravir** (422)
delight **réjouir** (270)
delist (Internet) **délister** (160)
deliver to **livrer à** (27)
demand **revendiquer** (256)
demand ransom **rançonner** (443)
demobilize **démobiliser** (486)
democratize **démocratiser** (486)
demolish **démolir**
demonstrate **démontrer** (299)
demote **destituer** (483)
denationalize **dénationaliser** (486)
denigrate **dénigrer** (21)
denote **dénoter** (498)
denounce **dénoncer** (371)
dent **cabosser** (79)
deny **nier**
deny **démentir** (291)
depart **partir**
depart from **se départir de** (434)
depend (on) **dépendre**
depend on **se fier**
depict **dépeindre**
depilate **épiler** (329)
deplore **déplorer** (22)
deploy **déployer** (187)
depoliticize **dépolitiser** (486)
depopulate **dépeupler** (326)
deport **déporter** (349)
deposit **consigner** (441)
deposit **déposer** (350)
deprave **dépraver** (276)
depreciate **déprécier** (41)
depress **déprimer** (220)
deprive **priver** (276)
derive from **dériver de** (329)
desalinate **dessaler** (326)
descend **descendre**
describe **décrire**
desert **déserter** (40)
deserve **mériter**
designate **désigner** (441)
desire **désirer**
despair **désespérer** (203)
despise **mépriser** (486)
destabilize **déstabiliser** (486)
destine/intend for **destiner à** (329)
destroy **détruire**
detail **détailler** (477)
detain **détenir** (463)
detect **détecter** (160)
deteriorate **détériorer** (27)
determine **déterminer** (329)
detest **détester**
detonate **détoner** (461)
detoxify **désintoxiquer** (219)
devalue **dévaluer** (114)
devastate **dévaster** (259)
devastate **saccager** (305)
develop **évoluer** (213)
develop **développer**
deviate **dévier** (41)
devote **dévouer** (269)
devote oneself to **se consacrer à** (54, 122)
devour **dévorer** (27)
diagnose **diagnostiquer** (219)
dial (a number) **composer** (350)
dictate **dicter** (253)
die **mourir**
die **périr**
differ **différer** (203)
dig **creuser** (32)
dig again **recreuser** (32)
dig out/up **bêcher** (285)
dig up **déterrer** (196)
dig, study hard **piocher** (82)
digest **digérer** (203)
digitize **numériser** (486)
dine **dîner**
direct **diriger** (119)
direct towards **acheminer** (465)
dirty **encrasser** (84)
dirty **souiller**
disabuse of **détromper de** (317) (See 480)
disadvantage **défavoriser** (486)
disadvantage **désavantager** (305)
disappear **disparaître**
disappoint **décevoir**
disapprove of **désapprouver** (44)
disarm **désarmer** (238)
discern **discerner** (27)
disconcert **déconcerter** (160)
disconnect **déconnecter** (27)
disconnect **débrancher** (285)
discontinue **discontinuer** (114)
discount (financial) **escompter** (103)
discourage from **décourager de** (305)
discover **découvrir**
discover, reveal **déceler** (297)
discredit **déconsidérer** (356)
discredit **discréditer** (215)
discriminate **discriminer** (465)
discuss **débattre** (67)
discuss **discuter**
disdain **dédaigner** (10)
disembark from **débarquer de** (219)
disentangle **débrouiller** (233)
disfigure **déparer** (27)
disguise oneself **se déguiser** (122, 486)
disgust **dégoûter** (244)
disgust **écoeurer**
dishevel **écheveler** (38)
dishonor **déshonorer** (22)

disillusioned, to become **déchanter** (90)
disinfect **désinfecter** (160)
disintegrate **désintégrer** (356)
disjoint **désarticuler** (81)
dislocate **démettre** (294)
dislodge **déloger** (305)
dismantle something **démonter qqch** (298) (aux. **avoir**)
dismay **consterner** (27)
dismiss **congédier** (212)
disobey **désobéir à** (314)
disorient **déboussoler** (498)
disorient **dépayser** (486)
dispatch **dépêcher** (27)
disperse **disperser** (478)
displace **déplacer** (342)
display **afficher** (94)
displease **déplaire**
dispossess **déposséder** (87)
dispute **contester** (160)
dispute something **disputer de qqch** (425)
disqualify **disqualifier** (212)
dissect **disséquer** (87, 284)
disseminate **disséminer** (465)
dissipate **dissiper** (251)
dissociate **dissocier** (41)
dissolve **dissoudre** (6)
dissuade from **dissuader de** (340)
distinguish **discriminer** (465)
distinguish **distinguer** (307)
distort **fausser** (353)
distract **distraire** (474)
distress **navrer** (27)
distress **chagriner** (329)
distribute **distribuer** (114)
disturb **déranger**
disturb **dérégler** (87)
diverge **diverger** (283)
diversify **diversifier** (41)
divert **dériver** (329)
divert **détourner** (470)
divide into **diviser en** (32)
divide up **lotir** (66)
divide up **répartir** (229)
divide up into pieces **morceler** (38)
divulge **divulguer** (307)
divulge a secret **ébruiter** (215)
do **faire**
do one's own hair **se coiffer** (122)
do someone's hair **coiffer qqn** (443)
do without something **se priver de qqch** (276)
document **documenter** (60)
dog someone **s'acharner contre qqn** (27, 33)
domesticate **domestiquer** (219)
dominant over, to be **primer sur** (220)
dominate **dominer** (329)
don (clothing) **affubler** (407)
doodle, scribble **crayonner** (171)
dose, to measure **doser** (321)
double **doubler** (481)
doubt **douter**
down, to go **descendre**
down, to go back **redescendre** (157)
down, to take **descendre**
download **télécharger** (91)
doze **sommeiller** (109)
doze **somnoler** (498)
drag **traîner** (167)
drain **drainer** (27)
drain **égoutter** (374)
drain, dry **assécher** (429)
draw **dessiner**
draw again **retirer**
draw from **puiser** (486)
draw up, erect **dresser** (23)
draw/incite a crowd **ameuter** (374)
dread, fear **redouter de** (173)
dream **rêver**
dream **songer**
dredge **draguer** (307)
dress (someone) **vêtir**
dress again **rhabiller** (477)
dress someone, something **habiller qqn, qqch** (477) (See 250; aux. **avoir**)
dressed again, to get **se rhabiller** (250)
dressed, to get **s'habiller**
dribble (sports) **dribbler** (326)
drink **boire**
drip **dégoutter** (244)
drive away **bouter** (28)
drivel **radoter** (96)
drizzle **bruiner** (27)
drone **ânonner** (171)
drool **baver** (276)
drown **se noyer**
drug **droguer** (307)
drum **tambouriner** (329)
drunk, to get **se soûler** (122, 421)
dry **sécher**
dry out **dessécher** (87)
dry out **essorer** (22)
dry up **tarir** (249)
dub (audio) **doubler** (481)
dull, to make **affadir** (229)
dupe **duper** (317)
duplicate **dupliquer** (219)
dust **épousseter** (267)
dye **teindre**
dynamite **dynamiter** (251)

E

earn **gagner**
ease **alléger** (52)
eat **manger**
economize **économiser** (486)
edit **éditer** (251)
educate **éduquer** (219)
effect **effectuer** (483)
egosurf **egosurfer** (27)
elect **élire**
electrify **électriser** (486)
elide **élider** (251)
eliminate **éliminer** (465)

elucidate **élucider** (26)
elude **éluder** (32)
emanate from **émaner de** (27)
emasculate **émasculer** (81)
embalm **embaumer** (27)
embark **embarquer** (219)
embarrass **embarrasser** (84)
embellish with **agrémenter de** (60)
embroider **broder** (96)
emigrate **émigrer** (21)
emit **émettre** (294)
emit **dégager**
empty **vidanger** (283)
empty **vider** (251)
empty out **dévaliser** (486)
enchant **enchanter** (90)
encircle **encercler** (27)
encircle with **ceindre de** (334)
encircle with **cercler de** (27)
enclose **enclaver** (276)
enclose **renfermer** (227)
encompass **englober** (27)
encourage **encourager**
encrust **encroûter** (244)
end **terminer**
end up in **aboutir à/dans** (229)
endorse **endosser** (79)
endow **douer** (269)
endure **endurer** (54)
engage **engager** (305)
engaged, to get **se fiancer** (122, 342)
engrave **buriner** (465)
engrave **graver** (276)
engulf **engloutir** (66)
enjoy **jouir**
enjoy oneself **s'amuser**
enlarge **agrandir** (245)
enlarge **élargir** (229)
enliven **aviver** (486)
ennoble **anoblir** (423)
enough, to be **suffire**
enraged, to be **enrager** (305)
enrich **enrichir** (229)
entangle **s'empêtrer** (33, 299)
enter **entrer**
entertain **divertir** (210)
entertain **récréer** (128)
entertain **égayer**
enthuse **enthousiasmer** (27)
entice **aguicher** (285)
entrust **confier** (212)
entwine **enlacer** (342)
enumerate **énumérer** (356)
envelope **envelopper** (235)
envisage **envisager** (305)
envy **envier** (212)
equal **égaler** (326)
equalize **égaliser** (486)
equip with **équiper de** (215)
equip with tools **outiller** (477)
equivalent, to be **équivaloir** (488)
eradicate **éradiquer** (219)
erase **effacer** (342)
erase **gommer** (310)
erect **ériger** (119)
erode **s'effriter** (33, 215)
erode **éroder** (96)
escape **s'échapper** (27, 33)
escape **échapper**
escape **s'enfuir**
escape **se sauver**
escape from **s'évader de** (26, 33)
establish **établir**
establish **fonder**
esteem **estimer** (27)
estimate **estimer** (27)
evacuate **évacuer** (114)
evade **escamoter** (96)
evaluate **évaluer**
evaporate **s'évaporer** (22, 33)
evoke **évoquer** (219)
exaggerate **exagérer** (356)
exalt **exalter** (28)
examine **examiner** (465)
exasperate **exaspérer** (203)
exceed **excéder** (87)
exceed **dépasser**
excel **exceller** (326)
except **excepter** (8)
exchange **échanger** (89)
excite **exciter** (251)
exclude **exclure** (105)
excommunicate **excommunier** (309)
excuse **excuser**
excuse oneself **s'excuser**
execute **exécuter** (169)
exempt **dispenser** (336)
exercise **exercer** (342)
exert **exercer** (342)
exhale **expirer** (466)
exhaust **abrutir** (229)
exhaust **épuiser** (486)
exhaust **éreinter** (90)
exhaust ***harasser** (183)
exhibit **exhiber** (251)
exhume **exhumer** (238)
exist **exister** (349)
exonerate **disculper** (27)
exonerate **exonérer** (203)
expect **s'attendre à** (208)
expect to **compter**
expel **expulser** (336)
experience **éprouver**
expire **expirer** (466)
expire **se périmer** (122, 220)
explain **expliquer**
explode **exploser** (321)
exploit **exploiter** (251)
explore **explorer** (22)
export **exporter** (349)
expose **exposer** (350)
express **exprimer**
expropriate **exproprier** (41)
exterminate **exterminer** (465)
extinguish **éteindre**
extract **extraire** (474)
extricate **dépêtrer** (349)
eye **lorgner** (441)
eye (someone) **zieuter** (27)

F

fabricate **fabuler** (81)
facilitate **faciliter** (225)
fact, to make a statement of **constater** (241)
fade **se faner** (122)
fade **flétrir** (383)
fail **recaler** (326)
fail **échouer**
fail **faillir**

faint **s'évanouir**
fake **truquer** (219)
fall **choir** (Def. and Imp.)
fall **tomber**
fall **chuter** (28)
fall again **retomber** (467)
fall asleep **s'endormir** (172, 257)
fall asleep again **se rendormir** (172) (aux. **être**)
fall for someone **s'éprendre de** (357)
falsify **falsifier** (212)
familiarize **familiariser** (486)
fan **éventer** (90)
fascinate **fasciner** (329)
fascinate **passionner** (171)
fashion **façonner** (171)
fast **jeûner** (146)
fat, to remove/trim **dégraisser** (274)
fatten **engraisser** (274)
favor **avantager** (305)
favor **favoriser** (486)
favor **privilégier** (41)
fax **télécopier** (212)
fear **craindre**
federate **fédérer** (203)
feed **nourrir**
feed with **alimenter de** (60)
feel **sentir**
feel **ressentir** (434)
feel an itch **démanger** (283)
feel by touching **tâter** (241)
feel well/unwell **se porter** (122, 349)
feign **feindre**
ferment (wine) **cuver** (32)
ferret out **fureter** (17)
fertilize **fertiliser** (486)
fiddle with **tripoter** (96)
fight **se battre**
fight **combattre**
file **limer** (220)
fill **emplir** (95)
fill **remplir**
fill (a place) with smoke **enfumer** (238)
fill up with **combler de** (407)
filling, to put in a **plomber** (240)
film **filmer** (227)
filter **filtrer** (299)
filter **épurer** (54)
finance **commanditer** (215)
find **trouver**
find (again) **retrouver** (481)
finish **achever**
finish **finir**
fire **licencier** (41)
fire **sacquer** (284)
fire **débaucher** (285)
fish **pêcher**
fish out **repêcher** (332)
fit (something) in **caser** (32)
fit together **emboîter** (251)
fix **fixer** (27)
flabbergast **époustoufler** (445)
flame (Internet) **flinguer** (307)
flash **clignoter** (27)
flatten **aplatir** (229)
flatter **flatter** (27)
fleck **tacheter** (267)
flee **fuir**
fleece **entôler** (498)
flex **fléchir** (383)
flex **ployer** (187)
fling **flanquer** (284)
flirt **flirter** (425)
float **flotter** (79)
flood **inonder** (336)
flourish **fleurir** (249)
flow **couler** (421)
flower again **refleurir** (249)
flutter **voleter** (267)
flutter **voltiger** (218)
flutter around **papillonner** (171)
fly **voler**
fly away **s'envoler**
fly over **survoler**
foam **écumer** (27)
foil **déjouer** (269)
fold **plier**
fold again **replier** (129)
follow **s'ensuivre** (453) (3d p. sing. and pl.)
follow **suivre**
follow from (usually impers.) **découler de** (421)
follow on someone's heels **talonner** (171)
forage **fourrager** (305)
forbid **interdire**
force **forcer**
force oneself **s'efforcer** (33, 342)
foresee **prévoir**
forge **forger** (283)
forget **oublier**
fork **bifurquer** (284)
form **former** (227)
formalize **formaliser** (486)
format (computer) **formater** (176)
formulate **formuler** (32)
fortify **fortifier** (212)
found **instaurer** (54)
found **fonder**
fragment **fragmenter** (464)
frame **encadrer** (299)
fraternize **fraterniser** (486)
free from **libérer de** (203)
free up **décoincer** (342)
freelance **piger** (218)
freeze **congeler** (242)
freeze **glacer** (342)
freeze **surgeler** (242)
freeze **geler**
freeze again **regeler** (242)
freeze up **se figer** (119)
frequent **fréquenter** (60)
frighten **effrayer**
frost **givrer** (466)
froth **mousser** (353)
frown **se renfrogner** (122, 441)
frustrate **frustrer** (22)
fry **frire** (Def. and Imp.)

fun time, to have a **se marrer** (122)
fun, to have **se divertir** (210, 214)
fun, to make **se moquer**
function **fonctionner** (171)
furnish **fournir**
furnish with **meubler de** (27)
furrow **sillonner** (171)

G

gab **papoter** (96)
gag **bâillonner** (171)
gallicize **franciser** (486)
gallop **galoper** (163)
garden **jardiner** (167)
gargle **se gargariser** (85, 486)
garnish **garnir de** (229)
gather **cueillir**
gather **recueillir**
gauge **jauger** (76)
generate **engendrer** (299)
gesticulate **gesticuler** (32)
get along (with) **s'entendre (avec)** (195) (aux. **être**)
get bigger **grossir** (282)
get by **se débrouiller** (122, 233)
get on well with **sympathiser avec** (486)
get something for someone **procurer qqch à qqn** (54)
giggle **ricaner** (27)
gild **dorer** (22)
give **donner**
give a first name **prénommer** (310)
give a nickname **surnommer** (310)
give again **redonner** (171)
give back **redonner** (171)
give back **rendre**
give birth to **accoucher de** (121)
give someone responsibility **responsabiliser** (486)
gleam **rutiler** (27)
glean **glaner** (27)
glisten **reluire** (See **luire**) (Def. and Imp.)
glisten **luire** (Def. and Imp.)
glisten **chatoyer** (187)
glorify **glorifier** (212)
glorify **magnifier** (212)
gnaw **ronger** (442)
go **aller**
go along **longer** (283)
go away **s'en aller**
go boating **canoter** (26)
go out **sortir**
go out again **ressortir** (444)
go past, beyond **dépasser** (328)
go up again **remonter** (298)
goad **aiguillonner** (171)
gobble up **bouffer** (235)
gossip **potiner** (329)
gossip about **babiller sur** (27)
govern **gouverner** (167)
grab by the collar **colleter** (267)
grant **octroyer** (187)
grant **accorder**
grasp **serrer**
grasp **tenir**
grate **râper** (59)
graze **brouter** (28)
graze **pâturer** (54)
greet **saluer** (114)
grill (meat, fish), toast (bread) **griller** (477)
grimace (one's face) **grimacer** (342)
grind **piler** (27)
grind **moudre**
grip **agripper** (163)
groan **gémir** (229)
groan **geindre** (334)
groom **toiletter** (246)
grope **tâtonner** (171)
group **grouper** (124)
group together **regrouper** (59)
grow **croître**
grow **grandir**
grumble **grogner** (10)
grumble **bougonner** (171)
grumble **rechigner** (441)
guarantee **cautionner** (171)
guarantee **garantir** (229)
guard against **prémunir contre** (229)
guess **deviner** (329)
guide **guider** (26)
guillotine **guillotiner** (329)
gush forth **jaillir** (423)
gut **étriper** (215)
guzzle **bâfrer** (82)

H

habitual offender, to be an **récidiver** (276)
hack (computer) **pirater** (241)
haggle **marchander** (147)
haggle, quibble **chicaner** (147)
hail **grêler** (Def. and Imp.)
hail, call to ***héler** (87)
hallucinate **halluciner** (329)
hammer **marteler** (297)
handicap ***handicaper** (59)
handle **manier** (212)
handle roughly **maltraiter** (475)
handle roughly **malmener** (290)
hang **pendre**
hang (up) **accrocher**
hang around **poireauter** (27)
hang on **se cramponner** (122, 171)
hang on **s'accrocher** (13)
hang up **raccrocher** (469)
happen **advenir** (Def. and Imp.)
happen **se passer** (Def. and Imp.)
harass ***harceler** (297)
harden **durcir** (95)
harden, toughen **endurcir** (95)
harm **nuire**
harm **léser** (87)
harness (horses) **atteler** (38)

harp on, repeat over and over **rabâcher** (82)
harvest (grapes) **vendanger** (283)
harvest, gather **récolter** (27)
hassle someone **emmerder** (240)
hasten **s'empresser de** (361)
hatch **éclore** (See **clore**) (Def. and Imp.)
hatch (with hatch marks) ***hachurer** (54)
hate **détester**
hate **haïr**
haunt ***hanter** (90)
have **avoir**
have a slimming effect **amincir** (229)
have to **devoir**
hazard ***hasarder** (240)
heal **guérir**
healthier, to make **assainir** (229)
hear **entendre**
heat **échauffer** (171)
heat up **chauffer** (235)
hebraize **hébraïser** (486)
help **aider**
help **secourir**
help oneself **se servir**
help out **dépanner** (171)
hem **ourler** (326)
hesitate **hésiter**
hesitate **tergiverser** (492)
hide **cacher**
hide (something) **planquer** (284)
hide oneself **se cacher**
hierarchize ***hiérarchiser** (486)
hinder **entraver** (276)
hinder **empêcher**
hire **engager** (305)
hire **embaucher** (285)
hit **cogner** (10)
hit **frapper**
hit ***heurter** (246)
hoist ***hisser** (84)
hold **tenir**
hold **receler** (297)
hold back **endiguer** (307)
hold up **supporter**
hole, to make a **trouer** (269)
honor **honorer** (22)
hoot ***hululer, ululer** (81)
hoot, toot, sound a horn **klaxonner** (171)
hope **espérer**
horn, to remove a **décorner** (470)
horn, to sound a **corner** (349)
horrify **horrifier** (212)
hospitalize **hospitaliser** (486)
host (Internet) **héberger** (283)
hover over **planer sur** (71)
howl ***hurler** (326)
hug **étreindre** (334)
hum **fredonner** (171)
hum, buzz **vrombir** (229)
humble oneself **s'abaisser**
hunt **chasser**
hurry **se dépêcher**
hurry oneself **se *hâter** (74, 241)
hurry, to be in a **se presser**
hurt onself **se blesser**
hyperlink (Internet) **hyperlier** (454)
hypertrophy **s'hypertrophier** (212) (aux. **être**)
hypnotize **hypnotiser** (486)

I

idealize **idéaliser** (486)
identify **identifier** (212)
idolize **idolâtrer** (299)
illuminate **illuminer** (465)
illustrate **illustrer** (299)
imagine **imaginer** (329)
imitate **imiter** (251)
immerse **immerger** (91)
immigrate **immigrer** (93)
immobilize **immobiliser** (486)
immolate **immoler** (498)
immortalize **immortaliser** (486)
immunize **immuniser** (486)
impatient, to get **s'impatienter** (33, 464)
implicate **impliquer** (219)
implore **implorer** (22)
implore **supplier**
implore **adjurer** (272)
imply **impliquer** (219)
import **importer** (349)
importune **importuner** (32)
impose **imposer** (350)
impoverish **appauvrir** (229)
impress **impressionner** (171)
imprison **incarcérer** (203)
improve **bonifier** (41)
improve **améliorer** (22)
improvise **improviser** (486)
improvise **se débrouiller**
inaugurate **inaugurer** (54)
incinerate **incinérer** (356)
incite **inciter** (251)
incline **incliner** (329)
include **inclure**
incorporate in **incorporer à** (22)
increase **redoubler** (407)
increase **acroître**
increase **augmenter**
increase **croître**
increase the value **valoriser** (486)
incur **encourir** (125)
indicate **indiquer**
indifferent to, to become **se blaser de** (33, 122)
indignant, to become **s'indigner** (33, 441)
indoctrinate **endoctriner** (329)
induce (to) **induire (à)** (106)
industrialize **industrialiser** (486)

infect with **infecter de** (113)
infer from **inférer de** (356)
infest with **infester de** (259)
infiltrate **s'infiltrer dans** (299, 262)
inflate **gonfler** (445)
inflict on **infliger à** (218)
influence **influencer** (99)
inform **informer** (227)
inform **renseigner** (194)
inform oneself **s'informer**
infringe **enfreindre** (334)
infuse **infuser** (32)
ingest **ingérer** (203)
inhale **aspirer** (21)
inhale **inspirer** (466)
inherit **hériter** (293)
inhibit **inhiber** (215)
initiate into **initier à** (389)
inject **injecter** (8)
injure **blesser**
injure oneself **se blesser**
inoculate **inoculer** (81)
inquire about **s'enquérir de** (19) (aux. **être**)
inscribe **inscrire** (177)
insert **insérer** (203)
insert **intercaler** (326)
insinuate **insinuer** (114)
insist **insister**
inspect **inspecter** (113)
inspire **inspirer** (466)
install **installer** (27)
install glass **vitrer** (22)
install signals **signaliser** (486)
institute **instituer** (483)
instruct **instruire**
insulate **isoler** (498)
insult **insulter** (176)
integrate **intégrer** (203)
intensify **s'intensifier** (212) (aux. **être**)
intercede **intercéder** (87)
intercept **intercepter** (8)
interest someone in something **intéresser qqn à qqch** (88)
interested, to be **s'intéresser**
interfere **interférer** (356)
interfere in **s'ingérer dans** (33, 203)
intermingle **entremêler** (82)
interpolate **interpoler** (498)
interpose between **interposer entre** (350)
interpret **interpréter** (87)
interrogate **interroger**
interrupt **interrompre**
intersperse with **entrecouper de** (124)
intertwine **entrelacer** (342)
intervene **intervenir** (491)
intervene **s'entremettre** (295)
interview **interviewer** (27)
intimidate by **intimider par** (266)
intoxicate **griser** (486)
intoxicated, to become **s'enivrer** (33)
introduce **introduire**
invade **envahir** (229)
invalidate **invalider** (266)
invent **inventer** (90)
inventory **recenser** (27)
invert **invertir** (66)
invest **investir** (66)
investigate **enquêter (sur)** (47)
invite **convier** (41)
invite **inviter**
invoke, call upon **invoquer** (219)
iron **repasser**
irradiate, radiate **irradier** (389)
irritate **irriter** (266)
irritate, tingle **picoter** (96)
isolate **isoler** (498)
isolate (from) **isoler (de)** (498)
italianize **italianiser** (486)

J

jabber **jacter** (8)
jabber **jargonner** (171)
jabber **baragouiner** (329)
jam **coincer** (342)
join **joindre**
join **unir**
join (member) **adhérer** (87)
join in marriage **conjoindre** (268)
join tip to tip, end to end **abouter** (173)
joke **blaguer** (307)
joke **plaisanter**
joke **rigoler** (498)
jolt **cahoter** (28)
jolt, bounce around **ballotter** (171)
judge **juger**
juggle **jongler** (326)
jump **sauter**
jump **tressaillir** (50)
jump **sursauter** (425)
justify **justifier** (389)
jut out **saillir** (50) (3d pers.); (229) (if **saillir** means "mate," 3d pers.)

K

keep **garder**
keep away from **éloigner de** (194)
kidnap **kidnapper** (235)
kill **tuer**
kill each other **s'entretuer** (33, 483)
kiss **embrasser**
knead **pétrir** (249)
kneel **s'agenouiller** (233)
knit **tricoter** (96)
knit (brow) **froncer** (34)
knock **toquer** (219)
knock down **abattre**
knock down **défoncer** (371)
knock out **assommer** (310)
know **connaître**
know (how) **savoir**

L

label **étiqueter** (267)
lace **lacer** (342)
lacerate **lacérer** (356)
laicize **laïciser** (486)
lament **se lamenter sur qqch** (60)
land **atterrir** (229)
land on the moon **alunir** (229)
languish **languir** (229)
lapidate **lapider** (251)

last **durer** (272)
lather **mousser** (353)
latinize **latiniser** (486)
laugh **rire**
launch **lancer**
lay (eggs) **pondre** (394)
lay off **débaucher** (285)
lead **conduire**
lead **emmener**
lead **mener**
lead away **emmener**
leaf through **feuilleter** (267)
lean against **adosser** (79)
lean against **s'arc-bouter à** (33)
lean one's elbow on **s'accouder sur** (33, 421)
lean over **se pencher** (122)
leap **bondir** (229)
leap about **gambader** (26)
learn **apprendre**
learn again **rapprendre, réapprendre** (42)
lease **affermer** (227)
leave **laisser**
leave **partir**
leave **quitter**
leave **sortir**
legislate **légiférer** (356)
lend **prêter**
lengthen **rallonger** (442)
lessen **amoindrir** (229)
level **niveler** (38)
level, to make **aplanir** (229)
liberate **libérer** (203)
lick **lécher** (87)
lie **mentir**
lie down **se coucher**
lie down **gésir** (Def. and Imp.)
lie low **se terrer** (122, 196)
life to, to give **vivifier** (212)
lift **lever**
light **éclairer** (21)
light again **rallumer** (238)
light, turn on **allumer** (238)
liking for, to have a **affectionner** (171)
limit **borner** (27)
limit **limiter** (251)
limp **boiter** (26)
link together **rattacher** (82)
liquidate **liquider** (251)
lisp **zézayer** (330)
list **lister** (27)
listen (to) **écouter**
listen to someone's chest **ausculter** (28)
live **vivre**
live (in) **habiter**
live again, come alive again **revivre** (496)
live in **loger dans** (263)
live on **subsister de** (53)
live temporarily **séjourner**
live with **loger chez** (263)
liven up **corser** (336)
load **charger**
locate **localiser** (486)
locate **repérer** (203)
located, to be **se situer** (122, 483)
located, to be **se trouver**
lock **verrouiller** (233)
lock up **enfermer** (227)
lodge **héberger** (283)
look (at) **regarder**
look for **chercher**
loom up **surgir** (229)
loosen **lâcher** (82)
loosen **détendre** (462)
lose **paumer** (27)
lose **perdre**
lost, to get **se perdre** (122, 337)
lost, to get **s'égarer** (33, 101)
love **aimer**
low **beugler** (27)
lower **rebaisser** (63)
lower **surbaisser** (63)
lower **abaisser**
lower **baisser**
lukewarm (hotter or colder), to become **tiédir** (210)
lukewarm, to make **attiédir** (229)
lunch **déjeuner**
lynch **lyncher** (78)

M

machinate **machiner** (329)
machine-gun **mitrailler** (477)
magnetize **aimanter** (90)
magnetize **magnétiser** (486)
mail **poster** (27)
mail, to return/forward **réexpédier** (212)
maintain **maintenir** (463)
maintain **entretenir** (463)
make **confectionner** (171)
make **faire**
manage **se débrouiller** (122, 233)
manage **gérer** (203)
manage **se débrouiller**
maneuver **manoeuvrer** (26)
manipulate **manipuler** (81)
manufacture **fabriquer** (219)
manufacture **manufacturer** (54)
maraud **marauder** (27)
marginalize **marginaliser** (486)
mark a path **baliser** (486)
mark off **jalonner** (171)
mark with **marquer de** (219)
married to someone, to get **se marier à/avec qqn** (122)
marry **épouser**
marry (someone to someone) **marier** (389)
martyr **martyriser** (486)
mask **masquer à** (219)
massacre **massacrer** (299)
massage **masser** (84)
master **maîtriser** (486)
match **assortir** (229)
matter, to be the **s'agir** (Def. and Imp.)

maximize **maximaliser/maximiser** (486)
mean **signifier** (212)
measure **mesurer** (54)
measure time **minuter** (32)
mechanize **mécaniser** (486)
meddle in **se mêler de** (83)
meddle with **se mêler à** (83)
meditate **méditer** (251)
meet **rencontrer**
meet with **se retrouver** (122, 481)
melt **fondre**
membership, to renew one's **se réabonner** (122, 171)
memorize **mémoriser** (486)
mend **raccommoder** (147)
mention **mentionner** (171)
merit **mériter**
migrate **migrer** (22)
milder, to get **radoucir** (95)
milk **traire**
mime **mimer** (220)
mine **miner** (465)
minimize **minimaliser/minimiser** (486)
mint **monnayer** (330)
mirror **mirer**
misjudge **méconnaître**
mislead **fourvoyer** (187)
misrepresent **travestir** (66)
miss **manquer**
miss **louper** (124)
miss **rater** (241)
mist up **embuer** (114)
mistaken, to be **se méprendre**
mistaken, to be **se tromper**
mistreat **maltraiter** (475)
misuse **abuser de qqch** (32)
misuse **maltraiter** (475)
mix **mélanger** (283)
mix up **brouiller** (233)
mix with **mêler à/avec** (82)
mixed up, to get **cafouiller** (233)
moan **râler** (498)
mobilize **mobiliser** (486)
mock **se gausser** (122, 353)
mock **railler** (477)
mock **persifler** (439)
model **modeler**
moderate **modérer** (203)
modernize **moderniser** (486)
modify **modifier** (389)
modulate **moduler** (81)
moisten **humecter** (60)
moisturize **hydrater** (241)
mold **mouler** (421)
moldy, to make/go **moisir** (95)
molest **molester** (160)
molt **muer** (483)
monopolize **monopoliser** (486)
monopolize (manipulate the market) **truster** (27)
moo **meugler** (326)
moor **amarrer** (27)
moralize **moraliser** (486)
mortgage **hypothéquer** (87, 219)
mortify **mortifier** (389)
motivate **motiver** (26)
mount **enfourcher** (285)
move **bouger**
move **mouvoir**
move (emotionally) **émouvoir**
move away **s'éloigner**
move back **reculer** (81)
move belongings from one residence to another **déménager** (305)
move in **emménager** (305)
move out of line **décaler** (326)
move over (Qué.) **se tasser** (84, 122)
multiply **multiplier** (454)
mumble **bredouiller** (233)
mumble **marmonner** (171)
mummify **momifier** (212)
murmur **murmurer** (54)
must **devoir**
mutilate **mutiler** (27)
mutiny **se mutiner** (329)
muzzle **museler** (38)
mystify **mystifier** (129)

N

nail **clouer** (269)
name **dénommer** (310)
name **nommer**
named, to be **s'appeler**
nap, to take a **roupiller** (477)
narrate **narrer** (22)
narrate **conter**
navigate **naviguer**
necessary, to be **falloir** (Def. and Imp.)
neglect **négliger** (119)
negotiate **négocier** (389)
neutralize **neutraliser** (486)
next to, to be **côtoyer** (187)
nibble at; snack **grignoter** (96)
nod (one's head) ***hocher** (82)
nod off **s'assoupir** (229)
normalize **normaliser** (486)
note **noter** (176)
notice **remarquer**
notice **s'aviser** (32, 33)
notify **aviser** (32)
notify **notifier** (322)
nuance **nuancer**
numb **engourdir** (210)
number **chiffrer** (27)
number **numéroter** (96)
nurse (baby) **téter** (87)
nurse (infant) **allaiter** (27)

O

obey **obéir**
objectify **objectiver** (276)
objection, to make an **objecter** (160)
oblige **obliger**
obliterate **oblitérer** (356)
observe **observer** (481)
obsess **obséder** (87)
obstruct **obstruer** (114)
obtain **obtenir**

occupy **occuper**
offend **offenser** (336)
offend **offusquer** (219)
offer **offrir**
oil **huiler** (27)
old, to grow **vieillir**
omit **omettre**
ooze **suinter** (464)
open **ouvrir**
open halfway **entrouvrir** (323)
open halfway **entrebâiller** (477)
operate **opérer** (356)
operate by remote control **télécommander** (98)
oppose **opposer** (350)
oppress **opprimer** (220)
opt for **opter pour** (113)
orchestrate **orchestrer** (22)
order **commander**
order, to put in **ranger**
organize **ordonner** (171)
organize **organiser** (486)
orient towards **s'orienter vers** (113)
orient, steer **aiguiller** (477)
oscillate **osciller** (477)
outdistance **distancer** (342)
outrage **outrer** (22)
outrage **outrager** (305)
overestimate **surestimer** (220)
overexpose **surexposer** (350)
overflow **déborder** (26)
overhang **surplomber** (240)
overlap **s'imbriquer** (33, 219)
overload **surcharger** (283)
overpay **surpayer** (17)
overquip **suréquiper** (215)
overtax **surimposer** (350)
overturn **renverser** (492)
overvalue **surévaluer** (213)
overwhelm **accabler** (407)
overwhelm **bouleverser** (492)
overwork **surmener** (290)
own **posséder**

P

pacify **pacifier** (389)
package **empaqueter** (267)
pact, to make a **pactiser** (486)
pad **matelasser** (274)
paint **peindre**
palatalize **palataliser** (486)
pale, to become **blêmir** (229)
palpitate **palpiter** (251)
pamper **choyer** (187)
pamper **dorloter** (96)
panic **s'affoler** (33, 421)
panic **paniquer** (219)
pant, gasp ***haleter** (17)
parachute **parachuter** (425)
pardon **pardonner**
park **garer** (435)
park **stationner** (171)
park; confine **parquer** (284)
parody **parodier** (212)
participate in **participer à** (251)
partition **cloisonner** (171)
pass **dépasser**
pass **passer**
pass (auto) **doubler** (481)
pass again **repasser**
pass away **décéder** (87)
pass away **trépasser** (84) (aux. **être** or **avoir**)
pass on to **répercuter sur** (169)
pass through **transiter** (251)
patch up **rafistoler** (498)
patient, to be **patienter** (26)
patrol **patrouiller** (233)
patronize **patronner** (171)
pauperize **paupériser** (486)
pave **paver** (276)
pave **revêtir** (493)
pay **rétribuer** (114)
pay (for) **payer**
pay by money order **mandater** (241)
pay off (duty) **s'acquitter de** (33, 374)
peak **plafonner** (171)
peck **becqueter** (267)
pedal **pédaler** (326)
peddle **colporter** (349)
peel **éplucher** (82)
peel **peler** (297)
penetrate **pénétrer** (356)
pep up **activer** (26)
pepper **poivrer** (466)
perceive **percevoir** (379)
perceive **apercevoir**
perch **percher** (93)
perch on **jucher sur** (469)
perfect **parfaire** (223)
perfect **perfectionner** (171)
perforate **perforer** (22)
perfume **parfumer** (238)
perish **périr**
perk up **ragaillardir** (210)
permeate **imprégner** (87, 441)
permit **permettre**
permutate, swap **permuter** (32)
perpetrate **perpétrer** (356)
persecute **persécuter** (32)
persevere **persévérer** (356)
persist **persister** (259)
persist in **s'obstiner à** (318, 329)
persist in **s'entêter** (33, 47)
personalize **personnaliser** (486)
personify **personnifier** (389)
personify **incarner** (27)
persuade **persuader**
pervert **pervertir** (66)
pet (an animal) **flatter** (27)
petrify **pétrifier** (212)
philosophize **philosopher** (27)
phish **hameçonner** (171)
photocopy **photocopier** (212)
photograph **photographier** (212)

phrase (in music) **phraser** (32)
pick **cueillir**
pick someone up (fig.) **draguer** (307)
pick up **ramasser** (92)
pierce **percer** (275)
pierce **transpercer** (342)
pile up **amasser** (92)
pile up **amonceler** (38)
pile up **empiler** (329)
pilfer **chaparder** (27)
pillage **piller** (477)
pilot **piloter** (96)
pin **épingler** (326)
pinch **pincer** (99)
pirate **pirater** (241)
pity **plaindre**
pity, to inspire **apitoyer** (187)
pity, to inspire **attendrir** (229)
pivot **pivoter** (96)
place **mettre**
place **placer**
place **poser**
plagiarize **plagier** (389)
plan **planifier** (212)
plan **programmer**
plane **raboter** (96)
plant **planter** (90)
plaster **plâtrer** (22)
plaster, to remove **déplâtrer** (349)
play **jouer**
play the piano **pianoter** (96)
plead **plaider** (26)
please **plaire**
pleat **plisser** (73)
plot **comploter** (349)
plot **manigancer** (342)
plot **tramer** (71)
plow **labourer** (481)
plug **tamponner** (171)
plug in **brancher**
plug up **colmater** (28)
plumb **plomber** (240)
plunge **plonger** (442)
plunge in, smash down **enfoncer** (371)
poach (cooking) **pocher** (82)
pocket **empocher** (285)
pocket again **rempocher** (82)
point **pointer** (464)
poison **empoisonner** (171)
poison **intoxiquer** (219)
poison **envenimer** (27)
polish **dégrossir** (282)
polish **polir** (423)
polish **fignoler** (498)
polish **peaufiner** (329)
politicize **politiser** (486)
poll **sonder** (27)
pollute with **polluer de** (114)
pomade, to put on **pommader** (240)
pontificate **pontifier** (212)
populate **peupler** (326)
position **positionner** (171)
possess **posséder**
postpone **reporter** (349)
postpone **ajourner** (433)
pour **verser**
pour again **reverser** (492)
pour out **épancher** (78)
pour out **déverser** (492)
powder **poudrer** (299)
practice **pratiquer** (219)
praise **louanger** (283)
praise **louer**
pray **prier**
preach **prêcher** (332)
precede **précéder** (87)
predestine **prédestiner** (329)
predict **présager** (305)
predict **prédire**
predispose **prédisposer** (350)
preexist **préexister à** (27)
preface **préfacer** (342)
prefer **préférer**
prejudge **préjuger** (271)
premeditate **préméditer** (251)
preoccupy **préoccuper** (317)
prepare **apprêter** (363)
prepare **préparer**
prescribe **prescrire** (177)
prescribe (medical) **ordonner** (171)
present **présenter**
preserve **conserver** (27)
preserve from **préserver de** (426)
preside (over) **présider** (251)
press **appuyer** (192)
press **presser**
presume **présumer** (238)
presuppose **présupposer** (350)
pretend **prétendre**
pretend to **affecter de** (8)
prevail over **prédominer sur** (465)
prevail over **prévaloir sur** (488)
prick **piquer** (219)
print **imprimer** (220)
privatize **privatiser** (486)
proceed from **procéder** (87)
proclaim **proclamer** (71)
proclaim **clamer** (9)
produce **produire**
profane **profaner** (27)
profess **professer** (73)
profile **profiler** (27)
profit from **profiter de** (251)
profit from/by **bénéficier de** (389)
profitable, to make **rentabiliser** (486)
program **programmer**
progress **progresser** (73)
prohibit **prohiber** (251)
prohibit **défendre**
project **projeter** (267)
prolong by **prolonger de** (442)
promise **promettre**
promote **promouvoir** (304) (*part. passé* promu, promue)
promulgate **promulguer** (307)
pronounce **prononcer**
prop up **étayer** (330)
propagate **propager** (305)
proportionate, to make **proportionner** (171)
propose **proposer** (350)
proscribe **proscrire** (177)

prosper **prospérer** (203)
prostitute oneself **se prostituer** (122, 483)
protect **protéger** (52)
protest **protester** (160)
proud of (something), to be **enorgueillir de** (229)
prove **prouver**
prove/turn out be **s'avérer** (33, 87)
provide **pourvoir** (497) (except Tenses 4 & 5, stem: pourvoir-; Tense 3 pourvus, pourvus, pourvut...; Tense 7 pourvusse, pourvusses, pourvût...)
provide **nantir** (66)
provide for **subvenir à** (491)
provoke **provoquer** (219)
prowl **rôder** (96)
prune **émonder** (240)
psychoanalyze **psychanalyser** (32)
publish **publier** (212)
publish **éditer** (251)
pull **tirer**
pull again **retirer**
pull down **rabattre** (67)
pull off leaves **effeuiller** (477)
pull on **tirailler** (477)
pulverize **pulvériser** (486)
pump **pomper** (59)
punch (a ticket) **composter** (349)
punch (ticket) **poinçonner** (171)
punctuate **ponctuer** (483)
puncture **ponctionner** (171)
puncture (tire) **crever** (278)
punish **châtier** (212)
punish **punir**
purge **purger** (283)
purify **purifier** (212)
purple, to become **se violacer** (342)
pursue **pourchasser** (92)
pursue **chasser**
pursue **poursuivre**
push **pousser**
push away **repousser** (353)
push back **refouler** (421)
push further in **renfoncer** (342)
put **mettre**
put **poser**
put a slipcover on ***housser** (353)
put again **remettre**
put back **reposer** (350)
put makeup on one's face **se maquiller** (122)
put out of order **détraquer** (219)
put topspin on a ball **lifter** (27)
put up posters **placarder** (240)

Q

quadruple **quadrupler** (326)
qualify **qualifier** (212)
quantify **quantifier** (212)
quarrel with each other **se quereller** (122, 477)
quebecize, make Québécois **québéciser** (486)
question **questionner** (171)
question **interroger**
question (police) **interpeller** (27)
quibble **ergoter** (96)
quibble **ratiociner** (329)
quiet, to be **se taire**
quintuple **quintupler** (326)
quote **citer** (251)

R

radicalize **radicaliser** (486)
rage **rager** (305)
rain **pleuvoir** (Def. and Imp.)
raise **exhausser** (353)
raise ***hausser** (92)
raise **soulever** (278)
raise **surélever** (278)
raise **élever**
raise **rehausser** (353)
raise a bid **surenchérir** (94)
raise again **relever** (278)
rake **ratisser** (486)
rally **rallier** (212)
ramify **se ramifier** (212) (aux. **être**)
rancid, to get **rancir** (95)
rant and rave **déblatérer** (356)
rarefy **raréfier** (212)
ratify **homologuer** (307)
ratify **entériner** (329)
ratify **ratifier** (212)
ration **rationner** (171)
ravage **ravager** (305)
reaccustom **réaccoutumer** (238)
reach **parvenir à** (491)
react **réagir** (25)
read **lire**
read again **relire**
readjust **réadapter** (8)
readmit **réadmettre** (294)
ready, to get oneself **s'apprêter à qqch** (48, 363)
reappear **réapparaître** (324)
reappear **reparaître**
reappear **ressurgir/resurgir** (229)
reappoint **renommer** (310)
rear up **cabrer** (27)
rear up **regimber** (240)
rearm **réarmer** (227)
reason **raisonner** (443)
reassure **rassurer** (54)
reassure **sécuriser** (486)
reassure **tranquilliser** (486)
rebel **se rebeller** (122)
reborn, to be **renaître** (306)
rebroadcast **rediffuser** (32)
rebuild **reconstituer** (483)
recall **rappeler**
receive **recevoir**
recite **réciter** (251)

reclassify **reclasser** (84)
recognize **reconnaître**
recommend **recommander** (98)
reconcile **concilier** (212)
reconcile **réconcilier** (212)
reconcile (with) **rabibocher** (285)
reconquer **reconquérir** (19)
reconsider **reconsidérer** (203)
reconstruct **reconstruire** (111)
reconstruct **recomposer** (350)
reconvert **reconvertir** (229)
recorrect **recorriger** (218)
recount **retracer** (342)
recover **recouvrer** (466)
recreate **recréer** (128)
recross **retraverser** (492)
recruit **recruter** (32)
rectify **rectifier** (389)
recycle **recycler** (326)
redden **rougeoyer** (187)
redefine **redéfinir** (229)
rediscover **redécouvrir** (139)
redo **refaire** (223)
reduce **réduire**
reduce **rabaisser** (63)
redye **reteindre** (334)
reeducate **rééduquer** (219)
reelect **réélire** (280)
reembark **rembarquer** (284)
reemerge **ressurgir/resurgir** (229)
reestablish **rétablir** (206)
reexamine **réexaminer** (465)
refer to **se référer à** (122, 356)
referee **arbitrer** (27)
refine **raffiner** (329)
reflect **refléter** (87)
reflect (thought) **réfléchir**
refract **réfracter** (27)
refresh **rafraîchir** (383)
refresh **désaltérer** (356)
refrigerate **réfrigérer** (203)
refund **ristourner** (27)
refuse **refuser**
refute **démentir** (291)
refute **réfuter** (425)
regain **regagner** (239)
regenerate **régénérer** (356)
register **s'inscrire** (177) (aux. **être**)
register **enregistrer** (393)
register **immatriculer** (81)
regret **regretter**
regulate **régulariser** (486)
regulate **régler** (87)
rehabilitate **réhabiliter** (251)
rehearse **répéter**
reheat **réchauffer** (84)
reign **régner** (87)
reimburse **rembourser** (27)
reimprison **réincarcérer** (356)
reincarnated, to be **se réincarner** (122)
reinforce **renforcer** (342)
reinstall **réinstaller** (326)
reinstate **réintégrer** (356)
reinvent **réinventer** (464)
reiterate **réitérer** (356)
reject **rejeter** (267)
rejoin **rejoindre** (268)
rejuvenate **rajeunir** (229)
relapse **rechuter** (32)
relate **relater** (241)
relativize **relativiser** (486)
relaunch **relancer** (342)
relax **délasser** (79)
relax **se détendre** (394)
relax **relaxer** (27)
relay **relayer** (330)
relearn **rapprendre, réapprendre** (42)
release **lâcher** (82)
relet **relouer** (269)
relieve **atténuer** (114)
relieve of **soulager de** (305)
reload **recharger** (91)
remain **rester**
remark **remarquer**
remedy **remédier à** (212)
remelt, recast **refondre** (394)
remember **se remémorer** (22, 122)
remember **se rappeler**
remember **se souvenir**
remodel **refaçonner** (443)
remove **enlever**
remove **retrancher** (78)
remove bandages **débander** (27)
remove one's makeup **se démaquiller** (477)
remunerate **rémunérer** (203)
renew **renouveler** (38)
renounce **renier** (309)
renounce, give up **renoncer** (371)
renovate **rénover** (276)
rent **louer**
reopen **rouvrir** (323)
repaint **repeindre** (334)
repair **réparer**
repatriate **rapatrier** (212)
repave **repaver** (276)
repeat **répéter**
repel **rebuter** (32)
repent **se repentir**
replace **suppléer** (128)
replace **remettre**
replace **replacer** (342)
replay **rejouer** (269)
reply **répliquer** (219)
repolish **repolir** (229)
repopulate **repeupler** (326)
represent **figurer** (54)
represent **représenter** (60)
repress **réprimer** (220)
reprimand ***houspiller** (477)
reprimand **réprimander**
reprint **réimprimer** (220)
reproach someone for something **reprocher qqch à qqn** (43)
reproduce **reproduire**
reprogram **reprogrammer** (368)
reprove **réprouver** (481)
republish **rééditer** (215)
repudiate **répudier** (212)
request **demander**
require **nécessiter** (251)
require **exiger**

require, demand **requérir** (19)
requisition **réquisitionner** (171)
reread **relire**
reroute **dérouter** (28)
resell **revendre** (489)
resemble **ressembler**
reserve **réserver** (276)
resheath **rengainer** (329)
reside **résider** (251)
reside **demeurer**
resign from **démissionner de** (171)
resign oneself to **se résigner à** (122, 441)
resist **résister** (259)
resoak **retremper** (247)
resolder **ressouder** (27)
resolve **résoudre**
resonate **résonner** (443)
resort to something **recourir à qqch** (125)
respect **respecter** (8)
respond **répondre**
respond **riposter** (27)
rest **se reposer**
restick **recoller** (326)
restock **regarnir** (229)
restore **restaurer** (347)
restrict **restreindre** (334)
restring **recorder** (27)
result from **provenir de** (491)
result from **résulter de** (27)
retain **retenir**
retie **renouer** (269)
retighten **resserrer** (22)
retighten **retendre** (394)
retire **se retirer**
retort **rétorquer** (284)
retouch **retoucher** (469)
retract **rétracter** (60)
retranscribe **retranscrire** (177)
retread (tire) **rechaper** (59)
return **rentrer**
return **retourner**
return, restore **restituer** (483)
retype **retaper** (59)
reunify **réunifier** (212)
reunite with **réunir à** (485)
reuse **réemployer/remployer** (187)
reuse **réutiliser** (486)
revalue **revaloriser** (486)
reveal **révéler** (356)
reverberate **réverbérer** (203)
revere **révérer** (203)
reverse **inverser** (492)
revise **remanier** (309)
revise **réviser** (486)
revitalize **revitaliser** (486)
revive **ranimer** (220)
revive **raviver** (276)
revoke **révoquer** (219)
revolt **révolter** (27)
revolutionize **révolutionner** (171)
reward **récompenser** (336)
rewind **rembobiner** (329)
rewrap **remballer** (326)
rewrite **récrire** (177)
rewrite **réécrire** (177)
rhyme **rimer** (220)
ricochet **ricocher** (82)
rid of, to get **se débarrasser de** (79, 122)
ridicule **ridiculiser** (486)
rifle through **trifouiller dans** (233)
ring **carillonner** (171)
ring **tinter** (464)
ring **sonner**
rinse **rincer** (99)
ripen **mûrir** (249)
rise up against **s'insurger contre** (33, 283)
risk **risquer** (219)
rival **rivaliser** (486)
rivet **river** (276)
roam around **vadrouiller** (233)
roam, wander **vaguer** (307)
roar **mugir** (229)
roar **rugir** (229)
roar with laughter **se bidonner** (122, 171)
roast **rôtir** (229)
rock **bercer** (99)
rock climb **varapper** (235)
roll **bouler** (421)
roll **rouler**
roll up **enrouler** (421)
romanize **romaniser** (486)
round (off) **arrondir** (229)
row **ramer** (27)
rub **frotter** (79)
rub elbows with **coudoyer** (187)
rubberize **caoutchouter** (28)
ruin **bousiller** (477)
ruin **délabrer** (407)
ruin **ruiner** (329)
ruin, smash up **esquinter** (90)
rule over **régenter** (464)
run **courir**
run away **déguerpir** (95)
run away **fuguer** (307)
run away **se sauver**
run off **filer** (27)
run out of breath **s'essouffler** (122, 445)
run to **accourir**
rush **se précipiter** (122, 251)
rush **brusquer** (219)
rush forward **s'élancer** (33, 342)
rush toward **se ruer sur/vers** (114, 122)
rust **rouiller** (233)

S

sabotage **saboter** (96)
sacrifice **sacrifier** (212)
sadden **attrister** (28)
sadden **désoler** (421)
saddle **seller** (326)
safeguard **sauvegarder** (240)
sail **naviguer**
sail, drift **voguer** (307)
sale, to put on **solder** (27)
salivate **saliver** (426)
salt **saler** (326)
salvage **récupérer** (203)

sample **échantillonner** (171)
sanctify **sanctifier** (212)
sanction (law) **sanctionner** (443)
sand **poncer** (342)
sand, to get buried in **s'ensabler** (33, 407)
satisfy **satisfaire**
saturate **saturer** (54)
save **sauver**
save **épargner** (10)
save (computer) **sauvegarder** (240)
saw **scier** (41)
say **dire**
scaffolding, to put up **échafauder** (447)
scan (image) **scanner** (171)
scan (verse) **scander** (240)
scandalize **scandaliser** (486)
scare away **effaroucher** (285)
scatter **éparpiller** (477)
scatter **parsemer** (341)
schematize **schématiser** (486)
school **scolariser** (486)
scoff at **narguer** (307)
scold **quereller** (477)
scold **gronder**
scold **engueuler** (421)
scorn **bafouer qqn** (269)
scrape **racler** (326)
scratch **égratigner** (441)
scratch **érafler** (439)
scratch **griffer** (439)
scratch **gratter**
screen (medical) **dépister** (215)
screw on **visser** (486)
scribble **griffonner** (171)
scrub **briquer** (219)
scrub **récurer** (54)
scrutinize **scruter** (32)
sculpt **sculpter** (8)
scuttle **saborder** (27)
seal **cacheter** (267)
search **fureter** (17)
search **perquisitionner** (171)
search **fouiller**
search **rechercher** (93)
season **assaisonner** (171)
season (soldiers) **aguerrir** (229)
secrete **sécréter** (87)
seduce **séduire**
see **voir**
see again **revoir**
see someone home **reconduire** (106)
see someone off, home **raccompagner** (441)
seek **chercher**
seek after **quêter** (47)
seem **sembler** (Def. and Imp.)
seem **paraître**
seem **sembler** (Def. and Imp.)
segment **segmenter** (60)
seize **s'emparer de** (33, 101)
seize **saisir**
seize **pogner** (441)
select **sélectionner** (171)
sell **vendre**
sell out of **écouler** (421)
send **expédier** (212)
send **envoyer**
send back **renvoyer** (200)
sensitize **sensibiliser** (486)
separate **disjoindre** (268)
separate **séparer**
separate in two **dédoubler** (407)
sermonize **sermonner** (171)
serve **servir**
serve again **resservir** (437)
serve oneself **se servir**
session, to be in **siéger** (52)
set **fixer** (27)
set free **délivrer** (21)
set free **affranchir** (72)
set on fire **incendier** (212)
set up **aménager** (305)
settle (debt) **s'acquitter de** (33, 374)
settle down, subside; **se tasser** (84, 122)
settle in **s'implanter** (33, 90)
sew **coudre**
sew up again **recoudre** (123)
sextuple **sextupler** (326)
shade **ombrager** (189)
shade **ombrer** (22)
shake **ébranler** (326)
shake **secouer**
shake **branler** (498)
shake **agiter** (251)
share **partager** (501)
sharpen **affûter** (173)
sharpen **aiguiser** (486)
shave **raser** (86)
shave oneself **se raser** (86, 122)
shear **tondre** (394)
sheath **gainer** (329)
shell (military) **canonner** (171)
shell (remove a shell) **décortiquer** (219)
shelter from **abriter de/contre** (251)
shield **blinder** (27)
shift ahead/back (hour) **décaler** (326)
shine **briller** (477)
shine **resplendir** (229)
shine **rayonner** (171)
shine **luire** (Def. and Imp.)
shiny, to make **lustrer** (299)
shiver **frissonner** (171)
shiver **grelotter** (79)
shock **choquer** (284)
shock **estomaquer** (219)
shoes, to put back on **se rechausser** (85)
shoes, to put on **chausser** (79)
shoot **fusiller** (477)
shop **magasiner** (159)
shopping (online), to go **magasiner en ligne**
short-circuit **court-circuiter** (215)
shorten **écourter** (160)
shorten **raccourcir** (95)
shoulder **épauler** (421)
shout **crier**

shove, bump **bousculer** (81)
shovel **pelleter** (267)
show **montrer**
show **manifester** (299)
show again **remontrer** (299)
shrink **rétrécir** (95)
shrink **se ratatiner** (122, 329)
shrivel up **se rabougrir** (214, 249)
shudder **frémir**
sift **cribler** (326)
sift **tamiser** (486)
sigh **soupirer** (21)
sign **signer**
signal **signaler**
signify **signifier** (212)
silent, to be **se taire**
silhouette **silhouetter** (386)
simmer **mijoter** (96)
simplify **simplifier** (212)
simulate **simuler** (81)
sin **pécher**
sing **chanter**
sing oneself **chantonner** (171)
sink **s'affaisser** (33, 274)
sink **sombrer** (22)
sip **siroter** (96)
sit down **s'asseoir**
sit down again **se rasseoir** (51) (aux. **être**; *part. passé* rassis, rassise)
sit down at a table (for a meal) **s'attabler** (33)
sit on (eggs) **couver** (28)
situate **situer** (483)
skate **patiner**
sketch **ébaucher** (469)
sketch **esquisser** (183)
ski **skier** (129)
skim (reading) **parcourir** (125)
skim off **écrémer** (87)
skimp **mégoter** (96)
skimp on **lésiner sur** (159)
skip **sautiller** (477)
slalom **slalomer** (71)
slander **diffamer** (71)
slander **médire**
slander **calomnier** (212)
slap **gifler** (439)
slash **balafrer** (27)
slash **sabrer** (22)
slash **taillader** (27)
slaughter **abattre**
sled **luger** (271)
sleep **dormir**
slice **trancher** (78)
slide **glisser** (73)
slow down **ralentir** (95)
smaller, to make/get **rapetisser** (486)
smash in (car, train) **téléscoper** (163)
smash into **percuter** (169)
smash, shatter **fracasser** (84)
smear **enduire** (133)
smell **flairer** (22)
smell **sentir**
smell up **empuantir** (210)
smile **sourire**
smoke **fumer**
smooth **lisser** (73)
snake, meander **serpenter** (60)
sneak in without paying **resquiller** (477)
sneak through **se faufiler** (27, 122)
sneeze **éternuer** (114)
sniffle **renifler** (439)
snore **ronfler** (445)
snow **neiger** (Def. and Imp.)
snub **snober** (27)
soak **détremper** (464)
soak **imbiber** (215)
soak **tremper** (247)
sob **sangloter** (96)
sober up **dégriser** (486)
socialize **socialiser** (486)
soften **amollir** (229)
soften **assouplir** (423)
soften **mollir** (229)
soften **se velouter** (28, 122)
soften **adoucir** (229)
soften **ramollir** (229)
soil **entacher** (82)
soil **salir**
soil **souiller**
sojourn **séjourner**
solder **souder** (27)
solicit **solliciter** (251)
solidify **solidifier** (212)
solubilize **solubiliser** (486)
solve **résoudre**
somersault **culbuter** (28)
sort **trier** (129)
soundproof **insonoriser** (486)
sour **aigrir** (229)
sow **semer** (341)
space **échelonner** (171)
sparing in the use of, to be **ménager** (305)
sparkle **scintiller** (477)
spatialize **spatialiser** (486)
speak **parler**
speak patois **patoiser** (486)
speak with a nasal twang **nasiller** (477)
specialize **se spécialiser** (486)
specify **préciser** (486)
specify **spécifier** (212)
speculate **spéculer** (81)
spell **épeler** (38)
spell **orthographier** (212)
spend (money) **dépenser**
spend (time) **passer**
spend the night away from one's house **découcher** (121)
spice up **épicer** (342)
spin **vriller** (477)
spin around **virevolter** (27)
spiritualize **spiritualiser** (486)
spit **cracher** (82)
splash **éclabousser** (79)
split **scinder** (240)
split **fendre**
split up **désunir** (229)
split up **sectionner** (171)
spoil **gâcher** (82)
spoil **gâter**
spoil **pourrir** (249)
sponge **éponger** (283)

spool **embobiner** (329)
spool **bobiner** (329)
spray **vaporiser** (486)
spread **répandre**
spread (butter, pâté) **tartiner** (329)
spread apart **écarter** (69)
spread out **étendre** (462)
spread out, display **étaler** (326)
sprinkle **asperger** (283)
sprinkle **saupoudrer** (299)
sprint **sprinter** (464)
spurt **gicler** (326)
spurt up **rejaillir** (423)
spy on **épier** (212)
spy on **espionner** (171)
squat **s'accroupir** (214)
squeeze **serrer**
squint **loucher** (469)
stab **zigouiller** (233)
stab **poignarder** (240)
stabilize **stabiliser** (486)
stack **superposer** (350)
stagger **chanceler** (38)
stagger **tituber** (32)
stagnate **croupir** (229)
stagnate **stagner** (441)
stagnate **vivoter** (96)
stain **maculer** (81)
stain with **tacher de** (82)
stall **caler** (27)
stammer **bafouiller** (233)
stammer **balbutier** (212)
stammer **bégayer** (179)
stamp **estamper** (247)
stamp **timbrer** (466)
stand someone up **plaquer** (219)
stand up **se dresser** (23, 122)
staple **agrafer** (27)
staple (Qué.) **brocher** (285)
starch **amidonner** (171)
stare at someone **dévisager** (305)
start **commencer**
start **amorcer** (342)
start again **redémarrer** (22)
start again **repartir** (327) (aux. **être**)
start out **démarrer** (27)
starve **affamer** (71)
state **énoncer** (371)
stay **demeurer**
stay **rester**
stay up **veiller** (109)
steal **choper** (163)
steal **faucher** (82)
steal **chiper** (251)
steal **dérober** (498)
steal **subtiliser** (486)
steal **voler**
steep **macérer** (203)
step over **enjamber** (240)
sterilize **stériliser** (486)
stick to **coller à** (445)
stick together **agglutiner** (329)
stiffen **raidir** (229)
stigmatize **stigmatiser** (486)
stimulate **stimuler** (81)
stimulate someone's appetite **allécher** (87)
stink **puer** (Def. and Imp.)
stipulate **stipuler** (81)
stir **remuer** (483)
stitch **brocher** (285)
stock **stocker** (27)
stockpile **emmagasiner** (159)
stone **lapider** (251)
stop **stopper** (163)
stop **arrêter**
stop (oneself) **s'arrêter**
store in a warehouse **entreposer** (350)
storm **tempêter** (47)
straddle, ride **chevaucher** (285)
straighten up **redresser** (353)
strain **peiner** (329)
strangle **étrangler** (326)
stratify **stratifier** (212)
stream **ruisseler** (38)
strengthen **affermir** (229)
strengthen **raffermir** (229)
stress **stresser** (353)
stretch (**étirer** (466)
stretch **tendre**
stretch one's legs **se dégourdir** (210, 214)
stretch oneself **s'étirer** (182, 466)
stretch oneself **s'étendre**
stretch out **allonger** (442)
strew something with **joncher qqch de** (93)
striate **strier** (129)
strike (lightning) **foudroyer** (187)
strike down **terrasser** (84)
strip **dépouiller** (233)
strip (paint, wood) **décaper** (235)
stripe with **zébrer de** (356)
stroll **se balader** (26, 122)
stroll **flâner** (443)
structure **structurer** (54)
struggle **se démener** (122, 290)
struggle **lutter** (425)
struggle **vasouiller** (233)
strut around **se pavaner** (122)
stubborn, to be **s'opiniâtrer** (33)
stuck, to get **s'enliser** (33, 486)
study **étudier**
study hard **bûcher** (285)
stuff **bourrer** (22)
stuff oneself **s'empiffrer** (33, 466)
stuff with (cooking), cram with **farcir de** (229)
stumble, trip **trébucher** (82)
stun **ébahir** (95)
stun **sidérer** (203)
stun **abasoudir**
stun **étourdir**
stupefy **abasourdir**
stupefy **stupéfier** (212)
style, to go out of **se démoder** (27)
stylize **styliser** (486)
subjugate **asservir** (229)
sublimate **sublimer** (220)
submerge **submerger** (283)
submit **soumettre**
subordinate **subordonner** (171)

subscribe for someone to **abonner à** (171)
subscribe to **s'abonner à** (83, 171)
subscribe to **souscrire à** (177)
subsidize **subventionner** (171)
substitute for **substituer à** (483)
subtract **soustraire** (474) (no *passé simple* or imp. subj.)
subvert **subvertir** (229)
succeed **succéder à** (87)
succeed **réussir**
succumb **succomber** (240)
suck **suçoter** (96)
suck **sucer**
suckle (animal) **allaiter** (27)
suffer **souffrir**
suffice **suffire** (Def. and Imp.)
suffocate **asphyxier** (41)
suffocate **étouffer** (353)
suffocate **suffoquer (de)** (219)
suggest **suggérer** (356)
suit **convenir**
suit **seoir** (Def. and Imp.)
sulk **bouder** (240)
summarize **résumer** (238)
summon **sommer** (310)
supervise **superviser** (486)
supper, to have **souper** (124)
supply **approvisionner** (171)
supply **ravitailler** (477)
supply with **munir de** (229)
support **soutenir** (463)
suppose **supposer** (350)
suppress **supprimer** (220)
surcharge **surtaxer** (27)
sure, to make **s'assurer**
surf (Internet) **naviguer**
surf, netsurf (Internet) **surfer** (27)
surmount **surmonter** (298) (aux. **avoir**)
surpass **surpasser** (84)
surprise **surprendre**
surrender **capituler** (81)
surround **environner** (171)
surround with **entourer de** (21)
surround, define **cerner** (27)
survey (land) **arpenter** (28)
survive **survivre**
suspect **se douter** (122, 173)
suspect of **soupçonner de** (443)
suspect of **suspecter de** (113)
suspend **suspendre** (335)
suture **suturer** (54)
swaddle **langer** (283)
swallow **avaler** (27)
swallow **gober** (27)
swallow up **engouffrer** (445)
swap **troquer** (219)
swarm **grouiller** (233)
swarm **fourmiller** (477)
swear **jurer**
swear in **assermenter** (374)
sweat **suer** (483)
sweat **transpirer** (466)
sweep **balayer**
sweep a chimney **ramoner** (461)
sweeten **édulcorer** (22)
sweeten **sucrer** (21)
sweet-talk **baratiner** (329)
swell **s'enfler** (361, 445)
swell up **se tuméfier** (212 (aux. **être**))
swim **nager**
swipe **rafler** (439)
swirl **tourbillonner** (171)
switch off **couper**
swoon **se pâmer** (71, 122)
symbolize **symboliser** (486)
sympathize **compatir** (95)
synchronize **synchroniser** (486)
synthesize **synthétiser** (486)
systematize **systématiser** (486)

T

take **prendre**
take a sample **prélever** (278)
take again **reprendre**
take away decorations **dégarnir** (229)
take back **reprendre**
take back **remporter** (349)
take back **remmener** (290)
take back, resume **reprendre** (357)
take care of, look after someone **soigner qqn** (10)
take for a walk **balader** (26)
take for a walk **promener** (290)
take off **ôter** (498)
take off (airplane) **décoller** (385)
take off one's shoes **se déchausser** (80, 122)
take out the color **déteindre** (207)
take place **se passer** (Def. and Imp.)
take place **se dérouler** (421)
take root **s'enraciner** (33, 329)
take shelter (from) **s'abriter de** (122, 251)
take shorthand **sténographier** (212)
take the place of honor **trôner** (27)
talk **parler**
talk at length **discourir sur** (125)
tame **apprivoiser** (486)
tame **dompter** (107)
tamp down, pack down **tasser** (84)
tamper with **tripatouiller** (233)

tan (leather) **tanner** (171)
tangle **enchevêtrer** (299)
tangle up **embrouiller** (233)
tap **tapoter** (96)
tap **taper** (235)
target **cibler** (27)
tarnish **galvauder** (26)
tarnish **ternir** (229)
taste **goûter**
taste, sample food **déguster** (53)
tattoo **tatouer** (175)
tax **taxer** (27)
teach **enseigner**
teach someone to read and write **alphabétiser** (486)
tear **déchirer**
tear pieces **écharper** (59)
tease **taquiner** (329)
telegraph **télégraphier** (212)
telephone **téléphoner**
televise **télédiffuser** (32)
televise **téléviser** (486)
tell (a story) **raconter**
temper **tempérer** (203)
temper, to be in a bad **décolérer** (356)
tempt **tenter**
tense **crisper** (27)
tenure, to give **titulariser** (486)
terminate **terminer**
terrify **épouvanter** (90)
terrify **terrifier** (212)
terrorize **terroriser** (486)
test **expérimenter** (464)
test **éprouver**
test **tester** (160)
testify **attester** (160)
testify **témoigner** (10)
thank **remercier**
thaw **dégeler** (242)
theorize **théoriser** (486)
thicken **épaissir** (95)
thin, to make **amaigrir** (282)
think **penser**
think **réfléchir**
thinner, to get **mincir** (95)
thread **enfiler** (329)
threaten with **menacer de** (342)
throw **jeter**
throw **lancer**
thunder **fulminer** (465)
thunder **tonner** (Def. and Imp.)
tickle **chatouiller** (233)
tidy up **ranger**
tie **lier** (129)
tie **nouer** (269)
tie down **arrimer** (27)
tie up **attacher** (82)
tie up **ligoter** (96)
tile **carreler** (38)
tilt **pencher** (93)
time **chronométrer** (87)
tinker **bricoler** (32)
tint **teinter** (464)
tintinnabulate **tintinnabuler** (81)
tip off **tuyauter** (27)
tip off **rancarder** (27)
tire **fatiguer** (307)
tired, to get **se lasser** (84, 122)
title **titrer** (466)
toast (drink) **trinquer** (284)
tolerate **tolérer** (356)
tolerate **supporter**
tone up **tonifier** (212)
tonsure **tonsurer** (54)
topple over **basculer** (81)
torment **tenailler** (477)
torment **tourmenter** (60)
torpedo **torpiller** (477)
torture **supplicier** (41)
torture **torturer** (54)
toss around **tanguer** (307)
total **totaliser** (486)
touch **toucher**
tousle someone's hair **ébouriffer** (215)
tousle someone's hair **décoiffer qqn** (443)
tow **remorquer** (284)
tow **tracter**
trace **tracer** (342)
track **traquer** (219)
track **pister** (27)
trade with **commercer avec** (99)
traffic **trafiquer** (219)
trample **piétiner** (329)
trample on **fouler** (421)
transcribe **transcrire** (177)
transfer **transborder**
transfer **transférer** (356)
transfer (funds) **virer** (21)
transform into **transformer en** (227)
transfuse **transfuser** (32)
transgress **transgresser** (353)
translate **traduire**
transmit **transmettre**
transmute **transmuer** (483)
transplant **transhumer** (238)
transplant **transplanter** (90)
transport **transporter** (349)
transport **véhiculer** (81)
transpose **transposer** (350)
trap **piéger** (52)
traumatize **traumatiser** (486)
travel **voyager**
travel through **parcourir** (125)
traverse **traverser**
treat **traiter**
tremble **trembloter** (96)
tremble with **trembler de** (407)
trick **tricher**
trickle down **dégouliner** (329)
trigger **déclencher** (285)
trim **tailler** (477)
trim **rogner** (441)
trip **buter** (173)
triple **tripler** (326)
triumph **triompher** (27)
trivialize **banaliser** (486)
trot **trotter** (246)
trot along **trottiner** (329)
trumpet **trompeter** (267)
truncate **tronquer** (284)
truth about a matter, to see the **se détromper** (480)
try **tâcher** (82)
try **essayer**

try **tenter**
try again **réessayer** (204)
try one's best **s'ingénier à** (309) (aux. **être**)
try to please **complaire à** (345)
tu, to use **tutoyer**
tumble **dégringoler** (498)
tumble down **dévaler** (27)
turn **tourner**
turn aside **détourner**
turn back **rebrousser** (353)
turn blue **bleuir** (229)
turn brown **roussir** (95)
turn green again **reverdir**
turn oneself away from **se détourner** (122, 161)
turn over, collapse **capoter**
turn pale **pâlir** (423)
turn pink **rosir** (95)
turn up **retrousser** (353)
twist **entortiller** (477)
twist **tordre**
type **taper** (235)
type **dactylographier** (366)
tyrannize **tyranniser** (486)

U

ugly, to make **enlaidir** (210)
ulcerate **ulcérer** (203)
unaware of, to be **ignorer** (22)
unblock **dégorger** (283)
unblock **débloquer** (219)
unbolt **déboulonner** (171)
unbridle **débrider** (251)
unbuckle **déboucler** (326)
unbutton **déboutonner** (171)
unchain **déchaîner** (329)
unclench **décontracter** (160)
unclog **déboucher** (285)
uncross (arms, legs) **décroiser** (486)
undergo **subir** (95)
underline **souligner** (10)
undermine **saper** (59)
understand **comprendre**
undertake **entreprendre**
undo **défaire**
undress **dévêtir** (493)
undress oneself **se déshabiller** (250)
undress oneself **se dévêtir** (250, 493)
undulate **ondoyer** (187)
undulate **onduler** (81)
unearth **déterrer** (196)
unearth **dénicher** (285)
unemployed, to be **chômer** (27)
unfasten **dégrafer** (27)
unfold **déplier** (389)
unhook **décrocher** (82)
uniform, to make **uniformiser** (486)
unify **unifier** (212)
unionize **syndicaliser** (486)
unionize **syndiquer** (219)
unite **unir**
unlace **délacer** (342)
unlearn **désapprendre** (42)
unload **décharger** (91)
unlock **déverrouiller** (233)
unpack **déballer** (498)
unplug **débrancher** (285)
unroll **dérouler** (421)
unscrew **dévisser** (486)
unseal **décacheter** (267)
unstick **décoller** (385)
unstitch **découdre** (123)
untangle **démêler** (82)
untie **délier** (389)
untie **dénouer** (269)
untie **détacher** (285)
unveil **dévoiler** (498)
unwind **se défouler** (122, 421)
unwind **dévider** (251)
unworthy of, to show oneself **démériter de** (293)
up, to get **se lever**
up, to go **monter**
up, to take **monter**
upload **télécharger vers le serveur** (91)
uproot **déraciner** (159)
uproot **arracher**
upset **vexer** (27)
upset, to be **s'inquiéter**
urbanize **urbaniser** (486)
urinate **uriner** (465)
use **employer**
use **utiliser**
use trickery **ruser** (32)
use up **user** (32)
used again, to become **se réhabituer** (33, 483)
used to, to get **s'habituer** (33, 483)
used to, to get **accoutumer** (238)
usurp **usurper** (59)
utilize **utiliser**

V

vaccinate against **vacciner contre** (329)
vacillate **vaciller** (477)
validate **valider** (251)
value **priser** (486)
vanquish **vaincre**
vaporize **vaporiser** (486)
varnish **vernir** (229)
vary **varier** (129)
vaunt, praise **vanter** (90)
vegetate **végéter** (356)
veil **voiler** (27)
venerate **vénérer** (356)
ventilate **ventiler** (266)
venture **aventurer** (148)
verbalize **verbaliser** (486)
verify **vérifier** (212)
versify **versifier** (41)
vibrate **vibrer** (22)
view, look at **visionner** (171)
violate, rape **violer** (498)
visit **visiter**
visualize **visualiser** (486)
vituperate **vitupérer** (203)
vocalize **vocaliser** (486)
vomit **vomir** (229)
vote again **revoter** (96)
vote for/against **voter pour/contre** (96)
vous, to use **vouvoyer**
vow **vouer à** (269)
vulgarize, popularize **vulgariser** (486)

W

waddle like a duck **se dandiner** (122, 329)
wade **patauger** (305)
wait **attendre**
wake up **se réveiller**
wake up (someone who's asleep) **réveiller** (109) (See 414)
walk **marcher**
walk along **cheminer** (465)
walk, to take a **se promener**
wall in **emmurer** (32)
wall in/up **murer** (54)
wallow **se vautrer** (122)
waltz **valser** (492)
wander **errer** (27)
wander **vagabonder** (248)
want **vouloir**
warm oneself up **se chauffer** (122, 235)
warm up **se réchauffer** (85)
warn **prévenir**
warn about **alerter de** (173)
warn about **avertir de** (229)
wash **laver**
wash one's face (w/washcloth) **se débarbouiller** (33, 233)
wash oneself **se laver**
waste **dilapider** (215)
waste **gaspiller** (477)
watch **guetter** (386)
watch **surveiller** (109)
watch **regarder**
water **arroser** (79)
water (animals) **abreuver** (26)
water (eye) **larmoyer** (187)
water down **délayer** (330)
waterproof, to make **étancher** (78)
wax **cirer** (466)
weaken **affaiblir** (229)
weaken **faiblir** (392)
weaken **défaillir** (222)
wear **porter**
wear down **vanner** (171)
wear thin **élimer** (27)
weave **tisser** (73)
weed **désherber** (27)
weigh **peser**
weigh down **alourdir de** (229)
weigh down **appesantir** (229)
weigh down **oppresser** (360)
weight, to lose **maigrir**
weight, to put back on **regrossir** (282)
weight, to put on **grossir** (282)
welcome **accueillir**
westernize **occidentaliser** (486)
wet **mouiller** (233)
wet, to get oneself **se mouiller** (83, 233)
whimper **pleurnicher** (285)
whinny, bray ***hennir** (229)
whip **flageller** (326)
whip **fouetter** (447)
whirl **tournoyer** (308)
whisper **susurrer** (22)
whisper **chuchoter**
whistle **siffloter** (96)
whistle **siffler**
whiten **blanchir**
wiggle **tortiller** (477)
wiggle **frétiller** (477)
will, to make out a (legal term) **tester** (160)
win **remporter** (349)
win **gagner**
wipe **torcher** (285)
wipe **essuyer**
wish **souhaiter**
withdraw **se retirer**
withdraw (in someone's favor) **se désister de (en faveur de qqn)** (53)
wobble **flageoler** (498)
wonder **se demander** (122, 147)
word **libeller** (27)
work **travailler**
work hard **besogner** (441)
work hard **bosser** (79)
worry **s'inquiéter**
worry someone **inquiéter qqn** (87) (See 258)
worsen **empirer** (466)
worth, to be **valoir**
wrap **emballer** (421)
wriggle **gigoter** (96)
wrinkle **rider** (27)
write **écrire**
write **rédiger** (218)
write about **disserter sur** (160)
write badly **écrivasser** (84)
wrong, to be **clocher** (285)
wrong, to be **se tromper**

X

x-ray **radiographier** (212)

Y

yap, yelp **japper** (235)
yawn **bâiller** (477)
yell **gueuler** (421)
yell **vociférer** (356)
yell at the top of one's lungs **s'époumoner** (461)
yellow, turn yellow **jaunir** (229)
yield **céder**
yodel **yodler** (326)

Z

zigzag **zigzaguer** (307)
zip up **zipper** (235)
zone **zoner** (461)
zoom in, zoom out **zoomer** (71)

Index of 2,600 additional verbs keyed to listing of 501 French verbs

The number after each verb is the number of the fully conjugated model verb in the main section. If the French verb you want is reflexive (for example, **s'appeler** or **se lever**), you will find it listed alphabetically under the first letter of the verb. The reflexive pronoun **s'** or **se** is given in parentheses after the verb: **appeler (s'), lever (se).** Sometimes two verb numbers are listed for a reflexive verb. For example, **s'abonner** is keyed to verb 171 (**donner**) and to verb 83 (**se cacher**) because it is a reflexive regular **-er** verb. If a verb is in the Defective and Impersonal verb section it will be marked Def. and Imp. Several verbs in this list are keyed to two verbs because you need to make two spelling changes.

Note: The English definitions are a guide to the most common meanings. In some cases we have also included a preposition when it is likely that you will use it along with the verb. There are obviously many more definitions for the verbs in this list. Think of the definitions as a way to make sure you're looking up the right word!

A

abandonner to abandon (171)
abdiquer to abdicate (219)
abhorrer to abhor, loathe (27)
abîmer to damage, spoil (27)
abjurer to abjure, renounce (148)
abominer to abominate, loathe (465)
abonder en to abound in, be plentiful (26)
abonner (s') à to subscribe to (83, 171)
abonner à to subscribe for someone to (171)
aborder to accost, approach (26)
abouter to join tip to tip, end to end (173)
aboutir à/dans to succeed, end up in (229)
aboyer to bark (187)
abraser to abrade (27)
abréger to shorten, abridge (52)
abreuver to water (animals) (26)
abriter de/contre to shelter from (251)
abriter (s') de to take shelter (from) (122, 251)
abrutir to exhaust (229)
absenter (s') de to absent oneself from (26)
absorber to absorb (385)
abstraire to abstract, isolate (474) (no *passé simple* or imp. subj.)
abuser de qqch to abuse, misuse (32)
accabler to overwhelm (407)
accaparer to capture, monopolize (27)
accéder à to get to, attain (87)
accélérer to accelerate (356)
accentuer to accentuate, stress (483)
accessoiriser to accessorize (486)
accidenter to damage, injure (27)
acclimater to acclimate (27)
accommoder to accommodate (147)
accomplir to accomplish (392)
accoster to accost (160)
accoucher de to give birth to (121)
accouder (s') sur to lean one's elbow on (33, 421)
accoupler to couple (27)
accoutumer to get used to (238)
accréditer to accredit (251)
accrocher (s') to hang on, collide (13)
accroupir (s') to squat, crouch (214)
acculer to corner somebody (81)
acculturer to acculturate (27)
accumuler to accumulate (81)
accuser (s') to accuse oneself (16, 33)
acharner (s') contre qqn to dog someone (27, 33)
acheminer to direct towards (465)
acquiescer to agree, approve (342)

acquitter (de) to acquit, release (from) (374)
acquitter (s') de to pay off (duty), settle (debt) (33, 374)
actionner to activate (171)
activer to speed up, pep up (26)
actualiser to bring up to date (16)
adapter à to fit, adapt to (8)
additionner to add up (171)
adhérer to join, be a member (87)
adhérer à to adhere to (87)
adjoindre à to associate (with) (268)
adjuger to award (283)
adjurer to implore, beg (272)
administrer to administer (26)
admonester to admonish (27)
adopter to adopt (8)
adosser to lean against (79)
adoucir to soften, sweeten (229)
adresser (s') à qqn to speak to someone, address someone (33, 79)
aduler to adulate, flatter (81)
advenir to happen, occur, come to pass (Def. and Imp.)
aérer to air, aerate (87)
affadir to make (something) dull (229)
affaiblir to weaken (229)
affaisser (s') to collapse, sink (33, 274)
affamer to starve (71)
affecter de to pretend to (8)
affectionner to have a liking for (171)
affermer to lease, rent (227)
affermir to strengthen (229)
afficher to display (94)
affilier (s') à to affiliate to (33, 41)
affirmer to affirm (227)
affliger de to afflict with (119)
affluer to abound (114)
affoler (s') to panic (33, 421)
affranchir to set free; to stamp (frank) (72)
affréter to charter (boat, plane) (87)
affronter to confront (113)
affubler to don (clothing) (407)
affûter to hone, sharpen (173)
agencer to arrange, combine (342)
agenouiller (s') to kneel (233)
agglutiner to agglutinate, stick together (329)
aggraver to aggravate, make worse (276)
agiter to wag, wave, shake (251)
agrafer to staple, fasten (27)
agrandir to enlarge (245)
agréer to accept (128)
agrémenter de to embellish with (60)
agresser to attack (23)
agripper to grab, grip (163)
aguerrir to harden, season (soldiers) (229)
aguicher to entice, seduce (285)
aiguiser to sharpen (486)
ahurir to astound, stun (229)
aigrir to sour (229)
aiguiller to orient, steer (477)
aiguillonner to goad (171)
aimanter to magnetize (90)
ajourner to postpone (433)
ajuster to adjust (28)
alarmer to alarm (310)
alerter de to warn about (173)
aliéner to alienate (87)
aligner to align (26)
alimenter de to feed with (60)
allaiter to breast-feed, nurse (infant), suckle (animal) (27)
allécher to stimulate someone's appetite (87)
alléger to ease, lighten (52)
allier to ally, tie together (41)
allonger to stretch out (442)
allouer to allocate, grant (281)
allumer to light, turn on (238)
alourdir de to weigh down (229)
alphabétiser to teach someone to read and write (486)
altérer to alter, spoil (87)
alterner to alternate (27)
alunir to land on the moon (229)
amadouer to coax (269)
amaigrir to make thin (282)
amarrer to moor, tie down (27)
amasser to amass, pile up (92)
ambitionner de to aspire to (171)
améliorer to improve, ameliorate (22)
aménager to set up, install (305)
amender to amend, correct (27)
américaniser to Americanize (32)
ameuter to draw/incite a crowd (374)
amidonner to starch (171)
amincir to have a slimming effect (229)
amoindrir to lessen (229)
amollir to soften (229)

amonceler to amass, pile up (38)
amorcer to start, boot (computer) (342)
amortir to cushion, soften (229)
amplifier de to amplify with/by (322)
amputer to amputate (251)
analyser to analyze (32)
ancrer to anchor (27)
anéantir to annihilate (229)
angliciser to anglicize (23)
angoisser to cause anguish, distress (27)
animer to animate (27)
annexer to annex (27)
annihiler to annihilate (27)
annuler to annul, cancel (81)
anoblir to ennoble (423)
ânonner to drone, stumble through a public reading (171)
anticiper to anticipate (329)
antidater to antedate, backdate (28)
apaiser to calm down, pacify (27)
apitoyer to inspire pity (187)
aplanir to make level, smooth (229)
aplatir to flatten (229)
appauvrir to impoverish (229)
applaudir de to applaud for (229)
appliquer to apply (219)
appesantir to weigh down (229)
appréhender to fear, grasp, apprehend (legal term) (27)
apprêter (s') à qqch to get oneself ready for (48, 363)
apprêter to get ready, prepare (363)
apprivoiser to tame (486)
approcher (s') to approach, come near (33, 43)
approfondir to deepen (229)
approprier (s') to appropriate (83, 212)
approvisionner to supply (171)
appuyer to lean, press (192)
arabiser to arabize (486)
arbitrer to arbitrate, referee (27)
arc-bouter (s') à to lean against (33)
archiver to archive (27)
armer to arm (238)
arnaquer to cheat, swindle (284)
arpenter to pace, survey (land) (28)
arquer to arch, curve (284)
arranger (s') to come to an agreement (33, 46)
arrimer to secure, tie down (27)
arroger (s') to claim falsely (33, 305)
arrondir to round (off) (229)
arroser to water (79)
articuler to articulate (81)
asperger to spray, sprinkle (283)
asphyxier to asphyxiate, suffocate (41)
aspirer to inhale (21)
assainir to clean, make healthier (229)
assaisonner to season (171)
assassiner to murder, assassinate (159)
assécher to drain, dry (429)
assembler to assemble (407)
assermenter to swear in (374)
asservir to subjugate (229)
assigner to assign (441)
assimiler to assimilate, take in (27)
assimiler qqn/qqch à to compare someone/something to (27)
associer (qqch à) to link (something with), associate (41)
assombrir to darken (229)
assommer to knock out, stun (310)
assortir to match (229)
assoupir (s') to nod off (229)
assouplir to soften (423)
assourdir to deafen (229)
assumer to assume, accept (27)
atomiser to atomize (486)
attabler (s') to sit down at a table (for a meal) (33)
attacher to tie up (82)
attaquer to attack (219)
attarder to delay (240)
attarder (s') to dawdle, fall behind schedule (33)
atteler to harness (horses) (38)
attendre (s') à to expect (208)
attendrir to inspire pity, tenderize (meat) (229)
atténuer to relieve, lighten, ease (114)
atterrir to land (229)
attester to testify (160)
attiédir to make lukewarm (229)
attribuer à to attribute to (114)
attrister to sadden (28)
ausculter to auscultate, listen to someone's chest (28)
automatiser to automate (486)
autoriser to authorize (16)
avaler to swallow (27)
avancer (s') to advance (oneself) (33, 61)
avantager to favor (305)
aventurer to venture (148)

avérer (s') to prove/turn out to be (33, 87)
avertir de to warn about (229)
aveugler to blind (27)
avilir to degrade, depreciate (423)
aviser to notify (32)
aviser (s') to notice, become aware (32, 33)
aviver to enliven, excite (486)
avoisiner to be close to, border (159)
avorter to abort (27)
avouer to admit (269)

B

babiller sur to gossip about (27)
bachoter to cram for an exam (96)
bâcler to botch up (445)
badiner to exchange banter, jest (167)
bafouer qqn to flout, scorn (269)
bafouiller to stammer (233)
bâfrer to guzzle, eat like a pig (82)
bagarrer to argue, wrangle (435)
baigner to bathe (10)
bâiller to yawn (477)
bâillonner to gag, muzzle (171)
baiser to kiss, have intercourse (Watch out! Unless you're kissing someone's cheek or hand, avoid *baiser*!) (27)
balader to take for a walk (26)
balader (se) to stroll (26, 122)
balafrer to slash (27)
balbutier to stammer (212)
baliser to mark a path, mark off (486)
ballotter to jolt, bounce around (171)
banaliser to make commonplace, trivialize (486)
bander to bandage, blindfold (27)
bannir de to banish from (229)
baptiser to baptize (32)
baragouiner to jabber, speak badly (329)
baratiner to sweet-talk (329)
barber to bore (27)
barbouiller (de) to daub (with) (233)
barrer to bar (21)
basculer to topple over (81)
baser sur to base upon (32)
batailler to battle (477)
bâtonner to beat with a stick (171)
baver to drool, dribble (276)
bêcher to dig out/up (285)
becqueter to peck (267)
bégayer to stammer (179)
bénéficier de to profit from/by (389)
bercer to rock (99)
besogner to drudge, work hard (441)
beugler to low, bellow (27)
beurrer to butter (26)
bidonner (se) to roar with laughter (122, 171)
bifurquer to bifurcate, fork (284)
bivouaquer to bivouac (219)
blaguer to joke (307)
blaser (se) de to become indifferent to (33, 122)
blasphémer to blaspheme (356)
blêmir to become pale (229)
bleuir to turn blue (229)
blinder to shield, armor (27)
bloguer to blog (307)
blondir to become blond, bleach hair (210)
bloquer to block up (219)
blottir (se) to cuddle (214, 229)
bluffer to bluff (26)
bobiner to wind, spool (329)
boiter to limp (26)
bombarder to bombard (385)
bondir to leap (229)
bonifier to improve (41)
border to border (248)
borner to limit (27)
bosser to work hard (79)
boucher to block up (469)
boucler to buckle (469)
bouder to sulk (240)
bouffer to gobble up (235)
bougonner to grumble (171)
bouillonner to bubble (171)
bouler to roll (421)
bouleverser to overwhelm (492)
bouquiner to read (329)
bourdonner to buzz (171)
bourgeonner to bud (171)
bourrer to stuff (22)
boursoufler to bloat, puff up (445)
bousculer to shove, bump (81)
bousiller to ruin (477)
bouter to drive away (28)
boutonner to button (171)
boxer to box (26)
boycotter to boycott (373)
brailler to bawl, cry (477)
brandir to brandish (210)
branler to shake (Watch out! Avoid using this verb pronominally!) (498)
braquer to aim, point (284)
brasser to brew, stir (79)
braver to defy (276)
bredouiller to mumble (233)
bricoler to tinker, fix (32)
brider to bridle, restrain (329)
briller to shine (477)
brimer to bully (27)
briquer to scrub (219)

briser to break, smash (32)
brocher to stitch, staple (Qué.) (285)
broder to embroider (96)
bronzer to bronze, tan (134)
brouiller to blur, mix up (233)
brouter to graze (28)
broyer to crush, grind (187)
bruiner to drizzle (27)
brunir to brown (229)
brusquer to rush, hasten (219)
brutaliser to brutalize, bully (486)
bûcher to study hard, cut down trees (Qué.) (285)
buriner to engrave (465)
buter to trip (173)

C

cabosser to dent (79)
cabrer to rear up (27)
cacheter to seal (267)
cadrer to correspond (with) (27)
cafouiller to get mixed up (233)
cahoter to jolt (28)
cajoler to cajole, coax (27)
calcifier to calcify (41)
calciner to char (329)
calculer to calculate (81)
caler to stall, wedge (27)
calibrer to calibrate (27)
câliner to cuddle (329)
calmer to calm (27)
calmer (se) to calm down (27)
calomnier to slander, libel (in writing) (212)
cambrer to arch (27)
cambrioler to break into, burglarize (26)
camoufler to camouflage (445)
camper to camp (235)
canaliser to channel, funnel (26)
canoniser to canonize (486)
canonner to shell (military) (171)
canoter to go boating, rowing (26)
cantonner to station, billet (171)
caoutchouter to rubberize (28)
capitaliser to capitalize (486)
capoter to turn over, collapse, go crazy (Qué.)
capituler to capitulate, surrender (81)
captiver to captivate (167)
capturer to capture (27)
caqueter to cackle, gossip (267)
caractériser to characterize (486)
carboniser to carbonize, burn up (486)
caresser to caress (353)
caricaturer to caricature (21)
carillonner to ring (171)
carnavaler to celebrate at a carnival (Qué.) (27)
carreler to tile (38)
caser to fit (something) in (32)
castrer to castrate (27)
cataloguer to catalog (307)
catéchiser to catechize (486)
cautionner to guarantee (171)
caviarder to censor (27)
ceindre de to encircle with (334)
célébrer to celebrate (356)
celer to conceal (297)
censurer to censure (54)
centraliser to centralize (486)
cercler de to encircle with (27)
cerner to surround, define (27)
certifier to certify (212)
chagriner to grieve, distress (329)
chahuter to create an uproar (8)
chaîner to chain (167)
chanceler to stagger (38)
chantonner to sing to oneself (171)
chaparder to pilfer, swipe (27)
chaperonner to chaperon (171)
charmer to charm (238)
châtier to punish (212)
chatouiller to tickle (233)
chatoyer to glisten, glimmer (187)
chauffer to warm up, heat up (235)
chauffer (se) to warm oneself up (122, 235)
chausser to put on shoes (79)
chavirer to capsize (27)
cheminer to walk along (465)
chevaucher to straddle, ride (285)
chialer to bawl (421)
chicaner to haggle, quibble (147)
chiffonner to crumple (171)
chiffrer to number (27)
chiper to steal (251)
choir to fall (Def. and Imp.)
choper to catch, snatch, steal (163)
chloroformer to chloroform (227)
chômer to be unemployed (27)
choquer to shock (284)
choyer to pamper (187)
chronométrer to time (87)
chuter to fall, flop (28)
cibler to target (27)
cimenter to cement (464)
cintrer to arch, curve (27)

circonscrire to circumscribe, delimit, set limits (177)
circonvenir to circumvent (491)
circuler to circulate (81)
cirer to wax (466)
ciseler to chisel, engrave (297)
citer to quote (251)
civiliser to civilize (486)
clamer to proclaim, clamor (9)
clapper (de la langue) to click (one's tongue) (235)
claquer to bang, click (one's tongue) (284)
clarifier to clarify (212)
classer to classify (84)
classifier to classify (212)
clavarder to chat (Internet) (69)
cligner to blink (10)
clignoter to blink, flash, twinkle (27)
climatiser to air condition (486)
cliquer to click (219)
clocher to be wrong (285)
cloisonner to partition (171)
cloner to clone (461)
clouer to nail, tack down (269)
cocher to check off (121)
coder to code (26)
codifier to codify (41)
coexister to coexist (259)
cogiter to cogitate, ponder (215)
cogner to hit (10)
coiffer qqn to do someone's hair (443)
coiffer (se) to do one's own hair (122)
coincer to jam, corner (342)
collaborer to collaborate (22)
collationner to collate (171)
collectionner to collect (171)
coller à to stick to (445)
colleter to grab by the collar (267)
colmater to plug up (28)
coloniser to colonize, settle (486)
colorer to color (22)
colorier to color (in) (212)
colporter to peddle (349)
combiner to combine (329)
combler de to fill up with (407)
commanditer to finance (215)
commémorer to commemorate (22)
commercer avec to trade with (99)
commercialiser to commercialize (486)
commuer to commute (legal term) (114)
communier to receive communion (389)
communiquer to communicate (219)
commuter to commute (mathematics) (173)
comparaître to appear before court (324)
compatir to sympathize (95)
compenser to compensate, make up for (336)
compiler to compile (251)
complaire à to try to please (345)
compléter to complete (87)
complimenter to compliment (60)
compliquer to complicate (219)
comploter to plot (349)
comporter (se) to behave (80, 349)
comporter to comprise (349)
composer to compose, dial (a number) (350)
composter to punch (a ticket) (349)
compromettre to compromise (294)
compulser to consult (32)
concasser to crush (84)
concéder to concede (87)
concentrer (se) sur to concentrate (oneself) on (80, 299)
concentrer sur to concentrate on (299)
concilier to reconcile (212)
concocter to concoct (349)
concorder avec to agree with (11)
concourir avec to compete with (125)
concurrencer to compete (342)
condamner to condemn (98)
condescendre à to condescend to (394)
conditionner to condition (171)
confectionner to make (171)
conférer to confer, bestow on (356)
confesser to confess (73)
confier to entrust (212)
configurer to configure (27)
confiner to confine (329)
confirmer to confirm (227)
confisquer to confiscate (219)
confluer to converge, flow together (114)
confondre to confound (231)
conformer (se) à to conform to (122, 227)
confronter to confront (113)
congédier to dismiss (212)
congeler to freeze (242)
conjecturer to conjecture, speculate (54)
conjoindre to join in marriage (268)
conjuguer to conjugate (307)
conjurer to beseech (54)
connecter to connect (349)

connecter (se) à to connect to (Internet) (122, 349)
consacrer to consecrate, devote (54)
consacrer (se) à to devote oneself to (54, 122)
conserver to preserve (27)
considérer to consider (87)
consigner to deposit (441)
consister en to consist of (215)
consoler to console (27)
consolider to consolidate (329)
consommer to consume, use up (310)
conspirer to conspire (21)
constater to make a statement of fact (241)
consterner to appall, dismay (27)
constituer to constitute (483)
consulter to consult (375)
consumer to burn up (32)
contacter to contact (28)
contaminer to contaminate (329)
contempler to contemplate (407)
contenter to content (464)
contester to dispute (160)
contourner to bypass, circumvent (470)
contrarier to annoy, bother, frustrate (41)
contraster avec to contrast with (160)
contrefaire to counterfeit (223)
contribuer to contribute (114)
contrôler to control (498)
contusionner to bruise (171)
converger to converge (283)
converser to converse (492)
convertir to convert (229)
convier to invite (41)
convoiter to covet (447)
convoquer to convene, summon (219)
convulser to convulse (336)
coopérer to cooperate (356)
coordonner to coordinate (171)
copier to copy (212)
corner to sound a horn, turn down the corner of a page (349)
correspondre to correspond (401)
corroborer to corroborate (27)
corser to liven up, spice up (336)
corseter to corset, constrict (297)
cotiser to contribute (32)
côtoyer to be next to, mix with (187)
coudoyer to rub elbows with, mix with (187)
couler to flow (421)
coupler to couple (421)
courber to bend (481)
couronner to crown (171)
courroucer to anger (342)
court-circuiter to short-circuit (215)
coûter to cost (Def. and Imp.)
couver to sit on (eggs), to plot (28)
cracher to spit (82)
cramponner (se) to cling to, hang on (122, 171)
craqueler to crack, crackle (object) (38)
craquer to crack (219)
crayonner to doodle, scribble (171)
créditer de to credit with (251)
crépiter to crackle (sound), sputter (215)
creuser to dig (32)
crevasser to crack, chap (skin) (84)
crever to burst, puncture (tire) (278)
crever de to burst with (278)
cribler to screen, sift, riddle (with bullets) (326)
crisper to flex, tense (27)
cristalliser to crystallize (486)
critiquer to criticize (219)
crocheter to pick, to crochet (17)
croiser to cross, to bump into someone (86)
croquer to crunch (219)
crouler to collapse, crumble (421)
croupir to stagnate (229)
crucifier to crucify (212)
cuisiner to cook (159)
culbuter to somersault, tumble (28)
culminer to culminate, peak (329)
cultiver to cultivate (329)
curer to clean (ears, nails, teeth) by scraping (32)
cuver to ferment (wine) (32)

D

dactylographier to type (366)
daigner to deign, condescend (10)
damner to damn (239)
dandiner (se) to waddle like a duck (122, 329)
dater de to date from (241)
déballer to unpack (498)
débander to remove bandages (27)
débarbouiller (se) to wash one's face (usually w/washcloth) (33, 233)
débarquer de to disembark from (219)
débarrasser to clear off (183)
débarrasser (se) de to get rid of (79, 122)
débattre to discuss (67)
débaucher to fire, lay off (285)
débiter to debit, to sell retail (251)

déblatérer to rant and rave (356)
déblayer to clear off (snow, dirt) (330)
débloquer to unblock (219)
déboguer to debug (computer) (307)
déboiser to deforest (486)
déborder to overflow (26)
déboucher to uncork, unclog (285)
déboucler to unbuckle (326)
déboulonner to unbolt (171)
déboussoler to disorient (498)
déboutonner to unbutton (171)
débrancher to disconnect, unplug (285)
débrayer to disengage the clutch, declutch (330)
débrider to unbridle (251)
débrouiller to disentangle (233)
débrouiller (se) to cope, get by, manage (122, 233)
débuter to begin (173)
décacheter to unseal (267)
décalcifier to decalcify, delime (41)
décaler to move out of line, to shift ahead/back (hour) (326)
décamper to decamp, run away (27)
décaper to strip (paint, wood) (235)
décapiter to decapitate (251)
décéder to pass away (87)
déceler to discover, reveal (297)
décerner to award (470)
déchaîner to unchain (329)
déchanter to become disillusioned (90)
décharger to unload (91)
déchausser (se) to take off one's shoes (80, 122)
déchiffrer to decipher (27)
décimer to decimate (27)
déclamer to declaim (71)
déclarer to declare (69)
déclencher to trigger, set off (285)
décliner to decline (465)
décoiffer qqn to tousle, mess up someone's hair (443)
décoincer to free up, loosen (342)
décolérer to be in a (bad) temper (356)
décoller to unstick, take off (airplane) (385)
décolorer to decolorize, to bleach (22)
décommander to cancel an order (98)
décomposer to decompose (350)
déconcerter to disconcert (160)
décongestionner to decongest, relieve congestion (traffic) (171)
déconnecter to disconnect (27)
déconseiller to advise against (109)
déconsidérer to discredit (356)
déconstruire to deconstruct (133)
décontracter to unclench, relax (160)
décorer de to decorate with (22)
décorner to remove a horn, smooth out (paper) (470)
décortiquer to shell (remove a shell), analyze (219)
découcher to spend the night away from one's house (121)
découdre to unstitch (123)
découler de to follow from (usually impers.) (421)
découper to cut up (124)
décourager de to discourage from (305)
décrasser to clean, scrub (79)
décréter to decree (87)
décrier to decry (129)
décroiser to uncross (arms, legs) (486)
décrocher to unhook; to get; to drop out of school (82)
décrotter to clean mud off (163)
dédaigner to disdain (10)
dédicacer à to dedicate to (a book) (342)
dédier à to dedicate to (212)
dédommager to compensate, make up for (305)
dédoubler to separate in two (407)
défaillir to weaken, faint (222)
défavoriser to disadvantage (486)
déférer à to defer to (356)
déferler to break (wave), unfurl (326)
défier to challenge (212)
définir to define (229)
défoncer to push the bottom out, knock down (371)
déformer to deform (227)
défouler (se) to unwind (122, 421)
défricher to clear (land) (285)
dégarnir to empty, take away objects/decorations (229)
dégeler to thaw (242)
dégivrer to defrost, deice (27)
dégonfler to deflate, reduce swelling (498)
dégorger to disgorge, unblock (283)
dégouliner to drip, trickle down (329)
dégourdir (se) to stretch one's legs, relieve stiffness (210, 214)
dégoûter to disgust (244)
dégoutter to drip (244)
dégrader to damage, degrade (27)
dégrafer to unfasten, unstaple (27)

dégraisser to remove/trim fat (274)
dégringoler to tumble (498)
dégriser to sober up (486)
dégrossir to polish (282)
déguerpir to run away (95)
déguiser (se) to disguise oneself (122, 486)
déguster to taste, sample food (53)
déjouer to foil, thwart (269)
délabrer to ruin (407)
délacer to unlace (342)
délaisser to abandon, quit (274)
délasser to relax (79)
délayer to mix, water down (330)
déléguer to delegate (87, 307)
délibérer to deliberate (356)
délier to untie (389)
délister to delist (Internet) (160)
délivrer to set free (21)
déloger to dislodge, move out (305)
demander (se) to wonder (122, 147)
démanger to feel an itch (283)
démaquiller (se) to remove one's makeup (477)
démarrer to start out, to boot (computer) (27)
démêler to untangle (82)
déménager to move belongings from one residence to another (305)
démener (se) to struggle (122, 290)
démentir to deny, refute (291)
déméritер de to show oneself unworthy of (293)
démettre to dislocate (294)
démissionner de to resign from (171)
démobiliser to demobilize, demotivate (486)
démocratiser to democratize (486)
démoder (se) to go out of style (27)
démonter qqch to dismantle something (298) (aux. **avoir**)
démontrer to demonstrate (299)
dénationaliser to denationalize (486)
dénicher to unearth, spot (285)
dénigrer to denigrate (21)
dénombrer to count (407)
dénommer to name (310)
dénoncer to denounce (371)
dénoter to denote (498)
dénouer to untie (269)
dépanner to fix, help out (171)
déparer to spoil, disfigure (27)
départir de (se) to depart from, stray from (434)
dépasser to go past, beyond (328)
dépayser to make a change of scenery, to disorient (486)
dépêcher to dispatch (27)
dépêtrer to extricate, free someone (349)
dépeupler to depopulate (326)
dépister to track down, screen (medical) (215)
déplacer to move, shift, displace (342)
déplâtrer to remove plaster, remove a cast (medical) (349)
déplier to unfold (389)
déplorer to deplore (22)
déployer to deploy, spread out, exhibit (187)
dépolitiser to depoliticize (486)
déporter to deport (349)
déposer to put down, set down, deposit (350)
déposséder to dispossess, deprive (87)
dépouiller to strip, skim, despoil (233)
dépraver to corrupt, deprave (276)
déprécier to depreciate (41)
déprimer to depress (220)
déraciner to uproot (159)
dérégler to disturb, throw out of whack (87)
dériver to divert (329)
dériver de to derive from (329)
dérober to steal (498)
dérouler to unwind, roll out, unroll (421)
dérouler (se) to unwind, take place (421)
dérouter to reroute, disconcert (28)
désaltérer to refresh, slake/quench thirst (356)
désamorcer to defuse (342)
désapprendre to unlearn, forget (42)
désapprouver to disapprove of (44)
désarmer to disarm (238)
désarticuler to disjoint (81)
désavantager to disadvantage (305)
déserter to desert, abandon (40)
désespérer to despair (203)
déshabiller (se) to undress oneself (250)
désherber to weed (27)
déshonorer to dishonor (22)
déshydrater to dehydrate (241)
désigner to designate, point out (441)
désinfecter to disinfect (160)
désintégrer to disintegrate (356)
désintoxiquer to detoxify (219)

désister (se) de (en faveur de qqn) to withdraw (in someone's favor) (53)
désobéir à to disobey (314)
désoler to sadden (421)
désosser to bone (remove bones) (79)
dessaler to desalinate (326)
dessécher to dry out (87)
desservir to clear away (**la table**/the table); to provide a service (437)
déstabiliser to destabilize (486)
destiner à to destine/intend for (329)
destituer to dismiss, demote (483)
désunir to split up (229)
détacher to untie (285)
détailler to detail, sell retail (477)
détecter to detect (160)
déteindre to take out the color (207)
détendre to loosen, slacken (462)
détendre (se) to relax (394)
détenir to detain (463)
détériorer to deteriorate (27)
déterminer to determine (329)
déterrer to dig up, unearth (196)
détoner to detonate (461)
détourner to divert (470)
détourner (se) to turn oneself away from (122, 161)
détraquer to put out of order (219)
détremper to soak (464)
détromper (se) to see the truth about a matter (480)
détromper de to disabuse of, free someone from a misconception (317) (See 480)
dévaler to tumble down (27)
dévaliser to rob, empty out (486)
dévaluer to devalue (114)
devancer to arrive ahead of, precede, anticipate (61)
dévaster to devastate (259)
déverrouiller to unlock, unbolt (233)
déverser to pour, pour out (492)
dévêtir to undress (493)
dévêtir (se) to undress oneself (250, 493)
dévider to unwind, reel off (251)
dévier to deviate (41)
deviner to guess (329)
dévisager to stare at someone (305)
dévisser to unscrew (486)
dévoiler to unveil (498)
dévorer to devour (27)
dévouer to devote (269)
diagnostiquer to diagnose (219)
dialoguer (avec un ordinateur) to converse; to interact with a computer (307)
dicter to dictate (253)
diffamer to defame, slander (71)
différer to differ, defer (203)
diffuser to broadcast, diffuse (32)
digérer to digest (203)
dilapider to waste (215)
diriger to direct (119)
discerner to discern, distinguish (27)
discontinuer to discontinue (114)
discourir sur to expatiate on, talk at length (125)
discréditer to discredit (215)
discriminer to discriminate, distinguish (465)
disculper to exonerate (27)
disjoindre to separate (268)
dispenser to exempt, excuse (336)
disperser to disperse (478)
disposer to arrange (350)
disputer de qqch to dispute something (425)
disqualifier to disqualify (212)
disséminer to disseminate, scatter (465)
disséquer to dissect, analyze (87, 284)
disserter sur to write about (160)
dissimuler to conceal, hide (81)
dissiper to dissipate, disperse (251)
dissocier to separate, dissociate (41)
dissoudre to dissolve (6)
dissuader de to dissuade from (340)
distancer to outdistance (342)
distraire to distract, entertain (474)
distinguer to distinguish (307)
distribuer to distribute (114)
diverger to diverge (283)
diversifier to diversify (41)
divertir to amuse, entertain (210)
divertir (se) to have fun (210, 214)
diviser en to divide into (32)
divulguer to divulge (307)
documenter to document (60)
domestiquer to domesticate (219)
dominer to control, dominate (329)
dompter to tame (107)
dorer to gild (22)
dorloter to pamper (96)
doser to measure/determine a dose (321)
doubler to double, to pass (auto), to dub (audio) (481)
douer to endow (269)

douter (se) to suspect (122, 173)
draguer to dredge (literal), to try to pick someone up (figurative) (307)
drainer to drain (27)
dresser to draw up, erect (23)
dresser (se) to stand up (23, 122)
dribbler to dribble (sports) (326)
droguer to drug (307)
duper to dupe, trick (317)
dupliquer to duplicate (219)
durcir to harden (95)
durer to last (272)
dynamiter dynamite (251)

E

ébahir to stun (95)
ébaucher to sketch (469)
éblouir to dazzle (229)
ébouriffer to tousle someone's hair, stun (215)
ébranler to shake (326)
ébruiter to divulge a secret (215)
écarter to separate, spread apart (69)
échafauder to build up, put up scaffolding (447)
échanger to exchange (89)
échantillonner to sample (171)
échapper (s') to escape (27, 33)
écharper to tear to pieces (59)
échauffer to heat, overheat (171)
échelonner to space, spread out at even intervals (171)
écheveler to dishevel (38)
éclabousser to splash (79)
éclaircir to clear up (229)
éclairer to light (21)
éclater en to burst into (176)
éclore to hatch (See **clore**) (Def. and Imp.)
écoeurer to disgust, make someone sick (466)
économiser to save, economize (486)
écouler to sell out of (421)
écourter to shorten (160)
écrabouiller to crush (233)
écraser to crush (183)
écrémer to skim off (87)
écrier (s') to cry out (33, 41)
écrivasser to write badly (84)
écrouler (s') to collapse (33, 421)
écumer to foam, lather, skim off (27)
édifier to build, edify (41)
éditer to publish, edit (251)
édulcorer to sweeten (22)
éduquer to educate (219)
effacer to efface, erase (342)
effarer to alarm (22)
effaroucher to scare away (285)
effectuer to effect, bring about (483)
effeuiller to pull off leaves, petals (477)
effleurer to brush, touch lightly (466)
efforcer (s') to force oneself, try (33, 342)
effriter (s') to erode (33, 215)
égaler to equal (326)
égaliser to equalize (486)
égarer (s') to get lost, wander (33, 101)
égorger to cut the throat of (283)
egosurfer to egosurf (27)
égoutter to drain (374)
égratigner to scratch (441)
élancer (s') to rush forward (33, 342)
élargir to enlarge, widen (229)
électriser to electrify (486)
élider to elide (251)
élimer to wear out, wear thin (27)
éliminer to eliminate (465)
éloigner de to move, keep away from (194)
élucider to elucidate (26)
éluder to elude (32)
émaner de to emanate from (27)
émasculer to emasculate (81)
emballer to pack, wrap (421)
embarquer to embark (219)
embarrasser to embarrass, clutter, hinder (84)
embaucher to hire (285)
embaumer to embalm, make fragrant (27)
embellir to beautify, embellish (229)
embêter to annoy, bother, worry (47)
embobiner to spool, wind, wrap someone around one's finger (329)
emboîter to fit together (251)
embrayer to engage the clutch (330)
embrouiller to complicate, tangle up (233)
embuer to mist up (114)
embusquer (s') to ambush (33, 284)
émettre to emit (294)
émigrer to emigrate (21)
emmagasiner to store, stockpile (159)
emménager to move in (305)
emmerder to bother, hassle someone (240)
emmurer to wall in (32)
émonder to prune (240)
empaqueter to wrap up, package (267)
emparer (s') de to seize (33, 101)
empêtrer (s') to trap, entangle (33, 299)
empiffrer (s') to stuff oneself, make a pig of oneself (33, 466)

empiler to pile up (329)
empirer to worsen (466)
emplir to fill (95)
empocher to pocket (285)
empoisonner to poison (171)
emporter to carry away (349)
empresser (s') de to make haste, hasten (361)
empuantir to smell/stink up (210)
encadrer to frame (299)
encaisser to cash (274)
encercler to encircle (27)
enchaîner to put in chains, to link/string together (167)
enchanter to enchant (90)
enchevêtrer to tangle, confuse (299)
enclaver to enclose (276)
encourir to incur (125)
encrasser to dirty (84)
encroûter to encrust (244)
endiguer to hold back (307)
endoctriner to indoctrinate (329)
endommager to damage (305)
endormir (s') to fall asleep (172, 257)
endosser to put on, endorse (79)
enduire to smear (133)
endurcir to harden, toughen (95)
endurer to endure (54)
énerver (s') to become annoyed (33, 276)
enfermer to shut away, lock up (227)
enfiler to thread, put on (329)
enfler (s') to swell (361, 445)
enfoncer to plunge in, smash down (371)
enfouir to bury (270)
enfourcher to mount, straddle (285)
enfreindre to infringe (334)
enfumer to fill (a place) with smoke (238)
engager (s') to commit oneself to do (305, 318)
engager to engage, start up, to hire (305)
engendrer to generate, beget (299)
englober to encompass, include (27)
engloutir to engulf, swallow up (66)
engouffrer to swallow up (445)
engourdir to numb (210)
engraisser to fatten (274)
engueuler to scold, chew someone out (421)
enhardir to make bold (210)
enivrer (s') to become intoxicated (33)
enjamber to stride, step over (240)
enjoindre à qqn de faire to charge someone to do (268)
enjôler to cajole (498)
enlacer to entwine, embrace (342)
enlaidir to make ugly (210)
enliser (s') to get stuck, bogged down (33, 486)
ennuyer (s') to be bored (55, 192)
énoncer to state, express (371)
enorgueillir de to be proud of (something) (229)
enquérir (s') de to inquire about (19) (aux. **être**)
enquêter (sur) to investigate (47)
enquiquiner to annoy, bore (329)
enraciner (s') to take root (33, 329)
enrager to be enraged, furious (305)
enrayer to block, curb (330)
enregistrer to record, register (393)
enrhumer (s') to catch a cold (33, 238)
enrichir to enrich (229)
enrouler to wind, roll up (421)
ensabler to cover in sand (407)
ensabler (s') to get stuck, buried in sand (33, 407)
ensanglanter to bloody (90)
ensevelir to bury (229)
ensoleiller to brighten with sunlight (109)
ensorceler to bewitch (38)
ensuivre (s') to follow (453) (3d pers. sing. and pl.)
entacher to soil (82)
entamer to begin, start (71)
entendre (s') (avec) to get along (with) (195) (aux. **être**)
entériner to ratify (329)
entêter (s') to persist in, be stubborn (33, 47)
enthousiasmer to enthuse (27)
entôler to fleece (498)
entortiller to twist (477)
entourer de to surround with (21)
entraîner to carry away (27)
entraver to hinder (276)
entrebâiller to open halfway (477)
entrecouper de to intersperse, interrupt with (124)
entrelacer to intertwine, interlace (342)
entremêler to intermingle (82)
entremettre (s') to intervene, meddle (295)
entreposer to store in a warehouse (350)
entretenir to maintain, support (463)
entretuer (s') to kill each other (33, 483)
entrevoir to catch a glimpse (497)

entrouvrir to half open, open halfway (323)
énumérer to enumerate (356)
envahir to invade (229)
envelopper to envelope, wrap up (235)
envenimer to poison, inflame (27)
envier to envy (212)
environner to surround (171)
envisager to envisage, contemplate (305)
épaissir to thicken (95)
épancher to pour out, vent (78)
épanouir (s') to bloom, blossom (214)
épargner to save, economize (10)
éparpiller to scatter (477)
épater to amaze, shock (241)
épauler to shoulder, support (421)
épeler to spell (38)
épicer to spice up (342)
épier to spy on (212)
épiler to depilate, remove unwanted hair (329)
épingler to pin (326)
éplucher to peel (82)
éponger to sponge (283)
époumoner (s') to yell at the top of one's lungs (461)
épousseter to dust (267)
époustoufler to flabbergast, stun (445)
épouvanter to terrify (90)
éprendre de (s') to fall for someone (357)
épuiser to exhaust (486)
épurer to filter, refine (54)
équilibrer to balance (158)
équiper de to equip with (215)
équivaloir to be equivalent (488)
éradiquer to eradicate (219)
érafler to scratch (439)
éreinter to exhaust (90)
ergoter to quibble (96)
ériger to erect (119)
éroder to erode (96)
errer to wander (27)
éructer to belch, burp (28)
escamoter to evade, dodge (96)
escompter to discount (financial), to count on (103)
escroquer to cheat (219)
espionner to spy on (171)
esquinter to ruin, smash up (90)
esquisser to sketch (183)
esquiver to avoid (276)
essorer dry out (22)
essouffler (s') to run out of breath (122, 445)
estamper to stamp (247)
estimer to esteem, estimate (27)
estomaquer to shock (219)
estomper to blur (247)
étaler to spread out, display (326)
étancher to make something waterproof, watertight (78)
étayer to prop up (330)
étendre to roll out, spread out (462)
éternuer to sneeze (114)
étêter to cut the head off of something (47)
étiqueter to label (267)
étirer to stretch 466)
étirer (s') to stretch oneself (182, 466)
étouffer to suffocate (353)
étrangler to strangle (326)
étreindre to embrace, hug (334)
étriper to gut (215)
évacuer to evacuate (114)
évader (s') de to escape from (26, 33)
évaporer (s') to evaporate (22, 33)
éveiller to awaken (109)
éventer to fan (90)
évoluer to develop (213)
évoquer to evoke (219)
exacerber to aggravate, exacerbate (27)
exagérer to exaggerate (356)
exalter to exalt, excite (28)
examiner to examine (465)
exaspérer to exasperate (203)
excéder to exceed (87)
exceller to excel (326)
excepter to except (8)
exciter to excite (251)
exclamer (s') to cry out (9)
exclure to exclude (105)
excommunier to excommunicate (309)
exécrer to abhor, detest (203)
exécuter to execute, carry out (169)
exercer to exercise, exert (342)
exhausser to raise (353)
exhiber to exhibit (251)
exhumer to exhume (238)
exister to exist (349)
exonérer to exonerate, exempt (203)
expédier to send (212)
expérimenter test (464)
expirer to exhale; to expire, die (466)
exploiter to exploit (251)
explorer to explore (22)
exploser to explode (321)
exporter to export (349)
exposer to expose (350)
exproprier to expropriate (41)
expulser to expel (336)
exterminer to exterminate (465)
extraire to extract (474)

F

fabriquer to manufacture (219)
fabuler to fabricate, make up stories (81)
fâcher qqn to annoy, offend, anger someone (82) (See 216; aux. **avoir**)
faciliter to facilitate (225)

façonner to shape, fashion (171)
facturer to bill (54)
faiblir to weaken (392)
falloir to be necessary, must, to be lacking (*à*), to need (Def. and Imp.)
falsifier to falsify (212)
familiariser to familiarize (486)
faner (se) to fade, wither (122)
farcir de to stuff with (cooking), cram with (229)
farder to apply makeup to someone's face (240)
farder (se) to apply makeup to one's own face (83, 240)
fasciner to fascinate (329)
fatiguer to tire, get weary (307)
faucher to reap, mow; to steal (82)
faufiler (se) to sneak through, slip through (27, 122)
fausser to distort, twist (353)
favoriser to favor (486)
fédérer to federate (203)
féliciter to congratulate (251)
fendiller to crack (477)
fertiliser to fertilize (486)
fêter to celebrate (363)
feuilleter to leaf through (267)
fiancer (se) to get engaged (122, 342)
figer (se) to coagulate, freeze up (119)
fignoler to polish, perfect (498)
figurer to represent (54)
filer to spin, dash off, run off (27)
filmer to film (227)
filtrer to filter (299)
fixer to fix, set, arrange (27)
flageller whip (326)
flageoler to wobble (498)
flairer to smell (22)
flamber to burn (240)
flamboyer to blaze (187)
flâner to stroll (443)
flanquer to fling (284)
flatter to flatter, to stroke/pet (an animal) (27)
fléchir to bend, flex (383)
flétrir to fade, wither (383)
fleurir to flourish (249)
flinguer to blow away (slang), to flame (Internet) (307)
flirter to flirt (425)
flotter to float (79)
foisonner to abound (171)
foncer to dash along, run along, to darken (371)
fonctionner to function, work (171)
forger to forge (283)
formaliser to formalize (486)
formater to format (computer) (176)
former to form (227)
formuler to formulate (32)
fortifier to fortify (212)
foudroyer to strike (lightning), strike down (187)
fouetter to whip (447)
fouler to press, trample on (421)
fourmiller to swarm, tingle (477)
fourrager to forage, rummage (305)
fourrer to cram, shove in (22)
fourvoyer to mislead (187)
fracasser to smash, shatter (84)
fragmenter to fragment, split (464)
fraîchir to get cooler (383)
franchir to clear, cross (383)
franciser to gallicize (486)
fraterniser to fraternize (486)
frauder to defraud, cheat (27)
frayer to clear (330)
fredonner to hum (171)
freiner to brake, slow down (329)
fréquenter to frequent (60)
frétiller to wiggle (477)
friser to curl (486)
frissonner to shiver (171)
froisser to crumple, crease (353)
frôler to brush against, come close to (498)
froncer to knit (brow), wrinkle (nose) (34)
frotter to rub (79)
frustrer to frustrate (22)
fuguer to run away (307)
fulminer to fulminate, thunder (465)
fureter to ferret out, pry into, snoop, search (17)
fuser to burst forth, melt (32)
fusiller to shoot (477)

G

gâcher to spoil (82)
gager to bet, wager (305)
gainer to sheath (329)
galoper to gallop (163)
galvauder to tarnish (26)
gambader to leap about, gambol (26)
garantir to guarantee (229)
garer to park (435)
gargariser (se) to gargle (85, 486)
garnir de to garnish, provide with (229)
gaspiller to waste (477)
gausser (se) to mock (122, 353)
gazéifier to carbonate, aerate (212)
gazouiller to chirp, warble (233)
geindre to groan, moan (334)
gémir to groan (229)
gercer to chap (342)
gérer to manage (203)
gesticuler to gesticulate, make gestures while talking (32)

gicler to spurt (326)
gifler to slap (439)
gigoter to wriggle (96)
givrer to frost (466)
glacer to freeze (342)
glaner to glean (27)
glisser to glide, slide (73)
glorifier to glorify (212)
glousser to cluck (353)
gober to swallow (27)
gommer to erase; to gum (310)
gonfler to inflate (445)
gouverner to govern (167)
graver to engrave (276)
gravir to climb (95)
grelotter to shiver (79)
griffer to scratch (439)
griffonner to scribble (171)
grignoter to nibble at; to snack (96)
griller to grill (meat, fish), toast (bread) (477)
grimacer to grimace (one's face) (342)
grincer to creak, grind (99)
griser to intoxicate, make tipsy (486)
grogner to growl, grumble (10)
grossir to get bigger, put on weight (282)
grouiller to swarm (233)
grouper to group (124)
guetter to watch (386)
gueuler to yell (421)
guider to guide (26)
guillotiner to guillotine (329)

H

NOTE: The mark * in front of the letter *h* denotes that it is aspirate; make no liaison and use *je* instead of *j'*; *me* instead of *m'*.

habiliter to authorize (251)
habiller qqn, qqch to dress someone, something (477) (See 250; aux. **avoir**)
habituer (s') to accustom oneself, get used to (33, 483)
habituer to accustom (483)
***hacher** to chop up (285)
***hachurer** to hatch (with hatch marks) (54)
***haleter** to pant, gasp (17)
halluciner to hallucinate (329)
hameçonner to phish (171)
***handicaper** to handicap (59)
***hanter** to haunt (90)
***harasser** to exhaust (183)
***harceler** to harass (297)
***hasarder** to hazard, risk (240)
***hâter (se)** to hurry oneself (74, 241)
***hausser** to raise (92)
héberger to lodge; to host (Internet) (283)
hébraïser to hebraize (486)
***héler** to hail, call to (87)
***hennir** to whinny, to bray (229)
***hérisser (se)** to bristle, become annoyed (122, 486)
hériter to inherit (293)
***heurter** to hit, bump (246)
***hiérarchiser** to hierarchize, classify in a hierarchy (486)
***hisser** to hoist (84)
***hocher** to nod (one's head) (82)
homologuer to approve, ratify (307)
honorer to honor (22)
horrifier to horrify (212)
hospitaliser to hospitalize (486)
***houspiller** to reprimand (477)
***housser** to put a slipcover on (353)
***huer** to boo (483)
huiler to oil (27)
***hululer, ululer** to hoot, screech (81)
humecter to moisten, dampen (60)
***hurler** to howl, yell (326)
hydrater to moisturize, hydrate (241)
hyperlier to hyperlink (Internet) (454)
hypertrophier (s') to hypertrophy, develop excessively (212) (aux. **être**)
hypnotiser to hypnotize (486)
hypothéquer to mortgage (87, 219)

I

idéaliser to idealize (486)
identifier to identify (212)
idolâtrer to idolize (299)
ignorer to be unaware of, not to know (22)
illuminer to illuminate (465)
illustrer to illustrate (299)
imaginer to imagine (329)
imbiber to soak (215)
imbriquer (s') to overlap, imbricate (33, 219)
imiter to imitate (251)
immatriculer to register (81)
immerger to immerse (91)
immigrer to immigrate (93)
immobiliser to immobilize (486)
immoler to immolate (498)
immortaliser to immortalize (486)
immuniser to immunize (486)
impatienter (s') to get impatient (33, 464)
implanter (s') to settle in, be located (33, 90)
impliquer to imply, implicate (219)

implorer to implore (22)
importer to import, to matter (349)
importuner to importune, bother (32)
imposer to impose (350)
imprégner to permeate (87, 441)
impressionner to impress (171)
imprimer to print (220)
improviser to improvise (486)
inaugurer to inaugurate, initiate (54)
incarcérer to imprison (203)
incarner to personify, embody (27)
incendier to set on fire (212)
incinérer to incinerate (356)
inciter to incite (251)
incliner (s') devant to bow down before (33, 329)
incliner to incline (329)
incommoder to bother, inconvenience (96)
incorporer à to incorporate in (22)
indigner (s') to become indignant (33, 441)
induire (à) to induce (to) (106)
industrialiser to industrialize (486)
infecter de to infect with (113)
inférer de to infer from (356)
infester de to infest with (259)
infiltrer (s') dans to infiltrate, filter into (299, 262)
infliger à to inflict on (218)
influencer to influence (99)
informatiser to computerize (486)
informer to inform (227)
infuser to infuse (32)
ingénier (s') à to try one's best, use one's ingenuity (309) (aux. **être**)
ingérer to ingest (203)
ingérer (s') dans to interfere in (33, 203)
inhiber to inhibit (215)
inhumer to bury (238)
initier à to initiate into (389)
injecter to inject (8)
injurier to abuse (389)
inoculer to inoculate (81)
inonder to flood (336)
inquiéter qqn to worry, disturb someone (87) (See 258)
inscrire to inscribe, write down (177)
inscrire (s') to join, register (177) (aux. **être**)
insérer to insert (203)
insinuer to insinuate (114)
insonoriser to soundproof (486)
inspecter to inspect (113)
inspirer to inspire, to inhale (466)
installer to install (27)
instaurer to found (54)
instituer to institute (483)
insulter to insult (176)
insurger (s') contre to rise up against (33, 283)
intégrer to integrate, assimilate (203)
intensifier (s') to intensify (212) (aux. **être**)
intercaler to insert, intercalate (326)
intercéder to intercede (87)
intercepter to intercept (8)
intéresser qqn à qqch to interest someone in something (88)
interférer to interfere (356)
interpeller to hail, to question (police) (27)
interpoler to interpolate (498)
interposer entre to interpose between (350)
interpréter to interpret (87)
intervenir to intervene (491)
interviewer to interview (27)
intimider par to intimidate by (266)
intoxiquer to poison (219)
invalider to invalidate (266)
inventer to invent (90)
inverser to reverse (492)
invertir to invert (66)
investir to invest (66)
invoquer to invoke, call upon (219)
irradier to irradiate, radiate (389)
irriter to irritate (266)
isoler to isolate, insulate (498)
isoler (de) to isolate (from) (498)
italianiser to italianize (486)

J

jacasser to chatter, jabber (84)
jacter to jabber (8)
jaillir to gush forth, spurt out (423)
jalonner to mark off (171)
japper to yap, yelp (235)
jardiner to garden (167)
jargonner to jabber (171)
jaser to chatter, prattle (84)
jauger to gauge, size up (76)
jaunir to yellow, turn yellow (229)
javelliser to bleach, chlorinate (486)
jeûner to fast, go without food (146)
joncher qqch de to strew something with (93)
jongler to juggle (326)
jucher sur to perch on (469)
jumeler to twin, couple (38)
justifier to justify (389)

K

kidnapper to kidnap (235)
klaxonner to hoot, toot, sound a horn (171)

L

labourer to plow (481)
lacer to lace (342)
lacérer to lacerate (356)
lâcher to loosen, let go, release (82)
laïciser to laicize, secularize (486)
lambiner to dawdle, dillydally (329)
lamenter (se) sur qqch to lament, moan over something (60)
langer to swaddle (283)
languir to languish (229)
lapider to lapidate, stone (251)
larmoyer to water (eye), to whimper (187)
lasser (se) to get tired (84, 122)
latiniser to latinize (486)
lécher to lick (87)
légiférer to legislate (356)
léguer to bequeath (87, 307)
léser to harm, injure (87)
lésiner sur to skimp on (159)
leurrer to deceive (22)
libeller to word, draw up, make out a check (27)
libérer to liberate, to move out (203)
libérer de to free from (203)
licencier to fire (41)
lier to tie (129)
lifter to put topspin on a ball (27)
ligoter to tie up (96)
limer to file (220)
limiter to limit (251)
liquider to liquidate (251)
lisser to smooth (73)
lister to list (27)
livrer à to deliver to (27)
localiser to locate (486)
loger chez to live with (263)
loger dans to live in (263)
longer to go/run along, border (283)
lorgner to eye (441)
lotir to divide up (66)
louanger to praise (283)
loucher to squint (469)
louper to miss, fail (124)
luger to sled, toboggan (271)
luire to shine, gleam, glisten (Def. and Imp.)
lustrer to shine, make shiny (299)
lutter to struggle (425)
lyncher to lynch (78)

M

macérer to steep (203)
mâcher to chew (82)
machiner to machinate, plot (329)
mâchonner to chew (171)
mâchurer to stain black, blacken, blur (54)
maçonner to build (with masonry) (171)
maculer to stain, spatter (81)
magasiner (en ligne) to shop, go shopping (online) (159)
magnétiser to magnetize, hypnotize (486)
magnifier to glorify, magnify (exalt) (212)
maintenir to maintain (463)
maîtriser to control, master (486)
malaxer to blend, knead (27)
malmener to handle roughly (290)
maltraiter to abuse, misuse, handle roughly, mistreat (475)
mandater to appoint; to pay by money order (241)
mander to command, summon (147)
manier to handle (212)
manifester to show, demonstrate (299)
manigancer to plot (342)
manipuler to manipulate (81)
manoeuvrer to maneuver, operate a machine, manipulate a person (26)
manufacturer to manufacture (54)
maquiller (se) to put makeup on one's face (122)
marauder to maraud, prowl, cruise (27)
marchander to haggle, bargain over (147)
marginaliser to marginalize (486)
marier to marry (someone to someone) (389)
marier (se) à/avec qqn to get married to someone (122)
marivauder to banter (27)
marmonner to mumble (171)
marquer de to mark with (219)
marrer (se) to have a fun time, good time (122)
marteler to hammer (297)
martyriser to martyr, mistreat (486)
masquer à to mask, conceal from (219)
massacrer to massacre (299)
masser to massage, gather together (84)
mastiquer to chew (219)
matelasser to pad (274)
mater to checkmate, curb (241)
matraquer to club (219)
maximaliser/maximiser to maximize (486)
mécaniser to mechanize (486)
méditer to meditate (251)
mégoter to skimp (96)
mélanger to mix (283)

mêler à/avec to mix with (82)
mêler (se) à to join in, meddle with, get mixed up in (83)
mêler (se) de to meddle in (83)
mémoriser to memorize (486)
menacer de to threaten with (342)
ménager to be sparing in the use of (305)
mendier to beg (212)
mentionner to mention (171)
mépriser to despise, scorn (486)
mesurer to measure (54)
métisser to crossbreed (274)
meubler de to furnish with (27)
meugler to moo (326)
meurtrir to bruise (249)
migrer to migrate (22)
mijoter to simmer (96)
militer to be an activist/militant (251)
mimer to mime (220)
mincir to get thinner (95)
miner to mine, undermine, erode (465)
minimaliser/minimiser to minimize (486)
minuter to measure time (32)
miser to bet (486)
mitrailler to machine-gun (477)
mobiliser to mobilize (486)
modérer to moderate, reduce (203)
moderniser to modernize (486)
modifier to modify (389)
moduler to modulate (81)
moisir to make moldy; to go moldy (95)
molester to molest (160)
mollir to soften (229)
momifier to mummify (212)
monnayer to mint, sell (330)
monopoliser to monopolize (486)
moraliser to moralize (486)
morceler to divide up into pieces (38)
mortifier to mortify (389)
motiver to motivate (26)
moucher (se) to blow one's nose (122)
mouiller (se) to get oneself wet (83, 233)
mouiller to wet (233)
mouler to mold, make a cast (421)
mousser to bubble, lather, froth (353)
muer to molt; to have a change of voice (483)
mugir to moo, roar (229)
multiplier to multiply (454)
munir de to supply with (229)
murer to wall in/up (54)
mûrir to ripen (249)
murmurer to murmur (54)
museler to muzzle (38)
mutiler to mutilate (27)
mutiner (se) to mutiny (329)
mystifier to deceive, mystify (129)

N

nantir to provide, supply (66)
napper de to coat, top with (59)
narguer to scoff at (307)
narrer to narrate (22)
nasiller to speak with a nasal twang; to quack (477)
natter to braid, interweave (246)
navrer to distress (27)
nécessiter to require (251)
négliger to neglect (119)
négocier to negotiate (389)
neiger to snow (Def. and Imp.)
neutraliser to neutralize (486)
niveler to level (38)
noircir to blacken (229)
noliser to charter (boat, plane) (486)
nombrer to count (22)
normaliser to normalize, standardize (486)
noter to note (176)
notifier to notify (322)
nouer to tie (269)
nuancer to nuance (342)
numériser to digitize (486)
numéroter to number, paginate (96)

O

objecter to make an objection (160)
objectiver to objectify (276)
oblitérer to obliterate (356)
obscurcir to darken, make obscure (229)
obséder to obsess (87)
observer to observe (481)
obstiner (s') à to persist in (318, 329)
obstruer to obstruct (114)
obtempérer à to comply with (203)
occasionner to cause (171)
occidentaliser to westernize (486)
octroyer to grant (187)
offenser to offend (336)
offusquer to offend (219)
oindre to anoint, rub with oil (268)
ombrager to shade (189)
ombrer to shade (22)
ondoyer to undulate (187)
onduler to undulate (81)
opérer to operate (356)
opiniâtrer (s') to be stubborn, persist in (33)
opposer to oppose (350)
oppresser to weigh down, suffocate (360)
opprimer to oppress (220)
opter pour to opt for (113)
orchestrer to orchestrate (22)

ordonner to arrange, organize, order, to prescribe (medical) (171)
organiser to organize (486)
orienter (s') vers to orient, direct towards (113)
orner de to decorate with (470)
orthographier to spell (212)
osciller to oscillate (477)
ôter to take off, remove (498)
ourler to hem (326)
outiller to equip with tools (477)
outrager to outrage (305)
outrer to exaggerate, outrage (22)

P

pacifier to pacify (389)
pactiser to make a pact (486)
palataliser to palatalize (486)
pâlir to turn pale (423)
palpiter to palpitate (251)
pâmer (se) to swoon (71, 122)
paner to bread, coat with bread crumbs (27)
paniquer to panic (219)
panser to bandage (134)
papillonner to flutter around (171)
papoter to gab, chatter (96)
parachuter to parachute (425)
parcourir to travel through; to skim (reading) (125)
parer to adorn (435)
parfaire to perfect (223)
parfumer to perfume (238)
parier sur to bet on (129)
parjurer (se) to break one's pledge (122, 272)
parodier to parody (212)
parquer to park; to confine (284)
parsemer to scatter (341)
partager to share (501)
participer à to participate in (251)
parvenir à to get to, reach (491)
passer (se) to happen, take place (Def. and Imp.)
passionner to fascinate (171)
patauger to splash, wade (305)
patienter to be patient, wait (26)
patoiser to speak patois (486)
patronner to sponsor, patronize (171)
patrouiller to patrol (233)
pâturer to graze (54)
paumer to lose (27)
paupériser to pauperize, impoverish (486)
pavaner (se) to strut around (122)
paver to pave (276)
peaufiner to polish, put on the finishing touches (329)
pédaler to pedal (326)
peiner to upset; to strain (329)
peler to peel (297)
pelleter to shovel (267)
pencher (se) to lean over (122)
pencher to tilt, tip up (93)
pénétrer to penetrate (356)
percer to pierce (275)
percevoir to notice, perceive (379)
percher to perch (93)
percuter to strike, smash into (169)
perdre (se) to get lost, lose one's way (122, 337)
perfectionner to perfect (171)
perforer to perforate (22)
périmer (se) to expire, lapse (legal term) (122, 220)
perler to bead (326)
permuter to permutate, swap (32)
perpétrer to perpetrate (356)
perquisitionner to search (171)
persécuter to persecute (32)
persévérer to persevere (356)
persifler to mock, scoff (439)
persister to persist (259)
personnaliser to personalize (486)
personnifier to personify (389)
pervertir to pervert (66)
pester to complain, curse (27)
péter to break, blow up, break wind (87)
pétiller to bubble, crackle (477)
pétrifier to petrify (212)
pétrir to knead (249)
peupler to populate (326)
philosopher to philosophize (27)
photocopier to photocopy (212)
photographier to photograph (212)
phraser to phrase (in music) (32)
pianoter to play the piano, tickle the ivory (96)
picoter to irritate, tingle (96)
piéger to trap (52)
piétiner to trample (329)
piger to catch on, understand, freelance (218)
piler to grind (27)
piller to pillage (477)
piloter to pilot (96)
pincer to pinch (99)
piocher to dig, study hard (82)
piquer to prick, sting, to steal (219)
pirater to pirate, hack (computer) (241)
pister to track, follow (27)

pivoter to pivot, revolve (96)
placarder to put up posters, cover up (240)
plafonner to peak (171)
plagier to plagiarize (389)
plaider to plead (26)
planer sur to hover over (71)
planifier to plan (212)
planquer to hide (something) (284)
planter to plant (90)
plaquer to jilt, stand up (219)
plâtrer to plaster, put in a cast (medical) (22)
pleurnicher to whimper, whine (285)
pleuvoir to rain (Def. and Imp.)
plisser to pleat, crease (73)
plomber to plumb, put in a filling (dentist) (240)
plonger to plunge, dive (442)
ployer to bend, flex (187)
pocher to poach (cooking) (82)
pogner to take, seize, understand (Qué.) (441)
poignarder to stab (240)
poinçonner to punch (ticket) (171)
poindre to dawn, break through (268)
pointer to point (464)
poireauter to hang around (27)
poivrer to pepper (466)
polir to polish (423)
politiser to politicize (486)
polluer de to pollute with (114)
pommader to put on pomade, ointment (240)
pomper to pump (59)
poncer to sand (342)
ponctionner to puncture (171)
ponctuer to punctuate (483)
pondérer to balance (203)
pondre to lay (eggs), produce (394)
pontifier to pontificate (212)
porter (se) to feel well/unwell (122, 349)
positionner to position (171)
poster to mail (27)
postuler to apply for (a position), postulate (81)
potasser to cram (for a test) (84)
potiner to gossip (329)
poudrer to powder (299)
pourchasser to pursue (92)
pourrir to spoil, rot (249)
pourvoir to provide (497) (except Tenses 4 & 5, stem: pourvoir-; Tense 3 pourvus, pourvus, pourvut...; Tense 7 pourvusse, pourvusses, pourvût...)
pratiquer to practice, drill (a hole) (219)
précéder to precede (87)
prêcher to preach (332)
précipiter (se) to rush (122, 251)
préciser to specify (486)
préconiser to advocate (486)
prédestiner to predestine (329)
prédisposer to predispose (350)
prédominer sur to prevail over (465)
préexister à to preexist, come before (27)
préfacer to preface (342)
préjuger to prejudge (271)
prélever to take a sample (278)
préméditer to premeditate (251)
prémunir contre to guard against (229)
prénommer to give a first name (310)
préoccuper to preoccupy, worry (317)
préposer à to appoint to (350)
présager to predict (305)
prescrire to prescribe (177)
préserver de to preserve from (426)
présider to preside (over) (251)
présumer to presume (238)
présupposer to presuppose (350)
prévaloir sur to prevail over (488)
primer sur to be dominant over (220)
priser to value (486)
privatiser to privatize (486)
priver to deprive (276)
priver de (se) qqch to do without something (276)
privilégier to favor, give an advantage to (41)
procéder de to arise, proceed from (87)
proclamer to proclaim (71)
procurer qqch à qqn to get something for someone (54)
profaner to profane (27)
professer to profess (73)
profiler to profile, outline (27)
profiter de to profit from, enjoy (251)
progresser to progress (73)
prohiber to prohibit (251)
projeter to project (267)
prolonger de to prolong by (442)
promener to take for a walk (290)
promouvoir to promote (304) (*part. passé* promu, promue)
promulguer to promulgate (307)
prôner to advocate (27)
propager to propagate, spread (305)
proportionner to make something match/be proportionate (171)

proposer to propose (350)
proscrire to proscribe, ban, outlaw (177)
prospérer to prosper (203)
prostituer (se) to prostitute oneself (122, 483)
protéger to protect (52)
protester to protest (160)
provenir de to result from (491)
provoquer to provoke (219)
psalmodier to chant (212)
psychanalyser to psychoanalyze (32)
publier to publish (212)
puer to stink (Def. and Imp.)
puiser to draw from (486)
pulvériser to pulverize (486)
purger to purge (283)
purifier to purify (212)

Q

quadriller to crisscross (477)
quadrupler to quadruple (326)
qualifier to qualify, consider, describe as (212)
quantifier to quantify (212)
québéciser to quebecize, make Québécois (486)
quereller (se) to quarrel with each other (122, 477)
quereller to scold (477)
questionner to question (171)
quêter to collect (money); to seek after (47)
quintupler to quintuple (326)

R

rabâcher to harp on, repeat over and over (82)
rabaisser to reduce, decrease, devalue (63)
rabattre to pull down (67)
rabibocher to reconcile (with) (285)
raboter to plane (96)
rabougrir (se) to shrivel up (214, 249)
raccommoder to mend (147)
raccompagner to see someone off, home (441)
raccorder à to connect to, link up (11)
raccourcir to shorten (95)
raccrocher to hang up (469)
racheter to buy back (17)
racheter (se) to redeem oneself (17, 122)
racler to scrape (326)
radicaliser to radicalize (486)
radier to cross off (a list) (212)
radiodiffuser to broadcast, radiocast (32)
radiographier to x-ray (212)
radoter to drivel (96)
radoucir to soften, get milder (95)
raffermir to strengthen, tone up (229)
raffiner to refine (329)
raffoler de to be crazy about (498)
rafistoler to patch up (498)
rafler to swipe (439)
rafraîchir to cool, refresh (383)
ragaillardir to perk up (210)
rager to rage, be infuriated (305)
raidir to stiffen (229)
railler to mock, jeer at (477)
raisonner to reason (443)
rajeunir to rejuvenate (229)
rajouter to add more (28)
ralentir to slow down (95)
râler to moan (498)
rallier to rally (212)
rallonger to lengthen (442)
rallumer to light again (238)
ramasser to pick up (92)
ramener to bring back (31)
ramer to row (27)
ramifier (se) to ramify, split (212) (aux. **être**)
ramollir to soften, weaken (229)
ramoner to sweep a chimney (461)
ramper to crawl (247)
rancarder to tip off, arrange a meeting with (27)
rancir to get stale/rancid (95)
rançonner to demand ransom (443)
ranimer to revive (220)
rapatrier to repatriate (212)
râper to grate (59)
rapetisser to make/get smaller (486)
rappliquer to come back (219)
rapporter to bring back (40)
rapprendre, réapprendre to learn again, relearn (42)
rapprocher de to bring closer to (43)
raréfier to rarefy (212)
raser (se) to shave oneself (86, 122)
raser to shave (86)
rassembler to assemble (407)
rasseoir (se) to take one's seat again, sit down again (51) (aux. **être**; *part. passé* rassis, rassise)
rassurer to reassure (54)
ratatiner (se) to shrink, shrivel (122, 329)
rater to miss, fail (241)
ratifier to ratify (212)
ratiociner to quibble (329)
rationner to ration (171)

ratisser to rake (486)
rattacher to attach again, link together (82)
rattraper to catch up (59)
raturer to cross out (54)
ravager to ravage (305)
ravaler to clean; to swallow (326)
ravir to delight (422)
raviser (se) to change one's mind (122, 486)
ravitailler to supply (477)
raviver to revive (276)
rayer to cross out (330)
rayonner to shine, be radiant (171)
réabonner (se) to renew one's membership/ subscription (122, 171)
réaccoutumer to reaccustom (238)
réadapter to readjust (8)
réadmettre to readmit (294)
réagir to react (25)
réaliser to carry out, realize (486)
réapparaître to reappear (324)
réapprendre, rapprendre to learn again, relearn (42)
réarmer to rearm (227)
rebaisser to lower (63)
rebeller (se) to rebel (122)
rebrousser to turn back; to brush the wrong way (353)
rebuter to repel, put off (32)
recaler to fail (326)
receler to hold, receive, harbor (someone) (297)
recenser to inventory, take a census (27)
réceptionner to catch, trap (a ball) (443)
rechaper to retread (tire) (59)
recharger to reload, refill (91)
réchauffer to reheat (84)
réchauffer (se) to warm up (85)
rechausser (se) to put one's shoes back on (85)
rechercher to search, hunt for (93)
réciter to recite (251)
rechigner to grumble, frown (441)
rechuter to relapse (32)
récidiver to be an habitual offender/recidivist (276)
réclamer to ask for, reclaim (71)
reclasser to reclassify (84)
recoller to restick (326)
récolter to harvest, gather (27)
recommander to recommend; to register (a letter) (98)
recommencer to begin again (99)
récompenser to reward (336)
recomposer to reconstruct, to redial a number (350)
recompter to recount, count again (103)
réconcilier to reconcile (212)
reconduire to see someone home, escort (106)
réconforter to comfort (349)
reconquérir to reconquer (19)
reconsidérer to reconsider (203)
reconstituer to rebuild, reconstruct (483)
reconstruire to reconstruct (111)
reconvertir to reconvert (229)
recorder to restring (27)
recorriger to recorrect (218)
recoucher (se) to go back to bed (122)
recoudre to sew up again (123)
recouper to cut again (124)
recourber to bend (240)
recourir à qqn/qqch to turn to someone, resort to something (125)
recouvrer to recover (466)
recouvrir to cover, cover again (126)
recréer to recreate (128)
récréer to amuse, entertain (128)
recreuser to dig again (32)
récrire to rewrite (177)
recroqueviller (se) to curl up (414)
recruter to recruit (32)
rectifier to rectify, correct (389)
reculer to step back, move back (81)
récupérer to salvage, recover (203)
récurer to scrub (54)
recycler to recycle (326)
redécouvrir to rediscover (139)
redéfinir to redefine (229)
redemander to ask again (147)
redémarrer to start again (22)
redescendre to go back down (157)
redevenir to become again (164)
rediffuser to rebroadcast (32)
rédiger to write, compose (218)
redonner to give again, give back (171)
redoubler to increase (407)
redouter de to dread, fear (173)
redresser to straighten up (353)
réécrire to rewrite (177)
rééditer to republish (215)
rééduquer to reeducate (219)
réélire to reelect (280)
réemployer/remployer to reuse (187)
réessayer to try again (204)
réexaminer to reexamine (465)
réexpédier to return/forward mail (212)

refaçonner to remodel (443)
refaire to redo (223)
référer (se) à to refer to, consult (122, 356)
refléter to reflect (87)
refleurir to flower again (249)
refondre to remelt, recast (394)
refouler to push back, force back (421)
réfracter to refract (27)
réfrigérer to refrigerate (203)
refroidir to cool (229)
réfuter to refute (425)
regagner to regain, win back, get back (239)
regarnir to restock (229)
regeler to freeze again, refreeze (242)
régénérer to regenerate (356)
régenter to rule over (464)
regimber to rear up, rebel (240)
régler to regulate, settle (87)
régner to reign, rule (87)
regorger de to abound in, overflow with (283)
regrossir to put weight back on (282)
regrouper to group together (59)
régulariser to regulate (486)
réhabiliter to rehabilitate (251)
réhabituer (se) to become used to again (33, 483)
rehausser to raise, increase (353)
réimprimer to reprint (220)
réincarcérer to reimprison (356)
réincarner (se) to be reincarnated (122)
réinstaller to reinstall (326)
réintégrer to reinstate (356)
réinventer to reinvent (464)
réitérer to reiterate (356)
rejaillir to splash up, spurt up (423)
rejeter to reject, throw up, spew (267)
rejoindre to rejoin, meet up with (268)
rejouer to replay (269)
réjouir to delight, gladden (270)
relancer to throw again, relaunch (342)
relater to relate (241)
relativiser to relativize (486)
relaxer to relax, release (27)
relayer to relieve, relay (330)
relever to raise again (278)
relouer to relet (269)
reluire to glisten (See **luire**) (Def. and Imp.)
remanier to revise (309)
remballer to repack, rewrap (326)
rembarquer to reembark (284)
rembobiner to rewind (329)
rembourser to reimburse (27)
remédier à to remedy (212)
remémorer (se) to remember (22, 122)
remmener to take/bring back (290)
remonter to go up again; **à** date back to (298)
remontrer to show again (299)
remorquer to tow (284)
remployer/réemployer to reuse (187)
rempocher to pocket again (82)
remporter to take back, win (349)
remprunter to borrow again (188)
remuer to move, stir (483)
rémunérer to remunerate (203)
renaître to be reborn, recover (306)
renchérir to go further, increase a bid (94)
rendormir (se) to fall asleep again (172) (aux. **être**)
renfermer to enclose, shut again, contain (227)
renfoncer to plunge/push further in (342)
renforcer to reinforce (342)
renfrogner (se) to frown (122, 441)
rengainer to resheath (329)
renier to renounce (309)
renifler to sniff, sniffle (439)
renommer to reappoint (310)
renoncer to renounce, give up (371)
renouer to retie (269)
renouveler to renew (38)
rénover to renovate (276)
renseigner to inform (194)
rentabiliser to make something profitable (486)
renverser to knock over, turn upside down, overturn (492)
renvoyer to send back (200)
repartir to start again (aux. **être**); to reply (aux. **avoir**) (327)
répartir to divide up, share (229)
repaver to repave (276)
repêcher to fish out, recover (332)
repeindre to repaint (334)
repentir (se) to repent ()
répercuter sur to pass on to (169)
repérer to locate, discover (203)

repeupler to repopulate (326)
replacer to replace, put back (342)
replier to fold again (129)
répliquer to retort, reply (219)
repolir to repolish (229)
reporter to carry forward, postpone, take back (349)
reposer to put back, rest on, ask a question again (350)
repousser to push away (353)
reprendre to take back, resume (357)
représenter to represent (60)
réprimer to repress (220)
reprocher qqch à qqn to blame, reproach someone for something (43)
reprogrammer to reprogram (368)
réprouver to reprove, condemn (481)
répudier to repudiate (212)
requérir to require, demand (19)
réquisitionner to requisition (171)
réserver to reserve (276)
résider to reside (251)
résigner (se) à to resign oneself to (122, 441)
résister to resist (259)
résonner to resonate, resound (443)
résorber to reduce, absorb (240)
respecter to respect (8)
respirer to breathe (466)
resplendir to shine (229)
responsabiliser to give someone responsibility (486)
resquiller to sneak in without paying (477)
ressentir to feel, experience (434)
resserrer to retighten (22)
resservir to serve again (437)
ressortir to go out again, take out again (444)
ressouder to resolder (27)
ressurgir/resurgir to reemerge, reappear (229)
restaurer to restore (347)
restituer to return, restore (483)
restreindre to restrict (334)
résulter de to result from (27)
résumer to summarize (238)
resurgir/ressurgir to reemerge, reappear (229)
rétablir to reestablish (206)
retaper to retype, fix up (59)
retarder to delay (240)
reteindre to redye (334)
retendre to retighten (394)
retomber to fall again (467)
rétorquer to retort (284)
retoucher to retouch (469)
retracer to recount (342)
rétracter to retract (60)
retrancher to remove, deduct (78)
retranscrire to retranscribe (177)
retransmettre to broadcast (294)
retraverser to recross (492)
rétrécir to shrink (95)
retremper to resoak (247)
rétribuer to pay (114)
retrousser to roll up, turn up (353)
retrouver to find (again) (481)
retrouver (se) to meet with, get together (122, 481)
réunifier to reunify (212)
réunir à to reunite with (485)
réutiliser to reuse (486)
revaloriser to revalue (486)
rêvasser to daydream (84)
réveiller to wake up (someone who's asleep) (109) (See 414)
réveillonner to celebrate on Christmas Eve or New Year's Eve (171)
révéler to reveal (356)
revendiquer to claim, demand (256)
revendre to resell (489)
réverbérer to reverberate, reflect (203)
reverdir to turn green again (229)
révérer to revere (203)
reverser to pour again, pour back (492)
revêtir to pave, take on a certain appearance (493)
réviser to revise (486)
revitaliser to revitalize (486)
revivre to live again, come alive again (496)
révolter to revolt (27)
révolutionner to revolutionize (171)
révoquer to revoke (219)
revoter to vote again (96)
rhabiller to dress again (477)
rhabiller (se) to get dressed again (250)
ricaner to giggle (27)
ricocher to ricochet (82)
rider to wrinkle (27)
ridiculiser to ridicule (486)
rigoler to laugh, joke (498)
rimer to rhyme, create poetry (220)
rincer to rinse (99)
riposter to respond, answer (27)
risquer to risk (219)
rissoler to brown (498)
ristourner to refund (27)
rivaliser to rival (486)
river to rivet (276)
roder to break in (mechanical) (96)
rôder to prowl (96)
rogner to trim (441)

romaniser to romanize (486)
ronfler to snore (445)
ronger to gnaw (442)
rosir to turn pink (95)
roter to burp (96)
rôtir to roast (229)
roucouler to coo (421)
rouer (de coups) to beat up (269)
rougeoyer to redden (187)
rouiller to rust (233)
roupiller to take a nap, sleep (477)
rouspéter to complain (87)
roussir to turn brown (95)
rouvrir to reopen (323)
ruer (se) sur/vers to rush toward (114, 122)
rugir to roar (229)
ruiner to ruin (329)
ruisseler to stream (38)
ruser to use trickery (32)
rutiler to gleam (27)

S

saborder to scuttle (27)
saboter to sabotage (96)
sabrer to slash (22)
saccager to devastate (305)
sacquer to fire, flunk (284)
sacrer to consecrate, swear (22)
sacrifier to sacrifice (212)
saigner to bleed (441)
saillir to jut out (50) (3d pers.); (229) (if **saillir**, means "to mate," 3d pers.)
saler to salt (326)
saliver to salivate (426)
saluer to greet, salute (114)
sanctifier to sanctify (212)
sanctionner to punish, to sanction (law) (443)
sangloter to sob (96)
saper to undermine (59)
saturer to saturate (54)
saupoudrer to sprinkle (299)
sautiller to skip (477)
sauvegarder to safeguard, to safe (computer) (240)
scandaliser to scandalize (486)
scander to scan (verse) (240)
scanner to scan (image) (171)
schématiser to schematize (486)
scier to saw (41)
scinder to split (240)
scintiller to sparkle (477)
scolariser to school, educate (486)
scruter to scrutinize (32)
sculpter to sculpt (8)
seconder to assist (240)
sécréter to secrete (87)
sectionner to split up (171)
sécuriser to reassure (486)
segmenter to segment (60)
sélectionner to select (171)
seller to saddle (326)
sembler to seem (Def. and Imp.)
semer to sow (341)
sensibiliser to sensitize, make aware (486)
seoir to be becoming, suit (Def. and Imp.)
sermonner to sermonize (171)
serpenter to snake, meander (60)
sextupler to sextuple (326)
sidérer to stun (203)
siéger to be in session (52)
siffloter to whistle (96)
signaliser to install signals/markings (486)
signifier to mean, signify (212)
silhouetter to silhouette (386)
sillonner to furrow, crisscross (171)
simplifier to simplify (212)
simuler to simulate (81)
singer to ape (283)
siroter to sip (96)
situer to situate, locate (483)
situer (se) to be located (122, 483)
skier to ski (129)
slalomer to slalom (71)
snober to snub (27)
socialiser to socialize, collectivize (486)
soigner qqn to take care of, look after someone (10)
solder to settle a debt, put on sale (27)
solidifier to solidify (212)
solliciter to solicit (251)
solubiliser to solubilize (486)
sombrer to sink (22)
sommeiller to doze (109)
sommer to summon (310)
somnoler to doze (498)
sonder to poll (27)
sonoriser to add a sound track (486)
soucier (se) de to care about (41) (aux. **être**)
souder to solder (27)
soulager de to relieve of (305)
soûler (se) to get drunk (122, 421)
soulever to raise (278)
souligner to underline (10)
soupçonner de to suspect of (443)
souper to have supper (124)
soupirer to sigh (21)
souscrire à to subscribe to (177)
soustraire to subtract (474) (no *passé simple* or imp. subj.)
soutenir to support (463)
soutirer to decant (466)
spatialiser to spatialize (486)
spécialiser (se) to specialize (486)
spécifier to specify (212)
spéculer to speculate (81)

spiritualiser to spiritualize (486)
sprinter to sprint (464)
stabiliser to stabilize (486)
stagner to stagnate (441)
stationner to park (171)
sténographier to take shorthand (212)
stériliser to sterilize (486)
stigmatiser to stigmatize (486)
stimuler to stimulate (81)
stipuler to stipulate (81)
stocker to stock (27)
stopper to stop (163)
stratifier to stratify (212)
stresser to stress (353)
strier to striate (129)
structurer to structure (54)
stupéfier to stupefy, stun (212)
styliser to stylize (486)
subir to undergo (95)
sublimer to sublimate (220)
submerger to submerge (283)
subordonner to subordinate (171)
subsister de to live on (53)
subtiliser to steal (486)
substituer à to substitute for (483)
subvenir à to provide for (491)
subventionner to subsidize (171)
subvertir to subvert, overthrow (229)
succéder à to succeed (87)
succomber to succumb (240)
suçoter to suck (96)
sucrer to sweeten (21)
suer to sweat (483)
suffire to suffice, be sufficient, be enough (Def. and Imp.)
suffoquer (de) to suffocate, choke (with) (219)
suggérer to suggest (356)
suinter to ooze (464)
superposer to stack, superimpose (350)
superviser to supervise (486)
suppléer to replace (128)
supplicier to torture (41)
supposer to suppose (350)
supprimer to suppress (220)
surabonder to abound (27)
surbaisser to lower (63)
surcharger to overload (283)
surélever to raise (278)
surenchérir to raise a bid (94)
suréquiper to overquip (215)
surestimer to overestimate (220)
surévaluer to overvalue (213)
surexposer to overexpose (350)
surfer to surf, netsurf (Internet) (27)
surgeler to freeze (242)
surgir to loom up, spring up (229)
surimposer to overtax (350)
surmener to overwork (290)
surmonter to overcome, surmount (298) (aux. **avoir**)
surnommer to give a nickname (310)
surpasser to surpass (84)
surpayer to overpay (17)
surplomber to overhang (240)
sursauter to jump, give a start (425)
surtaxer to surcharge (27)
surveiller to watch (109)
survenir to arise, occur (491)
suspecter de to suspect of (113)
suspendre to suspend (335)
susurrer to whisper (22)
suturer to suture (54)
symboliser to symbolize (486)
sympathiser avec to get on well with (486)
synchroniser to synchronize (486)
syndicaliser to unionize (486)
syndiquer to unionize (219)
synthétiser to synthesize (486)
systématiser to systematize (486)

T

tabler sur to count on (407)
tacher de to stain with (82)
tâcher to try (82)
tacheter to fleck (267)
taillader to slash (27)
tailler to cut, sharpen, trim (477)
talonner to tail, follow on someone's heels (171)
tambouriner to drum (329)
tamiser to sift (486)
tamponner to dab, mop up, plug (171)
tanguer to toss around, rock (the boat) (307)
tanner to tan (leather) (171)
tanner qqn to badger, pester someone (171)
taper to tap, type, strike, slap (235)
tapir (se) to crouch, hunker down (66) (aux. **être**)
tapoter to tap, pat (96)
taquiner to tease (329)
tarder to delay (240)
targuer (se) de to boast (122, 307)
tarir to dry up (249)
tartiner to spread (butter, pâté) (329)
tasser to tamp down, pack down (84)
tasser (se) to settle down, subside; to move over, step aside (Qué.) (84, 122)

tâter to feel by touching (241)
tâtonner to grope (171)
tatouer to tattoo (175)
taxer to tax (27)
teinter to tint (464)
télécharger to download (91)
télécharger vers le serveur to upload (91)
télécommander to operate by remote control (98)
télécopier to fax (212)
télédiffuser to televise (32)
télégraphier to telegraph (212)
téléguider to control by radio (27)
téléscoper to smash into (car, train) (163)
téléviser to televise (486)
témoigner to testify, show (10)
tempérer to temper (203)
tempêter to rant, storm (47)
temporiser to delay (486)
tenailler to torment (477)
tergiverser to procrastinate, hesitate (492)
ternir to tarnish (229)
terrasser to strike down (84)
terrer (se) to lie low, hide (122, 196)
terrifier to terrify (212)
terroriser to terrorize (486)
tester to test, make out a will (legal term) (160)
téter to nurse (baby) (87)
théoriser to theorize (486)
tiédir to become lukewarm (hotter or colder) (210)
timbrer to stamp (466)
tinter to ring (464)
tintinnabuler to tintinnabulate, jingle (81)
tirailler to pull on (477)
tisser to weave (73)
titrer to title, entitle, titrate (466)
tituber to stagger (32)
titulariser to give tenure, a contract (486)
toiletter to groom (246)
tolérer to tolerate (356)
tondre to mow, shear (394)
tonifier to tone up (212)
tonsurer to tonsure (54)
toquer to knock, rap, tap (219)
torcher to wipe (Watch out! **se torcher** = to wipe one's bottom) (285)
torchonner to botch (171)
torpiller to torpedo (477)
tortiller to twiddle, wiggle (477)
torturer to torture (54)
totaliser to total (486)
tourbillonner to swirl, whirl (171)
tourmenter to torment (60)
tournebouler to confuse (421)
tournoyer to whirl (308)
toussailler to have a slight persistent cough (477)
toussoter to have a slight cough (96)
tracasser to bother, worry (84)
tracer to trace (342)
tracter to tow ()
trafiquer to traffic, tamper with something (219)
traîner to drag (167)
tramer to plot (71)
trancher to slice (78)
tranquilliser to reassure (486)
transborder to transfer (27)
transcrire to transcribe (177)
transférer to transfer (356)
transformer en to transform into (227)
transfuser to transfuse (32)
transgresser to transgress (353)
transhumer to move, transplant (238)
transiger to compromise (218)
transiter to pass through (251)
transmuer to transmute (483)
transpercer to pierce (342)
transpirer to sweat, perspire (466)
transplanter to transplant (90)
transporter to transport (349)
transposer to transpose (350)
traquer to track (219)
traumatiser to traumatize (486)
travestir to dress up, misrepresent (66)
trébucher to stumble, trip (82)
trembler de to tremble with (407)
trembloter to tremble (96)
tremper to soak (247)
trépasser to pass away (84) (aux. **être** or **avoir**)
tressaillir to jump, flinch (50)
tresser to braid (73)
tricoter to knit (96)
trier to select, sort (129)
trifouiller dans to rifle through (233)
trimbaler to cart (something) around (326)
trinquer to toast (drink) (284)
triompher to triumph (27)
tripatouiller to tamper with (233)
tripler to triple (326)
tripoter to fiddle with (96)
tromper to deceive (247) (See 480)
trompeter to trumpet (267)
tronçonner to cut into sections (483)

trôner to take the place of honor (27)
tronquer to truncate (284)
troquer to swap, trade (219)
trotter to trot (246)
trottiner to trot along (329)
troubler to confuse (407)
trouer to make a hole in (269)
truquer to fake, rig (219)
truster to monopolize (manipulate the market) (27)
tuméfier (se) to swell up (212) (aux. **être**)
tuyauter to tip off (27)
tyranniser to tyrannize (486)

U

ulcérer to ulcerate (203)
ululer, hululer to hoot, screech (81)
unifier to unify (212)
uniformiser to make uniform, standardize (486)
urbaniser to urbanize (486)
uriner to urinate (465)
user to wear out, use up (32)
usurper to usurp (59)

V

vacciner contre to vaccinate against (329)
vaciller to sway, stagger, vacillate (477)
vadrouiller to roam around, wander (233)
vagabonder to wander (248)
vaguer to roam, wander (307)
valider to validate (251)
valoriser to increase the value, standing of someone/thing (486)
valser to waltz (492)
vanner to winnow, wear down (171)
vanter to vaunt, praise (90)
vanter (se) to brag (90, 122)
vaporiser to spray, vaporize (486)
varapper to rock climb (235)
varier to vary (129)
vasouiller to struggle (233)
vautrer (se) to wallow (122)
végéter to vegetate (356)
véhiculer to transport (81)
veiller to stay up, keep watch (109)
velouter (se) to soften (28, 122)
vendanger to harvest (grapes) (283)
vénérer to venerate (356)
ventiler to ventilate (266)
verbaliser to verbalize (486)
verdoyer to be green (187)
vérifier to verify (212)
vernir to varnish (229)
verrouiller to lock (233)
versifier to versify (41)
vexer to annoy, offend, upset (27)
vibrer to vibrate (22)
vidanger to empty (283)
vider to empty (251)
violacer (se) to become purple (342)
violer to violate, rape (498)
virer to turn, transfer (funds) (21)
virevolter to spin around (27)
viser à to aim at (486)
visionner to view, look at (171)
visser to screw on (486)
visualiser to visualize (486)
vitrer to install glass (22)
vitupérer to vituperate (203)
vivifier to give/bring life to (212)
vivoter to stagnate, barely get by (96)
vocaliser to vocalize (486)
vociférer to yell (356)
voguer to sail, drift (307)
voiler to veil (27)
voisiner to be close to (159)
voleter to flutter (267)
voltiger to flutter (218)
vomir to vomit (229)
voter pour/contre to vote for/against (96)
vouer à to dedicate to, to vow (269)
vriller to spin, whirl (477)
vrombir to hum, buzz (229)
vulgariser to vulgarize, popularize (486)

Y

yodler to yodel (326)

Z

zapper to zap, change channels (235)
zébrer de to streak, stripe with (356)
zézayer to lisp (330)
zieuter to eye (someone) (27)
zigouiller to bump off, stab (233)
zigzaguer to zigzag (307)
zipper to zip up (235)
zoner to zone (461)
zoomer to zoom in, zoom out (71)

3 Foreign Language Series From Barron's!

The **VERB SERIES** offers more than 300 of the most frequently used verbs.
The **GRAMMAR SERIES** provides complete coverage of the elements of grammar.
The **VOCABULARY SERIES** offers more than 3500 words and phrases with their foreign language translations. Each book: paperback.

FRENCH GRAMMAR
ISBN: 0-7641-1351-8
$6.99, Can. $9.99

GERMAN GRAMMAR
ISBN: 0-8120-4296-4
$7.99, Can. $11.50

ITALIAN GRAMMAR
ISBN: 0-7641-2060-3
$6.99, Can. $9.99

JAPANESE GRAMMAR
ISBN: 0-7641-2061-1
$6.95, Can. $9.95

RUSSIAN GRAMMAR
ISBN: 0-8120-4902-0
$7.99, Can. $9.99

SPANISH GRAMMAR
ISBN: 0-7641-1615-0
$6.99, Can. $9.99

FRENCH VERBS
ISBN: 0-7641-1356-9
$6.99, Can. $9.99

GERMAN VERBS
ISBN: 0-8120-4310-3
$8.99, Can. $12.99

ITALIAN VERBS
ISBN: 0-7641-2063-8
$6.99, Can. $8.75

SPANISH VERBS
ISBN: 0-7641-1357-7
$5.95, Can. $8.50

FRENCH VOCABULARY
ISBN: 0-7641-1999-0
$6.99, Can. $9.99

GERMAN VOCABULARY
ISBN: 0-8120-4497-5
$7.95, Can. $11.50

ITALIAN VOCABULARY
ISBN: 0-7641-2190-1
$6.95, Can. $9.95

JAPANESE VOCABULARY
ISBN: 0-8120-4743-5
$8.99, Can. $11.99

RUSSIAN VOCABULARY
ISBN: 0-8120-1554-1
$6.95, Can. $8.95

SPANISH VOCABULARY
ISBN: 0-7641-1985-3
$6.95, Can. $9.95

Barron's Educational Series, Inc.
250 Wireless Blvd., Hauppauge, NY 11788 •
Call toll-free: 1-800-645-3476
In Canada: Georgetown Book Warehouse
34 Armstrong Ave., Georgetown, Ontario L7G 4R9 •
Call toll-free: 1-800-247-7160
www.barronseduc.com
Can. $ = Canadian dollars

Books may be purchased at your bookstore or by mail from Barron's. Enclose check or money order for total amount plus sales tax where applicable and 18% for postage and handling (minimum charge $5.95 U.S. and Canada). Prices subject to change without notice. New York, New Jersey, Michigan, Tennessee, and California residents, please add sales tax to total after postage and handling.

(#26) R 6/07

Minimum Systems Requirement for the Flash Standalone Executable

Windows:
- Pentium II or higher recommended
- Windows 98, ME, NT4, 2000, XP
- 64 MB of installed RAM, 128 MB recommended
- 1024 × 768 color display

Apple:
- Power Macintosh Power PC processor (G3 or higher recommended)
- Mac OS® X 10.2–10.4 64 MB of installed RAM
- 128 MB recommended
- CD-ROM drive
- 1024 × 768 color display

Launching Instructions for the PC

Windows Users:
Insert the CD-ROM into your CD-ROM drive. The application should start in a few moments. If it doesn't, follow the steps below.

1. Click on the Start button on the Desktop and select Run.
2. Type "D:/501Verbs" (where D is the letter of your CD-ROM drive).
3. Click OK.

Launching Instructions for the Mac

Macintosh Users:
The CD will open to the desktop automatically when inserted into the CD drive. Double click the 501 Verbs Flash icon to launch the program.